THE GOSPEL
ACCORDING TO
JOHN

This book is gratefully dedicated to
Kenneth and Ruth Kantzer

THE GOSPEL
ACCORDING TO
JOHN

D. A. Carson

Inter-Varsity Press
Leicester, England

William B. Eerdmans Publishing Company
Grand Rapids, Michigan

INTER-VARSITY PRESS
38 De Montfort Street, Leicester LE1 7GP, England

Wm. B. EERDMANS PUBLISHING COMPANY
255 Jefferson S.E., Grand Rapids, MI 49503

Unless otherwise stated, Scripture quotations in this publication are
from the Holy Bible, New International Version. Copyright © 1973,
1978, 1984 International Bible Society. Used in USA by permission of
Zondervan Bible Publishers, Grand Rapids, Michigan, and published in
Great Britain by Hodder and Stoughton Ltd.

First published 1991

British Library Cataloguing in Publication Data
Carson, D. A.
The gospel according to John.
1. Bible. O.T. John – Critical studies
I. Title
226.506

ISBN 0-85111-749-X

Eerdmans ISBN 0–8028–3683–6

Set in Linotron Palatino
Typeset in Great Britain by Parker Typesetting Service, Leicester
Printed in the United States of America

64

CONTENTS

PREFACE

Anyone who dares to write yet another commentary on the Gospel of John must give reasons for doing so.

The original impetus was the invitation to provide a volume for a series. But as I set to work, it became clear that I needed more reason than that. A new commentary needs to justify itself in broader terms: it needs to carve a niche for itself by aiming at a specific readership, or by tackling certain problems, or by its particular emphases.

As these matters were discussed with the publishers, both they and I originally thought that the extra length and detail my own aims demanded could be accommodated within the series. Eventually, however, it was thought otherwise, and so we amicably agreed to publish this commentary on its own. This history largely explains why the format of this work is as it is.

This commentary seeks above all to explain the text of John's Gospel to those whose privilege and responsibility it is to minister the Word of God to others, to preach and to lead Bible studies. I have tried to include the kind of information they need to know, but to do so in such a way that the informed layperson could also use the work in personal study of the Bible, exclusively for purposes of personal growth in edification and understanding.

In particular, I have attempted:

(1) To make clear the *flow* of the text. Instead of offering detailed word studies and comments on Greek syntax, I have kept such remarks to the minimum required to make sense of the book, and have focused on the movement of thought.

(2) To engage a small but representative part of the massive secondary literature on John. Doubtless many who read this commentary will be informed pastors and theological students who need some kind of map of contemporary studies on John. Without permitting such interaction to become intrusive, I have tried to indicate what is valuable in such work, and where (and why) I depart from some of it.

(3) To draw a few lines towards establishing how the Fourth Gospel contributes to biblical and systematic theology. There is, of course, no point in deriding such syntheses; any thinking Christian is in some sense a systematician. But if all of us consciously or unconsciously systematize what we learn from the Scriptures, it may be a help to pause

now and then in the course of an exegetical and expository commentary and reflect on the contribution of the text to a mature and holistic Christian faith.

(4) To offer a consistent exposition of John's Gospel as an *evangelistic* Gospel. This is out of step, I confess, with what is in vogue in current scholarship: the majority opinion understands the Fourth Gospel to have been written with Christian readers in mind. In the past I have written the odd article poking away at this synthesis, trying to establish the minority opinion; but this commentary attempts, in part, to provide a global (if still entirely preliminary) defence of this reading.

No-one is more aware than I how far I have proved unable to achieve these goals as I would have liked. I am grateful for the careful reading and thoughtful suggestions of Leon Morris and David Kingdon. That I have not always agreed with them must not detract from the fact that because of their wisdom and attention to detail this work is better than it would have been without them. I am also grateful to the publishers, not least for their continued enthusiasm for the work even when it became clear that it could not be accommodated within the series for which it was originally planned. Finally, I want to express my thanks to Steve Bryan for compiling the Scripture index.

Above all, if this commentary helps some to honour the Son just as they honour the Father (5:23), and to believe that the Christ, the Son of God, is Jesus (20:30–31), and thus to discern both the love (3:16) and the wrath (3:36) of God that have been brought near in the coming of the Son, I shall be profoundly grateful.

Soli Deo gloria.

D. A. Carson

ABBREVIATIONS

AB	Anchor Bible.
Abbott	E. A. Abbott, *Johannine Grammar* (Adam and Charles Black, 1905).
An. Bib.	Analecta Biblica.
ANRW	*Aufstieg und Niedergang der römischen Welt.*
Appold	Mark L. Appold, *The Oneness Motif in the Fourth Gospel* (WUNT 1; Tübingen: J. C. B. Mohr [Paul Siebeck], 1976).
Aram.	Aramaic.
AusBibRev	*Australian Biblical Review.*
AV	Authorized Version (=King James Version).
B.	Babylonian Talmud.
BA	*Biblical Archaeologist.*
BAGD	W. Bauer, *A Greek-English Lexicon of the New Testament and Other Early Christian Literature*, translated and adapted by W. F. Arndt and F. W. Gingrich; fourth edition revised and augmented by F. W. Danker (Cambridge University Press, 1952/University of Chicago, 1979).
Barclay	William Barclay, *The Gospel of John*, 2 vols. (St Andrew Press 1955, ²1975).
Barrett	C. K. Barrett, *The Gospel according to St John: An Introduction with Commentary and notes on the Greek Text* (SPCK, ²1978).
Barrett, *Essays*	C. K. Barrett, *Essays on John* (SPCK, 1982).
Barrett, *GJJ*	C. K. Barrett, *The Gospel of John and Judaism* (SPCK, 1975).
Barrett, *HSGT*	C. K. Barrett, *The Holy Spirit and the Gospel Tradition* (SPCK, 1947).
Barth	Karl Barth, *Witness to the Word: A Commentary on John 1*, ed. W. Fürst, tr. G. W. Bromiley (Eerdmans, 1986).
Bauer	Walter Bauer, *Das Johannes-Evangelium* (Tübingen: J. C. B. Mohr [Paul Siebeck], 1933).
BBB	Bonner Biblische Beiträge.
BDF	F. Blass and A. Debrunner, *A Greek Grammar of the New Testament and Other Early Christian Literature*, tr.

9

and ed. R. W. Funk (Cambridge University Press/ University of Chicago, 1961).

Beasley-Murray G. R. Beasley-Murray, *John* (WBC 36; Word Books, 1987).

Becker J. Becker, *Das Evangelium des Johannes*, 2 vols. (Gütersloh: G. Mohn, 1979–81).

Bengel Johann Albrecht Bengel, *Gnomon on the New Testament*, vol. 2, tr. Andrew R. Fausset (T. & T. Clark, 1877).

Bernard J. H. Bernard, *The Gospel according to St John*, 2 vols. (ICC; T. & T. Clark, 1928).

BETL M. de Jonge (ed.), *L'Évangile de Jean: Sources, rédaction, théologie* (Leuven: Leuven University, 1977).

Betz Otto Betz, *Jesus: Des Messias Israels. Aufsätze zum biblischen Theologie* (WUNT 42; Tübingen: J. C. B. Mohr [Paul Siebeck], 1987).

Bib *Biblica.*

BJRL *Bulletin of the John Rylands Library.*

Blank Josef Blank, *Krisis: Untersuchungen zur johanneischen Christologie und Eschatologie* (Freiburg: Lambertus, 1964).

Blinzler J. Blinzler, *Der Prozeß Jesu* (Regensburg: Pustet, [4]1969).

Blomberg Craig L. Blomberg, *The Historical Reliability of the Gospels* (IVP, 1987).

Boers Hendrikus Boers, *Neither on this Mountain Nor in Jerusalem: A Study of John 4* (SBLMS 35; Atlanta: SP, 1988).

Boice J. M. Boice, *Witness and Revelation in the Gospel of John* (Zondervan, 1970).

Borgen P. Borgen, *Bread from Heaven* (SNT 10; Leiden: E. J. Brill, 1965).

Borgen, *Logos* P. Borgen, *LOGOS Was the True Light and Other Essays on the Gospel of John* (Trondheim: Tapir Publishers, 1983).

Borig R. Borig, *Der wahre Weinstock: Untersuchungen zu Jo 15, 1–10* (München: Kösel-Verlag, 1967).

Bornhäuser K. Bornhäuser, *Das Johannesevangelium: eine Missionsschrift für Israel* (Gütersloh: C. Bertelsmann, 1928).

Braun F.-M. Braun, *Jean le théologien*, 4 vols. (Paris: J. Gabalda, 1959–72).

Brown R. E. Brown, *The Gospel according to John: Introduction, Translation and Notes*, 2 vols. (Geoffrey Chapman/ Doubleday, 1966–71).

Brown, *Comm* R. E. Brown, *The Community of the Beloved Disciple* Geoffrey Chapman/Paulist, 1979).

Bruce F. F. Bruce, *The Gospel of John: Introduction, Exposition and Notes* (Pickering and Inglis, 1983).

BSac *Bibliotheca Sacra.*

BT	*The Bible Translator.*
BTB	*Biblical Theology Bulletin.*
Bühner	J.-A. Bühner, *Der Gesandte und sein Weg im 4. Evangelium: Die kultur- und religionsgeschichtlichen Grundlagen der johanneischen Sendungschristologie sowie ihre traditionsgeschichtliche Entwicklung* (Tübingen: J. C. B. Mohr [Paul Siebeck], 1977).
Bultmann	R. Bultmann, *The Gospel of John: A Commentary*, translated by G. R. Beasley-Murray, R. W. N. Hoare, and J. K. Riches (Blackwell, 1971).
Burge	G. M. Burge, *The Anointed Community. The Holy Spirit in the Johannine Tradition* (Eerdmans, 1987).
BZ	*Biblische Zeitschrift.*
Calvin	John Calvin, *Calvin's Commentaries: The Gospel according to St John*, 2 vols., tr. T. H. C. Parker (Oliver and Boyd, 1959–61).
Carson	D. A. Carson, *Divine Sovereignty and Human Responsibility: Biblical Perspectives in Tension* (Marshall, Morgan and Scott, 1981).
Carson, *FWD*	D. A. Carson, *The Farewell Discourse and Final Prayer of Jesus* (Baker, 1980).
Carson, *Matt*	D. A. Carson, 'Matthew', *The Expositor's Bible Commentary*, vol. 8 (Zondervan, 1984).
Carson, 'Mis'	D. A. Carson, 'Understanding Misunderstandings in the Fourth Gospel', *TynB* 33 (1982), pp. 59–89.
Carson, 'OT'	D. A. Carson, 'John and the Johannine Epistles', in D. A. Carson and H. G. M. Williamson (eds.), *It Is Written: Scripture Citing Scripture. Essays in Honour of Barnabas Lindars, SSF* (Cambridge University Press, 1988), pp. 245–264.
Carson, 'Purpose'	D. A. Carson, 'The Purpose of the Fourth Gospel: John 20:30–31 Reconsidered', *JBL* 108 (1987), pp. 639–651.
Carson/Woodbridge I, II	D. A. Carson and John D. Woodbridge (eds.), *Scripture and Truth* (IVP/Zondervan, 1983); *idem, Hermeneutics, Authority, and Canon* (IVP/Zondervan, 1986).
CBA	Catholic Biblical Association.
CBQ	*Catholic Biblical Quarterly.*
CBQMS	Catholic Biblical Quarterly Monograph Series.
Clark	G. H. Clark, *The Johannine Logos* (Presbyterian and Reformed Publishing Company, 1972).
ConNT	*Coniectanea Neotestamentica.*
CTM	*Concordia Theological Monthly.*
CTR	*Criswell Theological Review.*
Cullmann	O. Cullmann, *The Johannine Circle* (ET SCM, 1976).
Culpepper	R. A. Culpepper, *Anatomy of the Fourth Gospel: A Study in Literary Design* (Fortress, 1983).

11

Culpepper, *JS*	R. A. Culpepper, *The Johannine School* (Scholars Press, 1975).
Daube	D. Daube, *The New Testament and Rabbinic Judaism* (Athlone Press, 1956).
Dauer	A. Dauer, *Die Passionsgeschichte im Johannesevangelium: Eine traditionsgeschichtliche und theologische Untersuchung zu Joh 18,1–19,30* (München: Kösel Verlag, 1972).
Davey	J. E. Davey, *The Jesus of St John* (Lutterworth, 1958).
Davies	W. D. Davies, *The Gospel and the Land: Early Christianity and Jewish Territorial Doctrine* (University of California, 1974).
de Jonge	M. de Jonge, *Jesus: Stranger from Heaven and Son of God* (Scholars Press, 1977).
de la Potterie	I. de la Potterie, *La vérité dans Saint Jean*, 2 vols. (Rome: Biblical Institute Press, 1977).
Derrett	J. Duncan M. Derrett, *Law in the New Testament* (Darton, Longman and Todd, 1970).
Dodd, *HTFG*	C. H. Dodd, *Historical Tradition in the Fourth Gospel* (Cambridge University Press, 1963).
Dodd, *IFG*	C. H. Dodd, *The Interpretation of the Fourth Gospel* (Cambridge University Press, 1953)
Dods	Marcus Dods, *The Gospel of St. John, EGT.*
Duke	P. Duke, *Irony in the Fourth Gospel* (John Knox Press, 1985).
Dunn, *Making*	J. D. G. Dunn, *Christology in the Making: A New Testament Inquiry into the Origins of the Doctrine of the Incarnation* (SCM, 1980).
Edersheim	Alfred Edersheim, *The Life and Times of Jesus the Messiah*, 2 vols. (Longman, Green and Co., 1900).
EDT	W. Elwell (ed.), *Evangelical Dictionary of Theology* (Marshall, Morgan and Scott, 1985/Baker, 1984).
EGT	W. Robertson Nicoll (ed.), *The Expositor's Greek New Testament*, 5 vols. (Hodder and Stoughton, 1897–1910).
Eller	Vernard Eller, *Beloved Disciples: His Name, His Story, His Thought* (Eerdmans, 1988).
EphThLov	*Ephemerides Theologicae Lovaniensis.*
ET	English Translation
ExpT	*Expository Times.*
Fenton	J. C. Fenton, *The Gospel According to John* (Clarendon, 1970).
Ferrarro	Giuseppe Ferrarro, *L'«ora» di Cristo nel quarto vangelo* (Rome: Herder, 1974).
Ferrarro, *Spirito*	Giuseppe Ferrarro, *Lo Spirito nel vangelo di Giovanni* (Brescia: Paideia, 1986).

Fischer	G. Fischer, *Die himmlische Wohnungen: Untersuchungen zu Joh 14.2f* (Bern/Frankfurt: Lang, 1975).
fn.	footnote.
FN	*Filologia Neotestamentaria.*
Forestell	J. T. Forestell, *The Word of the Cross: Salvation as Revelation in the Fourth Gospel* (An. Bib. 57; Rome: Biblical Institute Press, 1974).
Fortna	R. Fortna, *The Gospel of Signs* (SNTSMS 11; Cambridge University Press, 1970).
Franck	E. Franck, *Revelation Taught: The Paraclete in the Gospel of John* (Lund: Gleerup, 1985).
Freed	E. D. Freed, *Old Testament Quotations in the Gospel of John* (SNT 11; Leiden: Brill, 1965).
Fs.	*Festschrift* (including all books written in honour or in memory of someone else).
Gardner-Smith	P. Gardner-Smith, *St John and the Synoptic Gospels* (Cambridge University Press, 1938).
Gk.	Greek.
GNB	Good News Bible.
Gnilka	J. Gnilka, *Johannesevangelium* (Würzburg: Echter Verlag, 1983).
Godet	F. Godet, *Commentary on the Gospel of St. John, with a Critical Introduction*, 2 vols., tr. M. D. Cusin (T. & T. Clark, 1887).
GP	R. T. France, D. Wenham and C. Blomberg (eds.), *Gospel Perspectives*, 6 vols. (JSOT Press, 1980–86).
Gruenler	R. G. Gruenler, *The Trinity in the Gospel of John: A Thematic Commentary on the Fourth Gospel* (Baker, 1986).
Guilding	A. Guilding, *The Fourth Gospel and Jewish Worship* (Clarendon, 1960).
Guthrie	D. Guthrie, *New Testament Introduction* (IVP, [4]1990).
Guthrie, *NTT*	D. Guthrie, *New Testament Theology* (IVP, 1981).
Haenchen	E. Haenchen, *A Commentary on the Gospel of John*, translated by R. W. Funk, edited by R. W. Funk and U. Busse, 2 vols. (SCM/Fortress, 1984).
Hanson	A. T. Hanson, *Grace and Truth: A Study in the Doctrine of the Incarnation* (SPCK, 1975).
Harvey	A. E. Harvey, *Jesus on Trial: A Study in the Fourth Gospel* (SPCK, 1976).
H. E.	*Ecclesiastical History* (Eusebius).
Heb.	Hebrew.
Hedrick/ Hodgson	Charles W. Hedrick and Robert Hodgson (eds.), *Nag Hammadi, Gnosticism, and Early Christianity* (Hendrickson, 1986).
Hendriksen	W. Hendriksen, *Exposition of the Gospel according to John*, 2 vols. (Baker, 1953–54).

Hengstenberg	E. W. Hengstenberg, *Commentary on the Gospel of John*, 2 vols. (ET T. & T. Clark, 1865–71).
Hennecke	E. Hennecke, *New Testament Apocrypha*, 2 vols., ed. W. Schneemelcher, tr. R. McL. Wilson (Lutterworth, 1963–65).
Holtzmann	H. J. Holtzmann, *Evangelium, Briefe und Offenbarung des Johannes* (Tübingen: J. C. B. Mohr [Paul Siebeck], ³1908).
Hoskyns	E. C. Hoskyns, *The Fourth Gospel*, edited by F. N. Davey (Faber and Faber, 1954).
Howard	W. F. Howard, 'The Gospel according to John', *The Interpreter's Bible*, vol. 8 (Abingdon, 1952).
Howard, *CSJ*	W. F. Howard, *Christianity According to St John* (Duckworth, 1943).
HTR	*Harvard Theological Review*.
Hunter	A. M. Hunter, *According to John* (SCM, 1968).
IBS	*Irish Biblical Studies*.
Ibuki	Yu Ibuki, *Die Wahrheit im Johannesevangelium* (BBB 39; Bonn: Peter Hanstein, 1972).
ICC	International Critical Commentaries.
IEJ	*Israel Exploration Journal*.
Int	*Interpretation*.
ISBE	G. W. Bromiley (ed.), *The International Standard Bible Encyclopedia*, revised edition (Eerdmans, 1979–88).
j.	Jerusalem Talmud.
JB	The Jerusalem Bible.
JBL	*Journal of Biblical Literature*.
Jeremias	J. Jeremias, *The Eucharistic Words of Jesus*, tr. Norman Perrin (SCM, 1966).
JETS	*Journal of the Evangelical Theological Society*.
JNES	*Journal of Near Eastern Studies*.
Jos.	Josephus (*Ant.*: Antiquities; *Ap.*: Against Apion; *Bel.*: War; *Vita*: Life).
Johnston	G. Johnston, *The Spirit-Paraclete in the Gospel of John* (SNTSMS 12; Cambridge University Press, 1970).
JSNT	*Journal for the Study of the New Testament*.
JTS	*Journal of Theological Studies*.
Käsemann	E. Käsemann, *The Testament of Jesus: A Study of the Gospel of John in the Light of Chapter 17*, tr. Gerhard Krodel (ET SCM, 1968).
Kremer	J. Kremer, *Lazarus: Die Geschichte einer Auferstehung. Text, Wirkungsgeschichte und Botschaft von Joh 11,1–46* (Stuttgart: Verlag Katholisches Bibelwerk GmbH, 1985).
Kümmel	W. G. Kümmel, *Introduction to the New Testament*, tr. H. C. Kee (ET SCM, 1975).
Kysar	R. Kysar, *John* (Augsburg, 1986).

Kysar, *Fourth*	R. Kysar, *The Fourth Evangelist and His Gospel: An Examination of Contemporary Scholarship* (Augsburg, 1975).
Ladd	George E. Ladd, *A Theology of the New Testament* (Lutterworth, 1975/Eerdmans, 1974).
Lagrange	M.-J. Lagrange, *Evangile selon Saint Jean* (Paris: J. Gabalda, 1925).
Lat.	Latin.
Lattke	M. Lattke, *Einheit in Wort: Die spezifische Bedeutung von ἀγάπη, ἀγαπᾶν und φιλεῖν im Johannesevangelium* (München: Kösel-Verlag, 1975).
Leistner	Reinhold Leistner, *Antijudaismus im Johannesevangelium? Darstellung des Problems in der neueren Auslegungsgeschichte und Untersuchung der Leidengeschichte* (Bern: Herbert Lang, 1974).
Léon-Dufour	X. Léon-Dufour, *The Gospels and the Jesus of History*, tr. and ed. J. McHugh (Collins, 1968).
Lightfoot	R. H. Lightfoot, *St John's Gospel: A Commentary* (Oxford University Press, 1956).
Lightfoot, *BE*	J. B. Lightfoot, *Biblical Essays* (Macmillan, 1893).
Lindars	B. Lindars, *The Gospel of John* (Oliphants, 1972).
Lindars, *BFG*	B. Lindars, *Behind the Fourth Gospel* (SPCK, 1971).
Lindars, *NTA*	B. Lindars, *New Testament Apologetic: the Doctrinal Significance of the Old Testament Quotations* (SCM, 1961).
Loisy	Alfred Loisy, *Le quatrième évangile* (Paris: Emile Nourry, 1921).
Lona	H. E. Lona, *Abraham in Johannes 8: Ein Beitrag zur Methodenfrage* (Bern: Herbert Lang, 1976).
LSJ	H. G. Liddell and R. Scott, *A Greek-English Lexicon*, new edition revised by H. S. Jones and R. Mackenzie, 2 vols. (Oxford University Press, 1940).
LXX	The Septuagint (pre-Christian Greek version of the Old Testament).
M. I, II, III, IV	J. H. Moulton, W. F. Howard, and Nigel Turner, *Grammar of New Testament Greek*, 4 vols. (T. & T. Clark, 1908–76).
Macgregor	G. H. C. Macgregor, *The Gospel of John* (Hodder and Stoughton, n.d.).
Manson	T. W. Manson, *On Paul and John: Some Selected Theological Themes*, ed. Matthew Black (SCM, 1963).
Marsh	J. Marsh, *The Gospel of St John* (Penguin, 1968).
Martin	Ralph P. Martin, *New Testament Foundations*, vol. 1: *The Four Gospels* (Paternoster, 1976/Eerdmans, 1975).
Martyn, *GJCH*	J. L. Martyn, *The Gospel of John in Christian History* (Paulist, 1978).
Martyn, *HTFG*	J. L. Martyn, *History and Theology in the Fourth Gospel* (Abingdon, [2]1979).

Metzger   B. M. Metzger, *A Textual Commentary on the Greek New Testament* (UBS, 1971).

Meeks   Wayne A. Meeks, *The Prophet-King: Moses Traditions and the Johannine Christology* (SNT 14; Leiden: E. J. Brill, 1967).

Meyer   H. A. W. Meyer, *Critical and Exegetical Hand-Book to the Gospel of John* (ET 1874–78; repr. Winona Lake, IN: Alpha Publications, 1979).

Michaels   J. Ramsey Michaels, *John* (Harper and Row, 1983).

Minear   P. S. Minear, *John: The Martyr's Gospel* (The Pilgrim Press, 1984).

MM   J. H. Moulton and G. Milligan, *The Vocabulary of the Greek New Testament, illustrated from the Papyri and other Non-Literary Sources* (Hodder and Stoughton 1930, repr. 1949).

Moloney   F. J. Moloney, *The Johannine Son of Man* (Rome: LAS, ²1978).

Moo   Douglas J. Moo, *The Old Testament in the Gospel Passion Narratives* (Almond, 1983).

Morris   L. Morris, *The Gospel according to John* (Eerdmans, 1971).

Morris, *JC*   L. Morris, *Jesus is the Christ: Studies in the Theology of John* (IVP, 1989).

Morris, *SFG*   L. Morris, *Studies in the Fourth Gospel* (Paternoster, 1969).

MT   Masoretic Text (the 'standard' Hebrew text of the Old Testament).

Mussner   F. Mussner, *The Historical Jesus in the Gospel of St John* (ET Burns and Oates, 1967).

NA²⁶   Nestle-Aland Greek New Testament, 26th edition.

NASB   New American Standard Bible.

NBD   J. D. Douglas and N. Hillyer (eds.), *New Bible Dictionary* (IVP, ²1982).

NEB   The New English Bible, Old Testament, 1970; New Testament, ²1970.

Neot   *Neotestamentica*.

NewDocs   G. H. R. Horsley, *New Documents Illustrating Early Christianity*, vols. 1–4 (Macquarie University, 1981–86).

Newbigin   Lesslie Newbigin, *The Light Has Come: An Exposition of the Fourth Gospel* (Handsel/Eerdmans, 1982).

Nicholson   G. C. Nicholson, *Death as Departure: The Johannine Descent-Ascent Schema* (SBLDS 63; Scholars Press, 1983).

NIDNTT   C. Brown (ed.), *The New International Dictionary of New Testament Theology*, vols. 1–4 (Paternoster, 1975–78).

NIGTC   New International Greek Testament Commentary.

NIV	New International Version.
NOT	*Notes on Translation.*
NovT	*Novum Testamentum.*
NRT	*Nouvelle Revue Théologique.*
NTS	*New Testament Studies.*
O'Day	G. R. O'Day, *Revelation in the Fourth Gospel: Narrative Mode and Theological Claim* (Fortress, 1986).
Odeberg	Hugo Odeberg, *The Fourth Gospel* (repr. Amsterdam: B. R. Grüner, 1968 [1929]).
Okure	Teresa Okure, *The Johannine Approach to Mission* (WUNT 31; Tübingen: J. C. B. Mohr [Paul Siebeck], 1988).
Olsson	B. Olsson, *Structure and Meaning of the Fourth Gospel* (Lund: Gleerup, 1974).
Painter	J. Painter, *John: Witness and Theologian* (SPCK, 1975).
Pancaro	Severino Pancaro, *The Law in the Fourth Gospel* (SNT 42; Leiden: E. J. Brill, 1975).
Panimolle	Salvatore Alberto Panimolle, *L'evangelista Giovanni: penserio e opera lettereria del quarto evangelista* (Rome: Borla, 1985).
par.	and parallel(s).
PEQ	*Palestine Exploration Quarterly.*
Petzer/Hartin	J. H. Petzer and P. J. Hartin (eds.), *A South African Perspective on the New Testament* (*Fs.* B. M. Metzger; Leiden: E. J. Brill, 1986).
Phillips	J. B. Phillips, *The New Testament in Modern English* (Bles/Collins, 1960).
Philo	Philo (*De Cher.*: On the Cherubim; *De Fug. et Inv.*: On Flight and Finding; *De Post. Caini*: On the Posterity of Cain; *Leg. Gaium*: On the Embassy to Gaius; *Legum Alleg.*: Allegorical Interpretation of Genesis; *Mut.*: On the Change of Names; *Som.*: On Dreams).
PL	J. P. Migne (ed.), *Patrologia Latina.*
Plummer	A. Plummer, *The Gospel according to St. John* (Cambridge University Press, 1882).
Pollard	T. E. Pollard, *Johannine Christology and the Early Church* (SNTSMS 13; Cambridge University Press, 1970).
Porsch	Felix Porsch, *Johannes-Evangelium* (Stuttgart: KBW, 1988).
Porter	Stanley E. Porter, *Verbal Aspect in the Greek of the New Testament, with Reference to Tense and Mood* (SBG 1; Bern: Peter Lang, 1989).
RB	*Revue Biblique.*
Reim	G. Reim, *Studien zum alttestamentlichen Hintergrund des Johannesevangeliums* (SNTSMS 22; Cambridge University Press, 1974).
RevQum	*Revue de Qumran.*

Reynolds	H. R. Reynolds, *The Gospel of St. John*, 2 vols. (London: Funk and Wagnalls, 1906).
Richter	G. Richter, *Die Fußwaschung im Johannesevangelium: Geschichte ihrer Deutung* (Regensburg: Friedrich Pustet, 1967).
Richter, *Studien*	G. Richter, *Studien zum Johannesevangelium* (Regensburg: Verlag Friedrich Pustet, 1977)
Ridderbos	Herman Ridderbos, *Het evangelie naar Johannes*, 2 vols. (Kampen: J. H. Kok, 1987–).
Riedl	J. Riedl, *Das Heilswerk Jesu nach Johannes* (Freiburg: Herder, 1973).
Ritt	H. Ritt, *Das Gebet zum Vater: Zur Interpretation von Joh 17* (Würzburg: Echter Verlag, 1979).
Rob	A. T. Robertson, *A Grammar of the Greek New Testament in Light of Historical Research* (Broadman, 1934).
Robinson, *John*	J. A. T. Robinson, *The Priority of John* (SCM, 1985).
Robinson, *More*	J. A. T. Robinson, *Twelve More New Testament Studies* SCM, 1984).
Robinson, *Red*	J. A. T. Robinson, *Redating the New Testament* (SCM, 1976).
Robinson, *Twelve*	J. A. T. Robinson, *Twelve New Testament Studies* (SCM, 1962).
RSV	(American) Revised Standard Version.
RTR	*Reformed Theological Review.*
RV	Revised Version.
Sanders	J. N. Sanders, *A Commentary on the Gospel according to St John*, ed. and completed by B. A. Mastin (Black, 1968).
SB	H. L. Strack and P. Billerbeck, *Kommentar zum neuen Testament aus Talmud und Midrasch* (München: C. H. Beck, 1926–61).
SBG	Studies in Biblical Greek.
SBLDS	Society of Biblical Literature Dissertation Series.
SBLMS	Society of Biblical Literature Monograph Series.
Schlatter	A. Schlatter, *Der Evanglist Johannes* (Stuttgart: Calwer, [4]1975).
Schnackenburg	R. Schnackenburg, *The Gospel according to St John*, tr. by K. Smyth, C. Hastings and others, 3 vols. (Burns and Oates, 1968–82); vol. 4 only in German, subtitled *Ergänzende Auslegungen und Exkurse* (Freiburg: Herder, 1984).
Schürer	Emil Schürer, *The History of the Jewish People in the Age of Jesus Christ (175 BC – AD 135)*, 4 vols.; revised and ed. by Geza Vermes, Fergus Millar, Martin Goodman, and Matthew Black (T. & T. Clark, 1973–87).
SE	*Studia Evangelica*, 6 vols.; ed. K. Aland, F. L. Cross, E. A. Livingston and others (1959–73).

Segovia	F. F. Segovia, *Love Relationships in the Johannine Tradition: Agapē/Agapan in 1 John and the Fourth Gospel* (SBLDS 58; Scholars Press, 1982).
Sevenster	M. C. Rientsma *et al.*, *Studies in John* (*Fs.* J. N. Sevenster; SNT 24; Leiden: E. J. Brill, 1970).
Sherwin-White	A. N. Sherwin-White, *Roman Society and Roman Law in the New Testament* (Oxford University Press, 1963).
Sidebottom	E. M. Sidebottom, *The Christ of the Fourth Gospel* (SPCK, 1961).
Simoens	Y. Simoens, *La gloire d'aimer: Structures stylistiques et interprétatives dans le Discours de la Cène (Jn 13–17)* (Rome: Biblical Institute Press, 1981).
Simonis	A. J. Simonis, *Die Hirtenrede im Johannes-Evangelium: Versuch einer Analyse von Johannes 10,1–18 nach Entstehung, Hintergrund und Inhalt* (Rome: Päpstliches Bibelinstitut, 1967).
SJT	*Scottish Journal of Theology.*
Smalley	S. S. Smalley, *John: Evangelist and Interpreter* (Paternoster, 1978).
Smith, *Essays*	D. M. Smith, *Johannine Christianity: Essays on its Setting, Sources, and Theology* (University of South Carolina Press, 1984).
SNT	Supplements to Novum Testamentum.
SNTSMS	Society for New Testament Studies Monograph Series.
SNTU	*Studien zum Neuen Testament und seiner Umwelt.*
SP	Scholars Press.
ST	*Studia Theologica.*
Strachan	R. H. Strachan, *The Fourth Gospel: Its Significance and Environment* (SCM, [3]1941).
Tasker	R. V. G. Tasker, *The Gospel according to St. John* (Tyndale Press, 1960).
TDNT	G. Kittel and G. Friedrich (eds.), *Theological Dictionary of the New Testament*, 10 vols. (ET Eerdmans, 1964–74).
Temple	W. Temple, *Readings in St John's Gospel* (1939–40; repr. Macmillan, 1968).
TheolBeit	*Theologische Beiträge.*
Thompson	Marianne M. Thompson, *The Humanity of Jesus in the Fourth Gospel* (Fortress, 1988).
ThR	*Theologische Rundschau.*
Thüsing	W. Thüsing, *Die Erhöhung und Verherrlichung Jesu im Johannesevangelium* (Münster: Aschendorff, [3]1979).
ThZ	*Theologische Zeitschrift.*
TLZ	*Theologische Literaturzeitung.*
Tragan	P.-R. Tragan, *La parabole du 'Pasteur' et ses explications: Jean, 10,1–18* (Rome: Editrice Anselmiana, 1980).

TrinJ	*Trinity Journal.*
Trites	Allison A. Trites, *The New Testament Concept of Witness* (SNTSMS 31; Cambridge University Press, 1977).
TU	*Texte und Untersuchungen.*
TynB	*Tyndale Bulletin.*
van Belle	G. van Belle, *Les parenthèses dans l'évangile de Jean: Aperçu historique et classification. Texte Grec de Jean* (Leuven University Press, 1985).
Vanderlip	D. George Vanderlip, *Christianity According to John* (Westminster, 1975).
van Hartings-veld	L. van Hartingsveld, *Die Eschatologie des Johannesevangeliums* (Assen: Van Gorcum, 1962).
VE	*Vox Evangelica.*
Vellanickal	M. Vellanickal, *The Divine Sonship of Christians in the Johannine Writings* (Rome: Biblical Institute Press, 1977).
v.l.	variant reading.
VT	*Vetus Testamentum.*
WBC	Word Biblical Commentary.
Westcott	B. F. Westcott, *The Gospel according to St John: The Greek Text with Introduction and Notes*, 2 vols. (John Murray, 1908).
Whitacre	Rodney A. Whitacre, *Johannine Polemic: The Role of Tradition and Theology* (SBLDS 67; Scholars Press, 1982).
Wiles	M. F. Wiles, *The Spiritual Gospel: The Interpretation of the Fourth Gospel in the Early Church* (Cambridge University Press, 1960).
Wilkens	W. Wilkens, *Zeichen und Werke: Ein Beitrag zur Theologie des 4. Evangeliums in Erzählungs- und Redestoff* (Zürich: Zwinglie, 1968).
Wilkinson	John Wilkinson, *The Jerusalem Jesus Knew: An Archaeological Guide to the Gospels* (Thames and Hudson, 1978).
WTJ	*Westminster Theological Journal.*
WUNT	Wissenschaftliche Untersuchungen zum Neuen Testament.
Zerwick	Maximilian Zerwick, *Biblical Greek Illustrated by Examples*, tr. Joseph Smith (Rome: Pontifical Biblical Institute, 1963).
ZNW	*Zeitschrift für die neutestamentliche Wissenschaft.*
ZWT	*Zeitschrift für wissenschaftliche Theologie.*

INTRODUCTION

I. SOME DISTINCTIVE CHARACTERISTICS OF THE GOSPEL OF JOHN

Perhaps more than any other, the Gospel of John has been used by Christians in every age, and for the greatest array of purposes. University students distribute free copies to their friends in the hope of introducing them to the Saviour. Elderly Christians on their deathbed ask that parts of this Gospel be read to them. Academics write learned dissertations on the relationship between John and some ancient corpus of literature. Children memorize entire chapters, and sing choruses based on its truth. Countless courses of sermons have been based on this book or on some part of it. It stood near the centre of Christological controversy in the fourth century, and for the last 150 years it has been at the heart of debate about the relation between history and theology. Until recently, the best known verse in the Bible was John 3:16 (possibly displaced today by Mt. 7:1!): a toddler could recite it. In this Gospel the love of God is dramatically mediated through Jesus Christ – so much so that Karl Barth is alleged to have commented that the most profound truth he had ever heard was 'Jesus loves me, this I know / For the Bible tells me so.'

Even so, a thoughtful reader does not have to work at this book very long before noticing remarkable differences between the Fourth Gospel (as the Gospel of John is often called) and the Synoptics.

First, John's Gospel leaves out a great deal of material that is characteristic of the Synoptics. There are no narrative parables in John, no account of the transfiguration, no record of the institution of the Lord's supper, no report of Jesus casting out a demon, no mention of Jesus' temptations. There are fewer brief, pithy utterances and more discourses, but some discourses found in the Synoptics (*e.g.* the Olivet Discourse, Mk. 13 par.) are not found in John. Although Jesus' baptism and the calling of the Twelve are doubtless presupposed, they are not actually described. Even themes central to the Synoptics have almost disappeared: in particular, the kingdom of God or the kingdom of heaven, so much a part of the preaching of Jesus in the Synoptic Gospels and the central theme of his narrative parables, is scarcely mentioned as such (*cf.* notes on 3:3, 5; 18:36).

Second, John includes a fair amount of material of which the Synoptists make no mention. All of the material in John 2 – 4, for instance, including his miraculous transformation of water into wine, his dialogue with Nicodemus and his ministry in Samaria, find no Synoptic counterpart. Further, the resurrection of Lazarus, Jesus' frequent visits to Jerusalem, and his extended dialogues or discourses in the temple and in various synagogues, not to mention much of his private instruction to his disciples, are all exclusive to the Fourth Gospel.

Doubtless some of this can be accounted for on the basis that John reports far more of Jesus' ministry in the south, in Judea and Samaria, than in Galilee; but the differences between John and the Synoptics are not all attributable to geographical focus. No less striking are the forcefully presented themes that dominate John but that are largely absent from the Synoptics. Only in John is Jesus *explicitly* identified with God (1:1, 18; 20:28). Here, too, Jesus makes a series of important 'I am' statements: I am the light of the world, the resurrection and the life, the good shepherd, the vine, the living water, the way, the truth and the life. These culminate in a series of absolute 'I am' statements that are redolent of God himself (*cf.* notes on 6:20; 8:24, 28, 58). The Fourth Gospel maintains a series of 'opposites', dualisms if you will, that are much stronger than in the Synoptics: life and death, from above and from below, light and dark, truth and lie, sight and blindness, and more.

Third, these themes become still more problematic for some readers when, formally at least, they contradict the treatment of similar themes in the Synoptic Gospels. Here, for instance, John the Baptist denies that he is Elijah (1:21), even though according to the Synoptists Jesus insists that he is (Mk. 9:11–13 par.). What shall we make of the bestowal of the Spirit (Jn. 20:22) and its relation to Acts 2? Above all, how do we account for the fact that in the Synoptics the disciples seem to grow from small beginnings in their understanding of who Jesus is, with various highpoints along the way, such as Caesarea Philippi (Mk. 8:27–30 par.), while in John the very first chapter finds various individuals confessing Jesus not only as Rabbi, but as Messiah, Son of God, Son of Man, Lamb of God and King of Israel?

Fourth, there are several chronological difficulties that must be addressed. In addition to the obvious questions, such as the relation between the cleansing of the temple at the beginning (Jn. 2:14–22) and at the end (Mk. 11:15–17 par.) of Jesus' public ministry, or the length of that ministry as attested by the number of Passovers it embraces (John reports at least three, the Synoptists only one); there are one or two questions of great difficulty that are precipitated in part by a knowledge of background ritual and circumstance. In particular, the chronology of the passion in the Fourth Gospel, as compared with that of the Synoptics, seems so idiosyncratic that it has generated complex theories about independent calendars, or about theological motifs that John is self-consciously allowing to skew the naked chronology. Did Jesus and his disciples eat the Passover, so that he was arrested the evening of Passover and crucified the next day, or was he crucified at the same time the Passover lambs were being slaughtered? And how does one account for the fact that the Synoptics picture Jesus being crucified about the third hour (9.00 a.m.), while in John Pilate's final decision is not reached until the sixth hour (19:14)?

Fifth, students of Greek, perhaps more readily than those who read the text only in translation, observe that the style of writing is quite different from that of the Synoptics. For instance, the vocabulary is smaller, there is frequent parataxis (the use of co-ordinate clauses instead of subordinating expressions, which elegant Greek much prefers), peculiar uses of pronouns (*e.g. ekeinos*, 'that one', frequently no more than 'he' in John), and many instances of asyndeton (simply laying out clauses beside each other, without connecting them with particles or conjunctions, as Greek prefers). More importantly, there is little discernible difference in style between the words that are ascribed to Jesus and the Evangelist's own comments. John has re-written the whole.

Finally, several historical anachronisms or other discrepancies are often alleged. 'Come now; let us leave', Jesus says in 14:31; yet there follow two more chapters of material before it becomes unambiguously clear that anyone has moved. Most scholars hold that John 21 is something of an afterthought appended to the original conclusion (20:30–31). In one place, at least, it is less than clear where Jesus' words end and those of John begin (3:10–21). Above all, the threat of synagogue excommunication (9:22) is widely regarded as anachronistic, since (it is argued) such discipline was not put into place until the late 80s of the first century.

Most of these features of John's Gospel are discussed at some length in the commentary, and need not detain us here. Even so, it is clear that John's independence is one of the reasons why this Gospel has precipitated such varied treatment during the history of the church.

II. HOW JOHN'S GOSPEL HAS BEEN UNDERSTOOD: SELECT SOUNDINGS

1. The early church

It could not have been long after the Fourth Gospel was published before it was collected with the other three to form the fourfold Gospel. In other words, for the most part the Gospel of John early circulated as part of one book. This book was not a scroll, as the first manuscripts doubtless were, but a 'codex', a book with separate leaves like ours, and sewn or glued on one side. It was known simply as 'The Gospel', containing the four canonical Gospels. This 'Gospel' was then divided into the parts that were thought to be 'According to Matthew', 'According to Mark', 'According to Luke' and 'According to John'.

It is usually assumed that these traditional ascriptions of authorship were attached to the books not before AD 125. Recently, however, Martin Hengel has mounted a plausible defence of the view that these 'titles' were attached to their respective individual books from the beginning, *i.e.* the four canonical Gospels are no more anonymous than any other book with a title page that includes the name of the author.[1] Hengel's arguments have not so far been accorded the attention they deserve. Although I shall not here assume that they are convincing, they must be borne in mind by those who too quickly dismiss the evidence of Papias, shortly to be discussed.

Probably the earliest New Testament fragment that has come down to us is a fragment of John, Papyrus 52, dating from AD 130 and containing a few words from John 18. Two other papyrus codices spring from the end of the second century: Papyrus 66 includes most of chs. 1 – 14 and parts of the remaining chapters, while Papyrus 75 contains most of Luke, followed by John 1 – 11 and parts of chs. 12 – 15. From the beginning of the third century comes Papyrus 45, which contains parts of all four Gospels plus Acts, though the mutilated state of the manuscript ensures that no book is complete. Thereafter the manuscript evidence becomes richer, the great fourth century uncials (manuscripts written in capital letters) followed by the many miniscules in succeeding centuries.

The thought and language of John's Gospel find affinities both in the *Odes of Solomon*, a collection of hymns from about the same period, and in the epistles of Ignatius, bishop of Antioch (*c.* AD 110–115), but no direct dependence has been proved to everyone's satisfaction.[2] Polycarp, bishop of Smyrna and writing *c.* AD 120, clearly quotes from 1 John (in *To the Philippians* 1:7, loosely citing 1 Jn. 4:2–3). If one concludes (as I do) that the Johannine Epistles were written after the Fourth Gospel, and by the same author, it is reasonable to suppose that Polycarp also knew the Fourth Gospel; but there is no conclusive literary evidence. Apparently the gnostic Basilides (*c.* AD 130) quotes John 1:9 ('The true light that gives light to every man was coming into the world') as a comment on Genesis 1:3 ('Let there be light'), but this information is dependent on Hyppolytus (*Refutation of Heresies* vii. 22. 4). If he is right, this is the first explicit quotation from John that has come down to us.

---

[1]Martin Hengel, *Studies in the Gospel of Mark* (London, 1985), pp. 66–84. For discussion, *cf.* D. A. Carson, Leon Morris and Douglas J. Moo, *New Testament Introduction* (Zondervan, forthcoming), ch. 2.

[2]It must be also said that, in the case of the *Odes of Solomon*, no convincing arguments have yet been advanced to demonstrate the opposite dependence either.

Indeed, gnostic interest in John continues strong throughout the second and third centuries. Gnosticism was not an orderly system of thought with well-defined borders, but (as one scholar has put it) 'a theosophical hotch-potch'. It sprang in part from the neo-Platonism that developed more than two centuries before Jesus. This world-view pitted what is 'spirit' or 'real' against what is merely material, temporal and without significance. Gnosticism went farther, and held to some kind of gnostic-redeemer who came to 'spiritual' people and explained to them their true genesis in the spiritual world, thereby freeing them from their bondage to the material world by this 'knowledge' (Gk. *gnōsis*) of their true being. Those who were truly 'spiritual' received their message; those who were entirely material dismissed them. In some forms of Gnosticism there were intervening categories. But in any case, the nature of bondage, in this system, is enslavement to matter, ignorance of one's true origins; the nature of redemption is the special 'knowledge' imparted by the gnostic-redeemer. In full-blown second-century Gnosticism, Jesus was identified as this gnostic-redeemer, and John's Gospel was interpreted (or mis-interpreted) to justify this claim.

Thus the *Gospel of Truth* (*c.* AD 140), the product of either the gnostic Valentinus or of one of his disciples, apparently alludes to the Fourth Gospel several times, even if it does not explicitly quote it. We are told (26:4–8) that when the Word appeared 'it became a body (*sōma*)' – which is more than most Gnostics would concede, but probably 'body' was judged less material and offensive than John's 'flesh' (*sarx*, Jn. 1:14). A little later, Valentinus displays his true colours when he says of the Word that 'those who were material were strangers and did not see his form or recognize him. For he came forth in flesh (*sarx*) of such a kind that nothing could block his progress' (31:1–7): apparently there is a confusion between Jesus' body during his ministry and his resurrection body (Jn. 20:19). Heracleon, one of the disciples of Valentinus, wrote the first commentary on John of which we have any knowledge. It has not come down to us independently, but is constantly quoted by Origen in his third-century commentary on the Fourth Gospel.

Of course, the Gnostics were not the only ones to use John's Gospel. Although several Fathers from the first half of the second century probably allude to the Fourth Gospel (*cf.* discussion below), the first writer in the orthodox stream actually to quote John, so far as our records go, is probably Justin Martyr, who at one point comments, 'Christ indeed said, "Unless you are born again you shall not enter into the kingdom of heaven." It is evident to all that those who have once been born cannot re-enter their mothers' wombs' (*First Apology* 61. 4–5). This is almost certainly a reference to John 3:3–5, though John is not actually named. Some scholars have wondered if this is merely a reference to oral tradition that came to Justin independently of the Gospel of John, since at a number of points where he might have usefully referred to John (*e.g.* in his teaching about the pre-existence of the Word of God) he fails to do so. Justin does not explicitly assign any of the canonical

Gospels to a specific author, but he does refer to them as the 'memoirs of the apostles'.

The first unambiguous quotation from the Fourth Gospel that ascribes the work to John is from Theophilus of Antioch (*c.* AD 181), but even before this date several writers, including Tatian (a student of Justin), Claudius Apollinaris (bishop of Hierapolis) and Athenagoras, unambiguously quote from the Fourth Gospel as from an authoritative source. This pushes us back to Polycarp and Papias, information about whom derives primarily from Irenaeus (end of the second century) and Eusebius the historian of the early church (fourth century). Polycarp was martyred in AD 156 at the age of eighty-six. There is no reason therefore to deny the truth of the claims that he associated with the apostles in Asia (John, Andrew, Philip) and was 'entrusted with the oversight of the Church in Smyrna by those who were eye-witnesses and ministers of the Lord' (*H. E.* III. xxxvi).

Irenaeus knew Polycarp personally, and it is Polycarp who mediates to us the most important information about the Fourth Gospel. Writing to Florinus, Irenaeus recalls:

> I remember the events of those days more clearly than those which have happened recently, for what we learn as children grows up with the soul and becomes united to it, so I can speak even of the place in which the blessed Polycarp sat and disputed, how he came in and went out, the character of his life, the appearance of his body, the discourse which he made to the people, how he reported his converse with John and with the others who had seen the Lord, how he remembered their words, and what were the things concerning the Lord which he had heard from them, including his miracles and his teaching,[1] and how Polycarp had received them from the eyewitnesses of the word of life, and reported all things in agreement with the Scriptures (*H. E.* V. xx. 5–6).

Most scholars recognize that this 'John', certainly a reference to John the apostle, the son of Zebedee, is in the mind of Irenaeus none other than the John whom he emphatically insists is the fourth Evangelist. For Irenaeus, that the Gospel should be 'fourfold' (in the sense described above) was as natural as that there should be four winds. As for the Fourth Gospel itself, he wrote: 'John the disciple of the Lord, who leaned back on his breast, published the Gospel while he was resident at Ephesus in Asia' (*Against Heresies* iii. 1. 2). In other words, the name of the fourth Evangelist is John, and is to be identified with the beloved disciple of John 13:23.

The evidence of Papias similarly depends on secondary sources.

---

[1]The translation is from the Loeb edition of Eusebius, except for this clause, where that edition clearly errs.

Papias was a contemporary of Polycarp, and may himself have been a student of John (Irenaeus, *Against Heresies* v. 33. 4, affirms it; Eusebius, *H. E.* III. xxxix. 2, denies it). Certainly Eusebius insists that Papias quoted from 1 John (*H. E.* III. xxxix). That Eusebius does not mention that Papias cited the Fourth Gospel is irrelevant: Eusebius' stated purpose was to discuss the disputed parts of the New Testament, as well as some of those people who linked the first century with what follows, rather than to provide a list of citations regarding 'acknowledged' books.[1]

Another piece of evidence regarding Papias is harder to evaluate. About AD 140 an extreme follower of the writings of Paul, Marcion by name, who had become convinced that only this apostle had truly followed the teachings of Jesus while all the others had relapsed into Judaism, went to Rome to try to convince the church there of his views. He argued, unsuccessfully, that the proper New Testament canon was comprised of ten letters of Paul and one Gospel, a mutilated version of Luke. Marcion was sufficiently dangerous that he succeeded in arousing responses. In particular, the so-called anti-Marcionite prologues to the Gospels have been viewed as part of these responses (though it must be admitted that some scholars think they emerged at a later period). The anti-Marcionite prologue to John has come down to us in a rather corrupt Latin version. It informs us that the Gospel of John was published while John was still alive, and was written down at John's dictation by Papias, a man from Hierapolis and one of John's near disciples. As for Marcion, he had been expelled by John himself. This information, the prologue argues, derives from the five exegetical books of Papias himself: the reference is to his *Exegesis of the Dominical Logia*, which survived into the Middle Ages in some libraries in Europe, but which is, regrettably, no longer extant.

Some of the information provided by the anti-Marcionite prologue is clearly mistaken. It is overwhelmingly doubtful that John excommunicated Marcion: the chronology is stretched too thin. Moreover, as Bruce (p. 10) points out, Papias for his part may have said that the churches or certain disciples 'wrote down' what John said, and was subsequently misquoted as meaning 'I wrote down', since in Greek the latter is formally indistinguishable from 'they wrote down'. Even so, there is no doubt in this document that John himself was responsible for the Fourth Gospel.

Not only Irenaeus, but Clement of Alexandria and Tertullian as well, provide firm second-century evidence for the belief that the apostle John wrote the Gospel. According to Eusebius (*H. E.* VI. xiv. 7), Clement wrote: 'But that John, last of all, conscious that the outward facts had

---

[1] In this connection, however, it is rather remarkable that 1 John should be mentioned, since it was universally accepted. Perhaps, as Westcott (1. lxiii–lxiv) suggests, it is because it belongs to the 'general' or 'catholic' epistles, which constituted a rather exceptional group of writings.

been set forth in the Gospels, was urged on by his disciples, and, divinely moved by the Spirit, composed a spiritual Gospel.' A more enigmatic, and in its details less believable, version of the same development is preserved in the Muratorian Canon, the earliest orthodox list of New Testament books to come down to us, probably from the end of the second century. It tells us not only that John's fellow-disciples and bishops urged him to write, but that by a dream or prophecy it was revealed to Andrew that John should in fact take up the task, writing in his own name, but that the others should review his work and contribute to it. Most scholars take this to be someone's deduction from John 21:24.

Some indirect evidence is in certain respects still more impressive. Tatian, a student of Justin Martyr, composed the first 'harmony' of the fourfold Gospel: he took the books apart and weaved them together into one continuous narrative. This *Diatessaron* (as it is called), first prepared in Greek, exerted enormous influence in its Syriac translation. But the crucial point to observe is that it is the Gospel of John that provides the framework into which the other three Gospels are fitted. That could not have been the case had there been questions about the authenticity of the book.

Indeed, by the end of the second century the only people who denied Johannine authorship to the Fourth Gospel were the so-called *Alogoi* – a substantivized adjective meaning 'witless ones', but used by the orthodox as a pun to refer to those who rejected the *logos* ('Word': *cf.* notes on 1:1) doctrine expounded in the Fourth Gospel, and therefore the Fourth Gospel itself. Further, an elder by the name of Gaius in the Roman church, who was one of the *Alogoi*, maintained orthodoxy at every point except in his rejection of John's Gospel and the Apocalypse. At least part of his motivation, however, was his virulent opposition to Montanism, an uncontrolled 'charismatic' movement arising in the middle of the second century that was wont to claim that its leader, Montanus, was the mouthpiece of the promised Paraclete. Since all of the Paraclete sayings that refer to the Spirit are found in John's Gospel (14:16, 26; 15:26; 16:7–15), Gaius did not need much persuading to side with the *Alogoi* on this point.

Certainly from the end of the second century on, there is virtual agreement in the church as to the authority, canonicity and authorship of the Gospel of John. An argument from silence in this case proves impressive (because we would otherwise have expected the person in question to make a lot of noise!): 'it is most significant that Eusebius, who had access to many works which are now lost, speaks without reserve of the fourth Gospel as the unquestioned work of St. John' (Westcott, 1. lix). The silence is 'most significant' precisely because it was Eusebius' concern to discuss the doubtful cases.

It should not be thought that the differences between John and the Synoptics (§ I, above) were unnoticed by the early church Fathers (*cf.* Wiles, pp. 13–40). The remark of Clement of Alexandria, to the effect that John composed 'a spiritual Gospel', is teasing. It certainly does not mean 'spiritual' as opposed to 'historical'; it may mean 'allegorical' or 'symbol-laden'. Irenaeus (*Against Heresies* ii. 22. 3) appeals to the length of Jesus' ministry in John's chronology to combat connections that gnostics drew between Jesus' passion, which they claimed took place in the twelfth month after his baptism, and the twelfth aeon, important in their cosmology. Eusebius, Epiphanius and Augustine set themselves the task of explaining other difficulties between John and the Synoptics, sometimes resorting to tortuous ingenuity. Origen does not think that the chronologies can be reconciled at the historical level, but argues that material falsehood may be the means, through allegory, of preserving and presenting spiritual truth. Theodore, by contrast, seeks to resolve chronological difficulties by arguing that the Synoptics do not really present a chronology with which to conflict: much of their presentation is piecemeal, and can be fitted into the Johannine schema. If there are differences between John and the Synoptics on the passion, for instance, it must be remembered not only that John was actually present for much of the period (unlike the other disciples, who had fled), but that any complex event remembered by a variety of people is bound to be described in independent but complementary fashion. This proves, in Theodore's view, that the witnesses were not in collusion, and are therefore all the more credible. Thus, his attempts at resolution operate at the *historical* level.

2. More recent discussion

Limitations of space forbid me from embarking on a summary of the larger interpretative achievements and failures of the Fathers.[1] The same holds true for commentaries of the Middle Ages and of the Reformation. Whether the Fourth Gospel was interpreted so as to ground some form of Christian mysticism, or so as to make clear the truth of justification by faith, there was at least no doubt that it was the product of the apostle John, that in some ways it is the most focused of the four canonical Gospels,[2] and that fundamental reconciliation between John and the Synoptics can be achieved.

With the onset of the Enlightenment, historical consciousness came into its own. In the major European universities doubt regarding the historical trustworthiness of the Gospels rose like a tide from about 1750

---

[1]For a useful summary, *cf.* Thomas Aquinas, *Commentary on the Four Gospels Collected out of the Works of the Fathers* (ET John Henry Parker, 1845). For a brief survey of medieval commentaries on John, *cf.* Panimolle, pp. 447–449.

[2]Calvin (I. 6) argues that John 'emphasizes more [than do the Synoptists] the doctrine in which Christ's office and the power of His death and resurrection are explained'. He adds: 'And since they all had the same object, to show Christ, the first three exhibit His body, if I may be permitted to put it like that, but John shows His soul. For this reason I am accustomed to say that this Gospel is a key to open the door to understanding the others, for whoever grasps the power of Christ as it is here graphically portrayed, will afterwards read with advantage what the others relate about the manifested Redeemer.'

on (though its antecedents were still earlier). Until 1835, however, John's Gospel fared somewhat better than did the Synoptics, though for doubtful reasons. Critics noted that John reports no exorcisms. He rapidly turns from miracles to discourse: indeed, his preferred word is 'sign', not 'wonder' or 'work of power'. All this suited an intellectual environment less and less open to the frankly supernatural, and more and more enamoured with notions of root ideas or core ideas that expressed themselves in various 'myths'.

The turning point came in 1835 with the publication of the first edition of *Das Leben Jesu. Kritisch bearbeitet*,[1] by David Friedrich Strauss.[2] In some ways, Strauss was merely carrying a little farther the scepticism of many of his colleagues. He was a rigorous antisupernaturalist, and generously appealed to the category of 'myth', at that point more commonly deployed in Old Testament studies than in New, to explain how some idea could be expressed by an ancient civilization in concrete forms that Strauss's generation (he felt) could no longer accept at the merely historical level. So far as Johannine studies are concerned, his major significance was that he applied this approach to Christology, with the result that John's presentation of Jesus as genuinely and simultaneously God and man also falls under the category of 'myth', and John's Gospel becomes the *least* historically credible of the canonical Gospels. For a Christ at the centre of Christology, Strauss substituted an idea, the idea that in humanity 'the divine Spirit [certainly not understood as the personal-transcendent God of the Bible!] manifests itself, and it is humanity which is to be regarded as the true Christ'.[3] At one blow Strauss laid waste any historical understanding of Christianity. The same blow relegated the Fourth Gospel, in the eyes of a growing number of critics, to the least useful work in the New Testament, from the perspective of the historian.

Strauss's book touched off a fire-storm. He was sacked from his post, and vilified in the press. Some of the opprobrium he faced was hypocritical, for the *kinds* of scepticism he expressed were already well entrenched. But most biblical scholars of sceptical bent had managed to cloak their scepticism in piety, and most of them had left the person of Jesus as presented in the Gospels uncriticized. Strauss refused to play the game, and so the pent-up suspicions of a society still largely controlled by Christian beliefs fell on him. Many of his fellow academics distanced themselves from him, at least for a time, fearing for their own jobs.

Nevertheless the work of Strauss became extraordinarily influential, even amongst those who could not go quite as far as he went. Before

---

[1]The work has only recently been translated into English, as *The Life of Jesus Critically Examined* (SCM, 1973).
[2]For an excellent assessment of Strauss's significance, *cf.* Horton Harris, *David Friedrich Strauss and His Theology* (Cambridge University Press, 1973).
[3]*Ibid.*, p. 55.

sketching in the developments that sprang up in his wake, however, it is important to recognize that not all scholars thought he was on the right track. During the next 150 years, major figures contributed to Johannine studies within an orthodox framework. One thinks of the major commentaries of E. Hengstenberg, B. F. Westcott and Leon Morris, and of the conservative critical introductions by Theodor Zahn, J. Gresham Machen and Donald Guthrie – not to mention hundreds of less eminent contributors to the discussion who have retained their intellectual integrity while reading the Gospel of John with the conviction that they were hearing the words of an apostle of Jesus who understood his role to be that of a witness to the truth.

Even so, the mainstream of Johannine scholarship ran in another direction. At the end of the last century and the beginning of this one, the most influential movement was the 'history-of-religions' school. This attempted to tie the rise and development of all religions to purely naturalistic and historical developments. Christianity was variously construed as some sort of amalgam of ancient mystery cult coupled with vestiges of Judaism, or as the result of a fecund union between Jewish thought and Greek or gnostic thought. In this light, John's Gospel was read as the tail end of this development, the evidence of what happened when a Palestinian sect established itself in the broader hellenistic world. Much of the power of this movement has drained away, as later scholarship has shown again and again that the simple disjunction between Jewish and hellenistic thought did not exist in the first century, that the philosophical commitment to antisupernaturalism cannot possibly listen adequately to the texts, and that theories about straight lines of religious and historical development are both artificial and empirically negated by the rise of every religious movement that can be studied at close range. Most contemporary scholars have benefited from the 'school', in that they have learned to ask *historical* questions with more rigour than would otherwise have been the case. A few still operate largely within the constraints of the movement as it manifested itself at the turn of the century.[1]

So far as John is concerned, the most influential scholar to emerge from this camp in the twentieth century was Rudolf Bultmann. His major commentary on John, a wealth of learning on countless details, was characterized by four features:

(1) He insisted that the most influential background to Johannine Christianity was Mandaen Gnosticism. Certainly he was able to adduce many intriguing parallels. The difficulty with the thesis, however, is that Mandaen Gnosticism, so far as extant sources go, is a late phenomenon. None of our written sources is earlier than about the seventh century

---

[1]One thinks especially of Helmut Koester, *Einführung in das Neuen Testament im Rahmen der Religionsgeschichte und Kulturgeschichte der hellenistischen und römischen Zeit* (de Gruyter, 1980 [ET Fortress, 1982]); and of some of the commentators in the prestigious Hermeneia series.

AD. Nevertheless, Bultmann held that Mandaen Gnosticism antedates Christianity and is determinative in the shaping of Johannine Christianity.

(2) Bultmann deployed systematic source-criticism on the Fourth Gospel, and separated out not only a 'signs source' (more on this later) and a discourse source, but other pieces as well, including the late work of a postulated 'ecclesiastical redactor' who tried to shape the book into more conventional forms of Christianity. Bultmann's judgments extended to separating words and phrases from their present context. In one of his more famous judgments, for instance, he argued that the words 'water and' in John 3:5 are attributable to the ecclesiastical redactor.

(3) Bultmann himself was rigorously committed to antisupernaturalism, as his famous 1941[1] essay makes clear. Inevitably this affects his judgment as to the *historical* reliability of much of John. For that matter, the essence of his judgment about what historians can really know about Jesus is that he was, that he existed – a brute *daß* ('that'), and no more.

(4) But according to his own lights, that did not matter. Christianity was best after being 'demythologized' (shades of Strauss) and therefore presented to contemporary humanity shorn of the beliefs that modern science (in his view) could not accept. This kernel, the real Christianity, turned out on close inspection to be very close to one form of existentialism. God is no longer the personal-transcendent God of the Bible, but the 'ground of all being'. Faith is no longer trust in a God who is there and who speaks truth that must be believed and obeyed, but a thoughtful self-abandonment to the claims of 'authentic existence'. When preaching, Bultmann used the traditional language of Christian spirituality, but what he meant was far removed from what was historically understood by such expressions. The Gospel of John was the closest of the four canonical Gospels to displaying the kind of 'demythologized' Christianity of which Bultmann approved (shades of the pre-Strauss praise of John), so he felt the greatest affinity for that Gospel. From his perspective, Bultmann was saving Christianity for modern men and women; from the perspective of his firmest critics, Bultmann had sacrificed the faith 'once for all entrusted to the saints' (Jude 3).

A number of factors have conspired to make Bultmann less influential than he once was. First, although some scholars, especially in Germany, still think that Gnosticism is the single greatest influence on the Fourth Gospel (one thinks of Haenchen's commentary), virtually no one argues for Mandaen Gnosticism. The evidence against the theory is too strong. Moreover, a strong (and in my judgment convincing) case can be made for the view that although neo-Platonism exerted a strong influence on some of the early churches, full-blown Gnosticism, complete with a gnostic-redeemer myth, does not put in an appearance until the very

---

[1]*Cf.* Rudolf Bultmann, 'New Testament and Mythology', in Hans Werner Bartsch (ed.), *Kerygma and Myth: A Theological Debate*, tr. Reginald H. Fuller (SPCK, 1953), pp. 1–44.

end of the first century, and that in many of its forms it is parasitic on Judaism and/or on Christianity.[1] It is disconcerting when these realities are not adequately weighed. For instance, in a recent essay evaluating 'Gnostic Sayings and Controversy Traditions in John 8:12–59' (in Hedrick/Hodgson, pp. 97–110), Helmut Koester draws a number of interesting parallels and simply *assumes* that the Evangelist knew of these or similar sayings, without addressing the possibility that in at least some instances the dependency may have gone the other way. This is reinforced by the recent work by Tuckett,[2] who offers convincing evidence that where the Synoptics can be paralleled in some measure by the gnostic documents from Nag Hammadi, the movement is from the Synoptics to Nag Hammadi. Although work of similar detail has not yet been done on John, it is doubtful if the outcome will be very different.[3] In any case, verbal parallels are of little significance unless the conceptual affinities are carefully sorted out.

Second, D. Moody Smith's decisive response to Bultmann's source-criticism[4] has meant that no-one follows Bultmann unhesitatingly in this respect. The source-criticism of John still has its supporters (*cf.* comments below, and in § III), but the detailed work of Bultmann has rightly suffered eclipse.

Third, the particularly virulent antisupernaturalism espoused by Bultmann has been mitigated by two factors. (1) However much the scholarly conventions of the time constrain many writers into a dispassionate, understated style (which of course has many advantages in academic debate), the fact of the matter is that many biblical scholars are firm believers. (2) Current scholarly interest on John is veering toward literary approaches that ask few *historical* questions (*i.e.* question about what really happened) in favour of asking *literary* questions (*i.e.* questions about how the text hangs together and conveys meaning). This focus has both advantages and disadvantages, as we shall see; but it certainly tends to mask the belief or unbelief of the interpreter, since the relevant historical questions are not posed.

Fourth, the radical scepticism about how much we can know of the historical Jesus has been dealt some dramatic blows. Quite apart from the fact that several of Bultmann's students launched a new quest for the historical Jesus (which many of us find rather reductionistic, but is a considerable improvement on its precursor), there were two developments that exercised major influence on the study of John.

First, in 1947 some bedouin boys stumbled across what came to be

---

[1]See especially E. M. Yamauchi, 'Pre-Christian Gnosticism in the Nag-Hammadi Texts?' *Church History* 48, 1979, pp. 129–141; *idem, Pre-Christian Gnosticism* (Baker, [2]1983).

[2]C. M. Tuckett, *Nag Hammadi and the Gospel Tradition: Synoptic Tradition in the Nag Hammadi Library* (T. & T. Clark, 1983).

[3]A few bits and pieces have been prudently assessed: *cf.* Craig A. Evans on the bearing of the *Trimorphic Protennoia* on the Prologue, in *NTS* 27, 1981, pp. 395–401.

[4]D. Moody Smith, *The Composition and Order of the Fourth Gospel: Bultmann's Literary Theory* (Yale University Press, 1965).

called the Dead Sea Scrolls of the Qumran community. Whatever significance they have in other areas of biblical study, so far as John is
concerned they provide countless parallels to the language and thought
of the Fourth Gospel. This is not to say that John borrows from Qumran,
or that the fourth Evangelist was once a monastic Jew living in a
Qumran-like hermitage himself: scholarly enthusiasm for such hypotheses has largely (and rightly) waned. The parallels between the Dead
Sea Scrolls and the Fourth Gospel are not of the sort that encourage
theories of direct dependence. What they do show, however, is that it is
altogether unnecessary to account for John's language, for his linguistic
dualisms (light/dark, from above/from below, *etc.*), even for some of his
choice expressions (*e.g.* 'Spirit of truth', 'the light of life', 'the sons of
light', 'doing the truth', 'the works of God') by appealing to a late
hellenistic environment. The closest parallels are often at Qumran, a
conservative, Jewish world that operated from about 150 BC to the fall of
Jerusalem and Judea. These parallels, then, have generated a 'new look'
at the Fourth Gospel (*cf.* Robinson, *Twelve*, pp. 94ff.). There remains a
considerable gulf between John and Qumran, as one of the earliest
scholars to draw connections between the two rightly noted.[1] But the
Qumran finds have touched off other studies that show, for instance,
how the form of argument in John and his exposition of Old Testament
Scripture draw from essentially Jewish streams of thought, so that the
number of scholars who confidently assign the Fourth Gospel to a
predominantly gnostic or hellenistic world is declining. Those who
continue in this path tend to proceed by way of pronouncement rather
than by way of detailed interaction with those more knowledgeable in
the Jewish sources.[2]

Second, the thesis of Gardner-Smith has taken hold of much of Johannine scholarship. Gardner-Smith argued that John is quite independent
of the Synoptics, *i.e.* that there is no evidence that the Fourth Gospel
was written as a theological 'correction' or 'addendum' to one or more of
the Synoptic Gospels. Much of the scepticism applied to John was built
on the assumption that because this Gospel was late and derivative, it
was correspondingly less reliable from the historical perspective. But if it
could be shown that this Gospel is *not* derivative, then perhaps it might
be argued that it preserves *independent* tradition regarding the original
events. In that case, what it preserves should be set over against the
Synoptics without prejudice. Dodd developed the argument into a
rigorous case in 1963 (*HTFG*), and has been followed by most commentators ever since (including Morris, *SFG*, pp. 15ff.). The position is
not without its weakness, as we shall see, but it has tended to diminish

---

[1] W. F. Albright, 'Recent Discoveries in Palestine and the Gospel of St John', in W. D.
Davies and D. Daube (eds.), *The Background of the New Testament and its Eschatology* (*Fs.*
C. H. Dodd; Cambridge University Press, 1954), esp. p. 170.
[2] To some extent this is true of the commentary by Haenchen, and of Helmut Koester, *op.
cit.*; and unequivocally true of the relevant essays in Hedrick/Hodgson.

the scepticism of the initial approach to John that many scholars at one time deployed.

3. The present position

The present position is characterized by considerable diversity not only of result but of method. I shall not attempt to survey the entire field: excellent surveys of the literature are readily available.[1] Instead, I shall limit myself to remarks in two areas. First, I shall briefly outline the views of a few of the dominant voices. Failure to mention certain figures does not mean their work is not valuable: *e.g.* there is no mention of the commentaries by R. H. Lightfoot and by Hoskyns and Davey. The latter is particularly suggestive, both from a theological perspective and on account of their treatment of the use of the Old Testament in John. But they are not discussed here (though they are cited in the commentary that follows) because, rightly or wrongly their work neither controls the present discussion nor represents a sizeable block of opinion. Second, I shall briefly outline the rising trend in Johannine studies, the application of 'literary criticism' or 'new criticism' to the Gospel of John. Evaluation can be postponed until the next section. This minimal survey is important if only to be able to appreciate the vantage points of the various authors to whom reference is made in the commentary that follows.

In the area of source-criticism, the most articulate voice is that of Fortna, who does not attempt to assign every word to one source or another, but who argues at great length for a coherent 'signs source' that can be retrieved from the Fourth Gospel. Like many others, he holds that the enumeration of the first two signs (2:11; 4:54) supplies substantial evidence that the signs themselves were once part of an enumerated list, a source that originally closed with 20:30–31. By and large, he has convinced few people that he is right in the hundreds of details about what should be included in this alleged source, but he has helped to convince many that there was indeed a signs source, even if its contents cannot be delineated with precision. Fortna's confidence in his details remains so strong that he has written a second book that attempts to distinguish between the theology of the source, as he reconstructs it, and the theology of the Gospel of John as it has come down to us.[2]

A rather different sort of source-criticism has been advanced by Brown. He is rather reluctant to apply the term 'source-criticism' to his own work. Even so, he holds that he has uncovered five layers of traditions that reflect the developing history of the Johannine community. He thinks of the Fourth Gospel as comprising an independent

---

[1] In addition to the technical bibliographies by H. Thyen (*ThR* 39, 1974, pp. 1–69, 222–252, 289–330; 42, 1977, pp. 211–270; 44, 1979, pp. 97–134) and Jürgen Becker (*ThR* 47, 1982, pp. 279–347), one might usefully consult Rudolf Schnackenburg, in *BETL*, pp. 19ff.; James McPolin, *IBS* 2, 1980, pp. 3–26; Kysar, *Fourth; idem, Int* 31, 1977, pp. 355–366; D. A. Carson, *Themelios* 9, 1983, pp. 8–18; *idem, Themelios* 14, 1989, pp. 57–64.

[2] Robert Fortna, *The Fourth Gospel and its Predecessor* (T. & T. Clark, 1989/Fortress, 1988).

tradition about Jesus (*i.e.* independent of the Synoptic Gospels) which was shaped into a distinctive Johannine presentation of the gospel. This was worked into a written Gospel, which was subsequently revised at least twice. Brown's views have developed since writing his commentary on the Fourth Gospel. These have been published both in popular form[1] and in a major commentary on the Johannine Epistles.[2] From his species of source-criticism, coupled with the extrapolations that are made possible by appealing to the Epistles of John, he suggests that the final product of the Fourth Gospel was associated with Christians interacting with six definable (and partially overlapping) groups: (1) Christians from apostolic churches whose Christology was perceived to be inadequate by the Johannine community. These other Christians could make the confessions of ch. 1; the Johannine community wanted to make the further confession that Jesus is God. Nevertheless unity with these Christians was perceived to be both possible and desirable (Jn. 17). (2) Jewish Christians whose faith depended heavily on signs and who rejected Christ's deity. The Johannine community did not view these as true believers (*cf.* Jn. 6:60–66). (3) 'Crypto-Christians', Jews who thought of themselves as Christians but who had not broken from the synagogue (some scholars, but not Brown, think of Nicodemus as the prototypical example). (4) Followers of John the Baptist who viewed him as more important than Jesus. Hence the polemic of 1:8; 3:30. (5) 'The Jews', *i.e.* unbelieving members of the synagogue in active opposition to the church, and now excommunicating any synagogue adherent who confessed Jesus to be the Messiah (9:22, 34). (6) The 'world', all those who reject the message of Jesus, Jews and Gentiles alike.

Those who follow Brown in all the details are few; those who think he is largely right, even if questionable on some of the details, are many. I shall say a little more about his reconstruction in the next section. For the moment, I would argue that, if John's Gospel was indeed put together from pieces, the view of Lindars is far more believable than that of Fortna or Brown. Much of John's Gospel, Lindars suggests, was originally sermonic material that the Evangelist successively put together. One does not have to agree with every suggestion Lindars has made about the way these sermons came together to see the intrinsic plausibility of the theory. It is tempting to postulate 'that the organizing of the traditions to form the Gospel took place through preaching, especially the preaching of the Evangelist' (Beasley-Murray, pp. xli–xlii). Indeed, there is much to be said for the view that each of the unambiguous narrative-discourse combinations in the first twelve chapters is constructed to present the good news of Jesus Christ as a complete overview, an evangelistic wholeness repeated from a wealth of different perspectives as the Fourth Gospel brings the various units together.

---

[1]Raymond E. Brown, *The Community of the Beloved Disciple* (Geoffrey Chapman/Paulist, 1979). For an alternative (though comparable) trajectory, *cf.* Martyn, *GJCH*.

[2]*Idem*, *The Epistles of John* (AB: Geoffrey Chapman, 1983/Doubleday, 1982).

Although the majority of commentators hold that John is independent of the Synoptic Gospels, this consensus is by no means universal. Owing primarily to the work of Neirynck[1] and de Solages[2], not to mention the detailed commentary by Barrett, a substantial minority of opinion is less than convinced that John's independence from the Synoptics can be so confidently affirmed. Perhaps the most careful evaluation is by Smith (*Essays*, pp. 97–172). The bearing of this debate on one's understanding of John's historical value will be probed a little in the next section.

As for the perceived background of the book, there is considerable diversity of opinion. It ranges from a decidedly Jewish and semitic background (*e.g.* Odeberg; Schlatter) to the various forms of Gnosticism preferred by Bultmann and Haenchen. Dodd (*IFG*) opts for the primary influence of the Hermetica, which our sources suggest are the writings of a second century AD gnosticizing movement. These purport to convey the instructions of Hermes Trismegistos (otherwise known as the Egyptian god Thoth). Dodd is followed by almost no one. Barrett is exceedingly eclectic, arguing that Jewish, hellenistic, gnostic and other influences all had their part to play in the shaping of the Fourth Gospel. Insofar as there is any consensus, it turns on what is most commonly perceived to be the *Sitz im Leben* ('setting-in-life') of the Fourth Gospel. Many scholars today hold that the Gospel of John was written toward the end of the first century to strengthen a church, probably in Asia Minor, that was either in dialogue with the local synagogue, or had just broken off such dialogue (though 'dialogue' may be too weak: 'evangelistic confrontation' is closer to what most scholars have in mind). If this reconstruction is correct (and I shall argue below, § VI, that it is not quite correct), then one must expect as part of the background of thought all the varieties of sources and belief that went into hellenistic Judaism at the end of the first century. This approach, more or less, is championed by Brown, Schnackenburg, and especially Martyn (*HTFG*).

As for the approach of modern commentators to the question of the historical value of the Fourth Gospel, there is no consensus at all. The field ranges from Morris, who argues that, however interested in theology John might be, he is interested in the trustworthiness of the witnesses, and committed to being historically accurate (even if necessarily selective); to Bultmann, who holds that on the historical front we can learn no more from John's Gospel than from the Synoptic Gospels, the bare *dass* ('that') of Jesus' existence. Along the way we might pause at Beasley-Murray, who thinks much good history is preserved in John, but that the Evangelist sometimes says things that are not *historically* true in order to preserve certain *theological* truth. Brown, Lindars and

---

[1]F. Neirynck in *BETL*, pp. 73–106; *idem*, in collaboration with Joël Delobel, Thierry Snoy, Gilbert van Belle, Frans van Segbroeck, *Jean et les synoptiques: Examen critique de l'exégèse de M.-E. Boismard* (BETL 49; Louvain University Press, 1979).

[2]Mgr. de Solages, *Jean et les synoptiques* (E. J. Brill, 1979).

Schnackenburg try to assess each pericope on its own, and emerge with somewhat disparate visions as to how much history is preserved in the Fourth Gospel. However conservative he is in much of his theology, Barrett insists that the Evangelist is simply not interested in historical questions, but is telling a story, in line with the traditions he received (and sometimes departing from them) in order to make various theological points. Especially in the passion narrative is Barrett convinced that John is almost worthless as a document that might inform us as to what actually happened. Martyn (*HTFG*) is so sceptical that he dissolves the tension between the claims of history and the claims of theology by thinking of 'history' as the history of the Johannine community: the Fourth Gospel, he thinks, tells us a fair bit about the history and the theology of *that community*, but virtually nothing about the history or the theology of Jesus himself.

Perhaps it should also be added that some authors, notably Dodd (*HTFG*), *sound* much more conservative in their historical judgments than they really are. In almost every pericope, Dodd finds some 'kernel' of historical truth, but it is usually very distant from what the text actually says. This distance is usually hidden behind the demonstrably reverent tone of the presentation, but the fact remains that, once Dodd's judgments are actually put together in hard light, it transpires that the total picture of Jesus in the Fourth Gospel is judged to be very unreal, as measured by the useful 'history' that Dodd actually 'uncovers' there. As one acute reviewer of Dodd has written, 'After all has been said, and every last particle of primitive gold-dust extracted, the Fourth Gospel is in its total character a much less reliable source of historical (especially biographical) information than Mark. . . .'[1]

If there is any 'cutting edge' to current studies on John, it belongs to those engaged in 'rhetorical criticism', 'new criticism', 'literary criticism': the labels vary. What is common in the diverse approaches represented by the works about to be mentioned is the primacy of a synchronic approach to the text: *i.e.* the scholars concerned do not ask, at least primarily, questions about the history of the text, the state of the Johannine community, the degree of John's historical trustworthiness, what sources can be detected, or the like. Rather, they ask how to make sense of the text as it stands, apart from any extra-textual reference it might make, and utilize a number of quite different models to answer that question.

Some of these studies examine only part of the Gospel. Olsson, for example, subjects John 2 – 4 to minute 'structural' examination to emerge with generally sane observations that nevertheless do not take us very far beyond what traditional exegesis produced. By contrast, Lona adopts a rather different approach to his chosen passage, John

---

[1] F. W. Beare, *NTS* 10, 1964, pp. 517–522. *Cf.* also D. A. Carson, 'Historical Tradition in the Fourth Gospel: After Dodd, What?' in *GP* 2, pp. 83–145.

8:33–56. He runs through it twice, the first time deploying the more or less standard critical tools, the second adopting the models of 'literary semiotics'. By this he means that he approaches the text synchronically, using models in communication theory and structuralist theory, in an attempt to establish a convergence of interpretations regarding the significance of Abraham. Kermode[1] provides an excellent example of how a literary critic can make sense of the Prologue (1:1–18) *as a text that is part of the Fourth Gospel* without resorting to the rather uncontrolled speculations about an original poem that John has allegedly borrowed, what bits are intrusions, what can be inferred about the *Sitz im Leben* that produced the Prologue, and so forth.

Others focus on a particular rhetorical device – Duke, for instance, on irony, and van Belle on the parenthetical 'asides' in John. O'Day pursues John's use of irony to the point where it becomes the locus of revelation, the 'how' of the way Jesus revealed the Father.[2]

But by far the most important and influential book in this area has been R. Alan Culpepper's *Anatomy of the Fourth Gospel* (1983). His aim is to provide the first comprehensive analysis of the Fourth Gospel using the categories of rhetorical criticism. He insists that meaning 'is produced in the mental moves the text calls for its reader to make, quite apart from questions concerning its sources and origin'. In successive chapters, then, Culpepper takes us through considerations of 'Narrator and Point of View', 'Narrative Time', 'Plot', 'Characters', 'Implicit Commentary' and 'The Implied Reader'. All the categories are drawn from the poetics (*i.e.* the 'rules' of literary-critical analysis) of the novel.

How this works out in practice is perhaps best conveyed by an example. In his second chapter, Culpepper distinguishes three terms. The *real author* refers to the person or persons who actually wrote the Fourth Gospel. The *implied author* 'is always distinct from the real author and is always evoked by a narrative. The Gospel of John, therefore, has an implied author simply by virtue of its being a narrative.' This *implied author* is an ideal or literary figure who may be inferred from the sum of the choices that constitute the narrative. He or she is a created version of the real author, and sometimes a subset of the real. The *narrator* is a rhetorical device, the voice that actually tells the story. The narrator *may* be dramatized as a character in the story; alternatively, the narrator may be undramatized, in which case the line between the narrator and the implied author becomes thin, though never entirely obliterated. The narrator actually tells the story, addresses the reader and resorts to explanatory asides – in short, the narrator is *intrusive* in the narrative.

The narrator of the Fourth Gospel, Culpepper argues, adopts omniscience as his psychological point of view. In literary criticism, this does

---

[1]Frank Kermode, *JSNT* 28, 1986, pp. 3–16. He has adopted something of the same approach, with only marginal success, while introducing the entire Gospel: *cf.* Robert Alter and Frank Kermode, *The Literary Guide to the Bible* (Collins, 1987), pp. 440–466.

[2]Not only in her book (*cf.* Abbreviations), but also in *JBL* 105, 1986, pp. 657–668.

not mean that the narrator is, like God, literally omniscient, but that he adopts a stance that enables him to provide inside information and views on what the characters are thinking, feeling, intending, believing, and so forth. Culpepper finds evidence for this in passages like 6:61; 13:28; 19:8. Similarly, there is a kind of 'omnipresence' to the narrator; he is 'present' in some sense as an unseen observer at the interview between the Samaritan woman and Jesus, because he is able to record what went on, to tell 'what no historical person could know'. Moreover, this narrator clearly writes retrospectively (*e.g.* 2:20–22; 7:39).

Based on this analysis, Culpepper proceeds to examine relationships between the narrator and Jesus (*e.g.* he finds both 'omniscient', and notes how the narrator so determines the language and idiom that both persons speak with exactly the same voice), and between the narrator and the implied author. Here Culpepper embarks on a rather important study of 21:24–25. He takes 21:24 to mean that the Evangelist (the real author) chooses to identify the implied author with the beloved disciple. 'When the narrator dramatically pulls the curtain on the implied author in the closing verses of the gospel, the reader recognizes that the Beloved Disciple fits the image the gospel projects of the implied author as one who knew Jesus intimately' (Culpepper, p. 47).

There is much more of the same, all of it worthy of lengthy discussion. But the dominant impression of the field of Johannine studies today is of considerable disagreement as to what the text says or implies, and disarray as to the best methods for studying the book. So perhaps this is the right place to offer a brief evaluation of some of these developments.

III. THE AUTHENTICITY OF THE FOURTH GOSPEL

Under the 'authenticity' of John's Gospel I mean to include a brief discussion of five topics that bear on one's evaluation as to how far the Fourth Gospel can be accepted as what it manifestly purports to be: a reliable witness to the origins, ministry, death, resurrection and exaltation of Jesus the Messiah. Such a witness does not have to be dispassionate, merely truthful. One accepts, for instance, that the first witnesses of Auschwitz were both truthful and passionate, even if in some circles they were at first easily dismissed because of their passion. But in retrospect, merely dispassionate witness regarding Auschwitz would be obscene. Similarly, a dispassionate witness to the person, teaching and work of Christ would necessarily be profane. To set theological commitment and historical reliability against each other as *necessarily* mutually incompatible is unrealistic; worse, it is an invitation to profanity. To put the matter another way:

One cannot therefore dissociate in John the witness of the past and the witness of the present, any more than one can dissociate in Jesus of Nazareth the man and the Word: the earthly life of Jesus cannot be reduced to that of an ordinary man, because a dimension of eternity will always smash the mould into which men try to force that earthly life. Yet the Gospel according to John is not just a theological meditation by a pious Christian living at the end of the first century; rather, it is a work in which the testimony of man and the testimony of the Spirit have been fused into one, to bring out the true meaning of Jesus' earthly life (Léon-Dufour, p. 106).

1. The possibility of effective source-criticism in John's Gospel

The retrieval of sources from the Gospel of John must be viewed as an extremely problematic endeavour.[1] There is no need to doubt that John used sources: his fellow-Evangelist Luke certainly did (Lk. 1:1–4), and there is no need to think that the fourth Evangelist followed some different course. Even here, however, caution is needed: Luke does not purport to be the result of eyewitness testimony, while John does. Quibbles about John's memory being a 'source' are beside the point: that is in one sense true, but entirely irrelevant, since the point of source-criticism is not to separate out memories from material obtained some other way, but to separate out *written* documents and external *oral* traditions that allegedly served as sources for the Gospel as we now have it.

Regardless of who wrote the Fourth Gospel, however, the presumption that the Evengelist used written sources is quite different from the assumption that we can retrieve them. One of the features of John's Gospel on which all sides agree is that stylistically it is cut from one cloth. The very feature that raises a difficulty – that John's comments and Jesus' speeches can sound so much the same – should also serve as a warning to those who think they can distinguish separate sources buried in the text. The stylistic unity of the book has been demonstrated again and again as concrete evidence against this or that source theory.[2] Elsewhere I have canvassed the major source theories produced this century and showed that the methods used and the results obtained are inconsistent, and that at countless junctures evidence that is adduced to support a source is better understood a different way.[3] Hengel rightly questions the likelihood that the Evangelist took over something like the

---

[1]For a useful survey of the application of source-criticism to the Fourth Gospel, cf. Smith, *Essays*, pp. 39–93.

[2]*E.g.* E. Schweizer, *Ego Eimi: Die religionsgeschichtliche Bedeutung der johanneischen Bildreden, zugleich ein Beitrag zur Quellenfrage des vierten Evangeliums* (Vandenhoeck und Ruprecht, 1939); E. Ruckstuhl, *Die literarische Einheit des Johannesevangeliums* (Paulus, 1951); *idem*, 'Johannine Language and Style', in *BETL*, pp. 125–147; G. van Belle, *De semeia–bron in het vierde evangilie: Ontstaan en groei van een hypothese* (Leuven University Press, 1975).

[3]D. A. Carson, *JBL* 97, 1978, pp. 411–429.

alleged 'Signs Source', which all sides admit (if it ever existed) boasted a theology radically different from that of the Evangelist, and incorporated it so mechanically that it can be retrieved by contemporary scholarship.[1] Indeed, if John knew of the Synoptic Gospels (*cf.* further discussion below), the one point on which all sides agree is that modern scholarship could not possibly reconstruct any block of Synoptic material from the text of John before us.

One of the more recent and creative attempts to use stylistic features to probe the unity of the Fourth Gospel is the statistically informed and understated study by Poythress[2] of the Greek conjunctions *de, kai,* and *oun,* along with the syntactical phenomenon of asyndeton. The frequency of the conjunctions is abnormally low in John; the frequency of asyndeton is unusually high. He demonstrates, so far as such evidence will take him (and he is aware of the pitfalls of small samples and the like) that this test argues for unified authorship of the Fourth Gospel, and common authorship between the Fourth Gospel and the Johannine Epistles.

It is this sort of evidence that has convinced commentators like Brown, Lindars and Haenchen that the pursuit of separable sources in the Fourth Gospel is a lost cause. That is why Brown prefers his pursuit of separable *traditions* that have allegedly evolved over the length of a certain trajectory of theological development (summarized in the last section); that is why Lindars prefers to think of a series of homilies that were collected, published, edited and added to over a period of time. But as influential as is, say, the five-step theory of Brown, it is important to see that it too is a kind of source theory, compounded with speculation about the *Sitz im Leben* ('setting-in-life') of each source – only in his case the sources are much fuzzier around the edges than the source postulated by Fortna. Brown of course prefers to talk about the development of 'traditions' rather than the delineation of 'sources.' Still, someone has to enter John's text with a literary scalpel and retrieve those traditions. It transpires that some of these lie on the surface, and are tied to certain words and expressions (which make them very similar indeed to literary 'sources'), while others are the reconstructions Brown offers to explain what he thinks must have generated this or that bit of text.

In other words, the source-criticism of Bultmann and Fortna has fallen on hard times because their hard evidence turns out to be patient of far simpler explanations, while the tradition-probing of Brown, which is far more speculative and much less controlled than Fortna's work, has exerted wide influence – presumably, one has to say, because it is self-coherent and therefore satisfying, but also utterly untestable. It must be remembered that the six groups Brown thinks the Gospel of John is confronting are mere inferences from the Gospel's text. Again

---

[1] Martin Hengel, 'The Wine Miracle at Cana', in L. D. Hurst and N. T. Wright (eds.), *The Glory of Christ in the New Testament* (*Fs.* G. B. Caird; Clarendon, 1987), p. 92.
[2] Vern Poythress, *NovT* 26, 1984, pp. 312–340; *idem, WTJ* 46, 1984, pp. 350–369.

and again, other inferences are possible, indeed preferable. And all of Brown's six groups, inferences as they are, are based on the prior inference, that it is relatively easy to read off from a text that purports to be about *Jesus* the life and circumstances and opponents of the group (!) that produces the document. Small wonder that Kysar (*Fourth*, p. 53) concludes, 'If the gospel evolved in a manner comparable to that offered by Brown and Lindars, it is totally beyond the grasp of the Johannine scholar and historian to produce even tentative proof that such was the case.'

There are philosophical questions related to this uncontrolled pursuit of sources and traditions that must be raised. In historical reconstruction, it is important not to assume an evolutionary 'developmental' model, and brilliant minds should not be multiplied beyond what is strictly necessary. Too many of the contemporary reconstructions begin with a hazy and barely discernible Jesus, followed by a number of sources, and climaxed by a brilliant Evangelist. One writer can go so far as to laud the Evangelists' brilliance for writing what sounds like history when everyone knows it is not: 'The Gospels sound like history, and that they do so is the consequence of an extraordinary rhetorical feat.'[1] One can think of a simpler explanation. As for the assumption of straightforward evolutionary development, the exasperation of Ratzinger is understandable:

> One can easily see how questionable the criteria have been by using a few examples. Who would hold that Clement of Rome is more developed or complex than Paul? Is James any more advanced than the Epistle to the Romans? Is the Didache more encompassing than the Pastoral Epistles? Take a look at later times: whole generations of Thomistic scholars have not been able to take in the greatness of his thought. Lutheran orthodoxy is far more medieval than was Luther himself. Even between great figures there is nothing to support this kind of developmental theory.
>
> Gregory the Great, for example, wrote long after Augustine, and knew of him, but for Gregory, the bold Augustinian vision is translated into the simplicity of religious understanding. Another example: what standard could one use to determine whether Pascal should be classified as before or after Descartes? Which of their philosophies should be judged the more developed? Further examples could be mentioned to illustrate the whole of human history. All judgments based on the theory of discontinuity in the tradition and on the assertion of an evolutionary priority of the 'simple' over the 'complex' can

---

[1] Frank Kermode, *The Genesis of Secrecy* (Harvard University Press, 1979), p. 113; cited also by Robinson, *John*, p. 26 n. 89.

thus be immediately called into question as lacking foundation.[1]

This is not to argue that even the most brilliant minds do not resort to
historical antecedents. Nor is it to say that sequences of development
cannot on occasion be traced out. But it is to warn against facile reconstructions of the development of Christian thought which at the end of
the day are no more than one possible set of inferences. From the
perspective of John himself, there was a remarkable development in the
disciples' *understanding* of who Jesus was, and much of this took place
after the resurrection and exaltation of their Lord. But it is a development of *understanding*, not of fresh theological invention. By constantly
drawing attention to the *mis*understandings of observers and disciples
alike during the days of Jesus' ministry, John shows he is able to
distinguish what he and others understood 'back then' and what he
came to understand only later. Indeed, he *insists* on the distinction: I
have catalogued the data elsewhere (Carson, 'Mis'), and this catalogue
constitutes a remarkably strong piece of evidence that the Evangelist
was self-consciously aware of the possibility of anachronism, and for his
own reasons studiously avoided it.

Of course, there is no *necessary* connection between source-criticism
and historical value. A coherent piece of literature could be written by
one author and be entirely fictive; an editor could piece together quite
different sources, checking them out carefully, and produce a piece of
front-rank historical reportage. But as actually practised, the pursuit of
sources and traditions in the study of John is rarely an end in itself, but a
proposed means of access to the development of Christian thought, or
to the history of the Johannine community. However insightful some of
these studies may be, at times it is necessary not only to question the
source-critical methods, but to demonstrate the remarkable fragility of
the underlying assumptions.

None of this discussion is meant to suggest that all problems in the
Fourth Gospel are purely in the eye of the beholder. It is merely to
suggest that comprehensive source theories are unacceptably speculative, and too frequently end up contradicting the only textual evidence
we actually have. The most prominent theories of dislocation or major
editorial insertion are briefly discussed in the notes on 6:1, 22; 7:1;
13:31ff.; 14:31; 21:1ff., 24–25; the significance of the enumeration of the
first two signs is discussed in the notes on 4:43–45, 54.

It seems far more likely that the Evangelist, himself a Christian
preacher, proclaimed the gospel for years. Doubtless he made notes;
doubtless he learned from others, and incorporated the work of others.
But whatever he took from other sources, like any good preacher he
made it his own: the high degree of uniformity of style demonstrates

---

[1]Joseph Cardinal Ratzinger, *Biblical Interpretation in Crisis* (The Fourth Annual Erasmus
Lecture; The Rockford Institute, 1988), p. 10.

that much. Eventually he put the material together, and published it as a book. It is quite conceivable that he produced the work in stages; it is unlikely that the work was released in stages, at least in stages with long delays between them, since there is no textual evidence of a distinction between earlier and later editions. There is in any case a sureness of touch, a simplicity of diction, and a unity of theme and development, that rhetorical criticism rightly applauds, and that testifies to a mature Christian witness and theologian. There is no need whatsoever to posit a later ecclesiastical redactor: the awkward jumps of one sort or another are exactly the sort of thing an author may leave in and a redactor is supposed to smooth out. In source-critical theory, of course, the redactor does not succeed in smoothing out everything, since once again it is the awkwardness of his redactional work that provides the clues to his existence; but how one can adequately distinguish between the aporias (as the 'awkward jumps' are called) of the Evangelist and the aporias of a hypothetical redactor in a work as stylistically uniform as this one has never been adequately explained. 'To put the same point in another way, if it was possible for a redactor to leave the Gospel in this form, it was equally possible for the evangelist to do so. We have no need to postulate a redactor.'[1]

2. The challenge of the stylistic unity

If the stylistic unity spells *finis* to source-critical approaches to John, the converse problem must be explored: Why should the Evangelist present his Gospel in this way, *i.e.* so as to betray little *stylistic* distinction between his own words and those of his Lord? Seven things may be said:

(a) Although the style of the Fourth Gospel is remarkably uniform throughout, the point must not be overstated. Reynolds (pp. cxxiii–cxxv) lists about 150 words that are placed on Jesus' lips in John but are never used elsewhere by the Evangelist. Not a few of these are sufficiently general that they would have been as appropriate in the Evangelist's narrative as in Jesus' discourse. This does not provide impetus for renewing efforts at source-criticism: no one suggests that the words placed on Jesus' lips were drawn from an independent source. Moreover, it has also been shown that where the distribution of a stylistic marker is *uneven* (*e.g.* in the relative frequency of the 'historic present' in non-discourse material, and its relative infrequency in the discourses) the pattern of scattering is so independent that it gives no support to any of the current source theories.[2]

Still, the relative stylistic uniformity of the book should not be ignored. Other factors must be considered.

---

[1]Leon Morris, 'The Composition of the Fourth Gospel', in W. Ward Gasque and William Sanford LaSor (eds.), *Scripture, Tradition, and Interpretation* (Fs. Everett F. Harrison; Eerdmans, 1978), p. 172. *Cf.* also Robinson, *Red*, p. 310.
[2]John J. O'Rourke, *JBL* 93, 1974, pp. 585–590.

(b) Westcott (1. cxv–cxix) argues at some length that there are different ways of reporting a discourse or an extensive dialogue, and his point has rightly been taken up by many. It is not simply a question of length: verbatim versus condensed version. It is also a question of the style and purpose of the reportage. At some point capturing the flavour of a discourse by including an array of verbatim phrases and quips may be important; at another, it may be far more strategic to zero in on the essential argument and outline it fairly, even if the language used is quite different from that of the original address. 'A many-sided speaker will . . . furnish materials for very different studies. But it would be wholly wrong to conclude that the sketch which preserves most literally those fragments of his words, which are capable of being so preserved, is more true than the sketch which gives a view of the ultimate principles of his doctrine. The former may give the manner and even the outward characteristics: the latter may reveal the soul' (Westcott, 1. cxv). Westcott goes on to provide useful examples.

(c) The general point may perhaps be strengthened if we think of the material in John's Gospel as first of all sermonic. A number of features are probably best explained by supposing we are 'listening' to a preacher's revised sermons. The doubled 'Amen!' on Jesus' lips, for instance (*cf.* notes on 1:51), found only in John, is just such a homiletical device, and causes no umbrage unless for some strange reason we suppose that preachers in the ancient world could appeal only to verbatim quotations. Some of what is included in or excluded from John's Gospel is much better accounted for by reflecting on the Evangelist's situation *as a Christian preacher*, so far as we can reconstruct it from both internal and external evidence, than by supposing that the Evangelist is including all he knows, or is attempting to correct some other Gospel, or is simply ignorant of some vital fact preserved elsewhere. The absence of narrative parables, especially parables about the kingdom, suggests that this preacher's audience is not steeped in apocalyptic and not linguistically semitic. The prevalence of so much terminology that has almost *universal* religious appeal (*cf.* comments below) suggests the Evangelist is trying to use language that will present the fewest barriers.

This does not mean that John is uninterested in, say, the kingdom of God. Quite apart from the cruciality of the few places where he *does* use the expression (3:3, 5; *cf.* 18:36), the *theme* of the kingdom is very powerfully presented in certain passages (*cf.* this commentary on chs. 18 – 19, for instance). Moreover, the kingdom in the Synoptic Gospels is often a 'tensive symbol' that can bear an extraordinary number of overtones.[1] This ensures that in some passages, for instance, 'entering

---

[1] *Cf.* J. Jeremias, *New Testament Theology 1: The Proclamation of Jesus* (SCM, 1971), pp. 32–34; Norman Perrin, *Jesus and the Language of the Kingdom* (SCM/Fortress, 1976), esp. pp. 29–34; R. T. France, 'The Church and the Kingdom of God: Some Hermeneutical Issues', in D. A. Carson (ed.), *Biblical Interpretation and the Church: Text and Context* (Paternoster, 1984), pp. 30–44.

the kingdom' is indistinguishable from 'entering into life' (*e.g.* Mt. 7:14, 21) – and John certainly has a great deal to say about life. In short, the fourth Evangelist is interested in presenting certain truths to certain people, and he exercises the preacher's prerogative of shaping his message accordingly. It has often been remarked that John's Gospel, however profound it may be, is narrower in focus than the Synoptics. When this narrowness of focus fills the entire page, certain things come to light that would not otherwise be seen, but a certain sense of dislocation in the reader is understandable. Once what the preacher (*i.e.* the Evangelist) is doing becomes clear, *i.e.* when the *scale* of his vision is clarified, the sense of dislocation largely evaporates.

(d) Of course, this preacher is not *just* a preacher. He presents himself as an eyewitness, a reliable (*cf.* notes on 19:35; 21:24) intermediary between the events themselves and the people who now need to hear them. Nor is he alone: he is conscious of the continuity of Christian truth (*cf.* notes on 1:14–18) and especially of the Spirit's role in equipping him for this task (15:26–27; 16:12–15). So far as John's understanding of his task goes, we may speak of the liberty he felt to use his own language, of the principles of selection that governed his choices of material, of the nature of the audience (and now the readership) that he envisioned, of the focus of his interests, of his remarkable habit of getting at the heart of an issue. But we may not glibly suppose that one who felt so strongly about the importance of fidelity in witnesses (*cf.* 10:40–42) could simply invent narrative and dialogue and pass it off as history. As for the way these observations bear on the literary genre of the 'Gospel' form, *cf.* § VI, on the purpose of the Fourth Gospel, below.

(e) Because the Spirit who helps the disciples of Jesus bear witness to him after the resurrection is none other than the Spirit of Jesus, some conclude that for the Evangelist the teaching he conveys from the Spirit is so much of a piece with the teaching of Jesus that questions of anachronism do not worry him. That is why John feels free to use the same language and style throughout his book. Put so clumsily, this says too much. We have already seen that John constantly distinguishes between what Jesus' disciples understood in the days of his flesh, and what they understood only later. That is not simply a point of antiquarian interest for the Evangelist: it is a theological axiom, since no New Testament writer insists more strongly than he that the disciples understood very little until after the resurrection of Jesus and the descent of the Spirit whom he bequeathed (*cf.* Carson, 'Mis').[1]

Even so, the point can be made less clumsily, and therefore more

---

[1] *Cf.* van Belle's nearly exhaustive study of John's 'parentheses' or asides, designed, he says, to make the reader follow everything, even when the people in the narrative cannot. For a supplementary list, *cf.* F. Neirynck, *EphThLov* 65, 1989, pp. 119–123. More important yet, Carl J. Bjerkelund (*Tauta Egeneto: Die Präzisierungssätze im Johannesevangelium* [WUNT 40; J. C. B. Mohr (Paul Siebeck), 1987] esp. pp. 133–145) argues that the explanatory asides and the fulfilment citations are so linked as to show John's profound commitment to both historical and salvation-historical distinctions.

acceptably. For John, there is only one, supreme revelation: the revelation of God in Jesus Christ. Whatever revelation *preceded* the revelation of Jesus merely anticipated him; whatever revelation is provided *after* Jesus' death and exaltation is still the revelation of the Son: the Spirit takes of what is his and makes it known to the disciples (16:14), bringing to their minds the things that Jesus himself taught and helping them to understand their meaning (14:26). To use the language of Hebrews, the climactic revelation is the Son-revelation (Heb. 1:1–2). Thus, although John is perfectly capable of making historical distinctions between what was understood earlier and what was grasped only later, nevertheless the revelation itself is all of a piece: it is the revelation of the Son of God. Without sacrificing the historical integrity of an account that insists on the development of understanding over time, the Evangelist may therefore have felt freer to couch his Gospel in one style, his own style, precisely because he undertakes to present the entire Son-revelation, including the graduated understanding of those who received it, from the vantage of one who had received the Spirit and been commissioned to pass on the good news.

(f) The differences between John and the Synoptics, significant as they are, should not be exaggerated. There is of course the 'Johannine thunderbolt' (Mt. 11:27 par.), *i.e.* the passage that sounds very Johannine buried in the Synoptics: it is altogether plausible that Jesus sometimes spoke in nothing less than what we think of as 'Johannine' style, and that John's style was to some degree influenced by Jesus himself. Beyond this, however, numerous subtle parallels between John and the Synoptics repeatedly recur. Some of these will be noted in the commentary. But mention of the Synoptics brings up the next point.

(g) Several of the discourses have been shown, with some degree of plausibility, to be modelled on the rabbinic commentaries of the day. These 'midrashim' (as they are called) are so tightly knit that it is very difficult to believe they are nothing more than isolated (and retrievable!) sayings of Jesus onto which a pastiche of commentary has been patched. This leads to one of two conclusions. Borgen, who has demonstrated the finely-wrought nature of the 'bread of life' discourse (6:26–59) as in part an exposition of Exodus 16, argues for the unity of the discourse but does not attribute it to Jesus. Hunter (pp. 97–98) likewise recognizes the unity, but thinks there is no evidence to prevent us from concluding the discourse is authentic. What must be added is that, granted its essential authenticity, the discourse has been cast into its shape and place in the Gospel by the Evangelist, whose style so largely stamps the whole. Similar things could be said about the midrashic nature of parts of John 12, the chiastic structure of 5:19–30, the cohesiveness of the dialogue with Nicodemus, and much more.

In other words, the Fourth Gospel's stylistic unity, considered at the level of vocabulary and syntax, argues for a unified authorial stamp that makes the pursuit of sources a dubious enterprise. Its compositional integrity, considered at the level of the cohesiveness of the argumentation in many of its narratives and discourses, argues for a similar conclusion, and suggests that the pursuit of merely brief, aphoristic utterances of Jesus (Did Jesus never utter more than an aphorism?) is similarly ephemeral. Grant to the Evangelist all stylistic licence: when all the evidence is taken together, it is not hard to believe that when we listen to the voice of the Evangelist in his description of what Jesus said, we are listening to the voice of Jesus himself.[1]

3. The relation between the Fourth Gospel and the Synoptics

The debate on the relationship between John and the Synoptics has often been cast in terms of simple disjunction: either John knows the Synoptics and depends upon them, or he does not. But we must not succumb to the tendency 'to speak of John's knowledge and use of the synoptics as if one necessarily meant the same as, or followed from, the other' (Smith, *Essays*, p. 148). No-one argues that John used Mark in the way that Matthew used Mark (assuming the dependence of the first two Gospels ran that way). But if the work of Dodd (*HTFG*) and others is right, and John preserves independent tradition, then the places where John and Mark seem to be very close (*e.g.* in the ordering of events in Jn. 6/Mk. 6) could be taken as evidence not of direct literary dependence but of common dependence on oral tradition, and ultimately on the order of the events themselves.

To put it like this, however, immediately exposes the complexity of the issue. The matter cannot be resolved simply by a close examination of John and the other Gospels. Irretrievably bound up with the question of literary dependence are several other issues, all of them disputed: (a) relative dates of composition: *e.g.* if Mark and John were both written during the 60s of the first century, there is intrinsically less likelihood of literary dependence than if Mark were written in, say, AD 50 or 55, and John were written in AD 90; (b) authorship: if we are not talking about lengthy descent of traditions in relative isolation from each other, but of apostolic authorship, *i.e.* of Peter standing behind the work of John Mark (as external evidence argues) and of John behind the Fourth Gospel, then explanations that rely on 'oral tradition' appear less plausible, while the likelihood of continued communication between friends like Peter and John is increased; (c) the relationship between the *events themselves* and what is found in the Gospels: for regardless of whether John depends on Mark, the easiest explanation as to why John 6 and Mark 6 preserve the same order of events *is that they actually occurred in that order*.

It is important to remember that the Gospels were written within the

---

[1] For useful reflection on the historical value of the discourses (or, better, the dialogues) in John, *cf.* Robinson, *Priority*, ch. 7.

lifetime of some who knew Jesus himself. The studies on which so much form- and redaction-criticism have been based, the works on which so much effort to delineate the 'descent of the oral tradition' turn, were careful examinations of the passing on of traditions within a pre-literate society (the Maoris) over three hundred years or more.[1] But in the Gospels we are dealing with a literate society (as the prologue of Luke attests), with books written within decades, not centuries, of the matters they describe. The observations of Green-Armytage (quoted also by Robinson, *Red*, p. 356) are a bit cheeky and reductionistic, but bear repeating:

> There is a world – I do not say a world in which all scholars live but one at any rate into which all of them sometimes stray, and which some of them seem permanently to inhabit – which is not the world in which I live. In my world, if *The Times* and *The Telegraph* both tell one story in somewhat different terms, nobody concludes that one of them must have copied the other, nor that the variations in the story have some esoteric significance. But in the world of which I am speaking this would be taken for granted. There, no story is ever derived from facts but always from somebody else's version of the same story. . . . In my world, almost every book, except some of those produced by Government departments, is written by one author. In that world almost every book is produced by a committee, and some of them by a whole series of committees. In my world, if I read that Mr Churchill, in 1935, said that Europe was heading for a disastrous war, I applaud his foresight. In that world, no prophecy, however vaguely worded, is ever made except after the event. In my world we say, 'The first world-war took place in 1914–1918.' In that world they say, 'The world-war narrative took shape in the third decade of the twentieth century.' In my world men and women live for considerable time – seventy, eighty, even a hundred years – and they are equipped with a thing called memory. In that world (it would appear) they come into being, write a book, and forthwith perish, all in a flash, and it is noted of them with astonishment that they 'preserve traces of primitive tradition' about things which happened well within their own adult lifetime.[2]

Where so much ink has been spilled on complex questions, it would be invidious to attempt rigorous analysis of the problem in so short a commentary as this. I can do no more than summarize my conclusions:

---

[1] *Cf.* D. A. Carson, 'Redaction Criticism: On the Legitimacy and Illegitimacy of a Literary Tool', in Carson/Woodbridge I, pp. 119–142, 376–381.

[2] A. H. N. Green-Armytage, *John Who Saw: a Layman's Essay on the Authorship of the Fourth Gospel* (Faber and Faber, 1952), pp. 12–13.

(a) The thesis that John is *literarily* dependent on one or more of the Synoptic Gospels has not been demonstrated beyond reasonable doubt, but neither has the thesis that John is literarily *in*dependent of the Synoptics.

(b) Direct literary dependence should not in any case be the exclusive issue. When we see how free John is when citing or alluding to the Old Testament, we perceive that if he adopted a similar practice when citing or alluding to other written works it would be exceedingly difficult to reconstruct any part of them from the Gospel he has written. My views on the dating and authorship of the various Gospels, coupled with the alignment of such literary evidence as we have (in particular the parallels between John and Mark, and to some extent between John and Luke),[1] suggest that John had read Mark, and probably Luke. It is not impossible that he read Matthew, but that is harder to prove.[2] But if he had them before him as he wrote, he did not consult them, or at least he did not make verbatim use of them. John wrote his own book. The *reasons* why he left out so much of their material will be probed below, for Smith is right when he says that if John knew one or more of the Synoptics, 'the question of why he made no greater use of them requires a convincing answer'(*Essays*, p. 148).

(c) The relationship between John and the Synoptics should not be evaluated exclusively in terms of the dependence one may have on the other, nor in terms of their divergences, but also in terms of their similarities and their *interlocking* connections. As for their similarities (on which cf. Blomberg, pp. 156–157), one thinks not only of parallel incidents and sayings, but of subtle touches. Parallel incidents include the Spirit's anointing of Jesus as testified by John the Baptist (Mk. 1:10 par. / Jn. 1:32), the contrast between the Baptist's baptism with water and the Messiah's anticipated baptism with the Spirit (Mk. 1:7–8 par. / Jn. 1:23), the feeding of the five thousand (Mk. 6:32–44 par. / Jn. 6:1–15),[3] and the walking on the water (Mk. 6:45–52 par. / Jn. 6:16–21). Many sayings (including Mt. 9:37–38 par. / Jn. 4:35; Mk. 6:4 par. / Jn. 4:44; Mt. 25:46 / Jn. 5:29; Mt. 11:25–27 par. / Jn. 10:14–15; Mk. 4:12 par. / Jn. 12:39–40; Mt. 18:12–14 / Lk. 15:3–7 / Jn. 10:1–15; Mt. 10:40 / Mk. 9:37 / Jn.

---

[1]In addition to the works of Barrett, Neirynck and de Solages, already cited, useful information and reflection can be found in J. Blinzler, *Johannes und die Synoptiker* (Katholisches Bibelwerk, 1965); E. F. Seigman, 'St John's Use of the Synoptic Material', *CBQ* 30, 1968, pp. 182–198; and especially M. E. Glasswell, 'The Relationship between John and Mark', *JSNT* 23, 1985, pp. 99–115.

[2]But cf. Gerhard Maier, 'Johannes und Matthäus – Zweispalt oder Viergestalt des Evangeliums?' in *GP* 2, pp. 267–291, who argues that there are numerous suggestive links between Matthew and John, especially in the passion narrative. For a summary, cf. Blomberg, p. 159.

[3]The sequence of events surrounding the feeding of the five thousand and the walking on the water is particularly rich in parallels between John and Mark, and much appealed to by those who insist John is directly dependent on Mark. For the contrary view, cf. the detailed comparison offered by P. W. Barnett, 'The Feeding of the Multitude in Mark 6/John 6', in *GP* 6, pp. 273–293.

12:44–45) are at least partially parallel, though not decisively attesting literary dependence. Some of them are detailed in the commentary that follows.

But the more subtle parallels are no less significant. Although John reports no narrative parables, he, no less than the Synoptists, describes a Jesus given to colourful metaphors and proverbs, many drawn from the world of nature (*e.g.* sowing and reaping, 4:37; the apprenticeship of the Son, 5:19–20a; slavery versus sonship, 8:35; working in the daylight, 9:4; 11:9–10; the shepherd, the thief, the gatekeeper, the sheep pen, 10:1ff.; the grain of wheat, 12:24; the vine and the vinedresser, 15:1–6; the woman in labour, 16:21). Whatever is made of the 'messianic secret' motif in Mark, the obvious parallel is the 'misunderstanding' theme in John. All four Gospels depict a Jesus with a unique sense of sonship to his heavenly Father, including the atypical form of personal address to God, '*Abba*, Father.' All the Gospels note the distinctive authority Jesus displays in his teaching; all of them show Jesus referring to himself as the 'Son of Man', with no-one else using that title to refer to him or to anyone else (Jn. 12:34 is no real exception). And, contrary to those who argue that in the Synoptics the miracles are simply the product of faith, while in John the 'signs' are what induce faith, in fact both the Synoptics and John have overlapping perspectives. In the Synoptics, miracles are not merely the result of faith: they are the consequence of Jesus' compassion (Mt. 9:36; 14:14; Mk. 1:41; Lk. 7:13), a means for accrediting Jesus (Mt. 11:4ff.), and a pointer to the cross (Mt. 8:17; *cf.* Carson, *Matt*, pp. 204–207). Meanwhile, if in John the signs should function to call faith into being (*e.g.* 10:38), the people can be rebuked for relying on them (4:48), much as in the Synoptics (*e.g.* Mt. 16:1–4), while faith based on the word of the witness is to be preferred (Jn. 20:29).[1]

But more impressive yet are the many places where John and the Synoptics represent an *interlocking* tradition, *i.e.* where they mutually reinforce or explain each other, without betraying overt literary dependence (*cf.* especially Morris, *SFG*, pp. 40–63; Robinson, *John*, chs. 4 – 6). An incomplete list might mention the following.

(i) John's report of an extensive Judean ministry is needed to explain several features in the Synoptics, which record a fairly brief Galilean ministry (about a year) and only a few days in Jerusalem prior to Jesus' death. Why, then, even in Mark (14:49) does Jesus say he taught in the temple courts 'every day' (NEB 'day after day')? How could the authorities have become so angry with him as to plot his execution, unless he had spent earlier periods in Judea? Similarly, why should the final trip southward have been viewed with such trepidation (Mk. 10:32; *cf.* Mt. 20:17; Lk. 18:31), unless Jesus had been south on earlier occasions and the animus of the Jewish leaders was already apparent? The Fourth

---

[1]For a balanced treatment, *cf.* R. Kysar, *John: The Maverick Gospel* (John Knox, 1976), pp. 65–83.

Gospel provides a concrete occasion (Jn. 11:1ff.). Even Jesus' ability to round up an ass (Mk. 11:1ff.) and to secure a furnished upper room (Mk. 14:12–16) is much easier to understand if we presuppose that he had numerous contacts in Judea from previous trips to that province. In the Synoptics, Jesus *knows* the family of Mary and Martha (Lk. 10:38–42), but only John's depiction of Jesus' ministry in the south explains how intimacy could be maintained with a family living in Bethany. *Cf.* also Hunter, pp. 57ff.

(ii) One of the charges levelled against Jesus at his trial was that he had threatened the destruction of the temple (Mk. 14:58 par.). Although there was insufficient evidence on the point to do Jesus any damage, the same charge was mockingly tripped out on Calvary (Mk. 15:29 par.). It even appears in the charges against Stephen (Acts 6:14). But it is only John who reports Jesus saying anything like this (Jn. 2:19), and at a period toward the *beginning* of his ministry, perhaps two years before his trial – which helps to explain why the witnesses could not get their stories together.

(iii) Still on the subject of the trial, Mark gives no reason as to why the Jewish authorities should reach their decision (14:64) and then carry Jesus off to Pilate. It is John who insists that they had no power to execute a prisoner (18:31). Some of the difficult historical questions relating to this point are treated in the commentary. What must be noted, however, is that John alone gives an explanation of what is reported by the Synoptists, and provides the rationale that makes sense of their texts.

(iv) Still related to the passion narrative, only John provides a reason as to why Peter can be placed within the high priest's courtyard (a point attested by the Synoptics, Mk. 14:54, 66ff. par.) at the time he disowns his Lord (Jn. 18:15–16).

(v) At the other end of Jesus' ministry, the Synoptic accounts of the call of some of Jesus' disciples (Mt. 4:18ff. par.) are more easily understood, from the historical point of view, if we presuppose, with John 1, that Jesus had prior contact with them, and that the fundamental shift in allegiance had already taken place.

(vi) If the speed and insistence with which Jesus compels his disciples to leave, after the feeding of the five thousand, while he himself retreats into the mountains to pray, seems somewhat incongruous (Mk. 6:45–46 par.), it is John who provides a ready explanation: the people were on the verge of proclaiming Jesus king, a king shaped by their hopes and expectations but not the kind of king Jesus really was (Jn. 6:15).

(vii) At several points, John provides explicit theological justification for actions or motifs common in the Synoptics, but relatively unexplained. Consider, for instance, the commonly noted fact that the Synoptics report many exorcisms while John records none. It is true that the Synoptics provide some theological reflection on what Jesus is doing when he eliminates demons from human personalities (*e.g.* Mt. 12:25–28; Lk. 11:14–26); but it is the Fourth Gospel that provides 'a theology of the devil' (Bishop Cassian, *SE* I, p. 146; also cited by Morris, *SFG*, p. 56). Jesus' opponents in John's Gospel trace their paternity to the devil himself (8:44). The betrayer is moved and inspired by the devil (6:70; 13:2). Although the devil is three times referred to as 'the prince of this world', in the climactic struggle he has no hold on Jesus (14:30) and is defeated by him (12:31; 16:11). In short, John as usual, is profoundly interested in the undergirding theology. If he reports no exorcisms, it may be less because he is ignorant of any such reports (!), or that he finds them distasteful, as that in the circles in which he is preaching most exorcists belonged to a well-known class of pagan miracle-workers from which he specifically wants to distance Jesus.[1] Again, although the Synoptics (especially Luke) devote quite a bit of space to prayer, passages such as Matthew 7:7–8; 17:20; Mark 11:22–24 which promise such enormous benefits from prayer are theologically deepened and constrained by passages such as John 14:13–14; 15:7–8, 16; 16:23, 26, where the blessings and promises and benefits of prayer, though not at all diminished, are more integrally tried to the 'name' of Jesus, to intimate union with him, to the ultimate goal of prayer – that the Father might be glorified in the Son.[2]

This interlocking pattern cuts the other way, though so far as I know it has never been adequately explored. In other words, if John often usefully explains something in the Synoptic Gospels, the Synoptists frequently provide information that enables us to make better sense of something in the Fourth Gospel. In John 18 – 19, the narrative plunges so quickly from the Jewish setting to the Roman court that it is difficult to see just what judicial action the Jews have taken, if any. The Synoptics provide the answer. Although John's Prologue pronounces that Jesus is the Word that was with God and was God, and that has now become flesh, and although his Gospel happily refers to Jesus' mother (2:1–5, 12; 19:25–27) and even to his 'father and mother' (6:42), nothing begins even remotely to explain by what means the one who shared glory with the Father before the world began (17:5) somehow became the son of Mary. For that, the birth narratives in Matthew and Luke are far more helpful; indeed, it is quite possible (though not provable) that they are presupposed by John, and used by him to inject irony into his text at 6:42; 7:27, 42. Even a saying like that reported in 4:44 ('Now Jesus himself had pointed out that a prophet has no honour in his own country') which has so many difficulties in its context in John's Gospel (*cf.* the commentary notes), is adjudged a hard saying because it is already found in Matthew 13:57. Why is it that Philip apparently hesitates to bring the Gentiles to Jesus in John 12:21–22, consulting with

---

[1]Incidentally, this suggestion does not jeopardize the thesis of this commentary that the Fourth Gospel was written to evangelize diaspora Jews, proselytes and God-fearers (*cf.* § VI, below); *cf.* Sceva and his sons, Acts 19:13–16.

[2]*Cf.* M. M. B. Turner, 'Prayer in the Gospels and Acts', in D. A. Carson (ed.), *Teach Us To Pray: Prayer in the Bible and the World* (Paternoster/Baker, 1989), ch. 4.

Andrew before actually approaching Jesus? The Fourth Gospel provides no clear answer. But it is quite possible that Jesus' earlier restriction of his disciples' ministry to Jews, not reported in John (*cf*. Mt. 10:5, 'Do not go among the Gentiles'), still lurks in Philip's mind and urges restraint.

Far more could be said about the interlocking nature of the relationship between the Fourth Gospel and the Synoptics. Precisely because it cuts both ways, because no direct, literary dependence can be proved, because no collusion can be demonstrated, it is far-fetched to think that John provides the information he does in order to escape from some difficulty he finds with the Synoptics. Nor is this an instance of perversely conservative harmonization, as if John cannot properly be read without referring to the Synoptics, and vice versa, resulting in a reductionistic flattening of the individual witness of each Gospel.[1] Rather, it is the *incidental* nature of these interlocking patterns that proves of such value to the historian. I am not arguing that John's *theological* thrusts connected with his passion narrative cannot be appreciated without reading the Synoptics, or that the *theological* points the individual Synoptists make when they describe the call of the disciples cannot be grasped without referring to what John has to say on the matter. Rather, I am suggesting that at the historical level the pattern is much bigger and much more complex than any one Gospel intimates. Something of that complexity can be sketched in by sympathetically examining the interlocking nature of the diverse Gospel presentations. The result makes good historical sense of many passages that have too quickly been written off by critics prone to disjunctive thinking.

(d) The lessons gleaned from this pattern of interlocking traditions have some bearing on the larger array of perceived chronological and other contradictions that lie between John and the Synoptics. In particular, one must constantly ask whether there is some larger historical reality that supports both the witness of John and the witness of one or more of the Synoptics. These sorts of considerations are borne in mind in the commentary that follows. For discussion of John the Baptist's understanding of who he is, *cf*. notes on 1:21; of the 'Johannine Pentecost', *cf*. notes on 20:17–23; of the cleansing of the temple, *cf*. notes on 2:12–22; of the difficulties surrounding the passion narrative, *cf*. notes on John 18 – 19; and particularly of the chronological problems of relating John's passion narrative with those of the Synoptics, *cf*. notes on 13:1, 27; 18:28; 19:14, 31, 36, 42.

Two or three illustrations may be useful. We have observed that the long list of Christological confessions in John 1 are variously explained. Certainly these early confessions are rather different from the witness of the Synoptics, where the confession of Caesarea Philippi (Mk. 8:27–30 par.) is much more central to the developing narrative. We recall

---

[1]For a useful treatment of the *proper* use of harmonization, *cf*. Craig L. Blomberg, 'The Legitimacy and Limits of Harmonization', in Carson/Woodbridge II, pp. 135–174.

Brown's theory that John puts all of these Christological confessions into his first chapter because he is quietly reproving the other Christian communities for holding *only* these confessional standards, while he himself is insisting on something more, on confessing Jesus as God – the climactic confession of his own work (20:28).

Brown's theory introduces more difficulties than it solves. In any case, if we listen to John and to the Synoptics with both theological *and* *historical* sympathy, a simpler resolution presents itself. On its own, John's account makes good historical sense. For disciples of the Baptist to dissociate themselves from him while he is at the height of his power and influence, and transfer their allegiance to someone from Galilee, still unknown and unsought, is most readily explained as the Evangelist explains it: John the Baptist himself pointed out who Jesus was, insisting that he came as his precursor, his forerunner. Those most in tune with the Baptist, most sympathetic to his message, would then prove most likely to become the followers of Jesus, and for the reason given: they believed him to be the promised Messiah, the King of Israel, the Son of God (a category which our sources show could serve as a designation of 'Messiah': *cf.* notes on 1:49). None of this means that Jesus' fledgling followers enjoyed a full, Christian understanding of these titles: of all four Evangelists, it is John who most persistently catalogues how much the early disciples *mis*understood. And all of this, as I have said, makes good intrinsic sense.

But so does the Synoptic presentation. It is only to be expected that Jesus' disciples grew in their understanding of who he was. Constantly astonished by the kind of 'messiah' he was turning out to be, they nevertheless came with time to settled conviction: he was none less than the Messiah, the hope of Israel. Even this was less than full, Christian belief: Peter's next step (Mk. 8:31–34 par.) is to tell Jesus that predictions about his imminent death are inappropriate to the Messiah they are following. Thus, the Synoptics portray rising understanding, but still expose the massive *mis*understanding that stood at the core of all belief in Jesus exercised before his death and resurrection.

Superimposing both views of reality also makes good intrinsic sense. The Evangelist who most quickly introduces the Christological titles most heavily stresses the lack of understanding and the sheer misunderstanding of Jesus' followers; the Evangelists who track their rising comprehension say less about the disciples' initial false steps, but some point out the profundity of their lingering misapprehensions. John's presentation no longer appears unhistorical; it is merely part of the undergirding historical realities.

But this does not mean we must constantly refer to the Synoptics to make sense of John. Superimposing the two visions gives us access to certain *historical* realities. Rightly handled, it may also enable us to discern what is peculiarly Johannine, and thus to understand with greater sensitivity just what the Evangelist is saying. His decision to structure his presentation this way – with the Evangelist himself constantly drawing attention to the misunderstanding of the disciples and of others, and explaining what was understood only later (*e.g.* 2:19–22; 3:3–5, 10; 6:32–35, 41, 42; 7:33–36; 8:18–20, 27–28; 10:1–6; 11:21–44, 49–53; 12:12–17; 13:6–10, 27–30; 16:1–4, 12–15; 18:10–11; 19:14; 20:3–9) enables him to operate at two levels, utilizing irony to make his readers see, again and again, that the disciples believed better than they knew, that Caiaphas prophesied better than he thought, that Pilate gave verdicts more just than he could have imagined. The narrative unfolds like a Greek tragedy, every step followed by the reader even when the participants cannot possibly understand what they rightly confess. And then, unlike the Greek tragedy, there is triumph, there is glorification: the supreme irony is that in the ignominy and defeat of the cross the plan of God achieved its greatest conquest, a conquest planned before the world began.

More generally, though the Christological distinctiveness of John's Gospel should not be denied, it should not be exaggerated. True, only this Gospel explicitly designates Jesus 'God' (1:1, 18; 20:28); but this Gospel also insists not only on Jesus' humanity but on his profound subordination to the Father (*cf.* especially the notes on 5:16–30).[1] Conversely, the Synoptists, for all their portrayal of Jesus as a man, portray him as the one who has the right to forgive sins (Mk. 2:1–12 par. – and who can forgive sins but God alone?), and relate parables in which Jesus transparently takes on the metaphorical role most commonly assigned to God in the Old Testament. Matthew and Luke cannot possibly think of Jesus as a mere mortal: their respective accounts of his virginal conception demonstrate that their most profound understanding of what it means for Jesus to be the 'Son of God' is tied up with the mystery of his birth (*cf.* Lk. 1:32, 35). Son of David Jesus may be (Mt. 1:1), but he is also 'Immanuel', 'God with us' (Mt. 1:23). The Synoptic Gospels present in seed form the full flowering of the incarnational understanding that would develop only later; but the seed is there, the entire genetic coding for the growth that later takes place.[2] If John lets us see a little more of the opening flower, it is in part because he indulges in more explanatory asides that unpack for the reader what is really going on.

Even the 'I am' statements constitute less of an historical problem than at first meets the eye. They are, of course, quite varied,[3] as the commentary will show. Jesus' plain affirmation of his messianic status in

---

[1]On the humanity of Jesus in John's Gospel, *cf.* P. Pokorny, *NTS* 30, 1984, pp. 217–228; Thompson; Carson, pp. 146–160; Panimolle, pp. 100–118; Morris, *JC*, pp. 43–67; over against Käsemann, who argues the evidence for Jesus' humanity in John is nothing more than the trappings necessary to secure a docetic Christology.

[2]For a responsible treatment of this organic growth of Christology, *cf.* I. Howard Marshall, *The Origins of New Testament Christology* (IVP, 1976; Apollos, ²1990); C. F. D. Moule, *The Origin of Christology* (Cambridge University Press, 1977); and many essays in H. H. Rowdon (ed.), *Christ the Lord* (IVP, 1982).

[3]*Cf.* Philip B. Harner, *The 'I Am' of the Fourth Gospel* (Fortress, 1970).

4:26 ('I who speak to you am he'), contrasting sharply with the circum-
locutions and symbol-laden language of so many Synoptics sayings,
may turn on the identity of his interlocutor: she is a Samaritan woman,
and unlikely to harbour exactly the same political expectations bound up
with ideas of messiahship in many strands of first-century Judaism.
After all, John reports that Jesus resorts to circumspect language when
he is in Judea (*e.g.* 7:28–44; 10:24–29). The majority of the 'I am' statements in John have some sort of completion: 'I am the bread of life'
(6:35). 'I am the good shepherd' (10:11), 'I am the true vine' (15:1) or the
like. These are plainly metaphorical, and although they are reasonably
transparent to later readers, they were confusing and difficult for the
first hearers (*e.g.* 6:60; 10:19; 16:30–32): religious leaders did not customarily say that sort of thing.[1] As for the occurrences of an absolute form
of 'I am', which can ultimately be traced back to Isaiah's use of the same
expression as a reference for God (*e.g.* Is. 43:10; 47:8, 10, especially LXX),
they are mixed in their clarity (*cf.* notes on 6:20; 8:28, 58), and are in any
case partly paralleled by Mark 6:50; 13:6. And if the most dramatic of the
sayings in John, 'Before Abraham was born, I am' (8:58) is without
explicit parallel, it is hard to see how it makes a claim radically superior
to the Synoptic portrayal of a Jesus who can not only adjudicate Jewish
interpretations of the law but radically abrogate parts of it (Mk. 7:15–19)
while claiming that all of it is fulfilled by him (Mt. 5:17ff.); who forgives
sin (Mt. 9:1ff.) and insists that an individual's eternal destiny turns on
obedience to him (Mt. 7:21–23); who demands loyalty that outstrips the
sanctity of family ties (Mt. 10:37–39; Mk. 10:29–30) and insists that
no-one knows the Father except those to whom the Son discloses him
(Lk. 10:22); who offers rest for the weary (Mt. 11:28–30) and salvation for
the lost (Lk. 15); who muzzles nature (Mk. 4:39) and raises the dead (Mt.
9:18–26). Individual deeds from such a list may in some cases find
parallels in the prophets or in the apostles; the combination finds its
only adequate parallel in God alone.[2]

In short, the variegated relationship that John enjoys with the Synoptic Gospels, far from calling into question the Fourth Gospel's essential
authenticity, on close inspection either supports it or allows for it on
every hand.

4. Reflections on the conceptual background
The wealth of suggestions that various scholars have offered as to the

[1]Most of the alleged parallels are from second and third century (or even later) gnostic
and hermetic sources. Those closest in time to John, drawn from the first half of the first
century, are claims of the mythical Egyptian goddess Isis, who was popular in the
Greek-speaking world: 'I am the one who discovered fruit for men'; 'I am the one who is
called the goddess among women'; *cf. NewDocs* 1. §2). These are, however, remarkably
*un*metaphorical, and in any case do not bear the Old Testament resonances of the
utterances in John.

[2]For a useful defence of the 'I am' sayings in John, *cf.* E. Stauffer, *Jesus and His Story*
(SCM, 1960), pp. 142–159. On the much larger question of how the contemporary scholar

'background' of the Fourth Gospel – Gnosticism, the Hermetica, Philo, one strand or another of Palestinian Judaism, hellenistic Judaism and more – have an important bearing on how we view John's ostensible setting, the Palestine of Jesus' day. Gone are the days (as we have seen) when the Fourth Gospel can be confidently ascribed to the syncretistic influence of Hellenism on nascent Christianity: the 'new look' prompted by the discovery of the Dead Sea Scrolls has forced all but the most enthusiastic supporters of hellenistic influence to pause. Even so, many scholars would be comfortable with the approach of Barrett, who both in his introduction (pp. 27–41) and repeatedly in his commentary argues that a rich diversity of non-Christian influences was incorporated into the very substance of this Gospel, providing it with its peculiar emphases and form.[1]

This is surely partly right, and yet potentially misleading. One reason why scholars are able to find parallels to John in so diverse an array of literature lies in John's vocabulary and pithy sayings. Words like light, darkness, life, death, spirit, word, love, believing, water, bread, clean, birth, children of God, can be found in almost any religion into which one probes. Frequently they have very different referents as one moves from religion to religion, but the vocabulary is as popular as religion itself. Nowhere, perhaps, has the importance of this phenomenon been more clearly set forth than in a little-known essay by Kysar.[2] Kysar compares the studies of C. H. Dodd and Rudolf Bultmann on the Prologue (Jn. 1:1–18), noting in particular the list of possible parallels each of the two scholars draws up to every conceivable phrase in those verses. Dodd and Bultmann each advance over three hundred parallels, *but the overlap in their lists is only 7%*. The dangers of what Sandmel calls 'parallelomania' become depressingly obvious.[3] Manson goes so far as to write:

> In fact, when one considers the material, cited to explain John, one might well begin to think that John was nothing less than a vision of the entire culture and religion of the ancient world. I venture to doubt the value of this comparative method. . . . [The] mere heaping up of verbal parallels may be more of a hindrance than a help. . . .

The fundamentally Jewish and Old Testament background to John's

---

can properly speak of the 'historical Jesus' and reconstruct something of his 'history', *cf.* the thoughtful essay by N. T. Wright, *SJT* 39, 1986, pp. 189–210.

[1]For a helpful summary of the most commonly drawn parallels, *cf.* Beasley-Murray, pp. liii–lxv; for useful analysis of changing scholarly opinion on the background to John, *cf.* W. F. Howard, *The Fourth Gospel in Recent Criticism and Interpretation* (revised by C. K. Barrett; Epworth, 1955), pp. 144–163; and especially Kysar, *Fourth*, pp. 102–146.

[2]Robert Kysar, *Canadian Journal of Theology* 16, 1970, pp. 250–255.

[3]Samuel Sandmel, *JBL* 81, 1962, pp. 2–13.

Gospel is increasingly recognized.[1] What we call the Old Testament is what he repeatedly quotes, and that to which he repeatedly and explicitly alludes (*e.g.* with references to the tabernacle, Jacob's ladder, Jacob's well, manna, Sabbath and so forth). The sheer accuracy of the Evangelist's topographical notes, all set in Palestine,[2] argues *at the least* for exposure to Jewish thought of Palestine. Barrett (p. 121) thinks it indicates no more than that the Evangelist used some Palestinian source that was itself remarkably accurate. Apart from the complex questions about the authorship of this Gospel, however (*cf.* § IV, below), if we assume that the Evangelist himself did not have detailed knowledge of Palestinian topography, nevertheless the fact that he had access to good topographical information on Palestine place names and descriptions such as references to the pool near the Sheep Gate, 5:2, to Siloam, 9:7, or Aenon near Salim, 3:23, warrants our supposing he could well have good information on other features relating to Jesus's ministry. It is easier yet to believe the author was himself a Jew from Palestine.

Scarcely less important is the way the Evangelist repeatedly insists that what he is writing is the product not only of theology but of *witness* (on which *cf.* especially Boice). The question of what a 'Gospel' is, to what genre it belongs, is extraordinarily difficult,[3] but the ease with which many modern scholars simply assume that all ancient 'biographers' and 'historians' felt free to manufacture speeches and put them on the lips of their heroes, and mingle historical and anachronistic references without any sense of what we would judge to be responsible historiography, is a little disconcerting. Although some ancient writers took such liberties, there was already in the first century a rather sophisticated scholarship on the nature of history, even if it was rather differently conceived than it is in the modern guild of historians. These more conservative approaches to history emphasized the importance of eyewitness participation in the events described, the importance of interviewing other eyewitnesses, travel to the scene of events to be narrated in an effort to gain an adequate grasp of the situation, checking details by documentary research, limitation of coverage to material where one has reliable information, even occasional insistence on the use of sources for speeches, and certainly the idea of 'truth' in history writing, conforming to what actually took place.[4] Moreover, many of the

---

[1]In addition to the larger commentaries, *cf.* F.-M. Braun, *RB* 62, 1955, pp. 5–44 (still useful, though somewhat dated); G. D. Kilpatrick in Sevenster, pp. 75–87; Robinson, *John*, esp. ch. 2.

[2]*Cf.* R. D. Potter, *SE I* (= *TU* 73), pp. 329–337 (though rightly criticized at points by Barrett, *GJJ*, pp. 36–38); W. F. Albright, *art. cit.*, pp. 153–171; Bruce E. Schein, *Following the Way: The Setting of John's Gospel* (Augsburg, 1980), the imaginative constructions in which must not be allowed to undermine the demonstration of John's detailed knowledge of the country; J. Finegan, *The Archaeology of the New Testament* (Princeton University Press, 1969), *passim;* Smalley, pp. 34–37; Robinson, *John*, pp. 52ff.

[3]From the large and growing literature, *cf.* especially D. E. Aune, *GP* 2, pp. 9–60; or, more popularly, *idem*, in *Mosaic* 20, 1987, pp. 1–10.

[4]*Cf.* Colin J. Hemer, *The Book of Acts in the Setting of Hellenistic History*, ed. Conrad H.

distinctive emphases of the Fourth Gospel, including the ascription of deity to Jesus, are most readily accounted for within the framework of *Jewish* Christianity.[1]

Of course, none of this proves that other influences are not also present. It is at this point that we must think through in what way we may rightly speak of the participation of other influences in the substance of the Fourth Gospel. The aligment of possible parallels in other literature is not enough, unless one can show that in concept (and not just in vocabulary) they are indistinguishable from what John says and the *only* explanation of it. Few argue that John is writing to a community in Palestine. Granted that his readers think in Greek, and that they are steeped in Old Testament thought as mediated through the LXX or something much like it, but that they live in the larger hellenistic world and that their heritage of Judaism is even more impregnated with the surrounding culture than that of Jews in Palestine, what moves is John likely to make in order to communicate his message? And how would such moves, taken to ensure effective communication, differ from the assumption that the Evangelist has himself succumbed to naive syncretism? To put the matter another way, what teaching *does John ascribe to Jesus* in the Fourth Gospel that can *only* be explained by resorting to, say, the syncretistic influence of Gnosticism on the Evangelist's thought?

This is not to say that Barrett is entirely wrong. The early Christians were aware that they were expanding outward into a frequently hostile set of world-views, and the most farsighted of them, however evangelistic their vision, were quick to distinguish between the 'world' and those whom the Father had given to the Son (to use John's expressions). But even such polarization means that influence has been exerted. John's effort to communicate the truth to men and women far removed from Palestine ensured that, if he was at all thoughtful in his task, he would not simply parrot the received traditions, but try to cast them in ways that would make them most easily understood. The question to be asked, then, is whether his attempt has succumbed, wittingly or unwittingly, to a syncretism that has admitted strands of thought essentially *alien* to the historic gospel, or has simply transposed the good news, as it were, to another key.

It is surely just here that John has proved to be not only a faithful witness but a gifted preacher. We have already noted a few of the dozens of markers he has left in the text to assure us that he distinguishes between what happened 'back then' in Jesus' day, and what was understood of it only later. In the same way, as Léon-Dufour has rightly argued, John resorts to rich symbolism, in part to show the

---

Gempf (WUNT 49; J. C. B. Mohr [Paul Siebeck], 1989), ch. 3, and with special reference to the work of Loveday Alexander and G. Schepens. *Cf.* also A. W. Mosley, *NTS* 12, 1965–66, pp. 10–26.

[1]On this particular point, *cf.* Richard N. Longenecker, *The Christology of Early Jewish Christianity* (SCM, 1970), pp. 136–141.

reader where the symbol-laden teaching of Jesus *back then* was heading.[1]

For instance, Jesus says, 'Destroy this temple, and I will raise it again in three days' (2:19). When uttered, this saying was incomprehensible both to Jesus' interlocutors and to his disciples. Jesus was, after all, standing in the temple complex as he spoke: the referent to 'temple' was at hand. Yet the Evangelist says that after the resurrection his disciples believed his words and the Scriptures, and understood the referent to be Jesus' body. The unfolding pattern by which so much in ancient Jewish religion finds its ultimate fulfilment in Jesus dominates not a little of John's appeal to the Scriptures. At the same time, however, the destruction of Jesus' body and its resurrection to life in three days did betoken, in John's eyes, the destruction of Jerusalem's temple and its replacement by the resurrected Lord, the true and utimate meeting place between God and human beings. The Romans *did* come and take away the place of the authorities and destroy the nation (11:50) and its religious institutions; what Jesus raised in three days proved to be their fulfilment. Nor is this reading into the text what is not there: the careful reader of the Fourth Gospel finds the clues liberally scattered along the way, as the commentary will show.

In exactly the same way, the Prologue opens with language that could be taken in several different ways, largely depending on the religious background of the interpreter. But as the Prologue proceeds, what the Evangelist is truly saying becomes more and more constrained, until only a distinctively Christian voice is heard. Better still, if the Prologue is read again after the entire Gospel has been read in a reflective manner, new insights spring to light. The language that once seemed so diffuse now appears decisively Christian much earlier in the text. John has written a subtle book that he *expects* to be read more than once.

Writing of other parts of John, Léon-Dufour put the matter well:

> A first principle of symbolic reading would therefore be to discover the coherence of the dialogues and the relevance of the speeches by placing them in the Jewish context of the first century. If we end up failing to recognize all this, it is because we allow ourselves to be dazzled by the light of Easter. The Christian present would contribute to erasing the roots of the Christian faith in that unique event which was the encounter of Jesus with men. . . . If, in his writing, John has actualised the past of Jesus of Nazareth by showing its relevance for the present time, the 'reading' of this written document does not consist in bringing the past into the present, but in developing a deeper understanding of the present in the light of the past.[2]

---

[1]*NTS* 27, 1980–81, pp. 439–456. More generally in the Gospels, *cf.* Ben F. Meyer, *The Aims of Jesus* (SCM, 1979).
[2]*Art cit.*, pp. 445–446.

Within some such framework as this, there can be little doubt that John betrays the influence on his writing of the world he seeks to influence with the good news of Jesus Christ. That such influence is at the expense of his faithfulness as a witness we have every reason to doubt.[1] And the dominant influences, the things that *constrain* his thought and theology, are the Old Testament, the heritage of Judaism, his knowledge both of first-century Palestine and of the culture and heritage of those for whom he is writing, and above all his grasp of the person, ministry and work of Jesus the Messiah, and the Christian understanding that was mediated to him through the work of the Spirit in the life of the church.

The question of the conceptual background to the Fourth Gospel is considered a little further when the purpose of the book is discussed below (§ VI).

5. An assessment of the 'new criticism'

The application of the 'new criticism' to the Fourth Gospel demands careful evaluation. To keep the discussion focused, what follows assesses the work of Culpepper (briefly described in § II, above), which is certainly the best and most comprehensive in the field.[2]

The most obvious questions arise from the unqualified transfer of categories developed in the poetics of the *novel* to Gospel literature. Culpepper is not entirely insensitive to the problem, of course; but his defence of his methods is not very convincing. The heart of his answer is twofold. First, although he concedes that '[the] danger of distortion must be faced constantly when techniques developed for the study of one genre are applied to another', nevertheless he insists that 'in principle the question of whether there can be a separate set of hermeneutical principles for the study of Scripture should have been settled as long ago as Schleiermacher' (pp. 9–10). In one sense this is entirely correct; but in no sense is it relevant to the problem posed. The question at stake is not whether or not we may examine the literary conventions of Scripture in the light of the literary conventions of other literature, but whether the modern novel is the best parallel to first-century Gospels. True, as Culpepper points out, there are indeed parallels between the Gospel of John and 'novelistic, realistic narrative', but Culpepper makes no attempt whatever to isolate the *dis*continuities. To take one example, Culpepper subsumes discussion of the eyewitness themes in John under the narrative categories of *narrator* and *implied author*, without seriously considering that if the witness themes are given force within some narrative framework other than the novel, the shape of the discussion

---

[1]By all means 'Let John be John', to use the title of an article by James D. G. Dunn, in Peter Stuhlmacher (ed.), *Das Evangelium und die Evangelien* (WUNT 28; J. C. B. Mohr [Paul Siebeck], 1983), pp. 309–339; but, *contra* Dunn, we may doubt that this means that the fourth Evangelist has succumbed to massive theological anachronism.

[2]Part of what follows is taken from my review of Culpepper in *TrinJ* 4, 1983, pp. 122–126.

inevitably swings to *some* consideration of the kind and quality of the *history* purportedly being told, and therefore to truth claims – and not just to the shape of the *story* being narrated.

Culpepper's second line of defence is the argument of Hans Frei in his influential work, *The Eclipse of Biblical Narrative*.[1] Frei argues that the Enlightenment drove Western thought to assess the truthfulness of narratives in exclusively *historical* terms. This 'crisis of historical narrative', Frei argues, led the Germans to develop higher criticism and thus to question the *truthfulness* of the Gospel narratives; but it led the English to invent the novel, which conveys its own kind of 'truth' – not truth *qua* historical facts or chronicle, but some deep insight into reality, constructed in historically more or less specific contexts. Therefore the way forward, Culpepper argues, in an age when many thoughtful people 'cannot accept as historically plausible [the Gospel's] characterization of Jesus as a miracle worker with full recollection of his pre-existence and knowledge of his life after death' (p. 236), is not to restrict truth to *historical* truth and therefore the truth claims of the Gospel, but to recognize the peculiar nature of *narrative* truth. Culpepper is not saying that the Fourth Gospel's narratives convey *nothing* of history; rather, he wants to preserve some sort of blend: 'The future of the Gospel in the life of the church will depend on the church's ability to relate both story and history to truth in such a way that neither has an exclusive claim to truth and one is not incompatible with the other' (p. 236). Yet not only does his example of miracles in the life of Jesus fail to inspire confidence (Could the resurrection be thrown into the list of negotiables? If not, why not?), but he gives no criteria to guide us, as if the division were immaterial.

Far more sophisticated is the work of Meir Sternberg, *The Poetics of Biblical Narrative*.[2] For a start, he displays care in making necessary distinctions. Both 'history' and 'fiction' are confusing terms, partly because both can refer to the world, *i.e.* to the represented object, and to the word, *i.e.* to the discourse that represents it. Sternberg goes on:

> This terminological wavering between world and word would remain a minor affair – most of us perpetuate it, if only for stylistic reasons – did it not tend to get out of hand. No longer innocuous, it then reinforces a conceptual fallacy that is potent and widespread enough anyway. The shift of meaning leads to a symbiosis of meaning, whereby history-writing is wedded to and fiction-writing opposed to factual truth. Now this double identification forms a category-mistake of the first order. For history-writing is not a record of fact – of what 'really happened' – but a discourse that claims to be a record of fact. Nor is fiction-writing a tissue of free inventions

[1] Yale University Press, 1974.
[2] Indiana University Press, 1985. Pp. 23–35 are of special relevance.

but a discourse that claims freedom of invention. The antithesis lies not in the presence or absence of truth value but of
the commitment to truth value.

The difference between truth value and truth claim is
fundamental.[1]

Sternberg's point is that bad historiography is still historiography,
even if it gets many facts wrong; it is not transmuted into fiction.
Meanwhile, a piece of fiction that utilizes many factually accurate loca-
tions and events and even descriptions of persons is not thereby transformed into a work of history. At stake in both instances is the nature of
the *truth claim* that is being made, not the truth value of the particular
work. 'Both historiography and fiction are genres of writing, not
bundles of fact or nonfact in verbal shape.'[2] The question that must be
faced, then, is this: What kind of truth claim does John make? Does the
work commend itself to the reader as belonging to the genre of fiction
(regardless of how much factual truth and/or theological truth it may
contain, *i.e.* regardless of its truth value), or belonging to the genre of
history (again, regardless of its truth value)? Or does it belong to some
other genre?

It is at this point that Culpepper's work is so uncontrolled. Because he
has already decided to use the poetics of the novel as his model in
discussing the Gospel of John, he has committed himself to a form of
writing whose truth claims, on the face of it, are fundamentally at odds
with the truth claims of the Fourth Gospel.

The problem is best seen in Culpepper's favourite analogy. He does
not want the Gospel of John to be thought of as a window on the
ministry of Jesus, enabling us to see *through* the text to that life and
ministry, but as a mirror in which we see not only ourselves but also the
meaning of the text that lies somewhere *between* the text and ourselves,
'and belief in the gospel can mean openness to the ways it calls readers
to interact with it, with life, and with their own world. It can mean
believing that the narrative is not only reliable but right and that Jesus'
life and our response mean for us what the story has led us to believe
they mean' (p. 237). But 'reliable' and 'right' in what sense? If in *some*
historical sense, we have been returned to the window – *i.e.* the narrator
'reliably' tells us some things about Jesus' ministry; but if purely in the
sense of the 'reliability' of the novelist, we have sacrificed the Gospel's
claims to certain historical specificity, to eyewitness credibility, to the
truth claims of this Gospel, and set sail on the shoreless sea of existential
subjectivity, all on the grounds that we may legitimately treat John as a
novel – the very point that remains to be proved. In that case the
meaning may be in the story, the story that *we* perceive, the story that
stands on *our* side of the text; but it tells us nothing of the ministry of

---

[1]*Ibid.*, p. 25.   [2]*Ibid.*, p. 26.

Jesus on the *other* side. The Gospel of John becomes a fascinating document of stimulating ideas, but it tells us nothing about an objective Saviour who is actually there, who died and rose again as the Lamb of God who takes away our sins.

This is not of course to argue for the positivist view of history associated with von Ranke. But it is to argue that 'the eclipse of biblical narrative' cannot be overcome by appealing to the novel. In any case, not a few historians are persuaded Frei's analysis of the rise of biblical criticism is *historically* mistaken: pre-Enlightenment Christians were *not* confused over the distinction between stories with extra-textual (*i.e.* historical) referents and stories without such referents.[1] Indeed, if Culpepper's approach prevailed in its strongest form, what would be communicated to the reader would not be the gospel at all, for the gospel is irretrievably bound up with God's self-disclosure and redemptive sacrifice in the person of his Son within the space-time continuum that constitutes history. The 'narrative truth' that a novel conveys is judged in terms of its universality (*e.g.* the depiction of *universal* human foibles, tensions, fears, loves, hates, relationships, *etc.*, found in every age and society). The historically specific contexts of such literature establish frameworks of more or less verisimilitude but do not constitute the 'universal' element for which the writing is praised.

By contrast, the Gospels are universally applicable to human beings, *not* because they portray a central figure who is just like the rest of us, but precisely the reverse: they depict a unique figure who alone can save us, and who scandalously invades humanity's existence at a specific point in the space-time continuum. Doubtless he is continuous with us in many ways, but to say only this is to say too little. To have faith in the gospel message is not the same thing as responding positively to the story of Superman, who is also said to invade our turf from beyond. Although biblical faith has a major 'subjective' or 'personal' or 'existential' component, it depends even more on its object – on the other side of the 'window'. Biblical Christianity cannot outlive the 'scandal of historical particularity'. By contrast, the novel thrives on the universals of human existence.

The dominant influence of the poetics of the novel on Culpepper's thinking and the consequent clouding of his exegetical judgment can be traced at scores of points. For instance, the treatment of the so-called 'omniscience' of the writer is slanted to fit the patterns generated by fiction writers; but on the face of it, any responsible observer could draw reasonable conclusions about what Jesus knew, or his disciples did not, or what Pilate feared, from the actions they took and/or the words they

[1]*E.g.* John D. Woodbridge, *Biblical Authority: A Critique of the Rogers/McKim Proposal* (Zondervan, 1982). For a compelling study of the relationship between truth and literary genres found in the Bible, *cf.* Kevin J. Vanhoozer, 'The Semantics of Biblical Literature: Truth and Scripture's Diverse Literary Forms', in Carson/Woodbridge II, pp. 51–104, 374–383.

spoke. To cite another modern literary genre, many modern biographies do not hesitate, on responsible grounds, to tell us what their subjects feared, thought, loved, supposed. And if the narrator of the Fourth Gospel was not historically privy to the conversation between Jesus and the Samaritan woman, this scarcely means he should be classed as an 'omnipresent' narrator in a fiction story; for after all, there are other ways of learning about a conversation between two people besides being there, the more so in this case where we are specifically told how freely the woman talked about the entire episode (4:29, 39, 42). Certainly the fourth Evangelist is far more reserved in these matters than, say, a nineteenth-century Victorian *novelist*, many of whom were given to the most minute probing of their subject's psyche. Or again, although Culpepper, as we have seen, says some very insightful things about John 21:24–25, some of his judgments spring from his adoption of fiction poetics as a Procrustean bed on which every scrap of evidence must be forced to lie. So firmly is he committed to the model of the analysis of the novel that the 'implied author' and the 'narrator' are no longer artifices that enable us to perform certain types of close analysis, within the poetics of the novel: they are almost hypostatized. But if the Gospel of John is not *a priori* condemned to the poetics of nineteenth-century fiction, the same evidence and arguments that Culpepper finely adduces might be used to forge the conclusion that the Evangelist *actually is* the beloved disciple.

But there is an unforeseen benefit that flows from Culpepper's work. Any approach, like his, that treats the text *as a finished literary product* and analyses it on that basis calls into question the legitimacy of the claim that layers of tradition can be peeled off the Gospel in order to lay bare the history of the community. If aporias, say, can be integrated into the source-critical approach of R. T. Fortna, they can also be integrated into the literary unity of R. A. Culpepper. If aporias may be literary devices they are not *necessary* evidence of seams.

In other words, Fortna and Culpepper represent divergent streams of contemporary biblical scholarship, so divergent, in fact, that a debate has begun about which approach to the text should take precedence. Culpepper has no doubts: 'Once the effort has been made to understand the narrative character of the gospels, some rapprochment with the traditional, historical issues will be necessary' (p. 11). But the problem is deeper than mere precedence. If the material can be responsibly integrated into the unity Culpepper envisages, or something like it, what right do we have to say the same evidence testifies to *disunity*, seams, disparate sources and the like?[1] Conversely, if the latter are justified, should we not conclude Culpepper's discovery of unity *must* have been artificially imposed? The unforeseen benefit from this debate, then, is

---

[1]One thinks, for instance, of the recent 'semiotic' study on Jn. 4 by Boers. At every turn Boers appeals to the very evidence adduced by source-criticism, to argue instead for deep unity.

that it may free up the rather rigid critical orthodoxy of the day and open up possibilities that have illegitimately been ruled out of court.

In short, Culpepper's work is important, not because it has all the answers, but because it is the most comprehensive treatment of the Fourth Gospel from the perspective of the new criticism, and will set much of the agenda for years to come. It cannot be thought to represent much of a threat to the authenticity of John's Gospel; indeed, it goes some way to establishing John's literary integrity, even if it deploys doubtful means to achieve this end.

IV. THE AUTHORSHIP OF THE FOURTH GOSPEL

The Fourth Gospel does not bear its author's name: like the Synoptics, it is formally anonymous. As far as we know, the title 'According to John' was attached to it as soon as the four canonical Gospels began to circulate together as 'the fourfold Gospel' (cf. § II, above), in part, no doubt, to distinguish it from the rest of the collection. Bruce (p. 1) observes, rather suggestively, 'It is noteworthy that, while the four canonical Gospels could afford to be published anonymously, the apocryphal Gospels which began to appear from the mid-second century onwards claimed (falsely) to be written by apostles or other persons associated with the Lord.'

We have already traced the principal 'external evidence' (*i.e.* evidence outside the Fourth Gospel itself) that maintains the Evangelist was none other than the apostle John, the son of Zebedee. That evidence, such as it is, is virtually unanimous. Even if Irenaeus, toward the end of the second century, is amongst the strongest, totally unambiguous witnesses, his personal connection with Polycarp, who knew John, means the distance in terms of personal memories is not very great. Even Dodd, who discounts the view that the apostle John wrote the Fourth Gospel, considers the external evidence 'formidable', adding, 'Of any external evidence to the contrary that could be called cogent I am not aware' (*HTFG*, p. 2; *cf.* also Robinson, *John*, pp. 99–104).

The fact remains that, despite support for Johannine authorship by a few front-rank scholars in this century,[1] and by many popular writers, a large majority of contemporary scholars reject this view. As we shall see, much of their argumentation turns on their reading of the *internal* evidence. It also requires their virtual dismissal of the external evidence. This is particularly regrettable. Most scholars of antiquity, were they

---

[1]*E.g.* Theodor Zahn, *Introduction to the New Testament*, 3 vols. (ET Kregel, 1953 [from 3rd German ed., 1909]), 3. 174ff.; Westcott, 1. ix–lxvii; Morris, *SFG*, pp. 139–192; Bruce, pp. 1–6; Michaels, pp. xv–xxiv; Robinson, *Red*, pp. 254ff.; *idem, John*, pp. 93ff.; E. Earle Ellis, *Southwestern Journal of Theology* 31, 1988, pp. 24–31.

assessing the authorship of some other document, could not so easily set aside evidence as plentiful, consistent and plainly tied to the source as is the external evidence that supports Johannine authorship. The majority of contemporary biblical scholars do not rest nearly as much weight on external evidence as do their colleagues in classical scholarship.[1]

One way of circumventing the force of the external evidence, still common but no longer quite as popular as it used to be, is by appealing to the words of Papias, as reported and interpreted by Eusebius, in support of the hypothesis that there were *two* Johns. Papias writes (according to Eusebius):

> And if anyone chanced to come who had actually been a follower of the elders, I would enquire as to the discourses of the elders, what Andrew or what Peter said, or what Philip, or what Thomas or James, or what John or Matthew or any other of the Lord's disciples; and things which Aristion and John the elder, disciples of the Lord, say.

Eusebius then comments:

> Here it is worth noting that twice in his enumeration he mentions the name of John: the former of these Johns he puts in the same list with Peter and James and Matthew and the other apostles, clearly indicating the evangelist; but the latter he places with the others, in a separate clause, outside the number of the apostles, placing Aristion before him; and he clearly calls him 'elder' (*H. E.* III. xxxix. 4–5).[2]

From this passage, many have inferred that perhaps it was this second John, a disciple of John the son of Zebedee, who wrote the Fourth Gospel. Perhaps, indeed, Irenaeus and Theophilus and other early Fathers confused their Johns. After all, Irenaeus can be shown to err at other points.

But recent study has shown that this appeal to Papias is precarious. In particular:

(1) It is now widely recognized that whereas Eusebius makes a distinction between 'apostles' and 'elders', understanding that the latter are disciples of the former and therefore second-generation Christians, Papias himself makes no such distinction. In the terms of Papias, 'the discourses of the elders' means the teaching of Andrew, Peter, *etc.* and

---

[1]*Cf.* G. Kennedy, 'Classical and Christian Source Criticism', in W. W. Walker, Jr. (ed.), *The Relationship among the Gospels: An Interdisciplinary Dialogue* (Trinity University Press, 1978), pp. 125–155.

[2]In this instance I have followed the translation of H. J. Lawlor and J. E. L. Oulton, *Eusebius: The Ecclesiastical History and the Martyrs of Palestine*, 2 vols. (repr. SPCK, 1954 [1927]), 1. 89, since it observes distinctions in the Gk. text overlooked by the Loeb edition.

the other apostles. It is Eusebius who elsewhere writes, 'Papias, of whom we are now speaking, acknowledges that he received the discourses of the apostles from those who had been their followers' (*H. E.* III. xxxix. 7). Transparently, that is not what Papias said. *Cf.* Lightfoot, *BE*, pp. 58ff.

(2) In the Papias quotation the most obvious reason why John is designated 'the elder' is precisely because he is being grouped with the elders just mentioned, *i.e.* with the apostles (*cf.* David Smith in *EGT*, 5. 161). It is worth noting that 'apostle' and 'elder' come together with a common referent in 1 Peter 5:1. Indeed, the particular Greek syntax Papias employs may well favour the view that 'Aristion *and John the elder'* means something like 'Aristion *and the aforementioned elder John'*.[1] Not only here but in *H. E.* III. xxxix. 14 it is John and not Aristion who is designated 'the elder'. In choosing to refer to the apostles as 'elders', Papias may well be echoing the language of 3 John 1 (on the assumption that Papias thought that epistle was written by the apostle John).

(3) It appears that the distinction Papias is making, in his two lists, is not between apostles and elders of the next generation, but between first-generation witnesses who have died (what they *said*) and first-generation witness who are still alive (what they *say*). Aristion, then, can be linked with John, not because neither is an apostle, but because both are first-generation disciples of the Lord. And this supports the witness of Irenaeus, who says that Papias, not less than Polycarp, was 'a hearer of John'.

(4) In any case, Eusebius had his own agenda. He so disliked the apocalyptic language of Revelation that he was only too glad to find it possible to assign its authorship to a John other than the apostle, and he seizes on 'John the elder' as he has 'retrieved' him from Papias.[2]

In short, it is far from certain that there was an 'elder John' independent of the apostle, and if there was, it is still less certain that he wrote anything. And if against the evidence we accept Eusebius' interpretation of Papias, we will assign the Fourth Gospel to the apostle John, and the Apocalypse to the elder John – while mainstream biblical scholarship assigns neither book to the apostle. If there is one eighth-century Syriac manuscript[3] that also suggests there were two Johns, and that the Fourth Gospel was written by the elder rather than the apostle, it may suggest that the modern misinterpretation of Eusebius was anticipated by a scholar working a millennium earlier.

The witness of Theophilus, Irenaeus and other second-century writers on the authorship of the Fourth Gospel is indeed 'formidable', though not absolutely decisive. Still more important is the internal evidence, *i.e.* what the Fourth Gospel says about itself.

The classic approach of Westcott, updated by Morris (*SFG*, pp. 218ff.),

---

[1] So C. S. Petrie, *NTS* 14, 1967–68, p. 21.
[2] *Cf.* G. Lee, *SE VI* (=*TU* 112), pp. 311–320.
[3] *Cf.* A. Mingana, *BJRL* 14, 1930, pp. 333–339.

was to establish five points: the author of the Fourth Gospel was (a) a Jew, (b) of Palestine, (c) an eyewitness, (d) an apostle, *i.e.* one of the Twelve, (e) the apostle John. The first two points are today rarely disputed,[1] and need not detain us here, not least since they are so admirably handled by Morris. In any case, the line of inquiry is already implicit in earlier remarks in this introduction regarding the significance of the Dead Sea Scrolls (which at the least compel us to recognize that it is unnecessary to resort to a period of expansion into the hellenistic world to account for John's characteristic expressions) and of the Evangelist's detailed knowledge of Palestinian topography and of the features of conservative Jewish debate. To this we must add the widely accepted fact, already appealed to by Lightfoot in the last century (*BE*, pp. 20f.), that at least in some instances John's quotations are closer in form to the Hebrew or Aramaic than to the Greek (esp. 12:40; 13:18; 19:37).

The other three points are all debated, and turn in large part on the identity of the 'beloved disciple', the now standard way of referring to the one whom the NIV more prosaically describes as 'the disciple whom Jesus loved' (*e.g.* 13:23). The raw information is quickly canvassed. The beloved disciple first appears as such at the last supper, where he is reclining next to Jesus and mediating Peter's question to the Master (13:23). He is found at the cross, where he receives a special commission to do with Jesus' mother (19:26–27), and at the empty tomb, where he outstrips Peter in speed but not in boldness (20:2–9). In the Epilogue to the Fourth Gospel (ch. 21), he is said to be the one who wrote 'these things': if 'wrote' means that he wrote the material himself (and did not simply cause the material to be written, as some have suggested), and 'these things' refers to the entire book and not just to ch. 21, then the beloved disciple is the Evangelist. If that is correct, then it is natural to identify the eyewitness who saw the blood and water flow from Jesus' side as the beloved disciple, even though he is not so described.

But who is the beloved disciple? The traditional view, that he is John the son of Zebedee, has been advanced for reasons of quite different weight. That the beloved disciple was at the last supper is not disputed (13:23). The Synoptics insist that only the apostles joined Jesus for this meal (Mk. 14:17 par.),[2] which places the beloved disciple within the band of the Twelve. He is repeatedly distinguished from Peter (Jn. 13:23–24; 20:2–9; 21:20), and by the same token should not be confused

---

[1]An exception is Margaret Pamment, *ExpT* 94, 1983, pp. 363–367, who holds that the beloved disciple is a Gentile believer. The heart of her argument is that 21:1ff. is concerned with the Gentile mission (in this she is partly right), and 'This suggests the beloved disciple [who appears in this chapter] is a gentile' (p. 367). This is a classic *non sequitur*. Granted that all the first believers were Jews, at least *some* of the first witnesses to Gentiles had to be Jews!

[2]Strangely, Robinson (*John*, p. 107 n. 307), thinks that the linking of Lk. 22:14 and Lk. 24:33 may call this into question. But the latter speaks of others with the apostles at a time after the resurrection, not at the last supper.

with any of the other apostles named in John 13 – 16. That he is one of the seven who go fishing in ch. 21, and by implication not Peter, Thomas or Nathanael, suggests he is one of the sons of Zebedee or one of the other two unnamed disciples (21:2). Of the sons of Zebedee, he cannot be James, since he was the first of the apostolic band to be martyred (during the reign of Herod Agrippa I, AD 41–44; cf. Acts 12:1–2), while the beloved disciple lived long enough to give weight to the rumour that he would not die (21:23). The fact that neither John nor James is mentioned by name in the Fourth Gospel, which nevertheless has place not only for prominent apostles like Peter and Andrew but also for relatively obscure members of the apostolic band like Philip and 'Judas (not Judas Iscariot)' (14:22) is passing strange, unless there is some reason for it. The traditional reason seems most plausible: the beloved disciple is none other than John, and he deliberately avoids using his personal name. This becomes more likely when we remember that the beloved disciple is constantly in the company of Peter, while both the Synoptics (Mk. 5:37; 9:2; 14:33; par.) and Acts (3:1 – 4:23; 8:15–25), not to mention Paul (Gal. 2:9), link Peter and John in friendship and shared experience. It has been noted (Westcott, 1. xlvii) that in this Gospel most of the important characters are designated with rather full expressions: Simon Peter, Thomas Didymus, Judas son of Simon Iscariot, Caiaphas the high priest that year. Strangely, however, John the Baptist is simply called 'John', even when he is first introduced (1:6; contrast Mk. 1:4 par.). The simplest explanation is that John the son of Zebedee is the one person who would *not* feel it necessary to distinguish the other John from himself.

Once again, the evidence is not entirely conclusive. For instance, it is just possible that the beloved disciple is one of the unnamed pair of disciples in John 21:2. But once the logical possibility has been duly noted, it seems to be a rather desperate expedient that stands against the force of the cumulative internal evidence and the substantial external evidence. Other identifications have been advanced. Some, for instance, have suggested Lazarus, on the grounds that 'beloved disciple' would be an appropriate form of self-reference for one of whom it is elsewhere said that Jesus loved him (11:5, 36).[1] Others have suggested the rich young man of Mark 10:21, on much the same ground.[2] Still others argue for the owner of the upper room, arguing that the reason he could lay his head on Jesus' breast was that, as the host, he was placed in a position of honour next to Jesus;[3] perhaps he was John Mark.[4] None of this is convincing, and all of it notoriously speculative. According to the Synoptic evidence, only the Twelve were present at the last supper with

---

[1]E.g. F. V. Filson, *JBL* 68, 1949, pp. 83–88; Eller.
[2]E.g. H. B. Swete, *JTS* 17, 1916, pp. 371–374.
[3]E.g. Eugen Ruckstuhl, *SNTU* 11, 1986, pp. 131–167.
[4]E.g. Marsh, p. 24; Pierson Parker, *JBL* 79, 1960, pp. 97–110. Sanders (pp. 29–52) thinks John Mark is the Evangelist but not the beloved disciple.

Jesus: that alone rules out all three suggestions. There is nothing to be said for the first two, other than that Jesus loved them; but that is surely an insufficient ground for identifying the beloved disciple, presupposing as it does that the circle of those whom Jesus loved was extremely limited. As for the second suggestion, to appeal to the Gospel of Mark to sort out the identity of the beloved disciple in John seems to be a dubious procedure. And if the owner of the upper room was present as host in any sense, why is it that all four Gospels present Jesus taking the initiative at the meal, serving, in fact, as the host? Moreover, there is no patristic evidence that John the son of Zebedee and John Mark were ever confused.

In his commentary, Brown strongly argues that the beloved disciple is John the son of Zebedee (though he does not identify him with the Evangelist), largely along the lines just taken. By the time of his more popular book outlining his understanding of the history of the Johannine community (Brown, *Comm*), however, he has changed his mind (pp. 33–34), without answering his own evidence. He now thinks the beloved disciple is an outsider, not one of the Twelve, but a Judean with access to the high priest's court (18:15–16), possibly the unnamed disciple in 1:35–40. Others have advanced extensive lists of reasons why the beloved disciple could not be John the son of Zebedee.[1] These vary considerably in quality, but they include such entries as these: John the son of Zebedee was a Galilean, yet much of the narrative of the Fourth Gospel takes place in Judea; John and Peter are elsewhere described as 'unschooled, ordinary men' (Acts 4:13), so John could not be expected to write a book of subtlety and depth; John and James are elsewhere described as 'Sons of Thunder' (Mk. 3:17), presumably suggesting impetuosity, intemperance and anger, yet this book is the most placid, even mystical, of the canonical Gospels; John was vengeful against the Samaritans (Lk. 9:54), so it is hard to imagine him writing a book that treats them so kindly (Jn. 4).

None of these arguments seems to carry much weight against the mass on the other side:

(1) Although John the son of Zebedee was a Galilean, by the time he wrote he had not only lived for years in Judea (during the earliest period of the church) but (on any traditional view) in the great metropolitan centre of Ephesus. To restrict John's focus of interest to the place of his origin, when at the time of writing he had not lived there for decades, seems a bit harsh. I would not want to be thought entirely ignorant of Vancouver (Canada), Cambridge (England) and Chicago (USA), where I have spent most of the last twenty years, because I was brought up in Drummondville, Québec (Canada).

(2) It has long been pointed out that the expression in Acts 4:13 does not mean that Peter and John were illiterate, or profoundly ignorant,

---

[1] *E.g.* Pierson Parker, *JBL* 81, 1962, pp. 35–43.

but, from the point of view of contemporary theological proficiency, 'untrained laymen' (NEB), not unlike Jesus himself (Jn. 7:15). The astonishment of the authorities was in any case occasioned by the competence of Peter and John when they should have been (relatively) ignorant, not by their ignorance when they should have been more competent. Jewish boys learned to read. Since John sprang from a family that was certainly not poor (they owned their own boats, Lk. 5:3, and employed others, Mk. 1:20), he may well have enjoyed an education that was better than average. Rabbi Akiba was apparently unlettered until the age of forty, and then became one of the greatest rabbis of his generation; it would not be surprising if some of the leaders of the church, decades after its founding, had devoted themselves to some serious study.

(3) The suggestion that a 'son of thunder' could not have become the apostle of love, or that a man steeped in racial bias against the Samaritans could not have written John 4, is an implicit denial of the power of the gospel and the mellowing effect of years of Christian leadership in an age when the Spirit's transforming might was so largely displayed. The argument is as convincing as the view that Saul the persecutor of the church could not have become the apostle to the Gentiles.

(4) Although the 'other disciple' who arranges for Peter to be admitted to the high priest's courtyard (18:15–16) is not explicitly said to be the beloved disciple, and may be someone else, yet the connection with John has more to be said for it than some think. It appears that this 'other disciple' was in the band of those who were with Jesus when he was arrested, and therefore one of the Eleven who had emerged from the upper room and had accompanied Jesus up the slopes of the Mount of Olives. His close association with Peter supports (though it does not prove) the view that he is none other than John. That a Galilean fisherman could have access to the high priest's court is frequently dismissed on the ground that a fishmonger could not enter unquestioned into the waiting room of the prime minister. In fact, the social model is all wrong. We have already seen that John's family enjoyed some substance; it may have been rich, and in many societies money breaks down social barriers. The relevant social barriers of first-century Palestine may not have been that strong in any case: rabbis were expected to gain a skilled trade apart from their study (thus Paul was a leather-worker), so that the stratification that divided the teacher from the manual labourer in Stoic and other circles of the hellenistic world was not a significant factor in much of Palestine. Galilee supplied the fish for all of the country except for the coast, and it was brought into Jerusalem through the Fish Gate (*cf.* Ne. 3:3; Zp. 1:10). As Robinson (*John*, p. 117) comments, that tradition may not be entirely fanciful which says that John's acquaintance with the girl at the gate and with the high priest's household stemmed from his familiarity with the tradesman's entrance.[1] He may have had a place in the city (19:27) and

---

[1] *Gospel of the Nazaraeans*, Fragment 33, in Hennecke, 1. 152.

served on occasion as his father's 'agent' (a role that crops up in the saying of 13:16). It has been pointed out that the peculiar term for cooked fish (*opsarion*), the form in which much of the trade would be conducted, occurs five times in the Fourth Gospel (*cf.* notes on 6:9, 11; 21:9, 10, 13) and not elsewhere in the New Testament.

(5) Although it has been argued in the past that a Palestinian could not write such fluent Greek, the argument no longer stands. There is now a powerful consensus that at least in Galilee, and perhaps elsewhere in first-century Palestine, the populace was at least bilingual, and in some cases trilingual. Aramaic was used for everyday speech. Hebrew may have been used for some formal and cultic occasions, but how many people could *speak* it is uncertain. And judging by the number of Greek coins and the amount of Greek inscriptional evidence uncovered, Greek was a common enough alternative language that linked the Jews not only to the Mediterranean world in general but to the Jewish diaspora and (in Galilee) to the Decapolis in particular. Some whose work brought them into close relationship with the army may also have attained a working knowledge of Latin. One does not have to visit many countries with a multi-lingual populace, like Norway or Switzerland or Kenya, before recognizing that multi-lingualism is scarcely a rare phenomenon. In any case, if John lived abroad for years before writing, he had ample time to practise his Greek. Moreover, although the Greek of John's Gospel is reasonably competent, it is not elegant, and it betrays a fair number of semitizing 'enhancements'.[1] It is, 'with little exception, the language of the Septuagint'.[2] This sort of evidence is perfectly consonant with what little we know of the background of John the son of Zebedee.[3]

In short, the internal evidence is very strong, though not beyond dispute, that the beloved disciple is John the apostle, the son of Zebedee. Who, then, is the Evangelist? To put the matter another way, what is the relationship between the beloved disciple and the fourth Evangelist?

The traditional answer is that they are one and the same. Ironically, once allowance is made for the misleading categories he uses, Culpepper's treatment of 21:24–25 assumes the same thing: the 'narrator'

---

[1] In recent years, linguistics has rightly distinguished between a semitism (in Greek, an expression or construction unparalleled in Greek and which makes good sense *only* if we assume the background of a semitic language) and semitic enhancement (an expression or construction which normally occurs rather rarely in Greek and whose frequency in a particular Greek document is best accounted for by appealing to underlying semitic influence). John's Gospel undoubtedly betrays both Aramaic and Hebraic enhancements; whether it betrays any Aramisms or Hebraisms is disputed.

[2] G. D. Kilpatrick, 'The Religious Background of the Fourth Gospel', in F. L. Cross (ed.), *Studies in the Fourth Gospel* (Mowbray, 1957), p. 43.

[3] *Cf.* Ellis, *art. cit.*, p. 25: 'A Palestinian Jew might well know the Greek language and Hellenistic thought, but a Jew native to the diaspora would not likely reflect such a close geographical knowledge of Palestine and would certainly not write Greek with the pervasive Semitic idiom observable in the Gospel of John.'

lets the reader know that the 'implied author' is none other than the beloved disciple. But for various reasons this view has been strenuously opposed. The resulting scenarios differ considerably. Some think that John the son of Zebedee probably in some way stands behind the tradition in the Fourth Gospel, but that the material went through lengthy adaptations, finally winding up in the hands of the Evangelist (whose identity is unknown – unless he is the 'elder' John!), whose work was subsequently touched up by a redactor, whose hand, perhaps, is betrayed in 21:24–25. Others think that the influence of John the son of Zebedee is more immediate and pervasive: he did not actually write the book, but caused it to be written (*cf.* notes on 21:24), perhaps through the hands of an amanuensis who enjoyed certain liberties of expression, and who might appropriately be called the Evangelist. The most important factors to be assessed are these:

(1) Perhaps the most frequently advanced reason for denying that the beloved disciple is the Evangelist lies in the expression 'beloved disciple' itself. It is argued that no Christian would call *himself* 'the disciple whom Jesus loved': the expression is strong, and is better thought of as something someone else would say *about* another disciple, than as something any believer would say about himself. Similarly, the person who wrote (lit.) that Jesus was in the bosom of the Father (*eis ton kolpon tou patros*, 1:18) would be loathe to say *of himself* that he reclined in the bosom of Jesus (*en tō kolpō tou Iēsou*, 13:23).

But these arguments, often repeated, should be abandoned. When a New Testament writer thinks of himself as someone whom Jesus loves, it is *never* to suggest that other believers are *not* loved, or are somehow loved less. Thus Paul, in describing the saving work of the Son of God, can suddenly make that work personal: he 'loved me, and gave himself for me' (Gal. 2:20): in no way does this imply that Paul thinks the Galatians are loved less. The suggestion betrays a profound ignorance of the psychological dynamics of Christian experience: those who are most profoundly aware of their own sin and need, and who in consequence most deeply feel the wonders of the grace of God that has reached out and saved them, *even them*, are those who are most likely to talk about themselves as the objects of God's love in Christ Jesus. Those who do not think of themselves in such terms ought to: their failure to do so reflects the paucity of their own spiritual experience, as the prayer of Ephesians 3:14–21 makes clear. If a 'son of thunder' has become the apostle of love, small wonder he thinks of himself as the peculiar object of the love of Jesus. But that is scarcely the mark of arrogance; it is, rather, the mark of brokenness. It is precisely why Christians still sing, in the first person singular:

> *Loved with everlasting love,*
> *Led by grace that love to know,*
> *Spirit, breathing from above,*
> *Thou hast taught me it is so!*

O this full and perfect peace!
O this transport all divine!
In a love which cannot cease,
I am his and he is mine.

> George W. Robinson (1838–77)

And if we are to hear overtones of 1:18 in the description of John lying on Jesus' bosom (13:23), it is no more than a suggestive example of a pattern that is constantly *prescribed* in the Fourth Gospel: Jesus is the mediator of his Father's love, his Father's judgment, his Father's redemption, his Father's knowledge, his Father's covenant.

The same sort of reasoning probably explains why the Evangelist does not name himself. He prefers to refer to himself obliquely, the better to focus on the One whom he serves; and his purposes in writing are not such that he needs explicitly to stand on his apostolic dignity. He is already well known by his intended readership (21:24, 25), and, like Paul when he is writing without strong polemical intent, does not need to call himself an 'apostle' (Phil. 1:1; contrast Gal. 1:1). As most scholars agree, the beloved disciple is no mere idealization, but an historical figure; yet even so, in certain respects he serves as a model for his readers to follow. They, too, are to serve as witnesses to the truth, and to make much of the love of Jesus in their lives.

Even if someone were to protest that this sort of reasoning does not seem to provide an *adequate* reason for the refusal of the beloved disciple to identify himself, what must surely be admitted is that if the Evangelist is someone other than John the son of Zebedee, his failure to mention the apostle John by name, when he mentions so many others, is even more difficult to explain. The point may be pressed a little further. The suggestion that the expression 'the disciple whom Jesus loved' is more easily thought of as something someone might say about someone else than as something someone might say about himself is not only without merit, it is self-defeating. It implies that the Evangelist (someone other than the beloved disciple, on this view) thought Jesus loved certain disciples and not others. Whatever the reason why Jesus nurtured an inner three (Peter, James and John), according to the Synoptic witness, it is very doubtful that it had much to do with arbitrarily dispensed love on Jesus' part.

(2) Some think that 'these things' which the beloved disciple is said to have written (21:24) refers only to the contents of ch. 21, not to the book as a whole. Quite apart from the fact that this view depends on a certain reading of ch. 21 (*cf.* notes there), it results in an anomaly: the beloved disciple, apparently the apostle John, wrote only ch. 21, while someone else wrote the rest – even though 'beloved disciple' occurs much earlier than ch. 21.

(3) It is frequently argued that wherever John appears with Peter the superiority of his insight is stressed. In John 13, for instance, Peter merely signals to the beloved disciple to ask Jesus the fateful question; in

John 20, not only does the beloved disciple reach the tomb before Peter, but only he is said to believe. Would John have said such things about himself? But more careful expositors have argued, rightly, that there is no question of inferiority or superiority in these descriptions, but of different gifts and characters. Barrett (pp. 118–119, 587–588), for instance, quite convincingly argues that 21:24 must be read with the verses that precede it: it is given to Peter to feed the flock of God and to glorify God by his death, while it is given to the beloved disciple to live a long time and to serve as the one who writes this book, serving as a witness to the truth. If the beloved disciple arrives at the tomb first, Peter enters first. If the beloved disciple is said to believe, it is not said that Peter fails to believe: the statement is part of the description that is moving towards his authentication as the author of this book.

(4) Some think that 21:22–23 must be taken to mean that the beloved disciple has died by the time the Fourth Gospel was published, and that one of the reasons for publication was to alleviate the crisis that had consequently arisen. But it is as easy to suppose that the widely-circulating rumour had come to the ears of the aging apostle, who consequently feared what might happen to the faith of some after he died, since their faith was resting on a false interpretation of something Jesus had actually said.

(5) The suggestion that the beloved disciple merely caused these things to be written, apparently through a disciple who served as an amanuensis of sorts (Tertius is commonly cited, Rom. 16:22), receives minor support from John 19:19–22: it is doubtful if Pilate actually wrote the *titulus* on the cross himself, but simply caused it to be written. Certainly it is far from clear just how much freedom an amanuensis in the ancient world might be permitted (*cf.* the discussion of Richard N. Longenecker, in Carson/Woodbridge I, pp. 101–114). Nevertheless, the example of Pilate suggests that what he caused to be written was *exactly* what he wanted written, and the verb 'testifies' in 21:24 suggests that the influence of the beloved disciple is not remote (*cf.* notes on 21:24). This is not to say that John could not have used an amanuensis; it is certainly not to argue that only authorship by the apostle John can be squared with the internal and external evidence. It is to argue, however, that this rather traditional view squares most easily with the evidence, and offers least tortuous explanations of difficulties that all of the relevant hypotheses must face.

Over against Brown, then, who (at least in his commentary) sees the beloved disciple as the apostle John but not as the Evangelist, and Cullmann (pp. 74–85), who sees the beloved disciple as the Evanglist but not the apostle John, the evidence here seems to favour Robinson (*Red*, p. 310), who writes, 'I believe that both men are right in what they assert and wrong in what they deny.' Yet Barrett (p. 132) insists it is a 'moral certainty' that the Fourth Gospel was not written by John the son of Zebedee, while Kümmel (p. 245) says Johannine authorship is 'out of the question'. One is frankly puzzled by their degree of dogmatism. Barrett writes (p. 132 n. 2):

Apostolic authorship has been defended at length and with learning by L. Morris . . . and his arguments should be carefully considered. It must be allowed to be not impossible that John the apostle wrote the gospel; this is why I use the term 'moral certainty'. The apostle may have lived to a very great age; he may have seen fit to draw on other sources in addition to his own memory; he may have learnt to write Greek correctly; he may have learnt not only the language but the thought-forms of his new environment (in Ephesus, Antioch, or Alexandria); he may have pondered the words of Jesus so long that they took shape in a new idiom; he may have become such an obscure figure that for some time orthodox Christians took little or no notice of his work. These are all possible, but the balance of probability is against their having all actually happened.

This is a mixed list. Assessment of the 'very great age' turns on one's dating of the book. If one opts for about AD 80 (cf. § V, below), John need only have been, say, seventy-five. Dodd published *HTFG* when he was in his eighties; Goodspeed wrote his work on Matthew when he was ninety; Sir Norman Anderson is still writing books at eighty. And it is not impossible that the Fourth Gospel was written before AD 70. Why it should be thought at all improbable that an apostle should 'draw on sources in addition to his own memory' I cannot imagine. The question of Greek and thought-forms I have already treated. It may be worth adding that when I first served as an assistant pastor in a French-speaking church in Québec, my senior, who was about forty years of age, was someone whose mother tongue was English, and who had not begun to learn French until his late twenties. I recall one particular evening when we drove home together, chatting in English after a tiring day of pastoral calls. He suddenly turned to me and said, 'I'm sorry, Don, I'm going to have to revert to French. I'm too tired to think in English.'

As for making Jesus' words come home in his own idiom, that is the preacher's *métier*, especially if involved in cross-cultural ministry. And the suggestion that the author of the Fourth Gospel was obscure or unknown is, as we have seen, somewhat overstated. Scholars differ as to whether John is alluded to in the *Epistle of Barnabas*, the *Didache*, and the *Shepherd of Hermas*. Probably a majority find echoes of the Fourth Gospel in Ignatius (c. AD 110). The pattern of recognition is not too surprising if the Gospel of John was published toward the end of the first century. We should not then expect it in, say, Clement of Rome (c. AD 95). There is perhaps more of a problem if the Fourth Gospel was published before AD 70 (as Morris and Robinson think). Even so, especially if the evidence of Irenaeus regarding Papias and Polycarp is read sympathetically, it is hard to credit the view that 'orthodox Christians took little or no notice' of this Gospel. Moreover, Christians then, as now, had their 'favourite' books. Matthew was an early favourite; John was not. In John's case, this may have had a little to do with the fact that the Fourth Gospel was early used (and abused) by the Gnostics: it takes a while to get a counter-polemic going.

For at least some contemporary scholars, there is such a matrix of inherited beliefs, judgments and commitments about the provenance of the Fourth Gospel that it is difficult to postulate apostolic authorship without abandoning the inherited web.[1] This matrix turns on the existence of a Johannine circle (Cullmann) or a Johannine school (Culpepper, JS), the core of a Johannine community whose existence and history can to some extent be delineated by inferences drawn from the Fourth Gospel, and (in the case of, say, Brown) by inferences drawn from layers of tradition that can be peeled back. In my view, as this introduction suggests, this web rests on merely possible inferences, not particularly plausible ones, the resulting matrix being used as a grid to eliminate the most natural inferences from both internal and external evidence.

Consider, for instance, Culpepper's attempt to put the theory of a Johannine school on a rigorous footing (JS). His work is largely given over to a delineation of various 'schools' in the ancient world: the Pythagorean school, the Greek academy, the lyceum, the 'school' at Qumran, the house of Hillel, Philo's 'school', and so forth. It transpires that Culpepper's understanding of a 'school' is undifferentiable from a sect, except that a 'school' has an additional characteristic: it is preoccupied with studying, learning, teaching and writing (p. 213). Even here, of course, his model runs into difficulty. He has earlier been forced to admit:

> Nothing is known of the history of the synagogue-school in which Philo worked, and none of the names of his students has survived. The inference that his writings continued to be studied arises from the use made of them by the later Christian school in Alexandria and the evident popularity of allegorical exegesis there. . . . Perhaps the reason for the complete silence of our sources on the history of Philo's school is that he actually exerted little influence on his community (p. 213).

Here, then, is speculation on the reason for the silence of the sources regarding a school the existence of which is an inference drawn from the later Christian use of an earlier Jewish writer! Out of this model emerges the construct of a Johannine school, with the beloved disciple serving as its head, functioning for the community as the Paraclete does in the

---

[1]For instance, in what is the most extensive critique of Robinson (John), P. Grelot (RB 94, 1987, pp. 519–573) presupposes that source-criticism can peel back the various layers that expose the existence of an entire school of disciples with developing traditions (e.g. pp. 543–545); he does not bother to *argue* his case.

Gospel of John (pp. 261–290). But Culpepper offers no criteria what-soever to distinguish how this 'school' could be distinguished from a group of Christians who cherish the Evangelist's writings and com-mend them to others. The history of the Johannine community (he now flips back and forth between 'community' and 'school') will, he assures us, be traced when there is greater consensus on the 'composition-history' of the Fourth Gospel (p. 279): the assumption is massive. He adds that the Johannine epistles constitute evidence for the existence of 'more than one community of believers which shared the same traditions, vocabulary, doctrines, and ethical principles' – though on the face of it this too invokes a massive assumption about community participation in the writing, for the simpler inference is that the Johannine epistles constitute evidence that their author wrote several pieces to several communities that were known to him. They *may* have constituted a collegial grouping of churches around one authority-figure; in my view, they probably did. But that is still a long way from delineating a 'school' of writers and students who were responsible for *the composition* of the Fourth Gospel. Even the 'we' in John 21:24, a difficult pronoun on any view (*cf.* commentary), does not unambiguously argue for a 'school' of writers. It could as easily refer to a group of attesting elders.

If, then, we tentatively affirm that the beloved disciple is both John the son of Zebedee and the fourth Evangelist, what difference does it make to our interpretation of the Fourth Gospel? At one level, very little. A New Testament book is not more authoritative or more trans-parent because it has an apostle as its writer; nor are Greek grammar and lexicography thereby transformed. At another level, however, there may be a very important result. Just as commitment to a hypo-thetical Johannine 'school' or 'circle' tends to prompt scholars to evalu-ate both internal and external evidence regarding Johannine authorship rather differently from what is advanced in this commentary, conver-sely the view that this Gospel was written by John the son of Zebedee (whether with an amanuensis or not) tends to prompt a fairly sceptical evaluation of the evidence advanced to offer a detailed delineation of the Johannine community. That shifts the focus of discussion quite a bit, as will become clear (see § VI, below), when the purpose of the book is considered. While still trying to understand the circumstances that would call forth from John this sort of book, as opposed to some other, we are freed from the suffocating burden of trying to reconstruct the Johannine community out of merely possible inferences from verse after verse in the Gospel, and are driven to listen more acutely to what the Evangelist says about Jesus. On the face of it, that is how we ought to read this book.

V. THE DATE AND PROVENANCE OF THE FOURTH GOSPEL

Suggestions during the last 150 years as to the date of this Gospel have varied from pre-AD 70 to the final quarter of the second century. Dates in the second century are now pretty well ruled out of court by the discovery of Papyrus Egerton 2 (*cf.* § II, above).

Beyond that limitation, none of the arguments is entirely convincing, and almost any date between about AD 55 and AD 95 is possible. Even so, 21:23 'suggests it was probably nearer the end of that period than the beginning' (Michaels, p. xxix). More by way of default than anything else, I tentatively hold to a date about AD 80.

It is worth briefly canvassing some of the arguments used to fix the date at some point along the spectrum. Some dates, it must be said, seem impossibly early. The inference to be drawn from 21:19 is that Peter had by his death glorified God when ch. 21 was composed. Peter died in AD 64 or 65; dates earlier than that seem unlikely for the Fourth Gospel. Those who hold to a pre-AD 70 (but post-AD 65) date point to details of Palestine written about as if Jerusalem and its temple complex were still standing. 'Now there is in Jerusalem near the Sheep Gate a pool' (Jn. 5:2), the Evangelist writes. The argument would be conclusive were it not for the fact that John uses the Greek present tense with 'historic' force (*i.e.* to refer to something in the past) more frequently than any other New Testament writer. Some find in the repeated use of 'disciples' to refer to the Twelve, rather than 'apostles', a hint of an early, less hierarchically-structured church life; those who think the Gospel is late use the same date to suggest that this Gospel is being written after the apostles have all died.

Some have suggested that the political clout ascribed to 'the Jews' reflects an early stage in Jewish-Christian relations, when the Christians were very much in the minority. Contrast, for instance, the relative positions of power reflected in Justyn Martyr's second-century *Dialogue with Trypho*. Again, there is some force to the argument, but in many communities Jews held the numerical advantage and could pull the political levers well beyond the end of the first century. In any case, the Fourth Gospel sets out to tell us what things were like *in Jesus' day*, and it is far from clear just how much of the Evangelist's description we may legitimately read back into his own situation. The silence of the Fourth Gospel on the destruction of the temple is considered powerful evidence for a pre-AD 70 date by some authors. Arguments from silence are tricky things. At first glance, however, there is some force to it, since the theme of the Evangelist in, say, 2:19–22 could have been strengthened if the overthrow of the temple had been mentioned. Does his silence, then, mean it has not yet occurred? But the evidence is far from compelling. How prominent the temple was in the thinking of Jews in the diaspora varied a great deal. If some time had elapsed, perhaps a decade, so that the initial shock of the reports of its destruction had passed, there is no reason to think that the Evangelist should have brought it up. Indeed, he is a writer who loves subtle allusions. If he wrote in, say, AD 80, he may have taken the destruction of the temple as a given, and let the given make its own contribution to his theological argument.

Apart from these and several similar reasons for a pre-AD 70 date, much of the energy of those who hold this position focuses on calling into question the reasons for a post-AD 70 date.[1] In this they are almost as successful as are those who defend a later date by criticizing an early one.

The dominant reasons for defending a date toward the end of the first century, say between AD 85 and AD 95, are basically four:

(1) There is very strong agreement amongst theologians of almost all stripes as to the strength of the tradition that the Gospel was written under the reign of Emperor Domitian (AD 81–96). But Robinson (*Red*, pp. 256–258) has shown that this tradition rests on very little. There is good, early tradition that the apostle John *lived* to a great age, surviving even into the reign of Emperor Trajan (AD 98–117; Irenaeus, *Adv. Haer.* 2. 22. 5; 3. 3. 4; quoted by Eusebius, *H. E.* III. xxiii. 3–4). Jerome, admittedly in the fourth century, places John's death in the sixty-eighth year 'after our Lord's passion' (*De. vir. ill.* 9), *i.e.* about AD 98.[2] There is also good patristic evidence that John was the last of the Evangelists to *write* his book (Irenaeus, *Adv. Haer.* 3. 1. 1; Clement, as cited by Eusebius, *H. E.* VI. xiv. 7; Eusebius himself, *H. E.* III. xxiv. 7). 'But that he wrote as a very old man is an inference which only appears late and accompanied by other statements which show that it is clearly secondary and unreliable' (Robinson, *Red*, p. 257).

(2) There is a strong contingent of scholars (dominated by Martyn, *HTFG*) who argue that both the concept and the term for 'to be put *out of the synagogue*' (9:22; *cf.* 12:42; 16:2; *aposynagōgos*) betrays a period after the decision of the Council of Jamnia to ban Christians from the synagogue. Entire theses have been based on this assumption (*e.g.* Whitacre, pp. 6ff.). In other words, they find in this expression an irreducible anachronism that dates the Gospel of John to a period after AD 85. Yet at every point their thesis has been challenged (*cf.* notes on 9:22), and today this argument wields less influence than it did a bare decade or so ago.

In more general terms, despite the frequency with which it is said that the Fourth Gospel reflects relations between Jews and Christians in the period AD 70–100, we have almost no documentation that can be *certainly* dated to that period, and there is nothing suggested by the Fourth Gospel that could not have been found in some communities

---

[1]In particular, Morris, pp. 35–40; F. L. Cribbs, *JBL* 89, 1970, pp. 38–55; Robinson, *Red*, pp. 254–311.
[2]On the very slight evidence that the apostle John was early martyred, almost universally (and rightly) dismissed by most scholars, *cf.* Guthrie, pp. 272–273.

at a much earlier (or later!) date.

(3) There are numerous details that are often taken as evidence of a late date. For instance, this Gospel is silent on the Sadducees, who contributed much to the religious life of Jerusalem and Judea before AD 70 but withered and became of marginal importance after that date. The argument would be weighty, were it not for the fact that John is similarly silent on the scribes, whose influence *increased* after AD 70. And John does make it clear that the priests, with rapidly diminishing influence after AD 70, were largely in control of the Sanhedrin in the run-up to Jesus' passion. Many similar details are briefly discussed in the notes on chs. 18 – 19.

(4) In the contemporary climate, perhaps the most pervasive reason for a date at the end of the first century is the implicit reconstruction of the development of Christian doctrine so many scholars adopt, a reconstruction that places the Fourth Gospel toward the end of the process reflected in the New Testament. Many commentators think that the theology reflected in the Fourth Gospel could not have developed much before the end of the first century. This view comes to concrete expression in a book like that of Dunn (*Making*), who argues that only at the end of the first century do we find articulated a full-blown notion of a personal, pre-existent Christ and a corresponding notion of incarnation.

But many are unconvinced by these reconstructions. There is ample evidence for far earlier support of these truths. The most natural reading of Rom. 9:5 is that Christ himself is called 'God over all',[1] and Romans was written not later than the mid 50s. However disputed that reference might be, recent study has vindicated the view that in Philippians 2:5ff., written not later than the early 60s and possibly reflecting a hymn of long standing in the church, Christ is said not to have viewed his equality with God as something to be exploited, but emptied himself and became a man and suffered the ignominy of the cross.[2] If the 'organic' view of the development of Christology outlined earlier (§ III) is correct, the elements of the church's Christology, the seed, the genetic coding if you will, was already present in Jesus himself. This is not to deny that development in the church's understanding took place over several decades. But it is very doubtful that this development was in a straight line, or that it was as slow as is often postulated.[3] As Ellis argues, 'From the resurrection of Jesus onward, there is no stage of early

---

[1] *Cf.* especially B. M. Metzger, 'The Punctuation of Rom. 9:5', in Barnabas Lindars and Stephen S. Smalley (eds.), *Christ and Spirit in the New Testament* (*Fs.* C. F. D. Moule; Cambridge University Press, 1973), pp. 95–112.

[2] *Cf.* especially N. T. Wright, *JTS* 37, 1986, pp. 321–352.

[3] Many have argued for this point, and it is well put by Robinson, *John*, ch. 8. But his own solution is exegetically unconvincing. After arguing, rightly, that 'high' Christology developed remarkably early, he expounds his understanding of John's 'high' Christology in categories that show that what he calls 'high' Christology is what everybody else would call 'low' Christology. In John's Gospel, he says, Jesus often calls himself the 'Son', but only once the 'Son of God'. If the reading 'unique God' is original in 1:18, and applied to Jesus, it was a slip that the Evangelist himself would have gladly corrected had it been

Christian history known to us in which the (implicit or explicit) confession of Jesus as God is absent.'[1]

Moreover, no Gospel stresses the functional *subordination* of Jesus to his Father more strongly than John (*cf.* especially the notes on 5:16–30). In other words, the emphasis in the Fourth Gospel on the deity of Christ must not be allowed to eclipse complementary emphases. If F. C. Conybeare could argue, 'If Athanasius had not had the Fourth Gospel to draw texts from Arius would not have been confuted',[2] the response of Pollard (p. 3) is only slightly exaggerated: 'That is however only part of the truth, for it would also be true to say that if Arius had not had the Fourth Gospel to draw texts from, he would not have needed confuting.' In short, attempts to date the Fourth Gospel by charting Christological trajectories do not appear very convincing.

Having criticized so many arguments dealing with dates, I must now offer two or three that lead me to think, very tentatively, that the Fourth Gospel was published around AD 80–85. None of these is conclusive; a rebuttal could be given to each one. Yet bundled together they provide at least a little weight.

First, there is no convincing pressure to place the Gospel of John as early on the spectrum as possible, but there is a little pressure to place John as late on it as possible, *viz.* the relatively late date at which it is cited with certainty by the Fathers.

Secondly, although the arguments for dating John based on trajectories of theological development are, as I have suggested, extremely weak, yet if any weight is to be given to them at all, at several points John's Gospel uses language that is on its way toward the less restrained and theologically less nuanced speech of Ignatius. I am thinking in particular of the ease and frequency with which Ignatius refers to Jesus as God, of his sacramental language (where in my view he has misunderstood John rather badly), and of his sharp antitheses.

Thirdly, although the fall of the temple did not have as much impact in the diaspora as in Palestinian Judaism, yet it is hard to believe that, if the Fourth Gospel were written after AD 70, the date was *immediately* after AD 70, say AD 72 (a year before Masada fell). The reverberations around the Empire, for both Jews and Christians, were doubtless still too powerful. A little time needed to elapse (one might reasonably expect) before a document like the Fourth Gospel could be free *not* to make an *explicit* allusion to the destruction of the temple.

Fourthly, although the point is disputed, at least 1 John of the Johannine epistles is best understood to be countering Gnostic influences.

---

pointed out to him. If in 1:14 the 'Word' becomes flesh, before this 'incarnation' the 'Word' was impersonal. There is much more of this, none of it compelling (*cf.* the commentary at the appropriate places). It is the error at the opposite extreme of Käsemann: the one argues that Jesus in John has a merely 'human face' (*cf.* J. A. T. Robinson, *The Human Face of God* [SCM, 1972]), while the other argues that he is so thoroughly divine that the human touches are merely docetic veneer.

[1] E. Earle Ellis, *art. cit.*, p. 27.   [2] *Hibbert Journal*, 1903, p. 620, in his review of Loisy.

Although some have argued that the Fourth Gospel has similar aims, while others have suggested that the Fourth Gospel is itself Gnostic, the truth, it appears, is simpler. John's Gospel has its own aims, and these are largely unconcerned with Gnosticism *per se*. That is not to say that the Fourth Gospel has no bearing on Gnosticism; rather, it is to say that its author does not demonstrably set out to confront it, nor does he succumb to it. It is a reasonable deduction that at least some of the heretics who depart from the Johannine community (1 Jn. 2:19) have read their gnostic interpretations into John's Gospel. But whether this is so or not, the concern that 1 John displays to confront Gnosticism suggests it is a later document than the Fourth Gospel. If it comes from the same hand as that which composed John's Gospel (as I think likely), or even from the same school (as is today more commonly suggested), then one must conclude that Gnosticism was *not* perceived as a great danger when the Fourth Gospel was written, or at several points it would have been cast in other terms. In other words, without suggesting that the Fourth Gospel has capsized to Gnosticism, and in fact insisting that it embraces several features that can usefully function as ammunition *against* Gnosticism, the fact remains that it does not read as a book that is concerned to combat gnosticizing tendencies. This difference in theological focus between John and 1 John demands a gap of time. If we allow a decade, the Fourth Gospel must be pushed back a little from the upper end of the spectrum, either because 1 John was written by an apostle who died before the end of the century, or because, as we have noted, 1 John is early cited by the sub-apostolic Fathers. A date of AD 80–85 for the publication of the Gospel of John seems reasonable.

The provenance of this Gospel is no less uncertain. Four places are most commonly proposed. Alexandria is championed by some, on the ground that John has certain affinities to Philo. These are considerably overstated (*cf.* notes on 1:1), and in any case one must assume that Philo was read outside Alexandria. Antioch has been put forward, on the ground that the Fourth Gospel has some affinities with the Syriac *Odes of Solomon*, presumed to come from this region, and with Ignatius, who served Antioch as its bishop. Again, however, the assumption that literary influence is possible only in the place of literary origin is seen to be unconvincing as soon as it is stated in such bald terms. The view that the Fourth Gospel must have been written in Palestine because of its close familiarity with cultural and topographical details peculiar to the region entails the view, strange on its very surface, that any book about the historical Jesus must have been written in Palestine. Both then and now, authors have been known to move around.

The traditional view is that the Fourth Gospel was written in Ephesus. In large part this view depends on the weight given to the uniform but sometimes difficult patristic evidence. Eusebius (*H. E.* III. i. 1) says that Asia (*i.e.* Asia Minor, approximately the western third of modern Turkey) was allotted to John when the apostles were dispersed at the outbreak of the Jewish War (AD 66–70). Some of the allotments or assignments that Eusebius lists are likely legendary, but perhaps this one is reliable since it agrees with other sources, *e.g.* Irenaeus (*Adv. Haer.* 3. 1. 2), who says that 'John, the disciple of the Lord . . . published the gospel while living at Ephesus in Asia.' Some hold, however, that Irenaeus confuses John the apostle with another John, the John who writes the Apocalypse. The issues are too complex to be aired here. The fact that the Montanists used John, and the Montanists were largely based on Phrygia, not too far from Ephesus, is often taken to support the case for Ephesian provenance; but again, John's Gospel could have been circulating in Phrygia half a century and more after it was written, *regardless* of where it was first published. What must be acknowledged is that no other location has the support of the church Fathers; rightly or wrongly, they point to Ephesus.

VI. THE PURPOSE OF THE GOSPEL OF JOHN

This topic, too, has generated highly diverse conclusions. Part of the discussion, at least, has depended on questionable assumptions or procedures, of which four are particularly common:

(1) Many earlier discussions of the purpose of the Fourth Gospel turned on the assumption that John depends on the Synoptic Gospels.[1] That means the governing purpose of John's Gospel should be uncovered by contrasting what John does with what the Synoptists do. He wrote a 'spiritual' Gospel, it is argued; or he wrote to supplement the earlier efforts, or even to supersede them. These theories refuse to let John be John; he must be John-compared-with-Mark, say, or with another Synoptist. Earlier discussion in this introduction regarding the relationship between John and the Synoptics enables us to dismiss these theories.

(2) A substantial number of modern proposals has sprung from some scholar's reconstruction of the Johannine community that is alleged to have called this book forth (*e.g.* Brown; Schnackenburg; Porsch). Inevitably a degree of circularity is set up: the community is reconstructed by drawing inferences from the Fourth Gospel, and, once this background is sufficiently widely accepted, the next generation of scholars tends to build on it, or modify it only slightly, by showing how the Fourth Gospel achieves its purpose by addressing that situation so tellingly. The circularity is not necessarily vicious, but it is far weaker

---

[1]In one form, the theory is as old as Clement of Alexandria (Eusebius, *H. E.* VI. xiv. 7). In this century it was made famous by Hans Windisch, *Johannes und die Synoptiker* (J. C. Hinrichs'sche Buchhandlung, 1926).

than is often assumed, owing to the very high number of merely possible but by no means compelling inferences that are invoked to delineate the community in the first place.

Meeks, for instance, argues that the Johannine community is sectarian, an isolated conventicle in struggling opposition against a powerful synagogue.[1] The Fourth Gospel, then, is a summary of these Jewish polemics, possibly even a handbook for new converts, certainly something to strengthen the community in its continuing conflict. Martyn (*HTFG*) offers a species of the same scenario (discussed in the notes on Jn. 9). But major components of this reconstruction may be called into question. To think of the Johannine community as isolated and sectarian is to miss the grand vision of John 17, not to mention the fact that John's Christology finds its closest parallels in the New Testament in the so-called hymns (*e.g.* Phil. 2:5–11; Col. 1:15–20), which suggests that the fourth Evangelist is thoroughly in touch with the wider church.

By contrast, Strachan (pp. 44–45) argues that one of John's major purposes was to combat Gnosticism. Ultimately careful exegesis of several parts of this Gospel did prove helpful in the church's struggle against Gnosticism, but it is doubtful that this aim was uppermost in the Evangelist's mind (*cf.* esp. Smalley, pp. 132–135). The categories are too Jewish. As compared with 1 John, the Fourth Gospel, if measured against the goal of responding to Gnosticism, is decidedly weak. One might even conclude it is a resounding failure, judging by the number of Gnostics who tried to use it to support their claims.

(3) Similarly, some statements of John's purpose depend rather narrowly on a single theme, feature, or even literary tool. Mussner,[2] for instance, examines all expressions dealing with knowledge, hearing the word of Jesus, and the like, and suggests that the Evangelist is effecting a transfer of reference from the time of Jesus to his own time. In this merged vision, the past is not annulled, but the angle of vision is from the present. The audience is invited to share the Evangelist's vision. The merging of visions, however, is so strong, in Mussner's view, that the distinctive word of the historical Jesus cannot be distinguished at all. Whence, then, the Evangelist's constant distinction between what Jesus' disciples understood at the time, and what they understood only later (*cf.* discussion above, § III)? What starts off as a suggestive entry-point for considering the purpose of the Fourth Gospel ends up disowning too many features integral to the book.

In the same way, Freed[3] wonders if John 4 does not constitute evidence that the Fourth Gospel was written, at least in part, to win Samaritan converts. One may well ask what methodological steps warrant the leap from circumstances ostensibly set in Jesus' day to identical

---

[1]Not only his book, listed in the abbreviations, but also his important article in *JBL* 91, 1972, pp. 44–72.

[2]F. Mussner, *The Historical Jesus and the Gospel of St. John* (ET Burns and Oates, 1967).

[3]E. D. Freed, *NovT* 12, 1970, pp. 241–256.

circumstances set in the Evangelist's day. Again, Malina attempts to locate the Johannine community by reading the Fourth Gospel in the framework of two models provided by sociolinguistics. However, as subsequent debate demonstrated (at the colloquy where Malina's paper was presented),[1] not only the adequacy of the sociolinguistic models may be questioned (they are, after all, projections of *our* minds), but the extent to which data on the Johannine community are obtained to feed into the models by 'mirror-reading' the text and seeing what is not really there. In another vein, David Rensberger[2] largely accepts modern reconstructions of the Johannine community (based, as we have seen, on a number of merely possible inferences), and then makes a number of further inferences to plot primarily sociological dimensions in John's purpose: the Evangelist is a kind of liberation theologian. At some point the text of the Gospel is swamped by the rush of inferences. This is not to deny that there are ethical implications in John's message; it is to say that if all attention is devoted to the alleged community, and almost none to the Christ John is concerned to proclaim, even naive intuitions begin to raise warning flags. Yet again, Käsemann has argued that the Fourth Gospel embraces a docetic Christology, largely on the grounds that human elements in the picture of Christ seem to serve as a vehicle for communication of revelation, and are therefore nothing more than a mere show of humanity to make communication from the Johannine Christ possible. He has been criticized on many grounds, but above all because the actual data he isolates in John fit better into a larger explanatory framework in which the glory of the divine self-disclosure in Christ is manifested in the realm of the human, the mundane, and ultimately in the realm of shame and apparent defeat (*cf*. Carson, esp. pp. 154ff.; and notes above).

(4) Finally, several commentators adopt what might be called a synthetic approach. What appear to be the best suggestions of others are blended together, so that the purpose of John's Gospel is to evangelize Jews, to evangelize Hellenists, to strengthen the church, to catechize new converts, to provide materials for the evangelization of Jews, and so forth.[3] Part of the problem here is the confusion between purpose and plausible effect. Just because John's Gospel can be used to offer comfort to the bereaved in the twentieth century does not mean that is why the Evangelist wrote it. In the same way, just because this Gospel could help Jewish Christians witnessing to unconverted Jews and proselytes in the nearby synagogue does not *itself* mean that is why the Evangelist wrote it. To think through all the plausibly good effects various parts of this book could have does not provide adequate reason for thinking that

---

[1]Bruce J. Malina *et al.*, *The Gospel of John in Sociolinguistic Perspective*, ed. Herman C. Waetjen (Protocol of the Forty–Eighth Colloquy; Center for Hermeneutical Studies in Hellenistic and Modern Culture, 1984).

[2]*Overcoming the World: Politics and Community in the Gospel of John* (SPCK, 1988).

[3]Beasley–Murray, pp. lxxxvii–xc, comes close to this range.

any one of them, or all of them together, was the purpose the Evangelist had in mind when he put pen to paper.

Other unconvincing purposes can be scanned in the major introductions.

The proper place to begin is with John's own statement of his purpose: 'Jesus did many other miraculous signs in the presence of his disciples, which are not recorded in this book. But these are written that you may believe that Jesus is the Christ, the Son of God, and that by believing you may have life in his name' (20:30–31). The words rendered 'that you may believe' hide a textual variant: either *hina pisteuēte* (present subjunctive) or *hina pisteusēte* (aorist subjunctive). Some have argued that the latter expression supports an evangelistic purpose: that you may come to faith, come to believe. The former, then, supports an edificatory purpose: that you may continue in faith, continue to believe. In fact, it can easily be shown that both expressions are used for both initial faith and continuing in faith (*cf.* Carson, 'Purpose', pp. 640–641), so that nothing can be resolved by the appeal to one textual variant or the other.

It is worth comparing these verses with the stated purpose of 1 John: 'I write these things to you who believe in the name of the Son of God so that you may know that you have eternal life' (1 Jn. 5:13). This verse was clearly written to encourage Christians; by the contrasting form of its expression, John 20:30–31 sounds evangelistic.

This impression is confirmed by the firm syntactical evidence that the first purpose clause in 20:31 must be rendered 'that you may believe that the Christ, the Son of God, is Jesus'. Thus the fundamental question the Fourth Gospel addresses is not 'Who is Jesus?' but 'Who is the Messiah? Who is the Christ? Who is the Son of God?'[1] In their context, these are questions of identity, not of kind: *i.e.* the question 'Who is the Christ?' should *not* here be taken to mean 'What kind of "Christ" are you talking about?' but 'So you claim that you know who the Christ is. Prove it, then: Who is he?'

These matters are discussed in the commentary on 20:31, and the technical warrants are provided in Carson ('Purpose'). For now it is sufficient to observe that Christians *would not ask that kind of question*, because they already knew the answer. The most likely people to ask that sort of question would be Jews and Jewish proselytes who know what 'the Christ' means, have some sort of messianic expectation, and

---

[1] It can be shown that, before Christianity made any headway, 'Son of God' was used in Jewish circles in parallel to expressions referring to the Davidic Messiah (*cf.* notes on 20:30–31). Even within the Fourth Gospel, of the eleven occurrences of 'Son of God' (two of which are variants), three are in parallel to Messiah or Christ (1:49; 11:27; 20:31), one is connected with the resurrection, a decidedly Jewish notion (5:25), two are bound up with the Old Testament and/or Jewish tradition (10:36; 19:37), and the remaining five are entirely comprehensible within a Jewish framework. Therefore the view that says the addition of 'Son of God' in 20:31 suggests an extension of the message to the hellenistic world, outside the Jewish framework, is without warrant.

are perhaps in dialogue with Christians and want to know more. In short, John's Gospel is not only evangelistic in its purpose (which was a dominant view until this century, when only a few have defended it),[1] but aims in particular to evangelize Jews and Jewish proselytes. This view has not been popular, but is gradually gaining influence,[2] and much can be said for it. It may even receive indirect support from some recent studies that try to interpret the Fourth Gospel as a piece of mission literature. The best of these[3] display generally excellent exegesis, but give little attention to the fact that with very little adaptation the same exegesis could justify the thesis that the Gospel of John was not written *to* believers *about* mission but *to* outsiders to *perform* mission.

The translation of semitic words (*e.g.* 1:38, 41; 4:25; 19:13, 17) has little bearing on the race and religion of the intended audience; it reflects solely on that audience's linguistic competence. Far more important is the combination of biblical quotations and especially allusions to the Old Testament that presuppose considerable familiarity with the Greek Old Testament.[4] These allusions may be explicit (*e.g.* the snake in the desert, 3:14; the manna from heaven, 6:31ff.), but they are even more impressive when they are implicit. One thinks, for instance, of the way Jesus' person and work are tied to elements in the Jewish feasts, or to the way that Jesus replaces 'holy space' (*cf.* Davies, pp. 288–335). Culpepper (p. 221) has rightly noted how no explanation is offered of 'the Son of Man' (*cf.* notes on 1:51), of 'the Prophet' (1:21, 25; 6:14), of the devil (13:2) or Satan (13:27). The story of Jacob's ladder is presupposed (1:51), the opening words 'In the beginning' conjure up memories of the opening words of Genesis 1:1. These and scores of similar features rule out the view that the Evangelist had a biblically-illiterate readership in mind. If the work is evangelistic, and intended for those who enjoy some competence in what we today call the Old Testament, diaspora Jews and proselytes to Judaism constitute the only possibility. When this is combined with the sheer individualism of the Fourth Gospel[5] – *i.e.* with the emphasis on the *individual's* coming to faith and responding properly to

---

[1]*E.g.* W. Oehler, *Das Johannesevangelium eine Missionsschrift für die Welt* (Bertelsmann, 1936; *idem, Zum Missionscharackter des Johannesevangeliums* (Bertelsmann, 1941); Dodd, *IFG*, p. 9; C. F. D. Moule, *The Birth of the New Testament* (Black, ³1982), pp. 136–137; Guthrie, pp. 284–285; Morris, pp. 855–857; *cf.* Martin, pp. 274ff.

[2]K. Bornhäuser; W. C. van Unnik, *SE* I, 1959, pp. 382–411; J. A. T. Robinson, *NTS* 6, 1959–60, pp. 117–131 (repr. Robinson, *Twelve*, pp. 107–125); David D. C. Braine, *SNTU* 13, 1988, pp. 101–155, especially pp. 105–111; George J. Brooke, 'Christ and the Law in John 7–10', in Barnabas Lindars (ed.), *Law and Religion: Essays in the Place of the Law in Israel and Early Christianity* (SPCK, 1988), pp. 102–112; Carson, 'Purpose'.

[3]*Cf.* esp. Okure, *passim*. Something similar could be said for Miguel Rodriguez Ruiz, *Das Missionsgedanke des Johannesevangeliums: Ein Beitrag zur johanneischen Soteriologie and Ekklesiologie* (Echter Verlag, 1987). For a survey of recent studies of John along this vein, *cf.* Schnackenburg, 4. 58–72.

[4]*Cf.* D. A. Carson, 'John and the Johannine Epistles'.

[5]*Cf.* Moule, *op. cit.*, pp. 136–137.

God's gracious self-disclosure in Jesus – the picture is compelling.

If John is profoundly interested in preventing the diaspora Jews from committing the same errors and sins that so many Jews of Palestine committed, it is not altogether surprising that he should use such strong language to denounce 'the Jews' (cf. notes on 1:19ff.). John may well have an interest in driving a wedge between ordinary Jews and (at least) some of their leaders. The Fourth Gospel is not as anti-Jewish as some people think anyway: salvation is still said to be 'from the Jews' (4:22), and often the referent of 'the Jews' is 'the Jews in Judea' or 'the Jewish leaders' or the like.[1] 'Anti-semitic' is simply the wrong category to apply to the Fourth Gospel: whatever hostilities are present turn on *theological* issues related to the acceptance or rejection of revelation, and not on race. How could it be, when all of the first Christians were Jews, and when, on this reading, both the fourth Evangelist and his readers were Jews? Those who respond to Jesus, whether Jews, Samaritans or 'other sheep' (10:16) to be added to Jesus' fold, are blessed; those who ignore him or reject him do so out of unbelief, disobedience (3:36) and culpable blindness (9:39–41), not genes.

The commentary that follows occasionally pauses to show how one passage or another fits nicely into this purpose. Some have argued, for instance, that John 14 – 17 cannot possibly be viewed as primarily evangelistic. Such judgment is premature, for at least two reasons. First, the evangelism of the early church was not merely existential. It had to explain, as it were, 'how we got from there to here', *especially* if the targeted audience was Jewish. Second, the best evangelistic literature not only explains *why* one should become a Christian, and *how* to become a Christian, but *what it means* to be a Christian. John 14 – 17 addresses those concerns rather pointedly, and numerous details within those chapters likewise suggest an evangelistic thrust (*e.g.* 14:6).

Barrett (*GJJ*, pp. 1–19) objects to this thesis largely because he finds other emphases than Jewish ones in the Fourth Gospel. But that is scarcely an impediment to the thesis. Diaspora Judaism was nothing if not syncretistic. Barrett's evidence is carefully marshalled; his conclusion is not entailed by it.

These brief reflections on the purpose of the Gospel of John have a bearing on our earlier discussions of the relationship between John and the Synoptics. If John is aware of the existence of even one or more of the Synoptic Gospels, why does he not use more of their material? It is not that he must use everything, but is it not surprising when he does not make use of themes within them that are perfectly compatible with his own? Why, for instance, does he not mention the transfiguration, with its anticipation of Jesus' final glorification, Jesus' superiority over Moses and Elijah ('*This* is my beloved Son; hear *him!*'), the 'sonship'

---

[1]*Cf.* especially Reinhold Leistner, *Antijudaismus im Johannesevangelium? Darstellung des Problems in der neueren Auslegungsgeschichte und Untersuchung des Leidengeschichte* (Herbert Lang, 1974); S. Wilson, *IBS* 1, 1978, pp. 28–50.

motif itself, and its connection with Jesus' suffering (*cf.* Mt. 17:1–13; Mk. 9:2–13; Lk. 9:28–36) – all themes dear to John's heart?

Certainly John knew of a lot more material that he could have used, but chose not to (20:31; 21:25). One must not assume that silence on some topic signals ignorance. But if we assume that the Evangelist was John the son of Zebedee, and if we assume, still more tentatively, that he had read one or more of the Synoptic Gospels, and if his purpose in writing was to evangelize Jews and proselytes in the diaspora, then several conclusions suggest themselves: (a) he wrote not to supersede or correct Gospels that were already circulating, but because he found them inadequate *for his purpose*; and (b) it was *his own purpose* that largely determined what he included or excluded in his own Gospel. Without here probing the purpose of each of the Synoptic Gospels, it is possible that one or more of them had been read by some in his targeted audience. But John gives his own witness. Years of preaching to Jews, both in Palestine and in the diaspora, had given him some ideas about how it should be done. Here he puts his ideas on paper; the result is the Gospel of John.

This makes sense of so much of the Fourth Gospel: the move from sign to discourse, the powerful reiteration of a relatively small range of themes largely dealing with the most fundamental issues, the careful enunciation of how the first disciples came to distinctly Christian faith, the pattern of relationships between the Old Testament Scriptures and this new covenant community, the carefully-wrought warnings against unbelief, and explanations of such unbelief, against the background of analogous Old Testament texts (esp. ch. 12), the manner in which Jesus' presence is still mediated through the Holy Spirit whom the Old Testament Scriptures themselves had promised would characterize the messianic age, the distinctive handling of Jesus' death, resurrection and exaltation, the particular emphases bound up with the resurrection narratives, and much more.

Omissions are perhaps harder to account for, not because this delineation of John's purpose does not fit, but because explanations for silence are inevitably speculative. If we consider what many judge to be the hardest one, the omission of the transfiguration narrative, perhaps the following things could be said:

(1) This is not the only such omission: the failure to report the institution of the Lord's supper has generated enormous discussion, not a little of it relevant to the transfiguration: *cf.* notes on 6:25ff.

(2) It is possible, though certainly not provable, that many in his readership were already familiar with one account or other of the transfiguration – just as many scholars assume that many of the readers were familiar with the Lord's supper, and therefore of its institution. The same thing could be said for other surprising omissions, especially if one or more of the Synoptic Gospels was circulating. Indeed, it is remarkable *how few* Synoptic episodes crop up in John, and those that do could scarcely be omitted (*e.g.* the feeding of the five thousand could not easily be dropped, if John is set on including the bread of life discourse).

93

Without suggesting that the Evangelist sets out to correct or to supplement the Synoptics (such a characterization is too abstract, makes John merely parasitic on the Synoptics, and does not listen to John's stated intent, 20:30–31), this means that if John chooses to write his own book for his own ends he may do so without feeling the pressure merely to repeat what has already been done.

(3) The important themes connected with the transfiguration (outlined above) are all present in John, but:

(4) John may well have decided to omit the narrative because it does not fit well with his emphasis on Jesus' cross/exaltation as the ultimate glorification of the Son. Of course, the transfiguration could be *made* to fit. For those with eyes to see, Jesus' signs displayed Jesus' glory (2:11) even before the cross; presumably the transfiguration could have been treated similarly. Even so, John lays stress on the glory of the Son *in the context* of his humanity, culminating in the cross and his return to the glory he had with the Father before the world began; he does not report glimpses of glory somewhat abstracted from that mission, a foretaste of what was to come apart from the mission itself. Thus in the closest parallel to the transfiguration, the voice from heaven in John 12:28, everything turns on the imminence of the 'hour' that is nothing less than the cross/exaltation itself. The hour for the Son to be glorified is 'here', *i.e.* it is the next item in God's gracious and sovereign timing; but it is *not* a visible display of glory *before* the climax toward which John's Gospel has been building.

(5) If then John's purpose is to evangelize Jews and proselytes, he is doubtless aware just how big a 'stumbling-block' the cross is to Jews (*cf.* 1 Cor. 1:23). Part of his goal, then, in writing an evangelistic book for Jews and proselytes, is to make the notion of a crucified Messiah coherent. The *intrinsic* offence of the cross he cannot remove. What he can do, what he feels he must do, is to show that the cross was there from the beginning of Jesus' ministry (Jesus is early announced as the Lamb of God, 1:29), and that the cross is at one and the same time nothing less than God's own plan, the evidence of the people's rejection of their Messiah, the means of returning Jesus to his Father's presence, the heart of God's inscrutable purposes to bring cleansing (Jn. 13) and life to his people, the dawning of the promised eschatological age, God's astonishing plan to bring glory to himself by being glorified in his Messiah. And if this is John's concern, it is not entirely surprising that he decided to say nothing about the transfiguration. His purpose was too finely honed to admit it.

This approach may be supported by reflecting on the Fourth Gospel's 'plot'. The 'plot' is not mere sequence of events. '"The king died, and then the queen died" is a story. "The king died and then the queen died of grief" is a plot. The time-sequence is preserved, but the sense of causality overshadows it.'[1] So the plot of John's Gospel is very tight, and is tied,

---

[1] E. M. Forster, *Aspects of the Novel* (1927, repr. Penguin, 1962), p. 87; cited in Culpepper, p. 80. *Cf.* also J. A. du Rand, 'Plot and Point of View in the Gospel of John', in Petzer/Hartin, pp. 149–169.

finally, to the 'hour', the purpose of God in the crucial redemptive event in all Christian witness, the death, resurrection and exaltation of Jesus Christ, and the urgency of true faith in the wake of that event. Nothing will deter John from pressing to that point – indeed, from pressing men and women to come to terms with that point.

VII. SOME THEOLOGICAL EMPHASES IN JOHN

Some of John's emphases have already been introduced. His theology is so wonderfully integrated, however, that attempts to compartmentalize his thought by itemizing its components are destined in some measure to misrepresent it. The commentaries with the best theological summaries are probably those of Barrett (pp. 67–99) and Schnackenburg (in its various excursuses). Several studies at the intermediate level are useful,[1] as are the sections on John in some of the standard New Testament theologies.[2] Although there are countless volumes that examine this or that aspect of his thought, there is no full-scale treatment of Johannine theology that is worthy of the name.

Since the commentary attempts to offer some theological comment (not simply remarks on words and historical settings and the like), what follows is not so much an exposition of various theological emphases in the Fourth Gospel as a list of the briefest summaries of such emphases and an indication where they are treated at greater length in the commentary.

(1) John's presentation of *who Jesus is* lies at the heart of all that is distinctive in this Gospel. It is not just a question of some titles being ascribed to Jesus that are not found outside the Johannine corpus (*e.g.* 'Lamb of God', 'Word', 'I am'). Rather, fundamental to all else that is said of him, Jesus is peculiarly the Son of God, or simply the Son. Although 'Son of God' can serve as a rough synonymn for 'Messiah', it is enriched by the unique manner in which Jesus as God's Son relates to his Father. He is functionally subordinate to him, and does only those things that the Father gives him to say and do, but he does *everything* that the Father does, since the Father shows him everything that he himself does. The perfection of Jesus' obedience and the unqualified nature of his dependence thereby become the loci in which Jesus discloses nothing less than the words and deeds of God. Although 'Son of God' could be used in extraordinarily diverse ways in the ancient world, this distinctive emphasis in John casts back its glow on many of the

---

[1]*E.g.* Howard, *CSJ*; Vanderlip; Morris, *JC*; and *cf.* Kysar, *Fourth*, pp. 173–263; Smith, *Essays*, pp. 175–222.

[2]*E.g.* W. G. Kümmel, *The Theology of the New Testament* (SCM, 1974), pp. 255–319; George E. Ladd, *A Theology of the New Testament* (Lutterworth, 1975/Eerdmans, 1974), pp. 213–308.

other Christological titles. 'Son of God', as we have seen, can be parallel to 'Messiah'; but so powerfully is it constrained by this relation between the Father and the Son that 'Messiah' itself becomes not *merely* a prophetic category bound up with the line of David and the expectation of the prophets, but *also* a title that connotes the profoundly *revelatory* work of God's promised servant.

Similarly, although 'Son of Man' can bear something of the shadings it enjoys in the Synoptics, where it characteristically falls into one of three categories (the Son of Man ministering on earth, suffering in humiliation and death, and coming in apocalyptic glory to inaugurate the consummated kingdom), the *configuration* of sayings in John is quite independent. Typically, the Son of Man is 'lifted up' in death, glorified through death, so that those who believe in him will have eternal life. But this title, too, has overtones of revelation: only the Son of Man has been to heaven, and therefore can speak what no other human being knows; only he is the link between heaven and earth (1:51; 3:11–13).

Small wonder, then, that John's summarizing title for Jesus is the 'Word'. It is a brilliant choice. In the beginning was the Word; in the beginning God expressed himself, if you will. And that Self-Expression, God's own Word, identified with God yet distinguishable from him, has now become flesh, the culmination of the prophetic hope.

For 'Son of God' or 'Son', *cf.* notes on 1:14, 34, 49; 3:16–18; 5:16–30, 37–38, 43–46; 8:36ff.; 10:31–39; 11:27; 14:10; 15:22–24; 17:1ff.; 19:7; 20:17, 30–31.

For 'Son of Man', *cf.* notes on 1:51; 3:13–14; 5:27; 6:27, 53–54, 62; 8:28–29; 9:35; 12:23–34; 13:31–32.

For 'Rabbi' or 'Teacher', *cf.* notes on 1:38, 49; 3:2, 26; 4:31–32; 6:25; [8:4]; 11:3, 8, 28; 13:13; 20:16.

For 'Messiah' or 'the Christ', *cf.* notes on 1:19–20, 29ff., 40–42; 3:1–3; 4:25–26, 28–29; 6:60–62; 7:30–32, 40–42; 9:22, 39; 10:22–30; 11:27; 12:34; 20:30–31.

For 'Lamb of God', *cf.* notes on 1:28, 29–36; 10:14–18; 11:51–52; 12:1; 15:13; 19:14; and *cf.* notes on the topic of 'salvation', below.

For the use of 'I am', with or without a predicate, *cf.* notes on 4:26; 6:20, 35; 8:12, 18, 23, 24, 28, 58; 10:7, 9, 11, 14; 11:25–26; 13:19; 14:6; 15:1, 5; 18:6, 8.

For Jesus as the King of Israel or of the Jews, *cf.* notes on 1:49; 12:13–18; 18:33–38; 19:2–3, 12, 15, 19–22.

For the way Jesus as the 'Word' illuminates this Gospel, *cf.* notes on 1:1–18; 3:3; 5:19–30; 6:63; 10:34–36; 12:44–50; 13:31–32; 14:6; 16:12; 17:6, 17; 19:5; 21:25.

For Jesus as God, *cf.* notes on 1:1, 14, 18; 5:19–30; 8:24, 28, 58; 10:33–36; 18:5–6, 8; 20:28.

For other Christological titles and emphases (except those implicit under other Johannine emphases, below), *cf.* notes on 1:25–27, 34, 38–39; 3:1–2, 16–21; 4:19, 24, 33–34, 42; 5:9–10, 26, 31–32, 45–46; 6:14–15, 46, 61, 68; 7:7–9, 18, 45–46, 52; 8:14, 30; 9:7, 16–17; 10:1ff.; 11:32–35;

12:7–8, 12–15, 44–50; 13:1ff., 36–37; 14:6–7, 9–11, 28–31; 15:1–5; 16:2–3; 17:1ff.; 18:4, 11.

(2) Both in the ancient world and our own, *salvation* was not a transparent category: it needed to be filled out. Salvation from what, we might ask, and by what means? That Jesus came not to judge the world but to save it (3:17; 12:47) demands that we think through the nature of the salvation he has achieved. Salvation, he insists, is of the Jews (4:22): the framework for Jesus' understanding of his own mission is shaped by the Scriptures mediated by the Jews, not by Samaritan distinctives, still less by Gnosticism.

If Jesus is the Lamb of God, it is that he might take away the world's sin (1:29, 36). The slavery from which he sets men and women free is slavery to sin (8:34ff). Despite the heavy emphasis on Jesus as the one who reveals his Father, salvation does not come (as in Gnosticism) by *mere* revelation. John's work is a Gospel: all the movement of the plot is toward the cross and the resurrection. The cross is not *merely* a revelatory moment (*contra* Forestell): it is the death of the shepherd for his sheep, the sacrifice of one man for his nation, the life that is given for the world, the victory of the Lamb of God, the triumph of the obedient Son who in consequence of his obedience bequeaths his life, his peace, his joy, his Spirit.

For John's development of the theme of salvation, and related notions of sin, atonement, life and knowledge of God, *cf.* notes on 1:4–5, 8–11, 16–17, 29–34; 2:12–17, 23–25; 3:1–2, 14–15, 16–21, 36; 4:10, 13–26, 44, 48, 53; 5:14, 22–23, 24, 39–40; 6:27, 33, 36, 51–58, 62–63; 7:17, 18; [8:1–11]; 8:15, 21–26, 31ff.; 9:5, 25, 38–41; 10:11–18; 11:49–52; 12:14–15, 44, 50; 13:5–10; 15:21–25; 17:1ff.; 18:15–18, 25–27; 19:11, 34–37; 20:23, 30–31.

(3) Few areas of John's thought have been more widely disputed, and with more divergent results, than *eschatology* (*cf.* Carson, pp. 134–146). John's development of this theme is tightly bound up with his distinctive use of 'the hour' (often rendered 'time' in NIV: *e.g.* 2:4; 7:6). All major New Testament corpora display the tension of trying simultaneously to express the wonderful truth that in the ministry, death, resurrection and exaltation of Jesus God's promised 'last days' have already arrived, and to insist that the fulness of that hope is still to come. Different authors set out the tension in different ways. The kingdom of God has come, but we must wait for it to come. The Holy Spirit is given to us as the downpayment and guarantee of the new heaven and the new earth, of the promised new creation with its resurrection hope; but meanwhile we groan in our earthly bodies waiting for the redemption that will be ours some day. The same tension is found in John: the hour 'is coming and has now come' (4:23; 5:25). Jesus has bequeathed his peace, but in this world we will have trouble (16:33).

Above all, in the wake of Jesus' exaltation and his gift of the Spirit, we can possess eternal life even now: that is a characteristic of John, who tilts his emphasis to the *present* enjoyment of eschatological blessings. But this is never at the expense of any future hope: the time is coming when those who are in the graves will come out to face the judgment of the One to whom all judgment has been entrusted by the Father (5:28–30). This is neither an aberration in John's thought, nor a piece of unassimilated tradition clumsily added by an incompetent redactor. It is part of what makes it possible for Christians to think of themselves as living between the 'already' and the 'not yet', between D-day and V-day (to use Cullmann's famous analogy). If John insists that Jesus even now makes himself present amongst his followers in the person of his Spirit (*e.g.* 14:23), he also insists Jesus himself is coming back to gather his own to the dwelling he has prepared for them (14:1–3).

For the Johannine distinctives on eschatology, *cf.* notes on 1:31–33; 2:4; 3:3, 5, 15–16; 4:23–24, 37–38; 5:21, 24–29; 6:14–15, 25; 8:15–16, 51; 11:23–26; 12:20–36; 13:1, 31–32, 36–37; 14:1–4, 11, 18–20, 22–23, 27; 16:6–7, 13; 16:19ff.; 17:1ff., 12, 24–26; 19:25–27, 34–35; 20:17; 21:20–23.

(4) John's teaching on the *Holy Spirit* has important similarities to Synoptic emphases. The Spirit is given to Jesus at his baptism; Jesus, in contrast to John the Baptist, is the one who will baptize his people 'in Holy Spirit'. But Jesus himself is uniquely endowed with the Spirit (3:34; *cf.* Lk. 4:14–21). He is not only the one who bears and bestows the Spirit, but by bequeathing the eschatological Spirit he discharges his role as the one who introduces what is characteristic under the promised new covenant (3:5; 7:37–39; though that terminology is not used). In the farewell discourse, the Holy Spirit is repeatedly described as the *paraklētos* – a pregnant expression that gives as much substance to the Spirit's work amongst believers as any in the New Testament. Above all, John ties the gift of the Spirit to the death and exaltation of the Son. The result is the elements of what came to be known as the doctrine of the Trinity. *Cf.* notes on 1:31–34; 3:3, 5, 6, 33–34; 4:23–24; 6:63; 7:37–39; 14:16–17, 23, 25–26; 15:26–27; 16:7–15; 20:21–23.

(5) Although John's *use of the Old Testament* is not as frequent or as explicit as that of Matthew, it is not slight (despite charges to that effect), and it is enriched by an extraordinarily frequent and subtle number of *allusions* to the Old Testament. One of the features of these allusions is the manner in which Jesus is assumed to *replace* Old Testament figures and institutions. He is the new temple, the one of whom Moses wrote, the true bread from heaven, the true Son, the genuine vine, the tabernacle, the serpent in the wilderness, the passover. Rarely articulated, there is nevertheless an underlying *hermeneutic* at work, a way of reading the Old Testament that goes back to Jesus himself. For some consideration of these matters, *cf.* notes on 1:14–18, 22–23, 34, 45, 47, 51; 2:1, 17–22, 23; 3:5, 14, 29–30; 4:21–22, 33–34; 5:17, 35, 38–40, 45, 46–47; 6:27–34, 35, 45, 49–50, 51; 7:19, 22–24, 37–39; [8:5–8]; 9:7, 28–29; 10:1–2, 3, 10, 11, 34–36; 12:13–14, 28, 34, 37–43; 13:18, 34–35; 15:1ff., 20, 25; 17:6, 12, 19; 19:18, 19–22, 28–29, 34, 36–37.

(6) No Gospel preserves more instances of *misunderstanding* and of failures to understand than does John. As we have already seen (§ III, above), the Gospel that is most explicit in its high Christology is most

insistent that the original disciples understood very little of it at the time. This polarity provides us with a remarkable approach to John's handling of history: many of the misunderstandings he attributes to the disciples of Jesus in the days of his flesh could not possibly have occurred in the days when the Evangelist wrote his Gospel. John not only *can* make the distinction between 'back then' and 'now', the structure of his theology demands that he do so. Otherwise the salvation-historical pattern of progressive revelation with which he himself operates would dissolve. *Cf.* notes on 2:19–22; 3:4; 4:11, 33–34; 6:34–35, 52, 60–62; 7:24ff., 41–42; 8:13ff., 19, 27, 31ff.; 10:6, 19–21, 24, 31–33, 39; 11:16; 12:16, 29–30; 13:28, 36–37; 14:5, 8; 16:17–18; introduction to 20:1ff., 9.

(7) Because so much scholarly interest has focused on the delineation of the Johannine community, there has been a corresponding emphasis on *the people of God* in this Gospel, on the church. Some of this discussion has been misguided: *e.g.* there has been considerable speculation as to why there is no mention of church officers such as elders and deacons. This, of course, is an instance of a theory running amok: however much we think we can infer about John's community, the fact remains that John set out to write a *Gospel*, to write about Jesus' ministry, death, resurrection and exaltation, not to write on the aftermath of that ministry. Those parts of the book that bear most immediately on the church are therefore cast in terms of what will take place after Jesus has returned to his Father.

This said, the elements of what it means to belong to the people of God, what it means, in fact, to be the church, are richly present (*cf.* Guthrie, *NTT*, pp. 720–730). If there is nothing on the ordering of the church's life or on the mechanics of organization and administration, there is much on the church's election, life, origin, nature, witness, suffering, fruit-bearing, prayer and unity, for these things are irrefragably tied to the person and mission of the Son. *Cf.* notes on 1:10–13; 3:3, 5, 19–21, 33, 36; 4:23–24; 5:24; 6:33, 37–40, 63–65; 7:37–39; 8:30ff.; 10:1ff.; 11:50–52; 12:24–26; 13:1, 8, 12–17, 34–35; 14:1–4, 6–7, 12–14, 21–23; 15:1ff.; 17:1ff; 19:23–24, 28–29; 21:1–14, 15–23.

(8) Of a quite different order is what John says (or does not say!) about *sacraments*. On the one hand, there is no record of the institution of the Lord's supper; on the other, the bread of life discourse is richly endowed with expressions that millions of Christians have happily applied to holy communion. The Fourth Gospel, I shall argue, is neither sacramentarian nor anti-sacramentarian: the categories are wrong. But by its consummately careful use of language, it drives people to the reality, to Christ himself, refusing to stop at that which points to the reality. *Cf.* notes on 1:24–26; 3:5, 22ff.; 4:2; 6:11, 22ff.; 7:37–39; 9:7; 13:10–11, 14–15; 15:1ff.; introduction to 17:1ff.; 19:34; 21:13.

(9) The complexities that bind together *election, faith and the function of signs* deserve some reflection. John holds men and women responsible for believing; unbelief is morally culpable. If faith bursts forth in consequence of what is revealed in the 'signs', well and good: they

legitimately serve as a basis for faith (*e.g.* 10:38). On the other hand, people are excoriated for their dependence on signs (4:48). It is a better faith that hears and believes rather than sees and believes (20:29). But in the last analysis, faith turns on sovereign election by the Son (15:16), on being part of the gift from the Father to the Son (6:37–44). And this, it must be insisted, drums at the heart of a book that is persistently evangelistic. God's will is not finally breached, even in the hardness of human hearts (12:37ff.), yet never is there the faintest hint of raw determination or fatalism, and always is there every inducement to trust 'the Saviour of the world' (4:42).

No New Testament book more acutely focuses attention on these essentially biblical polarities than the Gospel of John. *Cf.* notes on 1:12–13; 2:1–11, 23; 3:1–5, 19–21, 27, 36; 4:53–54; 5:5–6, 37–38; 6:1–21, 26, 29, 30–31, 37–44, 63–70; 7:1–5, 31; 8:45–47; 9:1–12, 35–41; 10:3–5, 14–15, 25–29, 37–38; 11:1–44, 45–48; 12:10–11, 17–19, 37–44; 13:1; 14:11; 15:16; 16:22; 17:2, 6, 11–16; 20:1ff., 29, 30–31; 21:1–14.

VIII. PREACHING FROM THE FOURTH GOSPEL

Because many who read this commentary will be preachers or Bible study leaders, two or three comments for them seem in order. These comments arise, in part, out of concern that the kinds of theological topics canvassed in the last section have been so abstracted from the text that they somehow lose the life and power of the Gospel narratives and discourses themselves. But these comments may also be necessary because many young preachers (and some not so young!) find it relatively easy to preach from an epistle, but find little to say when they turn to the Gospels.

Of the three comments that follow the first two pertain to preaching from any of the Gospels, and the last has to do with the peculiar challenge of preaching from John. In all of them, I assume that the reader has already devoted a fair bit of thought to the relations between ancient text and contemporary context, between expository lecture and expository preaching (where men and women are made to feel the text's bite and balm), between rigorous exegetical accuracy and colourful presentation.

(1) The challenge of preaching from the Gospels is, in part, the challenge of preaching from narrative. The best of Western seminaries and theological colleges reinforce the cultural bent toward the abstract, and fill students' heads with the importance of grammatical, lexicographical exegesis. Such exegesis is, of course, of enormous importance. But in students who do not have a feel for literature, it can have the unwitting effect of so focusing on the tree, indeed on the third knot of the fourth branch from the bottom of the sixth tree from the left, that the

entire forest remains unseen, except perhaps as a vague and ominous challenge.

The antidote is to direct attention to the *narrative* – not only the narrative of the entire Gospel, but each narrative within it. The precise meaning of, say, John 3:5 cannot properly be abstracted from the meaning of John 3:1–21; the meaning of John 2:4 cannot properly be sorted out without thinking through the meaning of John 2:1–11. Of course, the converse must also be said: the meaning of John 3:1–21 turns on John 3:5 (and a lot of other things as well). And the meaning of the pericope (as an individual unit within a Gospel is called) John 2:1–11 also depends on its place within the Gospel as a whole, *i.e.* what comes immediately before it and after it, the flow of the text and surrounding context, the place of the individual pericope within the entire Gospel.

Theoretically, most of us recognize these things. In my experience, however, too few preachers wrestle with their implications. They too often work exclusively from atomistic points of grammar outward to the pericope; they almost never work from the Gospel down through the pericope to the individual points of grammar. Both kinds of work are needed in reading any text, but the need is especially urgent in narrative texts.

(2) The challenge of preaching from the Gospels is the challenge of unpacking their place within redemptive history. It is at this point, I fear, that a certain amount of preaching in rather conservative contexts unwittingly tumbles into the same sort of error as some rather radical brands of Gospel criticism.

Gospel criticism, as we have seen, devotes so much attention to imaginative and detailed reconstructions of the communities of the Evangelists that what the Evangelists say about Jesus or claim that he himself said or did receives fairly short shrift. For quite different reasons, many conservative preachers are so busy drawing applications for their own congregations that they skip the prior question, 'What does this passage tell us about Jesus?' This is not the question of unreflective pietism. It is the question that must be asked *precisely because the material we are studying is a Gospel*.

To put the matter more positively, it is essential to locate the Gospels in their proper place in the stream of redemptive history. Although the Gospels were written after most of the epistles, what they purport to describe occurred before them. To use an analogy, doubtless two competent historians describing the Second World War, one writing in 1950 and the other in 1990, will differ in their visions as to what took place. In some measure, it ought to be possible to say something about their respective visions from the way their works proceed. But in both instances the topic of their exposition is the Second World War, not the intellectual communities out of which each historian has emerged. The analogy is imperfect, of course, since a Gospel-writer is likely to be far more interested in confessional witness and the immediate edification of his readers than a contemporary historian. Even so, the point is important, not only for the sake of Gospel criticism, but also for the preacher. John writes his book from his own vantage point, but he does not forget that he is writing about Jesus, the Jesus of history, the Jesus who ministered, died and rose again. We have already seen ample evidence that John distinguished between what the disciples grasped of Jesus during the days of his ministry, and what they understood only later. This means that the preacher must constantly reflect on what the Evangelist is telling him about Jesus, both what took place 'back then' and what Christians, aided by the Spirit, came to understand of that unparalleled revelation.

Although there are many passages in the Gospels that enable the preacher to make a direct application to the congregation or to contemporary society (*e.g.* the love command, Jn. 13:34–35), there are still more whose proper application awaits reflection on what the passage says about Jesus. By 'what the passage says about Jesus' I do not refer exclusively to Jesus' person and words and deeds (though I do not mean less than that), but to all that can be known of Jesus *and his place in the sweep of redemptive history*. How does Jesus fit into the Bible's 'story'? Rightly done, preaching from the Gospels enables a congregation to put its Bible together, and then to find the Bible's deepest and most transforming application emerging from this vision. To put the matter another way, John's stated purpose in composing the Fourth Gospel is not that his readers might believe, but that his readers might believe that the Christ, the Son of God, is Jesus, and that in believing they might have life in his name. To hammer away at the urgency of belief without pausing to think through *what* it is John wants his readers to believe and *whom* it is he wants them to trust is to betray the Gospel of John. Preaching from the Gospels is above all an exercise in the exposition and application of Christology.

(3) Even so, those who set out to expound John's Gospel, as opposed to one of the Synoptics, often find themselves enmeshed in 'vain repetition'. John's vision is more narrowly focused than that of the Synoptists. For all the wealth of his presentation of Jesus, his own application, made again and again with driving force, is that his readers should believe. Many a preacher has begun a series on this book only to find that his application is becoming boring even to his own ears, and abandoned the series at ch. 7 or ch. 9 or the like.

Two suggestions will largely dissolve this problem. The first was articulated under the last point: the series should concentrate on Jesus himself, on the fathomless Christological wealth bound up in this Gospel. The second suggestion is to select a fairly large unit of text as the basis for each sermon. If a preacher takes six weeks to expound the Prologue (1:1–18), and is actually saying anything that has much content, almost inevitably a great deal of later material in John has been dragged in. Far better to deliver one's soul on the Prologue in one sermon, complete ch. 1 the next week, and proceed at a good pace through the text so that while the slower preacher is polishing closing remarks on 1:51 you are already well into the farewell discourse.

IX. THE STRUCTURE OF JOHN'S GOSPEL

Like many other facets of the Gospel of John, its basic structure seems fairly simple until one starts to think about it. Doubtless this complexity wrapped in simplicity is the reason why scores of studies on John's structure have been published in the last two or three decades.

On the face of it, the Fourth Gospel offers a prologue (1:1–18) and an epilogue or appendix (21:1–25), between which are the two central sections, 1:19 – 12:50 and 13:1 – 20:31. Under the influence of two or three influential scholars, these are now frequently designated, respectively, 'Book of Signs' and 'Book of Glory' (Brown, 1. cxxxviii–cxxxix), or 'Book of Signs' and 'Book of the Passion' (Dodd, *IFG*, p. 289). The advantages are obvious.

Nevertheless, 'Book of Signs' makes it sound as if the signs are restricted to 1:19 – 12:50, whereas 20:30–31 makes it clear that from the Evangelist's perspective the *entire* Gospel is a book of signs. Moreover, although it is true that Jesus' passion is related in chs. 13 – 20, the passion narrative itself does not begin until ch. 18. If chs. 13 – 17 can be included on the ground that they are thematically tied to the passion, so also are many passages in chs. 1 – 12 (*e.g.* 1:29, 36; 6:35ff.; 11:49–52).

Others have advocated a quite different structure. Wyller,[1] for example, holds that 10:22–29 is the 'structural summit' of the work, the 'change of fate' of the hero, around which the rest of the material is organized. Despite the superficial plausibility of his argument, it is difficult to believe, on thematic grounds, that these verses have quite the structural importance Wyller assigns to them, and almost impossible to believe that Plato's Simile of the Cave is the most plausible model for the structure of a Gospel. Another scholar has detected a massive concentric structure patterned to match the concentric structure in the Prologue.[2] However, structures that are so complex and disputed as not to be *intuitively* obvious should be held rather loosely.

Trying to account for all the complexity in John, the latest major discussion of the structure of John's Gospel[3] finds major chiasms and what the author calls 'bridge-pericopes' and 'bridge-sections'. For instance, he suggests that 2:1 – 12:50 might be called the 'Book of Jesus' Signs', that 11:1 – 20:29 is the 'Book of Jesus' Hour', and that the overlapping chapters, John 11 – 12, constitute a 'bridge-section'. Although this or that detail may be disputed, he does succeed in showing how unified and tightly organized the Fourth Gospel is. It is anything but haphazard. Many have pointed out, for instance, that

---

[1]Egil A. Wyller, *ST* 42, 1988, pp. 151–167.

[2]Jeffrey Lloyd Staley, *The Print's First Kiss: A Rhetorical Investigation of the Implied Reader in the Fourth Gospel* (SBLDS 82; SP, 1985).

[3]George Mlakushyil, *The Christocentric Literary Structure of the Fourth Gospel* (An. Bib. 117; Pontifical Biblical Institute, 1987).

individual sections of various length are neatly brought to a close (*e.g.* 1:18; 4:42; 4:53–54; 10:40–42; 12:44–50; 20:30–31; 21:25).

One of the reasons why critics find so many mutually exclusive structures in John is that his repeated handling of only a few themes makes it possible to 'find' all kinds of parallels and chiasms.

The analysis that follows attempts to weigh the development of the Gospel *as a narrative* against the more formal considerations of structure. For instance, it has often been noted that the section 2:1 – 4:54 reflects a geographical *inclusio* (*i.e.* a literary device by which a passage is bounded by the same literary feature): the action moves from Cana to Cana. But although that is noted in the commentary, and the *inclusio* itself helps us discern that 2:1 – 4:54 does constitute a unit, it is less than clear that Cana *per se* is so important in Johannine thought it should be accorded paramount *theological* significance, beyond its minor role in helping readers to follow the movement of the text.

I am reasonably confident that the analysis follows the movement of thought that the Evangelist intended, but it must be stressed that this outline is no more authoritative than the chapter and verse divisions with which we are more familiar, and which formed no part of the original writing. It is not so much the basis of the exposition that follows, as its result. If it helps readers to follow the commentary, and thus in measure to follow John's thought as he bears witness to the Messiah the Son of God, it is amply justified.

ANALYSIS

COMMENTARY

I. THE PROLOGUE (1:1–18)

The Prologue is a foyer to the rest of the Fourth Gospel (as John's Gospel is often called), simultaneously drawing the reader in and introducing the major themes. The following parallels between the Prologue and the rest of the book immediately stand out,[1] although as we shall see there are many others of a more subtle nature:

	Prologue	Gospel
the pre-existence of the Logos or Son	1:1–2	17:5
in him was life	1:4	5:26
life is light	1:4	8:12
light rejected by darkness	1:5	3:19
yet not quenched by it	1:5	12:35
light coming into the world	1:9	3:19; 12:46
Christ not received by his own	1:11	4:44
being born to God and not of flesh	1:13	3:6; 8:41–42
seeing his glory	1:14	12:41
the 'one and only' Son	1:14, 18	3:16
truth in Jesus Christ	1:17	14:6
no-one has seen God, except the one who comes from God's side	1:18	6:46

Not only so, but many of the central, thematic words of this Gospel are first introduced in these verses: life, light (1:4), witness (1:7), true (in the sense of 'genuine' or 'ultimate', 1:9), world (1:10), glory, truth (1:14). But supremely, the Prologue summarizes how the 'Word' which was with God in the very beginning came into the sphere of time, history, tangibility[2] – in other words, how the Son of God was sent into the world to become the Jesus of history, so that the glory and grace of God might be uniquely and perfectly disclosed. The rest of the book is nothing other than an expansion of this theme.

The tightness of the connections between the Prologue and the Gospel render unlikely the view that the Prologue was composed by

---

[1] Adapted from Robinson, *More*, p. 68.
[2] *Cf.* Frank Kermode, *JSNT* 28, 1986, pp. 3–16.

someone other than the Evangelist. Suggestions that the Prologue, though written by the Evangelist, was composed later than the rest of the book (as the introduction of this commentary was written last!) are realistic, but speculative.

Many suggestions have been made that the Prologue was originally a poem from some other religious tradition (perhaps gnostic,[1] though there is no shortage of theories) that John took over and adapted for his own ends. Every writer uses sources in some sense, but the strong form of this hypothesis goes so far as to try to strip away John's alleged accretions in the hope of exposing the 'original'. The more specific the suggestions as to the shape and content of this 'original', the more speculative the arguments seem to be, with the result that few adopt so strong a form of the theory today. If John has used sources in the Prologue we cannot isolate them, for they have been so thoroughly re-worked and woven into a fabric of fresh design that there are no unambiguous seams.

The term 'poem' can be applied to the Prologue only with hesitation. Many have argued that the Prologue is poetry interrupted by two prose insertions (1:6-8, 15). The great diversity of the suggestions about how the 'poem' hangs together (cf. Brown, 1. 22) confirms what classical scholars are quick to point out on other grounds: these verses do not reflect the structure and rhythm of Greek poetry. Some therefore propose that the poetical features of the Prologue be explained by appealing to the poetic characteristics of Hebrew or Aramaic, on the assumption that the Prologue is a Greek translation of an underlying semitic work. But the characteristics in question – parallelism of various kinds, short clauses, frequent chiasms and the like – are found throughout the prose text of the entire Gospel. The most that can be concluded is that the *frequency* of such features in 1:1-18 enables us to speak of 'rhythmical prose'.

In particular, especially in the first half of the Prologue (1:1-12a) there is a set of linking words that lend deliberate pacing and dignity to the text. For example (using English words but the word order of the Greek text), we find in vv. 1-2, 'In the beginning . . . Word . . . Word . . . God . . . God . . . Word . . . in the beginning . . . God'; in v. 3, 'were made . . . were made'; in vv. 4-5, 'life . . . life . . . light . . . light . . . darkness . . . darkness'; in vv. 7-9, 'as a witness [testimony] . . . to testify concerning that light . . . not the light . . . as a witness [testimony] to the light . . . The true light that gives light'; in vv. 10-12, 'the world . . . the world . . . the world . . . that which was his own . . . his own . . . did not receive him . . . received him'. From v. 12b on there are few such links, and the rise in pace adds forward movement as the text with increasing explicitness drives deeper into the realm of history.

---

[1]For a prudent assessment of the relation between the Prologue and the *Trimorphic Protennoia* (the gnostic document to which appeal is currently most frequently made), *cf.* Craig A. Evans, *NTS* 27, 1981, pp. 395-401.

The structure of the Prologue is also disputed. Of the large number of proposals advanced by various writers, one of the most believable (though still not entirely free of difficulty) is the large chiasm put forward by Culpepper.[1] If one begins with both ends of the Prologue and works toward the middle, then at certain levels 1:1–2 parallels 1:18, 1:3 parallels 1:17, 1:4–5 parallels 1:16, 1:6–8 parallels 1:15, 1:9–10 parallels 1:14, 1:11 parallels 1:13, 1:12a parallels 1:12c, making 1:12b ('he gave them the right to become children of God') the 'pivot' on which the chiasm turns, the centre of attention. If the Prologue focuses on God's self-disclosure in the Word who becomes flesh (1:14) and thereby reveals glory and makes God known (1:18), it also introduces us to the result of this gracious revelation: certain people and not others become children of God. The rest of the Gospel is much concerned to spell out who the real children of God are, who truly are the children of Abraham, which people receive the Spirit and are born again.

Whether or not John intended his readers to find a chiasm in his Prologue, he clearly expected them to detect a certain progression in his line of thought. This in turn suggests that the two references to John the Baptist (1:6–8, 15) are not accidentally placed or somewhat repetitious. In 1:1–5, John traces his account of Jesus farther back than the beginning of the ministry, farther back than the virgin birth, farther back even than the creation. The account must reach back to the eternal, divine Word, God's agent in creation and the fount of life and light. Having established that absolute starting-point, the Evangelist then turns to the starting-point common to all early Christian tradition: the ministry of John the Baptist (1:6–8), whose transitoriness and function as a witness qualify him to be cast as a foil for the true light coming into the world. It is the coming of this light, and the reactions to him, that are then stressed (1:9–13). Although he was almost universally rejected, some people, born of God, did receive the right to become children of God. The coming of the light, of the Word, that made this possible was nothing less than incarnation, the 'in-fleshing' of the Word so that his grace and truth could be seen by human beings in a human being (1:14). Appropriately, it is at this point that the witness of John the Baptist is again introduced (1:15), and rises to the level of historical particularity. Precisely because the Evangelist's readers are familiar with the Old Testament, he concludes by briefly articulating the relationship between Jesus Christ and the revelation that has already been given, especially in the covenant mediated through Moses (1:16–18).

1. *In the beginning* immediately reminds any reader of the Old Testament of the opening verse of the Bible: 'In the beginning God created the heavens and the earth.' Genesis begins with creation; John refers to creation (vv. 3–4), but soon turns to what Paul calls 'new creation' (Jn. 3;

---

[1]R. Alan Culpepper, *NTS* 27, 1980–81, pp. 1–31. For a slightly different chiasm, *cf.* Jeff Staley, *CBQ* 48, 1986, pp. 241–263.

cf. 2 Cor. 5:17). Both in Genesis and here, the context shows that the *beginning* is absolute: the beginning of all things, the beginning of the universe. The Greek word behind 'beginning', *archē*, often bears the meaning 'origin' (cf. BAGD), and there may be echoes of that here, for the Word who already was 'in the beginning' is soon shown to be God's agent of creation (vv. 3–4), what we might call the 'originator' of all things. Granted that the Word enjoyed this role, it was inevitable that at the origin of everything he already was. Since Mark begins his Gospel with the same word, '*The beginning* of the gospel about Jesus Christ', it is also possible that John is making an allusion to his colleague's work, saying in effect, 'Mark has told you about the *beginning* of Jesus' public ministry; I want to show you that the starting point of the gospel can be traced farther back than that, before the *beginning* of the entire universe.'

Although the meanings of *ēn* ('was') and *egeneto* (rendered 'were made' in v. 3, 'came' in v. 6 and 'became' in v. 14) often overlap, John repeatedly uses the two verbs side by side to establish something of a contrast. For example, in 8:58 Jesus insists, '[Before] Abraham *was born* [a form of the second verb], *I am* [a form of the first verb].' In other words, when John uses the two verbs in the same context, *ēn* frequently signals existence, whereas *egeneto* signals 'coming into being' or 'coming into use'. In the beginning, the Word was already in existence.[1] Stretch our imagination backward as we will, we can find no point in time where we may agree with Arius, who, speaking of the Word, said, 'There was once when he was not.'[2]

But what is meant by 'Word'? The underlying term, *logos*, was used so widely and in such different contexts in first-century Greek (cf. LSJ) that many suggestions as to what it might mean here have been put forward.[3] The Stoics understood *logos* to be the rational principle by which everything exists, and which is of the essence of the rational human soul. As far as they were concerned, there is no other god than *logos*, and all that exists has sprung from seminal *logoi*, seeds of this *logos*. Others have suggested a background in Gnosticism, a widespread, ill-defined movement in the Mediterranean world of the first three centuries; but it must be admitted that, so far as our sources go, there is little evidence for the existence of full-blown Gnosticism before John wrote his Gospel (cf. the Introduction, §§ II–III). Still others think John has borrowed from Philo, a first-century Jew who was much influenced by Plato and his successors. Philo makes a distinction between the ideal world, which he calls 'the *logos* of God', and the real or phenomenal

---

[1] The other two uses of 'was' in v. 1 are less loaded, theologically speaking, for the verb there functions as a 'copula', *i.e.* as a connective joining the subject with its completion. Thus, in 'the Word *was* with God', the verb connects 'the Word' and 'with God' to establish a relationship, while in 'the Word *was* God' the verb connects 'the Word' and 'God' so as to predicate something of the Word.

[2] Socrates, *Ecclesiastical History*, I. v. 2.

[3] For useful surveys cf. NIDNTT, 3. 1081–1119; H. Bietenard, *ANRW* II 19. 2, pp. 580–618; NBD, pp. 703–704.

world which is but its copy. In particular, *logos* for Philo can refer to the ideal man, the primal man, from which all empirical human beings derive. But Philo's *logos* has no distinct personality, and does not itself *become* incarnate. John's *logos* doctrine, by contrast, is not tied to such dualism. More generally, *logos* can refer to inner thought, hence 'reason', even 'science'. That is one reason why some have advocated 'Reason' as a translation of *logos* (*e.g.* Clark). Alternatively, *logos* can refer to outward expression, hence 'speech' or 'message', which is why 'Word' is still thought by many to be the most appropriate term, provided it does not narrowly refer to a mere linguistic sign but is understood to mean something like 'message' (as in 1 Cor. 1:18).

However the Greek term is understood, there is a more readily available background than that provided by Philo or the Greek philosophical schools. Considering how frequently John quotes or alludes to the Old Testament, that is the place to begin. There, 'the word' (Heb. *dābār*) of God is connected with God's powerful activity in creation (*cf.* Gn. 1:3ff.; Ps. 33:6), revelation (Je. 1:4; Is. 9:8; Ezk. 33:7; Am. 3:1, 8) and deliverance (Ps. 107:20; Is. 55:1). If the LORD is said to *speak* to the prophet Isaiah (*e.g.* Is. 7:3), elsewhere we read that 'the *word of the* LORD came to Isaiah' (Is. 38:4; *cf.* Je. 1:4; Ezk. 1:6). It was by 'the word of the LORD' that the heavens were made (Ps. 33:6): in Gn. 1:3, 6, 9, *etc.* God simply speaks, and his powerful word creates. That same word effects deliverance and judgment (Is. 55:11; *cf.* Ps. 29:3ff.). When some of his people faced illness that brought them to the brink of death, God 'sent forth his word and healed them; he rescued them from the grave' (Ps. 107:20). This personification of the 'word' becomes even more colourful in Jewish writing composed after the Old Testament (*e.g. Wisdom* 18:14, 15). Whether this heritage was mediated to John by the Greek version of the Old Testament that many early Christians used, or even by an Aramaic paraphrase (called a 'Targum'), the ultimate fountain for this choice of language cannot be in serious doubt.

There are other components in the Old Testament background to the term *logos*. The 'Wisdom' of God is highly personified in some passages (especially Pr. 8:22ff.), becoming the agent of creation and a wonderful gift. This personification is again extended in later Jewish writings (*e.g. Wisdom* 7:22 – 8:1; *Ecclus.* 24). Many scholars, finding frequent parallels to John in Wisdom literature,[1] hold that the Evangelist assigns to *logos* some of the attributes of Wisdom. Something similar could be argued for the place of *Torah* (roughly, the law or teaching of God) in rabbinic thought; and again, the Word whom John is announcing picks up such themes and in certain respects transcends them (see below on vv. 16–18). There is much to be said for both views. However, the lack of Wisdom *terminology* in John's Gospel suggests that the parallels between

---

[1] *E.g.* Craig Koester, *The Dwelling of God: The Tabernacle in the Old Testament, Intertestamental Jewish Literature, and the New Testament* (CBQMS 24; CBA, 1989), pp. 108–110; Dodd, *IFG*, pp. 274–277; Haenchen, 1. 138–140.

Wisdom and John's *Logos* may stem less from direct dependence than from common dependence on Old Testament uses of 'word' and *Torah*, from which both have borrowed.

In short, God's 'Word' in the Old Testament is his powerful self-expression in creation, revelation and salvation, and the personification of that 'Word' makes it suitable for John to apply it as a title to God's ultimate self-disclosure, the person of his own Son. But if the expression would prove richest for Jewish readers, it would also resonate in the minds of some readers with entirely pagan backgrounds. In their case, however, they would soon discover that whatever they had understood the term to mean in the past, the author whose work they were then reading was forcing them into fresh thought (see on v. 14).

One must go farther. The wealth of possible backgrounds to the term *logos* in John's Prologue suggests that the determining factor is not this or that background but the church's experience of Jesus Christ. This is not to say the background is irrelevant. It is to say, rather, that when Christians looked around for suitable categories to express what they had come to know of Jesus Christ, many that they applied to him necessarily enjoyed a plethora of antecedent associations. The terms had to be semantically related to what the Christians wanted to say, or they could not have communicated with their own age. Nevertheless, many of the terms they chose, including this one, had semantic ranges so broad that they could shape the term *by their own usage* to make it convey, *in the context of their own work*, what they knew to be true of Jesus Christ (*cf.* Boice, p. 163). In that sense, as helpful as the background study may be, it cannot by itself determine exactly what John means by *logos*. For that information, while thinking through the background uses, we must above all listen to the Evangelist himself.

Because this Word, this divine self-expression, existed in the beginning, one might suppose that it was either with God, or nothing less than God himself. John insists the Word was both. The Word, he says, was *with God*. The preposition translated 'with' is *pros*, which commonly means 'to' or 'toward'. On that basis, many writers say John is trying to express a peculiar intimacy between the Word and God: the Word is oriented *toward* God, like lovers perpetually running *toward* each other in a beach scene from a sentimental film. That surely claims too much. In first-century Greek *pros* was encroaching on the territory normally occupied by other words for 'with'. In the NIV, the following instances of 'with' all have *pros* behind them: 'Aren't his sisters here *with* us?' (Mk. 6:3); 'Every day I was *with* you' (Mk. 14:49); 'at home *with* the Lord' (2 Cor. 5:8); 'I would have liked to keep him *with* me' (Phm. 13); 'the eternal life, which was *with* the Father' (1 Jn. 1:2). What we notice about all these examples, however, is that in all but one or two peculiar constructions (*e.g.* 1 Pet. 3:15), *pros* may mean 'with' only when a person is *with* a person, usually in some fairly intimate relationship. And that suggests that John may already be pointing out, rather subtly, that the

'Word' he is talking about is a person, *with* God and therefore distinguishable from God, and enjoying a personal relationship with him.

More, *the Word was God*. That is the translation demanded by the Greek structure, *theos ēn ho logos*. A long string of writers has argued that because *theos*, 'God', here has no article, John is not referring to God as a specific being, but to mere qualities of 'God-ness'. The Word, they say, was not God, but divine. This will not do. There is a perfectly serviceable word in Greek for 'divine' (namely *theios*). More importantly, there are many places in the New Testament where the predicate noun has no article, and yet is specific. Even in this chapter, 'you are the King of Israel' (1:49) has no article before 'King' in the original (*cf.* also Jn. 8:39; 17:17; Rom. 14:17; Gal. 4:25; Rev. 1:20). It has been shown that it is common for a definite predicate noun in this construction, placed before the verb, to be anarthrous (that is, to have no article; *cf.* Additional Note). Indeed, the effect of ordering the words this way is to emphasize 'God', as if John were saying, 'and the word was *God*!' In fact, if John had included the article, he would have been saying something quite untrue. He would have been so identifying the Word with God that no divine being could exist apart from the Word. In that case, it would be nonsense to say (in the words of the second clause of this verse) that the Word was *with* God. The 'Word does not by Himself make up the entire Godhead; nevertheless the divinity that belongs to the rest of the Godhead belongs also to Him' (Tasker, p. 45). 'The Word was *with* God, God's eternal Fellow; the Word *was* God, God's own Self.'[1]

Here then are some of the crucial constituents of a full-blown doctrine of the Trinity. 'John intends that the whole of his gospel shall be read in the light of this verse. The deeds and words of Jesus are the deeds and words of God; if this be not true the book is blasphemous' (Barrett, p. 156). It may well be that the Old Testament authority for this ascription of deity to the Messiah was Psalm 45 (as it was for the writer of Heb. 1), where the most obvious understanding of the text is that God himself addresses the messianic king as 'God'.[2] Others have suggested Isaiah 9:7. Certainly there is ample evidence that the early Christians were not slow in coming to confess Jesus not only as Messiah but also as God (Rom. 9:5; Phil. 2:5–11; Col. 1:15–20 – though in each instance some critics read the evidence another way). John is the most straightforward of all the New Testament writers in this respect (*cf.* also 20:28).

2. In one sense this verse is simply a repetition of the first two clauses of v. 1. But John includes these words to make sure what he has already said is understood. After all, v. 1 is very condensed. Now John works backward, saying in effect: 'This Word who is God, is the very one of whom I have also said that he was in the beginning, and that he was

---

[1]Edmund P. Clowney, 'A Biblical Theology of Prayer', in D. A. Carson (ed.), *Teach Us to Pray: Prayer in the Bible and the World* (Paternoster/Baker, 1990).
[2]*Cf.* G. Reim, *NTS* 30, 1984, pp. 158–160; M. J. Harris, *TynB* 35, 1984, pp. 65–89.

with (*pros*) God.' In particular, v. 2 reiterates the middle clause of v. 1, and thus prepares the way for v. 3.

3–4. Assuming that the NIV accurately represents the relation between v. 3 and v. 4 (see Additional Notes), and rightly renders the Greek, then v. 3 simply insists, both positively and negatively, that the Word was God's Agent in the creation of all that exists. Positively, *Through him all things were made*; negatively, *without him nothing was made that has been made.*The change in tense from *were made* to *has been made* is then the change in reference from the act of creation to the state of creation. Even so, the latter is a strange form of expression. It may be better to render the Greek, 'All things were made by him, and what was made (taking *ho gegonen* as the subject of the second clause) was in no way (taking *ouden* adverbially) made without him.'[1] Either way, the point is powerfully made. Just as in Genesis, where everything that came into being did so because of God's spoken word, and just as in Proverbs 3:19; 8:30, where Wisdom is the (personified) means by which all exists, so here: God's Word, understood in the Prologue to be a personal agent, created everything.

That the pre-existent Christ created everything is a common theme in the New Testament, even though the title 'Word' in this connection is restricted to the present passage. Referring to Jesus Christ, Paul says that all things were created 'by him' and even 'for him', and that 'in him all things hold together' (Col. 1:16–17). The writer of Hebrews speaks of the Son as the one through whom God made the universe (Heb. 1:2); the Apocalypse presents him as 'the Amen, the faithful and true witness, the *archē* (beginning? originator? ruler?) of God's creation' (Rev. 3:14) – and here 'Amen' may be an attempt to render the Hebrew '*āmôn* in Proverbs 8:30, where Wisdom is the 'craftsman'. 'No literary dependence is probable between one and another of these passages: the teaching which they convey is antecedent to them all and therefore impressively primitive' (Bruce, p. 32). John may share the language of some hellenistic philosophy, but his strong doctrine of creation radically avoids the dualism in which much of that tradition is steeped.

'Life' and 'light' are almost universal religious symbols. In John's usage they are not sentimental props but ways of focusing on the excellencies of the 'Word': *In him was life, and that life was the light of men.* Many commentators draw attention to the formal parallel in 5:26: 'For as the Father has life in himself, so he has granted the Son to have life in himself.' The relationship between God and the Word in the Prologue is identical with the relationship between the Father and the Son in the rest of the Gospel. Both 1:4 and 5:26 insist the Word/Son shares in the self-existing life of God. Later on Jesus claims that he is both the light of the world (8:12; 9:5) and the life (11:25; 14:6). Both Wisdom and Torah are commonly associated with life and light in the

[1]Georg Korting, *BZ* 33, 1989, pp. 97–104.

Jewish sources; John ties them in with Christ, the Word.

Nevertheless there is a difference between this passage and most of the rest of the Gospel where light and life come to the fore. In the rest of his book, John is largely interested in 'light' and 'life' as they relate to salvation: the 'light' is revelation which people may receive in active faith and be saved, the 'life' is either resurrection life or spiritual life that is its foretaste. If 1:4, by contrast, is read in the context of the first three verses, it is more likely that the life inhering in the Word is related not to salvation but to creation. The self-existing life of the Word was so dispensed at creation that it became the light of the human race (*tōn anthrōpōn*, 'of human beings'). It is not clear whether John is thinking of our essential constitution, the fact that we have been made 'in the image of God' (*cf.* Gn. 1:27, continuing the creation theme), or of the reflection of himself in the universe he has created (what theologians sometimes call 'natural' or 'general' revelation; *cf.* Rom. 1:20), or even of more specific revelation bound up with the coming of the Son. At least in this verse, John is more interested in the source of the light (the life of the Word) and its purpose (for the human race) than in the mode or purpose of its dispersal.

5. This verse is a masterpiece of planned ambiguity. If a hellenistic Jew, or for that matter even a pagan Greek, read through the opening verses to this point, and had no personal experience of Christianity, he or she might well take v. 5 to refer exclusively to creation, without moral overtones. Light and darkness are not simply opposites; darkness is nothing other than the absence of light. At the first creation, 'darkness was over the surface of the deep' (Gn. 1:2) until God said, 'Let there be light' (Gn. 1:3). At no time other than creation could it more appropriately be said, *The light shines in the darkness*. Precisely because John is talking about creation, and is not describing a dualistic universe in which light and darkness, goodness and evil, are matched opposites, he can describe the victory of the light: *the darkness did not overcome it* (as the verb *katelaben* can be translated). This understanding of v. 5 is in line with those who say that the Prologue makes no mention of the incarnation, or even of the personal, saving revelation of the Word, until v. 14.[1]

But any reader who had entered into sustained dialogue with Christians, and, more importantly, any reader who had read through this Gospel once and was now re-reading it, could not fail to see in v. 5 an anticipation of the light/darkness duality that dominates much of the rest of the book. The 'darkness' in John is not only absence of light, but positive evil (*cf.* 3:19; 8:12; 12:35, 46; 1 Jn. 1:5, 6; 2:8, 9, 11); the light is not only revelation bound up with creation, but with salvation. Apart from the light brought by the Messiah, the incarnate Word, people love darkness because their deeds are evil (3:19), and when the light does put

---

[1]*E.g.* Dunn, *Making,* pp. 239–243; Dodd, *IFG,* pp. 268–272. The suggestion of Sanders, p. 75, that there is included here a reference to the failure of persecution to stifle the gospel, is needlessly anachronistic, and contributes nothing to the flow of the Prologue.

in an appearance, they hate it, because they do not want their deeds to be exposed (3:20). In fact, wherever it is true that *the light shines in the darkness*, it is also true that *the darkness has not understood it* (taking *katelaben* as in the NIV). Reading v. 5 this way anticipates the rejection theme that becomes explicit in vv. 10–11. Alternatively, even if *katelaben* means something like *'did not overcome* it' (see Additional Note), it is quite possible that John, subtle writer that he is, wants his readers to see in the Word both the light of creation and the light of the redemption the Word brings in his incarnation.

6–8. The ultimate origins of Jesus Messiah, John will insist, are in the pre-incarnate Word who was with God and who was God. But when he comes to the account of Jesus' public ministry on the stage of human history, the Evangelist, in common with the Synoptics and with early Christian preaching, begins with the witness of John the Baptist (1:19ff.; *cf.* Acts 1:21–22; 10:37; 13:24–25). That is why it is entirely appropriate for him to introduce the Baptist here. The Word in whom inheres the life that is the light of men was first displayed in the public arena of history when a man sent from God bore witness to him. The name of that man *was John*. Interestingly, it is only in this Gospel that there is no additional description such as 'the Baptist', even though the Evangelist is careful to distinguish other characters who bear the same name (*e.g.* 'Then Judas (not Judas Iscariot)', 14:22; 'he gave it to Judas Iscariot, son of Simon' (13:26). The Evangelist does not need to identify John as 'the Baptist', because he never mentions by name the only other John in Jesus' circle, John the son of Zebedee, the brother of James and intimate of Peter. The traditional explanation for this silence is still the best one: John the son of Zebedee was responsible for this Gospel, and preferred to refer to himself only obliquely (*cf.* Introduction, § IV).

The forerunner's significance to the story is grounded in the fact that he was *sent from God*, assigned to this specific task. That he was commissioned by the Almighty places him in the same category as Moses (Ex. 3:10–15) and the prophets (*e.g.* Is. 6:8; Je. 1:4ff.) – indeed, in this respect, he is like Jesus himself, who was also sent from God (3:17; a frequent theme in the Fourth Gospel. *Cf.* the Additional Notes.). Obedient to his commission, he *came as a witness to testify* concerning the light. The courtroom language of 'witness' and 'testimony' is common in the New Testament (*cf.* Trites, esp. pp. 78–127),[1] but especially in this Gospel. A fuller description of the Baptist's witness appears in vv. 19–34; 3:27–30; 5:35, with a marvellous summary in 10:40–42. But other witness to the truth of God's self-disclosure in the Word abounds: there is the witness of the Samaritan woman (4:39), of the works of Jesus (5:36; 10:25), of the

---

[1]Similarly Harvey, and to some extent Boice. Nevertheless such 'witness' language is used in the ancient world in many contexts outside the courtroom: *cf.* J. Beutler, *Martyria: Traditionsgeschichtliche Untersuchungen zum Zeugnisthema bei Johannes* (Josef Knecht, 1972). In consequence, the courtroom scene forcefully advanced by Trites and Harvey needs substantial qualification.

Father (5:32, 37; 8:18), of the Old Testament (5:39–40), of the crowd (12:17), and of the Holy Spirit and the apostles (15:26–27). All these bear witness to Jesus, who himself bears witness to the truth (18:37), in conjunction with the Father (8:13–18).

The purpose of John the Baptist's witness, though of course not its result, was *so that through him all men might believe*. John 1:35–37 provides an instance where John's witness was not only effective but particularly fruitful in its result. Derivatively, because the Baptist's witness has been bound up in all four canonical Gospels with the beginning of Jesus' ministry, like Abel 'he still speaks, even though he is dead' (Heb. 11:4). All who have ever come to faith are indirectly dependent on his opening proclamation of the identity and saving purpose of Jesus Messiah.

Verse 8, with its negative insistence that the Baptist *was not the light*, has prompted many to speculate that the Evangelist wrote these words to refute a group of people who contended that John the Baptist was himself the final revelation of God to mankind, and that Christians had wrongly elevated Jesus to that status. That some people did associate themselves with John's baptism is clear from Acts 19:1–7, and from later sources; that they actually opposed the claims of Christians is not clear. John may have written v. 8a with such a group in mind, but it is important to remember that by and large the portrait of the Baptist in the Fourth Gospel is highly favourable (*cf*. Barth, pp. 50ff.), and quite in line with Matthew 11:2–15, which also grounds the significance of the Baptist's place in redemptive history in the peculiar testimony he bore to Jesus Christ (*cf*. Carson, *Matt*, pp. 260–269). Moreover the negative assertion of v. 8a may simply pave the way for v. 9. In any case, the negative clause in v. 8a is part of a construction that may be designed to stress the certainty of the divine plan. At the risk of overtranslation, we might render the verse, 'He was not the light, but it was necessary that he bear witness to the light.'[1]

9. If the phrase 'coming into the world' is understood to be masculine and attached to 'every man', then we must translate this verse as in NIV fn.: 'This was the true light that gives light to every man who comes into the world' (similarly AV). If this is the correct rendering, then there is nothing here or in v. 10 that requires us to go beyond the illumination granted to the entire race in the Word's creative activity (*cf*. vv. 4–5). This view is reinforced by a common rabbinic expression, 'all who come into the world', used to describe 'every man'. But that expression is always plural; the construction here is singular. It is best to take 'coming into the world' as a neuter form attached to 'light', adopting the translation of NIV: *The true light that gives light to every man was coming into the world*. The most convincing support for this rendering is the fact that 'coming into the world' or being sent into the world is in this Gospel repeatedly predicated of him who is the Word. Moreover the peculiar

---

[1]*Cf*. E. Delebeque, *Etudes Classiques* 54, 1986, pp. 147–158.

Greek syntax this translation presupposes is a common feature of John's style (*cf.* 1:28; 2:6; 3:23; 10:40; 11:1; 13:23; 18:18, 25).[1] What this means is that in this verse it is the Word, the light, that is coming into the world, in some act distinct from creation. If incarnation is not spelled out as forcefully as in v. 14, it is the same special visitation that is in view. Few could read the Fourth Gospel for the second time without recognizing that the coming of the Word into the world, described in the Prologue, is nothing other than the sending of the Son into the world, described in the rest of the book.

The word for 'true' (*alēthinos*), here and often in John, means 'real' or 'genuine'. Occasionally the word simply means 'veracious' as opposed to 'untrue', applicable to statements, witness, opinions (*e.g.* 4:37; 19:35); but characteristically it is applied to light (here), worshippers (4:23), bread from heaven (6:32), the vine (15:1), and even to God himself (7:28; 17:3). Other persons or institutions may claim to be the light, to be worshippers, to be the vine, to be bread from heaven, even to be 'god'; John sets out to present the *true* light, vine, bread and so forth.

In some passages this notion of 'true' or 'genuine' shades off into 'ultimate', because the contrast is not simply with what is false but with what is earlier and provisional or anticipatory in the history of God's gracious self-disclosure. 'The Johannine use of *alēthinos* does carry something of the Greek meaning of "real", but it is the real because it is the full revelation of God's truth' (Ladd, p. 167). Thus the manna provided in the Old Testament was genuinely from God; but Jesus is the *true* bread, the ultimate and therefore the genuine bread from heaven. Israel was God's chosen vine, and John would happily acknowledge the fact; but now Jesus himself is the locus or stalk of God's covenant community, whose members must be related to him as branches. So also here: any reader of the Old Testament would know that the law and Wisdom give light (*cf.* on 8:12), but John's point is that the Word who came into the world is *the* light, the *true* light, the genuine and ultimate self-disclosure of God to man.

Because John has insisted that the Word was the agent of creation, it might be thought that when he now describes that Word as coming *into the world* he means nothing more than that the Word has invaded the created order he himself made. But *world* for John has more specific overtones. Although some have argued that for John the word *kosmos* ('world') sometimes has positive overtones ('God so loved the world', 3:16), sometimes neutral overtones (as here; *cf.* also 21:24–25, where the 'world' is simply a big place that can hold a lot of books), and frequently negative overtones ('the world did not recognise him', 1:10), closer inspection shows that although a handful of passages preserve a neutral emphasis the vast majority are decidedly negative. There are no unambiguously positive occurrences. The 'world', or frequently 'this world'

---

[1]For another possibility, *cf.* Borgen, *Logos*, p. 103.

(*e.g.* 8:23; 9:39; 11:9; 18:36), is not the universe, but the created order (especially of human beings and human affairs) in rebellion against its Maker (*e.g.* 1:10; 7:7; 14:17, 22, 27, 30; 15:18–19; 16:8, 20, 33; 17:6, 9, 14). Therefore when John tells us that God loves the world (3:16), far from being an endorsement of the world, it is a testimony to the character of God. God's love is to be admired not because the world is so big but because the world is so bad. Barrett (pp. 161–162) thinks that in 3:16 the world can be 'split up into its components', those who believe and those who do not. In fact, the 'world' in John's usage comprises no believers at all. Those who come to faith are no longer of this world; they have been chosen out of this world (15:19). If Jesus is the Saviour of the world (4:42), that says a great deal about Jesus, but nothing positive about the world. In fact, it tells us the world is in need of a Saviour.

This structure is quite at odds with any gnostic or other interpretation that divides up the human race on the grounds of constitutional difference, some people being constitutionally able to receive the light because something of that light has been captured in their own beings. Even in v. 9, where 'world' might at first be taken as an instance of *kosmos* with neutral force, John is setting the stage for the massive rejection recorded in v. 10. Moreover, if the light comes *into the world*, it is because the proper abode of life is quite outside it; it does not belong to this world (8:23; 18:36), which is characterized by darkness. What is proper to this world is utterly repugnant to God (1 Jn. 2:16).

What then does John mean by saying that this light which comes into the world *gives light* (*phōtizei*) *to every man*? The complexities are several:

(1) The verb *phōtizei* may mean 'to illuminate (inwardly)', *i.e.* 'to give knowledge'. Though lexically secondary, this meaning is common in the LXX (*e.g.* Ps. 19[18]:8), and is known in the New Testament (*e.g.* Eph. 1:18). The possible interpretations are then three: (a) The true light shone on 'every man' without exception before coming into the world (at the incarnation), and continues to do so. The idea is akin to what systematic theologians call 'general revelation', which strips human beings of excuse (as Paul argues, Rom. 1:20; so Calvin, 1.15; Morris, p. 95). The thought is parallel to 1:4 as read in the light of 1:3 (*cf.* notes, above). But it is a little late in the Prologue to be harking back to that theme. (b) Alternatively, the true light may be understood to be shining in the context of the incarnation, illuminating not 'every man' without exception but 'every man' without distinction (*i.e.* not Jews only; *cf.* Acts 1:8; Col. 3:11). The thought is then parallel to 1:4 as read in the light of 1:5 (*cf.* notes, above; Bruce, p. 36). Lindars sees a parallel to *Wisdom* 9:9–18, 'where Wisdom, identified with the Holy Spirit, is the source of revelation, which man may too easily fail to perceive' (p. 89). But it is doubtful that John ever eliminates distinctions between the Word and the Holy Spirit, who in any case has not yet been introduced. More important, there are reasons for thinking that 'light' in John has a more discriminating function (*cf.* below). (c) A variation on the second interpretation is an appeal to Augustine's famous illustration of a town with

only one teacher. Though not all the citizens are the teacher's students, he is nevertheless the teacher for everyone. So Christ is the only true light God has given to the world, and therefore the light for every man. But however theologically true this is, it is not what the text says. It speaks not of the Word serving as (potential) light *for* every man, but of giving light *to* every man.

(2) The verb *phōtizei* may have its primary lexical meaning 'to shed light upon', *i.e.* 'to make visible', 'to bring to light'. Inner illumination is then not in view (whether of general revelation or of the special light that attends salvation). What is at stake, rather, is the objective revelation, the 'light', that comes into the world with the incarnation of the Word, the invasion of the 'true light'. It shines on every man, and divides the race: those who hate the light respond as the world does (1:10): they flee lest their deeds should be exposed by this light (3:19–21). But some receive this revelation (1:12–13), and thereby testify that their deeds have been done through God (3:21). In John's Gospel it is repeatedly the case that the light shines on all, and forces a distinction (*e.g.* 3:19–21; 8:12; 9:39–41). This light '"shines upon every man" (whether he sees it or not)' (Barrett, p. 161).

10. The Word, then, *was in the world* as a result of his special coming into it. Our decision regarding the meaning of 'world' in v. 9 has its bearing on the interpretation of v. 10. This was the world that *was made through him* – not a mere repetition of vv. 3–4, since 'world', as we have seen, has a narrower focus than 'everything that has been made'. The point is that John will not allow ontological dualism, the view that there exists a principle of evil entirely independent of the universe God created. Far from it: apart from the Word, 'nothing was made that has been made' (1:3). That includes the *kosmos*, the world of human beings and their affairs in rebellion against the Word. Instead of allowing dualism, John grounds the moral responsibility of the race in the doctrine of creation. This world created through the 'Word' *did not recognise him*, they did not 'know' him (*cf.* the Additional Notes).

11. This verse is not merely a poignant repetition of v. 10, even though its pathos stamps the coming of the Word as more personal and loving than the coming of the *logos* in pagan and gnostic thought. Indeed, for this reason the verse was instrumental in the conversion of Augustine (*Confessions*, VII, 9). The Word *came to that which was his own*: this is an attempt to translate *eis ta idia*: the neuter *ta idia* might mean 'his own property', or, better, 'his own home' (as in 16:32; 19:27; *cf.* Howard, p. 470; Thucydides, I. 141),[1] The former could be referring to the world as the Word's 'property'; the latter tilts the meaning in favour of a reference to the Jewish nation and heritage.[2]

---

[1]Although *ta idia* can refer either to possessions or home/homeland, the fuller expression, *eis ta idia*, always in the LXX and the NT means 'to one's home/homeland'.

[2]J. Jervell (*ST* 10, 1956, p. 21), however, though he accepts that *eis ta idia* here means 'to his own home', thinks the *world* is the proper homeland of the *Logos*, not the Jewish

If the Word of God came to fallen mankind in the general terms earlier described in v. 5, he came in law, prophecy, and wisdom, in deeds of deliverance, judgment, and mercy, and in sheer, brilliant theophany. Now the Word comes in personal self-disclosure 'to his own home', but his own people (as the masculine *hoi idioi* must be translated) *did not receive him*. Because of the universality of the Word's creative work, there is of course a sense in which *all* people are his own people; but in the light of the rest of the Gospel, the Evangelist is probably here thinking of the Jewish nation from which salvation comes (4:22). Indeed, the expression used, *hoi idioi*, is for John a characteristically (*cf.* esp. 1:41; 5:18; 10:3, 4, 12) *relational* term. John focuses not on the mere *status* of the covenant community, but on their proper *relationship* to the Word.

Again and again under the old covenant, the prophets describe the recalcitrance of the people of God. 'All day long I have held out my hands to an obstinate people, who walk in ways not good, pursuing their own imaginations – a people who continually provoke me to my very face' (Is. 65:2–3), declares the LORD. 'From the time your forefathers left Egypt until now [the onset of the Babylonian exile], day after day, again and again I sent you my servants the prophets. But they did not listen to me or pay attention. They were stiff-necked and did more evil than their forefathers' (Je. 7:25–26). This is the theme that John is picking up, and will develop in his own way;[1] for if there was one, dominant point that Christians had to make in their evangelism of first-century Jews (whether Jews steeped in a semitic tradition or those more orientated to the hellenistic world), it was the proposition that the Scriptures themselves require that the man they proclaimed as Saviour and Lord be crucified and largely rejected by his own people. That theme, as we shall see, reaches a climax in 12:37–41.

12–13. By themselves, vv. 10–11 would be grim indeed; but vv. 12–13 immediately soften the sweeping rejection of the Word by indicating that, as in Old Testament times, there remains a believing remnant. Many have pointed out that the words 'his own did not receive him' (1:11) could be placarded over the first twelve chapters of this book, but over chs. 13 – 21 we might raise the banner, '*Yet to all who received him* . . .'. Another way of describing these people is to say that they *believed in his name*. The 'name' is more than a label; it is the character of the person, or even the person himself. The entire expression does not guarantee that those who exercise such faith are genuine believers (see comments on 2:23–25); but at its best, such faith yields allegiance to the Word, trusts him completely, acknowledges his claims and confesses

---

nation. That would be entirely contrary to Johannine usage of 'world' (*kosmos*; *cf.* notes on v. 9). *Cf.* further J. W. Pryor, 'Jesus and Israel in the Fourth Gospel – John 1:11', *NovT* 32, 1990, pp. 201–218.

[1]Yet at the same time, 'the Jews' (*cf.* notes on 1:19) so commonly *represent* the world in the Fourth Gospel that even after we have concluded that v. 11 articulates a narrower and more emotional focus than v. 10, the broader pattern of rejection, encompassing the entire 'world', is never far away.

him with gratitude. That is what it means to 'receive' him.

To people who received him, to those who displayed such faith the Word *gave the right* (*exousia*; not 'power' as in AV) *to become children of God*. These people enjoy the privilege of becoming the covenant people of God, a privilege lost by the Messiah's own people (1:11), those related to him by nature and by the grace of the old covenant (*cf.* notes on vv. 16, 17).[1] In John the believer becomes a 'child' (*teknon*) of God, but only Jesus is the 'son' (*huios*) of God. The language is unlike that of Paul, who describes both Jesus and the believer as 'son' of God, but believers are 'sons' only by adoption. Thus both writers presume a distinction between the 'sonship' of believers and the unique 'sonship' of Jesus.

Another way of describing those who receive the Word is suggested by the 'children of God' metaphor: they are *children born not of natural descent, nor of human decision or a husband's will, but born of God*. The Prologue thus introduces us to the 'new birth' theme of ch. 3. The series of negations makes the same general point as 3:6: 'Flesh gives birth to flesh, but the Spirit gives birth to spirit.' Being born into the family of God is quite different from being born into a human family. 'Natural descent' (lit. 'of bloods', *i.e.* a blood relationship, on the assumption that natural procreation involves the mixing of bloods) avails nothing – which means that heritage and race, even the Jewish race, are irrelevant to spiritual birth. In John 8 the Evangelist enlarges on this theme, showing that physical descent from Abraham is of no significance if one does not reproduce Abraham's faith (*cf.* also Rom. 4; Gal. 3). Spiritual birth is not the product of sexual desire, 'the will of the flesh', here rendered 'of human decision'; it is certainly not the result of a husband's will (who is understood to take a 'lead' in sexual matters). New birth is, finally, nothing other than an act of God.

Some have argued that faith (v. 12) is the logical and temporal *condition* of the new birth (1:13; *e.g.* Barrett, p. 164); others have argued precisely the reverse (*e.g.* Holtzmann, pp. 40–42). In fact, these verses refrain from spelling out the connection between faith and new birth. Those who receive the Word are identical with those who believe in his name, and they are identical with those who are born of God (*cf.* further discussion in Carson, pp. 181–182).

14. For the first time since v. 1, the term *ho logos*, 'the Word', reappears. At this point the incarnation, the 'in-fleshing' of the Word, is articulated in the boldest way. If the Evangelist had said only that the eternal Word assumed manhood or adopted the form of a body, the reader steeped in the popular dualism of the hellenistic world might have missed the point. But John is unambiguous, almost shocking in the expressions he uses (*cf.* especially Barth, pp. 85ff.): *the Word became flesh*. Because succeeding clauses in this verse allude to Exodus 33:7 – 34:35, it is tempting to think this first clause does the same. The 'tent of meeting'

---

[1] J. W. Pryor, *RTR* 47, 1988, p. 48.

was the place where the LORD 'would *speak* to Moses face to face, as a man speaks with his friend' (Ex. 33:11). In Exodus Moses hears the divine name spoken by God himself, and this is followed by God's *word* written on two stone tablets. Now, John tells us, God's Word, his Self-expression, has become flesh.

This is the supreme revelation. If we are to know God, neither rationalism nor irrational mysticism will suffice: the former reduces God to mere object, and the latter abandons all controls. Even the revelation of antecedent Scripture cannot match this revelation, as the Epistle to the Hebrews also affirms in strikingly similar categories: 'In the past God spoke to our forefathers through the prophets at many times and in various ways, but in these last days he has spoken to us by his Son' (Heb. 1:1–2). The Word, God's very Self-expression, who was both with God and who was God, became flesh: he donned our humanity, save only our sin. God chose to make himself known, finally and ultimately, in a real, historical man: 'when "the Word became flesh", God became man' (Bruce, p. 40).[1]

The Word *made his dwelling among us*. More literally translated, the Greek verb *skēnoō* means that the Word pitched his tabernacle, or lived in his tent, amongst us. For Greek-speaking Jews and other readers of the Greek Old Testament, the term would call to mind the *skēnē*, the tabernacle where God met with Israel before the temple was built. The tabernacle was erected at God's command: 'Then have them make a sanctuary for me, and I will dwell among them' (Ex. 25:8). The people were to make this 'tabernacle' (Ex. 25:9; Heb. *miškān*; Gk. *skēnē*) and all its furnishings in exact accord with the pattern God had provided. Still later, the 'tent of meeting' (Heb. *'ōhel mē'ōḏ*, Ex. 33:7) is called, in the LXX, *hē skēnē martyriou* (lit. 'the tent [tabernacle] of witness').[2] Whether the allusion in John 1:14 is to the tabernacle or to the tent of meeting, the result is the same: now, the Evangelist implies, God has chosen to dwell amongst his people in a yet more personal way, in the Word-become-flesh.

Hellenistic Jews with at least a smattering of Hebrew would be quick to see another connection between John's words and the Old Testament. The corresponding Hebrew verb for 'to dwell', *šākan*, sometimes used of God 'dwelling' with Israel (*e.g.* Ex. 25:8; 29:46; Zc. 2:13), and the noun for 'tabernacle', *miškān*, are cognate with the post-biblical term *šᵉḵînā*. This word, strictly speaking, means 'residence', but most commonly refers to the glory of God who made himself present in the

---

[1]Käsemann has argued that this is nothing more than the modicum of human form required for the Word to be perceived at all, and that the Gospel is in fact docetic – *i.e.* that it adopts a Christology in which the Word only *appears* to be human. For more detailed discussion, *cf.* Carson, pp. 154ff.; Thompson, *passim*. On source theories like that of Richter, *Studien*, pp. 149–198, who judges this verse to be an interpolation, *cf.* the Introduction, § III.

[2]This is the connection drawn by Henry Mowvley, *ExpT* 95, 1983–84, p. 136. The words 'of witness' rather than 'of meeting' depend on a different pointing of the Hebrew.

tabernacle and the temple. The bright cloud of the presence of God settled (*šākan*) on the tabernacle, and the glory of the Lord filled it (Ex. 24:16; 40:34–35; similarly the temple, 1 Ki. 8:10–11). In post-biblical Hebrew, the *š^ekînā*-glory was nothing less than the visible manifestation of God. By alluding to such themes, John may be telling his readers that God manifested himself most clearly when the Word became flesh. The incarnate Word is the true *š^ekînā*, the ultimate manifestation of the presence of God amongst human beings, for this Word became a man. But this connection is less than certain, since it depends on some knowledge of Hebrew, and elsewhere John apparently assumes his readers enjoy no knowledge of that language (*cf.* 1:38, 41, 42; 9:7; 20:16).[1]

Whatever the connection with the *š^ekînā*, John draws an explicit line to 'glory': *We have seen his glory*. In the LXX, the word for 'glory', *doxa*, commonly renders Hebrew *kābôd*, a word used to denote the visible manifestation of God's self-disclosure in a theophany (Ex. 33:22; Dt. 5:22), or even of the 'glorious' status of God's people when he rises to save them (Is. 60:1). Small wonder that all in the temple, aware of the presence of the LORD, cry 'Glory!' (Ps. 29:9) – which also shows how the word almost means 'praise' in some contexts (*e.g.* Jn. 5:41). Jesus' glory was displayed in his 'signs' (2:11; 11:4, 40); he was supremely 'glorified' in his death and exaltation (7:39; 12:16, 23; 13:31–32). This does not mean he had no glory before he began his public ministry, for in fact he enjoyed glory with the Father before the incarnation, and returned to take up that glory again after his resurrection (17:5, 24). Other men seek their own glory (5:44; 12:43); by contrast, the peculiar relationship the incarnate Word had with the Father was such that he never sought glory for himself, but only God's glory (5:41; 7:18; 8:50). In the context of incarnation, the *we* who saw the Word's glory must refer to the Evangelist and other Christians who actually saw Jesus in the days of his earthly life. *Cf.* Stephen in Acts 7:55, where *kai* may mean 'even': Stephen, 'full of the Holy Spirit, looked up to heaven and saw the glory of God, *even* Jesus standing at the right hand of God.'

The glory John and others saw was *the glory of the One and Only*. The underlying expression was rendered 'only-begotten' Son in earlier translations, but despite the efforts of some to restore that rendering,[2] the NIV is a little closer to what is meant. The glory displayed in the incarnate Word is the kind of glory a father grants to his *one and only, best-loved* Son – and this 'father' is God himself. Thus it is nothing less than God's glory that John and his friends witnessed in the Word-made-flesh.

---

[1] *Cf.* Craig Koester, *op. cit.*, pp. 105f.

[2] *E.g.* J. V. Dahms, *NTS* 29, 1983, pp. 222–232; Dodd, *IFG*, p. 305. The term *monogenēs* is one of several terms used in the LXX to render Hebrew *yāḥîd*, referring to an 'only' child (*e.g.* Jdg. 11:34; *Tobit* 3:15; 6:14; 8:17; *cf.* Lk. 7:12; 8:42; 9:38; and especially Heb. 11:17 of Isaac, who was not Abraham's *only* son but was his 'only/dearest' son. This 'dearest' or 'beloved' component to the word's meaning is reflected in Gn. 22:2 where Isaac is called Abraham's *yāḥîd* son, and the LXX translates the word by *agapētos*, 'beloved'.

The words *full of grace and truth* may be descriptive of the Word, especially if *plērēs*, 'full', is understood to be nominative, agreeing with *logos*, 'Word'; but because 'full' is regularly indeclinable (that is, it does not formally 'agree' with any particular word form), it seems best to take the expression as a modifier of 'glory'. The glory of God manifest in the incarnate Word was *full of grace and truth*. In that case John is almost certainly directing his readers to Exodus 33 – 34 (*cf.* Hanson, pp. 5ff.). There Moses begs God, 'Now show me your glory' (Ex. 33:18). The LORD replies, 'I will cause all my goodness to pass in front of you, and I will proclaim my name, the LORD,[1] in your presence. I will have mercy on whom I will have mercy, and I will have compassion on whom I will have compassion' (Ex. 33:19). God's glory, then, is supremely his goodness. So Moses stands on Mount Sinai, and, we are told, 'the LORD came down in the cloud and stood there with him and proclaimed his name, the LORD. And he passed in front of Moses, proclaiming, "The LORD, the LORD, the compassionate and gracious God, slow to anger, abounding *in love and faithfulness*, maintaining love to thousands, and forgiving wickedness, rebellion and sin"' (Ex. 34:5–7).

The italicized words spell out the nature of that goodness which is God's glory. The two crucial words in Hebrew are *ḥesed* (variously rendered 'steadfast love', 'mercy', 'covenant love' – but it has recently been shown quite clearly that it is the *graciousness* of the love that is at stake[2]) and *'emet* ('truth' or 'faithfulness'). This pair of expressions recurs again and again in the Old Testament. The two words that John uses, 'full of *grace* and *truth*', are his ways of summing up the same ideas (on truth, *cf.* Schnackenburg, 2. 225–237; Ibuki, pp. 176–207). The glory revealed to Moses when the Lord passed in front of him and sounded his name, displaying that divine goodness characterized by ineffable grace and truth, was the very same glory John and his friends saw in the Word-made-flesh.

It is sometimes objected that in the LXX the characteristic expression for 'grace and truth' is *eleos* ['mercy'] *kai alētheia*, not (as in Jn. 1:14) *charis kai alētheia*. Indeed, *charis* ('grace') is never used to render Heb. *ḥesed* except in Esther 2:9. It is not impossible that John, working directly from the Hebrew, simply preferred *charis* (so Lindars, p. 95; Sanders, p. 82). Alternatively (though less likely), we may suppose that in John 1:14 'truth' is logically subordinate to grace, and the entire expression means something like 'truly full of grace'. In that case, we may think not of Exodus 34:6 but of Exodus 33:16, where Moses asks, 'How will anyone know that you are pleased with me and with your people unless you go

---

[1]The capitalized 'LORD' is an attempt to capture the four consonants YHWH, traditionally transliterated 'Yahweh' or 'Jehovah'. Questions as to the 'meaning' of the name are resolved less by etymology than by the way that name, reflecting the very character of God, is disclosed in God's dealing with his people. At the end of his ministry, Jesus can declare that he has made known the Father's 'name', and will make it known (17:26, RSV).

[2]*Cf.* Francis I. Andersen, 'Yahweh, the Kind and Sensitive God', in Peter T. O'Brien and David Peterson (eds.), *God Who Is Rich in Mercy* (*Fs.* D. B. Knox; Anzea, 1986), pp. 41–88.

with us?' The LXX renders this, 'And how will it be *truly* (*alēthōs*, the cognate adverb) known that I have found *grace* (*charin*) with you . . .?'

It is also possible that the Evangelist is echoing some words from the prophets. The LORD declares, 'Shout and be glad, O Daughter of Zion. For I am coming, and I will live (*kataskēnōsō*) among you' (Zc. 2:10 [LXX 2:14]). 'Then you will know that I, the LORD your God, dwell (*kataskēnōn*) in Zion, my holy hill' (Joel 3:17). 'My dwelling-place (*kataskēnōsis*) will be with them; I will be their God, and they will be my people. Then the nations will know that I the LORD make Israel holy, when my sanctuary is among them forever' (Ezk. 37:27–28; *cf.* Lv. 26:11 MT; Rev. 21:22–23).

Up to this point, a reader might be excused for thinking that the glory manifest in the incarnate Word was openly visible – that the Jesus who is about to be introduced by name went around Galilee and Judea with a kind of luminescence that marked him out as no ordinary mortal, as nothing less than the Son of God. But as John proceeds with his Gospel, it becomes clearer and clearer that the glory Christ displayed was not perceived by everyone. When he performed a miracle, a 'sign', he 'revealed his glory' (2:11), but only his disciples put their faith in him. The miraculous sign was not itself unshielded glory; the eyes of faith were necessary to 'see' the glory that was revealed by the sign. Then, as the book progresses, the revelation of Jesus' glory is especially tied to Jesus' cross and the exaltation that ensues (*cf.* Thüsing) – and certainly only those who have faith 'see' the glory of God in the Word-made-flesh in events such as these. There is a hiddenness to the display of glory in the incarnate Word, a hiddenness penetrated by the Evangelist and the early witnesses who could say, *We have seen his glory*. In a profound passage, Bultmann (pp. 60ff.) rightly emphasizes that the glory appears in *human* form; but his emphasis on the human becomes so extreme that one wonders if he thinks there is any divine being who has become incarnated. In John's Prologue, once the identity of the Word is grasped, the incarnation is seen as a stupendous act of revelation, of divine self-disclosure; but if the identity of the Word is not grasped, the incarnation itself is a nonsense. *Cf.* de la Potterie, pp. 76–78.

15. Because v. 16 would follow nicely on v. 14, some have seen v. 15 as an interpolation. It would be fairer to conclude that v. 15 is a planned parenthetical remark. The earlier mention of the witness of John the Baptist (vv. 6–8) dealt with the coming of the pre-existent light into the world; this verse abandons that theme and grounds the glory of the incarnate Word in a concrete individual, a concrete 'he' attested by another individual. Thus it prepares the way for the detailed account of the Baptist's witness, which immediately succeeds the Prologue .

The present tense (*John testifies concerning him*) followed immediately by the perfect tense (lit. 'he has cried out') combine to suggest the Evangelist is presenting John the Baptist's witness both vividly, as if it were in progress, and comprehensively, summing it up as a set-piece. Before the Baptist was able to point to a specific individual (*cf.* v. 33), he was able to announce in general terms the advent of the long-awaited

Coming One: *He who comes after me has surpassed me because he was before me*. In all four Gospels, Jesus entered public ministry *after* John. In a society where age and precedence bestowed peculiar honour, that might have been taken by superficial observers to mean John the Baptist was greater than Jesus. Not so, insists the Baptist: Jesus has *surpassed* him (lit., 'became before me'), precisely *because he was before* him. The peculiar expression means 'because he was first with respect to me'. It includes not only temporal priority (*cf.* NEB, 'before I was born, he already was'), which picks up the pre-existence emphasized at the beginning of the chapter, but also absolute primacy. That was the Baptist's proclamation before he knew of whom he spoke. Then, after identifying him, he could say, *This was he of whom I said*, *etc*. And by placing this summary of the Baptist's witness here, the Evangelist by anticipation is identifying Jesus with the Word-made-flesh: 'This was he of whom I spoke.'

16–17. Verse 14 described the glory of God manifest in the incarnate Word as *full* of grace and truth. Picking up on the term, John says that it is from this *fulness* that we have received grace after grace. Thus 'fulness' here bears no technical, gnostic sense.

The meaning of the last three words of v. 16, *charin anti charitos*, frequently rendered 'grace upon grace', principally turns on the force of the preposition *anti*. In addition to a number of highly improbable options, the most important interpretations are these:

(1) The word *anti* means 'corresponds to' (*e.g.* Bernard, 1. 29): the grace the Christian receives in some sense *corresponds to* the grace of Christ. This view does not adequately treat the way v. 17 is cast as the explanation of v. 16. Moreover, *anti* never unambiguously bears the meaning 'corresponds to', except in certain compounds (*e.g. antitypos*, lit. 'counterblow', a blow corresponding to another one, and hence 'antitype').

(2) The word *anti* means 'in return for': one grace is given *in return for* another. But the idea of grace being given 'in return for' something else, a kind of *quid pro quo*, is alien to the New Testament in general and to John in particular. Attempts to get around this point – such as Augustine's that the grace in which we live by faith is given in return for another, the grace of immortality (*In Johan. Tract*. iii. 8) – are alien to the context, and ignore the connection between v. 16 and v. 17.

(3) By far the most popular modern interpretation holds that *anti* means 'upon' or 'in addition to' (*e.g.* Schnackenburg, 1. 275–276; Bultmann, p. 78; Bruce, p. 43; M. J. Harris in *NIDNTT* 3. 1179–1180): hence the renderings 'grace upon grace' (NEB, RSV) and 'one blessing after another' (GNB, NIV). 'As the days come and go a new supply takes the place of the grace already bestowed as wave follows wave upon the shore' (Rob, p. 574; *cf.* Zerwick § 95). That is theologically true, of course, but it is very doubtful if that is John's point. The normal preposition for such meaning is *epi*, not *anti*.There is one parallel everyone cites (Philo, *de Post. Caini* 145), but on close inspection it proves unhelpful. Philo speaks of 'graces', not 'grace'; for him, there is

not an accumulation of graces, one 'upon' another, but a substitution of graces, one kind replacing another. His point, quite unlike John's, is that God is wise in dispensing his 'graces' in small doses, so that people do not receive more than they can cope with; John is emphasizing the superabundance of God's grace.[1]

(4) The most convincing view takes *anti* in one of its most common uses (and by far the most common in the LXX) to mean 'instead of': from Christ's fulness we have all received grace *instead of* grace.

But what does this mean? Some have argued that the grace received through Christ in the days of his flesh is replaced by the grace of the Holy Spirit after Christ's ascension, but this view is entirely alien to the context, and again ignores the tight link between v. 16 and v. 17. The latter follows hard on the 'grace instead of grace' (v. 16) with an explanatory 'For' or 'Because': *For the law was given through Moses; grace and truth came through Jesus Christ.* On the face of it, then, it appears that the grace and truth that came through Jesus Christ is what replaces the law; the law itself is understood to be an earlier display of grace.

The chief objections against this understanding of the flow of the text deserve mention:

(1) The most common is that 'the point of the present passage is that grace did not come by Moses' (Barrett, p. 168), and therefore we cannot imagine John speaking of the grace of the gospel replacing the *grace* of law. Certainly in Paul grace and law are often contrasted, but that is not the only way in which their relationship may be conceived. Paul himself can call the law 'holy' and 'good' (Rom. 7:12, 16). Moreover, this objection presupposes that the two halves of v. 17 are set over against each other (*e.g.* Gnilka, p. 16; Haenchen, 1.120; Pancaro, p. 541); but there is nothing in the Greek text that requires antithesis. As some have noted (Lindars, p. 98; J. Jeremias, *TDNT* 4. 873), it makes just as much sense of the original to see a comparison: 'Just as the law was given through Moses, so grace and truth came through Jesus Christ.' The covenant of law, then, is seen as a gracious gift from God, now replaced by a further gracious gift, the 'grace and truth' embodied in Jesus Christ – here named for the first time as the human being who is nothing other than the Word-made-flesh.

(2) Some have insisted that the Fourth Gospel is deeply opposed to the law, and could not possibly have seen it as a display of God's grace. This is largely based on two references to 'your Law' (8:17; 10:34), understood to be the Evangelist's way of distancing himself from the law. But that is a serious misreading of the evidence. In both instances the authority of the law is accepted, and serves as the justification of something Jesus himself was teaching. In both instances the words are ascribed to Jesus. In context, the crucial expressions mean something

---

[1]For this point and the subsequent discussion I am indebted to Ruth B. Edwards, *JSNT* 32, 1988, pp. 3–15. *Cf.* also de la Potterie, 1. 145–150).

like this: *Your own law*, yours in the sense that you claim it for yourselves, yours despite the fact that you hide behind its authority and try to use it against me and my teaching, yours even though it turns out on inspection to support me. That scarcely hints at rejection of the law! Moreover, that Jesus is the true bread of life (ch. 6) does not mean that the original manna was not a gracious gift; that Jesus can be likened to the snake in the desert (3:14) presupposes that the original was itself a fine display of grace. For John, the Law and the prophets wrote about Jesus (1:45); the Jews are rebuked for not believing what Moses wrote, for if they had believed Moses they would have believed Christ (4:45–54; 7:19, 22–23). Barrett's (p. 168) dismissive comment, 'nor is the grace of God available in two grades', rather misses the point; even Paul can speak of God's grace being 'made perfect' (2 Cor. 12:9).

(3) Conversely, others argue that for John the law in some sense continues in force: the Scripture cannot be broken (10:34), and therefore it is unreasonable to think that John in 1:16–17 can view the grace of the gospel, the grace that has come in Jesus Christ, as *replacing* law. But again, close attention to the way the Fourth Gospel treats the Old Testament alleviates the difficulty. In the passages already mentioned, and in a large number of others, the Old Testament Scriptures are understood to point forward to Jesus, to anticipate him, and thus to prophesy of him. In that sense he fulfils them. If even the covenant of law is 'prophetic' in this sense (*cf.* Mt. 11:13), then when that to which it points has arrived, it is in some sense displaced. It may continue in force as a continual pointer to that which it predicted, but its valid authority lies primarily in that which it announced and which has now arrived. The law, *i.e.* the law-covenant, was given by grace, and anticipated the incarnate Word, Jesus Christ; now that he has come, that same prophetic law-covenant is necessarily superseded by that which it 'prophesied' would come. The thought is not dissimilar to Matthew 5:17–20 (*cf.* Carson, *Matt*, pp. 140–147). It is this prophecy/fulfilment motif that explains why the two displays of grace are not precisely identical. The flow of the passage and the burden of the book as a whole magnify the fresh 'grace' that has come in Jesus Christ. That grace is necessarily greater than the 'grace' of the law whose function, in John's view, was primarily to anticipate the coming of the Word. This interpretation is reinforced if we accept the parallelism between v. 17 and v. 18 (suggested by Ibuki, p. 205): v. 17b is to v. 17a what v. 18b is to v. 18a.

'In Judaism, the law became an end in itself, something that could be separated from Moses through whom it was given. The *grace and truth* which *came by Jesus Christ* can never be dissociated from Himself' (Tasker, pp. 44–45). That point may lie behind the choice of verbs: the law 'was given' (*edothē*), grace and truth 'came' (*egeneto*), 'as if, according to the orderly and due course of the divine plan, this was the natural issue of all that had gone before' (*cf.* Westcott, 1. 127; Hanson, p. 7). This cannot mean there is *no* contrast between law and Jesus Christ: that contrast is explicit, on the surface of the text.[1] But the law that was *given* through Moses, and the grace and truth that *came* through Jesus Christ (v. 17), alike sprang from the fulness of the Word (v. 16), whether in his pre-existent oneness with the Father, or in his status as the Word-made-flesh. It is from that 'fulness' that we have received 'one grace replacing another'. It is in this sense that v. 16 is an explanation of v. 14 (it begins with *hoti*, 'for' or 'because'): we have seen his glory, John writes, *because* from the fulness of his grace and truth we have received grace that replaces the earlier grace – the grace of the incarnation, of the Word-made-flesh, of the glory of the Son 'tabernacling' with us, now replacing the grace of the antecedent but essentially promissory revelation. The 'we' who have received this new grace may have begun with John and the earliest eyewitnesses (*cf.* 1:14), but it now includes all who share the same faith (*cf.* 20:29).

18. *No-one has ever seen God*, John writes, as if to remind his readers not only of a commonplace of Judaism, but also of the fact that in the episode where Moses saw the LORD's glory (Ex. 33 – 34), to which allusion has just been made (1:14), Moses himself was not allowed to see God (Ex. 33:20). 'We should perhaps say, less anthropomorphically but equally metaphorically, that Moses saw, so to speak, the afterglow of the divine glory' (Bruce, p. 44). In that diminished sense, God speaks with Moses 'face to face', and Moses 'sees the form of the LORD' (Nu. 12:8). The vision of the LORD seated on his throne that Isaiah saw was so vivid and terrifying, so close to the 'real thing', even though it was but the hem[2] of the LORD's garment that filled the temple, that he could cry, 'Woe to me! . . . ¡ am ruined! For I am a man of unclean lips . . . and my eyes have seen the King, the LORD Almighty' (Is. 6:5). Such language is so startling that the translators of later Judaism toned it down. The fact remains that the consistent Old Testament assumption is that God cannot be seen, or, more precisely, that for a sinful human being to see him would bring death (Ex. 33:20; Dt. 4:12; Ps. 97:2). Apparent exceptions are always qualified in some way.

But, John adds, the unique and beloved one (the term is *monogenēs*: see notes on 1:14), [himself] God, has made him known. That is probably the correct text (see Additional Note). What it means is that the beloved Son, the incarnate Word (1:14), himself God while being *at the Father's side* – just as in v. 1 the Word was simultaneously God and with God – has broken the barrier that made it impossible for human beings to see God, and *has made him known*. This prepares the way for 6:46 and 14:9: 'Anyone who has seen me has seen the Father.'

The words translated *who is at the Father's side* in the NIV might more

---

[1] It is rightly emphasized but overstated in Klaus Haacker, *Die Stiftung des Heils: Untersuchung zur Struktur der johanneischen Theologie* (Stuttgart: Calwer, 1972).

[2] The Heb. word *šûl* (Is. 6:1) should be rendered 'hem', not 'train'. The word can refer to either, but there does not appear to be evidence that near-eastern monarchs of this period wore trains.

literally be rendered 'who is in the bosom of the Father'. A similar expression is found elsewhere: Lazarus is in Abraham's bosom (Lk. 16:22–23), and John rests on Jesus' bosom at the last supper (13:23). It apparently conveys an aura of intimacy, mutual love and knowledge. 'No-one has ever seen God', John has told us, but he will go on to add, 'except the one who is from God' (6:46), the one who is in the bosom of the Father. It is this intimacy that makes it possible for Jesus to know and speak about heavenly things (3:12–13; cf. Mt. 11:27). This Word-made-flesh, himself God, is nevertheless differentiable from God, and as such is intimate with God; as man, as God's incarnate Self-expression, he *has made* God *known*. Ben Sirach could ask who could describe (*ekdiēgēsetai*) God (*Ecclus.* 43:31); John declares that the incarnate Word made him known (*exēgēsato*). From this Greek term we derive 'exegesis': we might almost say that Jesus is the exegesis of God. Elsewhere in the New Testament the verb means 'to tell a narrative' or 'to narrate' (Lk. 24:35; Acts 10:8; 15:12, 14; 21:19). In that sense we might say that Jesus is the narration of God.[1] 'As Jesus gives life and is life, raises the dead and is the resurrection, gives bread and is bread, speaks truth and is the truth, so as he speaks the word he is the Word' (C. H. Dodd in oral tradition: cf. Beasley-Murray, p. 10).

The emphasis of the Prologue, then, is on the revelation of the Word as the ultimate disclosure of God himself. That theme is dramatically reinforced by the remarkable parallels between v. 1 and v. 18, constituting an *inclusio*, a kind of literary envelope that subtly clasps all of 1:1–18 in its embrace. Thus 'in the bosom of the Father' is parallel to 'with God'; 'the unique one, [himself] God', is parallel to 'was God'; and to say that this unique and beloved Person has made God known is to say that he is 'the Word', God's Self-expression.

The Prologue anticipates many of the themes and terms in the rest of the book. If 'Word' itself does not recur in this Christological sense (though cf. Rev. 19:13; perhaps 1 Jn. 1:1), it is probably because the Evangelist consciously looked for a term that neatly summed up his principal Christological emphases. A term that recurred throughout the Gospel might well have been taken as merely one title amongst many, rather than a summary of the whole. To use the language of Paul, Jesus is the visible 'image of the invisible God' (Col. 1:15).

It is important to note that the closest *conceptual* parallels in the New Testament to the Prologue are probably the so-called 'Christological hymns' (*e.g.* Phil. 2:5–11; Col. 1:15–20), material almost universally dated early, and certainly widely scattered. This suggests that John's

[1]So J. P. Louw, *Neot* 2, 1968, pp. 32–40. The suggestion of M.-E. Boismard (*RB* 59, 1952, pp. 23–39) that the verb means 'to lead the way' and the preposition *eis* means 'into' ('he has led the way into the bosom of the Father') depends on highly improbable Greek, and overlooks the fact that at this period the preposition *eis* was beginning to encroach on *en* (hence '*in* the bosom of the Father' rather than *into*).

Prologue is less innovative than some have thought.[1] The form of the presentation is fresh; the underlying Christology is not. And that in turn argues that John and his circle are not 'sectarians' fundamentally out of touch with the rest of the church (so Meeks). The connections between the Prologue and other parts of the New Testament are intuitively picked up in Christian hymnody, as in this hymn of praise by Josiah Condor (1789–1855):

> *Thou art the everlasting Word,*
> *The Father's only Son;*
> *God manifestly seen and heard,*
> *And Heaven's beloved One.*
> > *Worthy, O Lamb of God, art Thou*
> > *That every knee to Thee should bow.*
>
> *In Thee most perfectly expressed*
> *The Father's glories shine;*
> *Of the full Deity possessed,*
> *Eternally divine:*
> > *Worthy, O Lamb of God, art Thou*
> > *That every knee to Thee should bow.*
>
> *True image of the Infinite,*
> *Whose essence is concealed;*
> *Brightness of uncreated light;*
> *The heart of God revealed:*
> > *Worthy, O Lamb of God, art Thou*
> > *That every knee to Thee should bow.*
>
> *But the high mysteries of Thy name*
> *An angel's grasp transcend;*
> *The Father only – glorious claim! –*
> *The Son can comprehend:*
> > *Worthy, O Lamb of God, art Thou*
> > *That every knee to Thee should bow.*
>
> *Throughout the universe of bliss,*
> *The centre Thou, and sun;*
> *The eternal theme of praise is this,*
> *To Heaven's beloved One:*
> > *Worthy, O Lamb of God, art Thou*
> > *That every knee to Thee should bow.*

---

[1]Peter Hofrichter, *Im Anfang war der 'Johannesprolog'* (Verlag Friedrich Pustet, 1986), in a remarkable *tour de force*, argues that the 'original' Prologue, which he 'recovers' with source-criticism, is the conceptual source behind *all* New Testament Christology. His presentation is not convincing (*cf.* the blistering review of Raymond E. Brown, *CBQ* 49, 1987, pp. 668–669); but that he can make any sort of case at all shows that John's Prologue is not fundamentally out of step with at least some other emphases in the New Testament.

How the Son, the Word-made-flesh, 'narrated' or 'exegeted' God to man, John now proceeds to tell us.

Additional notes

1. Dunn, *Making*, p. 241, cites Philo, *Som*. i. 227–230, who in discussing the relationship of the *logos* to God also makes his argument depend on the presence or absence of an article: 'He that is truly God is One, but those that are improperly so called are more than one. Accordingly the holy word in the present instance has indicated him who is truly God by means of the articles saying "I am the God", while it omits the article when mentioning him who is improperly so called, saying "Who appeared to thee in the place" not "of the God", but simply "of God" [Gn. 31:13 LXX – *en tropō theou*]. Here it gives the title of "God" to his chief Word . . .'. Dunn does not argue that John borrows from Philo, but that Philo 'demonstrates that a distinction between *ho theos* and *theos* such as we find in John 1.1b–c, would be deliberate by the author and significant for the Greek reader.' But the parallel between Philo's self-conscious observations on the article and John's syntax are not close. Philo's *logos*, impersonal as it is, never really threatens the personal/transcendent God of Jewish monotheism anyway, and the syntactical distinction he draws is an argument of expedience, frequently contradicted by the exigencies of Greek grammar itself. By contrast, John's omission of the article is not part of an elaborate, syntactically ill-conceived argument to prove a point, but common Greek usage, and not even demonstrably self-conscious. Syntactically, the question does not turn simply on the presence or absence of the article, but on the presence or absence of the article with definite nominative predicate nouns preceding a finite copula[1] – which makes the alleged parallel in Philo irrelevant.

3–4. It is very difficult to decide whether the last two words of the Greek text of v. 3 should be read with what precedes (NIV: 'without him nothing was made *that has been made*'; similarly AV) or with what succeeds in the next verse (NEB: 'no single thing was created without him. All that came to be was alive with his life . . .'). K. Aland[2] argues strongly for the latter punctuation, which certainly prevailed in the early church amongst both the orthodox and the heterodox. On balance, however, the arguments of Schnackenburg (1. 239–240) in favour of reading the words with the rest of v. 3 seem persuasive. In particular, John regularly begins his sentences with the preposition 'in', which is how v. 4 begins. Moreover, it is very difficult to fathom exactly what 'That which came to be was life in him' (a rather literal rendering of the

---

[1]*Cf*. E. C. Colwell, *JBL* 52, 1933, pp. 12ff.; L. E. McGaughy, *Toward a Descriptive Analysis of EINAI as Linking Verb in New Testament Greek* (SBLDS 6; Society of Biblical Literature, 1972).

[2]*ZNW* 59, 1968, pp. 174–209.

second option) could mean; and the objection that the NIV reading is tautological ('nothing was made that has been made') can carry little force amongst those who have noted how frequently John resorts to repetition (*e.g.* vv. 1–2). In any case, as the main notes on this verse suggest (above), there is another way of rendering the text, even with this punctuation, that sidesteps this charge.

5. The verb *katalambanō* (from which *katalaben* derives) means 'to seize', and hence derivatively 'to overcome' or, alternatively, 'to seize with the mind' and therefore 'to understand'. John may be playing with the two meanings, as other authors of the time did (*cf.* Barrett, p. 158). In the only other passage in the Fourth Gospel where the verb is used with the light/darkness metaphor, however, the meaning 'to overcome' is required by the context (rendered 'overtakes' in the NIV, Jn. 12:35), which may have some bearing here. That the tense is aorist is of little significance in itself, since that tense merely establishes that the writer looks on the action holistically, not that the action took place at a specific time, more than once, instantaneously or the like. The suggestion of BAGD preserves the ambiguity: the darkness did not *master* the light.

6. That both John the Baptist and Jesus are said to be sent from God has prompted some to deny that the expression, when used of Jesus, is any indication of his pre-existence, since such pre-existence could scarcely be predicated of John. But apart from the fact that the passive form of the verb is used for John the Baptist (1:6; 3:28) while the active is reserved for Jesus (Morris, p. 89), it is the broader context that is determinative. The pre-existence of Jesus is already established by the Prologue on other grounds, so that when we are told that the Father sent his Son *into the world* (3:17) we are pre-conditioned by the text to think of pre-existence and incarnation.

10. The verb rendered 'recognise' by the NIV is *ginōskō*; the other common verb dealing with 'knowledge' is *oida*. 'Knowledge' is an important theme in the Fourth Gospel, though the noun itself is found neither in the Fourth Gospel nor in the Johannine Epistles. Unlike earlier Greek, the two verbs seem to be used synonymously (*cf.* 7:27; 8:55; 13:7; 21:17). Although both terms can be used for knowledge of facts (7:49; 9:20; 11:57; 18:2), in John they are more characteristically used of human knowledge of the divine persons and of the relationship amongst those persons. *Cf.* Barrett, pp. 162–163. For the relationship between knowledge and faith, *cf.* Painter, pp. 86–100.

13. A surprising number of (mostly Roman Catholic) scholars, along with JB, follow the Old Latin and some Syriac manuscripts, which read a singular verb 'who was born' instead of the plural 'who were born' (*e.g.* Vellanickal, pp. 112–132; especially J. Galot, *Etre né de Dieu* [Rome: Pontifical Biblical Institute, 1969]). The text in that case would support the virginal conception and birth of Jesus. The flow would then be: '. . . to those who believe in the name of him who was born, not from blood. . . .' No Greek manuscript supports this reading. No less important, one can imagine how copyists might move from the plural to the singular by adopting an *a fortiori* argument: If Christians are born of God, how much more true is this of Jesus? It is hard to imagine a reason for so thorough a textual corruption the other way. *Cf.* Metzger, p. 197.

18. The nest of textual variants is rather complicated, but probably the right reading is *monogenēs theos*, 'the unique and beloved one, [himself] God' – taking 'God' appositionally. No other passage puts these words together like this, which probably accounts for the change made by many copyists to *monogenēs huios*, 'the unique and beloved Son' (or, in more traditional language, 'the only begotten Son'). That is so common an expression in John that it is hard to imagine any copyist changing 'Son' to 'God'. Similarly, it is possible to explain the weakly-attested *monogenēs*, without either 'Son' or 'God' added, as an attempt to clear up the difficult reading with 'God' by simply dropping the latter; it is hard to imagine why any copyist would have *added* 'God' to *monogenēs* if this short form had been original. *Cf.* Metzger, p. 198.

II. JESUS' SELF-DISCLOSURE IN WORD AND DEED (1:19 – 10:42)

A. PRELUDE TO JESUS' PUBLIC MINISTRY (1:19–51)

1. John the Baptist's relation to Jesus (1:19–28)

19. As in the Synoptic Gospels, so here: the ministry of John the Baptist is presented before the Evangelist details the ways in which Jesus 'narrated' God. The Prologue has told us that the Baptist 'came as a witness to testify concerning that light' (1:7); now the Evangelist fleshes out John's testimony. The testimony on which the Evangelist focuses is the witness John the Baptist gave to the official delegations sent from Jerusalem. The other Gospel writers make no mention of this official probing, but there is nothing intrinsically improbable in the account. Granted the wide influence the Baptist exerted (*cf.* Mt. 3:5, 7), it would have been irresponsible of the leaders if they had failed to check him out.

This is the first use of the expression 'the Jews'. It is frequent in the Fourth Gospel, and because it commonly occurs as the designation of those who oppose Jesus, it has attracted much discussion. Some see in the expression evidence of Christian anti-Semitism; others think it refers primarily to Jewish leaders, not to the people at large; some think it reflects geography (a Galilean might well refer to his fellow Israelites from Judea as 'Jews'); still others think the diversity of usage in John betrays different sources used by the Evangelist, with only the most antagonistic use being his own.[1]

In fact, careful examination of the seventy or so occurrences suggests John uses 'the Jews' in a variety of ways. Sometimes the expression is rather neutral, explaining a ritual for readers removed from Palestine (*e.g.* 2:6). Elsewhere the expression bears decidedly positive overtones ('salvation is from the Jews', 4:22; Jesus himself is a Jew, 4:9). Some Jews believe (11:45; 12:11); others, unfortunately, seem to come to faith, and then turn away again (8.30ff). In 7:1, the expression takes on

---

[1]So Urban C. von Wahlde, *NTS* 28, 1982, pp. 33–60, whose review is otherwise extremely useful.

geographical colouring: the people of Judea. Most commonly it refers to the Jewish leaders, especially those of Jerusalem and Judea (as here in 1:19), and usually they are cast as those who actively oppose Jesus, fail to understand him, and who finally seek his death. Pre-eminently, they constitute the focal point of opposition to Jesus, the concretization of the 'world' (cf. notes on 1:10). Not all Jewish leaders, however, are presented negatively: Nicodemus and Joseph of Arimathea fare much better (3:1ff.; 7:50; 19:38–42).

This diversity of usage excludes interpretations that pit John's church against all 'Jews' of his day, for in that case the instances that are neutral, positive or dictated by the geography of Palestine would make little sense. The only context where the diversity of uses makes sense is the context of the historical Jesus. This does not mean that John's choice of terminology has not been influenced by his own context at the time of writing: apparently John is seeking to press the claims of Jesus Messiah on his own hellenistic Jewish readers, and the failures of the Jewish leaders who were Jesus' contemporaries constitute an admirably clear warning. Certainly 'anti-Semitism' is scarcely a reasonable charge against the Evangelist in any case, granted that he himself was a Jew. Even the charge of 'anti-Judaism' rather misses the mark, for the Evangelist is not motivated by a desire to destroy what he understands to be right and good in Judaism, but to controvert those who have so failed to appreciate their own heritage that they have failed to see its fulfilment in Jesus Christ.[1]

The *Jews of Jerusalem*, then, possibly leaders of the Sanhedrin (cf. notes on 11:47), *sent priests and Levites* to ask John the Baptist *who he was*. The Sanhedrin was largely controlled by the family of the high priest, and so it was natural enough that the envoys be priests and Levites, who would in any case be interested in questions of ritual purification and therefore in John's baptism. Levites belonged to the tribe of Levi, but had not descended from the family of Aaron the Levite, and could therefore not be priests. In Jesus' day they assisted in temple worship, primarily as musicians, and served as the temple police. John the Baptist himself was a Levite, and the son of a priest (though there is no evidence John himself ever exercised any distinctly priestly roles), and it is hard to think these facts would not have been known of one whose ministry was so influential.

20. The exact question from the interlocutors is not preserved. However, granted John's straightforward answer, *I am not the Christ*, it is not hard to see what they were after. First-century Palestine was rife with messianic expectations. Some expected a Davidic Messiah; others (as at Qumran) expected a priestly Messiah as well, not to mention the

---

[1] On this question, cf. Leistner; S. Wilson, *IBS* 1, 1979, pp. 28–50. Less careful, but still useful, is David Granskou, 'Anti-Judaism in the Passion Accounts of the Fourth Gospel', in Peter Richardson (ed.), *Anti-Judaism in Early Christianity* (Wilfrid Laurier University, 1986), pp. 201–216.

coming of 'the prophet' (1QS 9:11). But if they think he is a 'Messiah' at all, an 'Anointed One' long prophesied by the Scriptures, they are wrong. 'I am not *the Christ'*, the Baptist insists: here the Evangelist introduces us to the term which, in Greek (*christos*), is the verbal adjective of *chriō*, the verb 'to anoint', making 'Christ' the equivalent of Hebrew 'Messiah' (*cf.* further on vv. 40–42).

The forceful way this is presented, *He did not fail to confess, but confessed freely*, is the Evangelist's way of saying that even the Baptist's denials that he was the Christ constituted part of his positive witness to (his confession of) the true Christ. As to whether there were followers of the Baptist in John's day who thought he was the Messiah, *cf.* notes on 1:6–9, 15.

21. If John the Baptist was not the Messiah, perhaps he was some other figure popularly associated with the end-time. *Are you Elijah?* he is asked. After all, God had promised, through the prophet Malachi (4:5), 'See, I will send you the prophet Elijah before that great and dreadful day of the LORD comes.' False prophets had sometimes aped Elijah's dress (Zc. 13:14): was the Baptist's similarity in dress to Elijah (Mk. 1:6; 2 Ki. 1:8) a sign that he was a usurper, or the promised Elijah? Certainly Elijah and the Baptist both sternly insisted on the urgency of repentance. But to the question of the Jerusalem delegation, John firmly replies, *I am not*.

The Synoptic Gospels report that Jesus identified John the Baptist with the promised Elijah (Mt. 11:14; 17:12; Mk. 9:13; *cf.* Lk. 1:17), but they never suggest that the Baptist himself made the connection. Here he refuses to make it – a refusal which, when placed beside the Synoptic evidence, suggests that he did not detect as much significance in his own ministry as Jesus did.[1]

If he is not the Messiah and not Elijah, the delegation will try another possibility: *Are you the Prophet?* The promise of a prophet like Moses who would speak the words of God (Dt. 18:15–18) was early taken to refer to a special end-time figure; indeed, the Samaritans identified this prophet with the promised Messiah. However conceived, the promise of such a prophet was not fulfilled in himself: *He answered, 'No'*.

22–23. The delegates from the leaders in Jerusalem knew they had to return with more than a series of denials. If John the Baptist denies that he is one of the commonly expected end-time figures, then the least he can do is articulate what he makes of himself, and what significance he attaches to his own ministry: *What do you say about yourself?* (v. 22).

John replies *in the words of Isaiah the prophet*, applying Is. 40:3 to himself (as the Synoptists apply it to him: *cf.* Mt. 3:3; Mk. 1:3; Lk. 3:4). The

---

[1]Other explanations are possible, but in my judgment less likely; *cf.* Michaels, pp. 11–13; C. Blomberg, *CTR* 2, 1987, pp. 105–108. In particular, the notion that John the Baptist saw himself as the one who was preparing the way for Elijah, and that Jesus at least for a while accepted this Elijah role for himself (J. A. T. Robinson, *NTS* 4, 1957–58, esp. pp. 264–265, 270) is without adequate exegetical warrant.

Baptist may refuse to identify himself with any expected eschatological figure, but that does not mean he is simply another itinerant preacher. He may not be the Messiah or the prophet, but he is the *voice* predicted by Isaiah, the voice *of one calling in the desert, 'Make straight the way for the Lord.'*[1] In the original context, the Old Testament prophet is calling for a (metaphorical) improvement in the road system of the desert to the east, a levelling of hills and valleys and a straightening of the curves, to accommodate the return of the covenant people from exile. But even in Isaiah, the end of the exile begins to serve as a model, a literary 'type', of the final return to the Lord far greater than a return to geographical Jerusalem. If Isaiah 40 – 66 begins by announcing good news to Zion (= Jerusalem), it goes on to anticipate a still greater redemption effected by the suffering Servant of the Lord (Is. 52:13 – 53:12), climaxed by a new heaven and a new earth (Is. 65 – 66). It is this 'typological' connection, already established in the book of Isaiah, that the New Testament writers take up and understand to be fulfilled in the voice of John the Baptist, who cried in the desert, preparing a way for the Lord, and thereby announcing the coming of Jesus Messiah.

24–25. Traditionally v. 24 has been interpreted to mean 'they which were sent were of the Pharisees' (AV). This rendering depends on the inclusion of a Greek article which most text critics rightly omit. It is in any case highly improbable: the Pharisees were not strong enough to control the Sanhedrin (though they were influential members of it), still less to send a delegation of priests and Levites. If the article is omitted, v. 24 can still be taken in one of three ways. It could mean they had been sent 'from the Pharisees' (Bernard, 1. 38), in the sense that the entire delegation was made up of Pharisees. This is extremely unlikely: some priests and Levites held Pharisaic convictions, but they were relatively few. We might side with Phillips: 'Now some of the Pharisees had been sent to John' – which suggests a second deputation, different from the one introduced in v. 19. That is unlikely, however, since the question they ask (v. 25) presupposes knowledge of the previous exchange. By far the best alternative is that of the NEB: 'Some Pharisees who were in the deputation asked him'. This is entirely credible, for although the Pharisees did not control the Sanhedrin and other Jewish leadership in Jerusalem, they were sufficiently influential that an official delegation could scarcely have been sent without some representation from their wing.

The Pharisees (*cf. NBD*, pp. 924–925) were spiritual descendants of pious groups that had successfully opposed the notoriously cruel government of Antiochus Epiphanes (175–163 BC). This Syrian monarch had attempted to obliterate the Jewish faith. The Pharisees were extremely scrupulous about observing every minute detail of the law of

---

[1]On the text form, *cf.* M. J. J. Menken, *Bib* 66, 1985, pp. 190–205 (though his explanation as to why John changes 'prepare' [LXX *hetoimasate*] to 'make straight' [*euthynate*] is unconvincing).

God as they understood it, and were engaged in establishing an oral tradition about how that law was to be obeyed. At the same time they were in certain respects innovators, not mere traditionalists, for the creative and innovative manipulation of the oral tradition meant they were able to meet new challenges and situations more imaginatively than could mere traditionalists. Josephus, a first-century soldier-historian, tells us that there were about six thousand Pharisees in his day (Jos., *Ant.* xvii. 42). They met in 'fellowship groups' and controlled the teaching of many synagogues around the country. Most priests and Levites, however, belonged to the party of the Sadducees (whom John does not explicitly mention, probably in part because they were no longer a significant power at the time of writing). The Sadducees held to the authority of the written word alone, and judged the Pharisees to be both too innovative and too particular on many fronts. Their power was centred in Jerusalem and its temple – and therefore in the priests and Levites.

The question put to John the Baptist by the Pharisees in the deputation reflects one of their concerns: *Why then do you baptise if you are not the Christ, nor Elijah, nor the Prophet?* Their interest is in what authorizes John's baptismal practices. It is not that baptism was unknown. Some Jewish groups practised 'proselyte baptism', *i.e.* proselytes were baptized in the process of converting to Judaism. In the monastic community at Qumram, members invoked passages such as Ezekiel 36:25 to justify their daily baptism, a sign that they were the righteous community of the end-time. But in both instances baptism was *self-*administered. Candidates baptized *themselves.* One of the things that characterized the baptism of John the Baptist is that he himself administered it. It may even be that the authority implicit in such an innovative step triggered the assumption in the minds of at least some Pharisees that John's baptism was an end-time rite administered by an end-time figure with great authority.[1]

Nevertheless, their question should not be interpreted to mean that they have all unambiguously identified John's baptism as an eschatological rite: there is no good evidence to support such a view (*contra* Bultmann, p. 88). Rather, they want to discover by what authority John is baptizing *Jewish* people as part of their preparation for the kingdom he is announcing. Looking around for an adequate authority to sanction so extraordinary a practice, they wonder if he is an eschatological figure. And if he is not the Christ, nor Elijah, nor the Prophet (principal eschatological figures), then what could possibly justify his baptism?

The Synoptic Gospels preserve more details about the scope of John the Baptist's preaching and the significance of his baptism. Unlike those who held themselves to be adequately related to God by virtue of their

---

[1]For an evenhanded assessment of possible connections between baptism at Qumran and the baptism of John the Baptist, *cf.* Robinson, *Twelve*, pp. 11–27; *cf.* further, on the significance of Elijah in John, Richter, pp. 1–41.

descent from Abraham (Mt. 3:9; Lk. 3:8), John insisted that personal and individual repentance and faith were necessary (Mt. 3:1–10; Mk. 1:2–5; Lk. 3:3–14). In this he resembled the Old Testament prophets who sought to call out a holy remnant from the descendants of Abraham, and anticipated Jesus' insistence that his messianic community would transcend the barriers of race and depend on *personal* faith and new birth (*e.g.* Mt. 8:5–12; Jn. 3:1–16).

26–27. The Fourth Gospel, however, though in the preceding verses it presupposes that the Baptist dealt with such matters, immediately turns to the Christological bearing of his preaching. The emphatic '*I* baptise with water' (v. 26) might make the unwary reader remember Synoptic parallels (Mt. 3:11; Mk. 1:7–8; Lk. 3:16) and conclude that the *I* will serve as a foil for the One who will baptize in another medium, the Holy Spirit. Certainly the Baptist will make that point later (v. 33); but here he focuses on the authority question raised by the Pharisees, and immediately turns it into a matter of bearing witness to the hidden Messiah. His baptism is designed to prepare the people for *him*. John is well aware of the very real authority he enjoys: he will shortly speak of 'the one [*i.e.* God] who sent [him] to baptise' (v. 33). But whatever stature he has, enabling him to affirm '*I* baptise with water', it is nothing compared with the stature of One who is still unrecognized amongst the people, *one you do not know* (v. 26).

The Pharisees were interested in the warrant and authority behind John's baptism, wondering if the Baptist could be one of the promised eschatological figures. Yes, John replies in effect, I do indeed baptize, I have authority from God to do so; but I am nothing compared with the one to whom I bear witness. *He is the one who comes after me, the thongs of whose sandals I am not worthy to untie* (v. 27). The Baptist's words continue a theme in the Prologue (1:6–8, 15), and betray extraordinary humility in the context of a society where a student was expected to do for his teacher whatever a slave would do – except take off his shoes (*cf.* Daube, pp. 266–267). John the Baptist makes no exceptions, not even this one, and thereby defines his relation to Jesus the Messiah in a moving way that anticipates 3:30–36.

28. The *Bethany* most commonly mentioned in the Gospels lies a short distance east and slightly south of Jerusalem, on the road to Jericho, and is best known as the home of Jesus' friends, Mary, Martha and Lazarus (11:1). The Bethany mentioned here, however, is located *on the other side of the Jordan*, from the vantage point of the western side. Because there is no known Bethany on the east bank, numerous theories have been advanced. Some adopt the reading 'Bethabara' – a known village but almost certainly not the original text. Apart from the textual evidence, which strongly supports 'Bethany', John takes equal pains to identify the other Bethany's proximity to Jerusalem (11:18), which suggests that in his own mind he is referring to two places with the same name.

Although a dozen other suggestions have been advanced, recent research indicates that the most plausible theory is that the text refers to

Batanea (called Bashan in the Old Testament), not a town or village but an area in the north-east of the country, to which Jesus himself withdrew toward the end of his ministry when opponents in Judea were trying to kill him (10:39–40). This is more likely than any site in the tetrarchy of Herod Antipas, since by the end of Jesus' ministry Herod had already executed John the Baptist and generally ruled with more paranoia and cruelty than did his easy-going relative Philip, who ruled over Batanea.[1]

If Batanea is what John had in mind, why does he write 'Bethany'? In the first century, however, much greater diversity in the spelling of proper names was tolerated than today (Josephus, for instance, offers three different spellings for 'Batanea'). In such names 'th' and 't' sounds were sometimes confused. Moreover the Targums (Aramaic paraphrases of the Old Testament) preserve spellings that are very close to 'Bethany'. It may well be that John uses these details to make a point: he opts for a particular spelling to point out that Jesus' ministry begins and ends at 'Bethany'. *At Bethany on the other side of the Jordan* Jesus is identified by the Baptist as the Lamb of God who takes away the sin of the world (1:28–29); at the end of his public ministry, he retreats to the same place, and the witness of the Baptist is reviewed (10:39–40). Then in the very next chapter, Jesus performs his last and greatest 'sign' before the cross, the raising of Lazarus – at Bethany near Jerusalem (Jn. 11). The result is the announcement of the need for Jesus to die as a sacrifice for the people (11:45–53) – the promised Lamb of God indeed. What begins as public witness in the North ends in public crucifixion in the South. Judea, Samaria, Galilee, and now the Transjordan (of which Batanea was a part), all the regions of the promised land, are mentioned;[2] for Jesus was not a regional Messiah, a parochial preacher, but the true Israel (*cf.* notes on Jn. 15). Subtle writer that he is, John's geographical note in this verse anticipates and links major themes in his Gospel.

2. John the Baptist's public witness concerning Jesus (1:29–34)

This section forms something of a bridge. On the one hand, these verses continue the theme of the witness of John the Baptist, begun in the preceding verses (vv. 19–28); on the other, they introduce a lengthy list of titles applied to Jesus, a list that takes up the rest of the chapter: Lamb of God (1:29, 36), the Elect One (the most likely variant of 1:34), Rabbi (1:38, 49), Messiah/Christ (1:41), Son of God (1:49), King of Israel (1:49), Son of Man (1:51) – not to mention 'the one Moses wrote about in the law, and about whom the prophets also wrote' (1:45). *Cf.* Schnackenburg, 1. 507–514.

The fact that Jesus is so fully and so early recognized to be the Messiah

---

[1]For a detailed survey and defence of this view, *cf.* Rainer Riesner, *TynB* 38, 1987, pp. 29–63.
[2]*Ibid.*

is judged by some to be evidence for the unhistorical nature of John 1:29–51. After all, in the Synoptic Gospels Peter and the others do not volunteer a formal confession that Jesus is the Messiah until Caesarea Philippi (Mt. 16:13–20 par.), well into the ministry. But several factors mitigate the tension between the accounts. If some of Jesus' first disciples had earlier followed John the Baptist, we must suppose that *something* encouraged them to abandon their old master at the peak of his influence, in order to follow a still unknown preacher from Galilee. The best reason is the obvious one: they changed their allegiance precisely because it was the Baptist himself who pointed Jesus out as the one who was coming to fulfil the promises of Scripture. In that case, the confessions of John 1 are not only plausible, but almost historically necessary.

This does not mean that the followers of Jesus portrayed in John 1 enjoyed a thoroughly Christian grasp of the titles they applied to Jesus. Doubtless they were first uttered more in hope than in faith. In fact, of the four Gospels it is John's that most insistently stresses how much the disciples *misunderstood* what they confessed (*cf.* Carson, 'Mis'). In other words, if John records early confessions, he also emphasizes how little the first confessors understood. This leaves scope for a rising under-standing, better portrayed in the Synoptic Gospels. Even there, after all, when Peter and the others come to God-revealed knowledge that Jesus is the Christ, the Son of God, the confession is promptly marred by massive misunderstanding: Peter at least sees no place for the Messiah to suffer, and rebukes Jesus accordingly (Mt. 16:21–23 par.). Every gain in fresh understanding, including the first steps of discipleship, masked major misunderstanding that remained in place until after the cross and resurrection. That is an important point for John to make, if he is interested in evangelizing Jews in his own day; for it simultaneously encourages his contemporaries to take *steps* of faith, and begins the detailed explanation (needed by all first-century Jews) as to how the first 'converts' came to accept that the promised Messiah had to be crucified, cursed like an abominated criminal.

29. *The next day* probably refers to the day after John's response to the Jerusalem delegation. It also initiates a sequence of days culminating in the miracle at Cana (*cf.* notes on 2:1). Probably the baptism of Jesus at the hands of John the Baptist (which the Fourth Gospel does not record) took place some time earlier (*cf.* notes on vv. 31–33). At this point *John saw Jesus coming toward him* and bore witness both public and startling: *Look, the Lamb of God, who takes away the sin of the world!*

Modern Christians are so familiar with the entire clause that it takes an effort of the imagination to recognize that, before the coming and death of Jesus, it was not an obvious messianic designation. That fact has prompted the majority of modern interpreters to deny that John the Baptist made any such declaration. In their view, the entire account is a literary creation by the Evangelist, who, writing as a Christian, understands that Jesus is the Lamb of God, and then projects this understanding back on the Baptist. If 'Lamb of God' has sacrificial overtones, this scepticism becomes the more plausible when we remember that Matthew reports, in the strongest terms, that John the Baptist was *not* prepared for a suffering Messiah. Indeed, the Baptist entertained some doubts about who Jesus was precisely *because* he lacked this understanding (*cf.* Mt. 11:2-19; Carson, *Matt*, pp. 260-272).

This stance prompts some contemporary interpreters not to consider what John the Baptist might have understood by the title (since they deny he used it), and to ask only what John the Evangelist thought. Even here there is little agreement. The standard options are listed in the commentaries (*e.g.* Morris, pp. 144-147): Jesus is the 'gentle lamb' of Jeremiah 11:19 (though Jeremiah makes no mention of taking away the sins of the world); Jesus is the lamb of the daily sacrifice (though there is no evidence that the the daily sacrifice was ever called 'God's lamb' or 'lamb of God'); Jesus is the scapegoat (Lv. 16), which was banished to the desert, symbolically bearing away the sins of the people (though that animal was a goat, while Jn. 1:29 speaks of a lamb); Jesus is the lamb of Genesis 22, which proved to be the substitute for Isaac (though in the context of Genesis there is no mention of bearing sin away); Jesus is the guilt offering (Lv. 14; Nu. 6), which was certainly understood as a sacrifice that dealt with sin (though it appears bulls and goats were commonly sacrificed, rather than lambs); Jesus is the Servant of the Lord of Isaiah 53, since the Aramaic word *ṭalyā* probably spoken by the Baptist can mean either 'servant' or 'lamb' (though this presupposes that whoever put this Aramaic expression into Greek somehow avoided a perfectly common and obvious expression, 'the servant of the Lord', in order to produce a new and rather strange expression, 'the lamb of God'); Jesus is the apocalyptic, triumphant lamb of Revelation 7:17; 17:14 (though the expression is found in but few other Jewish texts, and uses *arnion* for 'lamb', rather than *amnos*, found here – though John does use *arnion* in 21:15); Jesus is the Passover lamb, certainly a theme alluded to elsewhere in the Fourth Gospel (though even here there is no evidence that the Passover lamb was a sin offering); Jesus is the lamb led to the slaughter (Is. 53:7), whose death effectively deals with transgression (though it must be admitted that the lamb in the Isaiah passage is no more than a simile).

More recently it has been suggested that 'the Lamb of God' (1:29) is simply a parallel to 'the Son of God' (1:34), and means no more than that.[1] But the literary parallelism on which this reconstruction depends is unconvincing, and the theory still does not explain why the 'Lamb of God' should be chosen as the alternative to 'Son of God'. Beasley-Murray (pp. 24-25) attempts to resolve both the historical problem and the question of backgrounds by arguing that what the historical John the Baptist probably said was simply 'Look, the Lamb of God!' (as in 1:36),

---

[1]P. J. du Plessis, in Petzer/Hartin, pp. 136-148.

probably thinking of the powerful, apocalyptic lamb, while it was the Evangelist who added the words 'who takes away the sin of the world' in 1:29, to inject a sacrificial, expiatory note. But detailed distinctions between source and comment, culminating in fine distinctions within a single sentence, are methodologically ill-founded in this Gospel, where John has written up all the material as his own.

Where there are so many disputed points, certainty cannot reasonably be achieved. If we credit the Evangelist with making an historical statement about the witness of John the Baptist, however, then perhaps some such reconstruction as the following involves fewest difficulties. When the Baptist identified Jesus as *the Lamb of God, who takes away the sin of the world*, he probably had in mind the apocalyptic lamb, the warrior lamb, found in some Jewish texts (*1 Enoch* 90:9-12; *Testament of Joseph* 19:8; *Testament of Benjamin* 3:8 – the latter passages probably, but not certainly, pre-Christian) and picked up in the Apocalypse (Rev. 5:6, 12; 7:17; 13:8; 17:14; 19:7, 9; 21:22-23; 22:1-3). If 'Lamb of God' was not a well-recognized, technical expression, the fact that our text uses *amnos* instead of *arnion* offers no great difficulty. Whether we assume the category lay readily to hand for the Baptist to use, or that he was one of the first to think it up, the impression gleaned from the Synoptics is that he thought of the Messiah as one who would come in terrible judgment and clean up the sin in Israel. In this light, what John the Baptist meant by 'who takes away the sin of the world' may have had more to do with judgment and destruction than with expiatory sacrifice. Certainly the verb *airō* normally means 'remove', 'take away', not 'bear away in atoning death' or the like (for which the more common verb is *anapherō*; cf. Dodd, *IFG*, pp. 230-238).

But this does not necessarily mean that John the Evangelist limited himself to this understanding of 'Lamb of God'. Just as John insists that Caiaphas the high priest spoke better than he knew (11:49-52), so it is easy to suppose that the Evangelist understood the Baptist to be doing the same thing. It is not that he thought the Baptist wrong; rather, as a post-resurrection Christian John could grasp a fuller picture than was possible for the Baptist. In particular he understood a great deal more about the significance of the Messiah's sacrificial death. It is hard to imagine that he could use an expression such as 'Lamb of God' *without* thinking of the atoning sacrifice of his resurrected and ascended Saviour. He is sufficiently faithful to the ambiguity of the expression that he does not transform 'takes away' from *airō* to an unambiguously sacrificial *anapherō*, as that would explicitly ascribe something to the Baptist the latter probably did not mean. But as a writer who holds that all (Old Testament) Scripture points to Jesus (5:39-40), John might well see adequate warrant for the application of this title to Jesus, sacrificially understood, in the lamb of Isaiah 53:7, 10. The word for 'lamb' in the LXX of Isaiah 53:7 is *amnos*, as here. Moreover, John appeals to Isaiah 53 elsewhere, and certainly Isaiah is one of the books from which he most frequently quotes. John might also have found warrant for this understanding of the expression in the passover lamb, and in other Old Testament imagery and institutions. *Cf.* Additional Note.

Whatever the antecedents of the expression, the sacrifice envisaged is not restricted in its purpose or effectiveness to the Jewish race. This Lamb of God takes away the sin *of the world* – that is, of all human beings without distinction, though not, as the Prologue has already made clear (1:11–12), of all without exception. This is *God's* provision: Jesus is the Lamb *of God*.

30. The Baptist goes on to affirm that this Jesus is none other than the one he had earlier been announcing, one who outstripped the Baptist himself in importance because by virtue of his pre-existence he took absolute precedence, even though he appeared on the stage of history after him. The reference is to 1:15, thus tying this paragraph to the Prologue.

31–33. Apparently John the Baptist had baptized Jesus some time earlier. Up to that point, John himself *did not know him* (v. 31) – which does not mean that John did not know Jesus at all, but only that he did not know him as the Coming One. All John knew was that his own ministry of preaching and *baptising with water* (v. 31) was ordained by God to prepare the way for this Coming One, *that he might be revealed to Israel* (v. 31). But now the Baptist provides a testimony to Jesus that explains how he identified the Coming One. Referring to the aftermath of Jesus' baptism, he testifies, *I have seen* (the perfect tense reflects a settled conviction) *the Spirit come down from heaven as a dove and remain on him* (v. 32). In the Synoptic Gospels, the descent of the Spirit as a dove was something Jesus himself witnessed (Mt. 3:16; Mk. 1:10; Lk. 3:22), a symbol in tandem with the voice from heaven. Here in the Fourth Gospel, however, the dove assumes a different (though certainly complementary) role: it identifies the Coming One *to John the Baptist*. He had been told by God himself (*the one who sent me to baptise with water*, v. 33) who the Coming One, the promised Messiah, would be: *The man on whom you see the Spirit come down and remain is he who will baptise with the Holy Spirit* (v. 33).

The early church preached that 'God anointed Jesus of Nazareth with the Holy Spirit and power' (Acts 10:38). When Christians read their Bibles (what we call the 'Old Testament'), they saw in Jesus the fulfilment of God's promises to pour out his Spirit on the coming Davidic king (Is. 11:1ff.), on the Servant of the Lord (Is. 42:1) and on the prophet-figure who announces, 'The Spirit of the Sovereign LORD is on me, because the LORD has anointed me to preach good news to the poor' (Is. 61:1). Small wonder, then, that some visible descent of the Spirit on Jesus served as the God-given sign by which the Baptist would know that this was the long-awaited Coming One. The choice of a dove to symbolize the Spirit's descent is not obvious, though there is some evidence in Jewish sources for a connection between 'dove' and 'Holy Spirit' (*cf.* Additional Note).

The Spirit not only descends on Jesus, but *remains* (vv. 32, 33) on him.

To Jesus 'God gives the Spirit without limit' (3:34). Some, like King Saul, experienced the Spirit's presence and power temporarily; Jesus, the great antitype of David, never displeases his Father (8:29), whose love and whose Spirit rest on him permanently (cf. 1 Sa. 16:13; 2 Sa. 7:15). Small wonder, then, that Jesus is equipped to baptize others, not merely (as did John the Baptist) in the medium of water, but in the Holy Spirit. This too anticipates the fulfilment of Old Testament prophecies, which looked forward to the time when God's people would have the Spirit poured out on them (e.g. Ezk. 36:25–26). That Jesus would baptize his people in the Holy Spirit is therefore simultaneously an attestation of who he is, and an announcement that the promised age is dawning.

For the Evangelist, then, the aspect of Jesus' baptism that suited his purposes in writing was its role in bringing the Baptist to recognize who Jesus was, and therefore to bear witness specifically to him, and no longer to an unidentified 'Coming One'.

34. The Baptist's firm *I have seen and I have testified* (both verbs are in the perfect) underscore how, for him, the sight of the Spirit descending on Jesus in bodily form bore transforming significance. It enabled him to point to Jesus, with clarity and conviction, and declare (according to the NIV) that *this is the Son of God*. A very good case can be made for the view that the best reading here is 'this is the Chosen One of God' (*ho eklektos* instead of *ho huios*). Textual support for 'Chosen One' is significant,[1] even if not as strongly supported as one might wish (*e.g.* the two important papyri designated P[66] and P[75] preserve 'the Son'). But 'Son' is a common designation for Jesus in the Fourth Gospel (*cf.* notes on 1:49; 5:16–30); 'the Elect One' is not elsewhere attested in this book. Copyists were therefore more likely, on balance, to change 'the Elect One of God' into 'the Son of God' than the reverse, especially since the former could be construed to support adoptionism. If so, 'the Elect One of God' is original, and John is probably making a direct reference to Isaiah 42:1, where God promises to pour out his Spirit on his servant, his 'chosen one' (LXX *ho eklektos*). In John's Gospel, the theme that the disciples of Jesus are his elect, his chosen ones, is extremely strong, (*e.g.* 6:65, 70; 13:18; 15:16, 19). But this privilege of believers is ultimately grounded in the fact that Jesus himself is God's chosen one *par excellence* – chosen as the suffering servant, the Lamb of God who takes away the sin of the world.

Additional notes

29. Many have argued recently that in the Fourth Gospel the power of God issuing in salvation emerges from revelation, not redemption; from

---

[1]Although Metzger (p. 200) prefers 'the Son of God' on 'the basis of age and diversity of witnesses', more than a few 'chiefly Western' manuscripts support 'the Chosen One of God' (*cf.* G. Schrenk, *TDNT*, p. 189, n. 18). There are important internal reasons for

God's gracious self-disclosure in Jesus, not from expiation of sin; from the demonstration of God's love on the cross, not from a work of atoning significance on the cross (e.g. Forestell, pp. 157–166; Painter, p. 63; Smalley, p. 224). In its strongest form this view is exegetically doubtful, illogical, and reductionistic: exegetically doubtful, because there are too many passages in John whose most obvious meaning includes the notion of sins dealt with by means of Jesus' sacrificial death; illogical, because, as James Denney pointed out at the turn of the century, it is as meaningless to detect profound, revelatory love in a cross of Christ that achieved nothing as it would be to detect profound love in a man who tries to prove his devotion to his fellow human beings by jumping off Brighton pier and drowning, with no purpose in view and no result achieved; and reductionistic, because we are being forced into an 'either/or' argument when the Fourth Gospel itself demands a 'both/and'. If there is restraint in the language John uses for the cross-work of Christ (cf. notes on 6:51; 10:11, 14; 11:50–51; 15:13; 17:19; 18:14), it is because John is attempting a faithful record of some of the events and circumstances *during Jesus' ministry*, while still trying to address his own readership. Cf. George L. Carey, TynB 32, 1981, pp. 97–122; Bruce H. Grigsby, JSNT 15, 1982, pp. 51–80.

31–33. Cf. SB 1. 123; Barrett, HSGT, pp. 36–39 – though his suggestion that in John, unlike the Synoptics, the dove is no more than a detail of the tradition seems weak, in the light of the explicit references to the Spirit (v. 33; cf. Burge, pp. 56–59). G. F. Hasel (ISBE 1. 988) detects an allusion to Genesis 1:2, since Rabbi Ben Zoma, a younger contemporary of the apostle, cites a rabbinic tradition to the effect that 'the Spirit of God was brooding on the face of the waters like a dove which broods over her young but does not touch them' (B. *Hagigah* 15a). The suggestion of Stephen Gero[1] that the Gospel narratives depend on the emergence of two separate traditions, one in which the Spirit descends on Jesus and the other in which a dove descends on him, is too speculative. In light of the recent suggestion of C. T. Begg[2] that the dove in Psalm 74:19–20 is a symbol of the covenant, based on Genesis 15:9–18, it is tempting to see in John 1:32 an allusion to the promise of the new covenant (Je. 31:31–34). The evidence is not strong, however, and John's explicit emphasis on the Holy Spirit makes the dove/Spirit connection more plausible.

3. Jesus gains his first disciples (1:35–42)
It is often said that the 'call' of the disciples in these verses cannot be reconciled with the Synoptic accounts (Mt. 4:18–22; 9:9; Mk. 1:16–20; 2:13–14; Lk. 5:1–11, 27–28). Traditional harmonization, which postulates that John's account is a preliminary 'call', ratified by the later one

---

supporting the reading less widely distributed in the witnesses (cf. Schnackenburg, 1. 305–306; Gordon D. Fee, Bib 55, 1974, p. 453).

[1] NovT 17, 1976, pp. 17–35. [2] VT 37, 1987, pp. 78–81.

reported in the Synoptic Gospels, is ruled out of court on the ground that John leaves no room for a second call. But strictly speaking Jesus does not 'call' his disciples at all in these verses (except possibly Philip: *cf.* notes on v. 43). They attach themselves to him because of the witness of the Baptist, and then because of the witness of the Baptist's followers. Nor is this a representative abandonment of 'other religions' (Barrett, p. 179, referring to the work of E. Schweizer) in favour of Jesus: the first disciples are presented as rightly adhering to what the witness of John the Baptist means, not as abandoning him in favour of a new, 'Christian' religion. Indeed, the promptness with which the disciples, according to the Synoptic tradition, abandon their livelihood (whether the fishing business or a tax office) in response to Jesus' explicit call, is psychologically and historically more plausible if that was not their first exposure to him or their first demonstration of fealty toward him. At this point in John, however, these fledgling disciples are still at the 'Come and you will see' (v. 39) stage, the 'You shall see greater things than that' (v. 50) stage.

35–37. *The next day* (*cf.* notes on 2:1) John the Baptist, seeing Jesus passing by, again identifies him as *the Lamb of God* (v. 36; *cf.* notes on 1:29); but this time two of his own disciples hear their master's witness. One of them was Andrew, Simon Peter's brother (v. 40); the other is not named. The traditional identification of the unnamed disciple as the Evangelist, the 'beloved disciple', is plausible enough. A number of features in the account, such as the specification of the hour (v. 39), can be explained as details sharply etched on the mind of the writer when he first encountered Jesus Christ. But there is no proof of this identification.

The text does not tell us that the Baptist expected his followers to become disciples of Jesus. Certainly some remained attached to John even after his death (*cf.* Acts 19:1ff.). But in the light of John the Baptist's self-perception as the forerunner of the Coming One, it is reasonable to assume that at least some of his disciples, those perhaps who understood him best, discerned that their master was constantly pointing beyond himself to another. Once he had identified the Coming One, it was only to be expected that some of them would follow Jesus. In doing so, the two disciples mentioned here are not scurrilously abandoning the Baptist in favour of a more prestigious leader, but are being truest to the teaching of the forerunner. This John the Baptist understood (3:27–30).

In the Fourth Gospel, the verb 'to follow' often means 'to follow as a disciple' (*e.g.* 1:43; 8:12; 12:26; 21:19, 20, 22). But this is not invariably the case: sometimes the verb is quite neutral (*e.g.* 11:31). It is possible the Evangelist is playing with both meanings: at one level, these two men were 'following' Jesus in the most mundane of senses, but at another they were taking the first steps of genuine discipleship.

38–39. As with the verb 'to follow', so also with Jesus' question, *What do you want?* It appears that the Evangelist is writing on two levels. The question makes sense as straightforward narrative: Jesus asks the two men who are following him to articulate what is on their minds. But the Evangelist wants his readers to reflect on a deeper question: the Logos-Messiah confronts those who make any show of beginning to follow him and demands that they articulate what they really want in life.

The two disciples of the Baptist begin their response with *Rabbi*. The word literally means 'my great one', but was a common term of honour addressed by a student to his master, his teacher (as John's explanatory aside points out, for the sake of his Greek readers). By the end of the first century AD the word became restricted to certain 'ordained' teachers who had successfully completed an appropriate course of rabbinical instruction. But at this point in the century there was apparently no official ordination; the title was used as a courtesy honorific, applied by respectful people to those they recognized as public teachers of divine subject matter. It is commonly applied to Jesus (1:49; 3:2; 4:31; 6:25; 9:2; 11:8), even by Nicodemus, himself a scholarly 'rabbi' (3:1–2). Similarly, the disciples of the Baptist could address their master the same way (3:26).

The question asked by the two disciples again makes sense as part of the developing narrative. Feeling perhaps that it would be presumptuous to plunge right into their profoundly theological concerns, they restrain themselves and ask a question the answer to which would enable them to seek him out in private and at greater leisure: *Rabbi, where are you staying?* The verb rendered 'are staying', *viz. menō*, is often translated 'to remain' or 'to abide', and is so characteristic of John's Gospel (especially Jn. 15) that it may well be the Evangelist again assigns more symbolic depth to the question than the Baptist's disciples could have intended at the time.

Jesus' simple response – *Come, and you will see* (v. 39) – doubtless delighted the Baptist's disciples, and constituted the beginning of their intimate relationship with Jesus Christ. They spent the rest of the day with him (from about 4.00 p.m. on: *cf.* Additional Notes), and perhaps later they understood that his invitation was of a piece with the theological invitation he later extended more broadly: 'If anyone chooses to do God's will, he will find out whether my teaching comes from God or whether I speak on my own' (7:17).

40–42. Andrew *was one of the two who heard what John had said and who had followed Jesus.* Even though he is introduced into the narrative before Peter, he is presented as *Simon Peter's brother*, because by the time this Gospel was written Peter's name was widely known, even in non-Christian Jewish circles; Andrew's much less so. *The first thing Andrew did* (*cf.* Additional Notes) was to find his brother and announce, *We have found the Messiah.* He thus became the first in a long line of successors who have discovered that the most common and effective Christian testimony is the private witness of friend to friend, brother to brother.

The term *Messiah* is a transliteration of a Hebrew or Aramaic word, substantivized to mean 'anointed one'. In the Old Testament it denotes the king of Israel (in the expression 'the LORD's anointed', *e.g.* 1 Sa. 16:6;

2 Sa. 1:14), the high priest (*e.g.* Lv. 4:3), and, in one passage, the patriarchs, 'my anointed ones' (Ps. 105:15), probably in their role as prophets. Quite apart from the verbal adjective, the act of anointing was instrumental in the 'consecration', the setting apart, of Aaron the priest (Ex. 29:7), David the king (1 Sa. 16:1–13), and Elisha the prophet (1 Ki. 19:16) – to mention no others. While much early Christian preaching stressed the *royal* motif, presenting Jesus as the messianic (*i.e.* 'anointed') king of Israel, the New Testament documents cumulatively present Jesus as the Messiah, *i.e.* the Anointed One, *par excellence* – the anointed prophet, priest and king. At this stage Andrew cannot have understood so much, and probably saw in the term 'Messiah' a (perhaps royal) designation of the Coming One. The Evangelist translates the term for his Greek readers, rendering it by the corresponding Greek verbal adjective *christos* (from *chriō*, 'to anoint'); hence our 'the Christ', understood in the first instance as a title, not a name.

When Peter is brought to him, Jesus assigns a new name as a declaration of what Peter will become. This is not so much a merely predictive utterance as a declaration of what Jesus will make of him. His name up to this time has been *Simon son of John* (or 'son of Jonah' in Mt. 16:17, 'Jonah' in Aramaic being an abbreviated form of 'John'; the name recurs in Jn. 21:15–17). But, says Jesus, *You will be called Cephas*: doubtless in Aramaic the expression was *kêpā'*, a word meaning 'rock'. The terminal 's' in 'Cephas' reflects an attempt to give the Aramaic word a Greek spelling (a pattern also adopted by Paul, *e.g.* 1 Cor. 9:5; Gal. 1:18). Because most of his readers cannot be expected to know any semitic language, John provides the translation, 'Peter'. The Evangelist thus makes it clear that the assignation of the name 'Peter' to John occurred at the very outset of Jesus' ministry, a fact not contradicted by either Mark 3:16 or Matthew 16:18. Whether this change of name is meant to reflect a change in character or, as in Matthew 16, to grant Peter a certain foundational role in the establishment of the church (*cf.* Carson, *Matt*, pp. 363–375) is unclear. The Epilogue (Jn. 21:18–19) tells us a little of what would happen to Peter. Here in John 1, however, the focus is much less on what this name change means for Peter, than on the Jesus who knows people thoroughly (*cf.* vv. 43–51), and not only 'sees into' them (*cf.* 47–48) but so calls them that he makes them what he calls them to be.

Additional notes

39. The 'tenth hour' is understood by some to mean ten o'clock in the morning, counting the hours from midnight to noon and noon until midnight. This is alleged to be the 'Roman' system, unlike the Jewish system which counts from sunrise to sunset (roughly 6.00 a.m. to 6.00 p.m.). But the evidence in support of a Roman system for counting hours turns out to be unconvincing. The primary support is from Pliny the Elder; but all he says is that Roman priests and authorities, like the

Egyptians, counted the official day, the civil day, from midnight to midnight – useful information in leases and other documents that expire at day's end. Nowhere does he suggest that any of his contemporaries count the *hours* of a day from midnight; indeed, he says that 'the common people everywhere' think of the day running from dawn to dark. Jews, Romans and others divided the daylight 'day' into twelve hours; the Romans divided the night into four watches. Counter evidence advanced by Westcott (2. 324–326) is unconvincing: *cf.* Morris, pp. 800–801. Symbolic interpretations (*e.g.* Bultmann, p. 100, suggests that 'tenth hour' signifies the time of fulfilment; *cf.* Ferraro, pp. 96–99) lack rudimentary controls.

41. The NIV's *The first thing Andrew did* presupposes the reading *prōton*, 'first', an adverbial accusative modifying 'did' – that is, the text means that the first thing Andrew did was to find Peter. That is the most probable meaning. Two alternatives should be noted: (1) Two manuscripts have *prōtos*, the adjectival form of 'first', modifying Andrew – that is, *first* Andrew found his brother, implying that the other disciple then did so. That would support the view that the other disciple was John, as his brother James was another early recruit to the band of the Twelve. (2) Two early Latin manuscripts have *mane* – that is, Andrew finds his brother *the next morning*. Verse 43 then introduces still another new day, and the entire sequence of days is advanced by one. That in turn affects the interpretation of 2:1 (*cf.* notes there). But the strongest textual evidence supports *prōton*, and the adverbial accusative use of the word is common in John.

4. Jesus gains two more disciples, Philip and Nathaniel (1:43–51)

Two more are now added to the list of Jesus' disciples: Philip and Nathanael. In this way the chapter provides concrete examples of a point made in the Prologue: although in general his own people did not receive him, yet some did, believing on his name and gaining from him the authority to become children of God (1:11–12).

43–44. *The next day* (*cf.* notes on 2:1) he *decided to leave for Galilee.* But who is it that decides? The NIV supports 'Jesus' as the subject, although the Greek text leaves the matter open: (lit.) 'The next day he decided to leave for Galilee and found Philip. Jesus said to him. . . .' It is quite possible 'Andrew' is the subject of the first clause. In that case Andrew *first* (v. 41) found his brother Simon Peter, and *then* found Philip. This interpretation not only gives extra significance to that 'first' (*cf.* notes on v. 41), but also explains why 'Jesus' is actually named in the second sentence of v. 43. This suggestion cannot be proved, because the Evangelist does not actually say that the one who decided to enter Galilee, after finding Philip, actually brought him to Jesus: if Andrew is the subject, that has to be assumed (an assumption that is natural enough, considering how condensed the narrative is). But that this view is correct is supported by the fact that everyone else who comes to Jesus in this chapter does so because of someone else's witness; if Andrew is the subject, there are no exceptions. Theologically, the Evangelist is re-inforcing his theme of the importance of bearing witness; historically, Jesus does not at this time 'call' any of these fledgling disciples, as he (later) does according to the accounts in the Synoptic Gospels.

Introductions complete, Jesus issues the foundational challenge to Philip: *Follow me* (v. 43; on 'follow', *cf.* notes on v. 37).[1]

If 'Bethany' is the district of Batanea (*cf.* notes on 1:28), then the decision to leave for Galilee, whether made by Jesus or by Andrew, meant travelling west. A suitable entry point was Bethsaida, located on the north-east shore of the Lake, and nicely rendered by Bruce (p. 59) as 'Fishertown'. Just over three decades earlier, the town had been re-founded by Philip the tetrarch and named 'Julias' in honour of Julia, the daughter of Emperor Augustus (*cf.* Lk. 3:1). Strictly speaking therefore the town did not lie in the district of Galilee (despite 'Bethsaida in Galilee', 12:21) but in Gaulanitis. There is however ample evidence that the common folk used 'Galilee' to refer to some territory east of the Jordan. Thus 'Judas the Galilaean', according to Josephus (*Ant.* xviii. 4), came from Gamala on the east side of the Lake (Acts 5:37).

Philip is listed in the Synoptic lists of the twelve apostles (Mk. 3:18 par.) and in Acts (1:13), but it is John who tells us most about him (*cf.* 6:6ff.; 12:21–22; 14:8–9). It is possible that John maintains this interest in Philip because of continued contact with him later in life. Eusebius (*H. E.* III. xxxi. 3) cites Polycrates to the effect that Philip, one of the Twelve, was buried in Hierapolis, a city in Asia Minor, the province where the apostle John apparently ministered for the last twenty-five years of his life. But this evidence is of uncertain value; Polycrates may have confused Philip the apostle with Philip the evangelist (*cf.*Acts 6:5; 8:5ff.).

The Philip in John 1:43–44 *was from the town of Bethsaida*, likewise the home of *Andrew and Peter* (v. 44). This has often been judged irre-trievably contradictory to Mark 1:21, 29, which locates Peter's house in Capernaum. Unless we are tempted to argue that Andrew and Peter owned two homes, one in Bethsaida and the other in Capernaum, it is perhaps wiser to observe a comparison. Jesus is consistently said to be from Nazareth (Mt. 2:23; 4:13; 21:11; Mk. 1:9; Lk. 1:26; 2:4, 39, 51; Jn. 1:45; Acts 10:38), but early in his ministry he moved to Capernaum (Mt. 4:13). If Andrew and Peter were reared in Bethsaida, they would be viewed as from Bethsaida, irrespective of where their mature years found them living and working.

45. As Andrew brought Simon Peter and perhaps Philip to Jesus, so

---

[1]If this interpretation is correct, the criticism of Barrett (p. 183) is emptied of force: 'Those who think that the Marcan "call" of Simon and Andrew can be made more credible by the use of the Johannine narrative do not always observe that the Johannine "call" of Philip raises all the difficulties of the Marcan story.' Even if one were to decide that Jesus is the subject of v. 43a, however, the most it would prove is that Jesus took the initiative with Philip at this juncture, but not yet with the others. No other account of the recruitment of Philip is provided by the Synoptic Gospels.

Philip found Nathanael and witnessed to him. That has been the foundational principle of truly Christian expansion ever since: new followers of Jesus bear witness of him to others, who in turn become disciples and repeat the process. The name 'Nathanael' means 'God gives' or 'God has given'. Some have therefore argued that he is not an historical character but a symbol: disciples have been *given* by the Father to Jesus (6:37). But John's readers apparently could not decipher semitic names. Therefore when John wants them to detect some symbolic significance in such names, he provides a translation (*e.g.* 9:7); he provides nothing here. Moreover, because the other disciples mentioned in this chapter are known historical characters, it is natural to think of Nathanael the same way. Others suggest he is an unknown disciple, or that he represents Matthew (*cf.* K. Hanhart, in Sevenster, pp. 23–26). Certainly the other disciples mentioned in these verses belonged to the band of the twelve apostles. The most likely suggestion is that Nathanael is the personal name of 'Bartholomew', which is then understood to be an Aramaic patronymic (*i.e.* identifying the person as the son of someone: 'the son of Tholomaeus' or the like). In three of the four lists of apostles, this Bartholomew is linked with Philip (Mt. 10:3; Mk. 3:18; Lk. 6:14; but not Acts 1:13).

Philip's witness is of a piece with Andrew's (v. 41), except that he does not call Jesus the Messiah but *the one Moses wrote about in the Law, and about whom the prophets also wrote*. That is the stance of this entire Gospel: Jesus fulfils the Old Testament Scriptures (*cf.* 5:39). The earliest disciples could not have identified Jesus as the promised Coming One, the Messiah, without believing that the Scriptures pointed to him, for that was part of the common stock of Jewish messianic hope. In this stream of thought, not only the prophets but even 'the Law' – *i.e.* the Pentateuch – anticipated the coming of the Messiah. (For a list of pentateuchal passages the rabbis interpreted messianically, *cf.* Edersheim, 2. 710–715 – though some of his sources are late.) Philip refers to no specific passage, but in this chapter Deuteronomy 18:15–19 and Genesis 28 are alluded to (in v. 21 and v. 51 respectively). To this must be added the large stock of material from the rest of the Old Testament, here lumped together as what 'the prophets' wrote.[1]

In the words *Jesus of Nazareth, the son of Joseph*, Philip provides exactly the kind of information that positively identifies a man in first-century Palestine: the name of his village, and the name of his (reputed) father. Elsewhere in the Fourth Gospel the unbelieving Jews try to discredit his claim that he came down from heaven by identifying him as 'the son of Joseph' (6:42), and there the irony to which John frequently resorts is obvious. It is in accord with this frequent use of irony that John 'should

---

[1]On the status of the Old Testament canon at the time of Jesus, *cf.* Roger T. Beckwith, *The Old Testament Canon of the New Testament Church* (SPCK, 1986/Eerdmans, 1985); or more briefly, David G. Dunbar, 'The Biblical Canon', in Carson/Woodbridge II, pp. 295–360, 424–446.

allow Jesus to be ignorantly described as "son of Joseph" while himself believing that Jesus had no human father' (Barrett, p. 184). But here in 1:45, so early in the book, before patterns of irony have become obvious to the reader, irony would likely be detected only by the person who read the book more than once (cf. Duke, p. 58).

46. Nathanael was from Cana (21:2), another town in Galilee. As Galileans were frequently despised by people from Judea, so it appears that even fellow Galileans despised Nazareth. Nathanel's scathing question probably reflects more than local rivalry between villages. From John's perspective, the fact that Jesus was reared in Nazareth not only obscured his origins in Bethlehem for those who did not search very far (7:41–42, 52), but also reflected the self-abasement of the man from heaven. He was known as 'Jesus of Nazareth' or 'Jesus the Nazarene' (cf. Mt. 2:23), not 'Jesus the Bethlehemite', with all the royal, Davidic overtones that would have provided. Some years later, Christians could be contemptuously dismissed as the 'Nazarene sect' (Acts 24:5).

Philip responded with the only satisfactory response possible: *Come and see.* 'Honest inquiry is a sovereign cure for prejudice. Nazareth might be all that Nathanael thought, but there is an exception to prove every rule; and what an exception these young men had found!' (Bruce, p. 60). But as in v. 39, not only are these words a challenge to the person in the narrative, but an invitation to the reader.

47. *When Jesus saw Nathanael approaching,* he said in his hearing, 'Truly, an Israelite in whom there is no guile!' – not, as in NIV, 'Here is a true Israelite . . .'. The adjective 'true' (*alēthinos*) is an important word for John, but he does not use it here (cf. notes on 1:9). Instead, he uses the word 'truly' (*alēthōs*), consistently deployed in the Fourth Gospel as an adverb (4:42; 6:14, 55 [*v.l.*]; 7:26, 40; 8:31; 17:8). Jesus is not saying that Nathanael is a 'true Israelite', in terms reminiscent of Paul's discussion of the new Israel (Rom. 2:28–29; 9:6). After all, at this point Nathanael is not a convert in any sense; and if he became a disciple of Jesus after their next exchange, he still had to pass through a lengthy period characterized by considerable misunderstanding. That Jesus refers to him as an 'Israelite' is not surprising; Palestinian Jews commonly referred to one another that way (K. G. Kuhn, *TDNT* 3. 359ff.). Jesus' point is not that Nathanael is an Israelite, 'true' or otherwise, but that Nathanael is a certain kind of Israelite, an Israelite in whom there is no guile, no deceit (*dolos; cf.* J. Painter, in *BETL*, pp. 359–362). Nathanael may have been blunt in his criticism of Nazareth, but he was an Israelite without duplicitous motives who was willing to examine for himself the claims being made about Jesus.

The encomium achieves extra depth in the light of the explicit reference to the Jacob story in the following verses. Doubtless Esau despised his birthright, but in Isaac's view that did not make Jacob innocent. Isaac informs Esau, 'Your brother came deceitfully (LXX 'with deceit [*dolos*]') and took your blessing', to which Esau replies, 'Isn't he rightly named Jacob (Heb. *yaʻaqōb*)? He has deceived me (*yaʻaqᵉḇēnî*) these two times'

(Gn. 27:35–36).[1] But Jacob came to be called Israel, after receiving a vision of God that transformed his character (Gn. 28:10ff.; 32:24–30). Nathanael, then, was an Israelite without deceit, an 'Israel' and not a 'Jacob' (*cf.* Temple, p. 30). He was a man worthy of the blessing pronounced in Psalm 32:2: 'Blessed is the man . . . in whose spirit is no deceit.' Since Jesus is about to tell him of greater visions that will be his (1:50–51), there may also be an allusion to the popular etymology that related 'Israel' to *'iš rō'eh 'ēl*, 'the man who sees God' (*cf.* Philo, *Leg. Alleg.* iii. 186).[2]

48. Nathanael's question, *How do you know me?*, demonstrates that Jesus' brief summary of his character had hit the mark. Jesus replies by showing that his supernatural knowledge extends beyond this: he 'saw' Nathanael while he was still under the fig tree. What Nathanael was doing under the fig tree is open to conjecture. In the Old Testament the fig tree is sometimes almost a symbol for 'home' or for prosperity (*e.g.* 1 Ki. 4:25; Is. 36:16; Zc. 3:10); occasionally in rabbinic literature its shade is associated with a place for meditation and prayer (SB 2. 371). But John's chief point here is Jesus' supernatural knowledge (*cf.* 2:4; 4:17–18; 6:70; 9:3; 11:4, 11; 13:10–11, 38), not Nathanael's activity.

49. This display of special knowledge combined with the witness of Philip to remove Nathanael's doubts instantly. Now he addresses Jesus as *Rabbi* (*cf.* notes on 1:38), a far more respectful approach than his first blunt question (v. 48). But the titles he assigns to Jesus go far beyond what any disciple would normally ascribe to his rabbi: *you are the Son of God; you are the King of Israel.*

Clearly, Nathanael was acknowledging Jesus as the Messiah, the Promised One to whom the ancient Scriptures had borne witness. But the particular titles chosen tell us a little more. The expression 'the son of X' can have an extraordinarily wide range of meanings, owing in part to the influence of Hebrew on the Greek of the New Testament. Hebrew does not have as many adjectives as do some languages, and compensates for the lack by a variety of idiomatic structures, including this one. Thus 'a wicked man' might be called 'a son of wickedness' (Ps. 89:22); people in trouble are 'sons of affliction' (Pr. 31:5; NIV 'oppressed'); valorous men are 'sons of valour' (Dt. 3:18; NIV 'able-bodied men'). Those deserving execution are 'sons of death' (1 Sa. 26:16). Small wonder, then, that Judas Iscariot can be called (literally) a 'son of perdition' (*cf.* notes on Jn. 17:12). In the sermon on the mount, peacemakers are called 'sons of God' (Mt. 5:9), because their peacemaking attests that in this respect at least they are imitating God. Like father, like son: so it was in the ancient world, far more strongly than today (*cf.* notes on 5:19ff.).

---

[1]This was a kind of 'pun' on Jacob. The correct etymology connects 'Jacob' with *'āqēb*, 'heel'; hence, *ya'ʿqōb* means 'he seizes by the heel' (*cf.* Gn.25:26), and by extension 'he overreaches'.

[2]The correct etymology links 'Israel' with *śārāh*, 'strive' (*cf.* Gn. 32:28).

In the Old Testament, Israel is God's son (Ex. 4:22–23; Dt. 1:31; 32:6; Je. 31:9, 20; Ho. 11:1), and certainly Jesus is presented in the Fourth Gospel as the successor of Israel, or, better, as the true Israel.[1] In later Jewish literature, the 'righteous' are spoken of as God's sons (*e.g. Jubilees* 1:24–25; *Wisdom* 2:18; *Ecclus.* 4:10). But the use of *Son of God* to designate the Messiah ultimately depends on passages such as 1 Samuel 26:17, 21, 25; 2 Samuel 7:14; Psalm 2:7 (linking sonship and Davidic royalty). The link is retained in Jewish literature, some of it pre-Christian (4Q *Florilegium* 1:6–7; IQSa 2:11ff.; *1 Enoch* 105:2; *4 Ezra* 7:28–29; 13:52; 14:9; *cf. NIDNTT* 3. 637). That appears to be how Nathanael used it, but readers of John's Gospel will quickly learn that the categories 'Son' and 'Son of God' are used to depict the unique relation of oneness and intimacy between Jesus and his Father. Jesus' sonship to God, however functionally described, involves a metaphysical, not merely a messianic, relationship (*cf.* notes on 5:16–30; 10:33). Nathanael spoke better than he knew.

The title *King of Israel* was used by Palestinian Jews for the Messiah; it is again applied to Jesus in 12:13. In John 18 – 19 the similar 'King of the Jews' occurs several times. Jesus did not quickly adopt either title for himself, as both expressions were in the popular mind largely tied to expectations of a political liberator. Yet Jesus was the promised King, even if he would have to explain that his kingdom was not of this world (18:36).

50–51. Nathanael took a prodigious step of faith largely on the basis of Jesus' display of supernatural knowledge. His faith is grounded upon a miracle, and such a foundation can be insecure (4:48; 14:11; *cf.* Mt. 7:21–23), though certainly better than nothing (10:25, 38). Jesus promises Nathanael that, regardless of the present importance of this display of supernatural knowledge, he will *see greater things than that* (v. 50), including the signs reported in this Gospel, the first of which is about to unfold (2:1–11). Indeed, more generically, what Nathanael will see is the greatness of the Son of Man, far surpassing the vision of the patriarch Israel (1:51).

In introducing this promise, Jesus employs, for the first time, the double 'Amen, amen' expression variously rendered 'verily, verily' (AV), 'truly, truly' (RSV), or 'in truth, in very truth' (NEB). The NIV adapts the entire construction 'Amen, amen, I say to you', making it 'I tell you the truth.' The original Hebrew word for 'amen' comes from a root denoting certainty, steadfastness. It was sometimes appended to the end of prayers (*e.g.* Ps. 41:13) to voice hearty agreement and solemn wish that the prayer be fulfilled; Jesus uses it before an utterance to confirm and emphasize its trustworthiness and importance. In the Synoptics the expression always occurs singly; in John, always doubled. The term is so characteristic of Jesus that it appears in transliteration even for the

---

[1]*Cf.* John Howton, *NTS* 10, 1963–64, pp. 227–237.

Greek-speaking readers of the Gospels. For this reason, Lindars (p. 48) takes the 'Amen' in these sayings to be a mark of authenticity.

Although Jesus is addressing Nathanael, the 'you' to whom he promises the vision of v. 51 is plural: the vision is probably for all the disciples, and by extension, for those also who would follow them (see the Additional Note). The imagery is drawn from Jacob's vision of the ladder (NIV 'stairway') 'resting on the earth, with its top reaching to heaven, and the angels of God were ascending and descending on it' (Gn. 28:12). The last two words, 'on it' in the NIV, could equally well be rendered 'on him' – *i.e.* the angels of God were ascending and descending *on Jacob*. A rather late Jewish document preserves the record of certain rabbinical disputes on this point, some of which may date back to the time of Jesus (*Genesis Rabbah* 68:18; 69:7; *cf.* Odeberg, pp. 33ff.). Some rabbis who supported 'on it' did so in part because they understood the antecedent of 'it' to be the *ladder*; indeed, if the Hebrew word *bô* ('on him' or 'on it') is taken to refer to *a thing*, its antecedent *must* be the ladder, not the place, because of its masculine gender. (The LXX uses a feminine pronoun at this point, because the Gk. word for 'ladder' is feminine.) But the more likely rendering of Genesis 28:12, marginally, is 'on him': the focus is on the revelation graciously given to Jacob. Thus in the next verse, we are told, 'There above him stood the LORD' (Gn. 28:13). The rendering 'above him' (Heb. *'ālâw*) is to be preferred to 'above it', not least because a little later, when God again reveals himself to Joseph and changes his name to Israel, the recital climaxes with the words, 'Then God went up from him (Heb. *mē'ālâw*) at the place where he had talked with him' (Gn. 35:13).[1] It is unlikely that the words 'on it' in Genesis 28:12 refer to the *place* where Jacob lay: the gender is wrong. But the place nevertheless takes on great significance: 'Jacob called the place where God had talked with him Bethel' (*i.e.* 'house of God', Gn. 35:15).

Because Jesus explicitly alludes to these experiences in Jacob's life, it becomes clear what kind of vision he is promising. It is quite beside the point to say that the cross is now the ladder (Derrett, p. 416), since Jesus makes no mention of the ladder. Equally, it misses the point to say that 1:51 draws a parallel between Jacob and the disciples: both are accorded visions, and what the disciples are promised is what Jacob saw, *viz.* Jesus himself.[2] After all, the explicit parallel is drawn between Jacob and Jesus: the angels ascend and descend on the Son of Man, as they ascended and descended on Jacob (for clearly that is how John understands Gn. 28:12). To *see heaven opened* is to be accorded a vision of divine matters (*cf.* Acts 10:11; Rev. 4:1; 19:11). What the disciples are promised, then, is heaven-sent confirmation that the one they have acknowledged

---

[1] I am indebted to Edward Clowney, 'The Biblical Theology of the Church', in D. A. Carson (ed.), *The Church in the Bible and the World* (Paternoster, 1987), esp. pp. 24–25, for links between the prepositions of Gn. 28:13 and Gn. 35:13.

[2] So Jerome H. Neyrey, *CBQ* 44, 1982, pp. 589–594.

as the Messiah has been appointed by God. Every Jew honoured Jacob/ Israel, the father of the twelve tribes; now everyone must recognize that this same God has appointed Jesus as his Messiah. If there is a hint of the 'new Israel' theme, it is here, not in v. 47. Jesus is the new Israel. Even the old Bethel, the old 'house of God', has been superseded. It is no longer *there*, at Bethel, that God reveals himself, but in Jesus (*cf.* Davies, p. 298) – just as later on Jesus renders obsolete such holy places as the temple (2:19–22) and the sacred mountains of the Samaritans (4:20–24). Through him comes the fulness of grace that surpasses and replaces the earlier grace (1:16).

Jesus' self-designation, 'the Son of Man', was an ambiguous expression. Both in Hebrew and in Greek a 'son of man' could be a circumlocution for a human being, and on occasion Jesus apparently used it instead of 'I' or 'me' (*e.g.* 6:27; *cf.* 6:20). At the same time, the expression enjoyed obvious affinity with the 'one like a son of man' in Daniel's vision (Dn. 7:13–14), the one who is granted universal authority by the Ancient of Days. Precisely because the expression was not narrowly tied to one eschatological figure, Jesus could take it up and use it without fear of being misunderstood because of doubtful associations in his hearers' minds. Titles like 'the King of Israel' and 'the King of the Jews', while appropriate at a certain level, were so loaded with political messianism that they could not be adopted without restraint and appropriate caveats. 'Son of Man', on the other hand, lay ready to hand as an expression that could be filled with precisely the right content. In the New Testament the title refers only to Jesus, and occurs almost always on his lips. In other words, he himself shapes its content, and under its rubric fuses the authoritative figure of Daniel 7 with the righteous sufferer motif from the Old Testament, a motif that reached its high point in the 'servant songs' of Isaiah 42:1 – 53:12. In the Fourth Gospel, the expression occurs thirteen times, and is most commonly associated with the themes of crucifixion (*e.g.* 3:14, 8:28) and revelation (6:27, 53), but also with eschatological authority (5:27; 9:39). *Cf.* Guthrie, *NTT*, pp. 282–290.

Nathanael could not be expected to grasp all of this at the time. Nevertheless the effect of Jesus' self-designation as the Son of Man is gently to qualify and re-orientate the political expectations bound up with titles like 'King of Israel'. The full articulation of 'the Son of Man' demanded all of Jesus' ministry, including his life, resurrection and exaltation. Precisely parallel to this development, it will take John the rest of his book to 'unpack' the significance of the title (*cf.* Moloney, pp. 37–41). The fulfilment of the promise of 1:51, the culmination of the Father's attestation of the Son, the privilege of seeing the glory of the Son of Man – these transpire throughout the Fourth Gospel, and are climaxed by Jesus' death and resurrection. Thus, 'you shall see' relates

> not to a future beyond the death of Jesus (as in Mark 14:62),
> but to the entire gamut of the action of the Son of Man for the

kingdom of God: from the heaven that became open at his baptism, the blessings of the saving sovereignty will be poured out through him in the signs he performs, the revelation of his word, the life that he lives, the death and resurrection that he accomplishes . . . till the goal is attained when the Son of Man welcomes the redeemed to the Father's house (14:3) (Beasley-Murray, p. 28).

Indeed, unlike the Synoptic Gospels, where some Son of Man sayings are associated with Jesus' suffering, others with his ministry and still and others with his coming in glory (*cf.* Carson, *Matt*, pp. 209–213), John fuses the themes, not to create an entirely different picture,[1] but so that the climactic glorification of the Son of Man is achieved *through* his cross, resurrection and exaltation. It is the *combination* of associated themes that is characteristic of Jesus' use of the title. John's Gospel makes it clear that for Jesus there can be no glory without obedience, no glorification without the cross. Above all else, it is Jesus' death/exaltation that provides for Nathanael and the other disciples, as for countless followers of Jesus since then, the most powerful fulfilment of the promise in this verse (*cf.* 8:28).

Additional note

51. Brown (pp. 88–89) and others who have followed him offer five reasons for taking v. 51 as a 'detached saying', none of which is convincing.

(1) If the conversation of v. 50 is in progress, why the awkward 'He then added' (lit. 'And he says to him') at the beginning of v. 51? But this common feature in John's narratives (*cf.* 1:39; 4:16, 21, 26, 32, 34; 5:8; 6:20, 35; 8:58; 9:37, 39; 11:23; 14:9; 20:15–17, 28–29; 21:6, 22) does not normally provoke Brown to this conclusion.

(2) Jesus is talking to Nathanael, but the vision is promised to a plural 'you'. But may not Jesus seek to strengthen Nathanael's faith with a promise applicable also to other disciples? *Cf.* 3:7, where a similar transition occurs.

(3) Brown argues that the 'sign' of 2:1–11 would serve as a far better example of the 'greater things' promised in v. 50 than does the promise of a vision in v. 51. But the vision itself is a generalized summary of the content of the 'greater things'. As such, v. 51 fits well where it is: it anticipates what is coming while providing the climactic Christological assertion of the first chapter, advanced by the Lord himself in the wake of the witness of the Evangelist (v. 1), John the Baptist (vv. 15, 29, 34, 36), Andrew (v. 41), Philip (v. 45) and Nathanael (v. 49).

(4) Brown holds that v. 51 is nowhere literally fulfilled in the Fourth

---

[1]*Cf.* Robert Maddox, 'The Function of the Son of Man in the Gospel of John', in Robert Banks (ed.), *Reconciliation and Hope* (*Fs.* Leon Morris; Paternoster, 1974), pp. 186–204.

Gospel, and therefore must be an interpolation. But it is very doubtful that the prediction is meant to be taken literally (*cf.* comments above).

(5) Brown argues that 1:51 is so similar to Matthew 26:64, especially if the variant '*henceforth* you will see' is included (*cf.* also Mt. 16:27–28), that one must think of John 1:51 as coming from some other context than the one set out here. But the variant is best explained as an assimilation to Matthew, and the peculiar order of the words, the angels *ascending and descending*, reflects Genesis 28:12, not Matthew 26:64 or 16:27–28. Allusion to Genesis 28 is not unexpected, in light of the reference to Israel (v. 47).

B. EARLY MINISTRY: SIGNS, WORKS AND WORDS (2:1 – 4:54)

1. The first sign: Jesus changes water to wine (2:1–11)

The account of Jesus' public ministry now begins, although this first sign (2:1–11) might better be labelled 'semi-public', since apparently only the servants and the disciples gained any knowledge of the source of the wine (vv. 9–11). Jesus' public ministry extends from 2:1 to 12:50 (if we include chs. 11 – 12, which are in certain respects transitional). These eleven chapters are often called the 'book of signs'; in them, Jesus *reveals* his glory (*cf.* 1:14). The remaining chapters of this Gospel are often labelled 'the book of glory'. Here Jesus is glorified by God – *i.e.* he *receives* glory (Kysar, p. 44). There is some usefulness to this breakdown, but *cf.* the remarks on the structure of the Fourth Gospel in the Introduction, § IX.

At the same time, this shorter section (2:1 – 4:54) is bounded not only by paired references to Cana, but by a thematic wholeness. These three chapters are organized to convey what Paul says in 2 Corinthians 5:17: 'the old has gone, the new has come!' 'The three chapters present the replacement of the old purifications by the wine of the kingdom of God, the old temple by the new in the risen Lord, an exposition of new birth for new creation, a contrast between the water of Jacob's well and the living water from Christ, and the worship of Jerusalem and Gerizim with worship "in Spirit and in truth"' (Dodd, *IFG*, p. 297).

The marriage at Cana and the transformation of water into wine have been interpreted in many ways, including some that are highly speculative or allegorical. In part, this is due to the fact that, unlike some other signs in the Fourth Gospel, no discourse is tightly tied to it to explain its significance (though some cast 3:1–21 in that role: contrast the tight thematic connections in John 6 between the feeding of the five thousand and the bread of life discourse); in part it springs from what has been called the '*profane* nature of the miracle'.[1] Even so, the view that

---

[1]So Martin Hengel, 'The Interpretation of the Wine Miracle at Cana: John 2:1–11', in L. D. Hurst and N. T. Wright (eds.), *The Glory of Christ in the New Testament* (*Fs.* G. B. Caird; Clarendon, 1987), pp. 83–112, esp. p. 84. *Cf.* also the study of Olsson.

what really happened was that Jesus told the servants to dilute the remaining wine with water[1] (*What* remaining wine?!), or that the story was created out of a parable of Jesus (Lindars, pp. 123–133),[2] not only seems remarkably speculative but a long way from John's self-understanding as a *witness*. Older attempts to interpret this sign as a Christianized version of the Dionysus myth (Dionysus was the Greek god of wine, the one who supplied the abundance of life and joy associated with inebriation) or of related stories have largely been abandoned in the light of evidence that the alleged parallels are wholly inadequate.[3] Other backgrounds have been proposed, equally interesting and equally unconvincing.

Some control over the exegesis can be gained by observing three factors. First, this is the first of the *signs* John relates, and John himself insists that his purpose in recording these signs was to convince people that the Christ, the Son of God, is Jesus (*cf.* notes on 20:30–31). We shall not go far wrong in our understanding of these verses if we seek to discover how they breed faith in Jesus. Second, the fact that various theological themes are richly present should have little or no bearing on the value of the narrative as history (despite Brown, 1. 101). We have long eclipsed the day when we may allow ourselves to think that the only account that has any pretension of being of historical value is the one where the writer is theologically disinterested in what he or she is writing. More generally, *cf.* the Introduction, § III; and on the historical value of this story, *cf.* Stephen T. Davis (*GP* 6, pp. 419–442). Third, the obvious background is the Old Testament itself, mediated through first-century Judaism, if we may judge by the multiplication of relevant allusions in chs. 2 – 4.

1–2. *The third day* is to be counted from the last event narrated, the exchange between Jesus and Nathanael. Some have suggested that 'the third day' is such a stock phrase in the accounts of Jesus' resurrection that John is using the time reference symbolically: on the third day, on the day of Jesus' resurrection, the new age begins, represented here by the wine. This seems overly subtle in a Gospel that does not stress 'the third day' in the resurrection narratives themselves. More impressive is the running sequence of days from 1:19 on, climaxing in the miraculous transformation of water into wine. Some interpreters see no significance in the sequence (*cf.* Michaels, pp. 27–28), partly because they count only six days. Beginning on the day a delegation is sent to interrogate the Baptist (1:19–28), the second day finds the Baptist announcing Jesus as the Lamb of God (1:29), the third day brings two disciples to Jesus' residence (1:35–42), and the fourth day witnesses the incident with

---

[1] W. F. Howard, *The Fourth Gospel in Recent Criticism and Interpretation* (revised by C. K. Barrett; Epworth, 1955), p. 191.

[2] On the relationships between Gospel miracles and Gospel parables, *cf.* Craig L. Blomberg, in *GP* 6, pp. 327–359.

[3] *Cf.* H. Noetzel, *Christus und Dionysus* (Calwer, 1960).

Nathanael. The wedding of 2:1–11 takes place 'the third day' after that, which, by inclusive reckoning, means two days later. This total of six days does not seem very significant. In fact, another day should be added. This is achieved, not by appealing to the variant at 1:41 (*cf.* note), but by observing that when the Baptist's two disciples attach themselves to Jesus it is already 4.00 p.m. on the third day – and they spent the rest of that day with him (1:39).[1] That means Andrew's introduction of Simon Peter to Jesus takes place on the *next* day, the fourth; the Nathanael exchange occurs on the fifth; the changing of the water into wine on the seventh.

This analysis is not grasping at straws. Only here does John provide a careful record of a sequence of days. This may of course reflect eyewitness participation, which in turn supports the hypothesis that John himself is the unnamed disciple with Andrew who heard the Baptist's witness (*cf.* notes on 1:35). Even so, for a writer as subtle as John to set out a week of activity, culminating in the miracle of new wine on the seventh day, may reflect more than antiquarian precision. John has already drawn attention to creation: the good news he proclaims in this Gospel reflects a new creation (*cf.* notes on 1:1). The week of days climaxing in the miracle at Cana may provide an echo of creation-week (Gn. 1). That means the miracle itself takes place on the seventh day, the Sabbath. Jesus' performance of redemptive work on the Sabbath is later in this Gospel (5:16ff.; 7:21–24; 9:16) given the most suggestive theological treatment in the New Testament, apart from Hebrews 4. Although we cannot be certain that the seven days in 1:19 – 2:1 were intended to carry this weight, it seems likely, but only if we assume the Evangelist's readers are familiar with the Scriptures (our Old Testament), and are expected to read this Gospel, meditatively, more than once.

That Jesus' first miracle takes place at a wedding,[2] and is designed to prevent serious social embarrassment, marks Jesus out as far removed from the monastic asceticism of hermitic communities like Qumran. The ordinance of marriage was intrinsic to creation (Gn. 1 – 2); it does not seem far-fetched for modern marriage services to invoke the setting of this miracle as evidence for Jesus' approval of the institution. The wedding *took place at Cana in Galilee* – another link with the immediately preceding verses, since Nathanael was from Cana (21:2). Of the various sites proposed by archaeologists, the most likely is Khirbet Qana, an uninhabited ruin about nine miles north of Nazareth, and lying in the Plain of Asochis (Jos., *Vita* 86, 207).

Jesus' mother, never named in this Gospel (perhaps to avoid confusing her with other women by the name of Mary?), appears in two narratives (here and 19:25–27), and features in two other brief allusions (2:12; 6:42). Some interpreters have assigned her an allegorical role,

---

[1]*Cf.* Paul Trudinger, *The Downside Review* 104/354, 1986, pp. 41–43.
[2]For marriage customs of the day, *cf.* SB 1. 500–517; 2. 372–399; H. Granquist, *Marriage Conditions in a Palestinian Village*, 2 vols. (Centraltryckeriet, 1931–35); Derrett, pp. 228–238.

representing Israel or the church, or have detected in her successful request for a solution to the shortage of wine sufficient reason to treat her as a mediatrix between us and her Son. On this reasoning, one wonders why everyone who ever asked Jesus for help and found in him the solution to some pressing need, should not be elevated to the status of mediator or mediatrix. More importantly, the allegorical and other elements in this story used to defend such speculations cannot be anchored in obvious themes pulsating throughout the Gospel: they simply are not there. Simpler explanations of the details lie to hand.

That Jesus, his mother and his disciples were all invited to the same wedding suggests the wedding was for a relative or close family friend. It is not impossible that Mary had some responsibility for the organization of the catering: hence her attempt to deal with the shortage of wine (2:3). If the temporal links between ch. 1 and ch. 2 are as tight as they seem, the *disciples* who accompanied Jesus are probably the five already mentioned: Andrew, Simon Peter, Philip, Nathanael and the unnamed disciple of 1:35 (John?). 'The Twelve' are mentioned in 6:67, but John provides no information as to how or when the other seven became followers of Jesus. There is no evidence to support the speculation that the reason the wine ran out was because Jesus arrived at the last moment with a crowd of followers who had not been anticipated.

3. A wedding celebration could last as long as a week, and the financial responsibility lay with the groom (*cf.* 2:9–10). To run out of supplies would be a dreadful embarrassment in a 'shame' culture; there is some evidence it could also lay the groom open to a lawsuit from aggrieved relatives of the bride. The 'wine' (*oinos*) that was needed was not mere grape juice, generic 'fruit of the vine'. The idea is intrinsically silly as applied to countries whose agricultural tradition is so committed to viticulture. Besides, in v. 10 the head steward expects that at this point in the celebration some of the guests would *have had too much to drink*: the verb *methyskō* does not refer to consuming too much liquid, but to inebriation. On the other hand, wine in the ancient world was diluted with water to between one-third and one-tenth of its fermented strength, *i.e.* something less strong than American beer. Undiluted wine, about the strength of wine today, was viewed as 'strong drink', and earned much more disapprobation.

What Mary was expecting when she voiced her complaint, *They have no more wine*, has been hotly disputed. Some have suggested that she was merely passing on the sad news, without any expectations at all, somewhat like the paralytic in 5:7. But this view is belied by 2:5, where Mary's instructions to the servants prove she expected something from Jesus. At the other extreme, some have argued that Mary anticipated a miracle. But the section ends by insisting this is the first of Jesus' miracles (2:11). The second-century accounts of the toddler Jesus turning clay pigeons into living birds are universally recognized to be apocryphal. There does not seem adequate reason, then, to think Mary's expectations would have been so high. It is more likely that Mary turned to Jesus because she had learned to rely upon his resourcefulness. The traditions that make her a widow by this period are plausible enough: Joseph does not appear on the scene after the episode in the temple when Jesus was twelve years of age (Lk. 2:41–52; though *cf*. Jn. 6:42 and notes there), and Jesus himself was known not only as the carpenter's son (Mt. 13:55) but as the carpenter (Mk. 6:3). Apparently the family fortunes had, up to this point, depended on Jesus' manual labour. Like any widow, Mary had leaned hard on her firstborn son. How easy that must have been, with a son like him! Moreover, from a literary point of view, John repeatedly records Jesus' interlocutors operating at a purely human, natural level, while Jesus himself transcends their questions, demands or expectations (3:3, 4; 4:15, 47; 5:6–7; 6:32–33, 41; 11:22–24). This interpretation of 2:3 fits into the same pattern.[1]

4. Jesus' enigmatic response invites comment on three points.

(1) The form of address, *gynai* (NIV 'Dear woman'), though thoroughly courteous, is not normally an endearing term, nor the form of address preferred by a son addressing a much-loved mother. When Jesus addresses Mary from the cross, he uses the same expression (19:26). English equivalents are hard to come by. 'Woman' is too distant, and possibly too condescending; 'Dear woman' is too sentimental. 'Lady' is not much used, except as a formal title or on the lips of a New York cab driver telling a female passenger to hurry up ('Get in, lady!'). The expression can be invested with deep love (as the husband of Pheroras addresses his wife with great affection: Jos., *Ant*. xvii. 74), but is not characteristically used that way. Bruce (p. 69) suggests the Ulster expression 'Woman dear'; the expression much heard in the southern United States, 'Ma'am', has it almost exactly, except that well-brought-up children in the South address their mothers with that term – and that is precisely how the term does *not* function on Jesus' lips. NEB's 'Your concern, mother, is not mine', is unjustified.

(2) The question itself, *ti emoi kai soi* (lit. 'what to me and to you?') has generated a number of translations. The expression, common in semitic idiom (*e.g.* Jdg. 11:12; 2 Sa. 16:10), always distances the two parties, the speaker's tone overlaid with some degree of reproach (*cf*. the demons addressing Jesus, Mt. 8:29; Mk. 1:24; 5:7; Lk. 4:34; 8:28). The tone is not rude; it is certainly abrupt. Some protest or refusal is also found where the idiom occurs in classical and hellenistic Greek (*cf*. Abbott § 2229). Some interpreters say the expression means either 'what have I to do with thee?' (RV) or 'what have you to do with me?' (RSV), opting for the latter on the basis of context (*e.g.* Bruce, p. 69). Strictly speaking, however, the idiom simply asks what is common to you and me – *i.e.* 'What do you and I have in common (so far as the matter at hand is concerned)?' That has generated the more periphrastic renderings, largely right in substance: 'You have no claims on me' or *why do you*

---

[1]*Cf*. M. Gourgues, *NRT* 108, 1986, pp. 174–191, esp. pp. 179–180.

involve me? (NIV). The expression is, at the very least, a measured rebuke; the efforts of Lagrange (p. 56) and Schnackenburg (1. 328), to make it mean something like 'what would you have me do?' are groundless.

We must not avoid the conclusion that Jesus by rebuking his mother, however courteously, declares, at the beginning of his ministry, his utter freedom from any kind of human advice, agenda or manipulation. He has embarked on his ministry, the purpose of his coming; his only lodestar is his heavenly Father's will (5:30; 8:29). This must have been extremely difficult for Mary. She had borne him, nursed him, taught his baby fingers elementary skills, watched him fall over as he learned to walk; apparently she had also come to rely on him as the family provider. But now that he had entered into the purpose of his coming, everything, even family ties, had to be subordinated to his divine mission. She could no longer view him as other mothers viewed their sons; she must no longer be allowed the prerogatives of motherhood. It is a remarkable fact that everywhere Mary appears during the course of Jesus' ministry, Jesus is at pains to establish distance between them (*e.g.* Mt. 12:46–50). This is not callousness on Jesus' part: on the cross he makes provision for her future (19:25–27). But she, like every other person, must come to him as to the promised Messiah, the Lamb of God who takes away the sin of the world. Neither she nor anyone else dare presume to approach him on an 'inside track' – a lesson even Peter had to learn (Mk. 8:31–33). For no-one could this lesson have been more difficult than for Jesus' mother; perhaps that was part of the sword that would pierce her soul (Lk. 2:35). For this we should honour her the more.

(3) The reason Jesus gives for the distance he maintains between his mother and himself must be viewed in the light of the cross. *My time has not yet come*, he says: the word 'time', literally 'hour' (*hōra*), constantly refers to his death on the cross and the exaltation bound up with it (7:30; 8:20; 12:23, 27; 13:1; 17:1), or the consequences deriving from it (5:28–29), so it would be unnatural to take it in any other way here. But how could that have been a response to Mary? And what could the reader be expected to understand from so enigmatic a reference?

To answer the second question first, rhetoric would call this sort of reference an internal prolepsis, a reference to a theme that will be developed later or to an event that will occur later in the narrative. Such a device captures the reader's interest and asks questions: What does 'hour' mean? When does this 'hour' come? By whetting the reader's curiosity it encourages more thoughtful reading; moreover the book becomes deeper and more complex when it is read the second, third and subsequent times. Anticipating the development of the theme, then, we note that the 'hour' of Jesus' death, resurrection and exaltation to glory is in the first part of this Gospel constantly said to be 'not yet', until the arrival of the Gentiles (12:20ff.). From that point on, with Jesus on the brink of death, the hour is said to have arrived (13:1; 17:1).

That forces us back to the first question: How could Jesus' words have been a response to Mary? She is apparently asking that Jesus do something to remedy the shortage of wine; he replies that the hour of his death/exaltation has not yet come.[1] The point of connection is probably threefold. First, although Mary probably laid out the need for wine in mundane terms, it is typical of Jesus to detect more symbolism in various utterances than the speaker envisaged (*cf.* notes on 2:3). Mary wants the wedding to end without embarrassment; Jesus remembers that the prophets characterized the messianic age as a time when wine would flow liberally (*e.g.* Je. 31:12; Ho. 14:7; Am. 9:13–14; *cf.* 2 Baruch 29:5; 1 Enoch 10:19).[2] Elsewhere he himself adapts the wedding as a symbol for the consummation of the messianic age (*e.g.* Mt. 22:1–14; 25.1–13). Treating the developing circumstances as an acted parable, Jesus is entirely correct to say that the hour of great wine, the hour of his glorification, has not yet come.[3]

Second, although the entire Gospel moves towards the cross, toward Jesus' glorification, it must not be thought that Jesus' ministry before the cross was irrelevant, or mere preparation. Rather, individual elements in that ministry *anticipated* the glorification of Jesus on the cross, in much the same way that Jesus' healing miracles in the Synoptic Gospels are said to anticipate the cross (*cf.* Carson, *Matt*, pp. 204–207, on Mt. 8:16–17). That is why John reports, at the end of this first sign, that the disciples witnessed Jesus' *glory*, and believed on him (2:11; *cf.* 11:4; 20:29–30). Of course they could not at this point witness Jesus' glory in all its brightness, for the constant theme of the book is that before the cross Jesus was not yet glorified (*e.g.* 7:39); but already they glimpsed something of the glory still to be revealed. Any aspect of *this* ministry could never be in response to human schedules; it could reflect only the timing of the Father's will. In exactly the same way, Jesus' brothers encourage him to go to Judea, but he replies, 'The right time for me has not yet come; for you any time is right' (7:6) – yet he does make the trip a short time later.

Third, it is just possible that the Evangelist sees a connection with 3:27–30, where Jesus, Jesus alone, is emphatically identified as the

---

[1] It has been argued that the word *oupō* ('not yet') should be taken as introducing a question: 'Has my hour not yet come?' This reverses the meaning, and makes it virtually 'Has not my hour not come?' Certainly the word *oupō* can have that force (*cf.* Mk.8:17). But that meaning is rare. The term is found twelve times in John, but never introducing a question. Two of those twelve occurrences are also with 'hour' (7:30; 8:20). Above all, this suggested rendering makes nonsense of John's use of 'hour', which at this early stage is repeatedly said *not* to have come.

[2] For the wealth of such imagery in Judaism, *cf.* Hengel, *art. cit.*, pp. 100–102.

[3] On the basis of the allusions in this narrative to the messianic banquet, and of the use of Esther 1 in rabbinic reflections on the same theme, Roger Aus (*Water into Wine and the Beheading of John the Baptist* [SP, 1988], pp. 1–37) lists as many parallels as possible to argue that John's account is derivative of Est. 1 (*i.e.* what many would call a midrash on Est. 1). I cannot take up his case here, though I do not find his argument convincing. Even so, his work does have relevance to v. 10, below.

messianic bridegroom. As such, he will supply all the 'wine' that is needed for the messianic banquet, but his hour has not yet come. As this story unfolds, he graciously makes good the deficiencies of the unknown bridegroom of John 2, in anticipation of the perfect way he himself will fill the role of the messianic bridegroom.[1]

5. In saying to the servants, *Do whatever he tells you*, Jesus' mother shakes off the gentle rebuke and exemplifies the best kind of persevering faith. Like the Canaanite woman who was rebuked for her presumptuous approach, but who persevered and was praised for her faith (Mt. 15:21–28), so Mary is rebuked for presuming on the family tie, yet displays faith that is perfectly content to leave the matter in Jesus' hands. This sort of pattern occurs elsewhere in John: Jesus initially refuses a request for assistance, then proceeds to help in his own way, often in response to a further demonstration of faith (4:47–50; cf. 11:21–44[2]). In short, in 2:3 Mary approaches Jesus as his mother, and is reproached; in 2:5, she responds as a believer, and her faith is honoured. She still does not know what he would do; but she has committed the matter to him, and trusts him. Bruce (p. 70) wisely comments, 'The recorded words of Mary are few; these particular words have an application beyond the immediate occasion which called them forth.'

These two verses (2:4–5), as difficult as they are, help to shape this account of Jesus' first miracle, and ensure that the focus is on Jesus' glory (2:11), not Mary's, and on the disciples' faith (2:11), including Mary's (2:5).[3]

6. Each jar held two or three 'measures' (*metrētēs*), each measure the equal of eight or nine (imperial) gallons. The pots together held, roughly, between one hundred and one hundred and fifty gallons (between 500 and 750 litres). The six water jars were made of stone, because stone, being more impervious than earthenware, did not itself contract uncleanness. They were therefore the more suitable *for ceremonial washing*. In the context of a wedding feast, perhaps the ritual washing of certain utensils and of guests' hands is especially in view (cf. Mk. 7:3–4; for the regulations on washing cf. SB 1. 695–705), but if so John sees this as representative of the broader question of the place of all ceremonial washings (cf. 3:25). Their purpose provides a clue to one of the meanings of the story: the water represents the old order of Jewish law and custom, which Jesus was to replace with something better (cf. 1:16).

[1]Cf. J. Duncan M. Derrett, *FN* 2, 1989, p. 50.
[2]M. Gourgues, *NRT* 108, 1986, p. 184, nicely compares the progression of thought in 2:3–10 and 11:21–44: (a) level of expected intervention (11:21–22 / 2:3); (b) higher level where the intervention must be located (11:23–26 / 2:4); (c) the response of faith (11:27 / 2:5); (d) intervention (11:39–44 / 2:7–10).
[3]It is hard to avoid the impression that unwillingness to face these rather simple conclusions have led some Catholic scholars to postulate that vv. 4–5 are a later interpolation: cf. Raymond E. Brown, in de Jonge, *BETL*, pp. 307–310; John McHugh, *The Mother of Jesus in the New Testament* (Geoffrey Chapman/Doubleday, 1975), pp. 388ff.

Some see in the number *six* a reference to incompleteness, one less than seven: the Jewish dispensation was incomplete until the coming of Jesus, who performs this miracle on the seventh day (*cf.* notes on 2:1–2). That view may well be strained, for the miracle concerns the transformation of water, not the provision of an additional water jar.

7–8. The usual interpretation of these verses is that Jesus, after telling the servants to fill up the six water jars, performed the miracle and then asked the servants to take some of the freshly made wine from the water jars to the 'master of the banquet'. The sheer quantity of water turned into wine then becomes symbolic of the lavish provision of the new age. But Westcott (1. 84) and one or two others have rightly insisted that the verb 'draw' (*antleō*, v. 8) is commonly used for drawing water from a well (*cf.* 4:7, 15). In other words, the water turned into wine was freshly drawn from the well after the water jars had been filled. The word *Now* might be taken to support this view. Up to this time the servants had drawn water to fill the vessels used for ceremonial washing; *now* they are to draw for the feast that symbolizes the messianic banquet. Filling jars with such large capacity *to the brim* then indicates that the time for ceremonial purification is completely fulfilled; the new order, symbolized by the wine, could not be drawn from jars so intimately connected with merely ceremonial purification. If John has not used the verb loosely (and there is no reason for thinking he has), this latter interpretation prevails.

The person the NIV calls *the master of the banquet*, to whom the servants bring the wine, is probably a chief steward or head waiter, in charge of catering and perhaps of the place where the banquet was held (*architriklinos*, lit. 'ruler of the table').[1]

9–10. There is now some independent evidence that most hosts would serve the best wine first, reserving the inferior for the end of the feast;[2] but in any case the practice makes sense. The bridegroom is addressed by the head steward because the bridegroom was responsible for providing all the food and drink. The suggestion of some popular interpreters that Jesus simply provided water, and that the steward accepted the substitute with good humour and a witty remark about how Adam's ale is the best kind, is indefensible. The text says that *the water had been turned into wine* (v. 9). Besides, social expectation would have been outraged if the groom had proved so improvident as to run out of supplies before the end of the feast. However, although *methyskō* demonstrates some inebriation was involved (*cf.* notes on vv. 1–2), there is 'no ground here for conclusions regarding the degree of intoxication of the guests at this wedding' (Barrett, p. 193). John's point is simply that the wine Jesus provides is unqualifiedly superior, as must

---

[1] Jewish sources do not permit us to be certain whether the *architriklinos* was a steward, as suggested here, or a guest chosen as superintendent of the feast. What is clear is that he served as 'master of ceremonies'.

[2] Aus, *op. cit.*, p. 10.

everything be that is tied to the new, messianic age Jesus is introducing.

11. John brings the account to a close by an *inclusio*, a literary device that envelops a section by repeating something at the end of the section that has already been used at the beginning – in this instance, *Cana of Galilee* (2:1, 11). This was *the first of his miraculous signs*: on the enumeration of the first two signs, and its alleged significance for a 'signs source', *cf.* notes on 4:43–45, 54; Introduction, §§ II, III (1). The word for 'first' (*archē*) can also mean primary: it is just possible that John is saying this *first* sign is also *primary*, because it points to the new dispensation of grace and fulfilment that Jesus is inaugurating. It may also hint at the 'new creation' theme: *cf.* the use of the word in 1:1, and notes at 2:1.

The New Testament uses several words to denote what we call 'miracles'. One of the most common, *dynameis* ('mighty works') is not found in John; another, *terata* ('wonders', 'portents', 'miracles') is found only when linked with *sēmeia* ('signs'), as in 'signs and wonders'; but this combination is found only once in the Fourth Gospel (4:48). John prefers the simple word 'signs': Jesus' miracles are never simply naked displays of power, still less neat conjuring tricks to impress the masses, but *signs*, significant displays of power that point beyond themselves to the deeper realities that could be perceived with the eyes of faith. Jesus himself in this Gospel refers to his miracles and to his other activity as his 'work' or 'works' (*e.g.* 5:36; NIV 'miracle(s)' in 7:21; 10:25).

By this first sign, Jesus *revealed his glory*, 'the glory of the One and Only, who came from the Father, full of grace and truth' (1:14). His glory would be revealed in greatest measure in his cross, resurrection and exaltation, but every step along the course of his ministry was an adumbration of that glory. The glory was not visible to all who had seen the miracle; the glory cannot be identified with the miraculous display (*cf.* notes on 1:14). The servants saw the sign, but not the glory; the disciples by faith perceived Jesus' glory behind the sign, and they *put their faith in him* (*episteusan eis auton*: *cf.* notes on 2:23–25).

Some hold that John has a scheme of seven signs, culminating in the resurrection of Lazarus; others link the feeding of the five thousand and the walking on the water (Jn. 6) as one sign, making the seventh the resurrection of Jesus himself. Because John does not specifically label all the miracles 'signs', it is hard to be certain that John intended either outline (*cf.* notes introducting 6:11–21). What is clear is that this first sign is linked with the summary statement of the purpose of the book in 20:30–31. In both places, the disciples saw and believed (2:11; 20:29). The time would come when blessing would be pronounced on new generations of followers who could not possibly see these events, but who have nevertheless believed and seen something of the glory of the Son (20:29).

2. Jesus clears the temple (2:12–17)

12. *After this* (whether *meta touto* or *meta tauta*) is a frequent connective between narratives in John (2:12; 3:22; 5:1, 14; 6:1; 7:1; 11:7, 11; 19:28, 38), and is no indication of the length of the interval between the two events. On the other hand, the Synoptics also place this move of Jesus and his family from Nazareth to Capernaum at the beginning of his recorded ministry (Mt. 4:13; Lk. 4:31; *cf.* also Jn. 6:24, 59). Capernaum (probably a transliteration of *kᵉpar-naḥûm*, 'the village of Nahum') lay on the north-west shore of Galilee, about sixteen miles east-northeast of Cana: so travellers literally 'went *down*' to Capernaum. The modern site is Tell-Hum. That Jesus and his family stayed only *for a few days* suggests that it was not long before it was time to leave to celebrate the Jewish Passover in Jerusalem (2:13).

The 'disciples' are probably those mentioned in John 1 (*cf.* notes on 2:1); the 'brothers' of Jesus are most probably his half-brothers, children of Joseph and Mary and all younger than he (*cf.* Carson, *Matt*, p. 299).

13. John keeps meticulous track of Jewish feasts. In addition to other feasts, he mentions three Passovers (2:13; 6:4; 11:55), possibly a fourth (5:1). This one probably takes place in AD 28. That he calls it *the Jewish Passover* (lit. 'the Passover of the Jews') is taken by some to indicate that his readers are primarily Gentiles for whom the very elements of Judaism must be explained, and by others to indicate that, as a Christian toward the end of the first century, he is writing from a dismissive and censorious point of view, setting 'the Jews' over against Jesus and his church. Neither view is satisfactory. It is hard to believe that John's readers are Gentiles so ignorant of Judaism that they do not know the Passover is Jewish, when at several scores of points John's argument depends on his readers' grasp of subtle and detailed points of Old Testament history and Scripture. It is equally unjustified to detect in this reference to 'the Jews' a sweeping indictment of all things Jewish from the perspective of the late first century, when elsewhere John argues that salvation is from the Jews (4:22; *cf.* notes on 1:19) and uses various devices to portray Jesus as the one who fulfils the promise of Passover. It seems more likely in this instance that because the Passover was celebrated in the temple *in Judea*, and the residents of Judea were called 'Jews' by both Galileans and diaspora Hebrews, the Passover is called the Passover of the Jews. This geographical approach to the expression fits the context, since the verse's purpose is to explain why *Jesus went up to Jerusalem* in Judea. (People went *up* to Jerusalem, both because Jerusalem stood at a higher elevation than Galilee, and also because histori-cally Jerusalem was the capital city – just as people go *up* to London from all over Britain.)

The festival of Passover was celebrated on the 14th day of the lunar month Nisan (full moon at the end of March or beginning of April). It commemorated the night when the angel of death 'passed over' the homes daubed with blood in the prescribed manner, killing the firstborn in all other homes. In the consternation and revulsion that followed, the Jews escaped from Egypt (Ex. 12). Passover was immediately followed by the seven-day Festival of Unleavened Bread (15–22 Nisan). *Cf.* notes on 18:28.

Because the Synoptic Gospels report a temple-cleansing at the end of Jesus' ministry, during the final Passover week, the week that led to the crucifixion (Mt. 21:12–17; Mk. 11:15–18; Lk. 19:45–46), most scholars argue that John has moved the account to the beginning of Jesus' ministry, perhaps because he sees in this cleansing a prophetic and programmatic action that explicates so much of what he will develop. A minority of interpreters argue that John preserves the historical timing, ascribing the shift to the Synoptics. Only a very few judge it likely that there were two temple cleansings, one near the beginning of Jesus' public ministry and the other at the end (*e.g.* Hendriksen, p. 120; Morris, pp. 188–191). Certainly all four Evangelists frequently arrange their material in topical rather than chronological order; one should not rush to harmonize by addition. Nevertheless the natural if not conclusive reading of 2:11–13 makes the temporal connections pretty tight (*cf.* notes, above); something similar could be said for the Synoptic accounts.

The primary objections to a double cleansing of the temple are two. First, there is a deep-seated scholarly bias against doubles of anything in Scripture, primarily because of the desire to tease out trajectories of developments. If there was one event with two reports, then the differences between the reports provide evidence for the way the tradition developed. Most such trajectories are highly speculative; they remain uncontrolled as long as it is unclear what criteria distinguish this sort of interpretation from one that postulates two similar events with independent reports. On both sides appeal is made to John's distinctive language. Morris (pp. 188–189), for instance, provides a list of distinctive vocabulary and narrative detail to support his view that there were two events. Others note similarities: in both John and the Synoptics, the event occurs near a Passover, Jesus overturns the tables of the money-changers, and (at least within the proximate context) the question of his authority is raised. It is very doubtful if either argument proves very much. Against Morris, distinctiveness in detail and in vocabulary is so typical of John's handling of *any* event reported both by Synoptists and John that the independence of narrative detail and locutions in the Fourth Gospel can scarcely be called on to prove there were two events. Morris is on surer ground when he points out that all of John 1 – 5, apart from some material on John the Baptist, constitutes a great block of non-Synoptic material. Why or how an ancient editor managed to secure this pericope alone and insert it into his material is hard to fathom. Against more sceptical interpretations, it is also hard to imagine two cleansings of the temple without *some* similarities. That both should occur near a Passover festival is not too surprising, since only at the high feasts would we be likely to find Jesus in Jerusalem.

When interpreters of John who hold that the Evangelist has moved the narrative here for theological reasons try to articulate those reasons, they neither agree with each other nor prove intrinsically convincing (*e.g.* one commentator suggests the temple-cleansing was moved from

John 12 to make room for the story of Lazarus – though why both stories could not have been included at that point is unclear). Moreover, any argument that provides a reason why John 2:13ff. 'fits' into the thematic development of the Fourth Gospel could equally well serve to explain why, on the assumption there were two cleansings, John chose to report *this* cleansing instead of the *later* one.

Second, it is often argued that if Jesus had cleansed the temple once, the authorities would never have let him get away with it again. This is ingenuous. If there were two cleansings, they were separated by two years, possibly three. During that interval Jesus visited Jerusalem several times for other appointed festivals, without attempting another temple-cleansing. The authorities could not possibly be expected to keep their guard up against him indefinitely. If he was not arrested the first time, it may well be because a certain amount of public feeling sided with Jesus: is not that suggested by 2:23?

In short, it is not possible to resolve with certainty whether only one cleansing of the temple took place, or two; but the arguments for one are weak and subjective, while the most natural reading of the texts favours two. Meanwhile it is important to note (1) that a detail in *John's* account of the temple-cleansing provides crucial background to the *Synoptic* record of Jesus' trial (*cf.* notes on 2:19), and (2) that this *early* temple-cleansing does not issue immediately in a conspiracy by the authorities to have him arrested and killed, for Jesus has not yet established his reputation, whereas the *later* cleansing reported in the Synoptics is presented more or less as one of the last straws that call down the wrath of the religious establishment.

14. The *cattle, sheep and doves* were used in the sacrificial worship of the temple. Especially for worshippers coming from a distance, it was a convenience and a service to be able to purchase them on site instead of having to bring them from afar. At one time the animal merchants set up their stalls across the Kidron Valley on the slopes of the Mount of Olives, but at this point they were *in the temple courts*, doubtless in the Court of the Gentiles (the outermost court). Others who were *sitting at tables exchanging money* were also providing a service. People from all over the Roman Empire gathered to Jerusalem for the high festivals, bringing many different coins with them; but the temple tax, to be paid by every conscientious Jewish male of twenty years of age or over, had to be deposited in Tyrian coinage (because of the high purity of its silver). This annual half-shekel (to use the language of the Old Testament) was equal to half a Tyrian stater or tetradrachm, and so two Jews often joined together to pay the tax in one coin (*cf.* Mt. 17:27; *NBD*, p. 792). The money-changers converted money to the approved currency, charging a percentage for their service. The tables of the money-changers were not set up all year round, but only around the time when the temple tax was collected. In Jerusalem, this was from 25 Adar on (the lunar month before Nisan; *cf.* Mishnah *Shekalim* 1:1, 3).

15–16. There is no evidence that the animal merchants and money-changers or the priestly authorities who allowed them to use the outer court were corrupt companions in graft. Jesus' complaint is not that they are guilty of sharp business practices and should therefore reform their ethical life, but that they should not be in the temple area at all.[1] *How dare you turn my Father's house into a market!* he exclaims. Instead of solemn dignity and the murmur of prayer, there is the bellowing of cattle and the bleating of sheep. Instead of brokenness and contrition, holy adoration and prolonged petition, there is noisy commerce. It is in this sense that Bauckham[2] is right: what he calls 'Jesus' demonstration in the temple' was 'an attack on the whole of the financial arrangements for the sacrifical system',[3] and thus an enormous threat to the priestly authorities.

Dodd (*IFG*, p. 300) suggests there is an allusion to Zechariah 14:21: 'And on that day there will no longer be a merchant in the house of the LORD Almighty.' Equally, John may be alluding to Malachi 3:1, 3: 'Then suddenly the Lord you are seeking will come to his temple. . . . he will purify the Levites and refine them like gold and silver.' This means that this act of prophetic symbolism was a denunciation of worship that was not pure (*cf.* also Ezk. 10:15–19; 11:22–23). It was a prophetic invitation to worship God from the heart, without clamour or distracting influences. At the same time it leads into a related theme: the temple itself, the focal point where God and believers meet, where God accepts believers because of a bloody sacrifice, will be superseded by another 'temple', another sacrifice (vv. 18–22).

Jesus' physical action was forceful, but not cruel; one does not easily drive out cattle and sheep without *a whip of cords*. Still, his action could not have generated a riotous uproar, or there would have been swift reprisals from the Roman troops in the fortress of Antonia overlooking part of the temple complex.

Sanders (pp. 116–117) observes that Jesus' mention of God as his Father does not evoke the same response as in 5:17–18. That (he argues) is because John treats one thing at a time: here (2:18) he goes on to explore the question of Jesus' authority, while in John 5 he discusses Jesus' person. But reference to God as one's Father, though perhaps

---

[1] This is true even in the parallel Synoptic accounts (Mt. 21:12–17; Mk. 11:15–18; Lk. 19:45–46) where in most translations Jesus accuses the merchants and money-changers of turning the temple into 'a den of robbers'. The Greek expression does not suggest thievery but zealotry: by setting up in the court of the Gentiles, they have excluded Gentiles who might have come to pray, and have turned the temple into 'a nationalist stronghold' (to use the happy expression of C. K. Barrett, in E. Earle Ellis and Erich Gräßer (eds.), *Jesus und Paulus* [Vandenhoeck und Ruprecht, 1975], pp. 13–20; *cf.* Carson, *Matt*, pp. 440–443).

[2] Richard Bauckham, 'Jesus' Demonstration in the Temple', in Barnabas Lindars (ed.), *Law and Religion: Essays on the Place of the Law in Israel and Early Christianity* (SPCK, 1988), pp. 72–89.

[3] *Ibid.*, p. 88. The argument of E. P. Sanders (*Jesus and Judaism* [SCM/Fortress, 1985], pp. 61–76) to the effect that, against the evidence of the Gospels, Jesus was not in any sense 'cleansing' the temple but was providing a prophetic portent of the temple's destruction, has been competently refuted by Craig A. Evans, *CBQ* 51, 1989, pp. 237–270.

strange, was not itself tantamount to making oneself equal with God: everything depended on the context. Here the focal point is Jesus' authority, not because the Evangelist can only manage one topic at a time, but because the cleansing of the temple demanded that Jesus provide some credentials. In John 5, however, Jesus' reference to his Father is offered in a context where Jesus works along with his Father and *above* the law (*cf.* notes on 5:16ff.).

17. John does not make it clear whether Jesus' disciples remembered this Old Testament text then and there, or only after the resurrection (*cf.* v. 22). The text itself, Psalm 69:9, finds the psalmist crying to God because of the implacable opposition he has endured from his foes. A major source of this enmity is their failure to understand or be sympathetic with the psalmist's profound commitment to the temple. That is why he can say, '. . . zeal for your house consumes me', for it is his zeal for the temple that has placed him in this invidious position. With other New Testament writers, however, John detects in the experiences of David a prophetic paradigm that anticipates what must take place in the life of 'great David's greater Son'. That explains why the words in 2:17, quoted from the LXX, change the tense to the future: *Zeal for your house will consume me.*[1] Jesus' cleansing of the temple testifies to his concern for pure worship, a right relationship with God at the place supremely designated to serve as the focal point of the relationship between God and man. But it is that very concern that is attracting opposition. For John, the manner by which Jesus will be 'consumed' is doubtless his death. If his disciples *remembered* these words at the time, they probably focused on the zeal, not the manner of the 'consumption'. Only later would they detect in these words a reference to his death (*cf.* 2:22).

3. Jesus replaces the temple (2:18–22)

18. The *Jews* who now confront Jesus are doubtless either the temple authorities or representatives of the Sanhedrin (*cf.* notes on 1:19). They *demanded* (*apekrithēsan*, lit. 'answered', but the verb, reflecting semitic influence, can introduce speech that is not a response) of Jesus some *miraculous sign* (*sēmeion*; *cf.* 2:11) to justify such a display of authority as that which ventured to regulate the temple. As the legal authorities, these Jews had every right to question the credentials of someone who had taken such bold action in the temple complex (*cf.* similarly Mk. 11:28 par.). But the way they cast their question betrays two critical deficiencies. First, they display no reflection or self-examination over whether

---

[1] Ps. 69 is quoted or alluded to in several other New Testament texts: Mt. 27:34 (Ps. 69:21); Lk. 23:36 (Ps. 69:21); Jn. 15:25 (Ps. 69:4); Jn. 19:28 (Ps. 69:21); Rom. 15:3 (Ps. 69:9b). This is the sort of concerted citation from a single chapter of the Old Testament that prompts C. H. Dodd (*According to the Scriptures* [Nisbet, 1952], p. 58), basing himself on the suggestion of J. Rendel Harris, to postulate the existence of 'testimony' books circulating in the church in its earliest days, *i.e.* books of Old Testament 'prooftexts' by which the earliest Christians learned to think through and support their essentially Christological reading of the Old Testament.

Jesus' cleansing of the temple and related charges were foundationally *just*. They are therefore less concerned with pure worship and a right approach to God than they are with questions of precedent and authority. Second, if the authorities had been convinced that Jesus was merely some petty hooligan, or that he was emotionally unstable, there were adequate recourses; that they requested a miraculous sign demonstrates they harboured at least a suspicion that they were dealing with a heaven-sent prophet. But if so, they were asking the wrong sort of question – one that various authorities asked on other occasions (Mk. 8:11; Mt. 12:38–39 = Lk. 11:29). A sign that would satisfy them, presumably some sort of miraculous display performed on demand, would have signalled the domestication of God. That sort of 'God' does powerful stunts to maintain allegiance, and that kind of allegiance is not worth having. Indeed, if the authorities had eyes to see, the cleansing of the temple was already a 'sign' they should have thought through and deciphered in terms of Old Testament Scripture.

19. Jesus' enigmatic response was understood neither by his interlocutors (*cf.* v. 20) nor by his disciples (v. 22). On the face of it, Jesus was inviting the authorities to destroy the temple, and was promising to raise it again within three days of its destruction. At the literal level, they were unlikely to call his bluff. They were nevertheless stymied, since he was offering them a powerful 'miraculous sign' to justify his authority for cleansing the temple. Indeed, it was a marvellously appropriate sign: anyone who could restore the temple within three days of its complete destruction must be judged to have the authority to regulate its practices.

The Synoptists report that at Jesus' trial before the Sanhedrin false witnesses charged him with making the statement, 'I will destroy this man-made temple and in three days will build another, not made by man' (Mk. 14:58 par.; *cf.* Mk. 15:29). The only record of such a statement is in this account provided by John: the Fourth Gospel here provides a detail that corroborates the Synoptic evidence. The destruction or desecration of a temple or other place of worship was judged a capital offence in the Graeco-Roman world. But the testimony of the witnesses in their report of Jesus' words did not agree; probably for this reason it was labelled 'false' (though from the perspective of the New Testament writers it was false in substance, because (1) if John 2:19 records the words Jesus actually used, he never said, '*I will* destroy . . .' but rather '[You] destroy . . . and I will raise it again'; and (2) what Jesus was referring to had primary reference to his own body, not the temple).

The word rendered 'temple' (*naos*), found in John only here and in the next two verses, may refer to the sanctuary proper, and not to the entire temple complex (*hieron*, used elsewhere, *e.g.* v. 14). But the distinction between the two terms is not well preserved in the Greek of this period.

20. The Jews are naturally incredulous that a building under construction for forty-six years could be rebuilt in three days. Their misunderstanding arises because they focus on the purely material, the natural;

they miss what Jesus is really talking about. Irony and misunderstanding are reported in the Synoptic Gospels (*e.g.* Mk. 7:15ff.; 8:15ff.), but they are prominent features in John (*e.g.* 3:3ff.; 6:41ff.; 11:4–53; *cf.* Carson, 'Mis'). *Cf.* Additional Note.

21. Explanations that clear away misunderstandings are common in John (*e.g.* 6:64, 71; 7:5, 39; 11:13, 51–52; 12:6, 33; 20:9). John explains that what Jesus was really referring to (in v. 19) was his own body, that body in which the Word became flesh (1:14). The Father and the incarnate Son enjoy unique mutual indwelling (14:10–11). Therefore it is the human body of Jesus that uniquely manifests the Father, and becomes the focal point of the manifestation of God to man, the living abode of God on earth, the fulfilment of all the temple meant, and the centre of all true worship (over against all other claims of 'holy space', 4:20–24). In this 'temple' the ultimate sacrifice would take place; within three days of death and burial, Jesus Christ, the true temple, would rise from the dead.

Two important corollaries flow from this identification. First, interpretations that understand the body that is raised up to be the church (following one common metaphor in Paul, *e.g.* Rom. 12:5; 1 Cor. 12:12ff.) are without warrant, for *that* 'body' was not first destroyed before being raised up. The words 'his body' can refer only to the physical body of Jesus, crucified, buried, and raised from the dead. Second, for Jesus to make this identification, after cleansing the temple in Jerusalem, means that he himself saw the connection between the temple and his own body to be fundamentally typological. We are inclined to think of 'prophecy' as verbal prediction that is 'fulfilled' when the event predicted by the prophecy has come to pass. But there is ample evidence that at least some New Testament writers, ultimately learning their principles of interpretation from Jesus himself, understood that some things 'predicted' in the Old Testament were not set out as verbal predictions, but as pictures, events, people, institutions. The sacrifices mandated by the Mosaic law included some built-in features that forced the thoughtful reader to expect a sacrifice beyond themselves; the law anticipated holiness from the heart; the system of priests looked forward to a perfect mediator; David and his kingdom announced, in their very being, the promise of a perfect David (*cf.* notes on 2:17). Such links cannot be traced out in detail here; but it appears that the temple in Jerusalem is being viewed in such a typological way. It was important that worship of God in its precincts be pure (2:13–17); it is even more important to recognize that the temple itself pointed forward to a better and final meeting-point between God and human beings (*cf.* 1:51; 4:21–24). Jesus cleansed the temple; under this typological reading of the Old Testament, he also replaced it, fulfilling its purposes.

22. John is the first to admit that neither he nor the other disciples understood any of this at the time. It was only after Jesus *was raised from the dead* that they *recalled what he had said.* Even then his words would not have made much sense to them, unless they had believed *the words* (lit.

'the word', probably referring to the 'saying' of v. 20) *that Jesus had spoken* and integrated that memory with their newly discovered understanding of what the Scripture said. With Jesus' resurrection came the wonderful gift of the Holy Spirit, the 'Paraclete' (*cf.* chs. 14 – 16), who called to their minds what Jesus had said and enabled them to understand it (14:26; 16:14). No specific Scripture is cited; perhaps John is thinking of a number of passages that promise the vindication of the Messiah, or more specific ones (*e.g.* Ps. 16:8–11, cited by Peter in Acts 2:25–28) at which we can only guess.

The disciples *believed the Scripture*: the expression is *pisteuō* ('I believe') plus the dative of 'the Scripture'. The dative is John's preferred construction when the object of faith is a thing (4:50; 5:47; 10:38). When the object of faith is a person, John may use the dative, or he may resort to *pisteuō eis* plus the accusative. (Believing the light, using the *eis* expression [12:36], is not really an exception, since the light refers to Christ.) Since the verb *pisteuō* ('to believe') can take either the dative or *eis* plus the accusative when the object is a person, some have argued that the latter signifies genuine faith and the former spurious faith. This is quite unlikely: *cf.* notes on 2:23–25; 8:30–31). The two expressions are synonymous for John; whether or not the faith in any passage is genuine or spurious can be determined only by the context.

Although misunderstandings of various sorts are an important literary device in John's Gospel, the group of about thirty misunderstandings represented by this one (*cf.* Carson, 'Mis', p. 89) enjoys one important characteristic that impinges on the historical value of the book. All the misunderstandings in this group (*e.g.* 2:18–22; 6:32–35; 10:1–6) were removed with the passage of time – usually the period from the onset of the misunderstanding to the resurrection of Jesus. From that point on there is no misunderstanding. That does not mean that everyone *accepts* the postulate that Jesus is the true temple, or the true bread from heaven, or the good shepherd; what it means is that Christians have come to understand it and believe it, while those to whom they are witnessing understand the claims well enough but choose *not* to believe them (at least initially).

It will not do to say that John has created these 'misunderstandings' because he is attempting to address the misunderstandings of potential converts at the end of the first century. If they were in touch with the church's witness at all, they would not *misunderstand* the claims, even if they did not *accept* them. This constitutes significant evidence for the historical authenticity of the misunderstandings, for in their very nature they could not easily have taken place *after* the resurrection (for full discussion *cf.* Carson, 'Mis'). That means John's purpose in retelling the stories is not to remove misunderstandings from the minds of his readers, but to establish the Christological points at issue by tying such points to Jesus' resurrection.

Additional note

20. The construction of the Second Temple was begun in the eighteenth year of Herod the Great, *i.e.* 20/19 BC (Jos., *Ant.* xv. 380; though Jos., *Bel.* i. 401 stipulates the fifteenth year of Herod – possibly an error, perhaps the date of the beginning of planning and the acquisition of materials). Forty-six years brings us to AD 27/28. But the entire complex was not completed until AD 63 (Jos., *Ant.* xx. 219), a mere seven years before its destruction in the Jewish War (AD 66–70), even though some think the most natural reading of the Greek implies that the building had taken forty-six years and was *complete* at the time the Jews spoke. From this some deduce that John got his dates mixed up, others that the building project, which proceeded in stages, may have been temporarily halted about this time. It is still more likely that too much is being made of the aorist passive verb (*cf.* Porter, pp. 52, 183, 185).

4. Inadequate faith (2:23–25)

23. At the same Passover festival, *many people saw the miraculous signs he was doing and believed in his name.* We are thereby briefly reminded of the wide-ranging ministry Jesus had already undertaken, even if relatively few individual narratives have been preserved for us (*cf.* 20:30–31). The people 'believed in his name': the expression is *episteusan eis to onoma autou*, even though their faith is spurious (*cf.* notes on 2:22). To exercise faith on the grounds of having witnessed *miraculous signs* is precarious (4:48; *cf.* Mk. 8:11–13). Although miracles cannot command faith (10:32), it is better to believe on the ground of miracles than not at all (*cf.* 10:38).

24–25. Sadly, their faith was spurious, and Jesus knew it. Unlike other religious leaders, he cannot be duped by flattery, enticed by praise or caught off-guard in innocence. His knowledge of men's hearts is profound, and accounts in part for the diversity of his approaches to individuals in the Gospels. He therefore did not *entrust himself* to these spurious converts. (The Greek repeats the verb, but with a slightly different meaning: we might paraphrase, 'the people *trusted* in his name, but he did not *entrust* himself to them.') By implication, Jesus wonderfully promises to entrust himself to those who truly trust him (*cf.* 10:14, 15).

Many commentators note the partial parallel to v. 25 in the Jewish commentary on Exodus, *Mekhilta Exod.* 15:32: 'Seven things are hidden from man – the day of death, the day of consolation, the depths of judgment, one's reward, the time of restoration of the kingdom of David, the time when the guilty kingdom [*i.e.* Rome] will be destroyed, and *what is within another.*' Scriptural proof for this final 'unknown' is elsewhere provided in *Genesis Rabbah* 65, *viz.* Jeremiah 17:10, 'I the LORD search the heart and examine the mind.' Even in this regard, then, Jesus, far from being limited like other human beings, does what God does (5:19, *cf.* SB 2. 412).

5. Jesus and Nicodemus (3:1–15)

The one who 'knew all men', who 'did not need man's testimony about man' (2:24–25), now enters into a number of conversations in which he instantly gets to the heart of individuals with highly diverse backgrounds and needs – Nicodemus (3:1–15), the Samaritan woman (4:1–26), the Gentile official (4:43–53), the man at the pool of Bethesda (5:1–15), and more.

It has become popular to follow the lead of Martyn (*HTFG*, pp. 119–123, 161–163), to see in Nicodemus a symbolic figure representing a local Jewish leader *at the time John was writing*, a figure who secretly believed but who needed encouragement to step out and make his faith public. The 'inspiration' for Nicodemus, then, is a person like Gamaliel (Acts 5). Martyn needlessly forces the text into anachronism at point after point, even though, as we have already seen (*cf.* notes on 2:22), John is perfectly willing and able to make distinctions between what happened 'back then' in the days of Jesus and what happened only after Jesus had risen from the dead. In any case, other readings, including an elementary sociolinguistic reading (*i.e.* one that focuses on the discourse in its own literary, linguistic and sociological context)[1] makes admirable sense of the putative historical context, as the notes below will briefly demonstrate.

Schnackenburg (1. 380ff.) and others have argued that 3:31–36 has been displaced, and should be inserted between v. 12 and v. 13. Although sense can be made of the text that way, greater sense flows from the order preserved for us. Even at the structural level there is a certain symmetry about the chapter as it stands. In vv. 1–21, the words of Jesus probably trail off at the end of v. 15, to be followed by the meditation of the Evangelist in vv. 16–21 (*cf.* notes on vv. 16–21). Similarly in vv. 22–36: the words of John the Baptist probably terminate with v. 30, while vv. 31–36 preserve a balancing meditation by the Evangelist on what has just been reported.

1. The word that connects this narrative with the preceding chapter is *de*, commonly rendered 'and' (NIV's *Now* is an idiomatic adaptation) or 'but'. If some variation of 'and' is accepted, the idea is that Nicodemus exemplified those who in some sense believed in Jesus, but with a faith so inadequate that Jesus did not entrust himself to them (2:23–25).[2] This interpretation may be reinforced by the fact that Nicodemus approached Jesus by referring to his signs – the very things that evoked spurious faith in 2:23–25. On the other hand, if *de* has its more usual adversative force ('but'), it means that, in contrast to those with inadequate faith at the end of ch. 2, Nicodemus' approach was not so faulty and Jesus did entrust himself to him. The Evangelist displays a habit of describing a

---

[1] One does not have to agree with every detail of the essay by F. P. Cotterell (*ExpT* 96, 1985, pp. 237–242) to appreciate this point.
[2] *Cf.* M. de Jonge, *BJRL* 53, 1970–71, pp. 337–359.

bleak reception of the Son of God, followed by some alleviating exception (*e.g.* 1:10–13; 3:19–21; 6:66–69). In this instance a mediating position seems best. The most natural reading of 3:1–15 is that at this point Nicodemus, though interested, is not particularly open to the truth (after all, Jesus' signs serve Nicodemus as a conversation starter, not, as in 2:23–25, as a trigger for faith, spurious or otherwise), yet eventually he comes around to side with Jesus (7:45–52) and ultimately to take his place at Calvary (19:38–42).

The name Nicodemus was common in Greek, but transliterated and made into a Jewish name. This Nicodemus has sometimes been identified with Naqdimon ben Gorion, a wealthy citizen of Jerusalem who supplied water to pilgrims at the principal feasts, and who is known to have lived in Jerusalem at the time of its siege in the Jewish War (AD 70; B. *Ta'anith* 19*b*–20*a*; *Gittin* 56*a*; *Ketuboth* 66*b*). That would have made Naqdimon a very young man forty years earlier, during the ministry of Jesus, probably too young to have been *a member of the Jewish ruling council*, the Sanhedrin, unless he was a very exceptional person indeed. Moreover, we may reasonably infer from v. 4 that Nicodemus was already an old man when he encountered Jesus. Regardless of his identification with any person named in extra-biblical sources, Nicodemus was *a man of the Pharisees* (*cf.* notes on 1:19, 24–25), and a distinguished teacher (*cf.* notes on 1:10).

2. Why Nicodemus came to Jesus *at night* is uncertain. Some have thought this reference to 'night' is nothing more than a personal reminiscence of an historical detail. Others remind us of the texts demonstrating that rabbis studied and debated long into the night. Still others speculate that Nicodemus came to Jesus at night in order to benefit from the cloak of darkness, fearing to be identified in the public mind with the Galilean teacher and wonder-worker. The best clue lies in John's use of 'night' elsewhere: in each instance (3:2; 9:4; 11:10; 13:30) the word is either used metaphorically for moral and spiritual darkness, or, if it refers to the night-time hours, it bears the same moral and spiritual symbolism.[1] Doubtless Nicodemus approached Jesus at night, but his own 'night' was blacker than he knew (*cf.* Hengstenberg, 1. 157–158; Lightfoot, p. 116).

Though he was a distinguished teacher, Nicodemus addressed Jesus with a collegial *Rabbi*. In a sense this was worth more than when the same word was uttered by two untaught disciples of John the Baptist (1:38); it was certainly more respectful than the tone of some of Nicodemus' colleagues (7:15, 45–52). Nor was Nicodemus as dismissive of Jesus' miracles as those who assigned his works to the power of Satan (8:48, 52; *cf.* Mk. 3:22ff. par.). It is the evidence of the miraculous signs that convinces Nicodemus that Jesus is no ordinary teacher: he must be *a*

---

[1] Against Cotterell, *art. cit.*, this is true even when John does not emphasize the word by 'fronting' it, *i.e.* by placing it toward the beginning of the clause.

teacher who has come from God – which is certainly not a confession of Jesus' pre-existence, but a recognition that God was peculiarly *with him*, very much as he was with Moses or Jeremiah (Ex. 3:12; Je. 1:19).

At one level this assessment of Jesus must be judged disappointing. Nicodemus does not suggest Jesus is a prophet, still less *the* prophet or the Messiah, but simply a teacher mightily endowed with God's power. Nicodemus was openly curious about Jesus, but still fell a long way short of confession that he was uniquely the promised Coming One.

Two plurals in this verse demand notice. First, Nicodemus refers to 'miraculous signs' (plur.), even though only one has been reported so far in any detail (2:1–11). But John has just mentioned others (2:23), and in any case this Gospel informs its readers that Jesus performed many miracles other than the ones found here (20:30; 21:24–25). The samples the Evangelist includes are those that are *sig*nificant for his purposes (*cf.* notes on 2:1). Second, Nicodemus speaks in the first person plural '*we* know', not '*I* know'. Some think this 'we' makes Nicodemus a spokesman for the 'many people' whose faith was spurious (2:23–25). This view is in danger of making Nicodemus a mere cipher, a literary creation of the Evangelist, since it is quite clear that Nicodemus would not see *himself* as an exemplar of spurious faith. Cotterell (*art. cit.*) suggests Nicodemus approached Jesus with a group of his disciples in tow, and spoke for all of them; Jesus then replied with a similar plural form, speaking both for himself and his own disciples (v. 11). Disciples on one side or the other may have been present; but the text does not say so, and in any case this explanation will certainly not do for v. 11 (*cf.* notes below). It is most natural to think that Nicodemus saw himself speaking for at least some of the Pharisees or members of the Jewish ruling council (v. 1) who were in essential agreement with him. Nicodemus is likely hiding somewhat behind his colleagues, his 'we' betraying a touch of swagger or nervousness. (John is particularly adept at wielding deft strokes to flesh out his characters: compare, for instance, the two who are healed in Jn. 5 and Jn. 9 respectively.)

On the appropriateness of Nicodemus' assumption that Jesus' miracles testify to who he is, *cf.* notes on 9:16ff.; 10:38; 14:11.

3. Formally, Nicodemus has not yet asked anything, though the implied question seems to be something like, 'Who are you, then? We know you are a teacher from God, but are you more? Are you a prophet? Are you the Messiah?' (*Cf.* notes on 1:19ff.) But Jesus' words are more than a response to a merely implied question. The fundamental presupposition behind the opening sally of Nicodemus, as behind the demand for a sign (2:18), is the ability of the interlocutor to assess the evidence Jesus may care to advance. Nicodemus, like other Jews (*cf.* notes on 8:31ff.), wants to set up criteria by which to assess who Jesus is. Jesus rejects the priority of Nicodemus, and radically questions his qualification for sorting out 'heavenly things' (v. 11; *cf.* Carson, p. 180; Haenchen, 1. 200). Nicodemus claims he can 'see' something of who Jesus is in the miracles; Jesus insists no-one can 'see' the saving reign of God at all, including the display of miraculous signs, unless born again. Even more fundamentally, if there is any possibility at all that Jesus is the promised Messiah, it would be more fitting for Nicodemus to ask himself if he is ready for *him*, rather than to ask if a proper claimant has arrived on the scene. As Christians today contemplate the Lord's return aright only if in consequence they purify themselves (1 Jn. 3:1–3), so Jews in Jesus' day best anticipated the coming of the Messiah when they most wanted to be transformed in line with the promises of life under the messianic age – to enjoy a new heart for God, cleansing and the fulness of the Spirit (*e.g.* Je. 31:28ff.; Ezk. 36:25–27).

That, at least, is the drift of Jesus' response to Nicodemus, and the nature of its connection with v. 2; but closer inspection is necessary. Introducing his words with the solemn formula *I tell you the truth* (*cf.* notes on 1:51), Jesus declares that *unless* a man (the expression in Greek refers to a man or a woman) *is born again*, he cannot *see the kingdom of God*. The full expression 'the kingdom of God' is not found in the Old Testament, though a number of passages speak of the Lord's kingdom, or, more dynamically, insist that the Lord *reigns*, or that the Lord is *king* (*e.g.* Ex. 15:18; Ps. 93:1; 103:19). These texts speak of the universal sweep of God's sovereignty. Everyone is 'in' that kingdom, whether or not one knows it or likes it. But the prophets also foresaw the advent of a kingdom at the end of history, presided over by a son of David (Is. 9:1–7; 11; Zc. 9:9–10), by the Lord's servant (Is. 42:1ff.; 49:1ff.), by the Lord himself (Is. 9:1–7; 33:2; Zc. 14:9). The coming ruler was thus differentiated from the Lord, and in other passages identified with him – just as the Word is both differentiated from God, and identified with him (Jn. 1:1). Modelled on God's covenant relationship with the people of Israel (Ex. 19:5–6; Dt. 33:5), the kingdom concept received decisive shaping in the promise that David's line would be everlasting (2 Sa. 7:12–16). Future aspects of the kingdom are not neglected by Old Testament writers (Is. 11:1ff.; Dn. 2:44; 7:14, 27), including the prospect of resurrection life (Dn. 12:1–3).

To a Jew with the background and convictions of Nicodemus, 'to see the kingdom of God' was to participate in the kingdom at the end of the age, to experience eternal, resurrection life. The same equivalence is found in the Synoptics (*cf.* Mk. 9:43, 45 'to enter life', parallel to 9:47 'to enter the kingdom of God'); it is particularly strong in the Fourth Gospel, where 'kingdom' language crops up only here (3:3, 5) and at Jesus' trial (18:36), while 'life' language predominates. One of the most startling features of the kingdom announced in the Synoptics is that it is not exclusively future. The kingdom, God's saving and transforming reign, has in certain respects already been inaugurated in the person, works and message of Jesus. John stresses this 'inaugurated' or 'realized' component of the long-awaited salvation even more. True, he can refer to the resurrection (5:28–29) and speak unambiguously of what takes place at the last day (*e.g.* Jn. 6:40), but it is far more characteristic of him to stress entry into life and participation in the eternal life *now* (*e.g.* Jn. 3:16).

If the kingdom does not dawn until the end of the age, then of course one cannot enter it before it comes. Predominant religious thought in Jesus' day affirmed that all Jews would be admitted to that kingdom apart from those guilty of deliberate apostasy or extraordinary wickedness (*e.g.* Mishnah *Sanhedrin* 10:1). But here was Jesus telling Nicodemus, a respected and conscientious member not only of Israel but of the Sanhedrin, that he cannot enter the kingdom unless he is *born again*. The verb rendered 'to be born' (*gennan*) can refer to the action of the father ('to beget') or the mother ('to give birth to'): the common ingredient is 'generation' or 'regeneration'. The coming of the kingdom at the end can be described as the 'regeneration' of the world (Mt. 19:28, niv 'renewal'), but here what is required is the regeneration of the individual *before* the end of the world and *in order to enter* the kingdom.

This regeneration is *anōthen*, a word that can mean 'from above' or 'again'. Because Nicodemus understood it to mean 'again' (*cf.* 'a second time', v. 4), and Jesus did not correct him, some have argued that 'again' must stand. But Jesus also insists that this new birth, this new begetting, this new regeneration, must be the work of the Spirit, who comes from the realm of the 'above'. Certainly the other occurrences of *anōthen* in John mean 'from above' (3:31; 19:11, 23). As he does with other terms,[1] John may be choosing to extend double meaning to this one in John 3:3, 7, both 'from above' and 'again'; he certainly does not mean less than the former. Readers who have followed the Gospel to this point will instantly think (as Nicodemus couldn't) of John 1:12–13: 'to be born again' or 'to be born from above' must mean the same thing as 'to become children of God', to be 'born of God', by believing in the name of the incarnate Word.

But what stands behind this expression? And to what kind of experience does it refer? Many commentators have tried to trace the origin of 'born again' language to various branches of Gnosticism, mystery religions or other forms of paganism (for a useful discussion, *cf.* Bauer, pp. 51ff.). Certainly this chapter of the Fourth Gospel would speak to people with such backgrounds, saying, in effect, 'You talk about new birth. We can attest a new birth that is more fundamental, more important, more life-transforming and God-pleasing than anything you have experienced or heard about.' Other scholars bring up the Jewish sources that say a newly baptized proselyte is like a new-born child, or those that insist the daily sacrifices make Israel like a one-year-old child (*cf.* SB 2. 421ff.). Neither parallel is relevant. The former refers to the legal status of the proselyte-convert, but no idea of generation is present; the latter may attest quite remarkable faith in the atoning work of the daily sacrifices, but promise innocence, not regeneration. Many others think this chapter is a Johannine version of the Synoptic saying that allots the kingdom of heaven/God only to those who become like little children

---

[1]*E.g.* 'king' (19:14, 15, 19, 21); 'man' (19:5); 'sleep' (11:13); 'to die for' (11:50–51; *cf.* 18:14); 'to lift up' (3:14; 8:28; 12:32, 34); 'water' (4:10). *Cf.* O. Cullmann, *ThZ* 4, 1948, pp. 360–372.

(Mt. 18:3; Mk. 10:15; Lk. 18:17). This is unconvincing. Jesus' point in the 'little children' saying is that child-like trust in God is necessary to salvation. By contrast, the focus here is not on the potential convert's humility, brokenness or faith, but on the need for *transformation*, for new life from another realm, for the intervention of the Spirit of God.

The delineation of the most likely background can await v. 5 (*cf.* notes, below); it is sufficient for the moment to note that Jesus *expected Nicodemus to grasp the significance of the new birth out of his background as a distinguished teacher of Scripture* (vv. 7, 10). Thus it is to antecedent Scripture that we must look. Certainly we cannot dismiss the category of new birth as incidental, rare, or narrowly Johannine, since it recurs in Tit. 3:5; 1 Pet. 1:3, 23; 1 Jn. 2:29; 3:9; 4:7; 5:1, 4, 18). What must be seized from Jesus' insistence on the new birth as the prerequisite for entrance into the kingdom is the fact that this truth is applied to a man of the calibre of Nicodemus. If Nicodemus, with his knowledge, gifts, understanding, position and integrity cannot enter the promised kingdom by virtue of his standing and works, what hope is there for anyone who seeks salvation along such lines? Even for a Nicodemus, there must be a radical transformation, the generation of new life, comparable with physical birth. Barrett (p. 206) finely cites Calvin: 'by the term *born again* He means not the amendment of a part but the renewal of the whole nature. Hence it follows that there is nothing in us that is not defective' (Calvin, 1. 63).

4. Nicodemus's incredulous response is part of a recurring pattern of misunderstanding followed by further explanation in this Gospel (*cf.* notes on 2:20). It is far from certain Nicodemus was quite as obtuse as a casual reading of his response might suggest (*cf.* Meyer, 1. 163, 'of a somewhat slow temperament': is this likely of 'Israel's teacher' [3:10]?). Some have wondered if he was purposely setting a metaphorical problem against a metaphorical challenge – *i.e.* he understood that Jesus was demanding some sort of transformation of an individual's entire character, but he could not see how an old man, decisively shaped by his heritage and firmly set in his ways, could possibly turn the clock back and start all over again as a new person. He could not possibly *enter a second time into his mother's womb to be born!* This reconstruction is too subtle, and ignores the theme of the kingdom of God, introduced by Jesus' challenge (v. 3). For a man like Nicodemus, entering the kingdom of God did not have to do with the transformation of an individual's character but with participation in the resurrection life of the new order God would powerfully bring about at the end of history. There is no evidence he was wistfully feeling the force of Tennyson's famous sigh, 'Ah for a man to arise in me / That the man I am may cease to be.'

A more realistic view is that Nicodemus did not understand what Jesus was talking about at all. At this point he could not believe (v. 12) that new birth was a requirement for entrance into the kingdom and was amazed (v. 7) by the very category. His response in v. 4 is therefore marked with incredulousness, which prompts him to reply with a crassly literalistic interpretation of what Jesus said, as a way of expressing a certain degree of scorn. Even his decision to take *anōthen* (v. 3) to mean 'again' or *a second time* may be part of that determined literalism.[1]

5. Whatever the nature and degree of Nicodemus's misunderstanding, Jesus sets about to restate his challenge in slightly different form (v. 5), and with expansive comment (vv. 6–8). Again there is the solemn formula *I tell you the truth* (*cf.* notes on 1:51). This time *no-one can enter the kingdom of God* displaces 'no-one can see the kingdom of God' (v. 3). The meaning is much the same; inability even to 'enter' may be slightly stronger than inability to 'see' (*i.e.* experience). But the crucial difference in the wording is the change from 'born *anōthen*' ('from above' or 'again') to *born of water and the Spirit*. These words have generated a host of interpretations, the most important of which may be summarized as follows:

(1) Noting that v. 6 describes *two* births, one from flesh to flesh and the other from Spirit to Spirit, some interpreters propose that 'born of water and the Spirit' similarly refers to two births, one natural and the other supernatural. Natural procreation is not enough; there must be a second birth, a second begetting, this one of the Spirit. To support this view, 'water' has been understood to refer to the amniotic fluid that breaks from the womb shortly before childbirth, or to stand metaphorically for semen. But there are no ancient sources that picture natural birth as 'from water', and the few that use 'drops' to stand for semen are rare and late. It is true that in sources relevant to the Fourth Gospel water can be associated with fecundity and procreation in a general way (*e.g.* Song 4:12–13; Pr. 5:15–18),[2] but none is tied quite so clearly to semen or to amniotic fluid as to make the connection here an obvious one. The Greek construction does not favour two births here. Moreover the entire expression 'of water and the Spirit' cries out to be read as the equivalent of *anōthen*, 'from above', if there is genuine parallelism between v. 3 and v. 5, and this too argues that the expression should be taken as a reference to but one birth, not two.

(2) Many find in 'water' a reference to Christian baptism (*e.g.* Brown, 2. 139–141). For Bultmann (pp. 138–139 n. 3) and others who have followed him, this is so embarrassing that he suggests the words 'water and' were not part of the original text, but added by a later ecclesiastical

---

[1]In any case it would be wrong to conclude that because this conversation took place in Aramaic, which does not (so far as I know) boast a word parallel to *anōthen* in ambiguity, Jesus must have used a term meaning 'again' for Nicodemus to respond in this way. We cannot even be certain that the conversation took place in Aramaic: there is very good evidence many people in Palestine were trilingual. But if it did take place in Aramaic, the report in Jn. 3 is doubtless in condensed form and decidedly Johannine in style, so that Nicodemus' apparent misunderstanding over *anōthen* may in fact have developed in more extended and prosaic form. At the end of the day, the only text we have to examine is the Greek text of John.

[2]For a defence of this first option, *cf.* Ben Witherington III, *NTS* 35, 1989, pp. 155–160; Morris, *JC*, pp. 150–151.

editor much more interested in Christian ritual than the Evangelist himself. There is no textual support for the omission. At the other end of the spectrum, Vellanickal (pp. 170ff.) suggests that when the Evangelist received this account there was no mention of water, but that he added it to provide an explicit reference to the rite of Christian initiation. Added or not, the simple word 'water' is understood by the majority of contemporary commentators to refer to Christian baptism, though there is little agreement amongst them on the relation between 'water' and 'Spirit'. After all, reference is made in the near context to Jesus' own baptismal ministry (3:22; 4:1), and John has connected water and Spirit in a baptismal context before (1:33, 34). Moreover John's alleged interest in sacraments in ch. 6 encourages the suspicion he is making a sacramental allusion here. Many accordingly suggest the Spirit effects new birth *through* water (= baptism) (*e.g.* Ferraro, *Spirito*, pp. 59–67).

Those who adopt this position, of course, are forced to admit that John's words could have had no relevance to the historical Nicodemus. This part of the account, at least, becomes a narrative fiction designed to instruct the church on the importance of baptism. What is not always recognized is that this theory makes the Evangelist an extraordinarily incompetent story-teller, since in v. 10 he pictures Jesus berating Nicodemus for *not* understanding these things. If water = baptism is so important for entering the kingdom, it is surprising that the rest of the discussion never mentions it again: the entire focus is on the work of the Spirit (v. 8), the work of the Son (vv. 14–15), the work of God himself (vv. 16–17), and the place of faith (vv. 15–16). The analogy between the mysterious wind and the sovereign work of the Spirit (v. 8) becomes very strange if Spirit-birth is tied so firmly to baptism. Some doubt if there is any *explicit* reference to the eucharist in John 6 (*cf.* notes on 6:25ff.), casting doubt on the supposition that the Evangelist is deeply interested in sacramental questions. If he were, it is surpassingly strange that he fails to make explicit connections, neglecting even to mention the institution of the Lord's supper. The Spirit plays a powerful role in John 14 – 16; 20:22, but there is no hint of baptism. Moreover the allusions to Jesus' baptismal activity (3:22; 4:1), far from fostering sacramentalism, explicitly divert attention elsewhere (*cf.* notes on 3:25–26; 4:2; 6:22ff.). The conjunction of water and Spirit in 1:26, 33 is no support for this position, as there the two are contrasted, whereas in 3:5 they are co-ordinated.

The entire view seems to rest on an unarticulated prejudice that every mention of water evoked instant recognition, in the minds of first-century readers, that the real reference was to baptism, but it is very doubtful that this prejudice can be sustained by the sources. Even so, this conclusion does not preclude the possibility of a *secondary allusion* to baptism (*cf.* notes, below).

(3) A variation on this view is that 'water' refers not to Christian baptism but to John's baptism (Godet, 2. 49–52; Westcott, 1. 108–109, and others). In that case, Jesus is either saying that the baptism of

repentance, as important as it is, must not be thought sufficient: there must be Spirit-birth as well; or, if Nicodemus refused to be baptized by the Baptist, Jesus is rebuking him and saying that he must pass through repentance-baptism ('water') and new birth ('Spirit'). 'To receive the Spirit from the Messiah was no humiliation; on the contrary, it was a glorious privilege. But to go down into Jordan before a wondering crowd and own [his] need of cleansing and new birth was too much. Therefore to this Pharisee our Lord declares that an honest dying to the past is as needful as new life for the future' (Dods, *EGT*, 1. 713).

The argument presupposes that John the Baptist was so influential at the time that a mere mention of water would conjure up pictures of his ministry. If so, however, the response of Nicodemus is inappropriate. If the allusion to the Baptist were clear, why should Nicodemus respond with such incredulity, ignorance and unbelief (3:4, 9–10, 12), rather than mere distaste or hardened arrogance? Even if John's baptism is mentioned in near contexts, the burden of these contexts is to stress the *relative unimportance* of his rite (1: 23, 26; 3:23, 30). If John's baptism lies behind 'water' in 3:5, would not this suggest that Jesus was making the Baptist's rite a *requirement* for entrance into the kingdom, even though that rite was shortly to be superseded by Christian baptism? Moreover, as Dods sets out this proposed solution, it is assumed that Jesus is recognized as the Messiah who dispenses the Spirit, but it is far from clear that Nicodemus has progressed so far in his appreciation of Jesus.

(4) Several interpreters have argued that Jesus is arguing against the ritual washings of the Essenes (a conservative and frequently monastic Jewish movement), or perhaps against Jewish ceremonies in general. What is necessary is Spirit-birth, not mere water-purification. But 'water' and 'Spirit' are not contrasted in v. 5: they are linked, and together become the equivalent of 'from above' (v. 3).

(5) A number of less influential proposals have been advanced. Some have suggested that 'water' represents *Torah* (which can refer to the Pentateuch, or to the entire Jewish teaching and tradition about God, written and oral, or something between the two extremes). But though water is sometimes a symbol for Torah in rabbinic literature, 'birth of water' or the like does not occur. Moreover the stress in the Fourth Gospel is on the life-giving qualities of *Jesus'* words (6:63); the Scriptures point to *him* (5:39). Odeberg (p. 50), Morris (pp. 216–218) and others have seen in 'born of water and the Spirit' an hendiadys for spiritual seed or semen, in contrast with semen of the flesh (v. 6). The entire expression refers to God's engendering seed or efflux, cast over against the natural birth Nicodemus mentions in the preceding verse. But Odeberg's supporting citations are both late and unconvincing, demanding that the reader (not to mention Nicodemus!) make numerous doubtful connections. Jesus' indignation that Nicodemus had not grasped what he was saying (v. 10) suddenly sounds artificial and forced. Hodges has recently suggested that the two crucial terms, both without articles, should be rendered 'water and wind', together

symbolizing God's vivifying work,[1] since Greek *pneuma* can mean 'wind' or 'breath' as well as 'spirit' (*cf.* notes on 3:8). But this fails to reckon with the fact that *pneuma* almost always means 'spirit' in the New Testament. Only very powerful contextual clues can compel another rendering: the presence or absence of the article is certainly not an adequate clue (*cf.* v. 8 where *pneuma* = 'wind' is articular). The word *pneuma* in the very next verse (v. 6) cannot easily be understood to mean anything other than 'spirit', and it is this consistent meaning that prepares the way for the analogical argument of v. 8, where wind symbolizes spirit.

The most plausible interpretation of 'born of water and the Spirit'[2] turns on three factors. First, the expression is parallel to 'from above' (*anōthen*, v. 3), and so only one birth is in view. Second, the preposition 'of' governs both 'water' and 'spirit'. The most natural way of taking this construction is to see the phrase as a conceptual unity: there is a water-spirit source (*cf.* Murray J. Harris, *NIDNTT* 3. 1178) that stands as the origin of this regeneration.[3] Third, Jesus berates Nicodemus for not understanding these things in his role as 'Israel's teacher' (v. 10), a senior 'professor' of the Scriptures, and this in turn suggests we must turn to what Christians call the Old Testament to begin to discern what Jesus had in mind.

Although the full construction 'born of water and of the Spirit' is not found in the Old Testament, the ingredients are there. At a minor level, the idea that Israel, the covenant community, was properly called 'God's son' (Ex. 4:22; Dt. 32:6; Ho. 11:1) provides at least a little potential background for the notion of God 'begetting' people, enough, Brown thinks, that it should have enabled Nicodemus 'to understand that Jesus was proclaiming the arrival of the eschatological times when men would be God's children' (1. 139). Far more important is the Old Testament background to 'water' and 'spirit'. The 'spirit' is constantly God's principle of life, even in creation (*e.g.* Gn. 2:7; 6:3; Jb. 34:14); but many Old Testament writers look forward to a time when God's 'spirit' will be

---

[1]So Zane Hodges, *BSac* 135, 1978, pp. 206–220.

[2]I am indebted to the fine article by Linda Belleville, *TrinJ* 1, 1980, pp. 125–141, whom I follow with only occasional demurrals. *Cf.* also James D. G. Dunn, *Baptism in the Holy Spirit* (SBT 15; SCM, 1970), p. 192. The eclectic treatment by Burge (pp. 158ff., esp. p. 163) occasionally evidences insight into the Old Testament background, but ends up confusing that background with Qumran ritual, the lustrations of apocalyptic Judaism and the baptism of John the Baptist.

[3]This is rather different from the position of Westcott (1. 108) that makes 'water' and 'spirit' have the same *referent*, prompting him to offer the rendering 'born of spiritual water' and hence 'born of the spiritual element'. Though both nouns are governed by the one preposition, this does not constitute a reason to think that they have the same referent, as Ben Witherington III (*art. cit.*, p. 159) rightly points out. But Witherington's criticism of Westcott is irrelevant to the position adopted here. He cites 1 Jn. 5:6, 'came through water and blood', where both 'water' and 'blood' are anarthrous and are governed by one preposition. He plausibly asserts that this means Jesus came in two separate events: through water (his baptism) and through blood (his cross). But in Johannine thought, this does not represent two discrete comings, but *one* coming *through both events*. So also Jn. 3:3, 5: *one* birth is in view *of both water and spirit*.

poured out on humankind (Joel 2:28) with the result that there will be blessing and righteousness (Is. 32:15–20; 44:3; Ezk. 39:29), and inner renewal which cleanses God's covenant people from their idolatry and disobedience (Ezk. 11:19–20; 36:26–27). When water is used figuratively in the Old Testament, it habitually refers to renewal or cleansing, especially when it is found in conjunction with 'spirit'. This conjunction may be explicit, or may hide behind language depicting the 'pouring out' of the spirit (cf. Nu. 19:17–19; Ps. 51:9–10; Is. 32:15; 44:3–5; 55:1–3; Je. 2:13; 17:13; Ezk. 47:9; Joel 2:28–29; Zc. 14:8). Most important of all is Ezekiel 36:25–27, where water and spirit come together so forcefully, the first to signify cleansing from impurity, and the second to depict the transformation of heart that will enable people to follow God wholly. And it is no accident that the account of the valley of dry bones, where Ezekiel preaches and the Spirit brings life to dry bones, follows hard after Ezekiel's water/spirit passage (cf. Ezk. 37; and notes on 3:8, below). The language is reminiscent of the 'new heart' expressions that revolve around the promise of the new covenant (Je. 31:29ff.). Similar themes were sometimes picked up in later Judaism (e.g. Jubilees 1:23–25).

In short, *born of water and spirit* (the article and the capital 'S' in the NIV should be dropped: the focus is on the impartation of God's nature as 'spirit' [cf. 4:24], not on the Holy Spirit as such) signals a new begetting, a new birth that cleanses and renews, the eschatological cleansing and renewal promised by the Old Testament prophets. True, the prophets tended to focus on the corporate results, the restoration of the nation; but they also anticipated a transformation of individual 'hearts' – no longer hearts of stone but hearts that hunger to do God's will. It appears that individual regeneration is presupposed. Apparently Nicodemus had not thought of the Old Testament passages this way. If he was like some other Pharisees, he was too confident of the quality of his own obedience to think he needed much repentance (cf. Lk. 7:30), let alone to have his whole life cleansed and his heart transformed, to be born again.

Some have argued that if the flow of the passage is anything like what has been described then it is hopelessly anachronistic, for John's Gospel makes it abundantly clear (cf. esp. 7:37–39) that the Holy Spirit would not be given until after Jesus is glorified, and it is this Holy Spirit who must effect the new birth, even if the expression 'born of water and spirit' does not refer to the Holy Spirit *per se*. So how then can Jesus demand of Nicodemus such regeneration?

The charge is ill-conceived. Jesus is not presented as demanding that Nicodemus experience the new birth in the instant; rather, he is forcefully articulating what must be experienced if one is to enter the kingdom of God. The resulting tension is no different from the corresponding Synoptic tension as to when the kingdom dawns. In Matthew, for instance, Jesus is born the King (Mt. 1 – 2), he announces the kingdom and performs the powerful works of the kingdom (4:17; 12:28), but it is not until he has arisen from the dead that all authority becomes his (28:18–20). That is why *all* discipleship in all four Gospels is inevitably transitional. The coming-to-faith of the first followers of Jesus was in certain respects unique: they *could not* instantly become 'Christians' in the full-orbed sense, and experience the full sweep of the new birth, until *after* the resurrection and glorification of Jesus. If we take the Gospel records seriously, we must conclude that Jesus sometimes proclaimed truth the full significance and application of which could be fully appreciated and experienced only after he had risen from the dead. John 3 falls under this category.

It appears, then, that the passage makes good sense within the historical framework set out for us, *i.e.* as a lesson for Nicodemus within the context of the ministry of Jesus. But we must also ask how John expected *his* readers to understand it. If his targeted readers were hellenistic Jews and Jewish proselytes who had been exposed to Christianity and whom John was trying to evangelize (*cf.* Introduction, § VI, and notes on 20:30–31), then his primary message for them is clear. No matter how good their Jewish credentials, they too must be born again if they are to see or enter the kingdom of God. When John wrote this, Christian baptism had been practised for several decades (which was of course not the case when Jesus spoke with Nicodemus). *If* (and it is a quite uncertain 'if') the Evangelist expected his readers to detect some secondary allusion to Christian baptism in v. 5 (*cf.* Richter, *Studien*, pp. 327–345), the thrust of the passage treats such an allusion quite distantly. What is emphasized is the need for radical transformation, the fulfilment of Old Testament promises anticipating the outpouring of the Spirit, and not a particular rite. If baptism is associated in the readers' minds with entrance into the Christian faith, and therefore with new birth, then they are being told in the strongest terms that it is the new birth itself that is essential, not the rite.[1]

6–7. Like generates like. *Flesh gives birth to flesh.* The word *flesh* does not here bear the most frequent freight Paul assigns it, 'sinful nature' or the like. As in 1:14, 'flesh' refers to human nature. The point is that natural, human birth produces people who belong to the earthly family of humankind, but not to the children of God. Only *the Spirit gives birth to spirit.* Even though there is no similar distinction between capitals and lower-case letters in Greek, the capitalization of the first 'Spirit' rightly preserves the thought that it is God's Holy Spirit who produces a new nature, a spirit-nature where 'spirit' is related to the sphere of God and things divine (as in 4:24). The antithesis between flesh and spirit is therefore not the contrast between lower and higher aspects of human nature, but the distinction between human beings and God. The second

---

[1] It has been suggested that, just as Jesus in this Gospel can utter some enigmatic saying the meaning of which is unclear until after the resurrection (*cf.* notes on 2:19–22), so John here presents Jesus as using an ambiguous category the baptismal meaning of which could be appreciated only later. But this species of hidden utterance is customarily identified as such in the Fourth Gospel, and its theme is invariably interwoven into the larger fabric of Johannine theology. Neither of these conditions is met with the hypothesis that water here symbolizes baptism.

occurrence of 'spirit' is not an adjective: we are not to read, 'The Spirit gives birth to spiritual people', understanding 'spiritual people' in some vague or merely functional way. What is in view is a new nature, not turning over a new leaf.

For human beings, those born of the flesh, to experience this new birth that makes them children of God, the eternal Word, himself God (1:1, 18), became flesh (1:14). Nicodemus could not have been expected to know all that the readers of the Prologue have absorbed, but from his study of Scripture, his grasp of the distance between human beings and God, and the axiom that like produces like, he should have understood the need for a God-given new birth, and God's promise that he would give his people a new heart, a new nature, clean lives and a full measure of the Spirit on the last day. That is why Jesus told Nicodemus he *should not be surprised.*

Jesus' central challenge in this passage has universal application: *You* (plural) *must be born again.* This transition to the plural (*cf.* vv. 3, 5) is taken by some scholars to indicate that it is really John who is addressing his readers, rather than Jesus who is addressing Nicodemus. But the plural 'you' is simply a strengthened form of the generalizing 'anyone' or 'a man' (Gk. *tis*) in 3:3, 5, and may also hark back with irony to Nicodemus' 'we' (3:2; *cf.* notes on v. 11). The plural 'you' sets Jesus over against not just Nicodemus, but the entire human race.

8. Both the Hebrew word *rûaḥ* and the Greek word *pneuma* can mean 'breath' or 'wind' as well as 'spirit', though in the New Testament any meaning other than 'Spirit' is extremely rare. That is why some people translate the first clause of this verse, 'The Spirit breathes where he wills'. That is unlikely: the hearing of sound and the mention of origin and destination are in the first instance more appropriately applied to the wind. Jesus is drawing an analogy between wind and the Spirit, or, more precisely, between the effects of wind and the effects of the Spirit, and the internal cohesion of the analogy is tighter in the Greek text than in English, because there the same word is used.

The point is that the wind can be neither controlled nor understood by human beings (remembering of course that this was written before modern meteorology alleviated at least some of our lack of understanding). But that does not mean we cannot detect the wind's effects. We hear its sound, watch the swaying grasses, see the clouds scudding by, hide in fear before the worst wind storms. So it is with the Spirit. We can neither control him nor understand him. But that does not mean we cannot witness his effects. Where the Spirit works, the effects are undeniable and unmistakable.

How is this relevant to the nature of the new birth? Having drawn the implicit analogy through the ambiguous term 'wind/spirit', Jesus applies it to the new birth by creating a further explicit analogy: *So it is with everyone born of the Spirit.* The person who is 'born of the Spirit' can be neither controlled nor understood by persons of but one birth. As the 'water and spirit' birth is grounded in Ezekiel 36:25–27 (*cf.* notes on v. 5), so there may be an allusion here to Ezekiel 37. There God's breath/Spirit (*rûah/pneuma*) comes upon the valley of dry bones and the dry bones are revived; God's people come to life. Thus it is with everyone born of the Spirit: they have their 'origin and destiny in the unseen God' (Fenton, p. 54), not in 'human decision or a husband's will', for they are 'born of God' (1:13). Both the mysteriousness and the undeniable power of the Spirit of God are displayed in the Scriptures to which Nicodemus had devoted so many years of study.

9-10. Nicodemus' incredulous question is not *How can this be?* (NIV), but 'How can this happen?' Doubtless he himself had for years taught others the conditions of entrance to the kingdom of God, conditions cast in terms of obedience to God's commands, devotion to God, happy submission to his will; but here he is facing a condition he has never heard expressed, the absolute requirement of birth from above. Even after Jesus' explanation, he is frankly sceptical that such a birth can take place. Judging by Jesus' rather sharp retort (v. 10), the question of Nicodemus reflects, not wondering and probing ingenuousness, but frank incredulity. Jesus' response projects the blame in sharp focus: Nicodemus in his role as *Israel's teacher* should have understood these things. The article with this expression (lit. 'the teacher of Israel') suggests he was a recognized master, an established religious authority. 'You are the Reverend Professor Doctor, *and do you not understand these things?*' Nothing could make clearer the fact that Jesus' teaching on the new birth was built on the teaching of the Old Testament (*cf.* notes on 3:5).

11. There is no further report of Nicodemus' replies: dialogue becomes monologue, which in turn becomes a paragraph of reflection by the Evangelist (*cf.* notes on 3:15). Apart from the formulaic *I tell you the truth* (*cf.* notes on 1:51), Jesus speaks in the plural: *we speak . . . we know . . . we testify . . . we have seen.* As in v. 7, the 'you' also becomes plural: hence NIV's *you people.* A few commentators therefore conclude that the historical Jesus thereby identifies himself with his disciples. This is unlikely: at this point in their pilgrimage the disciples could not be described as speaking of what they know and testifying to what they have seen, *viz.* heavenly things (v. 12).

The majority of interpreters detect frank anachronism: v. 11 does not report what Jesus said to Nicodemus. but what the church of John's day said to the synagogue. Bruce (pp. 86-87) makes a virtue of this perceived necessity: the Evangelist does not care whether he relates the witness of Jesus, or the witness of the later church to Jesus, since at bottom the witness is all one and the same. But although it may be 'the same' in the sense that all of it ultimately relates to the same divine self-disclosure in Jesus Christ, the sameness stops there. John is persistently careful to distinguish between what the disciples understood during Jesus' ministry and what they understood only later (*cf.* notes on 2:22, and Carson, 'Mis').

The simplest explanation for the plurals in this verse is that Jesus is sardonically aping the plural that Nicodemus affected when he first approached Jesus (v. 2). 'Rabbi', Nicodemus said, '*we* know you are a teacher who has come from God. . . .' 'I tell you the truth', responds Jesus, '*we* speak of what *we* know, and *we* testify to what *we* have seen' – as if to say, '*We* know one or two things too, *we* do!'

Nicodemus has found Jesus' teaching hard to understand, but Jesus turns that incredulity into a fundamentally Christological question. Nicodemus had approached Jesus with a certain amount of respect (v. 2), but he had not even begun to appreciate who Jesus really was. At bottom, Nicodemus's failure was not a failure of intellect but a failure to believe Jesus' witness: *you people do not accept our testimony*. The failure to believe was more reprehensible than the failure to understand, since it betrayed a fundamentally inadequate appreciation of who Jesus is.

12. The contrast between the 'earthly things' and the 'heavenly things' is not easy to fathom. Some take the 'earthly things' to refer to physical elements such as wind and natural birth, while 'heavenly things' refers to the new birth. But no-one disbelieves in 'earthly things' such as wind and physical birth. A subtler variation of the same interpretation takes the 'earthly things' to refer to birth and the blowing of the wind, but takes the clause *and you do not believe* to mean 'you do not trust and recognize God in these events, nor see how they point parabolically to birth from above'. This seems an extraordinarily generous periphrasis. It is also tangential to the context, for natural birth and the blowing of the wind do not function in the narrative as the appropriate objects of faith by which to gain spiritual insight, but illustrations or analogies of spiritual realities.

On the face of it, the obvious candidate for 'earthly things' is the new birth itself, the subject of Jesus' conversation so far (hence *I have spoken to you of earthly things . . .; cf.* Blank, pp. 62–63). Some reject this interpretation because birth 'of water and the spirit' is 'from above' (*anōthen*), so it can scarcely be considered an 'earthly thing'. But it is 'earthly' in that it takes place here on earth when people are born again. More important, Jesus' teaching on the new birth is elementary. If Nicodemus had apocalyptic leanings, then he might have wanted to know what the new heavens and new earth (Is. 65:17) would be like, what the kingdom of God would be like when it finally dawned. Jesus says, in effect, that entrance into the kingdom depends absolutely on new birth; if Nicodemus stumbles over this elementary point of entry, then what is the use of going on to explain more of the details of life in the kingdom? The 'heavenly things' are then the splendours of the consummated kingdom, and what it means to live under such glorious, ineffable rule.

13. This verse, connected to the preceding verse by *kai* ('and'), provides the explanation for the fact that Jesus is able to speak authoritatively of 'heavenly things'. It is often misunderstood, primarily because it can be translated more than one way. The NIV is misleading: *No-one has ever gone into heaven except (ei mē) the one who came from heaven* – which sounds as if Jesus, the 'one who came from heaven', had previously ascended into heaven as an exception to the rule. This is then taken by many scholars to be a further indication that parts of this chapter are anachronistic. The Evangelist, it is claimed, is writing from the perspective of the church at the end of the first century, looking back on the ascension of Christ decades earlier (*e.g.* Bauer, p. 56; Brown, 1. 145; esp. Nicholson, pp. 91–98, and Borgen, *Logos*, pp. 133–148). But is it very likely that the Evangelist would create so clumsy an anachronism when he is frequently so careful to distinguish between events during Jesus' ministry and understanding that took place only after the resurrection/ exaltation? Even in the immediate context, he goes on to treat the resurrection of Jesus as *future* to the stance at which he has placed Jesus. Moreover this appeal to anachronism does not explain why the Evangelist has so tightly tied this verse to the preceding one.

Resolution is found in the fact that *ei mē*, often translated 'except', can introduce an exception to the general idea that has been introduced, without providing an exception to what is explicitly stated in the immediately preceding clause. English usage in such cases often demands 'but', 'but rather' or 'but only' rather than 'except'. Compare Revelation 21:27: 'Nothing impure will ever enter it, nor will anyone who does what is shameful or deceitful, but only (*ei mē*) those whose names are written in the Lamb's book of life.' Clearly those written in the Lamb's book of life are not thought to be impure, shameful or deceitful; the translation would be highly misleading in this context if *ei mē* were rendered by 'except' (*cf.* also Mt. 12:4; Lk. 4:27; Acts 27:22; probably Gal. 1:19). True, in all these instances the member in the *ei mē* clause proves to be the only one that does the action described in the first clause: in the example from Revelation 21:27, only those whose names are written in the book of life actually enter the holy city. Applied to John 3:13, that might be taken to mean that the only one who has ascended is the one who has descended. But the flow of the argument and the peculiar perfect *anabebēken* ('has ascended') conspire to focus the 'exception' rather differently. Jesus can speak of heavenly things (v. 12), and (*kai*) no-one [else] has ascended into heaven and remained there [so as to be able to speak authoritatively about heavenly things] but only the one who has come down from heaven [is equipped to do so] (*cf.* Lagrange, pp. 80–81; Westcott, 1. 53; Moloney, pp. 53–59).[1]

The Judaism of Jesus' day circulated many stories of bygone saints who had ascended into heaven and received special insight into God's ways and plans. Many of these stories focused on Moses (*cf.* Meeks, pp. 110–111, 192–195, 235–236; Odeberg, pp. 72–94). Jesus insists that no-one has ascended to heaven in such a way as to return to talk about

---

[1]Lest it be thought that this interpretation makes *ei mē* in 3:13 too anomalous, there are instances of still more anomalous uses of these particles, *e.g.* Gal. 1:6–7: 'I am astonished that you are so quickly deserting the one who called you by the grace of Christ and are turning to a different gospel – which is really no gospel at all; only (*ei mē* – NIV 'Evidently') some people are throwing you into confusion . . .'

heavenly things. Only in heaven can true wisdom be found (*cf.* Pr. 30:4). But Jesus can speak of heavenly things, not because he ascended to heaven from a home on earth and then descended to tell others of his experiences, but because heaven was his home in the first place, and therefore he has 'inherently the fulness of heavenly knowledge' (Westcott, 1. 53).[1] He is *the one who came from heaven*; he is the revelatory *Son of Man* (*cf.* notes on 1:51). (*Cf.* Additional Note.)

14. The connections between this verse and the preceding verses are two. First, Jesus moves from an explanation of the new birth in terms of the categories 'water' and 'spirit' used by Ezekiel (*cf.* notes on 3:5) to a narrative passage, the well-known account of the bronze snake in the desert (Nu. 21:4–9). That bronze snake on a pole was the means God used to give new (physical) life to the children of Israel if they were bitten in the plague of snakes that had been sent in as a punishment for the persistent murmuring. By God's provision, new life was graciously granted. Why then should it be thought so strange that by the gracious provision of this same God there should be new spiritual life, indeed 'eternal life' (v. 15)?

Second, the deepest point of connection between the bronze snake and Jesus was in the act of being 'lifted up'. Moses *lifted up* the snake on a pole so that all who were afflicted in the camp might look and live. In the same way, *the Son of Man must be lifted up*. The Greek verb for 'lifted up' (*hypsoō*) in its four occurrences in this Gospel (*cf.* 8:28; 12:32, 34) always combines the notions of being physically lifted up on the cross, with the notion of exaltation. This is a theological adaptation of the literal ('to lift up') and the figurative ('to enhance') meanings of the verb. Even Isaiah brings together the themes of being lifted up and being glorified, and this in the context of the suffering servant (Is. 52:13 – 53:12, esp. 52:13 LXX).[2] If Jesus is the 'one who came from heaven' (v. 13), how shall he return? The Synoptists think of the crucifixion and the exaltation as temporally discrete steps; John makes it clear that Jesus' return to the glory he had with the Father before the world began (17:5) is accomplished by being 'lifted up' on the cross. It is this exaltation that draws people to him (8:28; 12:32). If in v. 13 the Son of Man is the revealer, the one who came down from heaven, here he is the sufferer and the exalted one – but it transpires that it is precisely in the matrix of suffering and exaltation that God most clearly reveals himself in the person of his Son. The theological connection between resurrection and exaltation is not infrequent in the New Testament (*e.g.* Acts 2:32–33; Rom. 8:34; Eph. 1:20; 2:6; Col. 3:1; 1 Pet. 1:21). John goes farther, and

---

[1] Contrast the claims of the apocalyptical visionaries amongst Jesus' Jewish contemporaries: *cf.* C. Rowland, *The Open Heaven* (SPCK/Crossroad, 1982), pp. 52–58, *passim*.

[2] The connection between *hypsoō* and crucifixion may have suggested itself to the Evangelist in part because of the Aramaic term *zᵉqap* ('to lift up', 'to crucify'). *Cf.* G. Bertram, *TDNT* 8. 610. On a possible Hebrew parallel, *cf.* Dodd, *IFG*, p. 377, and esp. H. Hollis, *NTS* 35, 1989, pp. 475–478 (on Gn. 40:13, 19 – though the LXX does not there read *hypsoō*).

theologically ties together the crucifixion, the resurrection and the exaltation.

Nicodemus, of course, could not have been expected to grasp both of these connections at the time. But the first one should have been clear. Nicodemus was being challenged to turn to Jesus for new birth in much the same way as the ancient Israelites were commanded to turn to the bronze snake for new life. Only when Nicodemus saw Jesus on the cross, or perhaps only in still later reflection on the cross, would it become clear that the 'lifting up'/exaltation of Jesus took place on a brutal block of wood on a forsaken site outside Jerusalem.

In the Fourth Gospel these themes – the divine revelation, exaltation and the obedient suffering of the Son – constantly congregate around the title 'the Son of Man' (*cf.* notes on 1:51). He *must* be lifted up: that is the determined purpose of God (*cf.* Mk. 8:31; 10:45). By his being lifted up, Jesus the Son of Man will be returned to the glory he once shared with his Father, while those who turn to him, as the Israelites turned to the bronze snake, will experience new birth.

15. The purpose of Jesus' being lifted up is now made explicit: *that everyone who believes may have eternal life in him* (taking *en autō*, 'in him', to modify 'eternal life', since John uses a quite different expression, *eis auton*, in connection with belief 'in him'). The verb 'to believe' is used absolutely (*i.e.* without an object) elsewhere in John as the condition or ground of eternal life (6:47; 20:31). The belief is certainly belief in Jesus Christ, including confidence in the truthfulness of his teaching (*cf.* v. 12). Nicodemus began by saying he recognized that Jesus was a teacher 'come from God' (v. 2), but at this point he neither understands him (v. 10) nor believes him (v. 12). But many, probably including Nicodemus, will believe him once he has been 'lifted up', the very purpose of which is that those who believe in him might have eternal life, and have it *in him*.

These two words put Jesus in quite a different category from the bronze snake. Every reader of the Old Testament knew that eventually that snake had to be destroyed by King Hezekiah, because too many people treated it as if it had some inherent, magical power (2 Ki. 18:4). What spared the Israelites from the mortal threat of the desert snakes was God's grace; the means was the bronze snake. But we must say more than that about Jesus. The Father has granted the Son to have life in himself (5:26); he is himself the resurrection and the life (11:25), and those who believe have life *in him*. Here then is the frankest answer to Nicodemus' question. 'How can this happen?' (v. 9). The kingdom of God is seen or entered, new birth is experienced, and eternal life begins, through the saving cross-work of Christ, received by faith.

The expression *eternal life* (*zōē aiōnios*) here makes its first appearance in the Fourth Gospel. Properly it means 'life of the age (*aiōn*) to come', and therefore resurrection life. But in John's Gospel that life may in some measure be experienced before the end, just as in the Synoptics the kingdom dawns before the end. Moreover, those who have read the

Prologue will recall that life resides in the Word: 'in him was life' (1:4).[1]
The eternal life begun by the new birth is nothing less than the eternal
life of the eternal Word.

Additional note

13. Although the words 'who is in heaven', appended to 'the Son of
Man', are absent from the two oldest manuscripts of John (P[66] and P[75]),
they occur in many others, sometimes with minor variations. If original,
they constitute strong support for the anachronism many find in the
verse (discussed above). It is frequently argued that one can easily
understand why copyists might have found it difficult and left it out, but
one cannot easily think of a good reason for inserting it – *i.e.* it is the
'harder reading' which, all things being equal, is more likely original.
But if no sensible copyist would have put it in, one wonders why we
should think John would put it in. Must the author always be judged
less sensible than the copyist? It seems best to regard the additional
words as an interpretative gloss that reflected later Christological
developments at a time when dogmatics was more influential than
sensitivity to chronology and historical development (*cf.* Metzger, pp.
203–204).

6. Extended comment I (3:16–21)

In two passages in this Gospel, both in this chapter (3:15–21 and
3:31–36), the words of a speaker (Jesus and John the Baptist respectively)
are succeeded by the explanatory reflections of the Evangelist. Because
the ancient texts did not use quotation marks or other orthographical
equivalents, the exact point of transition is disputed. In the first
incident, Nicholson (p. 89) thinks the dialogue ends at v. 10, with all of
vv. 11–21 being the comment of the Evangelist. This is unlikely: the title
'Son of Man' is so characteristically reserved for Jesus' lips as a form of
self-identification that it is unthinkable that he ended before v. 15. The
same problem attends the view of Beasley-Murray (p. 46), and others
before him, that makes 3:12–21 structurally parallel to 3:31–36. Some
argue that Jesus' monologue extends to the end of v. 21. But vv. 16–21
read more plausibly as the Evangelist's meditation. For instance, the
expression 'one and only' (*monogenēs*) is a word used by the Evangelist
(1:14, 18; *cf.* 1 Jn. 4:9), and is not elsewhere placed on the lips of Jesus or
of anyone else in this Gospel. Nor does Jesus normally refer to God as *ho
theos* ('God').[2]

Segovia (p. 166) and others argue that since the advent of redaction

---

[1] J. G. van der Watt, *Neot* 31, 1989, pp. 217–228, has shown that 'life' and 'eternal life'
refer to the same thing and have the same meaning, but that there is a stylistic difference
between the two: the simple 'life', for instance, is used in grammatical constructions and
thematic associations where the larger expression does not occur.

[2] For these and other characteristics of 3:16–21, *cf.* Mary Steele, *NOT* 2/2, 1988, pp. 51–58.

criticism it has become futile to attempt to distinguish between the original voice of Jesus and 'passages that betray the evangelist's own viewpoint'. He is right, but misses the point. If the Evangelist's reportage captures the essence of Jesus' teaching, but customarily in the Evangelist's words, and if the Evangelist is in happy agreement with Jesus' teaching, then clearly the distinction Segovia identifies cannot be made. But if the Evangelist usually casts his Gospel in such a way as to distinguish between the reported speech of various individuals (however much cast in his own linguistic patterns), and his own reflective comments, then if he fails to do so in a couple of instances it is noteworthy.

16. As the new birth, the acquisition of eternal life, has been grounded in the 'lifting up' of the Son (vv. 14–15), so also that 'lifting up', the climax of the Son's mission, is itself grounded in the love of God. The mission of the Son and its consequences is the theme of this paragraph, but John begins by insisting that the Son's mission was itself the consequence of God's love. The Greek construction behind *so loved that he gave his one and only Son* (*houtōs* plus *hōste* plus the indicative instead of the infinitive) emphasizes the intensity of the love, and insists that the envisaged consequence really did ensue;[1] the words 'his one and only Son' (*cf.* notes on 1:14) stress the greatness of the gift. The Father gave his best, his unique and beloved Son (*cf.* Rom. 8:32).

Both the verb 'to love' (*agapaō*) and the noun 'love' (*agapē*) occur much more frequently in chs. 13 – 17 than anywhere else in the Fourth Gospel, reflecting the fact that John devotes special attention to the love relationships amongst the Father, the Son and the disciples. The Father loves the Son (3:35; 10:17; 15:9–10; 17:23–24, 26; using another verb, 5:20), the Son loves the Father (14:31); Jesus loves his own, his true disciples (11:5; 13:1, 33, 34; 14:21; 15:9–10, 12; 21:7, 20), and they must love him (14:15, 21, 23f., 28; 21:15–26). They must also love one another (13:34–35; 15:12–13, 17; 17:26). Sometimes John speaks of the Father's love for the disciples (14:21, 23; 17:23), but more frequently the Father's love for the disciples is mediated through his Son. The world, fallen and rebellious human beings in general, does not and cannot love God (3:19; 5:42; 8:42).

From this pattern of relationships it is clear that there is nothing in the words *agapaō* and *agapē* themselves to suggest that the love of which John speaks is invariably spontaneous, self-generated, without reference to the loved one. John 'uses the same words both for God's spontaneous, gracious, love for men, and also for the responsive relation of the disciple to God, to which man is moved not by free unmerited favour to God (which would be impossible), but by a sense of God's favour to him' (Barrett, p. 215). This does not mean that for John there is no such thing as spontaneous, self-generated love, only that it is not tied

---

[1] *Cf.* C. Spicq, *RB* 95, 1958, pp. 358–360.

to a single word-group. More than any New Testament writer, John develops a theology of the love relations between the Father and the Son, and makes it clear that, as applied to human beings, the love of God is not the consequence of their loveliness but of the sublime truth that 'God is love' (1 Jn. 4:16).

From this survey it is clear that it is atypical for John to speak of God's love for *the world*, but this truth is therefore made to stand out as all the more wonderful. Jews were familiar with the truth that God loved the children of Israel; here God's love is not restricted by race. Even so, God's love is to be admired not because the world is so big and includes so many people, but because the world is so bad: that is the customary connotation of *kosmos* ('world'; *cf.* notes on 1:9). The world is so wicked that John elsewhere forbids Christians to love it or anything in it (1 Jn. 2:15–17). There is no contradiction between this prohibition and the fact that God does love it. Christians are not to love the world with the selfish love of participation; God loves the world with the self-less, costly love of redemption.

Many scholars find it impossible to reconcile this verse with the more restrictive circle of love (the Father, the Son and the disciples) that dominates the rest of the book, and with the persistent threat of judgment that stands over the world (*e.g.* 3:36). They therefore postulate an interpolation or the influence of some other source not properly assimilated into the book. Segovia (pp. 166–170) attempts a reconciliation by postulating that the narrower circle of love represents the post-resurrection status, when the Christians are set over against 'the Jews' and 'the world', which by definition is under condemnation and cannot be loved. The statement that God 'loved the world' belongs to the pre-resurrection period when the radical polarization had not yet taken place. This analysis misunderstands John at several points; worse, it overlooks a dominant theme of many of the biblical books. All believers have been chosen out of the world (15:19); they are not something other than 'world' when the gospel first comes to them. They would not have become true disciples apart from the love of God for the world. Even after the circle of believers is formed and the resurrection has taken place, these Christians are mandated to continue their witness, aided by the Spirit, in hopes of winning others from the world (15:26–27; 20:21). In other words, God maintains the same stance toward the world after the resurrection that he had before: he pronounces terrifying condemnation on the grounds of the world's sin, while still loving the world so much that the gift he gave to the world, the gift of his Son, remains the world's only hope.

This dual stance of God is a commonplace of biblical theology. The holy God finds wicked actions to be detestable things (Ezk. 18:10–13), but that does not prevent him from crying out, 'Do I take any pleasure in the death of the wicked? declares the Sovereign LORD. Rather, am I not pleased when they turn from their ways and live?' (Ezk. 18:23). The same dual track is found in God's stance to other nations. Moab, for instance, is so wicked that God's decree has gone forth: 'Make her drunk, for she has defied the LORD. Let Moab wallow in her vomit; let her be an object of ridicule. . . . In Moab I will put an end to those who make offerings on the high places and burn incense to their gods. . . . I have broken Moab like a jar that no-one wants. . . . Moab will be destroyed as a nation because she defied the LORD' (Jer. 48:26, 35, 38, 42). At the same time, the God who takes no pleasure in the death of the wicked declares, 'Therefore I wail over Moab, for all Moab I cry out. . . . So my heart laments for Moab like a flute; it laments like a flute for the men of Kir Hareseth' (Je. 48:31, 36).

Similarly in the New Testament: if it is true that the 'wrath of God is being revealed from heaven against all the godlessness and wickedness of men who suppress the truth by their wickedness' (Rom. 1:18), and if 'the wages of sin is death' (Rom. 6:23), it is also true, wonderfully true, that 'the gift of God is eternal life in Christ Jesus our Lord' (Rom. 6:23). Christians were not born Christians; they 'were by nature objects of wrath' (Eph. 2:3). Despite this desperate status, they were made alive with Christ because of God's great love for them, this God 'who is rich in mercy' (Eph. 2:4-5). Examples of this paired stance of God could be multiplied. Apart from God's love for the world, the very world that stands under his wrath, no-one would be saved; where there is a redeemed community, it stands in a different and richer relationship of love with God than does the world, but that distinction cannot legitimately be made to call in question the love of God for a world under his judgment.

Because John 3:16 is sandwiched between vv. 14-15 and v. 17, the fact that God *gave* his one and only Son is tied both to the Son's incarnation (v. 17) and to his death (vv. 14-15). That is the immediate result of the love of God for the world: the mission of the Son. His ultimate purpose is the salvation of those in the world who believe in him (*eis auton*, not *en autō* as in v. 15). Whoever believes in him experiences new birth (3:3, 5), has eternal life (3:15, 16), is saved (3:17); the alternative is to perish (*cf.* also 10:28), to lose one's life (12:25), to be doomed to destruction (17:12, cognate with 'to perish'). There is no third option.

17. The theme of the mission of the Son is common enough in the Synoptics (*e.g.* Mt. 9:13; 15:24; Mk. 1:38; Lk. 4:18, 43). Here John aims to make a simple point, a clarification of the purpose of that mission, already articulated in v. 16. God's purpose in sending his Son *into the world* (a phrase that distinguishes the sending of Jesus from the sending of John the Baptist, 1:6) was not *to condemn the world, but to save the world through him* (*cf.* 12:47). The verb rendered 'to condemn', *krinō*, can mean simply 'to judge'; but in this and many other passages in John, the judgment is clearly adverse (since it stands over against 'to save'), hence 'to condemn'. Thus the believer is not condemned (*krinō*, 3:18) and will not be condemned (5:24, lit. 'does not come into judgment' [*krisis*]).

Some find it difficult to reconcile this verse with 9:39, where Jesus declares. 'For judgment (*krisis*) I have come into this world. . . .'; indeed,

John insists that God has given Jesus 'authority to judge (*krinō*) because he is the Son of Man' (5:27). Two factors alleviate the difficulty. First, in these two passages the meaning of *krinō/krisis* is neutral. Anyone familiar with Daniel 7:13–14 would not be surprised to learn that the Son of Man has authority to pronounce judgment, and that he came for that purpose. That is rather different from saying he came to pronounce condemnation. Second, and more important, the Son of Man came into an already lost and condemned world. He did not come into a neutral world in order to save some and condemn others; he came into a lost world (for that is the nature of the 'world', 1:9) in order to save some. That not all of the world will be saved is made perfectly clear by the next verses (vv. 18–21); but God's purpose in the mission of Jesus was to bring salvation to it. That is why Jesus is later called 'the Saviour of the world' (4:42; *cf.* 1 Jn. 4:14).

18. No longer does John speak of 'the world' holistically. Instead he distinguishes between the one who believes and is therefore not condemned, and the one who does not believe. The latter *stands condemned already (ēdē kekritai) because he has not believed in the name of God's one and only Son*. Already in need of a Saviour before God's Son comes on his saving mission, this person compounds his or her guilt by not believing in the name of that Son. As with the arrogant critic who mocks a masterpiece, it is not the masterpiece that is condemned, but the critic. There is no need to await the final day of judgment (though it will come, 5:26–29): the person who disbelieves in the Father's one and only Son *stands condemned already*, and God's wrath remains on him (3:36). Thus the potential for condemnation is bound up with the mission of the Son to bring salvation. Although John does not explicitly appeal to Paul's 'justification by faith' doctrine, the substance of the matter is found here.

19–21. The essence of this self-incurred condemnation is pictured in the metaphorical terms, light and darkness. The *verdict* (Gk. *krisis*) is entirely negative in vv. 19–20. *Light has come into the world*; with the incarnation of the Word, the light shone in the darkness (*cf.* notes on 1:4–5) even more brightly than at the creation. As the light of the world (8:12), Jesus is the revelation of God and the objectification of divine holiness and purity. But *men loved darkness instead of light*: they preferred to live without such knowledge of God, without such brilliant purity. The reason was fundamentally moral: *their deeds were evil*. They were not willing to live by the truth; they valued their pride more than their integrity, their prejudice more than contrite faith. Worse, anyone in this camp hates the light and refuses to come to it *for fear that his deeds will be exposed (elengchthē)*. The verb suggests not only exposure but shame and conviction (*cf.* notes on 16:8ff.).

The alternative is to do the truth (NIV *lives by the truth*), a Semitic expression which means 'to act faithfully', 'to act honourably' (*e.g.* Gn. 47:29, RV; Ne. 9:33). The person who acts this way happily *comes into the light*; there is no reason not to. Nevertheless it is important to notice that

v. 21 is not cast in strict antithetic parallelism to v. 20. There are two important differences. First, the person who loves the darkness practices evil, an indeterminate succession of worthless deeds (the object in Gk. is anarthrous, *ho phaula prassōn*); his counterpart does *the* truth (*ho de poiōn tēn alētheian*), which suggests adherence to the truth as it is in Jesus Christ. Second, and more important, while the lover of darkness shuns the light out of fear of exposure, shame and conviction, the lover of light does not prance forward to parade his wares with cocky self-righteousness, but *comes into the light, so that it may be seen plainly that what he has done has been done through God*. This strange expression makes it clear that the lover of light is not some intrinsically superior person. If he or she enjoys the light, it is because all that has been performed, for which there is no shame or conviction, has been done 'through God' – 'in union with Him, and therefore by His power' (Westcott, 1. 124). Nor will it do (with Lattke, pp. 64–85, and others), to suggest that these light-lovers are Gnostics or some other group who love the light from the beginning, who never did belong to the 'world', who have always responded positively to divine revelation. After all, even the Twelve were chosen out of the world (15:19). These verses do not tell us how one moves from the darkness to the light, *i.e.* how one becomes a true disciple, a 'Christian', but simply focuses on the fundamental distinction that must be made between those who at the moment are rejecting the ultimate revelation of God in Jesus Christ, and those who are delighting in it. The one follows its course because its deeds are evil; the other follows its course not because its deeds are righteous, but because it longs to show that its deeds have been done through God.

The purpose of these three verses, then, is not to encourage readers to think they fall into a deterministic category bound up with their intrinsic nature, but to make them see the imminence of their danger (the verdict is being declared), and the fundamentally moral reasons why people hate the light. John stresses these points in the hope that his readers will beseech God that all they do may be done through him – in short, that they will turn to the 'lifted up' Son of Man with the same simple, desperate, unqualified faith as the Israelites displayed who turned to the bronze snake in the desert (vv. 13–15). By such faith and such faith alone can anyone experience the new birth (vv. 3, 5) and thereby gain eternal life (vv. 15–16).

7. John the Baptist's continuing witness concerning Jesus (3:22–30)

This is the fourth successive section to point out ways in which Jesus fulfils and surpasses Judaism: in 2:1–11, Jesus provides new wine that vastly surpasses anything that contemporary Judaism could afford, and renders obsolete the stone jars of purification; in 2:12–25, Jesus displaces the temple and thereby intimates that the temple's proper role is best seen as an anticipation of the ultimate point of mediation between God and man; in 3:1–21, Jesus fulfils prophecies of a 'water and spirit' regeneration, and proves in his death to be the ultimate antitype of the snake 'lifted up' in the desert; and hence (3:22–30) Jesus surpasses John the Baptist and any baptism or rite of purification he may represent. In the next chapter (4:1ff.), the uniqueness of Jesus will be set against movements that extend beyond the boundaries of Palestinian Judaism.

Some estimate that the juxtaposition of the new birth section (3:1–21) and these next verses, with their mention of baptism, constitutes solid evidence that John understood 'born of water and spirit' to refer to baptism. But too much stands against such a view: (1) The most natural reading of 'born of water and spirit' lies elsewhere (*cf.* notes on 3:5). (2) Baptism is not a major theme of 3:22–36; Christology is. Insofar as baptism is mentioned, it is associated with the old covenant purification rites (*cf.* v. 25). (3) If 3:22–36 pictures Jesus baptizing more people than John the Baptist, the focus of interest lies in the relative stature of Jesus and of John, *not* in the nature of baptism itself; for on that topic, the Evangelist by a parenthetical note at 4:2 will shortly *distance* Jesus from the actual act of baptizing.

22. *After this* – the expression gives no indication of the length of the interval (*cf.* notes on 2:12) – Jesus and his disciples *went out into the Judean countryside*. That is the most likely translation of the Greek (lit. 'into the Judean land'). The previous episode took place in Jerusalem (2:23), which was part of Judea; Jesus therefore could not have entered Judea, for he was already in it. Some have therefore postulated various displacements of the text, or poorly executed connections between disparate sources; but each of these theories breeds new difficulties more serious than the one thereby resolved (*cf.* Barrett, p. 219). Certainly these verses prepare us for ch. 4 (*cf.* notes on 4:38). It seems best to render the phrase as in NIV, and assume that John simply means Jesus and his disciples went out from the urban to the rural areas of Judea.

Only the Fourth Gospel mentions that Jesus baptized, and 4:2 specifies that he himself did not perform the rite but left it to his disciples. The context requires that this be taken as water baptism, not the baptism in the Holy Spirit the Baptist promised Jesus would administer (1:33; *cf.* 7:37–39).

23. Jesus' preaching and baptizing ministry overlapped with that of John the Baptist. The location, *Aenon near Salim*, is disputed, but both of the principal possibilities, Salim near Shechem and Salim about six miles south of Bethshan, are within the region of Samaria, at that time part of the Roman province of Judea. 'Aenon' is a transliterated Semitic word meaning 'springs'; both potential sites are well endowed with *plenty of water* (lit. 'many waters', which doubtless means 'many springs'). If the explanation given in this commentary of the Baptist's location at his first appearance is correct (*cf.* notes on 1:28), this means he had moved south by this time. Despite the onset of Jesus' ministry, *people were constantly coming to be baptised* by John the Baptist.

24. The purpose of this remark is not to state the obvious (after all,

John could scarcely have been baptizing if he had already been incarcerated) but to explain that what is related here (and probably in all of chs. 2 – 4) takes place earlier than any ministry recorded in the Synoptic Gospels. The Synoptists adopt the stance of Mark 1:14, which places the opening of Jesus' *Galilean* ministry in the period *after* John the Baptist had been arrested, without reporting any earlier *Judean* ministry. Apparently the Evangelist is aware that such a construction had circulated widely, and he does not want his credibility diminished by failing to explain the apparent discrepancy. (This has some obvious bearing on whether John had read any other of the canonical Gospels [*cf.* Introduction, §§ II, III], and on when Jesus cleared the temple, 2:12–17.)

25. The argument that developed between John's disciples and *a certain Jew* (the plural reading, 'the Jews', is less likely: *cf.* Metzger, p. 205) was *over the matter of ceremonial washing* (same word as in 2:6). The debate, in other words, did not focus on the relative merits of the baptism administered by John versus the baptism administered by Jesus, but over distinctly Jewish purification rites. Possibly the clash arose over the relation between John's baptism and more traditional Jewish practices, or the practices of other prominent Jewish religious figures. In addition to the rites of purification that had evolved more or less in dependence on the Old Testament, there were various groups who bathed daily in cold water, with a view to purity (*e.g.* Jos., *Bel.* ii. 129; *Vita* 11; Tosefta, *Yadayim* 2:20). Certainly John's baptism was open to misunderstanding by Jewish observers. Josephus, for instance, in his description of John's rite, rather badly distorts the place of repentance in John's teaching and baptismal practice (*Ant.* xviii. 117).

26. Apparently the debate with the Jew fostered further reflections amongst some of John's disciples over the durability of their master's ministry, especially in light of the rising popularity of Jesus. That they addressed John as *Rabbi* is not inappropriate, considering the term bore no technical associations at the beginning of the first century (*cf.* notes on 1:38). Although it is possible to interpret their words as a joyful declaration that their master's prediction regarding the supremacy of Jesus (1:26–34) was coming to pass, it is far more likely that their words are resentful and embittered. Otherwise the tone of John's response to them (vv. 27–30) is incomprehensible. Moreover their *everyone is going to him* is doubtless exaggeration sponsored by resentment, since John was still attracting considerable crowds (v. 23), even if they were now smaller than those attending Jesus. The argument that the Evangelist includes this material because Christians are in his time opposing a continuing group of followers of John the Baptist[1] is not very convincing (*cf.* notes on 1:19ff.).

27. The wide range of interpretations of this verse (What is given –

---

[1]For the most recent defence of this view, *cf.* M. A. Chevallier, *NTS* 32, 1984, pp. 528–543.

truth, grace, or the capacity to receive either? To whom is the gift given, Christ or the believer? Does the verse explain why John's crowds are diminishing, or why Christ's are increasing?) arises from the fact that John casts his response in the form of a maxim, an aphorism. As such it is extremely broad: God's sovereignty stands hidden behind all human claims, for a human being does not have anything but what he has received (cf. 1 Cor. 4:7). In a genuinely theistic universe this must be true: as frequently forgotten as it is, the maxim is almost self-evident (cf. Carson, pp. 125–127). In the immediate context, John the Baptist is applying the aphorism to the situation brought to his attention by his disciples. All gifts come *from heaven* (a reverential circumlocution for 'from God'), including the call to a particular station in the stream of redemptive history. For John the Baptist to have wished he were someone else, called to serve in a way many would judge more prominent, would simply be covetousness by another name; if the person he envied were the Messiah himself, he would be annulling the excellent ministry God had given him. Deep discontent over God's wise, sovereign disposition of people and things would in that instance betray not only unbelief and faithfulness, but the worst form of the perennial human sin, the arrogance that wants to be God and stand where God stands.

28. But in fact, John the Baptist, unlike some of his followers, is not perturbed by news of Jesus' rising popularity. He had always made clear to his followers that he was not the Christ (1:20), but that he was sent as his herald (1:26–34). Unlike many preachers for whom humility is little more than an affectation, John meant what he said. Both John and Jesus were given their roles by heaven (v. 27), and John was entirely content with his. Small wonder that the assessment of John provided by both Jesus (Mt. 11:7–11) and the fourth Evangelist (10:40–42) is so positive.

29. This verse is a parable that explains John the Baptist's understanding of his own role. The *friend who attends the bridegroom*, the ancient equivalent of a 'best man' who organized the details and presided over a Judean wedding (Galilean weddings were ordered on somewhat different lines), found his greatest joy in watching the ceremony proceed without a problem, and in knowing that the groom and his bride were being united with great rejoicing.

We cannot imagine that John the Baptist was ignorant of the many Old Testament passages that depict Israel or the faithful within Israel as the bride of the LORD (*e.g.* Is. 62:4–5; Je. 2:2; Ho. 2:16–20). Rather obliquely John is therefore also saying that the Jesus he has introduced to the faithful remnant in Israel is none other than Israel's King and Messiah. Jesus may allude to the same heritage of understanding in Mark 2:19. The Evangelist could not have been unaware of the fact that the post-resurrection church would picture Christ as the bridegroom and his church as the bride – the continuation and transformation of the Old Testament theme (*e.g.* 2 Cor. 11:2; Eph. 5:25–27; Rev. 21:2, 9; 22:17). The joy of the 'best man' belongs to the Baptist, *and it is now complete*. This Gospel repeatedly associates 'joy' with the verb *plēroun* ('to fulfil', 'to complete'); here John the Baptist means that he has the final and ultimate satisfaction of knowing that his God-given (v. 27) ministry has been successful. The rising prominence of Jesus, as upsetting as it may have been to some of John's disciples, floods John himself with surpassing joy, because that was exactly what he himself had worked for. *Cf.* Additional Note.

30. In short, John says, *He must become greater; I must become less.* The 'must' (*dei*) is nothing less than the determined will of God. John finds his joy, not in grudgingly conceding victory to a superior opponent, but in wholeheartedly embracing God's will, and the supremacy it assigns to Jesus. A great deal of later Christian piety has turned on the same truth.

Additional note

29–30. There is good evidence that in ancient Sumerian and Babylonian law the best man was absolutely prohibited from marrying the bride. The influence of this view on the Old Testament period is probably to be traced in Judges 14 – 15, where even the Philistines recognize the rightness of Samson's grievance. If this perspective, mediated through the Old Testament, descends as far as John the Baptist, then the Baptist is saying that he is 'the last who could compete with the bridegroom, for under no circumstances is he allowed to marry the bride'.[1]

8. *Extended comment II* (3:31–36)

Like vv. 16–21 (*cf.* notes), these verses appear to be the reflective explanation of the Evangelist himself.

31–32. These verses bring together several of the themes from the entire chapter (which is one reason why the suggestion that they properly belong after v. 12 is without adequate defence). From the immediate context, the Evangelist is explaining *why* Jesus the incarnate Word must become greater (v. 30): he alone is *from above* and is therefore *above all*. The Greek for 'from above', *anōthen*, immediately recalls 3:3: the new birth from above can be experienced only by faith in the One who is from above. By contrast, all others are *from the earth*: the word is *gē*, and, unlike 'world' (*kosmos*; *cf.* notes on 1:9), betrays nothing of sinfulness but only of finitude and limitation. In the immediate context, John the Baptist 'must become less' (v. 30) because he is *from the earth* and therefore *belongs to the earth* (the two *ek* phrases signify origin and kind respectively). Inevitably, he *speaks as one from the earth*: he called people to repentance and to baptism in water, but he could not reveal heaven's counsels, nor could he offer regeneration from above, the

---

[1] *Cf.* A van Selms, *JNES* 9, 1950, pp. 65–75, esp. p. 75. I am indebted to Prof. Carl Armerding for this reference.

long-promised renewal of water and spirit (v. 5). His references to the Holy Spirit were cast as promises of what another would be and do (1:32–34). Thus although he was sent from God (1:6), he too fits into the restriction of v. 13: only the Son of Man can speak with supreme authority of heavenly things, for he alone *testifies to what he has seen and heard* in the heavenly sphere.

The last three words of v. 31, *is above all*, may well be a gloss. That they merely repeat something said at the opening of the verse is no evidence for omission: John is given to repetitions (*cf.* notes on 1:2). On the other hand, the shorter reading is early and widely spread. If the omission is original, the text reads, 'The one who comes from heaven testifies to what he has seen and heard'.

John pessimistically evaluates the reception of the one from above: *no-one accepts his testimony*. In this he is merely repeating the evaluation of Jesus himself (3:11).

33–34. As in 1:11–12, the negative generalization admits certain exceptions. By accepting Jesus' testimony as to what he has seen and heard, the believer *has certified that God is truthful* – not just that Jesus is truthful, but that *God* is truthful. *For* (an important logical connective) *the one whom God has sent speaks the words of God*. Jesus so completely says and does all that God says and does, and only what God says and does (*e.g.* 5:19–30; 6:37–40; 8:29), that to believe Jesus is to believe God. Conversely, not to believe Jesus is to call God a liar (*cf.* 12:44–50; 1 Jn. 5:10).

Throughout redemptive history, God spoke to his people through many accredited messengers. Each received that measure of the Spirit that was required for his or her assigned task. Three centuries after John wrote, Rabbi Aha rightly commented that the Holy Spirit who rested on the prophets did so according to the measure (*bᵉmišqal*) of each prophet's assignment (*Leviticus Rabbah* 15:2). Not so to Jesus: to him *God gives the Spirit without limit* (this is almost certainly the correct rendering).[1] John the Baptist had already testified that he had seen the Spirit descend *and remain* on Jesus (1:32–33), in fulfilment of Isaiah's prophecy (Is. 11:2; 42:1; 61:1); the same truth is repeated in new form. (*Cf.* also the notes on 4:23–24.)

35. That it is God who gives the Spirit without measure to the Son (v. 34) is reinforced by the development of the argument in v. 35: *The Father loves the Son and has placed everything in his hands* – which is the more generalizing comment of which the statement about the unlimited gift of the Spirit is its more particular outworking.

Though it is the Father who sends and the Son who is sent (3:16, 17), though it is the Son who invariably obeys the Father, not the reverse (*cf.* 8:29), their relationship is nevertheless one of love (*cf.* 5:20; 10:17; 15:9;

[1]The alternative is to construe the last clause of v. 34 as if Christ were the subject: Christ does not give the Spirit in merely measured fashion to his followers. That may be true, but it does not fit the context well, and it loses the close connection with v. 35, a connection nicely preserved on the assumption that God is the subject of this last clause in v. 34.

17:23–24, 26). For the verb *agapaō*, 'to love', *cf.* notes on 3:16. Another verb for 'to love', *phileō*, occurs in a similar declaration of the love of the Father for the Son, in 5:20. Because of his love for the Son, the Father has given the Spirit to him without limit, and *has placed everything in his hands* (*cf.* Mt. 11:27; Lk. 10:22). Even the unfolding of redemptive history finds its ultimate source in the loving relationships in the Godhead. 'The Son is the Father's envoy plenipotentiary, his perfect spokesman and revealer' (Bruce, p. 97).

36. This verse is a fitting climax to the entire chapter. By laying out the only two alternatives, genuine faith and defiant disobedience, this verse once more brings to the fore the threat of looming judgment (*cf.* vv. 19–21). *Whoever believes the Son* (*cf.* 1:12; 3:3, 5, 15, 16) *has eternal life*, i.e. the life of the age to come, experienced now even if consummated only later (*cf.* 5:20–21, 25–26; 17:2). But whoever disobeys the Son (that is what the verb means, though NIV's *whoever rejects the Son* is close enough) *will not see life* (*cf.* 'seeing' the kingdom of God, v. 3), *for God's wrath remains on him.* If faith in the Son is the only way to inherit eternal life, and is commanded by God himself, then failure to trust him is as much disobedience as unbelief. The antithesis to seeing life is seeing death (8:51). Judgment has already been threatened (vv. 19–20); now it is alarmingly explicit. *God's wrath* is not some impersonal principle of retribution, but the personal response of a holy God who comes to his own world, sadly fallen into rebellion, and finds few who want anything to do with him. Such people are 'condemned already' (*cf.* v. 18).

This does not collapse the notion of eschatological judgment into present, spiritual experience, since the future judgment remains (5:28–29). Rather, it is in line with the New Testament insistence that the age to come can no longer be set off absolutely from the present age, now that Jesus the Messiah has come. Believers already enjoy the eternal life that will be consummated in the resurrection of their bodies at the parousia; unbelievers stand under the looming wrath of God that will be consummated in their resurrection and condemnation (*cf.* Ladd, pp. 307f.).

9. Jesus and the Samaritan woman (4:1–42)

Although various outlines of these verses have been suggested (most recently, Okure in her excellent study proposes narration [vv. 1–26], exposition [vv. 31–38] and demonstration [vv. 28–30, 39–42]), the entire narrative hangs together so well as a unit of thought that even the best suggestions of discrete movements within the passages strike some readers as artificial (note that Okure has to break up the 'demonstration' section). On the unity and cohesion of the passage, *cf.* Boers.

1–3. The connections between this account and the preceding chapters occur at several levels. Water symbolism continues (*cf.* 2:6; 3:5; 4:10ff.). Jesus continues a series of dialogues, in each of which he discloses himself as the fulfilment of Old Testament promises and institutions, as understood by highly orthodox Judaism (represented by

Nicodemus, 3:1ff.) or by circles widely viewed as flawed and even heterodox (represented by the Samaritans, 4:1ff.). More immediately, the debate about purification and baptism in the preceding verses (3:22ff.), precipitated by Jesus' rising popularity, constitutes a specific link. If the disciples of John the Baptist had not failed to note the extent of Jesus' ministry, it was unlikely the Pharisees (*cf.* notes on 1:19, 24) would, in view of their reservations toward both preachers. So (*oun*, a loose 'so' or 'therefore', in this instance connecting the fact of Jesus' rising influence with his discovery that the Pharisees had heard of it – lit.) when Jesus (or possibly 'the Lord', as in some manuscripts) found out that the Pharisees had heard that he *was gaining and baptising more disciples than John . . . he left Judea and went back once more to Galilee* (v. 3). Although there were other 'baptizers' in Judea about this time, John the Baptist and Jesus doubtless endured peculiar official scrutiny not only because of their growing influence but because of their distinctive message and authority, not to mention their distinctive use of baptism as an exclusively *initiatory* rite *for Jews*. Probably Jesus, already aware of a certain reserve on the part of the Baptist's disciples, and now learning that the Pharisees were focusing on his own rising popularity, decided it was best to leave Judea (*cf.* 3:22) for the north. Fearful that there might be an attempt to polarize the two ministries, Jesus determines to minimize the potential damage by departing for Galilee.

In a parenthetical note typical of the Evangelist (*cf.* 3:24; 4:8, 9b), verse 2 points out that Jesus himself did not baptize, but his disciples did – or, more pedantically, Jesus baptized only by using his disciples as the agents (*cf.* 3:22). This distinction between preaching and baptizing was later to be emulated in large part by Paul (1 Cor. 1:14–17). Both this narrative and the end of ch. 3 presuppose that Jesus' ministry overlapped with that of the Baptist; the point is not reported by the Synoptists, who begin their record of Jesus' public ministry in Galilee (*cf.* notes on 2:13; 3:22). Some contemporary scholars concede that Jesus may well have exercised ministry in Judea before the Galilean service recorded in the Synoptics, but find a contradiction in the fact that the Synoptics report the calling of the disciples *after* the onset of the Galilean ministry (Mk. 1:14, 16–20 par.) while John records something of their activity even in the early, Judean stage of Jesus' ministry. The problem appears less acute to those who think Jesus started to work with at least some of his disciples in the early stage, and then called them in some climactic way, perhaps to 'full-time' service, near the beginning of the Galilean ministry. Protestations notwithstanding, the abruptness of the call reported in the Synoptics may support this (*cf.* notes on 1:35ff.).

4. The route normally followed by Jewish travellers heading north from Judea to Galilee passed through Samaria. Geography therefore dictated that *Jesus had to go through Samaria* when he embarked on the three-day walk to Galilee. The only alternative was to cross the Jordan near Jericho, travel north up the east bank (the Transjordan) through largely Gentile territory, and cross back to the west bank near the Lake of Galilee. Popular commentators have sometimes insisted that the longer route through the Transjordan was the customary route for Jewish travellers, so great was their aversion to Samaritans; this in turn suggests that the 'had to' language (*edei*) reflects the compulsion of divine appointment, not geography. Josephus, however, provides ample assurance not only that the antipathy between Jews and Samaritans was strong, but also that Jews passing from Judea to Galilee or back nevertheless preferred the shorter route through Samaria (*Ant.* xx. 118; *Bel.* ii. 232; *Vita* 269). This does not mean that the meeting between Jesus and the Samaritan woman was outside the sweep of divine providential appointments (indeed, the 'had to' may refer to God's will for Jesus), but only that Jesus' travel arrangements cannot be marshalled as evidence of divine compulsion.

Samaria had no separate political existence in Jesus' day: it was united with Judea under the Roman procurator. Nevertheless for both Jews and Samaritans the area was defined by both history and religion. King Omri named the new capital of the northern kingdom 'Samaria' (1 Ki. 16:24), which name was then transferred to the district and sometimes to the entire northern kingdom. After the Assyrians captured Samaria in 722–721 BC, they deported all the Israelites of substance and settled the land with foreigners, who intermarried with the surviving Israelites and adhered to some form of their ancient religion (2 Ki. 17 – 18). After the exile, Jews returning to their homeland, the remains of the southern kingdom, viewed the Samaritans not only as the children of political rebels but as racial half-breeds whose religion was tainted by various unacceptable elements (Ne. 13; *cf.* Jos., *Ant.* xi. 297–347, esp. 340). About 400 BC the Samaritans erected a rival temple on Mount Gerizim; toward the end of the second century BC this was destroyed by John Hyrcanus, the Hasmonean ruler in Judea. This combination of events fuelled religious and theological animosities. Certainly by the first century the Samaritans had developed their own religious heritage based on the Pentateuch (they did not accept the other books of the Hebrew Bible as canonical), continuing to focus their worship not on Jerusalem and its temple but on Mount Gerizim. A small number of Samaritans survives to this day.

John may intend a contrast between the woman of this narrative and Nicodemus of ch. 3. He was learned, powerful, respected, orthodox, theologically trained; she was unschooled, without influence, despised, capable only of folk religion. He was a man, a Jew, a ruler; she was a woman, a Samaritan, a moral outcast. And both needed Jesus.

5. *Sychar*, the name of the Samaritan town at which Jesus arrived, is not attested in earlier literature, but is probably to be identified with the modern village of 'Askar, on the shoulder of Mount Ebal, opposite Mount Gerizim. Jacob's well, attested by a continuous line of tradition, lies about a half mile to the south of the modern village. Sychar, John tells us, was *near the plot of ground Jacob had given to his son Joseph.* The reference is to Genesis 48:22, where Israel (= Jacob) on his deathbed tells

Joseph, 'And to you, as one who is over your brothers, I give the ridge of land [Heb. *š⁼kem*, lit. "shoulder" of a mountain] I took from the Amorites with my sword and my bow.' When the Israelites conquered and settled Canaan, they brought with them out of Egypt the bones of their ancestor Joseph, and buried them 'at Shechem in the tract of land that Jacob bought for a hundred pieces of silver from the sons of Hamor, the father of Shechem. This became the inheritance of Joseph's descendants.' Sychar (if it is to be identified with 'Askar) lies about a mile from the ancient town of Shechem (modern Balata). Joseph's tomb lies but a few hundred yards north-west of Jacob's well.

6. The site of Jacob's well is as certain as such things can be. At various periods churches were built there, but they were destroyed by the Muslims. Today the well lies in the shadow of the crypt of an unfinished Orthodox church. It is often pointed out that the word for 'well' in this verse is *pēgē*, denoting a running spring; in vv. 11, 12, the word is *phrear*, meaning a cistern or dug-out well. Jacob's well is both: it was dug out, but it is fed by an underground spring that is remarkably reliable to this day.

Jesus arrived at Jacob's well *about the sixth hour*, almost certainly about noon (beginning the count about sunrise; *cf.* notes on 1:39) when the heat of the day and the progress of the journey explain Jesus' thirst and tiredness. Such references to natural human weakness are taken by Käsemann to be nothing more than dramatic dressing on an essentially docetic Christology. That conclusion is possible only if one half of the evidence is wielded to dismiss the other half. If the one who becomes flesh is none other than the eternal Word, what that Word becomes is nothing less than 'flesh', fully human (1:14).

7-8. Apparently the woman came to the well alone. Women were more likely to come in groups to fetch water, and either earlier or later in the day when the heat of the sun was not so fierce. Possibly the woman's public shame (4:16ff.) contributed to her isolation. The connection between v. 7 and the parenthetical explanation of v. 8 suggests that normally Jesus' disciples would have helped him draw water, but their absence prompted Jesus to breach social custom (*cf.* notes below) and ask the Samaritan woman for a drink. That Jesus and his disciples were willing to purchase food from Samaritans betrays a certain freedom from the self-imposed regulations of the stricter sort of Jews, who would have been unwilling to eat food that had been handled by Samaritans. Some foods, however, especially dry foods, were considered less easily defiled than others (*cf.* notes on 2:6).

9. The inherited suspicions and animosities between Jews and Gentiles (*cf.* notes on v. 4) erupted at practical levels. Although some Jews could imagine eating with Samaritans (Mishnah *Berakoth* 7:1), doubtless many a Jew would not eat with a Samaritan on the latter's home turf for fear of incurring ritual defilement. Probably this fear was intensified when the Samaritan was a woman: within a generation Jewish leaders would codify a law (Mishnah *Niddah* 4:1) that reflected longstanding

217

popular sentiment, to the effect that all 'the daughters of the Samaritans are menstruants from their cradle' and therefore perpetually in a state of ceremonial uncleanness.

The Samaritan woman's surprise is therefore entirely understandable: Jesus was a Jew and she was both a Samaritan and a woman. From her perspective, she dismisses him as a Jew; later on, Jews will dismiss him as a Samaritan (8:48). But if Jesus cannot be other than alien, he nevertheless wins some Jews and some Samaritans. At this point, however, the woman is not about to be won: she cannot fathom what would possess a Jew to ask her for a drink. She does not know that, far from being defiled by what is unclean, Jesus sanctifies what he touches. Others who touch lepers become unclean; Jesus touches a leper and brings healing (Mt. 8:3). A religious, male, Jewish aristocrat like Nicodemus, or an untrained, female Samaritan peasant who had made a mess of her life – Jesus converses frankly with both, and happily breaks social and religious taboos to do so. Meanwhile, John parenthetically (cf. notes on 4:2) explains why the woman is so suspicious: *For Jews do not use dishes Samaritans have used* (NIV fn.). That is probably the meaning of the Greek text (as Augustine understood,[1] and as Daube, pp. 373–382 has recently argued): although the verb *sunchrasthai* can mean 'to associate with' (cf. Schnackenburg, 1. 425 n. 19), it more commonly means 'to use together with', the object being understood from the context.

10. Not only had Jesus' request of the woman proven him to be above the biases of strictly observant Jews, but he himself now proffers 'living water' of which she knows nothing. She sees in him a weary Jewish traveller; she does not yet perceive his glory (cf. 1:14). If she had known who it was that was asking her for a drink, she would have been pressing him for a far better drink. The 'gift of God' that she does not recognize is probably the eternal life that only Jesus can bestow. Alternatively, Jesus is making use of Jewish categories, where the supreme 'gift of God' is the Torah (cf. Odeberg, p. 150). If that is the referent here, Jesus is saying that if the woman really knew her Torah, and who it was speaking with her, her response would have been quite different (cf. the rebuke to Nicodemus, 3:10, cf. 5:39–40).

Either way, what he promises is 'living water'. The expression has been chosen to allow two levels of meaning. On the one hand, it denotes fresh, running water from springs. On the other hand, the expression belongs to a considerable network of metaphorical uses. This diversity in the proposed backgrounds (cf. Barrett, pp. 233–234) betrays the esteem attached to fresh water in a country where so much land is terribly arid, and where most of it is arid for much of the year. In such an environment 'living water' is an expression waiting to become a metaphor for highly diverse religious values. The obvious background,

---

[1] *In Johan. Tract.* xv. 11; cf. T. E. Pollard, *ExpT* 92, 1980–81, pp. 147–148.

however, is the Old Testament. There God declares: 'My people have committed two sins: They have forsaken me, the spring of living water, and have dug their own cisterns, broken cisterns that cannot hold water' (Je. 2:13) – that is, they have rejected the fresh, 'running' supply of God and his faithful goodness, choosing instead the stagnant waters of cisterns they themselves prepared, discovering even then that their cisterns were cracked, and leaving them with nothing to sustain life and blessing. But the prophets look forward to a time when 'living water will flow out from Jerusalem' (Zc. 14:8; *cf.* Ezk. 47:9). The metaphor speaks of God and his grace, knowledge of God, life, the transforming power of the Holy Spirit; in Isaiah 1:16–18; Ezekiel 36:25–27 water promises cleansing. All of these themes are picked up in John's use of 'water' or 'living water' in this gospel (*cf.* notes on 3:5; 4:10–15; 7:38; 19:34). In John's Gospel there are passages where Jesus *is* the living water as he *is* the bread from heaven (6:35), and other passages where he *gives* the living water to believers. In this chapter, the water is the satisfying eternal life mediated by the Spirit that only Jesus, the Messiah and Saviour of the world, can provide.

11–12. Because of the double meaning of 'living water' (*cf.* notes on v. 10), the woman finds it easy to think Jesus is talking about fresh, running water, like that of the spring that feeds the well. On the misunderstanding theme, *cf.* notes on 2:22; 3:4. '*Sir*' [an appropriate rendering of *kyrie*, which is not Christologically 'loaded' here or in vv. 15, 19], she comments, '*you have nothing to draw with* [*i.e.* no bucket, *antlēma*, cognate with the verb *antleō* in v. 15; *cf.* notes on 3:8] *and the well* [*phrear*; *cf.* notes on v. 6] *is deep*' – still over 100 feet, and probably deeper then. *Where can you get this living water?*

To obtain water on this spot, even the patriarch Jacob had found it necessary to dig a well and to provide the means for raising the water from the deep hole. If Jesus was offering fresh water without expending the energy to dig or using the means provided, he was greater than Jacob, or a cheap charlatan. The woman has little doubt Jesus is the latter: the form of her question (v. 12) implies the answer was a decisive 'No!' in her own mind. But misunderstanding combines with irony to make the woman twice wrong: the 'living water' Jesus offers does not come from an ordinary well, and Jesus is in fact far greater than the patriarch Jacob – a point John's readers can appreciate, even if the Samaritan woman has not yet grasped the point. (A similarly skeptical question compares Jesus with the patriarch Abraham in 8:53, with no less irony.)

There is no Old Testament record of Jacob digging this well. Probably it belongs to tradition associated with the account of Jacob's move to the Shechem area (Gn. 33:18–20). Some have wondered why Jacob should have dug a well here at all, since several fine springs are but a short distance away. From this distance we cannot be sure; but it is not unlikely that the best water supplies were already claimed by local tribes, prompting Jacob to conclude that it would be wise to secure an independent water supply. He may have remembered the experiences of his father Isaac (Gn. 26:15–33).

13–14. The woman's question (v. 12) is sceptical, perhaps slightly derisory, but Jesus answers it. Some measure of the relative greatness of Jacob and of himself can be found in the fact that the water provided by the venerated patriarch, as valuable as it was, quenched thirst only for a short while; the 'living water' (cf. notes on v. 10) Jesus gives bans thirst forever in the one who drinks it. This thirst is not for natural water, but for God, for eternal life in the presence of God; and the thirst is met not by removing this aching desire but by pouring out the Spirit. Indeed, this water *will become in him a spring of water welling up to eternal life* (v. 14) – clearly a reference to the Spirit who alone gives life (6:63).

Again there are echoes of Old Testament promises. In the day of God's salvation, with joy God's people 'will draw water from the wells of salvation' (Is. 12:3). 'They will neither hunger nor thirst' (Is. 49:10; cf. Rev. 7:16); the pouring out of God's Spirit will be like pouring 'water on the thirsty land, and streams on the dry ground' (Is. 44:3). The language of inner satisfaction and transformation calls to mind a string of prophecies anticipating new hearts, the exchange of failed formalism in religion for a heart that knows and experiences God, and that hungers to do his will (Je. 31:29–34; Ezk. 36:25–27; Joel 2:28–32; cf. notes on 3:5). It is hard not to think of Isaiah 55:1–3: 'Come, all you who are thirsty, come to the waters . . . that your soul may live.' Here God promises to make 'an everlasting covenant' with all who come – not only with Israel but with 'the peoples', 'nations that do not know you' (Is. 55:4, 5). The same passage demands that 'the wicked forsake his way and the evil man his thoughts', for then God will have mercy and 'will freely pardon' (Is. 55:6, 7) – and indeed it is to the woman's sin that Jesus is about to turn (4:16ff.). Samaritans who limited the canon to the Pentateuch might not have appreciated such allusions to the prophets (though John's Jewish readers would), but in the later Samaritan liturgy that has come down to us for the Day of Atonement, it is said of the Taheb (the Samaritan equivalent of the Messiah) that 'water shall flow from his buckets' (an adaptation of Nu. 24:7; cf. Bruce, p. 105).

15. The woman, like Nicodemus, continues to think on the purely naturalistic plane, as is made clear by her desire not to *keep coming here to draw water*. If the stranger is speaking the truth, he is indeed greater than Jacob. The Samaritan woman, with what degree of scepticism or hope we cannot ascertain (cf. Jn. 6:34), wants to get in on any blessing that will enable her to abandon these trips to Jacob's well.

16. The change of subject, though abrupt, is not artificial. The Samaritan woman has already failed to grasp who Jesus is, and misconstrued the nature of the living water he was promising. By this turn in the dialogue, Jesus is indicating that she has also misunderstood the true dimensions of her own need, the real nature of her self-confessed thirst. Of course, by displaying his knowledge of her morally messy past (vv. 17–18) Jesus is exhibiting his own more-than-human knowledge (cf.

notes on 1:48) – a point the woman understands (v. 19). Nevertheless his remark is not designed to be merely self-revealing: rather, it is designed to help the woman come to terms with the nature of the gift he is offering.

Both in the Fourth Gospel and in the Synoptics, the sheer flexibility of Jesus leaps from the pages as he deals with a wide array of different people and their varied needs. No less startling (though more often ignored) is the manner in which Jesus commonly drives to the individual's greatest sin, hopelessness, guilt, despair, need. This should not be surprising: if he is the Lamb of God who takes away the sin of the world (1:29, 34), inevitably he will deal with sin in those who express some interest in knowing and following him.

17–18. The woman's truculent *I have no husband* was formally true, if her five former husbands were all deceased or divorced; but doubtless her intention was to ward off any further probing of this sensitive area of her life, while masking the guilt and hurt. Jesus exposes the whole truth (as the woman herself later admits, vv. 29, 39), but in the gentlest possible way: he commends her for her formal truthfulness, while pointing out that she has had five husbands (presumably each had died or divorced her) and the man with whom she is now sleeping is not her legal husband at all. Rabbinic opinion disapproved more than three marriages, even though they were legally permissible; no body of religious opinion approved common law marriages. Attempts to interpret the five husbands and live-in companion in some symbolic fashion are not convincing (*cf.* Additional Note).

19. *Sir* (*cf.* notes on v. 11), the woman replies, *I can see that you are a prophet*. The least that the woman means is that Jesus' precise knowledge of her past proves him to be inspired. But the syntax of the Greek allows the translation 'I can see that you are *the* prophet.' Because the Samaritans accepted only the books of the Pentateuch as canonical (*cf.* notes on v. 4), they understood the words of Deuteronomy 34:10, 'no prophet has risen in Israel like Moses, whom the LORD knew face to face', to be absolute and in force until the coming of the prophet like Moses (Dt. 18:15–19; *cf.* notes on 1:21), the second Moses, the Taheb (as they called this promised 'messianic' figure). If there cannot be another prophet between the first Moses and the second Moses, then to call Jesus 'prophet' is virtually to call him '*the* prophet'. However, in view of v. 25 it is unlikely that the Samaritan woman is in v. 19 making so clear a confession. The word 'prophet' was used to refer to a wide range of 'gifted' people, and at this point may not, in the woman's mind, denote a full-orbed Old Testament prophet, let alone a messianic figure.

20. The sudden change of subject has prompted many interpreters to suggest that the woman raises a disputed point of theology as a means to distract Jesus from the sin-question she find so embarrassing. It is always easier to talk theology than to deal with truth that is personally distressing. But this interpretation may be guilty of too greatly 'psychologizing' the text. A simpler supposition is that the woman's discovery that Jesus is some kind of Jewish prophet prompts her to raise the outstanding point of theological contention between Jews and Samaritans, as much to demonstrate her religious awareness as to set the stranger a testing challenge. 'There are some people who cannot engage in a religious conversation with a person of a different persuasion without bringing up the points on which they differ' (Bruce, p. 108).

Both Jews and Samaritans recognized that God had commanded their forefathers 'to seek the place the LORD your God [would] choose from among all [their] tribes to put his Name there for his dwelling' (Dt. 12:5), but they drew conflicting conclusions from this authorization. Because they recognized the rest of the Hebrew canon and not just the Pentateuch, the Jews concluded Jerusalem was the place: there David determined to build a temple to God, and God solemnly authorized his son Solomon to do so. There sacrifice was divinely sanctioned, the temple site retaining its significance when Zerubbabel rebuilt it after it was destroyed, and when later still Herod embellished it. For their part, the Samaritans recognized none of this. Moreover, their own textual traditions of Deuteronomy 12:5 read 'to seek the place the LORD your God *has chosen*'. This prompted them to look to the Pentateuch itself to discover the place. They noted that Shechem, overlooked by Mount Gerizim, was the first place Abraham built an altar once he entered the promised land (Gn. 12:6–7). It was on Mount Gerizim that the blessings were to be shouted to the covenant community, once they had entered the promised land (Dt. 11:29–30; 27:2–7, 12; *cf.* Jos. 8:33). In the Samaritan Bible, both in Exodus 20:17 and in Deuteronomy 5:21, the ten commandments are followed by words very similar to those found in Deuteronomy 27:2–7, thus effectively tying the decalogue itself to Mount Gerizim. Granted these theological understandings, it is small wonder that the Samaritans built their temple there (*cf.* notes on v. 4) and insisted Mount Gerizim was the highest mountain in the world – even though Mount Ebal, just across the valley, was demonstrably higher.[1] Even after their temple was destroyed by John Hyrcanus, the Samaritans continued to perform their sacrifices and other rites on this mountain. These were the competing religious claims that the Samaritan woman was inviting Jesus to address.

21. Jesus' response to the woman (vv. 21–24) is given in three parts. First, he announces the impending obsolescence of both the Jerusalem temple and the Mount Gerizim site as definitive places of worship (v. 21). Nevertheless, he insists, salvation springs from the Jews, not the Samaritans (v. 22). And finally, he explains more positively the nature of the worship that forever renders obsolete the conflicting claims of Jerusalem and Gerizim (vv. 23–24).

The opening words, *Believe me* (*pisteuō* plus the dative; *cf.* notes on

---

[1] On Samaritan thought, *cf.* R. J. Coggins, *Samaritans and Jews: The Origins of Samaritanism Reconsidered* (Oxford University Press, 1975); and J. Macdonald, *The Theology of the Samaritans* (SCM, 1964).

2:22), are not an invitation to trust Jesus with saving faith, but a simple asseverative (like 'I tell you the truth'). As in 2:4, the word *woman* (*gynai*) is neutral; 'madam' might be a better translation. The words *a time is coming* might better be rendered 'the hour is coming', since 'hour' (*hōra*) when unqualified always points in John's Gospel to the hour of Jesus' cross, resurrection and exaltation, or to events related to Jesus' passion and exaltation (as in 16:32), or to the situation introduced by Jesus' passion and exaltation (*cf.* notes on 2:4).[1] When that hour comes, Jesus avers, *you* (plural: *i.e.*, you Samaritans) *will worship the Father neither on this mountain nor in Jerusalem*. In other words, there is little to be gained by a prolonged debate over the relative claims of Jerusalem and Gerizim, since both sites are about to be bypassed by those who truly worship the Father. *The Father* is Jesus' characteristic way of referring to God (*e.g.* 2:16; 11:41; 12:27-28; 17:1). Because God is first and foremost the Father of the Son, the ground is prepared for the Christological emphases that follow (vv. 26, 29, 34). Nevertheless Jesus also taught his followers to address God in the same way (20:17; *cf.* Rom. 8:15; Gal. 4:6), so that the title became characteristically Christian.

22. Strictly speaking, Jesus makes no direct pronouncement on the relative merits of the claims of Jerusalem and Mount Gerizim. Nevertheless the antithesis he articulates addresses those claims indirectly. *You Samaritans* (the Greek employs the plural pronoun; NIV makes this clear by adding 'Samaritans'), Jesus insists, *worship what you do not know*. Jesus is not saying that the Samaritans hold to a view of God that makes him utterly unknowable, still less that they worship what they do not *believe* – as if he were attacking their sincerity. Rather, he is saying that the object of their worship is in fact unknown to them. They stand outside the stream of God's revelation, so that what they worship cannot possibly be characterized by truth and knowledge.[2] By contrast, Jesus says, *we* [Jews] *worship what we do know*: *i.e.*, whatever else was wrong with Jewish worship, at least it could be said that the object of their worship was known to them. The Jews stand within the stream of God's saving revelation; they know the one they worship, *for salvation* (*cf.* notes on 3:17) *is from the Jews*.

This last statement does not mean that all Jews will be saved: the entire Gospel stands against such a thesis. Nor does it simply mean that the promised deliverer, whether labelled Messiah or Taheb, would come from Judah, even though both the Hebrew Bible and the Samaritan Pentateuch make that point (Gn. 49:10). Rather, the idea is that, just as the Jews stand within the stream of God's saving revelation, so also can

---

[1] *Cf.* J. Seynaeve, *Revue Africaine de Théologie* 9, 1985, pp. 43-85.

[2] At a later date Samaria became heavily influenced by Gnosticism. Those who think the influence of Gnosticism was already pervasive when John wrote are inclined to think that in these words there is a sharp rebuke of Gnosticism: the Gnostics prided themselves on their knowledge, but in fact they are ignorant of the true God. But *cf.* the Introduction, §§ II, III.

it be said that they are the vehicle of that revelation, the historical matrix out of which that revelation emerges. 'In Judah God is known; his name is great in Israel' (Ps. 76:1). The ultimate authority for both Jews and Samaritans lay in their respective Bibles; in this debate at least, Jesus comes down decisively on the side of the Jews. There are immediate implications for the resolution of the conflicting claims of Jerusalem and Mount Gerizim, but Jesus does not press the point.

This verse also provides strong evidence that the Fourth Gospel is not anti-Semitic or even anti-Jewish, as some aver. John's frequent and sharp denunciation of 'the Jews' (*cf.* notes on 1:19) finds its deepest motivation neither in racial bias nor in pathological sectarianism but in the firm conviction that salvation, for Jews and Gentiles alike, lies in the Messiah announced by the Jewish Scriptures, a Messiah whose claims cannot be ignored without peril.[1]

23–24. As strongly as Jesus insists that the Jews were appointed by God to unique privilege and responsibility as they passed on the oracles of God (*cf.* Rom. 3:2), he insists no less strongly that their privileged position is in the process of dissolution as that eschatological age dawns to which their own Scriptures point. In the period up to Jesus' ministry, it was entirely correct to say that 'salvation is from the Jews' (v. 22). *Yet a time is coming and has now come* (lit. 'the hour is coming and now is': *cf.* notes on 2:4; 4:21) *when the true worshippers will worship the Father in spirit and truth.*' There is an advance on v. 21: not only is the time coming, but it has come. This oxymoron is a powerful way of asserting not only that the period of worship 'in spirit and truth' is about to come and awaits only the dawning of the 'hour', *i.e.* Jesus' death, resurrection and exaltation, but also that this period of true worship is already proleptically present in the person and ministry of Jesus before the cross. This worship can take place only in and through him: he is the true temple (2:19–22), he is the resurrection and the life (11:25). The passion and exaltation of Jesus constitute the turning point upon which the gift of the Holy Spirit depends (7:38–39; 16:7); but that salvation-historical turning point is possible only because of who Jesus is. Precisely for that reason, the hour is not only 'coming' but also 'has now come'.

The expression *the true worshippers* does not make a distinction between worshippers *after* the ministry of Jesus (the *true* worshippers) and those *before* the ministry of Jesus (presumably the *false* worshippers). Both true and false worshipper could be found under the terms of the old covenant, and both can be found appealing to the new covenant as well. Rather, the point is that with the coming of the 'hour' the distinction between true worshippers and all others turns on factors that make the ancient dispute between the conflicting claims of the Jerusalem

---

[1]Some scholars are so convinced John is anti-Semitic that they dismiss v. 22b as a gloss. For a useful refutation, *cf.* O'Day, pp. 69ff.

temple and Mount Gerizim obsolete. Under the eschatological conditions of the dawning hour, the true worshippers cannot be identified by
their attachment to a particular shrine, but by their worship of the Father
in spirit and truth.

The force of this phrase clearly depends on what is meant by the
simple clause, *God is spirit,* for in v. 24 that clause serves as further
explication and grounding for the reiterated truth that God's *worshippers
must worship in spirit and in truth.* By 'God is spirit' (not 'God is *a* spirit',
as in AV: *cf.* 1 Jn. 1:5; 4:8), Jesus is not suggesting that God is one spirit
amongst many, nor simply that he is incorporeal in the Stoic sense, nor
that 'spirit' completely defines his metaphysical properties. In this context 'spirit' characterizes what God is like, in the same way that flesh,
location, and corporeality characterize what human beings and their
world are like: *cf.* the parallelism of Is. 31:3, 'But the Egyptians are men
and not God; their horses are flesh and not spirit' (though these words
are not found in the LXX). More commonly the 'spirit' in the Old Testament is renovative, creative, life-giving (*cf.* notes on Jn. 3:5; 7:38-39).
Barrett (p. 238) rightly draws attention to 3:8, where what is 'spirit'
cannot itself be fully apprehended, but its effect cannot be denied. It is
known through its 'sound' (*phōnē* – *cf.* 1:23; 5:25, 28, 37-38; 10:3-5, 16, 27;
11:43; 12:28, 30; 18:37). In the same way, 'God is spirit' means that God is
invisible, divine as opposed to human (*cf.* 3:6), life-giving and unknowable to human beings unless he chooses to reveal himself (*cf.* 1:18). As
'God is light' and 'God is love' (1 Jn. 1:5; 4:8), so 'God is spirit': these are
elements in the way God presents himself to human beings, in his
gracious self-disclosure in his Son (*cf.* Porsch, p. 49; *cf.* Ibuki, pp.
311-313). And he *has* chosen to reveal himself: he has uttered his Word,
his own Self-Expression. In that Word, now become flesh, he may be
known as truly as it is possible for human beings to know him (1:1-18).
That incarnate Word is the one who baptizes his people in Holy Spirit
(1:33), for unless they are born from above, unless they are born of the
Spirit, they cannot see the kingdom of God, they cannot worship God
truly. This provision of the Spirit is made possible by the work of him
who is the truth (14:6), and who by his glorification by way of the cross
pours out the Spirit, who is called the Spirit of truth (14:17; 15:26; 16:13).

This God who is spirit can be worshipped only *in spirit and truth.* Both
in v. 23 and in v. 24, the one preposition 'in' governs both nouns (a point
obscured by the NIV of v. 24). There are not two separable characteristics
of the worship that must be offered: it must be 'in spirit and truth', *i.e.*
essentially God-centred, made possible by the gift of the Holy Spirit,
and in personal knowledge of and conformity to God's Word-made-
flesh, the one who is God's 'truth', the faithful exposition and fulfilment
of God and his saving purposes (*cf.* esp. de la Potterie, 2. 673ff.). The
worshippers whom God seeks worship him out of the fullness of the
supernatural life they enjoy ('in spirit'), and on the basis of God's
incarnate Self-Expression, Christ Jesus himself, through whom God's
person and will are finally and ultimately disclosed ('in truth'); and these

two characteristics form one matrix, indivisible. Indeed, the association of 'word' and 'Spirit' is strong in the Old Testament (*e.g.* Ne. 9:20, 30; Ps. 33:6; 147:18; Is. 59:21),[1] and it is just possible that this connection is in the Evangelist's mind, since Jesus the 'Word made flesh' (1:14) and 'the truth' (14:6) is also the one to whom God gives the Spirit without limit (3:34).

To worship the Father 'in spirit and truth' clearly means much more than worship without necessary ties to particular holy places (though it cannot mean any less). The prophets spoke of a time when worship would no longer be focused on a single, central sanctuary, when the earth would be full of the knowledge of the Lord as the waters cover the sea. The Apocalypse concludes with a vision of the consummated kingdom, the new Jerusalem, in which there is no temple to be found, 'because the Lord God Almighty and the Lamb are its temple' (Rev. 21:22). The fulfilment of that vision has not yet arrived in its fullness. Even so, Jesus insists, through his own mission the hour was dawning when the principal ingredients of that vision would be set in operation, a foretaste of the consummation to come. 'God is spirit, and his worshippers must (Gk. *dei*, here the divine 'must') worship him in spirit and truth.'

25. How much of this the Samaritan woman understands is debatable. Doubtless she catches some messianic implications of what Jesus is saying, and replies, in effect, that these sorts of questions will be resolved once Messiah appears. *'I know that Messiah' (called Christ) 'is coming'*: as usual, John parenthetically translates the semitic expression (*cf.* 1:38, 41). So far as we know, the Samaritans did not regularly use the term 'Messiah' until the sixteenth century;[2] the woman may have done so here in deference to her Jewish interlocutor. Samaritans preferred 'Taheb' (*cf.* notes on 4:4, 11–12, 19–20), 'the Restorer', or possibly 'he who returns'. *When he comes, he will explain everything to us*: that is more typically a Samaritan than a Jewish expectation. By and large Jews did not think of the Messiah primarily as a teacher (except perhaps as a teacher of the Gentiles: SB 2. 348; though *cf.* CD 6:11). By contrast, Samaritans pictured the Taheb as one who would reveal the truth, in line with his role as the ultimate prophet (Dt. 18:15–19; *cf.* Schnackenburg, 1. 441). John himself understands that Jesus is the 'revealer' in ways that outstrip both Jewish and Samaritan expectation (1:18; 14:6; *etc.*).

26. The stranger had been talking about eschatological matters with utter authority; the Samaritan woman rightly insists that the Messiah, when he came, would make such matters plain (v. 25). She may well have begun to suspect the truth, voicing her confession of faith as a kind

---

[1]For this observation I am indebted to Dr John Woodhouse of Moore College, Sydney, in an unpublished paper, 'The Spirit of God and the Word of God in the Old Testament'.

[2]*Cf.* M. de Jonge, *NTS* 19, 1973, pp. 246–270. But it must constantly be borne in mind that reconstructions of Samaritan theology in the first century are based on late sources.

of test to see what he would say. Jesus needs no further invitation: *I who speak to you am he.*[1] The one who sat by the well and asked her for a drink was none other than the promised Messiah, the expected Taheb, the one who could indeed provide her with 'living water'.

It is entirely in line with this Gospel that Jesus should unambiguously declare himself to be the Messiah to a Samaritan, but not to his own people. For many Jews, the title 'Messiah' carried so much political and military baggage that his self-disclosure in such settings necessarily had to be more subdued and subtle (*cf.* notes on 6:15; 10:24). Similarly, in the Synoptics Jesus is far more likely to encourage the public testimony of those who have experienced his transforming power if they live in Gentile territory (*e.g.* Lk. 8:26–39).

27. Jesus' disciples interrupt the conversation by their return from Sychar, where they had gone to purchase food (v. 8). Their unvoiced surprise that he was talking with a Samaritan woman reflects the prejudices of the day. Some (though by no means all) Jewish thought held that for a rabbi to talk much with a woman, even his own wife, was at best a waste of time and at worst a diversion from the study of *Torah*, and therefore potentially a great evil that could lead to Gehenna, hell (*Pirke Aboth* 1:5). Some rabbis went so far as to suggest that to provide their daughters with a knowledge of the *Torah* was as inappropriate as to teach them lechery, *i.e.* to sell them into prostitution (Mishnah *Sotah* 3:4; the same passage also provides the contrary view). Add to this the fact that this woman was a Samaritan (*cf.* notes on v. 9), and the disciples' surprise is understandable.

Jesus himself was not hostage to the sexism of his day (*cf.* 7:53 – 8:11; 11:5; Lk. 7:36–50; 8:2–3; 10:38–42). The reason why his disciples did not ask her *What do you want?* or ask him *Why are you talking with her?* is not given. Of course, if they had asked her the first question they would have been guilty of doing the very thing that surprised them in Jesus' actions. At least initially they may have refrained from asking Jesus the second question until the woman had departed (v. 28); after that point other matters seemed more urgent (v. 31). It is unduly sentimental to suppose that they restrained themselves because they had learned from experience to trust their Master's good reasons for what he did: they do not consistently exercise similar restraint elsewhere.

28–30. Whether the woman left her water jar out of nothing more than haste as she hurried back to Sychar, or out of simple courtesy so that at last Jesus might have his drink, is not made clear. Many have suggested that, whatever her reason, John detects a profound symbolism: in her eagerness to enjoy the new and living water, she abandons the old water jar, and thus speaks of renunciation of the old ceremonial forms of religion in favour of worship in spirit and truth. It is far from clear,

---

[1]Gk. *egō eimi, ho lalōn soi*. This instance of *egō eimi* (lit. 'I am') is not theologically loaded: *cf.* notes on 6:20, 35; 8:24, 28, 58.

however, that John means to say so much; for, unlike the water jars of 2:6ff., this one has no ritual purification tied up with it.

More striking is her eagerness to bear witness before the townspeople whom she had previously had reason to avoid. From Jesus' knowledge of her personal life she had concluded he must be, at very least, a prophet (v. 19; *cf.* 1:48); from the ensuing discussion she had begun to perceive that he was *the* prophet. Now, relating the steps in her thinking to her people, she exhorts them, *Come, see a man who told me everything I ever did* – which may be hyperbole, but quietly attests how central her messy and sinful personal life was to her own thinking. But if a stranger knows so much, may he not know more? She asks, with evident excitement but still some hesitation (*mēti*), *Could this be the Christ?*

Perhaps the townspeople were as impressed by her excitement and candour as by her argument. At any rate, they decided to see for themselves, and began the walk to Jacob's well while Jesus was still conversing with his disciples.

31–32. The disciples for their part were urging Jesus to eat some of the food they had just brought from the town. On *Rabbi*, *cf.* notes on 1:38. But Jesus, though doubtless still thirsty (v. 7) and probably hungry, is apparently dwelling on the conversation he has just had with the Samaritan woman. He decides to use the circumstance to teach his followers something of his own priorities: *I have food to eat that you know nothing about.*

33–34. As is common in the Fourth Gospel (*cf.* notes on 2:20; 3:3), the argument moves on by way of a misunderstanding. Jesus' disciples think of literal food as quickly as the Samaritan woman thought of literal water. If their excursion into town was in order to buy food, and Jesus now claims to have food of which they know nothing, it must be (they reason) that someone else has brought him food (v. 33).

But Jesus promptly disabuses them: *My food is to do the will of him who sent me and to finish his work.* Almost certainly Jesus is echoing Deuteronomy 8:3, where Moses addresses Israel and seeks to explain God's way to them: 'He humbled you, causing you to hunger and then feeding you with manna, which neither you nor your fathers had known, to teach you that man does not live on bread alone but on every word that comes from the mouth of the LORD' (*cf.* Jesus' use of this passage in Mt. 4:4 = Lk. 4:4). Jesus came to do the Father's will (5:36; 6:38), and always did no less (8:29). His works were the works of God (9:3–4; 10:25, 32, 37–38; 14:10; 17:4). No-one has ever exemplified the truth of Deuteronomy 8:3 in anything like the degree Jesus has: man does not live on bread alone but on every word that comes from the mouth of the LORD. 'The creative will of God, realized in obedience, sustains life' (Barrett, p. 241). If in his dealings with the Samaritan woman Jesus was performing his Father's will, there was greater sustenance and satisfaction in that than in any food the disciples could offer him. Indeed, all of Jesus' ministry is nothing other than submission to and performance of the will of the one who sent him (a frequent designation for God: *e.g.* 5:23–24,

30, 37; 6:38–39; 7:16, 18, 28, 33; 8:16, 18, 26, 29; 9:4; 12:44–45, 49; 13:20; 14:24; 16:5). Once the cross is firmly in view, Jesus can pray, 'I have brought you glory on earth by completing the work you gave me to do' (17:4; *cf.* Riedl, pp. 43–68). This sense of the *mission* of the Son (*cf.* notes on 3:17; 20:21) becomes a dominant theme in 5:19–47, making the present passage an anticipatory link.

35. From the mention of *four months*, some have attempted to date this incident to December or January, four months before the normal spring harvest. In that case Jesus is saying, 'You think harvest is four months off; but I am telling you that there are fields that need reaping immediately.' In support of this view, Guilding (pp. 206–211) argues that the synagogue lectionary readings for this period include Exodus 1:1 – 2:25; Joshua 24; Isaiah 27:6ff.; Ezekiel 20, all bearing themes that allegedly constitute the background on this passage. Quite apart from the questionable assumption that the rather late evidence for the synagogue lectionary cycles can legitimately be read back into the first century, the parallels are not very close (*e.g.* the well in the Exodus cycle was in Midian, not Samaria; the mountain was Horeb, not Gerizim). Bowman[1] suggests the reference is to the minor Samaritan feast *Zimmuth Pesaḥ*, presumably the Sabbath nearest the vernal conjunction of sun and moon four months before Pentecost (= harvest). *Zimmuth Pesaḥ* in the Samaritan liturgy celebrates the occasion, after the burning bush episode, when Moses met Aaron and told him of Israel's impending salvation. Others detect a merely proverbial saying, justified by a certain rhythmical prose: *Four months more and then the harvest*. Jesus is then saying, 'You think a certain gap must exist between sowing and harvest, but I am telling you that I have just sown the seed and the harvest is already taking place' (referring either to the Samaritan woman or to the people of Sychar who are approaching). Unfortunately there is no other attestation of this alleged 'proverb'.

Contextually, the problem with Guilding's explanation, apart from the lateness of our sources on Jewish lectionary cycles, is that it presupposes a *Jewish* lectionary in a *Samaritan* context. Bowman's view is historically plausible enough, if we read the rather late Samaritan sources back into the first century; but this merely historical connection does not itself establish how the saying functions in the ensuing verses, where Moses-typology does not seem to be the issue. On the other hand, there is evidence that, for the Samaritans (but not for the Jews), *Zimmuth Pesaḥ* fixed the time when the Passover *and* Pentecost (harvest) feasts fell: *Zimmuth Pesaḥ* is called the gate of the festivals.[2] That fact could have generated a Samaritan 'proverb' that has not otherwise come down to us.

---

[1]John Bowman, 'The Identity and Date of the Unnamed Feast of John 5:1', in Hans Goedicke (ed.), *Near Eastern Studies* (Fs. W. F. Albright; Johns Hopkins, 1971), pp. 43–56, esp. p.49.

[2]*Cf.* J. van Goudoever, *Biblical Calendars* (E. J. Brill, 1959), p. 82.

On any view, Jesus at this juncture is simply pointing out that by ordinary reckoning (*Do you not say . . . ?*) there are four months remaining until harvest, but in the salvation-historical plane the harvest has already begun. He himself is engaged in that harvest; that is part and parcel of the work the Father gave him to do (v. 34). On this reading, the gap between *sowing* and harvest has not yet been introduced (*cf.* vv. 36–38).

36. The words *Even now* (*ēdē*) could be read with v. 35, but customary Johannine usage and the pungency of the argument prefer the place- ment of the NIV. *Even now the reaper draws his wages* – *i.e.* the reaper is employed; he is not simply waiting around for the harvest, for harvest time has already arrived. He is busy reaping *the crop for eternal life*. The 'crop' refers to the people who become followers of Jesus, in the first instance the Samaritans; 'eternal life' (*cf.* notes on 3:15) is that for which the crop is harvested.

All this is *so that the sower and the reaper may be glad together*. Up to this point the sower has not been mentioned. This last clause of v. 36, however, extends the agricultural metaphor in two new directions. First, it calls to mind the eschatological promise of Amos 9:13: '"The days are coming", declares the LORD, "when the reaper will be over- taken by the ploughman and the planter by the one treading grapes."' The colourful image betokens the blessing of miraculous and unceasing fertility and prosperity. Jesus may therefore be saying that the eschato- logical age has dawned in his ministry, in which sowing and reaping are coming together in the harvesting of the crop, the messianic com- munity. On the joy of harvest as an eschatological symbol, *cf.* Psalm 126:5–6; Isaiah 9:3. Second, it allows for other sowers than Jesus, thus preparing the way for vv. 37–38.

37. NIV's *Thus* is misleading. It implies that the saying of v. 37 offers the explanation of v. 36. But the Greek phrase *en toutō* (lit. 'in this') can refer forward (*e.g.* 9:30; 13:35; 15:8) or backward (in John, only 16:30). Contextually, pointing forward is more likely: the saying '*One sows and another reaps*' is offered as a true summary of v. 38. It is unclear why Bultmann (p. 198) and other commentators judge the proverb on its own to express the inevitable and tragic inequality of life: one sows but receives no reward, while another reaps what he has not sowed. It could equally be taken as a reference to the unity of life and the diversity of gifts that go into a good harvest yield: one sows and another reaps, and the work of both sower and reaper is essential. The sower labours in anticipation of what is to come; the reaper must never forget that the harvest he enjoys is the fruit of another's toil.

38. The proverb of v. 37, then, is true in this situation: Jesus sent his disciples to reap what they have not worked for. So far as the Samaritans from Sychar are concerned, we have not been told that the disciples were sent to do anything; but Jesus is now talking in more general terms about the purpose of their calling. Just as reference to Jesus' unique death can immediately be applied to the manner in which his followers must die (12:24–26), so reference to Jesus' reaping is here immediately applied to the manner in which his disciples must participate in the harvest. They have already been commissioned to significant ministry (4:2); here, they are told that their fruitfulness is possible because of the work of others before them. In one sense there was a long succession of prophets and righteous leaders who led up to the ministry of Jesus, and Jesus has already demonstrated his awareness of the point (v. 22). But granted the fact that John the Baptist had recently ministered in this area (3:23), it is hard to resist the conclusion that Jesus is insisting John is the last in the succession of prophets and of others who sowed the seed but did not live long enough to participate in the harvest (cf. Lk. 16:16; Robinson, *Twelve*, pp. 61–66). Jesus and his followers arrive at that moment in redemptive history when the eschatological harvest begins. This is far more plausible than the view that anachronistically sees in the 'others' the hellenists who evangelized the Samaritans in Acts 8, and whose work the apostles later assimilated (Acts 8:14–17).

Whatever the precise referents, no Christian 'harvester' can ever justly forget that (1) success in reaping normally depends on the work of those who have gone before; and that (2) in those rare instances where sowing and reaping seem to go hand in hand, it is but the foretaste of the eschatological blessings still to come.[1]

39. The Samaritans re-enter the narrative. Initially they believed in Jesus because *of the woman's testimony* (cf. v. 29). The witness of ordinary human beings is never despised (cf. 1:7; 15:27; 17:20)[2], even though v. 42 underscores the fact that the peculiar witness of Jesus himself is more powerful and wonderful yet.

40–42. That Samaritans should urge a Jewish rabbi to stay with them attests not only the degree of confidence he had earned, but their conviction that he was none less than the promised Taheb, the Messiah. Though he stayed but *two days*, during that time the 'harvest' extended beyond those who had come out to see him owing to the witness of the woman: it now included *many more* who *became believers* – and this *because of his words* (v. 41). When the Samaritans make the point to the woman who first introduced Jesus to them (v. 42), it is not to disparage her testimony but to confirm it: they have heard for themselves, and have judged her witness to be true. Bultmann's conclusion (p. 201), that the human proclamation without which no-one can be brought to Christ is itself so insignificant that true believers are freed from its tutelage and may therefore criticize it, entirely misses the point.

It is possible, but by no means certain, that the 'city of Samaria' that

---

[1]Christians who have meditated on the Fourth Gospel as a whole find it difficult not to think of Jesus as the one who has done 'the hard work'; for he is not only the sower, but the seed, the grain of wheat that falls into the ground and dies, bearing great fruit (12:24). True though that is, it is very doubtful that John is thinking in those categories at this point in his presentation.

[2]Cf. R. Walker, ZNW 75, 1966, pp. 49–54.

Philip evangelized a few years later (Acts 8:4–8) was Sychar or perhaps nearby Shechem. The ready acceptance of Philip's message might then find some explanation in the preparatory work accomplished in this visit by Jesus and his disciples. In that case, Philip, too, reaped the benefit of the labour of others (v. 38).

When the Samaritans confess that this man Jesus *really is the Saviour of the world*, it is difficult to be certain precisely what category they are calling up. Perhaps they are impressed by the fact that the Jewish Messiah is also their Taheb; perhaps it is their way of expressing confidence that he will extend his saving reign to farthest reaches of the earth. As John renders their thought, the title 'Saviour of the world' becomes his own (in the New Testament it is found only here and in 1 Jn. 4:14), a way of supplying a title to the thought of 3:17. Although in the Old Testament God is the one who saves his people, and is sometimes called Saviour, the expression is not the exclusive preserve of Jewish tradition. Numerous Greek deities were ascribed the same title: not only Zeus, but Asclepius the god of healing, various gods of the mystery cults, and others. Even the Roman emperors were called 'saviour'; Hadrian (AD 117–138) was called the 'saviour of the world'. All this suggests that when John wrote the expression was not a technical one with a univocal meaning. John could adopt it and say, in effect, that the true Saviour of the world was not Zeus or Serapis, and certainly not the Roman emperor, but the Lamb of God who takes away the sin of the world (1:29, 34). Those who read John in the light of antecedent Scripture cannot help but think of the prophecies that anticipate the extension of the saving reign of God to the farthest corner of the earth. It was appropriate that the title 'Saviour of the world' should be applied to Jesus in the context of ministry to Samaritans, representing the first cross-cultural evangelism, undertaken by Jesus himself and issuing in a pattern to be followed by the church: 'you will be my witnesses in Jerusalem, and in all Judea and Samaria, and to the ends of the earth' (Acts 1:8).

Additional notes

18. The most common allegorical interpretation of John 4 holds that the five husbands represent five pagan deities introduced to the residents of Samaria by the settlers who were transported there (*cf.* notes on 4:4) from five cities in Mesopotamia and Syria (2 Ki. 17:24); the Samaritan woman represents the mixed and religiously tainted Samaritan race; and the sixth man, to whom the woman was not legally married, represents either another false god or, more commonly, the true God to whom the Samaritans are connected only by an illicit union. In fact, the details do not work out. The transported settlers originally worshipped seven pagan deities, not five (2 Ki. 17:30–32, 41; Jos., *Ant*. ix. 288 appears to have his facts wrong, possibly confused, like some modern expositors, by the five named cities from which the settlers were drawn), and these gods were all worshipped at the same time, not serially. Moreover, although it is true that John frequently uses institutions and details in symbolic ways (*e.g. cf.* notes on 2:19–22; 8:12), his symbolism in such cases is not only commonly predicated upon larger typologies connecting Jesus with the Old Testament, but in any case the symbolic value is tied to broader and demonstrable themes in the Fourth Gospel. The proposed symbolism in this instance fails both tests.

20–26. An excellent discussion of the Old Testament allusions scattered through these verses, and of the seamless unity of the argument (thereby ruling out of court the division of these verses into several sources) is found in Betz, pp. 420–438. This essay from Betz has also appeared in English, as '"To Worship God in Spirit and Truth": Reflections on John 4, 20–26', in Asher Finkel and Lawrence Frizzel (eds.), *Standing before God: Studies on Prayer in Scriptures and Tradition with Essays* (*Fs.* John M. Oesterreicher; Ktav, 1981), pp. 53–72. *Cf.* especially the connections he draws with Joshua 24.

10. The second sign: Jesus heals the official's son (4:43–54)

This section, especially 4:46–54, often serves as a test case for the question whether or not John wrote in conscious dependence on one or more of the Synoptic Gospels. The healing of the official's son (*huios*), in these verses, bears some resemblance to the healing of the centurion's servant (*cf.* Mt. 8:5–13, *pais*, which could refer to his own child or to a servant; Lk. 7:2–10, *doulos*, which is used only of a servant/slave). The rebuff Jesus administers to the official in this passage (v. 48) may call to mind the cure of the Syro-Phoenician woman's daughter (Mk. 7:24–30; Mt. 15:21–28). Finally, the notoriously difficult saying in v. 44 has parallels in Mark 6:1–6 (*cf.* Mt. 13:54–58; Lk. 4:16–30).[1]

The details of the debate are technical, and cannot be discussed here, though one or two asides are introduced into the comments that follow. It is likely that John had read Mark, and possibly Luke, before he wrote his Gospel. But this does not mean he incorporated large parts of their material in the way that Matthew incorporated large parts of Mark: John wrote his own book, and it is very doubtful that he had Mark or any other gospel before him as he wrote. Moreover, whether or not John knew Mark has no *necessary* bearing on whether this is John's version of a healing reported by the Synoptists. Some critical scholarship has been too quick to suppose that any account of a healing that bears some similarities to another account of a healing reflects either (1) a single healing and a single trajectory of developing interpretation, some of

---

[1]The best defence of the position that John wrote in complete independence of the Synoptics, not least in this pericope, is still Dodd, *HTFG*, pp. 238–241, 187–195. Against this view we may list Barrett, Anton Dauer, *Johannes und Lukas. Untersuchungen zu den johanneisch-lukanischen Parallelperikopen Joh 4, 46/Lk 7, 1–10 – Joh 12, 1–8/Lk 7, 36–50; 10, 38–42 – Joh 20, 19/Lk 24, 36–49* (Echter Verlag, 1984), and F. Neirynck, *EphThLov* 60, 1984, pp. 367–375.

which has handled the hard facts of the case rather loosely; or (2) a single healing and independent traditions that have been shaped rather differently. Doubtless some accounts did descend in one of those two ways, but a third possibility must always be considered: there were two or more miracles in somewhat similar circumstances, and the similarities in the separate reports reflects, in part, the similarity of those circumstances, but even more the similarity in the forces that 'shaped' such stories as they were passed on.[1] If we reckon with the possibility that the Fourth Gospel was written by the apostle John (*cf.* Introduction, § III), then two further factors must be taken into account. Apostolic authorship would not of course ensure that what was written was more 'truthful' than what might have been written by someone else: after all, no-one argues that because Luke was not one of the twelve apostles he was necessarily *less* truthful! But apostolic authorship would mean (1) expressions like 'the descent of the tradition' must take into much greater account the memory of an eyewitness; and (2) it becomes less likely that the composition of the Fourth Gospel was undertaken in a context hermetically sealed against other developments and publications in the rapidly multiplying church.

In this instance, there is no evidence that the 'royal official' was a Gentile (unlike the centurion in Mt. 8:5–13; Lk. 7:2–10; *cf.* notes on Jn. 4:46). Here it is the official's *son*, not a servant, who is healed. Moreover, Jesus treats the request of this official far differently, far more negatively, than he treats the faith of the centurion in the 'parallel' passages. The simplest explanation is that this is a quite different incident from the one reported in the Synoptic Gospels.

As for the purpose of these verses, and the contribution that they make to John's Gospel and to the sequence of thought at this point in his narrative, the question is so tied up with the disputed interpretation of vv. 43–45 that it is best to turn to the text without further ado.

43–45. After two days in Samaria, Jesus *left for Galilee*, resuming the trip he began in v. 3. The difficulty crops up in the next two verses. The proverb of v. 44, *a prophet has no honour in his own country* (Gk. *patris;* the term can refer either to one's 'homeland' or to one's 'hometown'), is tightly tied with v. 45. The Greek particle *oun* connects the two: '*Therefore* when he arrived in Galilee, the Galileans welcomed him.' But when some form of this proverb is used in the Synoptics (*viz.* Mt. 13:57; Mk. 6:4; Lk. 4:24) the word *patris* always refers to Jesus 'hometown', Nazareth, in Galilee. On the face of it, however, that will not fit here. Nazareth is not mentioned; moreover, if the 'homeland' of Galilee is

---

[1]Speaking technically, there is little thought given to methodological grounds for distinguishing between: (1) a narrative that has been shaped by form-critical pressures along a single trajectory; and (2) two somewhat similar narratives that have suffered the same form-critical pressures. On this and related questions, *cf.* D. A. Carson, 'Redaction Criticism: On the Legitimacy and Illegitimacy of a Literary Tool', in Carson/Woodbridge I, pp. 411–429.

meant, then why are we told in v. 45 that the Galileans *therefore* welcomed him?

About ten different solutions to the problem have been proposed.[1] The two most common are these:

(1) The *patris* refers to Judea or perhaps Jerusalem (Westcott, 1. 77–78; Hoskyns, pp. 259–260; Lindars, pp. 200–201). Jesus has left Judea, not only his 'spiritual' homeland in that Jerusalem is the centre of inherited Jewish religion but also his birthplace (though John does not mention the fact that Jesus was born in Bethlehem of Judea; but *cf.* notes on 7:42); he has left because of the rising opposition of 'the Jews' (7:1–3), often a category for 'Judeans' or for Jewish leaders in Judea (*cf.* notes on 1:19). He could expect no honour there, for 'a prophet has no honour in his own country'. By contrast, the Galileans received him gladly. But this interpretation is not without its problems. In the first place, the Fourth Gospel repeatedly mentions Nazareth as the place from which Jesus sprang (1:45–46; 7:41, 52; 19:19). Second, and far more important, this suggests that Jesus' movements were determined by his attempts to be honoured. Jerusalem rejects him, and Jesus does not like it, so he departs for the more responsive Galilee. Certainly Jesus' movements are influenced by the opposition (4:1–3; 7:1–9); but it would be entirely out of character for Jesus to choose his next destination on the basis of where he would most be honoured: he is the one who does not accept praise from men (5:41–44; *cf.* 2:23–25; Brown, 1. 187). Hendriksen (1. 179–180) and Dods (1. 164–165) escape the force of this criticism by saying that Jesus left Judea to avoid premature collision with the Pharisees: *i.e.* he retreats to Galilee not to seek more honour for himself, but because the honour that would accrue to him there would at least protect him from a premature onslaught (*cf.* 7:1–13). But the proverb in v. 44 is not cast in terms of protecting oneself, but in terms of winning honour. Moreover, as we shall see, the difference between the attitudes to Jesus in Judea and in Galilee is exaggerated. Third, this view assumes that the welcome Jesus received in vv. 45–52 was entirely positive. As we shall see (below), there are reasons for doubting this assessment.

(2) The *patris* refers to heaven (Lightfoot, p. 35). No-one who has read the Prologue could doubt that in some sense that was true. But the immediate context abounds in geographical place names, and there is no hint in the immediate context that *patris* should be taken in some spiritualizing sense. Moreover, as we have seen, this Gospel is also happy to stress the fact that Jesus springs from Nazareth (1:45–46; 7:41, 52). Above all, this interpretation falters on the *oun* ('therefore') which in the Greek text begins v. 45.

A more plausible interpretation identifies *patris* with Galilee – indeed, not just with Galilee, but with Galilee as it represents Jewish soil over against Samaritan soil. Jesus' 'own country', then, is Galilee and Judea,

---

[1]For a list and documentation, *cf.* D. A. Carson, *JBL* 97, 1978, p. 424, n. 50.

Jewish turf, as opposed to Samaria, from which he has just come. This obviously suits the immediate context; there is no need to pit Galilee (v. 45) against Judea, not mentioned since 4:3.[1] In Samaria Jesus has just enjoyed his first unqualified, unopposed, and open-hearted success. Now he returns to his own people (*cf.* 1:11), and, consistent with the pattern developed so far, the response is at best ambiguous. Although in John 2 his disciples put their faith in him (2:11), nevertheless 'the Jews' challenge him (2:18, 20), his disciples do not understand him (2:22),and the many who appeared to believe in him were spurious converts (2:23-25) whose 'faith' was generated in no small measure by the miraculous signs he was doing (2:23). The spiritual status of Nicodemus is not very hopeful (3:10), though it appears to improve later in the book. In John 4:1-3 Jesus leaves Judea, not because of any active persecution against him, but because he has learned that the Pharisees have heard of his popularity relative to that of John the Baptist: apparently he retreats to avoid the potential for division.

The same uncertainty and hesitation characterize the response described in the passage before us. The 'therefore' (*oun*) that introduces v. 45 must be taken to apply not only to the clause that immediately ensues, but to the whole verse, indeed, to the entire pericope. Jesus himself has declared that 'a prophet has no honour in his own country' (unlike the reception he enjoyed in Samaria), and he determinedly and knowingly heads in that direction. *Therefore* when he arrives, the Galileans welcome him – not as the Messiah, but because they had seen all that he had done at the Passover Feast in Jerusalem. John has already let his readers know how Jesus viewed that kind of faith (2:23-25), that kind of welcome. The details of the healing that follows make the same point. Verse 46 again begins with *oun*, 'therefore', introducing not simply v. 46a, but the entire narrative: precisely because the welcome the Galileans displayed was so dependent on miracles (unlike the faith of the Samaritans!), *therefore* on visiting Cana and being petitioned to perform a healing, Jesus detects in the royal official a welcome and a faith that desires a cure but that does not truly trust him. Indeed, the royal official, in Jesus' view, exemplifies what is wrong with the Galileans as a whole: Jesus' rebuke (v. 48) is in the plural, addressed to the people at large. Other details in the account support this reading (*cf.* notes below). What this means is that when John tells us that *the Galileans welcomed him*, the context he develops shows that here, as so often, he is writing with deep irony.

The material that follows ch. 4 also justifies this interpretation. John 5 locates Jesus back in Jerusalem, where rising opposition is apparent. Back in Galilee in John 6, the crowds misunderstand his messiahship

---

[1]For this view, *cf.* John W. Pryor, *CBQ* 47, 1987, pp. 254-263; also Brown, 1. 187, who however ignores the strength of his own position and postulates as well that v. 44 was inserted by a later redactor.

(6:15), and many of his disciples abandon him (6:66). The drama continues to unfold until John pronounces the final summarizing verdict on the large-scale failure of the Jews to believe in Jesus (12:36–43). These stern words do not apply exclusively to leaders, for in v. 36 Jesus is addressing the vast crowds at the Feast (*cf.* also 12:42); nor is the denunciation aimed exclusively at Judeans (as opposed to Galileans), for John explicitly identifies the crowd as 'that [which] had come for the Feast' (12:12), certainly including Galileans. When John quotes Isaiah 6 and Isaiah 53, he has in mind the rejection of Messiah by Israel, not by Judeans.

If this interpretation is correct, the significance of vv. 43–54, and their place in the development of this Gospel, become clear. The Samaritan interlude reminds the reader again of who Jesus really is: the Messiah (4:25–26), the one who has been sent by his Father to reap a crop for eternal life (vv. 34, 36), the Saviour of the world (v. 42). It also makes the large-scale failure of Israel to come to terms with Jesus all the more tragic: despised Samaritans turn to Christ, while many of the historic covenant community either actively oppose him or cannot progress beyond a fascination for miracles and politics. He came to his own, and his own received him not (1:11). Thus, for the Evangelist vv. 43–54 round out a theme begun in ch. 2. Indeed, John provides several allusions to ch. 2, as if he is self-consciously completing an *inclusio*: the references to Cana (2:1; 4:46), the miracle of water-to-wine (2:1–11; 4:46), Capernaum (2:12; 4:46), faulty faith based on miracles (2:23–25; 4:45, 48), and even an explicit numbering of the miracles (1:11; 4:54) to draw attention to the closing circle. While once again Jesus is presented as the one who gives life, the dark colours that surround this healing, projected forward by the account of the Samaritan woman (4:1–42) and by the proverb that opens the pericope (v. 44), anticipates the rising polarization in Israel, the multiplying animus that ultimately drives toward the cross. He may have been popular in Samaria, but he presses on to his own *patris*, where public sentiment will finally take him to Calvary. That is his mission: to be the Lamb of God who takes away the sin of the world.

This interpretation helps to explain why the account of the Samaritan woman is included in a book whose principal purpose is to win hellenistic Jews and proselytes to Jesus Christ (*cf.* notes on 20:30–31; Introduction, § VI). The presence of John 4:1–42 does not reflect deep dependence on Samaritan theology, or a church heavily engaged in Samaritan evangelism;[1] rather, the emphasis on the receptivity of the Samaritans, the introduction of the title 'the Saviour of the world', and the interest of the Gentiles (12:20ff.), in line with the cosmic scale the Prologue has already established, conspire to warn Jewish readers not to miss out on the blessing to which they should be heir (*cf.* 12:37ff.). John

[1]*Cf.* Margaret Pamment, *ZNW* 73, 1982, pp. 221–230.

intends to attract some of his own people to the good news of Christ Jesus by making them envious (*cf*. Rom. 11:13–14): while Jesus' blessings of new life and forgiveness are going to others, they are in danger of being passed by. They urgently need to seek out Jesus the Messiah on *his* terms, not theirs. *Cf*. Additional Note.

46. On the Greek *oun* ('Therefore') that opens this verse, *cf*. notes on 4:43–45. In addition to the connections between this verse and 2:1–11 already discussed, it is possible John is drawing a further connection. The one who transformed water into wine, eclipsing the old rites of purification and announcing the dawning joy of the messianic banquet, is the one who continues his messianic work, whether he is rightly trusted or not, by bringing healing and snatching life back from the brink of death (*cf*. Is. 35:5–6; 53:4a [*cf*. Mt. 8:16–17]; 61:1).

The Greek word for 'royal official', *basilikos*, sometimes rendered 'nobleman', probably refers to someone officially attached to the service of a *basileus*, a 'king' – here doubtless referring to Herod Antipas. He was tetrarch of Galilee from 4 BC to AD 39, and not properly a 'king' at all; but he was popularly considered one (Mk. 6:14).[1] There is no evidence that this official was a Gentile. Unlike the Gentile centurion in Matthew 8:5–13 and Luke 7:2–10 to which he is often compared, it is his son, not his servant, who is at the point of death.

47. Both here and in v. 49, the official begs Jesus to *come* or *come down* (same verb in Greek) to his home to heal his son, unlike the centurion of Matthew 8:5–13 and Luke 7:2–10 whose faith in the efficacy of Jesus' words needs no reassurance from Jesus' presence or touch, and whose humility frankly acknowledges that his home is not worthy of Jesus. The official in the verses before us sounds as if he is approaching Jesus out of the desperation of need, but with little thought as to who Jesus is. As far as the official is concerned, he has heard that Jesus can perform miracles (v. 45), and such power holds out hope for his son. Not until after the miracle is any faith displayed that goes beyond desperation (v. 53).

48. These words, addressed to the Galileans at large and not just to the royal official (hence *you people* in NIV), dominate the account and reinforce the impression that the welcome the Galileans accorded Jesus was fundamentally flawed, based as it was on too great a focus on miraculous signs (v. 45; *cf*. 2:23–25). Only here in this Gospel is the word 'wonders' (*teras*) used, and even then it is linked with 'signs' (*cf*. notes on 2:11). The sweeping rebuke Jesus offers may also be uttered as an inducement to the official's faith (unlike the centurion in the parallels cited, whose faith is spontaneous and rich).

In John's Gospel, too much interest in the raw miracles themselves is spiritually dangerous (2:23–25; 6:26). Miracles cannot compel genuine

---

[1] It is unlikely that this official was attached to the service of the Emperor, who was also sometimes referred to as 'king' in this period (*e.g.* Jn. 19:15), for Galilee was not part of any imperial province at this time. The variant *basiliskos* ('petty king') is too poorly attested to warrant overturning 'royal official'.

faith (*e.g.* 11:45–46).[1] But the apologetic value of miracles, though often exaggerated, should not be despised: Jesus himself can encourage faith on that basis, especially amongst those too skeptical to trust his word (10:38; 14:11).

49–50. The royal official is not interested in Christology or fulfilled prophecy or even in signs and wonders: he is interested in the well-being of his child (*paidion*). His urgent prayer for help (including *come down*: *cf.* notes on. v. 47) wins the Master's healing powers. The man accepts Jesus' word and departs, thus demonstrating that he, unlike most Galileans, is not simply interested in signs and wonders (v. 48).

51. While he is still *on the way*, lit. 'on the way down' (one inevitably travels 'down' to any point on the lakefront of Galilee, since the level of the lake is almost 700 feet below sea level and the surrounding land is much higher), the official runs into his servants who are bearing news of the restoration of his son.

52–53. The timing of the sudden healing, *at the seventh hour* (probably reckoning from sunrise – *i.e.* about 1.00 p.m.: *cf.* notes on 1:39), only served to strengthen the faith of the *basilikos*, since that was the time at which Jesus had performed the miracle. Both he and his household believed (thereby setting a paradigm: *cf.* Acts 10:2; 11:14; 16:15, 31; 18:8). *Cf.* the response to the first miracle performed in Galilee (2:11).

54. John is not including the signs performed in Judea (2:23). Of those done in Galilee, this was but the second (*cf.* 2:11), though many Galileans had witnessed more while they themselves were in the south (2:23; 4:45). There is no compelling reason to detect in this numbering of the first two signs detailed in this Gospel a 'signs source' that the Evangelist has incorporated into the book. The fact that the remaining signs in the Fourth Gospel are not enumerated stands against the hypothesis. For an alternative explanation, *cf.* notes above on vv. 43–45.

Additional note

43–45. Jesus' positive experience at Sychar in Samaria, presupposed in the interpretation of these verses sketched in above, may elucidate the Synoptic prohibition against going to any town of the Samaritans (Mt. 10:5–6). There Jesus sends the Twelve on a trainee mission. Since according to John his disciples had earlier witnessed Jesus' success amongst the Samaritans, they may have been tempted to see whether they could duplicate it. Quite apart from the fact that at this point their responsibility was exclusively 'to the lost sheep of Israel' (Mt. 10:6), the Twelve were still far too immature to attempt cross-cultural evangelism of a people they would accept only when the welcome mat was out: *cf.* Luke 9:52–56, where at least some disciples are eager to call down fire

---

[1]*Cf.* G. van Belle, *EphThLov* 61, 1985, pp. 167–169.

from heaven on another Samaritan town that shut its doors against Jesus and his followers.

C. RISING OPPOSITION: MORE SIGNS, WORKS AND WORDS (5:1 – 7:52)

1. The healing at the Pool of Bethesda (5:1-15)

For the view that chs. 5 and 6 were originally in the inverted order, or that ch. 6 was a later addition to the book, cf. notes on 6:1; 7:1. Chapters 3, 5 and 9 have served as the primary evidence for the thesis that the Fourth Gospel was written at two levels, that of Jesus and that of the church. There is a form of the theory that is demonstrably true (cf. Introduction, esp. §§ II, III and VI). Though describing what took place in the ministry of Jesus, John repeatedly points out what his followers grasped only later, and in any case writes so as to serve his contemporaries. But another form of this theory (e.g. Martyn, HTFG) feels it can read off this history of John's church from the surface of the text. It deserves healthy scepticism, and is discussed in the notes on ch. 9.

The three chapters of this section, John 5 – 7, record the shift from mere reservation and hesitation about Jesus to outright and sometimes official opposition. The first point of controversy is the Sabbath (5:9ff.), but this is soon displaced by a fundamentally Christological issue arising out of the dispute over the Sabbath (5:16–18), and this in turn leads to an extended discourse concerning Jesus' relationship with the Father, and the Scriptures that bear witness to him (5:19–47). Although the miracles of ch. 6 evoke superficial acclaim (6:14–15, 26), that allegiance cannot endure Jesus' teaching: even many of his disciples abandon him (6:66). By ch. 7, he is being charged with demon-possession (7:20), and, amidst profound confusion in the masses, the authorities try to arrest him (7:30), but without success (7:45–52). Throughout this rising clamour, Jesus progressively reveals himself to be the obedient Son of God, his Father (5:19ff.); the bread of life, the true manna which alone can give life to the world (6:51); the one who alone can provide the thirst-quenching drink of the Spirit (7:37–39).

1. John repeatedly ties his narrative to various Jewish feasts: cf. 2:13 (Passover); 6:4 (Passover); 7:2 (Tabernacles); 10:22 (Dedication); 11:55 (Passover). This is the only one that is not identified more precisely. A variant reading makes it 'the feast of the Jews', which would probably suggest Tabernacles or Passover; but the anarthrous reading is better attested. If Passover is intended, it might be argued that Jesus' public ministry extended to a period of about three and one-half years; if not, there is no particular reason why two and one-half years would not suffice. Some have strongly advocated Rosh ha-Shanah (the Feast of Trumpets, Lv. 23:23–25); but the strongest defence of this view, that of Guilding (pp. 70–92), depends in part on the inversion of chs. 5 and 6, and on rather late sources for the thesis that the lectionary of Jewish synagogues was full of judgment themes at that time of the year, themes parallel to those in John 5. The view that this unnamed feast is Purim, established in connection with the deliverance the Jews experienced in the time of Esther,[1] depends on too many speculative connections to be considered plausible.

The truth of the matter is that we do not know what feast John has in mind. If the other feasts are named, it is because the context in each case finds Jesus doing or saying something that picks up a theme related to it. By implication, if the feast in John 5 is not named, it is probably because the material in John 5 is not meant to be thematically related to it. Mention of *a feast of the Jews* in that case becomes little more than an historical marker to explain Jesus' presence in Jerusalem.

2. The words *there is in Jerusalem . . . a pool* have been taken by some as evidence that John wrote his Gospel before the siege and destruction of Jerusalem (AD 66–70). That is possible, but far from certain: John frequently uses the present tense to refer to past events (the so-called 'historic present'). The Greek word *probatikē* is an adjective, lit. 'having to do with sheep'; what it is modifying is uncertain. In the best reading (for the variants, *cf.* Barrett, pp. 251–252; Metzger, pp. 207–208), the word rendered 'a pool' (*kolymbēthra*) could be nominative or dative. If the latter, it is modified by the preceding phrase: *epi tē probatikē kolymbēthra* means 'near the sheep pool'. In that case the verb is left without a subject, and it remains unclear what it is that is called Bethesda. It is better to take *kolymbēthra* as a nominative. If so, the adjective *probatikē* is not explicitly modifying anything, presumably because in the days which the Evangelist is describing everyone knew what the word was attached to. The AV suggests 'sheep market'; but in the light of Nehemiah 3:1, 32; 12:39, 'near the Sheep Gate' (NIV) seems best. If John is referring to the same thing as Nehemiah, he has in mind a little opening in the north wall of the city, a little way west of the north-east corner.

The name of the pool is variously attested in the manuscripts as Bethesda, Bethzatha, Belzetha and Bethsaida. The first of these is almost certainly right, not only on various transcriptional grounds, but because it is now supported by the corresponding Hebrew name in the Copper Scroll from Qumran, first published in 1960. 'Bethesda' is the Greek transliteration of the Hebrew *bêt̠ 'ešdâ*, 'house of outpouring'; the Copper Scroll attests *bêt̠ 'ešdāṯayin*, the dual form of the same expression: 'house of twin outpourings'. (The Gk. word rendered 'Aramaic' in the NIV,

---

[1] John Bowman, *art. cit.*, tries to establish this identification as a consequence of the 'Four months and then the harvest' passage (4:35; *cf.* notes, above), where his suggestions are entirely plausible. This further step, however, turns on too many uncontrolled and merely 'possible' connections to assign it much credence. His case is not helped by his subsequent attempt to find many ties between Esther (connected with Purim) and the Fourth Gospel: *cf.* his *The Fourth Gospel and the Jews: A Study in R. Akiba, Esther and the Gospel of John* (Pickwick, 1975).

hebraïs, can refer to either Hebrew or Aramaic, and in its five occurrences in this Gospel always refers to the latter: *cf.* 19:13, 17, 20; 20:16).[1] A Bordeaux pilgrim visited Jerusalem in AD 333, and described a pair of pools with five arcades (though he called the pools 'Betsaida'). Sporadic excavations have probed the site for more than a century. It is located near the Church of St Anne, in the north-east quarter of the Old City (near Nehemiah's 'Sheep Gate'). There were two pools, lying north and south, surrounded by four covered colonnades in a rough trapezoid, with a fifth colonnade separating the two pools.[2] This hard evidence excludes the suggestion that the five colonnades are merely symbolic representations of the five books of Moses, now ineffective for healing and salvation.

3a. In the shelter of these colonnades *a great number of disabled people used to lie* (the imperfect tense in this context describing what was customary at the time).

A number of manuscripts support part or all of the NIV footnote: 'and they waited for the moving of the waters. From time to time an angel of the Lord would come down and stir up the waters. The first one into the pool after each such disturbance would be cured of whatever disease he had.' That the waters were disturbed on occasion is clear from v. 7, where the text is firm. Probably the lines in vv. 3b–4 were first introduced as marginal glosses (not every clause was introduced at the same time), reflecting popular belief about the cause of the water's disturbance. Although the twin pools were fed by the large reservoirs called Solomon's pools, they may also have been fed by intermittent springs which caused the disturbance. Some ancient witnesses speak of the redness of the water, popularly thought to be medicinal: the spring may have been chalybeate.

5. John tells us that the man had been *an invalid for thirty-eight years*. Although he may have been brought to the colonnades every day for all those years, it is perhaps more probable that he was brought there when the stirring of the water was expected. John does not identify the invalid's illness, but from v. 7 we must think of him as paralysed, lame or exceedingly weak. On the relation between his illness and his sin, *cf.* notes on v. 14.

Some have seen in these 'thirty-eight years' an allusion to the thirty-eight unnecessary years the Israelites spent in the desert, banished there because of their fear and unbelief at the first approach to the promised land (Dt. 2:14). This interpretation is unlikely: there is no interlocking symbolism between the two events. If John intends any symbolism, it may be along the following lines: just as the water from the purification pots of the orthodox could neither produce nor be mistaken for the new

[1]*Cf.* Paul Ellingworth, *BT* 37, 1986, pp. 338–341.
[2]So Origen, in his commentary on Jn. 5:2. *Cf.* J. Jeremias, *The Rediscovery of Bethesda* (Southern Baptist Theological Seminary, 1966); Wilkinson, pp. 95–104; Davies, pp. 302–313.

wine of the kingdom (2:1–11), and just as the water from Jacob's well could not satiate the ultimate thirst of religious people who may have looked to genuine revelation but whose views were widely viewed as aberrant (4:1–42), so the promises of merely superstitious religion have no power to transform the truly needy. It is not easy to understand why Dodd (*IFG*, p. 319) thinks the pool symbolizes the law. Those steeped in the Old Testament may think of this healing as a messianic fulfilment of Isaiah 35:6.

6. NIV's *learned* suggests Jesus found out about the invalid's sad condition by diligent inquiry, but the Greek participle *gnous* could equally suggest supernatural knowledge (*cf.* 1:47–48; 4:17; that it is aorist does not prove it is inceptive, 'became aware' or the like). Unlike the paralytic in Mark 2:1–12 who is dropped in front of Jesus through a hole in the roof, this one is picked out by Jesus from amongst the many other invalids. The sovereign initiative is with Jesus; no reason is given for his choice. Jesus' question, '*Do you want to get well?*', is often given a 'psychologizing' interpretation: Jesus is establishing that the first step toward wholeness is always deep desire for it (*e.g.* Barclay). But John does not develop the narrative in that direction (*cf.* following note). Jesus' question is best taken as one of the elliptical offers he is constantly making in this Gospel (*e.g.* 4:10; 6:32, 33).

7. The invalid apparently held to a popular belief that the first person into the pool after the waters had been disturbed, and only the first person, would be miraculously healed. There is no other attestation of this belief in sources roughly contemporaneous with Jesus, but analogous superstitions both ancient and modern are easy to come by. A very charitable reading of the invalid's response might take it as a direct response to Jesus' question (v. 6): the depth of his desire for healing can be measured by his persistent presence at the pool when the waters are stirred, even though he has no close friend who will ensure he is first into the water. That charitable reading would in turn reinforce the view that in v. 6 Jesus is testing the man's willingness; the test is now passed with flying colours. But John's deft portrait of the invalid throughout this chapter paints him in far more dour hues. He tries to avoid difficulties with the authorities by blaming the one who has healed him (v. 11); he is so dull he has not even discovered his benefactor's name (v. 13); once he finds out he reports Jesus to the authorities (v. 15). In this light, v. 7 reads less as an apt and subtle response to Jesus' question than as the crotchety grumblings of an old and not very perceptive man who thinks he is answering a stupid question. As in 4:11, 15, *kyrie* means no more than a civil 'Sir'. In terms of initiative, quick-wittedness, eager faith and a questing mind, this invalid is the painful opposite of everything that characterizes the wonderful character in John 9.

8. Jesus' powerful word heals the man: *Get up!* (*egeire*) anticipates the powerful voice of the Son of God on the last day (vv. 28–29), even as it exemplifies that powerful voice now (v. 25). Jesus' word also instructs the man: *Pick up your mat and walk*. The 'mat', normally made of straw, was light enough to be rolled up and easily carried on the shoulder of a well person. Jesus' command is nicely paralleled by Mark 2:11, though many other features of the two narratives differ. Probably the command was particularly suited to healed paralytics: the healed individual was not staggering off in ambiguous health, but leaving with the bodily strength necessary to carry his mat!

9a. 'Just as the thirty-eight years prove the gravity of the disease, so the carrying of the bed and the walking prove the completeness of the cure' (Barrett, p. 254).

9b–10. John briefly mentions that the healing took place on a Sabbath (v. 9b), thereby setting the stage for the confrontation and discourse that follow. There is ample evidence that numerous events in Jesus' ministry triggered controversy over the Sabbath (see below); this healing is among them. Indeed, in the larger scheme of the Fourth Gospel, this particular story has been included in John's Gospel partly because it illustrates the powerful voice of the Son of God (*cf.* notes on vv. 8, 25, 28–29), and partly because of its connection with a Sabbath dispute, and the Christological dialogue it precipitates.

The Synoptic Gospels record a number of incidents in which Jesus' activity on the Sabbath becomes the focus of controversy (Mk. 2:23 – 3:6; Lk. 13:10–17; 14:1–6; *cf.* Mt. 12:1–14). All the Gospels report that disputes between Jesus and the Jewish authorities over the Sabbath were so sharp that they figured prominently in the rising desire to kill Jesus. The reasons reported by the Synoptics for justifying Jesus' apparently lenient approach to the Sabbath include the argument that because Jesus and his followers constitute a messianic and Davidic community, the promised new age has dawned in which the Sabbath and other laws and institutions have been reinterpreted and fulfilled; that Jesus' presence means that something more than the temple has arrived; that elementary considerations of compassion warrant setting aside rigorous application of Sabbath provisions where those provisions and compassion conflict. The very diversity of the arguments attests the frequency with which the subject arose. Only here does the issue quickly develop into the relation between Jesus and his Father, in particular Jesus' right to work on the Sabbath if his Father does (5:17ff.).

The Old Testament had forbidden work on the Sabbath. But what is 'work'? The assumption in the Scripture seems to be that 'work' refers to one's customary employment; but judging by Mishnah (*Shabbath* 7:2; 10:5), dominant rabbinic opinion had analysed the prohibition into thirty-nine classes of work, including taking or carrying anything from one domain to another (except for cases of compassion, such as carrying a paralytic). By Old Testament standards, it is not clear the healed man was contravening the law, since he did not normally carry mats around for a living; according to the 'tradition of the elders' the man *was* breaking the law, since he was contravening one of the prohibited thirty-nine categories of work to which the law was understood to refer. It is not yet Jesus who is charged with breaking the law (*e.g.* for healing the man on a Sabbath, as in Mk. 3:1–6), though that will come (v. 18): for the moment, it is the healed man who must face the indignation of *the Jews* – here referring to the religious authorities in Jerusalem (*cf.* notes on 1:19).

11–13. The man defends himself by blaming the one who told him to do it. It is a doubtful exegesis that understands the man to be defending Jesus, as if he were saying that anyone with the authority to heal certainly has the authority to interpret the law authoritatively. He is simply 'ducking' the authorities; he will shortly go so far as to try to ingratiate himself with them (v. 15). For their part, the authorities perceive that anyone going around *telling* people to contravene one of the thirty-nine prohibited categories of work is far more dangerous than the odd individual who does so. They therefore inquire who the healer was (v. 12), but the healed man has no idea. There may also be a hint of irony (much more strongly developed in the healing of Jn. 9): the Jews hear of the wonderful healing and of the formal breach of their code, and are interested only in the latter. They think they see what is important, but in religious matters there are none so blind as those who are always certain that they see (*cf.* 9:39–41). Jesus himself had quickly slipped away (v. 13), acting in accordance with what became a consistent policy (*cf.* notes on 6:15).

14. *Later* (we do not know how much: on *meta tauta, cf.* notes on 2:12), Jesus finds the cured man *at the temple* (*i.e.* somewhere in the temple precincts, just south of the Bethesda pools) and explicitly connects the healing (*See, you are well again*) with the urgent need for moral reformation (*Stop sinning or something worse may happen to you*). Various scholars have insisted John is not implying that the man's illness was a consequence of a particular sin or pattern of sin. The most common reasons are: (1) 'Stop sinning' doubtless implies that the man was not chosen for healing because of his moral perfection, but it does not imply more. (2) Elsewhere in the Fourth Gospel, illness and death seem to be tied to the glory of God (9:3; 11:4); indeed, in the former of these two passages, any connection with a specific, individual sin is denied. (3) The clause 'something worse may happen to you' should be understood in line with Luke 13:1–5 – the Galileans who suffered so badly at Pilate's hands, and those on whom the tower of Siloam fell, were not pre-eminently guilty, and in the same way the thirty-eight years of paralysing illness cannot serve as an index of this man's guilt.

These arguments do not hold up to close scrutiny. (1) The issue is not whether this man was a *pre-eminent* sinner, but whether some tragedies in Scripture (and this one in particular) are seen as the outcome of specific sin. The answer is surely affirmative (*e.g.* Acts 5:1–11; 1 Cor. 11:30; 1 Jn. 5:16). This does not mean that everyone who commits these sins will inevitably fall ill or die; it does mean that some instances of suffering are the direct results of specific sin. (2) Syntactically, the two clauses, 'Stop sinning' and 'something worse may happen to you', cannot be interpreted independently. They are tied together: the meaning is 'Stop sinning *lest* something worse happen to you'. The unavoidable implication is that the bad thing that has already happened was occasioned by the sin which the person must not repeat. (3) Luke 13:1–5 has its own message for those who look on the tragedy of others: they must not interpret such tragedy as signifying that those who have suffered are morally inferior. We are all guilty; unless we repent, we too will perish. Meanwhile, it is of the Lord's mercies that we are not consumed. But Luke 13:1–5 says nothing *to the person who is suffering*, and is therefore irrelevant here. (4) It is a commonplace in many strands of Jewish and Christian theology that suffering and tragedy are the effluent of the fall, the corollary of life lived in a fallen and rebellious universe. In that sense, all sickness is the result of sin, but not necessarily of some specific, individual sin. In Matthew, Jesus' healing ministry functions in part as a sign that the deadly effects of the fall are being rolled back (Mt. 8:16–17; *cf.* Carson, *Matt*, pp. 204–207) by the one who came to save his people from their sin (Mt. 1:21). But although suffering and illness have this deep, theological connection with sin, in general, and although John elsewhere insists that a specific ailment is not *necessarily* the result of a specific sin (9:3), there is nothing in any of this that precludes the possibility that *some* ailments are the *direct* consequences of *specific* sins. And that is the most natural reading of this verse. (5) If so, it is just possible John is also telling us that the reason Jesus chose *this* invalid out of all the others who were waiting for the waters to be stirred, was precisely because his illness, and his alone, was tied to a specific sin.

If this interpretation is right, the syntax of *Stop sinning* is chosen to stress urgency.[1] The *something worse* must be final judgment (*cf.* v. 29).

15. Guilty of dullness rather than treachery, the man goes away and tells *the Jews* (*cf.* notes on v. 10) *that it was Jesus who had made him well*. It will not do to suppose he is innocently giving credit where credit is due, like the healed man in 9:11. In the latter case, credit is given when it is still a question of establishing the reality and credibility of the miracle; in the present context, the motive can hardly be a desire to assign appropriate praise to Jesus, for the hostile opposition has already manifested itself (vv. 11–13).

2. Jesus' response to opposition *(5:16–47)*

a. The relation of Jesus to his Father *(5:16–30)*

16. Exactly what is meant by *Jesus was doing these things on the Sabbath* is

---

[1]Gk. *mēketi hamartane*, lit. 'sin no more'. A prohibition using a present imperative, as here, is often taken to mean 'stop sinning' (thereby assuming the healed man had been sinning all along) rather than 'don't sin [again]' (thereby assuming he had not committed this particular sin since the fateful rebellion that had earned him the illness). That may be a correct interpretation in this instance, but there are too many exceptions to this grammatical 'rule' to base the interpretation on the present sense. It has been shown that the

not clear. The only breach recorded so far is not something Jesus himself did, but something he commanded and another did (vv. 9b–11). But the tense of the verb (imperfect in the best witnesses) may suggest that from John's perspective this particular Sabbath controversy was of a piece with a larger set of Sabbath disputes John does not find it necessary to record. That is why *the Jews* (*cf.* notes on 5:10) were persecuting him (the imperfect tense is again used).

17. The Greek says 'Jesus *answered* them', not simply 'Jesus *said* to them': no word from Jesus' opponents has been recorded, but he responds to their opposition and plots. Indeed, the verb behind 'answered' (*apekrinato*) is in the aorist middle – in John, found only here and in v. 19 (the aorist deponent passive, *apekrithē*, might be expected). Abbott (§ 2537) argues that this verbal form has legal overtones: Jesus responds to their charge, he offers his defence. The fact that the middle voice of this verb is so regularly attested in legal documents (MM, pp. 64–65) may provide some support for this view.

Jesus' response is quite unlike any he offers in other recorded Sabbath controversies (*cf.* notes on vv. 9b–10). At one level, he adopts common Jewish opinion. According to Genesis 2:2–3, on the seventh day of creation week God rested (the Heb. verb is *šābat*) from his creative work. Does God, then, keep the Sabbath law? If not, does not God himself become a law-breaker? But if he observes the Sabbath, who keeps the universe in running order while he rests? Philo, a Greek-speaking Jew heavily influenced by hellenistic writers, frankly denies that God has ever ceased his work of creation. The consensus amongst the rabbis, too, was that God works on the Sabbath, for otherwise providence itself would weekly go into abeyance. About the end of the first century, four eminent rabbis (Rabban Gamaliel II, R. Joshua, R. Eleazar b. Azariah, and R. Akiba) discussed the point, and concluded that although God works constantly, he cannot rightly be charged with violating the Sabbath law, since (1) the entire universe is his domain (Is. 6:3), and therefore he never carries anything outside it; (2) otherwise put, God fills the whole world (Je. 23:24); and in any case (3) God lifts nothing to a height greater than his own stature (*Exodus Rabbah* 30:9; *cf. Genesis Rabbah* 11:10).

Whether he breaks the Sabbath or not, God works continuously: all were agreed on that point. Assuming it, Jesus applies it to himself: *My father is always at work to this very day, and I, too, am working*. For this self-defence to be valid, the same factors that apply to God must apply to Jesus: either he is above the law given to mere mortals, or, if he operates within the law, it is because the entire universe is his. Jesus does not here argue, as he might have, that the Jews' interpretation of the Sabbath was incorrect – *e.g.* that in the Old Testament the

---

present imperative, the more highly 'marked' tense, regularly stresses urgency (*cf.* Porter, esp. pp. 335ff.).

prohibition of work on the Sabbath had reference to work normally done the other six days of the week, and therefore scarcely applied to the situation where a man, an invalid for thirty-eight years, carried his mat home after a miraculous cure! Instead, Jesus insists that whatever factors justify God's continuous work from creation on also justify his.

But what are Jesus' works? Because Jesus' response has been cast in terms of *his* works, the issue is no longer simply a matter of carrying something between domiciles on the Sabbath day. Jesus was not guilty of that 'work'. More important, his answer generalizes: the work Jesus does includes telling the healed invalid to carry his mat, but it also includes the healing itself, and, principally, all the redemptive activity Jesus undertakes. In the minute circumstances of the immediate crisis, the healed man is justified in carrying his mat because Jesus has ordered him to, and in doing so Jesus is 'working', just like the Father. Just as the fact that the Son of Man is Lord of the Sabbath can be used to defend the actions of Jesus' disciples (Mk. 2:23–28), so the fact that Jesus' works fall into the same category as his Father's works serves to exonerate the man who carries his mat.

There is perhaps another Sabbath allusion here. This confrontation leads to the ensuing discourse, which includes the affirmation that the Scriptures testify about Jesus (v. 39). *How* the Scriptures point to Jesus is not here explained; it can be deduced only from the rich diversity of the ways in which Old Testament passages are cited or alluded to in connection with Jesus' ministry. But just as the Fourth Gospel suggests that the various Jewish feasts, rightly understood, anticipated Jesus and thereby 'testify' to him, so it may be that the Sabbath festival is understood to point to him. The possibility is strengthened if Jesus is presupposing (as also Heb. 4:3–10)[1] that God's seventh-day rest (*sabbatismos*) at creation has never ended. In the Hebrews passage this 'sabbath-rest' is part of a pattern of 'rests' in the Old Testament: the seventh day, the rest of entering into the Promised Land, the promise of rest in the Psalms. The conclusion is drawn that there is still a rest for the people of God, a rest that can be entered and enjoyed by faith in Christ. This is a rest from dead works, a joyful participation in the salvation that has already dawned in Christ. None of these details is spelled out in the Fourth Gospel; but all careful readers of the ten commandments would understand that each Sabbath rest is a pointed commemoration of God's original seventh-day rest (Ex. 20:11). If the Father's work continues without pause alongside his unbroken seventh-day rest, and if Jesus' work is of a piece with his Father's work, may it not also be that his rest

---

[1] Many scholars also refer to Philo, *de Cher*. 87, for the same point. Although a parallel can be drawn, Philo's point is a little different: 'But Moses does not give the name of rest to mere inactivity. The cause of all things is by its nature active; it never ceases to work all that is best and most beautiful. God's rest is rather a working with absolute ease, without toil and without suffering.' Philo's focus is metaphysical; that of Heb.4:3–10, teleological and eschatological.

is of a piece with his Father's rest? We cannot be certain John intended to suggest so much; but it cannot escape attention that in John 7:21–24 the Sabbath which under the old covenant was subservient to circumcision becomes under Jesus' ministry subservient to the restoration of 'the whole man'.

Even Jesus' use of *my Father* adds to the pointedness of what he is saying. In corporate worship Jews sometimes spoke of God as 'our Father', but the individual way Jesus spoke of God as his own father displayed the unique Father-Son relationship Jesus claimed as his own.[1]

18. Jesus' opponents instantly grasp the implications of his remark, including the fact that he was *calling God his own Father*. Perceived infractions against Sabbath laws were serious, and might provoke murderous intent; but a man *making himself equal with God* was challenging the fundamental distinction between the holy, infinite God and finite, fallen human beings. *For this reason the Jews* (cf. notes on 1:19; 5:10) *tried all the harder to kill him.*

Various first-century pagan religions were quite happy to obliterate distinctions between God and humankind. If the exile had convinced the Jews of anything, it was that idolatry was always wrong and that God was wholly Other. 'To whom, then, will you compare God?' Isaiah asks; '"To whom will you compare me? Or who is my equal?" says the Holy One' (Is. 40:18, 25). Even a Jew as hellenized as Philo can insist, 'The mind is self-centred and godless when it deems itself to be equal to God' (*Legum Alleg.* i. 49; cf. Dodd, *IFG*, pp. 320–328). The rabbis acknowledge that God may make some like himself (chiefly Moses, Ex. 7:1) inasmuch as they represent God to others, but the four who according to Scripture *make themselves* like God all stand under terrible judgment: Pharaoh (Ezk. 29:3), Joash (2 Ch. 24:24), Hiram (Ezk. 28:2) and Nebuchadnezzar (Is. 14:14; Dn. 4; cf. SB 2. 462–465). That did not mean it was easy to arrest Jesus on a capital charge for what he had said. From their perspective he had in some sense blasphemed, but the laws regarding blasphemy (at least, a little later) were tightly defined. By the time Mishnah (*Sanhedrin* 7:5) was written (c. AD 200) blasphemy was defined as taking on one's lips the sacred name of God, YHWH ('Yahweh', 'LORD' or 'Jehovah' in English Bibles), though what passed for blasphemy may have been more loosely interpreted in Jesus' day. It may have been sufficient that Jesus, a mere mortal (from the perspective of the Jews), was saying things that made him God's equal (cf. 10:33).

Some have thought the Jews misunderstood what Jesus was saying – that Jesus was not really making himself 'equal (*isos*) with God'. In the light of the argument from 1:1 to 20:28, it is hard to believe John took

---

[1]Cf. J. Jeremias, *Abba: Studien zur neutestamentliche Theologie und Zeitgeschichte* (Vandenhoeck und Ruprecht, 1966), pp. 15–67; *idem, New Testament Theology I* (SCM, 1971), pp. 61–67. The point stands, regardless of whether there were isolated cases where individual Jews addressed God as 'Father', for Jesus' usage of this expression is set in sentences, dialogues and discourses that mark it as unique.

him that way. At the same time, John would be the first to insist that what the Jews understood by 'equal with God' was not exactly what either Jesus or John meant by it. The ensuing verses set out some of the parameters by which we may rightly understand that Jesus is equal with God (cf. Paul's remarks, also with respect to *isos*, in Phil. 2:6).[1] Jesus is not equal with God as *another* God or as a *competing* God: the functional subordination of the Son to the Father, the utter dependence of the Son upon the Father, are about to be explicated. So once again there is irony: the Jews take umbrage at Jesus' implicit claim to deity, having rightly detected the drift of Jesus' argument; but their understanding of Jesus' equality with God needs serious modification, for Christians will not accept di-theism or tri-theism any more than the Jews themselves. The ensuing verses may therefore be seen, in part, as a defence of a distinctly Christian form of monotheism (cf. Lightfoot, p. 141), as much as an explication of the nature of Jesus' equality with his Father.

19. Several scholars have argued that vv. 19–20a constitute a reworked parable: a son (the article in 'the son' is understood generically) who is an apprentice in his father's trade does only what he sees his father doing, and the father, out of love for his son, shows him all that he does. Such a parable might have been formed in Jesus' mind as he grew up learning the trade of carpentry from Joseph, until he in turn became known as the carpenter of Nazareth. It might be better to say that such a view of sonship is presupposed by Jesus' words: most sons grew up in the trade or profession served by their fathers. However, it is doubtful that vv. 19–20a at one time constituted an independent parable, not least because 'the Son' is a standard Christological expression, not easily taken generically by either first-century or modern readers.[2]

The principal thrust of v. 19 is that whatever 'making himself equal with God' (v. 18) might mean, for Jesus it does not mean complete or even partial independence from his Father (cf. 7:18). The truth is that *the Son can do nothing by himself* – or, better, 'on his own initiative' (*aph' heautou*, lit. 'from himself'). Though he is the unique Son of God (cf. notes on 1:49), and may truly be called God (1:1, 18; 20:28) and take to himself divine titles (*e.g.* 8:58) and, as in this context, divine rights (5:17), yet is he always submissive to the Father. Not only does the Son always do what pleases the Father (8:29), but he *can do only what he sees his Father doing*.[3] In this sense the relationship between the Father and the Son is

---

[1]*Cf.* now the fine essay by N. T. Wright, *JTS* 37, 1986, pp. 321–353. On the apparent discrepancy between the notion of Jesus being 'equal' with God and Jesus' statement, 'My Father is greater than I', *cf.* notes on 14:28.

[2]Although he overstates the case, Albert Vanhoye ('La composition de Jn. 5:19–30', in A. Descamps and A. de Halleux [eds.], *Mélanges Bibliques* [*Fs.* Béda Rigaux; Duculot, 1970], pp. 259–274) rightly highlights the chiasm (*i.e.* the inverted parallelism) in vv. 19–30. There are fairly close verbal and thematic correspondences between v. 19 and v. 30, v. 20 and vv. 28–29, v. 21 and v. 26, v. 22 and v. 27, and v. 24 and v. 25.

[3]On the sweep of the Son's dependence on his Father in John's Gospel, *cf.* Davey (esp. pp. 90–157), and esp. C. K. Barrett, '"The Father is greater than I" (Jo. 14,28):

250

not reciprocal. It is inconceivable that John could say that the Father does only what he sees the Son doing. That would be preposterous not only in the cultural understanding of father-son relationships, but also in John's understanding of the relationship between Jesus and his heavenly Father (against Gruenler, who tries to make the Father/Son relationship perfectly reciprocal by saying that each 'defers' to the other – but this is a 'fudge' category that blurs the obvious distinctions). The Father initiates, sends, commands, commissions, grants; the Son responds, obeys, performs his Father's will, receives authority. In this sense, the Son is the Father's agent (cf. Bühner),[1] though, as John goes on to insist, much more than an agent.

The Greek text of verses 19–23 is structured around four gar ('for' or 'because') statements. The first introduces the last clause of v. 19. The thought runs like this: It is impossible for the Son to take independent, self-determined action that would set him over against the Father as another God, for all the Son does is both coincident with and co-extensive with all that the Father does. 'Perfect Sonship involves perfect identity of will and action with the Father' (Westcott, 1. 189). It follows that separate, self-determined action would be a denial of his sonship. But if this last clause of v. 19 takes the impossibility of the Son operating independently and grounds it in the perfection of Jesus' sonship, it also constitutes another oblique claim to deity; for the only one who could conceivably do whatever the Father does must be as great as the Father, as divine as the Father.

20. The second For (gar) explains how it is that the Son can do whatever the Father does: it is because the Father loves the Son and shows him all he does. That the Father loves the Son has already been articulated in 3:35, there with the verb agapaō, here with the verb phileō. There is no difference in meaning: cf. the shifts in 11:3, 5, 36, and the notes on 3:16, 35; 21:15–17. If it is true that the Father loves the Son, it is no less true that the Son loves the Father. The love of the Father for the Son is displayed in the continuous disclosure of all he does to the Son (here in v. 20); the love of the Son for the Father is displayed in the perfect obedience that issues in the cross (14:31). The love of the Father and of the Son may be perfectly reciprocal in its purity, but not in the way the love of each is displayed.

If the Father out of love for his Son shows him all he does, and the Son in consequence and out of love for his Father obeys him perfectly and does whatever the Father does, such that people observe the Son and wonder at what he does, then two important truths follow: (1) The Son by his obedience to his Father is acting in such a way that he is *revealing* the Father, doing the Father's deeds, performing the Father's will. The

---

Subordinationist Christology in the New Testament', in J. Gnilka (ed.), *Neues Testament und Kirche* (Fs. R. Schnackenburg; Herder, 1974), pp. 140–159.

[1]Cf. also A. E. Harvey, 'Christ as Agent', in L. D. Hurst and N. T. Wright (eds.), *The Glory of Christ in the New Testament* (Fs. G. B. Caird; Clarendon, 1987), pp. 238–250.

Son is 'exegeting' or 'narrating' the Father (*cf.* notes on 1:18). (2) This marvellous disclosure of the nature and character of God utterly depends, in the first instance, not on God's love of us, but on the love of the Father for the Son and on the love of the Son for the Father. The same theme is developed in chs. 14 – 17: the achievement of the divine self-disclosure in Jesus, climaxed in the cross, was supremely the outflow of the reciprocal love of the Father and the Son within the Godhead.

To put the matter another way, if Jesus the Son of God stands with human beings, over against God, in dependence and obedience, he stands with God, over against human beings, in authority and revelation. Granted the incarnation, it is hard to see how God-made-flesh could reveal himself in any other way. The very obedience and dependence that characterize Jesus' utter subordination to the Father are themselves so perfect that all Jesus does is what the Father wills and does, so it is nothing less than the revelation of God. Small wonder that Jesus will later declare, 'Anyone who has seen me has seen the Father' (14:9; *cf.* Carson, pp. 146–162). In the immediate context, this means that Jesus' implicitly claimed 'equality with God' (vv. 17–18), as real as it is, must never be taken to mean (as the Jews apparently assumed) that God himself was compromised (if the claim were given any credence) or demeaned (assuming it were false). Far from it: the claim was true, but God was thereby revealed.

Indeed, the Father will show the Son *even greater things than these* that have been done: the healing of a particular disease (vv. 1–9), his teaching on this point, his instruction regarding the Sabbath. The Son, in obedience to what the Father shows him, will perform 'greater things': he will assume the authority and prerogatives of God himself and give life to the dead (v. 21) and pronounce final judgment (v. 22).

All this, Jesus says, will be *to your amazement* – or, more accurately put, 'in order that you may marvel'. This does not mean that Jesus derives some sort of cheap thrill at people's astonishment, and therefore shapes his mission to generate more of it, like a second-class illusionist who lives for the next round of applause. Jesus is here dealing with opponents. Because they are opponents they do not rest their faith in him. How then shall he communicate to them more of the Father's gracious self-disclosure in the Son? His progressively revelatory 'works', including his 'signs', teaching and divine authority as life-giver and judge, are designed in part to make his opponents marvel (*cf.* 10:38). That may be their first step toward faith.

21. The third *For* (*gar*) introduces an exemplification of the principal truth articulated in vv. 19–20. That the Son does whatever the Father does, owing to the Father's perfect self-disclosure to the Son, is nowhere better seen than in the perfect parallelism expressed here: *just as the Father raises the dead and gives them life, even so the Son gives life to whom he is pleased to give it*. The Old Testament writers presupposed that the raising of the dead was a prerogative belonging to God alone: 'Am I God? Can I kill and bring back to life' (2 Ki. 5:7). The same presupposition is amply attested in later Jewish tradition. Rabbi Johanan asserted that three keys remained in God's hand and were not entrusted to representatives: the key of the rain (cf. Dt. 28:12), the key of the womb (cf. Gn. 30:22), and the key of the resurrection of the dead (cf. Ezk. 37:13, SB 1. 523–524, 737, 895). Elijah was sometimes recognized as an exception: he served as a representative of God in raising the dead. But Jesus' authority in this regard goes beyond that of Elijah, for the Son gives life *to whom he is pleased to give it*. Although the Son 'can do nothing by himself' (v. 19), his will, his pleasure, his choices are so completely at one with the Father that it is no less true to say the crucial decisions are his. Unlike Elijah, Jesus is no mere instrument of divine power. (The point is further enlarged in v. 22.) Just as he chose one man out of the crowd of ill people by Bethesda (v. 6), so he chooses those to whom he gives life (cf. 15:16).

The two clauses of this verse are so parallel that 'raises the dead' must in the first instance refer to the same thing as 'gives life'. In Jewish literature of the period, resurrection from the dead belongs to the age to come: not even God himself characteristically contravenes that restriction (cf. notes on 11:24). Inevitably therefore, this verse assigns *eschatological* resurrection to Jesus (cf. vv. 25, 28–29; 1 Thes. 4:16). The person who has read this entire Gospel cannot help but think of John 11 as an anticipatory picture of the end – but still only a picture, since Lazarus is raised to a resumption of his earthly, mortal life, while the eschatological resurrection is to the life of the age to come.

Bultmann (pp. 256–257) understands vv. 21–23 to expound one simple thought, *viz.* that Jesus on behalf of his Father serves as eschatological judge, with power both to give life and to condemn. This right is certainly affirmed by the text, but the interpretation is too narrow, for it overlooks the emphasis John lays on the Son's *redemptive* work. Both the miracle of 4:46ff. and the one in this chapter display Jesus' power to grant life and strength, to bring wholeness to those at the point of death. If the Son does *all* that the Father gives him to do, that work is not *merely* revelatory and judicial; it is also atoning (1:29; 6:51; 11:49–52; 12:23–24) and quickening (5:21–24).

At the same time, Jesus' authority to 'give life' on the last day cannot be abstracted from the spiritual life he provides immediately to those who hear his word and believe him (cf. vv. 24, 25; 3:15, 16, 36). Both are contextually required. That in turn demands that we see in the life the believer may now obtain from Jesus not only a foretaste and an anticipation of the resurrection life to come, but something of its real substance – a downpayment of it (even if that category comes from Paul's pen).

22. This verse begins with the last of the four *gar* ('For') connectives. If this one is taken as parallel to the one that begins v. 23, NIV's *Moreover* is correct: *i.e.*, the demonstration that the Son does whatever the Father does (vv. 19–20) is found not only in the Son's authority to give life to the dead (v. 21) but also in his authority to give judgment on the last day (v. 22). However, it is more likely that v. 22 provides further reason and ground for the great claims of v. 21. The two clauses of v. 22, unlike the pair of clauses in v. 21, are not strictly parallel. In v. 21, *just as* the Father raises the dead, *even so* the Son gives life; but in v. 22, *the Father judges no-one*, for the sufficient reason that he *has entrusted all judgment to the Son*. The roles of Father and Son are parallel in v. 21; there is a distinction introduced in their roles in v. 22, determined by the Father. The flow of thought between the two verses, then, can be put like this: The Father and the Son both enjoy the prerogative of giving life (v. 21), *for* the Father has determined that it will not be his direct task to judge anyone, but has instead entrusted all judgment to the Son. Seen in this light, the authority to give resurrection life is the entailment of the authority to judge on the last day. Once articulated, the connection is obvious. *Cf.* also the relation between v. 26 and v. 27.

God had long been recognized as 'the Judge of all the earth' (Gn. 18:25). Throughout the pages of the Old Testament God had frequently exercised judgment in the lives of his covenant people and in the surrounding nations. But at the end of the age, there would be the last, great assize, when all would be judged, both small and great (*cf.* Rev. 20:11–15). Here, however, the Son insists that the office of judge, whether in the present or at the last day, has been entrusted to him. This does not mean Jesus will exercise judgment independently of the Father, for even the judgment he exercises is a reflection of his consistent determination to please the one who sent him (v. 30).

There exists a certain tension between 3:17 and 5:22, but it is more formal than real. The Father does not send the Son into the world to condemn (*krinō*) the world, but he does entrust all judgment (*krisis*) to the Son. The resolution turns in part on the semantic range of *krinō* and its cognates: it can refer to a (usually judicial) principle of discrimination, or to outright condemnation. John 3:17 speaks of the latter; John 5:22 refers more broadly to the former – though, clearly, any judicial discrimination issues in *some* condemnation. More importantly, John 3:17 refers to the *purpose* of the Son's coming: it was *not* to bring condemnation. By contrast, John 5:22 refers to the distinctive roles of Father and Son: the Father entrusts all judgment to the Son. That leaves room for the *purpose* of the Son's coming to be primarily salvific (3:16, 17), even though all must face him as their judge, and even though the inevitable *result* of his coming is that some will be condemned. *Cf.* also 5:26–27; 8:15–16.

23. The reason why the Father has entrusted all judgment to the Son is now disclosed: it is so *that all may honour the Son just as they honour the Father*. Whatever functional subordination may be stressed in this section, it guarantees, as we have seen, that the Son does everything that the Father does (*cf.* notes on vv. 19–20); and now Jesus declares that its purpose is that the Son may be at one with the Father not only in activity but in honour. This goes far beyond making Jesus a mere ambassador who acts in the name of the monarch who sent him, an envoy plenipotentiary whose derived authority is the equivalent of his master's.

That analogue breaks down precisely here, for the honour given to an envoy is never that given to the head of state. The Jews were right in detecting that Jesus was 'making himself equal with God' (vv. 17–18). But this does not diminish God. Indeed, the glorification of the Son is precisely what glorifies the Father (*cf.* notes on 12:28), just as in Philippians 2:9–11, where at the name of *Jesus* every knee bows and every tongue confesses that Jesus Christ is Lord, and all this is to the glory of God the Father. Because of the unique relation between the Father and the Son, the God who declares 'I am the LORD; that is my name! I will not give my glory to another' (Is. 42:8; *cf.* Is. 48:11) is not compromised or diminished when divine honours crown the head of the Son.

Granted that the purpose of the Father is that all should honour the Son, it is but a small step to Jesus' conclusion: *He who does not honour the Son does not honour the Father, who sent him.* In a theistic universe, such a statement belongs to one who is himself to be addressed as God (*cf.* 20:28), or to stark insanity. The one who utters such things is to be dismissed with pity or scorn, or worshipped as Lord. If with much current scholarship we retreat to seeing in such material less the claims of the Son than the beliefs and witness of the Evangelist and his church, the same options confront us. Either John is supremely deluded and must be dismissed as a fool, or his witness is true and Jesus is to be ascribed the honours due God alone. There is no rational middle ground.

Such a statement also betrays a strong salvation-historical perspective (as the church Fathers of the first three centuries understood).[1] Jesus is not saying that Abraham, Moses and David were not truly honouring the Father because they failed to honour the Son who had not yet been sent. Rather, he is focusing on the latest development in the history of redemption: the incarnation of the Word, the sending of the Son. Just as there were many who did not listen to the prophets of old, leaving but a remnant who faithfully obeyed Yahweh's gracious disclosures, so now with the coming of the Son there will be some who think they honour God while disowning God's Word, his gracious Self-Expression, his own Son. But they are deluded. Now that the Son has come, the person who withholds the honour due the Son similarly dishonours the Father (*cf.* 14:6; Acts 4:12). The statement not only makes an unyielding Christological claim, but prepares the way for the obduracy motif that dominates ch. 12.

24. This verse, introduced by the solemn formula *I tell you the truth* (*cf.* notes on 1:51), develops one theme introduced in the preceding verses. The Son, John has told us, 'gives life to whom he is pleased to give it' (v. 21). Who these people are is now presented in different terms: *whoever hears my word and believes him who sent me* (the Gk. construction makes

---

[1] *Cf.* M. Mees, *EphThLov* 62, 1986, pp. 102–117. After that period, the study of this passage tended to generate speculation on the metaphysical properties of the Trinity.

this a single, co-ordinate description) *has eternal life and will not be condemned*. Just as the Son healed the invalid by the pool of Bethesda by his *word*, so also is it his word that brings eternal life (*cf.* 6:63, 68) and cleansing (15:3), or judgment (12:47). The one who belongs to God hears what God says (8:47). Hearing Jesus' word is identical to hearing God's word, since the Son speaks only what the Father gives him to say. Hearing in this context, as often elsewhere, includes belief and obedience. The belief is spelled out, and its object is the one who sent Jesus – not because it would be inappropriate to specify Jesus as the object of faith (*e.g.* 3:16; 14:1), but because the immediate context is concerned to show how the Son in all he says and does mediates the Father to us. As the words and deeds of the Son are the words and deeds of the Father, so faith placed in the Son is placed in the Father who sent him.

The one who hears and believes in this way *has eternal life and will not be condemned* (*krinō*, here meaning 'judged adversely', as in 3:18). The idea is virtually indistinguishable from the negative component of Paul's doctrine of justification: the believer does not come to the final judgment, but leaves the court already acquitted. Nor is it necessary for the believer to wait until the last day to experience something of resurrection life: the believer *has eternal life* and *has crossed over from death to life* (*cf.* Col. 1:13). This is perhaps the strongest affirmation of inaugurated eschatology in the Fourth Gospel. Nevertheless, it does not mean the Evangelist has adopted the error of Hymenaeus and Philetus (2 Tim. 2:17–18), who insisted the resurrection had already taken place. The following verses (especially vv. 28–29) demonstrate that John still anticipates a final resurrection. But the stress on realized eschatology is typically Johannine.

25. The tension inherent in Christian eschatology between what belongs to the 'already' and what belongs to the 'not yet' is teased out in this and the following verses. For the expression *a time is coming and has now come*, *cf.* notes on 4:23. By v. 28, where the eschatology is orientated entirely toward the future, the 'time' or 'hour' *is coming*; John does not say it 'now is'. Here, however, the coming hour already is: the resurrection life for the physically dead in the end time is already being manifest as life for the spiritually dead. It is the voice of the Son of God (or his word: *cf.* v. 24; 6:63, 68; 11:43) that calls forth the dead, *and those who hear* (*cf.* notes on v. 24) *will live*. Such a voice, such a life-giving word, is nothing other than the voice of God (*cf.* Is. 55:3), whose vivifying power mediates the life-giving Spirit (*cf.* 3:3, 5; 7:37–39) even to dry bones (Ezk. 37).

26. The logical *For* (*gar*) is important: this verse explains how it is that the Son can exercise divine judgment and generate resurrection life by his powerful word. It is because, like God, he has life-in-himself. God is self-existent; he is always 'the living God'. Mere human beings are derived creatures; our life comes from God, and he can remove it as easily as he gave it. But to the Son, and to the Son alone, God has imparted life-in-himself. This cannot mean that the Son gained this prerogative only after the incarnation. The Prologue has already asserted of the pre-incarnate Word, 'In him was life' (1:4). The impartation of life-in-himself to the Son must be an act belonging to eternity, of a piece with the eternal Father/Son relationship, which is itself of a piece with the relationship between the Word and God, a relationship that existed 'in the beginning' (1:1). That is why the Son himself can be proclaimed as 'the eternal life, which was with the Father and has appeared to us' (1 Jn. 1:2). Many systematicians have tied this teaching to what they call 'the eternal generation of the Son'. This is unobjectionable, though 'the eternal generation of the Son' should probably not be connected with the term *monogenēs* (sometimes translated 'only begotten': *cf.* notes on 1:18). In the immediate context, it is this eternal impartation of life-in-himself to the Son that grounds his authority and power to call the dead to life by his powerful word.

27. As the Father has imparted life-in-himself to the Son (v. 26), so has he also *given him authority to judge* (cf. vv. 21–22). But an additional ground for this gift is provided: the Father has granted this authority to Jesus *because he is the Son of Man*. Because the title is anarthrous (*cf.* Additional Note), some have taken its meaning to be 'man', 'human being': Jesus is qualified to be the judge of human beings because he himself is a human being. He is one of us, and has shared our experiences. By itself that is wholly inadequate, for this condition would be met by every other human being. It is hard to believe that at this point John is neglecting the common heritage of Christian use (*cf.* notes on 1:51; 3:14–15); an allusion to the apocalyptic Son of Man of Daniel 7:13–14 is altogether likely, though here as elsewhere the title is not so stereotyped that it was instantly clear. In other uses (*e.g.* Ezekiel) it is God's way of addressing a very human prophet. Jesus could therefore shape the title to suit his own understanding of his role.

In this context three strands come together. Jesus is the apocalyptic Son of Man who receives from the Ancient of Days the prerogatives of Deity, a kingdom that entails total dominion. At the same time he belongs to humanity and has walked where humans walk (*cf.* Schlatter, p. 152). It is the *combination* of these features that make him uniquely qualified to judge. Third, judgment in the Fourth Gospel is often linked with revelation (3:19, 8:16; 12:31; 16:8, 11). Judgment descends because men love darkness rather than light. Now 'the Son of Man' has already been used in *revelatory* contexts in this Gospel (1:51; 3:14–15). The entailment of rejected revelation is judgment. Throughout this section (5:19ff.) Jesus' revelatory role has been emphasized, primarily under the title 'the Son [of God]'. But he who is the Son is also the Son of Man. His authority to judge becomes all the more understandable if it is based not only on his apocalyptic identity and his oneness with the human race, but also on the revelation he has so graciously imparted and which has so often been ignored and rejected (*cf.* Moloney, pp. 84–86). For these reasons God 'has given him authority to judge'. One could almost say this authority is but an entailment of his revelatory and life-giving functions in the midst of a dark and dying world (*cf.* notes on v. 22).

28-29. *Do not be amazed at this* refers to the teaching of the preceding verses, in particular Jesus' insistence that it is *his* voice that will call forth *all who are in their graves* on the last day. The words *for a time* (lit. 'hour', *hōra*) *is coming* are no longer qualified by 'and now is' (*cf.* notes on v. 25): the future, final apocalyptic resurrection is in view. The voice of the Son is powerful enough to generate spiritual life now; it will be powerful enough to call forth the dead then.

It has been argued that the resurrection envisaged here does not include believers, since they have already been 'raised' spiritually and do not come into judgment. Only the unbelievers are raised, and they are then divided into *those who have done good* and *those who have done evil* (*cf.* Barrett, p. 263). This will not do. Elsewhere John draws a close connection between those who experience spiritual life now and those who *will rise to live* at the last day: it is precisely they who enjoy eternal life now, by faith in Jesus and in the one who has sent him, whom Jesus will raise to life at the last day (6:40, 54). In the context of the Fourth Gospel, 'those who have done good' (or better, 'good things') are those who have come to the light so that it may be plainly seen that what they have done they have done through God (*cf.* 3:21). Conversely, 'those who have done evil [things]' 'loved darkness instead of light because their deeds were evil' (3:19). John is not juxtaposing salvation by works with salvation by faith: he will shortly insist, 'The work of God is this: to believe in the one he has sent' (6:29).[1]

Some have assigned these two verses to the hand of a later ecclesiastical redactor, largely on the ground that the futurist eschatology reflected here is out of step with the main stream of realized eschatology in this Gospel. That assignation is severely mistaken: the interweaving of the two strands lies near the heart of all Christian eschatology, including this book. That believers who already experience eternal life must rise on the last day is not incoherent: their new, resurrection-life existence will be the ratification[2] and confirmation of the life and freedom from condemnation they already enjoy. Others, Jesus insists, *will rise to be condemned* (lit. 'to the resurrection of judgment'), for in fact they have been 'condemned already' (3:18). And if realized eschatology predominates in the Fourth Gospel, it is partly because John emphasizes what Jesus actually accomplished during his ministry and by his death/exaltation, partly because of his strong

---

[1]J. G. van der Watt (*Neot* 19, 1985, pp. 71-86) proposes that 'all who are in their graves' refers to believers who lived and died before the incarnation and who will in consequence be judged according to their works. But there is nothing in the context to support such a restriction, and in any case it is doubtful if any New Testament writer holds that salvation before the coming of Jesus is based on 'works' in the absolute sense demanded by van der Watt.

[2]*Cf.* John T. Carroll (*BTB* 19, 1989, pp. 63-69) who speaks of futurist eschatology as the 'validation' of persevering belief in John's Gospel.

emphasis on *individual* renewal,[1] and partly because he focuses on the transformation of *people* (including their ultimate resurrection) and not of the universe.[2]

30. John's readers may be sure that the judgment Jesus will exercise is perfectly just, for, like everything else he says and does, in his judgment he is completely dependent on the word and will of his Father. In other words, this verse is a reiteration of vv. 19–20, specifically applied to Jesus' authority in judgment. Once again it is the very submission of Jesus to his Father, his unqualified commitment not to please himself but the one who sent him, that guarantees that all he says and does, even on the last day, is completely in accord with the Father's will.

Additional note

27. Every other occurrence of the title 'the Son of Man' in the New Testament uses a pair of articles, *ho huios tou anthrōpou*; only here is it anarthrous, *huios anthrōpou*. Of the many suggested reasons for this anomaly, the most likely two converge. The first is grammatical. It has been shown[3] that a definite predicative nominative noun that precedes the verb is most likely to be anarthrous. Moreover, both the LXX and Theodotion, Greek versions of the Old Testament, preserve the anarthrous construction in Daniel 7:13, the most dominant well-spring of 'Son of Man' motifs in the New Testament.

b. The witnesses concerning Jesus (5:31–47)

31–32. The preceding verses have emphasized that 'the Son can do nothing by himself' (v. 19; *cf.* v. 30). That is true even when the Son bears witness. *If I testify about myself*, Jesus insists, *my testimony is not valid* (v. 31). The Greek word behind 'valid' is *alēthēs*; it might be better to preserve the customary rendering, 'true'. It is a mistake to think Jesus is here discussing the conditions under which his testimony may be admitted as legally 'valid'. There are overtones of such a presentation in 8:17, but not here (so, rightly, Odeberg, p. 219, and Temple, p. 113 – though partly for the wrong reasons). Jesus certainly does not mean that if he says anything about himself it must be false (which is apparently what some Jews later understood him to be saying: *cf.* notes on 8:13ff., another instance of misunderstanding), but that if the burden of evidence to support the tremendous claims he has been making exclusively depends on his own self-attestation, his witness must be false. How could it be otherwise? He has already said in the strongest terms that all he says and does – including therefore his witness – is nothing other

---

[1] On this point, *cf.* C. F. D. Moule, 'A Neglected Factor in the Interpretation of Johannine Eschataology', in Sevenster, pp. 155–160.
[2] For John, the *kosmos* ('world') is characteristically the world of fallen *human* society, not a reference to the universe. *Cf.* Margaret Pamment, *JSNT* 15, 1982, pp. 81–85.
[3] E. C. Colwell, *JBL* 52, 1933, pp. 12–31.

than a reflection of his perfect obedience to his Father. He says and does only what the Father wants him to say and do. His witness is therefore *not* simply his own witness; it is the witness of the Father. *There is another who testifies in my favour* (v. 32), he declares, and in the light of the preceding verses this 'another' (*cf.* Additional Note) must be the Father.

At this point in the argument, then, Jesus is not claiming the Father is a witness entirely external to himself who is bearing witness for the sake of the opponents. In other contexts the Father may offer independent testimony for the sake of others (*e.g.* 12:28–30), but not here. The Father who testifies in this passage does so for Jesus' sake, to establish the content of Jesus' own utterance about himself: *I know that his testimony about me is valid.* This is of a piece with the perfect, inward awareness of his Father's will that Jesus displays elsewhere. He is the one who speaks what he knows, the one who is able to disclose heavenly things (*cf.* notes on 3:11, 12). He knows where he came from and where he is going (8:14), and stands with the Father who sent him (8:16). Jesus knows that he does not speak of his own accord: 'the Father who sent me commanded me what to say and how to say it. I know that his command leads to eternal life. So whatever I say is just what the Father has told me to say' (12:49–50). That is precisely what ensures that Jesus is not simply testifying about himself. In this context the Father's witness is for others only indirectly, *i.e.* through Jesus, who speaks and does what his Father wishes.

33–34. Jesus's hearers clearly need corroborative testimony (*cf.* notes on 1:6), and to this Jesus now turns. The first witness he mentions is John the Baptist, who came into the world to bear witness to the true light (1:7). Not only had he borne witness to the delegation sent by the religious leaders in Jerusalem (1:19–28), but he had also publicly identified Jesus as the Lamb of God, the Spirit-anointed Son of God (1:29–34). The perfect tenses ('You have sent . . . he has testified') 'present his testimony as an established datum' (Barrett, p. 264).

Although everything John the Baptist said about Jesus was true (*cf.* 10:40–41), Jesus himself did not, could not, *accept human testimony* – *i.e.*, he himself did not depend on it to establish who he was in his own mind. The preceding verses (5:19–30) have emphasized Jesus' intimate knowledge of the Father: he is able to say everything the Father gives him to say, he is able to do all that the Father does. As far as Jesus' self-consciousness is concerned, the 'another' (v. 32) who testifies in his favour is God himself. How could the witness of John the Baptist add to that? Jesus mentions the Baptist's witness, not for his own sake, but for the sake of his hearers, that they may be saved. People are saved by believing in Jesus; John the Baptist's witness may help them believe: that was its purpose (*cf.* 1:7), and hence Jesus' appeal to such witness is justified.

35. As in Matthew 11:7–15, Jesus evaluates the ministry of John the Baptist. Once more it is possible that the Evangelist includes these words to rebut followers of the Baptist who were raising him to too high a plane, but that is far from certain (cf. notes on 1:7). Although the Baptist was not the true light (1:8), he was *a lamp that burned and gave light*. Though not the light (*phōs*), he was a light-bearer, a lamp (*lychnos*). There is probably an allusion to Psalm 132:17: 'Here [at Zion] I will make a horn grow for David, and set up a lamp for my anointed one' (a *lychnos* for my *christos* in LXX 131:17).[1] The connection becomes all the tighter when it is noted that the word for 'enjoy' (*agalliathēnai*) occurs in the preceding verse of the psalm: Zion's 'saints will ever *sing for joy*' (LXX *agalliasei agalliasontai*). As a lamp, John 'burned and gave light' – or, as the Greek may suggest, 'was ignited and gave light', suggesting that John's light, his witness, was derivative of a higher source (cf. 1:33). The Jewish people generally, and even many of the leaders, *chose for a time to enjoy his light*. Both the New Testament and Josephus record that the ministry of John the Baptist generated considerable messianic excitement. His announcement that 'the Coming One' (1:27, Gk.) was near, his insistence that the people of God prepare for his coming, his implicit announcement of the dawning of the promised kingdom, the divine salvation and the pouring out of the Holy Spirit, however mingled with threats of judgment, provoked enthusiastic joy (the Greek word for 'enjoy', mentioned above, is very strong, and is used elsewhere in John only at 8:56).[2] If the Jews would remember that healthy response to John's preaching and recognize in Jesus the one whom the Baptist announced, then John's witness would prove extraordinarily fruitful. The sad reality, however, was that far too many chose to enjoy his light only *for a time*. The integrity of commitment was no greater than the depth of belief of those described in 2:23-25.

36. However valuable the testimony of John the Baptist to Jesus, before a watching world Jesus enjoys *testimony* to his person and mission that is far *weightier*.[3] This weightier testimony is the witness of the Father, which takes several forms. For a start, the works (plural, *contra* NIV) which the Father has given Jesus to finish, and which he is in process of completing, testify that the Father has sent him. These 'works' include all of Jesus' ministry, including the 'signs' (cf. notes on 2:11) which point to the climactic work, the work of redemption achieved in the cross and exaltation of the Lamb of God. Anyone who has followed John's Gospel this far will know that these works are not some mere demonstration that Jesus is a notable human being, perhaps

---

[1]Cf. F. Neugebauer, *ZNW* 52, 1961, p. 130. Cf. *Ecclus*, 48:1, which says that the word of Elijah 'burned like a torch' (*hōs lampas ekaieto*).

[2]*Contra* R. Mörchen (*BZ* 30, 1986, pp. 248-250), the use of the Greek verb in these two passages must be judged too isolated and incidental a factor to think that it signals a contrast in the text: the people's joy in John the Baptist would *not* be fulfilled, whereas Abraham's joy in seeing Jesus' day (8:56) *was* fulfilled.

[3]Some manuscripts read *meizōn* instead of *meizō*, apparently requiring the rendering, 'I who am greater than John have the witness'. That makes little sense: in the context Jesus is not comparing himself with John the Baptist. The longer form of the word may be an anomalous spelling (cf. M. I. 49).

a prophet, following the conclusion of Nicodemus (3:2). The argument in this verse turns on the exposition of the Father/Son relationship found in 5:19–30. All that Jesus does is nothing more and nothing less than what the Father gives him to do. The works he does are thus peculiarly divine: they are the works of God. Once this Father/Son relationship is grasped, everything Jesus does simultaneously attests who he is and who the Father is.

37–38. The witness the Father bears to Jesus in Jesus' works is of course indirect. But, Jesus insists, this same Father *has himself testified concerning me*. The personal nature of this divine witness to the Son is clear; the precise referent is not. The reference is probably not to the Father's witness to Jesus in the Scriptures, since they are not explicitly introduced until v. 39. Although it could be to the voice from heaven at Jesus' baptism (Mk. 1:11 par.), that event is not recorded in the Fourth Gospel (*cf.* notes on 1:32–34). It would be necessary to suppose, with Bruce (p. 136), that the readers were sufficiently familiar with that narrative that John could allude to it without narrating it himself. Some suppose this refers to the internal witness of the Spirit in the life of the believer, and cite 1 John 5:9–10 as a parallel – though it seems rather far removed from the present context. It might be better to take these words as a general reference to all of the Father's revealing work (*cf.* Lightfoot, pp. 146–147) – in antecedent redemptive event, in Scripture, in peculiar attestation of Jesus (as at the baptism), in the life of those who come to recognize who Jesus is. All such gracious revelation from the Father is understood by the New Testament writers, not least John, to serve as witness to the Son (*e.g. cf.* notes on 2:20–22; 5:39–40; 8:12; 12:41). John goes farther and points out that it is *the Father's* witness.

But Jesus' assessment of his hearers' openness to God's revelation is not sanguine. The damning indictment that follows runs along three lines. First, *You have never heard his voice* – unlike Moses, who heard God's voice (Ex. 33:11). Since Jesus speaks the words of God (3:34, 17:8), and the Jews do not hear God's voice in Jesus, it follows that they are not true followers of Moses. In fact, Moses turns out to be their accuser: if they had believed Moses, they would have believed Jesus (*cf.* notes on vv. 45–47). Second, *You have never . . . seen his form* – unlike Jacob (Israel), who saw God's form (*eidos*, both here and in LXX Gn. 32:30, 31). Since Jesus is the very manifestation of God (1:18; 14:9), and the Jews do not see God in Jesus, it follows that they are not true Israelites. Third, *nor does his* [God's] *word dwell in you* – unlike, say, Joshua (Jos. 1:8–9) or the psalmist (Ps. 119:11), who hid God's word in their hearts, meditating on it, learning not to sin against God, understanding that divine blessing in their lives was vitally dependent on the indwelling of this word. Since Jesus is the very word of God (1:1), and the Jews have no time for him, it follows that they share neither in the experience of nor the blessings upon Joshua and the psalmist.

The presupposition of this triple indictment is that Jesus' opponents had not really grasped the import of the antecedent revelation. God had spoken to the Fathers 'at many times and in various ways' (Heb. 1:1), but all of them had been anticipatory of the supreme revelation, the Son revelation (Heb. 1:2), the Word incarnate (1:14) that narrated God (1:18). Jesus is the fulfilment of all the antecedent revelation. Failure to believe in Jesus is therefore compelling evidence that, however exacting the scholarship that was studying that revelation, the revelation itself had not been absorbed, understood, obeyed. In the last clause of v. 38, *for you do not believe the one he sent*, the conjunction *for* should therefore be taken as introducing the conclusive *evidence* in support of the triple indictment, rather than as the *cause* of the spiritual and moral failure of Jesus' interlocutors.

39–40. Their tragic failure to grasp God's truth was nowhere more clearly manifest than in their approach to the Scriptures. It was not that they were negligent of this magnificent deposit. Jesus himself acknowledges, *You diligently study the Scriptures*. The form of the verb could be taken as an imperative (*cf.* AV 'Search the Scriptures'), but the context demands the indicative (*cf.* Dodd, *IFG*, pp. 329–330). The Jewish leaders of Jesus' day were undoubtedly diligent students of the Scriptures; they needed no exhortation along these lines. The verb rendered 'diligently study' corresponds to the Hebrew verb *dāraš*, a technical term used to refer to their study and exposition of the Bible and of 'oral Torah', the body of oral traditions that had also come down to them. But Jesus points out that their primary motivation in such diligent study was the hope of final acceptance by God: *you think that by them you possess eternal life*. Certainly there is ample external evidence that supports this reading of Jewish motivation: *e.g.* Hillel affirms that the more study of the law, the more life, and that if a man gains for himself words of the law he has gained for himself life in the world to come (*Pirke Aboth* 2:7).

By contrast, Jesus insists that there is nothing intrinsically life-giving about studying the Scriptures, if one fails to discern their true content and purpose. *These are the Scriptures*, Jesus says, *that testify about me*. This is one of six passages in the Fourth Gospel where Scripture or some writer of Old Testament Scripture is said to speak or write of Christ, even though no specific passage is adduced (*cf.* 1:45; 2:22; 3:10; 5:45–46; 20:9). What is at stake is a comprehensive hermeneutical key. By predictive prophecy, by type, by revelatory event and by anticipatory statute, what we call the Old Testament is understood to point to Christ, his ministry, his teaching, his death and resurrection.

Jesus makes a similar point in numerous passages in the Synoptic Gospels: *e.g.* both the law and the prophets prophesy until John (Mt. 11:13), and Jesus has come to fulfil the law and the prophets (Mt. 5:17ff.). Paul discovered that the law was not life-giving in itself (Rom. 7:10), and argues that, granted the sinfulness of the human race, no such life-giving law was possible (Gal. 3:21). Jesus Christ is the one to whom the Father has granted the right to have life in himself and to impart it to others (5:21, 26), as the Prologue has already suggested (1:4). He is 'the end of the law so that there may be righteousness for everyone who believes' (Rom. 10:4). Like John the Baptist (vv. 33–35), the Scriptures, rightly understood, point away from themselves to Jesus.

If therefore some of the Jews refuse to come to Jesus for life, that refusal constitutes evidence that they are not reading their Scriptures as they were meant to be read. No independence is more arrogant and more delusive than religious independence, which reaches its tragic apogee when the central meaning of Scripture is perverted. 'The world's resistance to God is based on its imagined security, which reaches its highest and most subversive form in religion and thus, for the Jews in their pattern of life based on Scripture. Their "searching" in the Scriptures makes them deaf to Jesus' word' (Bultmann, pp. 267–268).

Living as we do in a day rightly sensitive to anti-Semitism, it must be noted that Jews are far from being the only people who have read Scripture and supposed that its life-transforming power depends on much study but not particularly on Jesus. Moreover, the firm judgment against Jesus' interlocutors in these verses is no reflection of racial bias but of hermeneutical values (*cf.* Lk. 24:27, 45).

41–42. Jesus has already said that he does not accept human testimony (v. 34); now he adds that he does not accept human glory (*doxa*; *cf.* notes on 1:14), *praise from men*. The works that he does, including the signs, testify to who he is (5:36); in so doing, they manifest his glory (*doxa*; *cf.* notes on 2:11). With testimony of such calibre supporting him, his opponents must not think that he is scolding them out of petty pique, desperate to win their acclaim. If he stooped to become the kind of Messiah they wanted, doubtless he could attract their praise. But his entire commitment is to please his Father (5:19ff.), receiving the honour that only the Father can bestow (5:23), enjoying the 'glory' (*doxa*) of the one and only Son from the Father (1:14).

By contrast, Jesus' opponents 'accept praise from one another' (v. 44). *I know you*, Jesus says: not only does he know that the love of God is not in their hearts, but he knows *them*, with the all-seeing perception already attested in 2:24–25. The expression *the love of God* could be taken two ways: either Jesus is saying that they are not men whom God loves, or that they are not men who love God. The latter makes more sense in the context: they are people who love the darkness rather than the light (3:19). This interpretation also explains the *but* at the beginning of the verse: Jesus does not accept praise from men (v. 41), for his single-eyed vision is to do what pleases his Father (*cf.* 8:29) as his expression of filial love for the Father (*cf.* 14:31); *but*, by contrast with Jesus, his interlocutors do not love God.

43. Further evidence of their failure is found in their refusal to accept Jesus. Although he has come in his Father's name (a re-articulation of the theme of 5:19ff.: the Son's status as an emissary of the Father, with all the functional subordination that entails, is conjoined with the authority of the Father), his opponents do not accept him. Had they truly loved God, they could not have failed to love God's Son. As John elsewhere puts it, love for God is demonstrated in the keeping of his commandments, one of the chief of which is the command to believe in his Son Jesus Christ (1 Jn. 3:23; 5:3).

The chief punishment of the liar is not so much that he is not believed but that he does not believe; similarly, the chief judgment on those who deny that Jesus is the promised Messiah, the Son of God, is not so much that they have no Messiah, but that they follow false messiahs: *if someone else comes in his own name, you will accept him.* The reason is provided in the next verse. Josephus reports a string of messianic pretenders in the years before AD 70 (*Ant.* xx. 97–99, 171–172; *Bel.* ii. 258–265);[1] some scholars have suggested that a particular claimant is in view, such as Bar Kochba, who led an unsuccessful revolt about AD 132, and whom no less than the great Rabbi Akiba viewed as the 'star out of Jacob' prophesied by Balaam (Nu. 24:17) until he and his followers were routed and killed by the Romans. But the text is less interested in identifying a particular charlatan than in contrasting all messianic pretenders with Jesus.

44. The reason why Jesus' interlocutors were eager to accept messianic claimants who came in their own name but were unwilling to receive the one who came in the Father's name is now made clear. Like most people then and now, they were heavily dependent on accepting *praise* (*doxa*) *from one another*; they made *no effort to obtain the praise* (*doxa*) *that comes from God* (see Additional Note). Inevitably, that meant they were open to messianic claimants who used flattery or who panted after great reputations or whose values were so closely attuned to their audience that their audience felt they were very wise and farsighted; they were not open to the Messiah that Jesus was turning out to be, one who thought the only *doxa* ('glory'/'praise') worth pursuing was the glory of God. John sums up the tragic situation of most of his fellow Jews a little farther on: 'they loved praise (*doxa*) from men more than praise (*doxa*) from God' (12:43). How then could they believe? *Cf.* the apostle Paul's conclusion that a true Jew, circumcised in the heart, is one whose 'praise (*epainos*) is not from men, but from God' (Rom. 2:29).

45. In the great assize on the last day, it will not be Jesus who presses the charges and prosecutes the Jews he is addressing. His primary purpose is to save, not condemn (3:17). In any case there is no need for him to assume this role: Moses will be their accuser, the very Moses whom they esteem so highly as the mediator of the Sinai covenant, the one through whom God had given the law they so highly venerated (*cf.* Rom. 2:17). Indeed, there is evidence that at least some Jews thought that Moses continued to serve as a mediating intercessor, praying for them in heaven as he had prayed for them on earth in connection with the episode of the golden calf (Ex. 32:30–32; *cf. Assumption of Moses* 12:6, Meeks, p. 161). But whether the Jews 'set their hope' on Moses on account of their belief in his continued mediatorial role, or on account of his service in bringing the Sinai covenant to them (while it was the

---

[1] *Cf.* P. W. Barnett, *NTS* 27, 1980–81, pp. 679–697.

covenant itself that gave them confidence), they are, Jesus insists, deluded.

In this context (cf. especially vv. 39–40), it is clear that any accusation Moses brings will not be based on failure to obey this or that command, this or that provision of the covenant (cf. Rom. 2:12), but on their failure to understand the law-covenant. They take it as an end in itself, the final epitome of right religion, and not, as Jesus insists it was, as witness to Christ himself. If scupulous adherence to the law brings people to hope for salvation in the law itself and to reject the Messiah to whom the law pointed, then the law itself, and its human author, Moses, must stand up in outraged accusation.

46. The Greek text begins this verse with 'For' (*gar*): *For if you believed Moses, you would believe me*. They pinned their hopes on Moses (v. 45), not in the one of whom Moses wrote. No specific passage from the books of Moses is mentioned (cf. notes on v. 39). If a particular one is in view, perhaps it is Dt. 18:15 (cf. notes on Jn. 1:21; 4:19; 6:14; 7:40, 52). But it is perhaps more likely that this verse is referring to a certain *way* of reading the books of Moses (cf. notes on 1:51; 2:19) than to a specific passage (cf. Carson, 'OT').

47. The writings of Moses and the words of Jesus are closely linked. It is assumed that they have similar authority; but they are linked in another way, such that to believe one is to believe the other, and to reject one is to reject the other. It could scarcely be otherwise, if, in the terms of the sermon on the mount, Jesus came to fulfil the law and the prophets (Mt. 5:17). The Jews' failure to grasp what Moses and his writings were about is described as not *believing* what he wrote: *i.e.* this favourite term of the Evangelist includes more than mere credence, but right understanding and hearty obedience as well (cf. Lk. 16:31).

The opposition against Jesus is rising, and will culminate in his crucifixion, an execution publically justified, ironically, by an appeal to the law itself (19:7). But for the reader, there is an implicit invitation to understand and believe in Jesus and the law of Moses in a way that many Jews of Jesus' day did not.

Additional notes

31–32. It has often been noticed that the word for *another* (v. 32) is *allos*, which in classical Greek frequently denoted 'one in addition to the one(s) mentioned', and usually of the same sort – as opposed to *heteros*, which denoted one of two, and sometimes (though by no means always) with an implied contrast (cf. LSJ *s.v.*). If the distinction holds here, then Jesus is being placed on the same level as his Father. But the distinction is rare in the New Testament (though cf. Gal. 1:6–7). The word *heteros* occurs only once in the Fourth Gospel (19:37), and there it is indistinguishable from the classical use of *allos*! Moreover the use of *allos* in 5:43 (NIV 'someone else'), in the same discourse as the occurrence being examined, clearly must not be taken to mean 'another of the same sort'.

In short, no Christological weight can rest on this choice of pronoun. *Cf.* also the notes on 14:16.

39. In a few Old Latin and Old Syriac manuscripts, and in Papyrus Egerton 2, there is a variant in the punctuation that reads v. 39 as follows: 'You search the Scriptures in which you think you have eternal life.' This is almost certainly secondary. The central point is in any case secured: the Scriptures testify to Jesus Christ.

44. The AV offers 'the honour that cometh from God only', but this is an unsupported translation: NIV's 'only God' is correct. Some manuscripts omit 'God': 'the glory that comes from the Only One'. The meaning is but little affected. The shorter reading probably developed by the accidental dropping of $\overline{\Theta Y}$ in an early uncial manuscript reading TOYMONOY$\overline{\Theta Y}$OY.

3. The feeding of the five thousand *(6:1–15)*

This is the only miracle during Jesus' ministry that is recorded in all four Gospels. In one sense that is not surprising, since this is the only chapter in John that treats the Galilean phase of Jesus' ministry with which the Synoptists are so concerned. Several scholars have argued at length that John wrote his account completely independently of the written accounts that have come down to us in the Synoptics (Mt. 14:13–21; Mk. 6:35–44; Lk. 9:10–17; *cf.* also the feeding of the four thousand, Mt. 15:21–28; Mk. 8:1–9). But as elsewhere, a good case can be made that John knew of Mark's account (*cf.* Barrett, pp. 271ff.) – not that he copied him slavishly, but that he was familiar with his record of the details. The differences are minor, and can usually be explained in terms of the themes John wishes to emphasize. At one point, John and Mark provide clarifying details that help to explain the other's text (*cf.* notes on 6:5, 15).

1. *Some time after this* renders the same Greek expression, *meta tauta*, that introduces 5:1 and 6:1 (*cf.* notes on 2:12). The expression is vague: it establishes sequence, but not tight chronology. The next words establish that Jesus travelled to the east side of *the Sea of Galilee*, since *the far shore* is normally determined from the west side, the dominantly Jewish side. Because ch. 5 is set in Jerusalem, while 4:43–54 is set in Galilee, some have suggested that chs. 5 and 6 have somehow been displaced: ch. 5 should be set between chs. 6 and 7. This is only a marginal geographic 'improvement': there would still be a leap from the end of ch. 5 (set in Jerusalem) to the beginning of ch. 7 (set in Galilee). Moreover the motivation for the remark of Jesus' brothers in 7:3 largely disappears if ch. 7 is preceded by ch. 5 and not ch. 6. Other chronological difficulties, connected with the feasts, are also introduced. Moreover in the opening period of Jesus' ministry (1:19 – 4:54), the sudden shifts in location are rather striking. On the assumption that the order of the text is correct as it is, readers will not be surprised that the Evangelist now maintains the same kind of rapid oscillation. Rather oddly, Schnackenburg, 2.8, who argues for the transposition, appeals to the 'frequency of movement' in

1:19 – 4:54 as a reason why later editors might have set the chapters in the order we have them – 'to keep the impression of a constant shift in Jesus' activity between Galilee and Judea.' It is difficult to understand how an editor could be sensitive to such fine literary subtleties while being such a dimwit that he failed to perceive the geographical problem that the alleged transposition introduced.

The *Sea of Galilee* was in Old Testament times called Kinnereth ('lyre') because of its shape. About AD 20 Herod Antipas founded a city on the west shore and called it Tiberias, after the Roman emperor Tiberius Caesar. Gradually the name Tiberias was transferred to the lake, though probably the change was not common in poplar parlance until much later in the century, when John wrote. Hence John's parenthetical explanation (assuming that is the correct text, which is likely).[1]

2. A *great crowd of people* (*cf.* Mk. 6:33–34) followed him, not so much because they wanted to obey him, but, like those described in 2:23–25, *because they saw the miraculous signs he had performed on the sick*.

3. The Greek *to oros* does not necessarily refer to a particular mountain or hillside, but may simply mean 'the hill country' or 'the high ground', referring to the area east of the lake and well known today as the Golan Heights. Mark's 'a solitary place' (6:32) is not in conflict with this description, but is presupposed by it: Jesus *sat down with his disciples*, apparently intending to be alone with them (as Mark makes clear), and only then observes the great crowd closing in on him (v. 5).

4. Although this is the second of three Passovers mentioned by John (*cf.* 2:13, 23; 11:55ff.), his reason for including this aside is not so much chronological as theological. The Jewish Passover celebrated the exodus from Egypt. Intrinsic to the celebration was the slaughter of a lamb in each household, which then ate it. In this Gospel Jesus is the Lamb of God (1:29, 36). The first Passover to be mentioned (2:13, 23) is in the context of Jesus' self-designation as the temple that would have to be destroyed – a way of pointing to his death; the third Passover (11:55ff.) is at the time of his death. This intermediate one occurs about (John says it was *near*) the time of the feeding of the five thousand, which precipitates the bread of life discourse, in which Jesus identifies his flesh as the true bread that must be given for the life of the world (6:33, 51), the bread that must be eaten if people are to have eternal life. The connections become complex: the sacrifice of the lamb anticipates Jesus' death, the Old Testament manna is superseded by the real bread of life, the exodus typologically sets forth the eternal life that delivers us from sin and destruction, the Passover feast is taken over by the eucharist (both of which point to Jesus and his redemptive cross-work). 'The movement from the miracle to the discourse, from Moses to Jesus (*vv.* 32–5, *cf.*

---

[1]Some manuscripts omit 'of Galilee', leaving only (in Greek) 'the Sea of Tiberias'. Others add *eis ta merē* after 'of Galilee', *i.e.* 'of the Sea of Galilee to the regions of Tiberias'. Apart from its weak external attestation, however, it is difficult to imagine how this reading could have generated the text as it stands.

i. 17), and, above all, from *bread* to *flesh*, is almost unintelligible unless the reference in *v.* 4 to the Passover picks up i. 29, 36, anticipates xix. 36 (Exod. xii. 46; Num. ix. 12), and governs the whole narrative' (Hoskyns, p. 281). At the same time, the Passover Feast was to Palestinian Jews what the fourth of July is to Americans, or, better, what the anniversary of the Battle of the Boyne is to loyalist Protestants in Northern Ireland. It was a rallying point for intense, nationalistic zeal. This goes some way to explaining the fervour that tried to force Jesus to become king (*cf.* notes on v. 15).

5. Just as John sometimes provides details that help to explain puzzles in the Synoptic narrative (*cf.* notes on v. 15), so the reverse is sometimes true. Mark 6:33–35 explains that, after the crowd had run around the north end of the lake in order to catch up with him, Jesus taught them at some length – and that is why he felt concern about feeding them. Entirely within the normal range of Gospel reportage is the variability that assigns first mention of the problem to the disciples (Mark) or to Jesus (John). John's purpose is doubtless to preserve the initiative with Jesus. Only John specifies Philip (v. 5) and Andrew (v. 8); the Synoptics speak rather vaguely of 'the disciples'. Many have taken this as a sign of lateness, a piece of over-specification added by an author for verisimilitude. But B. M. Metzger has shown that names are as frequently omitted by later writers as added by them,[1] making any *a priori* charge presumptuous. In this instance Philip was the obvious person to ask: he came from the nearby town of Bethsaida (1:44). Specification of such details may therefore more reasonably be taken as evidence for the recollection of an eyewitness.

6. John adds this comment to forestall any reader from thinking that Jesus was stumped, surprised by the miracle that was eventually performed. The Evangelist avers that Jesus already had his own plan, but that the problem itself gave him a further opportunity to test Philip. The verb *peirazō* ('test') is commonly used by the Evangelists in the bad sense of 'tempt', to solicit to do evil. The word itself, however, is neutral, and is entirely appropriate here.

7–9. Philip's response betrays the fact that he can think only at the level of the marketplace, the natural world. One *denarius* was a day's pay for a common labourer; two hundred *denarii* (also specified at Mk. 6:37) therefore represents *eight months' wages* (NIV). Since a substantial proportion of a worker's wage went into daily food, this was, presumably, enough to provide for a family for eight months or a little longer. But the crowd was so large (v. 10) that even such a large sum of money *would not buy enough bread for each one to have a bite!*

Andrew's contribution is to introduce *a boy with five small barley loaves and two small fish* (v. 9). Only the Fourth Gospel specifies that these were

---

[1]'Names for the Nameless in the New Testament: a Study in the Growth of Christian Tradition', in *New Testament Studies: Philogical, Versional, and Patristic* (E. J. Brill, 1980), ch. 2.

barley loaves, the inexpensive bread of the poorer classes (*cf.* Philo, *Spec. Leg.* iii. 57). Some have seen in this detail an allusion to the miraculous feeding reported in 2 Kings 4:42–44: Jesus is a prophet greater than Elijah or Elisha. The Greek word *paidarion*, rendered 'a boy', can refer to a young man or a young slave (*cf.* BAGD and MM, *s.v.*; *NewDocs* 1. § 45). Elisha's servant is twice called a *paidarion* in the same chapter where he assists his master with the miraculous feeding (2 Ki. 4:38, 41 LXX; *cf.* Barrett, p. 275). The 'small fish' (*opsaria*) were probably pickled fish to be eaten as a side dish with the small cakes (scarcely 'loaves') of barley bread (though *cf.* notes on 21:9, 10, 13). Andrew's point, of course, was that this tiny meal was ludicrously inadequate to the need. John mentions it to heighten the miracle.

10. Despite the size of the crowd, Jesus proceeds in an orderly fashion, seating the people in preparation for the meal. Mark 6:39–40 mentions that they 'sat down in groups of hundreds and fifties', and that the grass was 'green' – another personal recollection of detail, and confirmation that the event took place in March or April (*i.e.* near Passover) when the grass is still green, before the hot summer sun burns it brown. Jesus has *the people* (*hoi anthrōpoi*) sit down; the number of the *men* (*hoi andres*) was *about five thousand*. The same distinction appears in all four Gospels, with Matthew 14:21 emphasizing the point. The total number of people may well have exceeded twenty thousand or more. In the light of v. 15, where the people try to make Jesus king by force, it is easy to think that, at least in John, the specification of five thousand *men* is a way of drawing attention to a potential guerrilla force of eager recruits willing and able to serve the right leader.

11. If Jesus used the common form of Jewish thanksgiving, he said something like this: 'Blessed art thou, O Lord our God, King of the universe, who bringest forth bread from the earth.' Jesus 'blesses' God, *i.e.* he thanks God; he does not 'bless' the food. The verb rendered *gave thanks* is the participle *eucharistēsas*, clearly cognate with the ecclesiastical term 'eucharist' by which many Christians refer to the Lord's supper, holy communion. The verb itself, however, is insufficient evidence to suppose that John is either anachronistic, or trying to portray the feeding as a eucharistic celebration. It is perfectly appropriate in the Jewish setting described here, and is in fact used in many different 'thanks' situations in the New Testament. Moreover if John were trying to project eucharistic symbolism, he missed many good opportunities: he does not mention the breaking of the bread, or the distribution of the pieces (unlike Mark). What John stresses, instead, is the lavishness of the supply: the people ate *as much as they wanted*, far outstripping the titbit that even two hundred *denarii* would have failed to supply (v. 7). So also the true bread from heaven who gives life to the world far outstrips the manna in the desert (vv. 30–33).

12–13. All are satisfied; *all had enough to eat*. John portrays this as a miracle, not a eucharistic mouthful, still less an ethical lesson on how to shame people into sharing their lunches. This is the ample provision of the Lord who declares, 'My people will be filled with my bounty' (Je. 31:14). Though the Lord has lavish abundance to meet the needs of the people, he will let *nothing be wasted*. Collecting what was left over at the end of the meal was a Jewish custom (SB 4. 625–626). Nevertheless in this injunction there is doubtless an ethical note of social responsibility that is patient of many applications. Twelve baskets are filled with leftovers: 'after all have been satisfied there is more left over than there was at the beginning!' (Bultmann, p. 213). That there were *twelve* baskets is almost certainly significant: the Lord has enough to supply the needs of the twelve tribes of Israel. All four Gospels draw attention to the number. From the time of Hilary of Poitiers (fourth century AD), it has been common to argue that the feeding of the five thousand represents the Lord's provision for the Jews, and the feeding of the four thousand, with seven baskets left over, represents the Lord's provision for the Gentiles. Certainly the word for 'basket' (*kophinos*) used in all four accounts of the feeding of the five thousand has peculiarly Jewish associations, whereas the 'basket' (*spyris*) used in the feeding of the four thousand (Mt. 15:37; Mk. 8:8) does not. It strains credulity, however, to suppose that John saw in the leftovers a symbol of the 'food that endures' (6:27).

14. It is uncertain whether the text speaks of 'the miraculous signs that Jesus did' or *the miraculous sign that Jesus did* (*cf.* Additional Note). Either way, the people find in the *miraculous sign* (*cf.* notes on 2:11) sufficient evidence to argue that Jesus is the expected *Prophet who is to come into the world* (*cf.* notes on 1:21). The reference is to Deuteronomy 18: 15–19 and the promise of a prophet like Moses. Certainly some first-century Jews interpreted that passage messianically, though admittedly there was diversity of opinion (*cf.* Meeks, pp. 91–98). Doubtless Jesus' provision of so much bread to so many people in a wilderness area prompted some to think of Moses' role in providing manna. Toward the end of the third century AD, Rabbi Isaac argued that 'as the former redeemer caused manna to descend . . . so will the latter Redeemer cause manna to descend' (cited in *Ecclesiastes Rabbah* on Ec. 1:9); perhaps the same sentiment coursed through some circles in the first century (*cf.* notes on v. 31). Against some contemporary commentators, it is important to note that John does not argue that the people are wrong in this judgment, but only in their estimate of its significance. Their attention was focused on food (v. 26) and victory (v. 15) – not on the divine self-disclosure mediated through the incarnate Son, not on the Son as the bread of life, not on a realistic assessment of their own need.

15. The reason Jesus *withdrew* (or 'fled': the witnesses vary) *to a mountain* (farther up the Golan Heights) by *himself*, leaving his disciples to cross the lake on their own (vv. 16ff.) was his knowledge, supernatural or merely insightful, that the crowds *intended to come and make him king by force*. The juxtaposition of v. 14 and v. 15 presupposes that the people who think Jesus may well be the eschatological *Prophet* (v. 14) understand this Prophet's role to be simultaneously kingly. If the first prophet, Moses, had led the people out of slavery to Egypt, surely the second would help them escape servitude to Rome. The Galileans themselves, of course, were not directly under a Roman governor, as were the Judeans, but Herod Antipas, their ruler, was merely a Roman puppet. This does not necessarily mean that they understand Jesus to stand in the Davidic line. Elsewhere in the Fourth Gospel we find some people distinguishing between the promised prophet and the Davidic Messiah (1:19–25; 7:40–42). Certainly such distinctions are attested in some Jewish sources (*e.g.* IQS 9:11). The desires of this crowd do not constitute evidence for a well-formulated theological structure. Rather, they had witnessed or heard of Jesus' miracles of healing, and they had been fed from food provided by his miraculous power. Surely nothing could prevent such a person from being the powerful liberator that so many children of Israel longed for. And if he was unwilling to assume the prerogatives and responsibilities of such leadership, they were more than willing to force the issue by fomenting a rebellion, crowning him king and daring the authorities to respond – thus forcing him to assume the mantle they had in mind for him.

Mark and John are mutually supportive: each makes clear certain features of the other's account. Mark points out that just before the feeding of the five thousand, Jesus sent the Twelve on a trainee mission throughout Galilee. The results were so spectacular that Herod Antipas was terribly upset, and wondered if John the Baptist, whom he had beheaded, had come back to life (Mk. 6:7–30). In the light of his popularity with the crowds, Jesus crossed over to the east bank of the lake, along with his disciples, in order to gain some respite from their pressing attentions, and perhaps also to escape Herod's jurisdiction. But the surging crowd ran around the north end of the lake and met Jesus on the east bank: escaping from Herod was easier than escaping from the crowd. Jesus taught them and fed them, for 'he had compassion on them, because they were like sheep without a shepherd' (Mk. 6:34). This does not so much mean that Jesus viewed them as a congregation without a pastor, as that he saw them as an army without a general (1 Ki. 22:17).[1] He well knew that the wrong sort of 'king' would not only divert them from the things that really mattered, but could lead them into a conflict with Rome from which they could not escape without a disastrous beating. All of this background, made clear in Mark, explains John 6:15. John does not bother to provide more details, most likely because they were largely irrelevant when he wrote: Jerusalem had already fallen, and the political setting was vastly different from when Jesus ministered and Mark wrote. Yet ironically, it is John, not Mark, that preserves the conclusion that Jesus knew the people were going to try to make him king by force – a fitting capstone for, and corroboration

---

[1] *Cf.* T. W. Manson, *The Servant-Messiah* (Cambridge University Press, 1953), p. 70; Bruce, p. 147.

of, Mark's account, and a compelling explanation of Mark 6:45.

The real nature of Jesus' kingship becomes a major issue in the passion narrative (18:33ff.). The truth of the matter is that Jesus' kingdom was like no other (18:36). Jesus himself knew that the way his kingdom would triumph would not be by beating the enemy in siege warfare, but by dying and rising from the dead; 'he would go to Jerusalem not to wield the spear and bring the judgment, but to receive the spear thrust and bear the judgment'.[1] Perhaps he recognized in the mob's enthusiastic but unwelcome attention the same temptation that he had confronted in the wilderness (Mt. 4:8–10; Lk. 4:5–8). And so he fled, abandoning the crowd and (according to Mark) sending even his own disciples away, back across the lake, perhaps in fear that they too might become contaminated by the crowd's irrepressible but misguided enthusiasm.

Additional note

14. The difference between 'sign' and 'signs' is the difference between *ho . . . sēmeion* and *ha . . . sēmeia*. The plural is supported by a small number of witnesses, but they are a powerful combination. Metzger (p. 211) argues that the plural is a scribal assimilation to the plurals in 2:23 and 6:2. That may be, but one might equally argue that the singular is a scribal 'correction' to align John's comment with the single miracle that had just been performed (an argument that Metzger himself uses in relation to 11:45). On balance, it is probably wise to adopt, rather tentatively, the singular reading, attested by the overwhelming majority of witnesses.

4. Jesus walks on the water (6:16–21)

The reasons why John included this paragraph, even though there is no dialogue or discourse that is thematically directly dependent upon it, include the following: (a) the story was apparently linked with the feeding of the five thousand in much early Christian transmission (Mt. 14:22–34; Mk. 6:45–52; though it is not found in Lk. 9); (b) it explains how Jesus and his disciples returned to Capernaum on the western side of the Lake (*cf.* vv. 24, 59); (c) it is tied to the exodus theme (*cf.* notes, below), which has already been introduced (*cf.* notes on vv. 14–15); and (d) structurally, it is tied to vv. 1–15 in much the same way that vv. 59–71 are tied to vv. 22–58 to form an ABCAB structure – *i.e.* A = 6:1–15; B = 6:16–21; C = 6:22–26; A = 6:27–58; B = 6:59–71. In both instances the 'B' is shorter than its corresponding 'A', it contracts from a focus on the crowds and the opponents to the disciples, and in both even the disciples themselves prove inadequate, in need of the sovereign intervention of Jesus.

[1] Edmund P. Clowney, *art. cit.* (*cf.* fn. on 1:1).

Alternatively, some hold that *each* of the seven 'signs' in John's Gospel (not including Jesus' death and resurrection) is paired with a discourse. The discourse may precede or succeed its corresponding sign. The list cautiously suggested by Morris (*JC*, p. 23) is as follows:

Signs	Discourses
1. Water into wine (2:1–11)	1. The new birth (3:1–21)
2. Healing the nobleman's son (4:46–54)	2. The water of life (4:1–42)
3. Healing the lame man (5:1–18)	3. The divine Son (5:19–47)
4. Feeding the multitude (6:1–15)	4. The bread of life (6:22–65)
5. Walking on the water (6:16–22)	5. The life-giving Spirit (7:1–52)
6. Sight to the man born blind (9:1–41)	6. The light of the world (8:12–59)
7. Raising of Lazarus (11:1–57)	7. The good shepherd (10:1–42)

To this one might add the passion and resurrection of Jesus (chs. 18 – 20), paired with chs. 14 – 17. On this view, the discourse that corresponds to the walking on the water, where Jesus makes himself known to his disciples on *his* terms, immediately after rejecting the groundswell of enthusiasm to crown him king (6:15), is the discourse where Jesus makes his presence known in Jerusalem, on his own terms (and not as a response to his brothers' demands), and promises that 'in the person of the Spirit' he would 'be present to meet the need of his own' (Morris, *JC*, p. 35; *cf.* 7:37–39).

This is not quite convincing. For instance, on any reading of 7:37–39 Jesus does *not* talk about being present with his people in the person of his Spirit: that is to read the *Paraclete*-passages of John 14 – 16 into 7:37–39. Moreover, if this were the only awkward pairing in Morris' list, we might be inclined to accept it; but one or two other pairs are still less convincing. For instance, Jn. 8:12–59 (Discourse 6) is not in reality a discourse on Jesus as the light of the world. Rather, it begins that way (8:12) and is then immediately side-tracked for the rest of ch. 8. The light/darkness theme resumes in the sign of the blind man who receives his sight in ch. 9. Morris himself concedes (*JC*, p. 35) that in the end the right conclusion may be that the walking on the water and the discourse of ch. 7 are not meant to be linked (*cf.* also Schnackenburg, 1. 67).

16–18. Mk. 6:46 tells us that Jesus went off to the high hills to pray. Although John does not mention that detail, he has certainly related the pressures (v. 15) that might well prompt him to seek secret intercession in his Father's presence. In the evening the disciples *went down to the lake*, re-embarked into the boat, and set off, toward the west, toward Capernaum. The words *By now it was dark, and Jesus had not yet joined them*, though doubtless prosaically true, may also be symbol-laden: as in 3:2; 13:30, the darkness of night and the absence of Jesus are powerfully linked. Difficult questions regarding chronological and geographical harmonization of the Gospel accounts are treated else-where (Carson, *Matt*, pp. 342–344).

The Sea of Galilee lies about six hundred feet below sea level. Cool air from the south-eastern tablelands can rush in to displace the warm moist air over the lake, churning up the water in a violent squall.

19. The Greek *stadion* was 606.75 feet, just under an English furlong. The disciples rowed twenty-five or thirty *stadia*, between 2.87 and 3.45 miles (which apparently accounts for NIV's *three or three and a half miles; cf.* Mk. 6:47, 'in the middle of the lake'). The disciples *saw Jesus approaching the boat, walking on the water*: the last phrase renders *epi tēs thalassēs*. Because the preposition *epi* plus the genitive can mean 'by' rather than 'on', some (*e.g.* Bernard, 1. 186, followed by Barclay) have suggested that the disciples rowed three miles or so hugging the shore, and the disciples saw Jesus walking *by* the sea rather than walking *on* it. But the phrase can mean 'on the sea' (*cf. epi* with the genitive in Rev. 10:5), and certainly Matthew and Mark make the site 'in the middle' of the lake. John may have had extra reason for avoiding *epi* plus the accusative, the customary way of expression 'on': he had already used that expression in 6:16 in the expression '*to* the lake'. The nice distinctions in preposi-tional use found in classical Greek were disappearing in the hellenistic Greek of the New Testament period. Context becomes the dominant criterion. If the disciples simply saw Jesus walking *by* the lake, it is hard to imagine why they were terrified. There can be no reasonable doubt that the Synoptists and John alike portray this event as a miracle.

20. Unlike Mark 6:49, John does not tell us that the disciples were afraid because they thought they were seeing a ghost. He is less interested in dissecting their fear than in portraying its alleviation. Jesus calms their fears by identifying himself: *It is I*. The Greek behind this expression is *egō eimi* (lit. 'I am'). The expression is sometimes used with an explicit predicate (*e.g.* 6:35; 10:14; 15:1), sometimes with a predicate that is implicit in the context (*cf.* notes on 8:24), and sometimes absolutely (*cf.* notes on 8:58). But the expression bears no necessary theological baggage: it is the perfectly normal way to say 'It is I' – a point made clear when it appears on the lips of the man born blind, after he is healed (9:9). 'If in the present passage there is any hint of the epiphany of a divine figure it is not because the words *egō eimi* are used but because in the gospel as a whole Jesus is a divine figure' (Barrett, p. 281). For this reason the suggestion of Bruce Grigsby[1] (following on the work of Schnackenburg, 2. 27) that the dropping of the prefatory words 'Take courage', attested by both Mark (6:50) and Matthew (14:27), was done in order to give the 'It is I' expression an 'aura of majesty', seems over-drawn. The words make perfectly good sense in Greek as a form of self-identification, simply 'It is I' – and doubtless that is how the disciples understood them. Thus, formally nothing is 'heightened'. We

[1]*ExpT* 100, 1989, p. 296.

are not to suppose that John's readers were supposed to compare his account of this episode, word for word, with that preserved in Mark, in order to ascertain John's meaning. On the other hand, the thoughtful reader who has read through this Gospel two or three times ought to observe the number and varied forms of 'I am' sayings (*cf.* notes on 6:35), and wonder if this occurrence in v. 20 may not be an anticipation of a clearer self-disclosure by Jesus. To that end, the Evangelist has contributed something by reducing the dialogue to the bare minimum. But it is important to see that the Evangelist has achieved this not by distorting the history but by subtly sharpening its foci so that the meditative reader will observe, once again, that he or she is privileged to grasp what the first disciples could not understand until later.

21. Once reassured, the disciples *were willing to take him into the boat,* which *immediately . . . reached the shore where they were heading.* If the language is taken strictly, this suggests another miracle, possibly with an allusion to Psalm 107:23–32 (especially v. 30, 'and he guided them to their desired haven'). This interpretation goes back at least as far as Origen. Those amongst John's readers who knew their Scriptures might well remember that the sea often stands for chaos and disorder, and it is God who controls it and stills it (*cf.* Jb. 38:8–11; Pss. 29:3–4, 10–11; 65:5–7; 89:9; and 107:23–32, just cited).

5. The 'Bread of Life' discourse (6:22–58)

Three disputed matters have governed much recent discussion of this discourse: the unity of the passage, the meaning of the discourse, and the origin of the argument.

(i) *The unity of the passage.* Those who deny the unity of the passage commonly point to two features. First, the recurring refrain 'and I will raise him up at the last day', or something similar (6:39, 40, 44, 54), is taken to reflect futurist eschatology inconsistent with the thrust of the rest of the book; second, vv. 51c–58 are understood to refer to the eucharist (*i.e.* the Lord's supper, or holy communion: different wings of the church prefer different labels), and are judged heavily sacramentarian in a book judged largely anti-sacramentarian. Therefore sections like these must have been added by a later 'ecclesiastical redactor'.

Neither argument withstands close scrutiny. Although John lays more stress on realized eschatology than on apocalyptic or futurist eschatology, he certainly does not abandon the latter. The resurrection from the grave on the last day has already been mentioned (5:28); Jesus' promise to come back and bring his own to the place he has prepared for them is best taken as a reference to the second advent (14:3); the final chapter records a specific reference to Jesus' personal return (21:22). Critics of a more sceptical turn try to excise all these passages from the alleged original document, understanding them to be late additions as well. But in fact, the futurist references are too widely scattered to be dismissed so arbitrarily. The references in John 6 to resurrection on the last day are part of an eschatological perspective that the Evangelist is quite unwilling to abandon.

Similarly, the argument that vv. 51c–58 are out of step with the alleged anti-sacramentarian stance of the rest of the Gospel presupposes that the verses in question are profoundly sacramentarian. Reasons will be advanced (below) for thinking that, just as it is doubtful John is vigorously *anti*-sacramentarian', it is even more doubtful that vv. 51c–58 are profoundly sacramentarian. Moreover, on stylistic and rhetorical grounds there is no reason for analysing the chapter into discrete, identifiable sources.[1] In the notes that follow, we shall try to show that these verses provide a striking metaphor that makes the teaching of the previous verses more vivid, but can scarcely be taken to introduce fundamentally new (and 'sacramental') meaning.[2]

(ii) *The meaning of the discourse.* Although there are numerous 'minority reports', such as the one that attempts to understand these words as Christian equivalents to pagan magic, the dominant approaches to this discourse today are three. The *first* interprets this discourse in fundamentally sacramental terms, especially (but not exclusively) vv. 52–59. This passage, it is argued, is talking about how the Christian ought to view the eucharist, the 'sacrament' (*cf.* Extended Note) of the Lord's supper. The very strong language of eating Jesus' flesh and drinking his blood is taken to support this. Many think that early Christian readers, for whom the eucharist was a central rite, could not have failed to interpret the passage that way. Moreover Ignatius, who probably knew the Evangelist, and who wrote between twenty five and forty years after this Gospel was published, adopts a sacramentarian stance:

> Stand fast, brethren, in the faith of Jesus Christ, and in His love, and in His passion, and in his resurrection. Do ye all come together in common, and individually . . . breaking one and the same bread, which is the medicine of immortality, and the antidote which prevents us from dying, but a cleansing remedy driving away evil, [which causes] that we should live in God through Jesus Christ (*ad Eph.* 20:2; *cf. ad Rom.* 7; *ad Smyrn.* 7:1).

If John was not a sacramentarian, how could so near a contemporary and (presumably) a disciple use such language?

But the argument is not convincing. Ignatius betrays a number of shifts that take us beyond anything the New Testament says. For instance, he introduces us to monarchial bishops who oversee several churches, though there is no evidence of such an office in the New

---

[1]*Cf.* E. Ruckstuhl, *Die literarische Einheit des Johannesevangeliums* (St. Paul, 1951); J. D. G. Dunn, 'John VI – A. Eucharistic Discourse?' *NTS* 17, 1970–71, pp. 328–338, esp. pp. 329–330; Borgen.

[2]For yet another partition theory, *cf.* the notes introducing vv. 27–34.

Testament. He insists that where the bishop is, there is the church, though the New Testament writers would be unhappy with such a statement. In this and several other areas, Ignatius can be no sure guide to what John thought. Anyone who has followed theological developments in the twentieth century, let alone the sixteenth or the first, does not need convincing that major changes can be introduced in the space of twenty years, even by disciples of a revered leader. In any case, it is quite possible that even Ignatius is a great deal less sacramentarian than his language might at first suggest: *cf.* discussion in Morris, p. 375, n. 118.

Moreover, if the Evangelist's intent is to provide sacramentarian theology, the language of John 6 misses several fine opportunities to echo the institution of the Lord's supper. In the unambiguous witnesses to the institution, we read 'this is my *body*', not 'this is my *flesh*'; John, however, speaks only of flesh, not of body (vv. 51ff.). Further, if John were so committed to sacramentarian theology as some suppose, it is passing strange that he fails to record the institution of the eucharist at the appropriate place in John 13,[1] and that he specifically draws attention to the fact that Jesus himself did not baptize people (4:2). What is promised to the person who eats Jesus' flesh and drinks his blood is eternal life and resurrection at the last day (6:54), and such things are elsewhere in the Fourth Gospel promised to those who believe in the Son, or receive him. It begins to sound as if the language should be taken metaphorically, not sacramentally (in the most theologically 'loaded' sense of 'sacrament').

Most contemporary writers who find the sacrament in John 6 do not worry about the built-in anachronism such an interpretation presupposes, as they do not give the chapter very high marks for authenticity anyway. The chapter, they suppose, represents *John's* theology, not that of Jesus. But however much the Evangelist has cast the discourse in his own terms, to argue that he created so much out of so little assumes he is such a dullard that he does not mind introducing blatant anachronisms, when in fact he is constantly drawing attention to what was understood in Jesus' day over against what was understood only later (*e.g.* 2:19-22; 20:9). Nor does it help to suggest that the material is basically authentic, but that Jesus himself meant to refer to something that could be understood only later, namely, the eucharist. In other passages where Jesus is understood only later (*e.g.* 2:19-22), his utterance is plain enough in its ostensible historical context once what he has been referring to is made clear after the resurrection. The same cannot be said for a eucharistic interpretation of this passage. Does not 6:63 itself insist that 'the flesh counts for nothing'?

These considerations lead some to adopt a *second* interpretation. The

---

[1] The argument that the institution of the Lord's supper is in fact recorded in Jn. 13, in the words 'he loved them to the end' (rsv; so R. M. Ball, *JSNT* 23, 1985, pp. 59-68), is both speculative and linguistically artificial.

language of John 6, they say, is metaphorical, and the theology is *anti*-sacramentarian. In many respects this argument is sound. Eating the flesh of the Son of Man is a striking, metaphorical way of saying that the gift of God's real 'bread of life' (v. 35) is appropriated by faith (v. 47). We must appropriate him into our inmost being. Indeed, as Beasley-Murray (p. 99) points out, we are more familiar with this kind of 'eating' metaphor than we may realize: we devour books, drink in lectures, swallow stories, ruminate on ideas, chew over a matter, and eat our own words. Doting grandparents declare they could eat up their grandchildren. On the very face of it, 'The theme of John 6 is Christology.'[1]

But that John 6 is understood in a metaphorical, non-sacramentarian fashion does not mean it should be read as *anti*-sacramentarian polemic. That presupposes we know far more about John's addressees than we do. If the Gospel is understood to be written for Christians (which is the majority view, though I judge it unlikely), we must assume that informed Christian readers might well detect overtones of the eucharist in this chapter. That in turn suggests that the Evangelist could scarcely have written such words at the end of the first century without reckoning with the fact that Christian readers would be tempted to see an allusion to the eucharist. Even then, however, if they were careful readers who took the setting of the narrative seriously, they would most likely conclude that the eucharist itself, so far as this passage may allude to it, points to him who is the bread of life, who came down from heaven to give his life for the world. If, however, John's intended readers are *not* Christians, the purpose of this chapter appears in a fresh light. But before turning to that point, it is necessary to mention one other interpretation.

The *third* view, found with increasing frequency in recent literature, is that although this discourse is primarily metaphorical and Christological, it is *also* sacramental and eucharistic, moving increasingly from the one to the other as the chapter progresses (*cf.* Léon-Dufour, pp. 91–92). That bread is necessary for life is often taken as proof positive of this interpretation, but all that such a bare axiom suggests is that the metaphor is eminently appropriate. It remains difficult to see what evidence there is in the text to justify a primarily eucharistic or sacramental interpretation. All sides acknowledge the language is richly metaphorical, but that fact does not itself sanction a sacramental reading. In other words, if the arguments against a thoroughly sacramentarian interpretation of this chapter are so strong, and the coherence of a metaphorical approach so commanding, what is to be gained by bringing in a eucharistic interpretation through the back door, as a kind of second layer of meaning?

Yet this critique, as we have seen, does not rule out another possibility: it is hard to imagine that the Evangelist, writing several decades

---

[1] H. Thyen, 'Aus der Literatur des Johannesevangelium', *ThR* 44, 1979, p. 109.

after the institution of the Lord's supper, could produce these words without noticing that many readers, even if they understood the passage aright, would in all likelihood detect some parallels with the eucharist. Fair enough – but this depends on the assumption that the intended readers are Christians. However, if the purpose of the Fourth Gospel is primarily evangelistic (cf. Introduction, § VI; notes on 20:30–31), a primarily metaphorical and Christological interpretation makes good sense, the more so if the primary target readership is comprised of curious Jews and Jewish proselytes, for they would be interested to see displayed an interpretation of Jesus' role as the antitype of Old Testament manna, as the antitype of Old Testament Moses. Insofar as there *may* be an allusion to the Christian eucharist, these readers, if in dialogue with the church and therefore somewhat aware of the church's regular celebration of the Lord's supper, would be likely to see in the rite itself a pictorial pointer to the central object of faith, the Lord Jesus himself.[1] 'John 6 is not about the Lord's Supper; rather, the Lord's Supper is about what is described in John 6.'[2]

(iii) The origin of the argument. While some have treated this chapter as a pastiche of disparate sources, Borgen and others have argued strongly for the unity of the chapter, largely on the parallels they draw between this chapter and Jewish exegesis of the Old Testament miracle of the manna. Some have taken this entire chapter as a Jewish-Christian exegesis of Psalm 78:24. Certain details of this approach are more convincing than others (cf. notes, below). What must be made clear, however, is that there is no entailment from such a position to the conclusion that the discourse is inauthentic: if the four canonical Gospels bear witness to anything about Jesus, it is that he himself was a gifted, telling and creative exegete of the Old Testament Scriptures.

---

[1]This view can be made to cohere with the suggestion of R. Wade Paschal, Jr., *TynB* 32, 1981, pp. 151–176, that in John the 'sacramental elements' are themselves used in *symbolic*, not sacramental, ways. C. K. Barrett (*Church Ministry, and Sacraments in the New Testament* [Paternoster/Eerdmans, 1985], pp. 74–75) may well be right when he suggests that John was written at a time

> when the Christian rite was in danger of becoming a mechanical repetition of the Last Supper, which was believed to secure, *ex opere operato*, eternal life for the recipient. Thus John, first, focused Paschal significance not on a meal but on Jesus crucified himself . . .; secondly, detached what he had to say about eating the flesh and drinking the blood of the Son of man from the Last Supper; and, thirdly, embedded these references to eating and drinking in a discourse which made it clear that receiving Christ, the bread of life, by faith belonged to a wider setting than a cult act, even though the cult act (which is clearly in mind in John 6) might be a particularly clear focusing of this receiving . . . [This] makes as clear as anyone could hope that sacraments . . . display with special clarity that paradox of centrality and peripherality which I have said is characteristic of the church, its members and its actions, in the New Testament.

[2]Colin Brown, *NIDNTT* 2. 535.

Extended note

22ff. A substantial part of the contemporary debate lies hidden behind the terminology. Some define 'sacrament' as a 'religious rite or ceremony instituted . . . by Jesus Christ' (R. S. Wallace, *EDT*, p. 965; in a regrettable lapse, Wallace says 'instituted *or recognized* by Jesus Christ', but that would transform Jewish rites, such as the Passover, into Christian sacraments!). With so simple a definition, few would find theological difficulty. But the history of the church shows that three linguistic mishaps contributed to the contemporary muddle.

First, the term *mystērion* was applied to the Lord's supper and to baptism, even though no such use is found in the New Testament. Almost certainly this designation developed because in common parlance the word *mystērion* was used to refer to the secret ceremonies that lay at the heart of the popular 'mystery religions'. These rites were thought to mediate divine benefits to the worshipper, and were more personal and much warmer in devotion than official exercises of religion. Superficial similarities between such rites and the Lord's supper made the transfer of terminology all but inevitable.

Second, an attempt was made to relate this new usage to New Testament teaching. The argument was one of analogy: just as miracles and signs are the visible manifestation of the powerful presence of the *mystery* of the kingdom, and just as Jesus' physical body is the visible demonstration of the *mystery* of the Word made flesh (1 Tim. 3:16), and just as the church is the 'bodily' manifestation of Christ, expressing the *mystery* of the relationship between Christ and the church (Eph. 5:32), so also the bread and wine are the visible manifestations of the presence of Christ in the eucharist, the Lord's supper – and therefore another 'mystery'. That link is not made in the New Testament (where the term refers almost exclusively to divine revelation in some measure hidden in previous ages but now disclosed in the person and teaching of Jesus Christ and his Spirit-anointed disciples), though it is explicit in none less than Calvin (*Tracts* II, 577).

Third, *mystērion* came in time to be translated into Latin by *sacramentum*; hence our word 'sacrament'. But the Latin *sacramentum* meant both 'a thing set apart as sacred' and 'a military oath of obedience as administered by the commander', with the result that, as applied to baptism and the Lord's supper, the 'sacraments' came to be thought of, in many branches of the church, as conveying grace in and of themselves. Augustine defined a sacrament as a 'visible word' or an 'outward and visible sign of an inward and spiritual grace', while at the same time being a form of pledged oath. In this latter sense, the word *sacramentum* was used very early to refer to Christian baptism (*cf.* Pliny, *Letters* X. xcvi. 7, describing what he has learned from apostate Christians of early Christian faith and practice: '. . . they had met regularly before dawn on a fixed day to chant verses alternately among themselves in honour of Christ as if to a god, *and also to bind themselves by oath* [Lat. *dicere secum invicem seque sacramento*], not for any criminal purpose but to abstain from theft . . .': the 'oath' [*sacramentum*] refers to baptismal vows). What was first used by a persecutor of the church (so far as our records go) came to be used by the church itself, and was especially congenial to Christians who thought of the church as the 'militia of Christ'. As the rendering for *mystērion*, however, 'sacrament' took over various associations of the Greek word, and the idea of ritual efficacy, both for salvation and for blessing, become attached to it. That was reinforced by the association with sacredness. Later generations within the Roman Catholic and Orthodox branches of the church not only elevated the sacraments to a place of prominence in the church's worship, but increasingly held that sacraments are efficacious signs, conveying by virtue of the rite itself the grace that they contain.[1]

The consequences of such developments prompt some Christians to prefer to refer to baptism and the Lord's supper as 'ordinances', *i.e.* things which the Lord has ordained. But if 'sacrament' be defined as at the beginning of this note, there can be no great objection.

Further, no small debate turns on the force of 'is' in 'This *is* my body', 'This *is* my blood' – on the assumption that the verb either does, or does not, bear ontological overtones. The debate is properly treated in commentaries on the Synoptics and Paul. But this much must be said: the verb 'to be' has a broad semantic range in the New Testament, including at least five distinguishable meanings (*cf.* D. A. Carson, *Exegetical Fallacies* [Baker, 1984], pp. 58–62). Nothing is gained by *assuming* that one particular meaning occurs here. The case must be *argued*.

a. Searching for Jesus (6:22–26)

22–24. The syntax of these verses is difficult, though the general sense is fairly plain; NIV has smoothed out the difficulties. It appears that the crowd *on the opposite shore of the lake* – *i.e.* on the east side, where the miracle had occurred, *opposite* to where the boat in v. 21 had just landed on the west bank – recognized that only one boat had brought over Jesus and his disciples. The crowd itself had come by foot; the disciples had left in the only boat, and without Jesus (*they had gone away alone*). So where was he? Their uncertainty doubtless accounts for their continued presence: perhaps many had walked home, but some at least were reluctant to return without him. Meanwhile *some boats from* (the city of) *Tiberias* (*cf.* notes on v. 1), on the north-west shore of the lake, landed near the people. Whether we are to think they were blown there by the storm, or that some folk from Tiberias piloted their boats across to fetch friends and neighbours, cannot be determined. By this time the remaining crowd has recognized that neither Jesus nor his disciples are

---

[1]Much of the wording of this discussion is my own; some has been taken over from 'An Evangelical Response to *Baptism, Eucharist and Ministry*', a paper prepared by a Task Force of the World Evangelical Fellowship, in which I was a participant. Source critics are welcome to isolate the parts I wrote; I myself cannot manage it.

still on the east bank: somehow Jesus himself has left. They therefore embark in the boats and cross the lake, landing at Capernaum, on the west bank, still *in search of Jesus*. Capernaum was at this point the 'home town' of Jesus and his family (*cf.* notes on 2:12). The ensuing discourse is set in Capernaum's synagogue (6:59).

25. When the crowds found Jesus *on the other side of the lake* (from which they had set out in the boats; the phrase may also emphasize the miraculous nature of Jesus' crossing), they are naturally curious about how he had got across. They address him as *Rabbi* (*cf.* notes on 1:38), betraying their own confusion and uncertainty: they acknowledge him as teacher though they are about to dispute his teaching, they clamour for him as king (v. 15) though they understand little of the nature of his reign. The question they ask means both *when did you get here?* (NIV) and 'How long have you been here?' (not unlike questions in French beginning with 'Depuis quand . . .?').

26. The strong asseverative *I tell you the truth* (*cf.* notes on 1:51) draws attention to Jesus' next words, but he does not answer their question. Had he told them the nature of his crossing, doubtless they would have been impressed; but what follows shows that mere miracles can be corrosive of genuine faith. Instead, Jesus questions their motives in looking for him. Jesus' charge is that their pursuit was not because they saw *miraculous signs,* but for crasser motives. A superficial reader might detect an unbearable contradiction with v. 14, which says that the people 'saw the miraculous sign that Jesus did' and concluded he was at least the Prophet and potentially a desirable king. But in v. 14 what the people see is the actual miracle, the multiplication of the bread and fish, the 'miraculous sign' (*sēmeion; cf.* notes on 2:11); what they failed to see is what the sign truly *signified*. At a superficial level, the signs attest that Jesus has remarkable powers; but the signs must never be assessed as nothing more than attesting portents. This particular miracle had filled the bellies of the people, and the crowd loved it (*you ate the loaves and had your fill*) and were willing on that basis to sign up immediately. Mark insists that even the Twelve 'had not understood about the loaves; their hearts were hardened' (Mk. 6:52; *cf.* 8:14–21). How much less had the crowds understood that the sign bore parabolic significance. It was a symbol-laden miracle, a 'sign' that pointed to the gospel itself, to Jesus himself. John sets himself the task of expounding that hidden meaning, by reporting Jesus' bread of life discourse in the following verses.

b. The true manna (6:27–34)

John later reports that the bread of life discourse was delivered 'in the synagogue in Capernaum' (6:59), but he nowhere makes clear where the transition to the synagogue takes place: at v. 27 is as good a guess as any.[1] The 'discourse' itself is in reality dialogue in which one side

[1] John Painter (*NTS* 35, 1989, pp. 421–450) argues that the transition comes at v. 41, where Jesus' interlocutors are no longer 'the crowd[s]' or 'the people' but 'the Jews'. But to

provides such extended answers that they become monologue. Such exchanges were not uncommon in synagogues.

27. When Jesus tells the people not to work *for food that spoils*, he is rebuking their purely materialistic notions of the kingdom (*cf.* v. 15). Like the woman at the well who was eager to be supplied with an endless supply of natural water, a supply that would eliminate the need to make frequent trips to the well (4:15), so these people hanker after a miracle-worker who will fill their stomachs with bread (6:26). Though the bread they had eaten the day before was miraculously produced, it was after all merely physical, 'destined to perish with use' (Col. 2:22). Men and women should pour their energy into pursuing (*i.e.* they should 'work for') *food that endures to eternal life* (*cf.* 'a spring of water welling up into eternal life', 4:14). The continuing discourse shows that the 'food' is Jesus himself, but the idea is not so much that Jesus endures forever as that, because this food endures, the life it sustains goes on into eternity. On *eternal life, cf.* notes on 3:15.

It is not entirely clear whether the antecedent of *which* is the 'food' or the 'eternal life'. If the former, it will shortly become clear that Jesus not only *gives* the food, he *is himself* the bread of life (vv. 35, 53). Either way, it is the Son of Man who *will give* it. If the tense is genuinely future-referring, it is looking to the time after Jesus' glorification when the Son's gifts, mediated by the Spirit, are richly bestowed (7:39; 14:15ff.; 16:7). If they ought to 'work for' the food that endures unto eternal life, they must also recognize that it is the Son alone who can give it. Jesus prefers not to use a term such as 'Messiah' in the context of such heated messianic/political expectations; he opts for *Son of Man*, a more ambiguous term which nevertheless is increasingly laden, in John, with associations of revelation brought from heaven to earth (*cf.* notes on 1:51; 3:13; 5:27). This Son of Man, Jesus insists, is the one on whom *the Father has placed his seal of approval*. The idea is that God has certified the Son as his own agent, authorizing him as the one who alone can bestow this food. God has attested the Son, in much the same way that someone who accepts the Son's testimony thereby attests or certifies (the same verb) that God himself is truthful. *When* God 'placed his seal of approval' on the Son is not specified. If we are to think of a specific time (though the aorist tense of the verb does not require that we so limit ourselves), perhaps the reference is to Jesus' baptism (*cf.* 1:31–34).

28. The crowd misunderstands the thrust of Jesus' prohibition. His words 'Do not work for food that spoils' (v. 27) did not focus on the nature of work, but on what is or is not an appropriate goal. His point was not that they should attempt some novel form of work, but that

---

elevate this signal above the many indications of cohesion in the plot line (*e.g.* 'At this', *oun,* v. 41; the intelligible flow of discussion on Jesus as the bread from heaven) is not only methodologically reductionistic, but assumes that 'the Jews' *always* serves as a marker for a certain kind of opposition, when actual usage is far more variable (*cf.* notes on 1:19ff.).

merely material notions of blessing are not worth pursuing. They respond by focusing all attention on work: (lit.) 'What must we do in order to work the works of God?' The expression 'the works of God' does not refer to the works that God performs, but (as in NIV) to *the works God requires*. Their question therefore resolves into this: Tell us what works God requires, and we will perform them. From John's perspective, their naïveté is formidable. They display no doubt about their intrinsic ability to meet any challenge God may set them; they evince no sensitivity to the fact that eternal life is first and foremost a gift within the purview of the Son of Man (v. 27).

29. Jesus sets them straight: *The work of God* – i.e. what God requires – is faith. This is not faith in the abstract, an existential trust without a coherent object. Rather, they must *believe in the one [God] has sent*. Such language may reflect a specific Old Testament passage, such as Malachi 3:1 where God promises to send, in due time, the 'messenger of the covenant', but in fact the language is reminiscent of the entire 'sentness' theme in the Fourth Gospel. Jesus is supremely the one who reveals God to us, precisely because, unlike any other person, he has been in the courts of heaven and has been sent from there so that the world might be saved through him (*e.g.* 3:11–17). Faith, faith with proper Christological object, is what God requires, not 'works' in any modern sense of the term. And even the faith that we must exercise is the fruit of God's activity (*cf.* notes on vv. 44, 65). Although the noun 'faith' is not used, this 'work of God' turns out to be nothing else than faith, making this 'work of God' diametrically opposed to what Paul means by 'the works of the law'. As a result, the thought of the passage is almost indistinguishable from Paul: 'For we maintain that a man is justified by faith apart from observing the law' (Rom. 3:28).

30–31. On 'sign', *cf.* notes on 2:11; on the demand for a sign, *cf.* notes on 2:18; 4:47, 48. Jesus has been teaching with naked authority; the synagogue crowd demands an attesting, validating sign. One might have thought that the feeding of the five thousand was sign enough. In fact, it was enough to prompt speculation that Jesus was the promised Prophet like Moses (v. 14).That in turn suggested to the crowd that they therefore had a right to expect more spectacular signs than Moses himself provided.

What sign, then, should they ask for? *What will you do?* they ask Jesus. It is just possible that the Scripture reading in the synagogue that Sabbath was Exodus 16:11–36, the account of God's provision of manna (*cf.* Guilding, pp. 61–65). Even if that were not so, the combination of Jesus' feeding of the multitude, plus his mention of 'food that endures to eternal life' over against 'food that spoils' (v. 27; *cf.* Ex. 16:20), might well be enough to trigger in them their reflection on manna. Their forefathers ate manna in the desert; there is even an Old Testament text to prove it. True, that manna spoiled with time. But that means, for the crowd, that if Jesus is promising to provide something better, then he had better be prepared to display an even more dramatic miracle than the miracle of the manna itself. If Jesus is superior to Moses, as his tone and claims suggest, then should not his followers be privileged to witness mightier works than those seen by the disciples of Moses?

Later rabbis argued that the Messiah, the 'latter Redeemer', would call down manna from heaven, as did the 'first redeemer' (*i.e.* Moses; see notes on v. 14). There is at least a little evidence that such beliefs were not unknown in the first century (*cf.* the reference to 'hidden manna' in Rev. 2:17, and 2 *Baruch* 29:8, dated about AD 100). If this is what the synagogue crowd means, it is a demand that Jesus prove his messianic status by duplicating or surpassing the miracle of the manna. But Jesus could not possibly acquiesce to such a demand. With the crowd's interest in a primarily political messiah, for Jesus to give in to their demand would have been to acknowledge the rightness of the aspirations they had displayed the day before, aspirations he had then rejected (vv. 14, 15). Worse still, it would have meant the domestication of his revealing and saving work: he would have become captive to the whims of a demanding crowd (*cf.* notes on 2:18ff.).

The exact source of the quotation is disputed. The most likely passage is Psalm 78:24 (LXX 77:24), but the Greek has echoes also of Nehemiah 9:15 and perhaps Exodus 16:4, 15; Psalm 105:40. Perhaps John is quoting the Old Testament loosely and alluding to all three passages.[1] *Cf.* Additional Note.

32. Again there is the strong asseverative, *I tell you the truth* (*cf.* v. 26; notes on 1:51): Jesus is persuaded that far too much attention has been lavished on Moses, and far too little on God himself, the ultimate supplier of the *bread from heaven*. In the last clause, *but it is my Father who gives you the true bread from heaven*, the shift to the present tense may be significant. Present tenses, especially in John, are often past-referring (the so-called 'historic present'), but if this one is present-referring, then Jesus is not only saying that his Father has been ignored while Moses has gained centre stage in the thought of his opponents, but that the *true* bread is in any case not the manna in the wilderness but what the Father is *now giving*. This paves the way for v. 33.

Based on Proverbs 9:5, where personified Wisdom cries out, 'Come, eat my food [lit. "my bread"] and drink the wine I have mixed', some Jewish authorities figuratively referred to the law of Moses, Torah, as 'bread' (*cf.* SB 2. 483-484; Odeberg, p. 243). If such symbolism is operative here, then the thought is something like this: the manna God provided through Moses is not the true bread from heaven, nor is the Torah God revealed through Moses the true Torah, though both pointed, in parabolic form, in the right direction (*cf.* also similar claims with respect to the temple, 2:18ff.; the various feasts, 4:21; the shepherd, 10:1ff.; the vine of God, 15:1ff.). The true bread from heaven, the true Torah, is Jesus himself (vv. 35, 47ff.). This does not mean that the

---

[1] *Cf.* discussion in Richter, pp. 199ff.; M. J. J. Menken, *NovT* 30, 1988, pp. 39-56.

manna was not in any sense bread from heaven, or that the Torah was not truly given by God. But the manna from heaven was comparatively crude: it perished with time, and the people who ate it perished with time. One of its chief functions was to serve as a type of the *true* bread from heaven. Similarly the law of Moses, as important and true as it was, would be replaced (*cf.* notes on 1:16) by that to which it pointed, that which fulfilled it. *Cf.* Dodd, *IFG*, pp.336–337.

The form of the argument has subtle parallels to forms of Jewish exegesis (*cf.* Borgen, pp. 61–67).

33. The *bread of God* is synonymous with the 'bread of heaven' (*cf.* 'kingdom of heaven' in Mt., *versus* 'kingdom of God' in Mk. and Lk.). In the Old Testament 'the bread of God' refers on occasion to the 'show-bread' (NIV, 'food of God', Lv. 21:6, 8, 17, 21, 22; 22:25); here it refers to Jesus, *he who comes down from heaven and gives life to the world.* In addition to establishing a typological reading of the Old Testament, this clause accomplishes three things: (1) it serves as a transition from the thought that Jesus *provides* the true bread from heaven (vv. 27ff.) to the thought that Jesus *is* the true bread from heaven (vv. 35ff.); (2) it expands the recipients from Jews to the world, *i.e.* to lost men and women without distinction, opening up the way to the proposition that the decisive factor is not whether or not one is a member of the Jewish race, an heir of the Mosaic covenant, but whether or not one is taught by God (v. 45), whether or not one believes in Jesus (v. 35) and has been given by the Father to the Son (vv. 37–40); (3) it reminds us that *this* bread of God is the revealer, the one who has narrated God to us (1:18), the one who alone can tell us heavenly things (3:11–13), the one whose words, because he is the obedient Son, are nothing less than the words of God (5:19ff.).

34. The synagogue crowd understands little of this. Like the woman at the well with her 'Sir, give me this water' (4:15), this request operates at a mundane level. The people take Jesus' words in v. 33 to mean 'the bread of God is that which comes down from heaven' – a grammatically possible rendering that misses the point: Jesus himself is the bread of God. Jesus therefore ventures, in the next section, to make the identification explicit.

Additional note

31. Borgen has compared the use made of this Old Testament text ('He gave them bread from heaven to eat') in John 6, with similar uses of the Old Testament in a variety of Jewish sources. Borgen argues that this chapter reflects a wide-spread homiletical pattern, a pattern that can be traced through most of the chapter and therefore contributes to the argument for its unity. Many features of his argument are convincing, even though only a few points are noted in this commentary. Less convincing, however, is his suggestion John was employing these 'midrashic' methods (*i.e.* these methods of commenting on an Old Testament text) in order to counter docetism, a heresy clearly established in the second century that denies the full humanity of Christ. Christ only *appeared* to become a man. *Cf.* Introduction, §§ II, III, VI; Martyn, pp. 122–128. In particular, the discussion of Borgen and those who follow him does not sufficiently allow for the revelatory stance that Jesus adopts in this chapter, quite unlike any of the teachers in the Jewish parallels that are commonly adduced.

c. Jesus the bread of life *(6:35–48)*

35. In view of his opponents' misunderstanding of his claim to be the bread of God (vv. 34–35), Jesus now speaks plainly: *I am the bread of life,*[1] a claim repeated at the end of this section (v. 48). Most of the intervening verses are an exposition of this theme and its entailments, cast for the most part in terms that are relatively independent of the bread-metaphor.[2] The verse at hand not only specifies that Jesus is the bread of life, but removes another of his opponents' implicit misunderstandings. When they said *'from now on* give us this bread' (v. 34), they were suggesting that the bread of heaven needed to be given again and again. But Jesus insists, *He who comes to me will never go hungry*. The thought is not unlike 13:9–10: the person who has been washed by Jesus does not need another bath, but only 'to wash his feet'. So the hungry and thirsty person who comes to Jesus finds his hunger satisfied and his thirst quenched. This does not mean there is no need for continued dependence upon him, for continued feeding upon him; it does mean there is no longer that core emptiness that the initial encounter with Jesus has met. The consummating satiation occurs when those 'who have washed their robes . . . in the blood of the Lamb' stand 'before the throne of God' and experience the oracle: 'Never again will they hunger; never again will they thirst' (Rev. 7:14–16).

Four further notes are in order:

(1) The image of 'thirst' is added to 'hunger', thereby anticipating vv. 53ff. In other words, the vivid language of vv. 53ff. is not as removed from the rest of the discourse as some have supposed. *Cf.* notes on 6:49ff.; 7:37–39.

(2) The essentially symbolic nature of 'bread of life' and related expressions in this discourse is disclosed by the mingling of metaphorical and non-metaphorical elements. Jesus is the bread of life, but it is the person who *comes to* him who does not hunger, not the person who *eats* him; similarly, it is the person who *believes in* him who does not thirst,[3] not the person who drinks him. Thus, when the language

---

[1]The genitive *tēs zōēs* ('of life') is what has been called a verbal genitive (*cf.* Henry Waterman, 'The Greek "Verbal Genitive"', in Gerald F. Hawthorne [ed.], *Current Issues in Biblical and Patristic Interpretation* [Eerdmans, 1975], pp. 289–293).

[2]For the most compelling treatment of metaphor in recent literature, *cf.* Janet Martin Soskice, *Metaphor and Religious Language* (Cambridge University Press, 1987).

[3]On the semantic difference between *will never go hungry* (*ou mē peinasē*, aorist subjunctive) and *will never be thirsty* (*ou mē dipsēsei pōpote*, future indicative), *cf.* Porter,

becomes more rigorously metaphorical in vv. 49ff., and we read of eating Jesus' flesh and drinking his blood, the meaning of the metaphors has already been established. *Cf.* the opening notes on 6:22ff., above.

(3) The expression *I am the bread of life* is the first of seven similar claims, each with *egō eimi* ('I am') and a predicate. The other six (plus minor variations) are: I am the light of the world (8:12), the gate (10:7, 9), the good shepherd (10:11, 14), the resurrection and the life (11:25), the way and the truth and the life (14:6), the true vine (15:1, 5). Two other expressions with 'I am' plus a predicate are structured rather differently in Greek (8:18, 23). The precise form is unique to the Fourth Gospel, but as Barrett (p. 292) notes, the Synoptists display other forms of 'I' utterances, while Synoptic parables 'provide much of the subject matter of the Johannine "I-sayings".' In addition, of course, John preserves a number of *egō eimi* ('I am') sayings without any predicate: *cf.* notes on 6:20; 8:24, 28, 58; 18:6; D. A. Carson, *EDT*, pp. 541–542; Introduction, § III (3).

(4) The Old Testament background to the parallelism of this verse may lie in Isaiah 55:1 (with respect to the eschatological salvation brought about by the word of God) and in Proverbs 8:5 (with respect to Wisdom). Contemporary writers often cite *Ecclesiasticus* 24:21, where Wisdom says: 'Those who eat me will hunger for more, and those who drink me will thirst for more.' If John is thinking of this passage at all, what he writes is in marked contrast. Because of Proverbs 8:5 and *Ecclesiasticus* 24:21, many commentators have understood much of John 6 as sapiential, *i.e.* as presenting Jesus as Wisdom incarnate, Wisdom *par excellence*. However, the connection with Isaiah 55:1 is more likely, not only because Isaiah is the most frequently quoted Old Testament book in the Fourth Gospel, but also because Isaiah 55 deals explicitly with the dawning of eschatological salvation, of a new and everlasting covenant, in the context of the word which effectively proceeds from the mouth of God (*cf.* 1:1). And even the Wisdom of *Ecclesiasticus* 24:21 is quickly identified with Torah (24:23), while (as noted above on v. 32) Wisdom in Proverbs 8:5 was understood in some Jewish circles to refer to Torah. The so-called sapiential interpretation of John 6 is not so much wrong as peripheral. John's approach is fundamentally Christological, and, so far as these Christological claims awaken echoes of old covenant religion, the connections are in terms of prophecy and fulfilment, along typological lines.

36. As Jesus charged the citizens of Jerusalem with unbelief (5:36–38), so now he repeatedly charges his fellow Galileans with the same sin (*cf.* v. 26). True, in one sense Jesus can acknowledge to them, *you have seen me* (the *me* should probably be admitted, even though it is missing from

---

p. 416. Against many who claim there is no difference in meaning, Porter rightly insists that the latter clause focuses on expectation: at the risk of overtranslation: 'may never hunger . . . can expect never to thirst'. The adverb *pōpote* reinforces the point; faith eliminates any sense of lack.

some manuscripts: *cf.* Carson, p. 249, n. 34), but they have seen only a mightily endowed man, a potential king (6:14, 15), not the Son of God who perfectly expresses the Father's word and deed (5:19ff.); they have seen only bread and power, not what they signify. This crowd has witnessed the divine revealer at work, but only their curiosity, appetites and political ambitions have been aroused, not their faith.

37. But if some can see Jesus and his miraculous signs, and yet still not come to faith, does that not suggest his mission is in some measure a failure? The question returns in ch. 12, where it is treated at some length. Already the answer is provided here: however many people do not believe, God's saving purposes cannot be thought to be frustrated. Jesus' confidence does not rest in the potential for positive response amongst well-meaning people. Far from it: his confidence is in his Father to bring to pass the Father's redemptive purposes: *All that the Father gives me will come to me.* Jesus' confidence in the success of his mission is frankly predestinarian.

The second part of this verse is frequently misunderstood. Formally it is a 'litotes', a figure of speech in which something is affirmed by negating its contrary. Thus, 'a citizen of no mean city' means 'a citizen of a rather important city'. When Jesus says *whoever comes to me I will never drive away*, the affirmative that he is expressing in this fashion is often taken to mean 'whoever comes to me I will certainly welcome'. The second part of the verse then becomes a softening of the predestinarianism in the first part. But in fact, the affirmation expressed by this litotes is rather different: 'whoever comes to me I will certainly keep in, preserve'. The flow of the verse is then as follows: All that (a singular neuter is used to refer to the elect collectively) the Father gives to Jesus, as his gift to his Son, will surely come to him; and whoever in fact comes (by virtue of being given by the Father to the Son), Jesus undertakes to keep in, to preserve. The second part of the verse moves from the collective whole to the individual, and from the actual coming (consequent on being part of the gift) to preservation. This interpretation is suggested by the verb *ekballō*, 'drive away' or 'cast out'. In almost all of its parallel occurrences, it is presupposed that what is driven out or cast out is already 'in'. 'I will never drive away' therefore means 'I will certainly keep in'. This interpretation, however strongly supported by the verb, is *required* by the context, the next three verses.[1]

38–40. The *For* (*hoti*) introduces the reason *why* Jesus will perfectly preserve all those whom the Father has given him. The heart of his response is this: The entire purpose of the incarnation, of his coming *down from heaven*, was not to do his own will, but the will of the Father who sent him (v. 38), and that will was that the Son should lose none (*i.e.* no individual) of all that the Father had given him (v. 39, with the same play between the individual and the collective singular as in v. 37).

---

[1] *Cf.* O. Hofius, *TheolBeit* 8, 1977, pp. 24–29.

This preservation of each individual in the collective of the elect includes resurrection at the last day. The argument is then reiterated in v. 40, with minor variations in emphasis, and one important one: the one whom the Son does not lose, whom he raises up at the last day, is here described not in terms of the gift of the Father to the Son (as in vv. 37, 39), but in terms of personal faith: *everyone who looks to the Son and believes in him shall have eternal life.*

Several observations will clarify the argument further:

(1) Divine sovereignty in salvation is a major theme in the Fourth Gospel. Morever, the form of it in these verses, that there exists a group of people who have been given by the Father to the Son, and that this group will inevitably come to the Son and be preserved by him, not only recurs in this chapter (v. 65) and perhaps in 10:29, but is strikingly central to the Lord's prayer in ch. 17 (vv. 1, 6, 9, 24; *cf.* Carson, pp. 186ff.). John is not embarrassed by this theme, because unlike many contemporary philosophers and theologians, he does not think that human responsibility is thereby mitigated. Thus, he can speak with equal ease of those who look to the Son and believe in him: this they must do, if they are to enjoy eternal life. But this responsibility to exercise faith does not, for the Evangelist, make God contingent. In short, John is quite happy with the position that modern philosophy calls 'compatibilism'.

(2) The obedience of the Son (v. 38), a theme extrapolated from 5:19ff., stands behind the assurance that those whom the Father has given to the Son will be preserved to the end, and will be resurrected on the last day. In other words, if any of them failed to achieve this goal, it would be the Son's everlasting shame: it would mean either that he was incapable of performing what the Father willed him to do, or that he was flagrantly disobedient to his Father. Both alternatives are unthinkable, not because he never experienced the temptation to disobey, but because succumbing to the temptation, however acute that temptation might be, was itself unthinkable to him. The Fourth Gospel does not record the agony of Gethsemane (*cf.* Mt. 26:36–46; though *cf.* notes on 12:27–28), including the resolute 'Yet not as I will, but as you will', but its entire Christology is an expression of that same resolution.

(3) In the first instance, those whom the Father has given to the Son are the immediate band of sincere disciples. At that level, it is possible to record at least the initial fulfilment of the Son's duty in 17:11–12, where Jesus avers that he has kept them all safe while he was with them, and now asks his Father to take over the task in view of the Son's imminent 'departure'. But that is not the end of the Son's task; it is only the *initial* fulfilment. He must still raise them at the last day. Moreover it becomes clear, especially in chs. 10 and 17, that the Father gave to Jesus others than the first disciples. These other sheep (ch. 10) must also come, those who would believe through the message of the first believers. All these the Son undertakes to resurrect on the last day. He loses none of them.

(4) The one exception is Judas Iscariot. This turns out not to be an

exception at all. It was not that the Son's preserving power broke down in this one instance; rather, Judas was the son of perdition from the beginning (*cf.* notes on 17:12). Jesus *chose* him to be one of the Twelve, but knew from the beginning that he was 'a devil' (*cf.* notes on 6:70–71).

(5) The futurist eschatology, in clear references to the final resurrection (vv. 39, 40, 44, 54), is not at all out of place (*cf.* notes prefacing vv. 22ff., above), but the culmination of the eternal life (v. 40) granted to everyone 'who looks to the Son and believes in him'. This 'eternal life' is more than mere unending existence: it is primarily the passing over from condemnation to acceptance, from death to life (5:24), and then it is a foretaste, the full banquet of which occurs in resurrection life (*cf.* 5:28–29).

(6) The verb 'looks' (v. 40) renders *theōreō*. In earlier Greek the verb was frequently used of a particularly perceptive and discerning 'looking'. In John, however, such use is not consistent. If there is particular perception here, it is because the context, and especially the next clause 'and believes in him', specifies the meaning.

(7) All of this explanation is part of the bread of life discourse. These verses not only contribute to the explanation as to why some believe and some do not, but, culminating in the promise of eternal, resurrection life, they unpack in non-metaphorical categories just what kind of life the 'bread of God' provides (vv. 33, 35).

41–42. 'The Jews' (*cf.* on 1:19) who grumble must be either the synagogue congregation of Capernaum (*cf.* v. 59), or at least its leaders. Their grumbling shows them to be of the same spirit as that displayed by their fathers in the wilderness who complained before (Ex. 16:2, 8–9) and after (Nu. 11:4ff.) the manna was provided. 'The Jews' in Jerusalem (5:18ff.) were incensed because they recognized Jesus said things that put him on a par with God; these Galilean Jews are incensed because they think they know a fellow Galilean, and take umbrage at his claims. It is not so much his claim to be bread that offends them, as his claim to be bread *from heaven*, his claim that he *came down from heaven*. How could this be so, when his family had moved to Capernaum and he was known there (*cf.* notes on 2:12)? Parallel suspicions were raised in Nazareth (Mk. 6:2–3; Lk. 4:22).

The language does not necessarily mean that Joseph was still alive. The crowd's point is simpler. They say, in effect, 'We know who Jesus' parents are. What right then does he have to claim nobler, even divine, heritage?' John's record of their question is steeped in irony (*cf.* Duke, pp. 64–65). The Jews think they know all there is to know about Jesus' paternity, but they speak in ignorance not only of his virginal conception but of his true identity. Repeatedly Jesus insists that his opponents do not know his (heavenly) Father at all (4:22; 8:19, 55; 15:21; 16:3; 17:25). Indeed, it will transpire that Jesus knows their 'father' (8:42ff.) far better than they know his! Unlike the readers of this Gospel, they do not know the Prologue – that the eternal Word became flesh (1:14)

43–44. The grumbling was not only insulting, but dangerous: it presupposed that divine revelation could be sorted out by talking the matter over, and thus diverted attention from the grace of God. 'So long as a man remains, and is content to remain, confident of his own ability, without divine help, to assess experience and the meaning of experience, he cannot "come to" the Lord, he cannot "believe"; only the Father can move him to this step, with its incalculable and final results' (Lightfoot, pp. 160–161).

The thought of v. 44 is the negative counterpart to v. 37a. The latter tells us that all whom the Father gives to the Son will come to him; here we are told that no-one can come to him unless the Father draws him (*cf.* Mk. 10:23ff.). And again, it will be Jesus himself who raises such a person up at the last day. The combination of v. 37a and v. 44 prove that this 'drawing' activity of the Father cannot be reduced to what theologians sometimes call 'prevenient grace' dispensed to every individual, for this 'drawing' is selective, or else the negative note in v. 44 is meaningless. Many attempt to dilute the force of the claim by referring to 12:32, where the same verb for 'to draw' (*helkyō*) occurs: Jesus there claims he will draw 'all men' to himself. The context shows rather clearly, however, that 12:32 refers to 'all men without distinction' (*i.e.* not just Jews) rather than to 'all men without exception'. Yet despite the strong predestinarian strain, it must be insisted with no less vigour that John emphasizes the responsibility of people to come to Jesus, and can excoriate them for refusing to do so (*e.g.* 5:40).

45. Jesus proceeds to explain what kind of 'drawing' (v. 44) the Father exercises. When he compels belief, it is not by the savage constraint of a rapist, but by the wonderful wooing of a lover. Otherwise put, it is by an insight, a teaching, an illumination implanted within the individual, in fulfilment of the Old Testament promise, *They will all be taught by God.* This is a paraphrase of Isaiah 54:13, addressed to the restored city of Jerusalem that the prophet foresees: 'All your sons will be taught by the LORD, and great will be your children's peace.' The passage is here applied typologically: in the New Testament the messianic community and the dawning of the saving reign of God are the typological fulfilments of the restoration of Jerusalem after the Babylonian exile.

In fact, this need for internal illumination is a commonplace of both Testaments. Jeremiah looks forward to a new covenant when God will put his law in the minds of his people, and write it on their hearts (Je. 31:31–34).In Ezekiel, God promises a new heart and a new spirit (Ezk. 36:24–26). The prophet Joel anticipates the time when God will pour out his Spirit not only on Jews but on all people (2:28ff.). In the Fourth Gospel, the new-birth language of John 3 announces the fulfilment of these prospects (*cf.* notes on 3:5). Jesus in the Farewell Discourse promises the coming of the Holy Spirit – with a *teaching* role (14:26–27; 16:12–15). This is equivalent to the 'anointing from the Holy One' (1 Jn. 2:20, 26–27). *Cf.* also 1 Corinthians 2:9–16; 2 Corinthians 3:4 – 4:6; Hebrews 8:6 – 10:18. Even the confession of Peter at Caesarea Philippi owed everything to the revelation of the Father (Mt. 16:17 par.). 'Those who receive this divine illumination and respond to it show by their coming to Christ that they are children and citizens of the new Jerusalem, as the prophet foretold' (Bruce, p. 157).

46. Some take this verse to be a parenthetical remark by the Evangelist, since at first glance its connection with the preceding is obscure. But the connection, once seen, is profound. Verse 45 must not be interpreted to mean that a person may enjoy a direct, personal, mystical knowledge of God *apart from the revelation that has been given in Jesus*, not even if in consequence of such an experience he or she then becomes a follower of Jesus. Only Jesus *has seen the Father*; no-one has seen God *except the one who is from God* (*cf.* 1:18; 3:13; 14:7ff.). Jesus himself is the mediator of such knowledge: he is the one who 'narrates' God (*cf.* 1:18; 12:45). Thus, however much people are unable to 'hear' Jesus because of their moral delinquency (8:43), however much they can hear him only if they are 'taught by God', it is simultaneously true to say that they are 'taught by God' if and only if they truly 'hear' Jesus. Only then will they be truly attracted to him. The argument is of course circular, but not vicious.

47–48. With yet another strong asseverative (*cf.* on 1:51), Jesus repeats the thought of 3:15. Notwithstanding the strong note of predestinarian thought in the preceding verses, this is an implicit invitation to believe, an implicit warning against unbelief. In this context, however, it strips the would-be disciple of all pretensions, of all self-congratulation, of all agendas save those laid down by Jesus himself. Those who believe, in a context like this, cannot approach Jesus as if they are doing him a favour, or, worse, as if they know what is best for him (as in 6:14–15). They *must* believe – but they do so on his terms, and by his grace. And their immediate inheritance and possession is *everlasting life* (NIV – the same Gk. expression stands behind 'eternal life' in v. 40).

All this, then, is what Jesus meant by saying *I am the bread of life* (v. 48; *cf.* v. 35). These two verses form 'the natural conclusion of this pattern of exegetical debate' (Borgen, p. 86).

d. Eating the flesh of the Son of Man (6:49–58)

The remainder of the discourse resorts to metaphor. If Jesus' opponents find his words unacceptable when he unpacks his 'I am the bread of life' claim in non-metaphorical fashion (vv. 35–48), he will revert to the metaphor itself, and extend it. Now the terms 'eat' and 'feed' dominate the passage (vv. 49, 50, 51, 52, 53, 54, 56, 57, 58). This makes attempts to see a major break at v. 51 or v. 52 (or, with Bultmann, pp. 234–235, and others, at v. 51c) rather speculative (on the unity of the passage, *cf.* notes preceding vv. 22ff., above).

49–50. The contrast between the Old Testament manna and Jesus the bread from heaven has already been introduced (vv. 30–33). Now one further aspect of that contrast is developed: the manna in the wilderness, heaven-sent though it was, and useful for sustaining natural life under desert conditions, could not bestow *eternal* life. The proof is irrefutable: all the Fathers died. By contrast, Jesus is the bread come down from heaven such that, if anyone *eats of this bread* (*i.e.* appropriates Jesus by faith, as in the preceding verses), eternal life is the assured result.

51. The first two sentences of this verse forcefully recapitulate the last two verses, and again (*cf.* vv. 35, 48) portray Jesus identifying himself as *the living bread*, an expression synonymous with 'the bread of life'. In the third sentence, the term 'bread' is further elucidated: *This bread is my flesh, which I will give for the life of the world*. Both clauses have generated much discussion.

The first of these two clauses inevitably calls to mind the institution of the eucharist: 'This is my body' (Mk. 14:22 par.). That John uses the term 'flesh' (*sarx*) rather than 'body' (*sōma*), found everywhere else in the New Testament when the Lord's supper is clearly in view, suggests (though it does not prove) that John is not making any *direct* reference to it. Those who argue that John's thought is here primarily or exclusively eucharistic suppose that John is simply following another linguistic custom, or even that 'flesh' was the more primitive form (an argument that can be refuted: *cf.* the sources in Beasley-Murray, p. 94). But the alert reader will think of 1:14: the Word became 'flesh' (*sarx*). 'It is as the incarnate logos that Jesus is able to give his "flesh" for the life of the world' (Moloney, p. 115). *Cf.* also the discussion on v. 54, below. That there may be a secondary allusion to the Lord's supper is another matter (*cf.* notes introducing 6:22ff.).

The second clause must be taken in a sacrificial sense, the more so since, if the bread of life is Jesus, what Jesus is giving is himself. The preposition in '*for* the life of the world' (*hyper*) is repeatedly found in a sacrificial context in the Fourth Gospel (*cf.* 10:11, 15; 11:51–52; 15:13; 17:19; 18:14; *cf.* also 13:37–38). Readers could not help but remember that Jesus has already been presented as the Lamb of God who takes away the sin of the world (1:29, 36). Jesus himself is the one who gives his flesh: his sacrifice is voluntary (*cf.* Heb. 9:13–14). And since it is *for the life of the world*, his sacrifice is vicarious.[1] It is hard not to think of the Suffering Servant (Is. 52: 13 – 53:12), the more so since Isaiah 54 has just been quoted (Jn. 6:45) and becomes quite central to the thought of John 12. Isaiah's 'Servant' reaches out to Jews and Gentiles alike (Is. 49:6); the same emphasis is struck here, in that Jesus gives himself for the life *of the world* (*cf.* 3:15–17; 4:42).

52. The Jews *began to argue sharply among themselves.* The verb (*emachonto*) is very strong. Any dullard could see that Jesus was not speaking literally: no-one would suppose Jesus was seriously advocating cannibalism and offering himself as the first meal. But if his language was figurative, what did he mean? Perhaps one argued for this view, another

[1]Strangely, G. D. Kilpatrick, *The Eucharist in Bible and Liturgy* (Cambridge University Press, 1983), p. 62, toys with the suggestion that a vicarious transaction ('I surrender life, others gain life') stands over against the notion of sacrifice.

for that, all of them repeating the same literal, unintelligent question to get at the point: *How can this man give us his flesh to eat?* *Cf.* notes on 3:4.

53–54. In response, Jesus repeats the truth of v. 51c, but now puts it in a conditional form: *unless you can eat the flesh of the Son of Man . . . you have no life in you.* Verse 54 puts the same truth positively, *Whoever eats my flesh . . . has eternal life*; and again, Jesus promises to raise such a person up at the last day. In addition to the repetition of a basic theme, several fresh points are added.

(1) The one whose flesh is eaten bears the title *the Son of Man* (*cf.* notes on 1:51; in this discourse, vv. 27, 62). In one sense, he is simply a *man*, *i.e.* someone with flesh and blood; but he is also the one on whom God has set his seal of approval (v. 27), the bread from heaven, the one who descends and then ascends 'to where he was before' (v. 62). 'Son of Man' is thus a title that speaks of Jesus as the man where God is supremely revealed, and the flesh of this 'Son of Man', unlike the flesh of any other, must be eaten if one is to gain eternal life.

(2) The words *and drink his (my) blood* are added in v. 53, and repeated in v. 54. The Jews had found Jesus' statement in v. 51c impenetrable at best, blatantly offensive at worst, but in this expansion Jesus in their view is even more offensive. The law of Moses forbade the drinking of blood, and even the eating of meat with the blood still in it. To drink the blood of the Son of Man was therefore, for them, an intuitively abhorrent notion. The net effect is to make Jesus' claim all the more scandalous, thereby preparing the way for vv. 61–62 (*cf.* notes, below). The primary symbolic reference of 'blood' in the Bible is not to life but to violent death, *i.e.* to life violently and often sacrificially ended.[1] It would be hard for any reader in the decades immediately after the cross not to think of Jesus' supreme sacrifice. At the same time, readers living toward the end of the first century, with any awareness of the church's ritual, might well be disposed to ponder the connection between this utterance and the Lord's table.

(3) In v. 54 and again in vv. 56, 57, 58, the verb for 'to eat' becomes *trōgō* (as opposed to *esthiō*, or more precisely its aorist stem *phag-*, the customary verb found elsewhere in this passage). In earlier Greek, *trōgō* was used for the munching of (especially herbivorous) animals; from the classical period on, the verb was also used of human beings. Some have taken its presence here as a sign of the literalness of 'eating' that occurs in the eucharist. It is far more likely that John injects no new meaning by selecting this verb, but prefers this verb when he opts for the Greek present tense (similarly in 13:18).

If any part of the bread of life discourse has been understood sacramentally, it is these two verses. Before leaping too hastily to this conclusion, however, certain points must be noted (in addition to those discussed in vv. 22ff. and v. 51).

[1] *Cf.* A. M. Stibbs, *The Meaning of the Word 'Blood' in Scripture* (Tyndale Press, 1947).

(1) Verses 54 and 40 are closely parallel: 'Whoever eats my flesh and drinks my blood has eternal life, and I will raise him up at the last day' (v. 54); '. . . everyone who looks to the Son and believes in him shall have eternal life, and I will raise him up at the last day' (v. 40). The only substantial difference is that one speaks of eating Jesus' flesh and drinking Jesus' blood, while the other, in precisely the same conceptual location, speaks of looking to the Son and believing in him. The conclusion is obvious: the former is the metaphorical way of referring to the latter. Indeed, we have seen that this link is supported by the structure of the entire discourse. Small wonder that Augustine of Hippo wrote, *Crede, et manducasti* ('Believe, and you have eaten').[1]

(2) Moreover, the language of vv. 53–54 is so completely unqualified that if its primary reference is to the eucharist we must conclude that the *one* thing necessary to eternal life is participation at the Lord's table. This interpretation of course actually *contradicts* the earlier parts of the discourse, not least v. 40. The only reasonable alternative is to understand these verses as a *repetition* of the earlier truth, but now in metaphorical form.

(3) The passage goes on to insist that 'the flesh counts for nothing' (v. 63). The verse is not self-evident, but its meaning becomes clear when it is carefully read in its context (*cf.* notes on vv. 61–63, below). Then what is really scandalous is not the ostensibly 'cannibalistic' metaphor, but the cross to which it points.

(4) That John must still add *and I will raise him up at the last day* (v. 54) proves he does not think that eating the flesh and drinking the blood themselves immediately confer resurrection/immortality. 'The eater still has to be raised up at the last day; the Eucharist, indeed the spiritual communion also to which it points, is not a recipe for immortality' (Barrett, *Essays*, p. 43). This establishes that the view of Ignatius, that the eucharist is the medicine of immortality (if his language is taken at face value: *cf.* notes on vv. 22ff.), is ruled out of court.

None of this means there is *no* allusion in these verses to the Lord's table. But such allusions as exist prompt the thoughtful reader to look behind the eucharist, to that to which the eucharist itself points. In other words, eucharistic allusions are set in the broader framework of Jesus' saving work, in particular his cross-work. Moreover, by the repeated stress in this discourse on Jesus' initiative, no room is left for a magical understanding of the Lord's table that would place God under constraint: submit to the rite, and win eternal life! Both the feeding miracle and the Lord's table, rightly understood, parabolically set out what it means to receive Jesus Christ by faith. Both Augustine and Cranmer have it right. The former sees in this passage 'a figure, enjoining that we should have a share in the sufferings of our Lord, and that we should retain a sweet and profitable memory of the fact that His flesh was

---

[1] Augustine, *In Johan. Tract.* xxvi. 1.

wounded and crucified for us'.[1] The latter maintains that 'figuratively he [Christ] is in the bread and wine, and spiritually he is in them that worthily eat and drink the bread and wine; but really, carnally, and corporally he is only in heaven, from whence he shall come to judge the quick and the dead'.[2]

If we assume that the first intended readers of this Gospel were Jews and Jewish proselytes in touch with Christians (cf. Introduction, § VI), this interpretation makes particularly good sense. If such readers know little of this Christian ordinance, John 6 makes sense as it stands. Within the matrix of thought of the Fourth Gospel, which boasts no overt reference to the Lord's table, the obvious references in this vivid language are to Jesus himself, including his cross-work. If such readers are in rather more intimate contact with Christians, and therefore know more of their rites, then they might well think of the eucharist, but find dispelled in this book any suggestion of mere magic, let alone gory cannibalism, since, whether one begins with the feeding miracle, the words of Jesus or the eucharistic rite, the text drives us back to Jesus and the saving significance of his life and death and life. Indeed, thoughtful *Christian* readers who might be tempted by untamed magical, mystical or sacramental notions could scarcely fail to learn the same lesson. In short, John 6 does not directly speak of the eucharist; it does expose the true meaning of the Lord's supper as clearly as any passage in Scripture.

55–56. Other foods, including the Old Testament manna, had certain value, but Jesus' flesh and blood really are food and drink – they are really what food and drink should be in an ideal, archetypical sense (cf. Additional Note). They provide eternal life. Whoever eats and drinks them (in the sense unpacked in the preceding verses), Jesus insists, *remains in me, and I in him*. That is *why* his flesh and blood really are food and drink. The verb 'remains' or 'abides' (*menō*) is important to John, defining not only relationships amongst Father, Son and Holy Spirit (1:32–33; 14:10; 15:10), but between believers and Christ (*e.g.* 5:38; 8:31; 15:4, 7, 9–10). The mutual indwelling pictured here (theologians call it 'co-inherence') is obviously not precisely reciprocal. That the believer remains in Jesus means he or she continues to be identified with Jesus, continues as a Christian (to use a later term), continues in saving faith and consequent transformation of life. That Jesus remains in the believer means that Jesus identifies himself with the believer, but not in reciprocal trust and transformation (that would be absurd) but in help, blessing, life, and personal presence by the Spirit (cf. 14:23–27).

57. The Father *sent* Jesus (cf. notes on 3:17; 20:21), and he is the *living Father*, the God who has life-in-himself (as in 5:26). This living God, in sending the Son, established that he would also have life-in-himself: the argument is a compressed form of 5:21, 24–27. In an analogous way,

---

[1] Augustine, *On Christian Doctrine* iii. 16.
[2] Archbishop Cranmer, *A Defence of the True and Catholick Doctrine of the Sacrament* (1550, repr. Christian Ministries Trust, 1987), p. 163.

Jesus says, the one who *feeds* (*trōgō; cf.* notes on vv. 53–54) *on me* (the use of the pronoun *me*, replacing 'my flesh' and 'my blood' in v. 56, confirms that the whole person of Christ is in view, not merely eucharistic elements) *will live because of me.* Jesus lives *because of the Father, i.e.* because of the Father's determination that Jesus should have life-in-himself (5:26); those who feed on Jesus live (Jesus says) *because of me*: there is both parallelism and breach of parallelism. Clearly, they live because of the Son's determination, but unlike him they never have life-in-themselves, but only in him. For the Christian, eternal life is always mediated through Jesus. However mystical the language of the Fourth Gospel, John cannot imagine any genuine spiritual life that is independent of Jesus.

58. Just as the preceding section was bracketed by an *inclusio*, a literary device that opens and closes a passage with the same or similar words (*cf.* vv. 35, 48, 'I am the bread of life'), so this section is similarly bracketed (*cf.* vv. 49, 58). Jesus reverts to the contrast between the Old Testament manna, which the Jews so greatly revered and wanted to use as a criterion for assessing Jesus (vv. 30–31), and the true bread from heaven, which alone enables the one who feeds to *live for ever.*

Additional notes

55. The witnesses vary between *alēthēs*, the adjective 'true', and *alēthōs*, the adverb 'truly' or 'really'. In statements with symbolic predicates such as 'food' and 'drink', John never uses the adjective *alēthēs*. If he wants an adjective, he uses *alēthinos* (*e.g.* 1:9). The adverb conforms to John's style elsewhere (1:47; 4:42; 6:14; 7:40; 8:31).

56. At the end of v. 56, some Western manuscripts add all or part of the following: 'As the Father is in me, I also am in the Father. I tell you the truth, if you do not receive the body of the Son of Man as the bread of life, you have no life in him.' This is almost certainly secondary, a homiletical expansion for which the Western text is well known.

6. Divided opinion and divine initiative (6:59–71)

The action in this section, depicting an exchange between Jesus and some Galilean Jews, takes place at the Passover feast one year before the Passover at which he dies. This is the last public, Galilean ministry recorded in the Fourth Gospel. Some scholars, wanting to dissociate v. 63 from vv. 51ff., suggest that this section originally followed v. 50, making vv. 51ff. an eucharistic interpolation. The unsuperable objection is that the word 'flesh', on which v. 63 depends, does not occur in vv. 35–50, but occurs repeatedly in vv. 51–58.

59. John has already established that this discourse took place at Capernaum (v. 24), the current home of Jesus' family (*cf.* notes on 2:12; 6:41–42). Now he tells us that Jesus said *this* (probably referring to the entire discourse and exchanges, vv. 27–58) *in the synagogue in Capernaum.* There is evidence that some synagogue services allowed such exchanges.[1] Certainly the topic would have been all the more appropriate if the lectionary readings at that time of year included both Exodus 16 and Isaiah 54 (regarding manna and being taught by God respectively; so Guilding, pp. 61–65).

60. Not only 'the Jews' (v. 52) but *many of his disciples* were finding Jesus' teaching hard to take. The dividing line, for John, is never race (*cf.* notes on 1:19) but response to Jesus. 'Disciples' must be distinguished from 'the Twelve' (*cf.* vv. 66, 67). More importantly, just as there is faith and faith (2:23–25), so are there disciples and disciples. At the most elementary level, a disciple is someone who is at that point following Jesus, either literally by joining the group that pursued him from place to place, or metaphorically in regarding him as the authoritative teacher. Such a 'disciple' is not necessarily a 'Christian', someone who has savingly trusted Jesus and sworn allegiance to him, given by the Father to the Son, drawn by the Father and born again by the Spirit. Jesus will make it clear in due course that only those who *continue* in his word are *truly* his 'disciples' (8:31). The 'disciples' described here do not remain in his word; they find it to be *hard teaching* (lit. 'word', *logos*; *cf.* notes on 1:1) and wonder *who can accept it*. The adjective rendered 'hard' in the NIV (*sklēros*) does not mean 'hard to understand' but 'harsh', 'offensive'. These 'disciples' will not long remain disciples, because they find Jesus' word intolerable.

What was it that offended their sensibilities? Judging by the preceding discourse, there were four features in Jesus' word at which they took umbrage. (1) They were more interested in food (v. 26), political messianism (vv. 14–15) and manipulative miracles (vv. 30–31) than in the spiritual realities to which the feeding miracle had pointed. (2) They were unprepared to relinquish their own sovereign authority even in matters religious, and therefore were incapable of taking the first steps of genuine faith (vv. 41–46). (3) In particular they were offended at the claims Jesus advanced, claiming to be greater than Moses, uniquely sent by God and authorized to give life (vv. 32ff., 58). (4) The extended metaphor of the 'bread' is itself offensive to them, especially when it assaults clear taboos and becomes a matter of 'eating flesh' and 'drinking blood'.

61. The brief remarks Jesus now offers touch on all these points. Probably his awareness of his disciples' grumbling springs from supernatural knowledge (*cf.* notes on 1:47–48; 2:24–25).

62. Jesus had earlier spoken of his coming down from heaven (v. 38). Now he asks what their reaction will be if they see him *ascend to where he was before*. The Greek preserves the condition but no conclusion, so it is possible to understand the argument in one of two ways: (1) Jesus' ascension will make the offence even greater; or (2) Jesus' ascension will

---

[1]*Cf.* I. Abrahams, *Studies in Pharisaism and the Gospels* (Cambridge University Press, 1917), 1. 1–17.

reduce or remove the offence. When we remember what Jesus' 'ascending' and his 'lifting up' (*cf.* notes on 3:14) mean in the Fourth Gospel, we may conclude that the alternatives are not mutually exclusive (*cf.* Westcott, 1. 247). If the disciples find Jesus' claims, authority and even his language offensive, what will they think when they see Jesus on the cross, his way of 'ascending' to the place where he was before? That is the supreme scandal. However offensive the linguistic expression 'eating flesh and drinking blood' may be, how much more offensive is the crucifixion of an alleged Messiah! The very idea is outrageous, bordering on blasphemous obscenity, 'a stumbling-block to Jews and foolishness to Gentiles' (1 Cor. 1:23). Yet this stands at the very heart of the divine self-disclosure. The moment of Jesus' greatest degradation and shame is the moment of his glorification, the path of his return to the glory he had with the Father before the world began (17:5). The hour when the Servant of the Lord is despised and rejected by men, when he is pierced for our transgressions and crushed for our iniquities (Is. 53:3–5) is the very portal to the time when 'he will be raised and lifted up and highly exalted' (Is. 52:13).

That is why the condition of this verse is left open. How men and women respond to this supreme scandal determines their destiny. Other religious leaders were said to have ascended to heaven at the end of their life, but Jesus the Son of Man (the title especially connected with his function as the revealer from heaven) first *descended* (v. 38; *cf.* notes on 1:51; 6:27, 53), and so in ascending is merely returning *to where he was before* (*cf.* 17:5). This not only affirms Jesus' pre-existence, but places him in a class quite different from antecedent Jewish religious heroes.

63. To take the words of the preceding discourse literally, without penetrating their symbolic meaning, is useless. It causes offence; it does not arrive at Jesus' meaning, for *the flesh counts for nothing*. Although this clause does not rule out all allusion in the preceding verses to the Lord's supper, it is impossible not to see in 'flesh' a direct reference to the preceding discussion, and therefore a dismissal of all *primarily* sacramental interpretations. It is not as if the flesh is of no significance: after all, the Word became flesh (1:14). But when all the focus of attention is on the flesh, then the real significance of Jesus is missed, and the kinds of objections raised both by 'the Jews' and by ostensible disciples quickly surface.

But if flesh does not give life, what does? One of the clearest characteristics of the Spirit in the Old Testament is the giving of life (*e.g.* Gn. 1:2; Ezk. 37:1ff.; *cf.* Barrett, *HSGT*, pp. 18–23). In this Gospel we have already been introduced to the Spirit's role in the new birth (Jn. 3); there the contrast between flesh and spirit is no less sharp. So here: *The Spirit gives life*. Strictly speaking, the Spirit does not come upon the disciples until after Jesus' ascension (7:37–39); but already Jesus himself is the bearer of the Spirit (1:32f.), the one to whom God gives the Spirit without limit and who therefore speaks the words of God (3:34). That is why Jesus can now say, *The words I have spoken to you are spirit* (*i.e.* they are the product of the life-giving Spirit) *and they are life* (*i.e.* Jesus' words, rightly understood and absorbed, generate life – *cf.* 5:24). If the words of Jesus in this discourse are rightly grasped, then instead of rejecting Jesus people will see him as the bread from heaven, the one who gives his flesh for the life of the world, the one who alone provides eternal life, and they will receive him and believe in him, taste eternal life even now, and enjoy the promise that he will raise them up on the last day.

It is hard not to see in the last clause an allusion to Jeremiah 15:16, where the prophet addresses God: 'When your words came, I ate them; they were my joy and my heart's delight' (*cf.* also Ezk. 2:8 – 3:3; Rev. 10:9ff.). In short, Jeremiah's assessment of God's words is the same as Jesus' assessment of his own words. One cannot feed on Christ without feeding on Christ's words, for truly believing Jesus cannot be separated from truly believing Jesus' words (5:46–47). Human beings live by every word that proceeds from the mouth of God (Dt. 8:3). The identical claim is now made for the words of Jesus, precisely because he is the Word incarnate (1:1–18; *cf.* 5:19–30).

The connection between v. 63 and vv. 61–62 is now clear. Already Jesus is establishing the link between his own ascension/glorification (v. 62) and the coming of the Spirit (v. 63; *cf.* 7:37–39). Moreover, all the points that had offended these shallow disciples find their answer here – a critically divisive answer. Here is sharp insistence on the priority of spiritual life, unrelenting stress on Jesus' authority and superiority over Moses, and above all the promise of eternal life engendered by the Spirit and the Word, consequent upon Jesus 'ascending' by a means more offensive than the harshest metaphor.

64. However great the revelation and the promises, some *do not believe*. If they do not combine the message with faith, it is of no value to them (Heb. 4:2). The pattern of unbelief came as no surprise to Jesus. He knew *from the beginning* (John means either 'from the beginning' of Jesus' ministry or possibly, as in 1:1, 'from the beginning' absolutely) not only who did not believe (*cf.* notes on v. 61) but also the supreme example of unbelief, the betrayer himself. The final words of the verse anticipate vv. 70–71. The rather rare future participial construction (*ho paradōsōn auton*, 'who would betray him') depicts the speaker's firm expectation (*cf.* Rob, p. 1118; Porter, p. 418). Jesus was going toward his God-appointed task with his eyes wide open.

65. 'This' in *This is why* refers to the phenomenon of unbelief – *i.e.* Jesus knew in advance that he would be rejected by many, and, knowing this, he earlier explained (vv. 37, 44) the need for the divine initiative which draws those whom the Father has given to the Son and enables them to believe. This advance explanation prepares the true believers themselves to face the attacks of unbelievers, without finding their own faith threatened (*cf.* 13:18–19). However much men and women are commanded to believe, and are held accountable for their unbelief, genuine coming to faith is never finally a matter of autonomous human decision. The remaining verses in the chapter show this is true even of the Twelve.

66. *From this time* (or 'For this reason': *ek toutou* could mean either) *many of his disciples* (*cf.* notes on v. 60) abandoned him decisively. Doubtless these *many . . . disciples* are those who found his earlier discourse intolerable (v. 60). Jesus' additional remarks have done nothing to remove the offence they have found in his words; he did not expect it to be otherwise, and would not shape his comments to pander to their taste. 'What they wanted, he would not give; what he offered, they would not receive' (Bruce, p. 164). These Galileans thus joined the earlier Jerusalem followers who failed to pass the test of unqualified allegiance and perseverance grounded in grace-prompted faith.

67. Jesus' question to the Twelve (here introduced as such for the first time; *cf.* Carson, *Matt*, pp. 236-240) opens with the interrogative *mē*. In non-rhetorical questions, this particle either demands the answer *No* or else puts the question in a hesitating, tentative fashion (M. 1. 193). Granted the certainty of Jesus' knowledge regarding those who are his, it is unlikely the latter applies here. The question is not moody, glum, but a challenging 'Surely *you* don't want to go away too, do you?' The question is asked more for their sake than his. They need to articulate a response more than he needs to hear it. One might guess from the flow of the narrative that the defection has been so substantial on this occasion that not many more than the Twelve actually remain.

68-69. As usual, *Simon Peter* (*cf.* notes on 1:40, 42) speaks his mind. His response has certain similarities to the confession at Caesarea Philippi (Mk. 8:29 par.), though it is not at all clear that the two passages refer to the same incident. Here, Peter's response is in two differentiable parts. (1) He asks, *Lord, to whom* [else] *shall we go?* What alternatives are there, granted that *You have the words of eternal life*? Peter may not have understood all that much of the preceding discourse, but he here picks up on v. 63: the words Jesus has spoken 'are spirit and they are life'. (2) *We believe and know* [the Gk. perfects are properly stative, *i.e.* expressing the state of the disciples' faith and knowledge: *cf.* Porter, pp. 251ff.] *that you are the Holy One of God*. The additional words found in the AV ('the Christ, the Son of the living God') are not original, but are due to assimilation to Matthew 16:16. The verbs 'to believe' and 'to know' are extremely common in John, and are frequently roughly synonymous (*cf.* the parallelism in 17:8). There is one absolute distinction: Jesus himself is said to know God (7:29; 8:55; 10:15; 17:25), but never to believe in him. To believe apparently has overtones of dependence appropriate to creatures, redeemed creatures, but not to the one who is both the agent of creation (1:3) and their redeemer. Knowledge in the Fourth Gospel is frequently personal (it is knowledge of God and of Jesus Christ that constitutes eternal life, 17:3), but no less frequently propositional (as here: the disciples know *that* Jesus is such and such).

The full title *the Holy One of God* occurs elsewhere in Mark 1:24 (= Luke 4:34) in the mouth of a demon. Probably it is a messianic title, though clear evidence of such usage is lacking. At the same time, the adjective 'holy' groups Jesus with his 'Holy Father' (17:11). Jesus is the one whom the Father has 'set apart [lit. "sanctified", same root as "holy"] as his very own' (10:36). Indeed, Jesus sanctifies himself (17:19). He could not but be the Holy One if he was to deal effectively with 'the sin of the world' (1:29).[1] Doubtless Peter and the other members of the Twelve entertained at that time a significantly muddier conception of what the expression meant than they did after Jesus' resurrection and exaltation. It was enough that their first messianic hopes (1:41, 45) were being confirmed, that they saw in Jesus one who was greater than a prophet, greater than Moses, none less than 'the Holy One of God'.

70. Nevertheless, Peter's way of expressing himself appears somewhat pretentious, as if he and his fellows are a cut above the fickle 'disciples' who have turned away, superior at least in insight. Indeed, Peter's words might almost be taken to mean that he is doing Jesus a favour. But Jesus will not allow even a whisper of human pretensions. Ultimately, the Twelve did not choose Jesus; he chose them (though alone amongst the Evangelists, John does not record their actual appointment). Even there, the one catastrophic failure amongst the Twelve was not unforeseen. One of them was a *diabolos*: the word in common Greek means 'slanderer' or 'false accuser', but in the New Testament it always refers, when it is a substantive, to Satan, the prince of darkness (*e.g.* 8:44; 13:2; *cf.* 13:27). Indeed the Greek should probably not be rendered *one of you is a devil* but 'one of you is the devil'. The meaning is clear from 13:2, clearer yet from Mark 8:33 par., where Jesus addresses Peter as 'Satan'. The supreme adversary (Heb. *śāṭān*) of God so operates behind failing human beings that his malice becomes theirs. Jesus can discern the source, and labels it appropriately.

71. The Evangelist, writing long after Jesus' announcement, makes the identification for his readers. At least six interpretations of *Iscariot* have been advanced (*cf.* Carson, *Matt*, pp. 239f.), but the most likely is that the term is a transliteration of Hebrew *'îš qᵉrîyôṯ*, 'man of Kerioth' (there are at least two eligible villages with that name). Such a designation would be appropriate not only for Judas but (as here) for his father Simon, assuming both sprang from the one region. As in the other three Gospels (Mt. 10:4; Mk. 3:19; Lk. 6:16), Judas is no sooner named than he is labelled as the betrayer. The nature of the betrayal is described in 18:2.

7. *Scepticism and uncertainty* (7:1–13)

Themes are so intricately interwoven in the Fourth Gospel that several quite different outlines of the book are possible. In particular, it is

---

[1]For a useful discussion of the title, *cf.* H. L. N. Joubert, *Neot* 2, 1968, pp. 52–69. The suggestion of W. R. Domeris (*Neot* 19, 1985, pp. 9–17) that 'Peter speaks from the *post-resurrection* standpoint of the Johannine community' (p. 15, emphasis his) is a fine example of assertion without evidence.

possible to link chs. 7 and 8 together (omitting 7:53 – 8:11: *cf.* notes, below) under the heading, 'Jesus at the Feast of Tabernacles'. Certainly two of the major themes associated with Tabernacles, water and light, surface in these chapters (7:37–39; 8:12), and the links from pericope to pericope are natural enough that the two chapters do constitute a unity. Nevertheless, other topics – deep uncertainty as to who Jesus is, a return to controversy over the Sabbath, further exploration of the theme of the Holy Spirit, hints about outreach beyond Jewish circles, paternity to Abraham, God and the devil, and above all the sustained theme of rising opposition – so firmly link each pericope into the larger argument of the book that to group these chapters under 'The Feast of Tabernacles' or the like seems vaguely reductionistic. Even so, the setting of the Feast will not be forgotten in the following notes.

1. Assuming that chs. 5 – 7 are in the right order as they stand (*cf.* notes on 5:1; 6:1), *After this* (*meta tauta*; *cf.* notes on 2:12) does not establish tight connections, merely sequence: *i.e.* in the period after the feeding miracle and the bread of life discourse, Jesus *went around* (in context the imperfect *periepatei* is probably to be understood 'continued to go around') *Galilee*. The reason for this geographical restriction was his desire to avoid Judea, *because the Jews were there waiting to take his life*. This is a clear reference to 5:18, where in the wake of the Sabbath controversy and Jesus' dramatic Christological claims, 'the Jews sought to kill him'. Both 5:18 and here, 'the Jews' (*cf.* notes on 1:19) refers to 'the Judeans' or, more precisely, the Jewish authorities in Judea. Jesus spent about a year in Galilee, the year of ministry on which the Synoptists focus most of their attention.

2. That year was about to end, occasioned by the impending Feast of Tabernacles. The institution of the Feast was associated in the Old Testament with the ingathering of harvest (Ex. 23:16; Lv. 23:33–36, 39–43; Dt. 16:13–15; not grain, which was reaped between April and June, but grapes and olives). The Feast ran for seven days, 15–21 Tishri, the Jewish lunar month that falls in September–October. A special festival assembly took place on the eighth day, 22 Tishri (Lv. 23:36; *cf.* SB 2. 774; Mishnah *Sukkah*). The time, therefore, is about six months after the feeding of the five thousand. According to Josephus, this Feast was the most popular of the three principal Jewish feasts that brought the faithful flocking to Jerusalem ('especially sacred and important', Jos., *Ant.* viii. 100). People living in rural areas built makeshift structures of light branches and leaves to live in for the week (hence 'booths' or 'tabernacles'; *cf.* Lv. 23:42); town dwellers put up similar structures on their flat roofs or in their courtyards. The Feast was known for a water-drawing rite and a lamp-lighting rite to which Jesus quite clearly refers (*cf.* 7:37ff.; 8:12).[1]

3–4. As in 2:1, *Jesus' brothers* most likely refers to the sons of Mary and

---

[1]For details of the Feast, *cf.* G. W. MacRae, *CBQ* 22, 1960, pp. 251–276.

Joseph, all younger than Jesus himself. At this point they are unbelievers (v. 5), a point attested by the Synoptics (cf. Mk. 3:21, 31–35 par.), and a small indication of John's care in avoiding anachronism: he does not at this point assume their subsequent conversion.

Not infrequently it is argued that this report of their challenge to Jesus is, for two reasons, historically implausible. First, the words *so that your disciples may see the miracles you do* make it sound as if his disciples have *not* seen his miracles, even though, by any definition of 'disciples' (cf. notes on 6:60), at least some disciples have been present on every occasion. Second, *You ought to leave here and go to Judea* has been taken to mean that the bulk of Jesus' disciples were in Judea, not Galilee, when the Synoptic Gospels leave the opposite impression.

But several considerations alleviate the difficulties. (1) If Jesus' brothers are aware of the large-scale defections besetting Jesus' 'disciples', attested at the end of ch. 6, then their suggestion that he perform miracles for his 'disciples' may mean no more than that he ought to satisfy them before his cause is entirely lost. (2) The Feast of Tabernacles was a popular attraction that drew countless thousands to Jerusalem. If Jesus went there to perform his miracles, not only would he enjoy the biggest crowds of his career, but the word would spread very quickly. Better still, in the nature of the case the most religious people of the nation would be the most likely to be there. What better place for a religious leader to parade his wares? (3) Jerusalem was central to the religious life of observant Jews, not only because of its long heritage but even more because the temple was there. Because the various forms of modern Judaism cannot follow the law of Moses so far as its sacrificial stipulations are concerned (since modern Judaism has no temple), we must make a mental effort to grasp how central the temple and Jerusalem were for the vast majority of Palestinian and even Diaspora Jews in Jesus' day. Even the reclusive monks of the Qumran community, by the Dead Sea, who wrote off the temple as impossibly apostate, thus indirectly confirm its centrality to contemporary thought and religious observance. If Jesus is interested in religious prominence, his brothers reason, sooner or later he must prove the master of Jerusalem. Otherwise he will always be regarded by the authorities and by the upper echelons of society as no more than a rustic, rural preacher (cf. 7:52).

What the brothers want, then, is that he should act *en parrēsia* (v. 4): the expression sometimes means 'plainly', 'clearly', *i.e.* without the oscurity of metaphor (10:24; 11:14; 16:25, 29), but here means 'publicly' (NIV), 'openly' (cf. 7:13, 26; 11:54; 18:20).[1] A public figure who wants to advance must make an impact on the capital. Jesus ought to *show [himself] to the world*, by which they mean 'to everybody'. But John the Evangelist doubtless sees irony in their request. Jesus' brothers want

---

[1] Cf. W. C. van Unnik, *BJRL* 44, 1962, pp. 466–488.

Jesus to put on a display; John's readers already know that such a display would pander to corrupt motives (6:14, 15, 26ff.) and in any case would not ensure genuine faith (2:23–25; 4:48). The brothers want Jesus to show himself to the *world*, but in John's most characteristic sense of that word (*cf.* notes on 1:9) the 'world' is precisely that which *cannot* receive him without ceasing to be the 'world'. In one sense, Jesus has no intention of showing himself to the 'world' (*cf.* note on 14:22). And yet in another sense, the reader who presses on to the rest of this Gospel discovers that it is in Jerusalem where Jesus reveals himself most dramatically – not in the spectacular miracles the brothers want but in the ignominy of the cross, the very cross by which Jesus draws all men to himself (12:32) and becomes the Saviour of the world (4:42).

5. The conjunction *For* introduces John's explanation as to *why* Jesus' brothers spoke as they did in vv. 3–4: they *did not believe in him*. The point is confirmed by the Synoptics (Mk. 3:21, 31 par.). Apparently Jesus' brothers did not become his followers until after the resurrection (Acts 1:14), and this because Jesus revealed himself to at least one of them personally (1 Cor. 15:7). We ought not to think the brothers' scepticism extended to doubt that he could perform dazzling miracles, otherwise their challenge that he should perform his works of power in Jerusalem would be incoherent. But they, like so many of the superficial disciples in 2:23–25; 6:60ff., could not perceive the *sig*nificance of what they saw, and therefore did not penetrate to Jesus' real identity and entrust themselves entirely to him. There is no evidence that their unbelief went as far as that of some opponents who credited Jesus with the power to perform remarkable miracles, while ascribing this power to Beelzebub, the prince of demons (Mk. 3:22 par.).

6. His brothers did not believe in him. *Therefore* Jesus gave further explanation as to why their judgments were so faulty. In brief, they had projected onto him what *they* would have done under similar circumstances, without reckoning with the uniqueness that stamped him. *The right time (kairos) for me has not yet come; for you any time is right* (lit. 'but your time [*kairos*] is always ready'). This calls to mind Jesus' response to his mother: 'My time (*hōra*) has not yet come' (2:4). The similarity in expression prompts most commentators to conclude that the difference in actual terms is incidental: *kairos* and *hōra*, on this view, mean the same thing. If so, *kairos* (which in John occurs only here and in v. 8) refers to the 'hour' (*hōra*) when Jesus is glorified by being lifted up on the cross, on the way to his Father's presence (*cf.* notes on 2:4). But another analysis seems preferable. The Greek word for 'hour' (*hōra*), often rendered 'time' in NIV, always bears the theological content just indicated, provided it is not modified by a number (as in 'the tenth hour' or the like). *Chronos*, another word rendered 'time', always focuses on the *extent* of time, not the point or specific hour of time (used in John only in 5:6; 7:33; 12:35; 14:9). The word *kairos*, found in vv. 6, 8, unlike *chronos* but like *hōra*, refers in this Gospel to a point of time, but unlike *hōra* does not refer to Christ's 'being lifted up', to his glorification by way of the cross. If that is the case, then unlike 2:4, Jesus is *not* saying that the time for unrestrained messianic blessings has not yet dawned because the 'time' of his glorification is not yet at hand (the final Passover was still more than six months away). Rather he is saying that the 'time' for his going up to Jerusalem for this Feast of Tabernacles is not yet at hand.

This interpretation is well-nigh necessitated by the final words of the verse: *for you any time (kairos) is right.* In this reading, *kairos* makes sense: *i.e.* Jesus' brothers are free to go up to Jerusalem for the Feast any time they like, while Jesus is under special constraint (*cf.* v. 8). Jesus' words become more biting when Odeberg's evidence (pp. 270–281) is taken into account. He lists numerous Jewish sources which, largely building upon Ecclesiastes 3:1ff. ('There is a time for everything, and a season for every activity under heaven. . . .'), delight to appeal to divine sovereignty to give significance to the diversity of things that can befall both the created order in general and the individual in particular. In that light, Jesus' brothers would not be upset to hear Jesus say his time had not come, but they may well have been scandalized to hear him say *for you any time is right.* It is almost as if they are being excluded from divine sovereignty – not that God suspended his providential reign in their case, but that what they did was utterly without significance as far as God is concerned. This interpretation is confirmed by the next verse.

7. Jesus' brothers lack an appointed time because they belong to the 'world' (*kosmos; cf.* notes on 1:9, 7:4). *The world cannot hate you,* Jesus tells them, for they belong to it, and the world loves its own (15:19). By contrast, the world hates Jesus, not only because he does not belong to it, but because he testifies that *what it does is evil* (*cf.* 3:19–20; 7:19; 8:31–59; 9:39–41; 16:8–9). The world always hates to have its evil exposed, to be convicted of its sin. That is why the brother's suggestion, that Jesus should show himself to the world (v. 4), was so misplaced. By 'the world', they mean 'everybody', but Jesus knows that 'everybody' belongs to 'the world' in a far more negative sense, already summarized in the Prologue (1:10).

Thus v. 7 simultaneously explains why Jesus will not rise to the challenge set him in v. 4, and why, for the brothers, *any time is right.* Their alignment with 'the world' means they know nothing of God's agenda. They do not listen to his word, do not recognize it when it comes, and cannot perceive the Word incarnate before them. They are divorced from God's *kairos*, his divine appointments,[1] and so any time will do. All appointments that ignore God's *kairos* are in the eternal scheme of things equally insignificant.

8–9. So let the brothers go to the Feast whenever they will. Their decision is without significance. But Jesus, whose itinerary is regulated by the Father, must at this point decline, because (he says) *for me the right*

---

[1]This interpretation must be distinguished from the one criticized by James Barr, *Biblical Words for Time* (SCM, ²1969), pp. 66–67, who rightly objects to any attempt to invest the meaning of *kairos* itself with salvation-historical significance.

time (kairos; cf. v. 6) *has not yet come.* The early textual witnesses are divided between *I am not yet (oupō) going up to this Feast* (NIV), and 'I am not *(ouk)* going up to the Feast'. The word *oupō* may have been an early scribal 'correction' to remove the obvious difficulty that arises in v. 10: Jesus does go up. But even if the reading *ouk* ('not') is correct, the difficulty is superficial because the context supplies a condition. Jesus' response to his brothers is not that he is planning to stay in Galilee forever, but that because his life is regulated by his heavenly Father's appointments he is *not* going to the Feast when they say he should. The 'counsel of the wicked' (Ps. 1:1) cannot be permitted to set his agenda. His 'not' turns down his brothers' request; it does not promise he will not go to the Feast when the Father sanctions the trip.

The verb rendered 'going up' *(anabainō)* is also used to refer to Jesus' ascent to the Father through death (3:13; 6:62; 20:17), and some see a similar allusion here. That is just possible, even though the brothers also 'go up' to the Feast, in the purely mundane sense that anyone travelling to Jerusalem from any point on the compass was said to be 'going up' to the capital. If such an allusion is intended, the idea is that Jesus' 'going up' cannot possibly be like the 'going up' of other pilgrims.

10. The assumption in this verse is that the Father has signalled Jesus in some way, so Jesus goes to Jerusalem, leaving Galilee for the last time before the cross. Even so, his journey is marked by maximum discretion, exactly the opposite of what the brothers had in mind. Bruce (p. 173) remarks that in the third-century work *Against the Christians,* the neo-platonist Porphyry on the basis of this incident disparages Jesus for his irresoluteness.[1] But John the Evangelist, far from depicting fickleness, is in fact portraying Jesus' firm resolve to do exactly what the Father gives him to do, and at the Father's time *(cf.* 5:19ff.).

11. Since there seems to be a difference between 'the Jews' in this verse, and 'the crowds' in the next, 'the Jews' *(cf.* notes on 1:19) here refers to the Jewish authorities in Judea, especially in Jerusalem. Doubtless we are to understand their search to be hostile: they hope the occasion of the Feast will draw Jesus out of Galilee, where he was in the jurisdiction of Herod Antipas, and thus bring Jesus into their hands. The words *that man (ekeinos)* probably reflect scorn or exasperation, possibly both.

12–13. The crowds, made up not only of Judeans but of Galileans and of diaspora Jews, adopt a milder stance. They are frankly curious about Jesus, and clearly divided in their opinions. Some, doubtless because they remember the good results of his miracles, simply conclude, *He is a good man,* even if their categories prevent them from concluding anything very profound about him. Others, of a more cynical disposition (for the punishment of the liar is not so much that he is not believed but that he does not believe), suspect he is a charlatan: *No, he deceives the*

[1] Referred to by Jerome, *Dialogues against the Pelagians,* 2. 17.

people. The latter view became dominant in some Jewish circles after the resurrection.[1] The Evangelist is doubtless aware of it, and, seeking to win Jews and proselytes to the Christian faith, here attempts to explain it by tracing it to its origin. Whatever their opinions, however, the crowds discuss them in whispers *for fear of the Jews* (*cf.* v. 11). Apparently the antipathy of the authorities has reached the point where they do not want Jesus discussed *publicly* (*parrēsia*; *cf.* notes on v. 4). Their displeasure with Jesus is boiling over to affect his followers (*cf.* 9:22; 16:1–2), and even those who, by their topic of conversation, make Jesus a more important figure than 'the Jews' wanted him to be.

Additional note

4. For the several linguistic connections between this verse and Matthew 10:26 = Luke 12:2; Mark 4:22 = Luke 8:17, *cf.* Lindars, p. 283. But the meaning of v. 4 is quite distinct from either pair of references. Nevertheless there are conceptual links between this verse and the 'messianic secret' theme in Mark, rightly understood. In both John and Mark, Jesus *necessarily* passes through a period in which his true identity is wholly or partially hidden from all witnesses, for were it otherwise his opponents *could not* have crucified him, his faithful followers *could not* have been crushed by his death and burial.

8. At the Feast of Tabernacles I (7:14–44)

In the notes on 7:1ff., the relative merits of an outline that tightly links ch. 7 and ch. 8 over against the more thematically comprehensive outline adopted here were indicated. If v. 14 is tightly tied to vv. 1–13, another structure can be discerned in the rest of the chapter, *viz.* a pair of cycles, each with three points: (1) Jesus teaches, vv. 15–24, 37–39; (2) Jesus' teaching calls forth debate and speculation among the people, vv. 25–31, 40–44; (3) the Jewish leaders' mission to arrest Jesus, and its results, vv. 32–36, 45–52.[2] This pair of cycles constitutes no evidence for separate sources, but is the fruit of John's artistic skill. Others have argued that vv. 15–24 originally followed 5:47 (*e.g.* Bernard, 1. 258–259; Bultmann, pp. 237ff.). Brief counter-arguments are registered below. Guilding (p. 98) argues that the argument of John 7 – 9 is determined by the Jewish lectionary cycle. This is rather overstated. If (and it is a substantial 'if') the lectionary cycles preserved for us in later sources extended back into the first century, it is not at all unlikely that John, and for that matter Jesus himself, would make use of them to support their arguments. But the lectionaries certainly do not *determine* John's agenda, which is his own; at most they support it. Some see the

---

[1] The Babylonian Talmud (*Sanhedrin* 43a) preserves a tradition that says Jesus was executed on Passover Eve because he was a deceiver who practised sorcery and led Israel astray. Similar opinions are found in Justin Martyr's *Dialogue with Trypho*, 69, 108.

[2] *Cf.* J. Schneider, *ZNW* 45, 1954, pp. 108–119.

narrative of John 7 operating at two levels, one being John's historical circumstance and the other being the level of Jesus' ministry. This theory is briefly discussed in the notes on 9:1ff.

a. Jesus' authoritative teaching (7:14-24)

14. The words *Not until halfway through the Feast* do not express the exact time Jesus went up to Jerusalem, but they eliminate the beginning, when his brothers wanted him to go, and the last day, by which time he was already present (v. 37). Owing to the renewed Sabbath controversy recorded in 7:21-24, it has been suggested that he arrived on a Sabbath, but the Sabbath is presented in this text as an item on a theological, not a chronological, agenda. On the verb 'go up', *cf.* notes on v. 8.

It might be asked why, if Jesus was trying to maintain anonymity, he chose to go to the temple courts and teach. Certainly the setting was right for teaching: other rabbis taught their followers there as well. But drawing vast crowds as it did, the temple was not a site that fostered privacy. We must recall, however, that the focus of Jesus' concern was not privacy but obedience to his Father. Even so, had he gone publicly with the other pilgrims at the beginning of the Feast, it is not unlikely that a premature 'triumphal entry' might have been forced on him, an event the authorities would have judged all the more destabilizing if this Feast occurred shortly after the slaughter of the Galileans in the temple courts (Lk. 13:1).

15. Like the Galilean crowds that 'were amazed at his teaching, because he taught as one who had authority, and not as their teachers of the law' (Mt. 7:28-29), so *the Jews* (*cf.* on 1:19; probably here referring to the Judean crowds, not excluding the Judean authorities) of Jerusalem *were amazed*. Like Mt. 7:29, John's underlying concern is the question of Jesus' authority; unlike Mt. 7:29, however, John does not link the astonishment of the people to a contrast between Jesus' teaching and that of the scribes (who found it difficult to teach for long without citing lengthy lists of authoritative sources, while Jesus kept saying, 'But I say to you . . .', or 'I tell you the truth'), but chooses to link their astonishment to Jesus' lack of formal training: *How did this man get such learning without having studied?* The question in Greek (lit. 'How does this man know letters [*grammata*] . . .?') could mean, 'How is it that he can read and write?' But in fact, such basic attainments were commonplace amongst Jews (especially males), and would evoke no amazement. Rather, they were astonished that someone who had not studied in one of the great rabbinical centres of learning, or with one of the famous rabbis, could have such a command of Scripture, such telling mastery in his exposition. About a year later, Peter and John similarly confounded the religious authorities, who were compelled to observe that although they were 'unschooled (*agrammatoi*), ordinary men' (Acts 4:13), they had been with Jesus and apparently drew their knowledge and authority from that exposure.

Those who think 7:15-24 originally followed 5:47 note that in the latter passage Jesus accuses his opponents of not believing 'what [Moses] wrote', literally, not believing his *grammata*, his writings. One might equally argue that John is purposefully drawing attention to the events that took place during Jesus' previously recorded visit to Jerusalem, as he also does by reporting Jesus' allusion to the earlier attempt to kill him (7:19). Such allusive links, however, do not jeopardize the plausibility of the setting established within ch. 7: mention of Jesus' teaching in the temple courts (7:14) prepares the way for discussion of Jesus' learning, and mention of the Jews' determination to take Jesus' life (7:1) prepares the way for his accusing question (v. 19). *Cf.* also Lindars, *BFG*, p. 54.

16. One of the consequences of studying for years in the rabbinical centres was the tendency to substantiate every pronouncement by appealing to precedent, to earlier rabbinic judgments. Not to do so might indicate a certain arrogance, an independence of spirit in danger of drifting from the weight of tradition. Jesus too insists he is no inventive upstart: *My teaching is not my own.* But unlike his rabbinic contemporaries, neither is his teaching based on a long chain of human tradition: it comes (he insists) *from him who sent me*, a particularly Johannine way of referring to his heavenly Father, although the expression is found in the Synoptics (Mt. 10:40; Mk. 9:37; Lk. 9:48). At one level, all the prophets who came before Jesus would have wanted to insist that their teaching was not their own, but came from the one who sent them. But in the light of earlier discussions in this book (5:19–30; 6:57; *cf.* 8:26, 38; 14:9–10), we must conclude that Jesus is claiming something rather more than they. Earlier prophets could thunder, 'Thus says the LORD!' But Jesus' words and deeds are so much at one with the Father's, not only because of his unqualified obedience but also because he does *everything* the Father does (5:19ff.), that Jesus can legitimately and repeatedly presage his remarks with an authoritative, '*I* tell you the truth' (*cf.* notes on 1:51).

17. Whether or not Jesus' claims are true is another matter. Here he insists that the question cannot be decided by the rigorous debating procedures of the rabbinic schools. There is a moral dimension involved. Jesus has already insisted that free human decisions about his claims are impossible (6:44); now he articulates what, from the human side, is necessary to a right assessment of his teaching. *If anyone chooses to do God's will, he will find out. . . .* The point is not that a seeker must attain a certain God-approved level of ethical achievement before venturing an assessment as to whether or not Jesus' teaching comes from God, but that a seeker must be fundamentally committed to *doing* God's will. This is a faith commitment. God then fills the seeker's horizon. God's will is not simply to be thought about and assessed, as if God is the object we may politely examine, dissect and discuss, picking and choosing what we like of him. The faith commitment envisaged here, this moral choice, is properly basic, and renders impossible any attitude that sets us up as judges of God's ways. This means that the truth is self-authenticating – not with vicious circularity, as if it has no meshing-points with the

312

external, examinable world (Does not Jesus himself invite us to believe on the evidence of the signs, 10:38?), but in the sense that finite and fallen human beings cannot set themselves up on some sure ground *outside* the truth and thus gain the vantage from which they may assess it. Divine revelation can only be assessed, as it were, from the inside. From that perspective the person who *chooses to do God's will* discovers that Jesus' teaching articulates it, that Jesus does not speak on his own but as the Word of God.

18. The maxims of this verse not only confirm that Jesus is *a man of truth*, but they exhibit the real reason why his opponents are unable to assess him rightly. The one who prides himself on being his own man, on speaking *on his own*, has his ego bound up with his witness, and so at least in part he speaks *to gain honour* (*doxa; cf.* notes on 1:14) *for himself*. Jesus is quite unlike that. He is totally committed to working for *the honour* (*doxa*) *of the one who sent him*. As a result he can be trusted. He is neither a religious charlatan nor a respected religious leader with inevitably mixed motives. He is as trustworthy as his motives are unmixed. If Jesus were simply trying to persuade others to his views, he would seek whatever means seemed most effective. In fact he has utterly rejected such pragmatism (vv. 3–8) in favour of his Father's agenda. The flow of the chapter is further evidence that vv. 15ff. rightly follow vv. 1–14. Meanwhile his opponents cannot believe because they accept praise (*doxa*) from one another (5:44).

19. Those who argue that vv. 15–24 originally followed 5:47 find supporting evidence in the mention of Moses in both passages. But the introduction of Moses here is natural enough in the sequence of thought as we find it in the present order. The reference to Moses stems from two needs: (1) The need to develop more thoroughly what 'God's will' (v. 17) is. For both Jesus and his interlocutors, the will of God is revealed in the law: 'I desire to do your will, O my God; your law is within my heart' (Ps. 40:8; *cf.* Hoskyns, pp. 357–358). The question *Has not Moses given you the law?* is rhetorical, but its form in Greek anticipates an enthusiastic mental affirmative, making the question itself a statement: Moses has indeed given you the law.[1] (2) The need to give substance to the argument that the reason why people do not find out that Jesus' teaching comes from God is that they have not chosen to do God's will,

---

[1]That Jesus speaks of Moses giving *you* the law, instead of *us*, is judged by many to be an irrefutable evidence of historical anachronism, reflecting the time when Christians felt somewhat distanced from the law of Moses. That readers toward the end of the first century might well feel at home with the distance (especially in the wake of the destruction of the temple and therefore of the entire sacrificial system) few would deny. Nevertheless the *you* makes sense even within the ministry of Jesus as John presents him, for two reasons: (1) It anticipates the next clause, 'not one of *you* keeps the law'. Neither the Jesus of the Synoptic Gospels nor the Jesus of the Fourth Gospel could be expected to say 'not one of *us* keeps the law'. (2) If we grant that Jesus knows he is the *fulfilment* of the law – a position for which there is substantial evidence – then he must have distanced himself from the law on some occasions.

i.e. to obey the law (v. 17). Jesus is about to mention specific elements of the law that Jesus' opponents do not keep. Put differently, Jesus needs to demonstrate that his opponents do not share the purity of motive that characterizes his own service for the Father (v. 18). They have the law: Moses gave it to them (*cf.* 1:17) and they delight in it. But, like Paul, this passage insists that mere possession of the law cannot guarantee sanctity. Ironically, it guarantees condemnation: *not one of you keeps the law*.

The only evidence that Jesus adduces to support this contention is the hatred that stands behind the desire to kill him: *Why are you trying to kill me?* He does not mean that every Jew breaks the law *at this point*, but any large crowd in the temple precincts inevitably includes some of the authorities (*cf.* note on v. 15) who are guilty at this very point (*cf.* 5:18; 7:1). The law of Moses says, 'You shall not murder' (Ex. 20:13), but since their attempts to execute him are the attempts to execute an innocent man, it is nothing less than attempted murder, an effort to break this law.

20. The crowd, made up of more than the authorities (*cf.* notes on vv. 15, 19), instantly repudiates the charge. Their counter-accusation, *You are demon-possessed* (lit. 'You have a demon'), is probably their explanation for what they judge to be insane behaviour, a connection that others later make (*cf.* 10:20, 'He is demon-possessed *and raving mad.*'). Their assumption is that he is paranoid, suffering also perhaps from delusions of grandeur (*cf.* also the notes on 8:48ff.). The charge, made elsewhere, that he is actively in league with the prince of demons (Mk. 3:22 par.) betrays a blacker vision.

21. Rather than offer further evidence for the universality of law-breaking amongst his opponents, Jesus chooses to shore up the one point he has raised so far: he reminds them of the antipathy he evoked the last time he was in Jerusalem. The *one miracle* (lit. 'one work') to which he refers is doubtless the healing of the man paralysed for thirty-eight years (5:1ff.). That one work evoked astonishment – not the astonishment that leads to praise, but the astonishment that someone would actually tell another to carry his mat on the Sabbath day, openly flouting the accepted norms for Sabbath conduct.

22. The NIV rather botches the Greek, which, admittedly, is somewhat difficult. It opens with *dia touto*, 'on account of this'. Because no connection is transparent, some (*e.g.* Sanders, p. 207; RSV; Bruce, p. 177) have suggested that the words should be read with the preceding verse (there was little or no punctuation in the original manuscripts, so in theory such rearrangements involve no tampering with the text): 'you are all astonished *on account of this*'. That makes good sense, but it is opposed to Johannine usage, which always places the phrase *first* in its clause. This view must therefore be discounted. If *dia touto* is read with v. 22, a problem remains, for the expression usually refers to a reason already given, *i.e.* 'on account of this [that I have just mentioned]. . .'. The most likely explanation is that 'this' refers to the work of healing, of the restoration to full health, that Jesus has just referred to, but here considered paradigmatically: it was on account of precisely *such* thorough renewal that Moses gave the circumcision law.

The rest of this verse and all of the next combine to support this interpretation. Before tracing it out, it is important to observe the parenthetical aside: circumcision *did not come from Moses, but from the patriarchs*. Historically, that is correct: circumcision was instituted as a covenant sign while Abraham was still alive (Gn. 17:10ff.), and was formalized as part of the Mosaic code at Sinai (Ex. 12:44ff.). But John does not include the aside in order to foster interest in arcane historical details. The observation tends to depreciate Moses a little, and, more importantly, establish that this rite was antecedent to the Mosaic law, and therefore took precedence over it (*cf.* Gal. 3:17).

The threads now come together. Whether the circumcision law came from Moses or from the time of the patriarchs, the result was the same: *you circumcise a child on the Sabbath*. The law required that circumcision take place on the eighth day. If a child were born on the Sabbath, the eighth day (in an inclusive system of reckoning) fell on the subsequent Sabbath. The question, then, is which law takes precedence: the command that the child be circumcised on the eighth day, or the prohibition against all regular work on the Sabbath day. Jesus' words record the conclusion: the Jews regularly circumcised their children on the Sabbath, if the Sabbath was the eighth day (*cf.* Mishnah *Shabbath* 18:3; 19:2–3; *Nedarim* 3:11).

23. So here were Jesus' opponents, then, formally 'breaking' the Sabbath *so that the law of Moses* in respect to circumcision *may not be broken*. They did this regularly; Jesus performed but the one work, the 'one miracle' (v. 21), yet it called forth deep resentment. Why then are they so *angry* (*cholaō*, exceedingly rare; *cf. NewDocs* 4. § 91)? Some (*e.g.* Beasley-Murray, pp. 109–110) think that Jesus by this reasoning is proving his point in v. 19, that all of his opponents break the law since all of them sanction circumcision on the Sabbath. This is an unlikely interpretation, for two reasons. First, it would mean that Jesus was conceding he was himself a lawbreaker, even if, unlike his opponents, he breached the Sabbath law only once. Second, the point in the text is that the Jews establish a hierarchy of precedence amongst the detailed prescriptions of the Mosaic code, precisely in order to *keep* the law. The same principle of a hierarchy of precedence is displayed in Matthew 12:5, where Jesus points out that the priests who carry out their sacred duties on the Sabbath incur no guilt as Sabbath violators. The conclusion in this passage is not that the Jews by this principle actually *break* the law (though formally they do, *cf.* Carson, *Matt, in loc.*), but that Jesus' one miracle implicitly appeals to a similar hierarchy of precedence.

But although it is similar, it is not the same hierarchy. Jewish thinkers of about this time argued, on the basis of the precedence of eighth day circumcision over Sabbath, that any *necessary* act of mercy could be lawfully performed on the Sabbath. Circumcision was viewed as a perfecting rite: one member of the body, by this rite, was perfected, and had to be perfected on the eighth day; how much more, then, must an act be undertaken, even on the Sabbath, if it perfects the whole body, *i.e.* if it saves a life (*cf.* Tosephta *Shabbath* 15:16; *Mekhilta* [a rabbinical commentary] on Ex. 31:13). Jesus establishes a slightly different hierarchy by removing the criterion of urgency or necessity. The Jews might well reason that a man who has been paralysed for thirty-eight years can surely wait one more day to be healed. But by eliminating necessity from consideration, Jesus' hierarchy of precedence forges the tightest possible link between circumcision and the *healing of the whole man* – and this in a context that has just reminded us that circumcision antedates the law of Moses, and therefore the Sabbath laws, anyway (v. 22). Jesus' healing of the whole man thereby becomes a fulfilment of Old Testament circumcision, on the very day that served as a signal of God's Old Testament purposes of redemption and rest. Jesus' reasoning is not the pettifogging exegesis of a theologian determined to exonerate his own mistaken practice at all costs, but insistence that his activity is the fulfilment of the redemptive purposes of God set forth in the old covenant, and therefore an anticipation of the argument not only in Galatians 3 but also in Hebrews 4. It is further evidence that Moses wrote of Christ (Jn. 5:46).

Although the details of this argument are not found in any of the numerous Sabbath conflicts reported by the Synoptists, that is scarcely ground for suspecting John's record to be inauthentic, since the dominant feature of the Synoptic Sabbath pericopae is the sheer diversity of the arguments presented. In other words, John simply adds one more, one that is at least in line with some Synoptic arguments (*e.g.* the assertion that Jesus stands *above* the Sabbath as its Lord, Mk. 2:28 par.),[1] and an anticipation of the theological argument presumed in Hebrews 4.

24. Jesus' opponents have been judging *by mere appearances*. They should *stop judging* (*mē* plus present imperative *krinete* here has the force of requiring the cessation of the action, not merely the prohibition of the action) by superficial criteria, *and make a right judgment*. This appeal has many formal Old Testament parallels (*e.g.* Dt. 16:18–19; Is. 11:3–4; Zc. 7:9), all of them dealing with the administration of public justice (in the Isaiah passage, under messianic conditions). Jesus' appeal is more personal, eschatological and redemptive. They have misconstrued his character by a fundamentally flawed set of deductions from Old Testament law, an approach that turns out to be superficial, far too committed to 'mere appearances'. If their approach to God's will were one of faith (*cf.* notes on v. 17), they would soon discern that Jesus is not a Sabbath-breaker, but the one who fulfils both Sabbath and circumcision.

---

[1]For fuller discussion, *cf.* the essays in D. A. Carson (ed.), *From Sabbath to Lord's Day: A Biblical, Historical and Theological Investigation* (Paternoster/Zondervan, 1982).

Additional note

24. In an age when Matthew 7:1 ('Do not judge, or you too will be judged') has displaced John 3:16 as the only verse in the Bible the man in the street is likely to know, it is perhaps worth adding that Matthew 7:1 forbids judgmentalism, not moral discernment. By contrast, John 7:24 demands moral and theological discernment in the context of obedient faith (7:17), while excoriating self-righteous legalism and offering no sanction for censorious heresy-hunting.

b. Who is Jesus Christ? *(7:25-36)*

25. The discussion now abandons the subject of the Sabbath, and returns to the uncertainty amongst the people described earlier (vv. 11–13) and now evoked again (*At that point*, *oun*, 'therefore') by the claims implicit in Jesus' bold public teaching (vv. 14–24). Those who ask the question are *the people of Jerusalem*. They are far more likely than the Galileans and other pilgrims to know the mind and machinations of the Jerusalem authorities. While some in their naïveté might doubt that anyone was trying to kill Jesus (7:19, 20), these people knew better (*cf.* 5:16, 18; 7:1). What took them by surprise was the public nature of his proclamation, even in the face of such a threat.

26. But if Jesus' boldness in *speaking publicly* (*parrēsia*, *cf.* notes on v. 4) is surprising to these sophisticated Jerusalemites, what is no less surprising is the silence of *the authorities*. Why do they not arrest Jesus forthwith? A possible explanation suggests itself: perhaps (the Gk. interrogative participle *mēpote* indicates a tentative question: *cf.* M. 1. 192–193) the authorities themselves have weighed the evidence, perhaps even know of fresh evidence, concluding, at least in private, that Jesus really is the Christ, the Messiah (*cf.* notes on 1:41). In John's Gospel, this is the first time such a possibility has been articulated in Jerusalem.

27. No sooner has the suggestion been ventilated than it is dismissed. The reason lies in the first of three popularly-held notions of what the Messiah would be like that are mentioned in this chapter (*cf.* further on vv. 31, 42). The Jerusalemites are convinced that they know *where this man is from; when the Christ comes, no-one will know where he is from*. This cannot mean that they think the biblical revelation provides no hint of Messiah's ultimate origins (*cf.* Mi. 5:2; Mt. 2:4–6; *cf.* Dn. 7:13). These Jerusalemites are not like those who thought in apocalyptic terms and assumed the Messiah would be hidden from before the creation until the moment of his self-disclosure (*1 Enoch* 48:6; *4 Ezra* 13:51–52; the former source is probably post-Christian, the latter certainly so). Rather, the Jerusalemites hold the view, attested elsewhere (Justin Martyr, *Dialogue with Trypho* 8. 7; probably presupposed in some rabbinic language about the Messiah 'appearing', SB 2. 489), that the Messiah would be born of flesh and blood yet would be wholly unknown until he appeared to effect Israel's redemption. The same perspective is presupposed in

Matthew 24:26–27; Mark 13:21–22; Luke 17:23–24. With such expectations, there could be none of this 'perhaps he is, perhaps he isn't' speculation. As far as they were concerned, they know where Jesus came from: he sprang from Nazareth, and his family home was now in Capernaum, and he had been engaged in an itinerant ministry for some time. This is of course another instance of the celebrated 'Johannine irony': the Jerusalemites are not as informed of Jesus' true origins as they think. On possible differences between the two instances of the verb 'to know' in this verse (*oidamen* and *ginōskei* respectively), *cf.* Porter, pp. 281–287.

28–29. Whether Jesus had supernatural knowledge of their discussion (*cf.* notes on 1:47), or, more likely in this context, has overheard it, he *cried out* (the verb *krazō* is always used by John to introduce a public pronouncement: *cf.* 1:15; 7:37; 12:44), *Yes, you know me, and you know where I am from.* Read this way, Jesus acknowledges a certain soundness to their judgment, even though his next words show they understand less than they think. Alternatively, the words could be read as a question: 'You know me, and you know where I am from?' – *i.e.* a fundamental challenge to their pretensions. Either way, their deep ignorance is exposed. *I am not here* (*elēlutha*, lit. 'I have not come') *on my own, but he who sent me* [a standard way of referring to God in the Fourth Gospel] *is true* (*alēthinos*)', *i.e.* 'real'. Jesus is not saying that God, the one who sent him, is 'true', *i.e.* 'faithful', but that he is 'real'. Jesus' point is not that God exists (none of his interlocutors would have doubted it) but that God, as the one who sent him, is real – or, in modern idiom, he really is the one who sent Jesus, regardless of what the Jerusalemites might think of Jesus' origins. But, sadly (Jesus tells them), *You do not know him.* The Jews prided themselves in knowing the one true God, unlike the pagans around them (*cf.* Rom. 2:17–19). Certainly that was their privileged heritage (*cf.* notes on Jn. 4:22). They especially thought that God had made himself known to them in the law. But the law, Jesus has already insisted, points to himself (5:46). If the Jews do not recognize who Jesus is, it must be that they do not really understand the law, they do not really know the God who gave the law, for if they had really known him they would not have rejected his Son (*cf.* notes on 8:42). Jesus does know him, knows him uniquely (*cf.* notes on 3:12–13; 5:19ff.; 6:38, 57). Indeed, now that Jesus has come, sent by the Father, his very presence serves as a test of antecedent pretensions about knowing God. The implication is that those who recognize who he is really do know God; those who cannot discern who he is cannot possibly know God, especially not now when the very focal point of the divine self-disclosure is the incarnate Word before them (*cf.* 5:19–30). The cumulative Christological thought to this point in the Gospel is very similar to Matthew 11:27; Luke 10:22.

30–31. Taken together, these verses bear witness to the division that takes place whenever the revelation of God in Christ Jesus confronts human beings (*e.g.* 1:11–12; 3:18–21). In this instance, some of the

Jerusalemites who had been disputing with him tried to seize him, apparently in a spontaneous decision rather different from the formal effort to arrest Jesus that follows (vv. 32, 45). How Jesus escaped from them is unclear; the reason why he was able to escape was *because his time* (*hōra*, 'hour', cf. notes on 2:4) *had not yet come*, the 'hour' when he would be seized and crucified according to the Father's will had not arrived. Even so, many others in the crowd *put their faith in him* – with what seriousness and perseverance we are not told (cf. notes on 2:23–25; 6:60), unless they are those mentioned in 8:31ff. Their reasoning, however, is recorded: *When the Christ comes, will he do more miraculous signs than this man?* Faith based on signs is not strongly encouraged (2:11, 23; 4:48; *etc.*), though it is better than nothing (10:38). There is no hint, however, that these people developed any deep understanding of the significance of the signs, thereby grasping who Jesus really was. Popular messianism did not, apparently, commonly associate Messiah with miracles, but if this crowd brought together in their minds the Messiah and the eschatological prophet (who was expected to perform miracles (cf. Meeks, pp. 162ff.), the genesis of their question is adequately explained (and is a more plausible suggestion than that this is an anachronistic *Christian* formulation: so Schnackenburg, 2. 149; de Jonge, pp. 91–92). It is the second of the three popular tests that are raised in this chapter (cf. notes on vv. 27, 42).

32. The authorities have already indicated that they do not want Jesus to be the topic of conversation (vv. 12–13), let alone venerated as Messiah. The whispered and tentative faith of those described in v. 31, once it reached the ears of the Pharisees and chief priests, therefore served as a signal that it was time to sign an arrest warrant. Some (*e.g.* Barrett, p. 324) find the link between Pharisees and chief priests (who were almost all Sadducees) historically problematic: surely they did not get along very well, so the repeated links in John (7:32, 45; 11:47, 57; 18:3) betray the Evangelist's ignorance of the party lines that existed in the days of Jesus. This criticism is naïve. Common enemies make strange bedfellows (witness Lk. 23:12!). More important, if this arrest warrant was the official action of the Sanhedrin, some agreement amongst the three groups that made up the Sanhedrin (*viz.* the Pharisees, the Sadducees/priests and the elders – cf. notes on 1:19, 24; 11:47) would have been not only desirable but necessary.

The *temple guards* were a kind of temple police force, drawn from the Levites, with primary responsibility for maintaining order in the temple area. But since the Sanhedrin governed the internal affairs of the country in all matters of little interest to the Roman prefect, the temple police could be used at the pleasure of that high court in matters quite removed from the sacred precincts. If Jesus was still teaching somewhere in the temple area, however, they would not have had to go far. These guards were under a commanding officer, 'the captain of the temple', who was also drawn from one of the priestly families and whose authority in a wide range of practical matters was second only to that of the high priest (*cf.* Schürer 2. 277f.).

33–34. Good writer that he is, the Evangelist, knowing how to build up suspense, refuses to tell us the outcome of the guards' mission right away (*cf.* vv. 45ff.). Instead he tells us what Jesus is saying and doing at the same moment the guards are seeking an appropriate time to arrest him, a time that will cause minimum commotion in a crowded city bursting with messianic expectations. Hearing of the official warrant (the Gk. of v. 33 opens with a 'therefore'), Jesus speaks of his imminent departure in words that are clear to any reader (especially after the entire book has been read at least once). He has but a short time before the cross (once again the Father's foreordained schedule is presupposed: *cf.* notes on 7:6), the means by which he returns to the one who sent him. Death is not, for Jesus, the end, but the return to the glory he had with the Father before the world began (17:5), his being lifted up to where he was before (*cf.* notes on 3:14). Once Jesus reached that point, others could not join him, not even the faithful disciples (13:33). Indeed, for some there is implicit threat: the time would come when some would look for him and die in their sins (8:21).

35–36. Once again Jesus' words are misunderstood. *The Jews* (whether the authorities or all those most opposed to him within the crowd) who think they know all there is to know about his origins (v. 27) cannot imagine that Jesus can take himself somewhere where they could not find him if they chose to do so. The most likely explanation of his words (the tentative *mē* introduces their deliberative question), they conclude, is that he will go to where *our people* (Gk. *diaspora*) *live scattered among the Greeks, and teach the Greeks.* It is unclear whether the last three words, 'and teach the Greeks', picture a further step in the argument: *i.e.* does Jesus go (in their question) to the diaspora and teach Greek-speaking Jews, or does he go to the diaspora (made up of Greek-speaking Jews) and also teach Greeks, *i.e.* Gentiles? The latter is marginally more likely, but probably Gentile *proselytes* are in view (as in 12:20). Once again the 'Johannine irony' is very thickly laid on. Not only will serious readers of this Gospel remember that within six months the question of visiting proselytes will signal for Jesus the onset of the last 'hour' (12:20ff.), but that after the cross, resurrection and ascension the truth of the gospel Jesus proclaimed would in fact be spread in Jewish and Gentile circles throughout the Roman Empire and beyond. Indeed, there is even more irony if, as has been suggested in this commentary (*cf.* Introduction, § VI; notes on 20:30–31), the Fourth Gospel was in the first instance penned as an evangelistic treatise aimed at diaspora Jews and Greek-speaking proselytes.

Additional note

34. The words *where I am* end with *egō eimi* (*cf.* notes on 6:20), prompting some (*e.g.* Brown, p. 314) to think this is the divine *egō eimi* of 8:58 and perhaps of 8:24, 28. This interpretation is very doubtful. The

Greek expression makes good sense without importing theological over-tones from elsewhere. Moreover, when the expression *does* have maximum weight, it is either absolute (8:58) or the object of what ought to be believed ('if you do not believe that *I am*' or the like, 8:24, 28); it does not follow the locative conjunction 'where'.

c. The promise of the Spirit (7:37–44)

The proclamation of Jesus recorded in these verses, with its dependence on a water metaphor, is entirely appropriate to its setting in the Feast of Tabernacles with its well-known water-pouring rite. There is another thematic connection with the immediately preceding verses. Jesus has just spoken of his departure, of going to a place where his opponents cannot come (vv. 33–36). Those who have read this Gospel before will recognize that the bestowal of the Spirit is directly consequent upon Jesus' departure – a theme developed in John 14 – 16, but now coming to explicit articulation here.

37–38. The opening words, *On the last and greatest day of the Feast*, suggest a different and later day from that on which the events des-cribed in the previous verses occurred. Perhaps once word of the arrest warrant became known (vv. 32–34), Jesus kept quiet and out of sight until the time came for this dramatic pronouncement, and then its audacious authority prevented the temple guards from carrying out their assignment (vv. 45–46).

But on what day did Jesus so speak? It could have been the seventh day, the final day of the Feast proper, or the eighth day, the closing festival (*cf.* notes on v. 2). In favour of the former is the fact that, so far as we know, the water-pouring rite (*cf.* notes below) and the lights cere-mony (*cf.* notes on 8:12) did not extend beyond the seventh day. More-over, by Old Testament standards the Feast of Tabernacles itself lasted seven days: it seems odd to refer to the eighth day as the 'last and greatest day *of the Feast'*. On the other hand, in favour of the eighth day is the fact that at least some Jews in the first century so linked the eighth day with the preceding seven that they thought of the Feast of Taber-nacles as an eight-day feast (Jos., *Ant.* iii. 245). Moreover, on any reckoning the eighth day really was a great day, distinct from the others, a rest day (*i.e.* a special Sabbath) distinguished by particular sacrifices, the joyful dismantling of the booths, and the repeated singing of the *Hallel* (Pss. 113 – 118). Moreover, if Jesus' public pronouncements (7:37–38; 8:12) are informed by the rites of the Feast of Tabernacles, there may have been special force to his words if he spoke them on the eighth day, immediately *after* the ceremonies themselves had ceased. The water and the light of the Tabernacles rites pass into memory, year after year; his claim to provide living water and light for the world is continuously valid.

On the seven days of the Feast, a golden flagon was filled with water from the pool of Siloam and was carried in a procession led by the High Priest back to the temple. As the procession approached the watergate on the south side of the inner court three blasts from the *šôp̄ār* – a trumpet connected with joyful occasions – were sounded. While the pilgrims watched, the priests processed around the altar with the flagon, the temple choir singing the *Hallel* (Pss. 113 – 118; *cf.* Mishnah *Sukkah* 4:9). When the choir reached Psalm 118, every male pilgrim shook a *lûlāḇ* (willow and myrtle twigs tied with palm) in his right hand, while his left raised a piece of citrus fruit (a sign of the ingathered harvest), and all cried 'Give thanks to the LORD!' three times. The water was offered to God at the time of the morning sacrifice, along with the daily drink-offering (of wine). The wine and the water were poured into their respective silver bowls, and then poured out before the LORD. Moreover, these ceremonies of the Feast of Tabernacles were related in Jewish thought both to the LORD's provision of water in the desert and to the LORD's pouring out of the Spirit in the last days. Pouring at the Feast of Tabernacles refers symbolically to the messianic age in which a stream from the sacred rock would flow over the whole earth (*cf.* J. Jeremias, *TDNT*, 4. 277f.).

Thus, although the words *If anyone is thirsty, let him come to me and drink* inevitably call to mind Isaiah 55:1 (*cf.* also Rev. 22:1–2; Jn. 4:10–14; 6:35), the particular association of the water rite with this Feast demands that we seek more focused significance. It is clear that this Feast was associated with adequate rainfall (*cf.* Zc. 14:16–17 – and interestingly enough, this chapter from Zechariah was read on the first day of the Feast of Tabernacles in the liturgy prescribed in B. *Megillah* 31*a*), not surprisingly in light of the harvest connections. Although the water rite was not prescribed by Old Testament law, its roots go back at least a couple of hundred years before Christ, and perhaps earlier (*cf.* 1 Sa. 7:6). Thus in addition to the numerous 'water' passages in the Old Testament, some of them associated with this Feast (*cf.* Is. 12:3, 'With joy you will draw water from the wells of salvation'), the water rite itself symbolized the fertility and fruitfulness that only rain could bring. This would be especially clear if we could be certain that a number of Jewish beliefs, recorded later, reflect traditions that reach back to the first century.[1] These specifically connect the eighth day with great joy in the light of God's faithful provision of rain, and also interpret the day as a festive anticipation of God's promises to pour out spiritual 'rains' in the messianic age. The water-pouring ceremony is interpreted in these traditions as a foretaste of the eschatological rivers of living water foreseen by Ezekiel (47:1–9) and Zechariah (13:1). In these traditions the water miracle in the wilderness (Ex. 17:1–7; Nu. 20:8–13; *cf.* Ps. 78:16–20) is in turn a forerunner of the water rite of the Feast of Tabernacles.

In general terms, then, Jesus' pronouncement is clear: he is the fulfilment of all that the Feast of Tabernacles anticipated. If Isaiah could

---

[1]*Pesiqta Rabbati* 52:3–6; Tosephta *Sukkah* 3:3–12. *Cf.* Bruce H. Grigsby, *Bib* 67, 1986, pp. 101–108.

invite the thirsty to drink from the waters (Is. 55:1), Jesus announces that he is the one who can provide the waters. But the details of these words turn on a difficult decision regarding the punctuation of the Greek text. The principal options are two. (1) The traditional interpretation places a full stop at the end of v. 37 (as in the NIV). The result is that it is most natural to take the 'streams of living water' (v. 38) to be flowing from within the believer (*i.e.* 'from within him', referring back to 'whoever believes in me'). (2) The more recent, so-called 'Christological interpretation' places a comma after 'to me' (v. 37), with no full stop after 'and drink'. This results in rough parallelism:

> If a man is thirsty, let him come to me,
> And let him drink who believes in me.

The result is that the next words, 'as the Scripture has said', need not be taken with what precedes; they may just as easily be the introduction to the *following* words. If that is the case, the text from 'As the Scripture has said' to the end of v. 38 may be an explanatory aside provided by the Evangelist, and the 'streams of living water' might then be thought to be flowing from within *Christ* (*i.e.* 'him' then refers to Christ – which is why this is called the 'Christological' interpretation).

Decision is difficult, and there are several mediating positions, but these two dominate the landscape. Before deciding what interpretation seems best, however, it is important to appreciate how much the two options have in common. Both interpret the water as the Spirit, both insist that the blessing is something believers will enjoy only later (from the standpoint of Jesus' ministry), both relate the promise of the Spirit to Jesus' invitation at the Feast of Tabernacles, and both make Jesus the one who supplies the 'drink' and quenches thirst. The principal differences between the two are that the first says that streams of living water will flow *from the believer*, while the second says they will flow *from Christ*; and the first continues Jesus' words to the end of v. 38, while the second sees them ending with the first clause of v. 38.

Even here, the difference must not be exaggerated. Perhaps the greatest strength of the second view, as the two are commonly set forth, is that in the Fourth Gospel believers are never the source of 'living water', the Spirit who will come on them after Jesus is glorified. The Holy Spirit comes from God or Christ. The nearest thing to an exception is 15:26–27, but here all that is said is that believers witness to the world with the Spirit's help. Only in this very derivative sense are believers said to be the source of the Spirit for others. The extraordinarily strong Christological focus of the entire Gospel therefore commonly serves in many modern commentaries to rule out the first view and justify the second.

But this is probably a false antithesis. Even under the first view, there is nothing in the text to necessitate the conclusion that believers are the *source* of the Spirit *to others*. This point is more easily appreciated in the

323

Greek text. Whether 'from within him' refers to Christ or to the believer, it is the NIV's rendering of *ek tēs koilias autou*, lit. 'from within his belly'. As the Greek expression here refers to the centre of human personality, NIV's paraphrasis is acceptable and reasonable. In terms of the two major interpretative options before us, the question becomes, 'Whose belly?' The believer's, or Christ's? Those who favour the second view are inclined to see a partial fulfilment in 19:34 – when Jesus' side was pierced the spear brought forth 'a sudden flow of blood and water'. But the word *koilia* ('belly') does not show up in 19:34, and the LXX provides ample evidence that *koilia* had become by this time a fairly close synonym for *kardia*, 'heart' – and that word surely applies to believers as well as to Jesus. If on grounds still to be provided we conclude that the 'belly' is that of the believer, the closest parallel is 4:13–14: 'Everyone who drinks this water will be thirsty again, but whoever drinks the water I give him will never thirst. Indeed, the water I give him *will become in him a spring of water welling up to eternal life.*' Here there is no suggestion of the believer supplying water to other people. Similarly on the first interpretation of 7:37–39: the image of streams of water from the believer's heart or belly places the accent 'on the rich abundance of the Spirit's life and power in the heart of the believer, like a self-replenishing stream' (Michaels, p. 126). On this reading, the source of the stream is Jesus, regardless of whose 'belly' is in view in v. 38, regardless (in the NIV text) of the antecedent of 'from within *him*'.[1]

If it is agreed, then, that the first view does not make the believer the *source* of the Spirit *for others* any more than the second view, then on a variety of grounds the first option seems preferable. Although the second provides a chiasm (a literary form favoured by John), yet in the Greek text it is rather rough (as even Dodd, *IFG*, p. 349, who favours this view, admits). Conceptually, the parallelism required by the second view makes 'anyone who is thirsty' to parallel 'anyone who believes in me' – a peculiar (though certainly not impossible) pairing, for one would have thought that thirst better describes an individual's life *before* belief, at which point the thirst is quenched (*cf.* 4:13–14; 6:35). Moreover, it is a peculiarly Johannine feature to begin a clause or sentence with 'Whoever believes in me' (*ho pisteuōn*) or the like (forty-one occurrences), a feature preserved under the first interpretation. There is no instance of *ho pisteuōn* attaching itself to a previous conditional clause, as the second interpretation requires. The textual evidence supports the first view, including the important papyrus P[66], and all modern critical editions of the Greek New Testament adopt it. So, too, do virtually all the Greek Fathers. Many other arguments could be adduced in favour of the first view. Most telling, perhaps, is the observation by Fee,[2] that the first

---

[1]This point is regularly overlooked by the majority of those who adopt the second view. *Cf.* Juan B. Cortés, *CBQ* 29, 1967, pp. 75–86, rightly arguing against, amongst others, Brown, 1. 320.

[2]Gordon D. Fee, *ExpT* 89, 1978, pp. 116–118.

words of v. 39 ('By this he meant', *touto de eipen*) typically in John refer to *Jesus'* words, not the words of someone else or of Scripture. And if it is Jesus and not the Evangelist who is speaking in v. 38, then the words 'from within him' *cannot* refer to Jesus but to someone else – and the only other candidate is 'whoever believes in him'.

It has been objected to the first view that it is grammatically awkward: *'Whoever believes* . . . streams of living water will flow from within *him'* – an instance of anacolouthon, resumption of a suspended case by a pronoun in another case. But this is fairly common in the New Testament, more common in John than in the Synoptic Gospels. For instance, a literal rendering of John 8:45 is, 'But *I*, because I tell you the truth, you do not believe in *me*.' Moreover, of the twenty-eight examples of this construction in the Fourth Gospel, twenty-two are found in the words of Jesus, two in the Prologue (1:12, 18), two in the words of John the Baptist (1:33; 3:32), one in the discussion of the Baptist's disciples (3:26), one in the mouth of the paralytic (5:11; *cf.* BDF § 466(2)), leaving none for the Evangelist in his own comments (unless the second interpretation, against the evidence, is adopted here).

It has also been objected, against the first view, that when the preposition *kathōs* ('as' or 'just as') introduces a quotation from Scripture, it always immediately *follows* its main clause, and the Scripture quotation itself follows *kathōs* – a fact that favours the second interpretation (as in 6:31; 12:14). But to this we may reply: (1) there are only two other instances in John, just listed, and neither of them uses the word 'Scripture' (*graphē*) as this passage does; (2) of all the New Testament writers, John is the most notorious for varying the forms of the introductory formulae by which he introduces Scripture (*cf.* Carson, 'OT', pp. 247f.); (3) although the exact Scripture reference here is disputed (*cf.* discussion, below) it probably *does* begin only *after* the *kathōs* clause ('*as* the Scripture has said'); (4) if we consider the *total* number of occurrences in the Fourth Gospel, regardless of whether or not Scripture is thereby introduced, then, as Morris (p. 425) observes, *kathōs* follows its main clause nineteen times, and does not follow it thirteen times. This defence of the second interpretation therefore has no statistical merit.[1]

In short, vv. 37–38 preserve a powerful Christological claim, and an invitation entirely congruent with similar invitations elsewhere (4:10–14; 6:35). But if (with this commentary) we accept the first interpretation, we must still ask what Scripture is in mind. Certainly John can elsewhere refer to the Old Testament without making it at all clear what passage he has in mind (*e.g.* 20:9). What is often overlooked is that, even under the first interpretation, it may not be necessary to hunt for a text that narrowly describes streams of water flowing from the believer. Scripture

---

[1]Thus the contention of Brown (1. 321) that the grammatical argument favouring *ho pisteuōn* ('whoever believes') at the head of the clause, and the grammatical argument regarding *kathōs* (summarized above), 'really cancel one another out', seems vastly overstated.

may be cited to ground *the entire matrix of thought* found in vv. 37–38: *i.e.* we may need to look for a passage that is related to the Feast of Tabernacles, and that looks to the promise of the Spirit in the messianic age and the consequent blessing on the messianic community, not for a passage that describes water flowing from someone's belly. This essentially Christological focus is thus as justifiable under the first interpretation as under the second.

If for the moment we concentrate on texts that use the metaphor of water to speak of spiritual blessing enjoyed by believers, perhaps the most striking is Isaiah 58:11: 'The LORD will guide you always; . . . You will be like a well-watered garden, like a spring whose waters never fail' (*cf.* also Pr. 4:23; 5:15; Zc. 14:8). If we enlarge our search and take in texts that promise the blessing of the Spirit, perhaps related to the coming Davidic monarch or to the new covenant, we might think of Isaiah 12:3; 44:3; 49:10; Ezekiel 36:25–27; 47:1; Joel 3:18; Amos 9:11–15; Zechariah 13:1.

But our search for an Old Testament background can be made more precise.[1] In Nehemiah 8:5–18,[2] those who have returned from exile are pictured obeying the command of Deuteronomy 31:10–11: 'At the end of every seven years . . . during the Feast of Tabernacles, when all Israel comes to appear before the LORD your God . . . you shall read this law before them in their hearing . . . so that they can listen and learn to fear the LORD your God and follow carefully all the words of this law.' The people were in great distress as Ezra and the Levites 'instructed the people in the Law while the people were standing there. They read from the Book of the Law, making it clear and giving the meaning so that the people could understand what was being read' (Ne. 8:7–8). Part of what they learned was that at this time of the year, the seventh month, they were to make 'booths' or tabernacles and celebrate the Feast of Tabernacles (*cf.* Lv. 23:33–43). This they obeyed, and the celebration lasted the entire month, not merely the prescribed seven days. 'Day after day, from the first day to the last, Ezra read from the Book of the Law of God' (Ne. 8:18). Toward the end of the month, some Levites led the people in an extended prayer of praise and confession. That prayer includes an historical recital of many of the principal events during the wilderness wanderings. In particular, the people pray,

> In their hunger you gave them bread from heaven, and in their thirst you brought them water from the rock . . . Because of your great compassion you did not abandon them in the

---

[1] I am indebted for some of what follows to my colleague Dr John Sailhamer and my doctoral student Rev. David Johnson, though neither would want to be associated with all of my conclusions.

[2] Freed (p. 37) notes that Ne. 9 is the only Old Testament passage where spirit, manna and water all come together (and, we might add, in connection with the Feast of Tabernacles), but he makes nothing of it.

desert. By day the pillar of cloud did not cease to guide them on their path, nor the pillar of fire by night to shine on the way they were to take. You gave your good Spirit to instruct them. You did not withhold your manna from their mouths, and you gave them water for their thirst (Ne. 9:15, 19–20).

Clearly, the initial reference here is to the two instances of water from the rock (Ex. 17; Nu. 20). The links are many. The water-from-the-rock episodes are set forth as in some ways parallel to the provision of manna (Ne. 9:15, 20), the 'bread from heaven' as it is called (cf. Ex. 16:4; Ps. 78:24; Jn. 6:31). Both the manna and the water are in turn linked with the giving of the law – the manna because it is tied to the word of God in Deuteronomy 8:3, a passage clearly in mind (cf. Ne. 9:21; and note that Dt. 8:15–16 also makes mention of water from the rock, and links it with manna), and the water because Nehemiah 9:15 is syntactically linked (in Hebrew) to Nehemiah 9:13: 'You came down on Mount Sinai; you spoke to them from heaven. You gave them regulations and laws that are just and right. . . .'[1] By Nehemiah 9:20, however, the manna and the water, elsewhere in this chapter linked with the law, are now tied to the provision of the Spirit: 'You gave your good Spirit to instruct them'. The last three words demonstrate that the provision of the Spirit, according to Nehemiah, was bound up with the *instruction* of the people (*i.e.* in the law). So the gift of the law/Spirit is symbolized by the provision of manna/water.

It is to this set of associations that John 7:37–38 makes reference. Jesus has already insisted that Moses (in the law) wrote about him (5:46). In John 6 the Evangelist has argued that the Old Testament manna is properly fulfilled in the true bread from heaven, Jesus himself, the Word incarnate (6:29ff.). In that chapter the tie with thirst (and therefore implicitly with water) is already briefly drawn (6:35), but the 'drink' in John 6 soon turns out to be Jesus' blood, and the food his flesh. Here in John 7, however, partly because of its eminent suitability in connection with the Feast of Tabernacles, the water/thirst motif returns, and the tie with the Spirit which has already been established in the book of Nehemiah is explicitly drawn.

Some other Old Testament passages that link water and Spirit also probably hark back to the water-from-the-rock episodes (*e.g.* Is. 44:3). That the water in John 7:37–38 is 'living' (*i.e.* running; *cf.* notes on 4:10) may owe something to Ezekiel 47:1–12, where the river flows from the eschatological temple to bring life wherever it goes. Some of this imagery appears to build on the oracle of Numbers 24:6–9, which again makes an allusion to Numbers 20:11 (the second instance of water

---

[1]It is also just possible that Ne. 9:15 alludes to Ex. 17:6, where at the first provision of water the Lord stands by the rock *at Horeb* (= Sinai).

gushing from the rock).[1] Other secondary passages linking water and Spirit may be in view, where neither the Feast of Tabernacles nor the episodes of the provision of water from rock are a central issue (Pr. 4:23; 5:15; Is. 12:3; 49:10; Ezk. 36:25–27; 47:1ff.; Joel 3:18; Am. 9:11–15; Zc. 13:1; 14:8). Indeed, one of them (Ezk. 36:25–27) John has used in John 3:5 (cf. notes there). Taken together, they richly anticipate the eschatological blessing of the Spirit on the believer's life, like 'a spring of water welling up to eternal life' (4:14), like 'streams of living water [that] will flow from within him' (7:38).

If this is correct, Jesus in John 7:37–39, prompted perhaps by the Feast of Tabernacles, thinks of that Feast in Nehemiah 9, and that chapter's use of the accounts of the provision of water from the rock, and the connection Nehemiah draws between water/manna and law/Spirit. But he takes one further step, the same Christological step he has taken when talking of worship with the woman at the well, or when talking of manna with the crowds in John 6: he insists he alone can provide the real drink, the satisfying Spirit. 'If anyone is thirsty, let him come to me and drink' (v. 37). The Scripture has itself promised this bountiful provision of living water welling up in believers: all the Old Testament portrayals of this rich bounty are understood to be at bottom anticipations that point to the richest provision of all. John himself explicitly confirms the connection between water and Spirit (v. 39).

On this reading of John 7:37–39, the awkwardness in finding a satisfying solution to the complexities of the passage springs from the attempt, on the one hand, to follow the second interpretation (when the textual and stylistic evidence strongly favour the first), and, on the other, to find an Old Testament background that refers to water from a believer's belly. But if the Scripture in view is meant to ground the thought of vv. 37–38 within the context of the Feast of Tabernacles, the interpretation suggested here commends itself.[2]

39. For the significance of the words *By this he meant, cf.* the notes above. John now makes it clear, lest any of his readers should fail to comprehend, that what Jesus was talking about by this metaphor, and concomitantly what the Old Testament texts were really anticipating, was the gift of the Holy Spirit. Water sometimes served as a symbol for the Holy Spirit (SB 2. 434–435), and, in at least one Jewish interpretation, the ceremony in question was called the 'water-*drawing*' ceremony because 'from there they *draw* the inspiration of the Holy Spirit, as it is written, "With joy you *will draw* water from the wells of salvation" [Is. 12:3]' (emphasis added; cf. j. Sukkah 5:1; cf. Ruth Rabbah 4:8 [a rabbinical

---

[1]In particular, both Nu. 20:11 and Nu. 24:7 include the Heb. expression *mayim rābîm* ('abundant waters') – though this is not so rare (about twenty-nine occurrences in the Old Testament) as to authorize certainty that a connection is being drawn by the author.

[2]Those who follow the second interpretation sometimes suggest that 'out of [Christ's] belly' makes Christ an antitype of the rock, *out of* which water flowed. But the linguistic connections are not to be found in this passage; and rocks do not have bellies.

commentary on Ruth 2:9]). John agrees, but sees the source of the promised Holy Spirit to be Jesus himself, once he had been 'glorified', *i.e.* once he had died, risen and ascended to his Father. By *those who believed in him* John is referring not only to those who had believed in Jesus during the days of his flesh, but also to those who would later believe (*cf.* 17:20; 20:29).

Up to this point in Jesus' ministry, *the Spirit had not yet been given*. This paraphrase has the meaning right, though the reading most likely original is, literally, 'for the Spirit was not yet'. Of course John cannot possibly mean the Spirit was not yet in existence, or operative in the prophets. John himself has already spoken of the Spirit's operation upon and in Jesus himself (1:32; 3:34). What the Evangelist means is that the Spirit of the dawning kingdom comes as the result – indeed, the entailment – of the Son's completed work, and up to that point the Holy Spirit was *not* given in the full, Christian sense of the term (*cf.* also the notes on 3:1–15).

40–42. When Jesus fed the crowds in the wilderness, some immediately thought he must be the Prophet like Moses predicted in Deuteronomy 18:15–18 (*cf.* notes on 6:14), doubtless owing to the fact that the closest Old Testament equivalent to this miracle was the provision of manna under Moses' ministry. Perhaps Jesus' most recent pronouncement (vv. 37–39) prompted some to think of Moses again, this time in connection with the miraculous provision of water from the rock (Ex. 17:6; Nu. 20:11). That is why some reflected on Deuteronomy 18 once again, and concluded, *Surely this man is the Prophet*.

Others were not sure, and surmised instead, *He is the Christ* (v. 41). A contemporary Christian reader might find it difficult to imagine how these two confessions could be divided. In the first century, however, many Jews thought of the promised Prophet and of the Messiah as two separate individuals. John 1:19ff. demonstrates further that by 'the Prophet' is not meant the one who comes in the spirit and power of Elijah. It is possible (though not certain) that Christians were the first to identify the Davidic Messiah with the Prophet like Moses, precisely because they recognized in Jesus the one who perfectly fulfilled both prophecies – just as it is doubtful that anyone systematically linked the suffering servant prophecies with the royal messianic prophecies until Jesus himself came on the scene (on the complex evidence, *cf.* Schürer, 2. 547–549).

Still others found difficulty believing that Jesus was the Messiah. They were doubtless Jerusalemites, or at least Judeans, and had been brought up to believe not only that the Messiah would *come from David's family* (2 Sa. 7:12–16; Ps. 89:3–4; Is. 9:7; 55:3) but that he would be born in Bethlehem (Mi. 5:2). As far as they were concerned, Jesus was a Galilean: he could not possibly qualify. In this way the third publicly-voiced criterion for messiahship in this chapter is introduced (*cf.* notes on vv. 27, 31). But this is once again an instance of superb irony. John knows, and any of his readers who have been in touch with Christians at all knew, that Jesus 'as to his human nature was a descendant of David' (Rom. 1:3), indeed that he was born in Bethlehem. This is a superb instance of 'Johannine irony'. 'If we infer from this passage that the fourth Evangelist either did not know or did not accept Jesus' Davidic descent or nativity in Bethlehem, we expose our own failure to appreciate his delicate handling of this situation' (Bruce, p. 184). The objection that other 'ambiguous or ironic "misunderstandings" by Jesus' opponents in John are eventually exposed in the development of the gospel' (Meeks, p. 37) while neither David nor Bethlehem is mentioned again, is entirely without weight. The Johannine 'misunderstandings' are always explained, but Johannine irony is often left without explicit exposition (*e.g.* 7:35; 11:48; 13:38 – as Duke, pp. 66–67 and n. 12, ably points out). Indeed, explicit exposition on some occasions would be heavy-handed, destructive of the irony itself. In any case, beyond the irony connected with David and Bethlehem, John's readers are also aware that Jesus came from heaven (*cf.* 3:8; 8:14, 23). For his opponents to be questioning him is for them to be siding with the world that does not recognize him (1:10, 11).

43–44. The three positions about Jesus just outlined (vv. 40–42) doubtless represent a far broader spectrum of opinion. *The people were divided because of Jesus*: lit. there was a *schisma* because of him, a recurring theme (the same word recurs in 9:16; 10:19; *cf.* also 3:19–21; 12:31–32, 46–49; Schnackenburg, 2. 159). Christians may expect similar division to result from their witness (15:18ff.; *cf.* Mt. 10:32ff.); those contemplating the possibility of becoming Christians need to be warned about the possible costs (*cf.* notes on 15:18 – 16:4; *cf.* Lk. 9:57–62; 14:25–33). Some who leaned toward quick, political answers *wanted to seize him*, but as in v. 30, *no-one laid a hand on him*: his hour had not yet come.

9. The unbelief of Jewish leaders (7:45–52)

45–46. The abortive attempt to seize Jesus in the previous verse reminds the reader that an official arrest warrant has already been authorized (v. 32). The Greek text of v. 45 begins with *oun*, which most commonly means 'therefore' (NIV's 'Finally' is without justification). Occasionally *oun* has resumptive force (BAGD *s.v.*), and if that is the meaning here the word points back to v. 32. But if *oun* has its more common inferential force, the idea is that because the crowds were so divided that 'no-one laid a hand on him' (v. 44), *therefore* the temple guards became disoriented and abandoned their assignment and *went back to the chief priests and Pharisees* (*i.e.* to the Sanhedrin; *cf.* notes on v. 32). Naturally enough these authorities wanted to know why the temple police had not performed the task assigned them. The response of the guards sharpens up the reasons for their hesitation: *No-one ever spoke the way this man does*.

Their problem lay partly in the fact that they were not brutal thugs, mercenaries trained to perform any barbarous act provided the pay was right. They were themselves drawn from the Levites; they were religiously trained, and could feel themselves torn apart at the deepest level of their being by the same deeds and words of Jesus that were tearing apart the population at large. Evidence for the incomparable wisdom and authority Jesus displayed in his speech is not hard to find (*e.g.* Mk. 1:22; 12:17, 32–34, 37; par.; *cf.* notes on 8:7–9; 18:3–6). The witness of the guards was not borne of genuine faith, but John intends his readers to perceive that the guards spoke better than they knew. Literally rendered, their words mean, 'No man (*anthrōpos*, "human being") ever spoke as he does' – for John's readers know, as the guards did not, that Jesus is not merely a human being, but the incarnate Word (1:14), the one whose every word and deed is the revelation of the Father (5:19–30; 8:28–29).

47–48. The sneering question of the Pharisees does not mock the guards on the ground that, as police officers, they should have followed orders, but on the ground that, as Levites who should follow the religious authorities, they have compromised their theological integrity and been seduced by a transparent imposter who could never manage to deceive the *real* thinkers. This of course is more 'Johannine irony', for one of the religious authorities is about to step forward on Jesus' behalf. Even if Nicodemus is not a genuine disciple at this point (*cf.* notes on 3:1ff.), nevertheless he, 'Israel's teacher' (3:10), had addressed Jesus as 'a teacher who has come from God' (3:2). Indeed, a little farther on John will report that 'many even among the leaders believed in him' (12:42). Perhaps the intuitions of the temple guards were not so misguided after all. The irony cuts another way. It is a commonplace of the Christian gospel that not many wise and noble are chosen: God makes it a practice to go after the weak, the foolish, the ignorant, the despised (*e.g.* Mt. 11:25; Lk. 10:21; 1 Cor. 1:26–31). The religious authorities boast that they have not been duped; their very boasting is precisely what has duped them.

49. Over against the rulers and the Pharisees (v. 48) stand *this mob* (*ochlos*, 'crowd') *that knows nothing of the law*. This is an exact representation of the way many learned rabbis viewed the common folk, 'the people of the land' (Heb. *'am hā'āreṣ*) as they condescendingly labelled them. The label had originally been applied to the entire nation of Israel (*e.g.* Ezk. 22:29), but came in time to refer to the common people over against the leaders (Je. 1:18), and then to the mixed population that settled in Samaria and Judea during the exile, in distinction from the pureblood Jews who returned after the exile (Ezr. 10:2, 11). Amongst the rabbis 'the people of the land' always refers to the people who do not know the law, *i.e.* the law of Moses both as it is found in the Hebrew Scriptures and as it was thought to be preserved in oral tradition; and if they do not know it, they cannot keep it. Since the law is the law of God, the 'people of the land' are characterized by both ignorance and impiety.[1]

---

[1]For a convenient summary of the sources and discussion, *cf.* SB 2. 494–519; and esp. Appendix E, by George F. Moore, in F. J. Foakes Jackson and Kirsopp Lake, *The Beginnings of Christianity*, 5 vols. (1920–1933, repr. Baker, 1979), 1. 439–445.

The school of Rabbi Meir said, 'If anyone has learned the Scripture and the Mishnah [a large corpus of Jewish tradition] but has not served as a student of the Learned he is one of the people of the land. If he has learned the Scripture but not the Mishnah he is an uneducated man; if he has learned neither the Scripture nor the Mishnah the Scripture says of him: "I sow the house of Israel and the house of Judah with seed of men and seed of cattle [*i.e.* he is indistinguishable from an animal]"' (*cf.* SB 2. 486). Even the more liberally-minded Rabbi Hillel, a generation before Christ, insisted, 'A brutish man does not fear sin, and no people of the land ('*am hā'āreṣ*) is pious' (*Pirke Aboth* 2:6). The sentiment could take on extreme form amongst the Qumran sectaries (*e.g.* 1QS 10:19–21).

Small wonder, then, that under the exasperation of discovering that Jesus has not yet been arrested, the religious authorities vent their spleen on the temple guards, implicitly condemning them for acting like the '*am hā'āreṣ*, who can be instantly and sweepingly damned with the words, *there is a curse on them*. The sheer ignorance of these people ensured that they could be easily deceived. And still John's irony is quietly chuckling in the background.

50–51. When Nicodemus (*cf.* on 3:1ff.) speaks up, it is not to defend Jesus directly, but to raise a procedural point which, if observed, would work in his favour. There is no explicit Old Testament text that makes the point Nicodemus raises (though *cf.* Dt. 1:16); the closest rabbinic rule that has come down to us is probably this: 'Unless a mortal hears the pleas that a man can put forward, he is not able to give judgment' (*Exodus Rabbah* 21:3, a rabbinical commentary on Ex. 14:15). Roman law agreed with the point (*cf.* Acts 25:16). In Acts 5:34–39 another rabbi, Gamaliel, perhaps only two years or less later, again attempts to inject a cooler rationalism into the Sanhedrin's heated proceedings.

52. But the colleagues of Nicodemus were too worked up and too hostile to listen to mere reason. Where argument fails, they reply with contempt: *Are you from Galilee, too?* – *i.e.* the only explanation for your strange outburst in defence of a Galilean, Nicodemus, is that you must have sprung from such inferior stock yourself! *Look into it* probably means 'Search [*sc.* the Scriptures]'. The notion that no prophet comes from Galilee is not independently attested in Jewish sources. Indeed, Rabbi Eliezer (*c.* AD 90) said that there was no tribe of Israel that failed to produce a prophet (B. *Sukkah* 27b). It is just barely possible that the Jewish authorities say this out of sheer frustration at their inability to curtail the activities and teaching of Jesus, this despised teacher from Galilee. In more sober moments they would have gladly recognized that the prophets Jonah and Nahum sprang from Galilee, and probably others as well. It is also possible that the original reading is not 'a prophet' but 'the prophet', *i.e.* the prophet like Moses (*cf.* notes on 6:14; 7:40): some of the earliest and best manuscripts support this reading, though admittedly the bulk of the textual attestation goes the other way. If the definite article is retained, then all the 'Johannine irony' found in v. 42 returns. The Old Testament does not tell us exactly where the eschatological prophet would be born. The officials of the Sanhedrin, reflecting the deep biases against Galilee entertained by Judeans, simply cannot believe that the prophet could come from such an area. But in reality, Jesus is not so much a son of Galilee as the authorities think. By voicing themselves so strongly, they succeed only in displaying their ignorance of his true origins.

EXCURSUS: THE WOMAN CAUGHT IN ADULTERY (7:53 – 8:11)

Despite the best efforts of Zane Hodges[1] to prove that this narrative was originally part of John's Gospel, the evidence is against him, and modern English versions are right to rule it off from the rest of the text (NIV) or to relegate it to a footnote (RSV). These verses are present in most of the medieval Greek miniscule manuscripts, but they are absent from virtually all early Greek manuscripts that have come down to us, representing great diversity of textual traditions. The most notable exception is the Western uncial D, known for its independence in numerous other places. They are also missing from the earliest forms of the Syriac and Coptic Gospels, and from many Old Latin, Old Georgian and Armenian manuscripts. All the early church Fathers omit this narrative: in commenting on John, they pass immediately from 7:52 to 8:12. No Eastern Father cites the passage before the tenth century. Didymus the Blind (a fourth-century exegete from Alexandria) reports a variation on this narrative,[2] not the narrative as we have it here. Moreover, a number of (later) manuscripts that include the narrative mark it off with asterisks or obeli, indicating hesitation as to its authenticity, while those that do include it display a rather high frequency of textual variants. Although most of the manuscripts that include the story place it here (*i.e.* at 7:53 – 8:11), some place it instead after Luke 21:38, and other witnesses variously place it after John 7:44, John 7:36 or John 21:25.[3] The diversity of placement confirms the inauthenticity of the verses. Finally, even if someone should decide that the material is authentic, it would be very difficult to justify the view that the material is authentically *Johannine*: there are numerous expressions and constructions that are found nowhere in John, but which are characteristic of the Synoptic Gospels, Luke in particular (*cf.* notes, below).

On the other hand, there is little reason for doubting that the event here described occurred, even if in its written form it did not in the beginning belong to the canonical books. Similar stories are found in

---

[1]*BSac* 136, 1979, pp. 318–372; 137, 1980, pp. 41–53.
[2]*Cf.* Bart D. Ehrman, *NTS* 34, 1988, pp. 24–44.
[3]For a convenient summary of the evidence, *cf.* Metzger, pp. 219–222.

other sources. One of the best known, reported by Papias (and recorded by the historian Eusebius, *H. E.* III. xxxix. 16), is the account of a woman, accused in the Lord's presence of many sins (unlike the woman here who is accused of but one). The narrative before us also has a number of parallels (some of them noted below) with stories in the Synoptic Gospels. The reason for its insertion here may have been to illustrate 7:24 and 8:15 or, conceivably, the Jews' sinfulness over against Jesus' sinlessness (8:21, 24, 46).

7:53 – 8:1. The abrupt opening is reminiscent of Jesus' pattern during the week before his passion, the week in which Jesus spent the nights in Bethany, travelling to and from Jerusalem each day, with pauses along the way at the Mount of Olives (*cf.* Mk. 11:11–12, 19–20, and esp. Lk. 21:37). That is as plausible a setting for this incident as any other suggestion.

2. Several expressions in this verse are typical of Luke-Acts (or in one case of Matthew as well): *orthos* ('dawn') is found in the New Testament elsewhere only in Luke 24:1; Acts 5:21; *paraginomai* ('appear') and *laos* ('people') are common in Luke-Acts, rare in John; and for *he sat down to teach them cf.* Matthew 5:1–2; Luke 4:20; 5:3. The content of this verse is closely paralleled by Luke 21:38, again referring to the week of Jesus' passion: 'and all the people came early in the morning to hear him at the temple'. The outer court served as the venue for many scribes to gather their students around them and expound the law to them. Jesus used the same facilities, even if his content could not easily be compared with what the others taught.

3–4. Because the venue was so public, it was easy enough for officials and opponents to mingle with disciples and bring up hard cases. *The teachers of the law* (lit. 'scribes') *and the Pharisees* are often mentioned together in the Synoptics, but never in the genuine text of John. The scribes were the recognized students and expositors of the law of Moses, but so central was the law in the life and thought of first-century Palestinian Jews that the scribes came to assume something of the roles of lawyer, ethicist, theologian, catechist, and jurist. Most of them, but certainly not all, were Pharisees by conviction (*cf.* notes on 1:19ff.).

These religious authorities, then, approach Jesus with nominal respect: *Teacher* is doubtless the equivalent of 'Rabbi' (*cf.* notes on 1:38). The woman they bring with them *was caught in the act of adultery.* Adultery is not a sin one commits in splendid isolation: one wonders why the man was not brought with her. Either he was fleeter of foot than she, and escaped, leaving her to face hostile accusers on her own; or the accusers themselves were sufficiently chauvinistic to focus exclusively on the woman. The inequity of the situation arouses our feelings of compassion, however guilty she herself was. In any case, the next verses suggest that the authorities in this case are less interested in ensuring that evenhanded justice be meted out than in hoisting Jesus onto the horns of a dilemma.

5–6a. The authorities' quotation of the law (*Moses commanded us to stone* *such women*) raises a widely disputed question: Was the woman married, or single and betrothed? Stoning is the biblically prescribed punishment for a betrothed virgin who is sexually unfaithful to her fiancé, a punishment to be meted out to both sexual partners (Dt. 22:23–24). Elsewhere (Lv. 20:10; Dt. 22:22) death is prescribed for all unfaithful wives and their lovers, but no mode (such as stoning) is laid down. In the Mishnah (*Sanhedrin* 7:4), however, the two cases are sharply differentiated: the offence in the first instance is punishable by stoning (it is viewed as the more serious of the two), and the second by strangling. That would mean the woman in this passage was betrothed, not married. It is rather doubtful, however, that the distinction existed in Jesus' day.[1]

Although capital punishment by stoning is still meted out today in some Muslim countries for the offence of adultery, there is little evidence that it was carried out very often in first-century Palestine, especially in urban areas. John suggests as much: the authorities were not interested in the intrinsic merits of this case, still less in assuring that justice be done and be seen to be done, but *were using this question as a trap, in order to have a basis for accusing him.* There are several Synoptic parallels (Mk. 3:2; 10:2 par.; Lk. 6:7). If Jesus disavowed the law of Moses, his credibility would be instantly undermined: he could be dismissed as a lawless person and perhaps be charged in the courts with serious offences. If he upheld the law of Moses, he would not only be supporting a position that was largely unpopular but one that was probably not carried out in public life, and, worse, which would have been hard to square with his well-known compassion for the broken and disreputable, his quickness to forgive and restore, and his announcement of the life-transforming power bound up with the new birth. It is even possible, as Jeremias suggests,[2] that formal agreement with the law of Moses could have been interpreted in such a way as to get him into serious difficulty with the Roman overlord. If in the name of Moses he pronounced the death sentence on this woman, and it was actually carried out, he would have been infringing the exclusive rights of the Roman prefect, who alone at this period had the authority to impose capital sentences (*cf.* notes on 18:31–32). If this is part of the dilemma the authorities planned for Jesus, this narrative takes on the flavour of the trap recorded in Mark 12:13–17 par.

6b–8. Why and what Jesus wrote on the ground cannot be ascertained. A longstanding interpretation in the church has been that he wrote part of Jeremiah 17:13: 'Those who turn away from you will be written in the dust because they have forsaken the LORD, the spring of living water.' T. W. Manson[3] was the first to suggest that Jesus was imitating the practice of Roman magistrates who first wrote their sentence and then read it; but it is far from clear that Jesus wrote a sentence

---

[1]*Cf.* J. Blinzler, *NTS* 4, 1957, pp. 32–47; Daube, p. 307.
[2]J. Jeremias, *ZNW* 43, 1950–51, pp. 148–150.
[3]T. W. Manson, *ZNW* 44, 1952–53, pp. 255–256.

(at least, a sentence for the woman), and in any case this explanation is less than satisfactory for v. 8. Derrett (p. 187) suggests that the first time Jesus stooped down he wrote, 'Do not help a wicked man by being a malicious witness' (Ex. 23:1b), and the second time, 'Have nothing to do with a false charge and do not put an innocent or honest person to death, for I will not acquit the guilty' (Ex. 23:7). This seems to give the woman more than her due. (Derrett avoids this problem by hypothesizing that the accusers could have prevented the adultery, but failed to do so in a disgusting conspiracy that was aimed at embarrassing Jesus.) Some have suggested that what Jesus wrote is entirely incidental. The action of writing was itself parabolic, and what really counted – as if Jesus were saying, in effect, 'You are the people of whom Scripture speaks!' In the absence of parallels, however, it is hard to see how the opponents would have read so much into Jesus' action. The truth is that we do not know.

At one level, his writing on the ground was a delaying action that failed to satisfy Jesus' opponents, so *they kept on questioning him.* However ambiguous his writing may be to us today, the words with which he finally responded are clear enough: *If any one of you is without sin, let him be the first to throw a stone at her.* This is a direct reference to Deuteronomy 13:9; 17:7 (*cf.* Lv. 24:14) – the witnesses of the crime must be the first to throw the stones, and they must not be participants in the crime itself. Jesus' saying does not mean that the authorities must be paragons of sinless perfection before the death sentence can properly be meted out, nor does it mean that one must be free even from lust before one can legitimately condemn adultery (even though lust and adultery belong to the same genus, Mt. 5:28). It means, rather, that they must not be guilty of this particular sin. As in many societies around the world, so here: when it comes to sexual sins, the woman was much more likely to be in legal and social jeopardy than her paramour. The man could lead a 'respectable' life while masking the same sexual sins with a knowing wink. Jesus' simple condition, without calling into question the Mosaic code, cuts through the double standard and drives hard to reach the conscience.

9. Many manuscripts specifically say that the accusers were 'convicted by their own conscience' (AV), but their stunned departure testifies as much. Those who had come to shame Jesus now leave in shame. When they have gone, the woman is still said to be 'in the midst' (AV; Gk. *en mesō*). All John means is that the ring around her has melted away, and she was *still standing there* (NIV).

10–11. Alone with the woman, Jesus addresses her for the first time. His form of address, *Woman* (*gynai*), is entirely respectful (*cf.* notes on 2:4; 4:21; 19:26; 20:13). He does not here ask if she is guilty, but if there are others who condemn her. That she is guilty is presupposed by the final words of v. 11: *Go now and leave your life of sin.* But she answers his question with a direct *No-one, sir* (Gk. *kyrie*, which means 'sir' as readily as 'lord' or 'Lord'). Only now does Jesus come close to answering the question that was first set him. Regardless of the exigencies of the law of Moses, in this instance Jesus says *neither do I condemn you*. The confidence and personal absoluteness of Jesus' words not only call to mind that Jesus came not to condemn but to save (3:17; 12:47), but prompt us to remember the Synoptic accounts that assign Jesus, like God himself, the right to forgive sin (Mt. 9:1–8 par.). The proper response to mercy received on account of past sins is purity in the future. NIV's *leave your life of sin* establishes the point directly, even if the expression almost paints the woman as an habitual whore (though the Greek bears no such overtones).

D. RADICAL CONFRONTATION: CLIMACTIC SIGNS, WORKS AND WORDS *(8:12 – 10:42)*

1. At the Feast of Tabernacles II: Jesus' debate with 'the Jews' *(8:12–59)*

a. The authority of Jesus' testimony *(8:12–20)*

12. If we assume that when John wrote his Gospel he did not include (and may not have known the material of) 7:53 – 8:11, then 8:12 attaches itself to 7:52. Further, if the uncertainty that finds expression in 7:40–44 and the sharp exchanges in the Sanhedrin in 7:45–52 are removed from Jesus' public utterances, then 8:12 follows on nicely from 7:37–39. That is what is indicated by the word *again* (*palin*, which is the first word in the Gk. text of 8:12): *again* he spoke to the people, still in the context of the Feast of Tabernacles.

'He who has not seen the joy of the place of water-drawing has never in his life seen joy': this extravagant claim stands just before the description of the lighting of the four huge lamps in the temple's court of women and of the exuberant celebration that took place under their light (Mishnah *Sukkah* 5:1–4). 'Men of piety and good works' danced through the night, holding burning torches in their hands and singing songs and praises. The Levitical orchestras cut loose, and some sources attest that this went on every night of the Feast of Tabernacles, with the light from the temple area shedding its glow all over Jerusalem. In this context Jesus declares to the people, *I am the light of the world*.

This is the second of the 'I am' statements that are followed by a predicate (*cf.* notes on 6:35). Of the incarnate Word we have already learned that the life 'was the light of men' (*cf.* notes on 1:4). The light metaphor is steeped in Old Testament allusions. The glory of the very presence of God in the cloud led the people to the promised land (Ex. 13:21–22) and protected them from those who would destroy them (Ex. 14:19–25). The Israelites were trained to sing, 'The LORD is my light and my salvation' (Ps. 27:1). The word of God, the law of God, is a light to guide the path of those who cherish instruction (Ps. 119:105; Pr. 6:23);

God's light is shed abroad in revelation (Ezk. 1:4, 13, 26–28) and salvation (Hab. 3:3–4). 'Light is Yahweh in action, Ps. 44:3' (H. Conzelmann, *TDNT* 9, 320). Isaiah tells us that the servant of the LORD was appointed as a light to the Gentiles, that he might bring God's salvation to the ends of the earth (Is. 49:6). The coming eschatological age would be a time when the LORD himself would be the light for his people (Is. 60:19–22; *cf.* Rev. 21:23–24). Perhaps Zechariah 14:5b–7 is especially significant, with its promise of continual light on the last day, followed by the promise of living waters flowing from Jerusalem – this passage probably forming part of the liturgical readings of this Feast (*cf.* notes on 7:37–39). The great, burning lights of the Feast of Tabernacles resonate with such strains. Already in the Fourth Gospel the dawning of the light in the coming of Jesus has been a significant theme. In this age of an inaugurated but not yet consummated kingdom, however, the light is still in mortal combat with darkness (1:4, 9; 3:19–21).

In fact, light is so common a religious symbol that commentators can find roughly parallel passages in a wide diversity of religious backgrounds that John may well have been exposed to (*cf.* Barrett, pp. 335–337; Dodd, *IFG*, pp. 201–298; Odeberg, pp. 286–292; Bultmann, pp. 40–44, 342–343).[1] Insofar as some of his readers have been reared in one or more of these religious contexts, John would not be adverse to pointing out the ways in which Jesus is the *true* light. But the Gospel is strongly Jewish, and the struggle over claims to authority are with Jews who wish to maintain as paramount their received tradition. That must be the primary locus of the debate that interests the Evangelist, as well as the locus of debate during Jesus' life and ministry.

In the context of such powerful ritual, Jesus' declaration must have come with stunning force. He does not let it hang in the air as an abstract dictum. There is an immediate consequence: *Whoever follows me* (an appropriate thing to do with light if it is the glorious pillar of cloud setting out the way in the wilderness) *will never walk in darkness* (*cf.* 1:5, 9; 3:19–21; 12:35, 46) *but will have the light of life* – i.e. the light that produces life (*cf.* notes on 'bread of life', 6:35; *cf.* Ps. 36:9, 'For with you is the fountain of life; in your light we see light.').

That is as far as the theme is explicitly taken in this chapter. The interest now turns to the authority of Jesus in making such a claim. Nevertheless the verse is strategically placed, for it not only rounds out Jesus' claims in connection with the Feast of Tabernacles, but prepares the way for ch. 9, where the outworking of Jesus' claim to be the light (*cf.* 9:5) is depicted in a miracle by which a blind man is made to see, while others who think they see remain blind to the light. More important to

---

[1]Helmut Koester (in Hedrick/Hodgson, pp. 97–110, esp. pp. 99–100), finds numerous ostensible parallels in a variety of gnostic sources. Most of them are not close. When they are closer in form, they are frequently worlds apart in conception. Above all, Koester addresses neither the question as to who borrowed from whom, nor the questions raised by the multiplicity of backgrounds from which similar 'parallels' may be drawn.

the immediate context, the theme of light is not unrelated to the question of truthfulness and witness in the following verses, for light cannot but attest to its own presence; otherwise put, it bears witness to itself, and its source is entirely supportive of that witness.

13. When *the Pharisees* (*cf.* notes on 1:19, 24) challenge him, they bring up Jesus' own words. 'If I testify about myself, my testimony is not valid' (5:31). Certainly the law of Moses required multiple attestation in capital cases (Dt. 17:6), and in other criminal proceedings as well (Dt. 19:15). In the Mishnah (*Ketuboth* 2:9) the principle is adopted and applied to other legal situations.

14. But in fact, the Pharisees have misunderstood Jesus' earlier utterance (*cf.* notes on 5:31). He was certainly not saying that if he spoke without supporting witness he was necessarily a liar, but that if he testified about himself – *i.e.* outside the framework he had just established, in which everything he says is nothing more and nothing less than what the Father gives him to say – then of course the kind of claims he was making could not possibly be true. Sadly, the Pharisees have understood his words in a purely juridical sense, as if he were interested in nothing more than establishing the legal criteria for acceptable testimony. So Jesus goes over the same ground he has been over before (5:19–30, 36–37), using slightly different terms. He can, he says, offer true (*alēthēs*, *cf.* notes on 5:31) testimony concerning himself, because he knows his unique origin and destiny (an important theme in the Fourth Gospel: *cf.* 3:11–13; 7:27–28, 34–35; 9:29–30; 13:1, 36–47; 14:4ff.; 16:5, 28; 19:9). His opponents have no right to speak, since they do not know where he came from (*viz.* the Father, 5:36–37; 16:28) nor where he is going (*viz.* the Father, 13:1; 16:28; 17:5). He will shortly point out once more that even in these claims he is not speaking in naked independence, but is speaking in perfect conformity with the Father's will (vv. 16, 18).

15. Sadly, in assessing who Jesus is, his opponents are judging *by human standards* (*kata tēn sarka*, lit. 'according to the flesh'). This is probably even worse than judging 'by mere appearances' (7:24); here they are resorting to the criteria of flesh, of fallen mankind in a fallen world, without the compelling control of the Spirit (*cf.* 3:3–7). They see his 'flesh', as it were, but never contemplate the possibility that he could be the Word made flesh (1:14). To regard Christ by so limited a set of criteria is to weigh him 'from a worldly point of view' (2 Cor. 5:16; *kata sarka*). As for himself, Jesus declares, *I pass judgment on no-one.* It will not do (with Bruce, p. 189, and others) to argue that Jesus changes the meaning of the verb *krinō* here from 'assess' to 'pass judicial sentence', and conclude that Jesus does *not* judge in the sense that he came into the world to save, not to condemn 3:17. That is true, of course, but the line of thought would be the merest pun. Jesus means, rather, that he does not judge anyone at all *the way his opponents do* – *i.e.* he does not appeal to superficial, 'fleshly' criteria, and accordingly mark people up or down. If that is what his opponents mean by judging, Jesus does not do any of it.

Indeed, as Bernard (1.295) remarks, the Synoptics record the charge that Jesus was not discriminating enough (Mk. 2:16; Lk. 7:39; 15:2; *cf.* Jn. 8:11).

16. But that does not mean that Jesus does not judge in *any* sense. His purpose was to save, not to condemn, but his very presence guarantees that humanity divides around him, and a large part of it is correspondingly judged by him (*cf.* 9:39). Indeed, the Son of Man has been given unique authority to judge (5:27), precisely because of who he is. And quite apart from eschatological judgment, if Jesus assesses, even now, a person or situation, his judgment will inevitably prove *right* (*alēthinē, i.e.* genuine, ultimate, and therefore right), because in this area as in every other Jesus does not stand alone but with the Father who sent him. Jesus judges only as he hears from the Father, and thus his judgment is just (*cf.* notes on 5:30).

17–18. Because of this, even the formal conditions of the law (*cf.* notes on v. 13) are met: the Father and the Son, in perfect agreement, both bear testimony, in the sense already established (*cf.* notes on 5:19–30, 36–37).

Not a few commentators think it historically implausible that Jesus could ever have so distanced himself from the law of Moses as to refer to it as *your law*. In their view the terminology betrays the growing hostility between the church and the synagogue. But as in 7:19 (*cf.* notes there), *your* law seems appropriate precisely because the Pharisees are appealing to that law to question Jesus' practice, while Jesus is claiming to be the new locus of revelation from the Father such that the law finds fulfilment in him. Unless one is arbitrarily prepared to argue that Jesus had no consciousness of his unique role in the sweep of redemptive history, in his role as the agent of creation (1:3), in his pre-existence (8:58), it would be astonishing if he had *not* distanced himself from the law at certain points.

The words *I am one who testifies* formally constitutes another 'I am' saying, but in Greek it is structurally rather different from those listed in the notes on 6:35. The words do not so much identify Jesus as a particular individual (someone called 'the testifier' or the like) as they identify his peculiar qualifications: he is peculiarly the *one who testifies*, with full qualifications for doing so, for the reasons specified in vv. 14, 16. The other one qualified to do so is the Father (the Holy Spirit will be added as a qualified witness in chs. 14 – 16).

19. Not infrequently in John, Jesus says something profound only to have it misinterpreted by others. So here: Jesus has been explicating the unique relation he enjoys with his heavenly Father as he bears witness to the truth, and his opponents want the Father identified, apparently thinking on a purely human plane. As elsewhere, the misunderstanding leads to further explanations, though in this instance they are delayed for a few verses. Nevertheless, the 'Father' theme, and the corresponding question as to what paternity Jesus and the Pharisees may legitimately claim, dominates the rest of the chapter. For the moment, Jesus responds with an accusation akin to 5:37–38. By their question the Pharisees are admitting that they really do not know who Jesus is, despite the earlier claims of some Jerusalemites (7:27). Worse, their inability to recognize Jesus testifies that they really do not know God himself (*cf.* 1:18; 5:38; 14:7, 9). How could they? They were still judging 'by human standards' (v. 15). If they had really recognized who he was, they would have known the Father also – not only because Jesus reveals the Father, so that truly to know Jesus is to know the Father, but also because special revelation from God is required to know who Jesus is (6:44, 45).

20. The Evangelist rounds off this exchange by identifying the setting (a pattern he has followed elsewhere: *cf.* 6:59). The *place where the offerings were put* probably refers to the thirteen 'shofar-chests' (probably so named because the 'chests' were shaped like shofars (Heb. *šôpār*), a trumpet; *cf.* Mishnah *Shekalim* 2:1; 6:1, 5). Each was inscribed with the use to which the money collected in it was ostensibly put. Nowhere do we learn explicitly where they were placed, but probably they were located in the Court of the Women, if we may judge from access women had to them (*cf.* Mk. 12:41–42; *cf.* SB 2. 37–45). John's principal point is that *no-one seized him, because his time (hōra) had not yet come.* Cf. notes on 2:4; 7:6, 30. The assumption, of course, is that the animus against Jesus in some circles had not abated, but had increased, and was biding its time. But the right 'hour' (*hōra*) would be determined by God himself.

b. The origin of Jesus' authority *(8:21–30)*

21. As in v. 12, so here: the Greek word for 'again' (NIV *Once more*) indicates a pause, yet a fundamental continuity with what precedes. The themes developed in vv. 12–20 are enlarged upon throughout the rest of this chapter. They include: where Jesus comes from (vv. 23, 26, 29); where he is going (vv. 21–22, 28); who the Father is (vv. 26–27, 38, 54–55); who Jesus is (vv. 23–26, 38, 54–55). Further (as Barrett, p. 340, rightly observes), the opposite of each of these themes is applied to the Jews. Jesus is from above, they are from below; they are from this world, he is not from this world (v. 23); where he goes, they cannot come (v. 21); God is his Father, theirs is the devil (vv. 26–27, 41–44, 54–55).

In large measure, Jesus in v. 21 repeats the thought of 7:33–34 (*cf.* notes), but is more threatening. Worse, he is no more understood this time than the last. By *I am going away* (*hypagō*) Jesus refers to his death, the means by which he 'goes away' to his Father. It is unlikely John thinks the Jews will then seek Jesus personally. He knows perfectly well that most of the leadership were only too glad to see him go, and did their best to quell the persistent accounts of his resurrection. What is meant, rather, is that they will go on looking for the Messiah (which is why Jesus says *you will look for me*). If they do, they cannot possibly find him; they are chasing an ephemeral wisp, for they have rejected the only Messiah there is. They will die in their sin: the singular *sin* refers to the particular sin of unbelief, of rejecting Jesus and the revelation he is and brings (cf. 9:41). *Where I go*, Jesus says, *you cannot come*. How could it be otherwise? To reject the Son is to reject the Father (5:23); how then shall they enter the Father's presence on the last day? When Jesus later tells his own disciples that they cannot go where he is, their prospect is entirely different to that of the Jews: they will follow him later (13:33, 36).

22. For *the Jews*, cf. notes on 1:19. Here the reference is to the crowds who are largely sceptical or confused, some of whom may believe in him but even then only with an unsatisfactory faith (vv. 31, 37). As in 7:34–35, they are unable to fathom what Jesus means by 'going away' (v. 21). There they wondered if he was contemplating a mission to the Gentiles; here they wonder if he is contemplating suicide (thought to be a dark sin by most Jewish scholars: cf. Jos., *Bel.* iii. 375). This is almost certainly an ironic prophecy of Jesus' death, akin to 11:49–50 (cf. Hoskyns, p. 334). His opponents are wrong to think he will achieve his departure by killing himself; unwittingly they are nevertheless profoundly right, for he 'goes away' by voluntarily laying down his life (10:18), not in suicide but in submission to his Father's will, in a violent death meted out by his enemies.

23. Jesus cuts through their misguided speculation by declaring that he and they emerge from two entirely antithetical realms. He is *from above*, i.e. *not of this world*, but from heaven, sent by his Father. They are *from below*, which does not mean 'from hell' or 'from the underworld' or the like, but *of this world*, this fallen moral order in conscious rebellion against its creator (cf. notes on 1:9, 10; 3:16). The contrast is not between a spiritual world and a material world (John is not a neoplatonist), but between the realm of God himself and the realm of his fallen and rebellious creation, the 'world' which hates Jesus because he testifies that 'what it does is evil' (7:7). That is the fundamental reason why Jesus' opponents can neither recognize who he is nor understand his teaching. Nothing will suffice to remove such blindness but being 'taught by God' (6:45), being born again (3:3, 5), finding the one who is himself the way, the truth and the life (14:6).

24. Because the realm from which Jesus' opponents spring is not only rebellious but morally culpable, they will (as Jesus had already insisted, v. 21) die in their sins. The plural *sins* contrasts with the singular in v. 21, and refers to the diverse and ugly forms of corruption that mushroom from the one sin of unbelief. That is why Jesus adds, *If you do not believe . . . you will indeed die in your sins*. The assumption, of course, is that the only possibility of escape lies in genuine belief. Under this condition, men and women will *not die* in their sins.

But what are they to believe? The conditional clause provides the proper object of faith: 'If you do not believe that *egō eimi*'. In 6:20, where the expression first occurs (though cf. notes on 4:26), it means 'It is I'. More commonly it is the first part of a revelatory formula that is filled out with an appropriate completion: *I am* the bread of life, or the like (cf. notes on 6:35). But the absolute usage in this passage (also in vv. 28, 58;

13:19; possibly 18:6) certainly has more theological weight to it. In this sort of context, it does not appear to be a normal Greek expression at all: it would be considered such only if the surrounding verses supplied an implicit completion – which is why the NIV, rather hopefully, supplies 'I am *the one I claim to be*'. Nicholson (p.113), attempting greater precision, suggests 'Unless you believe that I am not of this world/that I am from above, you will die in your sins' (with a similar approach in v. 28). But this probably confuses the proper object of faith with what it is that grounds Jesus' authority. That the expression is somewhat obscure in this context is supported by the mystified question of Jesus' opponents in the next verse: 'Who are you?' To that extent the kind of completion envisaged by Nicholson is a *possible* way of understanding the text. The question, however, is whether it is an *adequate* way of understanding the text. The answer comes later in the chapter: that the expression is in fact to be taken absolutely becomes progressively clear, culminating in v. 58 – and once the expression becomes that clear, Jesus' opponents take up stones to kill him (v. 59)

It has been argued that the background to the expression lies in pagan religious descriptions of 'heroized mortals', human beings who become much like pagan deities because of some great achievement. Quite apart from the numerous flaws in the alleged parallelism, the entire context of John 8 is Jewish, not least in the repeated references to Abraham and his children. More plausibly, some have suggested that *egō eimi* depends on Exodus 3:13–14. There Moses asks God to identify himself with a name, a name he can use when he tells the leaders of the Israelies that the God of their fathers has sent him. God replies, 'I AM WHO I AM. This is what you are to say to the Israelites: "I AM has sent me to you."' In the LXX, the Greek version of the Old Testament, the text reads: '"*Egō eimi ho ōn* ['I am the one who is', or 'I am the existent one']"; tell them that "*ho ōn* ['the existent one', or 'the one who is']" has sent you.' If the Evangelist had intended a direct reference to Exodus 3:14, one might have expected *ho ōn* instead of *egō eimi*.

That is why the majority of interpreters today rightly see that, however ambiguous the expression remains in vv. 24, 28 (but not in v. 58), the proper background to *egō eimi* in John 8:24, 28, 58 is the use of *egō eimi* in Isaiah 40 – 55 (*cf.* especially Is. 41:4; 43:10, 13, 25; 46:4; 48:12; *cf.* also Dt. 32:39). In the Hebrew original, God discloses himself in the repeated declaration, 'I am he' (Heb. *'ªnî hû'*);[1] it is this expression that the LXX consistently renders by *egō eimi*, formally 'I am'. Isaiah 43:10 is especially close to Johannine language: '"You are my witnesses,"

---

[1]The words 'I am he' (Heb. *'ªnî hû'*) are probably the origin of a late and rather strange variation on the divine name, lit. 'I and he' (Heb. *'ªnî wᵉhû'*), a variation used at the Feast of Tabernacles when the priests chanted Ps. 118 (*cf.* Dodd, *IFG*, pp. 93–96). Instead of singing 'I am Yahweh', they sang 'I and he', apparently as a mark of the close identification of the God of Israel and his covenant people. It is not obvious, however, that a similar association should be read into John.

declares the Lord, "and my servant whom I have chosen, so that you may know and believe me and understand that *I am he*."' In Isaiah, the contexts demand that 'I am he' means 'I am the same', 'I am forever the same', and perhaps even 'I am Yahweh', with a direct allusion to Exodus 3:14 (*cf.* Is. 43:11–13). For others to apply this title to themselves was blasphemous, an invitation to face the wrath of God (Is. 47:8; Zp. 2:15). For Jesus to apply such words to himself is tantamount to a claim to deity, once it is clear that the other potential meanings of *egō eimi* are contextually impossible. This does not mean that Jesus and Yahweh of the Old Testament are identified without remainder, since v. 28 (where this title next occurs) is immediately followed by v. 29, where Jesus again distinguishes himself from the Father (similarly 13:19–20). But this tension between unqualified statements affirming the full deity of the Word or of the Son, and those which distinguish the Word or the Son from the Father, are typical of the Fourth Gospel and are present from the very first verse (*cf.* notes on 1:1, 18; 5:19–30).[1]

25. The ambiguity bound up with *egō eimi* (v. 24) prompts Jesus' opponents to ask, *Who are you?* Assuming the next sentence is best rendered, 'Just what I told you at the beginning' (*cf.* Additional Note), what Jesus means is that his revelatory witness has been consistent from the beginning. What he is now claiming, however hard it is for them to understand it, is of a piece with the claims he made and the declarations he offered at the beginning of his ministry.

26. Far from being reluctant to speak, Jesus tells his opponents *I have much to say*. His task is to take what he has heard from the one who has sent him and *tell the world*; in doing so, he inevitably testifies that what the world does is evil (7:7). The contrast between the revelation he mediates from the Father and the stance of his hearers is so great that what he is saying is *about* them, but inevitably *in judgment* of them. The contrast between the two parts of the verse, indicated by the word *But*, turns on the source of his utterances. His opponents have asked him who he is; Jesus replies that he is just what he said he was in the beginning (v. 25). Moreover he has much more to say to them, even if his word will be a word of judgment. *But* this does not mean he is now speaking on his own, for all that Jesus tells to the world he has heard from the one who sent him (*cf.* 3:34; 5:19–30; 8:15–16), and that one is true.

27. By 'he who sent me' (v. 26), the Jews *did not understand that he was telling them about his Father*. One might have thought that the point had been made pretty clear in 5:16–30. Certainly John does not report what the Jews thought Jesus actually meant. Possibly the fact that Jesus refers to God as the one who sent him instead of as his Father (*cf.* 5:18) confused a few of his hearers. In any case, the Evangelist leaves his

---

[1] The numerous parallels between the 'I am' passages in Jn. 8 – 9 and the 'Servant of the Lord' in Is. 42 – 43 have been helpfully set out by J. G. Coetzee, in Petzer/Hartin, pp. 170–177.

readers in no doubt as to what Jesus meant, while casting doubt on the spiritual discernment of 'the Jews'.

28–29. When will the full disclosure of who Jesus is take place? When will his glory be most fully revealed? That will occur when the *Son of Man* (*cf.* notes on 1:51; 3:14) is *lifted up* (*cf.* notes on 3:14). The double force of the verb is maintained. When Jesus is 'lifted up' on the cross, he is being 'lifted up' to his Father's presence, returned to the glory he enjoyed with the Father before the world began (17:5). This does not mean that the cross is merely the first stage on the way to the real exaltation, however, since the cross itself is the glorification of Jesus (*cf.* notes on 1:14; 12:23–33). The exaltation of Jesus by means of the cross is also the exaltation of Jesus on the cross. That is the event which, though perpetrated by his enemies ('when *you* have lifted up the Son of Man'), establishes Jesus' claim most forcefully: *then you will know that egō eimi* (*cf.* notes on v. 24). One of the functions of the cross is to reveal who Jesus is. That is when the Jews will know the truth. By this John is not saying that all of Jesus' opponents will be converted in the wake of the cross. But if they do come to know who Jesus is, they will know it most surely because of the cross. And even those who do not believe stand at the last day condemned by him whom they 'lifted up' on the cross, blinded to the glory that shone around them, yet one day forced to kneel and confess that Jesus is Lord (*cf.* Phil. 2:10–11).

Probably we should read a full stop after 'I am'. In the next words, nothing in the Greek text corresponds to NIV's 'that'. Rather, Jesus goes on to say, 'And I do nothing on my own . . .', recapitulating the argument of 3:34; 5:30; 6:38; 8:16; *etc.* Both Jesus' teaching about the cross, and his actual going to the cross, are nothing other than the Father's will. Jesus' profound sense of the Father's presence (*he has not left me alone*), even on the eve of the cross itself (*cf.* 16:32), is the direct consequence of his perfect, self-conscious submission to his Father's will (*I always do what pleases him*).

30. So compelling was Jesus' teaching, even without the full comprehension that depended on the cross and resurrection, that *many put their faith in him*. That had happened before, at another Jerusalem feast, in consequence of Jesus' miracles (2:23); but that faith had turned out to be spurious (2:24–25). What of this faith?

Additional notes

25. The difficult point in the Greek text of this verse turns on the expression *tēn archēn*, which is the accusative case of words normally meaning 'the beginning'. The accusative case is often used to signify a direct object, but that makes no sense here. The words must therefore be taken as an adverbial accusative (not an uncommon use of this noun: *cf.* LSJ, *s.v.*). That still leaves a number of options. The most important of these are: (1) The sentence in which *tēn archēn* is found is to be taken as a question (there were few punctuation marks in the original text to discriminate between affirmations and questions; context must decide), the Greek word *hoti* must be rendered 'Why?' (as in Mk. 9:28, an admittedly uncommon use), and *tēn archēn* means 'at all' – *i.e.* 'Why do I speak to you at all?' This makes sense of the grammar, but ill suits the context, since the next verse finds Jesus saying that he has much more to say in judgment of them. (2) The sentence may be an affirmation, with *hoti* broken up into two words, *ho ti* (since the original manuscripts rarely left spaces between words, and so context must decide where the breaks come), and *tēn archēn* means 'at first' or 'in the beginning'. It helps, then, to supply, mentally, *egō eimi* ('I am' – a perfectly legitimate procedure in Greek, which tends to drop out expressions that the writer judges obvious from the context). This generates 'Just what I told you at the beginning.' The verb here translated 'I told you' (*lalō*) is a present form, but here it is past-referring, a not uncommon use of the verb, clearly required by the phrase 'at the beginning'. This interpretation is probably right, and is supported by a variant reading that tries to force the issue by 'correcting' the sentence to read, 'I told you in the beginning that which also I am telling you' (*cf.* Metzger, pp. 223–224). What does not seem appropriate is any attempt to make *tēn archēn* mean 'from the beginning'. There is another phrase to express that thought (*ap'archēs*). The NIV rendering, 'Just what I have been claiming all along', is a periphrastic way of supporting this unlikely interpretation.

c. The children of Abraham (8:31–59)

31. The opening clause seems innocuous, until it becomes apparent in the ensuing verses that *the Jews who had believed him*, apparently referring to the 'many' who 'put their faith in him' in the preceding verse, turn out to be, in Jesus' view, slaves to sin (v. 34), indifferent to Jesus' word (v. 37), children of the devil (v. 44), liars (v. 55), and guilty of mob tactics, including attempted murder of the one in whom they have professed to believe (v. 59). Explanations for this anomaly have been many, and include the following:

(1) Verse 31, or some part of it, is a gloss, *i.e.* a later insertion into the text. There is no manuscript evidence for this suggestion. Moreover, glossators are known for their tendency to *remove* ostensible difficulties from the text by additional explanation, not for any tendency to *add* fresh difficulties.

(2) Some argue that there is a difference in meaning between *pisteuō* (the verb 'to believe') plus the preposition *eis* ('to', 'into'), plus the accusative, used in v. 30, and *pisteuō* plus the dative, used in v. 31. In this view, the first construction is reserved for genuine, saving faith; the second describes inadequate, superficial faith. That means v. 31 introduces a new group of people. The problem is that the linguistic distinction does not stand up. The former construction, ostensibly referring to saving faith, is used in 2:23 of spurious faith; the latter construction, allegedly reserved for superficial faith, clearly refers to genuine faith in 5:24. Whatever distinction there may be between the two expressions

does not lie in the distinction between the genuine and the spurious (*cf.* Bultmann, p. 252, n. 2).

(3) Others suggest that these 'believers' are Judaizing Christians, those who hold to the necessity of adhering to circumcision and the constraints of the Mosaic code while nevertheless confessing Jesus as the Messiah. John therefore presents them as children of the devil, in much the same way that Paul pronounces his *anathema* on the Judaizers with whom he had to deal (Gal. 1:6-9). But this not only makes John's Gospel hopelessly anachronistic, it misconstrues the terms of the debate in this chapter. The focus here is on the authority of Jesus, his unique relation to his Father and consequent revelatory stance – not on competing opinions regarding the conditions of entrance to the messianic community, focusing on the place of the law in the stream of redemptive history.

(4) Still others (*e.g.* Schnackenburg, and esp. Erich Gräßer[1]) argue that vv. 30-31 refer to genuine believers, but that the polemics of the succeeding verses are not directed *against* them but against Jewish controversialists in *John*'s day who were a continual threat against the fledgling faith of new Jewish converts. In other words, the sharp exchanges of 8:33ff. are not designed to put down spurious converts, but to strengthen new converts by putting down those most likely to damage them. However, it must be frankly acknowledged that the text itself does not support this view. The problem of the text is 'resolved' by manufacturing a group that is not actually mentioned, a group whose existence is finally dependent on a synthetic *Sitz im Leben* (life-setting) in John's church, a *Sitz im Leben* characterized by unnecessary anachronism and historical reconstruction of a sort that comports well with certain scholarly fads but is little based on exegesis. *Cf.* Introduction, § III.

(5) The component of anachronism in the latter reconstruction can be removed by postulating that, in addition to genuine believers in vv. 30-31, there are others present in the temple precincts *in the time of Jesus* who had no room for his word (v. 37), and that Jesus' harshest condemnations were reserved for them. That others were present in so public a setting is undoubtedly true, but this 'solution' fails to account for v. 31, which stubbornly insists that Jesus' ensuing remarks were directed 'to the Jews who had believed him'.[2]

It seems wiser to observe that John has already introduced the theme of fickle faith. In 2:23, the many people who believed in his name when they saw the miraculous signs Jesus was doing turn out to have untrustworthy faith (2:24-25). Some seek to exclude this parallel on the

---

[1]*Der Alte Bund im Neuen* (J. C. B. Mohr [Paul Siebeck], 1980), pp. 154-167.

[2]James Swetnam, *Bib* 61, 1980, pp. 106-109, supports this fifth interpretation by arguing that the perfect participle *pepisteukotas* has pluperfect force, *i.e.* 'who had believed in him (*sc.* but no longer did so).' The perfect participle can, rather rarely, refer to action that no longer continues, but that is far from what the perfect participle, in itself, actually means (*cf.* Porter, ch. 5). In other instances where the perfect participle is alleged to take on such referential force, the context makes it clear.

ground that the faith in question is the fruit of signs, not words, and signs are elsewhere deprecated (4:48). But the signs *can* foster an *acceptable* faith (10:38). More important, the same theme of fickle faith recurs in 6:60, where many of Jesus' disciples turn away from him *after a discourse of which they disapprove*, not after a sign. A similar situation develops here. Some believe in Jesus: whether or not their faith is genuine cannot be determined by the linguistic expression selected by the Evangelist. But Jesus now lays down exactly what it is that separates spurious faith from true faith, fickle disciples from genuine disciples: *If you hold to my teaching, you are really my disciples*. The verb rendered 'hold' is *menō*, to abide, to remain – a theme of critical importance that returns in a concentrated way in ch. 15. In short, perseverance is the mark of true faith, of real disciples. A genuine believer remains in Jesus' 'word' (*logos*), his teaching (*cf*. notes on 1:1): *i.e.* such a person obeys it, seeks to understand it better, and finds it more precious, more controlling, precisely when other forces flatly oppose it. It is the one who continues in the teaching who has both the Father and the Son (2 Jn. 9; *cf*. Heb. 3:14; Rev. 2:26).

This interpretation makes sense of the literary context, and suits the purpose of the book. To the Jews who have professed faith in him, Jesus, understandably enough, indicates what genuine faith does: it perseveres, it holds tight to Jesus' teaching, with some glorious consequences (v. 32). But such faith costs not less than everything, and the freedom it brings presupposes that life before such faith is pitiful slavery. By sketching genuine faith in such stark terms, Jesus is standing true to a pattern we find elsewhere: he is never interested in multiplying numbers of converts if they are not genuine believers, and therefore he insists on forcing would-be disciples to count the cost (*cf*. Lk. 9:57–62; 14:25–33). Up to this point in the text it is unclear to the reader whether these 'believers' will prove true or false. Verses 33ff. settle the matter: they cannot follow Jesus' teaching unhesitatingly, they cannot believe that he is necessary to their true freedom, they will not recognize their own slavery to sin, not even the fickleness that oscillates between hero-worship and massive discontent. The movement in reactions to Jesus is entirely parallel to the flow from 6:14–15 to 6:60ff. The Evangelist includes all of this material not because he is trying to nurture the faith of fledgling believers, but because he is trying to evangelize Jews and proselytes who must carefully understand what faith in Jesus Christ entails. They, too, must count the cost, and John, like Jesus, must present the gospel in such a way that spurious professions of faith are soon unmasked before they flood the ranks of the messianic community with people who have never been born again.

32. Holding to Jesus' teaching (v. 31) not only establishes the genuineness of faith, it also has its own authenticating power. We come to know the truth, not simply by intellectual assessment, but by moral commitment (*cf*. notes on 7:17). On 'truth', *cf*. notes on 1:14; 14:6; here it is close to the meaning of 'gospel', the truth that has been revealed in and by

Jesus. Because of truth's intimate connection with Jesus, true disciples 'must not only hear his words: they must in some sort be united with him who is the truth' (Dodd, *IFG*, p. 178). Judaism taught that study of the law makes a man free (*e.g. Pirke Aboth* 3:5); the Fourth Gospel insists that the law points to Jesus (5:39, 46), himself the truth (14:6) and the one who is full of grace and truth (1:14), if true freedom is to be enjoyed. The nature of that freedom depends on the nature of the slavery Jesus has in mind, and that point is what is next clarified by the turn of the discussion.

33. If Jesus is offering freedom, the assumption is that the Jews are currently slaves. This they emphatically deny: how can they be considered slaves to anyone or anything when they are *Abraham's descendants* (lit. 'seed')? It is unlikely that the objection means the Jews have never been in political subjection to anyone. That would be absurd: there was scarcely a major power whom the Jews had *not* served: Egypt, Assyria, Babylon, Greece, Syria and Rome had all held the Jews in political captivity. True, their relative freedom and especially their religious independence under the Romans (whether in the days of Jesus or when John most likely wrote his book) was substantial; yet the fact remains that they were in service to Caesar. It is much more probable that the Jews are talking about spiritual, inward freedom and privilege. Thus, Rabbi Akiba is credited with saying that all Israelites are kings' sons, *i.e.* the descendants of Abraham, Isaac and Jacob (B. *Shabbath* 128*a*).[1] The Jews saw themselves as 'sons of the kingdom' (*cf.* Mt. 8:12). Bauer (p. 125) and Barrett (p. 345) rightly compare Mark 2:17, where the Jews are convinced they are whole and therefore need no physician – just as they are here convinced they are free and therefore need no liberation (*cf.* also 9:40–41). The final sentence of this verse, *How can you say that we shall be set free?*, has an ugly, challenging tone to it that anticipates v. 53. These 'believers' are already demonstrating their unwillingness to hold to Jesus' teaching (v. 31), for their sense of inherited privilege is so strong they can neither acknowledge their own need nor recognize the divine Word incarnate before them. Their very words demonstrate their slavery in the categories of the next verse.

Jesus thus finds himself in the place where he must explain what he means by freedom and slavery (vv. 34–36), disabuse his interlocutors of any sense of privilege that depends on merely physical lineage to Abraham (vv. 37–44; *cf.* notes on 3:3, 5), and reassert his own unique authority (vv. 45ff.).

34. With the strong asseveration *I tell you the truth* (*cf.* notes on 1:51),

---

[1] A list of privileges that some saw as the inevitable heritage of every Jew is found in SB 1. 116–121 (though the sources are of various dates). The passage from Josephus (*Bel.* vii. 323) that testifies that Jews 'determined neither to serve the Romans nor any other save God', and cited by some commentators (*e.g.* Barrett, p. 345), is irrelevant, because it is a statement justifying continued revolt in the Jewish war, not the kind of freedom claimed in Jn. 8:33, a freedom which stands *despite* continued and uncontested political subjugation.

Jesus makes plain the kind of slavery (and, implicitly, the kind of freedom) he has in mind: *everyone who sins is a slave to sin* (*cf.* Rom. 6:12, 13, 17). Not only does the practice of sin (the Greek is literally 'the one who does sin'; *cf.* 1 Jn. 3:4, 8, 9) prove that one is a slave to sin, but the practice of sin actively enslaves. For Jesus , then, the ultimate bondage is not enslavement to a political or economic system, but vicious slavery to moral failure, to rebellion against the God who has made us. The despotic master is not Caesar, but shameful self-centredness, an evil and enslaving devotion to created things at the expense of worship of the Creator. This is why Jesus would not let himself be reduced to the level of a merely political Messiah (6:14, 15). It is not that his claims have no bearing on questions of social justice, but that the pursuit of social justice alone will always prove vain and ephemeral unless the deeper enslavement is recognized and handled. In Jesus' view, Caesar himself is a slave.

35–36. From the notion of slavery (v. 34) the thought progresses to the status of slaves. Dodd (*HTFG*, pp. 379–382), followed by others, has argued that these two verses originally constituted a parable about the different spiritual circumstances of people and about the possibility of change. In this context, the application is clear: the Jews think of themselves as sons (of Abraham), but in reality they are slaves (to sin). As sons of Abraham, the Jews felt spiritually confident, not to say self-assured; to be told they are but slaves strikes at the root of their assurance, for *a slave has no permanent place in the family* (*cf.* Mt. 3:9; 8:11–12; Mk. 12:9). The genuine son in this context is not the Christian, but Christ himself (the Gk. word for 'son' is *ho huios*, always used in John for Jesus Christ; believers are *ta tekna tou theou*, 'children of God').[1] Whether or not these verses ever constituted a separable parable may be open to dispute. The picture of the son belonging to the house *forever* (*eis ton aiōna*) may be against it, though this may mean no more than that a son cannot ever be anything other than a son, while a slave can be sold or given away. *So if the Son sets you free* – now not simply the son of the householder, but the Son of God, as that title is repeatedly used in this Gospel (*cf.* notes on 5:19ff.) – *you will be free indeed*. Jesus not only enjoys inalienable rights as the unique Son of God, but exercises full authority, vested in him by the Father (3:35), to liberate slaves. Those whom Jesus liberates from the tyranny of sin are really (*ontōs*) free (*cf.* Rom. 8:2; Gal. 5:1). True freedom is not the liberty to do anything we please, but the liberty to do what we ought; and it is genuine liberty because doing what we ought now pleases us.

37. The Jews have tied their self-professed freedom to their status as the 'seed' of Abraham (v. 33), so Jesus now turns to that question. Even in the Old Testament, physical descent from Abraham was not sufficient

---

[1] It goes beyond the text, and in direct opposition to this distinction, to argue, with Vellanickal (pp. 286ff.), that the Son elevates the slaves to his own level of sonship.

to determine the line of the seed, the real heirs of Abraham (Gn. 21:9–10) – a point Paul observes and makes use of (Rom. 9:7; Gal. 4:21–31). 'A man is not a Jew if he is only one outwardly, nor is circumcision merely outward and physical. No, a man is a Jew if he is one inwardly: and circumcision is circumcision of the heart, by the Spirit, not by the written code. Such a man's praise is not from men, but from God' (Rom. 2:28–29; contrast Jn. 5:44!). So writes Paul, but Jeremiah (9:25–26) had made a similar point, and John himself would later elaborate on the fact that paternity, in the spiritual realm, is established by right conduct, right belief, transparent love (*e.g.* 1 Jn. 3:10). In short, Jesus resorts to a moral and ethical notion of descent as being of far more importance than merely physical descent, and as being already supported by Scripture.

At one level, therefore, Jesus can happily acknowledge that the Jews *are Abraham's descendants*, but it is the level of least interest and importance. Far more significant is their fickle mob psychology that can believe Jesus only (vv. 30, 31) when his teachings do not clash with their prejudices, and can turn murderous when their fundamental religious biases are called into question (7:32; 8:20, 37, 59). That is not conduct that attests spiritual descent from Abraham. Worse, it betrays a willingness to abandon Jesus' teaching (v. 31), thereby calling into question the integrity of their profession of faith: *you have no room for my word.*[1]

38. If the Jews are falsely claiming Abraham as their father, Jesus is rightly claiming God as his: he is passing on what he has seen in his Father's presence (*i.e.* he always acts just like his Father: *cf.* 3:11–13, 34; 5:19ff.; 6:46). Jesus' conduct displays his true paternity. Sadly, the same is true of the Jews: they do what they have heard from their father[2] – only they have not yet grasped that Jesus is referring to the devil himself (v. 44).

39–41a. The stern protest, *Abraham is our father*, doubtless misses the proleptic allusion to the devil. It is not mere repetition of a biological fact. The Jews are advancing the argument by saying, in effect, that even in the moral and ethical realm, they measure up well enough to be considered the descendants of Abraham. Jesus does not respond by again reiterating that spiritual and moral kinship is the only kind that matters – that point is now common ground between him and his opponents – but by highlighting the peculiar aspects of their conduct that are diametrically opposed to Abraham's. Abraham obeyed God's

---

[1]Lit. 'my word has no place (*ou chōrei*) in you', or 'my word does not operate in you'. Some commentators opt very strongly for one translation or the other, thinking the connection with vv. 30, 31 is thereby greatly improved, or, conversely, so thoroughly broken that v. 37 *must* be dealing with people other than the believers of vv. 30, 31 (*cf.* notes on v. 31). In fact, the choice makes very little difference.

[2]The possessive pronoun 'your' is omitted by some early witnesses. If we accept the omission as authentic, it is possible (though not necessary) to read the verb in the last clause as an imperative: 'do (*poieite*) the things that you have heard from the Father [*i.e.* God]'). But the evidence for omission of the pronoun is far from compelling, while the parallel in v. 41a strongly favours a statement rather than a command.

voice and followed his requirements, commandments, decrees and laws (Gn. 26:5). By contrast, the rising antipathy Jesus' interlocutors display to the one who has passed on the truth that he heard from God can only mean that, unlike Abraham, they have no real heart for God, no sensitivity to his voice. Their 'father' must therefore be someone else.

41b. Naturally enough, the Jews do not appreciate Jesus' insistence that their conduct disallows their claim to Abraham as their father. His charge makes them spiritual bastards: *We are not illegitimate children*, they protest. There may be one or both of two other overtones in these words:

(1) It is not at all impossible that the Jews are alluding to the irregularities connected with Jesus' birth. From their perspective, he displays considerable cheek to talk about paternity: *they* were not born of fornication (wink, wink). If this is a correct reading, then it is a further instance of Johannine irony, irony which extends beyond the virginal conception of Christ (*cf.* notes on 6:42) to the question of his ultimate origin in the Father (1:1–18; 3:17).

(2) It is also possible that this verse anticipates v. 48, where Jesus is charged with being a 'Samaritan'. Samaritans and Jews each fostered mutually antithetical accounts of the dubious origins of the other group. Unfortunately, the Samaritan views of the origins of the Jews are not well preserved. There is some evidence, however, that they thought Satan seduced Eve to produce Cain. If they also thought of these Jews as descendants of Cain rather than of Seth, then it is just possible that the Jews in this passage, thinking that Jesus is siding with the Samaritans against them, respond to the charge and deny that their origins lay in fornication.[1]

In any case, if Jesus will not allow them Abraham as their father, surely he cannot deny them God. Had not the LORD himself declared, 'Israel is my firstborn son' (Ex. 4:22), and 'I am Israel's father' (Je. 31:9; *cf.* Dt. 14:1–2)? In one sense, this is, for the Jews in this context, both a proud claim and the ultimate defiance: there is no turning back in the debate at this point. That the Evangelist records it may be in part his own wry way of referring to the unique origins of Jesus.

42. Jesus does not deny the truth of the Old Testament texts, but denies their applicability to his opponents. The implicit reason has already been given: spiritual sonship in the only sense that matters is attested by likeness and conduct, whether the 'father' is Abraham or God. The explicit criterion in this verse, however, is love for Jesus. Knowing with absolute certainty that he himself has come from God and has been sent by him (this recurring emphasis on Jesus' functional subordination harks back to 5:19ff.), Jesus can only conclude that if the Jews do not enthusiastically embrace him and love him, it must be because they themselves do not know the Father (*cf.* 1 Jn. 5:1). By

---

[1]*Cf.* J. Bowman, *BJRL* 40, 1957–58, pp. 306–308; Bruce, p. 199.

implication, of course, that means God's word about being a Father to Israel must apply to others.

43. The words of v. 42 have already hinted that there exists a fatal flaw in the character of Jesus' opponents even before he comes to them; vv. 44–45 now make the point explicit. If Jesus' 'language' (*lalia*, his 'spoken speech', what linguists would call his 'parole') is unclear to them, it is *because* they are unable to hear (*akouein*, almost with the sense 'to obey') his word (*logos*; NIV, 'what I say'). It is not that his idiom, the peculiar way Jesus dresses his message, is so difficult that they cannot comprehend what he is trying to say. That would suggest the fault is with him: he is a poor communicator. Rather, because they cannot truly 'hear' (including 'obey'!) his message, *i.e.* the thrust of his word, the content of the revelation of the incarnate Word, therefore they are unable to grasp the meaning of his outward speech. The flaw is therefore not with the communicator, but with those whose values and prejudices make them constitutionally unable to 'hear'.

44. Jesus has already established that if God were the 'Father' of these Jews, they would love him (v. 42). Since they do not, another paternity (once again an ethical and moral relationship) is attested. For the first time, the father of his opponents (under his analysis) is specifically identified: *You belong to your father, the devil.*[1] Precisely because this kind of sonship is predicated on kinship of behaviour and values, it is not surprising that Jesus' opponents want to carry out their father's desires (*epithymiai*, sometimes negatively, 'lusts'; sometimes neutrally, 'desires'). What are they? Two are mentioned: (1) The devil *was a murderer from the beginning*, probably a reference to the fall of Adam and Eve. By the success of his temptation, he robbed Adam of spiritual life, and through him brought death to the entire race (*cf.* Rom. 5:12). (2) He abandoned the truth, *for there is no truth in him. When he lies, he speaks his native language, for he is a liar and the father of lies.* Like his murder, the devil's lies are evident from the Garden of Eden on; for in the Garden God said, 'You will surely die' (Gn. 2:17), while the devil promptly retorted, 'You will not surely die'. Either God or the devil was lying; John accepts the given that 'it is impossible for God to lie' (Heb. 6:18). Just as God inevitably speaks the truth, the devil spontaneously gravitates to lying: *When he lies, he speaks his native language* (lit. 'he speaks out of his own [*sc.* nature or essential characteristics]').

45. The tragedy of the liar is not only that he deceives others, but that he does not hold to the truth (v. 44). Jesus' words in this verse are therefore very sombre. The first clause is not concessive ('*although* I tell the truth') but causal: '*because* I tell the truth, you do not believe in me'. The children of God will so love the truth that they will believe in Jesus; the children of the devil will be so characterized by lies that they will not

---

[1]The Greek of the first clause could be translated, 'You are of the father of the devil.' Some early Gnostics doubtless preferred to take it that way. The traditional rendering is correct (*cf.* 1 Jn. 3:8), with 'the devil' standing in apposition to 'the father'.

be able to accept the truth, precisely *because it is the truth*.

This explains unbelief. What is *not* explained in this verse is belief. If even the genuine disciples were once members of the fallen and rebellious world, until 'chosen out of the world' by Jesus (15:19), how did *they* come to believe the truth at a time in their lives when the truth itself would have evoked unbelief? The passage does not say; the answer has in fact been provided in John 6, and will be repeated in 8:47. What was necessary was that the Father draw them (6:44), that they be given to the Son (6:37), that they be taught by God (6:45) and chosen by Jesus (6:70). The need for the strong divine initiative emphasized in John 6 is powerfully explained in John 8. From an evangelistic point of view, this combination of themes strips away any ground of boasting or arrogance from those who do believe, while it challenges and threatens unbelievers at the very core of their being, insistently demanding that they reconsider the direction and entire array of values that have stamped their life to this point.

46–47. The first rhetorical question of v. 46 must not be misunderstood. Jesus does not ask whether anyone *thinks* he is guilty of sin. Clearly, many did (*e.g.* 5:18, where some thought he was guilty not only of breaking the Sabbath, but also of blasphemy by making himself equal with God). The question, rather, is whether anyone can *prove* him guilty of sin.[1] Jesus can raise a similar sort of challenge at his trial (18:23); probably the assumption of his question is that before the high court of heaven, his opponents cannot prove him guilty of sin. This is not because he has been sinning with a wonderful degree of underhandedness, but because he has never been guilty of sin. At one level, as Godet (2. 350) remarks, 'The *perfect* holiness of Christ is in this passage demonstrated, not by the silence of the Jews, who might have ignored the sins of their questioner, but by the assurance with which His direct consciousness of the purity of His whole life is in this question affirmed.' But at the level at which Jesus' rhetorical question is actually taken up in the rest of the verse, the challenge before Jesus' opponents is simpler. If the best theological minds, however much they may dislike Jesus' claims and dispute his teachings, find it impossible to marshall convincing reasons that would convict him of sin in (the heavenly) court, should they not begin to question themselves? Perhaps he is telling the truth, truth that is identified both with what Jesus says (v. 43) and with what God says (v. 47; *cf.* de la Potterie, 1. 61–64). And if he is, why do they not believe him? The reason is that only the one who *belongs to God hears what God says*. The conclusion is inevitable: *The reason you do not hear is that you do not belong to God* (*cf.* notes on v. 45).

48. When their theological argument fails, Jesus' opponents turn to personal abuse. Jews and Samaritans did not enjoy easy dealings (*cf.*

---

[1] The Greek construction could be taken to mean 'convict me [*i.e.* psychologically, personally] of sin', but in this context 'prove me guilty of sin' seems more appropriate. For further notes on the construction, *cf.* 16:8–11.

notes on 4:4, 9). As has been indicated, it is possible that some of Jesus' opponents thought that by casting aspersions on their paternity he was rather traitorously siding with the despised Samaritans (*cf.* notes on v. 41). The charge that Jesus was a Samaritan is found only here in the four Gospels. The charge of being demon-possessed is common enough (in John, *cf.* also 7:20; 8:52; 10:20), but its precise link with the accusation of being a Samaritan is uncertain. It may simply be that Jesus' accusers thought that for a *Jew* to question the paternity of other Jews was so despicable that only demon-possession could explain it.

49. But Jesus denies he is demon-possessed. His claims and behaviour are not the fruit of arrogance, dementia, Samaritanism or the occult, but simply of obedience to the Father (*cf.* 3:34; 5:19ff.; 8:38; 17:8, 14). By saying and doing always and only what the Father gives him to say and do, he honours the Father. By refusing to respond positively to those same words and deeds, his hearers dishonour him, and therefore the one who sent him (5:23).

50. Jesus can truly say that he honours the Father (v. 49) only if he can also truly say that he does not seek glory (*cf.* notes on 1:14, 5:44) for himself. Unlike others, he pursues only the glory that comes from God. What others think is immaterial; God's approval is everything, for *he is the judge* (*cf.* 1 Cor. 4:2–5).

51. Although Jesus has briefly responded to the charge of his opponents, the purpose of his coming and of all he has had to say has been the salvation of his hearers (*cf.* 3:16, 17), not personal self-promotion. Perhaps it is the mention of God as judge (v. 50) that triggers his return to the central purpose of his mission. With the strong asseveration *I tell you the truth* (*cf.* notes on 1:51), Jesus again declares that if someone keeps his word, *i.e.* believes it, cleaves to it, obeys and lives by it (equivalent to *remaining* in Jesus' word: *cf.* notes on v. 31), *he will never see death*. After all, Jesus has the words of eternal life (*cf.* 6:63, 68). 'The assurance relates to life which physical death cannot extinguish, and so to the death of the spirit; the believer receives eternal life, i.e., the life of the kingdom of God, over which death has no power and which is destined for resurrection' (Beasley-Murray, p. 137).[1] The thought is similar to 5:24; 6:40, 47; 11:25–26.

52. 'To taste death' (*cf.* Mk. 9:1; Heb. 2:9) and 'to see death' (v. 51) simply mean 'to die', *i.e.* to experience death. To the Jews, thinking at the level of the strictly literal and physical, these expressions all refer to the death of the body, a matter of relatively small moment to John. They reason that Abraham heard and obeyed the word of God, yet died; the prophets heard, obeyed and taught the word of God, and they too died. For Jesus to suggest that Jesus' word is superior to what Abraham and the prophets mediated to others, so that if someone keeps Jesus' word

---

[1]*Contra* Haenchen (2. 32), who states, without warrant, that this hope *replaces* the expectation of a future parousia.

he or she will never taste death, is so preposterous that only a demonic illusion could account for it.

53. The form of their question, *Are you greater than our father Abraham?*, expects a negative answer (as in 4:12). Johannine irony strikes again, for his readers know that the correct answer is the opposite of what the Jews expect. NIV's *Who do you think you are?* is too periphrastic to catch the flavour of the original, which might better be rendered, 'Whom do you make yourself?' or 'Whom do you make yourself out to be?' (so Bruce, p. 203). The truth of the matter, of course, is that their question completely misses the central points Jesus (and this Gospel) have been making. Jesus does not make himself or exalt himself to be anything. Far from it: he is the most obedient and dependent of men, uniquely submissive to his Father (*cf*. vv. 28, 38, 42, 50; *cf*. notes on 5:16–30).

54. Jesus refutes any suggestion that he has promoted himself. He well understands that any self-praise, any self-glory, independent of the glory of God, *means nothing* (*cf*. Heb. 5:5). That is why his own submission is so absolute. At the same time, however, Jesus insists that the Father *is the one who glorifies me* (*cf*. notes on 5:23; 8:50; 17:1, 4–5). From Jesus' perspective, the irony is that his opponents claim this God as their own, but they display no knowledge of this God's profound commitment to glorify his unique Son (*cf*. 5:37ff.) . The nature of that glorification (*cf*. notes on 1:14), of course, is not in the public display some might have appreciated, but in the ignominy of the cross and consequent return to the glory the Son enjoyed with the Father before the world began (17:5).

55. In one sense, the charge that these Jews do not know God is of a piece with some Old Testament prophetic denunciations (*e.g.* Ho. 4:1; 6:6), and is implicit in Old Testament prophecies that predict a time when the people *would* know God (*e.g.* Je. 31:31ff.). But the sharp contrast between the people and Jesus cannot be paralleled in the Old Testament. Isaiah could lament that he was a man of unclean lips and lived amongst a people of unclean lips (Is. 6:5), but Jesus insists that, quite unlike his opponents, he truly does know God (*cf*. 3:11–13). For him to deny such knowledge of God would make him the liar his opponents become when they claim they do know him. (On the verbs for 'to know', *cf*. notes on 7:27.) Jesus knows God, and invariably keeps his word (*cf*. v. 29, 'I always do what pleases him'). In John, knowledge of God cannot be separated from obedience.

56. If the truth be told, the Abraham to whom the Jews have made such frequent appeal in this chapter (hence *Your father Abraham* rather than 'our father Abraham'; *cf*. 'your own Law', v. 17) *rejoiced at the thought of seeing my day; he saw it and was glad*. The verb rendered 'rejoiced' (*agalliaomai*) does not necessarily bear overtones of the Jubilee (*cf*. notes on 5:35), but it is strong. To what event or stance in Abraham's life could such strong 'exultation' rightly be ascribed?

Based on Genesis 15:17–21, Rabbi Akiba argued that God disclosed to Abraham the secrets of the age to come (*i.e.* of the messianic age), though other rabbis preferred to think that God revealed to Abraham the secrets of this world only (cf. *Genesis Rabbah* 44:25ff.; 59:6). Some scholars (*e.g.* Lindars, p. 335) propose that John 8:56 means Abraham was already in paradise, seeing Jesus in his ministry. There is no biblical sanction for this perspective, and the development of the argument in vv. 57–58 makes it unlikely. It has also been suggested that Abraham rejoiced when he announced to Isaac, on the way to the sacrifice, 'God himself will provide a lamb for the burnt offering, my son' (Gn. 22:8).[1] Certainly the *Akedah*, the 'binding of Isaac', played a significant role in Jewish and Christian thought about sacrifice and atonement. That Abraham 'rejoiced' is taken by some to refer to his laughter at the prospect of a son (Gn. 17:17, interpreted as joy, not scorn, as in Philo, *Mut.* 154–169). Certainly there was a Jewish tradition, based partly on Genesis 17:17 and partly on Genesis 21:6, and reflected in Targum Onkelos (an Aramaic paraphrase), *Jubilees* 16:16–29 and elsewhere, that Abraham rejoiced greatly at the birth of his son Isaac.[2] If this birth is understood as the onset of the promise that through Abraham all the nations of the earth would be blessed, then Abraham's laughter/joy is connected with his perception that the promised blessings still to come were in process of realization in the birth of his son.

Whatever the allusion, it is unlikely that Jesus' opponents took umbrage because they heard him ascribing powers of foresight to the patriarch Abraham. It is altogether likely that some of them, at least, believed that Abraham knew in advance of the messianic age. The point of tension arose because of the way Jesus phrases this: not 'Your father Abraham rejoiced to see the messianic age', but 'Your father Abraham rejoiced to see my day'. The 'day' or the 'day of the Lord' becomes *Jesus'* day. Even if 'to see my day' does not mean some prophetic vision of the literal fulfilment of prophecy in Jesus and his ministry, but some vision, however vague, of the promise inherent in the binding of Isaac or (better) of the covenant promising that in him all the nations of the earth would be blessed (Gn. 12:1ff. *et al.* – hence NIV's addition of 'at the thought of'), the fact remains that Jesus identifies the ultimate fulfilment of all Abraham's hopes and joys with his own person and work.

57. A claim like that of v. 56, if valid, would mean the overthrow of all the points they had been arguing. It was easier to interpret Jesus' words rather crassly, as if Jesus had claimed to be Abraham's natural contemporary. Then it could be handily dismissed: Jesus was not yet

---

[1]Bruce (p. 207, n. 19) draws attention to the *Testament of Levi* 18:6, where Levi predicts the coming of a 'new priest' for whom 'the heavens shall be opened, and from the temple of glory shall come upon him sanctification, with the Father's voice as from Abraham to Isaac' (apparently referring to Gn. 22:8, since this is the only text in the Bible that records words spoken by Abraham to Isaac).

[2]Pierre Grelot, *RevQum* 13, 1988, pp. 621–628.

fifty (a round figure, and no indication of Jesus' age at the time, despite the deductions made by a number of church Fathers), while Abraham had been dead for two millennia.

58. Once more Jesus solemnly announces, *I tell you the truth* (*cf.* notes on 1:51). If he had wanted to claim only that he existed before Abraham, it would have been simpler to say, 'Before Abraham was, I was.' Instead, bringing forward the use of *egō eimi* found in vv. 24, 28, Jesus says, 'Before Abraham was born, *I am.*' Whatever doubts may attach themselves to whether or not *egō eimi* should be taken absolutely in vv. 24, 28, here there can be none. Moreover, the strong linguistic connections with Isaiah 40 – 55 are supported by obvious conceptual links: *cf.* 'I, the LORD – with the first of them and with the last – *I am he*' (Is. 41:4); 'Yes, and from ancient days I am he' (Is. 43:13). *Cf.* Ps. 90:2. That the Jews take up stones to kill him presupposes that they understand these words as some kind of blasphemous claim to deity. Nevertheless, as in 1:1, so here: neither the Word nor the Son is so identified with God that there is no remainder. *Cf.* notes on v. 24.

Abraham looked forward to the messianic age, the age that was, in John's understanding, inaugurated by the incarnation of the Word who already was 'in the beginning' (1:1), like God, eternal. In conformity with John's Prologue, Jesus takes to himself one of the most sacred of divine expressions of self-reference, and makes the *assumption* of that expression the proof of his superiority over Abraham (a point rather muddied by Bultmann, pp. 327–328; Schnackenburg, 2. 88–89; 223–224).

59. Stoning was prescribed for blasphemy (Lv. 24:16; *cf.* Mishnah *Sanhedrin* 7:4), though of course such stoning was supposed to be the result of a calm judicial decision, not the fruit of mob violence. Jesus is saying things that only God should say. On the assumption that he has no right whatsoever to speak this way, the Jews are scandalized.

Jesus repeatedly escapes arrest, until the appointed hour of the Father arrives (7:30, 44; 8:20; *cf.* 18:6). How Jesus slipped away, and with what degree of supernatural intervention, is not made clear. Davies (pp. 290–296) continues his study of the way Jesus in the Fourth Gospel displaces and fulfils 'holy space' by noting how, after Jesus replaces Bethel, Sabbath, manna, the water and light ceremonies of the Feast of Tabernacles, yet before he is actually consecrated (at the Feast of Dedication in 10:22ff.) to replace the tabernacle and the temple, he here symbolically leaves *the temple grounds*, like the *šᵉkînâ*-glory (*cf.* notes on 1:14) abandoning the temple. Schnackenburg (2. 224) cites Augustine: 'As man [Jesus] flees from the stones, but woe to those from whose heart of stone God flees!' (*In Johan. Tract.* xliii. 18).

Additional notes

42. Westcott (2. 19–20), followed by Dodd (*IFG*, p. 259), suggests the words 'for I came from God (*ek tou theou exēlthon*) and now am here (*kai hēkō*)' may refer to more than the incarnation and immediate mission respectively. Westcott assigns full classical force to the preposition *ek* ('out of'); he takes a similar step in 16:28, where Jesus says, 'I came forth from (*para* plus the genitive) the Father'. By contrast, the preposition *apo* ('from') is used in 13:3; 16:30, clearly referring to the incarnation. Westcott and Dodd therefore conclude that here and in 16:28, the words explain the true divinity of the Son: the Father is the 'source and fountain' of his Son. Jesus 'had his origin in the being of the Father' (Dodd), not of course suggesting that there was a time when he was not (*cf.* notes on 1:1) but referring to that which later came to be known as the eternal generation of the Son. The argument is plausible, but cannot rest securely on distinctions in the prepositions themselves. Hellenistic usage of the prepositions tended to blur many fine distinctions that classical Greek preserved.

57. A good case can be made for arguing that the Jews' incredulous question should be rendered, 'You have seen Abraham for fewer than fifty years!' – as if they are prepared to grant the possibility that Jesus has communed with Abraham, but not for long. *Cf.* Edouard Delebecque, *RB* 93, 1986, pp. 85–92.

2. Jesus heals a man born blind (9:1-41)

Thematically, this chapter is tied to the Feast of Tabernacles (ch. 8) through the explicit reference to Jesus as the light of the world (9:5; *cf.* 8:12). This chapter portrays what happens when the light shines: some are made to see, like this man born blind, while others, who think they see, turn away, blinded, as it were, by the light (9:39-41). At the same time, this chapter prepares the way for ch. 10, where a sharp contrast is drawn between the good shepherd, who gives his life for his sheep, and other religious leaders, like those in ch. 9, who are nothing but thieves and hirelings. The shepherd/sheep theme runs beyond the first part (10:1–21) to the second part of the chapter (10:22ff.), which is unambiguously tied to the feast of Dedication (10:22), about three months later than the Feast of Tabernacles. This has the effect of making it unclear just when the miracle of ch. 9 took place, though apparently at some point between the two Feasts (*cf.* Brown, 1. 388–390).

John 9 has been a favourite test case for source critics and others who have attempted to delineate what was going on in John's community. Haenchen (2. 41), for instance, argues that the Evangelist composed only vv. 4–5, 39–41, all the rest stemming from a source. The 'source' uses signs to show that Jesus is the Messiah, whereas the Evangelist views the signs as pointing beyond themselves to the spiritual realm. This antithesis is without merit; John's Gospel is far more nuanced. The signs attest who Jesus is precisely *because* they point beyond themselves, and even then they do not guarantee insight. Even if Haenchen's antithesis were accepted, Painter has shown that there are numerous symbolic elements within the alleged 'source' that invite the thoughtful reader to look beyond the raw material.[1] Fortna (p. 71) sees in vv. 1–8 a conflation of parts of a miracle story and a pronouncement story (a narrative whose form and content are designed to make a 'pronouncement' as to who Jesus is, or the nature of the kingdom, or the like). Again, however, the criteria for such source-critical work are not very convincing.[2] That John may have used written sources in the composition of his work, few would doubt (cf. Lk. 1:1–4). That he so miserably failed to integrate them into the finished Gospel that they can now be retrieved, piece by piece, demands an inordinate amount of faith in the skills of the source critic, especially in a book as homogenous as this (cf. Introduction, § III).

By far the most influential work on this chapter in recent years is that of J. Louis Martyn (HTFG, pp. 24ff.), who uses John 9 as the critical 'test case' for his overarching thesis. Martyn believes that John's Gospel was written to help the church, probably in Ephesus, in its degenerating relationships with the local synagogue. To that end, John composed several of his chapters on two tiers, or at two levels. The first level takes place 'back there', during the ministry of Jesus; the second takes place in the life of the church in Ephesus. In ch. 9, Martyn thinks that vv. 1–5 operate on both levels: Jesus was doubtless believed to have performed a miracle much like this (whether he did or not Martyn judges to be of little importance), but at the same time there was a Christian preacher ministering in the Jewish quarters of Ephesus who performed a similar miracle (again, whether it actually occurred is judged of little significance) whom Jesus symbolizes in these verses. From v. 6 on, however, all reference to the 'back there' level, the level of the historical Jesus, vanishes from view, as the Evangelist devotes all his energy to sorting out the church/synagogue disputes in his own day. Martyn then adopts a similar approach in several other chapters of John.

What is it in Martyn's mind that warrants the theory? In part, of course, his work fits into a broader stream of Johannine study that devotes most of its attention to working out what the 'Johannine community' is like. The prevalence of Old Testament themes and motifs impels many to suppose that this Gospel has emerged out of the matrix of church/synagogue controversy. But the definitive evidence, for Martyn, lies in parts of the text that he judges decisively anachronisitic. In this chapter, his prime example is in the Greek word rendered 'put out of the synagogue'. Many have disputed his conclusions (cf. notes on v. 22), but even if undoubted anachronisms were found, it is hard to see how such evidence could justify two-tier readings of parts of the chapter, or the assumption that large parts are necessarily descriptive of what took place only in John's day. And in fact, most commentators who

[1]John Painter, JSNT 28, 1986, pp. 31–61 – although unfortunately Painter accepts Haenchen's fundamental antithesis, and merely argues for a more restricted source.
[2]Cf. D. A. Carson, JBL 97, 1978, pp. 411–429.

praise Martyn's work quickly concede that the details of his reconstruction are so finely spun that they prove unconvincing. Then, after such sweeping disavowals, they credit Martyn with supporting the currently dominant reconstruction of the *Sitz im Leben* ('life-setting') of the Johannine community. The truth seems to be that, had Martyn restricted himself to generalizations about the Johannine community, his book would have provoked little stir, but would have been registered as one more opinion in support of the currently dominant view. Instead, he has attempted a detailed reconstruction, supposing that such a reconstruction may legitimately be read off the surface of a text ostensibly written about the Christ who had left this world's scene six decades earlier. The irony is that most scholars discount the details, yet still hail the work as a valuable support of the received tradition.

Detailed criticism of Martyn's thesis cannot be attempted here. Occasional remarks intrude into the following notes, especially at v. 22. The major concern of what follows is to make sense of the text as it stands, to show how it should be taken as a responsible description of what took place in the life of Jesus, and to demonstrate how it fits into the dominant purpose of the Evangelist, that the readers may believe that the Christ, the Son of God, is Jesus (*cf.* notes on 20:30–31).

a. The sign (*9:1–12*)

1. *As he went along* is sufficiently vague as a connector that very little precise information about time and place can be deduced. Because of the connections ch. 9 has with chs. 8 and 10 (*cf.* notes, above), we must suppose Jesus is still in Jerusalem, presumably at some point between the Feast of Tabernacles and the Feast of Dedication. How it became known that the man was *blind from birth* is not disclosed. Granted the symbolism of the chapter, it is likely that this detail, in addition to heightening the effect of the miracle, signals that human beings are spiritually blind from birth. *Cf.* notes on 12:37ff.

2. The disciples assume, like most Palestinian Jews of their day, that sin and suffering are intimately connected. In one sense, they are correct; they are simply working out the entailments of the fall (Gn. 3). If rabbis argued that there is no death without sin (B. *Shabbath* 55a; proved by referring to Ezk. 18:20) and no suffering without guilt (citing Ps. 89:32), Paul in the New Testament would certainly agree (Rom. 1 – 2; 3:10ff.). But once theologians move from generalizing statements about the origin of the human race's maladies to tight connections between the sins and the sufferings *of an individual*, they go beyond the biblical evidence (whether from the Old Testament or the New). That a specific illness or experience of suffering *can* be the direct consequence of a specific sin, few would deny (*e.g.* Miriam's revolt, Nu. 12; notes on Jn. 5:14; *cf.* 1 Cor. 11:30). That it is invariably so, numerous biblical texts flatly deny (*e.g.* Job; Gal. 4:13; 2 Cor. 12:7).

In this instance, the disciples presuppose the tightest possible connection. This specific individual is suffering from blindness; therefore some specific, individual sin must have been the antecedent cause. Because he was born blind, it must be that either he sinned in the womb (certainly regarded as possible by some Jews),[1] or his parent sinned in some way that implicated him (*e.g.* when a pregnant woman worships in a pagan temple her unborn foetus was regarded as participating in the pagan rite, *Canticles Rabbah* I, 6, § 3). On this point, the disciples have not progressed beyond Job's 'miserable comforters'.

3. Although Jesus does not disavow the generalizing connection between sin and suffering, he completely disavows a universalizing of *particular* connections. In this instance, he insists that *neither this man nor his parents sinned*. Rather, *this happened so that the work* [lit. 'works'] *of God might be displayed in his life*. Formally, the concluding clause could be taken as a result clause ('with the result that') or a purpose clause ('in order that'); either way, John certainly does not think that the occurrence of blindness from birth was outside the sweep of God's control, and therefore of his purpose. The attempt to read this as an imperatival clause ('Let the works of God be displayed in him!') is just barely possible, but rendered highly unlikely by the parallel in 11:4.

4–5. The combination of a plural pronoun and a singular pronoun ('*we* must do the work of him who sent *me*') emphasizes the exclusiveness of Jesus as the sent one (*cf.* 6:38) in preparation for v. 7, while associating his disciples with him in the work. Martyn (pp. 7–8) takes this as evidence of a post-resurrection perspective. In one sense, that is correct, for elsewhere Jesus looks forward to the continuation of his ministry through his disciples (14:12). That surely does not mean, however, that there was no sense in which his disciples were associated with his ministry while Jesus was still on the way to the cross – a point well attested in the Synoptics (Mt. 10; Lk. 10). (The plural at Jn. 3:11 probably has another explanation: *cf.* notes there.)

There is special urgency in performing the works of God (NIV again offers the sing. form) *as long as it is day*, *i.e.* while Jesus is still with them. He is himself the light of the world (v. 5) – a repetition of 8:12, without the dramatic *egō eimi*. This does not mean that Jesus stops being the light of the world once he has ascended. It means, rather, that the light shines brightly while he lives out his human life up to the moment of his glorification. Throughout that period he is the light that exposes the world, judges the world, saves the world. Those who enjoy his light will be engulfed by darkness when he is taken away (12:35). Then night descends, when *no-one can work*. 'Night' regularly bears metaphorical freight in John, akin to 'darkness' (*cf.* notes on 3:2 [*cf.* 19:39]; 11:10; 13:30). Once Jesus has been glorified, the Holy Spirit, the 'Paraclete', continues many of the functions Jesus performed in the days of his flesh (chs. 14 – 16). Jesus' stance towards the world remains salvific: he has

---

[1]Thus in *Genesis Rabbah* 63:6 (a rabbinical commentary) on Gn. 25:22, various disputants discuss the ante-natal conduct of Esau and Jacob, and Ps. 58:3 is cited to prove that Esau displayed sinful inclinations from the womb. *Cf.* further SB 2. 527–529.

more sheep to bring , not of this sheep pen (10:16), more people to bring into perfect oneness, people who will believe through the witness of the Holy Spirit (15:26–27) and the first believers (17:20–26). In that mediated sense, the light continues to shine.

The focus here, however, is not what prevails after Jesus is glorified and has poured out his Spirit (7:37–39), but the darkness of the period when Jesus is first taken from his disciples. The association of the disciples with Jesus' work ('we must do . . .') refers to the period before Jesus is taken away by the cross, not to the period when, empowered by the Spirit, they will work until he returns. Against those who see vv. 4–5 as a late insertion into the flow of the argument, it must be said that these verses are crucial precisely because they signal to the reader how the healing of the blind man is to be understood. It is not just a miracle; it is a sign, the work of the Father, mediated through the sent one, to shed light on those who live in darkness. The Evangelist is thus telling his readers that the long-awaited Messiah really is Jesus (cf. notes on vv. 30, 31), that Jesus' symbol-laden miracles attest the point, and that his departure brought down a 'night' on many Jewish leaders who refused to open their eyes to the light, but also, by implication, that it would be disastrous for people still to disbelieve at the time of writing, compounding the sinful blindness of the original rejection of the Messiah by a continued rejection of the Messiah's messengers.

6. The words *Having said this* tightly tie v. 6 to vv. 4–5. Jesus has just declared that he is the light of the world (v. 5); he now proceeds to illustrate the point by giving light to the man born blind. He is thereby obeying the one who sent him (v. 4), while many around him are shutting out the light.

Unlike 4:47 or 11:3, but much as in 5:6, Jesus here takes the initiative. 'The blind man, introduced as the theme of a theological debate, becomes the object of divine mercy and a place of revelation' (Barrett, p. 358). The use of saliva calls to mind the healing of the deaf and dumb man in the Decapolis (Mk. 7:33) and of the blind man in Bethsaida (Mk. 8:23). In both those instances, however, the saliva was apparently directly applied; here a mud pack is made with the saliva, and applied to the man's eyes. It is extremely difficult to decide just what this signifies. Scholars often cite rabbinic opinion to the effect that the saliva of the firstborn of a father has healing properties, but not the saliva of the firstborn of a mother (B. *Baba Bathra* 126b). But because the use of spittle in the surrounding pagan culture was so often associated with magical practices,[1] it appears that rabbis more commonly condemned the use of saliva (so, for instance, Rabbi Akiba, in Tosephta, *Sanhedrin* 12:10; cf. SB 2. 15). Not a few church Fathers saw an allusion to Genesis 2:7: since

---

[1]There are many examples listed in the major commentaries. The one most commonly cited is the healing of the blind soldier, Valerius Aper, apparently by Asclepius, in which no spittle was used, but an eye-salve made of the blood of a white cock and honey (cf. A. Deissmann, *Light from the Ancient East* [Hodder and Stoughton, 1910], p. 132).

God made human beings out of the dust of the ground, Jesus, in an act of creation, used a little dust to make eyes that were otherwise lacking. Calvin (1. 241) suggests the mudpack was designed to double the intensity of the blindness in order to magnify the cure (not unlike the water poured over Elijah's altar on Mount Carmel). Still others think there is some sort of faith-inducing symbolism here.

Another suggestion, recently put forward by David Smith,[1] has its attractions. Building on the work of the cultural anthropologist Mary Douglas,[2] Smith notes that, judging by the Old Testament and by later Jewish tradition, Palestinian Jews, like people in many other cultures around the world, believed that human excreta (including urine, breast milk, saliva, menstrual flow, *etc.*) were all forms of (ceremonial) pollutant, 'dirt'. In such tribes, under certain conditions that same 'dirt', in the hands of people authorized with the appropriate power, could be transformed into an instrument of blessing. Thus blood and saliva pollute, but in the right context blood cleanses and saliva cures. Certainly uncleanness in the Old Testament can be conveyed by saliva (Lv. 15:8). If the reversal of the taboos also applies (and here the evidence is admittedly scanty), then by using spittle as part of his treatment Jesus is making a claim to have religious authority. The situation is not entirely unlike the healing of a man with leprosy: by touching him Jesus does not contract the leper's uncleanness, but heals the leper of his disease (Mt. 8:1–4).

In this context, the Pharisees certainly express inordinate interest in *how* the blind man was healed (vv. 15, 19, 26). Elsewhere there is ample evidence that Jesus was prepared to break various ritual taboos (Mt. 8:1–4; 23:23–26; Lk. 11:37–38). Considerable anthropological evidence indicates that where prevailing religious values focus centrally on pollution and taboos expressed in terms of human excreta, there is corresponding anxiety about the social and political structures. In other words, the taboos surrounding the human body give symbolic expression to massive social constraints. To attack the symbols, as Jesus clearly did on some occasions (whether or not this be judged to be one of them), would be perceived as an attack on the social, political, and religious system. This interpretation squares with at least one major reading of who the Pharisees were and what interested them, and with the witness of the Fourth Gospel that records the fear gripping the authorities over the possibility that their fiefdom could be overthrown (11:48, 50).

7. When the mud paste made of Jesus' spittle and a bit of dirt had been applied to the man's eyes, he was told to wash it off in the pool of Siloam. If the significance of the saliva is somewhat obscure, John will not allow 'Siloam' the same freedom. As he elsewhere explains semitic words (*cf.* notes on 1:38), so here: *this word means Sent.* 'Siloam' is

---

[1] David Smith, *TrinJ* 6, 1985, pp. 151–156.

[2] Mary Douglas, *Purity and Danger: An Analysis of the Concepts of Pollution and Taboo* (Ark, 1984).

transliteration for Heb. *šilôah̬*, which is itself derived from the verb *šālah̬*, 'to send'. Isaiah speaks of 'the gently flowing waters of Shiloah' (Is. 8:6; *cf.* Ne. 3:15). The pool of Siloam, south-west of the City of David, received its water through a channel which carried (or 'sent') it from the spring of Gihon in the Kidron valley. Probably it is to be identified with the 'Lower Pool' (Is. 22:9) or 'Old Pool' (Is. 22:11), a little way to the south-east of what tourist guides refer to as the pool of Siloam. The latter has enjoyed this name at least since the time of Constantine, but it is the 'Upper Pool' (*cf.* Is. 7:3; 36:2) which receives its water from the Gihon through the tunnel Hezekiah had built before the attack of 701 BC (2 Ki. 20:20; 2 Ch. 32:4, 30; Is. 22:11; *cf.* Wilkinson, pp. 104–108).

The suitability of drawing attention to Siloam may have depended simply on its name. As it was called 'Sent', so Jesus was supremely the sent one (*cf.* notes on 20:21). Moreover, in Isaiah 8:6 the Jews reject the waters of Shiloah; here they reject Jesus. Both Jewish and Christian interpreters have understood Genesis 49:10 messianically, where a similar term appears: the sceptre will not depart from Judah until *Shiloh* comes. Further, the water for the water-pouring rites of the Feast of Tabernacles (*cf.* notes on 7:37–39) was drawn from the pool of Siloam. All of these associations prompt Grigsby to see in the washing in the pool a symbol of the believer's salvific 'bath', an implicit and 'universal command to all unbelievers to wash in the fountain of cleansing waters at Calvary'.[1] Granted that Jesus himself is the sent one, and that the granting of sight to this blind man symbolizes the spiritual illumination without which one cannot see the true light from God, these extensions do not seem farfetched.

Attempts to see in this washing an elaboration of baptism (*e.g.* Brown, 1. 380–382) are far less convincing (*cf.* especially Schnackenburg, 2. 257–258). 'The Evangelist's profound use of symbolism in his delineation of the word and works of Jesus should not be extended to an allegorizing of details of which the Evangelist himself provides no hint' (Beasley-Murray, p. 162).

So far the initiative has been entirely with Jesus. Now the man (who of course has still not seen Jesus) obeys and washes, *and came home seeing*. John's readers know that, although the healing is as thorough as the blind man's obedience, the power itself came not from the obedience, nor from a pool called 'Sent', but from the 'sent one' himself.

Formally, Jesus now drops out of the narrative until v. 35, while the healed man stands in centre stage; yet the healed man is merely the occasion of the discussion, the stone of offence, while at the heart of the ensuing debate is Jesus himself (*cf.* Blank, p. 255).

8–9. A congenitally blind man was unlikely to be able to support himself by any means other than begging. His neighbours had become

---

[1]Bruce Grigsby, *NovT* 27, 1985, pp. 227–235. He is on more doubtful grounds, however, when he wants to draw in baptism as well: *cf.* John Painter, *art. cit.*, pp. 44–46.

so used to the sight of him doing so that they were flabbergasted to think the blind beggar could now see. Some found it easier to believe that the blind man had somehow disappeared, and the fellow before them was someone else, someone who bore a remarkable resemblance to their blind neighbour. As elsewhere, John summarizes the buzzing intercourse of astonished but ignorant opinion (*cf.* 7:12, 25–27, 31). It is all cut short by the insistent witness of the one who had been blind: *I am the man*.

10–12. Naturally, the man's neighbours (not the Pharisees: they are not introduced until v. 13) want to know what happened, and the healed man accurately summarizes what took place. Unlike the healed paralytic in ch. 5, this man appears sharp, quick-witted, and eventually quite sardonic toward religious leaders who would not face facts. The colour in the two personalities testifies not only to the Evangelist's stylistic versatility, but to the differences in people to whom Jesus ministered.

The only testimony that the man born blind can offer at this point is his summary of the bare facts of the case. He refers to the one who gave him light as 'the man they call Jesus' – *i.e.* he had learned of his name from the talk of the time, but had not yet seen him, and still had little theological opinion about him. That his friends ask, *Where is this man?*, does not betray a desire to check their neighbour's story, but a natural desire to meet the man who had performed such an astonishing miracle. But not even the healed man could answer the question.

b. The investigation by the Pharisees (9:13–34)

i. The first interrogation of the healed man (9:13–17)
13. There is no need to ascribe malice to those who *brought to the Pharisees the man who had been blind*. They could not have known that the healed man would be subjected to interrogation and expulsion from the synagogue. In a day when almost all events bore religious overtones, the extraordinary healing cried out for comment by the religious authorities – much more so than the way that, in today's world, after a significant international event millions of people will expect the Foreign Office or the State Department to express an opinion.

But why to the Pharisees? Why not mention the Sanhedrin, or at least the scribes and Sadducees (*cf.* notes on 1:19, 24)? But it is unlikely that the crowds were attempting to elicit a judicial opinion from the highest court in the land. They simply wanted advice from their local synagogue leaders. At that level, the Sadducees counted for relatively little; the Pharisees counted for far more. If scribes (the finest experts in the law, and those who taught it in the synagogues and in private) are not explicitly mentioned, it may be because most scribes were, theologically, Pharisees; indeed, by the time John wrote, all scribes belonged to that party (which had changed quite a bit, owing not least to the devastation of Jerusalem in AD 70). In short, John pictures the healed man's neighbours turning to their local religious leaders and asking them what they should make of the healing. For the same reason, the threatened excommunication (v. 22) is from the local synagogue: there is no evidence it is a national ban from every synagogue, or a ban from the temple.

14. For the first time, John mentions that the healing had taken place on a Sabbath. Though some see this as a late intrusion into the narrative (*e.g.* Becker, p. 315), the suggestion overlooks the fact that this detail governs much of the ensuing discussion. As in 5:9, 16ff., however, the Evangelist does not linger long on Sabbath issues *per se*, but on the weightier Christological issues to which a Sabbath healing gives rise.

From the point of view of some Pharisees, at least, Jesus had transgressed the oral law regarding the Sabbath on two, and perhaps three, points. Healing itself was forbidden, except for cases where life itself was in danger (*cf.* notes on 5:9, 16; 7:21ff.; SB 1. 623–629) – an exception inapplicable here, since the man was born blind. Moreover, amongst the prohibited categories of work was kneading (Mishnah *Shabbath* 7:2), and making mud from spittle and dirt might well have struck the leaders as falling under that prohibition. And finally, there was a division of opinion amongst the authorities as to whether or not anointing the eyes was legal on a Sabbath (B. *Abodah Zarah* 28b). The combination of these factors transformed the sense of open, probing amazement they should have experienced into suspicion, doubt, and theological umbrage.

15. Apparently the Pharisees launched a serious inquiry. Doubtless the healed man gave them a full report. John records only a condensed version. Interestingly enough, the focus of this condensation is on the 'how' of the miracle (*cf.* notes at the beginning of the chapter).

16. Earlier, the crowd was divided over Jesus (7:40–43); now the authorities are similarly at odds.[1] They are divided into two groups. The first, beginning their reasoning by focusing on the Sabbath, and convinced that their interpretation of the Sabbath is correct and that therefore Jesus is in violation of the law of God, judges that the healing miracle itself is not an adequate attestation of his authority. After all, the law of Moses warns against false prophets and those who foretell by dreams, insisting that even if what they predict comes true they must nevertheless be put to death if by their teaching they are drawing people away from the LORD (Dt. 13:1–5). They have no choice: they must conclude that *This man is not from God.* In this context, *from God* does not refer to Jesus' metaphysical origins. What this group is denying is much simpler: Jesus has not been sent 'from God' in any sense, *i.e.* he is not God's messenger, not even in the way John the Baptist was 'sent from God' (1:6).

---

[1]Schlatter (p. 227) presents evidence that the division of opinion roughly followed the schools of Shammai and Hillel respectively, the former arguing from first theological principles ('anyone who breaks the law is a sinner'), the latter from the established facts of the case ('Jesus has performed a good work').

The other group, astounded at the healing miracle itself, finds it hard to believe that Jesus is a sinner. Only the power of God can heal a man born blind. If Jesus performed the miracle, it must be the power of God at work – and surely God does not use as the agent of his power a public sinner. By implication, this means that whatever Jesus has done on the Sabbath needs to be weighed again.

The verse is steeped in irony. Taken in its strongest form, the second argument is worthless, even if the conclusion is sound. Not only the Old Testament (Dt. 13:1–5) but also the New (*e.g.* Mt. 7:21–23; 2 Thes. 2:9) insists that miracles cannot be an infallible guide to spiritual authority. If Moses' rod could become a snake, so could the rods of the Egyptian magicians. This does not mean miracles have *no* attesting force. They are sometimes seen as 'signs of the apostles' (*cf.* 2 Cor. 12:12). In the Fourth Gospel, although any demand for signs is rebuked (*cf.* notes on 4:48), yet Jesus prefers faith based on signs to no faith at all (10:38; 14:11). In other words, the second group employs at best a weak argument, but comes up with the truth, however hestitantly expressed. The first group presents an argument that is logically far more compelling, *provided* their interpretation of the Sabbath is correct. John's sympathetic readers know that the first group's conclusion is wrong: Jesus is indeed *from God*, in ways far more profound than the religious authorities of Jesus' day could imagine. Inevitably, that means their understanding of the Sabbath is also wrong (*cf.* notes on 5:16ff.; 7:21ff.).

17. The division of opinion amongst the religious authorities prompts them to question the man who had been healed. He had no particular expertise in law, theology or Scripture, but, as the Pharisees remark, *it was your eyes he opened*. The question forces him to take sides, and, unlike the man in ch. 5, he instantly sides with Jesus. The confession *He is a prophet* may reflect a man in his spiritual infancy, but it is a step in the right direction, an improvement over his 'the man they call Jesus' (v. 11). Others had judged Jesus to be a prophet (4:19) or even *the* prophet (6:14). Probably the healed man means the former. The niceties of Sabbath regulations do not concern him. He knows that a work of God was done in his life (*cf.* vv. 25, 32–33), and therefore the human agent must be an extraordinary individual, a prophet, someone sent with God's word. This man's eyes are opening wider: he is beginning to see still more clearly, while the eyes of his judges are becoming clouded over with blinding, theological mist.

ii. The interrogation of the man's parents (9:18–23)

18–19. *The Jews* mentioned here are still the Pharisees of v. 13. John likes to vary his terms, and his use of 'the Jews' has different referents in different contexts (*cf.* notes on 1:19). The Jews confront a serious dilemma (v. 16). They cannot unify their ranks, and without such unity they cannot present a united front against Jesus. They decide to go over the facts of the case again, hoping that the discovery of some mistake will resolve their dilemma. The most minute points are probed.

(1) Neighbours might be mistaken as to the man's identity, but surely his parents could not be fooled. They must be called. (2) Granted that he is their son, can they testify that he was blind before the alleged miracle? (3) Can they testify that he was *born* blind? Here, presumably, the witness of the healed man was worthless. He could perhaps testify that he could not remember ever seeing; only his parents could testify unambiguously to the fact that their son was afflicted with blindness from birth. (4) If they insist that this man is their son, and that he was born blind, what is their explanation for the healing? That the authorities press the healed man's *parents* on these points suggests that they are prepared to doubt the healed man's witness on the first two points, that he was unreliable on the third, and theologically confused or naïve on the fourth.

20–21. For reasons still to be explained (vv. 22–23), the parents are uncomfortable with the Jews' line of attack. They are prepared to affirm that this is indeed their son, and that he was blind, indeed, born blind. Those answers will not get them into trouble. As for the last question, *how he can see now, or who opened his eyes,* they defer to their son. *He is of age* probably means he is old enough to give legal testimony himself, *i.e.* at least thirteen. It is unreasonable to think that they did not know who had performed the healing, even though there is no indication that they were present at the cure itself. Although the parents thereby preserve their own relations with the authorities, the answers they did provide must have been pretty unpalatable. Their witness established that a notable miracle had occurred.

22–23. These verses disclose the reason why the healed man's parents were so reticent when it came to answering the Jews' final question: they did not want to be expelled from the synagogue. But these two verses have become the focal point of much modern debate. They are judged hopelessly anachronistic by many interpreters. Barrett writes, 'That the synagogue had already at that time applied a test of Christian heresy is unthinkable' (p. 361). For Martyn, as we have seen (*cf.* notes at the beginning of this chapter), this verse becomes the critical justification for his detailed 'two level' reading of the chapter.

In brief, their reasoning is as follows:

(1) The word rendered 'put out of the synagogue' (*aposynagōgos*) occurs in the Greek Bible only in John 9:22; 12:42; 16:2. The notion is late.

(2) The text says that the Jews had 'already . . . decided' to expel those who confessed Jesus as the Christ – and that suggests an even earlier date. It is so anachronistic that it is easier to think this time reference dates back from *John's* stance at the end of the first century, to a time that post-dates the ministry of Jesus.

(3) The obvious candidate, it is argued, is the Twelfth Benediction, re-written by Samuel the Small for the Sanhedrin reconstituted after the devastating fall of Jerusalem in AD 70. All pious Jews would recite the liturgical Eighteen Benedictions (*cf.* Schürer, 2. 459–463) three times a day. The Twelfth, re-written (it is thought) to exclude Christian Jews

from the synagogue by including in the liturgy a snippet that no Christian could utter, ran something like the following:[1] 'For the renegades let there be no hope, and may the arrogant kingdom soon be rooted out in our days, and the Nazarenes [*i.e.* Christians] and the *mînîm* ['heretics'] perish as in a moment and be rooted out from the book of life and with the righteous may they not be inscribed. Blessed art thou, O Lord, who humblest the arrogant.' This is often ironically called 'the benediction of the heretics' (*birkat ha-mînîm*). The date of this form of the 'Benediction' is customarily put at about AD 85–90, prepared during the Council of Jamnia, and written by Samuel the Small in response to an appeal by Rabbi Gamaliel, who led the Council (*cf.* B. *Berakoth* 28*b*). If that is what the Evangelist is referring to, then of course the text of 9:22 is anachronistic, and in principle raises the possibility that there are other anachronisms that litter the chapter.

(4) Although there were in Jesus' day already suspensions and expulsions for various periods of time (conveniently summarized in Brown, 2. 374), some argue that what John refers to could not be any of them. The most serious, the *ḥērem* ('ban'), was judged more severe a punishment than flogging by the synagogue authorities. Anyone under this 'ban' was forbidden all contact with Jews except his spouse and children; but he was still permitted to participate in religious exercises (Mishnah *Middoth* 2:2). It is this latter feature, permission to continue participating in religious exercises, that makes it unlikely that the *ḥērem* is what John is referring to: the expulsion he has in mind is *from the synagogue*. That is best met, not by the *ḥērem*, but by the *birkat ha-mînîm*.

(5) The confession 'Jesus is the Christ' is distinctly Christian (*i.e.* post-resurrection), judging by Romans 10:9. According to Mark, Jesus was not publicly confessed as the Messiah, the Christ, except by demons.

Nevertheless, many scholars cast doubt on parts or all of this reconstruction. The most important considerations are these:

(1) The Synoptic Gospels, including Mark, insist that Jesus, during his ministry, enunciated a test of discipleship that included public confession of Jesus (Mt. 10:32–33 = Lk. 12:8–9; *cf.* Mk. 8:33ff.). The question of the High Priest to Jesus at his trial (Mk. 14:61) shows that the confession of Jesus as the Christ was already current – and upsetting to the religious authorities. The beatitude in Matthew 5:11–12 = Luke 6:22–23 promises blessing on the disciples of Jesus who are persecuted and reviled, and (in Luke's account) who are excluded from the synagogue. Although Barrett, as we have seen, thinks a test of Christian heresy is 'unthinkable' during the ministry of Jesus, others judge it 'not intrinsically improbable' (Sanders, p. 242), the more so if it is local – *i.e.* the decision of local synagogue leaders.

---

[1]It is important to note that even this is based on a Hebrew manuscript found in the Cairo *genizah* (a place for storing old, sacred manuscripts) and on one fifteenth-century

(2) What we know of synagogue expulsions in Jesus' day is fragmentary, but the evidence admitted to the discussion must go beyond the *ḥērem* ('ban'), or we are simply knocking down a straw man. Some forms of excommunication existed from the days of Ezra (10:8) on. According to Mishnah (*Taanith* 3:8), about 80 BC Simon b. Shetah spoke of pronouncing a ban against Onias the Circle-maker. Paul could be thrown out of a synagogue (Acts 13:50) long before the *birkat ha-mînîm* was composed.

(3) It must be pointed out that the evidence in favour of a re-written Twelfth Benediction designed to ferret out Christians in the synagogues is partially reconstruction. Another reconstruction is possible, one that denies that there ever was an anti-Christian Jewish prayer[1] (though this view is still a minority report). Some argue that the prayer was directed exclusively against Jewish sectarians.

(4) Moreover, W. Horbury, in an article that examines the evidence exhaustively,[2] argues rather convincingly that there had long been a benediction against heretics in the synagogues, and that the Twelfth Benediction could not and did not itself evict the Christians from the synagogues, but merely reinforced an earlier and much more drastic expulsion. It is not even certain that whatever strengthening of the Twelfth Benediction took place at the hand of Samuel the Small was related to any expulsion whatsoever. It appears far more likely that the aim of the rewriting was to prevent those reckoned to be heretics from serving as precentors or in some other official capacity, not to prevent them from attending.[3]

(5) It might be argued that the word 'already' (Jn. 9:22) favours this interpretation. Both John and his readers know of drastic expulsions that forced many Christians out of the synagogues at various points after the resurrection, but his point is that *already*, during the life of Jesus, the first threats of expulsion, at local levels, were taking place. That is not unlikely, granted the degree of hostility that Jesus evoked during the later stages of his public ministry (he was, after all, crucified!).

(6) The confession that Jesus is the Christ is certainly important to Paul (Rom. 10:9). But must we assume that it arose out of nowhere immediately after the resurrection? Evidence has already been advanced that

---

manuscript in the Bodleian library. The re-wording of the Twelfth Benediction lapsed (it is argued) once the urgency of excluding Christian Jews from the synagogue had passed.

[1] Cf. R. Kimelman, 'Birkat Ha-Minim and the Lack of Evidence for an anti-Christian Jewish Prayer in Late Antiquity', in E. P. Sanders *et al.* (eds.), *Jewish and Christian Self-Definition, vol. 2, Aspects of Judaism in the Graeco-Roman Period* (SCM/Fortress, 1981), pp. 226–244, 391–403.

[2] W. Horbury, *JTS* 33, 1982, pp. 19–61.

[3] For useful discussion of this point and related matters, *cf.* Robinson, *John*, pp. 72ff.; Beasley-Murray, pp. lxxvi–lxxviii; Harvey, p. 89; D. R. A. Hare, *The Theme of Jewish Persecution in the Gospel according to St Matthew* (Cambridge University Press, 1967), pp. 54–55; Ridderbos, 1. 395–398.

the earliest disciples must have had some inkling of Jesus' messianic status (*cf.* notes on 1:41, *etc.*); it was the *nature* of his messiahship that gave them (not to mention the crowds and the religious authorities) so much trouble. Messianic fever was in the air; it would have been astonishing if some groups had *not* ascribed messianic status of one sort or another to Jesus (*cf.* notes on 6:14–15). That might well have been enough for some authorities to invoke bans and threats of excommunication in various local synagogues.

In short, the evidence in favour of an anachronism in 9:22 is at best inconclusive. This does not mean that, even if the description is historically authentic, the text has no direct bearing on John's readers. The 'already' hints at opposition still going on. The parents of the healed man may be sketched in with such detail so that John's readers will see an example of people who know the truth but who will not boldly step over the line with courageous witness. If the setting of this book is as proposed in this commentary – written toward the end of the first century with the primary aim of evangelizing Jews and Jewish proselytes – then John's readers, if they are becoming sympathetic to Jesus at all, must now identify themselves either with the parents, whose faith was not strong enough to act with courage, or with the healed man, who comes to a growing understanding of who Jesus is. His eyes were opened, physically and spiritually, and the frank confession of his new faith, even in the face of distinguished opposition, provides a model for a new generation of Jews and Jewish proselytes who are coming to faith.[1]

iii. The second interrogation of the healed man (9:24–34)

24–25. The religious authorities now face a serious conundrum. Apparently they have reached enough unanimity to agree that *this man* (a contemptuous reference to Jesus) *is a sinner.* If theological reasoning and the introduction of testimony have failed to unite the divided opinion of the authorities expressed earlier (v. 16), the sheer pressure to sort the matter out, and the groundswell of antipathy against Jesus, have succeeded. But their interrogation of the healed man's parents has not budged the testimony of the man himself: a notable miracle has taken place, and if God is behind it why should the human agent be judged sinful? Once more the authorities suspect that something has been kept hidden from them, and they adjure the man to tell the truth. *Give glory to God* does not mean something like 'Praise God for what he has done in your life', still less 'Praise God and not Jesus', but, as in Joshua 7:19, something like 'Before God, own up and admit the truth'. That 'truth' they want confessed, of course, is that Jesus is a sinner, a

---

[1] Horbury, *ibid.*, pp. 51–53, suggests that the *Sitz im Leben* ('life-setting') of the Twelfth Benediction was not the need to expel Christians, whether Jews or Gentiles, but the desire to win over Gentiles who might be present, to vie for converts with the Christian church.

transgressor of the law (by which they mean the oral law, which many conservative Jews understood to have the same divine, binding force as the written code); therefore there must be some other fragment of information that the man is hiding from them, something that would enable them to be at ease with their 'given', the sinfulness of Jesus.

The healed man professes no competence to judge whether or not Jesus is a sinner. At least to this point in the discussion, he is prepared to leave that question to the theological experts. But one thing he does know, and this point he will not relinquish: he was blind, and now sees. Granted the importance of the witness theme to the Fourth Gospel, John may also be telling his readers that decisive faith is characterized by the testimony of personal witness. Certainly countless Christians throughout the ages have applied the same words to their own transformation, their own experience of the move from darkness to light: *One thing I do know. I was blind but now I see!*

26–27. If the religious authorities are to maintain their view that Jesus is a sinner, they have no recourse but to go over the same ground yet again. The healed man, hitherto polite, now discovers that the professed impartiality of his interlocutors is nothing more than show. As a result he begins to deploy a quite marvellous gift for sardonic repartee. Since he has already answered all their questions before, what could possibly prompt them to hear his answers all over again? Mere cynicism with judicial procedure might suggest that they were trying to trip him up in his testimony. Instead, with a show of innocence he asks if their desire to hear a repetition of his testimony is bound up with a secret desire to become disciples of Jesus themselves.

28–29. The suggestion incenses them, and they respond by hurling insults. Their rudeness doubtless springs in part from pricked consciences: the man they are questioning has seen through their efforts to trip him up. His ironic, taunting question strips off all pretence of evenhanded evaluation. The bottom line is an authority question: they are *disciples of Moses!* They *know that God spoke to Moses* face to face, and gave him the law (Ex. 33:11; Nu. 12:8). As far as they are concerned, the conflict between Moses and Jesus is irreconcilable; so if the healed man is siding with Jesus, it must be because he is *this fellow's* [again contemptuous] *disciple*. As for Jesus, the authorities are not even certain *where he comes from* (*cf.* notes on v. 16). Formally, of course, this is in contradiction with the claims of 7:27. But it is futile for the modern critic to appeal to different sources. Some of their confessed uncertainty as to Jesus' origin may stem from Jesus' repeated insistence that, despite their earlier claims that they *do* know where he is from, in fact they know nothing of the kind (*cf.* 3:8; 8:14). His claims are confusing them. More important, both 7:27 and 9:29 are simultaneously false and ironically true.

The Pharisees' self-designation as *the disciples of Moses* is not common, though *cf.* Mt. 23:2 and B. *Yoma* 4a, where it is applied to Pharisees as opposed to Sadducees.[1] Nevertheless, these verses encapsulate the heart of the dispute between Judaism and Christianity, and in particular between Pharisaic Judaism (which dominated the scene after AD 70) and Christianity. The Pharisees knew that God had revealed his will through Moses. This law of God embraced not only the written word (what we refer to as the Pentateuch), but also a mass of oral tradition handed on from generation to generation.[2] By the standards of the latter, Jesus was certainly a transgressor. The Pharisees therefore preferred to remain 'disciples of Moses', *i.e.* to remain with the given, rather than to attach themselves to some upstart about whom they knew all too little. But John's readers know what answer the Evangelist provides to such a stance. It is this: If the Jews rightly understood what Moses wrote, they would grasp that he wrote of Jesus (5:39–40). On the last day, Moses himself will be their accuser (5:45–46). What is at stake, then, is a profoundly hermeneutical question: How is the antecedent revelation to be understood with reference to the new revelation in the person and teaching of Jesus the Messiah? The same question permeates all the Gospels (*e.g.* Mt. 5:17ff.). John himself happily concedes that 'the law was given through Moses' (1:17), but he insists that the fulness of divine revelation came exclusively through Jesus Christ (*cf.* notes on 1:17–18).[3]

30–33. We are not to think that the healed man grasped all of these points. His increasing boldness and sardonic wit stem from his most uncommon gift, common sense. What he finds *remarkable* is not his own belief, but the unbelief of the officials. Jesus has performed an astonishing miracle of healing, and they cannot decide *where he comes from* (which on the man's lips does not have metaphysical overtones: *cf.* notes on v. 16). Healing of the blind is extremely rare in the Old Testament, and connected with extraordinary circumstances (*e.g.* 2 Ki. 6:8–23). Jewish tradition reports one or two instances of the blind being healed (*Tobit* 2:10; 11:10–13). But nowhere is there a report of a healing *of a man born blind* (v. 32). That fact is linked by the healed man to the second of the two lines of argument developed in v. 16, now cast in terms of prayer: *God does not listen to sinners. He listens to the godly man who does his will.* The relation between the righteousness of the one praying and God's attentiveness is amply attested in Scripture (*e.g.* Jb. 27:9; 35:13; Pss. 66:18; 109:7; Pr. 15:29; Is. 1:15; *cf.* Jn. 14:13–14; 16:23–27; 1 Jn. 3:21–22).

---

[1]*Cf.* also *Pirke Aboth* 5:19, where Jews are referred to as 'the disciples of Abraham', while Christians are dismissed as 'the disciples of Balaam the wicked [= Jesus!]' (SB 2. 535).

[2]So *Pirke Aboth* 1:1: 'Moses received the [oral] Law from Sinai and committed it to Joshua, and Joshua to the elders, and the elders to the Prophets; and the Prophets committed it to the men of the great Synagogue.'

[3]The Jews made the law the interpretative centre of their thought, assuming for instance that Abraham kept the law (though the law had not yet been given in his time). Interestingly, part of Paul's *hermeneutical* response – *i.e.* his response at the level of how the Scriptures ought to be interpreted – is that what we call the Old Testament must be read in chronological sequence, or else God's progressive, redemptive purposes will be obscured (*cf.* especially Gal. 3). In other words, the Bible must be read salvation-historically.

Strictly speaking, even this does not *prove* that Jesus is a righteous man, since the example of the Egyptian magicians and others (*cf.* notes on v. 16) suggests that there are other spiritual powers beside God that may be at work. It is always risky to identify spiritual power with divine power. But such theological niceties do not trouble the healed man. His spiritual instincts are good, even if his theological argumentation is not entirely convincing. His 'givens' are simple: his congenital blindness has been healed, and the God who performed the healing does not answer the prayers of sinners. The conclusion is obvious: *if this man were not from God, he could do nothing* (v. 33).

34. The Pharisees are so outraged by what they perceive as ignorant insolence that they neither weigh the applicability of the principle the healed man has cited, nor articulate a possible theological exception. So convinced are they that Jesus is at best a charlatan, at worst a dangerous sinner, that they do not remember the ancient promises that one of the signs of the dawning of the messianic age is the restoration of sight to the blind (Is. 29:18; 35:5; 42:7). But, stung by the impertinence of this untrained member of the common herd (*cf.* notes on 7:49) arguing with them and besting them at their own game, they opt for personal abuse instead of evenhanded evaluation. In so doing they unwittingly confirm one of the points their interrogation aimed to overthrow: *You were steeped in sin at birth* is a cruel reference to the man's congenital blindness, not a theological statement about the universality of original sin. So the man was born blind after all! So Jesus must have opened his eyes! But the irony of their rage quite escapes them, so great is their own blindness (*cf.* 3:19–21; 9:39–41). The context of John's final coment, *And they threw him out*, suggests this was the excommunication feared by the man's parents (*cf.* notes on v. 22), not merely physical expulsion from the place where the discussion took place.

c. The sight of the blind and the blindness of the sighted (9:35–41)

35. 'Though my father and mother' – or for that matter, the religious authorities – 'forsake me, the Lord will receive me' (Ps. 27:10). In part, the Evangelist is simply completing the story. A preliminary division between the children of light and the children of darkness has occurred, insofar as the Pharisees have rejected the light and the healed man has been open to it. But the latter still does not understand very much about the light (*cf.* v. 36), so Jesus, taking the initiative, *found him* (*cf.* 5:14) and brought him to decisive and knowledgeable faith. At the same time, the Evangelist is driving home some important lessons for readers who are on the verge of conversion: opposition from the Jewish authorities is to be expected – it has always been that way; such opposition is best met with courage, and with transparent openness to the revelation of Jesus Christ. Opposition by the authorities, even excommunication, testifies that they are blind, not right; and, most importantly, mature and know-ledgeable faith are frequently the *consequence* of such a decisive break, rather than the condition.

The healed man had never seen Jesus, and had not met him since he had departed to go and wash in the pool of Siloam (v. 7). Once Jesus finds him, he asks the question, *Do you believe in the Son of Man?* In this context, the question must not be taken to mean 'Do you believe that the Son of Man exists?' but 'Do you place your trust in the Son of Man?' But why is the object of faith *the Son of Man*, when simply 'the Son' is the more common Christological title in the Fourth Gospel? The anomaly prompted many later copyists to change 'Son of Man' to 'Son of God', but it is almost universally acknowledged that 'Son of Man' is original, not only because the earliest manuscripts support this reading, but also because it is hard to see why in this instance copyists would have introduced a harder reading.

But what is significant about *the Son of Man* here? Not a few commentators see the term as indistinguishable from 'the Son of God' in this context, or the equivalent of 'the Christ' or 'the Lord' (*cf.* the confessions of Acts 8:37; Rom. 10:9; 1 Cor. 12:3; Phil. 2:11; 1 Jn. 2:22–23). But then why was not one of those titles chosen? The significance of 'Son of Man' in this verse must be deduced primarily by the usage of the term in the Fourth Gospel. In that light, Jesus is inviting the man to put his trust in the one who is the revelation of God to man (*cf.* notes on 1:51; 3:13–14; 5:27; 6:27, 53, 62; 8:28; and especially Moloney, pp. 149–159). Jesus himself is the Word incarnate, the one who uniquely reveals God. Indeed, in the context of ch. 9, the fundamental conflict is between the view that Jesus must be interpreted in terms of the law (as understood by the Pharisees), and the view that Jesus is the ultimate divine self-disclosure by whom and through whom the deepest significance of the law can be discerned. At the same time, the term in John is connected with a judging role: Jesus is assigned final responsibility at the great assize because he is the Son of Man (5:27). It is no accident, then, that the present paragraph culminates in vv. 39–41: 'For judgment I have come into this world . . .' Because John 9 also deals with the importance of public confession of Jesus, one is also tempted to think of Luke 12:8: 'I tell you, whoever acknowledges me before men, the Son of Man will also acknowledge him before the angels of God.'

36. In this context, unlike 12:34, the question *Who is he, sir?* is probably not a request for information as to the Son of Man's characteristics and functions, but a request that the Son of Man be identified. Judging by the end of the verse, the man is eager to believe in him: he has come to the end of his confidence in the traditional religious authorities. The Greek word *kyrie* is rightly rendered 'sir' (NIV).

37–38. In words reminiscent of his self-disclosure to the Samaritan woman (4:26), Jesus identifies himself as the Son of Man whom the formerly blind man has *now seen*. On the occasion that he first sees Jesus, he sees him as the Son of Man, in marked contrast not only to others who see for a much longer period of time but who 'see' nothing (6:36), but also to the high priest who will see the Son of Man only on the last day, and then in the terrible contours of judgment (Mk. 14:62). The man's response (*cf*. Additional Note) is instantaneous: *Lord* (*kyrie*, here rightly rendered 'Lord' rather than 'Sir'). *I believe*. The NIV reports that *he worshipped him*: the Greek verb *proskyneō* means to prostrate oneself before', 'to do obeissance to', and frequently occurs in contexts where there is no notion of worship or adoration. The verb takes on the force of 'to worship' when the person before whom one prostrates oneself is God. It is not clear that the healed man is yet ready to address Jesus as Thomas did after the resurrection, 'My Lord and my God' (20:28). It is likely that the healed man is offering obeissance to Jesus as the redeemer from God, the revealer of God. That is already a great step forward from his earlier references to Jesus (vv. 11, 17, 33). But the Evangelist, who knows that the Christological confessions in his Gospel will climax with 20:28 (*cf*. 1:1, 18), doubtless understands that the healed man is 'worshipping' better than he knew.

39. Apparently Jesus found the healed man in a public place, for although his comments to him were personal, some Pharisees were able to listen in (v. 40). Jesus' remarks in v. 39 are thus cast as a summarizing statement to the healed man of what has taken place, enabling him to grasp that the miracle that opened his eyes, and the ensuing debate with the religious authorities, constituted an acted parable about sight and blindness in the spiritual realm. The words *I have come*, or something similar, recur in this Gospel to express the purpose of Jesus' mission. Although the words themselves do not necessarily presuppose pre-existence, it would be wrong to overlook that overtone in the context of Johannine theology (*cf*. 5:43; 7:28; 8:42; 10:10; 12:27, 46–47; 16:28; 17:8). On *world*, *cf*. notes on 1:10.

Formally, the entire clause *For judgment* (*krima*) *I have come into this world* stands in contradiction with 3:17, 'For God did not send his Son into the world to condemn (*krinō*) the world' (*cf*. also 12:47). The charge is superficial. Even 3:17 is immediately followed by 3:18–21, with its contrast between darkness and light and its implicit threat of judgment (*cf*. also 3:36). Jesus' point in 9:39 is not that the very purpose of his coming was to condemn, nor even simply to divide the human race. He came to save, not condemn (12:47). But saving some entails condemning others. In that derivative sense, Jesus has indeed come *for judgment*. 'This is the paradox of the revelation, that in order to bring grace it must also give offence, and so can turn to judgment. In order to be grace it must uncover sin; he who resists this binds himself to his sin, and so through the revelation sin for the first time becomes definitive' (Bult-mann, pp. 341–342).

In this sense, the second half of the verse must be understood as a purpose clause, not merely 'so that' but 'in order that *the blind will see and those who see will become blind*'. The language is borrowed from two texts in Isaiah (6:10; 42:19; *cf*. Mk. 4:12, where parables are assigned the same purpose), the first of which is quoted by John in 12:40 (*cf*. notes there); but the immediate reference is to the healing of the blind man that has just taken place, and to the symbolic significance of that healing that has already been introduced (v. 5). At the spiritual level, *the blind* refers to those who are in spiritual darkness, and are therefore lost, and know it (just as the blind man repeatedly emphasizes how little he knows, vv. 25, 36). Jesus came to open their eyes, to give them the 'light' of revelation that will enable them to see. But *those who see* (which is Jesus' cryptic and ironic way of saying 'those who think they see'), like the Pharisees in this chapter who make so many confident pronouncements but who are profoundly wrong (vv. 16, 22, 24, 29, 34), inevitably reject the true light when it comes. So certain are they that they can see, they utterly reject any suggestion to the contrary, and thereby confirm their own darkness. That tragic conclusion is the *foreseen* result of Jesus' coming, and in that sense part of its purpose. Pastorally speaking, John is again stressing the point that a certain poverty of spirit (*cf.* Mt. 5:3), an abasement of personal pride (especially over one's religious opinions), and a candid acknowledgment of spiritual blindness are indispensable characteristics of the person who receives spiritual sight, true revelation, at the hands of Jesus (*cf.* notes on 7:17).

40–41. Sadly, some Pharisees who were listening in on this assessment understood little of it, and, utterly self-centred, they wanted only to find out whether Jesus thought his statements about the blind applied to them. With profound irony, Jesus replies, *If you were blind*, *i.e.* in the sense that I have spoken of blindness as a lost condition that cries out for illumination, *you would not be guilty of sin*, in particular the sin of unbelief that rejects the revelation of the Son; *but now that you claim you can see*, you are satisfied with the light of the law as interpreted by your received traditions, and consequently you reject the true light when it shines upon you (*cf.* notes on 15:22; *cf.* Pr. 26:12, 'Do you see a man wise in his own eyes? There is more hope for a fool than for him'). And so *your guilt remains*. Although the verb 'to remain' (*menō*) normally has positive overtones in the Fourth Gospel (*e.g.* 15:5), both here and in 3:36 the picture is negative, and frightening. This concluding pronouncement, *your guilt remains*, is of a piece with the irrevocable punishments that await those who blaspheme against the Holy Spirit (Mk. 3:29 par.), those who seek repentance after crucifying afresh the Son of God (Heb. 6:4–6; 10:26–31), those who sin unto death (1 Jn. 5:16–17).

Jesus did not come to a world of sinners aware of their need, and eager to be rid of their sin. Even those who entirely rely on genuine but inadequate light (the Old Testament revelation, 5:39–40) may prove too arrogant to admit the depth of their blindness. The brilliant shining of the true light only blinds them further. Their guilt remains. This is an evangelistic appeal as forthright as 3:36, a warning specifically shaped to apply to Jews and Jewish proselytes who from the 'given' of the Old Testament revelation are contemplating the claims of the gospel; and it has been rightly applied, in a derivative sense, to countless generations of men and women from every race ever since this Gospel was first published.

Additional note

38–39a. Several manuscripts omit all of v. 38, and 'Jesus said' from v.
39. Some scholars have justified the omission, partly on the ground that
the verb for 'said' in v. 38 (*ephē*) is rare in John (only at 1:23 and some
variants at 9:36), while the verb rendered 'worshipped' is found only in
4:20–24 (where God is the object; Metzger, p. 229, wrongly says the verb
is found only here). These scholars suggest that the words were added
for liturgical reasons, perhaps as part of a baptismal catechesis, where
the candidate would respond in the terms of v. 38. This presupposes
that liturgical forces were influential in shaping the transmission of the
text at an astonishingly early date, since one very early papyrus (P^{75})
omits it. In view of the overwhelming textual evidence supporting
inclusion of the words, it is best to judge them original. One might as
easily hypothesize that the omission, if it did not occur accidentally,
originated in a lectionary that sought to unify Jesus' teaching by jumping from v. 37 to v. 39.

3. Jesus as the shepherd of the sheep (10:1–21)
Two matters deserve preliminary attention:

(1) Many scholars have advocated some major displacement or other.
(For a history of scholarly opnion, *cf.* Tragan, pp. 55–175.) For instance,
since vv. 19–21 refer to the healing of the blind man, some propose that
these verses should immediately follow ch. 9. If vv. 22ff. follow hard
after this, then the Feast of Dedication (v. 22) is introduced before all of
the shepherd/sheep theme of ch. 10, smoothing out (it is argued) the
present arrangement, in which vv. 1–18 appear to be connected with ch.
9, located at the time of the Feast of Tabernacles (7:1ff.), while vv. 22ff.,
still dealing with the sheep theme, is tied to the Feast of Dedication,
three months later.

But recent study, wisely, has been far more cautious about proposing
such dislocations. Apart from the difficulty of imagining how such
chunks of material might get moved around when being copied, and
how, say, v. 27 could ever be thought to stand before v. 4, John 10
makes sense as it stands, both internally and in relation to ch. 9. The
thematic break between ch. 9 and ch. 10 is not as radical as first appears
(*e.g.* Simonis). The healed man has been roughly treated by the religious
authorities, and thrown out of the synagogue. What John next writes,
then, is that many thieves and robbers destroy the sheep, while the
good shepherd leads his own out from the sheep pen and into his own
flock. And if the bare juxtaposition of 10:1–18 with the end of ch. 9 is not
enough to establish the connection, John reports the continuing uncertainty of 'the Jews' over the healing of the blind man (10:19–21) in order
to tie the two passages together. At the same time, vv. 1–18 offer more
than comment on the fate of the blind man. The shepherd/sheep theme
not only brings its own rich allusions to the Old Testament, but re-
introduces the subject of Jesus' death into the discussion, in preparation

for 11:49–52; 12:23ff.; 13:1ff. The second half of ch. 10 (vv. 22ff.), set at the Feast of Dedication, deals with a number of messianic themes, of which the shepherd motif is but one. From an historical point of view, it is not at all unlikely that an itinerant preacher like Jesus recycled his themes again and again; from a literary point of view, we have already found that the Evangelist favours returning to themes already brought up and exploring them a little further (*e.g.* the Sabbath question crops up in chs. 5, 7, 9; *cf.* notes on v. 7). Brown (1. 389) goes farther, and notes that there is nothing to exclude the possibility that both ch. 9 and 10:1–18 took place *between* the two Feasts, thus constituting a kind of chronological bridge between them.

(2) Amongst the many attempts to penetrate behind ch. 10 in order to retrieve underlying sources are those that distinguish between vv. 1–5 and vv. 7–18, the latter judged to be an editorial expansion on the parable itself. That it is an explanation and expansion is clear; that it is on such grounds secondary by no means follows. Derrett[1] constructs a highly original narrative parable which (he claims) John had in front of him, but which John chose to 'decode' by going back to the original allusions to Scripture. These scriptural allusions John then treated to standard Jewish interpretative techniques in order to create his own message. Derrett lays out numerous interesting parallels; his reconstruction as a whole is nonetheless so speculative as to prove unbelievable.

More influential is the essay by Robinson,[2] who argues that vv. 1–5 constitute a fusion of two simpler parables. The first (vv. 1–3a) offers a challenge to the watchmen, the gate-keepers of Israel, to recognize who Jesus is and that he therefore has the right of entry. The second (vv. 3b–5) has as its point that Jesus' authority cannot be authenticated by signs; rather, it is self-authenticating and is demonstrated when his sheep hear his voice. Tragan (pp. 191ff.) prefers to think of vv. 1–2 as the parable, and vv. 3–5 as allegorizing commentary. These and similar attempts presuppose that this must be a 'parable' (or more than one 'parable'), and that parables have certain identifiable forms. But formal criteria must not be imported from the Synoptic Gospels (*cf.* Schnackenburg, 2. 279–281). John preserves no Synoptic-style narrative parables. This 'figure of speech' (*cf.* notes on v. 6) is distinctly Johannine. Just as John 15, far from offering a parable of a vine, simply provides observations on viticulture with various symbolic connections spelled out, so this chapter provides observations on sheep-farming, not as an end in itself but as a vehicle to get across the desired message in symbolic ways. But it is the message that controls the sheep-farming symbols, not vice versa. *Cf.* notes on vv. 4ff.

a. The 'figure of speech' *(10:1–5)*

1–2. The solemn *I tell you the truth* (*cf.* notes on 1:51) opens the

---

[1]J. D. M. Derrett, *ST* 27, 1973, pp. 25–50.
[2]John A. T. Robinson, *ZNW* 46, 1955, pp. 233–240; repr. Robinson, *Twelve*, pp. 67–75.

sustained metaphors that follow, all based on first-century sheep farming. The conceptual connection with the previous chapter is strengthened by focusing at once on thieves and robbers (cf. 9:39–41); the shepherd's introduction to the scene awaits v. 2.

The details would be familiar to John's readers. The sheep are in a fold, a sheep pen. This might be part of a family courtyard; in view of v. 3, it is better to think of a larger, independent enclosure, where several families kept their sheep, hiring an undershepherd (the 'watchman' of v. 2) to guard the gate. Those who were authorized to enter would of course do so through the gate. He whose interest is stealing or wounding the sheep would avoid the gate; he *climbs in by some other way*. The words *a thief and a robber* are virtually synonomous in English; *kleptēs* and *lēstēs* suggest, respectively, thief (like Judas, 12:6) and insurrectionist (18:40) – though it is not clear that John means any great difference. His point is that these unauthorized people enter and brutalize the sheep. By contrast, the shepherd knows his sheep, is recognized by the watchman and by the sheep alike, and leads them out for their own good.

It is hard to read these words without thinking of several backgrounds. By far the most important is Ezekiel 34. There the LORD berates 'the shepherds of Israel', the religious leaders of Ezekiel's day, for slaughtering the choice animals, clothing themselves with wool, yet utterly failing to look after the flock. 'You have not strengthened the weak or healed the sick or bound up the injured. You have not brought back the strays or searched for the lost. You have ruled them harshly and brutally' (Ezk. 34:4). God insists they are *his* sheep, *his* flock. In common with other Old Testament passages where both the LORD and his servant David are set forth as the ultimate solution to the problems of the people of God, so here. The LORD says, 'I will rescue my flock . . . I will bring them out from the nations . . . I will pasture them on the mountains of Israel . . . I myself will tend my sheep . . . I will bind up the injured and strengthen the weak . . . I will shepherd the flock with justice' (34:10–16). Nevertheless, the alternative note is sounded: 'I will place over them one shepherd, my servant David, and he will tend them; he will tend them and be their shepherd. I the LORD will be their God, and my servant David will be prince among them. I the LORD have spoken. I will make a covenant of peace with them and rid the land of wild beasts so that they may live in the desert and sleep in the forests in safety' (vv. 23–25). The same themes – God's servant David ruling over his people in the constraints of a new covenant, 'a covenant of peace' and 'an everlasting covenant', and serving as their shepherd – recur in Ezekiel 37 as the climactic expanation of the miracle of revivification in the valley of dry bones. This in turn follows hard on the promise of cleansing water and transforming spirit (Ezk. 36:25–27), already picked up in John 3 (cf. notes on 3:5). Other Old Testament passages castigate the shepherds of Israel for their dereliction of duty (e.g. Is. 56:9–12; Je. 23:1–4; 25:32–38; Zc. 11), or portray God as the ultimate shepherd of

Israel (Ps. 80:1; Is. 40:11; *cf.* Ps. 23:1). The mingling of the foci – the promised shepherd is the LORD, or the promised shepherd is the LORD's servant David – is peculiarly appropriate in a book where the Word is God, and the Word is God's emissary, distinguishable from him.

If this background is primary, then in the context of Jesus' ministry the thieves and robbers are the religious leaders who are more interested in fleecing the sheep than in guiding, nurturing and guarding them. They are the leaders of ch. 9, who should have had ears to hear Jesus' claims and recognize him as the revelation from God, but who instead belittle and expel the sheep. This seems more likely than hypotheses that restrict the referent of 'robber' to the Zealots (so Simonis, pp. 127–142). By v. 8, the focus changes a little to settle on those religious leaders who are messianic pretenders.

In addition to this Old Testament background, one can scarcely ignore the extensive use of sheep/shepherd imagery in the Synoptic Gospels (*e.g.* Mt. 9:36; 18:12–14; Mk. 6:34; 14:27 [*cf.* Zc. 13:7–9]; Lk. 15:1–7). So endemic to the culture of first-century Palestinian Judaism were sheep that multiple metaphorical use is to be expected.[1] To detect direct dependence on one or more Synoptic account is therefore a dubious enterprise. Bultmann (pp. 371f.) suggests that the thieves and robbers are the many 'saviours' of the hellenistic world. Jesus himself would scarcely have had that world in view. Despite the penetration of Judaism by Hellenism at many levels, this did *not* include, in Judea, the importation and popularization of numerous Greek deities. That some of John's readers might have discerned hellenistic parallels depends in large part on who we think his readers were. If, as has been argued in this commentary, they were primarily Jews and proselytes in the diaspora, the most natural identification they could have made would have been Jewish leaders, especially those who continued to reject the claim that the Messiah was Jesus, but including also various Jewish messianic pretenders – including those whose pretensions had brought about the destruction of Jerusalem.

3. The *watchman* or 'porter', probably a hired undershepherd (*cf.* notes on vv. 1–2), recognizes the shepherd and *opens the gate for him*. The sheep listen to the shepherd's voice. That he calls his *own sheep* presupposes that several flocks are in the fold; the shepherd calls out his own. Near-Eastern shepherds have been known to stand at different spots outside the enclosure and sound out their own peculiar calls, their own sheep responding and gathering around their shepherd. This shepherd goes further: he calls his own sheep *by name*, which at the least means

---

[1]More important, it is of the nature of metaphor that it is a literary device that speaks of one thing *in terms that are suggestive of another* (*cf.* Janet Martin Soskice, as in the fn. to 6:35). That sheep farming was widespread in the largely agrarian cultures of the first-century Mediterranean basin ensures that *many* associations would commend themselves to both writer and readers. To demand that these constitute a single, self-consistent mental picture, or a story with a unified plot, is to be unnecessarily restrictive on the natures of both metaphor and parable.

that he calls them individually (*cf.* 3 Jn. 15 for the same expression), and thus *leads them out*. Jesus comes to the sheep pen of Judaism, and calls his own sheep out individually to constitute his own messianic 'flock'. The assumption is that they are in some way 'his' before he calls them (*cf.* notes on vv. 25–29; 6:37, 39, 44, 64–65; 17:6, 9, 24; 18:9).

That this shepherd leads his sheep out (in v. 9, in and out, to find pasture) may allude, typologically, to Numbers 27:15–17, where Moses prays for a successor who will lead the people of God out and bring them in, 'so that the LORD's people will not be like sheep without a shepherd'. The next verse in Numbers 27 makes clear that the successor is Joshua, which name, in Greek, is 'Jesus'.

4–5. Unlike Western shepherds who drive the sheep, often using a sheep dog, the shepherds of the Near East, both now and in Jesus' day, lead their flocks, their voice calling them on. That such a shepherd goes ahead of his sheep and draws them constitutes an admirable picture of the master/disciple relationship. The sheep follow simply *because they know his voice*; by the same token, they will run from anyone else because *they do not recognise a stranger's voice*. The 'stranger' is probably a thief or robber; the 'hired hand' is not introduced until v. 12. Christ's elect sheep inevitably follow him (*cf.* notes on v. 3).

b. Misunderstanding (10:6)

6. The word rendered 'figure of speech' is *paroimia*, an expression that occurs again in 16:25, 29 but never in the Synoptic Gospels. The favoured term there is *parabolē* ('parable'), which never occurs in John. Both words render Hebrew *māšāl*, and all three words can refer to an extraordinarily wide variety of literary forms, including proverbs, parables, maxims, similes, allegories, fables, riddles, narratives embodying certain truths, taunts and more (*cf.* Carson, *Matt*, pp. 301–304). The common feature in these quite different genres is that there is something enigmatic or cryptic about them: hence NIV's 'figure of speech'. Whatever the form (and Jesus used many forms), Jesus' opponents *did not understand what he was telling them*. How could they? They were not of his sheep (*cf.* v. 26). And when they do begin to grasp what he says, their limited understanding only serves as the basis for rejecting him (*e.g.* 5:16ff.; 6:60; 7:20, 45ff.; 8:31ff.; 9:39–41). John's comment in this verse is therefore simultaneously a theological indictment and a step toward the further explanations in the next verses. Misunderstanding is frequently followed by explication in this Gospel.

c. Expansion (10:7–18)

The fuller explanation in these verses cannot easily be accommodated as long as we think of vv. 1–5 as a cohesive narrative parable, and the verses before us as mere explanation of them. Now Jesus is not the shepherd who goes through the gate; rather, he *is* the gate (v. 7). Before, the shepherd led the sheep out of the fold; now he leads them in and out (v. 9). Hired hands are introduced (v. 12), along with sheep from other sheep pens (v. 16), and the death of the shepherd (v. 15). The tensions are largely alleviated when we recognize that the expansions in these verses are not predicated on a single, narrative parable, but are further metaphorical uses of the three dominant features of the shepherding language introduced in vv. 1–5 – *viz.* the gate, which generates further metaphorical expansion in vv. 7–10; the shepherd, whose parallels with Jesus are further elucidated in vv. 11–18; and the notion of his own sheep, further expanded in vv. 26–30. This last section is placed a little further on in the chapter because it admirably explains the Jews' unbelief of Jesus' messianic claims.[1] In short, John 10 makes sense as it stands, as long as we do not approach it with false expectations of a formally coherent *narrative*.

7–8. Both here and in v. 9, Jesus claims, *I am the gate* (*cf.* Additional Note). (On the 'I am' formula with a predicate, *cf.* notes on 6:35; on the asseveration *I tell you the truth*, *cf.* notes on 1:51; 10:1.) In vv. 1–5, Jesus the shepherd enters the sheep pen through the gate; here, he is the gate. Even if we allow for the various sources that demonstrate that some Near-Eastern shepherds slept in the gateway of their own sheep pens, keeping marauders out and sheep in (*cf.* Beasley-Murray, p. 169), the tensions are not entirely alleviated. For although such background allows the reader to link the gate and the shepherd, the framework is still quite different from vv. 1–5, where a watchman presides at the gate, sanctioning the entrance of the shepherd, and several flocks are assumed to be in the fold. Here, the watchman has disappeared, and the only flock in the enclosure belongs to the shepherd who serves as the gate. In short, this is not an explanation of vv. 1–5, so much as an expansion of some of the metaphors found in those verses.

Some scholars suppose that in v. 7 Jesus is the gate *to* the sheep, deciding which putative shepherd may gain access to the sheep, while in v. 9 he becomes the gate *for* the sheep, allowing them ready entrance and egress. (The Greek is ambiguous.) The distinction is too clever; it assumes a continuation of the watchman motif from v. 3, even though that metaphor has been left behind. Verse 8 does not sanction a continuation of the motif. Rather, the earlier contrast between the shepherd and the thieves and robbers (vv. 1–5) is now slightly transformed into a contrast between the gate (which may also be the shepherd) and the thieves and robbers: *i.e.* the latter come with selfish motives and brutal tactics to ravage the flock, while the former serves as a symbol of security and plenty (*cf.* vv. 9–10). The ensuing verses suggest that *All who ever came before me* excludes from the indictment such leaders as Moses, Isaiah, Jeremiah and others who heard God's voice in former times, and who served him faithfully in the terms of the covenant to which they had sworn allegiance. Nevertheless, the expression surely

---

[1] *Cf.* J. Schneider, 'Zur Komposition von Joh. 10', in *Coniectanea Neotestamentica XI* (Fs. A. Fridrichsen; Gleerup, 1947), pp. 220–225.

hints at more than despotic local leaders who care more for their own gain than for the sheep in their care (*cf.* 'thieves and robbers' in v. 8). It sounds, rather, as if reference is being made to messianic pretenders who promise the people freedom but who lead them into war, suffering and slavery. The freedom Jesus wins for his people (*cf.* notes on 8:34) will be achieved not by sword and shield, but by a cross. If large crowds are taken up with the pretenders, the real sheep do not listen to them (*cf.* v. 5).

9–10. Barrett (pp. 371–373) provides an impressive list of 'gate' expressions in Jewish, Christian and hellenistic sources. But the lavishness of the list defeats its purpose. All that is demonstrated is that 'gate' is a common metaphor in various religions. What significance it has in any particular passage must be determined by the contextual and conceptual parameters of the text at hand. Here, the idea is not that Jesus the shepherd draws out his own flock from a rather mixed fold (vv. 1–5), but that Jesus the gate is the sole means by which the sheep may enter the safety of the fold (v. 9a) or the luxurious forage of the pasture (v. 9b). The thought is akin to 14:6: 'I am the way and the truth and the life. No-one comes to the Father except through me.' While the thief comes *only to steal and kill and destroy,* Jesus comes *that they may have life, and have it to the full.* This is a proverbial way of insisting that there is only one means of receiving eternal life (the Synoptics might have preferred to speak of entering the kingdom, although entering into life is also attested there), only one source of knowledge of God, only one fount of spiritual nourishment, only one basis for spiritual security – Jesus alone. The world still seeks its humanistic, political saviours – its Hitlers, its Stalins, its Maos, its Pol Pots – and only too late does it learn that they blatantly confiscate personal property (they come 'only to steal'), ruthlessly trample human life under foot (they come 'only . . . to kill'), and contemptuously savage all that is valuable (they come 'only . . . to destroy'). 'Jesus is right. It is not the Christian doctrine of heaven that is the myth, but the humanist dream of utopia.'[1]

Within the metaphorical world, *life . . . to the full* suggests fat, contented, flourishing sheep, not terrorized by brigands; outside the narrative world, it means that the life Jesus' true disciples enjoy is not to be construed as more time to fill (merely 'everlasting' life), but life at its scarcely imagined best, life to be lived. It is tempting to see here an allusion to Psalm 118:20, 'This is the gate of the Lord through which the righteous may enter.' Certainly the subsequent verses (118:22–24) are happily applied to Christ elsewhere in the New Testament (Mt. 21:42; 2 Pet. 2:7).

11. As vv. 7–10 depict Jesus as the gate for the sheep, so vv. 11–18, picking up on another expression from vv. 1–5, portray Jesus as the shepherd – indeed, the 'good' (*kalos*) shepherd. Many people in the

---

[1]Roy Clements, *Introducing Jesus* (Kingsway, 1986), p. 103.

industrialized West (though not Australians!) are inclined to think of shepherds as sentimental beings, perhaps somewhat effeminate, with their arms full of cuddly lambs, and the English adjective 'good' does nothing to dissuade us from these misconceptions. But the shepherd's job was tiring, manly and sometimes dangerous. The word *kalos* suggests perhaps nobility or worth: the noble shepherd or the worthy shepherd (though Lindars' 'ideal shepherd', p. 361, reaches a bit beyond the semantic range of the word). Elsewhere Jesus is said to be the *true* light, the *true* vine, the *true* manna, and so forth, always with reference to a temporal and perhaps failed type. The expression serves to identify him as the *genuine* antitype, with roots in eternity. Here, however, Jesus is not contrasting himself with temporal types, successful or otherwise, but with hired hands who have no real attachment to the sheep. Over against their deep self-interest, he is the noble shepherd. On the 'I am' formula with a predicate, *cf.* notes on 6:35; on the Old Testament background, *cf.* the notes on vv. 1–2; there may also be a self-conscious allusion to the worthless shepherd of Zechariah 11:17. The numerous parallels drawn from hellenistic and gnostic sources (*cf.* especially Bauer, pp. 143–144) belong to a quite different world, and are possible only because they too draw from the universals of first-century experience.

Within the metaphorical world, that *the good shepherd lays down his life for the sheep* means no more than that he is prepared to do so. He is willing to risk his life for the sheep, perhaps by beating back a marauding bear (*cf.* 1 Sa. 17:34–36). But the death of shepherds for such reasons must have been fairly rare, and even then it would never be the *intention* of the shepherd to die. That would leave his flock entirely exposed. But by the strong language Jesus uses, he points beyond the metaphorical world to himself. He does not merely risk his life, he lays it down, in line with the Father's will (vv. 17, 18). Far from being accidental, Jesus' death is precisely what qualifies him to be the good shepherd – a point presupposed in Hebrews 13:20, which acknowledges Jesus to be 'that great Shepherd of the sheep'. And by his death, far from exposing his flock to further ravages, he draws them to himself (12:32).

The words 'for (*hyper*) the sheep' suggest sacrifice. The preposition, itself ambiguous, in John always occurs in a sacrificial context, whether referring to the death of Jesus (6:51; 10:11, 15; 11:50ff.; 17:19; 18:14), of Peter (13:37–38), or of a man prepared to die for his friend (15:13). In no case does this suggest a death with merely exemplary significance; in each case the death envisaged is on behalf of someone else. The shepherd does not die for his sheep to serve as an example, throwing himself off a cliff in a grotesque and futile display while bellowing, 'See how much I love you!' No, the assumption is that the sheep are in mortal danger; that in their defence the shepherd loses his life; that by his death they are saved. That, and that alone, is what makes him *the good shepherd*. He carries a cross, not plastic explosives or an Uzi sub-machine-gun. Moreover, Jesus' death is here presented as a sacrifice peculiarly directed to the redemption *of his sheep*, whether of this (Jewish) sheep pen or of others (v. 16). This emphasis on the *intentionality* of Jesus' sacrifice is itself grounded on Jesus' peculiar intimacy with his sheep, an intimacy whose proper analogy is the mutual knowledge of the Father and the Son (vv. 14–15 and notes there).

12–13. Thieves and robbers (vv. 1, 8) are obviously wicked; the hired hand is not wicked, simply more committed to his own well-being than to the well-being of the sheep. When care for the flock is neither too arduous nor too dangerous, he is willing to work and receive his pay; but *when he sees the wolf coming*, when there is danger to his own skin, he retires forthwith and abandons the sheep to their devices. This cannot be surprising: the man *is a hired hand and cares nothing for the sheep*. It is uncertain whether or not the hired hand refers to certain religious leaders who perform their duty well enough in normal times, always provided they are paid, but who never display personal care for the sheep in times of danger, occupied as they are with their own safety and advancement. It may be that the hired hand is primarily a foil to emphasize what is characteristic about the good shepherd (in the next verses).

14–15. The repetition of *I am the good shepherd* (*cf.* notes on v. 11) not only lays emphasis on the sacrificial theme already introduced and about to be enlarged upon (vv. 15, 17, 18), but signals to the reader that what immediately follows, the theme of the mutual knowledge of the shepherd and the sheep (vv. 14, 15), is also of great importance. This mutual recognition, or better, mutual knowledge, is clearly experiential, and is analogous to the mutual knowledge of the Father and the Son (v. 15). That the shepherd knows his sheep, and the sheep know their shepherd, is presupposed by vv. 3–4; this mutual knowledge is precisely what ensures that they follow their shepherd, and only him. But the intimacy of this relationship is mirrored on the intimacy between the Father and the Son (*cf.* also notes on 15:9–11); indeed, the intimacy of the sheep/shepherd relationship is *grounded upon* the intimacy between the Father and the Son (*cf.* notes on 17:21; *cf.* also Mt. 11:27). However clearly this Gospel portrays Jesus as the Saviour of the world (4:42), the Lamb of God who takes away the sin of the world (1:29, 36), it insists no less emphatically that Jesus has a peculiar relation with those the Father has given him (6:37ff.), with those he has chosen out of the world (15:16, 19). So here: Jesus' death is peculiarly for his sheep, just as we elsewhere read that 'Christ loved the church and gave himself up for her' (Eph. 5:25).

Because of the clarity of the later passages (15:9–11; 17:21), not to mention the theme of sacrifice in this passage ('I lay down my life for the sheep' is repeated in v. 15), the intimacy envisaged here cannot legitimately be confused with the hellenistic mysticism of the magical papyri, still less with the vagaries of the modern 'new age' movement.

John envisages no *identification* between God and the believer; 'man is not deified but delivered' (Barrett, p. 376).

16. *I have other sheep* is tied to the previous two verses by the assumption that, however many sheep Jesus has, they are known to Jesus and ultimately respond to his voice. At the same time, this verse refers back to vv. 1–5. There the sheep pen represents Judaism. Jesus calls his own sheep out of that fold, thereby constituting his own flock; the sheep that remain in that pen are, presumably, the unbelieving Jews. If Jesus has *other sheep that are not of this sheep pen*, the reference must be to Gentiles. When he calls them, they, too, will respond to his voice, *and there shall be one flock and one shepherd* (cf. Additional Note). Thus, salvation which is 'from the Jews' (4:22) must first be announced to the Jews, but opens to enlist Gentiles as well (cf. Rom. 1:16). Jesus' death was not only 'for the Jewish nation' but also 'for the scattered children of God, to bring them together and make them one' (11:51–52). This is the fulfilment of messianic prophecy, and the ground of the Gentile mission. Indeed, if it is Jesus himself who must gather these sheep from other pens, it is assumed that it is Jesus himself who is operative in the Gentile mission (cf. the closing words of Mt. 28:18–20). The vision of unity in the words *one flock and one shepherd* not only prepares the reader for the dominant theme of ch. 17, but receives major treatment in other New Testament books (*e.g.* 1 Cor. 12; 2 Cor. 5:14–21; Gal. 3:28; Eph. 2:11–22; 4:3–6).

17. Jesus has just set out the relationship between the Father and the Son as the analogue of the relationship between the sheep and the shepherd. But the relationship between the Father and the Son is more fundamental than that. The love of the Father for the Son, and the love of the Son for the Father, are logically prior to the love of God for the world, and the basis that makes salvation possible (cf. notes on 3:35; 5:20; 8:29; 14:31). If Jesus has just mentioned the unique intimacy he enjoys with his Father, he is now at pains to elucidate *why* the Father loves him. It is not that the Father withholds his love until Jesus agrees to give up his life on the cross and rise again. Rather, the love of the Father for the Son is eternally linked with the unqualified obedience of the Son to the Father, his utter dependence upon him, culminating in this greatest act of obedience now just before him: willingness to bear the shame and ignominy of Golgotha, the isolation and rejection of death, the sin and curse reserved for the Lamb of God.

The last clause of the verse should probably be read as a purpose clause: Jesus lays down his life *in order to* take it up again. Jesus' sacrificial death was not an end in itself, and his resurrection an afterthought. His death was with the resurrection in view. He died in order to rise, and by his rising to proceed toward his ultimate glorification (12:23; 17:5) and the pouring out of the Spirit (7:37–39) so that others, too, might live.

18. In one sense, of course, Jesus' enemies conspired against him and killed him. But if that is all that can be said, it is unclear how his death could be construed as anything more heroic than a martyr's commitment – certainly not a God-ordained sacrifice whose moral significance is bound up with the willingness of the sacrifice to submit to God's will. The early Christians, understanding these issues well, simultaneously reproached the official executioners, and confidently prayed, 'They did what your power and will had decided beforehand should happen' (Acts 4:27–28). So here: not only Jesus' disciples before the cross, but any who are interested in becoming Christians after the event, must understand that looking at the crucifixion from God's perspective assures us that no part of it took place outside God's plan. How could the most significant event in redemptive history be construed in any other way?

However these difficult questions are weighed (*cf.* Carson), Jesus' point is that the sacrificial death of the shepherd, when it occurs, must not be taken as an accident of fate or merely as a tragedy perpetrated by misguided men, but as the Father's plan. Part of the Son's obedience to that plan is his consummate awareness that he lays down his life of his own accord. The authority he has received from his Father sanctions not only this, but his own resurrection. So at one are the Father and the Son in this plan that, 'When, in rising from the dead, Jesus takes up his life again, nothing occurs other than that the Father glorifies him' (Schnackenburg, 2. 302).

Nevertheless, though the Father and Son are at one, it is the oneness of command and obedience: *This command I received from my Father* (*cf.* notes on 5:16ff.). The theme of Jesus' obedience is already well established; the language of command is common from here on in John (and in 1 Jn. and 2 Jn. as well), whether the commands of the Father to the Son (10:18; 12:49–50; 14:31; 15:10), or of the Son to his disciples (13:34; 14:15, 21; 15:10, 12, 14, 17). *Cf.* especially the notes on 15:9–11.

Additional notes

7. Precisely because we might have expected some expansion of the theme that Jesus is the shepherd, the words 'I am the gate for the sheep' come as a bit of a surprise. For this reason, and because the identification of Jesus with the gate introduces a little tension with the earlier metaphors (vv. 1–5), some early manuscripts change 'gate' to 'shepherd'. Though attested early, the 'shepherd' reading is found in only one Greek manuscript and a few versions.

9. According to Hegesippus, a second-century writer, James the half-brother of Jesus was executed by Jewish opponents, in part because of his answer to the question, 'What is the gate (*thyra*, as in Jn. 10:7, 9) of Jesus?' (by which they probably meant the gate of which Jesus spoke). When James answered in terms reminiscent of Matthew 26:64, he was thrown off the temple and, still alive, was stoned to death (*H. E.* II. xxiii. 12–19). Whatever the reliability of this report, it attests that Jesus did indeed speak of himself as the door or gate.

16. The AV's 'one fold' instead of 'one flock' is based on the Latin

Vulgate's error, *unum ovile*. The revisers of King James were without excuse, not only because of the Greek, but also because the earlier work of William Tyndale had got it right ('one flock'). The context itself demands 'flock': the sheep are drawn out of the 'fold' or 'sheep pen' of Judaism, and from other pens as well, attracted by the voice of the shepherd, and constitute one new flock, the messianic community.

Although the vast majority of commentators adopt the interpretation outlined in the notes (above), two groups contest it: (1) A few, such as Martyn (*GJCH*, p. 15), and those who follow him, argue that the 'other sheep' are Christians in other Christian communities who have been scattered by the persecution of the 80s. This view is both needlessly anachronistic and hopelessly speculative: *cf.* John Pryor, *RTR* 47, 1988, pp. 44–51, esp. p. 46. (2) Some of those who hold that this Gospel was written to evangelize Jews of the diaspora, rather than to nurture the churches, argue that 'other sheep' refers not to Gentiles but to hellenized Jews, Jews living outside Palestine (*e.g.* Robinson, *Twelve*, pp. 114–115; van Hartingsveld, pp. 94–98). This is unlikely (*cf.* further notes on 'some Greeks' in 12:20). The *category* presupposed by 'other sheep' is *Gentiles*, even if *in practice* the Gentiles most open to evangelism were God-fearers and others profoundly sympathetic to the Jewish heritage of monotheistic revealed religion. They are amongst those John is seeking to evangelize.

d. The reactions of the Jews (10:19–21)

19. Again the words *the Jews* (*cf.* notes on 1:19) are ambiguous. Here the reference is probably to the crowds at large, leaders and lay alike, who are divided over him (*cf.* 7:12, 13). Despite the reference to the blind man in v. 21, it seems especially unwarranted to make vv. 19–21 follow after 9:41 (*cf.* notes on 10:1) since the division is caused by *these words* of Jesus.

20–21. Some are convinced that talk identifying Jesus as the Davidic shepherd, yet one determined to lay down his life for the sheep, proves he is *demon-possessed and raving mad*. The charge is not double-barrelled: the idea is that he is demon-possessed (*cf.* 7:20; 8:48) and therefore raving mad. Others conclude that even if Jesus' words are obscure, they are compelling, gracious, searching, sane; they *are not the sayings of a man possessed by a demon*. Moreover, this discourse has taken place in Jerusalem, where the man born blind had been healed, and the less critical auditors, recalling the arguments recorded in 9:16, 30, 32, are unable to leap to a damning conclusion when they cannot imagine how a demon could open the eyes of the blind. And the division remains.

4. At the Feast of Dedication: Christological claims and open opposition (10:22–39)

The governing themes of this chapter, indeed of this Gospel, are Christological, leading up to the moving conclusion of 20:30–31.[1] Thus

---

[1]*Cf.* Ulrich Busse, *NTS* 33, 1987, p. 525.

although the next two subsections develop topics already introduced in this chapter, above all they focus on two Christological titles.

a. Jesus the Messiah *(10:22–30)*

22–23. The *Feast of Dedication* was not authorized by the Hebrew Scriptures; it was a relatively recent institution. In 167 BC the Syrian Antiochus Epiphanes overran Jerusalem and polluted the temple, setting up a pagan altar to displace the altar of Israel's God. Chafing under the brutal repression, under which possession of any part of the Hebrew Scriptures was a capital offence, many Jews revolted and developed the fine art of guerilla warfare. Eventually they grew strong enough to overthrow the oppressor, and, under the leadership of Judas Maccabaeus ('Judas the Hammer'), they recaptured the temple and reconsecrated it to God on 25 Kislev (the lunar month that approximately coincides with December), 164 BC. The people celebrated the re-dedication of the temple for eight days, and it was decreed that a similar eight-day Feast of Dedication (*Hanukkah*) should be held every year, beginning on 25 Kislev (*cf.* 1 *Macc.* 4:36–59; 2 *Macc.* 1:9, 18; 10:1–8). Whether or not they took over an earlier festival of the winter solstice is disputed; certainly the celebration was religious (and necessarily political!) from this time on. It was also called the Feast of Lights, because of the lighting of lamps and candles in Jewish homes to celebrate the Feast, symbols deployed because the right to worship 'appeared to us (*hēmin phanēnai*, perhaps "shone upon us") at a time when we hardly dared hope for it' (Jos., *Ant.* xii. 325). Both the use of lights and the joyousness of the occasion ensured that it would be compared with the Feast of Tabernacles (*cf.* 7:2); indeed, it was called 'a Feast of Tabernacles in the month Kislev' (2 *Macc.* 1:9). Unlike Tabernacles, however, it could be celebrated at home.

In part, specification of the Feast is John's way of moving the narrative along: it is a chronological marker. But as with other feasts, this one, too, is understood to be fulfilled in Jesus the Son of God (*cf.* notes on v. 36).

John's comment that *It was winter* is probably in anticipation of the fact that *Jesus was in the temple area walking in Solomon's Colonnade* on the eastern side of the temple – *i.e.* the cold weather drove him to walk and teach in Solomon's porch, and not in an open court. John may have chosen to mention this detail not so much out of interest in arcane topography (though even here less suspicious interpreters detect the testimony of an eye-witness), but because he saw it was an anticipation of where the first believers, after the resurrection, would regularly gather to proclaim that Jesus is the Christ (Acts 3:11; 5:12). Beasley-Murray (p. 173) and others suggest that, like the cryptic 'it was night' (13:30), this identification of the season of the year has spiritual significance: 'A great deliverance from an Antichrist and the triumph of true religion was being celebrated, but the frosty temperature without corresponded to the frozen spirits of "the Jews".' Although this interpretation is possible, there is no recurring hot/cold contrast in the Fourth

Gospel to support it, quite unlike the light/darkness contrast that under-girds the symbolic interpretation of 13:30.

24. *The Jews* (*cf.* notes on 1:19) are often the opponents of Christ in this Gospel, but not always. The uncertainty is of pressing interest here, because the Greek behind the first question could be rendered, as in the NIV, *How long will you keep us in suspense?*, or, more negatively, 'How long are you going to annoy us?' If the latter is the question, 'the Jews' are clearly antagonistic; if the former, 'the Jews' may not be adversaries, but those who would like the question of his status cleared up once and for all. In the context of what follows, the former meaning is far more likely. This suggests that the Jews are not seeking for clarity in order to worship him without restraint; rather they want to obtain from him an unambiguous statement that would provide an adequate basis for their attack.

Jesus was unlikely to oblige them. Not once in public discourse in a Jewish context had he explicitly declared himself to be the Messiah. In private conversation with the Samaritan woman he was prepared to do so (4:26). According to the Synoptic Gospels, at some point in his public ministry he was also prepared to disclose himself to his immediate circle of disciples (Mt. 16:13ff. par.). But it was quite another matter to make such a declaration in a public, Jewish environment, whether before opponents or would-be disciples. The term 'Messiah' or its Greek equivalent 'Christ' had too many political and military connotations in first-century Palestine (*cf.* notes on 6:14–15; 11:48), and such overtones Jesus was always careful to avoid. More importantly, even if Jesus had spoken with utmost clarity, 'the Jews' would not have believed on him. John himself is convinced that the actual record of Jesus' words and works, with all its restraint, was more than enough to bring people to believe that the Son of God was Jesus (20:30–31). Indeed, for those with eyes to see (John informs his readers), so deft had been Jesus' self-references, his use of the Old Testament, his handling of titles, his discussions of the relation between God and himself, that he has vir-tually pointed himself out as the Messiah. The Jews demand that he tell them *plainly* (the same word as used in 7:4, 13, 26); the reader can see that even Jesus' description of himself as the good shepherd (vv. 1–18) was tantamount to such plain speaking. Jesus himself is about to make the same point.

25. When Jesus says *I did tell you*, he is not referring to an explicit statement. Had he spoken that plainly, they would have misunderstood him, for their notions of messiahship could not embrace a suffering servant or a kingdom not immediately political and military. If he had tried to speak plainly and publicly both about his messiahship and the necessity of his suffering, he would have been dismissed as a knave and a fool, if we may judge by the confused and dismissive reactions of his closest disciples when he opened up to them. At the same time, all of his ministry, both words and deeds, pointed in the one direction: in that sense he *had* told them. Even his works (*erga*, which includes his miracles), done in the Father's name as the revelation of the Father's will and the embodiment of the Father's power (*cf.* notes on 5:16ff.), taken cumulatively, testify that the Father has sent him (*cf.* notes on 5:36). It is not that miracles cannot be performed by others (*cf.* notes on 9:16), but that the array of his deeds – including the restoration of a man paralysed for thirty-eight years, the thoroughly attested healing of a man born blind, and, shortly, the resurrection of a man indisputably dead – along with the tone and content of his teaching, speak volumes on his behalf.

26–27. What then can explain the obtuseness of so many hearers? It is that they do not belong to Jesus' sheep. It is not just that his own sheep *do* hear his voice, that he knows them, and that they follow him (points made in vv. 1–18 and here repeated), but that those who are *not* his sheep do *not* hear his voice, that he does *not* know them, and that therefore they do *not* follow him. Neither Jesus nor John means to reduce the moral responsibility of the opponents in the slightest. That they are not Jesus' sheep does not excuse them; it indicts them. But the predestinarian note ensures that even their massive unbelief is not surprising: it is to be expected, and falls under the umbrella of God's sovereignty (*cf.* notes on 6:44; 12:37ff.).

28. To his own sheep, then, Jesus gives eternal life (*cf.* notes on 1:4; 3:15). In terms of the sheep metaphor, Jesus has already said that he gives them 'life . . . to the full', abundant life (v. 10); now he plainly states that such life is his own eternal life, frequently 'hidden' in the Gospel under the figures of water, bread, light, good pasture. The consequence of his knowing his sheep, and of his gift to them of eternal life, is that *they shall never perish*. It could not be otherwise, if they have eternal life (*cf.* notes on 6:51, 58; 8:51, 52; 11:26). Even so, the focus is not on the power of the life itself, but on Jesus' power: *no-one can snatch them out of my hand*,[1] not the marauding wolf (v. 12), not the thieves and robbers (vv. 1, 8), not anyone. To think otherwise would entail the conclusion that Jesus had failed in the explicit assignment given him by the Father, to preserve all those given to him (*cf.* notes on 6:37–40). The ultimate security of Jesus' sheep rests with the good shepherd.

29. Like everything that Jesus does, however, even this preserving action is not independent of the Father. All that Jesus says and does is merely the embodiment of the Father's will; this activity is explicitly so (6:37–40). This means that it is the Father himself who ultimately stands behind the preservation of Jesus' sheep. If some think Jesus to be too frail for so lofty an assignment, they must surely recognize that it is the Father's commitment no less than his. Who then can steal from God? Who has strength or subtlety sufficient to overpower or outwit the sovereign Father? *My Father, who has given them to me, is greater than all.*[2]

---

[1]The Greek employs the future tense, *ouch harpasei*, used in connection with its semantic force of 'expectation' to stress that no-one should expect to seize them from Jesus' hand (*cf.* Porter, pp. 403–439, esp. p. 416).

[2]This assumes that the NIV rightly preserves the best reading of the Greek. There is a

Indeed, at certain junctions in the history of redemption, the preservation of those the Father has given to the Son is explicitly and immediately assigned to the Father. In particular, when Jesus is about to undergo the isolation and grim agony of the cross, he formally hands over the responsibility for the preservation of his own to his Father (17:12). If the Father is greater than all things or persons, there is no force or being sufficient to sever the relation between the true believer and Jesus Christ. In short, as Paul would say to the Colossian believers, 'your life is now hidden with Christ in God' (Col. 3:3). There can be no greater security.

30. Verses 28–29 affirm that both the Father and the Son are engaged in the perfect preservation of Jesus' sheep. Small wonder, then, that Jesus can say, *I and the Father are one*. The word for 'one' is the neuter *hen*, not the masculine *heis*: Jesus and his Father are not one person, as the masculine would suggest, for then the *distinction* between Jesus and God already introduced in 1:1b would be obliterated, and John could not refer to Jesus praying to his Father, being commissioned by and obedient to his Father, and so on. Rather, Jesus and his Father are perfectly one in action, in what they do: what Jesus does, the Father does, and vice versa (*cf.* notes on 5:19ff.).

This verse has generated profound and complex controversies over the question of Jesus' nature. Arians (those who deny that Jesus is truly God) both ancient[1] and modern have entered the lists, while many scholars of orthodox conviction nevertheless hold that this verse supports only a functional oneness. The following five points may help to clarify the issues:

(1) The language of 'oneness' itself is not decisive. This is made clear by 17:22, where Jesus prays that his disciples 'may be one as we are one'.

(2) On the other hand, an appeal to 17:22 cannot decisively prove that the claim 'I and the Father are one', in this passage, refers *merely* to a oneness of will or action, and stands utterly devoid of metaphysical overtones. After all, this is a book in which the Word is openly declared to be God (1:1, 18), in which the climactic confession is 'My Lord and my God!' (20:28), in which Jesus takes on his own lips the name of God (8:58), in which numerous Old Testament references and especially allusions portray Jesus standing where God alone stands (*e.g.* 12:41). The reader should therefore hesitate before denying that there is any claim to deity whatsoever in these words.

(3) The immediate context is the most important single control. This includes not only the clearly functional categories of vv. 28–29 (*viz.* Jesus

---

nest of variants here, and more than one way to translate several of them. The reading chosen is that of the Byzantine tradition, more recently supported by an early papyrus, P[66]. It makes the most sense in the context, and various reasonable conjectures have been advanced to explain how this obvious reading might well have been corrupted so thoroughly in the manuscript tradition.

[1]*Cf.* T. E. Pollard, *NTS* 3, 1956–57, pp. 334–349.

and his Father share the same will and task, the preservation of Jesus' sheep), but two other factors. *First,* this is of a piece with 5:16ff. There, too, the Jews understood Jesus to be speaking blasphemy, because he claimed to be God. As we saw, they were partly right and partly wrong. They were wrong in that they envisaged another God, a competing God; they were right in that Jesus not only claimed that he could do only what his Father gave him to do, but that he did *everything* the Father did (5:19). No other human being in the stream of Jewish monotheism could meaningfully make such a claim. *Second,* the oneness of will and task, in this context, is so transparently a *divine* will, a *divine* task (*viz.* the saving and preserving of men and women for the kingdom) that although the categories are *formally* functional some deeper union is presupposed.

(4) It is important to remember that in the Fourth Gospel Jesus is the *unique* Son. Others are children of God; only he is the Son, the revealer, the one who has come down from heaven, the good shepherd who gives his life for his sheep, the true vine, the light of the world, the Word made flesh. The reader brings this sort of information to the interpretation of 10:30, and ought to.

(5) In 17:22, the order of the comparison is not reciprocal. The unity of the Father and the Son is the reality against which the unity of believers is to be measured, not the reverse (*cf.* Schnackenburg, 2. 308). And like any analogy that generates a comparison, the analogy cannot be pushed to exhaustion.

In short, although the words *I and the Father are one* do not affirm complete identity, in the context of this book they certainly suggest more than that Jesus' will was one with the will of his Father, at least in the weak sense that a human being may at times regulate his own will and deed by the will of God. If instead Jesus' will is exhaustively one with his Father's will, some kind of metaphysical unity is presupposed, even if not articulated. Though the focus is on the common commitment of Father and Son to display protective power toward what they commonly own (17:10), John's development of Christology to this point demands that some more essential unity be presupposed, quite in line with the first verse of the Gospel. Even from a structural point of view, this verse constitutes a 'shattering statement' (Lindars, *BFG*, p. 52), the climax to this part of the chapter, every bit as much as 'before Abraham was born, I am!' forms the climax to ch. 8. The Jews had asked for a plain statement that would clarify whether or not he was the Messiah. He gave them far more, and the response was the same as in 5:18; 8:59.

b. Jesus the Son of God *(10:31–39)*

31–33. *Cf.* 5:18, where stoning as the means of execution is probably presupposed, and 8:59. In all three instances, the desire to execute Jesus sprang from the perception that he was claiming equality or oneness with God – which of course was correct, though certainly not as an additional deity. In theory, stoning was to be performed in the wake of a judicial sentence. But because the Roman authorities reserved capital cases to their own discretion (*cf.* 18:31), and preferred crucifixion, and because mob emotions could easily get out of hand in a populace both oppressed and fiercely proud of its religious heritage, lynch law could easily prevail (*cf.* Acts 7:54ff.).

It is often pointed out that the technical definition of blasphemy recorded in Mishnah (*Sanhedrin* 7:5) requires that to be guilty a person had to pronounce the name of God, the Tetragrammeton (often transcribed as 'Yahweh' today). Because there is no evidence that Jesus ever defied that prohibition, some scholars argue that the Evangelist displays considerable ignorance of first-century Judaism. But the problem is not so simple. The Mishnah was compiled about AD 200, and incorporates not a few regulations modified by the relatively more humane and sophisticated heirs to the Pharisees. There is no evidence whatsoever that the Sadducees ever adopted so narrow a definition of blasphemy, and they largely controlled the Sanhedrin and influenced not a little of religious opinion in and around Jerusalem. The hotch-potch of competing and fervent religious opinions in Palestine before the fall of Jerusalem in AD 70 sometimes mocks the streamlined, restrained and largely univocal vision preserved in the Mishnah. In addition to charges of blasphemy raised against Jesus at his trials (*cf.* 19:7), the Synoptics also preserve evidence of the same charge levelled against him during the course of his ministry (Mk. 2:7 par.).

Unlike the situation in 8:59, Jesus does not immediately withdraw (though *cf.* v. 39) but stays long enough to confront his opponents. By asking which of the *many great miracles from the Father* have earned their wrath, Jesus is simultaneously claiming that all he has done has been the work of God himself (*cf.* 5:19–23), attesting to the truth of v. 30, and demanding that his accusers think through his life: is there not something incongruous about religion that *objects* to the healing of long-term paralytics and the curing of someone born blind? The irony is sharpened in Greek, where *erga kala* (NIV 'great works') suggests noble works or beautiful works (*cf.* notes on *kalos*, v. 11).

But the Jews cannot see their way to thinking through the implications of Jesus' works. They could always explain them away, one way or another. The immovable point of offence lies in what Jesus *says*: from their perspective, he has spoken blasphemy. Jesus, a mere mortal, claims to be (literally, 'makes himself') God, lining himself up on the other side of the unbridgeable chasm that separates the transcendent, infinite creator from his finite and fallen creatures. For the reader, the irony is palpable. Jesus has not 'made himself' God. He is himself the eternal Word, the Word that was with God and was God. He is the unique Son, utterly obedient to his Father and doing everything the Father does (5:19ff.). As the Son, there has indeed been a change in his status, but one that is almost the reverse of what the Jews thinks: he has obediently and humbly accepted the incarnation. The Word became flesh (1:14), the Son became a man.

34–36. Jesus appeals to *your* (though this word is omitted in some manuscripts) *Law,* which is not an anachronistic Christian disavowal of the Old Testament, since the Old Testament was the Bible of the first Christians. The point, rather, is that the truth of Jesus' claims, and, from the Evangelist's perspective, of the Christians' claims, was substantiated by the Scripture of the Jews themselves. *Law* here refers to the entire Old Testament canon, of which the law (the Pentateuch) is the most important part. (Similar usage is found in 12:34; 15:25; 1 Cor. 14:21; contrast Lk. 24:44.)

Jesus defends his claims by quoting Psalm 82:6, here drawn exactly from the LXX. The entire verse, and the next (Ps. 82:7), develops a single line of argument: 'I said, "You are 'gods'; you are all sons of the Most High." But you will die like mere men; you will fall like every other ruler' (NIV). As Jesus uses the text, the general line of his argument is clear. This Scripture proves that the word 'god' is legitimately used to refer to others than God himself. If there are others whom God (the author of Scripture) can address as 'god' and 'sons of the Most High' (*i.e.* sons of God), on what biblical basis should anyone object when Jesus says, *I am God's Son*? The argument gains extra force when it is remembered that Jesus is *the one whom the Father set apart as his very own and sent into the world.*

Although this much is clear, uncertainty abounds as to the identity of those whom God is addressing in Psalm 82. The chief options are:

(1) God is addressing Israel's judges, who are corrupting justice in the courts of the land (Ps. 82:1–4). They are called 'gods' because to exercise justice is fundamentally a divine prerogative vouchsafed to certain individuals (Dt. 1:17). Sadly, they do not begin to live up to their responsibilities, so they will be wiped out. The chief difficulty with the assumption that John 10 understands Psalm 82 in this way is that Jesus characterizes those who are addressed in Psalm 82 as those *to whom the word of God came.* Although this expression could refer to the word that came to the (alleged) angels *in the Psalm,* there is good evidence that Jewish leaders understood *all of Israel* to be the people to whom the word of the Lord came (*cf.* the third interpretation, below).

Jungkuntz[1] offers an embellishment on this first interpretation. He argues that the clause *and the Scripture cannot be broken* does not mean that Scriptures always tell the truth (though that is presupposed), but that this prophetic Scripture must be *fulfilled.* The only part of Psalm 82 that could be understood as prophecy is v. 8: 'Rise up, O God, judge the earth, for all the nations are your inheritance.' Jesus' citation of Psalm 82 is now interpreted to mean that he excoriates the judges of Israel for their utter failure, while he himself fulfils Psalm 82:8, claiming to be God in human form and therefore his people's perfect judge and deliverer. But as attractive as this is, it rests too much weight on the assumption that 'cannot be broken' (Gk. verb *lyō*) means 'is fulfilled'. Although the

---

[1]Richard Jungkuntz, *CTM* 35, 1964, pp. 556–565.

verb *lyō* can be set over against the verb 'to fulfil' in Matthew 5:17ff., that is not the case in John: *cf.* its use in 7:23, where to break the law of Moses means to transgress one of the law's requirements.

(2) God is addressing angelic powers who abused the authority God had given them over the nations. Emerton[1] has argued that the LXX version understood the Hebrew Psalm that way, as did the Syriac. Apart from some rather stunning modifications, the same line of thought is preserved in a document from Qumran (11Q *Melchizedek*). John 10 then presupposes, as Hebrews 1–2 argues, that Jesus is superior to all angelic beings. If fallen angelic beings can be addressed as 'gods', how much more appropriate is the application of the word to Jesus. The difficulty with this line of argument is that the Fourth Gospel fails to mention angels or Melchizedek. Moreover the setting for the quotation draws a sharp contrast between God and 'a mere man' (v. 38), not God and angels.

(3) God is addressing Israel at the time of the giving of the law. There is good evidence that many rabbis understood Psalm 82 this way. The curse that fell on the Israelites was then in consequence of the golden calf episode. The word of God pre-eminently came to Israel at Sinai (as virtually all Jewish leaders believed), but the subsequent rebellion, compounded by the failure to take the land at the first approach, led to the death of that entire generation. This interpretation is strengthened when it is remembered that Israel is also called God's firstborn son (Ex. 4:21–22), generating a typology which Jesus has already claimed to have fulfilled (*cf.* notes on 8:31ff.).

Hanson[2] offers a variation on this interpretation. Like Jungkuntz, he argues that the quotation from Psalm 82:6 carries along the entire Psalm, and that Psalm 82:8 is understood to be a prophecy fulfilled in the ministry of Jesus Christ. Unlike Jungkuntz, however, he holds that the word 'to whom *the word of God* came' (Jn. 10:35) refers to the pre-existent Word, the *Logos* (*cf.* notes on 1:1), and means 'to whom the (pre-existent) Word of God spoke'. The argument in John 10, then, is that if being addressed by the pre-existent Word justifies the usage in Psalm 82, where human beings are called gods, then we are amply justified in applying 'Son of God' to the man who is the human bearer of the pre-existent Word. In addition to the difficulties faced by Jungkuntz, this view, for all of its attractions, faces the considerable difficulty that the expression 'the word of God came' is such standard biblical fare (especially in Jeremiah and Ezekiel) for the message of God being declared to someone that it is hard to imagine why a first-century reader would take it to mean something else, unless there were substantial contextual clues.

It appears best, then, to adopt the unadorned third interpretation.

---

[1] J. A. Emerton, *JTS* 11, 1960, pp. 239–232; *idem*, *JTS* 17, 1966, pp. 399–401.
[2] A. T. Hanson, *NTS* 11, 1964–65, pp. 158–162; *idem*, *NTS* 13, 1967, pp. 363–367.

Three observations help to clarify the line of thought. *First*, the words *the Scripture cannot be broken* mean that the Scripture cannot be annulled or set aside or proved false (*cf.* Mk. 7:13). Conceptually, it complements *your Law*: it is reprehensible to set aside the authority of Scripture, the Scripture whose authority you yourselves accept, just because the text I have cited seems inconvenient to you at the moment.

Second, the clause *whom the Father set apart as his very own* (lit. 'sanctified', *hagiazō; cf.* notes on 17:17, 19) *and sent into the world* points to Jesus' entire mission as the Father's emissary, a mission culminating in the cross, resurrection and glorification. At the same time, it probably echoes the Feast of Dedication, which commemorates the sanctification of the temple after it had been desecrated. The Jews celebrate the sanctification of the temple, but they, like the disciples, remain unaware of the ways in which the temple points to Jesus (2:19–22), so that the really critical 'sanctification', the crucial act of setting something or someone aside for God's exclusive use, was the setting aside of the pre-incarnate Son to the work of the mission on which he was even then engaged. In this way Jesus outstrips and fulfils this Feast as he has the others. If this reference is allusive, it is of a piece with the development of the fulfilment motif in connection with the other feasts (*e.g. cf.* notes on 6:4; 7:21–24, 37–38; 8:12; 19:31–37).

Third, although the argument is *ad hominem* – *i.e.* it does not require Jesus to subscribe to the same literal exegesis as his opponents – it is not for that reason silly. Jesus is not using this argument to *prove* that he is God or the Son of God, in the full-blooded sense propounded in this Gospel. In that case the argumentation would be without merit. Rather, he recognizes that the animus of his opponents has not been thought through. In the heat of their opposition to what they hear Jesus to be saying, they are partly right (he does make himself equal with God), partly wrong (this fact does not establish a competing God), and profoundly mistaken (they have not grasped the drift of their own Scriptures to see how he fulfils them, nor have they known God well enough to perceive that the revelation he is and brings is in continuity with and the capstone of the revelation of God already provided). The stated context – mob humours heated to the threshold of explosive violence – does not provide him with the leisure for cool theological dialogue. So he administers a short, sharp shock, a *scriptural* reason why they should not take umbrage just because he calls himself the Son of God. That reason does not establish the nature of his unique sonship: that is presupposed, rather, by his self-reference as *the one whom the Father set apart . . . and sent into the world*. But the *ad hominem* rebuke stalls the crowd long enough for him to appeal once more to the testimony of his words and works (vv. 37–38).

37–38. Having secured a breathing space before the threat of mob violence would force him to retreat (v. 39), Jesus appeals to the evidence he wants his opponents to weigh. He does not expect to be believed on the basis of his own naked claims. But if what he does is those things that the Father does (*cf.* notes on 5:19–23), should not that fact give them pause? Or, by implication, are they so ignorant of God that they do not really know what he does? Even if they cannot yet bring themselves to believe Jesus, *i.e.* to absorb and believe his words, the least they should do is believe the works (*erga*), which include, but should probably not be restricted to, the 'miracles' (NIV). The argument is a reiteration of v. 25 (*cf.* notes), and it will surface again in 14:10–11.

The reason why the Jews should reflect on his deeds is that they might *learn and understand* (*gnōte kai ginōskēte* – the difference is 'between the act of knowing and the continuing progress in understanding'[1]) that the Father is in Jesus and Jesus is in the Father. This is offered in explanation of v. 30, which provoked the running debate of vv. 31–38. As a theme, it will not be developed thoroughly until 14:10–11; 17:21. There is between the Father and the Son what theologians call a 'mutual co-inherence': each is 'in' the other. This mutual co-inherence is the grounding of the teaching of 5:19ff. More important, it extends, in some derivative sense, to embrace believers, who are 'in' Christ while he is 'in' them (*cf.* notes on 14:20ff.).

39. However precious such teaching might be to later believers, it was further evidence of blasphemy to those who first heard it. But their attempt to seize him was as futile as the attempt recorded in 7:30, and doubtless for the same reason: his hour had not yet come.

5. Strategic retreat, continued advance (10:40–42)

40. In the light of the rising attacks (*cf.* 5:18; 7:30; 8:37, 59; 10:31), Jesus *went back across the Jordan*, to the east side, away from Jerusalem and Judea, *to the place where John had been baptising in the early days*. If the reasoning set out in the notes on 1:28 is correct, the reference is not to Perea, but to Batanea, in the tetrarchy of Philip, in the north-east. The symbolism is palpable. John the Baptist had prepared the way for the beginning of Jesus' public ministry, and now that public ministry is drawing to a close, while the Baptist's ministry is reviewed once more (vv. 41–42). For the theological symbolism, *cf.* notes on 1:28.

41–42. Though the authorities in Jerusalem are eager to see Jesus die, in rural Batanea the memory of the ministry of John the Baptist, who had been executed some time before, bore signal fruit. They remembered the Baptist's witness to Jesus, and now find Jesus' ministry so powerful that the Baptist's witness is confirmed. The fact that *John never performed a miraculous sign* has double significance. Bammel[2] has shown that Jewish sources do not invest energy in praising putatively great men *unless* some miracle or other is attributed to them. John's greatness, by contrast, consists in the faithfulness, clarity and veracity of his witness to Jesus. No witness could ask for a better epitaph: *all that John*

---

[1]Porter, p. 328. This way of putting it is to be preferred over Rob, p. 850.

[2]E. Bammel, 'John Did No Miracles: John 10:41', in C. F. D. Moule (ed.), *Miracles: Cambridge Studies in their Philosophy and History* (Mowbrays, 1965), pp. 197–202.

said about this man was true. Of course, some things that John the Baptist had said of Jesus had not yet been fulfilled. Jesus had not yet taken away the sin of the world (1:29, 34), nor had he yet baptized people with the Holy Spirit (1:33; *cf.* 7:39). Even so, the drift of John's pointed witness, his insistence that he was not worthy to untie the thongs of Jesus' sandals (1:27), had been so confirmed in the brief ministry of Jesus amongst them that *many believed in Jesus.* Their faith was an unwitting attestation of the fruitfulness of the Baptist's witness (1:7).

III. TRANSITION: LIFE AND DEATH, KING AND SUFFERING SERVANT (11:1 – 12:50)

Though many interpreters link ch. 11 with the previous chapters and view ch. 12 alone as the transition between Jesus' public ministry and his passion, it seems wiser to tie chs. 11 and 12 together. The final verses of ch. 10 close a giant *inclusio*: Jesus' public ministry begins and ends with the witness of the Baptist (1:19 – 10:42). The subsequent move to the region near Jerusalem is the last one. Up until now we have learned of the bread of life, the water of life, the light of life; now, in the last sign, Jesus gives life itself (11:25–26), an anticipation of the fruitfulness of his own death (12:23–24).

A. THE DEATH AND RESURRECTION OF LAZARUS (11:1–44)

Perhaps because this is the climactic and most dramatic miraculous sign in the Fourth Gospel, considerable doubt has been cast on its historical worth. This has come from various quarters. Some simply deny that supernatural events are possible (*e.g.* Bultmann); others insist that, even if there is some special activity of Jesus at the base of this account, literary criticism is fundamentally incapable of offering a reasoned decision as to the historical value of the report itself, if that report includes allegedly unique events (*e.g.* Kremer); still others think that this account is probably a historicizing of the parable Jesus told about the rich man and Lazarus (Lk. 16:19–31).

The matters raised by such doubts are too complex to be convincingly treated in a brief commentary. For those who think that supernatural intervention by a personal/transcendent God is impossible, profitable discussion must begin elsewhere than at this narrative. Those (like the present writer) who believe in the incarnation (an invasion of the personal/transcendent Word into *history*) and resurrection of Jesus find it rather useless to swallow a camel and strain out a gnat. Kremer's learned study of how this chapter has been interpreted in the past, and especially his moving appeal for an existentialist interpretation of the text, goes well beyond the effort to discover ways in which an ancient text may legitimately be applied to our existential situations (*i.e.* to the situations bound up with contemporary existence). For him, existential proclamation is the forceful preaching of the message he discovers in the text, after he has insisted that whether or not the text has an external referent is irrelevant. Far from being more biblical and spiritual an approach (as he thinks), this reduces proclamation from the joyful announcement of objective good news to the artistic depiction of myths that some find interesting and psychologically beneficial; it transforms faith from trust in a trustworthy object or person to a rather bland (some would say naïve) openness to authentic existence, all objective succour banished to the unknowable.[1] 'One should . . . keep steadfastly in mind that he who wrote the Gospel of the Word *made flesh* viewed history as of first importance; he would never have related a story of Jesus, still less created one, that he did not have reason to believe took place' (Beasley-Murray, p. 199).

As for the suggestion that this account is an historicizing of Luke 16:19–31, it is indeed remarkable that both stories centre on a man named Lazarus who dies. Parallels beyond that point, however, are immediately swamped by differences that are far more striking. The closest parallels to the parable reported by Luke are found in Egyptian and rabbinic sources. If he knew of such parallels, apparently (it is argued) Jesus took up one such story current in his day and adapted it for his own use. What is striking, however, is that he gives the man in his parable the name 'Lazarus', for in the overwhelming majority of Jesus' parables the actors bear no names. Moreover, the details concerning Lazarus in John 11 are not anomalous if the account is treated as historically credible. Even the names of Mary, Martha and Lazarus were discovered (in 1873) in ossuary inscriptions in a tomb near Bethany[2] – which of course does not prove that this was the tomb of the three siblings mentioned in John 11, but it does demonstrate that the names, at least, were common enough. To describe Lazarus as 'from Bethany' (11:1) is to locate him as firmly as Philip, who was 'from Bethsaida' (1:44). That the Evangelist himself is clearly not reporting bare 'facts' but is trying to make numerous theological points cannot detract from his own assurance that the points he is making rest on the reality of the stunning miracle that took place.[3] *Cf.* also Morris, pp. 532ff., and esp. Murray J. Harris, *GP 6*, pp. 310–317.

---

[1] For a stunning example of this approach, *cf.* Sandra M. Schneiders, *Int* 41, 1987, pp. 44–56.

[2] *Cf.* C. S. Clermont-Ganneau, *PEQ* 6, 1874, pp. 7–10; C. H. Kraeling, *BA* 9, 1946, p. 18. The name of Simon is also present. I am indebted to Bruce, p. 253, for these references.

[3] For the numerous source-critical theories relating to this chapter, *cf.* Kremer, pp. 82ff.;

1. *The death of Lazarus* (11:1–16)

1. This narrative begins without any formal link with ch. 10, but deep links are present nonetheless. Chapter 10 ends with a determined attempt to arrest Jesus, and with his successful escape and retreat into Batanea. What calls him south again is the appeal of Mary and Martha. That he comes is not only testimony to his love for the Bethany family (*cf.* vv. 5, 8), but also that he sees this challenge as some kind of signal from his heavenly Father (*cf.* notes on vv. 9, 10). Although he will withdraw from the authorities one more time before his arrest (v. 54), on that occasion Jesus remains within a few miles of Jerusalem. Thus in transparent irony it is his quest to bring his dead friend back to life that precipitates the Sanhedrin decision against him (vv. 45ff.) and therefore his own execution.

This Bethany, lying on the east side of the Mount of Olives less than two miles from Jerusalem along the road toward Jericho, has not been mentioned in the Fourth Gospel before, and must be distinguished from the Bethany of 1:28 and that alluded to in 10:40–42. That is why John characterizes it as the *village of Mary and her sister Martha*.

2. Only now do we learn that Lazarus is the brother of Mary and Martha. The family appears in John for the first time, but *cf.* Lk. 10:38ff. That John can identify Mary to his readers by alluding to the episode in which she *poured perfume on the Lord and wiped his feet with her hair*, even before he narrates that event (12:1–8), presupposes that he thinks his readers have already heard of it. From this, most commentators assume that his hearers are Christians. This does not necessarily follow. We need assume only two things, both reasonable: (1) that Christians and Jews are in steady contact with each other at this time, the Christians still trying to convert the Jews and ready at a moment's notice to tell their story again; (2) that the story of Mary was a high profile component of Christian witness. There may be a trace of that in John's reference to Jesus as *Lord*. John is very careful not to refer to Jesus as 'the Lord' in the pre-Easter setting, unless the remark, as here, is clearly the Evangelist's appropriate label, written from the vantage of his post-Easter comprehension. Moreover, even if John's readers had never heard of Mary, his proleptic reference to her is not bad form. We have seen evidence from time to time of John's intention that his Gospel be read more than once. It is not at all unrealistic to think that John (like many a good story-teller) should introduce a figure who is explained more thoroughly in a subsequent passage. For the first-time reader, the forward reference adds thrust to the incentive to press on; for the reader who is perusing the book for the second or third time, the early reference to Mary helps to tie the book together. As a parallel, one thinks of the reference to the

---

Schnackenburg, 2. 316ff.; Beasley-Murray, pp. 184–187; and especially Brian H. Henneberry, 'The Raising of Lazarus (John 11:1–44): An Evaluation of the Hypothesis that a Written Tradition Lies Behind the Narrative' (unpublished doctoral dissertation, University of Louvain, 1983).

Baptist's imprisonment before the account of that imprisonment (Mt. 4:12; 14:3–12). In short, this verse cannot be taken as evidence that John's intended readers were Christians.

3. The sisters' *kyrie* (NIV 'Lord') is the common Greek for 'sir' (*cf.* notes on 4:11). If (as seems likely) they spoke in Aramaic, the form of their address was probably 'Rabbi' (*cf.* notes on v. 28): *i.e.* 'Lord' acknowledges Jesus as their master, themselves as disciples, but is certainly not here a confession of his deity. The sister's reference to their brother as the one Jesus loves is touching. It hints at friendships and relationships that are barely explored in the Gospels, and it suggests that some at least felt peculiarly loved by him. Because the human authority behind this Gospel is 'the beloved disciple' (*cf.* notes on 13:23; 19:26–27; 20:2; 21:7, 21ff.), Eller (and others before him) have argued that Lazarus is the fourth Evangelist. The theory is not convincing (*cf.* notes on 13:23; Introduction, § IV). The verb for *loved* here is *phileō*; in v. 5, it is *agapaō*, without any discernible shift in meaning (*cf.* notes on 3:35; 5:20; 20:2; 21:15–17). If there is significance in the choice of *phileō* here, it may be that John is anticipating his use of the cognate *philos* in 15:14–15. (The expression 'the beloved disciple' renders *agapaō* four times, and *phileō* once [in 20:2].)

4. Jesus does not mean that this sickness is not fatal, but that it will not *end* – ultimately – in death. Far from it: it will end in resurrection from the dead, and that for God's glory. The thought is akin to 9:3, where the blind man's congenital handicap 'happened so that the work of God might be displayed in his life'. The death of Lazarus will prove to be *for God's glory* – not 'in order that God may be glorified, *i.e.* praised', but 'in order that God's glory may be revealed', since in John 'glory' (*cf.* notes on 1:14) is more commonly not the praise that is God's due but his revelation, his self-disclosure. But God's self-disclosure takes place preeminently in his Son (*cf.* 1:14–18). If the death of Lazarus came about so that God's glory might be revealed, this particular revelation of God's glory is *so that God's Son may be glorified through it: i.e.* the raising of Lazarus provides an opportunity for God, in revealing his glory, to glorify his Son, for it is the Father's express purpose that all should honour the Son even as they honour the Father (5:23). Elsewhere, Jesus for his part says that he has glorified his Father by completing the works the Father assigned him to perform (17:4). The Father and the Son are mutually committed to the other's glory. The irony is that if in this miracle of restoration to life both the Father and the Son are glorified (*i.e.* revealed for who they are), the supreme moment of glorification comes in Jesus' death (*cf.* notes on 12:28).

5–6. What Jesus has just said could be interpreted as callousness toward the Bethany family. John will have none of it: he insists that *Jesus loved* (on the verb, *cf.* notes on v. 3) *Martha and her sister and Lazarus*. That Martha is mentioned first and her sister left unnamed may suggest that Martha was the eldest. Be that as it may, John's point is that the glorification described in the previous verse is not harsh and thoughtless because devoid of affection for others, but entirely in keeping with Jesus' love for this family. Lazarus' death and the resurrection that follows are not only to glorify the Father and the Son, but are for the good of Lazarus and his sisters.

The NIV's rendering of the opening of v. 6 is without linguistic defence: *Yet when he heard* . . . The translators have set the affirmation of Jesus' love (v. 5) in dramatic tension with the two-day delay reported in v. 6. The obvious contribution of the particles *hōs oun*, however, suggests a rendering such as this: *When therefore he heard that Lazarus was sick, he stayed where he was two more days*. This means that the two-day delay was *motivated* by Jesus' love for Martha, Mary and Lazarus. How can this be?

On the customary reconstruction, the message that Lazarus was ill took one day to reach Jesus in the Transjordan, but Jesus knew immediately, by supernatural means (*cf.* notes on 1:47), that Lazarus had already died, presumably almost as soon as the messenger had left. Jesus' delay for two days did not, therefore, bring about the death of Lazarus. Following the delay, another day was taken up with the return trip, making a total of four days (v. 17). The decision to delay is therefore to be explained as the deliberate refusal to be manipulated (*cf.* 2:4; 7:3), but to await his Father's timing. Above all, the delay ensured that Lazarus had been dead long enough that no-one could misinterpret the miracle as a mere resuscitation, effected before the man's spirit had properly left the area (*cf.* notes on v. 17). The miracle that Jesus actually performed therefore confirmed the faith of his disciples and friends with dramatic power that would have been lacking if Jesus had responded immediately to the plea for help.

Although there are numerous valuable insights in this reconstruction, as a total synthesis it must be jettisoned if Jesus was not staying (as is commonly supposed) in the Transjordan, a mere day's journey from Bethany near Jerusalem, but (as has been argued in the notes at 1:28; 10:40–42) in the region of Batanea, approximately 150 kilometres to the north-east of Jerusalem. The traditional interpretation must presuppose that Lazarus died almost as soon as the messenger left Bethany with the news that Lazarus was ill. This overlooks the differences between 11:4 and 11:11. When the messenger first arrives, Jesus says, 'This sickness will not end in death' – which presupposes that as far as Jesus is concerned Lazarus was ill but still alive at the time. Only after the two-day delay does Jesus say, 'Our friend Lazarus has fallen asleep' – almost as if his supernaturally acquired knowledge of Lazarus' death is the divine signal that sends him and his disciples off to Bethany.[1] That means the four days that elapse between Lazarus' death and his resurrection (v. 17) begin just before Jesus sets out on the trip to Bethany. If Jesus were staying in the Transjordan, only one day, or at the most two,

---

[1] *Cf.* Rainer Riesner, *TynB* 38, 1987, pp. 44–45.

would be required for the journey. From Jewish sources it is well known that a day's journey for a healthy person was considered to be 40 or 45 kilometres. The 150 kilometres that separate Bethany near Jerusalem from Bethany/Batanea would require the four days suggested by v. 17. *Cf.* also the Additional Note on vv. 14–15.

It might be objected that this makes Jesus somehow responsible for the death of Lazarus. That is not so: if Jesus had left immediately, Lazarus would have been dead for two days before he arrived – not enough to offset possible superstitions associated with resuscitations within the first three days (*cf.* notes on v. 17). Jesus' timing was in any case regulated by his Father's will, and not by any request of friends, or even of family (*cf.* 2:4; 7:3–9; *cf.* Schlatter, p. 248). More important, by waiting to leave until Lazarus had died, and therefore ensuring that he could not arrive until the fourth day after the death, Jesus is accomplishing two things: he is powerfully demonstrating himself to be the resurrection and the life (v. 25), and he is powerfully establishing the faith not only of his disciples (v. 15) and of some Jews who were onlookers (v. 45), *but also of the Bethany family itself* (*cf.* notes on vv. 22ff.). As the narrative is cast, the delay is for the good of all concerned, including Lazarus, Mary and Martha.[1] How then can Jesus legitimately be cast as hard-hearted?

This is why the 'therefore' of v. 6 contributes to the flow of the argument. Lazarus' illness will not finally issue in death: it is for the glory of God (v. 4). This does not mean Jesus is indifferent to human suffering. Far from it: Jesus loves Martha, Mary and Lazarus (v. 5). Indeed, it is in consequence of that love that he delays his departure by two days, waiting for the divine signal, the news of Lazarus' death, before he sets out on the four-day journey (v. 6), for this delay will make a substantial contribution to the strengthening of the faith of the Bethany family.

7–8. When, after the two-day delay, Jesus announces his plans to return to Judea, and invites his disciples to join him, they are frankly aghast. It was only *a short while ago* (*nyn*, normally 'now', but here with the meaning 'recently', part of the semantic range of the word in classical Greek) that *the Jews* tried to stone him. The reference is to what took place at the Feast of Dedication (10:31, 39), after Jesus had announced, 'I and my Father are one.' If Jesus is in Batanea as he speaks, his reference to *the Jews* suggests the meaning 'the Judeans' (*cf.* notes on 1:19; 7:1). The disciples recognize that the animus against Jesus is now so great it could easily result in his death. They do not recognize that his death, however appalling an event, would also be his glorification and the consummation of his ministry.

9–10. In days before accurate time-pieces existed, both the Romans and the Jews divided the daylight period into twelve 'hours', which

---

[1]*Cf.* W. H. Cadman, *SE* I (= *TU* 73, 1959), pp. 423–434, especially p. 426.

therefore varied in length with the changing seasons. During those twelve daylight hours, most people did their work; once the darkness came, it was time to stop work. At the pedestrian level, these verses describe the obvious; *this world's light* refers to the sun.

At a deeper level, the context suggests two complementary meanings. As in 12:24ff., there is an application first to Jesus, and then to his disciples. As an answer to the question of the disciples as to why *Jesus* is determined to go up to Judea (v. 8), these verses metaphorically insist that Jesus is safe as long as he performs his Father's will. The daylight period of his ministry may be far advanced, but it is wrong to quit before the twelve hours have been filled up. The time will come soon enough when he will not be able to work. But because the disciples have been asked to accompany Jesus to Judea (v. 7), there is an obvious application to them as well. Jesus himself is the light of the world (8:12; *cf.* the last clause of v. 9) who is still with them. As long as they have him, for the full twelve hours of their 'daylight' they should perform the works assigned them. The time would come, all too soon, when the darkness of his departure would make such work impossible (*cf.* notes on 9:4).

11–13. As further explanation as to why he is determined to go up to Judea, Jesus informs his followers that Lazarus is *asleep*, but, says Jesus, *I am going there to wake him up*. The contrast between the plural *our friend* and *I am going* is not accidental: Jesus alone is the resurrection and the life (v. 25). At first glance, the failure of the disciples to discern the metaphorical significance of *asleep* is remarkable, prompting many commentators to label this an artificial literary device. Perhaps; but several factors must be borne in mind. *First*, the word used in v. 13 for 'sleep' (*koimēsis*, only here in the New Testament) is also found in hellenistic sources (*cf.* LSJ, *s.v.*; *NewDocs* 3. § 80). There is no reason why Jesus should not have referred to death as 'sleep', and no reason why the Evangelist should not have reported it using this word. Nevertheless, although sleep as a metaphor for death is common in Christian theology, it is less common (though not unknown) in the Old Testament and in the Judaism of the second temple period. In the Old Testament, it chiefly appears in the formula 'X slept with his fathers' (especially in the books of Kings and Chronicles), and suggests an irrevocable sleep which cannot be wakened (*cf.* also Jb 14:11–12). By contrast, the notion that death was a sleep from which one would one day be awakened (Dn. 12:2) was by no means commonplace amongst the people. Later Jewish sources track its ascendancy. *Second*, there is an independent record of a similar misunderstanding in the ministry of Jesus (Mk. 5:39 par. – though the Gk. word is different). *Third*, modern readers know how the story will come out; Jesus' disciples did not have that advantage. *Fourth*, the messenger had come announcing Lazarus' illness, not his death. The mind-set of the disciples was toward illness. *Fifth*, the context makes clear that the disciples did not want to return to Judea. It is not hard to imagine how such fear might well breed a small degree of obtuseness.

John intends his readers to associate v. 11 and vv. 25, 26: those who are Jesus' friends and who fall 'asleep' will one day be wakened by him who is the resurrection and the life. It is more doubtful that the word behind *he will get better* (v. 12), *viz. sōthēsetai* (lit. 'he will be saved'), cleverly hints at salvation, since the verb is quite commonly applied to full health (though the play on words is probably deliberate in Mk. 5:34; 10:52).

14–15. Jesus therefore speaks *plainly* (*parrēsia, cf.* notes on 7:4), *Lazarus is dead.* The relationships amongst the Greek clauses is difficult (*cf.* Additional Note). If the NIV has it right, Jesus is glad he was not present when Lazarus died, presumably because he would have prevented his death and therefore removed the opportunity to provide this faith-engendering resurrection.

16. The name *Thomas* has not so far been attested in literature earlier than the Fourth Gospel (Heb. *t'ōm* and Aram. *t'ōmā* mean 'twin'), but the Greek word *didymos*, though it means 'twin', is known to serve as a proper name.[1] There is no answer to the obvious question, 'Whose twin?' In some later Syriac-speaking churches, it was suggested that Thomas was to be identified with the Judas of Mark 6:3 and John 14:22 (*cf.* Additional Note *in loc.*), and was the twin brother of Jesus himself. Needless to say, that minority report has not prevailed.

Because of his role in ch. 20, the church has come to think of him as the doubter. The other New Testament books merely include his name in lists of apostles (Mt. 10:3; Mk. 3:18; Lk. 6:15; Acts 1:13); John alone fleshes out the man (here; 14:5; 20:24–29; 21:2). On this occasion Thomas reflects not doubt but raw devotion and courage, even though it was courage shot through with misunderstanding and incomprehension: misunderstanding, in that he had not grasped the assurance implicit in vv. 9–10, and incomprehension, in that the death Jesus had to face as the Lamb of God (1:29, 36) could not possibly be shared by his disciples. Yet there is another sense in which Thomas, like others in this Gospel, spoke better than he knew: his words have become a clarion call to would-be disciples, after the resurrection, to take up their cross daily and follow Jesus (*cf.* notes on 12:25; *cf.* Mk. 8:34; 2 Cor. 4:10).

Additional note

14–15. The verb behind *has died* (*apethanen*) is an aorist, and should not be taken as a perfect with stative force (*i.e.* Lazarus is in the state of death). If we take it to refer to 'what has just happened' (M. I, pp. 135, 139–140, 247), *i.e.* 'Lazarus has (just) died', it confirms the geography specified in the notes on v. 6. The NIV understands the clausal relationships in the Greek text as follows: the causal ground of Jesus' rejoicing is

---

[1] Another view is that *Thōmas* is a genuine Greek name chosen for its similar sound to the Hebrew or Aramaic equivalents (BDF § 53).

the fact that he was not present in Bethany when Lazarus died; this rejoicing is not for his sake but for the sake of his disciples; the purpose toward which Jesus' rejoicing is orientated is the belief of the disciples. All of this makes sense of some very condensed Greek. But several other reconstructions are possible. One of the most attractive begins with the observation that the aorist *apethanen* is not normally used in the New Testament to describe the state of death unless there is associated with the verb a qualifying or contrasting phrase or clause. This and one or two other observations have combined to treat the words *and for your sake I am glad* as parenthetical, generating the translation: 'Lazarus is dead – and I am glad, for your sake – dead in order that you may believe, dead because I was not there.'[1]

2. Jesus the resurrection and the life (11:17–27)

17. On the geography and time required for travel, *cf.* notes on v. 6. From a slightly later date there are sources attesting the rabbinic belief that the soul hovers over the body of the deceased person for the first three days, 'intending to re-enter it, but as soon as it sees its appearance change', *i.e.* that decomposition has set in, it departs (*Leviticus Rabbah* [a rabbinical commentary] 18:1 [on Lv. 15:1]; for other references *cf.* SB 2. 544f.). At that point death is irreversible. Though Lagrange (p. 307) doubts that this belief stretches back to the time of Jesus, it seems to be presupposed here. Together with v. 39, this verse establishes the awesome character of the sign about to be performed.

18–19. The text specifies that Bethany was fifteen *stadia* from Jerusalem. One *stadion* is approximately 202 yards 9 inches; fifteen *stadia* are therefore equivalent to 3033.75 yards, or just over 1.72 miles (hence NIV's *less than two miles*). The implication is that the *many Jews* who came to comfort Martha and Mary were from Jerusalem, which in turn suggests that the family was rather prominent. Although comforting the bereaved was almost universally regarded as a religious and social responsibility (on the customs, *cf.* Edersheim, 2. 320–321; SB 4. 592–607), not every villager would have been consoled by 'many' Jews from the nearby city. The same suggestion of prominence is supported by the expense of the perfume lavished on Jesus by Mary (12:1ff.). The *many Jews* (on the term, *cf.* notes on 1:19; there is no negative overtone here) become witnesses of the resurrection of Lazarus (vv. 45ff.). Mention of the proximity of Jerusalem also heightens the reader's awareness of the immense risks Jesus is taking by coming so close to the capital, and thus anticipates his death.

20. The picture of Martha as more active and perhaps more aggressive than Mary is in striking accord with the cameo found in Luke 10:38–42.[2]

21–22. Martha's opening *Lord* is probably to be taken as in v. 3. Her

---

[1] Edouard Delebecque, *Bib* 67, 1986, pp. 75–80.
[2] *Cf.* T. E. Pollard, *TU* 102, 1973, pp. 434–443, for a fresh study of John's portrayal of the two women.

first words to Jesus are not a rebuke, as if she were saying that Jesus ought to have been there. Rather, they are words of grief and of faith: she is confident that if Jesus had been present while her brother lay ill, Jesus would have healed him. Verse 22 has been taken by many to mean that Martha's faith runs deeper yet: she is confident that if Jesus asks his Father to raise her brother from the dead, his prayer will be answered. That is not quite what the text says, and the unbelief reported in v. 39 stands dramatically against that interpretation. Verse 22 must be taken more generally: Martha is not only persuaded that her brother would not have died had Jesus been present, but even now, in her bereavement, she has not lost her confidence in Jesus, and still recognizes the peculiar intimacy he enjoys with his Father, an intimacy that ensures unprecedented fruitfulness to his prayers.

23–24. Verse 23 is a masterpiece of planned ambiguity. At one level Jesus' words *Your brother will rise again* could be taken as no more than a devout, orthodox attempt to provide Martha with solace by drawing her attention to the resurrection at the end. Death will not have the last word: *at the last day* (v. 24),[1] the resurrection will take place and her brother will be restored to bodily life. That is the way Martha understands Jesus' words (v. 24). She shared with Jesus and with Pharisaic Judaism a belief in the resurrection (*cf.* Acts 23:8; Jos., *Bel.* ii. 163; Mishnah *Sanhedrin* 10:1), a view roundly denied by the Sadducees (Mk. 12:18–27; Acts 23:8). But at another level, Jesus is promising more immediate resurrection for Lazarus. That point escapes Martha; only the unfolding drama will disclose this meaning in Jesus' words.

25–26. On *I am* (*egō eimi*) with a predicate, *cf.* notes on 6:35. Jesus has repeatedly mentioned resurrection on the last day (5:21, 25–29; 6:39–40). In this he has been in line with mainstream Judaism. But these references have also insisted that he alone, under the express sanction of the Father, would raise the dead on the last day. The same truth is now repeated in the pithy claim, *I am the resurrection and the life.* Jesus' concern is to divert Martha's focus from an abstract belief in what takes place on the last day, to a personalized belief in him who alone can provide it. Just as he not only gives the bread from heaven (6:27) but is himself the bread of life (6:35), so also he not only raises the dead on the last day (5:21, 25ff.) but is himself the resurrection and the life. There is neither resurrection nor eternal life outside of him.

Assuming the firmness of the text,[2] the question is whether

---

[1] Amongst the New Testament writers, only John uses the expression 'the last day' (*cf.* 6:39, 40, 44, 54; 12:48). Other writers prefer the plural, 'the last days', usually referring (as Beasley-Murray, p. 190, points out) to the times *preceding* the end (*cf.* Acts 2:17; 2 Tim. 3:1; Jas. 5:3).

[2] The words 'and the life' are missing from one early Greek papyrus (P45), two versional witnesses and three early Fathers (though two of these make no attempt to cite the full text, so the value of their witness is disputed). The overwhelming external evidence favours inclusion. If the words are original, presumably they were either dropped accidentally, or else by someone who (wrongly) judged them to be redundant.

(1) *resurrection and life* refer to the same thing, making the mention of life a mere pleonasm, a preacher's way of reinforcing a point, or, better (with Schnackenburg, 2. 331), the word *life* adding little new meaning but nevertheless elucidating what is meant by *resurrection*; or (2) *resurrection and life* refer to two complementary things.

The second option is more credible (*cf.* Dodd, *IFG*, pp. 364–366), and it appears that the two components, 'I am the resurrection' and 'I am the life', are successively elucidated in the two ensuing clauses. The plain reference of *resurrection* is to the final resurrection of believers at the last day, through Christ whose power effects it. This part of Jesus' claim is elucidated by the next clause: the one who believes in Jesus will 'come to life' (NEB; this is the obvious meaning of the verb in 5:25 and elsewhere), *even though he dies.* These words ensure that it is the final resurrection that is in view. The elucidation of *I am . . . the life* appears in the clause after that: *whoever lives and believes in me will never die.* The verb *lives* cannot simply mean *is alive*, as the triteness would be unbearable; obviously only those who are alive can believe! We have repeatedly noticed that the background for these verses is 5:21ff., and there the notion of *life* is invariably the life of God, saving life, eternal life, the life of the kingdom. So also here: we might paraphrase, 'whoever has eternal life and believes in me will never die'. The two descriptions 'has eternal life' and 'believes in me' are not tautologous. The first stresses the internal change that must come about, wrought by the power of God (*viz.* he lives, he has eternal life); the second underlines what stance the individual must adopt (*viz.* he believes). In Greek they are lumped together (*pas ho zōn kai pisteuōn*), suggesting that both descriptions refer to one individual. This clause, then, is the elucidation of the truth that Jesus is the life. Doubtless it is theoretically possible to see this life as exclusively post-resurrection life, life lived in the resurrection body. But this is surely promising something more. If the last half of v. 25 stipulates that the believer, even though he or she dies, will nevertheless come to life at the resurrection, the first half of v. 26 stipulates that the believer, the one who already enjoys resurrection life this side of death, will in some sense never die. That is a recurring theme in this Gospel. In anticipation of Jesus' resurrection and the pouring out of the Spirit, there is the repeated promise that those who believe in him will immediately possess eternal life. 'I tell you the truth, if anyone keeps my word, he will never see death' (8:51; *cf.* 3:15, 16; 5:24). Ordinary, mortal life ebbs away; the life that Jesus gives never ends. It is in that sense that whoever lives and believes in Jesus will never die.

Such a degree of realized eschatology prompts Käsemann at one point (p. 75) to suggest that the Fourth Gospel displays the heresy of Hymenaeus and Philetus (2 Tim. 2:17–18), who taught that the resurrection had already taken place. That misunderstands John rather badly. Although John lays stress on the present experience of the life only Jesus can give, it is never at the expense of denying the prospect of ultimate resurrection – and in this instance, as in ch. 5, the two themes are juxtaposed. All the major New Testament writers maintain some sort of tension between futurist eschatology and inaugurated or realized eschatology. John lays more stress on the latter than some; unlike the heretics of 2 Timothy 2, he nevertheless insists that the resurrection will take place, and that the locus of both resurrection and eternal life is in Jesus.

When Jesus asks Martha *Do you believe this?*, he is not asking if she believes that he is about to raise her brother from the dead, but if her faith can go beyond quiet confidence that her brother will be resurrected at the last day to personal trust in Jesus as the resurrection and the life, the only person who can grant eternal life and promise the transformation of resurrection. If she answers positively, the raising of Lazarus becomes a paradigm, an acted parable of the life-giving power of Jesus. It is not *more* than that, *i.e.* it is not of a piece with the resurrection that takes place at the end of the age (*cf.* notes on vv. 43ff.), nor with the infusion of the life of the kingdom (since that is not normally accompanied by the reversal of the death of our mortal bodies).

27. Martha's *Yes, Lord* (*cf.* notes on v. 3) introduces more than a confession of the points Jesus has raised, but a personal confidence in Jesus as the Christ, the Messiah, the Son of God (*cf.* 20:30–31). Her confession is neither mere repetition, nor the pious but distracted and meandering response of someone who has not followed the argument. Her reply carries the argument forward, for she holds that the one who is 'the resurrection and the life' must be such by virtue of the fact that he is God's promised Messiah. Her firm *I believe* (Gk. perfect, *pepisteuka*) reflects the state of her confident trust (*cf.* notes on 6:69). Her faith is a rich mixture of personal trust (*fiducia*) and of confidence that certain things about Jesus are true (*assensus*), viz. that he is the Christ (*cf.* notes on 1:41), that he is the Son of God (*cf.* notes on 1:49), and that he is the one who was to come into the world (*cf.* notes on 1:9; 6:14).

3. *Jesus outraged and grief-stricken* (11:28–37)

28. Martha's confession (v. 27) terminates her conversation with Jesus: at this point there is no more to be said. In the light of the ensuing verses, Martha's care to draw Mary aside before announcing Jesus' arrival is an attempt to provide her sister with a private meeting. *The Teacher* is a natural way of referring to Jesus for any disciple in the pre-resurrection period (*cf.* notes on v. 3; 20:16). That Jesus was asking for Mary becomes clear only now; there is no record of his actual request – a salutary reminder of how condensed and fragmentary the records are.

The effort to secure a private meeting between Jesus and Mary should not be invested with too much theological significance. It is precarious to conclude, for instance, that the sisters were trying to protect him from his enemies (so Sanders, p. 270), for there is no evidence to support the view; or that Jesus chose to remain outside the village in order to preserve his anonymity (which would make little sense since he has already announced to his disciples that his purpose for taking this trip was to raise Lazarus from the dead [v. 11] – which could certainly not be done in obscurity). It is much more likely that both Jesus and the sisters were trying to preserve a little privacy in the midst of a house full of mourners, professional and otherwise.

29–32. Whatever the attempt at privacy, it was to no avail. Mary's departure is duly noted by the mourners, who, thinking she is heading for the tomb, decide to follow her, doubtless to lend their support. There is no negative overtone in this reference to *the Jews* (v. 31; *cf.* notes on 1:19).

When Mary reaches Jesus, she falls at his feet – indicating, perhaps, less emotional restraint than her sister displayed – and utters the same thing Martha had said (v.21).[1] This similarity surely makes it harsh to conclude (with Schnackenburg, 2. 333), that 'Mary gives the impression of being nothing but a complaining woman'. If unlike Martha she does not go on to affirm her continued faith in Jesus, her words nevertheless reveal her confidence that Jesus has power to heal. Her approach to Jesus is more emotional than that of her sister, and less private, and so the interchange now follows a different line.

33–35. Jewish funeral custom dictated that even a poor family was expected to hire at least two flute players and a professional wailing woman (Mishnah *Ketuboth* 4:4), and this family was anything but poor (*cf.* 12:1ff.). In addition to the tears of Mary and her grieving friends, therefore, doubtless there was quite a bit of professional grief. When Jesus saw all this, 'he was outraged in spirit, and troubled' (my transl.). To justify so radical a departure from the NIV's *he was deeply moved in spirit and troubled*, two questions must be addressed.

(1) What does the crucial word *embrimaomai* actually mean? In extra-biblical Greek, it can refer to the *snorting* of horses; as applied to human beings, it invariably suggests anger, outrage or emotional indignation. In the New Testament, it occurs twice in this chapter (*cf.* v. 38), and elsewhere only in Matthew 9:30; Mark 1:43; 14:5; and in a textual variant to Matthew 12:18. Not only this word but its cognates as well move in this sphere of meaning. Beasley-Murray (pp. 192–193) points out that German translations get it right; most English translations soften the passage to 'he groaned in spirit', 'he sighed heavily', 'he was deeply touched' or, as here, 'he was deeply moved in spirit' – all without linguistic justification. The phrase *in spirit* is not in dispute. It does not refer to the Holy Spirit, but is roughly equivalent to 'in himself': his inward reaction was anger or outrage or indignation. John adds that he *was troubled*,[2] the same strong verb used in 12:27; 13:21. It is lexically inexcusable to reduce this emotional upset to the effects of empathy, grief, pain or the like.

---

[1]The words are identical in the NIV (vv. 21, 22); there is a small change of word order in Greek.

[2]The text is enough of a 'hard saying' that some ancient authorities soften it by introducing an 'as': 'he was troubled in spirit as one who is outraged'.

415

(2) At what, then, was Jesus angry? The suggestion that the grief of the sisters and of the Jews is almost forcing a miracle upon him, arousing his wrath (so Barrett, p. 399; *cf.* 2:4; 4:48; 6:26) is countered by the fact that Jesus has already expressed his own determination to perform the miracle (v. 11). It is equally unjustified to think that Jesus is upset because he judges the mourning of the Jews to be hypocritical. The text does not cast their mourning in a different light to that of Mary, and in any case John, unlike the Synoptists, does not focus on the hypocrisy of the Jews (he never uses *hypokrisis* and related words). Even if we note that Jesus' visceral response occurs *when Jesus saw [Mary] weeping, and the Jews who had come along with her also weeping*, two interpretations are possible. Some think that Jesus is moved by their grief, and is consequently angry with the sin, sickness and death in this fallen world that wrecks so much havoc and generates so much sorrow. Others think that the anger is directed at the unbelief itself. The men and women before him were grieving like pagans, like 'the rest of men, who have no hope' (1 Thes. 4:13). Profound grief at such bereavement is natural enough; grief that degenerates to despair, that pours out its loss as if there were no resurrection, is an implicit denial of that resurrection.

Perhaps these two interpretations are not irreconcilable. With most of us, to be angry with someone is inconsistent with being loving and empathetic toward that person. With Jesus, as with his Father, the antithesis breaks down. This is the Jesus who could utter his terrible 'woes' (Mt. 23), yet grieve over the city of Jerusalem (Mt. 23:37–39). Christians themselves, 'like the rest ... were by nature objects of [God's] wrath' (Eph. 2:3), even though 'In love he predestined us to be adopted as his sons through Jesus Christ, in accordance with his pleasure and will' (Eph. 1:4–5). So also here. The one who always does what pleases his Father (8:29) is indignant when faced with attitudes that are not governed by the truths the Father has revealed. If sin, illness and death, all devastating features of this fallen world, excite his wrath, it is hard to see how unbelief is excluded. But the world that is at enmity with God is also the object of God's love (*cf.* notes on 3:16), so it is not surprising that when he was shown the tomb where the body lay, *Jesus wept*. The verb *wept* (*dakryō*) is different from that describing the weeping of Mary and the Jews (*klaiō*): it means 'to shed tears', but usually in lament before some calamity. It is unreasonable to think that Jesus' tears were shed for Lazarus, since he knew he was about to raise him from the dead (v. 11). Rather, the same sin and death, the same unbelief, that prompted his outrage, also generated his grief. Those who follow Jesus as his disciples today do well to learn the same tension – that grief and compassion without outrage reduce to mere sentiment, while outrage without grief hardens into self-righteous arrogance and irascibility.

36–37. Jesus' display of emotion is interpreted in two ways by the Jews, both interpretations curiously right and wrong. To some, Jesus' tears before Lazarus' tomb testified *how he loved* (*phileō*; *cf.* notes on v. 3) *him*. Their conclusion was true: Jesus did love Lazarus and his sisters (v.

5), but Jesus' tears were scarcely evidence of it in the way the Jews imagined it, for they understood his grief to be as despairing as their own. Others remembered the spectacular healing of the man born blind (ch. 9; Jerusalem was not far away, v. 18), and wondered why someone who could heal so powerfully could not have prevented the death of a friend he obviously loved. At one level their reasoning is sound: Jesus *did* heal the blind man, and he *could have prevented* Lazarus from dying. There is no need to suppose that their attitude was sneering, that their confidence that Jesus had healed the blind man was dissembled. They were puzzled and confused. Nevertheless, even to ask the question in this way betrays massive unbelief. It is the unbelief of the person whose faith does not rest on who Jesus is and what he has revealed of the Father, but on displays of power. Such inchoate 'faith' is so weak it constantly demands new signs and miracles (*cf.* notes on 4:48; 6:30–31). This unbelief is the reason the next verse reports that Jesus' quiet outrage flares up again (the verb is *embrimaomai*, as in v. 33).

4. The resurrection of Lazarus (11:38–44)

38. On this display of Jesus' emotion, *cf.* notes on v. 33. Many Jews buried their dead in caves, natural or hewn out of the rock. The cave might be either vertical or horizontal; in both cases it was commonly sealed by a stone. By the fourth century the site had become important enough for Christians for a church to be built over the crypt believed to be Lazarus' tomb, and called the Lazareion. From this word derives the modern Muslim name for Bethany, El-Azariyeh.[1] Even if the site is authentic, there have nevertheless been some major modifications (*e.g.* the present mosque blocks the ancient entrance: *cf.* Wilkinson, p. 110).

39–40. That Martha (who has apparently by this time joined her sister and the Jews) takes charge and issues the practical objection to Jesus' request that the stone be removed is entirely in character. Her objection confirms that she did not understand from her earlier conversation that Jesus was going to raise her brother immediately. There was no reason why she should have. On the significance of *four days*, *cf.* notes on v. 17. The fear of the stench of decomposition assumes the body was not embalmed. Some have argued that v. 44 contradicts this assumption. However, what is described in v. 44 (*cf.* notes) is much less than an embalming, and in any case aromatic spices were used in Jewish circles not to embalm bodies (as did the Egyptians) but to counteract repulsive odours from bodily decomposition (*cf.* Sanders, p. 274 n. 1).

Although Jesus had told his disciples that Lazarus' illness was for the glory of God (v. 4), he had not (so far as is recorded) referred to 'glory' in his conversation with Martha. His rhetorical question *Did I not tell you that if you believed, you would see the glory of God?* must therefore be taken

---

[1] The name 'Lazarus' derives from the Hebrew *laṣar*, an abbreviated form of Eleazar (= 'he whom God helps'); but there is little evidence that John plays with names in this way.

as a summary of what was promised in vv. 23–26 – *i.e.* to raise to life someone who has died is a revelatory act, the manifestation of the glory of God in Christ Jesus. Jesus' question should not be taken to imply that in vv. 23–26 he was somehow promising that he would indeed raise Lazarus immediately, but that if, as Martha herself confessed (v. 27), Jesus the Messiah is the resurrection and the life, then even in the face of this death he is to be trusted, for he will do nothing other than that which displays the glory of God.

41–42. Apparently Martha gave her consent, and *they took away the stone*. Jesus' prayer is remarkable for several reasons. *First*, his direct reference to God as 'Father' is characteristic of his praying (*cf.* 17:1, 11, 25). *Second*, the prayer assumes that Jesus has already asked for Lazarus' life, and that all he must do is to thank his Father for the answer. In itself, that is not surprising: v. 11 also assumes that the raising of Lazarus had been determined for some time. *Third*, the public nature of his prayer is not a matter of playing to the gallery (so Loisy, p. 353). Quite the reverse, for (1) the prayer seeks to draw his hearers into the intimacy of Jesus' own relationship with the Father; (2) the prayer demonstrates the truth of 5:19ff., *i.e.* that Jesus does nothing by himself, but is totally dependent on and obedient to his Father's will. The Son may ask; the Father grants. What Jesus is hoping will be accomplished is that some of his hearers will in consequence believe that he has been sent by God himself.

It is not foreign to the spirit of the passage to remark that public prayers, though like private prayers addressed to God, must be crafted with the public in mind as well.

43–44. Even before the last day, and in anticipation of it, Jesus' cry 'Lazarus, come out!' proved to be an instance when the dead heard the voice of the Son of God (5:25, 28–29) and sprang to life. Though it is not John's point, it has often been remarked that the authority of Jesus is so great that, had he not specified Lazarus, all the tombs would have given up their dead to resurrection life.

Many commentators cite Basil (*c.* AD 330–379), who, supposing that the graveclothes bound Lazarus so tightly he could not possibly, by himself, emerge from the tomb, speaks of 'a miracle within a miracle'. John does not think in such terms, and in any case the graveclothes were not so restrictive. The corpse was customarily laid on a sheet of linen, wide enough to envelop the body completely and more than twice the length of the corpse. The body was so placed on the sheet that the feet were at one end, and then the sheet was drawn over the head and back down to the feet. The feet were bound at the ankles, and the arms were tied to the body with linen strips. The face[1] was bound with another *cloth* (*soudarion*, a loan-word from the Latin *sudarium*, 'sweat-cloth', often

---

[1]Gk. *opsis*, which normally means 'appearance' (as in 7:24), but here means 'face', as often in the papyri (*cf.* MM, p. 471).

worn in life around the neck).[1] Jesus' body was apparently prepared for burial in the same way (*cf.* 19:40; 20:5, 7). A person so bound could hop and shuffle, but scarcely walk. Therefore when Jesus commanded Lazarus to come forth, and the *dead man came out*, Jesus promptly gave the order, *Take off the grave clothes and let him go.*

Readers cannot help but compare the resurrection of Jesus, after which the linen strips were still present and the *soudarion* was neatly 'folded up by itself, separate from the linen' (20:7). The differences are of a piece with the general New Testament witness to the uniqueness of Jesus' resurrection. Lazarus was called to a restoration of mortal life. Small wonder he groped blindly for the exit, and needed to be released from the graveclothes that bound him. Jesus rose with what Paul calls 'a spiritual body' (1 Cor. 15), leaving the graveclothes behind, materializing in closed rooms. Though his resurrected body bore the marks of his five wounds and was capable of eating and of being touched, it was raised with the power of endless life, the firstfruits of the resurrection at the end. Those who hear Jesus' shout on the last day will participate in his resurrection; the resurrection of Lazarus, occurring before that of Jesus, could only be a pale anticipation of what was yet to come. It was, in fact, a 'sign' (*cf.* notes on 2:11), rightly the climactic sign.

B. THE JUDICIAL DECISION TO KILL JESUS (11:45–54)

1. The plot and its paradox (11:45–53)

It is often argued that John substitutes this plot for the Synoptic accounts of the trial of Jesus before the High Priest, and that therefore its historical worth is dubious. Close reading of Mark 14:1, however, shows that even the Synoptists *presuppose* an earlier decision, here attested by John.

45–46. Jesus' words and deeds frequently divided the Jews (*e.g.* 6:14, 15; 7:10–13, 45–52). So again here. Of the considerable number of *the Jews* (again there is no negative overtone; *cf.* notes on 1:19) *who had come to visit Mary* (which presupposes that it was Mary rather than Martha who had an extensive circle of friends), and who witnessed the glory of God (*cf.* vv. 4, 40), *many . . . put their faith in him.* The calibre of their faith (*cf.* 2:23–25; 8:30–31) is not discussed. It is in any case superior to the conduct of those who *went to the Pharisees and told them what Jesus had done.* One might charitably hope that the motive of at least some of them was to win the Pharisees to the truth, but the contrast set up between those who believe and those who go to the Pharisees suggests that their intent was more malicious. That *the Pharisees* (*cf.* notes on 1:19, 24) are approached, rather than any other group, does not betray ignorance of

---

[1]*Cf.* Sanders, p. 276 – though his view that the *soudarion* was added 'to keep the jaw in place' is dubious. *Cf.* especially J. Blinzler, p. 396.

Jerusalem life before the destruction of the temple. Because so many of them were scribes, public teachers and synagogue leaders, they were frequently more in touch with the common people than were the priests.

There are clearly many other things we might have liked to learn: what Lazarus experienced in the grave, the nature and time of his subsequent death, what he did or did not say to his neighbours, and more. John reports none of it. Everything is sacrificed to the sign itself, to what it anticipates, and even to the way it precipitates it by arousing the animus of the authorities.

> Behold a man raised up by Christ!
> The rest remaineth unreveal'd;
> He told it not; or something seal'd
> The lips of the Evangelist.[1]

47–48. The Pharisees by themselves could not take decisive judicial action. The highest judicial body in the land was the Sanhedrin, which under Roman authority controlled all Jewish internal affairs. It was simultaneously a judiciary, a legislative body, and, through the high priest, an executive; and all of this authority was perceived to rest on a theocratic basis. In Jesus' day the (seventy?) members of the Sanhedrin were dominated by the chief priests, *i.e.* priests drawn from the extended family of the high priest, who presided over it (as the seventy-first member?). Virtually all the priests were Sadducees. The Pharisees constituted an influential minority; most of them were scribes. The rest of the members were elders, landed aristocrats of mixed (or few) theological views. *Cf.* notes on 1:19, 24; 3:1; 7:45ff.; Additional Note on 18:24. The Pharisees allied themselves with the chief priests, and the problem of Jesus was put on the Sanhedrin's agenda.

The answer to the rhetorical question *What are we accomplishing?* (*i.e.* by the paltry steps we have taken so far), is, of course, 'Nothing!' The religious authorities find it impossible to dispute that Jesus is performing *many miraculous signs*, especially after the embarrassment they endured in their exchange with the man born blind who had been healed (ch. 9), and now after the public raising of Lazarus. But this does not prompt them to re-assess their stance toward Jesus. Rather, they express their fear that popular messianic expectations will be fired to fever pitch, and, with or without Jesus' sanction, set off an uprising that would bring down the full weight of Rome upon their heads. They fear such reprisals could end in destruction of 'our *place*' (almost certainly a reference to the temple: *cf.* 2 Ezra 14:7 [LXX; *cf.* Ne. 4:7]; Je. 7:14; Acts 6:14) and nation (*i.e.* the semi-autonomous status of the Jewish nation). Nevertheless, the peculiar way this is worded shows they are above all

---

[1]Alfred Lord Tennyson, *In Memoriam*; also cited by Bruce, p. 249.

afraid that the Romans will come and take away *from them* the temple and nation (*cf.* Becker, pp. 367–368).[1] They are prompted less by dispassionate concern for the well-being of the nation than for their own positions of power and prestige. Note also the 'better for you' in v. 50. The rapid changes in power across the previous three centuries make such fears understandable, if not admirable.

49–50. Presiding over the Sanhedrin was *Caiaphas, who was high priest that year*. Joseph Caiaphas had been appointed high priest in AD 18 by the Roman prefect Valerius Gratus. His father-in-law was Annas, who himself filled the office during the years AD 6–15, and whose influence prevailed long after his term of office (*cf.* notes on 18:12ff.). Caiaphas remained in office until AD 36, when he and Pontius Pilate were both sacked at the same time. Only John and Matthew (26:57) mention Caiaphas by name in connection with Jesus' death (though *cf.* Lk. 3:2; Acts 4:6). It has often been suggested that because John stipulates that Caiaphas was high priest *that year*, he has been influenced by pagan priestly systems in the hellenistic world where priests were often appointed only for a year, and thus betrays his ignorance of Jewish custom (so Bauer, p. 151; Bultmann, p. 410 n. 10; Haenchen, 2. 75). But the conclusion is much too hasty. The demonstrative *that* may simply mean 'that fateful year' or 'that memorable year', referring to Jesus' death – a solution favoured by the repetition of the words in v. 51; 18:13, and one that can be traced back to Origen. Alternatively, it must be remembered that although the Old Testament specified that the high priest, once appointed, was to serve for life, in reality the office had long been a political football, high priests being appointed and deposed at the will (or whim) of the overlord. Caiaphas, in fact, displayed extraordinary sticking power for the times (eighteen years). John's remark may therefore reflect his intimate knowledge of the tenuousness of the office (so Lightfoot, *BE*, pp. 28–29; Schlatter, p. 258; Bammel, just cited).

Caiaphas' opening blast, *You know nothing at all!*, is the ancient equivalent of 'You don't know what you are talking about!' Even so, it is certainly not a reflection of the Dale Carnegie school of diplomacy, and it nicely confirms the judgment of Josephus that the Sadducees were barbarous and wild even toward those of their own party (*Bel.* ii. 166) – though it must be remembered that Josephus, as a Pharisee, was scarcely an unbiased observer. As the presiding officer, Caiaphas delivers his own opinion: *it is better for you that one man die for the people than that the whole nation perish.*

Double meanings run to the end of v. 52; Johannine irony reaches its apogee here. The legal precedents for Caiaphas' judgment are complex (*cf.* Beasley-Murray, pp. 196–197), his reasoning rather simple. Both from the perspective of political prudence in international realism (what

---

[1]*Cf.* E. Bammel, '"Ex illa itaque die consilium fecerunt . . ."', in E. Bammel (ed.), *The Trial of Jesus* (*Fs.* C. F. D. Moule; SCM, 1970), pp. 11–40, esp. pp. 23–24.

will save the nation), and from the perspective of what is best for the ruling party ('it is better for you': cf. notes on v. 48), the execution of Jesus is indicated. And so he died – but the nation perished anyway, not because of Jesus' activity but because of the constant mad search for political solutions where there was little spiritual renewal. Justice is sacrificed to expediency.

When Caiaphas argues that Jesus must die *for the people* (*hyper tou laou*), he is using sacrificial language (*cf.* notes on 10:11). He certainly did not mean this in a Christian sense; he probably meant that Jesus was to be 'devoted' to death, sacrificed as a scapegoat, in order to spare the nation and its leaders. Readers living after the cross could not help but see more. In this sentence, Jews are referred to both as a nation (*ethnos*) and as a people (*laos*), and both terms are later taken over by Christians and applied to the church.

51–52. John has often used irony or double meaning, and sometimes drawn attention to it (*cf.* notes on 2:19–22). Here he spells out his understanding of Caiaphas's words, and how the prophecy came about. Caiaphas *did not say this on his own.* This does not mean that God used Caiaphas as if he were a puppet, a creature like Balaam's ass, a mere mouthpiece. Caiaphas spoke his considered if calloused opinion. But when Caiaphas spoke, God was also speaking, even if they were not saying the same things (*cf.* Carson, pp. 128–129; *cf.* Acts 4:27–28). Caiaphas spoke as a prophet, partly by virtue of the fact that he was the high priest,[1] partly by virtue of the fact that it was 'that [fateful] year' when Jesus was to die. *What* he prophesied was:

(1) *that Jesus would die for the Jewish[2] nation* – and once again, 'for the nation' (*hyper tou ethnous*) is sacrificial language (*cf.* notes on vv. 49–50), frequently associated with a ransom. Both Caiaphas and John understand Jesus' death to be substitutionary: either Jesus dies, or the nation dies. 'If He dies the nation lives. It is His life instead of theirs' (Morris, p. 568). But while Caiaphas is thinking at the purely political level, John invites his readers to think in terms of the Lamb of God who takes away the sin of the world (1:29, 34).

(2) *that Jesus would die . . . not only for that nation but also for the scattered children of God, to bring them together and make them one.* In a purely Jewish context, 'the scattered children of God' would be understood to refer to the Jews of the diaspora, who would be gathered together in the promised land to share in the kingdom of God (*e.g.* Is. 43:5; Ezk. 34:12; 36:24ff.). Christians were quick to draw typological connections: the real children of God are those who receive the incarnate Word and believe in

---

[1] At one time the high priest revealed God's will by using the Urim and Thummim. Zadok the priest is assumed to be a 'seer' (2 Sa. 15:27). For the full range of evidence, *cf.* C. H. Dodd, 'The Prophecy of Caiaphas: John 11:47–53', *More New Testament Studies* (Manchester University Press, 1968), pp. 58–68. As for unconscious prophecy, *cf.* SB 2. 546.

[2] The word *Jewish* is not in the Greek, but is clearly understood, judging by the contrast John draws between 'that nation' and 'the scattered people of God' in v. 52.

422

his name (1:12, 13), and if they are dispersed in the world (*cf.* 1 Pet. 1:1) they will be gathered not only at the parousia, but into the one church, the community of the Messiah (*to bring them together and make them one* here seems to refer to the immediate effects of Jesus' death; *cf.* also 17:21). The 'oneness' motif anticipates chs. 14 – 17, esp. ch. 17, a foretaste of which has already been introduced in ch. 10. There we learn that Jesus must draw his sheep from many sheep pens into one flock, under one shepherd (10:16). The ultimate 'holy nation' is the church (*cf.* 1 Pet. 2:9). All of this anticipates the Gentile mission (*cf.* also 12:32), but it is heavily based in Jewish categories, and must have been a powerful inducement for the first Jewish readers and their proselytes to convert to Christianity.

Barrett (pp. 407–408) asks whether we are to think of the 'scattered children of God' as (1) those who are gathered together by the effects of Christ's cross on the grounds that they *are by nature* children of God, or as (2) those who are *made* children of God by the death of Christ and thus united together as one (in the church). Those who detect deterministic Stoic or gnostic thought as the background of John's theology opt for the former; Barrett himself decisively opts for the latter, on the grounds that 1:12–13; 3:3, 5 'make it clear that men *become* children of God only by receiving Christ, by birth of water and Spirit' (*cf.* also Vellanickal, pp. 214ff.). Why then are they called 'children of God' before they are regenerated and gathered? The answer is in line with the predestinarian strain in this Gospel: Jesus *already has* sheep in other pens whom he must bring (10:16); certain people have already been given to the Son by the Father (6:37ff., 44, 65), even if they have not yet become disciples. The thought is akin to Acts 18:9, 10. For them Jesus lays down his life, 'to bring them together and make them one'.

53. *Cf.* Matthew 26:3, 4. The advice of the high priest was accepted: *ebouleusanto* does not mean *they plotted* (NIV) but 'they resolved' (BAGD, p. 145). The decision has now been made; it remains only to carry it out, as efficiently as is compatible with political expediency. In short, Jesus is not to be arrested in order to be tried; he is to be tried because he has already been found guilty (as Mk. 14:1–2 presupposes). And this, John insists, has been precipitated by the raising of Lazarus (*cf.* also 12:10).

2. Jesus' response (11:54)

54. A large council (of seventy-one? *cf.* notes on vv. 47–48; Additional Note on 18:24) is unlikely to be secure, especially if there are sympathizers in it (*cf.* 7:45ff.; *cf.* also notes on v. 57). So it is not surprising that Jesus found out about the Sanhedrin's decision, and *therefore . . . no longer moved about publicly among the Jews.* To those with eyes to see he was making a theological statement: no human court could force him to the cross. Both the fact and the timing were simultaneously the Father's determination and his own willed act (10:17, 18; *cf.* notes on 12:23ff.). In this context *the Jews* must refer to the Judeans, for Jesus withdraws *to a village called Ephraim* (probably Old Testament Ephron, 2 Ch. 13:19), most likely the modern village of Et-Taiyibeh, four miles north-east of Bethel and about twelve miles from Jerusalem – far enough away to be safe for the time being, but close enough to be able to attend the culminating Passover (vv. 55ff.) at the hour determined by his Father (12:23).

C. TRIUMPH AND IMPENDING DEATH *(11:55 – 12:36)*

1. The setting: the Passover of the Jews *(11:55–57)*

55. This is the third Passover mentioned by John. The first (2:13ff.) took place during the period while the ministries of the Baptist and of Jesus overlapped (*cf.* 3:24). The second occurred during Jesus' Galilean ministry (6:4), and he did not go up to Jerusalem on that occasion. Nevertheless John 6 is replete with allusions to the Passover theme. It is just possible (though unlikely) that the unnamed feast of 5:1 refers to another Passover. More likely, however, the one mentioned here (11:55) is the third and last for the period of Jesus' ministry, which therefore establishes that his public ministry ran a little over two years. If the first Passover was in AD 28, forty-six years after the date Herod the Great began the rebuilding of the temple (2:20), the year of Jesus' death and resurrection is AD 30.[1] The reasons for calling it *the Jewish Passover* (lit. 'The Passover of the Jews') are much the same as in 2:13 (*cf.* notes).

Jerusalem was viewed as the capital of the nation, and so from every point on the compass pilgrims travelled *up from the country to Jerusalem*, much as in England one travels *up* to London.[2] The need for cere-monial purification before Passover is stipulated in Numbers 9:6ff. for those who had contracted ceremonial defilement of some sort (*e.g.* by touching a corpse), and was still operative in Jesus' day (*cf.* Schlatter, pp. 261–262). The appropriate purificatory rites occupied one week before Passover. Jesus himself felt no need to cleanse himself in this way: his movements are reported in 12:1ff.

56. The number of pilgrims already in Jerusalem to undergo the purificatory ceremonies fanned into flame the discussion as to what Jesus would do. Their debate is reminiscent of the one that took place at Tabernacles (*cf.* notes on 7:11). Since that time, however, the rising hostility of the authorities (*cf.* 7:25, 32; 8:59; 10:31, 39), culminating in the recent judicial decision (if it had become known to a wide circle, which is not unlikely: *cf.* notes on vv. 54, 57), made their debate the more acute. If there is no evidence of hostility on the part of the

---

[1] For an alternative reckoning, *cf.* Harold Hoehner, *Chronological Aspects of the Life of Christ* (Zondervan, 1977).

[2] Unless, of course, one is travelling from Cambridge or Oxford, but this is a peculiar conceit.

ordinary pilgrim, neither is there evidence of thoughtful discipleship – only of considerable enthusiasm (*cf.* 12:12ff.), some of it (as in 6:14–15) misplaced.

57. The circulation of the orders of *the chief priests and Pharisees* (*cf.* notes on 7:32; 11:47) was enough to alert residents and pilgrims alike that the Sanhedrin had decided to take decisive action against Jesus.

2. Mary anoints Jesus (12:1–11)

This chapter contains no miraculous 'sign', and no sustained discourse. The first two narrative sections (vv. 1–11, 12–19) report events in which others honour Jesus, even though many do not grasp the significance of what is happening. In the third section (vv. 20–36) the arrival of the Greeks seeking Jesus serves as a signal that the 'hour' (*cf.* notes on 2:4) is at hand, and this generates a mixture of dialogue and monologue. The chapter ends with a lengthy meditation, steeped in Old Testament Scripture, as to why so many Jews did not believe, and a reflective summary of Jesus' authority and of the urgency of belief. Every paragraph builds toward the farewell discourse, passion and resurrection which immediately follow.

The anointing of Jesus at Bethany demands comparison with Matthew 26:6–13 = Mark 14:3–9; Luke 7:36–38. Matthew and Mark tell of an anointing at Bethany, in the house of Simon the leper. Their incident is undated, but is placed toward the end of Jesus' public ministry. The woman is unnamed, but she anoints Jesus' head with ointment of nard, taken from an alabaster jar. The disciples (Mt.; Mk. has 'some of those present') were indignant. Jesus defends the woman, relates the anointing to his death and burial, mentions the fact that the poor will always be present, and promises that the woman's deed will always be remembered wherever the gospel is preached. By contrast, Luke reports a dinner at the home of a Pharisee (unnamed). An unnamed woman of immoral character, learning of Jesus' presence at the meal, brings an alabaster jar of perfume (not specified as nard). Overcome with remorse, she weeps so copiously that her tears wet Jesus' feet, which she wipes with her hair and then anoints with the perfume. The subsequent discussion centres neither on the poor nor on Jesus' impending burial, but on the unvoiced accusation of the Pharisee, who thinks that if Jesus were a prophet he would have known what kind of woman this was and forbidden her to touch him. Jesus detects in her tears the gratitude of one who had been forgiven much.

Although there are some critics who hold that one event stands behind the four reports, the discrepancies between Luke's account and the other three are so large that only unbridled imagination can offer adequate reasons to explain why so many differences would have been invented.[1]

---

[1]Thus Brown, 1. 449–452, and I. Howard Marshall, *The Gospel of Luke* (NIGTC; Paternoster, 1978), pp. 304–307, strongly argue for two separate incidents.

The parallels between John and Matthew/Mark are much closer. Both place the anointing in Bethany, though Matthew/Mark specify the home of Simon the leper while John does not say to whom it belonged (*cf.* notes on v. 2). In both, the ointment is pure nard (*cf.* notes on v. 3 for the peculiar expression used); in both the reaction of the onlookers is that the perfume should have been sold and given to the poor. Matthew specifies that this was the reaction of the disciples; John names one particular disciple, Judas Iscariot. Both mention the sum of three hundred denarii as the value of the perfume (Mark says 'more than' three hundred denarii). In both Jesus defends the woman, and makes a reference to his burial.

Nevertheless, there are differences between John and Matthew/Mark. The least important is the setting: in Matthew/Mark it is placed after the triumphal entry, in John it is placed before. It must be remembered, however, that the time indicators in Matthew/Mark are notoriously loose. These Evangelists often order their accounts according to topic, not chronology. In John's case the event is tied to the raising of Lazarus (vv. 1–2, 9–11), and the devotion of Mary serves, amongst other things, as a startling foil to the decision of the leaders to kill Jesus (*cf.* notes on 11:53). Apart from a number of details, none of which provides the remotest hint of contradiction (*e.g.* Mark does not name the woman, John specifies that it was Mary; Mark speaks of breaking the alabaster jar, John does not), the most startling difference is in the descriptions of the anointing. Mark speaks of an anointing on Jesus' head, John of an anointing on Jesus' feet followed by wiping of Jesus' feet with the woman's hair (*cf.* Luke's account, where the hair of the immoral woman was used to wipe her tears from Jesus' feet before the perfume was applied). This strange pattern of textual affinities has convinced many scholars that, assuming there were two separate incidents, there has been a 'crossover' of details as the stories were retold, resulting in clear errors in John's account.[1] Why would anyone wipe off perfume that had just been applied? And would a respectable woman let down her tresses in male company?

Nevertheless, several small details in the text encourage the reader to inject a small dose of historical imagination before resorting too quickly to the critic's knife. *First*, the amount of nard is noticed by John (*cf.* notes on v. 3), and is implied by Mark's reference to the breaking of the jar's neck (*i.e.* the jar was full, and breaking the neck was the way to pour all of it out). It is far too large a quantity to have been poured out over the head alone. *Second*, in both Matthew (26:12) and Mark (14:8), Jesus is reported as saying that the perfume was poured on *his body* in anticipation of his burial – a strange way of referring to his head alone. These two observations strongly suggest that the perfume was applied to more than Jesus' head or his feet. Indeed, if Jesus could see in its application a

[1]So Brown, *ibid.*; Marshall, *ibid.*; Beasley-Murray, p. 206; and many others.

prefiguring of the unguents applied at his burial, one must suppose that it was lavishly applied. *Third*, Matthew and Mark have thematic reasons for referring in particular to Jesus' head: they wish to show that he is being honoured, anointed as king. It would not have been inappropriate for John to make the same emphases, but by mentioning the anointing on *Jesus' feet* there is injected into the description a sense of the woman's self-perceived unworthiness. She thus becomes a foil not only of the religious authorities who were actively plotting Jesus' death, but of the disciples who, in the very next chapter, have to be *taught* to wash one another's feet, and by Jesus himself (13:1ff.). In short, it is reasonable to suppose that what actually happened was comprehensive enough to generate the accounts of both John and Matthew/Mark, including the divergences that initially seem so odd.

1. The words *Six days before the Passover* introduce a chronological problem that is discussed in the notes on 13:1. Anticipating the conclusion of that discussion, the view that insists John represents Passover as beginning on the following Friday evening (*i.e.* the onset of Saturday, by Jewish reckoning) appears incorrect. It is more likely that, with the Synoptics, he thinks of Passover beginning Thursday evening (*i.e.* the onset of Friday). *Six days before the Passover* most likely refers to the preceding Saturday, which began the Friday evening. If Jesus *arrived at Bethany* that evening, just as Sabbath began, the 'dinner' that is described (v. 2) probably occurred on the Sabbath, the Saturday evening. After sundown, when Sabbath had officially ended, the large crowd of Jews assembled (vv. 9–11), and the next day, Sunday, the triumphal entry took place (vv. 12ff.). It is less likely that the *six days* have symbolic force (*cf.* notes on 2:1).

Bethany, situated less than two miles from Jerusalem (*cf.* notes on 11:1), was the home of Mary, Martha and Lazarus, whose raising the Evangelist has just reported. At one level, the setting prepares the way for v. 2, and the introduction of the dinner and the anointing. But the anointing itself points to Jesus' death (v. 8); and meanwhile, at a subtler level, mention of Passover (*cf.* notes on 11:55) in this context reminds the reader that the one who raised Lazarus from the dead is about to go to his own death, as a sacrificial lamb, a passover lamb, the deliverer of his people.

2. If this *dinner* (*deipnon*, which can refer to a meal at any time of day) is in the evening of Saturday, the close of the Sabbath (*cf.* v. 1), it is probably connected with the ritual that separated the Sabbath from the rest of the week, including the *Habdalah*, the synagogue service that followed the meal (Mishnah *Berakoth* 8:5 suggests the rites were this early). However, this narrative lacks the concentration of suggestive elements that would support the hypothesis that the Evangelist is forging some sort of typological link – *e.g.* that Jesus himself is the true Sabbath-rest, or that proper Sabbath worship directs its devotion to Jesus.

The Greek literally reads, 'they made ... a supper' (*epoiēsan ...*

deipnon), without any specification of the antecedent of 'they'. One might surmise Mary, Martha and Lazarus, but the text does not say so. The third person plural 'they' may have indeterminate force, like French 'on' or German 'man': hence NIV's rendering in the passive, *a dinner was given*. That Lazarus *was among those reclining at the table*, or that *Martha served*, proves nothing: a village dinner honouring a celebrated guest might well draw in several families to do the work, and the presence of Lazarus at any Bethany dinner designed to honour Jesus would scarcely be surprising. It has been suggested that Simon the Leper (Mk. 14:3) was the father of Lazarus and his sisters, and therefore the real owner of their home, even though for all practical purposes they owned it. This is an attractive hypothesis, but completely without supporting evidence. The actions of Mary and Martha – the latter serving, the former adoring – are consistent with the picture of the two women preserved in Luke 10:38–42.

On the custom of *reclining at the table, cf.* notes on 13:2–5, 23.

3. The quantity of perfume is considerable, a *litra*, a measurement of weight apparently equivalent to the Latin *libra* (*cf.* MM, p. 377), approximately eleven ounces (*i.e.* a little less than three-quarters of a pound avoirdupois; *cf.* notes on 19:39). *Nard* is an oil extracted from the root and spike (hence 'spikenard' in some versions) of the nard plant, grown in India. It is modified by the adjective *pistikēs*, whose meaning is disputed. Some derive the term from the Aramaic word *pîstaqa'*, referring to the pistachio nut: *i.e.* 'pistic nard' is not really nard but a derivative of the pistachio. Others think it derives from *pinō* ('I drink'), so that 'pistic nard' means 'liquid nard'. Neither derivation is convincing. More likely it derives from *pistos* ('faithful' or 'genuine'), hence NIV's *pure nard*. Its purity, quantity and origin account for its appalling cost: when John labels it *an expensive perfume*, he is thinking on a scale far larger than what we might mean by the words (*cf.* notes on vv. 4–5; on the varieties of nard and their cost, *cf.* LSJ *s.v.*; *NewDocs* 1. § 41).

Since those who were eating were reclining, their feet extended away from the table, making it possible to anoint as much of the person as one might wish (*cf.* notes at the beginning of this chapter), including the feet. John focuses on Jesus' feet: in terms of the symbolism established in ch. 13, at the very least this signifies the utmost in self-humbling devotion and love, regardless of cost (the expense of the nard) or of what others might think (Mary let down the tresses of her hair to wipe Jesus' feet). Mention of the fact that *the house was filled with the fragrance of the perfume* suggests not only extravagant love (Lindars, p. 417), but suggests that the fragrance of the act will extend far beyond the event itself (*cf.* Mk. 14:9).

4–5. Although Judas Iscariot (*cf.* notes on 6:71) speaks, others doubtless had the same thought (Mk. 14:4), even amongst the disciples (Mt. 26:8). The persistent habit of the Evangelists to tag Judas as the traitor (here, *who was later to betray him*) does not spring from any prescience they enjoyed at the time, but from the shocking force of their hindsight. It is as if they cannot recollect anything he said and did without also remembering that he was the one who ultimately betrayed the Lord of Glory for thirty pieces of silver.

The objection Judas raises has a superficial plausibility to it. The sum of 'three hundred denarii' (RSV), the value of the perfume, must not be estimated according to the modern value of an equivalent amount of silver, but according to wages and purchasing power. One denarius was the daily wage given to a common day-labourer; three hundred denarii was therefore the equivalent of *a year's wages* for a fully employed labourer (no money would be earned on Sabbaths and other holy days). The sum was enormous. Either Mary and her family were very wealthy, or perhaps this was a family heirloom that had been passed down to her. Either way, Judas displays a certain utilitarianism that pits pragmatic compassion, concern for the poor, against extravagant, unqualified devotion. If self-righteous piety sometimes snuffs out genuine compassion, it must also be admitted, with shame, that social activism, even that which meets real needs, sometimes masks a spirit that knows nothing of worship and adoration.

6. With Judas Iscariot, the case is far worse: his personal greed for material things masquerades as altruism. Like the hired hand, he cares nothing for the sheep (10:13). Because he was the treasurer of the apostolic band, the *keeper of the money bag*, probably he hoped such gifts as this nard could in future be turned into cash, to which he could then help himself. The *money bag* was doubtless used to meet the disciples' needs, and also to provide alms to the poor. Normally it was replenished by disciples who cherished Jesus' ministry, like the women mentioned in Luke 8:2, 3. The last clause could almost be taken to mean that Judas used to 'carry' (*bastazō*) what was put in, but in the right contexts the verb means 'steal' or 'pilfer' – not unlike the verb 'lift' in the United Kingdom. This is the only place in the New Testament where Judas is called a thief – indeed, where any charge other than Judas' ultimate betrayal is levelled against him. Yet the charge is believable: anyone who would betray another person for thirty pieces of silver has an unhealthy avarice for material things.

7–8. The Greek of v. 7 could be taken several ways, the most important of which are: (1) 'Leave her alone, in order that she may keep it [*i.e.* the perfume] for the day of my burial.' But this assumes Mary has barely begun to pour the perfume on Jesus, whereas vv. 3, 5 suggest she had already emptied the lot onto him. (2) Elliptically: 'Leave her alone. [She has done this] in order to keep it for the day of my burial.' This will make sense only if what Mary has done, in the understood ellipsis, is not the anointing itself, but the keeping of the perfume for just such an occasion rather than selling it and distributing the proceeds to the poor. (3) The Greek construction could be taken imperatively, though this use of it is rare: 'Leave her alone. Let her keep it for the day of my burial.' But this makes sense only if 'keep' means something like 'keep in mind' or 'remember', and there is little lexicographical support for this meaning

(Lk. 2:19, 51 comes close). (4) Translating the Greek the same way, others nevertheless take the 'it' (*auto*) to mean 'Leave her alone. Let her keep *the credit* [of having poured out this perfume] for the day of my burial' – but this seems to be a rather generous paraphrase.

The second option seems best, but certainty is impossible. Nor is it necessary to argue, whether here or in Mark 14:6, 8, that Mary herself intended the anointing to be a prefiguring of Jesus' burial. There is no clear evidence that Mary or anyone else understood before the cross that Jesus had to die. She meant this to be an act of costly, humble devotion, but like Caiaphas (11:49–52) she signalled more than she knew. In the culture of the day, it was not thought inappropriate to spend lavish sums at a funeral, including the cost of the perfumes that were designed to stifle the smell of decay (*cf.* notes on 11:39). But here was Mary, lavishly pouring out perfume on Jesus while he was yet alive. Small wonder Jesus sees it as a prefiguring of the anointing that Joseph of Arimathea and Nicodemus performed (19:38–42).

Verse 8 is closely parallel to Matthew 26:11 = Mark 14:7, but because either the entire verse or some part of it is missing from a few manuscripts some commentators judge the omission to be original. The textual evidence in favour of inclusion is very strong (*cf.* Metzger, pp. 236–237), and the verse makes sense as part of the rebuke to Judas Iscariot. That the poor are always present (*cf.* Dt. 15:11) is not an excuse for stinginess in almsgiving, but a reminder that they would still be around to receive the alms distributed amongst them long after Jesus himself had been taken away: *you will not always have me.* Were a mere mortal to claim such priority, he would be very ill or unspeakably arrogant. Jesus speaks this way as a matter of course, not only because he sees his cross and burial on the near horizon, but also because he knows he is to receive the same honour that is due the Father (5:23).

Mark 14:10, 11 makes it clear that it is this episode, including Jesus' sharp rebuke, that finally prompts Judas to approach the religious authorities with the proposal of betrayal. Though John makes no such connection explicit, when the betrayal begins to unfold he makes it clear that the devil's prompting of Judas antedates the last supper itself (*cf.* notes on 13:2).

9. After Jesus had raised Lazarus, he left almost immediately for Ephraim (11:54). Probably few people apart from the family, mourners and his own disciples had seen him since that time. The report that he was back in Bethany provided an opportunity for *a large crowd of Jews* (= Judeans? *cf.* notes on 1:19) to come out and see him. Probably many came from Jerusalem; indeed, so close to the Feast of Passover, doubtless at least some were pilgrims. Lazarus himself drew spectators. If until this point he had shielded himself from much vulgar curiosity, the public nature of this dinner in Jesus' honour made such privacy impossible: the crowds wanted *also to see Lazarus.*

10–11. Thus Lazarus became a focus for the plots of the chief priests. His very life provided a ground for faith in Jesus, so he too had to be destroyed (cf. notes on 11:53). Although faith grounded on such a sign could not be as pure and strong as faith based on Jesus' word (cf. 10:38), it is far better than no faith. The calibre of their faith is not assessed (unlike the faith of those described in 2:23–25). What is clear is that the raising of Lazarus prompts many *Jews* (clearly there is no animus directed against those represented by the term here! cf. notes on 1:19) to 'go over' to Jesus and put their faith in him: the expressions assume a self-conscious conversion, a move away from the religion practised by the authorities and a move toward genuine trust in Jesus.

3. The triumphal entry (12:12–19)

Because this is one of relatively few incidents in the life of Jesus that is reported in all four Gospels (cf. Mt. 21:1–11; Mk. 11:1–11; Lk. 19:29–38), there has been much discussion not only on the peculiar emphases found in each Gospel but also on the question of whether John had Mark or some other Synoptic Gospel before him when he wrote. On the latter question, there is still no consensus.[1] As for the former, some of the more important divergences in John will be noted.

12. For the time reference *next day*, cf. notes on v. 1. This is presumably Sunday of passion week. The *great crowd* is made up of pilgrims who have come to Jerusalem *for the Feast*, i.e. for Passover. Josephus (*Bel.* vi. 422–425) describes one Passover, just before the Jewish War (AD 66–70), when 2,700,000 people took part, not counting the defiled and the foreigners who were present in the city. Even if his numbers are inflated, the crowds were undoubtedly immense. The assumption in this verse and the next is that Jesus was met on the road from Bethany by pilgrims who had already reached Jerusalem, and who went out to meet him once they heard he was approaching. Many of these pilgrims would have been Galileans who were familiar with his ministry; many others would have heard of the raising of Lazarus (cf. 11:55–57) and eagerly sought an opportunity to see Jesus. Dodd (*HTFG*, p. 156) and others suggest that John's account is the story that would be told by someone in Jerusalem who heard of Jesus' approach, and the Synoptic account is the story that would be told by one of the pilgrims on the road who accompanied Jesus. But this is too antithetical an approach: two of the Synoptics report that there were crowds before and behind (Mt. 11:9; Mk. 11:9; cf. Carson, *Matt*, p. 439), apparently an indirect confirmation of John's report (cf. especially vv. 17, 18).

13. There was little difficulty obtaining *palm branches*: date palms were plentiful around Jerusalem, and still grow there. But there is nothing in

---

[1] In favour of Johannine dependence on one or more of the Synoptics are Barrett, pp. 415ff.; and Edwin D. Freed, *JBL* 80, 1961, pp. 329–338. The best treatment against dependence is that of Smith, *Essays*, pp. 97–105. Both sides, regrettably, think only in terms of the descent of tradition through various intermediaries, and never consider the possibility of eyewitness reportage with its own theological bent. That possibility does not resolve the issue of dependence; indeed, it could be made to favour either view. But it must not be left out of the discussion. Cf. Introduction, §§ II, III.

the Old Testament that prescribes palm branches at Passover, whereas
the people were commanded to take 'palm fronds . . . and rejoice before
the LORD your God' at the Feast of Tabernacles. This is one of the factors
that prompted T. W. Manson to argue that the triumphal entry actually
took place six months earlier and was transferred to this setting.[1] In fact,
this expedient is unnecessary. From about two centuries earlier, palm
branches had already become a national (not to say nationalist) symbol.
When Simon the Maccabee drove the Syrian forces out of the Jerusalem
citadel he was fêted with music and the waving of palm branches (cf.
1 Macc. 13:51, 141 BC), which had also been prominent at the rededi-
cation of the temple (*2 Macc.* 10:7, 164 BC). Apocalyptic visions of the end
utilize palm branches (*Testament of Naphtali* 5). Palms appear on the coins
struck by the insurgents during the Jewish wars against Rome (AD
66–70, 132–135); indeed, the use of the palm as a symbol for Judea was
sufficiently well established that the coins struck by the Romans to
celebrate their victory also sported it.[2] In short, waving of palm branches
was no longer restrictively associated with Tabernacles. In this instance,
it may well have signalled nationalist hope that a messianic liberator was
arriving on the scene (cf. 6:14–15).

The cry *Hosanna!*, originally a transliteration of Hebrew *hôšî'â nā'* (lit.
'give salvation now'), had come to be a term of acclamation or praise.
Every Jew knew of its occurrence in Psalm 118:25, for Psalm 118 is part of
the Hallel (Pss. 113 – 118), sung each morning by the temple choir
during the Feast of Tabernacles (cf. notes on 7:37) but also associated at
this period with the Feast of Dedication (on which cf. 10:22; 2 *Macc.* 1:9;
10:6) and with the Passover (cf. Mishnah *Pesahim* 5:7; 9:3; 10:7). Indeed,
at Tabernacles at least (and possibly at the other Feasts), every man and
boy waved his *lûlāb* (a few shoots of willow and myrtle tied with palm)
when the choir reached the *Hosanna!* in Psalm 118:25. The connection
was so strong that many Jews referred to their lulabs as hosannas.

The succeeding words are also drawn from Psalm 118. *Blessed is he who
comes in the name of the Lord* (cf. Ps. 118:26) originally conferred a blessing
on the pilgrim heading up to Jerusalem: 'in the name of the Lord'
modified 'Blessed'. It is possible that in the psalm the welcome and
blessing were pronounced upon a Davidic king (though that is not
explicitly said). Certainly in the Midrash on Psalm 118 this line is
understood messianically: the one who comes is the Messiah (*Midrash
Tehillim* 244a; cf. SB 1. 150). So here; the crowds do not simply pronounce
a blessing in the name of the Lord on the one who comes, but pronounce a blessing on the one who comes in the name of the Lord. The
next line shows that this is the way the crowd understands their own
words: *Blessed is the King of Israel* is not a quotation from Psalm 118, but
messianic identification of 'he who comes in the name of the Lord'.

---

[1] *BJRL* 33, 1950–51, pp. 272–298.
[2] H. St. J. Hart, *JTS* 3, 1952, pp. 172–198; cf. Bruce, p. 176 n. 8.

Something similar is reported by Luke (19:38). For the title 'King of Israel', *cf.* notes on 1:49; 18:37; 19:19.

14–15. The Synoptists here preserve much more information, and make it clear that Jesus arranged for the ride on the ass, thereby self-consciously fulfilling the prophecy of Zechariah 9:9. John cuts out these arrangements, and briefly reports, *Jesus found a young donkey* (the verb certainly allows room for the meaning 'to find by the agency of others', as Barrett, p. 418, points out, but it shows no interest in it). The expression *young donkey* (*onarion*) confirms that he rode a young animal (Mark specifies that it was unbroken), but again John makes nothing of it. The text does not specify when Jesus began his ride. Perhaps Jesus set his arrangements in motion, then began his journey into Jerusalem on foot, with the clamour of the crowd on every side, only to be met by his disciples bringing the animal for him to ride. Whatever the exact sequence, to report the ride on the donkey immediately after the acclamation of the crowd has the effect of damping down nationalist expectations. He does not enter Jerusalem on a war horse (*cf.* Is. 31:1–3; 1 Ki. 4:26), which would have whipped the political aspirations of the vast crowds into insurrectionist frenzy, but he chooses to present himself as the king who comes in peace, 'gentle and riding on a donkey' (Zc. 9:9).

The quotation bears closer inspection. The opening words, *Do not be afraid*, are found neither in the Hebrew nor in any version of Zechariah 9:9, and replace 'Rejoice greatly'. Quite likely they are drawn from Isaiah 40:9, where they are addressed to the one who brings good tidings to Zion. It is not uncommon for New Testament quotations from the Old Testament to derive from two or more passages (*e.g.* Mt. 27:9–10; Mk. 1:2–3). *Daughter of Zion*, drawn from Zechariah 9:9, is a common way of referring to the people of Jerusalem, especially in their guise as the oppressed or fallen people of God. The rest of the quotation is an abridgment of Zechariah 9:9. Like many New Testament quotations from the Old, however, the entire Old Testament context must be borne in mind if the full force of the words is to be recognized. After the promise of the coming of the gentle king, God further promises, 'I will take away the chariots from Ephraim and the war-horses from Jerusalem, and the battle-bow will be broken. He will proclaim peace to the nations. His rule will extend from sea to sea and from the River [*i.e.* the Euphrates] to the ends of the earth. As for you, because of the blood of my covenant with you, I will free your prisoners from the waterless pit' (Zc. 9:10, 11). Three points stand out: (1) The coming of the gentle king is associated with the cessation of war: this, too, was understood by John as defining the work of Jesus in such a way that he could never be reduced to an enthusiastic Zealot. (2) The coming of the gentle king is associated with the proclamation of peace to the nations, extending his reign to the ends of the earth. The latter half of Zechariah 9:10 is itself a quotation from Psalm 72:8, which promises a world-wide reign for Zion's king, a son of David. (3) The coming of the gentle king is associated with the blood of God's covenant that spells release for prisoners – themes already precious to John (*cf.* 1:29, 34; 3:5; 6:35–58; 8:31–34), and associated with Passover and with the death of the servant-king that lies immediately ahead.

16. This verse closely resembles John's remark about what the disciples did not understand when Jesus talked about destroying the temple and raising it in three days: 'After he was raised from the dead, his disciples recalled what he had said. Then they believed the Scripture and the words that Jesus had spoken' (2:22). There, the crucial turning point in their understanding took place 'after he was raised from the dead'; here, it is *after Jesus was glorified*. But this amounts to virtually the same thing. Jesus' death marked the turning point. It was part of the movement that led on to his resurrection and exaltation, *i.e.* his glorification, and the bestowal of the Spirit that was conditioned by it (7:39; 16:7).

Barrett (pp. 416, 417) and others detect an intolerable contradiction. If the disciples did not understand that Jesus' use of the ass fulfils prophecy, making Jesus the promised messianic king, then how is it that the crowds hail him as the King of Israel (v. 13)? Surely it cannot be thought that their understanding is better than that of Jesus' most intimate followers? Barrett therefore reasons that John has composed this verse to stress the theological centrality of Jesus' glorification, but has failed to note that in so doing he has written incredible 'history'.

The cogency of this argument turns on identifying the *these things* that the disciples did not understand with the confession of Jesus as the messianic king. But in John's narrative the crowds confess Jesus as the King of Israel *before* Zechariah 9:9 is introduced. Jesus refuses to reinforce their political and nationalist aspirations by riding on a war horse or by stirring up insurrection against the Romans. Rather, he takes steps to enter Jerusalem on a donkey, fulfilling rather different Old Testament promises. The full significance of this parabolic action and the Scripture on which it was based (summarized in the notes on vv. 14–15) neither the disciples nor the crowd grasped until after Jesus had been glorified and the Holy Spirit poured out (14:26; 16:12–15).

As in 2:22 (*cf.* notes), far from decreasing the historical plausibility of the narrative, the disciples' misunderstanding increases it. Not only is their failure to comprehend the *nature* of Jesus' kingship and the inevitability of the cross universally attested in the Gospels, that failure was also something that *could not* be misunderstood *after* Jesus' death and glorification. Christians could scarcely be thought to be Christians without understanding these fundamentals, and Jews in any sort of intimate dialogue with Christians would also understand what Christians meant. They might not *believe* their interpretation of the Old Testament Scriptures, but there could not easily be a profound misunderstanding of what was meant by these things. For such readers, this passage comes not to relieve misunderstanding but better to ground fledgling understanding, and to explain the evolution of the thinking of the first Christians by basing their change of perspective and comprehension in the glorification of Jesus Christ.

17–18. Two crowds are depicted in these verses. The first crowd is the one *that was with him when he called Lazarus from the tomb*. This may have included a number of folk from Bethany, and perhaps a substantial number of others who had been present at the raising of Lazarus (11:45) and who had been invited back to the dinner in honour of Jesus (12:2). They would not be suppressed, and bore witness (Gk. *emartyrei*, NIV 'spread the word') to what they had seen, thus magnifying the witness borne by the sign itself (*cf.* 5:36; 10:38) and serving as models for all who bear witness to the truth. The other came out from Jerusalem to meet him (*cf.* 12:12), stimulated in part by the reports of the miracle.

19. Doubtless the scene was fraught with potential explosiveness. Jesus could have begun an armed revolt then and there. The Pharisees observe the crowds and are greatly disquieted. Less accommodating to the Roman overlords than the Sadducees, they nevertheless thought that the path of wisdom was to endure the occupation, and chafe under their perception of Jesus' rising popularity. The Sanhedrin has taken its decision (11:49–53), but has to execute it with stealth because of the crowds; meanwhile, so far as the Pharisees are concerned, Jesus goes from strength to strength, and the political stability becomes more and more fragile: *See, this is getting us nowhere.*

But in the report of their closing statement, there is not only hyperbole and exaggeration – *Look how the whole world has gone after him!* – but superb Johannine irony as well. By *the world*, the Pharisees mean 'everyone', *i.e.* everyone in the Jerusalem area, including the pilgrims from all over the Mediterranean basin and beyond. But *the world* (*kosmos; cf.* notes on 1:9) commonly refers in the Fourth Gospel to people everywhere without racial distinction but who are lost and in rebellion against God (*cf.* notes on 3:16, 17). In truth the aim of Jesus' mission was to save the world (3:17). The crowd that acclaims Jesus as the King of Israel anticipates the broader sweep of humanity that will enjoy Jesus' saving reign. As the plots of the Pharisees and their colleagues were not proving very effective in reducing Jesus' popularity, so the later attempts to stem the rising tide of Christianity proved exasperating. And nothing so confirms that the world was even then beginning to go after Jesus as the visit of 'some Greeks' (v. 20) whose request to meet Jesus triggers the onset of the 'hour'. At the same time, there is probably irony within irony. For by the end of the chapter John will insist that the overwhelming reaction to Jesus was unbelief (12:37ff.), so that here, as elsewhere (2:23–25; 6:60; 8:30ff.), the Evangelist does not accord a very high place to the crowd's positive response to Jesus. Thus, both levels of irony point forward to the dominant themes in the rest of John 12.

4. Gentiles trigger Jesus' announcement of the 'hour' (12:20–36)

20. The *Greeks* who request to see Jesus not only represent 'the whole world' (*cf.* notes on v. 19), but they stand in contrast to the Pharisees who are exasperated by Jesus' growing influence. Although several scholars have argued that these Greeks are Greek-speaking Jews, *i.e.* Jews of the diaspora (for the literature, *cf.* H. B. Kossen in Sevenster, pp. 97–110), it is strange that John should call them *Greeks* – a different term from that rendered 'Grecian Jews' in Acts 6:1. These Greeks were not necessarily from Greece: as elsewhere in the New Testament, the term refers to Gentiles who come from any part of the Greek-speaking world, possibly even a Greek city as near as the Decapolis. That they were God-fearing is intimated by John's remark that they *went up to worship at the Feast* (*sc.* of Passover, 12:1). It is possible that they were proselytes, *i.e.* fully fledged converts to Judaism who would have been permitted to worship with Jews, but this cannot be inferred from the text, since other Gentiles who are said to have gone up to worship could not possibly be proselytes (*e.g.* the Ethiopian eunuch, Acts 8:27; *cf.* Jos., *Bel.* vi. 427). Like Cornelius (Acts 10) or the centurion who loved the Jews and built them a synagogue (Lk. 7:5), such Greeks admired much that they saw in Judaism without becoming official converts, and sometimes attended the great Jewish festivals in Jerusalem, where they were admitted to the court of the Gentiles. The Greek construction suggests that these Gentiles were drawn from those who regularly made such pilgrimages. Entrance to the inner courts was forbidden, on pain of death, to all Gentiles save proselytes. Warning notices were posted on the barrier ('the dividing wall of hostility', Eph. 2:14) that separated the inner courts from the court of the Gentiles. Not even the Roman Governor of Syria, Vitellius, dared ignore the prohibition or test its sanction when he attended the feast seven years later (March AD 37; *cf.* Jos., *Ant.* xviii. 122).

21–22. Why they should ask to see Jesus is not clear. Their curiosity may have been stirred by no more than the buzz of conversation all around them. If a couple of days had elapsed between v. 19 and v. 20, then it is possible that the cleansing of the temple had taken place, described in Mark 11:15–17: Jesus drove out the traders and their merchandise and insisted that the temple was 'a house of prayer *for all nations*' (*cf.* Is. 56:7).[1] If this report of Jesus' words reached the ears of the Greeks, they may have been drawn to a religious leader who seemed to question the inferior status of Gentiles before God. Or they may have come from the Decapolis, and therefore been somewhat informed about Jesus' ministry in Galilee.

The last suggestion may find marginal support in the fact that they approach Philip. If they were from the Decapolis or from one of the territories north and east of Lake Galilee (*e.g.* Batanea, Gaulanitis, Trachonitis), it would not have taken much effort to find out which of the disciples came from the nearest town, and Philip's hometown, *Bethsaida in Galilee* (in fact, located in Gaulanitis; *cf.* notes on 1:44) qualified.

---

[1]For the relation between this and the temple cleansing reported in Jn. 2, *cf.* notes on 2:14ff.

Alternatively, they may have been drawn to Philip because, like Andrew, he had a Greek name (though both disciples were Jews). Why they approached one of the disciples instead of Jesus himself is not stated: perhaps it was because they were still uncertain as to how (or whether) Jesus would receive Gentiles. Apparently Philip shares their hesitation (owing, perhaps, to instruction such as that in Mt. 10:5, 6), and therefore consults with Andrew, who, though not as unhesitating as in his initial evangelistic zeal (1:40–42), initiates the inquiry to Jesus.

Whatever the dynamics, these Gentiles approach Philip and say, *Sir* (*kyrie*, clearly with no force of 'Lord'; *cf.* notes on 4:19; 9:36), *we would like to see Jesus*. The verb 'to see' in this context means 'to have an interview with': *cf.* Luke 8:20; 9:9; Acts 28:20.

23. Strictly speaking, Jesus does not respond to the direct request of the Gentiles, but to the situation that their request represents. At the very moment when the Jewish authorities are turning most virulently against him, some Gentiles begin to clamour for his attention. This is not unlike one of the great themes of Romans 9 – 11: apart from a remnant, Israel as a whole rejects their Messiah, but by his death and resurrection he sweeps into his covenant community large numbers of Gentiles who had earlier been excluded from the people of the covenant. In this instance, however, the approach of the Greeks is *for Jesus* a kind of trigger, a signal that the climactic hour has dawned. (One is reminded of the divine signal John the Baptist was given, 1:33.)

Up to this point, the 'hour' has always been future (2:4; 4:21, 23; 7:30; 8:20), the 'hour' that is nothing less than the appointed time for Jesus' death, resurrection and exaltation – in short, his glorification. Now, dramatically, the request of the Greeks changes the parameters: *The hour has come for the Son of Man to be glorified.* From now until the passion the 'hour' is in immediate prospect (12:27; 13:1; 17:1). In the Synoptic Gospels, the 'Son of Man' title is most commonly used by Jesus *either* in connection with his sufferings *or* in connection with his coming in glory. Here the two are fused, not only because Jesus' death (vv. 24, 32) is the first stage on his way to receiving glory (v. 16), *i.e.* on his way to returning to the glory he had with the Father before the world began (17:5), but also because Jesus' death was itself the supreme manifestation of Jesus' glory (*cf.* notes on 1:14; 8:50, 54; 12:28; 13:31–32).[1] It is not just that the shame of the cross is inevitably followed by the glory of the exaltation, but that the glory is already fully displayed in the shame. Moreover, in view of the numerous links between Isaiah 52:13 – 53:12, the fourth 'Servant Song', and John 12:37ff. (*cf.* notes below), we are probably justified even here in detecting an allusion to Isaiah 52:13, where we are told that the Servant 'will be raised and lifted up and

---

[1] *Cf.* Blank, pp. 134–142. The position of Nicholson, pp. 149ff. – that glorification in the Fourth Gospel never includes Jesus' death but refers exclusively to his exaltation – is too narrowly based on 17:5, and results in the strange conclusion that 12:24 does not refer to Jesus' death.

highly exalted' (LXX *doxasthēsetai*, 'will be glorified').

The Greeks whose pressing for an interview precipitated Jesus' response disappear from view. Whether or not their request was granted is not recorded; theologically speaking, the point is irrelevant (and therefore omitted), because even if they met with Jesus at this point there is a sense in which they could not yet 'see' him, they could not yet belong to him, until the 'hour' is over and Jesus has been 'lifted up from the earth' (v. 32). That is what is necessary for the gospel to be fully operative, the gospel that encompasses Jew and Gentile alike and draws together a new covenant community whose locus is no longer constrained by the parameters of Sinai.

24. If in v. 23 Jesus' death is subsumed under his glorification, in v. 24 it is depicted as a kernel of wheat that is sown in the ground, dying to bring forth a rich harvest. But the connection between the two verses is deeper. Jesus' glorification is tied to his refusal to seek his own glory (8:50, 54), to his commitment always to do what pleases his Father (8:29). The principled subordination of the Son to the Father (*cf.* notes on 5:19ff.; 6:37ff.) culminates in the spectacular obedience of self-sacrifice. Like the seed whose death is the germination of life for a great crop, so Jesus' death generates a plentiful harvest. The seed is thereby vindicated; the Son is thereby glorified. The Evangelist has already pictured the same truth in other terms: Jesus is the bread that came down from heaven and gave his life for others (6:35–59), he is the one who dies so that the people may survive (11:49–52).

In a largely agrarian society, the image of a seed dying in order to produce fruit could be exploited in many different contexts. Paul develops the image with respect to the resurrection (1 Cor. 15:36–38); the principle of multiplied fruitfulness crops up in several parables (*e.g.*Mk. 4:3–9, 26–29, 31–32; Mt. 13:24–30). Indeed, the cyclical pattern of sowing and reaping becomes a dominant motif in the various fertility cults and some of the mystery religions rife in antiquity. That does not mean either Jesus or John borrows from these sources. John may have been aware of Paul's use of this image (certainly the closest conceptual parallel), but in fact the image lay ready to hand for multiple application. The Christological use of it in this verse is perhaps heightened by the strong asseverative *I tell you the truth* (*cf.* notes on 1:51).

25. But if the principle modelled by the seed – that death is the necessary condition for the generation of life – is peculiarly applicable to Jesus, in a slightly different way it is properly applied to all of Jesus' followers. As 1 Peter 2:21ff. rapidly moves from the unique and redemptive sacrifice of Christ to its exemplary significance for Jesus' followers, so the movement of thought in this passage runs from Jesus' uniquely fruitful death (the death of one seed producing many living seeds) to the mandated death of Jesus' followers as the necessary condition of their *own* life. The person who *loves his life will lose it*: it could not be otherwise, for to love one's life is a fundamental denial of God's sovereignty, of God's rights, and a brazen elevation of self to the apogee of one's perception, and therefore an idolatrous focus on self, which is the heart of all sin. Such a person loses his life, *i.e.* causes his own perdition. By contrast, the one *who hates his life* (the love/hate contrast reflects a semitic idiom that articulates fundamental preference, not hatred on some absolute scale: *cf.* Gn. 29:31, 33; Dt. 21:15 AV, NASB mg.) *will keep it for eternal life* (*cf.* Mk. 8:35 par. – which also follows a passion prediction). This person denies himself, or, to use another of Jesus' metaphors, takes up his cross daily (Mk. 8:34 par.), *i.e.* he chooses not to pander to self-interest but at the deepest level of his being declines to make himself the focus of his interest and perception, thereby *dying*.

A second contrast emerges in v. 25. The man who hates his life *in this world* will keep it *for eternal life*. Indeed, the contrast is bipolar: not only *this* [present] *world* as opposed to *eternal life*, but this present *evil world* (*cf.* notes on 1:9), characterized by rebellion, death and judgment (3:19–21, 36), as opposed to the blessings of eternal *life* (*cf.* notes on 1:4; 3:15).

26. These choices cannot be acts of mere self-abnegation. Self must be displaced by another; the endless, shameless focus on self must be displaced by focus on Jesus Christ, who is the supreme revelation of God. That change of focus ensures both death and glorification, for the Jesus who says *where I am, my servant also will be* is on his way to the cross and to his Father (*cf.* 14:3). As Jesus' crucifixion is the path to his glorification, so the believer's 'death' is the path to vindication: *My Father will honour the one who serves me*.

27. But before Jesus' disciples can follow him in this way, Jesus himself must die and be glorified. As wonderful as the ultimate glorification of this 'hour' will be, the cross cannot be faced with equanimity: *Now* (*i.e.* at this 'hour', v. 23) *my heart is troubled*. Nicholson (pp. 127–129) thinks this being 'troubled', and that in 13:21, represent no fear and hesitation on Jesus' part as he faces the cross, but concern over whether his disciples will prove steadfast. The Jesus of John's Gospel, Nicholson maintains, undergoes no Gethsemane agony: he is on his way to reunion with his Father, and betrays no second thoughts. But if Jesus is troubled not by the prospect of the cross but out of anxiety for his disciples, his words in vv. 27–28, however interpreted, make little sense. Methodologically, Nicholson is aligning himself with those who establish a tyranny of the dominant theme. For example, everyone acknowledges that in John realized or inaugurated eschatology is dominant, but those who establish a tyranny of the dominant insist in consequence that the futurist eschatology of (say) 5:25–28 must be re-interpreted, or attributed to a later redactor. Almost everyone acknowledges that Jesus' deity dominates the Christological landscape of this Gospel, but Käsemann, seeking to establish a tyranny of the dominant, proves uncomfortable with passages like 4:6–7 (*cf.* notes). Similarly, most commentators agree, with Nicholson, that the resoluteness of Jesus as he goes to the cross is one of John's emphases, but Nicholson's effort to establish a tyranny of the dominant fails to listen to the minor chords, and descends to reductionism. Even in John, Jesus cannot contemplate the cross as a docetic actor, steeped in dispassionate unconcern. His heart is deeply troubled (*cf.* also notes on 11:33–35). The verb is a strong one, and signifies revulsion, horror, anxiety, agitation (*cf.* Thüsing, pp. 79–89).

On the other hand, there is little warrant for thinking that this account is merely a Johannine re-working of the agony of Gethsemane (Mk. 14:32–42 par.). Dodd (*HTFG*, pp. 69ff.) has demonstrated the independence of John's report. Surely it cannot be surprising that the prospect of the cross proved utterly daunting to Jesus on more than one occasion. This passage is tied to the themes of glorification (v. 28) and of the hour (v. 31), and provides incentive to follow (v. 26) the one whose death we must in some measure emulate, assured he did not find the path easy himself.

Deeply troubled, then, Jesus asks himself, *what shall I say*? The next sentence could be read as either a question or a prayer. If the former, then the deliberative question *what shall I say*? breeds a hypothetical possibility: 'Shall I say, "*Father, save me from his hour*"?' But this possibility is no sooner raised than it is jettisoned: *No* (*alla*, lit. 'but'), *it was for this very reason I came to this hour*. This rendering not only sounds faintly histrionic, but worse, it means that what is troubling Jesus in the first clause of the verse is given no substance. If the question is only hypothetical and instantly rejected, the 'trouble' is merely reported and then instantly resolved. After the deliberative question *what shall I say*? it seems better to take the next words as a positive prayer: *Father, save me from this hour*! Now Jesus' agony is fully revealed. This prayer is entirely analogous to Gethsemane's 'Take this cup from me' (Mk. 14:36). In both instances the strong adversative follows: *alla*, 'but' – in the one case, 'not what I will, but what you will' (Mk. 14:36), and here, *No* (*alla*), *it was for this very reason I came to this hour*. Jesus can no sooner pray to be spared this hour, to escape this cup, than he must face again his unswerving commitment to adhere to his Father's will (5:19ff.; 6:37ff.; 8:29; so, rightly, Hendriksen, pp. 198–200, though for doubtful reasons). That is why Jesus is so troubled. 'The horror of death, and the ardour of His obedience, were meeting together' (Bengel, 2. 408).

28. What, then, shall he pray? He prays, *Father, glorify your name*! This is not some compromise petition, since the glorification of the Father's name for which he asks turns on Jesus' willing obedience, even unto death. This request is nothing other than an articulation of the principle that has controlled his life and ministry (7:18; 8:29, 50). The servant who does not stoop to his own will, but who performs the will of the one who sent him – even to the death of the cross – is the one who glorifies God. But the focus of the prayer transcends *mere* acquiescence; it betrays acquiescence that is subsumed under the passionate desire to bring glory to God, in much the same way that the petition 'hallowed be your name' in the Lord's model prayer presupposes the active obedience of the one who is praying. And since Ezekiel 36 has already been referred to in John 3:5, it is tempting to think that Ezekiel 36:22, 32 are in mind here, thus subsuming all of Christ's redemptive work and the inauguration of the new covenant under God's solemn Old Testament pledge to glorify his own name.

And this time heaven answers his petition with an audible voice, one of only three instances during the ministry of Jesus when this took place (and the other two, Jesus' baptism and his transfiguration, are not reported in the Fourth Gospel). The voice (*phōnē*, 'voice' or 'sound') is presumably what the rabbis called the *baṭ qôl* (lit. 'the daughter [*i.e.* echo] of a voice'). In rabbinic understanding this heavenly voice was the most that could be expected, since the gift of prophecy, in the classic sense, had been withdrawn and would remain withdrawn until the onset of the messianic age.[1] He alone could distinguish exactly what the voice said: *I have glorified it* – apparently throughout Jesus' earthly ministry, in the incarnation (1:14) and especially in the powerful signs (*cf.* notes on 2:11; 11:40) – *and will glorify it again* – presumably in the death and exaltation of Jesus, which makes this promise a direct response to Jesus' petition.[2] The heavenly Father who has been glorifying his name throughout the ministry of his dear Son can be counted on to continue that glorification at the climactic hour.

29–30. If Jesus hears the heavenly voice distinctly, the *crowd that was there* does not. Some, presumably those less open to observable supernatural intervention, *said it had thundered*; others recognized that the sound was speech, a voice, and not just noise, but there is no evidence that they could make out what was being said (*cf.* Acts 9:7; 22:9). Moreover, they wrongly ascribed the voice to an angel, since the connection between 'Father' and 'I' in v. 28 makes it clear that the voice was God's.

But if the crowd does not understand what the voice from heaven utters, how can Jesus say, 'This voice was for your benefit, not mine'? Since it is Jesus' heart that is troubled (v. 27), and it is he alone who understands the heavenly message and (presumably) later conveys it to his disciples so that it comes to be recorded in this passage, must we not assume that, at least in part, the voice came for his benefit? Four factors alleviate the difficulty.

(1) Tasker (pp. 152–153) is probably right to see here a semitic contrast:

---

[1] *Cf.* Barrett, *HSGT*, pp. 39f. It is true, as D. E. Aune, *JBL* 101, 1982, pp. 419–421, points out, that Josephus, a first-century Jewish historian, can use the word 'prophet' to refer to people who display 'prophetic' phenomena contemporary to his own day. But in fact, 'prophet' and 'prophecy' had come by the first century to refer to an enormous range of phenomena, none of it with the form and authority status of classic, biblical prophecy. On that point, Jewish sources, it appears, are univocal: *cf.* D. A. Carson, *Showing the Spirit* (Paternoster, 1987), p. 154, esp. n. 27.

[2] It is far less likely that *I have glorified it* refers both to Jesus' ministry and to his death and glorification, while *[I] will glorify it again* refers to the drawing of all men to himself by the power of the Spirit (*cf.* v. 32). That would mean that the agony of Jesus' petition in v. 28a is rather summarily dismissed by a proleptic statement.

i.e. v. 30 means that the voice came more for the crowd's benefit than for his, not that there was no benefit for him whatsoever.

(2) Strictly speaking, Jesus did not need the voice from heaven. Doubtless the audible confirmation that his prayer was heard was comforting, but in fact the outcome of Jesus' troubled mind was already resolved by his final petition (v. 28a).

(3) Even if the message of the heavenly voice is mediated through Jesus and not grasped immediately by the bystanders, that message, recorded in v. 28, is for the enormous benefit of the disciples amongst the bystanders once they have lived through the period of the cross and find themselves in urgent need of making sense of it all. Some truths the disciples could not manage to digest at the time (*cf.* 16:12). The Evangelist makes much of these; that is one reason why he constantly plays on the theme of misunderstanding (*e.g. cf.* notes on 2:19–22; 6:32ff.; *etc.*). But eventually they would remember what Jesus had told them the voice had uttered, and it would be for them a divine confirmation that the shameful cross, and all that flowed from it, was not a defeat but a victory, not final destruction but ultimate glorification. Even in the Evangelist's day, Jews (and Gentile proselytes and God-fearers) most urgently needed to hear heaven's pronouncement – the pronouncement that the cross did not stamp Jesus out as irredeemably cursed and condemned, but proved to be the locus of his glorification.

(4) Even though the crowd did not understand the voice, the very fact that a voice from heaven spoke should have been sufficient to alert those with any spiritual sensitivity that a turning-point in redemptive history was impending. For those with ears to hear, Jesus' next words consequently take on fresh urgency. Jesus' unpacking of the implications of what the voice said – that is the burden of vv. 31–33 – inevitably gained extra authority and urgency in the minds of his followers.

31–33. The movement of thought is important. The arrival of the Greeks (v. 20) has triggered in Jesus' mind the recognition that his appointed 'hour' has arrived (v. 23). Because that hour encompasses the cross, he is deeply troubled (v. 27), but rises to his consuming concern: that the Father should glorify his own name, even in this hour (v. 28). Jesus' prayer, both simple and profound, evokes an audible response from heaven, the actual content of which only Jesus can understand, but which nevertheless serves as a supernatural attestation before the crowd of the transcendent importance of the sequence of events set off by the arrival of the Gentiles. What does all this mean? In vv. 31–32 Jesus unpacks the significance of these developments, with v. 33 providing an explanatory aside by the Evangelist to guide readers into the proper interpretation of one of the points Jesus makes. We may discern five emphases, all dealing with the significance of the impending passion/ glorification:

(1) The passion/glorification of the Son *is the time for judgment on this world*. Judgment (*krisis; cf.* notes on 3:17, 19–21; 5:22–30; 7:24; 8:16) is in one sense reserved for the end of the age, for the 'last judgment'. But the

texts just cited also show that judgment begins with the first coming of Christ, climaxing in his passion. As the light of the world, Jesus forces a division between those whose evil deeds are exposed by his brilliance, and those whose deeds prompt them to embrace the light in order to testify that what they have done 'has been done through God' (3:19–21). Similarly here: Jesus' passion/glorification draws people to himself (v. 32), but also constitutes judgment *on this world*, all of human society in rebellion against its creator. The world thought it was passing judgment on Jesus, not only as it perpetually debated who he was (*e.g.* 6:14, 42, 60; 7:15; 8:48, 52–53; 9:29; 10:19; 11:37), but climactically in the cross. In reality, the cross was passing judgment on them. Since Jesus was sent as his Father's representative, his agent and the supreme divine revelation, rejection of the Son is rejection of God himself (5:23). In the callous murder of the Son of God, sin displays itself in its most virulently evil form. But in that death, God was also giving his Son as a sacrifice, the Lamb of God; in that death, Jesus was securing the life of the 'many seeds' (v. 24). Thus Jesus' passion/glorification signifies judgment both positively and negatively. As far as 'the world' is concerned, however, it can only be negative. There can be no further reprieve, for there can be no hope for those who reject the one person whose death/exaltation is the epiphany of God's gracious, saving self-disclosure.

(2) The passion/glorification is also the time when *the prince of this world will be driven out*. The title 'prince [or "ruler"] of this world' recurs in John (14:30; 16:11), and similar titles are used elsewhere in the New Testament (Mt. 4:8, 9 [= Lk. 4:6, 7]; 2 Cor. 4:4; Eph. 2:2; 6:12) and in some Jewish literature of the period to refer to Satan (though in rabbinic literature 'prince of the world' never refers to Satan).[1] Although the cross might seem like Satan's triumph, it is in fact his defeat. In one sense Satan was defeated by the outbreaking power of the kingdom of God even within the ministry of Jesus (Lk. 10:18). But the fundamental smashing of his reign of tyranny takes place in the death/exaltation of Jesus. This is a brief statement analogous to the apocalyptic scene in Revelation: the followers of the Lamb overcome the dragon 'by [*i.e.* "on account of"] the blood of the Lamb' (Rev. 12:11). When Jesus was glorified, 'lifted up' to heaven by means of the cross, enthroned, then too was Satan dethroned. What residual power the prince of this world enjoys is further curtailed by the Holy Spirit, the Counsellor (16:11).

(3) The passion/glorification of Jesus is equivalent to Jesus' being *lifted up from the earth* (*cf.* notes on 3:14; 8:28). There is no justification for NIV's adversative *But*. The same victory, the same death/exaltation, is in view: 'And I (*kagō*), when I am lifted up. . . .' The precise Hebrew term behind 'to be lifted up' is debated (*cf.* Beasley-Murray, p. 214), but it is quite

---

[1]For the most comprehensive recent discussion, *cf.* Alan F. Segal, 'Ruler of This World: Attitudes about Mediator Figures and the Importance of Sociology for Self-Definition', in E. P. Sanders *et al.* (eds.), *Jewish and Christian Self-Definition*, vol. 2 (SCM/Fortress, 1981), pp. 245–268, 403–413.

certain that the verb used here has been chosen because it is ambiguous. Jesus is not only 'lifted up' on the cross, he is 'lifted up' (*i.e.* 'exalted') to glory. The notions of 'being lifted up' and 'glorification' come together in Isaiah 52:13, where 'being lifted up' refers to the exaltation of the Servant of the LORD, though the context lays emphasis on his sufferings. In the New Testament, Jesus' atoning death and his exaltation come together, with various degrees of explicitness, in Philippians 2:9; 1 Timothy 3:16; Hebrews 1:3 and possibly Luke 9:51. Lest the readers think exclusively of exaltation, the Evangelist in v. 33 makes an aside to connect the verb with Jesus' death (which is also the way the crowds seem to understand it in v. 34): Jesus said this *to show the kind of death he was going to die.* The words *kind of death* refer in the first instance to the nature of the execution itself (*i.e.* crucifixion, in which the victim is 'lifted up'; stoning, say, is excluded; *cf.* 21:19), but continue to hint at the point made throughout the passage: Jesus' death is the pathway to his glorification, indeed an integral part of it. 'His being glorified is not a reward or recompense for his crucifixion; it inheres in his crucifixion' (Bruce, p. 267).

(4) The consequence of this passion/glorification, this death/exaltation, is that Jesus will draw all men to himself – not to his cross, considered abstractly, but to himself, precisely as the incarnate Word who suffers and dies and is glorified in order to draw all men to himself. On the verb 'to draw', *cf.* notes on 6:44. There, the one who draws is the Father; here, it is the Son, but nothing much should be made of this (5:19). But the scope and efficacy of the drawing in the two places are quite different. There, the focus is on those individuals whom the Father gives to the Son, whom the Son infallibly preserves and raises up at the last day. Here, 'all men' reminds the reader of what triggered these statements, *viz.* the arrival of the Greeks, and means 'all people without distinction, Jews and Gentiles alike', not all individuals without exception, since the surrounding context has just established judgment as a major theme (v. 31), a time for distinguishing between those who love their lives (and therefore lose them) and those who hate their lives (and therefore keep them for eternal life, v. 25). The critical event in Jesus' ministry that sanctions his drawing of all people without distinction, and not Jews only (*cf.* 10:16; 11:52), is his cross/exaltation, his being 'lifted up'. This is the implicit answer to the Greeks: the hour has come for him to die and be exalted, and in the wake of that passion/glorification they will be able to approach him as freely as do the children of the old covenant.

(5) This dramatic development twice comes under the powerful *Now* (v. 31). This adverb not only ties these verses back to vv. 23, 27, but emphasizes the eschatological nature of the events that are impending. The judgment of the world, the destruction of Satan, the exaltation of the Son of Man, the drawing of men and women from the ends of the earth – these might all be reserved for the end times. But the end times have begun already. It is not that there is nothing reserved for the

consummation; rather, it is that the decisive step is about to be taken in the death/exaltation of Jesus.

34. Strictly speaking, the crowd's quotation of what Jesus said, so far as John has reported it, is inexact: Jesus has not said, *The Son of Man must be lifted up.* Nevertheless they are not wrong. In this tightly woven dialogue Jesus has referred to himself using the 'Son of Man' title (v. 23), and the crowd understands the self-reference. They draw two further connections, both presupposed by their question: (1) The glorification of the Son of Man (v. 23) and the 'lifting up' of Jesus (v. 32) are tied to Jesus' *death* (*cf.* also 3:14; 8:28). (2) Jesus' self-presentation as the 'Son of Man' is a messianic claim; hence they can preface their question with the observation that they have heard from the Law that *the Christ* (*i.e.* the Messiah; *cf.* notes on 1:41) will remain forever. Not everyone in Palestine could have made a confident connection between 'Son of Man' and 'Messiah'. Despite Jesus' frequent references to himself as the Son of Man, a brief four months earlier the authorities had entreated him to tell them plainly whether or not he was the Messiah (10:24). But the people were not as versed in the theology of eschatological figures as were their leaders. Some, for instance, could tie 'prophet' and 'king' together (6:14–15); others maintained a distinction between them (7:40–41). At this late stage in Jesus' public ministry, the messianic expectations were running high (*cf.* 12:12ff.); it is not surprising that this crowd connects 'Son of Man' and 'Messiah'.

From a Christian perspective, then, the crowd's intuitions on all these matters were sound. Their perplexity stemmed from the fact that in their understanding the promised Messiah would *remain for ever.* They based this belief on *the Law,* here a reference to the Hebrew Scriptures, of which the law of Moses, the Pentateuch, was the supremely important part (*cf.* 10:34, where a quotation from Ps. 82 is also said to be 'written in your Law'). What passage they have in mind is uncertain. Isaiah 9:7 promises that the kingdom of the expected Prince of the house of David will be established for ever; in Ezekiel 37:25 God promises that 'David my servant' will be Israel's prince for ever. Some scholars think of Psalm 72:17, where the name of the king, the royal son, the Messiah, will endure forever. Others think of Psalm 89:35–37, where the psalmist declares that David's seed, his line, will remain for ever.[1]

What is clear is that the Palestinian Judaism of the time expected the Messiah to be triumphant; most expected him to be eternal. Jewish sources amply attest this (*e.g.* 1 Enoch 49:1; 62:14; *Psalms of Solomon* 17:4). A slightly later Judaism speculated that the Messiah would be defeated and destroyed before the consummation (*e.g.* 4 Ezra 7:28–29), but that perspective had not invaded the thinking of Jesus' interlocutors. And so

---

[1]W. C. van Unnik, *NovT* 3, 1959, pp. 174–179. Several authors appeal to Targums (ancient Aramaic paraphrases): *e.g.* B. McNeil, *NovT* 19, 1977, pp. 22–33; B. Chilton, *NovT* 22, 1980, pp. 176–178. G. Bampfylde (*JSNT* 17, 1983, pp. 87–89) appeals to Ps. 61:6–7. *Cf.* also Moloney, p. 182.

they ask the question, *Who is this 'Son of Man'?* By this they do not seek simple identification, but demand to know what kind of Son of Man/ Messiah Jesus has in mind, of whom it can be said that he will die. That is not only the sort of question we might expect the crowds to ask the historical Jesus during the closing hours of his public ministry, it is also the sort of question that Jews and Jewish proselytes interested in Christianity at the end of the first century would need to have answered, before they could become Christians. The mere *identity* question would not be obscure in AD 85; Christians would affirm that Jesus is the Messiah, the Son of Man; Jews would deny it. But interested, thoughtful Jews and proselytes who were considering the claims of Christianity would ask the question reflected here: What kind of Son of Man are you claiming Jesus is, when we know he died in ignominy and under the curse of God?

35–36a. The historical Jesus declines to answer the question; those readers of the Fourth Gospel who have eyes to see now perceive that he has already done so. Certainly Jesus the Messiah and Son of Man 'remains forever', but this is in function of his glorification, which is achieved in and through the shame and pain of his death. But what Jesus does is *refer* to his impending death (*You are going to have the light just a little while longer*), and encourage the crowds to walk in that light as long as they have it.

The NIV's *before darkness overtakes you* makes the connection with the preceding clause merely temporal ('before'), and therefore implies that the darkness is as inevitable as the march of time. The RSV's 'lest the darkness overtake you' is somewhat closer to the Greek; or, better yet, the Greek might be rendered, 'lest the darkness master you' (*cf.* notes on 1:5). The 'light' will be with them only for a while: it (or rather, he) will be taken away by the cross. In that sense, the onset of 'darkness' is inevitable. But if they walk in the light as long as they have the light, then the darkness, when it comes, will not overpower them, master them. The alternative is ghastly: *The man who walks in the dark does not know where he is going.*

The light/darkness contrast is prevalent in John's Gospel (*cf.* 1:4–9; 3:19–21; 8:12; 9:1ff.). The crowds are strongly urged to trust Jesus, the light of the world, based on what they do know of him: *Put your trust in the light while you have it, so that you may become sons of light.* The last expression, 'sons of light', reflects idiomatic Hebrew: a 'son of light' displays the ethical qualities of 'light', and has become a disciple of the 'light' (*cf.* 1 Thes. 5:5; and Eph. 5:8, where the expression is 'children of light'). It will not be any easier to place trust in Jesus *after* the cross; the crowds should commit themselves to him in trust and discipleship now, before he, as the light of the world, is taken from them, and they find themselves in total darkness.

36b. That Jesus then *left and hid himself from them* recalls 8:59, but in this context it signifies much more. Not only is the public ministry of Jesus now drawing to a close (apart from 12:44–50, his next public act of self-disclosure is the death/exaltation itself), but by his withdrawal, his self-conscious hiding from the people, he is acting out the judicial warning he has just pronounced. This acted parable of judgment the Evangelist finds to be not only a suitable climax to the warnings and entreaties of the previous verses, but a telling introduction to his own theological reflections on the unbelief of so many amongst his own people (vv. 37ff.).

D. THEOLOGY OF UNBELIEF *(12:37–50)*

1. *The prediction of Scripture (12:37–43)*

37. In the remaining chapters before the trial and crucifixion, Jesus devotes himself to his own disciples. The great majority of the Jews are excluded, shut out by their unbelief. Not even the miraculous signs John has recounted, the very purpose of which was to engender belief (20:30–31), proved adequate to fire the faith of these people. They are like the ancient Israelites whom Moses addressed: 'With your own eyes you saw those great trials, those miraculous signs and great wonders. But to this day the LORD has not given you a mind that understands or eyes that see or ears that hear' (Dt. 29:3–4; *cf.* Brown, 1. 485). Faith based on signs may be inferior, but it is better than unbelief (2:11; 10:38; 14:11).

38. Some explanation must be given for such large-scale, catastrophic unbelief. There is ample evidence that the substantial unbelief of the Jewish people before the resurrection was a major hindrance to the conversion of Jews after the resurrection. Surely (it was argued) we may call into question the messianic claims of one so thoroughly rejected by the Jewish people by whom and for whom the prophetic Scriptures were written! The Christian answer, as clearly articulated in Paul (esp. Rom. 9 – 11) as here, is that this unbelief was not only foreseen by Scripture but on that very account *necessitated* by Scripture. Although the Greek conjunction *hina* sometimes has resultative force (the meaning here would then be that the unbelief of the people *resulted* in the fulfilment of Old Testament prophecy, not that it occurred *in order that* Old Testament prophecy might be fulfilled),[1] no such weakening can be legitimate here: v. 39 insists that it was for this reason that the people *could not* believe. On the other hand, such unambiguous predestinarianism is never set over against human responsibility: v. 37 presumes there is human culpability, and v. 43 articulates an utterly reprehensible human motive for the unbelief. Meanwhile, v. 32 draws attention to those Jews who do believe. Philosophically, like every major author in the canon, John is a compatibilist (*cf.* Carson). Theologically, John is summarizing a truth

---

[1] In this context, it does not help to distinguish between 'intended result' and 'unintended result'; *cf.* Iver Larsen, *NOT* 2/2, 1988, pp. 28–34.

presented throughout the Fourth Gospel: by and large the nation of Israel refused the regeneration through the Spirit that lay at the core of the promised new covenant (cf. 3:3–5). Israel's leaders thought they could see when they were blind (9:39–41). This emphasis was already set out in the Prologue (1:10, 11).

The Scripture John first cites to prove his point (cf. Rom. 10:16) is Isaiah 53:1 (LXX, which is close enough to the Hebrew). The question in Isaiah 53:1 is the prophet's report of the astonishment of the nations concerning the Servant of the Lord, who was rejected by people and exalted by God himself (the question immediately follows 52:13–15). If the supreme Servant of the Lord is Jesus the Messiah, the applicability of this passage is obvious. In John's context, *our message* focuses on the teaching of Jesus, while *the arm of the Lord* refers primarily to the miraculous signs.

39–41. Verse 39 ties the unbelief of the people to the texts cited in both v. 38 and v. 40. The inability of the people to believe is tied to Scripture's prediction, but that prediction is of a judicial hardening: God himself *has blinded their eyes and deadened their hearts.* The passage cited, Isaiah 6:10 (here somewhat closer to the Hebrew than to the LXX), appears also in Mark 4:12 par. and Acts 28:26–27, and probably underlies Romans 11:7–25. All three are concerned with divine, judicial hardening.

In Isaiah 6 the prophet, after being granted a vision of the LORD that has resulted in his profound repentance and cleansing, offers to serve as the LORD's messenger. And so he is commissioned – but with the chilling prospect of being ignored, scorned and rejected by the people to whom he is to speak. God commands Isaiah to undertake this ministry in the full knowledge that the results will be negative; indeed, such preaching to these people *evokes* a negative response, is in some sense the *cause* of the negative response.[1] In that sense God himself, through the prophet, hardens the heart of people – a point later recognized by the prophet when he begs the Almighty to display himself in more merciful ways (Is. 63:15–19). The assumption that God may judicially harden men and women frequently surfaces in the New Testament (*e.g.* Rom. 9:18; 2 Thes. 2:11). If a superficial reading finds this harsh, manipulative, even robotic, four things must constantly be borne in mind: (1) God's sovereignty in these matters is *never* pitted against human responsibility (cf. notes on v. 38); (2) God's judicial hardening is not presented as the capricious manipulation of an arbitrary potentate cursing morally neutral or even morally pure beings, but as a holy condemnation of a guilty people who are condemned to do and be what

---

[1]John Painter ('Eschatological Faith in the Gospel of John', in Robert Banks [ed.], *Reconciliation and Hope* [Fs. Leon Morris; Paternoster, 1974], pp. 46–47) argues that the 'he' who blinds the eyes and deadens the heart is the devil, the 'prince of the world' (v. 31), in distinction from the one who heals them. But despite Painter's appeal to 2 Cor. 4:4, the reference to 'the prince of this world' in Jn. 12 is too far away to admit this interpretation as very likely. Theologically, Painter's paper is keen to deny compatibilism (cf. notes on v. 38) and consequently depreciates the more obvious meaning.

they themselves have chosen; (3) God's sovereignty in these matters can also be a cause for hope, for if he is *not* sovereign in these areas there is little point in petitioning him for help, while if he is sovereign the anguished pleas of the prophet (Is. 63:15–19) – and of believers throughout the history of the church – make sense; (4) God's sovereign hardening of the people in Isaiah's day, his commissioning of Isaiah to apparently fruitless ministry, is a stage in God's 'strange work' (Is. 28:21–22) that brings God's ultimate redemptive purposes to pass. Paul argues rather similarly in Romans 9:22–33.

This passage from Isaiah 6 is not said to be fulfilled in Jesus' ministry. It may simply be listed as supporting evidence of the kind of judicial hardening that makes the prophecy of Isaiah 53:1 (Jn. 12:38) understandable. Nevertheless there are some points in the text that suggest direct application to Jesus. The Hebrew text of Isaiah moves from heart to ears to eyes, and then reverses the sequence, running from sight to hearing to understanding. John drops all reference to ears and hearing, and puts eyes first. Following hard on the mention of the miraculous signs (v. 37), the stress on sight is not surprising. Indeed, this emphasis also harks back to the miracle of John 9, with its concluding damning indictment (9:39–41). The emphasis on understanding with the heart stands over against merely superficial faith (*e.g.*2:23–25; 6:60; 8:30ff.). The last clause, *and I would heal them*, approximates the wording of the LXX , and probably includes an ironic reference to the inner meaning of the healing miracles.[1]

Perhaps the most difficult statement in John 12 occurs in v. 41: *Isaiah said this because he saw Jesus'* (lit. 'his', but the most natural antecedent is Jesus; but see below) *glory and spoke about him*. In the NIV (and most modern versions), this has two effects:

(1) It means that in his vision Isaiah saw (the pre-incarnate) Jesus. But there is a slightly different possibility. Targum Jonathan (an Aramaic paraphrase) to Isaiah 6:1 reads not 'I saw the LORD' but 'I saw the glory of the LORD', while the Targum to Is. 6:4 reads not 'the King, the LORD of hosts' but 'the glory of the *shekinah* of the King of the ages, the LORD of hosts'. It may not be necessary to appeal to the Targum; even in the Hebrew text Isaiah 6:3 already speaks of God's glory. If instead we are to take the pronoun, as in NIV, to refer to *Jesus'* glory, then John is unambiguously tying Jesus to Yahweh, the LORD of hosts, the Almighty – Isaiah saw Jesus in some pre-incarnate fashion. It is not the ascription of deity to Jesus that makes this a strange rendering, for such an ascription is commonplace in early Christianity, sometimes allusively and sometimes (especially in this Gospel) most explicitly (*cf.* 1:1, 18; 17:5; 20:28). What is remarkable, on this rendering of the passage, is the statement that *Isaiah* saw Jesus' glory. This may be no more than the conclusion of

---

[1]*Cf.* Judith M. Lieu, *NTS* 34, 1988, pp. 85–86. On the text form, which appears to make use of both the Hebrew and the LXX, *cf.* M. J. J. Menken, *BZ* 32, 1988, pp. 189–209.

a chain of Christian reasoning: if the Son, the Word, was with God in the beginning, and was God, and if he was God's agent of creation, and the perfect revelation of God to humankind, then it stands to reason that in those Old Testament passages where God is said to reveal himself rather spectacularly to someone, it must have been through the agency of his Son, his Word, however imperfectly the point was spelled out at the time. Therefore Isaiah said these words *because* (a stronger reading than 'when', AV) he saw Jesus' glory.

(2) On the assumption that the pronoun refers to *Jesus'* glory, v. 41 also makes Jesus himself the author of the judicial hardening, for the final *him* of the verse must refer to the same person as the pronoun. On this reading, the straightforward replacement of the LORD in Isaiah 6 with Jesus continues beyond vv. 1, 5, down to v. 10, making it *Jesus* who has blinded their eyes and deadened their hearts.

Alternatively, whether or not John appeals to the Targum, it is possible to think he is saying that Jesus *is* God's glory, *i.e.* that Isaiah 'saw his [*i.e.* God's] glory, namely, Christ'.[1] If we follow this suggestion, then the final clause, 'and spoke about *him*', may refer to God's glory, *i.e.* Jesus. At that point it is tempting to observe several tight connections between Isaiah 53:1 (cited in v. 38), and Isaiah 6:10 (cited in v. 40). The two passages from Isaiah are not connected by the obduracy motif alone, but also by the themes of being lifted up (Is. 6:1; 52:13), of glory (Is. 6:3; 52:13 LXX), and of sin (6:7; 53:12).[2] Especially the themes of being lifted up and of glorification would strike resonant chords with the Evangelist's Christology; the forgiveness of sin (Is. 6:7) or the bearing of sin (Is. 53:12) might resonate with 1:29, 34. Thus, when the Evangelist says that Isaiah saw God's glory, namely Jesus, *and spoke about him*, he may well be thinking of the Suffering Servant who was exalted. The linkages just outlined suggest it; what makes it very likely is the dozen or so overtones of Isaiah 52:13 – 53:12 found within John 12 that show the Evangelist had the Servant Song in mind when he composed this chapter.[3]

42–43. Just as the sweeping indictment of 1:10, 11 is followed by the exceptions of 1:12, 13, so the indictment of 12:37–41 is followed by these two verses. But these verses (vv. 42–43) refer to real exceptions only by implication: *i.e.* if *many even among the leaders believed in him*, however imperfect their faith, should we not think also of the many ordinary folk who put their faith in Jesus, often with much more candour and much less reserve than their leaders? The leaders themselves (same word as in 3:1) seem at this point to fit the pattern of inadequate, irresolute, even spurious faith that John repeatedly describes in this Gospel (*e.g.* 2:23–25;

---

[1]Craig A. Evans, 'Obduracy and the Lord's Servant: Some Observations on the Use of the Old Testament in the Fourth Gospel', in Craig A. Evans and William F. Stinespring (eds.), *Early Jewish and Christian Exegesis: Studies in Memory of William Hugh Brownlee* (Scholars Press, 1987), p. 232.

[2]*Ibid.*, pp. 231–232.   [3]*Ibid.*, pp. 232–236.

6:60; 8:30ff.). Nicodemus was willing to stand up for Jesus in the San-hedrin (7:50–52); he and Joseph of Arimathaea publicly identified them-selves with Jesus' cause by providing decent burial for him. Doubtless there were other leaders, less courageous even than this, who main-tained some distant attachment to Jesus, who believed in him in some sense, of whose faith the Pharisees knew nothing (7:48). Sadly, their faith was still so weak that they would not take any step that would threaten their position in the synagogue;[1] *they loved praise from men more than praise from God,* and therefore fell under Jesus' searing indictment (5:44), here repeated by the Evangelist (*cf.* Mt. 6:1–21; Rom. 2:29). They still knew nothing of the powerful new birth that could make them children of God and enable them to enter the messianic kingdom (3:3, 5; 1:12, 13; *cf.* 12:26). Perhaps after the resurrection they joined other Jewish leaders in becoming true Christians (*cf.* Acts 6:7). Almost cer-tainly the Evangelist knew of Jews and proselytes in his day who were happy enough to believe in Jesus in some sense, but who displayed similar hesitations. He wants them to know such secret faith will not do.

2. *The authority behind Jesus' promise – and threat (12:44–50)*
As the Evangelist offers his own extended theological comment in 3:16–21, 31–36, so he does the same here, with the additional factor that his comments constitute a summarizing paragraph powerfully drawing Jesus' public ministry to a close. Many of this paragraph's themes have already been introduced, and need not receive extended treatment again. Nevertheless the emphasis on the fact that God himself stands behind Jesus – whether as the object of faith or as the condemning judge – encourages the most serious consideration of the claims of Christ advanced to this point, and injects urgency into the Evangelist's reflec-tions on unbelief.

44–45. Jesus had said that the crowd would have the light 'just a little while longer' (12:35). Here, apparently, is his final public challenge to the crowds, a deft summary of many strands in his teaching (though it is overstating the evidence to call this, with Dodd, *IFG*, p. 382, the kerygma of Jesus). The idea that he is God's agent, so that those who believe in him actually believe in the one who sent him, finds sanction not only in John (13:20), but also in the Synoptics (Mt. 10:40; Mk. 9:37 = Lk. 9:48; Lk. 10:16). But the theme has been developed in special ways in the Fourth Gospel. In particular, the peculiar subordination of the Son to the Father is precisely what guarantees that all that the Son does is what the Father wants him to do, indeed, what the Father does (*cf.* notes on 3:31–36; 5:19ff.; 6:37–40; 7:27–29; 8:14–17, 28–29, 42–43; 10:34–36). More-over, because of the strong Christology of this Gospel, what Jesus is

---

[1] *Cf.* the threat of excommunication in 9:22. Once again Martyn, *HTFG*, p. 76, elaborates complex speculation that seeks to tie vv. 42–43 exclusively to the eighties and nineties of the first century (*cf.* notes on ch. 9). That the Evangelist himself is interested in Jewish

saying goes beyond the mere functionalism of the common Jewish maxim, 'One sent is as he who sent him.' Thus faith in Jesus (v. 44) is not faith in a merely human agent, one more prophet, but faith in God mediated by God's supreme self-disclosure, the Word incarnate, the God/man, his unique Son – or else it is not faith at all. And so closely is the Son, the Word, identified with the Father (1:1, 18), that to see Jesus is to see the Father who sent him (*cf.* 14:9).

46. As the Father's agent, the Father's Son, Jesus is the revealer of God (1:18). That is why he earlier claimed, 'I am the light of the world' (8:12). Here the thought is similar, the language less bold: Jesus has come into the world *as a light*. The Evangelist thus continues the theme of vv. 35, 36, using the light/darkness antithesis not only to invite belief by making darkness repulsive, but also to stress, in preparation for vv. 47–48, that the purpose of his coming was not to bring condemnation but transformation.

47–48. What then of men and women who, like those described in vv. 42–43, exercise only superficial faith, the faith that hears Jesus' words but does not keep them (*cf.* Mt. 7:24–27; Jas. 2:14ff.)? Jesus has already insisted that it is the one who keeps his word who will never taste death (8:31, 52); those who disobey the Son do not have eternal life, but the wrath of God remains on them (3:36). This does not mean that Jesus came with the express purpose of bringing condemnation (*cf.* notes on 3:17; 8:15), even though, from another perspective, judgment has been assigned to him (*cf.* notes on 5:22, 27; 8:16, 26). The idea is that the same message that proclaims life and forgiveness to the believer proclaims condemnation and wrath to the unbeliever, and this judgment on the world (v. 31) is now impending.

There is, however, a peculiar standard of judgment applied to those who hear Jesus' words but do not keep them. Just as those who were steeped in the words of Moses would be judged by them and find themselves condemned (5:45–47), so anyone who rejects Jesus – *i.e.* anyone who has heard his words but who does not accept them as they are to be taken – *that very word which I spoke will condemn him at the last day*.

49–50. The reason why the Son's words are so final and threaten unbelievers with judgment (vv. 47–48) is that they are the words of the Father (v. 49; *cf.* 5:19ff.). Many Jews saw the law of Moses as the source of life (*cf.* notes on 5:39; *cf.* Dt. 32:45ff.). Rightly understood, this was surely true (*cf.* Mk. 10:17–18; Lk. 10:28). But now the law of Moses, as gracious a gift of God as it was, is being replaced, or, better, fulfilled, by new grace (*cf.* notes on 1:16–17), bound up with the person and words of Jesus, the incarnate Word (1:14). All that Jesus says, and even how to say it, has been commanded by the Father (v. 49), and God's command, which stands behind the revelation Jesus is and brings, *leads to eternal*

---

evangelism at that period cannot easily be gainsaid; most of the rest of Martyn's argument is sheerest speculation.

life. For Jesus, the Father's command not only shapes and sanctions his speech, but leads inexorably to the cross (10:18; 12:20–33).

If John concludes Jesus' public ministry on this note, it is because Jesus' speech is a reflection of his person. Not only is what Jesus says just what the Father has told him to say, but he himself is the Word of God, God's self-expression (1:1). Jesus has lived in unqualified obedience to his Father; he is now about to die in the same unqualified obedience, for he who is the Word-made-flesh (1:14) is also the Lamb of God who takes away the sin of the world (1:29).

IV. JESUS' SELF-DISCLOSURE IN HIS CROSS AND EXALTATION (13:1 – 20:31)

A. THE LAST SUPPER (13:1–30)

Several of the signs in the first half of the Fourth Gospel are immediately followed by extended discourses that 'unpack' the significance of the sign. Here the order is reversed: one of the purposes of the chapters immediately before us, embracing the last supper, the farewell discourse and the final prayer of Jesus (Jn. 13 – 17), is to 'unpack', before the event, the significance of Jesus' departure – his death, burial, resurrection, exaltation and the consequent coming of the Holy Spirit.

Prefatory notes on the structure and content of the farewell discourse are reserved for the introduction to 13:31, below. At the moment it will suffice to comment briefly on two other questions:

(1) *How does John's chronology of the passion narrative relate to the chronology of the Synoptic Gospels?* The Synoptic Gospels clearly indicate that Jesus and his disciples celebrated the Passover together (Mk. 14:12; Lk. 22:15), apparently during the early hours of 15 Nisan (reckoning the beginning of each day at sundown). In that particular year, the Passover ran from about 6.00 p.m. Thursday to about 6.00 p.m. Friday. Seven verses in John's Gospel, however, have convinced most scholars that John places the last supper the night before, on Wednesday evening, 14 Nisan (Jn. 13:1, 27; 18:28; 19:14, 31, 36, 42). This reckoning assigns Jesus' crucifixion to Thursday afternoon, at the time of the slaughtering of the Passover lambs at the temple in preparation for the Passover that lay just ahead. Theologically, this means that the last supper cannot easily be construed as a paschal meal, even if the link between Jesus' death and the slaughter of the lambs might be considered a significant gain (cf. 1:29, 34); historically, this reckoning introduces such a jarring contradiction with the Synoptics that most commentators have felt it necessary either to approve one scheme while condemning the other, or to propose some kind of resolution.

Those like Bernard (p. cvii) who defend John's dating usually do so on the grounds that they find the evidence of the Synoptics self-contradictory, leaving them free to choose John almost by default. Their evaluation of the Synoptic texts is complex, and cannot be reviewed here; Barrett (pp. 48–50) has rightly shown that the Synoptic texts cannot bear the weight that is placed on them (*cf.* also Jeremias, pp. 41–62). A variation on this approach is defended by France[1] and others. France argues that John's chronology is right, and that the Synoptics do not contradict it. What Jesus ate was not the Passover but a meal that anticipated Passover, since he knew that at the time of the Passover he would be hanging on the cross. Of course, this means that Jesus and his disciples could not have eaten an appropriately sacrificed lamb, since the temple authorities were unlikely to accommodate themselves to his divinely sanctioned sense of timing. France does not find this point difficult, because he notes that none of the four Gospels explicitly mentions the eating of a lamb.

The most difficult point for France to circumnavigate is Mark 14:12, which in the view of most commentators inexorably ties the last supper to the Passover. France disagrees. Both France and his opponents agree that Mark 14:12 explicitly affirms that the preparations for the last supper were made on the day that the paschal lambs were slaughtered. The slaughter normally took place between 3.00 p.m. and 5.00 p.m. on 14 Nisan, falling on a Thursday in the year in question; Passover itself began about 6.00 p.m. on the same Thursday, the beginning of 15 Nisan. Most commentators think, rightly, that this means the disciples were busy all day Thursday in the various preparations required for the feast, and then ate the Passover meal that evening, 15 Nisan. France apparently wants the disciples to prepare for the feast, and all the disciples to eat this anticipatory meal, the night before, from 6.00 p.m. on Wednesday, already 14 Nisan. In other words, in France's view all the preparations would have had to be made, and the meal itself eaten, on the Wednesday evening after about 6.00 p.m. But not only is this an unnatural reading of Mark 14:12, it makes the chronology impossibly tight, when we bear in mind that the preparations included locating the room by following a man carrying a water jar, and then, presumably, purchasing and preparing the food, and arranging the room.

Conversely, most of those who think that the Synoptics have it historically right argue that John introduces an historical anomaly in order to gain a theological point: Jesus is not only the true temple, the true light, the true vine, but the true paschal lamb: John places Jesus' death at the time of the slaughtering of the paschal lambs in order to establish this next step in his replacement motif. 'This may not be good history; but it does seem to be Johannine theology' (Barrett, p. 51; *cf.* Lindars, p. 446). But not only does this theory leave the historical contradiction with the Synoptics unaddressed, it appears flimsy even at

---

[1] R. T. France, 'Chronological Aspects of "Gospel Harmony"', *VE* 16, 1986, pp. 50–54.

the theological level. John does not in these chapters draw attention to the slaughter of the lambs, nor does he here refer to Jesus as the true Lamb of God.

These difficulties have led to a number of suggested resolutions that turn on calendrical disputes in the first century. The most important of these reconstructions, that of Jaubert,[1] argues that Jesus and his disciples followed a solar calendar known to us from *Jubilees* and possibly adopted at Qumran (a monastic community by the Dead Sea). This calendar invariably places Passover on *Tuesday* evening (14-15 Nisan), so that is when Jesus and his disciples ate their Passover meal. But the 'official' calendar followed by the Pharisees and Sadducees in the Jerusalem establishment was lunar, and that fateful year Passover fell on Thursday-Friday (sundown to sundown). This and similar theories end up defending both John and the Synoptics: Jesus ate a Passover meal with his disciples (Synoptics), but it was at a time earlier in the week than the official Passover, which meant he could still be crucified during the slaughter of the Passover lambs according to the schedule of the lunar calendar (John).

But these calendrical theories all involve delicate historical judgments or a paucity of hard evidence. Jaubert's theory, for instance, turns in part on the interpretation of a third-century document (the *Didascalia*) which on the face of it is rather more concerned with justifying current fasting practices by appealing to Passion Week than with giving much useful historical information about that week. More seriously, it is altogether unlikely that the Jewish authorities in the time of Jesus sanctioned the slaughter of paschal lambs on any day other then the official lunar day. Thus even if Jesus and his disciples followed a sectarian calendar – a very doubtful suggestion – they would not have been able to eat an early paschal meal, since the paschal lamb had to be slaughtered at the temple, and the priestly classes were not noted for affable flexibility.

Most other approaches to the problem bear the burden of even greater ingenuity and even less historical likelihood.[2] The solution that carries fewest difficulties argues that the Synoptic chronology is correct: Jesus and his disciples did indeed eat a Passover meal on Thursday, the beginning of 15 Nisan. John's Gospel, rightly interpreted, does not contradict this chronology in any of the seven verses alleged to do so (13:1, 27; 18:28; 19:14, 31, 36, 42). This stance will briefly be defended in

[1]A. Jaubert, *The Date of the Last Supper* (Alba, 1965).

[2]*E.g.* Eugen Ruckstuhl, 'Zur Chronologie der Leidensgeschichte Jesu', *SNTU* 10, 1985, pp. 27–61; 11, 1986, pp. 97–129, argues that Jesus and his disciples ate an Essene paschal meal on Tuesday evening; that he was arrested and brought before the high priest's court on Wednesday; that on Thursday he was sentenced to death by that court; that he was executed on Friday. Ruckstuhl's reconstruction depends on the assumption of very tight links between Jesus and the Essenes.

the pages that follow, as these verses come up.[1] Not less important, the numerous hints *within John's narrative* that the Evangelist understood the supper he reports to be a Passover celebration will be noted.

(2) *Why does John omit explicit mention of the institution of what has come to be called 'the eucharist' or 'the Lord's supper'?* Some argue that this is evidence the Evangelist is explicitly anti-sacramentarian: so, for instance, Bultmann (pp. 485–486), who thinks that John displaces the institution of the Lord's supper with the prayer of John 17, in order to affirm that the blessings of eternal life stem from faithful response to the revelatory word, not from any alleged power in the sacrament. Other interpreters, themselves sacramentarian in their commitments, suppose that John omits the institution of the Lord's supper from John 13 because he has dealt with the subject so fully in John 6. That view, of course, entirely depends on reading John 6 that way.

Quite apart from the slipperiness of a term like 'sacrament', the exposition of John 6 in this commentary forbids so simplistic a reading of that chapter. Insofar as John allows echoes of the eucharist to flavour his language in the bread of life discourse, his point is that the ultimate saving act is the cross/exaltation of Jesus. Jesus himself is the bread of life. It is even possible that the view of the Lord's supper popular in John's day had become magical, that many people supposed 'that a rite recalling that solemn moment must be automatically salutary' (Barrett, p. 85). Far better then to detach eucharistic allusions from the Lord's supper (which in any case would surely have been widely known) and emphasize instead that to which such allusions point – Jesus himself, the true bread from heaven which alone can give eternal life. Jesus came and lived and died and rose again and was exalted not to bequeath to needy sinners a rite, but himself, and all the blessings that flow from that gift. The Evangelist, especially if his purpose is to evangelize men and women in his own generation, refuses to be distracted from this central and fundamental message.

1. Jesus washes his disciples' feet *(13:1–17)*

A quick reading of 13:1–17 (some prefer to think of 13:1–20 as the basic unit) shows that the episode of the footwashing is turned in two directions. On the one hand, it is symbolic of spiritual cleansing (*cf.* especially vv. 8–10); on the other, it serves as a standard of humble service and therefore as a call to all of Jesus' disciples to 'wash one another's feet' (vv. 12–17). This bifocal application has generated considerable discussion on the structure and provenance of the narrative. In an influential essay, Boismard[2] argued that underlying our text stand two entirely disparate interpretations of the event of the footwashing: a *sacramental*

---

[1]For a more detailed defence of the view briefly developed here, *cf.* Norval Geldenhuys, *The Gospel of Luke* (Marshall, Morgan and Scott, 1950), pp. 649–670; Carson, *Matt*, pp. 530–532; Blomberg, pp. 175–178.

[2]M. E. Boismard, *RB* 71, 1964, pp. 5–24.

interpretation (vv. 3, 4–5, 6–10, 21–30) and a *moralistic* interpretation (vv. 1–2, 4–5, 12–15, 17–19). More recently, others have offered variations on this theme.[1] Somewhat earlier, Bultmann (pp. 462–463), rejecting any sacramentalism in the 'original' Gospel, argued that the Evangelist's source consisted of vv. 4–5, 12–20; the Evangelist himself added vv. 6–10. Brown (2. 560–562) reverses the precedence. He views the first narrative as a prophetic action symbolizing the Lord's suffering for others, and suggests it derives from the Evangelist. The second narrative, he reasons, derives from a later editor in the 'Johannine school'. Many scholars follow Brown, with minor variations: *e.g.* Becker (2. 419–430) argues that the editor was the 'ecclesiastical redactor' originally postulated by Bultmann.[2]

It is impossible in this brief commentary to treat these theories in detail. Nevertheless, two countervailing lines of contemporary research should be noted.

(1) Many commentators, far from teasing out two competing traditions that have allegedly been slapped together by incompetent redactors, judge that this section is entirely the work of the Evangelist (Lindars, p. 447), that the combination of these two themes is characteristically Johannine (Barrett, p. 462), and even that the attempt to separate out the ethical or moralistic from the profoundly religious symbolism of the footwashing 'throws Johannine theology as a whole into confusion' (Haenchen, 2. 114). Already in John 12 the image of the dying kernel of wheat is applied first to the unique death of the Son of Man, and then derivatively to Jesus' disciples (12:24ff.). Similarly, in the Synoptic Gospels the announcement of Jesus' death and resurrection is immediately followed by the responsibility (and privilege!) of all disciples to take up their cross and follow Jesus (Mk. 8:13ff. par.). Peter exhibits no embarrassment in finding in Jesus' unique, sin-bearing suffering and death a model for Christian suffering (1 Pet. 2:13–25). In short, the link is common in Christian paraenesis, and the drive toward two entirely separate narratives in John 13 correspondingly unjustified. As with the crucifixion, so with the footwashing: each is simultaneously an act of God by which human beings are freed or cleansed – whether in reality (the cross) or in symbol (the footwashing) – and an example that Jesus' followers are to emulate. Indeed, we shall argue that John preserves *three* distinguishable but related uses of the footwashing, and attaches all of them to the teaching of the Master.

(2) A number of recent studies have appealed to structural and literary categories to demonstrate the unity and coherence of John 13, indeed

---

[1]Michal Wojciechowski, *NTS* 34, 1988, pp. 135–141; *cf.* also Richter, pp. 314–320.

[2]For a comprehensive survey and evaluation of modern interpretations of this passage, *cf.* Chris Thomas, 'Footwashing in John 13 and the Johannine Community' (Ph.D. dissertation, Sheffield University, forthcoming).

the unity and coherence of John 13 – 17.[1] Most of these studies are quick to aver that there must have been detachable sources underlying these chapters, that the search for a detailed 'life-setting' (*Sitz im Leben*) for each of these sources is a valuable one, and so forth, but that their own focus of interest is in demonstrating the unity and structure of the text *as it now stands*. The problem, of course, is that the various alleged sources and strata are uncovered by appealing to perceived breaks in thematic development ('aporias'), to apparent repetitions, grammatical breaks and other perceived incongruities. If all of these textual features are now subsumed under an overreaching structure, if all the bits fit into some literary unity, where is the evidence for the *dis*unity? Or conversely, if the evidence for the disparate sources is so strong, must we not conclude that the attempts to display fundamental literary unity are methodologically wrong-headed?

If it is the first responsibility of the interpreter to make sense of the text *as it now stands*, then the demonstrations of unity and internal coherence enjoy a certain methodological priority. Certainly at the level of language, John has so forcefully stamped his account with his own style, idiom and emphases that source-criticism at that level is vain. Of course, even after arguing for the unity of the passage, its authenticity and reliability are not thereby necessarily established. But it would be fair to say that a pastiche approach to John's Gospel not only depends on multiplying speculations but tends to reduce the Gospel's fundamental credibility, while a demonstration of essential literary and theological integrity not only attests the Evangelist's skill but enhances his reliability as a witness to Jesus Christ.

Although some see 13:1–3 as a lengthy introduction to the farewell discourse in general and to the footwashing in particular, opening up the narrative again after the meditative conclusion to the first major part of this Gospel (12:36–50),[2] it is better, from the perspective of both Greek syntax and theme, to see 13:1 as an introduction, with vv. 2–3 plunging into the first part of the demonstration of 'the full extent of [Christ's] love' (13:1).

1. If the opening words *It was just before the Passover Feast* are taken as a heading to chs. 13 – 17, it follows that the meal the disciples are about to have with Jesus could not itself have been the Passover meal. Taking the clause that way plunges us into the chronological problems discussed above. But there is nothing in the words themselves to discourage us from taking the clause as an introduction to the footwashing only, and not to the discourses that follow the meal. Chronologically, the opening words then place the footwashing before the Passover meal about to begin (and v. 2, in the best texts, does not contradict this point); theologically, the clause alerts the readers to the Passover theme developed

---

[1]E.g. Simoens, esp. pp. 81–104; Francis J. Moloney, *AusBibRev* 34, 1986, pp. 1–16; and, to some extent, Culpepper, pp. 79–98.

[2]W. K. Grossouw, *NovT* 8, 1966, pp. 124–131.

throughout the book (2:13, 23; 6:4; 11:55; 12:1; *cf.* 18:28, 39; 19:14), inviting them to see in the footwashing an anticipation of Jesus' own climactic Passover act as the Lamb of God who takes away the sin of the world (1:29; *cf.* notes on 13:6–9).

All along Jesus has indicated that his climactic hour, determined by his heavenly Father, had not yet arrived (*e.g.* 2:4; 7:8). More recently he had received the crucial 'signal' that indicated the last act was next, the hour of the Son of Man's glorification (12:23). Thus, *Jesus knew that the time had come for him to leave the world and go to the Father.* The 'world' (*cf.* notes on 1:10) is important in these chapters: it occurs forty times, primarily to draw a sharp contrast between Jesus' 'own', his disciples, and the mass of lost humanity, the 'world' from which they were drawn and in which they must live until their final vindication. If God loves the world (3:16), it is in order to draw men and women out of it. Those so drawn out constitute a new entity, set over against the world: the world loves its 'own', Jesus loves his 'own' (15:19). The object of the love of God in Christ, in these chapters, is therefore not the lost world, but the newly forming people of God, the disciples of the Messiah, the nascent church, the community of the elect. Jesus had loved his own all along; *he now showed them the full extent of his love.*

This wording is one possible rendering of the Greek, which might more literally be translated, 'he loved them to the end [*eis telos*]'. The words 'to the end' might be taken adverbially to mean 'to the uttermost', 'utterly', and hence the NIV's paraphrase. But if 'end' (*telos*) is taken temporally, the clause means that Jesus loved them to the very end of his life.[1] Either way, the text presupposes that the way Jesus displays his unflagging love for his own is in the cross immediately ahead, and in the act of self-abasing love, the foot-washing, that anticipates the cross. 'Greater love has no-one than this, that he lay down his life for his friends' (15:13).

2. Judging by the time marker in v. 30, the meal that is about to begin is an *evening meal* (*deipnon; cf.* notes on 12:2). Assuming that the opening clause means that this meal had just been served (*cf.* Additional Note), the stage is thereby set for Jesus to begin washing his disciples' feet. Before proceeding with the narrative, however, John ensures that his readers will grasp just how strongly this episode attests the loving character of Jesus. The disciples whose feet he was about to wash include Judas Iscariot, son of Simon (*cf.* Additional Note), whose treacherous plot had already been conceived.

The expression is awkward: 'the devil already having put it into the heart that Judas . . . should betray him'. Whose heart? One might assume the heart of Judas (for somewhat analogous language, *cf.* Rev. 17:17), and indeed some Greek manuscripts preserve the genitive of

---

[1]Lattke, pp. 143–145, argues that John wants both meanings to be understood, with the temporal one being primary.

Judas (*Iouda*) that sanctions such a rendering. The idea, then, is not that Judas was not responsible, for a heart incited by Satan actually wills what the devil wills (Schlatter, p. 279); rather, the plot against Jesus, however mediated by wicked human beings, was nothing less then satanic. Interpreters admit, however, that the genitive *Iouda* is an easier reading than the nominative *Ioudas*, and therefore, all other things being equal, somewhat less likely to be original. If we adopt the nominative, it is more natural (though, against Barrett, p. 439, surely not required) to understand the heart to be the devil's: the devil put it into *his own heart* that Judas would betray Jesus, *i.e.* the devil so decided. Despite alleged parallels, however (*viz.* 1 Sa. 29:10 LXX; Jb. 22:22), it is doubtful that 'to put into one's (own) heart' ever means 'to decide', so that this understanding of the nominative is intrinsically unlikely. One is tempted to think that the original was nominative, but was such an awkward way of saying that the devil put the thought into Judas' heart that some later copyists made the point clear by 'correcting' to the genitive. Either way, the devil and Judas are now in a conspiracy of evil to bring Jesus to the cross, a conspiracy fleshed out in vv. 18, 19, 21–30; ch. 18.

3–5. Jesus' special knowledge of his Father's will for him, articulated in v. 1, is now repeated, but with two significant additions: he knew not only that the time had come for him to leave this world, but that *he had come from God* and that *the Father had put all things under his power*. With such power and status at his disposal, we might have expected him to defeat the devil in an immediate and flashy confrontation, and to devastate Judas with an unstoppable blast of divine wrath. Instead, he washes his disciples' feet, including the feet of the betrayer.

Doubtless the disciples would have been happy to wash his feet; they could not conceive of washing one another's feet, since this was a task normally reserved for the lowliest of menial servants. Peers did not wash one another's feet, except very rarely and as a mark of great love. Some Jews insisted that Jewish slaves should not be required to wash the feet of others; this job should be reserved for Gentile slaves, or for women and children and pupils (*Mekhilta* § 1 on Ex. 21:2). In one well-known story, when Rabbi Ishmael returned home from synagogue one day and his mother wished to wash his feet, he refused on the ground that the task was too demeaning. She took the matter to the rabbinic court on the ground that she viewed the task, in his case, as an honour (*cf.* SB 1. 707). The reluctance of Jesus' disciples to volunteer for such a task is, to say the least, culturally understandable; their shock at his volunteering is not merely the result of being shamefaced, it is their response to finding their sense of the fitness of things shattered.[1] But here Jesus reverses normal roles. His act of humility is as unnecessary as it is stunning, and is simultaneously a display of love (v. 1), a symbol of

---

[1] There is no instance in either Jewish or Greco-Roman sources of a superior washing the feet of an inferior: *cf.* Chris Thomas, *op. cit.*, ch. 3.

saving cleansing (vv. 6–9), and a model of Christian conduct (vv. 12–17).

We must picture the disciples reclining on thin mats around a low table. Each is leaning on his arm, usually the left; the feet radiate outward from the table. Jesus pushes himself up from his own mat. The details are revealing: Jesus *took off his outer clothing, and wrapped a towel round his waist* – thus adopting the dress of a menial slave, dress that was looked down upon in both Jewish and Gentile circles (SB 2. 557; Suetonius, *Caligula*, 26). Thus he *began to wash his disciples' feet*, thereby demonstrating his claim, 'I am among you as one who serves' (Lk. 22:27; *cf.* Mk. 10:45 par.). The one who was 'in very nature God . . . made himself nothing' and took 'the very nature of a servant' (Phil. 2:6–7). Indeed, he 'became obedient to death – even death on a cross!' (Phil. 2:8). The matchless self-emptying of the eternal Son, the eternal Word, reaches its climax on the cross. This does not mean that the Word *exchanges* the form of God for the form of a servant; it means, rather, that he so dons our flesh and goes open-eyed to the cross that his deity is *revealed* in our flesh, supremely at the moment of greatest weakness, greatest service (*cf.* notes on 1:14).

6–7. Doubtless all of the disciples were extremely embarrassed by these proceedings. For most of them, their embarrassment bred beleaguered silence; for Peter, it meant he had to object. As at Caesarea Philippi (Mk. 8:32–33 par.), his objection is candid and well-motivated, but totally ignorant of his Master's course. The Greek construction of his question suggests indignant emphasis: 'Are *you* going to wash *my* feet?'[1]

But Jesus expects him to submit to the washing in faith. As the disciples cannot yet understand how the one whom they venerate as the Messiah must go to the cross, so they cannot understand the symbol-laden acts that anticipate it. Peter and the others will understand *later* – or, better, 'after these things' (Gk. *meta tauta*). This does not refer to the footwashing, but to the passion to which the footwashing points. After Jesus' death/exaltation, and certainly after the descent of the Spirit who comes in consequence of that tragic and glorious event, they will understand. Peter's failure to comprehend is of a piece with many such failures, on the part of enemies and disciples alike, during the period of Jesus' public ministry (*cf.* notes on 2:22; 7:37–39; 12:16; 16:13; 20:9; *cf.* Carson, 'Mis').

8–9. Peter demonstrates his incomprehension by his next words: *No . . . you shall never wash my feet*. His expression is strong, but despite his outrage he is still thinking at no higher level than what is socially fitting. If there were nothing more at stake then the naked act of footwashing, Jesus' response would seem petty, unbearably rigid. It would sound like fake humility: 'I command you to let me be humble and let me wash your feet – or you're fired!' But once the symbolism is seen, Jesus' words

---

[1] *Contra* BDF § 473. It is reading too much into the word order to say that 'the impression is given of Peter spluttering in astonishment and incomprehension' (Beasley–Murray, p. 233).

are almost inevitable: *Unless I wash you, you have no part with me.* That is always true: unless the Lamb of God has taken away a person's sin, has washed that person, he or she can have no part with him.

The notion of 'having a part (*meros*) in' something is regularly used with respect to inheritance (*e.g.* Lk. 15:12), and, in Jewish thought, can refer to participation in eschatological blessings (*cf.* Mt. 24:51; Rev. 20:6). The word is not infrequently tied to belonging to Jesus Christ or to the people of God, however conceived (*e.g.* Lk. 12:46; Rev. 22:19). Conceptually, having a 'part with Jesus' is given some content in the Fourth Gospel in 14:1–3 and 17:24. Perhaps Peter understood an eschatological reference in this verse; he certainly understood that he wanted to be linked with Jesus. It is very doubtful that he or anyone else other than Jesus himself grasped that the basis of the cleansing foreshadowed by the washing of his feet lay ahead in the hideous ignominy of the barbarous cross. But what Peter did understand was enough to prompt his typically unrestrained rejoinder: *not just my feet but my hands and my head as well!*

It does not seem wise to postulate (as some do) that 'hands' are mentioned because they are the part of the body that Jews would most naturally expect to contract ritual uncleanness first, since ritual cleanliness is not in view. Nor does the mention of 'head' serve by metonymy as a reference to the whole person – as if Peter wants a complete bath! In that case, why does Peter mention his hands as a separate part? Such interpretations are too heavy-handed. Peter's response sounds more like unrestrained exuberance.

10–11. Jesus' reply has been understood in two fundamentally different ways, with variations. The two ways turn on an exceedingly difficult textual variant.

(1) The majority of modern expositors[1] omit the Greek words *ei mē tous podas*, 'except his feet', generating a translation such as 'A person who has had a bath (*louō*) does not need a wash (*niptō*)' – assuming the two verbs *louō* and *niptō* must be sharply distinguished.[2] The verb *niptō* ('to wash') is also the verb used in v. 8, 'Unless I *wash* you . . .' The idea, then, is that the disciples had *already* 'had a bath', and their 'whole body is clean'. Peter therefore does not need a complete wash. The act of footwashing is a symbol of this complete washing, and not some additional cleansing. If it were a mere additional cleansing, it would be a *relatively* insignificant step, which is incompatible with v. 7. Later copyists, failing to understand this point, added the words 'except his feet', and drastically changed the meaning. The shorter reading must therefore be accepted as the original, and is attested by Codex Sinaiticus (Alexandrian text, fourth century), various Latin readings from the

---

[1]Too numerous to list, they are ably represented by Brown, 2. 567–568; Bultmann, p. 470; Beasley–Murray, pp. 229, 234–235; James D. G. Dunn, *ZNW* 61, 1970, p. 250.
[2]So F. Hauck, *TDNT*, 4. 946–947.

fourth to the twelfth centuries (Western text), and by the text known to Origen (Caesarean, third century).

(2) Nevertheless it must be admitted that the preponderance of textual evidence favours retention of the phrase, generating a rendering such as 'A person who has had a bath does not need to wash, *except his feet*' (or, more idiomatically with the NIV, '. . . needs only to wash his feet'). It is far from clear that the move from *louō* to *niptō* is critical to a proper interpretation, for not only is the older semantic distinction between the two verbs often ignored by hellenistic writers (as most scholars admit[1]), but John is particularly given to using pairs of verbs synonymously, for purely stylistic reasons (*e.g. oida* and *ginōskō* for 'to know'; *pempō* and *apostellō* for 'to send'; *agapaō* and *phileō* for 'to love'; *cf.* especially Morris, *SFG*, pp. 293–319). In this view, Jesus is going on to give a fresh lesson. In vv. 6–8 the footwashing symbolizes the cleansing that is the result of Christ's impending cross-work. But Peter's unrestrained (and thoughtless) exuberance (v. 9) opens up the opportunity to turn the footwashing to another point: the initial and fundamental cleansing that Christ provides is a once-for-all act. Individuals who have been cleansed by Christ's atoning work will doubtless need to have subsequent sins washed away, but the fundamental cleansing can never be repeated. It rather misses the point to charge that this view makes the footwashing a mere 'topping up', a symbol not of the fundamental cross-work of Christ and its effects but of progressive Christian experience. *In this verse* that may be so – but the point is that this verse has launched into a new application of the footwashing. The first application used the footwashing to symbolize Christ's atoning, cleansing death; this second application makes the points just elucidated; the third and final application teaches lessons in humility (vv. 12–17). One could not responsibly argue against the obvious meaning of vv. 12–15 by saying that this makes Jesus' disciples responsible to die a unique, atoning death: that would be to confuse the first and third applications. In the same way, the first and second applications must not be confused.

Some such view was defended by many older scholars, and is supported by some more recent ones.[2] Moreover, this changing, shifting use of a figure is methodologically much like the way John handles the sheep/shepherd metaphor in John 10, or the vine metaphor in John 15. The interpretation of John 13:10 affirmed here also fits the theology of 1 John, which, assuming common authorship (though this point is disputed), is not to be ignored. In his first epistle, addressed to Christians, to people who have already believed (1 Jn. 5:13) and received eternal life (2:25), John insists that continuing confession of sin is necessary (1:9), as

---

[1]Chris Thomas, *op. cit.*, ch. 2, is an exception.

[2]E.g. Westcott, 2. 150; Bernard, 2. 462; Schlatter, pp. 282–283; and more recently Haenchen, 2. 457 (though he thinks the text is full of confusion); Bruce, pp. 282–283; Metzger, p. 240; and, on the text-critical question, especially John Christopher Thomas, *NovT* 29, 1987, pp. 46–52.

is continued dependence upon Jesus Christ, who is the atoning sacrifice for our sins (2:1, 2). The thought of John 13:10 is not dissimilar.

If the longer reading is original, one must ask what might have prompted the early omission of the phrase. The best suggestion is that some early copyists wrongly detected a pedantic contradiction between this phrase and the next clause, *his whole body is clean*, and consequently decided to drop the phrase. But Jesus' point, granted the longer text, is that the common experience of natural life has its counterpoint in spiritual existence: the person who has taken a bath, and who is basically clean, may nevertheless need to have his feet washed after a short walk on dusty roads, even though another bath would be superfluous. In the same way, the disciples have received the cleansing salvation, prospectively, by faith: *you are clean*, Jesus comments, and then adds, *though not every one of you*.

John comments that Jesus said this in full consciousness of who *was going to betray him* (*cf.* 6:70, 71).

Doubtless when Jesus washed the disciples' feet he included the feet of Judas Iscariot. If this proves anything beyond the unfathomable love and forbearance of the Master, it is that no rite, even if performed by Jesus himself, ensures spiritual cleansing. Washed Judas may have been; cleansed he was not (*cf.* 6:63–64). The only other place in the Fourth Gospel where Jesus tells his disciples (minus Judas) that they are clean is 15:3: 'You are already clean because of the word I have spoken to you.' Real cleansing is effected both through Jesus' revelatory word and through the atoning sacrifice to which the footwashing pointed.

This becomes another small but telling reason why sacramentarian interpretations of the footwashing[1] must be firmly rejected – a point increasingly recognized by modern commentators.[2] Many connect the footwashing with baptism (but of course, some detect baptism every time water is mentioned). Some of those who retain the longer reading suggest that the secondary washing refers to the eucharist – though J. Michl has rightly protested that footwashing is a rather remarkable symbol for tasting Jesus' flesh and blood.[3] The focus of the entire chapter is on Christology and soteriology, *i.e.* on who Christ is and on what he does. The most that can be said is that insofar as the footwashing anticipates the cleansing cross-work of Christ, it is parallel to Christian rites that look back on the same climactic event.

12. The notes that serve as preface to this section, above, have argued that there is no reason to think that the new application of the footwashing, immediately before us (vv. 12–17), stems from a different hand. After donning his outer garment again, and returning to his own mat (*cf.* v. 4), Jesus asks, *Do you understand what I have done for you?* The

---

[1]*E.g.* J. N. Suggit, *Neot* 19, 1988, pp. 64–70.
[2]*E.g.* Richter, pp. 295–298; Becker, 2. 425; and especially Schnackenburg, 3. 19–20, who once espoused a baptismal interpretation of the footwashing and later abandoned it.
[3]J. Michl, *Bib* 50, 1959, pp. 697–708.

exemplary nature of the footwashing is then unpacked (vv. 13–17). But the links that tie these verses to the theme of cleansing that dominates the preceding verses are more than accidental. Even when the foot-washing is said to point, in various ways, to spiritual cleansing based on Christ's death, both the footwashing and that atoning death are the supreme displays of Jesus' love for his own (v. 1b). The footwashing was shocking to Jesus' disciples, but not half as shocking as the notion of a Messiah who would die the hideous and shameful death of crucifixion, the death of the damned. But the two events – the footwashing and the crucifixion – are truly of a piece: the revered and exalted Messiah assumes the role of the despised servant for the good of others. That, plus the notion of cleansing, explains why the footwashing can point so effectively to the cross. But service for others cannot be restricted to this unique act. If the footwashing and the cross are prompted by Jesus' daunting love (v. 1), the fellowship of the cleansed that he is creating is to be characterized by the same love (vv. 34–35), and therefore by the same self-abnegation for the sake of serving others. And that means that the footwashing is almost *bound* to have exemplary significance, just as Christ's death, however unique, has exemplary force (*e.g.* Mk. 10:35–45; Jn. 12:24–26; 1 Pet. 2).

13. Jesus now answers the question he set in v. 12: whether or not his followers understood, he will explain what he has done. *Teacher* (*didaskalos*) is the equivalent of 'Rabbi', the term regularly used by disciples addressing their teachers (as John the Baptist's followers addressed him, 3:26; *cf.* also 1:38, 49; 3:2; 4:31; 6:25; 9:21; 11:8). *Lord* (*kyrios*) was doubtless first applied to Jesus as a mark of respect for his teaching role, the equivalent of Aramaic *mar*; the expression is preserved in the New Testament in *marana tha*, lit. 'Our Lord, come!' (1 Cor. 16:22; NIV 'Come, O Lord') – clearly the influence of Aramaic-speaking Christians projecting one of their favourite sayings into the Greek-speaking world. 'Rabbi' and 'Mari' are known to have come together on the lips of rabbinic pupils addressing their masters (*cf.* SB 2. 558). But on the lips of Christians after the resurrection of Jesus Christ, 'Lord' took on richer meaning as the deepest reflections on who Jesus is took hold. 'Lord' became one of the important ways Christians referred to Jesus as the one whom God raised and exalted with 'the name that is above every name' (Phil. 2:9–11; *cf.* Acts 2:36). Indeed, readers of the Septuagint were used to referring to God himself as the 'Lord'. The Evangelist understands this; no-one who reported the confession of 20:28 could fail to do so. Thus he simultaneously remains faithful to the historical constraints of that fateful Passover night, and to the theology he wants to instil. Indeed, later readers could not help finding in Jesus' dramatic words – *and rightly so, for that is what I am* – at least an adumbration of a claim that goes way beyond what a rabbi might say. In its thrust, the verse echoes Lk. 6:46, 'Why do you call me "Lord, Lord," and do not do what I say?'

14–15. One of the ways human pride manifests itself in a stratified society is in refusing to take the lower rôle. But now that Jesus, their *Lord* *and Teacher*, has washed his disciples' feet – an unthinkable act! – there is every reason why they *also should wash one another's feet*, and no conceivable reason for refusing to do so. Jesus says, *I have set you an example* (*hypodeigma* – the word suggests both 'example' and 'pattern'; cf. Heb. 4:11; 8:5; 9:25; Jas. 5:10; 2 Pet. 2:6) *that you should do as I have done for you*. Little becomes Jesus' followers more than humility. Christian zeal divorced from transparent humility sounds hollow, even pathetic.

We may reasonably ask if those Christian communities that practise footwashing as a Christian sacrament on a par with baptism and the Lord's supper have understood this passage better than those who find they cannot elevate footwashing to the same plane. We may ask something similar of the formal act of footwashing on Maundy Thursday, when popes, bishops, abbots and others have often washed the feet of junior clergy and sometimes of paupers. Two factors have prevented most Christians, rightly, from so institutionalizing footwashing. First, nowhere else in the New Testament, or in the earliest extra-biblical documents of the church, is footwashing treated as an ecclesiastical rite, an ordinance, a sacrament. The mention of footwashing in 1 Timothy 5:10 is no exception: there it is not introduced as a universal rite, but is placed in a list of good deeds of open-hearted hospitality that qualify a widow to be included in the support list. Wise theologians and expositors have always been reluctant to raise to the level of universal rite something that appears only once in Scripture. Second, and perhaps more importantly, the heart of Jesus' command is a humility and helpfulness toward brothers and sisters in Christ that may be cruelly parodied by a mere 'rite' of footwashing that easily masks an unbroken spirit and a haughty heart.

16. Jesus drives the point home with an aphorism, one that was probably often repeated during his ministry, one that could easily be turned to several different applications (cf. Mt. 10:24; Lk. 6:40; Jn. 15:20). After the strong asseverative *I tell you the truth* (cf. notes on 1:51), Jesus deepens the teacher/pupil contrast by introducing two other pairs: master/servant (understood to be a slave) and superior (*i.e.* one who sends)/messenger. The word for 'messenger' is *apostolos*, the only time the word appears in the Fourth Gospel, and here without any overtones of the official 'twelve apostles': the word enjoyed a wide range of meaning throughout the New Testament period. This does not mean that the Evangelist had no concept of a special group of twelve disciples: he elsewhere repeatedly refers to 'the Twelve' (6:67, 70; 20:24). The point of the aphorism in this context is in any case painfully clear: no emissary has the right to think he is exempt from tasks cheerfully undertaken by the one who sent him, and no slave has the right to judge any menial task beneath him after his master has already performed it.

> Great God, in Christ you call our name
> and then receive us as your own,
> not through some merit, right or claim,

but by your gracious love alone.
We strain to glimpse your mercy-seat
and find you kneeling at our feet.

Then take the towel, and break the bread,
and humble us, and call us friends.
Suffer and serve till all are fed,
and show how grandly love intends
to work till all creation sings,
to fill all worlds, to crown all things.

Brian A. Wren (1936 –)[1]

17. The words *these things* probably refer back to vv. 14–15, with v. 16 a kind of aphoristic parenthesis. There is a form of religious piety that utters a hearty 'Amen!' to the most stringent demands of discipleship, but which rarely does anything about them. Jesus has already condemned those who hear his words but who fail to keep them (12:47–48; *cf.* 8:31). Now he emphasizes the truth again, in line with a repeated stress in the Gospels (*e.g.* Mt. 7:21–27; Mk. 3:35; Lk. 6:47–48) and elsewhere (*e.g.* Heb. 12:14; Jas. 1:22–25).

Additional note

2. Two textual variants control discussion of this verse: (a) the manuscript evidence for the present participle *ginomenou* and for the aorist participle *genomenou* is very evenly divided. The former is often taken to mean that the meal was 'in progress' (hence 'during supper', RSV), but might mean that it 'was being served' (NIV); the latter is often taken to mean that supper was over ('supper being ended', AV), but could be interpreted to mean that supper had just been served. Verses 4 and 26 make it impossible to believe that supper was over, and for that reason many prefer the present participle. Conversely, that makes the aorist participle the harder reading (especially if it is understood as in the AV), and for that reason intrinsically more likely to have been changed by a copyist. It is therefore attractive to suppose that the aorist is original, but that it should be understood to mean that supper had just been served (an instance of what has traditionally been called the 'ingressive aorist'). (b) There is a nest of variants surrounding the name 'Judas Iscariot, son of Simon', but none affects the basic identification of the man. On the bearing of the contest between the genitive and the nominative of 'Judas', *cf.* notes above; on 'Iscariot', *cf.* notes on 6:71.

[1] Reprinted by permission of Oxford University Press (USA and Canada; Hope Publishing Company, Illinois 60188, USA).

2. Jesus predicts his betrayal (13:18–30)

18. Jesus had repeatedly warned about the treachery of someone within the ranks of the Twelve (6:71; 12:4; 13:2). He has just made it clear, once again, that one of them is not at all clean (13:10). Now, referring to those who will be 'blessed' by doing what he has told them (v. 17), he says, *I am not referring to all of you; I know those I have chosen.* It is possible to understand these words to carry an implicit tail, *viz.* 'and Judas isn't one of them', making Judas stand outside the circle of the chosen. But Jesus' words in 6:70 ('Have I not chosen you, the Twelve? Yet one of you is a devil!') show that Judas is at this point to be counted amongst the Twelve; his words in 13:18 assume the same thing. The reason why he now takes the pains to show that inclusion of Judas was not an oversight or a sign of weakness on his part is so that their faith might be strengthened for the critical hour. As in 6:70, the argument assumes that not all election is to salvation.

The reason Jesus chose one who would betray him was to fulfil Scripture. The text cited, Psalm 41:9, ascribed to David, is part of a plaintive lament called forth by the painful experience of being mocked by enemies when already suffering debilitating and life-threatening illness. Worse yet is the treason of friends: 'Even my close friend, whom I trusted, he who shared my bread, has lifted up his heel against me.' By no stretch of the imagination can the entire psalm rightly be labelled 'messianic', for it includes lines such as these: 'O Lord, have mercy upon me; heal me, for I have sinned against you' (Ps. 41:4). The basis for seeing in this psalm a prophecy which is fulfilled in Jesus does not depend on designating the entire psalm 'messianic', but on two other features. First, because of 2 Samuel 7:12–16, Psalm 2 and other passages, David himself became a 'type', a model, of 'great David's greater Son', the promised Messiah. This did not mean that *everything* that happened to David had to find its echo in Jesus. It meant that many of the broad themes of his life were understood that way – especially where language was so hyperbolic when applied to David alone that many readers of Scripture, Jews and Christians alike, were driven to seeing in such texts an anticipation, an adumbration, of the coming King. That, in part, is the explanation behind the reasoning that quotes Psalm 16:8–11 in Acts 2:24ff., or Psalm 45:6–7 in Hebrews 1:8–9. Second, amongst the great themes of David's life that are repeatedly picked up in the New Testament are those that focus on his suffering, weakness, betrayal by friends, discouragement (*e.g.* the use of Ps. 22 in the passion narratives). Great David suffered; his greatness did not exempt him from pain and tears. Christians who came to see that the greatest display of the glory of the incarnate Word lay in the suffering and death so despised by the blind world, could not help but emphasize the similar strand in David's life, and see in it part of the mosaic that established a Davidic 'typology'.

John's recording of the text is closer to the MT than to the LXX. Near-Eastern notions of hospitality and courtesy meant that betrayal by one who is sharing bread is especially heinous. The final clause, *has lifted*

470

up his heel against me, literally means (in Hebrew) 'has made his heel great against me'. There have been many ingenious interpretations. The most likely is that it means 'has given me a great fall' or 'has taken cruel advantage of me' or 'has walked out on me'.[1] The precise point of betrayal is less important than that it was done by an intimate friend.

19. Although he is about to be betrayed, Jesus is not a hapless victim. Even the treachery of Judas can only serve the redemptive purposes of the mission on which Jesus has been sent. Here Jesus explains to his disciples that the reason why he is telling them of the impending betrayal is *so that when it does happen you will believe that I am He*. In the event, the disciples found it desperately difficult to come to terms with the cross; they would have found it impossible without this preparation, preparation that recurs in the next chapters (*e.g.* 14:29). Only Jesus' resurrection and exaltation and his gift of the Spirit would utterly clear their minds and answer their questions, but the careful groundwork Jesus here lays proved sufficiently strong to keep the disciples together. They did not scatter immediately after the crucifixion, but kept together until his resurrection fully vindicated him and established their faith.

The content of that faith could have been put in many ways. Here the object of Jesus' proleptic reassurance is that they might believe that *egō eimi* – an everyday expression that can be devoid of theological overtones (*cf.* notes on 6:20; 9:9), or can call to mind the ineffable name of God, the I AM, the I AM WHAT I AM (SO NEB; *cf.* notes on 8:24, 28, 58; *cf.* Ex. 3:14), the I AM HE of Is. 41:4; 43:10.

20. This verse is closely paralleled by Matthew 10:40 (*cf.* Mk. 9:37; Lk. 10:16); the basic notion itself is reflected in several other passages (*e.g.* Mt. 25:40; Jn. 5:19ff.). Its relevance in this context probably turns on three features: (1) The stunning Christological claim, 'I am He', in the previous verse, is filled out by the words *and whoever accepts me accepts the one who sent me*. This inevitably calls to mind 5:19ff., where the intimacy of the relationship between the Father and the Son has been spelled out in such detail. (2) This verse powerfully ties the disciples to Jesus, and therefore serves as a foil for the failure of Judas Iscariot. The mission of Jesus is here assigned the highest theological significance, the most absolutely binding authority – the authority of God himself. Failure to close with Christ is failure to know God. And because his disciples re-present him to the world, their mission, their ministry, takes on precisely the same absolute significance. (3) Thus Jesus anticipates the commission of 20:21 (see notes), where the parallels between his own mission and the mission of his disciples are explicitly drawn. To the disciples before the cross, this saying could be no more than a tantalizing hint at the work that would be theirs; to the same disciples after the resurrection, this became not only assurance that Jesus knew the direction he was taking (and therefore an incentive to their faith, as in v.

[1]Bruce, pp. 287, 296 and n. 14, citing A. R. Millard for the last suggestion.

16), but also a foretaste of the commission that would consume them to the end of their days.

21–22. Up to this point Jesus had spoken in fairly oblique terms of the impending betrayal (6:70; 13:10, 18). The Twelve were already somewhat disoriented by Jesus' allusions to his suffering and death, categories they still could not square with their conviction that he was the promised Messiah. Doubtless references to betrayal and treachery seemed similarly obscure. Perhaps some wondered if Jesus were referring to disciples just outside the ring of the Twelve; others might have wondered if betrayal would be inadvertent. Perhaps the notion of betrayal did not seem very threatening to them, since their Master could calm storms, raise the dead, feed the hungry, heal the sick. What possible disaster could befall him that he could not rectify?

But Jesus himself was deeply *troubled in spirit* (for the expression, *cf.* notes on 12:27). His anguish was visible, and caught the attention of his disciples. He *testified* (*martyreō*): the verb is usually associated in the Fourth Gospel with the witness of others to him, but in several passages he himself bears witness (*e.g.* 3:32; 7:7; 13:21). Here and in 7:7 the witness that he bears is a bold and public declaration of the world's evil – in this instance of the evil of one of his own intimate followers. His emphatic statement (for the asseverative, *cf.* notes on 1:51) *one of you is going to betray me* cannot be misunderstood. In the embarrassed silence that follows, they grasp his meaning but are *at a loss to know which of them he meant* (*cf.* Mk. 14:19). Simultaneously, the betrayer knows he is about to be exposed, and is confronted with the starkest choice: rush forward immediately to execute his wretched plot, or renounce his evil and beg forgiveness.

23. For the first time *the disciple whom Jesus loved* is introduced. He will reappear at Jesus' cross (19:26–27), at the empty tomb (20:2–9), by the Sea of Tiberias, when the risen Jesus appeared to seven of his disciples (21:1, 20–23), and in the final two verses that ascribe the authority of this Gospel to him (21:24, 25). Difficult questions concerning the authorship of the Fourth Gospel are briefly treated in the Introduction (§ IV). For the moment, it is worth summarizing the most important things that can be said about 'the disciple whom Jesus loved' (often referred to as 'the beloved disciple', owing to the phraseology of the AV):

(1) Assuming that only the Twelve joined Jesus at the last supper (as Mk. 14:17 affirms), he was one of the Twelve. John does not make the assumption explicit. The parallel between 13:18 and 6:70 rather suggests it.

(2) The verb 'to love' in the expression 'the disciple whom Jesus *loved*' can be either *phileō* (20:2) or *agapaō* (13:23; 19:26–27; 21:20ff.). Because Lazarus is also said to be loved by Jesus, again with the Greek verbs used interchangeably (11:3, 5, 36), some have suggested that Lazarus is the beloved disciple (*e.g.* Eller). But Lazarus was not one of the Twelve, and does not enjoy the studied anonymity that characterizes the beloved disciple.

(3) The beloved disciple appears in connection with Peter, and most of his subsequent appearances are also in association with Peter.

(4) At the last supper, the disciple whom Jesus loved reclined (*cf.* notes on vv. 4–5) next to Jesus – indeed, as the next verses suggest, on Jesus' right. Some have suggested that this is a fictionalized elevation of John over Peter. It is highly unlikely, however, that the Twelve reclined according to rank (especially in light of vv. 12–17), or for that matter that they always reclined in the same order. In any case, the place of highest honour was at the left hand of the host, not the right. Peter was in neither position (*cf.* vv. 24–26). We do not know who was at the left; it may have been Judas Iscariot (*cf.* v. 26).

(5) If we compare the four canonical Gospels, by a process of elimination we arrive at John the son of Zebedee as the most likely identity of 'the disciple whom Jesus loved'.

(6) The words 'was reclining next to him' are a rather periphrastic rendering of what literally means 'was reclining in his bosom'. The expression is literally correct (*cf.* vv. 24–26), but also calls to mind 1:18, where the Word of God, the unique one, himself God, is said to be in the bosom of the Father. The verse before us may therefore suggest that the beloved disciple was in a relationship with Jesus analogous to the relationship Jesus enjoyed with his heavenly Father. The centrality of such analogical relationships has already been hinted at by v. 20.

If we wonder why the beloved disciple chooses this form of anonymity, two answers are suggested by the emphases of the Fourth Gospel. Just as 'the beloved disciple', if a self-designation, implies not arrogance (as if to say 'I am more loved than others') but a profound sense of indebtedness to grace ('What a wonder – that I should be loved by the incarnate Word!': *cf.* Introduction, § IV), so the silence as to the identity of the beloved disciple may be a quiet way of refusing to give even the impression of sharing a platform with Jesus. 'Like the other John at the very beginning of the Gospel, the first witness to Jesus, he is only a voice. The identity of the speaker does not matter: what matters is the witness that he gives' (Newbigin, p. xiii). At the same time, the author thus serves as a model for his readers: becoming a Christian means a transforming relationship with Jesus Christ, such that he receives the glory.

It was customary to sit at most meals. Reclining at table, a hellenistic custom, was reserved for special meals. When first introduced into the Jewish world, it was probably a sign of extreme decadence (Am. 6:4–7), but by New Testament times it was normal at important banquets and feasts, and therefore was virtually required at the Passover celebration, almost as a mark of unhurried celebration and freedom, in self-conscious contrast with the haste with which the first Passover was eaten on the night of the exodus (Ex. 12:11; *cf.* B. *Pesahim* 108*a*; *NewDocs* 1. § 1; 2. § 26). In short, the posture of Jesus and his men is a small indicator that they were in fact eating the Passover meal (*cf.* notes at the beginning of this chapter).

24-25. Jesus' blunt prediction that one of the assembled disciples was going to betray him (v. 21) evoked stunned silence (v. 22). Typically, it was Peter who recovered first, and even he was sufficiently cowed that, instead of blurting out his question, he signalled to 'the disciple whom Jesus loved' to prompt him to ask the question discreetly. This disciple was reclining next to Jesus, but on his right. Therefore his back was to the Master. The easiest way for him to address Jesus was to lean back until his head literally rested on Jesus' breast. Neither the footwashing nor this resting of a head on Jesus' breast would have been possible if Leonardo da Vinci's conception of the last supper had been correct. Westerners may recoil at the physical proximity of two men. In many parts of the world, of course (*e.g.* the Philippines, the Arab world), men walk down the street holding hands. This is a sign of friendship, not homosexuality. Men and women in such cultures may *not* hold hands in public: that would be a sign of licentiousness. Addressing Jesus by one of the two titles introduced in v. 14, the beloved disciple quietly passes on Peter's question.

26. Apparently Jesus' answer was given in quiet tones: vv. 27-30 make it clear that the other disciples did not know why Judas Iscariot left. Why 'the disciple whom Jesus loved' did nothing is less clear, unless the momentous nature of Jesus' confidence left him temporarily paralysed – the more so since Jesus himself was clearly taking no remedial action. The host at a feast (whose role is here filled by Jesus) might well dip into a common bowl and pull out a particularly tasty bit and pass it to a guest as a mark of honour or friendship. The word behind *this piece of bread* (*psōmion*), used only here in the New Testament, means, literally, a morsel, and commonly referred to bread, though sometimes to meat. The Evangelist may well be thinking of an early point in the paschal meal when bitter herbs were dipped into a bowl of fruit puree, the ḥarōseṭ sauce of dates, raisins and sour wine. This 'sop' Jesus passed to Judas Iscariot. That Jesus could pass it so easily suggests Judas was close by, possibly on his left, the place of honour. On the form of Judas' name, *cf.* notes on 6:71; 13:2.

27. Although Haenchen (2. 111) dismissively refers to the piece of food given to Judas as 'the magical morsel with which Satan entered', and although some have seen the gesture as a sign of judgment, even as a 'Satanic sacrament' (so Wrede, cited by Bultmann, p. 482 n. 6), yet the gentleness and courtesy implicit in giving such a morsel must not be lost to view. It is more consistent with the picture of Jesus in this Gospel, and with the course of events in the life of Judas Iscariot, to think of this 'sop' as a final gesture of supreme love (*cf.* v. 1).

And that final act of love becomes, with a terrible immediacy, the decisive movement of judgment. At this moment we are witnessing the climax of that action of sifting, of separation, of judgment which has been the central theme in John's account of the public ministry of Jesus . . . (3:16-19). So the

> final gesture of affection precipitates the final surrender of
> Judas to the power of darkness. The light shines in the dark-
> ness, and the darkness has neither understood it nor
> mastered it. (Newbigin, p. 173)

Judas received the sop but not the love. Instead of breaking him and
urging him to contrition, it hardened his resolve. At that point Satan
(only here mentioned by name; *cf.* v. 2) *entered into him*: the expression
probably signifies thorough possession.

What you are about to do, do quickly, Jesus tells him in the hearing of all.
The Greek *tachion* may, as in 20:4, be a comparative, 'do *more quickly*
(than you were planning)'. If Judas' descent is complete, he may as well
get on with his treachery and be done with it.

28–29. Although *no-one at the meal understood why Jesus said this to him*,
the beloved disciple must have understood the significance of Jesus
giving Judas a choice morsel. For the reasons already stated, however
(*cf.* notes on v. 26), the disciple whom Jesus loved did nothing, and
joined the others in wondering what Jesus was talking about now. John
explains, in retrospect, what the other disciples thought: Judas was
being asked *to buy what was needed for the Feast, or to give something to the
poor*.

Many have taken these words as evidence that this meal took place
twenty-four hours before the Passover (*cf.* notes at the beginning of this
chapter). If not before the Passover, why send Judas out at this late
hour? And if this were Passover night, would any shops have remained
open?

These objections are far from convincing. One might wonder, on
these premises, why Jesus should send Judas out for purchases for a
feast still twenty-four hours away. The next day would have left ample
time. It is best to think of this taking place on the night of Passover, 15
Nisan. Judas was sent out (so the disciples thought) to purchase *what
was needed for the Feast, i.e.* not the feast of Passover, but the Feast of
Unleavened Bread (the *ḥagigah*), which began that night and lasted for
seven days. The next day, still Friday 15 Nisan, was a high feast day; the
following day was Sabbath. It might seem best to make necessary
purchases (*e.g.* more unleavened bread) immediately. Purchases on that
Thursday evening were in all likelihood possible, though inconvenient.
The rabbinic authorities were in dispute on the matter (*cf.* Mishnah
Pesahim 4:5). One could buy necessities even on a Sabbath if it fell before
Passover, provided it was done by leaving something in trust rather
than paying cash (Mishnah *Shabbath* 23:1). Moreover, it was customary
to give alms to the poor on Passover night, the temple gates being left
open from midnight on, allowing beggars to congregate there (Jeremias,
p. 54). On any night other than Passover it is hard to imagine why the
disciples might have thought Jesus was sending Judas out *to give something to the poor*: the next day would have done just as well.

30. Sold out to Satan though he was, Judas had no recourse but to obey the word of Jesus. Even in this detail, Jesus makes it clear that no-one takes his life from him: he voluntarily lays it down (*cf.* notes on 10:18).

Many modern commentators have speculated on Judas' motives. It has been argued that Judas was trying to precipitate a decision by Jesus to take political power; that he hated the thought of a political revolution and was being dismissed from the room before the planning for the final political coup began; that this Passover meal was illegal and that Judas was taking the 'sop' to the authorities to get Jesus into trouble; and much more. John's narrative is more succinct, and less speculative. If the morsel or sop (*psōmion*, NIV 'bread') is mentioned again, it is only to indicate the pace of the developments. Judas went out. *And it was night.* Doubtless this is historical reminiscence, but it is also profound theology. Even though 'the paschal moon was shining at the full' (Howard, p. 690), Judas was swallowed up by the most awful darkness, indeed by outer darkness (Mt. 8:12; 22:13; 25:30). Judas was heading to his own place (*cf.* 1:5; 3:19–21; Acts 1:25). But in another way it was also the night time for Jesus: it was the hour of the power of darkness (Lk. 22:53).

> Mine own Apostle, who the bag did beare,
> Though he had all I had did not forbeare
> To sell me also, and to put me there:
> > Was ever grief like mine?
>
> For thirtie pence he did my death devise,
> Who at three hundred did the ointment prize,
> Not half so sweet as my sweet sacrifice:
> > Was ever grief like mine?[1]

B. THE FAREWELL DISCOURSE: PART ONE
(13:31 – 14:31)

If the farewell discourse has been a favourite passage for Christians down through the ages to choose for study and meditation, it has also proved, in the last two centuries, the focal point for considerable debate. Six topics merit brief preliminary comment.

(1) Scholars have not agreed as to where the farewell discourse begins. Our common chapter divisions might suggest 14:1, but an excellent case can be made for 13:31.[2] In 13:30, Judas goes out into the night; at that

[1]George Herbert, in C. A. Patrides (ed.), *The English Poems of George Herbert* (Rowman and Littlefield, 1974), p. 48.

[2]For a minor variation, in which 13:31–32 is read with the preceding verses and 13:33 –

point Jesus begins to address those who will in the long term be faithful to him. If there is some dialogue in these verses (13:36–38), it is no more than one finds in chs. 14 – 16. This solution does not make a major impact on the interpretation of the farewell discourse, but it does see the departure of Judas as much more of a turning point in the plot, and it enhances the link between the end of ch. 13 and the beginning of ch. 14 (*cf.* notes, below).

(2)The major structural challenge of the entire discourse is occasioned by the closing sentence of 14:31: 'Come now; let us leave.' What is the relation between the material before and after that break?

(a) Several harmonizing suggestions have been put forward. The most common response throughout the church's history has been that the first two chapters, John 13 – 14, are set in the upper room, while chs. 15 – 17 continue the dialogue along the road to the Mount of Olives, culminating in the prayer of John 17. Most contemporary scholars dismiss this option: it 'seems incredible' (Barrett, p. 454), it is 'hardly to be countenanced' (Beasley-Murray, p. 223). If a reason is given for this judgment, it is the wording of 18:1: 'When he had finished praying, Jesus *left with his disciples and crossed the Kidron Valley.*' The natural way to take this, it is argued, is that Jesus and his disciples *left the upper room.* In that case, why the exhortation of 14:31? Are we to think of Jesus and his disciples standing around for three more chapters before they left? Indeed, this is almost as common a solution in the history of the church (*cf.* Meyer, 2. 235–237). Other proposals are often less convincing. It appears unjustified, with Dodd (see notes, below), to render the last clause of 14:31 in such a way that only a spiritual meaning is intended: 'Up, let us march to meet him [*i.e.* the prince of this world, 14:30]!'

(b) Various displacements of the text have been suggested, all of them with this in common, that 14:31 now comes much later in the discourse (Bernard: 13:1–31a; 15; 16; 13:31b–38; 14; 17; Bultmann: 13:1–30; 17; 13:31–35; 15; 16; 13:36 – 14:31), thereby easing the perceived clash between 14:31 and 18:1. But these suggestions of displacements, like those put forward regarding John 5 – 7 (*cf.* notes there), introduce more problems than they resolve. John 14 is particularly full of questions by the disciples, but these questions become less intelligible if we are to suppose that the material of John 15 – 16 comes before them. Moreover, it has often been noted that 14:16–17 reads like the introduction of the sayings about the Holy Spirit, the 'Paraclete'. These two verses are somewhat incongruous if they succeed all the other passages in the discourse about the Paraclete.

(c) Some have suggested that John 14 or John 13:31 – 14:31 constitutes the original record of a discourse, and that the Evangelist then gives his own meditations upon it in John 15 – 16. If so, it is hard to understand

---

14:3 is taken as a unit, *cf.* Xavier Léon-Dufour, 'Situation de Jean 13', in Ulrich Luz and Hans Weder (eds.), *Die Mitte des Neuen Testaments: Einheit und Vielfalt neutestamentlicher Theologie* (*Fs.* Eduard Schweizer; Vandenhoeck und Ruprecht, 1983), pp. 131–141.

why he did such a botched job in his final editing. Moreover, there is another weakness in this theory that the next option brings out.

(d) Another common hypothesis today is that John 14 or John 13:31 – 14:31 constitutes one version of a dominical discourse, and that John 15 – 16 (some say John 15 – 17) constitutes a second version. Neither is more primary than the other; they are simply alternative accounts and reflections. The evidence for this view (it is argued) lies in the common themes of the two sections: both parts talk of the departure of Jesus to the Father and of his coming again (14:2–3, 18–20, 22–23, 28; 16:5–7, 16–22, 28; 17:11, 13), of the revelation of the Father (14:9; 17:6, 26), of prayer in Jesus' name (14:13–15; 16:23–24, 26), of Jesus' relation to the Father (14:6–7, 9–11, 28; 15:10, 23–24; 16:15; 17:1–2, 4–5, 8, 10, 21–26), of keeping Jesus' commands (14:15, 21, 23; 15:10, 12–14, 17), of the Paraclete (14:16–17, 26; 15:26–27; 16:7–15), and of the judgment of the prince of the world (14:30; 16:11). The very fact that so much of the same ground is covered calls in question the third option (above), that makes so much of chs. 15 – 16 secondary, and favours the 'two version' theory. Of course, this means that the Evangelist was pretty clumsy at 14:31b, when he joined the alleged two versions together. That is why many scholars plump for the third option, but suggest that the Evangelist finished his work at 14:31b, and a *later* redactor put in the rest of the material. Presumably it is permissible to credit the redactor with clumsiness even when one is reluctant to charge the Evangelist with this crime.

There is no way of proving to the satisfaction of everyone the rightness or wrongness of any particular 'solution'. The multiplication of sources and redactors ought to be treated with particular suspicion: most writers will frankly acknowledge that their roughest drafts are their *first*, and that successive polishing, by the original author or someone else, reduces the number of apparent aporias and enhances the smoothness. The only time this is not so occurs when the final editor is notoriously incompetent. Incompetent or not, there is precious little evidence in the text, solid evidence, that interpreters two thousand years removed from the events may seize on to distinguish believably amongst five layers of tradition and redaction (so Brown).

The interpreter's first job is to make sense of the text as it stands. Not only the witness theme but also numerous bits of incidental evidence suggest that much of the Gospel depends on eyewitness memory (*cf.* Introduction, §§ III, IV). If we take these bits at their face value, 14:31b appears, on initial reading, to be a momentous instance of personal recollection: little of theological value turns on the words 'Come now; let us leave'; their inclusion can be justified only on the grounds of an incompetent editor or *simply on the grounds that personal memory of the events recalled them that way* (but *cf.* notes below). The memory was strong enough that no attempt was made to expunge the words, despite the little they add to the immediate context. If one discounts the suggestion that the Evangelist felt he had to include words like those found in Mark

14:42 ('Rise! Let us go! Here comes my betrayer!' – uttered in Geth-semane), and simply put them here because he couldn't think of a better place (as if this part of John were slavishly following Mark!), one can nevertheless imagine at least two plausible scenarios.

First, it is possible that Jesus and his disciples did *not* in fact leave until after John 17. Anyone who has frequently invited home ten to twenty graduate students (as has the present writer) knows how common it is, after someone has announced it is time to go, for another half hour to slip past before anyone makes a serious move to leave. There is no concrete evidence *against* this view; the link between 14:31 and 18:1 might be taken to support it. The troubling question is why the Evan-gelist should have bothered to report 14:31b at all. Apart from appeal to the power of memory, it might be argued that the decision to record a delay in departure is the Evangelist's attempt to depict yet again Jesus' profound love for his disciples (*cf.* 13:1), his concern to drill into them certain stabilizing truths that would see them through the crisis ahead (*cf.* 14:29), his desire to place before them, through his final prayer (Jn. 17), the cosmic sweep of the tragedy and triumph about to befall.

Alternatively, one could imagine Jesus and his disciples actually leaving at this point, and continuing their conversation in the narrow streets of the old city. Some have suggested a pause at the temple; others have ventured that the presence of vines along the way, or of frescoes of vines at the temple or on the gates of the wall,[1] might have triggered 'I am the true vine . . .' In this case, the departure in 18:1 is most likely departure from the city. Lest this approach to the interpreta-tion of 14:31b sound like the desperate expedient of an unteachable conservative, it must be pointed out that Haenchen, who can scarcely be called a conservative, thinks 14:31b pictures the disciples leaving (even though his approach to 18:1 is rather independent, 2. 128, 164), and does not see in 15:1ff. the beginning of a new farewell discourse or of a new version of the one farewell discourse.

(3) Fernando Segovia might be taken as the most painstaking pro-ponent amongst several recent writers who find many different levels of tradition, and corresponding ecclesiastical 'life-settings', *within* the farewell discourse. Paragraph by paragraph, half verse by half verse, they take the text apart to construct what they judge to be a profile of the development of the community. Such studies develop a certain internal plausibility: the parts are made to fit, and therefore such studies cannot be convincingly falsified. But it is exceedingly difficult to imagine how these competing bits were brought together to form a sustained dis-course. More importantly, if study of the discourse *as a whole* leads the student to the conclusion that the material fundamentally coheres, that there is some rationale to its development, the boundless enthusiasm of

---

[1]In particular, it is sometimes argued that the 'I am the vine' metaphor was triggered by the golden vine overhanging the main entrance to the temple proper (Jos., *Bel.* v. 210; *Ant.* xv. 395; Mishnah *Middoth* 3:8; Tacitus, *Histories* V. v).

some source critics must be judged not only speculative but finally indefensible. The problems of source-criticism in the Fourth Gospel are briefly mentioned in the Introduction (§§ II, III); here it is enough to make reasonable sense out of the text as it stands.

(4) Recent studies of these chapters have noted their formal similarities to other 'farewell discourses' or 'testaments' of famous men from the ancient world. The genre is known in the hellenistic world, but is even more common in Jewish literature. Attention has been drawn to Jacob's last words to his sons (Gn. 49), Joshua's final remarks to his people (Jos. 22 – 24), and David's address to Solomon and to the nation (1 Ch. 28 – 29). Written not long before or after the New Testament (its precise date is disputed), *The Testaments of the Twelve Patriarchs* is nothing other than the supposed final remarks of each of the patriarchs to their own progeny. Some argue, with some justification, that the book of Deuteronomy provides something of a literary model.[1] Just as Israel is about to enter the promised land, the departing Moses addresses the covenant community; just as Jesus' disciples are about to enter the age of the Spirit, the departing Jesus addresses the new covenant community.

Whatever the similarities between the farewell discourse and other pieces of similar genre, one fundamental distinction must be kept in mind. In all the other instances, the person saying farewell was not expecting to come back. When John writes up these chapters, both he and his readers know the outcome of the issue: Jesus departed, as he said, but he came back from the grave, made himself present through the Spirit he bequeathed, and promised to return personally at the end of the age. For this reason, this so-called 'farewell discourse' is close to being fundamentally misnamed. On the face of it, this discourse was delivered not merely by one about to die, but (as John and his readers know) by one who died and rose again and who continues to make himself known to his disciples. This does not mean the discourse as we have it is larded with anachronisms (*contra* Brown, 2. 582): as we shall see, the discourse coheres well *within the historical setting the Evangelist establishes for it*. Nevertheless many parts of it, like many symbol-laden sayings and events throughout Jesus' ministry, could be grasped in their fulness only after Jesus' death/exaltation and his gift of the Spirit.

(5) Mention of the Spirit introduces one of the themes peculiar to the farewell discourse – the five sayings about the 'Paraclete' (an attempt to transliterate *paraklētos*, variously rendered 'Counsellor', 'Helper', 'Advocate', 'Comforter': cf. notes at 14:16). All five passages (14:15–17, 25–26; 15:26–27; 16:7–11, 12–15) apply the term to the Holy Spirit. Elsewhere in the New Testament, the word appears only in 1 John 2:2, and there it refers to Jesus Christ. While some have proposed that these five passages were originally an independent block of material, others argue that their integration into their present contexts is so good that

---

[1]*Cf.* A. Lacomara, *CBQ* 36, 1974, pp. 65–84.

speculation as to an original block of Paraclete-material is unprofitable. Whatever the case, it is more important to recognize that these Paraclete passages have important parallels in other New Testament books,[1] that within the Fourth Gospel they build on antecedent remarks about the Holy Spirit (especially 1:32–34; 3:5, 34; 4:23–24; 7:37–39), and that they anticipate 20:22–23.[2]

(6) This commentary has consistently argued that the primary purpose of the Gospel of John was the evangelization of diaspora Jews – a thoroughly eclectic group – and of Gentile proselytes to Jewish faith. It has often been argued that John 14 – 17 stands decisively against such a thesis: these chapters were written for believers, not to win unbelievers. Despite the surface plausibility of this argument, a strong case can be made for the view that even in chs. 14 – 17 John has unbelievers primarily in view. The following points may be briefly made, in anticipation of the fuller exposition:

(a) Although it is true that these chapters report Jesus' words to and before Jesus' *disciples*, their primary focus is not the nature of discipleship, but the nature of Jesus' mission and what takes place after his impending departure. The emphasis is on understanding the significance of Jesus' death/exaltation, his glorification, the consequent coming of the Paraclete, the relationship of the post-resurrection, post-coming-of-the-Paraclete age to that depicted in these chapters. In other words, the focus is salvation-historical: *i.e.* it is a foundational explanation needed by any Jew or proselyte entertaining the possibility of becoming a Christian.

(b) To the extent that discipleship is in view at all, there is considerable emphasis on *remaining* in Jesus' word, on continuing in obedience to Jesus' teachings. That is clearly a critical aspect of proper *evangelistic* endeavour – a point already established by the Fourth Gospel (*cf.* notes on 8:31, 32).

(c) The best evangelistic literature is eager to make clear not only *how* to become a Christian, but also *what it is like* to live as a Christian. Themes detailing fruitfulness in the believer's life, the continued witness and explanations and comfort provided by the Holy Spirit, the prospect of final vindication – these can as easily be seen as incentives to becoming a Christian as edification or exposition for Christians.

(d) A passage such as 15:26–27 not only preserves proper location in the salvation–historical development, but it also accomplishes two more things: it authorizes the kind of evangelism that the Gospel as a whole seeks to accomplish (implicitly responding to critics who find nascent

---

[1]Cf. André Feuillet, *Divinitas* 33, 1989, pp. 16–43.

[2]Useful literature includes H. Windisch, *The Spirit–Paraclete in the Fourth Gospel* (ET Fortress, 1968); Johnston; Burge; de la Potterie, 1. 341ff.; and Franck; Otto Betz, *Der Paraklet* (E. J. Brill, 1963). For the treatment of the Paraclete in the early centuries of the church, *cf.* A. Casurella, *The Johannine Paraclete in the Church Fathers: A Study in the History of Exegesis* (J. C. B. Mohr [Paul Siebeck], 1983).

Christianity bumptious and fractious) and, in the larger context of 15:17 – 16:4, it openly demands that prospective Christians themselves get involved in witness and evangelism, detailing the cost of failure in this regard. There are only two groups of people: witnessing disciples of Jesus who are willing to suffer for their faith, and 'the world', evil and condemned. Thematically, there are echoes of Mark 8:34–38 par. The choices are polarized, blunt, demanding – and entirely appropriate to forceful evangelistic literature.

1. Jesus predicts Peter's denial (13:31–38)

31–32. It is almost as if, now that Judas has gone, the last barrier to the onset of the impending 'hour' has been removed, and Jesus signals the development: *God will glorify the Son . . . at once.* Already in ch. 12 the approach of the Gentiles signalled to Jesus that the period of public ministry and waiting was over, and the 'hour' had come (*cf.* notes on 12:23). Now the departure of Judas puts the actual machinery of arrest, trial and execution into motion. As troubling as that was, this was also the hour for the Son of Man to be glorified, indeed to be glorified in the presence of God with the glory he had with the Father before the world began (17:5). Even in the Prologue, the glorification of the incarnate Word occurs not in a spectacular display of blinding light but in the matrix of human existence (1:14). Now, bringing to a climax a theme developed throughout this Gospel, the Evangelist makes it clear that the supreme moment of divine self-disclosure, the greatest moment of displayed glory, was in the shame of the cross. That is the primary reason why the title *Son of Man* is employed here (*cf.* notes on 1:51; Moloney, pp. 194–202). Outside the New Testament, the title is associated with glory (especially Dn. 7; *1 Enoch*); within the Synoptics, the title is as frequently associated with suffering. In John, the two are dramatically brought together.

Caird[1] has shown that the aorist passive of *doxazō* ('to glorify'), used twice in v. 31 and once in the first clause of v. 32, was the expected way to translate the MT's use of the Hebrew niphal of *nik̲bad̲*, used of the revelation of God's splendid activity. We are driven to Isaiah 49:3, where God addresses the Servant of the LORD: 'You are my servant, Israel, in whom I will display my splendour.' But Jesus transcends Israel's role. In his impending death/exaltation, Jesus is glorified (*i.e.* God's splendour is displayed in the perfect obedience of the Son's sacrifice). To put the matter another way, Jesus, by perfectly revealing the Father to human beings, has brought glory to the Father (17:4). But so intertwined are the operations of the Father and the Son that the entire mission can be looked at another way. Instead of focusing on the glorification of the Son of Man and the correlative glorification of the Father in the Son's voluntary sacrifice, one may reverse the order. If God is glorified in the

[1]G. B. Caird, *NTS* 15, 1969, pp. 265–277.

Son,[1] it is no less true to say that God will glorify the Son in himself. Despite the future tense (see Additional Note), this does not refer to some event at the end of time, for (John reports) the Father expects to glorify the Son *at once*, *i.e.* in the death/exaltation now impending. The phrase *in himself* probably refers to the Father, *i.e.* 'in God the Father himself'; the entire clause has much the same force as 17:5. Christ's glorified humanity is taken up to have fellowship with the Father (Westcott, 2. 160). God is glorified in Jesus' temporal obedience, sacrifice, death, resurrection and exaltation – one event; Jesus is glorified in the same event, in the eternal presence and essence of his heavenly Father, partly because by this event he re-enters the glory he had with the Father before the Word became incarnate (1:14), before the world began (17:5). The entire event displays the saving sovereignty of God, God's dawning kingdom.

33. Explicit mention of Jesus' impending 'glorification' (vv. 31–32) prompts Jesus to embark on one of the dominant themes of the discourse: his concern to prepare his disciples for his departure. *My children*, he addresses them, fulfilling the paschal role of head of the family. The term used is the diminutive *teknia*, used only here in the Fourth Gospel, but seven times in 1 John by the same author when he addresses his readers (and once more in the New Testament in Gal. 4:19, again in the context of a gentle, not to say emotional, appeal). 'My dear children' would not be an over-translation. *I will be with you only a little longer* might refer either to Jesus' death or to his ascension. Both departures (which arc perceived as constituting a theological unity) are addressed in the chapters that follow. Twice before he had *told the Jews* that he was departing and that they would seek him and prove unable to find him (7:33–34; 8:21). *Jews* clearly refers to Jesus' opponents, primarily Jewish leaders, since his own disciples were also Jewish but are here differentiated from *the Jews* (*cf.* notes on 1:19). But although Jesus' followers must come to grips with his departure, the tone of this announcement to them is vastly different from the two passages where 'the Jews' are informed that they will not be able to find him (7:34); rather, they are told he is going to prepare a place for them (14:1–3). They are not told that they will die in their sin (8:21); rather, because he lives, they too will live (14:19).

34–35. Since the theme of these verses is taken up again in 15:9–16, many have argued that its presence here is the result of an awkward bit of redactional manipulation. On the contrary: it makes perfectly good sense. Having announced his departure, and having insisted that his disciples cannot now come with him (v. 33), Jesus begins to lay out what he expects of them while he is away. Unfortunately, they still cannot get over the unambiguous insistence that Jesus' departure is imminent, and

---

[1]Some good witnesses omit this conditional clause. Probably the clause is authentic, but even if omission were favoured some such clause as this must be understood to make sense of the flow of the passsage. *Cf.* Metzger, p. 242.

so Peter interrupts and presses the point (vv. 36–38). This in turn prompts Jesus to embark on an extended and comforting explanation regarding his departure, before returning to more detailed descriptions of what is expected of them, and what is promised to them, during the time he is absent from them. In other words, when these chapters are read with literary sensitivity and a modicum of historical realism (instead of treating them as a manual of systematic theology that must have all the points in an abstract and idealized order), passages which have been cursorily dismissed as late additions or awkward displacements make rather good sense where they stand.

The *new command*[1] is simple enough for a toddler to memorize and appreciate, profound enough that the most mature believers are repeatedly embarrassed at how poorly they comprehend it and put it into practice: *Love one another. As I have loved you, so you must love one another*. The standard of comparison is Jesus' love (*cf.* v. 1), just exemplified in the footwashing (*cf.* vv. 12–17); but since the footwashing points to his death (vv. 6–10), these same disciples but a few days later would begin to appreciate a standard of love they would explore throughout their pilgrimage. The more we recognize the depth of our own sin, the more we recognize the love of the Saviour; the more we appreciate the love of the Saviour, the higher his standard appears; the higher his standard appears, the more we recognize in our selfishness, our innate self-centredness, the depth of our own sin. With a standard like this, no thoughtful believer can ever say, this side of the parousia, 'I am perfectly keeping the basic stipulation of the new covenant.'

The *new* command is not 'new' because nothing like it had ever been said before. The Mosaic covenant had mandated two love commandments: 'Love the LORD your God with all your heart and with all your soul and with all your strength' (Dt. 6:5); 'Do not seek revenge or bear a grudge against one of your people, but love your neighbour as yourself. I am the LORD' (Lv. 19:18). Jesus taught that all the law and the prophets were summed up in these two commands (Mk. 12:28–33; *cf.* Rom. 13:8–10; Gal. 5:14). John himself can elsewhere recognize that in certain respects this is 'no new command' at all (1 Jn. 2:7–8). Why, then, should he here report that it is 'new'?

Its newness is bound up not only with the new standard ('As I have loved you') but with the new order it both mandates and exemplifies. It is possible that there is an indirect allusion to the new covenant that was inaugurated at the last supper (1 Cor 11:25; *cf.* Lk. 22:20; Lindars, p. 463), the new covenant that promised the transformation of heart and mind (Je. 31:29–34; Ezk. 36:24–26; *cf.* notes on 3:5). Whether or not that allusion can be sustained, this commandment is presented as the marching order for the newly gathering messianic community, brought into

---

[1]In the Latin Vulgate, 'new commandment' appears as *mandatum novum*, from which we derive '*Maundy* Thursday', the anniversary of the last supper when the new commandment was instituted.

existence by the redemption long purposed by God himself (*cf.* notes on vv. 31–32). It is not just that the standard is Christ and his love; more, it is a command designed to reflect the relationship of love that exists between the Father and the Son (*cf.* 8:29; 10:18; 12:49–50; 14:31; 15:10), designed to bring about amongst the members of the nascent messianic community the kind of unity that characterizes Jesus and his Father (Jn. 17). The new command is therefore not only the obligation of the new covenant community to respond to the God who has loved them and redeemed them by the oblation of his Son, and their response to his gracious election which constituted them his people, it is a privilege which, rightly lived out, proclaims the true God before a watching world. That is why Jesus ends his injunction with the words, *All men will know that you are my disciples, if you love one another*. Orthodoxy without principial obedience to this characteristic command of the new covenant is merely so much humbug.[1]

Not a few scholars (*e.g.* Fenton, p. 27) have suggested that the Fourth Gospel offers a *lower* standard of love than, say, the sermon on the mount, where love for enemies is mandated (Mt. 5:43–47), not simply love for the members of the new covenant community. This is taken as evidence that the Johannine community has become narrow and sectarian. In fact, the charge is poorly conceived. John's Gospel insists on the love of God for the world (3:16), to which Jesus' followers are also sent (20:21). After all, this Gospel confesses that Jesus is the Saviour of the world (4:42). It is not that this love is inferior to that demanded in the sermon on the mount; rather, it is focused rather differently. At the risk of confounding logic, it is not so much that Christians are to love the world less, as that they are to love one another more. Better put, their love for each other ought to be a reflection of their new status and experience as the children of God, reflecting the mutual love of the Father and the Son and imitating the love that has been shown them; their love for the world is the love of compassion, forbearance, evangelism, empathy – since all true Christians recognize they can never be more than mere beggars telling others where there is bread.[2] The New Testament as a whole concentrates sometimes on this focus of love, sometimes on that; it refuses to measure one against the other.

For notes on the words for 'to love', *cf.* 3:16; 13:23; 21:15–18.

36–38. Peter, and doubtless others amongst the Eleven who are slower to respond, are less interested in the new commandment than in the

---

[1]Many here cite the remarkable testimony of Tertullian, writing about a century later than John. The pagans of his day marvelled at the love of the Christian fellowship, especially as it faced sometimes ferocious persecution: 'See how they love one another! . . . how are they ready even to die for one another!' (*Apology* 39. 7; *cf.* Jn. 15:13; 1 Jn. 3:16).

[2]N. Lohfink, *Jesus and Community* (Fortress, 1984), III. 5, rightly insists that brotherly love within the Christian community can scarcely be viewed as a declension from the demand of Jesus to love neighbours and enemies, since Jesus himself gathered a believing community around him, called them 'brothers', and introduced many sharp distinctions between them and the mass of unbelievers.

threatened departure of their Master. Peter asks the obvious question: *Lord, where are you going?* Knowledge of the Master's plans and continued intimacy with him are more attractive than obedience. Like the Jews in 7:35, he does not properly understand Jesus' references to his departure, though, judging by v. 37, he has at least some intimation that death is threatening.

Jesus' reply is designed to discourage impetuous claims at the moment, and to be fully understood only later. Peter *cannot follow now*, not only because it is not the time for him to die (*cf.* 21:18–19), but because only Jesus, the Lamb of God, can offer the sacrifice that deals with the world's sins. Only he can reveal the Father perfectly, and be glorified in the presence of the Father with the glory he had before the world began. But Peter *will follow later*, not as a second lamb of God, but in the sense that he will follow Jesus in death, and join him in glory.

But Peter is unwilling to wait: *Lord, why can't I follow you now?* The question betrays fundamental ignorance of the eschatological shift even than taking place, of the utter uniqueness of the Master and his sacrifice. Nevertheless Peter should not be harshly judged. Peter speaks not out of angry pique so much as confused devotion: *I will lay down my life for you.* All four Gospels report Peter's protestation of willingness to die. Tragically, the boast that he would never deny his Lord, even to the point of death, displays not only gross ignorance of human weakness, but a certain haughty independence that is the seed of the denial itself. Moreover, in this context the words are rich in irony (*cf.* Duke, pp. 49–50; 50–51). Lest that irony be missed, they are repeated in Jesus' answering rhetorical question: *Will you really lay down your life for me?* Who, after all, is laying down his life for whom (*cf.* 10:15; 11:50–52)? Yet in another sense, Peter spoke better than he knew. He could not lay down his life for Jesus *then*; he would lay it down three decades later, and thereby glorify God (*cf.* notes on 21:18–19). In so doing he followed the example of the Master and displayed his love for his brothers and sisters in Christ (*cf.* 12:25–26; 15:13).

Sadly, good intentions in a secure room after good food are far less attractive in a darkened garden with a hostile mob. At this point in his pilgrimage, Peter's intentions and self-assessment vastly outstrip his strength. And so Jesus utters the fateful prediction: *I tell you the truth* (*cf.* 1:51), *before the cock crows, you will disown me three times!*

Additional notes

31–32. Commentators have often struggled with the tenses of the verb 'to glorify' in these two verses – a string of four aorists followed by two futures. The aorists, which many grammarians judge must refer to something in the past (if they are in the indicative mood, as here), prompt not a few commentators to think that John is confusing the situation in the church of his day with the ostensible setting, the night Jesus was betrayed. The two instances of the future are then understood either to be setting the record straight, *i.e.* reverting to the perspective of the ostensible setting; or to reflect a rather botched attempt at mingling futurist eschatology (reflected in the future tenses) with inaugurated eschatology (preserved in *at once*). However, it can easily be shown that verbs in the aorist tense, even when in the indicative mood, can be past-referring, present-referring, and even future-referring, as well as omnitemporal and atemporal (*cf.* Porter pp. 75–76, 233). A consistent aspect-theory of the Greek verb finds little difficulty here. Future tenses commonly express expectation, whether or not there is a temporal factor demanded by the context. Even traditional approaches to Greek grammar can successfully navigate the difficulty, however, by arguing that these aorists are 'proleptic' (*i.e.* future-referring!), viewing the decisive death/exaltation as virtually accomplished, since the decisive steps have already been taken and the redemptive purposes of God are secure.

38. The idea of *two* cock-crowings, preserved in some MSS of Mark 14:30, 68, 72, if original, is the difference between saying 'before the bell rings for dinner' and 'before the second bell rings for dinner' (*cf.* Carson, *Matt*, p. 542). Apparently it was usual for roosters in Palestine to crow about 12.30 a.m., 1.30 a.m., and 2.30 a.m., prompting the Romans to give the term 'cockcrow' to the watch between midnight and roughly 3.00 a.m.

2. The promise of a place where Jesus is going (14:1–4)

1. It is Jesus who is heading for the agony of the cross; it is Jesus who is deeply 'troubled' in heart (12:27) and spirit (13:21). Yet on this night of nights, when of all times it would have been appropriate for Jesus' followers to lend him emotional and spiritual support, he is still the one who gives, comforts, instructs. For they, too, are *troubled* (same verb as the verses just cited) – not because they are rushing toward pain, ignominy, shame, crucifixion, but because they are confused, uncertain of what Jesus means, and threatened by references to his imminent departure. However appropriate it may be to cite the words *Do not let your hearts be troubled* at Christian funerals, they were first addressed to disciples who under substantial emotional pressure were on the brink of catastrophic failure.

The links with the previous chapter, then, are two. First, there is an implicit tie to Peter: if *his* faith is about to shatter, will the other disciples prove more stable in their trust? Small wonder the Eleven are profoundly upset. Second, and more broadly, because of the disciples' turmoil Jesus unpacks at some length the implications of his impending departure (13:33, 36).

The way the disciples are to calm their hearts is spelled out in the second part of the verse: *Trust in God; trust also in me*. The two verbs rendered 'trust' (*pisteuō; cf.* notes on 1:12) could be either indicative or imperative, leading to the following principal translations: (a) indicative/indicative: 'You trust in God and you trust in me' – which at some marginal level is true, but not obviously appropriate in this context since the core problem of the disciples' felt turmoil is lack of trust; (b) indicative/imperative: 'You trust in God; trust also in me' (or the variation of Bultmann [p. 600], 'Do you believe in God? Then believe also in me') – which makes sense as an invitation to extend the object of their faith beyond God as they have known him in the past to Jesus as well, but it is not clear, from their troubled hearts, that their trust in God is very secure at this point; (c) imperative/imperative: 'Trust in God; trust also in me' (NIV). This is the way the verbs were taken in nearly all the Old Latin MSS, and it makes most sense of the context.[1]

Although the last option is best, all three assume a formidably high Christology, for they link Jesus with the Father as an appropriate object of faith. For thoughtful readers of the Gospel, however, the link is almost inevitable. If Jesus invariably speaks the words of God and performs the acts of God (5:19ff.), should he not be trusted like God? If *he* tells his followers not to let their hearts be troubled, must it not be because he has ample and justifiable reason?

2–3. The reason is now spelled out: Jesus' departure is for the disciples' advantage. True, he is going away, but he is going away to prepare a place for them, and he will come and get them so that they may be where he is. What more could they ask for?

Thus far all the commentators agree. But the language used of Jesus' 'coming back' and 'being with' his disciples refers at various places in these chapters to different things: sometimes to Jesus' return to his disciples after his resurrection, sometimes to Jesus' 'coming' to them by the Spirit after he has been exalted to the glory of the Father, and sometimes to his 'coming' at the end of the age (in this chapter, *cf.* notes on vv. 18–20 and 22–23). Indeed, in the view of some commentators, the language in vv. 2–3 is purposely ambiguous in order simultaneously to refer to more than one coming (so, for instance, Westcott, 2. 168; Lagrange, pp. 373–374; Strachan, p. 280; Barrett, p. 457). More idiosyncratic interpretations of vv. 2–3 have also been put forward. Some think that the Christian's death and departure to be with Jesus is in view (Lightfoot, pp. 275–276; Bultmann, p. 602). On the face of it, however, the only death in the context is that of Jesus, while the collective framing of the promise ('I will come back and take *you* [plural] to be with me') cannot easily be squared with such an interpretation (*cf.* Fischer, pp. 310–311). Gundry[2] argues that vv. 2–3 refer to the fellowship the disciples of Jesus will enjoy with Jesus through the Spirit, but this, as we shall see, largely turns on an unlikely rendering of the word translated *rooms*.

The details of the text argue that these two verses refer to the second advent of Jesus, when he comes to take his followers to be with him forever. The Greek word *monē*, cognate with the verb *menō* ('to remain',

---

[1]The fourth possibility, imperative/indicative, though syntactically possible, is incoherent: 'Trust in God; you trust also in me.'
[2]R. H. Gundry, *ZNW* 58, 1967, pp. 68–72.

'to stay', 'to dwell'), properly signifies a 'dwelling place'. Because the Latin Vulgate rendered it *mansiones*, the AV/KJV, followed by the RV used 'mansions'. However, since heaven is here pictured as the Father's *house*, it is more natural to think of 'dwelling-places' within a house as *rooms* (NIV) or suites or the like. The only other place the word occurs in the New Testament is in 14:23: 'My Father . . . [and I] will come to him and make our *home* with him' – *i.e.* the believer, indwelt by the Spirit, thus becomes the 'dwelling-place', and hence the 'home', of the Triune God. It is by reading this referent of the word in v. 23 back into v. 2 that Gundry finds warrant for his view that the coming of Jesus in vv. 2–3 is the bestowal of the Spirit. The fact remains that the world *monē* simply means 'dwelling-place'; there is no more reason to read the *referent* of that word (*i.e.* to what dwelling-place the word refers) in v. 23 back into v. 2 than the reverse: in both instances the context must decide. Further, there is no good reason to picture these dwelling-places in v. 2 as way-stations, temporary lodgings, even though the Latin *mansiones* can have that force. Against Origen and those who have followed him (*e.g.* Temple, p. 226), heaven is not here pictured as a series of progressive and temporary states up which one advances until perfection is finally attained. The word carries no such overtones, and there are no hints in the context to support such a view. Nor does *my Father's house* here . refer to the church as the spiritual house or temple of God (*cf.* 1 Cor. 3:16–17; Eph. 2:20–22; 1 Pet. 2:5): that metaphor is not found in the Fourth Gospel. Moreover, even in passages where the metaphor is teased out, the church is referred to as the house of God, but never 'the Father's house' or 'my Father's house'.

The simplest explanation is best: *my Father's house* refers to heaven, and in heaven are many *rooms*, many dwelling-places. The point is not the lavishness of each apartment, but the fact that such ample provision has been made that there is more than enough space for every one of Jesus' disciples to join him in his Father's home. Besides, have they not just been encouraged to trust him (v. 1), and always found strong reason to do so? Can they not therefore be assured that if heaven were other than what he has described, he would have told them (*cf.* Additional Note)?

I am going there to prepare a place for you: the words presuppose that the 'place' exists before Jesus gets there. It is not that he arrives on the scene and then begins to prepare the place; rather, in the context of Johannine theology, it is the going itself, via the cross and resurrection, that prepares the place for Jesus' disciples. And if he takes such trouble, all to prepare a place for his own, it is inconceivable that the rest should not follow: *I will come back and take you to be with me that you also may be where I am.* Unlike some other passages that look to the parousia, this one focuses less on apocalyptic elements and the winding-up of the cosmos (*cf.* Mk. 13:24–27; 2 Thes. 2) than on the comfort to be enjoyed by believers in the presence of God (*cf.* 1 Thes.

4:15–18) – which is different again from those passages that offer solace to the believers on *their* death (*e.g.* 2 Cor. 5:8; Phil. 1:23).

4. Although Jesus tells his disciples, *You know the way to the place where I am going* (*cf.* Additional Note), the next verse demonstrates that, at some level, they know nothing of the sort. John's point is not that Jesus has made some terrible error in assessing his disciples, but that precisely because they know him they *do* know the way to the place he has just prescribed. Once again it is by reading on and then coming back and re-reading the text that we find Jesus' anticipation of his clear, impending statement that he himself is the way (v. 6).

Additional notes

2. Some manuscripts insert *hoti* (here meaning 'that') before the last clause, generating either a statement or a question: 'If not, I would have told you *that* I go to prepare a place for you', a barely possible rendering; or 'If not, would I have told you *that* I go to prepare a place for you?', a slightly strange query since up to this point Jesus has made no such announcement. Alternatively, the *hoti* could mean 'because' or 'for' and be connected with the first part of v. 2: 'In my Father's house are many rooms (if it were not so I would have told you), *for* I am going there to prepare a place for you.' The logic of the latter is a bit stilted, and the parenthetical remark somewhat awkward. Although NIV represents the shorter text (*i.e.* omission of *hoti*), it is marginally more likely that *hoti* is original. If so, perhaps the second option, the question form, is least objectionable, understanding that John's report is meant to be so condensed that he has chosen not to record the fact that Jesus is going to prepare a place for his disciples other than by the rhetorical question itself. The thrust of such a rendering is in meaning only a whisker away from the NIV.

4. Some manuscripts preserve a longer reading, 'You know the place where I am going, and you know the way.' This makes for a slightly smoother transition to v. 5. Even if the longer reading is of doubtful authenticity, the shorter reading must be understood in much the same way.

3. Jesus as the way to the Father (14:5–14)

5. Thomas (*cf.* notes on 11:16; 20:24) appears in the Fourth Gospel as a loyal, even a courageous, disciple, but one who is liberally endowed with misapprehensions and doubts. His question sounds as if he interpreted Jesus' words in the most crassly natural way: he wants an unambiguous destination, for without such a destination how can one meaningfully speak of the route there? Dodd (*IFG*, p. 412, n. 1) goes beyond the evidence when he argues that the sequence runs like this: Jesus: 'You know the way; you do not need to know where it leads.' Thomas: 'If we do not know the destination, how can we know the way?' In fact, Jesus has just spelled out the destination (vv. 2–3) and advised them that they *also* know the way (v. 4). Thomas replies, in effect, that he (and the other disciples) have not really come to grips with what he has said about the destination, so how could Jesus' further insistence that they know the way bear coherent meaning?

6. The second half of this verse shows that the entire verse must be taken as the answer to Thomas's question. This means that *way* gains a little emphasis over *truth* and *life*. This is not to say that v. 6a should be interpreted as a semitism, the first noun governing the other two ('I am the way of truth and life', and hence 'I am the true and living way'); the three terms are syntactically co-ordinate, and Greek has other ways of expressing subordination. Still, if Thomas' question and v. 6a demonstrate that *way* is the principal theme, it follows that *truth* and *life* enjoy a supporting role: Jesus is the way to God, precisely because he is the truth of God (*cf.* notes on 1:14) and the life of God (*cf.* notes on 1:4; 3:15; 11:25). Jesus is the truth, because he embodies the supreme revelation of God – he himself 'narrates' God (1:18), says and does exclusively what the Father gives him to say and do (5:19ff; 8:29), indeed he is properly called 'God' (1:1, 18; 20:28). He is God's gracious self-disclosure, his 'Word', made flesh (1:14). Jesus is the life (1:4), the one who has 'life in himself' (5:26), 'the resurrection and the life' (11:25), 'the true God and eternal life' (1 Jn. 5:20). Only because he is the truth and the life can Jesus be the way for others to come to God, the way for his disciples to attain the many dwelling-places in the Father's house (vv. 2–3), and therefore the answer to Thomas's question (v. 5). In this context Jesus does not simply blaze a trail, commanding others to take the way that he himself takes; rather, he *is* the way. Nor is it adequate to say that Jesus 'is the Way in the sense that he is the whole background against which action must be performed, the atmosphere in which life must be lived' (Sidebottom, p. 146): that assigns Jesus far too passive a rôle. He is himself the Saviour (4:42), the Lamb of God (1:29, 34), the one who so speaks that those who are in the graves hear his voice and come forth (5:28–29). He so mediates God's truth and God's life that he is the very way to God (*cf.* de la Potterie, p. 938), the one who alone can say, *No-one comes to the Father except through me*.

In the framework of this Gospel, this exclusivism is directed in at least two directions. First, it is constrained by the salvation-historical consciousness of the Evangelist: *i.e.* now that Jesus has come as the culminating revelation of the Father, it is totally inadequate to claim that one knows God, on the basis of the *antecedent* revelation of bygone epochs, while disowning Jesus Christ. Indeed, the test of whether or not Jews in Jesus' day, and in John's day, *really* knew God through the revelation that had already been disclosed, lay in their response to the supreme revelation from the Father, Jesus Christ himself, to which the Scriptures, properly understood, invariably point (*cf.* notes on 5:39–46). Second, even if John's language utilizes metaphors and images common amongst the religions of the Roman world and well attested in diaspora Judaism, he does not mean for a moment to suggest that Christianity is merely one more religion amongst many. They are ineffective in bringing people to the true God. *No-one*, Jesus insists, *comes to the Father except through me.* That is the necessary stance behind all fervent evangelism (*cf.* notes on 20:30–31).[1]

The meditation of Thomas à Kempis is often quoted:

> Follow thou me. I am the way and the truth and the life. Without the way there is no going; without the truth there is no knowing; without the life there is no living. I am the way which thou must follow; the truth which thou must believe; the life for which thou must hope. I am the inviolable way; the infallible truth, the never-ending life. I am the straightest way; the sovereign truth; life true, life blessed, life uncreated.[2]

Or, in a triplet of sonnets:

> *I am the way to God: I did not come*
> *To light a path, to blaze a trail, that you*
> *May simply follow in my tracks, pursue*
> *My shadow like a prize that's cheaply won.*
> *My life reveals the life of God, the sum*
> *Of all he is and does. So how can you,*
> *The sons of night, look on me and construe*
> *My way as just the road for you to run?*
> > *My path takes in Gethsemane, the Cross,*
> > *And stark rejection draped in agony.*
> > *My way to God embraces utmost loss:*
> > *Your way to God is not my way, but me.*
> *Each other path is dismal swamp, or fraud.*
> *I stand alone: I am the way to God.*
>
> *I am the truth of God: I do not claim*
> *I merely speak the truth, as though I were*
> *A prophet (but no more), a channel, stirred*
> *By Spirit power, of purely human frame.*
> *Nor do I say that when I take his name*
> *Upon my lips, my teaching cannot err*
> *(Though that is true). A mere interpreter*
> *I'm not, some prophet-voice of special fame.*

---

[1] It is a strange judgment indeed that argues, 'Jesus' claim, understood in the light of the prologue, is inclusive, not exclusive' (Bruce, pp. 298–299; picked up by Beasley-Murray, p. 253). For although the Word, before his incarnation, stands behind all of creation, that 'inclusiveness' is immediately shattered by the sweeping rejection he faces by 'the world', by 'that which was his own' (1:10, 11). Only those who 'received him' and 'believed in his name' were given 'the right to become children of God' (1:12). In short, the prologue is as exclusive as 14:6, and offers scant support for Karl Rahner's theory of the 'anonymous Christian'.

[2] *The Imitation of Christ*, 56. 1.

In timeless reaches of eternity
The Triune God decided that the Word,
The self-expression of the Deity,
Would put on flesh and blood – and thus be heard.
The claim to speak the truth good men applaud.
I claim much more: I am the truth of God.

I am the resurrection life. It's not
As though I merely bear life-giving drink,
A magic elixir which (men might think)
Is cheap because though lavish it's not bought.
The price of life was fully paid: I fought
With death and black despair; for I'm the drink
Of life. The resurrection morn's the link
Between my death and endless life long sought.
I am the firstborn from the dead; and by
My triumph, I deal death to lusts and hates.
My life I now extend to men, and ply
Them with the draught that ever satiates.
Religion's page with empty boasts is rife:
But I'm the resurrection and the life.[1]

7. The meaning of the first part of v. 7 turns on a textual variant. The variant behind the NIV text is basically negative: *If you really knew me* [and you don't], *you would know my Father as well.* Although this reading is strongly attested, it appears to have been influenced by v. 8, where Philip reveals the depth of his ignorance, and by 8:19. The reading of the second-century papyrus P[66], the uncial Sinaiticus (ℵ), the first hand of Codex Bezae (D) and some other witnesses is more or less preserved in the NIV fn., and has good claims to authenticity: *If you have come to know me, you will know my Father also.* The assumption, in other words, is that at least the disciples have come to know Jesus ('really' in the NIV fn. casts doubt on this, and is textually unwarranted); what they must understand is that this knowledge of Jesus is the *entrée* to true knowledge of the Father. *From now on,* Jesus insists, *you do know him and have seen him.* The contracted pair of words rendered *From now on* (*ap'arti*), could be read as one word (there were usually no spaces between words in the early uncial manuscripts) with the meaning 'assuredly'. It is tempting to think that is what Jesus means here: 'and assuredly you do know him and have seen him.'[2] If we retain *From now on,* the reference is to the time the disciples have come to know Jesus during his ministry, and especially through the hour of his death and resurrection, now immediately upon them.

8. At one level Philip (*cf.* notes on 1:44; 11:21, 22) and the others truly

[1]Carson, *FWD*, pp. 29–30.
[2]*Cf.* A. Debrunner, *ConNT* 11, 1947, p. 48; Beasley-Murray, pp. 241, 243.

do know Jesus, and therefore in the Son they have seen the Father. But they do not recognize this yet. As highly as they think of Jesus, they do not yet grasp that in Jesus God has made himself known. To the extent that this is still beyond them, they do not know Jesus himself very well.

So Philip asks for direct access, as it were, an immediate display of God himself. He thus joins the queue of human beings through the ages who have rightly understood that there can be no higher experience, no greater good, than seeing God as he is, in unimaginable splendour and transcendent glory. We have been made in his image, and however much we have defaced that image, we still yearn for the *visio Dei*, the vision of God. Moses had begged, 'Now show me your glory' (Ex. 33:18; in the LXX, 'Show me yourself'). But the most he was allowed to glimpse was the trailing edge of the back of God's glory. The Evangelist has already made it clear in his Prologue that however mitigated God's gracious self-disclosure was in former times, in Jesus he has made himself known, definitively, gloriously, visibly (*cf.* notes on 1:14, 18; *cf.* 12:45).

9. Jesus' question (v. 9) is tinged with sadness. If his opponents do not recognize who he is, it is because they have not been taught by God, they have not listened to the Father (6:45). If those closest to him still display similar ignorance of who he is, despite loyalty to him, they attest their profound spiritual blindness. Even being with Jesus *such a long time* – the reference is to the duration of Jesus' ministry – does not guarantee the deepest insight, insight into the truth that all of Jesus' actions and words have supported and which he now articulates: *Anyone who has seen me has seen the Father.*

10. Jesus' question *Don't you believe . . . ?* presupposes that all disciples *ought* to believe that Jesus is in the Father and the Father in him. This mutual indwelling (*cf.* notes on 10:38) is 'a linguistic way of describing . . . the complete unity between Jesus and the Father' (Schnackenburg, 3. 69), articulated elsewhere in a statement such as 'I and the Father are one' (10:30). This does not obliterate all distinctions between them: the words and works of Jesus are given to him by the Father (5:19ff.; 8:28; 12:49), though the reverse cannot be said. Indeed, it is precisely this degree of unity that ensures Jesus reveals God to us (*cf.* notes on 5:19–30).

That is why it is inadequate, despite the popularity of the theory, to see behind vv. 9–11 nothing more than the rabbinic principle that 'a man's agent is like to himself' (Mishnah *Berakoth* 5:5). That kind of model is adequate to account for the language of, say, 13:20, and even to claim that Jesus' words and works are those of the one who sent him. But in the Fourth Gospel this 'envoy' model is suddenly outstripped when we are told that *everything* Jesus does is what the Father gives him to do, and that he does *everything* the Father does: now we are dealing in unique 'sonship' language (*cf.* notes on 5:19ff.). No mere envoy would refer to the one who sent him as his Father, claim that whoever has seen him has seen the Father, and affirm mutual indwelling between himself and the one who sent him.

Within the context of the Fourth Gospel as a whole, the supremely revealing event when God displays himself in Jesus with most startling glory, the moment when the Father is most powerfully glorified in his Son, lies in the glorification of Jesus, the death/exaltation of Jesus, now immediately ahead. And it is the consequence of that event, *viz.* the gift of the Spirit, that will finally enable Jesus' disciples to grasp the truth of which they are still but dimly aware.

11. *Believe me* in this context does not simply mean 'Trust me', but 'Believe that what I have just said [summarized in the next clause] is true'. If they still find it difficult to penetrate the meaning of his words, at the very least they should *believe on the evidence of the miracles* (Gk. *erga*, 'works', but the miracles are primarily in view) *themselves*. Similar appeal is made twice elsewhere (*cf.* notes on 5:36; 10:37-38), but the context of this passage makes it the most telling of the three. Jesus' point is not simply that displays of supernatural power frequently prove convincing, but that the miracles themselves are signs (*cf.* notes on 2:11). Thoughtful meditation on, say, the turning of the water into wine, the multiplication of the loaves or on the raising of Lazarus will disclose what these miracles signify: *viz.* that the saving kingdom *of God* is at work in the ministry of Jesus, and this in ways tied to his very person. The miracles are non-verbal Christological signposts.

12. Jesus has been appealing for faith. The appeal continues in vv. 12-14 by focusing on the fruitfulness that *anyone who has faith* in Jesus (*ho pisteuōn eis eme* – an expression that embraces all believers, not just the apostles) will enjoy. The promise is staggering: the person with such faith, Jesus says, *will do what I have been doing*. Indeed, *he will do even greater things than these* – not because he is greater, but *because I am going to the Father*.

The *things* (*erga*, 'works', *cf.* v. 11) Jesus has been doing, and the greater things that follow, cannot legitimately be restricted to deeds of humility (13:15) or acts of love (13:34-35), still less to proclamation of Jesus' 'words' (v. 10). Jesus' 'works' may include more than his miracles; they never exclude them. But even so, *greater works* is not a transparent expression. It cannot simply mean *more* works – *i.e.* the church will do more things than Jesus did, since it embraces so many people over such a long period of time – since there are perfectly good Greek ways of saying 'more', and since in any case the meaning would then be unbearably trite. Nor can *greater works* mean 'more spectacular' or 'more supernatural' works: it is hard to imagine works that are more spectacular or supernatural than the raising of Lazarus from the dead, the multiplication of bread and the turning of water into wine.

The clues to the expression's meaning are two: first, the final clause, *because I am going to the Father*, and second, the parallel in 5:20: 'For the Father loves the Son and shows him all he does. Yes, to your amazement he will show him even *greater things than these*' (*meizona toutōn*, as in

14:12). The two clues point in the same direction. Jesus' disciples will perform greater works because he is going to the Father: this cannot mean that they will have greater scope for their activity because he will have faded from the scene and relinquished the turf to them, but that the very basis for their greater works is his *going to the Father*. Their works become greater precisely because of the new order that has come about consequent on his going to the Father. Similarly, the context of 5:20 shows that the greater works the Father will show the Son, and that the Son will therefore manifest to his followers, are displays of resurrection and judgment (*cf.* 5:17, 24–26). This life-giving power of the Son depends in turn on the Son's death, resurrection and exaltation.

In short, the works that the disciples perform after the resurrection are greater than those done by Jesus before his death insofar as the former belong to an age of clarity and power introduced by Jesus' sacrifice and exaltation. Both Jesus' words and his deeds were somewhat veiled during the days of his flesh; even his closest followers, as the foregoing verses make clear, grasped only part of what he was saying. But Jesus is about to return to his Father, he is about to be glorified, and in the wake of his glorification his followers will know and make known all that Jesus is and does, and their every deed and word will belong to the new eschatological age that will then have dawned. The 'signs' and 'works' Jesus performed during his ministry *could not* fully accomplish their true end until *after* Jesus had risen from the dead and been exalted. Only at that point could they be seen for what they were. By contrast, the works believers are given to do through the power of the eschatological Spirit, *after* Jesus' glorification, will be set in the framework of Jesus' death and triumph, and will therefore more immediately and truly reveal the Son. Thus *greater things* is constrained by salvation-historical realities.[1] In consequence many more converts will be gathered into the messianic community, the nascent church, than were drawn in during Jesus' ministry (*cf.* 15:26–27; 17:20; 20:21, 29). The contrast itself, however, turns not on raw numbers but on the power and clarity that mushroom after the eschatological hinge has swung and the new day has dawned. The contrast between the greatness of John the Baptist and the greatness of the least in the kingdom is not entirely dissimilar (*cf.* Carson, *Matt*, pp. 262–269, on Mt. 11:7–15).

13–14. The reason why the 'greater things' are done consequent upon Jesus' going to the Father (v. 12) is now clarified further: the disciples'

---

[1]*Cf.* Christian Dietzfelbinger, *NTS* 35, 1989, pp. 27–47, whose analysis is very helpful until he begins to speculate on the nature of the Johannine community for whom such a passage might be relevant. These theological emphases would, transparently, prove equally potent in the evangelization of those with Jewish or proselyte background who needed to be convinced what Christian life was about. Dietzfelbinger also exaggerates the uniqueness of this Johannine contribution to the theology of the New Testament. When it is set against the salvation-historical background sketched in above, its analogues in the rest of the New Testament are to be found not in this or that deed, but in the transformation of perspective from, say, Luke to Acts.

fruitful conduct is the product of their prayers, prayers offered in Jesus' name. Whether this prayer is directed to the Father or to Jesus (*cf.* 'You may ask *me*', v. 14 – but *cf.* Additional Note, below), it is offered in Jesus' name, and he is the one who grants the request (*I will do it*, v. 14). This demonstrates that the contrast in v. 12 is not finally between Jesus' works and his disciples' works but between the works of Jesus that he himself performed during the days of his flesh, and the works that he performs through his disciples after his death and exaltation. Glorified with the glory he had with the Father before the world began (17:5), the Son is no longer limited by the pre-death humanness that characterized his ministry. At that point redemption is won, the kingdom of God is triumphantly invading the nations with saving and transforming power, the locus of the covenant community stretches outward from its Jewish confines to embrace the world, and the disciples themselves are empowered and equipped to engage in far-reaching ministry. The latter turns on the gift of the Holy Spirit, which gift is about to be introduced into the discussion (vv. 15ff.).

In the post-Easter situation, the Son's mediatorial role extends even to the prayers of his followers. Prayers in his name are prayers that are offered in thorough accord with all that his name stands for (*i.e.* his name is not used as a magical incantation: *cf.* 1 Jn. 5:14), and in recognition that the only approach to God those who pray enjoy, their only *way* to God (*cf.* vv. 4–6), is Jesus himself (*cf.* H. Bietenhard, *TDNT* 5. 258–261, 276). Such prayer is never abstracted from the Father; for the Son's purpose, even as he answers the prayers of his followers, is to *bring glory to the Father* (v. 13). During his ministry on earth, the Son's consistent aim, and his achievement, was to bring glory to his Father (5:41; 7:18; 8:50, 54). That was, no less, the Son's purpose in completing his mission by going to the cross (12:28) – which was simultaneously the means by which the Son would be supremely glorified (12:23). Now in the splendour of his exaltation, the Son's purpose does not change: he enables his own to do 'greater things' in order that he may bring glory to the Father.

Additional note

14. This verse is omitted by a minority of witnesses, some of them important, including a substantial number of ancient versions. Nevertheless the verse is almost certainly original. Reasons why it was omitted may have included the following: (1) A copyist's eye may have inadvertently dropped from the first word of v. 14 (*ean*) to the first word of v. 15 (*ean*), an accidental error called 'haplography'. (2) Alternatively, a copyist might have thought, wrongly, that the verse contradicts 16:23, and decided to drop it. (3) Someone may have omitted it on the ground that it was too repetitive of truth already expressed in v. 13a. Amongst the witnesses that support the verse are a minority that drop the *me* in the first clause, thereby giving the impression that the prayer is addressed to the Father in Jesus' name, rather than to Jesus in Jesus' name. Textual evidence favours the inclusion of the pronoun. The seeming awkwardness of 'ask *me* in *my* name' is paralleled elsewhere (Pss. 25:11; 31:3; 79:9). In any case, it is very doubtful that the Evangelist would be interested in drawing overly fine distinctions in the proper object of prayer, since he can happily refer to the gift of the Spirit as the result of the Son's request to the Father (vv. 16, 26), or as the Son's own emissary (15:26; 16:7). *Cf.* notes on 15:6–7, 16.

4. The departure of Jesus and the coming of the Spirit of Truth (14:15–31)

For a brief introduction to the five Paraclete passages (14:16–17, 26; 15:26–27; 16:7–11, 12–15), especially their cohesiveness within these chapters, *cf.* the notes introducing 13:31ff.

15. Two links tie this verse to what precedes. (1) The prospect of doing 'greater things' anticipates the need for enabling power, the manifestation of God himself by his Spirit. This verse is moving the discussion toward vv. 16–17. (2) The obedience theme is of a piece with asking for things in Jesus' name (vv. 13–14). None of the promised fruitfulness will come to those who think they can manipulate the exalted Christ, or use him for their own ends.

Barrett (p. 461) rightly observes that the protasis *If you love me* 'controls the grammar of the next two verses (15–17a), and the thought of the next six (15–21)'. Jesus has demonstrated his love for his own (13:1ff.), declared his love for them and commanded them to love one another (13:34–35); now for the first time in the Fourth Gospel he speaks of their love for him. The conditional is third class: Jesus neither assumes that his followers love him, nor assumes that they do not, even for the sake of the argument, but projects a condition and stipulates its entailment: they *will obey* (the future, not the imperative, is the correct reading: *cf.* Metzger, p. 245) what he commands.

The uncompromising connection between love for Christ and obedience to Christ repeatedly recurs in John's writings (*cf.* vv. 21, 23; 15:14). The linkage approaches the level of definition: 'This is love for God: to obey his commands' (1 Jn. 5:3). But what are his 'commands'? The parallels that tie together 'what I command' (v. 15, lit. 'my commands'), 'commands' (v. 21), and 'my teaching' (lit. 'my word' in v. 23, and 'my words' in v. 24) suggest to some that more is at stake than Jesus' ethical *commands*. What the one who loves Jesus will observe is not simply an array of discrete ethical injunctions, but the entire revelation from the Father, revelation holistically conceived (*cf.* 3:31–32; 12:47–49; 17:6). Nevertheless the plural forms ('commands', *entolai*) likely focus on the individual components of Jesus' requirements, while the singular 'teaching' (*logos*; *cf.* notes on 14:23; 17:6) focus on the Christ-revelation as a comprehensive whole. Of course, one of the principal ingredients of this revelation is the obligation Jesus' followers have under the new covenant to love one another (13:34–35). John sees this as so integrally tied to holistic devotion to God that he can elsewhere say, 'This is how we know that we love the children of God: by loving God and carrying out his commands' (1 Jn. 5:2).

16. The first entailment of the disciples' love for Jesus is their obedience (v. 15); the second is that Jesus will ask the Father to provide for them another Counsellor to be with them forever. The love of the disciples for Jesus should not be seen as the price paid for this gift, any more than it is the price paid for their obedience. Jesus is describing a set of essential relations, not a set of titillating conditions. His true followers will love him; they will obey him; and he on his part will secure for them, from the Father who denies nothing to his Son, *another Counsellor*. If in this passage the Counsellor is given by the Father at the Son's request, elsewhere he is sent by the Father in Christ's name (v. 26), sent by Christ from the Father (15:26), proceeds ('goes out') from the Father (15:26), or is sent by Christ (16:7). It is not that the Evangelist cannot distinguish these expressions one from the other, still less that the two ways of referring to the sending of the Spirit are 'in direct tension' (Burge, p. 203). Rather, the same sending can be described in various complementary ways, granted the tight cohesion of the Father and the Son (*cf.* 5:19–30).

The Greek term *paraklētos*, rendered 'Counsellor' in the NIV, is the verbal adjective of *parakaleō*, lit. 'to call alongside', and hence 'to encourage', 'to exhort'. The verbal adjective has passive force, and is roughly equivalent to *ho parakeklēmenos*, 'one who is called alongside'. In secular Greek, *paraklētos* primarily means 'legal assistant, advocate' (LSJ, *s.v.*) *i.e.* someone who helps another in court, whether as an advocate, a witness, or a representative. With this legal force it was transliterated into Hebrew and Aramaic (*cf.* Additional Note). In Greek, however, the term never had the restrictively technical force that Latin *advocatus* ('a legal advocate') had. Moreover, the passive form does not rule out the possibility that the Paraclete may be an active speaker on behalf of someone before someone else (*cf.* G. Behm, *TDNT* 5. 803).

In John's usage, the legal overtones are sharpest in 16:7–11, but there the Paraclete serves rather more as a prosecuting attorney than as counsel for the defence. NIV's 'Counsellor' is not wrong, so long as 'legal counsellor' is understood, not 'camp counsellor' or 'marriage counsellor' – and even so, the Paraclete's ministry extends beyond the legal sphere. The same limitation afflicts 'Advocate'. AV's 'Comforter' was not bad in Elizabethan English, when the verb 'to comfort' meant 'to strengthen, give succour to, to encourage, to aid' (from Latin *confortare*, 'to strengthen'). In today's ears, 'Comforter' sounds either like a quilt or like a do-gooder at a wake, and for most speakers of English should be abandoned. 'Helper' (GNB) is not bad, but has overtones of being subordinate or inferior, overtones clearly absent from John 14 – 16.

The one whom Jesus will ask the Father to send is called 'another Paraclete' (*allon paraklēton*). Although it is just possible to understand this expression to mean 'another one, *i.e.* a Paraclete', the arguments in favour of 'another Paraclete' are decisive (*cf.* Franck, p. 38). Some argue that *allon* here means '*another* Paraclete *of the same type*', but John's use of this term forbids us to rest so much weight on it (*cf.* Additional Note on 5:31–32). Nevertheless 'another Paraclete' in the context of Jesus' departure implies that the disciples already have one, the one who is departing. Although Jesus is never in the Fourth Gospel explicitly referred to as a *paraklētos*, the title is applied to him in 1 John 2:1 (NIV 'one who speaks . . . in our defence'). That means that Jesus' *present* advocacy is discharged in the courts of heaven; John 14 implies that *during his ministry* his role as Paraclete, strengthening and helping his disciples, was discharged on earth. 'Another Paraclete' is given to perform this latter task.

17. The identity of the other Paraclete is now made clear: he is *the Spirit of truth* (a title used here and in 15:26; 16:13). Although the expression itself is found in Judaism of the first century, it is customarily parallel to the 'spirit of perversity', the two spirits referring to two 'inclinations' that battle it out in every human being (*Testament of Judah* 20:1, 5; 1QS 3:18ff.; 4:23). It never has this dualistic force in John. Within the framework of the Fourth Gospel, the expression immediately calls up the sustained treatment of the Holy Spirit afforded in earlier chapters (*cf.* notes on 1:32–33; 3:5–8; 4:23–24; 6:63; 7:37–39). Judging by descriptions of his work, the Paraclete is the Spirit of truth primarily because he communicates the truth (*cf.* notes on v. 26; 16:12–15). Coming so soon after 14:6, where Jesus claims to be the truth, 'the Spirit of truth' may in part define the Paraclete as the Spirit who bears witness to the truth, *i.e.* to the truth that Jesus is (*cf.* Johnston, pp. 121–122).

The world (*kosmos*; *cf.* notes on 1:10), the moral order in rebellion against God, *cannot accept him, because it neither sees him nor knows him*. Profoundly materialistic, the world is suspicious of what it cannot see; but seeing in itself guarantees nothing, as the world's response to Jesus demonstrates. The truth is that the world does not know the Spirit of truth, and cannot accept him (*cf.* 1 Cor. 2:14), and if it could it would cease being the 'world' (*cf.* Bultmann, p. 626). Moreover, in terms of the Spirit's responsibility to replace Jesus as Paraclete to the disciples, it would be a profound contradiction of their fresh, eschatological, new covenant experiences of God mediated by the Spirit (*cf.* notes on 3:5; 7:37–39) if these experiences were shared with those who had not yet closed with Jesus. This does not mean the Spirit of truth has no task to discharge toward outsiders: that will be elucidated in due course (16:7–11); it does mean that there are peculiar ways in which the Spirit of truth remains with them already, and will be in them following Jesus' glorification (*cf.* Additional Note). The disciples therefore know him already, better than they think they do; they will know him more intimately, after Jesus has been exalted and has sent the Spirit of truth.

This must not be construed as a merely credal position. The Spirit is to be experienced; otherwise the promise (in the ensuing verses) of relief from the sense of abandonment is empty. Schnackenburg (3. 153) is right: 'In the twentieth century . . . consciousness of the presence of the

Spirit has to be [*sic*] a very great extent disappeared, even in the believing community. It is possible to say that the only person who will understand the words about the Spirit is the one who has already experienced the presence of the Spirit.'

18–20. Doubtless the disciples still feel abandoned. Jesus consoles them: *I will not leave you as orphans*, children bereft of parents who would support them – though in secular Greek the word *orphans* is also used of children stripped of only one parent or of disciples stripped of their master (*cf. NewDocs* 4. § 71). *I will come to you*, Jesus assures them; but which coming is in view?

Arguments have been advanced for all three 'comings' – Jesus' resurrection, the gift of the Spirit, the parousia – and for various combinations of them. Two of the resurrection appearances are explicitly cast in terms of Jesus' 'coming' (20:19, 26), and this well suits the personal language ('I will come to you . . . you will see me'). On the other hand, John 14:18–20 is framed by two passages that explicitly refer to the coming of the Spirit (vv. 16–17, 25–26). Again, some reflect on the 'coming' language of v. 3, with its reference to the parousia, and think that Jesus here talks about the same thing. Still other commentators think John has purposely collapsed these 'comings' so that differences amongst them are at a vanishing point, as if to say that it does not matter what 'coming' is in view, provided that Jesus remains with his followers and does not abandon them as orphans. More sceptical commentators argue that John represents a mature version of Christianity, where Jesus' personal resurrection and the promise of his apocalyptic coming at the end of time are effectively 'demythologized' in favour of an emphasis on the coming of the Spirit. Bultmann (pp. 617–618) argues that v. 18 originally referred to the parousia, but that the Evangelist by putting the verse in this context has changed its meaning to make it refer to the coming of the Spirit.

Much of the discussion seems much too uncontrolled. Some false steps have been taken because too much has been made to rest on parallels to single words such as 'coming' or a related form of the verb. When vv. 18–20 are read within the framework of the impending 'hour', a concatenation of small clues drives the reader to the conclusion that Jesus is referring to his departure in death and his return after his resurrection. The language is personal: *I will come to you . . . you will see me*. There is no reason to think that the Evangelist simply confuses the coming of the Spirit with the coming of Jesus. Indeed, it is not at all clear that John ever speaks of the coming of Jesus *in* the Spirit (*cf.* Beasley-Murray, p. 258; though *cf.* v. 23, below). After all, the time when the disciples come to recognize that Jesus is in the Father and the Father is in him is *that day* (v. 20) when Jesus has risen from the dead: that is the 'coming' in view. The consequence of Jesus' rising from the dead is new life for the disciples, new eschatological life mediated by the Spirit: *Because I live, you also will live*. This interpretation of vv. 18–20 is confirmed by the passage conceptually closest to it, 16:16–30 (*cf.* esp. 14:13–14 and 16:20, 22–23).

The primary reason why some interpreters detect in 14:18–20 a reference to the Paraclete is the proximity of two Paraclete passages (vv. 16–17, 25–26). In fact, this proximity is better explained another way. It is not that the two Paraclete passages force us to detect in these verses yet another reference to the Paraclete, this one somewhat veiled; rather, the coming of the Paraclete in the two unambiguous passages is conditioned by Jesus' death and resurrection. He cannot ask the Father (as he has promised) for 'another Counsellor' (v. 16) unless he rises from the dead – in short, unless he comes to his disciples again after his impending 'departure' in death.

The sequence of thought, then, runs as follows: Jesus has promised to ask the Father to send another Counsellor, the Spirit of truth, to be with his disciples forever (vv. 16–17). They should be encouraged: this Paraclete lives with them and will be in them (v. 17b). One can well imagine the implicit response of the disciples: This promise is all well and good, but what about *you*? Jesus' answer is that he himself will not leave them orphans; he will come to them (v. 18). The next two verses (vv. 19–20) unpack what this means. The world will not see Jesus any more. Even after the resurrection, Jesus never manifests himself to other than his disciples (or to those who, because of Jesus' self–disclosure to them, become his disciples).[1] Because he lives (surely a reference to his resurrection), they, too, will live, and *on that day* realize that Jesus is in the Father (*i.e.* they will comprehend what Jesus has briefly outlined of his relationship with the Father, in vv. 7–11), they are in him, and he is in them. It is important to remember that although the transformation of the disciples' understanding can be said to turn on the glorification of Jesus (12:16) or on the coming of the Paraclete (16:12–15), it can equally be said to turn on Jesus' resurrection (2:22). That is the turning point in view here.

As for the full significance of the disciples being in Jesus, and Jesus in them, there is fuller exposition not only in vv. 23ff., but also in ch. 17. Even here, it must be remarked that the transformation of the disciples goes on beyond Easter day. The resurrection of Jesus inaugurates the dawning kingdom; the disciples gain not only fresh understanding, but resurrection life (*Because I live, you also will live*). Eschatological terminology piles up (*Before long*, lit. 'yet a little while': *cf.* Is. 26:20; Hg. 2:33–34; Heb. 10:37; *On that day*, Is. 2:11; Je. 31:29; Mt. 24:36 par.), for this Evangelist is the undisputed master of inaugurated eschatology. Thus Jesus 'comes at Easter to be reunited with his disciples and to lift to a new plane his relationship with them, for which that in the ministry could be only a preparation' (Beasley-Murray, pp. 258–259).

21. Still focusing on the conditions that will prevail 'on that day' (v. 20) Jesus again articulates the truth of v. 15: love for Jesus is evidenced in

---

[1]Thus allowance is made for Saul who became ·Paul, and who was certainly not a believer when the Lord appeared to him. His companions heard noise but discerned no words, saw light but saw no Saviour. *Cf.* similarly the footnotes to the notes on 19:26–27.

having and obeying Jesus' commands. ('To have' in this context does not mean simply 'to be in receipt of', 'to possess', but, as elsewhere in Greek literature, 'to grasp with the mind'.) So at one are Jesus and the Father that according to Jesus the one who loves him *will be loved by my Father, and I too will love him.* The idea is not that the believer initiates this relation of love by demonstrating obedience, and that Jesus and his Father simply respond. After all, the Fourth Gospel repeatedly makes it clear that the initiative in the relationship between Jesus and his followers finally lies with Jesus (*cf.* notes on 6:70; 15:16) or with his Father (*cf.* notes on 6:37; 10:29). The idea, rather, is that the ongoing relationship between Jesus and his disciples is characterized by obedience on their part, and thus is logically conditioned by it. They love and obey Jesus, and he loves them, in exactly the same way that he loves and obeys his Father, and the Father loves him (*cf.* 3:35; 5:20; 8:29; 14:31). Moreover, as the Father in function of his love for the Son shows him all things (3:35; 5:20), so the Son in function of his love for his disciples says *I will . . . show myself to* [them]. The groundwork is being laid for the 'oneness' between Jesus and his disciples that mirrors the oneness between Jesus and his heavenly Father, a theme developed in ch. 17.

With the connection between obedience and love so explicit, it should be self-evident that the circle of love in view embraces all of Jesus' true disciples, but not the 'world', which falls within a rather different and more extended circle of love (*cf.* notes on 13:1, 34–35).

Thus Jesus is not only the mediator of the love of God for his own, but in consequence he 'shows himself' to them (*emphanizō*, 'to make manifest' and hence in the passive 'to appear before'). In the light of the argument of vv. 18–20, one thinks first of the passages where this verb and its related forms refer to the resurrection appearances (Mt. 27:53; Mk. 16:9; Acts 10:40); Jesus 'shows himself' to his own in his resurrection body (Jn. 20 – 21). Nevertheless the verb and its cognates are used to refer to several different types of concrete display. In the LXX the verb can refer to theophanies (*e.g.* Ex. 33:13, 18). In the New Testament the cognate noun can refer to the first coming of Jesus Christ in its entirety (2 Tim. 1:10), as well as to his second coming (2 Thes. 2:8; 1 Tim. 6:14; 2 Tim. 4:1, 8; Tit. 2:13). The verb is elsewhere used to refer to Christ's appearance in his Father's presence after his death and resurrection (Heb. 9:24), not to mention several theologically innocuous occurrences (Acts 23:15, 22; 24:1; 25:2, 15; Heb. 11:14). It is possible, then, that in the light of the developing argument (14:22–23) Jesus' words in 14:21 refer not only to the resurrection appearances to the first disciples but also to the corresponding self-disclosures of Jesus to his disciples in later times (*cf.* Mt. 28:20, 'And surely I am with you always, to the very end of the age.')

22. This Judas is probably the one identified as (lit.) 'Judas of James' in Luke 6:16; Acts 1:13 (whether his brother or his son; Carson, *Matt*, p. 239; *cf.* Additional Note). His question is not so much *why . . . ?* as *how is it . . . ?* In view of the fact that none of the disciples entertained very clear notions of the resurrection of Christ before the fact, it is unlikely that Judas is specifically asking how it is Jesus will show himself, in his resurrection body, to the disciples and not to the world. By the same reasoning, his question cannot be taken as a clear reference to the Holy Spirit (*cf.* v. 17). Rather, Judas hears these distinctions between what the world will perceive or be given, and what the disciples will enjoy, and in his mind he cannot square this distinction with his belief that the kingdom must arrive in undeniable and irresistible splendour. If Jesus is the messianic king, then he *must* startle the world with apocalyptic self-disclosure. Indeed, a select reading of some Old Testament passages (*e.g.* Is. 11; Dn. 7; Hab. 3:3–15; Zc. 9), without compensating reflection on passages that speak of suffering and atonement, might be taken to sanction just such a stance.

23. Jesus does not deny that there will be an apocalyptic dénouement at the end (*cf.* 5:28, 29; 6:39, 40; 14:1–3), but he insists that the theophany of which he has been speaking occurs within the circle of love that displays itself in obedience to the Son's *teaching* (*logos*; the singular suggests the Son's revelation as a whole: contrast v. 21). That is why he reiterates vv. 15 and 21. Of the person who so loves and obeys Jesus, Jesus himself promises, *My Father will love him, and we will come to him and make our home* (*monē; cf.* notes on v. 2) *with him.*

Thus, while Jesus leaves his disciples in order to prepare in his Father's house 'dwelling-places' (*cf.* v. 2) for his followers, he simultaneously joins with the Father (their equality is implicit) in making a 'dwelling-place' in the believer. Presumably this manifestation of the Father and the Son in the life of the believer is through the Spirit, although the text does not explicitly say so. Other New Testament passages testify to the dwelling of the Son in the Christian (*e.g.* Eph. 3:17); this is the only place where the Father and the Son are linked in this task. Those who think that the Father and the Son are present in the believer *only through* the Holy Spirit see the indwelling in this verse as indistinguishable from the gift of the Spirit. Others join with Augustine in thinking that this text coupled with vv. 25–26 argues for the indwelling of the Triune God in the believer (*In Johan. Tract.* lxxvi. 4).

However conceived, this is an anticipation, an inauguration, of the final, consummating experience of God after the parousia, when the words of the Apocalypse will be fulfilled: 'Now the dwelling of God is with men, and he will live with them. They will be his people, and God himself will be with them and be their God . . . I did not see a temple in the city, because the Lord God Almighty and the Lamb are its temple' (Rev. 21:3, 22; *cf.* 1 Ki. 8:27; Ezk. 37:26–27; Zc. 2:10). Many religions ancient and modern seek some kind of mystical intimacy with the Creator. John's thought is distinguished from the panentheistic framework that characterizes most of these religious quests by three features: (1) his insistence on the historical realities of the supreme revelation in Jesus Christ; (2) his unswerving theism, indeed, monotheism; (3) his frank links between, on the one hand, personal devotion to Christ that breeds obedience and therefore moral probity, and, on the other, his candid report of Jesus' promise that Christians will *experience* God.

24. The last point, the ethical one, is now reiterated in a statement that is the converse of vv. 15, 23a. Mere duty will not generate obedience to Christ; only love for him can do that. Meanwhile we must be reminded whose words are to be obeyed: the words of Jesus are the words of the Father who sent him (*cf.* notes on 5:19ff.).

25–26. Throughout these chapters Jesus repeatedly refers, in a reflective way, to his own teaching (*cf.* 16:1, 12, 25, 33). In this instance the clause *while still with you* not only maintains emphasis on the dominant theme, Jesus' impending departure, but serves to introduce the second of the five Paraclete passages (*cf.* notes on vv. 16–17), promising the Holy Spirit. That the Father sends him (see Additional Note) in Jesus' name may not be greatly different from saying that the Father will send him in response to Jesus' request (v. 16). There may, however, be a further point: if he is sent in Jesus' name, he is *Jesus'* emissary (not simply his substitute, *contra* Brown, 2. 653; Franck, p. 41). Just as Jesus came in his Father's name (5:43; 10:25), *i.e.* as his Father's emissary, so the Spirit comes in Jesus' name.

The task of the Paraclete in this passage extends beyond what is said of him in vv. 16–17. In John's Gospel the disciples are shown to fail, throughout Jesus' ministry, in their understanding of Jesus. One of the Spirit's principal tasks, after Jesus is glorified, is to remind the disciples of Jesus' teaching and thus, in the new situation after the resurrection, to help them grasp its significance and thus to teach them what it meant. Indeed, the Evangelist himself draws attention to some things that were remembered and understood only after the resurrection (2:19–22; 12:16; *cf.* 20:9). Granted the prominence of this theme, the promise of v. 26 has in view the Spirit's role to the first generation of disciples, not to all subsequent Christians. John's purpose in including this theme and this verse is not to explain how readers at the end of the first century may be taught by the Spirit, but to explain to readers at the end of the first century how the first witnesses, the first disciples, came to an accurate and full understanding of the truth of Jesus Christ. The Spirit's ministry in this respect was not to bring qualitatively new revelation, but to complete, to fill out, the revelation brought by Jesus himself.

27. *Peace* (*eirēnē*) reflects Hebrew *šâlôm*, the customary Jewish greeting and word of farewell. Here it is primarily farewell (*cf.* also 16:33). This peace he 'leaves' with his disciples: the verb (*aphienai*) probably here has the sense of 'bequeaths' (as in Ps. 16:14 LXX [MT 17:14]; Ec. 2:18). Yet this word of farewell becomes a word of greeting after the resurrection (20:19, 21, 26). The contexts of these twin uses are so pregnant with meaning that the underlying notion of peace must be fundamentally messianic and eschatological. *Peace* is one of the fundamental characteristics of the messianic kingdom anticipated in the Old Testament (Nu. 6:26; Ps. 29:11; Is. 9:6–7; 52:7; 54:13; 57:19; Ezk. 37:26; Hg. 2:9) and fulfilled in the New (Acts 10:36; Rom. 1:7; 5:1; 14:17). 'The new order is simply the peace of God in the world' (Hoskyns, p. 461). At the individual level, this peace secures composure in the midst of trouble, and dissolves fear, as the final injunction of this verse demonstrates. This is the peace which garrisons our hearts and minds against the invasion of anxiety (Phil. 4:7), and rules or arbitrates in the hearts of God's people to maintain harmony amongst them (Col. 3:15).

Of this peace Jesus says, *I do not give* it *to you as the world gives*. The world is powerless to give peace. There is sufficient hatred, selfishness, bitterness, malice, anxiety and fear that every attempt at peace is rapidly swamped. Within a biblical framework, attempts to achieve personal equanimity or merely political stability, whether by ritual, mysticism or propaganda, without dealing with the fundamental reasons for strife, are intrinsically loathsome. That is why God denounces 'prophets and priests alike' who 'practise deceit. They dress the wound of my people as though it were not serious. "Peace, peace," they say, where there is no peace. Are they ashamed of their loathsome conduct? No, they have no shame at all; they do not even know how to blush' (Je. 6:13–15). The world promises peace and waves the flag of peace as a greeting; it cannot give it.

But Jesus displays transcendent peace, his own peace, *my peace*, throughout his perilous hour of suffering and death. And by that death he absorbs in himself the malice of others, the sin of the world, and introduces the promised messianic peace in a way none of his contemporaries had envisaged. The *pax Romana* ('Roman peace') was won and maintained by a brutal sword; not a few Jews thought the messianic peace would have to be secured by a still mightier sword. Instead, it was secured by an innocent man who suffered and died at the hands of the Romans, of the Jews, and of all of us. And by his death he effected for his own followers peace with God, and therefore 'the peace of God, which transcends all understanding' (Phil. 4:7).

That peace, in Jesus' teaching, is to be as characteristic of the dawning kingdom as the presence and power of the Holy Spirit, and Jesus bequeaths both (vv. 26–27), thus fully providing all that is necessary to meet his disciples' fears (vv. 1, 27). Many have remarked that in this discourse Jesus imparts to his followers not only 'my peace' but also 'my love' (15:9, 10) and 'my joy' (15:11). Bruce (p. 305) goes further: 'When we recall that love, joy and peace are the first three graces in the fruit of the Spirit in Gal. 5:22, we may wonder if these three did not form a triad in primitive Christian thought comparable to faith, hope and love.' If so, the sanction is dominical, and the common element is love.

28. Jesus is still dealing with what is troubling his disciples and firing their fear, *viz.* his repeatedly announced departure (*You heard me say*; cf. vv. 2–4, 12, 18–19, 21, 23). But now he goes over to the offensive, however mildly: their failure to understand, their failure to trust him, is also a failure of love. If they truly loved him (and the clear implication is that they do not), they would be glad that he is going to the Father. After all, his departure ensures that he will take them to be with him for ever

(vv. 1–3): that alone should have been a cause for joy. Genuine love for Jesus would have found another cause for joy: *the Father is greater than I.*

At a popular level, this clause is often cited, out of context, by modern Arians who renew the controversy from the early centuries that is connected with the name of Arius (on which *cf.* Pollard; Wiles, pp. 122–125). The problem is how to put together that strand of Johannine (and New Testament) witness that places Jesus on a level with God (1:1, 18; 5:16–18; 10:30; 20:28), with that strand that emphatically insists upon Jesus' obedience to his Father and on his dependence upon his Father (4:34; 5:19–30; 8:29; 12:48–49), not to mention John's description of the origin and purpose of the Son's mediation in creation, revelation and redemption as being in the Father's will (1:3–4, 14, 18; 3:17; 5:21–27). It cannot be right to depreciate the truth of one strand by appeal to the other. Arians deploy the latter strand to deny the former: Jesus is less than fully God. Gnostics deploy the former to depreciate the latter: Jesus may in some sense be divine, but he is not fully human. In each passage the immediate context resolves most of the difficulties (*cf.* notes on the passages listed). In the clause before us, *the Father is greater than I* cannot be taken to mean that Jesus is not God, or that he is a lesser God: the historical context of Jewish monotheism forbids the latter, and the immediate literary context renders the former irrelevant. If the writer of this commentary were to say, 'Her Majesty Queen Elizabeth the Second is greater than I', no-one would take this to mean that she is more of a human being than I. The *greater than* category cannot legitimately be presumed to refer to ontology, apart from the controls imposed by context. The Queen is greater than I in wealth, authority, majesty, influence, renown and doubtless many more ways: only the surrounding discussion could clarify just what type of greatness may be in view.

What, then, does *for the Father is greater than I* mean in this context? Some have attached these words to those immediately preceding: 'I am going to the Father, *for* the Father is greater than I.' This is syntactically reasonable, but the precise logic inherent in *for* (*hoti*, 'because') is obscure. Presumably it would mean that Jesus is going back to the one who commissioned him, under the assumption that Jesus has all but completed his task, *for* the one who sent him is greater than the one who is sent (*cf.* 13:16). The connection is not tight, and it bears little on the rest of the verse.

It is better to take *for the Father is greater than I* to refer not to the immediately preceding clause, but to the main clause: 'If you loved me, *you would be glad* that I am going to the Father, *for* the Father is greater than I.' Some then take the intrinsic logic like this: 'you would be glad *for* everything is under control'. Doubtless the disciples would have lost some of their fear and anxiety if they had really believed that everything was under control, but it is very doubtful if the clause *for the Father is greater than I* can be reduced to nothing more than a generalized statement about the sovereignty of God. The comparison, after all, is between Jesus and his Father ('greater than I'), yet in v. 1 the assumption is that the disciples believe in God better than they believe in Jesus, making this kind of exhortation rather strange. Isn't God sovereign, and are not things under control, whether or not Jesus goes back to the Father? And how does this have any bearing on the conditional clause 'If you loved me, you would be glad . . .'?

The only interpretation that makes adequate sense of the context connects *for the Father is greater than I* with the main verb (as does the preceding option), but understands the logic of the *for* or *because* rather differently: If Jesus' disciples truly loved him, they would be glad that he is returning to his Father, *for* he is returning to the sphere where he belongs, to the glory he had with the Father before the world began (17:5), to the place where the Father is undiminished in glory, unquestionably greater than the Son in his incarnate state. To this point the disciples have responded emotionally entirely according to their perception of *their own* gain or loss. If they had loved Jesus, they would have perceived that his departure to his own 'home' was *his* gain and rejoiced with him at the prospect. As it is, their grief is an index of their self-centredness.

Theologically, two further points must be drawn. First, the failure of these first disciples, sad to say, has often been repeated in the history of the church, where Christians have been far more alert to their own griefs and sorrows than to the things that bring their Master joy. Second, although the interpretation of v. 28 advanced here turns on the distinction between the Father in his glory and the Son in his incarnation, nevertheless this verse also attests to the pattern of functional subordination of the Son to the Father, already alluded to, that extends backward into eternity past (*cf.* Barrett, *Essays*, pp. 19–36: Carson, pp. 146–160). 'The Father is *fons divinitatis* ["the divine fountainhead"] in which the being of the Son has its source; the Father is God sending and commanding, the Son is God sent and obedient. John's thought here is focused on the humiliation of the Son in his earthly life, a humiliation which now, in his death, reached both its climax and its end' (Barrett, p. 468).

29. If Jesus tells his disciples these things now, it is not to shame them but to ensure faith when the events of which he speaks actually occur. Jesus said the same thing with reference to the treason of Judas Iscariot (13:19).

30–31. *I will not speak with you much longer* should not be taken as the end of a discourse (*cf.* notes introducing 13:31ff.): similar expressions are scattered throughout John 14 – 16 (*e.g.* 14:25; 16:12) and cumulatively convey the impending onset of the 'hour'. Jesus cannot speak much longer, *for the prince of this world* (*cf.* notes on 12:31) *is coming*. Whatever role Judas Iscariot plays as a responsible agent, the devil himself precipitates Jesus' death (*cf.* notes on 6:70; 13:21, 27). In fact, though he does not know it, the devil is to be overthrown. *He has no hold on me* is an idiomatic rendering of 'he has nothing in me', recalling a Hebrew idiom frequently used in legal contexts, 'he has no claim on me', 'he has nothing over me'. How could he? Jesus is not of this world (8:23), and he has never sinned (8:46). The devil could have a hold on Jesus only if there were a justifiable charge against Jesus. Jesus' death would then be his due, and the devil's triumph.

But in actual fact Jesus' death, far from being the sign of his defeat at Satan's hand, is the culminating proof, as Jesus avers, *that I love the Father and that I do exactly what my Father has commanded me* (*cf.* Additional Note). As the love of Jesus' disciples for their Master is attested by their obedience (vv. 15, 21, 23), so also does the Son himself remain in his Father's love by keeping his commandments (8:29; 15:10). Jesus' love for and obedience toward his Father are supremely displayed in his willingness to sacrifice his own life (10:17–18).

And *the world must learn* this. The world may think, with the devil, that Jesus is defeated by his death. It must learn that Jesus is vindicated in his death, and that the cross, resurrection, and exaltation of Jesus Christ ultimately turn on the commitment of the Son to love and obey his heavenly Father at all costs. The love relationships within the Trinity (to use a term that developed later) are logically prior to the love of God for the world. Ironically, the very rebellion and sinful self-centredness that damns the world, that makes the world the world, is overthrown by the obedience and self-sacrificing love of the Son, who thereby not only displays what a proper relation to God consists in, but is vindicated and wins release and redemption for those the Father has given to him. The world itself will learn this – either when men and women discover the truth and cease to belong to the world, or at the time when 'every knee [shall] bow . . . and every tongue confess that Jesus Christ is Lord, to the glory of God the Father' (Phil. 2:10–11). These truths, cherished by every Christian, constitute the most profound evangelistic appeal.

On the final words of the chapter, *Come now; let us leave, cf.* notes introducing 13:31ff.

Additional notes

16. Not only was *paraklētos* transliterated into Hebrew and Aramaic (*pᵉraqlît*), so also was its rough synonym *synēgoros* and its antonym *katēgoros* (as *sanêgôr* and *qaṭēgôr* respectively). In later rabbinical commentaries, the role of the advocate, the *sanêgôr*, is assigned to the Holy Spirit (*Leviticus Rabbah* 6:1 on Lv. 5:1). Although the word *katēgoros* ('prosecutor', 'accuser') does not occur in the Fourth Gospel, the Paraclete takes on this role in John 16:8. The terms 'advocate' and 'accuser' appear together in the much-cited saying of Rabbi Eliezer ben Jacob, 'He that performs one precept gets for himself one advocate (*pᵉraqlît*) and he that commits one transgression gets for himself one accuser (*qaṭēgôr*)' (*Pirke Aboth* 4:11).

17. It is uncertain whether *menei* should be accented *ménei* ('he remains', NIV 'he lives') or *meneî* ('he will live'). Further, the textual evidence is finely divided between *estin* ('and *is* in you') and *estai* ('and *will be* in you', as in NIV). On the whole, it seems best to follow the NIV: the Holy Spirit, even as Jesus spoke with his disciples, was living with them inasmuch as Jesus was present with them, for to him the Father had given the Spirit without limit (3:34). But the time would come, after Jesus had been glorified and had petitioned his Father to send 'another Paraclete', when the Spirit himself would be in the disciples themselves.

22. The variants in this verse are very complex, engendering some confusion not only over 'Iscariot' (*cf.* notes on 6:71 and 13:2) but over the identity of Judas. Two Coptic versions read 'Judas the Cananite', apparently an attempt to identify him with Simon the Cananaean (Mt. 10:4; Mk. 3:18). The Sinaitic Syriac has 'Thomas' and the Curetonian Syriac 'Judas Thomas' for 'Judas not Iscariot'. Syriac Christians apparently regularly called the apostle Thomas 'Judas Thomas'; some of the same circles preserved the legend that Thomas was the twin brother of Jesus (*cf.* notes of 11:16). For useful discussion, *cf.* A. F. J. Klijn, 'John xiv and the Name Judas Thomas', in Sevenster, pp. 88–96.

26. These notes have consistently referred to the Holy Spirit, the Paraclete, as a person. The reasons for this decision have been summarized elsewhere (Carson, *FWD*, pp. 65–66). Inasmuch as the Paraclete is given as, in certain respects, a personal replacement for Jesus, and that John does not hesitate to use the personal masculine pronoun of him even though the word 'Spirit' in Greek is formally neuter, this approach is entirely justified.

30–31. The interpretation offered above follows the punctuation of the NIV, which places a comma at the end of v. 30 and therefore builds a contrast between the devil's futile attempt to bring a claim against Jesus and Jesus' resolute commitment to please his Father. Alternatively, one could read a full stop at the end of v. 30, and then begin, 'But that the world may know . . ., come now, let us leave.' Although both renderings are syntactically possible, the former makes better use of the strong Johannine theme of Jesus' consistent love for and obedience to his Father.

C. THE FAREWELL DISCOURSE: PART TWO *(15:1 – 16:33)*

1. *The vine and the branches* (15:1–16)

The links between vv. 1–8 and vv. 9–16 are intricate. Both sections speak of 'remaining', the first of remaining in the vine/Jesus, the second of remaining in Jesus' love (vv. 4–7, 9–10). Both hold up fruitfulness as the disciple's goal (vv. 5, 16); both tie such fruitfulness to prayer (vv. 7–8, 16). And both sections are built around a change in salvation-historical perspective, *i.e.* both depend on a self-conscious change from the old covenant to the new: under the image of the vine, Israel gives way to Jesus (*cf.* notes on v. 1), and under the impact of fresh revelation, 'servants' give way to 'friends' (v. 15).

Whatever the individual points of comparison between the two sections, the imagery of the vine and the branches becomes clearer as soon as it is recognized that vv. 9–16 serves as commentary on the metaphor, a recapitulation of some of the same themes without directly appealing to the metaphor.[1] At the same time, the metaphor enriches the exposition of vv. 9–16, for apart from the vine imagery in the first part of the chapter these verses might be interpreted in too mechanical a way – as if the relationship between Jesus and his disciples can be exhaustively described in terms of obedience, perseverance, revelation and love. What would then be missing is the panoply of associations connected with the vine: fruitfulness, dependence, vital union, pruning, and the Old Testament associations that present Jesus as a replacement for (or, better, the fulfilment of) Israel (cf. notes below).

Many commentators detect in the imagery of the vine a reference to the eucharist, since one of the two elements of that rite is wine. This view is perhaps marginally strengthened if chs. 15 – 16 are viewed as an alternative farewell discourse, and therefore thematically tied directly to ch. 13, the report of the last supper (cf. notes on 13:31ff.). Even so, there is precious little to support this interpretation. There is no hint of believers drinking the fruit of the vine (cf. Mt. 26:29; Mk. 14:25; Lk. 22:18); indeed, there is no mention of wine at all, still less a connection with Jesus' blood. 'The truth is that John is speaking of the union of believers with Christ, apart from whom they can do nothing. This union, originating in his initiative and sealed by his death on their behalf, is completed by the believers' responsive love and obedience, and is the essence of Christianity' (Barrett, p. 470). At most there may be an indirect allusion to the Lord's table, much as in ch. 6 (cf. notes on 6:25–59).

a. The extended metaphor (15:1–8)

Vines and vineyards crop up in several parables in the Synoptic Gospels (Mt. 21:23–41; Mk. 12:1–9; Lk. 20:9–16; Mt. 20:1–16; 21:28–32; Lk. 13:6–9). These parables have two things in common: (a) they all have narrative plot; (b) in each case the vineyard, or people connected with the vineyard, portray Israel, or a part of Israel, being far less fruitful than ought to have been the case. By contrast, the extended metaphor in John 15:1–8 shows no plot development, and Jesus himself is the vine. From these data various conclusions have been drawn: that John the Evangelist has transformed the largely futurist eschatology of the Synoptics into the inaugurated eschatology with which he is more comfortable; that he has transmuted the vine imagery to make it suit his own Christology, where Jesus, complete with 'I am . . .' saying, replaces Israel;

---

[1] The parallels between the two parts are less rich if, with Borig (p. 19), the passage is divided: vv. 1–10, vv. 11–17. But although this has its attractions, it overlooks the way in which *all* of vv. 9–16 constitute an exposition of vv. 1–8, while largely leaving the vine metaphor behind.

that the abolition of plot coheres with the omission of any plot-dominated parables in the Fourth Gospel. In short, these verses of John 15 are the product of the Evangelist's transforming meditation on earlier tradition, and correspondingly enjoy only the loosest connection with the historical Jesus.

These inferences prove to be weakly based. All the Synoptic passages focus on a vineyard or those associated with it; none of them centres on a vine. Even within the list of Synoptic passages that mention a vineyard there are considerable differences: the brief summary of similarities (above) conceals more than it reveals. The parable in Mark 12:1–9 par. is really about tenant farmers who refuse to recognize the owner's rights, issuing finally in the death of the owner's son and therefore in the owner's inexorable wrath. That the setting is a vineyard is relatively incidental. In Matthew 20:1–16 the plot turns on the generosity of the landowner who pays the various workers the same amount, regardless of the length of their service that day: once again, the plot has nothing to do with the *kind* of farming that frames the parable. Here, too, the plot has more to do with grace than with futurist eschatology. In short, John can be accused of transforming an earlier literary tradition only by claiming, falsely, that there was a uniform tradition waiting to be transformed, and that John's treatment is demonstrably parasitic on it.

It is clear from parallel texts that the vine/vineyard was one of the most common motifs in ancient religions (*cf.* note on v. 1); it is not surprising that a mind as creative and nimble as that of the Master should use it in a colourful variety of ways. The frequency with which vine imagery occurs in the ancient sources, and the diversity of uses to which it is put (*cf.* Borig, pp. 79–194), also tell against the creative proposal of Bauckham.[1] Bauckham links passages in *The Odes of Solomon, The Gospel of Thomas, The Acts of Thomas* and elsewhere to 'rediscover', however tentatively, an authentic parable of Jesus which, he thinks, is simply commented on here in John 15, without the parable itself being provided. But the strength of his case is not aided by the multiplication of partial parallels, especially when the parallels he adduces are sometimes verbal, sometimes thematic, and sometimes a mingling of vine imagery and the imagery of the world-tree (*cf.* Dn. 4 – which is not, in Scripture, a vine). The multiple 'parallels' attest the power of vine imagery, and confirm the tendency by which choice descriptions rapidly become clichés in other contexts; they offer little support for the common dependence that would justify a reconstructed parable. And if Jesus had told a parable along the line of Bauckham's reconstruction (in itself not implausible), it would be astonishing, not to say unprecedented, for the parable to be omitted and its 'interpretation' (Jn. 15:1ff.) to be retained.

That the extended metaphor in these verses has no plot has prompted

---

[1]Richard Bauckman, *NTS* 33, 1987, pp. 84–101.

some recent writers to designate this a *māšāl* (a wise or enigmatic saying) rather than a parable (*cf.* Brown, 2. 668–669). The distinction depends too much on modern definitions. Of the thirty-three occurrences of *māšāl* in the Old Testament, twenty-eight occurrences are rendered by the Greek *parabolē*, and cover what we would call proverbs, maxims, similes, allegories, fables, comparisons, riddles, taunts, stories embodying some truth. Much the same range can be found in the New Testament (*cf.* Carson, *Matt*, pp. 302–303; C. Brown, NIDNTT 2. 743–760). The vine imagery provides us with an extended metaphor without plot, an illustrative comparison – a form also known in the Synoptics (*e.g.* Mt. 15:15; 24:32).

1. This is the last of the 'I am . . .' sayings (*cf.* notes on 6:35), and the only one that runs on into an additional assertion, *and my Father is the gardener.* Although the Son's role is central in these verses, the Father's is not mere background: he trims and prunes the branches.

Vine imagery is so common in the ancient world that scholars have been able to discover parallels they find compelling in a wide range of literature – in Gnosticism, the Mandaean corpus, Philo, the literature of Palestinian Judaism, and more. The popularity of such imagery in ancient agrarian societies means that superficial similarities cannot themselves demonstrate dependence, at least until all competing claims are weighed. Two factors decisively decide the issue in favour of an Old Testament background: (a) the frequency of John's appeals to the Old Testament, both in allusions and in quotations; (b) the dominance in the Fourth Gospel of the 'replacement' motif (*cf.* notes on 2:19–22), for that motif strongly operates in this passage (*contra* Borig).

In the Old Testament the vine is a common symbol for Israel, the covenant people of God (Ps. 80:9–16; Is. 5:1–7; 27:2ff.; Je. 2:21; 12:10ff.; Ezk. 15:1–8; 17:1–21; 19:10–14; Ho. 10:1–2). Most remarkable is the fact that whenever historic Israel is referred to under this figure it is the vine's failure to produce good fruit that is emphasized, along with the corresponding threat of God's judgment on the nation. Now, in contrast to such failure, Jesus claims, 'I am the *true* vine', *i.e.* the one to whom Israel pointed, the one that brings forth good fruit. Jesus has already, in principle, superseded the temple, the Jewish feasts, Moses, various holy sites; here he supersedes Israel as the very locus of the people of God. (A similar contrast between Israel and Jesus is developed in various ways in the Synoptics: *e.g.* in the temptation narrative, Mt. 4:1–11 par.)

Perhaps the most important Old Testament passage is Psalm 80, in that it brings together the themes of vine and son of man:

> *Restore us, O God Almighty;*
> *make your face shine upon us,*
> *that we may be saved.*
> *You brought a vine out of Egypt;*
> *you drove out the nations and planted it. . . .*
> *Return to us, O God Almighty!*

> Look down from heaven and see!
> Watch over this vine,
> the root your right hand has planted,
> the son [the Heb. word may mean 'stock' or 'branch'] you have
>   raised up for yourself.
> Your vine is cut down, it is burned with fire;
> at your rebuke your people perish
> Let your hand rest on the man at your right hand,
> the son of man you have raised up for yourself.
>
> (Ps. 80:7-8, 14-17)

The true (*alēthinos*; *cf.* notes on 1:9) vine, then, is not the apostate people, but Jesus himself, and those who are incorporated in him. The theme would prove especially telling to diaspora Jews: if they wish to enjoy the status of being part of God's chosen vine, they must be rightly related to Jesus. Nevertheless the replacement theme does not exhaust the significance of the vine: the imagery itself suggests incorporation, mutual indwelling, fruitfulness. It is making the imagery walk on all fours to argue, with several commentators, that Jesus is the total vine, and not just the trunk over against the branches; *i.e.* the branches are truly in him. The image becomes ludicrous: not only does it then require that it is Jesus himself who is pruned, but it understands the branches not only to be 'in him' but to be him.

As in Psalm 80, God plants and cultivates the vine: he is the *gardener*: the Greek word (*geōrgos*) properly means 'farmer', though in English 'farmer' is not normally used to describe vinedressing. It is hard not to see in the relation between the vine and this gardener a reflection of the kind of subordination the Son displays toward his Father (*cf.* notes on 5:19ff.; Fenton, p. 158).

2. Chapter 14 has already introduced the mutual indwelling of the believer and Jesus ('you are in me, and I am in you', 14:20). Here the same notion is portrayed in the vine imagery. Jesus is the vine; his disciples are the branches (*klēma*; the word is particularly used of vine tendrils, though in other literature it is occasionally applied to heavier branches). The branches derive their life from the vine; the vine produces its fruit through the branches.

The role of the Father, the heavenly gardener, is twofold. To take them in reverse order: first, *he prunes* or trims *every branch that does bear fruit*. No fruit-bearing branch is exempt. Doubtless the Father's purpose is loving – it is so that each branch *will be even more fruitful* – but the procedure may be painful. The thought is not unlike Hebrews 12:4-11, cast in terms of another model: the Lord disciplines his own the way a father disciplines his children. All this is 'for our good, that we may share in his holiness' (Heb. 12:10).

Second, the Father (Jesus says) *cuts off every branch in me that bears no fruit*, *i.e.* he gets rid of the dead wood so that the living, fruit-bearing branches may be sharply distinguished from them, and may have more room for growth. The phrase *in me* has prompted considerable speculation as to whether John is thinking of Jews who were once in God's vine but who have now been cast off, or of apostate Christians. The former does not easily suit *in me*: it is hard to see in what sense Jews who never put their trust in Jesus were once 'in him', even if they once belonged to the vine of Israel before it was superseded by Jesus. But the latter view, that these dead branches are apostate Christians, must confront the strong evidence within John that true disciples are preserved to the end (*e.g.* notes on 6:37–40; 10:28). It is more satisfactory to recognize that asking the *in me* language to settle such disputes is to push the vine imagery too far. The transparent purpose of the verse is to insist that there are no true Christians without some measure of fruit. Fruitfulness is an infallible mark of true Christianity; the alternative is dead wood, and the exigencies of the vine metaphor make it necessary that such wood be connected to the vine. (Dead branches from some other tree, lying around in the vineyard dirt, could scarcely make the point.) These have no life in them; they have never borne fruit, or else they would have been pruned, not cut off. Because Jesus is the *true* vine, in contradistinction to the vine of Israel that bore either no fruit or rotten fruit, it is impossible to think that any branch that bears *no* fruit can long be considered part of him: his own credentials as the true vine would be called in question as fundamentally as the credentials of Israel. *Cf.* further on v. 6. If we must think of 'branches' with real contact with Jesus, we need go no further than Judas Iscariot (*cf.* notes on 6:70–71; 13:10). Indeed, there is a persistent strand of New Testament witness that depicts men and women with some degree of connection with Jesus, or with the Christian church, who nevertheless by failing to display the grace of perseverance finally testify that the transforming life of Christ has never pulsated within them (*e.g.* Mt. 13:18–23; 24:12; Jn. 8:31ff.; Heb. 3:14–19; 1 Jn. 2:19; 2 Jn. 9).

The Greek displays a play on words that is hard to render in English. The Father 'cuts off' (*airei*) every dead branch; he 'trims' (*kathairei*) every fruit-bearing branch; indeed the disciples listening to Jesus are already 'clean' (*katharoi*, v. 3) because of the word Jesus has spoken to them. The verb *kathairei* and its cognate adjective *katharoi* are appropriate to both an agricultural (*cf.* Barrett, p. 473) and a moral or religious context. *Cf.* Additional Note.

3. It is not clear if this verse provides the means of the purification – as if Jesus' word were pruning shears – or if Jesus' word is simply what started these branches off clean and fruitful, *already* clean. Probably the latter is in view, since the former rather confuses the work of the Father with that of the Son. The cleansing power of the word Jesus has spoken to his disciples, then, is equivalent to the life of the vine pulsating through the branches. Jesus' *word* (*logos*) is not assigned magical power. What is meant, rather, is that Jesus' 'teaching' (as *logos* is rendered in 14:23), in its entirety, including what he is and what he does (since he himself is the *logos* incarnate, 1:1, 14), has already taken hold in the life of these followers (*cf.* notes on 13:10).

4. The first sentence of v. 4 can be taken in one of three ways; all of them make sense. (1) Conditional: 'If you remain in me, I will remain in you' (which is the assumption of the NIV's rendering). Read in this way, the believer's perseverance in remaining in Jesus is the occasional cause, not the ultimate cause, of Jesus' remaining in the believer (*cf.* 8:31-32; 15:9-11). (2) Comparison: 'Remain in me, as I remain in you' (the Greek allows this: the second clause has no verb, but simply 'and I in you'). The thought is coherent enough; the 'and' (as opposed to 'as') is mildly surprising. In the context of the threats on both sides of the verse, it is indefensible to take the 'I in you' as an absolute promise *regardless* of the perseverance or fickleness of the ostensible believer. (3) Mutual imperative: 'Let us both remain in each other', 'Let there be mutual indwelling'. Again, however, the syntax is strange: the strong second person imperative in the first clause cannot easily be reduced to this mutual exhortation, and the normal Greek way of expressing this thought is by a hortatory subjunctive.

If the first reading, the conditional, has a slight edge, the general thought is in any case clear. No branch has life in itself; it is utterly dependent for life and fruitfulness on the vine to which it is attached. The living branch is thus truly 'in' the vine; the life of the vine is truly 'in' the branch. Lest the point be missed, Jesus steps away from the vine imagery a little and directly addresses his hearers (though he preserves the figure of 'fruit'): *Neither can you bear fruit unless you remain in me.* This is not the inorganic growth of external accretion, like the growth of an alum crystal in an alum solution; it is organic growth, internal growth, driven by the pulsating life of the vine in the branch, and only this kind of growth produces fruit. The imagery of the vine is stretched a little when the 'branches' are given the responsibility to remain in the vine, but the point is clear: continuous dependence on the vine, constant reliance upon him, persistent spiritual imbibing of his life – this is the *sine qua non* of spiritual fruitfulness. The Christian or Christian organization that expands by external accretion, that merely apes Christian conduct and witness, but is not impelled by life within, brings forth dead crystals, not fruit.

Malatesta has convincingly demonstrated that in 1 John 'to remain in' language and 'to be in' language are associated with new covenant theology.[1] If the same is true here, as has been argued,[2] we are not far from the Old Testament new covenant texts, all of which promise a renewed heart or a right mind or the presence of the Spirit in the new covenant people, such that they will obey what God says. Thus God remains among and in his people by renewing them with his life, with

---

[1]E. Malatesta, *Interiority and Covenant* (An. Bib. 69; Biblical Institute Press, 1978), esp. ch. 8.

[2]J. W. Pryor, *RTR* 48, 1988, pp. 49-50.

his Spirit, and making his presence known in them and among them (*cf.* 14:16, 23); they remain in him by obeying his commands, as the explanation in 15:9–11 makes clear.

5–6. The central thoughts of vv. 1–4 are here repeated, but without mention of the gardener (v. 1) or of the pruning (v. 2). The ultimate alternatives are set out with simple starkness: one either remains in the vine and is a fruit-bearing branch, or one is thrown away and burned.

There has been considerable dispute over the nature of the 'fruit' that is envisaged: the fruit, we are told, is obedience, or new converts, or love, or Christian character. These interpretations are reductionistic. The branch's purpose is to *bear much fruit* (v. 5), but the next verses show that this fruit is the consequence of prayer in Jesus' name, and is to the Father's glory (vv. 7, 8, 16). This suggests that the 'fruit' in the vine imagery represents everything that is the product of effective prayer in Jesus' name, including obedience to Jesus' commands (v. 10), experience of Jesus' joy (v. 11 – as earlier his peace, 14:27), love for one another (v. 12), and witness to the world (vv. 16, 27). This fruit is nothing less than the outcome of persevering dependence on the vine, driven by faith, embracing all of the believer's life and the product of his witness.

The tenses of two verbs in v. 6 are difficult (*cf.* Additional Note). What is clear is the imagery of destruction. When Ezekiel appealed to vine imagery, he warned that if a vine failed to produce fruit its wood was good for nothing but a fire (Ezk. 15:1–8); Jesus assumes the same thing, and by thus alluding to Ezekiel, where the vine stands for Israel, he is warning his contemporaries of their imminent danger, and reinforcing the replacement motif with which the chapter began. From the perspective of the Evangelist, both the threat and the promise still apply to the Jews to whom he is primarily writing. The fire symbolizes judgment, and attests the uselessness of what it consumes. Although the fire is part of the symbolism here associated with the vine, there can be little doubt that John and his readers perceived a similar fate for the faithless themselves (*cf.* 5:29; 1 Jn. 2:18–19; Mt. 13:37–42).

7. Many commentators hold that the vine imagery ends in v. 6, and that vv. 7–8 begin the explanation. It is true that Jesus now reverts to the second person ('If *you* remain in me . . .'), but such a change in person also takes place in the middle of the vine imagery (v. 4b), and therefore cannot be decisive. The continued reference to fruit (v. 8) suggests that the imagery of the vine, though it is being explained, is still in full view.

The mutual indwelling depicted by the vine imagery is not narrowly mystical. *If you remain in me* is teased out in vv. 9ff., and is there equivalent to doing all that Jesus commands; *If . . . my words remain in you* is another way of getting at the same truth. Jesus' *words* (*rhēmata*) are all the individual utterances that together constitute Jesus' 'word' (v. 3; *logos*). Such words must so lodge in the disciple's mind and heart that conformity to Christ, obedience to Christ, is the most natural (supernatural?) thing in the world. This does not mean that the mutual indwelling is reduced to obedience. Rather, 'Jesus and his revelation are virtually interchangeable, for he is incarnate revelation' (Brown, 2. 662). Conformity in one area ensures conformity in the other; a test in the observable area of obedience to Christ is a test of the unseen area of genuine spiritual vitality. All this is equivalent to remaining in the vine; that is the union out of which fruit is produced. To cast it in terms of prayer, such a truly obedient believer proves effective in prayer, since all he or she asks for conforms to the will of God (*cf.* notes on 14:12–14).

8. Such a fruitful prayer life, Jesus avers, *is to my Father's glory* (*edoxasthē*: on the aorist, *cf.* the Additional Note to v. 6). In the Fourth Gospel it is more common for the Son to be glorified; but God also glorifies himself in the Son (12:28), and is glorified in or through the Son (13:31; 14:13; 17:4). Since the fruit of believers is a consequence of the Son's redemptive work, the result of the vine's pulsating life (15:4), and the Son's response to the prayers of his followers (14:13), it follows that their fruitfulness brings glory to the Father through the Son. More precisely, the fruitfulness of believers is part and parcel of the way the Son glorifies his Father. In John's syntax, 'that you bear much fruit and [so] be my disciples' (*cf.* Additional Note) is in explanation of '*This* is to my Father's glory'. In short, Christians must remember that the fruit that issues out of their obedient faith-union with Christ lies at the heart of how Jesus brings glory to his Father. Those who are contemplating the claims of the gospel, like John's readers, must reckon with the fact that failure to honour the Son is failure to honour God (5:23). Fruitlessness not only threatens fire (v. 6), but robs God of the glory rightly his.

Additional notes

2. Several popular writers, going back directly or indirectly to A. W. Pink (*Exposition of the Gospel of John*, 3 vols. [Cleveland Bible Truth Depot, 1929] 3. 337), argue that *airō* does not here mean 'cuts off' (NIV) but 'lifts up [from the ground]' – *i.e.* the fruitless branches are 'lifted up' so that they may gain the exposure to sun that has been denied them, and thereby become abundantly fruitbearing. However, of its twenty-four occurrences in the Fourth Gospel, *airō* might be rendered 'take' or 'lift up' eight times (5:8–12; 8:59; 10:18, 24), and 'take away' or 'remove' sixteen times (1:29; 2:16; 11:39, 41, 48; 15:2; 16:22; 17–15; 19:15, 31, 38 [*bis*]; 20:1–2, 13, 15). More importantly, although the verb *by itself* may bear the meaning of 'lift up' (*cf.* J. Jeremias, *TDNT* 1. 185), yet in the context of viticulture it is not the most natural way to take it. Despite arguments to the contrary, there is no good evidence of which I am aware to confirm that lower stalks of grapevines were seasonally 'lifted up' from the ground. Moreover, the sharp contrast of v. 2, on the traditional interpretation, prepares the way for v. 6. This more recent interpretation sounds like an attempt to prevent embarrassment at the thought of branches 'in me' being cut off, in contradiction (it is thought) to such passages as 6:37–40. But as the exposition above shows, these fears are unfounded. *Cf.* J. Carl Laney, *BSac* 141, 1989, pp. 55–66, esp. pp. 58–60.

6. The combination of verb tenses in this verse has occasioned discussion: 'If anyone does not remain (*menē*, present subjunctive) . . . he is like a branch that is thrown away (*eblēthē*, aorist indicative) and withers (*exēranthē*, aorist indicative). Amongst the proposed solutions are the following:

(1) The distinctions are time-related, and are theologically important: 'If anyone *does not remain* (present tense), like a branch he *has been thrown away* and *has been withered* (past tenses)' – *i.e.* the reason why the branch does not remain is that it has already been rejected. This reading is then taken to demonstrate that if a branch does not remain it is not a failure in perseverance or in the Father's keeping power, but a sign of judgment. This will not do: Greek verbs are not so conveniently time-based, even in the indicative (*cf.* Porter, esp. chs. 2, 3, 4); and if they were one would have expected two perfects rather than two aorists, and the perseverance of believers is better handled another way (*cf.* notes on vv. 1–2). In any case, the logic of this reading is terribly strained: it is hard to see how a branch does not remain in the vine *in consequence* of having been thrown away and having withered.

(2) Some read the aorists as gnomic (a generalizing usage stating what always happens under the given conditions) or proleptic (treating with a past tense something that takes place in the future). Both of these observations are themselves correct: it is always true that if a branch does not remain in the vine it is thrown away and it withers, and, relative to the failure to remain in the vine, the actions of being thrown away and of withering are necessarily future. But neither 'solution' explains why the aorist tense was chosen.

(3) It is better, following aspectual theory of the Greek verb, to understand that the essential feature of the aorist form is the idea of completeness that the speaker or writer wishes to depict: the branch that does not remain in the vine is thrown away and withers – the judgment is complete, decisive.

8. One textual variant in this verse is one of the most difficult in the entire Gospel of John. (1) Reading the aorist subjunctive *genēsthe* ('[that] you be [or "become"] my disciples') makes the verb parallel to the verb in the previous clause, 'that (*hina*) you bear (*pherēte*) much fruit'; the text is then understood as in the notes above. This reading is supported by ancient and diverse manuscripts. (2) Alternatively, we may read the future indicative *genēsesthe* (lit. 'you will be [or "become"] my disciples'). This is also well attested, and is, syntactically, the harder reading, thus gaining some claim to authenticity. If original, the meaning might still be very similar, since there are other instances of the future indicative occurring after *hina*. Alternatively, this future indicative could be taken to introduce an entirely new clause. We might paraphrase, 'Bearing fruit is to my Father's glory, and [thus] you will be my disciples' – *i.e.* fruit-bearing is so bound up with genuine discipleship that the one stands by metonymy for the other.

b. Unpacking the metaphor *(15:9–16)*

These verses explicate and take further some of the themes introduced in vv. 1–8 (*cf.* notes introducing ch. 15).

9–10. The relationship between the Father and the Son is frequently set forth in chs. 13 – 17 as the paradigm for the relationship between Jesus and his disciples. The immediate link with the preceding verses is the 'remain' language. Remaining in the vine (v. 4) has already been tied to obedience to Jesus' words (v. 7); now the same point is made a different way. The agricultural metaphor has its limitations; it does not depict the unfathomable love that sets the disciples in this new intimacy. *As the Father has loved me*, Jesus says – and the aorist *ēgapēsen* ('has loved') probably signals the perfection, the completeness of the Father's love for his Son, including his love for him before time began[1] – *so have I loved you*. Again the aorist *ēgapēsa* ('I have loved') is used: Jesus depicts his love for his own as a completed thing, so imminently does the cross stand in view. Of course the Father himself loves the disciples (16:27), but there is a peculiar sense in which Jesus is the mediator of that love, a love whose only adequate analogy is the love of the Father for the Son.

The injunction to *remain* in Jesus' love (the aorist *meinate* does not require that we think of the moment of entrance into the act of remaining, but looks at remaining globally, as a complete act) presupposes that, however much God's love for us is gracious and undeserved, continued enjoyment of that love turns, at least in part, on our response to it. Lest we should fill the injunction to remain in Christ's love with some insipid, pious jargon, v. 11 immediately makes the issue clear. If we are the recipients of Jesus' love in a way analogous to his own reception of the Father's love, we must remain in Jesus' love by exactly the same means by which he has always remained in his Father's love: obedience, that total obedience which finds Jesus testifying, 'The one who sent me is with me; he has not left me alone, for I always do what pleases him' (8:29). The obedience of Jesus is one of the central Christological realities articulated by this Gospel (*e.g.* 4:34; 5:19ff.; 6:38; 8:29, 55; 10:17–18; 12:27–28; 14:31). Elsewhere that obedience ensures that Jesus' revelation is nothing less than divine (5:19ff.); here it serves as the supreme paradigm for the obedience we owe.

If obedience is the condition of continuously remaining in Jesus' love, it is no less important to remember that in 14:15, 21 our love for Jesus is the wellspring of our obedience to him, as our obedience is the demonstration of the reality of that love.

These two verses do not impose on the believer an absolute alternative, perfect obedience or utter apostasy; rather, they set up the only ultimate standard, the standard of Jesus himself. The practical tensions between this supreme standard and the faulty steps of obedience

---

[1]That the Father loves the Son is elsewhere expressed in other tenses (3:35; 5:20; 10:17); here and at 17:24, 26, the aorist occurs.

practised by Jesus' followers are more fully explored in 1 John.

11. Jesus has promised 'my peace' (14:27) and insisted that his followers remain in 'my love' (15:10); now he promises them 'my joy'. Lest the constraints of the unqualified obedience mandated by vv. 9–10 seem grey and joyless, Jesus insists that his own obedience to the Father is the ground of his joy; and he promises that those who obey him will share the same joy – indeed, that his very purpose in laying down such demands is that their *joy may be complete* (*cf.* 1 Jn. 1:4). What is presupposed is that human joy in a fallen world will at best be ephemeral, shallow, incomplete, until human existence is overtaken by an experience of the love of God in Christ Jesus, the love for which we were created, a mutual love that issues in obedience without reserve. The Son does not give his disciples his joy as a discrete package; he shares his joy insofar as they share his obedience, the obedience that willingly faces death to self-interest (12:24–26).

12. The individual commands that must be obeyed if a disciple of Jesus is to remain in his love (v. 10) are now subsumed under one command: *Love each other as I have loved you*. Love for God (Dt. 6:4–5; *cf.* Mk. 12:29–31 par.) or for Jesus himself (14:15) is presupposed. Jesus' point is not that love for fellow believers exempts one from the call to love God with heart and soul and mind and strength, but that genuine love for God ensures genuine love for his Son, who is the focal point of divine revelation; that genuine love for the Son ensures obedience to him (14:15); that obedience to him is especially tested by obedience to the new commandment, the command to love (13:34–35; 15:12). By an unbreakable chain, love for God is tied to and verified by love for other believers (*cf.* 1 Jn. 4:11–21). The words *as I have loved you* not only remind us of the immeasurably high standard Jesus himself provides, but explicitly tie this passage to the new commandment (13:34–35), and anticipate the next verse. As John says elsewhere, 'This is how we know what love is: Jesus Christ laid down his life for us. And we ought to lay down our lives for our brothers' (1 Jn. 3:16).

13. At one level, this axiom lays out the standard of love Jesus' disciples are to show to one another; at another, it refers to Jesus' death on behalf of his friends – even if the disciples could not have understood this point when they first heard the words. 'The eternal divine love reached its complete and unsurpassable expression in the death of Christ, which was at the same time the death of a man for his friends' (Barrett, p. 476). The saying thus becomes one of the things of which the Holy Spirit will remind them in due course (14:26). As the Lamb of God (1:29, 36), Jesus is supremely the one who gives his life for his friends (*philoi*). Because John does not normally distinguish the two most common roots for 'to love' (*agapaō* and *phileō*), we are probably justified in rendering this 'that one lay down his life for those he loves' (*cf.* 10:15).

Two reflections are called for to mute the concerns of some commentators. *First*, although it is true that many ancient writers expatiate on friendship and argue that laying down one's life for a friend is the final demonstration of true friendship, it is going too far to conclude that John is merely 'clothing an ancient rule of friendship in biblical speech in order to apply it to the relation of Jesus to His disciples and also to that of the disciples with one another' (G. Stählin, *TDNT* 9. 166). The background of the Old Testament, coupled with the supreme example of Jesus himself, provides all the inspiration that is needed. It is quite another thing, however, to say that this utterance and the example of Jesus would resonate widely amongst readers in the ancient world.

Second, many object that to call this life-sacrificing love *for friends* the greatest love is to lower the standard: surely life-sacrificing love *for enemies* is greater yet. The objection fails to lay enough weight on the context, presupposing, as it does, that Jesus ought to be setting out a comparison between love for friends and love for enemies, when in fact the historic context finds Jesus among friends, addressing friends, and concerned to set out a pattern for their future behaviour (*cf.* notes on 13:34–35). In different contexts we find Jesus enjoining love for enemies upon his disciples (Mt. 5:43–47), or Paul testifying that God's *enemies* were reconciled to him by the death of his Son (Rom. 5:8–10). In the context of such sacrifice, 'love has sunk below its proper level if it begins to ask who is my friend and who is my enemy'.[1]

14–15. Although there is a sense in which Jesus gives his life for the world (1:29, 34; 3:16; *etc.*), there is another in which he dies for his friends (*cf.* also notes on 10:15). Who then are his friends? *You are my friends if you do what I command.* This obedience is not what *makes* them friends; it is what *characterizes* his friends. Clearly, then, this 'friendship' is not strictly reciprocal: these friends of Jesus cannot turn around and say that Jesus will be their friend if he does what they say. Although Abraham (2 Chr. 20:7; Is. 41:8; Jas. 2:23) and Moses (Ex. 33:11) are called friends of God, God is never called their friend; although Jesus can refer to Lazarus as his friend (Jn. 11:11), Jesus is not called the friend of Lazarus. Neither God nor Jesus is ever referred to in Scripture as the 'friend' of anyone. Of course, this does not mean that either God or Jesus is an '*un*friend': if one measures friendship strictly on the basis of who loves most, guilty sinners can find no better and truer friend than in the God and Father of our Lord Jesus Christ, and in the Son whom he has sent. But mutual, reciprocal friendship of the modern variety is not in view, and cannot be without demeaning God.

Jesus' friends, then, are the objects of his love (v. 13), and are obedient to him (v. 14). If obedience is a necessary criterion, what distinguishes them from servants (*douloi*, 'slaves')? Modern notions of friendship and slavery would draw the line at the requirement of obedience. Jesus, more familiar with hierarchical structures than are we, makes revelation the distinguishing feature. Nor is this an arbitrary distinction. Abraham and Moses, the only Old Testament characters who are called 'friends of

---

[1]Philip Loyd, *The Life according to St. John* (Clarendon, 1936), *in loc.*

God', enjoyed extraordinary access to the mind of God – so much so that later Jews speculated on what unrecorded revelations they might have received (cf. SB 2. 525–526; Meeks, chs. 3 – 4).

An absolute potentate demands obedience in all his subjects. His slaves, however, are simply told what to do, while his friends are informed of his thinking, enjoy his confidence and learn to obey with a sense of privilege and with full understanding of their master's heart. So also here: Jesus' absolute right to command is in no way diminished, but he takes pains to inform his friends of his motives, plans, purposes. The words *no longer* inject a salvation-historical note (entirely appropriate, given the replacement theme bound up with the *true* vine; cf. notes on vv. 1–2). In times past God's covenant people were not informed of God's saving plan in the full measure now accorded Jesus' disciples. Although there is much they cannot grasp (16:12), within that constraint Jesus has told them everything he has learned from his Father. The Paraclete whom Jesus sends will in the wake of the cross and resurrection complete the revelation bound up with the person and work of Christ (14:26; 16:12–15), thereby making Jesus' disciples more informed, more privileged, more comprehending than any believers who ever came before (cf. 1 Pet. 1:10–12).

16. As so often in this Gospel, where there is the slightest danger that the disciples will puff themselves up because of the privileges they enjoy, Jesus immediately forestalls any pretensions they might have (cf. notes on 6:70, 71). In the final analysis, his followers are privy to such revelations not because they are wiser or better and consequently made the right choices, but because Christ chose them.

The best Greek texts record that Jesus chose them and *set them apart* (*ethēka*) that they might go and bear fruit. This verb also occurs in v. 13: Jesus 'sets apart' or 'sets aside' (NIV 'lays down') his life for others. The verb commonly occurs, with a personal object, in contexts where people are being 'set apart' for particular ministry (*e.g.* Acts 13:47 [citing Is. 49:6]; 1 Tim. 1:12). This fact, and the emphasis on *going* and bearing fruit, have suggested to many commentators, probably rightly, that the fruit primarily in view in this verse is the fruit that emerges from mission, from specific ministry to which the disciples have been sent. The fruit, in short, is new converts. One purpose of election, then, is that the disciples who have been so blessed with revelation and understanding, should win others to the faith – *fruit that will last* (cf. 8:31). With these references to fruit and to its enduring quality (the verb is again *menō*, 'to remain'), it becomes clear that these closing allusions to the vine imagery ensure that, however comprehensive the nature of the fruit that Christians bear, the focus on evangelism and mission is truly central. As in John's day, so now: this is simultaneously a mandate to Christ's followers and a summons to those who do not yet know him. That is why the union of love that joins believers with Jesus can never become a comfortable, exclusivistic huddle that only they can share. Doubtless it is a unique union, an extension of the union of the

Godhead; but by its very nature, it is a union, an intimacy, which, by the necessity of its own constitution, seeks to bring others into its orb.

The NIV's *Then*, introducing the last sentence of the verse, is unjustified. The Greek begins with *hina* ('that'), parallel to the previous *hina*: '*that* you should go and bear fruit, and [that] your fruit should remain; *that* whatever you ask of the Father in My name, He may give it to you' (NASB). In short, these closing words again remind the reader that the means of the fruitfulness for which they have been chosen is prayer in Jesus' name (*cf.* notes on 14:12–14; 15:7–8).

2. Opposition from the world *(15:17 – 16:4a)*

If the union of believers with Jesus constitutes a community of love, that community stands over against the world. Those more sociologically inclined could doubtless offer a reasonable explanation as to why Christians, who claim to know God and who belong to a society (the church) from which others are excluded, might well excite some animus. But the reasons listed in these verses to explain the world's hatred are not sociological but theological. In this case the two categories overlap, though the latter are more fundamental: the foundational theological differences between the community of Jesus' followers and the world not only open a window on the motives and reactions of those who can tolerate neither Jesus nor his followers, but they also generate sociological differences which are bound to multiply enmity. This enmity was well-developed by the time John wrote, and therefore not a little scholarly ingenuity has been devoted to delineating the precise circumstances that preserved this denunciation of the world. But because John writes primarily in theological categories rather than any other, these verses are relevant in any historical situation where the church faces the fires of persecution.[1]

From an evangelistic perspective, these verses demand decision, because the issues are of ultimate importance. Following Jesus costs something (*cf.* Lk. 9:57–62; 14:25–33), and may cost life itself. Yet not following Jesus means one is siding with a lost and hateful world. To warn prospective disciples of these unyielding realities serves to discourage spurious conversions and to foster true ones, just as Jesus told these things to the first disciples in order to ensure stability until the time of faith truly dawned (16:1).

17. This verse is transitional. On the one hand, it reiterates vv. 10, 12; on the other, it sets the stage for the contrasting hatred displayed by the world and discussed in the ensuing verses.

18–19. The purpose of these verses is to eliminate the surprise factor when persecution does break out, *i.e.* to accomplish what John more

---

[1]For a useful summary of similar passages in the Synoptic Gospels and some speculative suggestions on their inter-relations, *cf.* B. Lindars, 'The Persecution of Christians in John 15:18 – 16:4a', in W. Horbury and B. McNeil (eds.), *Suffering and Martyrdom in the New Testament* (Cambridge University Press, 1981), pp. 48–69.

prosaically accomplishes elsewhere by a simple warning: 'Do not be surprised, my brothers, if the world hates you' (1 Jn. 3:13). *If the world hates you* – and the assumption is that it will – *keep in mind that it hated me first.* The *world* (*kosmos*; *cf.* notes on 1:9), as commonly in John, refers to the created moral order in active rebellion against God. The ultimate reason for the world's hatred of Jesus is that he testifies that its deeds are evil (7:7). Christ's followers will be hated by the same world, partly because they are associated with the one who is supremely hated, and partly because, as they increase in the intimacy, love, obedience and fruitfulness depicted in the preceding verses, they will have the same effect on the world as their Master. They, too, will appear alien. The world loves its own: this is not a sociological remark about inborn suspicion of strangers, but a moral condemnation. The world is a society of rebels, and therefore finds it hard to tolerate those who are in joyful allegiance to the king to whom all loyalty is due. Christians *do not belong to the world*, not because they have never belonged, but because, Jesus avers, *I have chosen you out of the world* (*cf.* notes on 6:70–71; 15:16). Former rebels who have by the grace of the king been won back to loving allegiance to their rightful monarch are not likely to prove popular with those who persist in rebellion. Christians cannot think of themselves as intrinsically superior. They are ever conscious that by nature they are, with all others, 'objects of wrath' (Eph. 2:3). But having been chosen out of the world, having been drawn by the Messiah's love into the group referred to as the Messiah's 'own' who are still in the world (13:1), their newly found alien status makes them pariahs in that world, the world of rebels.

20. The 'words' that Jesus now exhorts his disciples to remember, *No servant is greater than his master*, are a quotation from 13:16. The principle was there applied to the primacy of humility and of mutual service: if the Master is content to wash his servants' feet, it is pathetically unbecoming for his servants to scramble for positions of honour, to disdain the lowly task that helps their peers. Here the same principle is applied to persecution: *If they persecuted me, they will persecute you also* (*cf.* Mt. 10:16–25; Mk. 13:9–13; *cf.* Lk. 6:40). Those who preach Jesus' gospel and live in progressive conformity to his own life and teaching will attract the same antagonism that he did.

The second 'if' statement has been understood in two ways:

(1) If the thought of the sentence is synonymously parallel to the preceding sentence, the protasis (the 'if' clause) may be taken as offering a merely hypothetical possibility that in fact never occurs. The argument then runs: 'If they persecuted me (and they did), they will persecute you also; if they obeyed my teaching (and they didn't), they will obey yours also (so of course they won't).' Hence NEB paraphrases '. . . they will follow your teaching as little as they have followed mine' (similarly Lagrange, p. 411; Becker, p. 490). The effect of this reading is to set the world in such antithesis to Christ and his gospel that conversion is impossible. That is a strange position, since the disciples themselves

were chosen *out of the world* (v. 19), and Jesus is about to pray for those who will believe through the message of his followers (17:20; *cf.* 3:16–17; 4:42; 6:33, 51; 17:21).

(2) If the thought of the last sentence in this verse is in contrastive parallelism to the preceding sentence, the protasis in the last sentence offers an alternative to the protasis of the preceding sentence. The argument then runs: 'If they persecuted me (and many of them did), they will persecute you also; if they obeyed my teaching (and some of them did), they will obey yours also.' This reading, more likely than the alternative, means that human beings belonging to the world divide around Jesus' followers and their message exactly as they divided around Jesus and his message (*cf.* 12:44–50).

21. The cause of the venomous opposition outlined in vv. 18–20 is now specified: Jesus says it is *because of my name*, here equivalent to 'because of me'. Responses to Jesus' disciples, whether for good or for ill, finally turn not on who they are but on who Jesus is. The people of the world *do not know the One who sent me*. The implication is that if they had truly known God, they would have recognized the revelation of God in Jesus. Failure to recognize who Jesus is therefore constitutes damning evidence that, protestations notwithstanding, these people enjoyed far less antecedent knowledge of God than they claimed. The thought is expanded in vv. 22–24.

22–24. The idea is not that if Jesus had not come the people would have continued in sinless perfection – as if the coming of Jesus introduced for the first time sin and its attendant guilt before God (the Greek behind 'they would not be guilty of sin' is, more simply, 'they would not have sin'). Rather, by coming and speaking to them Jesus incited the most central and controlling of sins: rejection of God's gracious revelation, rebellion against God, decisive preference for darkness rather than light (*cf.* notes on 3:19–21; 9:39–41). The thought parallels several denunciations in the Synoptic Gospels, where Jesus' Galilean contemporaries are excoriated for their lack of repentance, and told they will face more severe judgment than pagan cities like Tyre and Sidon, indeed worse punishment than Sodom, proverbial for wickedness (Mt. 11:20–24). The pagan queen of Sheba and the ancient city of Nineveh come off better than Jesus' favoured hearers, because they responded positively to the light that was given them (Lk. 11:31–32). So also here: Jesus has *done among them what no-one else did* (v. 24), yet despite so many signs 'they still would not believe in him' (12:37). Religious interest that pursues signs may be suspicious (4:48), and faith based on sight is intrinsically inferior (20:29); even so, it is infinitely better than no faith, and the signs and works of Jesus make a legitimate claim on faith (4:34; 5:36; 9:32–33; 10:38). Rejection of Jesus' words (v. 22) and works (v. 24) is thus the rejection of the clearest light, the fullest revelation; and therefore it incurs the most central, deep-stained guilt.

Whether the people recognized it or not, Jesus' work was nothing less than God's work. In Jesus' speech God's words were heard (5:19ff.); in

Jesus' works God's activity was seen (4:34); indeed, in Jesus God himself was seen (14:9). Jesus is the one who 'narrates' God on the plane of human existence (1:18). Thus to hate Jesus is to hate God (vv. 23, 24b; *cf.* 5:23b), just as to accept Jesus is to accept his Father (13:20). So tightly is Jesus bound up with his Father, both in his person (1:1, 18; 8:58; 20:28) and in his words and deeds (5:19–30), that every attitude directed toward him is no less directed toward God. This profound Christology, attested not only by the flow of the argument but also by the almost incidental 'my Father' (as opposed to 'the Father'), accounts for the persecution Jesus' followers will face (v. 21). It also means that the people of the world *have no excuse for their sin.* The word rendered *excuse* (*prophasis*) is perhaps a little stronger than 'excuse': they have no 'pretence', no 'pretext' for their sin.[1] Whatever pretence (and it is *only* pretence) the world might have conjured up to justify its evil before the coming of Christ, it has entirely lost now that this sublime revelation from God himself has come. This revelation simultaneously exposes sin and provides its remedy (a theme further developed in 16:8–11); the world that rejects it hates the exposure (3:19–21) and thus denies any need for a remedy.

25. None of the hatred displayed by the world should be thought of as jeopardizing God's redemptive plan. Even this hateful rejection[2] serves *to fulfil what is written in their Law.* Since the ensuing quotation is from the Psalms, the word *Law,* as in 12:34, refers to the antecedent Scriptures, and not just the Pentateuch. Insistence that it is '*their* Law' does not mean Jesus and his disciples fail to recognize its authority; indeed, Jesus repeatedly appeals to those same Scriptures in defence of his claims. The point, rather, is ironical: the Jews' *own Scriptures* condemn their position (*cf.* notes on '*your* Law', 10:34).

The quotation *They hated me without reason* has been drawn from Psalm 35:19 or Psalm 69:4. The latter is more likely, not only because Psalm 69 was widely regarded as messianic but also because it was frequently quarried by New Testament writers for appropriate quotations (*cf.* notes on 2:17). A Davidic typology is presupposed: If David could be hated for no reason, how much more the Messiah who would spring from his loins? Thus the hatred of the world against Jesus is not only unjustified (it is 'without reason'), but those who hate are condemned out of their own Bible (thus building toward mention of *synagogue* persecution, 16:2), even while they unwittingly fulfil their own Scriptures by the course they adopt.

26–27. It is often objected that this third Paraclete saying (*cf.* notes on 14:16–17, 26) so demonstrably breaks up the flow of the context that we

---

[1]As is clear from the other New Testament occurrences of the word: Mk. 12:40 par.; Acts 27:30; Phil. 1:18; 1 Thes. 2:5.

[2]This rendering reads the Greek construction as an ellipse, which is altogether likely, judging by John's style (*cf.* 9:3; 13:18). It is just possible to take this as an imperative: 'But let the word be fulfilled. . . .'

must suppose it was inserted here from some other source. In fact, its home is comfortabiy here. Although 16:1–4 continues the treatment of persecution, the focus shifts from the *cause* of persecution to the *response of Jesus' disciples* to persecution. Before taking that fresh step, there is another point that cries out for clarification. The preceding verses (15:18–25) have repeatedly insisted that hatred toward Jesus' disciples springs from hatred against Jesus himself, and that this in turn has been the world's response to the revelation that he is and brings. But if Jesus is going away – a theme already developed in ch. 14 – how will this confrontation with the world continue? And if it does not continue, how shall hatred from the world still be related to who Jesus is, what he says and what he does? The answer is briefly provided in these two verses: the Holy Spirit joins with the disciples in testifying about Jesus to the world. The world's opposition thus continues to revolve around the question of who Jesus is. The Holy Spirit and the witnessing community are then treated in reverse order in the ensuing verses: 16:1–4 focuses on the community of believers and their reaction to the world, and 16:5–11 summarizes how the Spirit continues the same convicting work that Jesus himself undertook during the days of his flesh.

On *Counsellor* and *the Spirit of truth, cf.* notes on 14:16, 17. Jesus will send the Paraclete from the Father to the disciples; so closely is Jesus tied to the Father that John sees no discrepancy between this way of putting it and other alternatives: Jesus asks the Father to send the Paraclete (14:16), or the Father sends the Paraclete in Jesus' name (14:26). Otherwise put, the Spirit of truth is the one *who goes out from the Father*: the verb (*ekporeuomai*) is somewhat unexpected, but probably means little more than an alternative, *exerchomai*, repeatedly applied to the Son (8:42; 13:3; 16:27, 28, 30; 17:8).

From earlier versions which speak of the Spirit *proceeding* from the Father (*e.g.* AV 'proceedeth from the Father') has come the habit of referring to a prolonged doctrinal debate as the debate over the *procession* of the Spirit. The *procession* of the Spirit was understood in metaphysical terms, *i.e.* this clause was understood to refer to the Spirit's ontological relationship with the Father, not to the mission on which he was sent. The creed of Nicaea and of Constantinople appeals to this clause. The Western version, however, added the words 'and the Son' (Lat. *filioque*): the Holy Spirit 'proceeds from the Father *and the Son*'. Thus the *filioque* phrase in the doctrine of the procession of the Spirit came to be a divisive point in the debates between Eastern and Western branches of Christendom, the former arguing that the addition of 'and the Son' is not only without textual warrant but was adopted by only one branch of the church, the latter arguing that the addition merely makes explicit the teaching of the surrounding context and is in any case needed to preserve the integrity of the doctrine of the Trinity.[1]

---

[1]For a useful summary, *cf.* G. Bray, *TynB* 34, 1983, pp. 91–144.

It would be easy to dismiss the debate as much ado about nothing, since it is almost certain that the words 'who goes out from the Father', set in synonymous parallelism with 'whom I will send to you from the Father', refer not to some ontological 'procession' but to the mission of the Spirit. But if the theological debate is divorced from the meaning of this one clause and allowed to stand on its own, then it becomes clear that tremendous issues are at stake after all, but were mistakenly connected with the interpretation of this clause. To speak of God 'sending' the Son, and of the Son 'going out' from the Father, in a context where the Son is nothing other than the pre-incarnate Word (1:1ff.), who is both with God and who is God (1:1), and who himself becomes flesh (1:14), and can still be addressed as God (20:28), raises extraordinarily complex ontological questions about the being of God. Some of these are addressed by the Evangelist himself (*cf.* notes on 5:16–30). Even if the 'sending' and 'going out' of the Son refer to his mission, this is not the mission of yet another merely human prophet, but of him who though one with the Father donned our flesh. With this strong Christology coursing through his work, the Evangelist who tells us that the Paraclete, the Holy Spirit, comes in certain respects as a *replacement* of the Son, and is sent by the Son, or at his request and by the Father, cannot be thought to be speaking without reflection. It is no accident that in 15:26, when Jesus goes on to say *'he will* testify about me', John uses the masculine pronoun *ekeinos*, even though it breaks concord with the (formally) neuter status of the preceding relative pronoun: *i.e.* 'the Spirit is thought of in personal terms' (Barrett, p. 482). Thus although the clause 'who goes out from the Father' refers to the mission of the Spirit, in analogy with the mission of the Son, this is the mission of the Spirit who in certain respects replaces the Son, is sent by the Father and the Son, and belongs (so far as we can meaningfully use such ambiguous terminology) to the Godhead every bit as much as the Son. In short, the elements of a full-blown doctrine of the Trinity crop up repeatedly in the Fourth Gospel; and the early creedal statement, complete with the *filioque* phrase, is eminently defensible, once we allow that this clause in 15:26 does not itself specify a certain ontological status, but joins with the matrix of Johannine Christology and pneumatology to presuppose it.

In the context of 15:18 – 16:4a, Jesus says the Spirit *will testify about me.* The verb is in the future tense, while the next 'testify' verb, of which the disciples ('you') are the subject, is either present indicative or imperative. The change prompts the reader to think that the imperative is meant; hence NIV's *you also must testify.* The reason is that they have been with Jesus *from the beginning*: here, in 16:4 and possibly in 6:64 and 8:25 the word *archē* ('beginning') has reference to the beginning of Jesus' ministry (though *cf.* also 2:11), rather than to the beginning of creation (1:1, 2; 8:44). This specific reference to Jesus' earthly ministry shows that the disciples primarily in view are the first eyewitnesses; only derivatively (though certainly derivatively) can this be applied to later Christians.

This is one of the small touches that locate the setting in the closing

529

hours of the ministry of Jesus. By the end of the first century, it could not be said of many that they had been with Jesus 'from the beginning'. Doubtless the first witnesses set something of a model for later ones. Even so, to cast the discourse this way means John is not simply telling his readers what to do and how to live, blithely ignoring anachronisms. Rather, his help for his readers is indirect, by explaining in some detail *what happened back there* – even if the details he selects are of particular relevance to his readers. This sort of passage, of course, is as relevant to prospective new converts as to mature Christians who are waning in their zeal or flagging under opposition. It sets out the historic basis on which Christianity is to be believed, and the kind of life and witness expected of all Christians. When the church is facing persecution, it is especially important for prospective converts to have some idea what conversion will let them in for.

Although the Spirit may bear witness to the world apart from Christians, it would be out of step with these chapters to think that Christians are thought of as those who bear witness apart from the Spirit. Whether we think of the Spirit's help in the crisis of acute persecution (Mk. 13:11) or in the context of sustained, faithful witness (Acts 5:32), the community's witness is to be empowered by the Paraclete himself. This witness must always be about Jesus: it brings before the world the truth of the revelation of God in Jesus Christ, in his word, his works, his death and resurrection, with all its potential for both blessing and judgment. As this witness proceeds, it will force a division in the world (v. 20) that is an extension of Jesus' own divisive ministry (3:19–21; 12:44–50) – a point Paul well understood (2 Cor. 2:14–17). Such a vision entails the expectation of opposition, and therefore the remaining verses in this section (16:1–4a) prepare the believers to face it.

16:1. The greatest danger the disciples will confront from the opposition of the world is not death but apostasy. The reason Jesus has said *All this* (*i.e.* 15:18–27) is *so that you will not go astray* (*skandalisthēte*; *cf.* note on this verb in 6:61; *cf.* Mk. 14:27–31). The danger was real when John wrote these words, though elsewhere he develops a theology to account for defection while maintaining the security of the believer (1 Jn. 2:19).

2. The nature of the most pressing threat is spelled out: vehement expulsion from the synagogue (on the complex historical questions, *cf.* notes on 9:22; 12:42–43). Certainly there are other reports of Jesus foreseeing the persecution his followers would face (Mt. 5:10–12; Lk. 6:22). The words *a time is coming* (lit. 'an hour is coming', *erchetai hōra*; *cf.* notes on 4:21, 23) refer to a time future to that of Jesus' ministry; but the 'hour' language (*cf.* notes on 2:4; 7:30; 8:20–21; 12:23, 27) suggests that this time is bound up with the death, resurrection and exaltation of Jesus. That is, after all, the crucial turning point after which the animus of the world will begin to be redirected from Jesus (in the flesh) to Jesus' disciples. The onset of the kingdom is also the onset of persecution for those who live under its rule.

There should be little doubt that the first virulent opposition Christians faced came from the Jews, precisely because the church sprang out of Judaism and all of its earliest members were Jews. It is not surprising that Paul five times received the thirty-nine lashes (2 Cor. 11:24) – a distinctive punishment meted out by synagogue authorities – or that Acts reports many forms of opposition stimulated by the opposition of Jewish authorities (e.g. ch. 7). That Christendom has heinously repaid the compliment must not blind us to the evidence of the first century, when Christianity was still relatively weak and some branches of Judaism were feeling highly threatened. There is certainly evidence that some rabbinic authorities held that slaying heretics could be an act of divine worship (e.g. Numbers Rabbah 21.3 (191a) [with reference to Nu. 25:13];[1] Mishnah Sanhedrin 9:6).

Even so, three historical and theological notes are needed to put this verse in perspective.

(1) As serious as the charge is, the Evangelist, not to say Jesus himself, can be credited with assigning honest, religious motives to the persecutors. That does not make what they did right, or the suffering they inflicted less painful; it does avoid the vengeful denunciation of another's motives. John is content to record that these people thought they were offering a service to God. Certainly that is how Paul analysed his own pre-Christian commitment to persecute the church.

(2) On the other hand, such religious motives do not ameliorate the problem, but make it worse. Whether in the first century or in the twentieth, Christians have often discovered that the most dangerous oppression comes not from careless pagans but from zealous adherents to religious faith, and from other ideologues. A sermon was preached when Cranmer was burned at the stake. Christians have faced severe persecution performed in the name of Yahweh, in the name of Allah, in the name of Marx – and in the name of Jesus.

(3) In any case, John treats the persecution with intense irony. These religious persecutors think they are offering a service (latreia, 'worship', 'spiritual service') to God. They are profoundly deluded – yet at the same time the death of Christians by persecution truly is an offering to God. Cf. the irony of 11:49–52, where the opposition spoke better than it knew.

---

[1] Nu. 25:13 reads: 'He [Phinehas, who turned aside God's wrath by slaying an idolator] and his descendants will have a covenant of a lasting priesthood, because he was zealous for the honour of his God and made atonement for the Israelites.' The Midrash Rabbah comments: 'But did he offer a sacrifice, to justify the expression ATONEMENT in this connection? No, but it serves to teach you that if a man sheds the blood of the wicked it is as though he had offered an offering.' It is not easy to determine how widespread this interpretation was; but in any case it was rare for exegetical judgments of this sort to be turned into public policy. What evidence there is for early Jewish persecution of Christians suggests it was spontaneous and undisciplined (though perhaps nurtured by such exegesis), while wiser, cooler heads, like that of Gamaliel (Acts 5:33–40), counselled patience.

3. The reason for such opposition is that the oppressors *have not known* (*ouk egnōsan*, possibly 'have not come to know', with Bruce, p. 317) either the Father or the Son (*cf.* Rev. 2:9; 3:9). To know the Son truly as the revelation of God is to know God (14:7), and to have such knowledge is to have eternal life (17:3). Not to know God is to spawn hostility toward those who do (15:18–21).

4a As in v. 1, the reason why Jesus is so explicit on these matters is so that when persecution does break out the disciples will not be taken by surprise and thus be tempted toward apostasy. Rather, they will remember what Jesus said, and their faith will be strengthened because they will be assured that what is happening to them is not outside either his knowledge or his control (*cf.* 13:19; 14:29).

Instead of *when the time comes*, the best reading is *when their hour comes* (*cf.* Lk. 22:53). In this context, *their hour* refers not only to the death of Jesus, but to the outbreak of persecution against his followers that will ensue. It is *their* hour because it will appear that the oppressors have the upper hand; from the perspective of faith, it is *their* hour only in the most ephemeral way, and ultimately the oppressors are working their own defeat. Indeed, because *hour* is so regularly tied up with Jesus' appointment with his death/exaltation (*cf.* notes on 2:4), it is hard not to see that the Evangelist has introduced another irony: what appears to be *their* hour has been introduced by *Jesus'* hour, but in his case, he seems to be suffering defeat in the very moment when he is winning the greatest of all victories, while at their hour they seem to be winning when they are suffering the greatest of all defeats.

3. The work of the Holy Spirit (16:4b–15)

4b. Jesus has not earlier spelled out the full dangers of persecution because he was still with them, and could largely protect them by absorbing all opposition himself, thus deflecting it from them. Indeed, his arrest proves to be the last time he serves them in this way (18:8, 9). At the same time, the words *because I was with you* bring up again Jesus' imminent departure (a dominant theme in ch. 14), and thus prepare the way for what follows.

5. The formal contradiction between this verse and 13:36; 14:5 is so flagrant that a large array of solutions has been proposed. Some (*e.g.* Bernard, 1. xx; Bultmann, pp. 459–461) have appealed to this contradiction in support of their respective theories of major dislocations in the text. Most scholars today concede that these theories introduce as many difficulties as they resolve (*cf.* notes introducing 13:31ff.). Others (*e.g.* Brown, 2. 710; Schnackenburg, 3. 126; Beasley-Murray, p. 279) assign the contradiction to an editor who had such reverence for his source material that he did not smooth out the difficulty, even if he noticed it. That means, of course, that the difficulty is a real one, and belongs to irreconcilable sources. The theory is not very believable: we are asked to hold that John held his sources in such high esteem he would not iron out a problem, when all the linguistic evidence argues that whatever sources John had he so handled them that the final text is stamped with a single unitary style (*cf.* Introduction, § III; for a detailed example, *cf.* notes on 20:1ff.).

Others deny there is any contradiction by appealing to one of several details in the text. Lagrange (pp. 417–418) puts the emphasis on the *Now*: the disciples have heard and understood Jesus' comments about his destination, so naturally, *now* no-one asks him where he is going. Even so, their sadness remains. This explanation would be more convincing if *now* clearly modified the verb *asks*, instead of *I am going*, as it appears to. Barrett (p. 485) emphasizes the present tense: Jesus is not saying that none of the disciples have ever asked this question, but that none of them *is asking* it *now*, when they really need to. Dodd (*IFG*, pp. 411–413, n. 1) insists that the disciples actually know where Jesus is going, and that Jesus is simply rebuking them for their unreasonable sadness – though on the face of it that is not what the text says.

It is hard to be certain what approach is best. One suspects that part of the problem lies in a fairly mechanical approach to the text, an approach that is sometimes insensitive to literary nuances. In the flow of the argument both in 13:36 and in 14:5, it is not clear that either Peter or Thomas was really asking the question formally represented by their words. A little boy, disappointed that his father is suddenly called away for an emergency meeting when both the boy and his Dad had expected to go fishing together, says, 'Aw, Dad, where are you going?', but cares nothing at all to learn the destination. The question is a protest; the unspoken question is 'Why are you leaving me?' The disciples have been asking several questions of that sort; they have not *really* asked thoughtful questions about where Jesus is going and what it means for them. They have been too self-absorbed in their own loss. Moreover the drift of all four Gospels assures us that none of the inner ring of disciples entertained the idea, before the cross, that the Messiah would simultaneously be conquering king, suffering, dying servant and resurrected Lord. So how much of Jesus' talk about his departure to the Father did they understand at this point?

6–7. What is undeniable is that the disciples are filled with deep grief over their impending loss: the word for *grief* (*lypē*) recurs in vv. 20, 21, 22. What they need to hold on to (for the strong asseverative *I tell you the truth*, *cf.* notes on 1:51) is this: *It is for your good* (same expression as in 11:50; 18:14) *that I am going away.* The reason for this judgment is then made clear: unless Jesus departs, the 'Counsellor', the Paraclete (*cf.* notes on 14:16) will not come to them; but if Jesus goes, he will send (*cf.* notes on 14:16, 26; 15:26) him to them. The thought is not that Jesus and the Holy Spirit cannot, for unarticulated metaphysical reasons, simultaneously minister to God's people, or any other such strange notion. Rather, the thought is eschatological. The many biblical promises that the Spirit will characterize the age of the kingdom of God (*e.g.* Is. 11:1–10; 32:14–18; 42:1–4; 44:1–5; Ezk. 11:17–20; 36:24–27; 37:1–14; Joel 2:28–32; *cf.* notes on Jn. 3:5; 7:37–39) breed anticipation. But this saving reign of God cannot be fully inaugurated until Jesus has died, risen from the dead, and been exalted to this Father's right hand, returned to the glory he enjoyed with the Father before the world began.

Jesus' valuation of what is for his disciples' 'good', indeed, for our good, ought to temper longings of the 'Oh-if-only-I-could-have-been-in-Galilee-when-Jesus-was-there!' sort. That same Jesus insists it is better to be alive now, after the coming of the Spirit. Before the triumphant in-breaking of God's saving reign, before the inauguration of the new covenant, millions ignored the claims of the true God. Pentecost transformed that limitation, and millions have been brought to happy submission to the Lord Jesus Christ and to growing obedience by the power of the Spirit whom he bequeathed. That is why the final two Paraclete utterances (vv. 8–11 and 12:15) are introduced at this point.

8–11. The Greek of these four verses is so compressed that it is difficult to decide exactly what is meant. On any reading vv. 9–11 constitute an expansion or explanation of the rather cryptic utterance of v. 8. This verse tells us that when the Paraclete (promised in v. 7) comes, *'he will convict* the world *of guilt in regard to'* (*elenxei peri*) several things. Disagreements regarding the interpretation of vv. 8–11 begin with disputes over the meaning of this verb. Some have argued that the basic meaning of *elenchō* in classical Greek is 'to expose', though this component of its meaning receives little emphasis in LSJ (p. 531). The focus rather in classical Greek is on putting to shame, treating with contempt, cross-examining, accusing, bringing to the test, proving, refuting. In the Greek most relevant to the period of the writing of the Fourth Gospel, the verb has a somewhat similar focus.

Commentators most commonly propose to render the verb in this passage by 'to expose', 'to convince', or 'to convict'. Although any of these might in theory be acceptable, part of the difficulty in securing a credible interpretation rests on the ambiguities of the *English* words. 'To expose' has no *necessarily* negative overtones (*e.g.* 'to expose one's body to the rays of the sun'), but it can be used in contexts where the exposure engenders profound shame. 'To convince' someone can sound like a merely intellectual exercise, and this seems a bit anaemic if there ought to be a personal, shamed recognition of personal guilt. 'To convict' could be understood in a purely judicial sense of bringing down a negative verdict, regardless of whether or not the convicted party admits any guilt; alternatively, it is used in religious contexts to mean something like 'to bring someone to an acknowledgment of personal guilt'.

The verb occurs eighteen times in the New Testament (*cf.* Mt. 18:15; Lk. 3:19; Jn. 3:20; 8:46; 1 Cor. 14:24; Eph. 5:11, 13; 1 Tim. 5:20; 2 Tim. 4:2; Tit. 1:9, 13; 2:15; Heb. 12:5; Jas. 2:9; Jude 15, 22; Rev. 3:19). Arguably, in every instance the verb has to do with showing someone his sin, usually as a summons to repentance (so, rightly, F. Büchsel, *TDNT* 2. 473–474). The two passages where the verb has most commonly been taken to mean 'to expose' (in a neutral sense) are John 3:20 and Ephesians 5:13. In the former, Schnackenburg (1. 406–407, n. 160) seeks to prove the point by arguing that 'his deeds *will be exposed*' (v. 20) is parallel to 'it *may be seen plainly*' (v. 21) – a parallelism with more potential merit in Greek than in English. Even so, close scrutiny of the parallelism, in Greek, shows that '*lest* his deeds *will be exposed*' (*mē elenchthē*) is antithetically parallel to the longer expression, 'his deeds *may be plainly seen* . . . that *they are wrought in God*' (*phanerōthē* . . . *hoti en theō estin eirgasmena*). The 'exposure,' then, is the exposure of one who does evil and who hates the light; it brings the shame that makes the evil person shrink from the light. Similarly, although Ephesians 5:13 ('But everything *exposed* by the light becomes visible') might at first glance be thought to offer a neutral instance of the verb, the larger context precludes such optimism, as the occurrence of the verb two verses earlier makes clear: 'Have nothing to do with the fruitless deeds of darkness, but rather *expose* them' (Eph. 5:11).

As for the longer prepositional expression *elenchō peri* ('to convict of [or "about"]'), in addition to its occurrence in John 16, it is found three times in the New Testament. Of these, the preposition is twice followed by some evil (Jn. 8:46; Jude 15), and once by the name of a person who occasioned the evil (Lk. 3:19).

With these constraints in mind, we may briefly outline some of the most important suggested interpretations of this passage:[1]

(1) Many take v. 8 to mean that the Spirit *will prove* the world *wrong about* sin, righteousness and judgment; the three *hoti* clauses in vv. 9–11 (NIV 'because') are then taken as instances of the '*hoti* explicative' – *i.e.* each of these clauses must begin with 'in that', and gives the substance of what is wrong with the world's thinking in each of the three areas. This sounds far too cerebral: the world merely holds wrong opinions which must be righted by argument. The one other place in the Fourth Gospel where the verb *elenchō* is linked to *peri* cannot be taken to support such a weak notion: Jesus' question in 8:46 certainly does not mean, 'Which of you can prove I have the wrong idea about sin?'

(2) Others agree that the three *hoti* clauses in vv. 9–11 are explicative and must be rendered by 'in that', but they take the verb to mean 'to convict'. This is often tied to the view that the *paraklētos* (*cf.* notes on 14:16) is fundamentally a legal figure – usually some sort of counsel for the defence, but here a prosecuting attorney. The entire scene is then understood to be modelled on the courtroom. But consistency demands that if this be 'conviction' in a judicial sense, the Paraclete as prosecuting attorney is not convincing *the world* of its guilt, but is proving to *the judge* that the world is guilty. That reading cannot be justified by New Testament usage of the verb; nor is there any judge in the context. Most of those who adopt this stance unwittingly slide over to the other sense of 'convict' in their exposition: the Paraclete is bringing about a sense of

---

[1]For detailed discussion, bibliography and defence of the position adopted here, *cf.* D. A. Carson, *JBL* 98, 1979, pp. 547–566.

guilt in the world. That accords well with the meaning of the verb. However, when the verb bears this sense, the preposition *peri* is normally followed by the sin which is being held up to elicit the sense of shame and guilt, or by the sinner who performs the evil. To return to 8:46, the question is 'Can any of you convict me *of* sin?', not 'in regard to' sin. Without question that is the way the first of the three elements 'sin and righteousness and judgment' would be taken, if it were not for the presence of the other two: *i.e.* we would happily read 'he will convict the world *of* sin'.[1] This could only be taken to mean 'he will convict the world of *its* [*i.e.*the world's] sin', not 'he will convict the world *in regard to sin*'. But then what shall we do with 'righteousness' and 'judgment'? By understanding *peri* to mean 'in regard to', it is possible to suppose that the references are to *the world*'s sin, *Christ*'s righteousness and *God*'s judgment – but that is simply not the natural way of understanding *peri* after the verb *elenchō*.

(3) Several scholars have modified the first interpretation. They take the verb to mean 'to prove [the world] wrong about', but they argue that this proof is directed neither to an independent judge, nor to the world itself, but to the disciples. The *hoti* clauses are then variously taken as explicative or causal. But this is certainly not the most obvious meaning of the verb: the most enthusiastic supporter of this position[2] can adduce only four instances of this meaning, one in Plato, two in pre-Christian papyri, one in a later church Father, with no examples from the New Testament or the LXX. The alleged structural reasons for supporting this view prove unsubstantial.

(4) Lindars (pp. 500–504), developing some suggestions advanced by others, proposes that John means the Paraclete will expose the world for a verdict of guilty (taking *hamartia* to refer to guilt, not sin), a verdict of innocence (Gk. *dikaiosynē*, normally rendered 'righteousness'), a verdict one way or the other (Gk. *krisis*, 'judgment'). This rendering of *elenchō peri*, however, entails no conclusion about the guilt of the world (Gk. *kosmos*). But the one certainty in every instance of the verb in the New Testament, and in the overwhelming majority of occurrences elsewhere, is the guilt of the party being 'convicted'. That is doubly the case here: in John the 'world' as a theological construct is invariably guilty (*cf.* notes on 1:9).

(5) These weaknesses and complexities have driven the present writer to consider another proposal, defended at length in the article to which reference has already been made. In common with other New Testament usages, *elenchō* means 'to convict [the world]' in the personal sense, *i.e.* not arguing the case for the world's objective guilt before God

---

[1]NIV's 'of guilt in regard to sin' is redundant and periphrastic: redundant in that 'to convict' does not need the addition of the words 'of guilt', since they are already presupposed; periphrastic in that the translators are merely setting up the sentence to make 'in regard to' acceptable.
[2]*Viz.* de la Potterie, 2. 399–421.

at the final Great Assize, but shaming the world and convincing it of its own guilt, thus calling it to repentance. The preposition *peri* then introduces what the world is guilty of: its sin, its righteousness and its judgment. The *hoti* clauses in vv. 9–11 are causal, each clause providing a reason why the Paraclete is engaged in this convicting work.

The meaning, then, is as follows. Just as Jesus forced a division in the world (15:20) by showing that what it does is evil (7:7; 15:22), so the Paraclete continues this work. Indeed, he most commonly does so through the witness of disciples (15:26, 27); he always does so in connection with the truth of the gospel of Jesus Christ, since his whole purpose is to bring glory to him (16:14).[1] By his 'departure', his death/exaltation, Jesus fulfils the conditions that must be met before he can send the Paraclete; and the gift of the Paraclete is so great that Jesus' 'departure' must be seen as for the disciples' good (vv. 6, 7). When the Paraclete comes, he extends the ministry of Jesus in ways the disciples could not have foreseen. In particular, he convicts the world of its sin, its righteousness, and its judgment.

He convicts the world of its sin *because* (*hoti*) the people who constitute the world do not believe in Jesus (v. 9). If they did believe in Jesus, they would believe his statements about their guilt and turn to him. As it is, their unbelief brings not only condemnation (3:18, 36) but wilful ignorance of their need. The world's unbelief not only ensures that it will not receive life, it ensures that it cannot perceive that it walks in death and *needs* life. The Holy Spirit presses home the world's sin *despite* the world's unbelief; he convicts the world of sin *because* they do not believe in Jesus. This convicting work of the Paraclete is therefore gracious: it is designed to bring men and women of the world to recognize their need, and so turn to Jesus, and thus stop being 'the world'.

He convicts the world of its righteousness *because* (*hoti*) Jesus is going to the Father (v. 10). It might be objected that it is passing strange to speak of convicting the world of *righteousness* at all. Nevertheless the syntactical parallel with 'sin' is plain enough, and this is the most straightforward way of taking *elenchō peri* (discussed above). This is in fact the only place in the Fourth Gospel where *dikaiosynē* (righteousness') occurs, and the context must determine its exact force. Certainly John can on occasion treat one of his favourite words negatively: although 'to believe' is normally a good thing, it can be quite spurious (2:23–25; 8:31ff.). John loves to quote or allude to Isaiah, and Isaiah 64:5 (LXX) establishes that all the *dikaiosynē* ('righteousness') of the people of Isaiah's day was as a menstruous cloth. Within the Fourth Gospel, this reading of 'righteousness' is eminently appropriate. For instance, the temple, the focus of Jewish worship and righteousness, must be

---

[1]Strangely, Beasley–Murray (p. 281) rejects the interpretation advanced here on the ground that it denies this point. In fact, I insist on it.

cleansed, and is in any case eclipsed by Jesus' body (2:13–23). The Sabbath regulations of the Pharisees are carefully observed, while Jesus is condemned for healing a paralytic of thirty-eight years (5:16). There is plenty of religious 'righteousness' (even where the word is not used): the leaders possess the law of Moses. Yet sadly they attempt to kill Jesus (7:19). Some Pharisees who did come to believe refused to profess their faith because they feared that they would be excommunicated from the synagogue (12:42–43). Is it not therefore thematically appropriate that the Paraclete should convict the world of its *righteousness*? Certainly there are other places in the New Testament where the *dikaiosynē* of the world is shown to be hopelessly inadequate (*e.g.* Mt. 5:20; Rom. 10:3; Phil. 3:6–9; Tit. 3:5).

The reason *why* the Paraclete convicts the world of its righteousness is *because* Jesus is going to the Father. As we have observed, one of Jesus' most startling roles with respect to the world was to show up the emptiness of its pretensions, to expose by his light the darkness of the world for what it is (3:19–21; 7:7; 15:22, 24). But now Jesus is going; how will that convicting work be continued? It is continued by the Paraclete, who drives home this conviction in the world precisely *because* Jesus is no longer present to discharge this task. Undoubtedly this kind of conviction is driven home to the world primarily through Jesus' followers who, empowered by the Holy Spirit, live their lives in such growing conformity to Christ that the same impact on the world is observed as when Jesus himself lived out his life before the world. Thus when Christians obey the 'new commandment', 'all men' learn that they are Jesus' disciples (13:35; *cf.* 1 Jn. 4:12). That this work of the Spirit is accomplished through the disciples is probably the reason for the shift to the second person in v. 10: 'because I am going to the Father, where *you* can see me no longer', rather than the expected *they*. The point is that Jesus was the paradigm, the model of behaviour, the 'master' who was to be followed. Now the Paraclete so empowers them, taking 'from what is mine and [making] it known to you' (v. 15), that they continue to follow Jesus and thus convict the world of its empty righteousness.

Finally, the Paraclete convicts the world of its judgment, *because* (*hoti*) *the prince of this world* [*cf.* notes on 12:31] *now stands condemned* (v. 11). The judgment of which the Spirit convicts the world is its multifaceted spiritual blindness, supremely displayed in its treatment of Jesus. Earlier Jesus had exhorted the 'world', 'Stop judging by mere appearances, and make a right judgment' (7:24). Jesus' judgment is righteous (*dikaia*, 5:30) and true (8:16). The world's judgment is profoundly wrong and morally perverse. And now, the Paraclete convicts the world of its false judgment, because in the impending triumph of Christ the prince of this world stands condemned. All false judgment is related to him who was a liar from the beginning, whose children we are if we echo his values (8:42–47). If *he* stands condemned by the triumph of the cross, the false judgment of those who follow in his train is doubly exposed. The need for conviction of this false judgment is all the more urgent; the world is condemned already (3:36) and in desperate need to learn of its plight.

12. This fifth and final Paraclete passage (vv. 12–15) is a suitable climax to the series, since it focuses on the completion of the revelation of Jesus Christ. That, however, is the very point at which some commentators stumble: they find this verse, which looks to revelation the disciples are not at this time able to bear, in flat contradiction with the second Paraclete passage (14:26), where the Spirit's work centres on enabling the disciples to remember what Jesus has *already* taught them (*e.g.* Becker, 2. 498). This rigid dichotomy is unwarranted. Both passages are more qualified. In 14:26, the Paraclete's task will not only be to 'remind you of everything I have said to you', but it is also to 'teach you all things'. Conversely, in 16:12–15 the Paraclete is the one who says more than Jesus can say at the time, more than the disciples can bear during the days of Jesus' ministry; yet this 'more than you can now bear' is constrained by a crucial preposition in v. 13 (*cf.* notes below) and is never more than taking what belongs to Jesus and making it known to the disciples (v. 14).

We are to understand that Jesus is the nodal point of revelation, God's culminating self-disclosure, God's final self-expression, God's 'Word' (1:1, 14). All antecedent revelation has pointed toward him, and reaches its climax in him. That does not mean he himself provides all the details his followers will need; it does mean that 'extra' bits the Holy Spirit provides after he is sent by Christ Jesus, consequent upon Jesus' death/exaltation, are nothing more than the filling out of the revelation nodally present in Jesus himself. The same thought is presented in different form in Hebrews 1:1–4: in times past God spoke through the prophets at many times and in various ways, 'but in these days he has spoken to us *by his Son*' (*en huiō*; the anarthrous construction focuses on the climactic *quality* of this revelation). When the Epistle to the Hebrews was written, the author certainly knew of the gift of the Spirit and of the writing of at least some of the New Testament books, but he sees such steps as no more than the unpacking of the Son-revelation. Similarly here: John 14:26 and 16:12–15 are mutually complementary. Because of this theme of the finality of the revelation of God in Jesus Christ, the church has always been rightly suspicious of claims of still further definitive revelation that is binding on the consciences of all Christians – whether in the claims, say, of Mormonism, or in the pretensions of the Rev. Moon – and rightly deems such stances as profoundly aberrant and cultic. *Cf.* further on v. 15.

13. For *Spirit of truth, cf.* notes on 14:16. The Paraclete *will guide you in* (Gk. *en* is the best reading; *eis*, 'into', as in NIV, is secondary: *cf.* Metzger, p. 247) all truth. If there is a distinction between '*in* all truth' and '*into* all truth', it is that the latter hints at truth the disciples have not yet in any sense penetrated, while '*in* all truth' suggests an exploration of truth already principially disclosed.[1] Jesus himself is the truth (14:6); now the

---

[1] If a distinction is to be maintained between the two prepositions, the one suggested

Spirit of truth leads the disciples into all the implications of the truth, the revelation, intrinsically bound up with Jesus Christ. There is no other locus of truth; this is *all truth*. The notion of 'guidance' (the Gk. verb is *hodēgeō*) in all truth has nothing to do with privileged information pertaining to one's choice of vocation or mate, but with understanding God as he has revealed himself, and with obeying that revelation – as the occurrence of this verb in the Psalms makes clear (*e.g.* Pss. 25:4–5 [LXX 24:4–5]; 143:10 [142:10]).

Just as Jesus never spoke or acted on his own initiative, but said and did exactly what the Father gave him to say and do (3:34–35; 5:19–20; 7:16–18; 8:26–29, 42–43; 12:47–50; 14:10), so also the Spirit *speaks only what he hears* – a point elucidated in vv. 14–15. As Jesus' absolute but exhaustive obedience to his Father ensures that he is not to be taken as either a mere mortal or as a competing deity, but as the very revelation of God himself (*cf.* notes on 5:19–30), so also the Spirit, by this utter dependence, ensures the unity of God and of the revelation God graciously grants.

The Spirit tells the disciples *what is yet to come*. This has often been understood to refer to revelation about the later stages of the kingdom, perhaps in apocalyptic form and exemplified in the book of Revelation (so Schlatter, p. 314; Bernard, 2. 511; Johnston, pp. 38–39). But there is nothing in the context that demands an essentially futurist eschatology, and the theme, though present in John, is scarcely central. By contrast, Thüsing (pp.149–153) argues that this refers to what is immediately future to the upper room setting, *i.e.* to Jesus' death, resurrection and exaltation. That is just barely possible, but if so the language and the timing are exceedingly strange. After all, the Paraclete cannot come until *after* Jesus' death/exaltation, so by the time he tells the disciples about it he would be announcing an event already behind them.

On the other hand, it makes sense to suppose that the Holy Spirit is unpacking some of that event's significance. The verb used here and repeated in vv. 14, 15 (*anangellō*, NIV 'tell' in v. 13, and 'make known' in vv. 14, 15) suggests an announcement, indeed in this context a revelatory declaration (as its use in 4:25 suggests), but it is a *reiterative* announcement (Brown, 2. 708). These features square best with the view that *what is yet to come* refers to all that transpires *in consequence* of the pivotal revelation bound up with Jesus' person, ministry, death, resurrection and exaltation. This includes the Paraclete's own witness to Jesus, his ministry to the world (16:8–11) primarily through the church (15:26, 27), the pattern of life and obedience under the inbreaking kingdom, up to and including the consummation.[1] All of this the Spirit

---

above seems much more likely than the alternative suggestion, that *eis* ('into') is original and here means 'into the very heart of the truth' – an instance of a rather periphrastic reading.

[1]F. Porsch, *Pneuma und Wort. Ein exegetischer Beitrag zur Pneumatologie des Johannesevangeliums* (Knecht, 1974), p. 298, especially emphasizes the eschatological dimensions of *what*

of truth 'announces', yet in making it known he is doing little more than fleshing out the implications of God's triumphant self-disclosure in the person and work of his Son.

14–15. Just as the Son by his ministry on earth brought glory to his Father (7:18; 17:4), so the Paraclete by his ministry brings glory to Jesus: that is his central aim. His means is the unfolding of Jesus' person and work: *i.e. taking from what is mine and making it known to you* does not simply mean that the Paraclete passes on what Jesus declares, but that all the revelation bound up in Jesus' person and mission are pressed home on the disciples. Of course, all that Jesus said and did is nothing more and nothing else than what the Father gave him to say and do. That finally includes all that the Father does, 'because whatever the Father does the Son also does. For the Father loves the Son and shows him all he does' (5:19, 20). Therefore if the Spirit takes *what is mine* and makes it known to the disciples, the content of *what is mine* is nothing less than the revelation of the Father himself, for Jesus declares, *All that belongs to the Father is mine* (v. 15). *That is why* Jesus has cast the Spirit's ministry in terms of the unfolding of what belongs to the Son: this is not a slighting of God, or undue elevation of the Son, since what belongs to the Father belongs to the Son. It is therefore entirely appropriate that the Spirit's ministry be designed to bring glory to the Son (v. 14). The Father himself has declared that all should honour the Son even as they honour the Father (5:23). And the Son, for his part, is no less concerned to bring glory to his Father (14:13; 17:1, 4).

It is important to recognize that the disciples who will directly benefit from these ministrations of the Spirit are *primarily* the apostles (*cf.* Additional Note). In two of the other Paraclete passages, explicit reference is made to *reminding* the disciples of what Jesus said during the days of his flesh (14:26) or to the fact that they had been *with Jesus* from the beginning of his ministry (15:27). Both references rule out later disciples. Here, too, the primary focus of the Spirit's ministry is doubtless on those who could not, when Jesus spoke, bear more than he was giving them (v. 12), but who would need to be guided in all the truth of the revelation of God in Christ Jesus that they had been privileged to witness. At least part of the consequence of that unfolding is this Gospel of John.

Derivatively, we may speak of the Spirit's continued work in the disciples of Jesus today. But that is not the primary emphasis of these verses; and in any case it is impossible to think of such continuing ministry of the Spirit leading men and women to stances *outside* the enriching and explanatory ministry he exercised amongst the first witnesses, which is crystallized in this book. That the emphasis is so transparently on the first witnesses, on how they came to what we

---

is yet to come, but understands them to be transmuted into realized eschatology, common to the Fourth Gospel. This is surely right, so long as a future consummation is not ruled out; *cf.* notes on 5:28–29; 6:39, 40; 14:1–3.

would call a fully Christian understanding of all that Jesus is and did, drives our attention *to Jesus himself*, and away from subsidiary themes like discipleship, the continuing work of the Spirit and the like: This almost self-evident fact greatly supports the view that John's Gospel is primarily evangelistic in its intent.

Additional note

12–15. The question of the possibility of continued 'revelation' amongst Jesus' disciples after the eyewitnesses have passed from the scene is not here directly addressed. Reflections on this question are better based on such data as the range of meanings that reside in the 'revelation' word group (*e.g.* note the use of *apokalyptō*, NIV 'make clear', in Phil. 3:15, in a context that most later theologians would prefer to assign to 'illumination' rather than to 'revelation'), or in the 'prophecy' word group: *cf.* D. A. Carson, *Showing the Spirit* (Paternoster, 1987), esp. pp. 91–100, 119–135. Burge (pp. 211–217) rather forces John to address such questions by describing the Paraclete's role in 14:26 as 'anamnesis' (essentially 'remembering') and in 16:12–15 as revelatory, and associating the former with 'tradition' and the latter with fresh revelation that is mediated through the Spirit from the risen Christ, and which is always controlled by the Spirit. But the categories are somewhat skewed, precisely because they are generated by the desire to answer modern questions of little direct interest to the Evangelist. That is also the reason why the specific references *to the first eyewitnesses* (especially 14:26; 15:27; 16:12) are skirted in Burge's treatment. In consequence the unique elements in the ministry of the first disciples, unique because under God these disciples alone mediate the transition in salvation-historical developments, are largely ignored in favour of finding immediate significance in each statement for the church at large. Such emphases reflect the contemporary scholarly mood, which tends to quarry the Gospels, including John, for lessons in ecclesiology and discipleship, largely ignoring the unique elements in the Gospel presentations that make them cry out to be read with other foci paramount: above all Christ and the dawning of the promised eschatological era, consequent upon his death and resurrection.

4. The prospect of joy beyond the trouble of this world
(16:16–33)

16. This verse is transitional. By referring to Jesus' departure, it simultaneously closes off the topic introduced in vv. 4b–6, and sets the stage for the confusion of the disciples in vv. 17–18, which leads on to Jesus' explicit treatment of his departure, as opposed to his treatment of the work of the Paraclete who comes in consequence of Jesus' departure.

But which departure and return are in view? Does the first 'little while' mark the time until Jesus' death, or until his ascension? Does the 'you will see me' after the second 'little while' refer to Jesus' resurrection, the descent of the Spirit (*cf.* 14:23), or the parousia (14:1–4)? Or should we join the many modern commentators who think John is cleverly deploying his language to include double or treble references?

Despite the popularity of this latter view, the notes on the following verses argue that each bit of evidence makes most sense if this verse refers to Jesus' departure in death and his return after his resurrection. The 'little while' after which the disciples will see Jesus no more has already been intimated both to the Jews (7:33) and to the disciples (13:33). Jesus will die. But then 'after a little while' his disciples will again see him: Jesus will rise from the dead. Some manuscripts add 'because I am going to the Father' to the end of the verse, probably to facilitate the transition to the second question in v. 17.

17–19. The disciples still have no category to allow them to make sense of a Messiah who would die, rise from the dead, and abandon his people in favour of 'another Counsellor' (14:16). Their perplexity provides the justification to the assessment Jesus has just rendered: they cannot yet bear all that Jesus wants to say to them (v. 12). They ask themselves what Jesus means by his words in v. 16, and link them to what Jesus had earlier[1] said about going to the Father (v. 17; *cf.* v. 5). In particular they are perplexed by the double use of a *little while* (v. 18).

Jesus is fully aware (*egnō*, 'knew'; NIV 'saw'; there is no reason to postulate supernatural knowledge) of their desire to question him, and repeats his comment while preparing to address their confusion. That John includes double repetition of the words in v. 16 (vv. 17, 19)[2] argues that he sees this departure 'in a little while' and return 'after a little while' as utterly central to the themes he has been developing in these chapters.

20. On the dramatic asseverative *I tell you the truth*, *cf.* notes on 1:51. This verse can only be referring to the grief of the disciples while Jesus was dead, and while the 'world' (*kosmos*; *cf.* notes on 1:9) was rejoicing at having disposed of him so decisively. The clause *your grief will turn to joy* refers to the transformation of the disciples' attitudes when they see the resurrected Jesus again. Arguments to the effect that this joy refers to the ecstasy Christians will experience at the parousia necessarily presuppose that grief characterizes them throughout this age until Jesus returns. That will not square with Jesus' promise of joy to his disciples *throughout* the Christian era (15:11), still less with John's report of the disciples' reactions when they saw the resurrected Christ: 'The disciples were overjoyed when they saw the Lord' (20:20).

The verb 'to mourn' (*thrēneō*) occurs only here in the Fourth Gospel; the verb 'to weep' (*klaiō*) also occurs in 11:31, 33; 20:11, 13, 15, always in connection with death. In Luke 7:32, the two verbs come together at a

---

[1]This assumes, of course, the shorter reading in v. 16: *cf.* notes, above.

[2]In all three verses, the first verb is *theōreō* and the second is *horaō*, apparently used here synonymously with the meaning 'to see'. John frequently varies his terms, with no discernible shift in meaning (*cf.* Morris, *SFG*, pp. 293–319).

funeral (even if it is a child's game). Similarly, 'grief' (*lypē*) is often caused by death (though not invariably: *e.g.* Rom. 9:2). Correspondingly, the joy the disciples are promised springs from Jesus' resurrection. This contrast controls the thought of the next four verses.

21. Jesus briefly illustrates the dramatic change from grief to joy by sketching in a non-narrative parable. The intense labour pains a woman[1] commonly suffers in delivering a baby give way to satisfied joy that 'a child' (*anthrōpos*, properly 'a human being') has been born into the world.

The combination of intense suffering and relieved joy at childbirth is in the Old Testament a common illustration of the travail God's people must suffer before the immense relief and joy brought about by the advent of the promised messianic salvation (*e.g.* Is. 21:2–3; 26:16–21; 66:7–14; Je. 13:21; Mi. 4:9–10). Isaiah 26:16–21 is particularly important: it combines the figure of the woman in childbirth, the words 'a little while' and the promise of resurrection. The model of a woman in childbirth generated a popular metaphor in the Judaism of Jesus' day: 'the birth pains of the Messiah' refers to a period of terrible trouble that must precede the consummation. It is not unlikely that this verse alludes to this eschatological theme, only here the intense suffering is borne by the Messiah himself. This interpretation is strengthened by the use of *hōra* (properly 'hour'; NIV 'time'): the word is pregnant with meaning in the Fourth Gospel, and is regularly related to Jesus' death and the dawning of the new age (*cf.* notes on 2:4). This means Jesus' death and resurrection are properly *eschatological* events. This does not mean that the Fourth Gospel confuses Easter and the parousia, or obliterates all distinction between them so that they mean the same thing (as Bultmann, p. 581, argues). Rather, John is here earthing his realized or inaugurated eschatology. By showing the coherence of Jesus' death/exaltation with the parousia, he not only declares the former to be a properly eschatological event, but makes the entire period between Easter and the consummation the onset of the eschaton (*cf.* Hoskyns, pp. 487–489; Lindars, pp. 506–510). The same theme is further developed in the next two verses.

22. *So with you:* the illustration is now applied specifically to the circumstances of the disciples. The *Now* is proleptic: it eliminates the first 'little while' (v. 16) and views the cross as impending. Once the disciples rejoice, after the resurrection, *no-one will take away [their] joy,* because the resurrection of Jesus is not merely a discrete event but the onset of the eschatological age, the dawning of the new creation (*cf.* notes on 20:22), the precursor to the age of the Paraclete. The Greek behind *and you will rejoice* might more literally be rendered 'and your heart will rejoice' (*kai charēsetai hymōn hē kardia*): exactly the same words

---

[1]The article with 'woman' in Greek (*hē gynē*) does not refer to a particular woman (suggestions have included the women mentioned in 2:4; 19:25ff.; Gn. 3:15–16; Rev. 12) but is generic. Hence the indefinite article in English.

are found in Isaiah 66:14, in the context of promises of the consummation. The change from the expected 'you will see me again' to *I will see
you again* is not meant to hint that the disciples will not *really* see him (for
that would contradict vv. 16, 17, 19), but that Jesus' 'seeing' of them is
far more foundational to the relationship than their seeing of him – a
point Paul well understood (*cf.* Gal. 4:9, 'But now that you know God –
or rather are known by God – . . .'). The thought is analogous to John
15:16: 'You did not choose me [though of course in one sense they did!],
but I chose you [for that is the properly fundamental perspective] . . .'

23. *In that day* or 'that day' or the like often in the New Testament
refers to the last days, the end of the age (*e.g.* Mk. 13:11, 17, 19 par.;
14:25; Acts 2:18; 2 Tim. 1:12, 18; Heb. 8:10; Rev. 9:15). This does not
mean that Jesus here refers to the end of history and *not* to the period
after his resurrection, but that he is referring to the period after his
resurrection *as* the end of history (*cf.* 1 Jn. 2:18, 'Dear children, this is the
last hour'). *Cf.* 14:20.

In that day, after Jesus has risen and ascended and the Holy Spirit has
been sent, *you will no longer ask me anything*. Rather, as the rest of the
verse shows, his followers will ask the Father in Jesus' name. Although
in classical Greek the verb 'to ask' (*erōtaō*) means 'to ask a question'
rather than 'to ask for [something]' (which meaning was reserved for
aiteō), in the Greek of the New Testament period *erōtaō* can have either
force. Even in John, *erōtaō* sometimes means 'to ask a question' (1:19, 21,
25; 9:2, 19, 21; 16:5, 19, 30), and sometimes 'to ask for [something]' (4:31,
40, 47; 14:16; 16:26; 17:9). In the verse before us, *erōtaō* is used in the first
clause ('you will no longer *ask* me anything'), and *aiteō* in the last clause
('my Father will give you whatever you *ask* in my name'). If the two
verbs are roughly synonymous, with the meaning 'to ask for [some-
thing]', then the only contrast in the verse is between the disciples
asking Jesus for things during the period of his public ministry, and
their asking the Father for things after Jesus has risen. That certainly
makes sense, and comports well with John's tendency to mix his verbs
(*cf.* the second fn. to v. 19). This verse is then taking up the theme of
prayer 'in Jesus' name', a theme already developed in this discourse (*cf.*
notes on 14:12–14; 15:7–8, 16).

It is just possible, however, that in addition to this theme, which in
any case is found in the last half of the verse, the first clause, with *erōtaō*,
may address a more immediate concern, *viz.* the disciples' repeated
requests *for information*. 'In that day, you will no longer ask me anything', as you have been doing, for then you will truly know and
understand. Christians are the ones who, by definition, truly know (*cf.*
1 Jn. 2:20), for it is a mark of the changing pattern of redemptive history
under the new covenant that they have been greatly informed as to what
God is doing: indeed, that is the very reason why Jesus has called them
his 'friends' (*cf.* notes on 15:14, 15). 'That . . . is *the eschatological situation:*
to have no more questions!' (Bultmann, p. 583; emphasis his).

In the historical setting of the farewell discourse, this clause then becomes an incentive to wait just a bit longer, until they enjoy the understanding thus promised to them. In the evangelistic setting in which John writes, this clause becomes an incentive to 'close with' Christ and become a Christian, for only then can one truly settle one's religious qualms and questions and rest with quietness in the eschatological community of those who know God and are satisfied. On this reading, the next words, *I tell you the truth* (*cf*. notes on 1:51) introduce a further entailment of belonging to the period of rejoicing, the attainment of the prayer life already described in the discourse.

24. The disciples had certainly asked for things, and asked questions; but up to this point they had not asked the Father (v.23) for things (the verb is *aiteō*; *cf*. notes on v. 23) *in Jesus' name* (*cf*. notes on 14:13): that was a privilege that belonged to the new order. Now, in anticipation of that new order, the disciples are exhorted, *Ask* (the verb is still *aiteō*) *and you will receive*. They are to do this in full recognition that this is the route to the joy Jesus had earlier promised them. If that joy is part of the matrix of consistent obedience (15:11), that obedience, that remaining in Jesus (15:4) and his love (15:9) and his word (8:31), is the matrix out of which fruitbearing springs, the fruitbearing that is the direct consequence of prayer (15:7, 8). Thus the connections amongst asking, receiving and complete joy in 16:24 turn out to be a compressed version of themes developed in ch. 15, but now more clearly set within the eschatological situation introduced by Jesus' death and resurrection.

25. Jesus has been speaking somewhat enigmatically, somewhat cryptically: *en paroimias* (NIV 'figuratively') does not necessarily mean 'in a figure' or 'in a metaphor' or 'in a parable', but has to do with the obscurity of his utterances (*cf*. notes on *paroimia* at 10:6). The reference is therefore not restricted to the illustration of the woman in childbirth (v. 21); it embraces the entire discourse, and confirms Jesus' assessment of his disciples' current ability (v. 12). However, *a time* (*hōra*, 'hour': the reference is eschatological; *cf*. notes on 2:4; 16:21) *is coming* (*cf*. notes on 4:21, 23) when Jesus will speak *plainly* about his Father. The word *plainly* renders *parrēsia*, and has been used to refer to the public nature of Jesus' ministry (7:4, 26; 11:54); but, of greater relevance here, it has also been used to refer to plain language as opposed to enigmatic or cryptic speech (10:24; 11:14).

This passage is often thought to be in irreconcilable conflict with Mark 4:33–34, where Jesus speaks to the crowds only in parables, but to his disciples privately 'explained everything'. Here it is the disciples who are confused by Jesus' utterances. In fact, the apparent discrepancy between John and Mark is superficial, and springs from quite different foci of interest. Here in John 16:25, the contrast is between what is enigmatic or cryptic during the ministry of Jesus, and what becomes plain or clear after Jesus' death/exaltation and gift of the Spirit. It is not simply a matter of unpacking a figure of speech, of explaining a parable (as in Mk. 4:33–34). After all, even in Mark the disciples who had the narrative parables explained to them display no place whatsoever for a *crucified* Messiah (Mk. 8:33ff.). *None* of the Gospel writers suggests that *any* of Jesus' disciples made much sense of the cross until *after* the resurrection. And it is in this most dramatic of divine self-disclosures, in this shame and triumph of death, in this eschatological victory of death and resurrection, that the ultimate significance of Jesus is to be found – and therefore also the clearest display of the character and purposes of God. Because John's Gospel focuses so narrowly and thoroughly on these central points, the theme of the disciples' misunderstanding or dim understanding is repeatedly underscored (*e.g.* notes on 2:22; 12:16; 13:7; Carson, 'Mis'). Although all of Jesus' life and ministry has been a manifestation of God (1:14, 18; 14:9), the veiling has been particularly acute because the disciples cannot fathom his references to his departure. With the dawning of the 'hour', with the coming of the new order, Jesus' language from the days of his flesh will become clearer (14:26); Jesus himself, after the resurrection, will speak words that will lose their enigmatic character, words about his Father (16:25; Lk. 24:27, 44–48; *cf.* 20:17); and after his ascension, the Paraclete will continue to unpack the meaning of the revelation bound up with Jesus the Messiah (16:12–15).

26–27. In addition to the increased understanding the disciples will enjoy after the resurrection (v. 25), *in that day* they will ask (*aiteō; cf.* notes on v. 23) the Father for things in Jesus' name. All these categories have been introduced (*cf.* 14:12–14; 15:7–8, 16; 16:23), but Jesus wants his followers to understand that the phrase *in my name* does not mean that they are thereby distanced from God. It does not mean that they are restricted to asking Jesus for things, and he conveys their requests to the Father; it does not mean (in Jesus' words) that *I will ask the Father on your behalf.* Far from it: the *Father himself loves you,* and needs no prompting from the Son. After all, it was the love of the Father for the world that initiated the mission of the Son (3:16). Nor is this truth in conflict with New Testament passages that emphasize the intercessory work of the exalted Christ (Rom. 8:34; Heb. 7:25; *cf.* 1 Jn. 2:1). Rightly understood, such passages focus on the mediatorial role of the Son in the plan of redemption, and therefore on the basis of the Christian's acceptance by God; they do not stipulate a mechanical conveyancing of the Christian's prayers, as if Jesus' purpose were to restrict the believer's access to the Father.

The love of the Father that is in view in these verses is peculiarly directed toward the believers. Just as Jesus remains in his Father's love by being obedient to him (8:29; 15:10), and just as believers remain in Jesus' love by being obedient to him (15:9–11), so this circle of love is large enough to include the Father himself: he loves (*philei; cf.* notes on 5:20; 11:3; 21:15–17) the disciples because they love Christ and believe that he came from God (v. 27). The thought, in short, is an extension of 15:9–16.

28. If we follow the text as it is represented in the NIV (see Additional Note), the words 'I came from God' in v. 27 are now expanded into what is almost a summary of Jesus' entire mission, in categories now familiar.

It runs from the mission of the Son as the envoy of the Father (*I came from the Father, cf.* 3:16, 17), through the incarnation and the humiliation meted out to him by the world (*and entered the world, cf.* 1:10–11, 14), to the departure from the world (*now I am leaving the world, cf.* 14:19) and his return to his Father (*I am . . . going back to the Father* – perhaps the dominant theme of chs. 14 – 17).

29–30. No misunderstanding is more pathetic than that which thinks it no longer exists. Ignoring or not comprehending Jesus' insistence that the time for speech without enigma lies just ahead, his disciples think he is already (note the repeated *Now* in vv. 29, 30) speaking 'without figures of speech' (*cf.* notes on v. 25). They happily confess that Jesus knows all things – which is probably not so much an affirmation of Jesus' omniscience as of his utter mastery of all he has to tell them about God and his ways. Implicitly, it is a confession that Jesus supremely reveals God, without rigorous thought as to the metaphysics of the situation. They add, *You do not even need to have anyone ask you questions* – whether to test his knowledge, or because he has often displayed supernatural knowledge of the thoughts of his interlocutors (*e.g.* 2:24–25; in this chapter, 16:19 is not a convincing instance). The final sentence, *This makes us believe that you came from God*, though formally embracing a true conclusion, betrays just how feeble a foundation supports the immature faith they have so far attained (*cf.* notes on 1:48–49; 4:19, 29). Even the over-confident *Now we can see* (*oidamen*, lit. 'we know') echoes other false claims to knowledge in this Gospel (*e.g.* 3:2; 6:42; 7:27; *cf.* Duke, pp. 57–59).

31–32. As in 6:68–70, human pretensions lead only to rebuke. Although Jesus' response in v. 31 could be taken as a quizzical question, richer irony is preserved if their words are repeated with heavy exasperation: lit. 'Now you believe!' Yet in one sense they had spoken more truly than they knew: Jesus did *not* need to question them to know what was in their minds, and he knew perfectly well that the coming test would find them all wanting. Peter had already been warned of his impending failure (13:38); now all the disciples are forced to face their fears as they hear a similar prediction that embraces them all.

The impending disaster is again announced in terms of the coming *hōra* ('hour'), but this hour *has come* – it is even nearer than the hour for plain speaking predicted in v. 25. The disciples' temporary defection is cast in the language of Zechariah 13:7, specifically quoted in Mark 14:27 par.; *cf.* Mark 14:50. But however badly he will be abandoned by his disciples, Jesus is assured of his Father's support: *Yet I am not alone, for my Father is with me* (*cf.* 8:16, 29). Even so, Dodd's comment (*IFG*, p. 416 n. 1) is astute:

> The damping down of an enthusiastic confession of faith might seem surprising, if we did not remember that it corresponds to a constant pattern, not only in the Fourth Gospel but elsewhere: cf. John vi. 68–70, viii. 38; Mark viii. 29–33

(and parallels), x. 28-31, 38-40, xiv. 29-31. It is part of the character and genius of the Church that its foundation members were discredited men; it owed its existence not to their faith, courage, or virtue, but to what Christ had done with them; and this they could never forget.

Commentators frequently find two jarring notes in this verse:

(1) Some find it incongruous that after stressing the universal scattering of the disciples, the Evangelist nevertheless manages to place the beloved disciple near the cross (19:26-27). But surely this is not more difficult than the Synoptic report that when Jesus was arrested all his disciples forsook him and fled, even though Peter (and John?) returned to the High Priest's residence. The point is that all of Jesus' disciples did flee, and not even the beloved disciple, who loitered near the cross (as did, after all, some who taunted the Master), so identified himself with Jesus as to be arrested and share in his suffering. In ch. 21 the disciple whom Jesus loves returns, with others, to the fishing boats – a sign, perhaps, that he had still not found his way back to whole-hearted loyalty to his Lord.

(2) Some find that v. 32b stands in contradiction to the cry of desolation recorded in Mark 15:34 par. Certainly John focuses more acutely on Jesus' obedience and sublime courage than do the Synoptists, who instead emphasize the depth of his agony. Even so, it is somewhat harsh to diagnose contradiction when less depressing diagnoses are ready to hand. John 16:32b contrasts the Father's faithfulness with the fickleness of his followers, as Jesus takes the path of suffering and is brutally crucified. It does not assess what depth of revulsion the Father himself may have known when his Son was made sin for us (2 Cor. 5:21), nor explore Jesus' sense of total abandonment, for some brief period of time, when only words quoted from Psalm 22:1 could begin to express his anguish. It is still less a 'solution' to argue that Jesus *felt* abandoned by his Father, but was not: so profound a mistake may please those determined to psychoanalyse people who have been off the scene for two thousand years, but it will prove unsatisfying to those who ponder what the cross achieved.[1]

33. However grave the temporary defection of his disciples may be, Jesus looks beyond their collapse to their restoration, and ends the discourse with encouragement. Doubtless *these things* refers to the entire discourse: his purpose in expatiating at some length is so that his disciples *may have peace*, the peace that only he can give (*cf.* notes on 14:27). The two spheres of existence mentioned in this verse are constantly at odds. Christians belong to both spheres. *In this world* Christians will face *thlipsis* (NIV 'trouble'), often a reference to eschatological woes (*e.g.* Mk. 13:9; Rom. 2:9), sometimes a reference to persecution (Jn.

---

[1]*Cf.* J. I. Packer, *TynB* 25, 1974, pp. 3-45.

15:18 – 16:4a; Acts 11:19; Eph. 3:13), and here (as in Mt. 24; Rev. 7:14) a reference to a combination of the two. By contrast, *in me*, Jesus assures them, they will have peace: this *in me* language is probably an extension of the metaphor of the vine (ch. 15). Whatever the trouble, the peace prevails, just as elsewhere the privilege of being more than a conqueror goes to those who are faithful under the most appalling opposition (Rom. 8:31–39).

The fundamental ground for perseverance of this order is the triumph of Jesus: *I have overcome the world* (*cf.* 12:31; 1 Cor. 15:57; 1 Jn. 2:13–14; 4:4; 5:4–5). Jesus is not so opposing the church and the world (*kosmos*; *cf.* notes on 1:9) that there can be no conversions from the latter to the former (17:20; 20:29). Nor does the verb rendered 'overcome' (*nikaō*) merely refer to a personal overcoming, the preservation of personal integrity in the face of protracted opposition. Rather, the verb indicates victory; Jesus has *conquered* the world, in the same way that he has defeated the prince of this world. Jesus' point is that by his death he has made the world's opposition pointless and beggarly. The decisive battle has been waged and won. The world continues its wretched attacks, but those who are in Christ share the victory he has won. They cannot be harmed by the world's evil, and they know who triumphs in the end. From this they take heart, and begin to share his peace.

Additional note

27–28. The words 'I came from the Father' at the beginning of v. 28 are omitted by a small but powerful combination of manuscripts. Verses 27–28 would then run together: '. . . that I came from God and entered the world . . .'. If the shorter reading is original, the expansion is meant as an improvement (as in 14:4). But the textual evidence for the short text is not as strong as in 14:4, and brief repetitions are so much a pattern of Johannine style that the longer reading is probably original. At the end of v. 27, some manuscripts attest 'from the Father' instead of 'from God'. The former is marginally more likely if we adopt the shorter reading in v. 28; the latter is more likely if we follow the longer reading reflected in the NIV and most other English versions. Other variants in these two verses are less consequential.

D. THE PRAYER OF JESUS (*17:1–26*)

This prayer is not free-standing; it is intimately connected by themes and link-words with the discourse that precedes it (chs. 14 – 16), as even the first words of 17:1 ('After Jesus said this . . .') intimate. Indeed, there is ample evidence that prayers of one sort or another were frequently connected with 'farewell discourses' in the ancient world, both in Jewish and in hellenistic literature (*e.g.* Gn. 49; Dt. 32 – 33; *Jubilees* 22:7–23).[1] What is unique about this prayer rests neither on form nor on literary associations but on him who offers it, and when. He is the incarnate Son of God, and he is returning to his Father by the route of a desperately shameful and painful death. He prays that the course on which he is embarked will bring glory to his Father, and that his followers, in consequence of his own death and exaltation, will be preserved *from* evil and *for* the priceless privilege of seeing Jesus' glory, all the while imitating in their own relationship the reciprocity of love displayed by the Father and the Son.

In some respects the prayer is a summary of the entire Fourth Gospel to this point. Its principal themes include Jesus' obedience to his Father, the glorification of his Father through his death/exaltation, the revelation of God in Christ Jesus, the choosing of the disciples out of the world, their mission to the world, their unity modelled on the unity of the Father and the Son, and their final destiny in the presence of the Father and the Son. To cast this summary in the form of a prayer is not only to anticipate Jesus' being 'lifted up' on the cross, but to contribute to the climax of the movement that brings Christ back to God – one of the central themes of the farewell discourse (*cf.* Dodd, *IFG*, pp. 419–420).

This is one of the features of John 17 that makes Käsemann's influential study of it so anomalous. Käsemann not only argues that John's Christology is profoundly docetic – a view adequately criticized elsewhere[2] – but that John has no theology of the death of Jesus. One is reminded of Martin Kähler's famous epigram describing Mark's Gospel: 'a passion story with a detailed introduction'. H. Thyen not only thinks that the same could be said of John, but argues that from the beginning to the end the Fourth Gospel portrays Jesus' passion as God's action in him.[3] In this light, John 17 is part of the crescendo to which such passages as 1:29, 34; 3:14–15; 6:51–58; 10:11; 11:49–52; 13:8 have been building, a crescendo that is climaxed in chs. 18 – 20 in the passion and triumph of Jesus the Messiah.

The Synoptic Evangelists, especially Luke, mention Jesus' prayers fairly often (Mt. 14:23; 19:13; 26:36–44; 27:46; Mk. 1:35; 6:46; 14:32–39; 15:34; Lk. 3:21; 5:16; 6:12; 9:18, 28–29; 11:1; 22:41–45; 23:46),[4] but, apart from the so-called 'Lord's Prayer' (Mt. 6:9–13; Lk. 11:2–4 – better thought of as the disciples' prayer, taught by the Lord), only rarely is the content of the prayers reported. These have to do with his passion: the prayers of Gethsemane and the cross. In the Fourth Gospel, there are two recorded prayers of Jesus in addition to the one before us. The first is at

---

[1]On the literary character of Jn. 17, *cf.* Appold, pp. 190–211; on its stylistic features, *cf.* David Alan Black, *CTR* 3, 1988, pp. 141–159.

[2]*Cf.* Carson, pp. 154–158; Ritt, pp. 118–123; Introduction, §§ III, VII; Thompson.

[3]Cited by Beasley-Murray, p. 306, from an unpublished paper.

[4]*Cf.* M. M. B. Turner, 'Prayer in the Gospels and Acts', in D. A. Carson (ed.), *Teach Us To Pray: Prayer in the Bible and the World* (Paternoster/Baker, 1990).

the tomb of Lazarus (11:41–42). Though a prayer, it was constructed with the needs of the people who heard it in mind ('but I said this for the benefit of the people standing here', 11:42). Something similar can be said about the prayers in John 12:27–28 and John 17: each is rightly labelled a prayer, but is at once petition, proclamation, even revelation.[1]

The relation of John 17 to the Synoptic reports of Jesus' anguished praying in Gethsemane is disputed. Fenton (p. 172) points out that the Synoptic descriptions of Jesus' prayers in Gethsemane (Mt. 26:36–44; Mk. 14:32–39; Lk. 22:41–45) focus on Jesus' obedience ('Yet not what I will, but what you will'), and especially on the suffering and personal cost to Jesus. His tears, sweat like drops of blood, and prolonged agonizing all contribute to the portrait. By contrast, although John 17 maintains the theme of Jesus' obedience (e.g. v. 4, 'I have brought you glory on earth by completing the work you gave me to do'), it yields no hint of suffering, personal agony or physical pain. Brown (2. 748) so strongly emphasizes these and other differences that any genuine reconciliation between Gethsemane and John 17 at first glance seems exceedingly difficult.

A more sympathetic reading both of the Synoptics and of John suggests several compelling points of connection. If the prayers of John 12:27–28 (cf. notes) and John 17 are put together, Jesus' obedience and his suffering coalesce. Psychologically it is altogether convincing that as he approached the cross Jesus should betray both resolution and horror, both filial obedience and personal agony. Both strands are found in John and in the Synoptics. For instance, if Luke records the anguish of Gethsemane (Lk. 22:41–45), he also insists, 'As the time approached for him to be taken up to heaven, Jesus resolutely set out for Jerusalem' (Lk. 9:51). The Synoptists, after all, are the ones who report Jesus' determined 'not as I will, but as you will' (Mt. 26:39; Mk. 14:36; Lk. 22:42).

Nor is there good reason to think that John 17 is the Evangelist's theological expansion of the last element of the petition 'Glorify your name!' (12:28), or a creative re-creation of the 'Gethsemane' prayers placed in a different location. However much the different Evangelists chose to emphasize distinct aspects of our Lord's prayers, and reported those prayers in their own idiom, it is surely too much to be asked to believe that Jesus prayed only once on his way to the cross. Did he wait for Gethsemane, as it were, before he got around to the business of prayer, thereby inciting the Evangelists, who were clearly more spiritual than their Master, to manufacture their own prayers and place them on Jesus' lips at discrete intervals in their narratives?

At least from the time of David Chytraeus (1530–1600), John 17 has commonly been referred to as Jesus' 'high priestly prayer'. The designation is not unfitting, inasmuch as Jesus prays for others in a distinctly

---

[1]Cf. S. C. Agourides, SE IV, 1968, pp. 137–143, who rightly observes that, for all that Jn. 17 is a prayer, it is also instruction. It is meant to be heard by the disciples and read by later readers. The 'consolatory discourse is changed into a prayer' (p. 137).

mediatorial way – a priestly task – while he prays for himself with his self-oblation in view (vv. 5, 19). Even so, sacrificial language is not strong; more importantly, Christians have often thought of Christ's 'high priestly ministry' in terms of his post-ascension intercession (*e.g.* Rom. 8:34; Heb. 7:25; 1 Jn. 2:1), while this chapter finds Christ praying on the way to the cross. Others have favoured 'Jesus' Prayer of Consecration', the consecration of Jesus to death and glorification, and of the disciples to mission and unity (*e.g.* Westcott, 2. 238; Hoskyns, p. 494). On the other hand, the theme of consecration by no means exhausts the prayer's themes, some of which are better explored under the (admittedly more generic) title adopted here.[1]

Of the many outlines that have been proposed for this chapter, the most widely adopted one is as follows: Jesus prays for himself (vv. 1–5), for his disciples (vv. 6–19), and for the church (vv. 20–26). Some prefer to link vv. 6–8 with the first section rather than with the second. Others divide the last section into two: vv. 20–23, Jesus prays that all believers may be one; vv. 24–26, Jesus prays that all believers may be perfected so as to see Jesus' glory. Other schemes are still more complicated.[2] The following exposition adapts the outline followed by Schnackenburg (3. 167–169) and Beasley-Murray (pp. 295–296).

1. Jesus prays for his glorification *(17:1–5)*

1. *After Jesus said this* links John 17 to the farewell discourse of John 14 – 16. As in the prayer recorded in 11:41, Jesus raises his eyes to heaven. In a book which makes so much of 'Son' Christology (*cf.* especially 5:16–30) it is altogether natural for Jesus to address God as *Father* (*cf.* 11:41; 12:27), even as he has constantly referred to him in that way. Farther on in the prayer, 'Father' gives way to 'Holy Father' (v. 11) and 'Righteous Father' (v. 25).

Repeatedly throughout the Gospel we are told that the 'hour' has not yet come (2:4; 7:6, 8, 30; 8:20). From the time 'some Greeks' (12:20) try to see him, the hour is impending, it 'has come' (12:23, 27–28, 31–32; 13:1, 31). The *time* (*hōra*, 'hour') is the appointed time for Jesus' death/ exaltation, for his glorification. That God's appointed hour has arrived does not strike Jesus as an excuse for resigned fatalism, but for prayer: precisely *because* the hour has come for the Son to be glorified, he prays that the glorification might take place. This is God's appointed hour; let God's will be done – indeed, Jesus prays that his Father will accomplish the purpose of this appointed hour. As so often in Scripture, emphasis

---

[1]It is far from clear, however, that those additional themes include any direct reference to the eucharist. True, the early second-century document *Didache* offers parallels to Jn. 17 in its eucharistic prayer (ch. 10), but this does not demonstrate the theological *provenance* of such themes in Jn. 17 but merely renders plausible the view that some second-century Christians *utilized* Jn. 17 at their celebration of the Lord's supper. Whatever allusions there may be to the Lord's supper, they are even more indirect than in Jn. 6.

[2]*Cf.* Rudolf Schnackenburg, *BZ* 17, 1973, pp. 67–78, 196–202.

on God's sovereignty functions as an incentive to prayer, not a disincentive.

Although Jesus prays for himself in vv. 1–5, his praying is scarcely analogous to what we do when we pray for ourselves (*cf.* Carson, *FWD*, p. 182). There is but one petition: *Glorify your Son* (*cf.* also v. 5). For the general thought, *cf.* notes on 12:23; on the 'glory' of the Son, *cf.* notes on 1:14. The associations here are complex. The verb 'to glorify' can mean 'to praise, to honour', and something of that meaning is suggested by the fact that God's purpose is that all should honour the Son even as they honour the Father (5:23). The very event by which the Son was being 'lifted up' in horrible ignominy and shame was that for which he would be praised around the world by men and women whose sins he had borne. But in this context the primary meaning of 'to glorify' is 'to clothe in splendour', as v. 5 makes clear. The petition asks the Father to reverse the self-emptying entailed in hs incarnation and to restore him to the splendour that he shared with the Father before the world began. The cross and Jesus' ascension/exaltation are thus inseparable. The hideous profanity of Golgotha means nothing less than the Son's glorification. That Jesus should pray that the Father might glorify the Son is therefore also a moving expression of his own willingness to obey the Father even unto death (*cf.* notes on v. 19).

From Jesus' perspective, even the glorification of the Son is not an end in itself. Jesus offers his petition (he says) in order *that your Son may glorify you*. As he seeks not the praise of men but the glory that comes from the only God (5:44), so Jesus seeks by his own glorification nothing less than the glory of his Father (*cf.* notes on 13:31–32). The distinctions between the Father and the Son that are so carefully maintained in the Fourth Gospel (*e.g.* 5:19–30; 12:20ff.; *cf.* 1:1b) happily give way on occasion to frank confessions of Jesus' deity (1:1c, 18; 8:58; 14:10; 20:28), so it is not entirely surprising that Jesus' crucifixion and exaltation issue not only in his own glorification but that of his Father as well. God is clothed in splendour as he brings about this death/exaltation of his Son.

2. The first word of v. 2 in the Greek text is *kathōs*, better rendered 'just as' than 'for'. In other words, v. 2 establishes the ground for the petition of v. 1b, and does so by establishing an analogical pattern. This can be schematized as follows:

17:1b		17:2
Glorify your Son		you granted him authority over all people
(purpose)	just as	*(purpose)*
that your Son may glorify you		that he might give eternal life to all those you have given him

All of v. 2 is the ground for v. 1b, but there are important horizontal parallels that can be observed in this schematization. The first part of v. 2 is best understood as referring to God's pre-temporal decision to give his Son authority (*exousia*; *cf.* notes on 1:12) over all people (*pasēs sarkōs*, lit. 'all flesh', a common Jewish way of referring to all of humanity). This is not the authority Jesus enjoys inherent in his being the Son, making the Father's gift of authority equivalent to the fact that the Father is the *fons divinitatis*, the source of deity, of the Son; for if that were in view, it is hard to see how it could serve as the basis for the prayer of v. 1b. Nor does v. 2a proleptically refer to the gift of authority the Father grants the Son consequent upon the Son's obedience unto death: again, it is hard to see how that still future grant could serve as the *ground* for the petition of v. 1. Rather, v. 2b refers to the Father's gift, *in eternity past*, of authority over all humanity, on the basis of the Son's *prospective* obedient humiliation, death, resurrection and exaltation. It is nothing less than the redemptive plan of God, for the second part of the verse makes the purpose of this grant clear: it is that the Son might give eternal life to those the Father has given him.

Thus, when Jesus petitions his Father to glorify the Son (v. 1b), he does so on the basis of the Father's pre-temporal plan to give all authority to the Son as a function of the Son's triumphant cross-work and exaltation. Jesus asks that he might be glorified in order that he might in turn glorify the Father (v. 1b) – which is congruent with the purpose clause in v. 2. As the Father is glorified before human beings, so they are brought to faith in the Son and in the one who sent him, and gain the eternal life that was the purpose of the grant of authority given to the Son. *Cf.* the numerous points of contact with Romans 1:1–5.

Although the grant of authority is 'over all people', the *purpose* of the grant is that those whom the Father has given to the Son might have eternal life. As in 6:37 and elsewhere, they are collectively grouped into a neuter plural (*pan ho*, lit. 'all which'), even while their individuality is preserved by the pronoun *autois* (lit. 'that he might give eternal life *to them*'). There is no embarrassment whatsoever between the assertion that God's sovereign purposes extend to the election of those who will be redeemed, and the twin assumptions that God's love extends to the 'world' (*cf.* notes on 1:9; 3:16), and that those who reject God's mercy stand under his wrath (3:36; *cf.* Carson, especially pp. 163–198). In Synoptic categories, this grant of universal authority to the Son is nothing less than the universal sovereignty of God, the universal kingdom of God, which is mediated exclusively through Christ once the cross, the resurrection and the exaltation have occurred (Mt. 28:18; *cf.* 1 Cor. 15:27–28). Everything and everyone in the universe is subject to this kingdom, whether the point is acknowledged or not. The saving subset of this universal reign, the 'kingdom' which one 'enters' only by the new birth (3:3, 5; *cf.* Mt. 7:21–23; 13:24–30), is the dynamic equivalent of that peculiar exercise of the Son's authority that issues in eternal life for all those the Father has given to the Son (*cf.* also 5:21–27). On 'eternal life', *cf.* notes on 1:4; 3:15.

3. Many commentators treat v. 3 as a parenthesis to the argument, a tangential explanation of 'eternal life' introduced in v. 2. Barrett (p. 503)

says it is the sort of material that would have been included in a footnote, had that orthographical device been available to the Evangelist. But if the links between v. 1 and v. 2, suggested above, fairly represent the flow of thought, then v. 3 constitutes a natural progression (cf. Ritt, pp. 345–353). The gift of authority to the Son, consequent upon his death and exaltation, has as its end that all those whom the Father has given to the Son should be given eternal life (v. 2). Otherwise put, the glorification of the Son entails the glorification of God (v. 1) – i.e. God is clothed in splendour in the eyes of those who perceive what has been achieved by God himself in the cross, resurrection and exaltation of his Son. To see God's glory, to be given eternal life – these are parallel, and, lest the reader miss the point, the two themes are drawn together in v. 3. Eternal life turns on nothing more and nothing less than knowledge of the true God. Eternal life is not so much everlasting life as personal knowledge of the Everlasting One.

Many religions tie eternal life to the knowledge of God or of gods. Long lists of partial parallels to various sources are cited in the larger commentaries. But the closest parallels are found in the Old Testament. We have already observed that an integral element of the promised new covenant is that all of God's new covenant people, from the least to the greatest, would know him personally, and without an intermediary so typical of the old covenant relationships (Je. 31:34; Heb. 8:11; cf. notes on Jn. 3:5). God's people are destroyed from lack of knowledge (Ho. 4:6); conversely, Habakkuk foresees a time when 'the earth will be filled with the knowledge of the glory of the LORD, as the waters cover the sea' (Hab. 2:14). We are to 'acknowledge him' (lit. 'know him'), and 'he will direct [our] paths' (Pr. 3:6); 'the LORD is your life' (Dt. 30:20). To know God is to be transformed, and thus to be introduced to a life that could not otherwise be experienced.

This is not knowledge of 'the divine' in some pantheistic or merely utilitarian sense. This is knowledge of the only true God (cf. 5:44; 1 Thes. 1:9; 1 Jn. 5:20). But because this one true God has supremely revealed himself in the person of his Son (1:18), knowledge of God cannot be divorced from knowledge of Jesus Christ. Indeed, knowledge of Jesus Christ, whom God has sent, is the ultimate access to knowledge of God (cf. 14:7; 20:31; especially Mt. 11:27). Nor is this knowledge of God and of Jesus Christ merely intellectual, mere information (though it invariably includes information). In a Gospel that ranks belief no less central than knowledge to the acquisition of eternal life (3:16; 20:31), it is clear that the knowledge of God and of Jesus Christ entails fellowship, trust, personal relationship, faith. There is no more powerful evangelistic theme.

4–5. Throughout his ministry Jesus has brought glory to God on earth – i.e. Jesus has so clothed the Father with splendour that many human beings (creatures of the earth, not of heaven) have come to praise him. After all, the incarnation itself was a display of glory (cf. notes on 1:14). The difficult point of this verse is the uncertainty as to whether the work that Jesus has completed refers to everything he has done *up to this point*, or proleptically includes his obedience unto death, the death that lies immediately ahead (*cf.* Riedl, pp. 69–186). Either interpretation can be made to 'fit' the passage. Some have argued for the former by appealing to the contrast implicit in the words *And now* (v. 5), which introduce the glorification of Jesus (= his death/exaltation). This misses the mark. There is certainly a contrast between v. 4 and v. 5, but it is not between previous work that Jesus has completed and his cross-work that lies immediately ahead. Rather, a contrast is drawn between the glory that Jesus by his work has brought to the Father on earth, and the glory he asks the Father to give him (*cf.* 13:31–32) in heaven. Once that is seen, it makes best sense if v. 4 includes *all* the work by which Jesus brings glory to his Father, and that includes his own death, resurrection and exaltation (*cf.* 4:34; 5:36; 19:30). So he is speaking proleptically (as in v. 12, 'While I was with them . . .'), oscillating with a more prosaic description of his place at this moment in the flow of redemptive history (*e.g.* v. 11, 'I am coming to you . . .').[1]

What is clear is that Jesus is asking to be returned to the glory that he shared with the Father before the world began, *i.e.* before creation (*cf.* notes on 1:1; 8:58). Haenchen (2. 502) rightly observes that this means the incarnation entailed a forfeiture of glory, and this ill accords with Käsemann's thesis (especially pp. 8–26) that the Fourth Gospel portrays no genuine incarnation at all, but thinks of Jesus in docetic terms as a 'god walking about the earth'. This does not mean that Jesus is asking for what might be called a 'de-incarnation' in order to be returned to the glory he once enjoyed. When the Word became flesh (1:14), this new condition was not designed to be temporary. When Jesus is glorified, he does not leave his body behind in a grave, but rises with a transformed, glorified body (to use a Pauline category; *cf.* notes on ch. 20) which returns to the Father (*cf.* 20:17) and thus to the glory the Son had with the Father 'before the world began'.

2. Jesus prays for his disciples (17:6–19)

a. Jesus' grounds for this prayer (17:6–11a)

Jesus has prayed for himself, in particular for his glorification (vv. 1–5). That glorification is integrally bound up with the benefit of all those the Father has given him (v. 2), so it is not surprising that he now turns from his single petition for himself to his several for his disciples. Before beginning them, Jesus advances the grounds for these petitions, *i.e.* the

---

[1]Part of the problem is introduced by the widespread tendency to translate certain Greek verbs rather rigidly by time-based English verbs, even though the differences among the 'tenses' of Greek verbs are best understood to be based on distinctions in 'verbal aspect', not time: *cf.* Porter. Thus 'I *have brought you glory* (*edoxasa*, aorist tense)' is not necessarily past-referring. Rather, the author chooses to view the work that brings the Father glory as a complete whole, and therefore selects the aorist.

reasons why he is praying for these people as opposed to others, and the reasons why the Father should meet his requests.

6. These people for whom Jesus now lifts his voice in prayer are those whom the Father has given to the Son (vv. 2, 6; *cf.* notes on 6:37). This gift was not rooted in anything intrinsic to the people themselves. They were part of the wicked world (*cf.* notes on 1:9), but God gave them to Jesus *out of the world* – apparently functionally equivalent to the fact that Jesus chose them out of the world (15:19). Thus in a profound sense they belonged to God antecedently to Jesus' ministry (*They were yours; you gave them to me*).

To these people, then, Jesus has revealed God's name (NIV fn.). The aorist *ephanerōsa* ('I have revealed', lit. 'I have manifested') doubtless sums up all of Jesus' ministry, including the cross that lies just ahead (*cf.* notes on v. 4). The revelation of God's name does not seem greatly different from the glorification of God on earth (v. 4); *cf.* Sidebottom, p. 40). God's 'name' embodies his character; to reveal God's name is to make God's character known. It is hard not to detect the hint of a reference to Ex. 3:13–15. Some have thought a particular 'name' of God is in view: 'I am' (8:58; Brown, 2. 755–756); 'I am he' (Dodd, *IFG*, p. 417); 'Father' (Schlatter, pp. 319–320). There is no need to choose. Jesus' disclosure of the name of God is coincident with his 'narration' of the invisible God (*cf.* notes on 1:18), in fulfilment of the biblical prophecy, 'Therefore my people will know my name' (Is. 52:6).

The ones for whom Jesus prays, then, antecedently belonged to God, who took them out of the world and gave them to his Son, who manifested God's name to them. From the human side, they can be described in terms of their response to God's gracious self-disclosure in Christ Jesus. At one level, Jesus and his teachings were in the public arena; of these people, however, Jesus can testify to his Father, *they have obeyed your word* (*logos*; *cf.* notes on 1:1; 14:23). That the revelation Jesus simultaneously is and delivers can be briefly summed up as *your word* is not surprising, for all of Jesus' words are God's words (5:19–30), and Jesus himself is God's self-expression, God's Word incarnate (1:1, 14). What is initially a little more surprising is that Jesus' disciples, before his cross and resurrection, should be described as those who have obeyed this revelatory word. Jesus keeps God's word (8:55), his commands (15:10), and he encourages his followers to observe *his* word (8:51–52; 14:23) or words (14:24), *his* commands (14:15, 21; 15:10). The failures of the disciples, to which Jesus himself has drawn sharp attention (*e.g.* 16:31–32), force us to ponder how Jesus can so readily characterize their response as obedience.

Many commentators find in this anomaly strong evidence that the Evangelist has (unwittingly?) slipped into anachronism, describing the competence of the apostles and of other early Christians long after the resurrection. This explanation is intrinsically unlikely, for no Evangelist exceeds John in his care to distinguish what the disciples understood during the ministry of Jesus and what they understood only later (*e.g.*

2:19–22; *cf.* Carson, 'Mis', for a chart of relevant passages and fairly detailed discussion). Moreover, a good case can be made that when in the Fourth Gospel Jesus refers to his *words* (plural) he is talking about the precepts he lays down, almost equivalent to his 'commands' (*entolai*, as in 14:21; 15:10), but when he refers to his *word* (singular) he is talking about his message as a whole, almost equivalent to 'gospel'. The disciples had not displayed mature conformity to the details of Jesus' teaching, but they had committed themselves unreservedly to Jesus as the Messiah, the one who truly reveals the Father. True, they did not yet enjoy the full understanding that would be theirs after Jesus had risen (2:22) and the Spirit had been given (16:12–15), but John does not claim they did. In this context, the proper comparison is not between the faith-status of the disciples *before* the resurrection and the faith-status of the disciples *after* the resurrection, but between the belief and obedience of the *disciples before* the resurrection and the unbelief and disobedience of the *world before* the resurrection. Judged by those standards – *i.e.* placing them at their proper location in the stream of redemptive history – the first disciples stand out. When other 'disciples' judge that Jesus teaches too many hard things, the Twelve stay with Jesus: 'You have the words of eternal life. We believe and know that you are the Holy One of God' (6:68–69). Even where there is risk to life and health, the closest disciples self-consciously choose to remain with Christ (11:16; 13:37), however flawed their courage might have been. At the fundamental level, Jesus' assessment of his closest followers is entirely realistic, and in no way a contradiction of 16:31–32. After all, despite the generous assessment in 17:6, Jesus goes on to ask the Father to keep them safe (17:11). That they have kept the revelatory 'word' that Jesus has mediated to them from the Father does not mean they have already become 'Christians' in the full post-Pentecostal, Antiochian sense (Acts 11:26). It simply means that, as compared with the world, they have been drawn out of it (v. 6), and constitute the nucleus of what will become the expanding messianic community, the church. Only this interpretation makes sense of the verses that follow.

7. *Now*, at the end of Jesus' ministry and just before his death, the disciples *know* (Jesus prays) *that everything you have given me comes from you*.

The verb *know* reflects the Greek *egnōkan*: assuming the perfect tense is the original reading (*cf.* Metzger, p. 249), it refers to the state of their knowledge at the time established by the *Now*. They may not have understood that their Messiah had to die and rise again; they may not have grasped how he was to embrace and fulfil in his own person Old Testament motifs of kingship, sacrifice, priesthood and suffering servant. But they had come to the deep conviction that Jesus was God's messenger, that he had been sent by God and that all he taught was God's truth. The strange way of putting the last point – *that everything you have given me comes from you*, which sounds complicated and tautologous compared with, say, 'that everything I have comes from you' –

carefully emphasizes Jesus' dependence upon his Father (*cf.* notes on 5:16–30).

8. This verse expands further on the themes of v. 7. The phrase 'everything you have given me' (v. 7) is here identified as *the words you gave me*. Here *words* renders the Greek *rhēmata*, neither Jesus' teaching as a whole nor his itemized precepts, but his actual 'words' or his 'utterances'. These were given to Jesus by God; the Son says only what the Father gives him to say. And the disciples *accepted* (*elabon*) these words. They may not always have understood them, but so attached had they become to Jesus that they accepted his words as true revelation from God. Moreover, however strong the predestinarianism in vv. 2, 6, it is important to insist that the disciples accepted Jesus' words, they obeyed Jesus' 'word' (v. 6), they believed that God sent Jesus (v. 8): the accepting, the obedience, the faith is *their* accepting, *their* obedience and *their* faith, regardless of how prevenient God's grace had been in their lives. This, too, becomes part of the ground of Jesus' prayer for them.

The upshot is that the disciples *have come to know* (in this context a better rendering of the aorist *egnōsan*[1] than NIV's 'knew') *with certainty* (*alēthōs, i.e.* 'truly', 'in truth') *that I came from you*; or, otherwise put, *they believed that you sent me*. In this verse there is little distinction between the knowledge and the belief of the disciples (*cf.* notes on v. 3).

9. For these disciples, then, Jesus prays (*erōtaō*, lit. 'I ask', here clearly with the sense 'I ask for something': *cf.* notes on 16:23). The Greek word order makes the contrast very sharp: 'not for the world (*cf.* notes on 1:9) I pray, but for those you have given me'. The next words summarize all the grounds adduced so far: *for they are yours*.

The antithesis between the disciples and the world is extremely sharp, but it should not be made absolute. The Father loves the world so much he sends his Son (3:16), who is designated the 'Saviour of the world' (4:42; *cf.* 3:17; 12:47). On the other hand, the distinction between the disciples and the world should not be reduced to the merely ultilitarian – as if Jesus restricts himself to praying for his disciples for no other reason than that they are his means for reaching the world. True, their mission is mentioned a few verses later (v. 18), and Jesus can pray for those who will believe in him through their message (v. 20). Even so, the fundamental reason for Jesus' self-imposed restriction as to whom he prays for at this point is not utilitarian or missiological but theological: *they are yours*. However wide is the love of God (3:16), however salvific the stance of Jesus toward the world (12:47), there is a peculiar relationship of love, intimacy, disclosure, obedience, faith, dependence, joy, peace, eschatological blessing and fruitfulness that binds the disciples together and with the Godhead. These themes have dominated the farewell

---

[1]A few manuscripts omit *kai egnōsan* ('and they have come to know'), possibly by copyists who thought the clause contradicted 6:69 (so Lagrange, p. 443; Metzger, p. 249). The flow then runs: '. . . and they accepted with certainty that I came from you . . .'. The longer reading is original.

discourse. The world can be prayed for only to the end that some who now belong to it might abandon it and join with others who have been chosen out of the world. There is nothing intrinsic to the 'world' itself, granted what John makes of the world (*cf.* notes on 1:9), that could sanction prayers on its behalf. To pray for the world, the created moral order in active rebellion against God, would be blasphemous; there is no hope for the world. There is hope only for some who now constitute the world but who will cease to be the world and will join those of whom Jesus says *for they are yours*.

10. What belongs to the Father, however, belongs no less to the Son, and vice versa: *All I have is yours, and all you have is mine.* The disciples already belonged to the Father when he gave them to the Son: 'they were yours' (v. 6). And because the Father has given them to the Son, they are no less his (vv. 2, 6). However much the reciprocal ownership expressed in v. 10a turns on the gift the Father extends to the Son, it is nevertheless a Christological claim of extraordinary reach (*cf.* notes on 5:19–30).

Perhaps this reciprocity of ownership calls to mind, much as in 5:23, the Father's intention that all should honour the Son. If so, it provides the link to the second half of v. 10: *And glory has come to me through them.* As in v. 6 (*cf.* notes), the extent to which Jesus has been glorified in the lives of his disciples is still pathetically slim compared with what will yet be (*cf.* 13:34–35; 14:13), but it is infinitely better than what he has received from 'the world'. This, too, becomes grounds for his prayer for them.

11a. The final reason Jesus advances to ground his prayer for the disciples is the fact that he is about to leave them. As so frequently in chs. 14 – 17, he describes his passion in terms of his going to the Father (*I am coming to you*). No longer will Jesus be 'in the world' (*cf.* notes on 1:10). The disciples, aided by the Holy Spirit, will have to face the world's temptations and the world's hostility (15:18 – 16:4) without the help of his immediate physical presence and protection.

b. Jesus prays that his disciples may be protected *(17:11b–16)*

11b. Jesus' petitions for his disciples are prefaced by *Holy Father*, a form of address found only here in the Fourth Gospel (though *cf.* vv. 1, 5, 25). It was not arbitrarily chosen. Not only does it preserve a view of God that combines awesome transcendence with familial intimacy (*cf.* Mt. 11:25), but, more importantly, it prepares the way for vv. 17–19 and the 'sanctification' or 'consecration' (the underlying Gk. term means 'to make *holy*': *cf.* notes below) of Jesus and of his disciples. The thought, as we shall see, is that the holiness of the Father establishes what it means for the Son and his followers to 'consecrate' themselves – the Johannine equivalent of 'I am the LORD your God; consecrate yourselves and be holy, because I am holy' (Lv. 11:44; *cf.* 1 Pet. 1:16; Mt. 5:48; Barrett, p. 507). The root of Jesus' 'holiness' and of ours is tied up in our respective relationships with the holy Father.

The basic petition could be understood in two ways. Literally translated, it reads 'keep them in your name' (*tēreson autous en tō onomati sou*). If the phrase *en tō onomati sou* ('in your name') is taken to have instrumental force (*i.e.* '*by* your name'), modifying *tēreson* ('keep'), the petition means 'protect them by your name' or, more periphrastically as in NIV, *protect them by the power of your name* (so, *e.g.*, Schlatter, p. 321; Bultmann, p. 503; Bruce, p. 332). In favour of this reading is the instrumental power of God's name in some Old Testament passages: 'Save me, O God, by your name; vindicate me by your might' (Ps. 54:1). The parallelism shows that God's name may stand not only for the manifestation of God's character, but also for his might (*cf.* also Ps. 20:1; Pr. 18:10). Alternatively, the phrase *en tō onomati sou* ('*in* your name') may be taken to have locative force ('*in* your name'), modifying *autous* ('them'). The passage must then be rendered 'keep them in your name', *i.e.* 'keep them in loyalty to you' or 'keep them in full adherence to your character' (so, *e.g.*, Lagrange, p. 445; Lindars, p. 524; Schnackenburg, 3. 180).

It is difficult to be certain which interpretation is right, and Brown (2. 759), amongst others, argues for both. But the context rather favours the second interpretation. The next clause, *the name you gave me*,[1] coheres better with the second interpretation than the first. If 'your name' in the disputed clause refers to God's power, then *the name you gave me* must mean, more or less, 'the power you gave me'. That would mean Jesus is asking his Father to protect his followers by using the same power that the Father had already given Jesus. The standard of comparison is the reverse of what one expects in the Fourth Gospel: Jesus is dependent upon his Father, and his power is meted out to him, and measured by, his Father's power (*e.g.* 5:19ff.), not the reverse.[2] Moreover, this use of 'name' ill accords with its occurrence in vv. 6–8. By contrast, if 'in your name' has locative force and modifies 'them', then God's 'name' has its most common connotation of the revelation of God's character, and *the name you gave me* assumes that God has supremely revealed himself in Jesus. That is not only a dominant theme in this Gospel (1:18; 14:9), but entirely suits vv. 6–8, 'I have revealed *your name* to those whom you gave me out of the world' (*cf.* notes, above).

In short, Jesus prays that God will keep his followers in firm fidelity to the revelation Jesus himself has mediated to them. The purpose of such faithful allegiance, Jesus avers, is *that they may be one as we are one*. Barrett (p. 508) comments that the 'disciples are to be kept by God not as units but as a unity', but that slightly misses the point. They are not kept *as* a unity; rather, their unity is the purpose of their being kept. They cannot

---

[1]On the textual variant, *cf.* Metzger, pp. 249–250. This reading is defended by the overwhelming majority of commentators and text critics.

[2]It is no help to compare the frequent appeals for power in the Pauline letters – *e.g.* passages that speak of the very same resurrection power that raised Jesus from the dead. Not only is Pauline language rather different from that of John on this point, but 'power' in such contexts is not connected with 'name'. More importantly, even in such passages the reference is to God's power raising *Jesus* from the dead, not divine power *given* to Jesus.

be one as Jesus and the Father are one unless they are kept in God's name, *i.e.* in loyal allegiance to his gracious self-disclosure in the person of his Son. A similar pattern prevails in vv. 17–19: persistence in the truth is the prerequisite to participation in Jesus' sanctification. On the nature of the unity, *cf.* notes on v. 21.

12. During his ministry Jesus *protected* the disciples and *kept them safe*,[1] not *by* the name God gave him, but *in* the name God gave him (*cf.* notes on v. 11) – *i.e.* in the revelation of God himself mediated in the person of Jesus. The only exception is Judas Iscariot, and this exception is merely apparent, since Jesus repeatedly indicates not only his awareness of the traitor's schemes, but that his choice of him was antedated by his awareness of what would take place (6:64, 70; 13:10–11, 18, 21–22). Verse 12b makes something of the same point. It establishes that Jesus has been utterly faithful to the task assigned him, *viz.* to keep and protect those that the Father has given him (*cf.* notes on 6:37–38). Jesus' prayer for his disciples, in this context, therefore *excludes* Judas Iscariot, for otherwise one would have to conclude that Jesus failed in the responsibility that had been assigned him.

The delicacy of getting this matter right is what prompts the inclusion of v. 12b. Judas Iscariot's exceptional status is established by two features:

(1) He is called 'the son of perdition' (NASB, and most versions; Gk. *ho huios tēs apōleias*). The expression could refer either to Judas' character (*e.g.* in Is. 57:4, MT's 'children of unrighteousness' [NIV's 'brood of rebels'] becomes, in the LXX, *tekna apōleias*, 'children of perdition'), or to Judas' destiny (*e.g.* in Is. 35:4 MT, 'the people I have totally destroyed' becomes, in the LXX, *ton laon tēs apōleias*, 'the people of perdition'). Both are true; probably the latter is dominant in this context. The noun *apōleia* ('perdition') in the New Testament commonly refers to eschatological damnation (Mt. 7:13; Acts 8:20; Rom. 9:22; Phil. 1:28; 3:19; 1 Tim. 6:9; Heb. 10:39; 2 Pet. 2:1; 3:7; Rev. 17:8, 11). The full expression found here, *ho huios tēs apōleias* ('the son of perdition') also occurs in 2 Thessalonians 2:3, where it is in apposition to the eschatological 'man of sin' (NIV fn.) who must be revealed before the end. Probably John 17:12 portrays Judas Iscariot as a horrible precursor belonging to the same genus as the eschatological 'son of perdition', just as in 1 Jn. 2:18, 22; 4:3 John portrays the heretical teachers he there confronts as of a piece with the antichrist.[2]

(2) The reference to the fulfilment of Scripture also assures the reader that the defection of Judas is foreseen by Scripture, and therefore no

---

[1] In v. 11 and at the beginning of v. 12, the verb is *tēreō* (lit. 'I keep'); the parallel verb in v. 12 is *phylassō* (lit. 'I guard'). Once again John displays his penchant for minor stylistic variations in parallel expressions.

[2] This is a far more likely analysis than the argument of Lightfoot (p. 301) to the effect that Judas Iscariot in John's presentation *is* the eschatological 'man of sin'. The parallel with the antichrist language in 1 Jn. 2 is striking: John makes the heretical teachers 'antichrist', but only while insisting that the definitive antichrist is still to come.

evidence of a failure on Jesus' part. The Scripture in view is probably Psalm 41:10, applied to Judas in John 13:18 (*cf.* notes), rather than Psalm 109:8 (*cf.* Acts 1:20).[1]

13. Although Jesus is saying these things while he is still *in the world*, no-one is more aware than he that his departure is imminent (*I am coming to you now*). If *these things* refers to the contents of his prayer (*i.e.* to Jn. 17 alone), then saying *these things* with the purpose of transmitting *the full measure of my joy* to the disciples calls to mind 11:42. There, too, Jesus prays out loud in such a way as to benefit those who heard his praying. This prayer demonstrates the depth of Jesus' communion with his Father, and this constitutes a paradigm for the intimate relationship with the Father that the disciples themselves will come to enjoy. Moreover, after the resurrection the truth of 17:1–5 will be freshly absorbed, and the wonder of who Jesus is will itself give birth to joy. But more probably *these things* refers to the entire farewell discourse. If so, *my joy* points unmistakably to 15:11, where Jesus' joy, like that of the disciples for whom he prays, turns on abiding in the Father's love, which itself turns on obedience to him. This interpretation makes best sense of the passage. Jesus is praying that the disciples may be kept safe, which is equivalent to praying that they may so be preserved that they remain in the Father's love, obedient to him and in hearty allegiance to the 'word' (v. 6) Jesus taught. What is now made clear is that Jesus' concern in such a prayer is not that the statistics on faithfulness be preserved, but that his disciples might share his joy.

14. The dangers from which Jesus is asking his Father to protect his disciples are real and urgent. He has given them his 'word', and they obeyed it (*cf.* notes on vv. 6, 8). That word is nothing less than the truth of the revelation of God (v. 17), the knowledge of which is eternal life (v. 3; 20:31). Therefore *the world has hated them* (*emisēsen*; on the aorist tense, *cf.* notes on v. 4–5). The reason (as in 15:18 – 16:4a) is that the disciples are now *not of the world any more than I am of the world*. Of course, this does not tie the disciples to Jesus' ontology. They have been chosen out of the world (15:19); Jesus never was of it, and had to enter it (1:10, 14). But for the disciples, the consequence of their having been chosen out of the world, of their having obeyed the word the Father gave Jesus, is that they, like Jesus, are aligned with the Father and his gracious self-disclosure in Christ Jesus. Insofar as they side with this revelation, the disciples infuriate the world. The world loves its own, and the disciples are *not of the world*, but are of God and his revelation. This revelation, in presenting the truth and commanding assent, condemns

---

[1] Wendy E. Sproston ('"The Scripture" in John 17:12', in Barry P. Thompson (ed.), *Scripture: Meaning and Method* [Fs. A. T. Hanson; Hull University Press, 1987], pp. 24–36) argues that 'the Scripture' refers to Jesus' comment on Judas in 6:69. That the Evangelist can cite Jesus' words and assign them the highest authority cannot be doubted; that he could place on Jesus' lips a citation of Jesus' own words and refer to them as Scripture is wholly implausible.

the world and exposes its evil (3:19–21; 7:7), and the world snarls in savage rage.

15–16. If in the light of this conflict Jesus prays for his own, he makes it clear that he is not praying that God would *take them out of the world* (as he himself is about to leave the world) but that God might *protect them from the evil one*. The last phrase in the original (*ek tou ponērou*) could be taken in an abstract sense ('from evil') or as a reference to the devil. The latter is almost certainly what is meant (*cf.* Mt. 6:13; 1 Jn. 2:13–14; 3:12; 5:18–19). The death/exaltation of the Master spells the principal defeat of the ruler of this world (12:31; 14:30; 16:11), but that does not rob him of all power to inflict terrible damage on the Lord's followers, if they are left without succour. Until the consummation, when the last enemy is destroyed, 'the whole world is under the control of the evil one' (1 Jn. 5:19). The Christians' task, then, is not to be withdrawn from the world, nor to be confused with the world (hence the reminder of v. 16, repeating the thought of v. 14b), but to remain in the world, maintaining witness to the truth by the help of the Paraclete (15:26–27), and absorbing all the malice that the world can muster, finally protected by the Father himself, in response to the prayer of Jesus.

Doubtless Christians in John's day were forced to ponder the implications of this prayer. So also were those who were contemplating the possibility of becoming Christians. The cosmic, spiritual nature of the conflict is laid bare. The followers of Jesus are permitted neither the luxury of compromise with a 'world' (*cf.* notes on 1:9) that is intrinsically evil and under the devil's power, nor the safety of disengagement. But if the Christian pilgrimage is inherently perilous, the safety that only God himself can provide is assured, as certainly as the prayers of God's own dear Son will be answered.

c. Jesus prays that his disciples may be sanctified (17:17–19)

17. The 'holiness' word-group from which *Sanctify* derives is rather rare in the Fourth Gospel. The verb occurs in 10:36; 17:17, 19; the adjective 'holy' is found in the expression 'Holy Spirit' in 1:33; 14:26; 20:22, and otherwise in 6:69; 17:11. At its most basic level of meaning, 'holy' is almost an adjective for God: he is transcendent, 'other', distinct, separate from his creation, and so the angels cry unceasingly in his presence, 'Holy! Holy! Holy!' (*cf.* Is. 6:3; Rev. 4:8). Derivatively, then, people and things that are reserved for him are also called holy – whether a censer for an altar in the temple of the old covenant, or a man set apart to be the high priest. The prophet Jeremiah, and Aaron and his sons, were all 'sanctified', *i.e.* set apart for sacred duty, reserved for God (Je. 1:5; Ex. 28:41). The moral overtones in our English words 'holy' and 'sanctification' emerge only at that point: *i.e.* ideally if someone is set apart for God and God's purposes alone, that person will do only what God wants, and hate all that God hates. That is what it means to be holy, as God is holy (Lv. 11:44–45; 1 Pet. 1:16).

Jesus is the one whom the Father 'set apart [*i.e.* "sanctified"; the verb is *hagiazō*] as his very own and sent into the world' (*cf.* notes on 10:36). That is, the Father reserved the Son for his own purposes in this mission into the world. Otherwise put, the Son sanctified himself (*cf.* v. 19, below) – *i.e.* he set himself apart to be and do exactly what the Father assigned him. Now he prays that God will *sanctify* (*hagiazō*) the disciples. In John's Gospel, such 'sanctification' is always for mission. The mission of the disciples is spelled out in the next verse; the present verse focuses on the *means* of the sanctification: 'Sanctify them *by the truth; your word is truth.*'

This can only mean that the means Jesus expects his Father to use as he sanctifies his Son's followers is *the truth.* The Father will immerse Jesus' followers in the revelation of himself in his Son; he will sanctify them by sending the Paraclete to guide them into all truth (15:13). Jesus' followers will be 'set apart' from the world, reserved for God's service, insofar as they think and live in conformity with the truth, the 'word' of revelation (v. 6) supremely mediated through Christ (himself the truth, 14:6, and the Word incarnate, 1:1, 14) – the revelation now embodied in the pages of this book. In practical terms, no-one can be 'sanctified' or set apart for the Lord's use without learning to think God's thoughts after him, without learning to live in conformity with the 'word' he has graciously given. By contrast, the heart of 'worldliness', of what makes the world the world (1:9), is fundamental suppression or denial of the truth, profound rejection of God's gracious 'word', his self-disclosure in Christ.

18. As Jesus was 'sanctified' and sent into the world (10:36), so the purpose of the 'sanctification' of his followers is that they are sent, by Jesus himself, into the world. This is an anticipation of the mission articulated in 20:21, the mission adumbrated in 13:20 and 15:26–27. The aorist tense ('*I have sent* them into the world') is often taken as firm evidence of anachronism, since the commission lies in the future with respect to this point in Jesus' ministry. This judgment is of a piece with the rather mechanical interpretation of the aorist in v. 4–5 (*cf.* notes).

There are four larger theological issues raised by comparing this verse with the broader context of the Fourth Gospel. (1) Comparison with v. 20, where Jesus extends the list of those for whom he is praying, attests that those for whom he prays in vv. 6–19 are primarily his original followers, and therefore that John is maintaining historical specificity, and remarkable freedom from anachronism. (2) Use of the phrase *into the world* for the mission of the disciples shows that there is no *necessary* overtone of incarnation or of invasion from another world. Only the broader descriptions of the coming of the Son 'into the world' betray the ontological gap that forever distances the origins of Jesus' mission from the origins of the disciples' mission. In the immediate context, all the emphasis is on the points of comparison, especially the invasion of the wicked 'world' from a stance that owes everything to God and nothing to the world. (3) That Jesus' prayer for his disciples has as its end their mission to the world demonstrates that this Gospel is not introducing an absolute cleavage between Jesus' followers and the world. Not only were they drawn from the world (15:19), but the prayer that they may be kept safe in the world and sanctified by the truth so as to engage in mission to the world is ample evidence that they are the continuing locus of 3:16: 'God so loved the world that he sent . . .' (*cf.* 1 Jn. 4:12). (4) Seekers reading this Gospel are thus introduced to the profound mandate and unique example that animate the witness of Christians. More, they are thus exposed to the mutually exclusive circles that demand a choice: the circle of the world, in all its rebellion and lostness, and the circle of the disciples of Jesus, in all the privilege of their relationship to the living, self-disclosing, mission-ordaining, sanctifying God.

19. As strange as *I sanctify myself* is, at one level it is nothing more than Jesus' determination to co-operate with the Father's sanctification of him (*cf.* notes on 10:36; 17:17). Jesus is as determined to set himself apart for his Father's exclusive service as the Father is to set him apart. Immediately, however, the context cries out with two additional themes.

(1) The sweep of the Fourth Gospel demonstrates that the central purpose of the mission of the Son is his death, resurrection and return to glory. If Jesus consecrates himself to perform the Father's will, he consecrates himself to the sacrifice of the cross – a theme he registers elsewhere (*cf.* notes on 10:17–18; 18:11; 19:30; *cf.* 1:29, 34; 11:49–52). The point is intimated in this verse by the fact that Jesus sanctifies himself *for them* (*hyper autōn*): the language is evocative of atonement passages elsewhere (*e.g.* Mk. 14:24; Lk. 22:19; Jn. 6:51; 1 Cor. 11:24). It is also evocative of Old Testament passages where the sacrificial animal was 'consecrated' or 'set apart' for death – indeed, of language where consecration becomes synonymous with the sacrificial death itself (*e.g.* Dt. 15:19, 21).

(2) At the same time, the second part of the verse, *that they too may be truly sanctified*, suggests that the sanctification of the believers consequent upon Jesus' sanctification of himself must be something akin to what he undergoes. Here it seems best to find a parallel in the notion of the consecration of prophet or priest to particular service (*cf.* references in the notes on v. 17). Jesus dedicates himself to the task of bringing in God's saving reign, as God's priest (*i.e.* his mediator) and prophet (*i.e.* revealer); but the purpose of this dedication is that his followers may dedicate themselves to the same saving reign, the same mission to the world (v. 18).

Thus in language that applies equally well to the consecration of a sacrifice and the consecration of a priest, Jesus is said to consecrate ('sanctify') himself. His sacrifice cannot be other than acceptable to his Father and efficacious in its effect, since as both victim and priest he who is one with the Father (1:1; 14:9–10) voluntarily sets himself apart to perform his Father's will (*cf.* Heb. 9:14; 10:9–10).

That prepares the way for the next turn in Jesus' prayer, his petitions for those who will believe through their message.

3. Jesus prays for those who will believe (17:20–23)

20–21. This extension to those who will believe through the witness of the original disciples assumes that their witness will in some measure prove effective. What Jesus prays for these believers-to-be is *that all of them may be one* (v. 21) – a petition that repeats what Jesus has prayed for his original disciples, a petition whose significance is further unpacked in the remaining clauses of the verse. This is not simply a 'unity of love'. It is a unity predicated on adherence to the revelation the Father mediated to the first disciples through his Son, the revelation they accepted (vv. 6, 8) and then passed on ('those who will believe in me *through their message'*, v. 20). It is analogous to the oneness Jesus enjoys with his Father, here fleshed out in the words *just as you are in me and I am in you*. The Father is actually in the Son, so much so that we can be told that it is the Father who is performing the Son's works (14:10); yet the Son is in the Father, not only in dependence upon and obedience to him, but his agent in creation (1:2–3) and his wholly concurring Son in the redemption and preservation of those the Father has given him (*e.g.* 6:37–40; 17:6, 19). The Father and the Son are distinguishable (the pre-incarnate Word is 'with' God, 1:1; the Son prays to his Father; the Father commissions and sends, while the Son obeys), yet they are one.

Similarly, the believers, still distinct, are to be one in purpose, in love, in action undertaken with and for one another, in joint submission to the revelation received. More: Jesus prays to his Father that these disciples may *also be in us*, probably alluding to the 'union' language of the vine metaphor (ch. 15). They are 'in' the Father and his Son, so identified with God and dependent upon him for life and fruitfulness, that they themselves become the locus of the Father's life and work *in them* (*cf.* 14:12; 15:7). All of this is to the end *that the world may believe that you have sent me*. As the display of genuine love amongst the believers attests that they are Jesus' disciples (13:34–35), so this display of unity is so compelling, so un-worldly, that their witness as to who Jesus is becomes explainable only if Jesus truly is the revealer whom the Father has sent.

Although the unity envisaged in this chapter is not institutional, this purpose clause at the end of v. 21 shows beyond possibility of doubt that the unity is meant to be observable. It is not achieved by hunting enthusiastically for the lowest common theological denominator, but by common adherence to the apostolic gospel, by love that is joyfully self-sacrificing, by undaunted commitment to the shared goals of the mission with which Jesus' followers have been charged, by self-conscious dependence on God himself for life and fruitfulness. It is a unity necessarily present, at least *in nuce*, amongst genuine believers; it is a unity that must be brought to perfection (v. 23).

22. The nature of the unity is further unpacked. The *glory* (*cf.* notes on 1:14) that the Father gave the Son he has transmitted to his followers. Exactly what is meant by these clauses is much disputed. Some tie this glory to that for which Jesus prays in vv. 1, 5, but this makes v. 22

necessarily anachronistic. On the whole, it seems best not to take *them* as a reference to the original disciples alone, but as a reference to all disciples, including those who will (later) believe through the witness of Jesus' first followers. If so, Jesus has given his *glory* to them in the sense that he has brought to completion his revelatory task (if, as in vv. 4-5 and repeatedly throughout the chapter, he may be permitted to speak proleptically and thus include his climactic cross-work). *Glory* commonly refers to the manifestation of God's character or person in a revelatory context; Jesus has mediated the glory of God, personally to his first followers and through them to those who believe on account of their message. And he has done all of this *that they may be one as we are one*.

23. *Cf.* v. 21. Some measure of unity in the disciples is assumed, but Jesus prays that they may *be brought to complete unity*, sharing richly in both the unity of purpose and the wealth of love that tie the Father and the Son together. The purpose, as in v. 21, is *to let the world know that you sent me*, to which is now added the further goal, *that you . . . have loved them even as you have loved me*. The thought is breathtakingly extravagant. The unity of the disciples, as it approaches the perfection that is its goal (*teteleiōmenoi; cf.* the use of this verb in 4:34; 5:36; 17:4), serves not only to convince many in the world that Christ is indeed the supreme locus of divine revelation as Christians claim (*that you sent me*), but that Christians themselves have been caught up into the love of the Father for the Son, secure and content and fulfilled because loved by the Almighty himself (*cf.* Eph. 3:17b-19), with the very same love he reserves for his Son. It is hard to imagine a more compelling evangelistic appeal.

4. Jesus prays that all believers may be perfected so as to see Jesus' glory (17:24-26)

24. Jesus frankly expresses his will to the Father (*I want . . .*, thelō, lit. 'I will'), but of course his will is nothing less than the will of his Father (4:34; 5:30; 6:38). What Jesus wants is *those you have given me* (*cf.* Additional Note) *to be with me where I am, and to see my glory*. *Those you have given me* includes all the elect, both the original followers and those who would believe on account of their message (*cf.* v. 2). The 'glory' Jesus wants his disciples to see is (he tells his Father) *the glory you have given me because you loved me before the creation of the world* (lit. 'before the foundation of the world': *cf.* Mt. 13:35; 25:34; Eph. 1:4; Heb. 4:3; 9:26; 1 Pet. 1:20; Rev. 13:8; 17:8) – an unambiguous reference to v. 5, where Jesus prays to be restored to the glory that he had with the Father before the world began. The first witnesses could testify that they had seen Jesus' glory (1:14), as indeed they had, not only in selected 'signs' (*e.g.* 2:11) but supremely in the cross and resurrection. Even so, they had not witnessed Jesus' glory in its unveiled splendour. Christians from every generation glimpse something of Jesus' glory even now (*cf.* 2 Cor. 3:18), but one day, when he appears, we shall be like him, for we shall see him as he is (1 Jn. 3:2). The glory of Christ that his followers will see is his glory as God, the glory he enjoyed before his mission because of the

Father's love for him. The ultimate hope of Jesus' followers thus turns on the love of the Father for the Son, as in 14:31 it turns on the love of the Son for the Father. Presumably those who share, with the Son, the delight of being loved by the Father (v. 23), share also in the glory to which the Son is restored in consequence of his triumphant death/ exaltation. We are thus brought back to the futurist eschatology of 14:2–3,[1] while creation and consummation meet in the glory of the Son.

25–26. Although it is possible to think of these two verses as a summary of the entire prayer, their connection with v. 24 is perhaps more compelling. They serve to ground the eschatological prospect of v. 24, not only by continuing the theme of the Father's love for the Son, but by emphasizing the continuing manifestation of the Father to the believers, the continuing 'making known' of the Father,[2] in anticipation of the consummating glory.

Jesus addresses God as *Righteous Father* (*cf.* v. 11) because God is acknowledged to be profoundly righteous in that judgment by which the 'world' (*cf.* notes on 1:9) is condemned for its ignorance, while Jesus and his followers are accepted. Jesus' mission is not a failure: although[3] *the world does not know you*, Jesus tells his Father, he himself does, and has made God known to his disciples. Jesus knows God intrinsically; because he has in turn made God known to his followers, they have come to recognize that the Father himself sent Jesus. Moreover, Jesus' revelatory work will continue (presumably through the Holy Spirit), so that God's gracious self-disclosure in his Son will not be reduced to a mere datum of history, but will be a lived experience (*cf.* 14:23). The purpose of this continuing manifestation of God himself is, first, that the love the Father has for the Son (*cf.* v. 24) may be *in them* – which may mean 'amongst them' (and displayed in their love for one another) or 'within them' (so that as individuals they become loving people). It is impossible to think of one without the other. The crucial point is that this text does not simply make these followers the objects of God's love (as in v. 23), but promises that they will be so transformed, as God is continually made known to them, that God's own love for his Son will become their love. The love with which they learn to love is nothing less than the love amongst the persons of the Godhead (*cf.* notes on 15:12–17).

The second purpose of Christ's continuing work in making known his Father is (Jesus avers) *that I myself may be in them* – and again *in them* might mean 'amongst them' or 'within them'. Either way, this is nothing

---

[1]In the light of our interpretation of 14:2–3, and of the plain statements of 5:28–29; 6:39–40, it is wholly inadequate to think that the eschatology in view in this verse refers to nothing more than what happens to the individual believer when he or she dies, without any window on the consummation.

[2]Once again John's penchant for near synonyms is evidenced in the parallel between 'I have revealed' (v. 6; *ephanerōsa*, lit. 'I have manifested') and 'I have made [you] known' (v. 26; *egnōrisa*).

[3]On the difficult Greek syntax, *cf.* Beasley-Murray, p. 293.

less than the fulfilment of the ancient hope that God would dwell in the midst of his people (*cf.* 14:20).

Additional note

24. In manuscripts from a compelling diversity of text types, the text literally reads 'what you have given me'. This reading has been 'corrected' in many manuscripts to the formally more coherent 'those you have given me'. English syntax may well demand that this be the translation in any case, but the neuter singular is fairly common in John when the elect are referred to as a group (*e.g.* 6:37; 17:2).

E. THE TRIAL AND PASSION OF JESUS *(18:1 – 19:42)*

All the canonical Gospels move inexorably toward the passion and resurrection of Jesus the Messiah; indeed, without this climax, a 'Gospel' would not be a Gospel. However widely individual stories about Jesus and his teaching and miracles circulated before the Evangelists wrote them down, there is little doubt that the first connected, running accounts of Jesus had to do with his passion.

Contemporary debates over John 18 – 19 tend to revolve around the following issues:

(1) The *literary* relation between John's passion narrative and those found in the Synoptics continues to excite discussion. Dauer, for instance, undertakes a minute examination, and feels he can strip off Johannine accretions and editorial changes to expose a pre-Johannine written source that was influenced by the Synoptic Gospels. M. Sabbe (*BETL*, pp. 203–234) examines Dauer's work for one section of the account (Jn. 18:1–11) and concludes that it is far simpler to conclude that John relied directly on the Synoptics: hypotheses about a written pre-Johannine source that mediates Synoptic influence he judges unwarranted. By contrast, Dodd (*HTFG*, esp. pp. 65ff.) argues that John writes in complete independence of the Synoptic tradition.

The issues are too complex to be probed here, although in the notes that follow attention will occasionally be drawn to Synoptic parallels. Conclusions about dependence and literary sources turn on evidence that will not support much weight; moreover, such conclusions are dependent in part on how we think of the entire development of first-century Christianity, and of such related questions as the authorship of the Gospels, the degree of communication amongst the churches of the first century, and much more. In this commentary it is assumed that John had read at least one and perhaps two of the Synoptic Gospels. For various reasons, however, he chose to write his own book, so that the *demonstration* of direct dependence is an uncertain business. Even the evidence that purports to show that John's account is secondary is not very reputable. For instance, it has been argued that the addition of specific names – the Kidron, Peter as the one who wields the sword, Malchus for the servant who loses his ear – is a late attempt to add verisimilitude to earlier accounts that even then could not fit names to the places or individuals involved. This is far too sceptical. Metzger[1] has shown from both biblical and extra-biblical parallels that later accounts sometimes add names, and sometimes drop them: adding or dropping therefore cannot be used to demonstrate the secondary nature of the account. In some instances the presence of added names might be used to argue for an independent source. As for the argument that the date of Jesus' death in John's Gospel is incompatible with the evidence of the Synoptics, *cf.* discussion introducing 13:1, and notes on 13:27; 18:28; 19:14, 31, 36, 42.

(2) The *theological* relation between the passion narrative in John and its parallels in the Synoptics can be traced out, but is often overstated. The most commonly raised differences are three.. (a) The Romans play a more central role in John than in the Synoptics: they appear even in the arrest scene (18:3), and Pilate takes up much more space. This is judged by some to be historically improbable, and nothing more than the Evangelist's desire to show that the entire world was arrayed against Jesus. (b) Not only is there no record in John of Jesus' agony in Gethsemane, but in general there are many efforts to show that Jesus is in control. There is no mention of Judas' traitorous kiss: Jesus goes forth to his arrest (18:1, 4) and controls the flow of events. He interrogates his captors, and displays enough of his glory that they fall backward to the ground (vv. 3–8). (c) There are several passages in John that have no parallel whatsoever in the Synoptics: bringing Jesus to Annas (18:12–14), his answer to the high priest and to the official who slapped him (18:19–24), conversations between Jesus and Pilate (18:28–37; 19:9–11) and between Pilate and the Jews (18:28–32; 19:4–7, 13–16), the statement that Jesus carried his own cross (19:17), an excursus on the significance of the inscription on the cross (19:20–22), the forging of the link between his mother and the beloved disciple (19:26–27), and the cry from the cross recorded in 19:30.

We consider these three in turn:

(a) Although the Romans are more important in John's narrative than in the Synoptics, that point can be exaggerated. Only in John 19:12, never in the Synoptics, are the *Jews* portrayed as manipulating Pilate in order to ensure a guilty verdict and a capital sentence. Moreover, sceptics writing on the Synoptic Gospels frequently charge them with downplaying the real part Pilate played, since (it is alleged) it was safer to blame the Jews than the Romans. That charge is misguided: by the time

[1]Bruce M. Metzger, *New Testament Studies: Philological, Versional, and Patristic* (E. J. Brill, 1980), ch. 2, 'Names for the Nameless in the New Testament: a Study in the Growth of Christian Tradition'.

the Gospels were written, Pilate had long since been deposed and banished by Rome. It does suggest, however, that chronic historical scepticism can find fault no matter what the evidence. John emphasizes Pilate's role, so sceptical wisdom maintains John is manufacturing evidence in order to justify his thesis that the entire world opposed Jesus. The charge bears its measure of irony: John is also frequently charged with anti-Semitism, and if that were his bias it is strange that Pilate should play so large a role.

In any case, so far as Jesus' execution is concerned there is, as we shall see, more than enough guilt to go around. Individual texts are treated below (*e.g.* notes on 18:3, 28ff.). For the moment it is enough to affirm that the additional material on Pilate is historically credible (so far as it can be tested), and provides complementary, not contradictory, information. Its net effect on the flow of John's narrative is not so much to condemn the entire world (since for John the 'world' is not so much big as bad, and therefore can be represented as easily by Jews as by Gentiles: *cf.* notes on 1:9; 3:16), but to weave a more detailed picture that leaves John room to present the nature of Jesus' kingdom (18:33–38; 19:12–16) and to demonstrate in narrative form the truth already articulated: Jesus is not a martyr but a voluntary sacrifice, obedient to his Father's will (10:17–18).

(b) Again, there is genuine insight in the observation that John portrays Jesus as in control of his destiny as he makes his way to the cross. On the other hand, far too much is made of some points. True, Judas' traitorous kiss is not reported, but it is John alone who makes it clear how the traitor knew where to find Jesus (v. 2), and thus to betray him. Although the agony of Gethsemane goes unreported in this Gospel, John preserves other signs of Jesus' struggle (*cf.* notes on 12:27–28; 18:11), while in the Synoptic Gospels the Gethsemane prayers end with the kind of firm resolution ('not my will, but yours be done') that is exemplified here at his arrest (*cf.* notes introducing ch. 17). Certainly the tone Jesus strikes with his interlocutors in this Gospel differs but little from the tone set by Jesus after his arrest in the Synoptics. Resolution and anguish, firm commitment to obey the Father and personal recoil at the cost – these are not mutually exclusive options even amongst believers suffering today. How much less are they mutually exclusive possibilities in one who is repeatedly described in both divine and human terms! In short, John's portrait of Jesus' arrest, interrogation, trials and death focuses on a different part of the spectrum than do the accounts by the Synoptists, but it is the same spectrum, and the portraits (as we shall see) prove mutually enriching and mutually explanatory.

(c) As for the numerous snippets that are found only in John, they are best treated in the notes (below). Some of them are tightly bound up with Johannine themes (*e.g.* the connection between Mary and the beloved disciple [19:26–27], or the cry 'It is finished' [19:30]). That fact cannot itself justify the view that the material is created out of whole cloth to make a point. In a book studded with witness themes, it is easier to believe, rather, that the Evangelist wants to bear witness himself – to make some points out of material he knows to be true but not yet published.

(3) Perhaps the most heated debate turns on the charge that all the Gospel accounts of the arrest, trials, crucifixion and death of Jesus are hopelessly ill-informed. They are nothing but the created smear campaign of Christians steeped in unconscionable anti-Semitism, an ugly bias starkly revealed in the numerous details that are historically impossible. In particular, there are so many illegalities in the proceedings that the narration can only be understood as a pathetic piece of religious propaganda. Although there is no consensus as to what actually happened, it is regularly pointed out that in the tractate *Sanhedrin* of the Jewish Mishnah it is stipulated that in capital cases there were to be no night trials, that the proceedings had to extend over at least two consecutive days, and that provision was made for the private interrogation of witnesses. More than one Jewish writer has gone so far as to argue that the Sanhedrin actually tried to save Jesus from the Roman tribunal. All contrary evidence is assigned to the bias of the later church.

Lengthy discussions and surveys of the literature are found elsewhere (*cf.* Carson, *Matt*, pp. 549–552; Beasley-Murray, pp. 308–313).[1] Particular problems relevant to the Fourth Gospel are briefly mentioned in the notes below. For now it is sufficient to observe the following points: (a) Many Mishnaic stipulations never had the force of obeyed law; they were theoretical formulations only. For instance, there is no independent evidence that the 'burnings' described in Mishnah *Sanhedrin* 7:2 ever took place. (b) There is ample historical evidence that many legal restrictions could be breached if the court decided that 'the hour demands it'. If the authorities feared mob violence, they would have strong incentive to increase the pace of the proceedings. Although executions could take place on feast days, they could not take place on the Sabbath. If Jesus was arrested Thursday evening (considered Friday by Jewish reckoning), things had to move swiftly if Jesus was to be executed and buried by dusk on Friday, the onset of the Sabbath. Roman officials like Pilate worked only from dawn until late morning: if the Jewish authorities were to approach him with their demand for judicial execution, they would have to prepare their case overnight. (c) In any case, the Gospel accounts themselves draw attention to certain irregularities. In most societies, strong religious conviction coupled with personal animus is not likely to be stifled by legal barriers: expedience can usually find a way. (d) Moreover, it is disputed just how many of the stipulations of Mishnah (compiled about AD 200) should be read back into Jesus' time; it is disputed just what relationship prevailed between the Pharisees of Jesus' day and the rabbis who figure most prominently

[1] To which should now also be added Ellis Rivkin, *What Crucified Jesus? The Political Execution of a Charismatic* (Abingdon, 1984).

in the Mishnah; it is disputed how many of the rabbinic concerns would have held sway in the pre-AD 70 Sanhedrin where *Sadducees* enjoyed more authority than Pharisees.

As painful as it is to bring the subject up, we must frankly suggest that the opinions of not a few historians have been coloured by the holocaust. The legacy of Western Christendom's persecution of Jews is so foul, and reached such horrifying, benumbing proportions in the Nazi terror, that almost by way of reaction many scholars, both Jewish and Christian, have gone to great lengths to blame the church and to distance Jews from any culpability in the death of Jesus. The hate-mongering charge of 'God-killer' has reflected so much animus and evoked so much pain that it is not surprising that historical even-handedness becomes extremely difficult, and can easily be interpreted as moral weakness. The best scholars from both sides have long recognized this. The Jewish scholar Samuel Sandmel writes: 'Perhaps we might be willing to say to ourselves that it is not at all impossible that some Jews, even leading Jews, recommended the death of Jesus to Pilate. We are averse to saying this to ourselves, for so total has been the charge against us that we have been constrained to make a total denial.'[1]

There is something here for Christians to ponder, something for Jews to think about, and something for everyone, regardless of religious or racial background, to contemplate. In reverse order: All of us must remember that it is the party in power that is most likely to do the persecuting, whether in the first century or in the sixteenth. Jews must recognize that most if not all of the New Testament writers were racially Jews, Jews who had become Christians. 'Anti-Semitism' is simply not the right category for such people.[2] The New Testament dividing line is theological, spiritual, historical – not racial. And most important of all, we who call ourselves Christians must constantly remember that our own theology insists that each of us is as guilty of putting Jesus on the cross as Caiaphas. It is our guilt that brought Jesus to the cross as the Lamb of God (1:29, 36). Theologically, this does not mitigate Jewish guilt, or Roman guilt. It does not excuse individuals like Caiaphas and Pilate. It does place Jesus' death against the backdrop of the more properly basic guilt: the guilt of ordinary sinners who would not have known pardon and forgiveness apart from the demonstration of the love of God in his Son Christ Jesus, the guilt of the world, my guilt, that called forth the unmerited love of God displayed in the mission of his Son. That means that any Christian, by virtue of the elemental theology he or she espouses as a Christian, is singularly ill-placed to point a finger of condescending condemnation in the direction of other sinners.

There are several ways by which the diverse Gospel accounts of Jesus'

---

[1]Samuel Sandmel, *We Jews and Jesus* (Oxford University Press, 1965), p. 141. There is some early Jewish evidence that suggests Jews condemned Jesus for being a sorcerer and an apostate (*cf.* esp. B. *Sanhedrin* 43a): *cf.* W. Horbury, *JTS* 33, 1982, pp. 56–58.

[2]*Cf.* Leistner; S. Wilson, *IBS* 1, 1979, pp. 28–50.

passion, especially his arrest and trials, can be brought into a single story-line. There were two trials, one Jewish and one Roman. The former began with informal examination by Annas (18:12–14, 19–23), possibly while members of the Sanhedrin were being hurriedly summoned. A session of the Sanhedrin (Mt. 26:57–68; Mk. 14:53–65) with frank consensus was followed by a formal decision at dawn and dispatch to Pilate (Mt. 27:1–2; Lk. 22:66–71). The Roman trial began with a first examination before Pilate (Mt. 27:11–14; Jn. 18:28–38a), which was followed by Herod's interrogation (Lk. 23:6–12) and Jesus' final appearance before Pilate (Mt. 27:15–31; Jn. 18:38b – 19:16). Other reconstructions are possible, but this one usefully co-ordinates the biblical data. Even so, in the notes that follow primary attention is devoted to John's story-line.

1. *Jesus arrested* (18:1–11)

1. *Tauta eipōn* (lit. 'having said these things') may refer to the prayer of ch. 17 (hence NIV's 'When he had finished praying'), but more probably it refers to all of chs. 14 – 17. Jesus now sets in motion the departure of which he has been speaking (14:2, *etc.*); he exemplifies the self-consecration that has been the burden of his prayer (17:19). *Jesus left* may mean that he and *his disciples* left the upper room; alternatively, it means they left the city (*cf.* notes on 13:31ff.; 14:31). Heading east, they crossed the *Kidron Valley*, the *Wadi en-Nar*, the bottom of which at this point falls two hundred feet below the base of the outer court of the temple. This wadi courses roughly south or south-east until it meets the Dead Sea (*cf.* Ezk. 47:1ff.; Zc. 14:8; *cf.* notes on Jn. 7:37–38). The Greek literally reads *ho cheimarros tou Kedrōn*: a *cheimarros* is an intermittent stream, one that is dry most of the year but that becomes a torrent during seasonal rains. NIV's 'Kidron' preserves Hebrew spelling; following the LXX, this passage (in the Greek) adopts *Kedrōn*, which some later copyists of the New Testament confused with the Greek word *kedros* ('cedar'), changing the form of the article before the word to generate the meaning 'valley of the cedars'. Rising to the east of the Kidron is the Mount of Olives. On its slopes *there was an olive grove* (*kēpos*, lit. 'garden'); Matthew (26:36) and Mark (14:32) call it 'Gethsemane' (= 'oil-press'). John says that Jesus and his disciples *went into it*; later he says that Jesus *went out*: the verbs suggest a walled enclosure.

2. That *Jesus had often met there with his disciples*, especially in the week leading up to Passover, is attested by Luke 21:37; 22:39 (which must not be taken to mean that Jesus did not on most nights eventually withdraw all the way to Bethany). On the night of Passover itself, Jewish law required that observing Jews remain within an extended city limit that included Gethsemane but excluded Bethany. Probably this walled olive grove was set aside by some wealthy supporter for the use of Jesus and his disciples. They resorted there sufficiently regularly that Judas *knew the place*. The time (at night) and location (away from the city itself, removed from crowds that could become mobs) provided the betrayer with an ideal venue in which to bring the arresting officers right up to

Jesus (*cf.* Lk. 22:6). Having 'sanctified himself' for the sacrificial death immediately ahead, Jesus does to seek to escape his opponents by changing his habits: he goes to the place where Judas Iscariot could count on finding him.

3. Only John specifies that, in addition to bringing the Jewish officials, Judas Iscariot also guided *a detachment of soldiers*. The Greek (*tēn speiran*) makes it clear that these were not Jews, but *'the cohort* (of Roman auxiliaries)'. A full auxiliary cohort had a paper strength of 1,000 men, *i.e.* 760 foot soldiers and 240 cavalry, and was led by a 'chiliarch' (lit. 'leader of a thousand', often translated 'tribune'; v. 12, 'commander'). In practice a cohort normally numbered 600 men; but in any case the noun *speira* can refer to a 'maniple' of only 200 men, and it is not necessary to assume that an entire maniple was present. Roman auxiliary troops were usually stationed at Caesarea, but during the feast days they were garrisoned in the fortress of Antonia to the north-west of the temple complex. This move to Jerusalem not only ensured more efficient policing of the huge throngs that swelled the population of Jerusalem during the high feasts, but guaranteed that any mob violence or incipient rebellion, bred by the crowding and the religious fervour, would be efficiently crushed. That is probably the reason why they were called out to support the temple officials: the risk of mob response was doubtless rather high in the case of an arrest of someone with Jesus' popularity.

It is mere pedantry that understands the participle *labōn* to mean that Judas was 'taking' the troops to Jesus, as if he had the authority to command them. He merely 'took' them through the darkness to the place where he thought it would be possible to arrest Jesus in relative privacy – *i.e.* he was *guiding* them. The *officials from the chief priests and Pharisees* were doubtless temple police, the primary arresting officers (if we may judge by Jesus' destination after his arrest). *Chief priests* and *Pharisees* are often linked (7:32, 45; 11:47, 57). The former expression refers to the priestly aristocracy that largely controlled the Sanhedrin; the latter are not mentioned again after this point (*cf.* notes on 1:19, 24). The combination of Jewish and Roman authorities in this arrest indicts the whole world. At the historical level, it reminds us that common foes generate strange friendships (*cf.* Lk. 23:6–12), and suggests that Pilate may well have been tipped off to the imminence of the arrest before Jesus was actually brought into his court.

The *torches, lanterns and weapons* are not anomalous, even though there was a full moon (since it was Passover): doubtless Judas had told them where they were going, and the prospect of scrambling around a mountainside in pursuit of one man prompted more than one official to bring a light.

4. All four Gospels present Jesus as knowing what would happen: *e.g.* in the Synoptics the passion predictions, the agonized praying in Gethsemane and the calm insistence that he could call on legions of angels for help are otherwise meaningless. But the theme is especially strong in John (*cf.* 10:18): Jesus offers up his life in obedience to his Father, not as a

pathetic martyr buffeted by the ill winds of a cruel fate. In full knowledge of what was to befall him, Jesus *went out* (of the enclosed olive
grove, apparently) and asked his question.

5–6. Perhaps it was at this point that Judas kissed Jesus: John does not
record the detail. The Evangelist's parenthetical remark *And Judas the
traitor was standing there with them* shows that he is not thereby exoner-
ating the betrayer. Considering Judas' rôle in leading the arresting
officials to the garden (v. 2) it seems arbitrary to argue that the kiss is
omitted to de-emphasize Judas' significance and underline Jesus' control
of events. More likely the Evangelist, omitting details, is simply driving
toward the Christological centre: 'Who is it you want?'

Jesus of Nazareth (lit. 'Jesus the Nazarene', an uncommon way of
saying the same thing), they reply. Jesus' answer, *I am he* (on the
variant, *cf.* the Additional Note), evokes a startling response: *they drew
back and fell to the ground.* The Greek form of Jesus' answer is ambiguous:
egō eimi (lit. 'I am') is often to be read as mere self-identification ('It is I'),
or as if the appropriate complement were inserted from the context (*i.e.*
'I am Jesus'), but can bear far richer overtones (*cf.* notes on 6:20; 8:24, 28,
58; 13:19). In Isaiah 40 – 55, it is God himself who repeatedly takes these
words on his lips. But precisely because the expression is indeed
ambiguous, and the context provides a perfectly adequate complement,
we must not conjecture that Jesus' interlocutors fell back for no other
reason than that Jesus uttered an expression that ought to be reserved
for the Almighty alone. For those with eyes to see as they read this book,
that hint, that overtone, is undoubtedly present; but if those who first
heard Jesus speak had so understood him, it is far more likely that their
reaction would have mirrored that recorded in 8:58–59, where Jesus
utters the same words without the covering ambiguity.

Others (*e.g.* Lindars, p. 541) have suggested this is a Johannine
creation of a theophany, in which the normal experience is to fall
prostrate (Ezk. 1:28; Dn. 10:9; Acts 9:4; Rev. 1:17). Yet such theophanies
do not depict the worshipper *drawing back* and falling to the ground.
More important, if John is creating a theophany, he is painfully clumsy:
in this view, the arresting officials experience a theophany as they gaze
on Jesus and hear his words, and then proceed to arrest him anyway!
Once again, the reader, after the fact, knows that the incarnate Word
manifested his glory in the veil of his flesh (*cf.* notes on 1:14), but John
does not need to resort to formally incomprehensible narrative in order
to score theological points. The Evangelist has already testified to the
effect of Jesus' words on temple officials sent to arrest him (7:45–46);
indeed, it is not at all unlikely that some of the same personnel are again
involved. If they have been awed by Jesus before, if they have been
dumbfounded by his teaching, his authority, his directness in the full
light of day in the precincts of the temple where they most feel at home,
it is not hard to believe that they are staggered by his open self-
disclosure on a sloping mountainside in the middle of the night – the
more so if some of them hear the overtones of God's self-disclosure in

the prophecy of Isaiah. It may take them a few seconds to pull them-selves together and regroup; in the Evangelist's eyes, their physical ineptitude was another instance of people responding better than they knew (*cf.* notes on 11:49–52).[1]

7–9. The scene is repeated, but before Jesus is taken away he ensures that his followers are not harmed. Just as events fulfil the authoritative and prophetic words of Scripture, so this event fulfils Jesus' own words, which cannot be less authoritative (*cf.* Mk. 13:31). The utterance that is here fulfilled, *I have not lost one of those you gave me,* is a summary of 17:12, itself based on 6:39; 10:28. The exception of Judas Iscariot, verbalized in these verses, is understood and not here repeated. Some have objected that the verbal claims of these verses relate to the eternal salvation of Jesus' followers, while this 'fulfilment' depicts nothing more than escape from arrest and (perhaps) physical death. Dodd (*IFG*, pp. 432–433) rightly rejects the criticism. In one sense, the disciples' safety is secured by Jesus' arrest and death. But this is not simply the substitution of physical safety for eternal salvation. Rather, it is the symbol of it, an illustration of it – more, it is the first step in securing the eschatological reality.

10–11. Although this incident is reported in the Synoptic Gospels (Mt. 26:51–52; Mk. 14:47; Lk. 22:49–51), only John names Simon Peter and Malchus (*cf.* notes introducing this chapter). The *sword* (*machaira*) may have been not much more than a dagger. The blow was as clumsy as Peter's courage was great; the tactic was as pointless as Peter's mis-understanding was total. John agrees with Luke in noting that it was Malchus' *right* ear that was severed, and with Matthew in recording Jesus' command to put away the sword (*cf.* also Je. 47:6). But in Matthew this command is followed by a paraenetic conclusion: 'for all who draw the sword will die by the sword'. Here John's report focuses all the attention on Jesus Christ himself: *Shall I not drink the cup the Father has given me?* Peter's bravery is not only useless, it is a denial of the work to which Jesus has just consecrated himself – and entirely in line with the Synoptic evidence as to the failure of the disciples to comprehend the passion when it was announced to them (Mk. 8:31–33 par.; *cf.* Jn. 13:6–10). Jesus' commitment to 'drink the cup' prepared for him by his Father calls to mind Jesus' prayer in Gethsemane (Mt. 26:39, 42; *cf.* also Mk. 14:36; Jn. 12:27–28), though the emphasis here – firm resolution to accept what the Father gives him – better reflects the *outcome* of the prayer in Gethsemane ('not my will, but yours be done') than the agonizing supplication that secured it.

Additional note

5. Some manuscripts read 'I am Jesus', with or without the article for

---

[1]Although it is frequently suggested, there is insufficient reason to think that the Evangelist has such passages as Pss. 27:2; 56:9 in mind.

Jesus. In the early uncial (*i.e.* written in capital letters) scripts, 'Jesus' was abbreviated IC. Words were run together without spaces between them, so that the previous word AYTOIC ('to them') plus the articular form of Jesus' name would have appeared as AYTOICOIC – and it is easy enough to imagine how the last part could have been dropped by a copyist. Something similar can be argued if the name of Jesus is placed after *egō eimi* (where it appears in some manuscripts). But it is more likely that some early copyist inserted the name, thinking that it clarified the flow of the narrative, and failing to recognize the intended ambiguity in Jesus' response (discussed above). In any case the simple answer *egō eimi* ('I am') is textually firm in v. 8.

2. Jesus before Annas *(18:12–14)*

12–14. Only John reports this preliminary interrogation before Annas. The fact that the words *the detachment of soldiers with its commander* (*cf.* notes on v. 3) precede *and the Jewish officials* may suggest that the Roman auxiliaries surged forward and took greater prominence after Peter's abortive strike. There was scarcely any reason to arrest Peter if Jesus had healed Malchus – although, apparently, John simply assumes the healing, for he does not report it. That the Jewish officials were the primary arresting officers is clear from the fact that John is brought to Annas, and then to Caiaphas; the Roman auxiliaries, their role of preventing trouble complete, doubtless returned to their barracks in the Fortress of Antonia.

The Greek behind 'the Jewish officials' might more literally be rendered 'the officers of the Jews'. *The Jews* is a notoriously slippery term in the Fourth Gospel (*cf.* notes on 1:19), but here the referent is the Jewish authorities, whose highest court was the Sanhedrin presided over by the high priest. Theologically, 'the Jews' in chs. 18 – 19 are presented as those who cling to the minutiae of the law while failing to understand how the law points to Jesus the Messiah (*e.g.* 18:28, 31–35; 19:7, 15; *cf.* Pancaro, pp. 307–310). They aim to execute Jesus as a law-breaker, whereas if they understood the law aright (*cf.* 5:39–40) they would become Jesus' followers.

Formally, the ensuing verses are confusing. Jesus is brought before Annas, who is distinguished from Caiaphas the high priest (v. 13). The high priest (Annas? Caiaphas?) questions Jesus (v. 19), and then Annas sends him to Caiaphas the high priest (v. 24). The formal incongruities have generated textual displacements in a few manuscripts, but these are certainly secondary (*cf.* Metzger, pp. 251–252; Bultmann, pp. 643–644). One or two suggested emendations are no less problematic.

The problem is largely resolved once the complexities surrounding the high priesthood in the first century are recognized. Annas held the office from AD 6 until AD 15, when Valerius Gratus, Pilate's predecessor, deposed him. Annas continued to hold enormous influence, not only because many Jews resented the arbitrary deposition and appointment of high priests by a foreign power (under the Mosaic legislation the appointment was for life!), but also because no fewer than five of Annas' sons, and his son-in-law Caiaphas, held the office at one time or another (Jos., *Ant.* xx. 198). Annas was thus the patriarch of a high priestly family, and doubtless many still considered him the 'real' high priest even though Caiaphas was the high priest by Roman lights. Luke preserves the same tension. He dates the opening of John the Baptist's ministry by locating it during the reigns of various monarchs, and 'during the high priesthood of Annas and Caiaphas' (Lk. 3:2; *cf.* Acts 4:6). So it is not surprising that Jesus should have been taken first to Annas; probably the matter was decided in advance, and Annas was to some extent the power behind Caiaphas. Thus the 'high priest' who questions Jesus in v. 19 is Annas. Caiaphas does not take his turn until after v. 24.

On *that year*, and the identification of Caiaphas as *the one who had advised the Jews that it would be good if one man died for the people*, *cf.* notes on 11:49–52. The theme surfaces again not merely for the sake of identifying Caiaphas, but to remind the reader of the full and tragic run of ironies that characterize the entire unfolding of the Father's wise purposes. That is also the primary reason why there is no report of formal Jewish deliberations. The mere chronicling of the event is of little interest to John; perhaps he judges that the essential facts have been adequately circulated elsewhere.

3. Peter's first denial of Jesus (18:15–18)

15–16. All four Gospels relate Peter's sad lapse. The point is not the raw fact that Peter disowned his Lord, but that he did so as a disciple, an intimate disciple (*cf.* Culpepper, p. 120). In the flow of the narrative, this has the double effect of demonstrating Jesus' advance knowledge of his passion, and therefore his control over the events (Jesus predicted this incident, 13:38), and of isolating Jesus even from his most intimate followers, thereby drawing attention to the uniqueness of his suffering and death.

Two difficult questions of identification in these verses divide the commentators.

(1) The person with Simon Peter, 'another disciple', is not identified. Traditionally this person has been identified with the 'beloved disciple' (*cf.* Introduction, § III; and notes on 13:23), presumably John the Apostle. Most contemporary scholars question this identification, partly because this 'other disciple' is not specifically called the 'beloved disciple', and partly because most judge it unlikely that a fisherman from Galilee would have such ready access to the high priest's court-yard. Both verses say he was 'known' to the high priest: indeed, the Greek word (*gnōstos*) suggests more than mere recognition, the way a prime minister might recognize his or her cobbler, but something of intimacy. In the LXX it can refer to a 'close friend' (*e.g.* 2 Ki. 10:11; Ps. 55:13); in Luke 2:44 the meaning is similar, referring to friends of such intimacy that they are associated with relatives (*cf.* also *NewDocs* 4. § 44).

In the nature of the case, the 'other disciple' could not have enjoyed such unchallenged access to the high priest's courtyard unless he were a great deal more than a nodding acquaintance. For this reason many scholars suggest this 'other disciple' is an unnamed Jerusalem disciple not otherwise known.

On the other hand, the traditional identification should not be ruled out too quickly. The fourth Evangelist does not hesitate to provide the names of other prominent inquirers and followers in the Jerusalem area, *viz.* Nicodemus and Joseph of Arimathea. The oblique manner of reference, 'another disciple', calls to mind the 'beloved disciple' who is so regularly unnamed. This is the more striking when we remember the close connection between the beloved disciple and Peter (13:23–24; 20:2–10; 21:20–24) – a close connection confirmed by the Synoptics (under the reasonable assumption that the beloved disciple is John the Apostle). Moreover, contemporary social stratification is not necessarily relevant to the first century: a modern prime minister may not be intimate with the family of the neighbourhood fishmonger, but it is far from clear that divisions ran along such lines in ancient Israel. John's father was wealthy enough to have hired hands (Mk. 1:19–20). A little wealth, perhaps a relative or two on the inside track in Jerusalem, and the connection between a Galilean fisherman and the Jerusalem high priest does not seem so far-fetched – especially in a society which, unlike parts of the Greek world, did not erect barriers between manual labour and educational or priestly roles. Rabbis were expected to gain a trade skill (as Paul was a journeyman leather worker). The most competent recent evaluation of the evidence concludes, rather tentatively, that the 'other disciple' is the beloved disciple.[1] Whoever he was, he was not only able to walk into the high priest's courtyard without being questioned, he was also able to speak to the servant-girl attending the gate and ensure that Peter was admitted as well.

(2) Who is the 'high priest', and what is meant by his 'courtyard' (*aulē*)? If 'high priest' were a reference to Caiaphas (v. 13), and the ensuing interrogation before the Sanhedrin, the *aulē* could be within the temple complex. The sequence of 'high priest' references in this chapter (esp. vv. 13–14, 19, 24), however, shows that Annas is in view, and that *aulē* is the courtyard, the atrium connected with his house. This becomes a virtual certainty with the mention of a *girl on duty* at the gate: only men held such assignments in the temple precincts. *Cf.* also notes on v. 18. It is not unlikely that the house of Caiaphas shared the same courtyard, and that the second stage of the investigation (v. 24) was also relatively private, though with at least some members of the Sanhedrin present, presaging the formal action of the Sanhedrin about dawn (the latter not recorded in the Fourth Gospel; *cf.* notes introducing 18:1).

---

[1] Frans Neirynck, *Evangelica: Gospel Studies – Etudes d'Evangile. Collected Essays*, ed. F. van Segbroeck (Leuven University Press, 1982), pp. 335–364.

17. Both here and in Mark 14:66, 69 par., it is a servant-girl who confronts Peter the first time. If she recognized the other disciple as someone who could be admitted, doubtless she knew him well enough to know he was a disciple of Jesus. Seeing Peter come in with him, she made the obvious connection and asked the obvious question: 'Are you *another* of this man's disciples?' (American NIV; *mē kai sy ek tōn mathētōn ei tou anthrōpou toutou*; lit. 'Surely you are not *also* [one] of this man's disciples, are you?' – expressing, perhaps, a disdainful disbelief that Peter, under the circumstances, felt to be intimidating).

The form of the question suggests either that the expected answer is 'No', or, more likely in this context, that the question is a 'cautious assertion' (M. I, pp. 192–193). The question may not have been hostile so much as cynical. But Peter, cowed by his surroundings (as the other disciple was not, being more familiar with them), and threatened by his own memory of the fact that he was the only disciple who had struck a servant of the high priest (v. 10), begins his shameful descent. He may have viewed this first instance of self-distancing from the Master as a rite of admission to the courtyard; but once performed, it was easy to repeat, with rising vehemence.

18. The detail of the fire (also reported in Mk. 14:54; Lk. 22:55–56) suggests eyewitness recollection. Only John mentions it was a charcoal fire (*anthrakia*; he offers the same detail in 21:9). There are two important historical implications. (1) Although a fire was kept burning in the Chamber of Immersion for the benefit of the priests whose duty it was to immerse themselves during the night (Mishnah *Tamid* 1:1), outsiders like Peter would not have had access to it. This confirms that the courtyard (v. 15) is private. (2) It is an 'accidental' confirmation that these preliminary proceedings against Jesus took place at night, when *it was cold* and the servants and officials made up a fire to keep warm. This was an exceedingly unlikely prospect during the day, especially around Passover season (*cf.* Sherwin-White, p. 45, who offers evidence that fires were not normally lit at night, when people were sleeping, unless there were extraordinary reasons for staying up). Night proceedings in normal cases were doubtless viewed as illegal. Where the case was exceptional and the pressure of time extraordinary, doubtless legal loopholes could be found (*cf.* notes introducing v. 1). And so it came about that *Peter also was standing with them, warming himself.*

4. The interrogation of Jesus before Annas *(18:19–24)*

19. The *high priest* (here surely Annas; *cf.* notes on v. 13) *questioned Jesus about* two matters, *his disciples and his teaching.* The former question may have dealt with the size of his following and the potential for any possible conspiracy; the latter question suggests that the fundamental concern of the Jewish authorities was theological, even though they presented the case to Pilate as primarily political (*cf.* 19:7, 12). At the core of their concern was Jesus' claim as to who he was (19:7), and consequently their fear that he was leading the people astray, into apostasy (*cf.* 7:12, 47).

In a formal Jewish hearing in the first century, it *may* have been illegal to question the defendant. A case had to rest on the weight of the testimony of witnesses. This was certainly the way Maimonides (in the Middle Ages) understood Mishnah (*Sanhedrin* 6:2). Those who argue that the inference of Maimonides is legitimate are inclined to argue that the prohibition prevailed in the first century.[1] Even so, if this interrogation is an informal procedure before the high priest emeritus, and not before the Sanhedrin, Annas may not have seen himself bound by such rules.

20-21. About his disciples, Jesus says nothing, determined as he is to protect them to the end (*cf.* v. 9). More generally, Jesus protests that he has always spoken *openly* (*parrēsia*; *cf.* notes on 7:4) *to the world* (*kosmos*; *cf.* notes on 1:9); he *said nothing in secret* (v. 20). This cannot mean that Jesus never spoke to his disciples in private; all four Gospels controvert the suggestion. But what he said to them in private was of a piece with what he said in public. He did not maintain one message for public consumption and another, more dangerous one for a secret group of initiates. His private discourses further unpacked what he said in public, or extrapolated his message a little farther according to his perception of his followers' willingness and capacity to understand and obey. But the heart of what he preached was in the public arena, the result of teaching *in synagogues or at the temple*. Therefore there was little point in questioning his disciples; any of the countless thousands who had heard him would do.

Jesus' challenge takes on extra bite if the legal requirements discussed above (v. 19) were in force in his day. Proper procedure was to interrogate the witnesses, not the defendant; indeed, witnesses *for* the defendant were heard before witness *against* him. *Ask those who heard me. Surely they know what I said.*

22-23. Some minor official, quick to take umbrage at Jesus' challenge to the high priest, slapped him on the face (the word *rhapisma* refers to a sharp blow with the flat of the hand). Jesus does not back down. If his response to the high priest was illegal or inappropriate, then appropriate contempt of court charges should be filed against him: *testify as to what is wrong.* But if he spoke the truth, especially if in challenge of an illicit form of interrogation, why the assault? In short, Jesus is asking for a fair trial, while his opponents are already unmasked as those who, unable to win their case by fair means, are perfectly happy to resort to foul.

Jesus' response is sometimes unfavourably compared with what of the Apostle Paul, who was also struck for challenging the high priest

---

[1]*E.g.* I. Abrahams, *Studies in Pharisaism and the Gospels II* (Cambridge University Press, 1924), pp. 58, 132-134; K. Bornhaüser, *The Death and Resurrection of Jesus Christ* (tr. A. Rumpus; Bangalore: C. L. Press, 1958), p. 98.

(Acts 23:2–5). That, of course, was in a formal session of the Sanhedrin. Paul apologized for calling the high priest 'you whitewashed wall' (*i.e.* a hypocrite, a dirty piece of work daubed with whitewash to preserve appearances), on the ground that it was a violation of Scripture (Ex. 22:28) to speak evil about the ruler of the people. But Jesus did not call anyone names; he had nothing for which to apologize. Nor was he refusing to 'turn the other cheek': that ought to be clear from the cross itself. But turning the other cheek without bearing witness to the truth is not the fruit of moral resolution but the terrorized cowardice of the wimp.

24. Annas recognizes that he will get nowhere with this man, and sends him to Caiaphas. If Jesus is to be brought before Pilate, the legal accusation must be brought by the *reigning* high priest, Caiaphas, in his capacity as chairman of the Sanhedrin (*cf.* Additional Note). The AV's pluperfect, 'Now Annas had sent him bound . . .', is an attempt to alleviate the difficulty inherent in having two 'high priests' (*cf.* notes on vv. 13–14, 15–16). Syntactically it is a possible but unlikely rendering of the Greek, and is in any case unwarranted once the complexities of the first-century high priesthood are grasped.

Additional note

24. In recent years there has been a great deal of discussion on the composition and authority of the Sanhedrin in the time of Jesus. Some have argued that there were *two* 'Sanhedrins' operating under the aegis of Roman law, one essentially religious and the other civil. The scholars who espouse this view say that Jesus must have been tried before the latter, and the Evangelists have got it wrong. The evidence involved, however, is largely inferential, and based on sources of widely scattered dates and uncertain interpretation. The majority of scholars, both Jewish and Christian, do not multiply Sanhedrins in AD 30. Alexander[1] offers an excellent summary of what was most likely the case.

5. Peter's second and third denials of Jesus (18:25–27)

For discussion of the relation between this report and those of the Synoptic Evangelists *cf.* Carson, *Matt*, pp. 557–558; for brief treatment of the essential historicity of Peter's denials, *cf.* Beasley-Murray, pp. 325–326.

25. John takes us back to the fire (v. 18) where Peter *stood warming himself*. The reason for interweaving Jesus' first replies to his accusers with Peter's denials is to make the contrast stand out: 'John has constructed a dramatic contrast wherein Jesus stands up to his questioners and denies nothing, while Peter cowers before his questioners and

---

[1]Philip S. Alexander, 'Jewish Law in the Time of Jesus: Towards a Clarification of the Problem', in Barnabas Lindars (ed.), *Law and Religion: Essays on the Place of the Law in Israel and Early Christianity* (SPCK, 1988), pp. 44–58, esp. pp. 46–49. *Cf.* also Schürer, 2. 199–226.

denies everything' (Brown, 2. 842). The clause *he was asked* is the NIV's periphrastic rendering of 'they said to him', possibly a generalizing construction that reflects one interlocutor while several other temple officials and retainers are standing around the fire within earshot. The question they put is virtually identical to that recorded in v. 17, including the reference to *'another* of his disciples' (which may suggest that the 'other disciple' was still present). Peter *denied it* (*ērnēsato*, repeated in v. 27), which calls to mind Jesus' saying about those who deny him before men (Mt. 10:33 = Lk. 12:9).

26–27. Only John specifies that the third person to challenge Peter was *a relative of the man whose ear Peter had cut off.* This can most sympathetically be read as evidence that the beloved disciple is none other than the 'another disciple' (v. 15), displaying detailed knowledge of the high priest's household. Perhaps the fire flared, and the man glimpsed Peter's features a little more clearly. But again Peter denied any knowledge of his Master. John makes no mention of the oaths and curses to which he resorted this third time (Mk. 14:71 par.), nor of the bitter tears that followed the crowing of the rooster. The account is leaner, quietly veiled. The effect is to emphasize the fulfilment of Jesus' words to Peter (13:36), and to make it clear that 'Peter cannot follow Jesus, until Jesus has died for him' (Fenton, p. 182).

Both for John's readers, and for the early church generally, this is not Peter's final scene. As serious as was his disowning of the Master, so greatly also must we esteem the grace that forgave him and restored him to fellowship and service. And that means – both in John's Gospel and in our lives – that there is hope for the rest of us.

Additional note

25. The repetition of *warming himself* (*cf.* vv. 18, 25) is often taken as evidence of a literary seam, the opening of an otherwise smooth narrative to let in the intervening material. The fact that a similar repetition is found in Mark's account of Peter's denials (Mk. 14:54, 67) has generated considerable scholarly dispute as to whether or not the parallels between Mark and John constitute proof of literary dependence, or at least of a common source. Craig A. Evans[1] surveys the evidence and convincingly argues that this kind of repetition, with intercalated material, is a stock literary device in Greek romances and histories, in particular where two lines of the plot are developing simultaneously (in this case, the interrogation of Jesus and Peter's denials). The differences between John and Mark are sufficient that direct literary dependence cannot be *proved*; on the other hand, the device is so standard that each Evangelist may have used it independently, or even codified in written form something of the way the

[1] *JBL* 101, 1982, pp. 245–249.

accounts of Jesus' passion were circulating in oral form as part of the church's preaching and teaching.

6. The trial of Jesus before Pilate (18:28 – 19:16a)

John reports far more details of this trial before Pilate than do the three Synoptists combined. Theologically, the dominant theme is the kingdom, the authority of Jesus (18:36; 19:11, 14). At numerous points, knowledge of the Synoptic material is (wittingly or unwittingly) presupposed. For instance, the formal decision of the Sanhedrin is not mentioned, but is clearly assumed (*cf.* the notes below). Some critics find it incredible that any report of what occurred in the privacy of Pilate's court should have slipped out to become part of John's narrative. It is simpler, they allege, to postulate that the Evangelist is indulging in creative writing to make theological points that have no reference in historical reality. Theological points he is doubtless making, but that is no reason to think he is creating a narrative *ex nihilo* ('out of nothing'). We do not know what sources John enjoyed to let him know what happened in the court the Jews would not enter. Possibly Jesus himself, after his resurrection, told some of the details. Perhaps some of the court attendants became Christians in the early years of rapid growth in the Christian church, and passed on their recollections to the apostolic leadership. Some court records were public, and therefore available to those willing to do some research (such as Luke: *cf.* Lk. 1:1–4). We do not know where John obtained his information, but our ignorance is not threatening unless some startling reason is advanced as to why John should have told us how he found out, or unless there is overwhelming reason to think that John *could not* have known. And neither condition applies.

Although Pilate is the only figure who appears in every scene, it is Jesus himself, and the nature of his kingdom, that occupy centre stage.[1]

a. Pilate questions the prosecution (18:28–32)

28. The Greek text does not supply a definite subject to the verb *led*. 'Then they led Jesus from Caiaphas . . .' has been clarified by the NIV to read 'Then *the Jews* led. . . .' This is not unjust, if by 'the Jews' is meant the Jewish authorities of the Sanhedrin under the leadership of Caiaphas (*cf.* 18:31; 19:6, 15). They led Jesus to the *praitōrion* (Gk. transliteration from the Lat. *praetorium*), which denotes the headquarters of the commanding officer of a Roman military camp, or the headquarters of a Roman military governor (as Pilate was). Pilate's normal headquarters was in Caesarea, in the palace Herod the Great had built for himself; but he and his predecessors and successors made it a point to be in Jerusalem on the high feasts, to be available to quell any untoward disturbance. While in Jerusalem, his abode became his Jerusalem *praetorium*.

---

[1] *Cf.* C. H. Giblin, *Bib* 67, 1986, pp. 221–239.

Archaeologists differ as to whether this headquarters was Herod's palace on the western wall, or the Fortress of Antonia (named after Mark Antony) north-west of the temple complex and connected by steps to the temple's outer court (*cf.* Acts 21:35, 40).[1] NIV's 'palace' rather begs the issue.

The word rendered 'early morning' (*prōï*) is ambiguous. The Romans gave to the last two watches of the night (roughly midnight to 3.00 a.m. and 3.00 a.m. to 6.00 a.m. respectively) the names *alectorophōnia* ('cockcrow') and *prōï* ('early morning' or 'dawning'). If the word is used in this technical sense, Jesus is brought to Pilate before 6.00 a.m. In itself this is unsurprising: as we have noted, many Roman officials began the day very early in the morning and finished their day's labours by 10.00 or 11.00 a.m. (*cf.* Sherwin-White, p. 45). More likely the word should be understood without this technical meaning. The formal session of the Sanhedrin, which passed judgment on Jesus before sending him on to Pilate, would have been happier to meet 'very early in the morning' (Mk. 15:1 par.) but *after* sunrise, than in the fourth watch of the night, since Jewish law forbade trying capital cases at night.

On arriving, the Jewish authorities refused to enter Pilate's headquarters, preferring to stand outside in the colonnade. They wished to avoid *ceremonial uncleanness*; they *wanted to be able to eat the Passover*. This statement calls for three comments:

(1) The Mishnah provides evidence that a Jew who entered the dwelling-places of Gentiles became ceremonially unclean (*Oholoth* 18:7, 9; *cf.* SB 2. 838–839); remaining outside in the colonnade avoided the pollution. Under normal circumstances most Jews with business in Gentile quarters would incur the defilement and follow established procedure to regain ritual purity. Such cleansing procedure took time, and therefore in this instance the Jews want to avoid the uncleanness so that they will still be *able to eat the Passover*. Some forms of defilement could be removed by taking a bath at the end of the day (*i.e.* at sundown; *cf.* Lv. 15:5–11, 16–18; 22:5–7). If that were the case here, the Jews would then have been free to eat the Passover the 'next' day, *i.e.* after sundown on the same day, by our reckoning. We must therefore assume that the defilement in view is of a kind that cannot be removed until seven days have elapsed. Bruce (p. 349) suggests it is the presence of yeast (*cf.* Ex. 12:19; 13:7; Mishnah *Pesahim* 1:1; 2:1); others have suggested contamination from road dust brought in by foreign visitors (Mishnah *Berakoth* 9:5). These were but one-day pollutions. The context of Mishnah *Oholoth* suggests rather that the reason why a Jew would contract uncleanness in a Gentile home was because Gentiles were believed to bury aborted fetuses (*i.e.* corpses) in their homes, or flush them down their drains, and Numbers 9:7–10 insists that anyone who is unclean on account of

---

[1]The latter is the traditional site, and marks the beginning of the Via Dolorosa that winds its course to the Church of the Holy Sepulchre.

contact with a dead body – a seven-day defilement, Numbers 9:6–11; 31:19 – at the time of Passover must not participate in the feast, but must keep a second Passover, held a month later to accommodate such hardship cases. The evidence is complex and the matter not certainly resolved.[1] Moreover, we shall note below, under (3), that the problem may be a false one, resolved another way.

(2) The effect of this statement in the flow of the narrative is twofold. First, it constitutes a formidable example of Johannine irony. The Jews take elaborate precautions to avoid ritual contamination in order to eat the Passover, at the very time they are busy manipulating the judicial system to secure the death of him who alone is the true Passover. Second, the effect of the Jews' scruples is to send Pilate scuttling back and forth, acting on two stages as it were, a front stage and a rear stage (so Dodd, *HTFG*, p. 96). This simultaneously enhances the drama of the narrative, ensures that the Jews do not hear Jesus' self-disclosing claims before Pilate, and 'portrays the human predicament in which one must choose between Jesus and the world' (Duke, p. 126).

(3) The general problem of reconciling this statement with the Synoptic insistence that Jesus himself ate the Passover meal, was betrayed that night and crucified the next day (by Western reckoning of days), has already been discussed (*cf.* notes introducing 13:1, and on 13:1, 27; 19:14, 31, 36). It is tempting here to understand *to eat the Passover* to refer, not to the Passover meal itself, but to the continuing Feast of Unleavened Bread, which continued for seven days. In particular, attention may be focused on the *ḥagigah*, the feast-offering offered on the morning of the first full paschal day (*cf.* Nu. 28:18–19). There is ample evidence that 'the Passover' could refer to the combined feast of the paschal meal itself plus the ensuing Feast of Unleavened bread (*e.g.* Lk. 22:1: 'Now the Feast of Unleavened Bread, called the Passover, was approaching'). If then the Jewish authorities wanted to continue full participation in the entire feast, they would have to avoid *all* ritual contamination. Even if they contracted a form of defilement that could be washed away at sundown, it would preclude them from participating that day. True, the *ḥagigah* could be eaten later in the week, but the Jewish leaders, conscious of their public position, would be eager to avoid any uncleanness that would force them to withdraw from the feast, however temporarily. At this point, distinctions between defilement that lasts until sundown and defilement that lasts seven days become irrelevant.

This interpretation becomes very convincing if our treatment of 19:31 (*cf.* notes) is correct. Morris (pp. 778–779) concedes that 'the Passover'

---

[1] Although Barrett (p. 532) and others say that the Synoptists place the priests inside the Governor's court (Mt. 27:11–12; Mk. 15:2–3; Lk. 23:1–2), this is not quite correct. In each instance, the Synoptic Evangelist says that the Jewish authorities accused Jesus before Pilate. But that could be said of John's Gospel as well! The Synoptists simply do not raise the question of Jewish scruples in this regard; they are less interested in pregnant irony than is John.

can refer to the Passover plus the Feast of Unleavened Bread, but insists that 'to eat the Passover' cannot refer to all or part of the Feast of Unleavened Bread *apart from* the Feast of Passover. The criticism has little weight: the interpretation here defended is not that 'the Passover' refers to the Feast of Unleavened Bread *apart from* Passover, but to the *entire Passover festival*. The Jews wanted to continue to participate in the entire feast; they wanted to eat the Passover.

29. Pontius Pilate, the governor of Judea, is introduced to the narrative. He received his appointment from the Emperor Tiberius in AD 26, probably about four years earlier than these events, and held the post until AD 37. He has often been thought of as a Roman Procurator, owing to the evidence of the Roman historian Tacitus (*Annals* XV. xliv. 4), but an inscription published in 1962, discovered in the Herodian theatre in Caesarea, calls him 'prefect (Lat. *praefectus*) of Judea'. The Gospels use the generic category 'governor' (*hēgemōn*). Both from biblical and extra-biblical sources, historians have come to know him as a morally weak and vacillating man who, like many of the same breed, tried to hide his flaws under shows of stubbornness and brutality. His rule earned him the loathing of the Jewish people, small groups of whom violently protested and were put down with savage ferocity (*cf.* Lk. 13:1).

Because the Jewish authorities refused to enter the praetorium (v. 28), the Governor *came out to them*. This is not historically incredible. Any Roman governor would have been aware of the Jews' deep religious sensitivities, and some of them, at least, he would have honoured, especially during the high feasts when it was more than usually necessary to avoid riots. It was an easy task to order his servants to move his judgment seat.

His question *What charges are you bringing against this man?* formally opened the judicial proceedings. The fact that Roman troops were used at the arrest (vv. 3, 12) proves that the Jewish authorities had communicated something of this case to Pilate in advance; the sparring that follows in the wake of his question confirms the point. They had expected Pilate to confirm their judgment and order the death sentence by crucifixion; instead, he orders a fresh hearing in his presence.

30. This explains the truculence of their reply; otherwise their words appear impossibly insolent. The fact that Pilate had sufficiently agreed with their legal briefs to sanction sending a detachment of troops had doubtless encouraged them to think that he would ratify the proceedings of the Sanhedrin and get on to other business. To find him opening up what was in fact a new trial made them sullen. Hence their terse remark. The course of the subsequent interrogation (v. 33) shows that, whether at this point or in earlier legal briefs, the Jews had cast their case in political categories that Pilate could understand, even though the categories that upset them the most were theological (19:7).

31. Resentful of their truculence, their disrespectful assumption that the Roman governor would fit into their plans, Pilate humiliated them yet further: *Take him yourselves and judge him by your own law.* Doubtless

Pilate knew what the Jewish authorities wanted. But if they were going to talk in vague generalities about law-breaking, they could handle the case within their own court system. By contrast, if they expected a capital sentence to be handed down they were going to have to speak up and convince him, since, as they themselves conceded, they could not legally proceed without him. The Pilate disclosed in the historical documents almost certainly acted like this not so much out of any passion for justice as out of the ego-building satisfaction he gained from making the Jewish authorities jump through legal hoops and recognize his authority.

A long line of scholars influenced by Lietzmann[1] (and cautiously represented by Barrett, pp. 533–535) have argued that John is historically inaccurate on this point, and that the Sanhedrin retained the power of execution. In fact, the evidence supporting John is rather strong. When Rome took over Judea and began direct rule through a prefect in AD 6, capital jurisdiction was taken away from the Jews and invested in the governor (Jos., *Bel.* ii. 117) – Rome's common practice in provincial administration. Indeed, 'the capital power was the most jealously guarded of all the attributes of government' (Sherwin-White, pp. 24–47, esp. p. 36). Second-century Jewish evidence (*j. Sanhedrin* 1:1; 7:2) says that this power was taken from the Jews forty years before the fall of the temple, *i.e.* in AD 30, about the time of Jesus' death. The date assigned is curious; according to Josephus' evidence, we might have expected sixty-four years before the destruction of the temple. Bruce's suggestion is attractive (p. 351): 'it may be that the remembrance persisted of a situation around AD 30 when the deprivation of this right was of special significance.'

Those who suspect John of inaccuracy focus most of their attention on Josephus (*Bel.* v. 193–194; vi. 124–126), who insists that the Jewish authorities had the right to execute any Gentile, even a Roman citizen, who trespassed into the inner part of the temple. But this is surely the exception that established the rule, especially since the Romans were not thereby conceding very much. Desecration of a temple was almost universally viewed as a heinous crime in the ancient world, frequently punishable by death. That may be the reason why, according to the Synoptists (Mk. 14:57–59), the Sanhedrin expended some energy in trying to prove that Jesus had threatened the temple (*cf.* notes on Jn. 2:18–22). The report of Stephen's death (Acts 6 – 7) is frequently cited as evidence that the Sanhedrin retained capital jurisdiction, but that sounds more like mob violence winked at by the court than officially sanctioned by the court. Barrett (p. 534) and others, rather strangely, refer to Josephus' report (*Ant.* xx. 200) of the execution by stoning of James the half-brother of Jesus, but Josephus makes a major point of the

---

[1] H. Lietzmann, 'Der Prozeß Jesu', in *Sitzungsberichte der Preussischen Akademie der Wissenschaftenen* 14, 1934, pp. 313–322; repr. *Kleine Schriften II* (Berlin: Akademie, 1958), pp. 251–263.

fact that Annas (he calls him 'Ananus') the high priest convened the Sanhedrin and secured a capital verdict in the interval between the administrations of Festus, who had died, and Albinus his successor, who was still on his way.

In short, the evidence of John is well supported by extra-biblical witness. But this means that not only the *Jewish* authorities had to secure a guilty verdict, they had to persuade *Pilate* to find Jesus guilty of a capital crime. Offences that were simply against the Jewish law (v. 31a) would be of little moment to Pilate. This forced the Jewish authorities to tinge their charges against Jesus with political overtones: these were the categories Pilate understood (*cf.* notes on v. 33; 19:6, 12).

32. Whatever the mix of religious and political motivation, John the Evangelist detects the hand of God himself. The political realities guaranteed that when sentence was finally passed Jesus would be executed by crucifixion, not by stoning. The text does not say that *the Jews* wanted Jesus crucified rather than stoned, ostensibly because they remembered that 'anyone who is hung on a tree is under God's curse' (Dt. 21:23), and they wanted to ensure that Jesus would be viewed as accursed (so Beasley-Murray, p. 328). Rather, John is saying that the flux of events, including the brute fact that the Romans had to sanction capital punishment, brought about the fulfilment of Jesus' words *indicating the kind of death he was going to die*, his being 'lifted up from the earth' (Jn. 12:32-33). And thus, too, Jesus' words are fulfilled in the same way that Scripture's words are fulfilled.

b. Pilate questions Jesus (18:33–38a)

33. Back inside the *praetorium* (*cf.* v. 28), Pilate begins his interrogation of Jesus. The question *Are you the king of the Jews?* is reported in all four Gospels (*cf.* Mk. 15:2 par.); in John's narrative, it presupposes that the charge the Sanhedrin levelled against Jesus before Pilate was cast in these terms (*cf.* 19:21).[1] Possibly Pilate asked it in a contemptuous manner: opening the question with 'you' (*sy*) may suggest it (though *cf.* M. III. 37). Apparently the rage of the Sanhedrin was roused by the theological threat they perceived in Jesus – a point made clear in the Synoptics and implied throughout John's account (*e.g.* 18:35; 19:7). Jesus claimed to be the Messiah, the Son of God; their problem was how to formulate this claim in a manner calculated to impress Pilate with how dangerous Jesus was, and therefore to bring down the death penalty. The solution lay ready to hand. In Jewish expectation, the Davidic Messiah was necessarily the promised king of Israel (*cf.* 1:49). Thus is introduced a theme of controlling importance to chs. 18 – 19 (*cf.* 18:33–37, 39; 19:3, 12, 15, 19–22).

34–35. In the Synoptics, Jesus replies to Pilate's question with a brief

---

[1]*Cf.* E. Bammel, 'The Trial before Pilate', in E. Bammel and C. F. D. Moule (eds.), *Jesus and the Politics of His Day* (Cambridge University Press 1984), esp. pp. 417–419.

sy legeis (NIV 'Yes, it is as you say': Mt. 27:11; Mk. 15:2; Lk. 23:3). The expression is 'affirmative in content, and reluctant or circumlocutory in formulation'.[1] That answer also appears in v. 37, but John reports an intervening exchange between Jesus and Pilate that sheds light on the nature of Jesus' kingship. John includes these details for two reasons. Not only does this raise the horizon from the plane of antiquarian interest (*Was* Jesus a pretender to the throne of a minor Roman province in AD 30?) to the level of universal appeal ('My kingdom is not of this world', v. 36), but, more importantly for Jewish readers in the diaspora, it clarifies the *nature* of the messianic reign. If Jesus' claims are to be believed, if faith is to be invested in Jesus, the essence of his kingship must be made clear.

Jesus cannot possibly answer with a simple 'Yes' or 'No' unless he knows what is meant by the question. He therefore asks Pilate if the question the governor has posed spontaneously springs from his own understanding and curiousity (*cf*. Hoskyns, p. 520), or is simply a repetition of the Sanhedrin's charge. If the former, then perhaps Jesus can lead him to better or deeper understanding; if the latter, then Pilate is already so profoundly misled that major clarification will be necessary if Jesus is to answer truthfully at all. At the same time Jesus, as it were, has become the interrogator; the prisoner has become the judge (*cf*. notes on 3:2).

Pilate's answer is indignant, perhaps contemptuous: literally 'Am I a Jew?' – expecting a strong negative answer. He is saying, in effect, that the royal pretensions of any Jew can mean nothing to him personally; he has no stake in their outcome, and could not possibly be seriously contemplating the claims of the man before him. *It was your people and your chief priests* [they are singled out, as the predominant voice in the Sanhedrin] *who handed you over* (*paredōken se*: the verb may have the force of 'betrayed you') *to me.*

Pilate's response also suggests that he is less than satisfied with the Sanhedrin's charges against Jesus. There must be *something* behind the virulence of their animosity, even if it is unclear; and a cynical Roman governor in a political hotbed like first-century Judea was unlikely to be swayed into thinking that the Jewish authorities would take such pains with someone intent on doing damage to Rome – unless their own interests were at risk. Hence the question: *What is it you have done?*

It is just possible that under Pilate's question 'Am I a Jew?' the Evangelist finds lurking deeper ironies. Pilate despises and distrusts the Jews, yet in the course of the narrative he is eventually forced to adopt their position. Insofar as the Jews here represent the 'world', Pilate joins them. And in any case, the reader knows that in a profound sense Pilate's question really means (though certainly not intended this way by Pilate), 'Are you my king?' (*cf*. Duke, pp. 129–130).

[1]David R. Catchpole, *NTS* 17, 1970–71, pp. 213–226.

36. If Pilate is simply conveying the charge laid against Jesus by the Sanhedrin, Jesus knows how to answer Pilate's first question (v. 33). He acknowledges that he is a king, but so defines his 'kingdom' (*basileia*; the word has primary overtones of 'reign', 'kingship', not territory; *cf.* notes on 3:3, 5) as to remove all possibility of offence against the Empire. That is why Jesus defines his reign negatively: it *is not of this world* (*kosmos; cf.* notes on 1:9). If Jesus were a king or king-pretender in any sense that concerned the governors of the Empire, he would have marshalled his followers to fight and protect him from arrest. The fact that he was arrested so easily – indeed, that he stifled the inclination of one of his followers to rely on the sword (18:10, 11) – proves that his kingship is of a different order. It is not *of this world*; it is not 'from here' (*enteuthen*; strangely, NIV opts for a positive statement, and says it is 'from another place'). Both expressions mean that Jesus' reign does not have its source or origin in this world (*cf.* 8:23) – this world which is both created by God through the agency of the pre-incarnate Word (1:2, 3) and locked in persistent rebellion against its creator (1:10, 11). It is the sphere of darkness, of rebellion, of blindness, of sin. The kingships of this world preserve themselves by force and violence; if Jesus' kingship finds its origin elsewhere, it will not be defended by the world's means. And if it resorts to no force and no fighting, it is hard to see how Rome's interests are in jeopardy.

It is important to see 'that Jesus' statement should not be misconstrued as meaning that his kingdom is not *active* in this world, or *has nothing to do with* this world' (Beasley-Murray, p. 331). John certainly expects the power of the inbreaking kingdom to affect this world; elsewhere he insists that the world is conquered by those who believe in Jesus (1 Jn. 5:4). But theirs is the sort of struggle, and victory, that cannot effectively be opposed by armed might.

37. Pilate has understood little. He knows that Jesus has spoken of his 'kingdom', and therefore that Jesus' pretensions as a king must be probed a little harder: *You are a king, then!* Jesus' answer, translated literally, reads, 'You say that I am a king', periphrastically rendered by Dodd as '"King" is *your* word, not mine' (*HTFG*, p. 99; similarly Bruce, pp. 353–354). But in fact the evidence is very strong that the expression is unambiguously affirmative (hence NIV's *You are right in saying I am a king*), even if, as in the simpler expression, it is reluctant or leads to circumlocution (*cf.* notes on vv. 34–35). In other words, Jesus has gone far enough in self-disclosure that he must frankly attest his own kingly status, but he would be profoundly misleading if he did not continue to spell out the peculiar nature of his reign. Having described his kingdom negatively (v. 36), he now defines his kingly mission positively. To be a king was the reason he was born, the reason he came into the world: in the context of the Fourth Gospel, this pair of expressions refers to the incarnation, his move from the glory he shared with the Father in his presence (17:5) to his manifestation in this fallen world to manifest something of that glory (1:14). Only here in this Gospel is the birth of

Jesus unambiguously mentioned. He came, in short, to be a king – or, otherwise put, *to testify to the truth* (*alētheia*; *cf*. notes on 1:14; 4:24; 14:6). The parallelism suggests his kingdom is the kingdom of truth; or, more precisely put, the exercise of his saving kingship is virtually indistinguishable from his testifying to the truth. In this context, *truth* is understood in more than an intellectual sense (*cf*. de la Potterie, 2. 624ff.); it is nothing less than the self-disclosure of God in his Son, who is the truth (14:6). Disclosing the truth of God, of salvation and of judgment, was the principal way of making subjects, of exercising his saving kingship (*cf*. Lagrange, p. 477).

Similarly, only those who are rightly related to God, to the truth itself, can grasp Jesus' witness to the truth (*cf*. 3:16–21). *Everyone* who is *on the side of truth* (lit. 'who is of the truth') listens to Jesus (*cf*. 10:3, 16, 27).

38a. If Jesus' kingship is indistinguishable from his testimony to the truth, and if his followers are characterized by allegiance to his testimony rather than by violent upheaval, Pilate is forced to recognize that Jesus is the victim of a Sanhedrin plot. Moreover, there is an implicit invitation in Jesus' words. The man in the dock invites his judge to be his follower, to align himself with those who are 'of the truth'. Jesus is not dangerous; he may also be getting under Pilate's skin. Either way, Pilate abruptly terminates the interrogation with a curt and cynical question: *What is truth?* – and just as abruptly turns away, either because he is convinced there is no answer, or, more likely, because he does not want to hear it. He thus proves he is not amongst those whom the Father has given to the Son (*cf*. Haenchen, 2. 180).

c. Barabbas (18:38b–40)

38b. Returning to the outer colonnade (*cf*. vv. 28–29), Pilate yields his verdict to 'the Jews' (*cf*. notes on 1:19), now apparently augmented by vociferous supporters (v. 40; 19:6, 12, 14, 15). His statement *I find no basis for a charge against him* (*cf*. Lk. 23:14) shows that he understood Jesus' answer well enough to grasp that the formal 'Yes, I am a king' really meant 'No, I am not a king in any merely political sense, a king who might endanger the Empire.'

39. If Pilate had been stamped with integrity, his verdict would have ended the matter: Jesus would have been released, and the Jewish authorities dismissed. For whatever reason (to help the Jews save face? to save his own skin, because he had already received private threats akin to the public threat of 19:12? to embarrass the authorities before the crowds, whom he thought would support Jesus?), he offered to release Jesus in accordance with the custom at that season of the year (*cf*. Additional Note). The cast of his question – *Do you want me to release 'the king of the Jews'?* – suggests he was still trying to antagonize the authorities, since this was the title they specifically denied could be rightly ascribed to Jesus.

40. All four canonical Gospels tell us a little of Barabbas (whose full name may have been Jesus Barabbas: there is a variant reading in support of the longer name in Mt. 27:16, 17). He was a *lēstēs* (lit. 'one who seizes plunder'). In the hands of some first-century authors, however, the word depicts not simply a brigand, but a terrorist (from the Roman point of view), a guerilla (from the nationalist perspective); hence NIV's *had taken part in a rebellion*. He had participated in bloody insurrection (Mk. 15:7).

Thus, at the instigation of the chief priests, who normally had nothing to do with Zealots and others interested in armed rebellion, the crowds call for the release of a man who has committed murder in his struggle against Rome, while condemning a man falsely accused of being a danger to Rome. Pilate cannot fail to see the irony. What will he do?

Additional note

39. There is no unambiguous extra-biblical evidence for this Passover custom, and this has led not a few scholars to doubt its historicity. One passage in the Mishnah, *Pesahim* 8:6, probably refers to it: they may slaughter the Passover lamb for a variety of people whose actual condition is uncertain (*e.g.* invalids), including 'one whom they have promised to bring out of prison'. Such a prisoner could scarcely have been under restraints by a Jewish court, since such a court would know about the demands of Passover and could be counted on to make a clean decision one way or another. A special promise of release, by a foreign court, at Passover season, seems to be in view; and the fact that legislation is required suggests that these releases occurred with some regularity. Although Mark 15:8 pictures the crowd asking for the release of a prisoner according to custom, while John has Pilate bringing the matter up, the custom itself is still assumed. It is not unlikely that some request was made to Pilate before his public offer, just as there must have been some formal charge laid against Jesus before Pilate began his interrogation (*cf.* notes on v. 33). In both instances John omits the details as irrelevant to his purposes.

d. Jesus sentenced *(19:1–16a)*

1. Since Pilate has already declared Jesus to be innocent (18:38), at first sight it is surprising to read, *Then Pilate took Jesus and had him flogged* (*emastigōsen*). The context shows, however, that this is nothing but a fresh strategy to set Jesus free (*cf.* notes on vv. 4–6). Pilate orders a flogging which, he thinks, will meet the Jews' demand that Jesus be punished, and perhaps evoke a little sympathy for him as well, and thus dissipate the clamour for his crucifixion. The scene parallels Luke 23:13–16: Pilate tells the Jewish officials that Jesus 'has done nothing to deserve death', and concludes, 'Therefore, I will punish (*paideusas*) him and then release him.'

Perhaps nowhere more than in the sufferings of the Master does it seem distracting and ungrateful to focus on perceived difficulties in relating John to the Synoptic Gospels. But reflection on some of these questions helps us to understand a little better just what he endured. The question, then, is how this flogging relates to the witness of Mark 15:15 (*cf.* Mt. 27:26), which affirms that Pilate had Jesus flogged (*phragellōsas*) *after* the capital sentence was passed.

Flogging administered by the Romans could take one of three forms: the *fustigatio*, a less severe beating meted out for relatively light offences such as hooliganism, and often accompanied by a severe warning; the *flagellatio*, a brutal flogging administered to criminals whose offences were more serious; and the *verberatio*, the most terrible scourging of all, and one that was always associated with other punishments, including crucifixion. In this last form, the victim was stripped and tied to a post, and then beaten by several torturers (in the Roman provinces they were soldiers) until they were exhausted, or their commanding officer called them off. For victims who, like Jesus, were neither Roman citizens nor soldiers, the favoured instrument was a whip whose leather thongs were fitted with pieces of bone or lead or other metal. The beatings were so savage that the victims sometimes died. Eyewitness records report that such brutal scourgings could leave victims with their bones and entrails exposed.

What beating, then, did Pilate administer to Jesus? There appear to be two possibilities.

(1) The scourging was the most brutal, the *verberatio*, Mark's *phragellōsas* (Mk. 15:15), commonly meted out to a victim about to be crucified to weaken and dehumanize him. But if John is referring to the same beating, then it is necessary to follow Blinzler (p. 334), who argues that the aorist participle in Mk. 15:15 refers to a scourging administered to Jesus *before* Pilate delivered the death sentence. Thus the discrepancy in time between John and Matthew/Mark is cleared up. But for three reasons, this is quite unlikely. First, when an aorist particle (like Mark's *phragellōsas*) follows the finite verb on which it depends (*paredōken*, 'handed him over'), it usually refers to a succeeding event; second, it is hard to imagine any Roman prefect administering the *verberatio* before sentencing; and third, it is so brutal that it ill accords with the theme of Luke and of John, that Pilate at first found Jesus innocent and merely wanted to administer enough punishment to be able to appease Jewish officialdom and then let Jesus go.

(2) It is better to follow Sherwin-White (pp. 27–28), who argues that the flogging threatened in Luke and reported here in John is the *fustigatio*, the least severe form, and was intended partly to appease the Jews and partly to teach Jesus a lesson (*cf.* Luke's *paideusas*; John's *emastigōsen*, 'had [him] flogged', is a more generic description) for being something of a trouble-maker. The chronology of Luke and John is correct. But this means that Jesus received a second scourging, the wretched *verberatio*, after the sentence of crucifixion was passed. This would hasten death, and the nearness of the special Sabbath of that week provided the officials with some pressure to ensure that the agony of crucifixion, which could go on for days, would not be permitted to

run on too long (Jn. 19:31–33). This also explains why he was too weak to carry his own cross very far (*cf.* notes on v. 17).

2–3. At one level the cruelty depicted in these verses is nothing other than barracks vulgarity. Probably the 'crown of thorns' was twisted together from the long spikes of the date palm,[1] fashioned into a mock imitation of the radiate crowns oriental god-kings were depicted as wearing. The intention of the soldiers was rough mockery, but the long thorns (up to twelve inches) added to the blood and the pain. The 'purple robe' was probably a military cloak flung around Jesus' shoulders, mocking dress-up for a royal robe (*cf.* Carson, *Matt*, p. 573). The soldiers line up to pay their homage, but as they bend the knee and cry *Hail, king of the Jews!* they strike him in the face (for the word *rhapisma, cf.* notes on 18:22). Cf. Isaiah 50:6.

At the same time, however, this scene provides indirect evidence that the charge the Sanhedrin preferred against Jesus before Pilate is that he claimed to be the king of the Jews – from their perspective, a messianic pretender, and in Pilate's eyes (they hoped), a rebel against Caesar. At a still deeper level, John is writing ironically: once again Jesus' opponents, in this case Gentiles, speak better than they know (*cf.* 11:49–52), for Jesus is in truth the king of Israel (1:49; 3:3, 5; 18:36; Dauer, pp. 262–263).

4–5. *Once more* Pilate steps out of the *praetorium* (*cf.* 18:28) to address the Jews. He delivers his verdict (*cf.* 18:38), and then dramatically presents Jesus – a sorry sight, swollen, bruised, bleeding from those cruel and ridiculous thorns. Aware as he is that it is *the people* who must choose the man who will receive the governor's amnesty, he presents Jesus as a beaten, harmless and rather pathetic figure to make their choice of him as easy as possible. In his dramatic utterance *Here is the man!* (in Latin, *Ecce homo!*), Pilate is speaking with dripping irony: here is the man you find so dangerous and threatening: can you not see he is harmless and somewhat ridiculous? If the governor is thereby mocking Jesus, he is ridiculing the Jewish authorities with no less venom. But the Evangelist records the event with still deeper irony: here indeed is the Man, the Word made flesh (1:14). All the witnesses were too blind to see it at the time, but this Man was displaying his glory, the glory of the one and only Son, in the very disgrace, pain, weakness and brutalization that Pilate advanced as suitable evidence that he was a judicial irrelevance.[2]

6. The chief priests (*cf.* notes on 7:32) and their officials cannot be so easily placated, partly, no doubt, because of their animus against Jesus, and partly because they resent Pilate's mockery of them. They will not be satisfied by anything other than Jesus' death. Indeed, they are aware that the charge they are bringing against him can have but one outcome

---

[1] H. St. J. Hart, *JTS* 3, 1952, pp. 71–74.

[2] For a detailed study, rich in allusions but sometimes uncontrolled, *cf.* Charles Panackel, *ΙΔOY O ANΘΡΩΠOΣ (John 19:5)* (Pontificia Università Gregoriana, 1988). He is far too certain that John openly engages in a polemic against docetism: *cf.* Introduction, § VI.

if he is found guilty. Anyone not a Roman citizen found guilty of sedition could expect crucifixion. Recent memory provided many examples both in Judea and in surrounding territories; only a slightly longer perspective would call to mind Alexander Jannaeus who in 88 BC crucified 800 rebels (Jos., *Bel.* i. 97). And so they cry, *Crucify! Crucify!*

Discovering that his strategem has failed, Pilate responds with dismissive indignation and disgust: *You take him and crucify him.* The pronouns have emphatic force: *You* take him . . . *I* find no basis for a charge against him (*cf.* 18:38; 19:4). Of course, this is not a formal transfer of his prerogatives to the Jewish court (*cf.* 18:31), as the reply of the Jews in the next verse demonstrates; rather, it is a sarcastic taunt: You bring him to me for trial but you will not accept my judgment.

7. At one level this does not report a change in the charge brought against Jesus, for as we have seen (*cf.* notes on 18:33), in the mind of the Jewish authorities Jesus' messianic pretensions were both religious and political in nature. They have judged it advisable, in their initial approach to Pilate, to stress the political elements in the case, thinking that these would prove most damaging to Jesus in the eyes of the Roman governor. Finding their strategy slipping away, they emphasize the religious elements – and thus expose their deepest motives. A Roman prefect was not only responsible for keeping the peace but, within the constraints of Rome's priorities, he was to maintain local law as well. So the Jews expound the point of law they want Pilate to grasp. *We have a law* does not refer to Torah as a whole but to one statue, presumably Leviticus 24:16: 'anyone who blasphemes the name of the LORD must be put to death. The entire assembly must stone him. Whether an alien or native-born, when he blasphemes the Name, he must be put to death.' By the time the Mishnah was codified, about AD 200, this statute was interpreted to mean that an essential element in blasphemy was the actual articulation of God's ineffable name (Mishnah *Sanhedrin* 7:5; *Kerithoth* 1:1–2), but apparently no such restriction was in force in Jesus' day. The charge of blasphemy figures largely in the trial before Caiaphas (Mk. 14:55–64 par.), so it is unsurprising to find it alluded to here. Moreover, in the Fourth Gospel the charge of blasphemy has been a rising theme (*e.g.* 5:18; 8:58, 59; 10:33, 36).

The language of the Jewish officials, 'he claimed to be *the Son of God*', almost sounds as if the claim itself was sufficient to presume guilt of blasphemy. In many contexts that was demonstrably untrue. The anointed king of Israel was sometimes referred to as God's Son in the Old Testament (Pss. 2:7; 89:26–27), and in some intertestamental sources 'Son of God' is parallel to 'Messiah' (4Q *Florilegium*; *cf.* notes on 1:49; *NIDNTT* 3. 637). But Jesus' opponents rightly recognize that as he uses the title there are overtones not only of messiahship but of sharing the rights and authority of God himself (*cf.* 1:34; 5:19–30).

8. When Pilate heard this slight revision of the charge the Sanhedrin was preferring against Jesus, *he was even more afraid.* Why *even more* (*mallon*)? It is possible to read some kind of fear or at least begrudging

awe into Pilate's question in 18:38 ('What is truth?'), but the flow of the narrative up to his point makes Pilate cynical and blunt, and more interested in putting the Jewish authorities in their place than in standing up for justice. Indeed, the Greek word *mallon* ('more' or 'even more' or 'rather') could be taken two other ways. Verse 8 may mean that when Pilate heard the revised charge 'he become afraid *rather than* (complying with their wish)'. As cynical as many senior Roman officials were, many of them were also deeply superstitious. To a Jewish ear, the charge that Jesus claimed to be the Son of God would be taken as a messianic pretension, and perhaps also, in the light of the continuing debate between Jesus and Jewish officials, as a blasphemous excuse to claim prerogatives that belong to God alone; but to a Graeco-Roman ear, the charge sounded quite different. It had nothing to do with blasphemy, and presented no threat to the Roman Empire; rather, it placed Jesus in an ill-defined category of 'divine men', gifted individuals who were believed to enjoy certain 'divine' powers. If Jesus was a 'son of God' in this sense, Pilate might well feel a twinge of fear; he had just had Jesus whipped. Moreover, the Greek word *mallon* may simply have elative rather than comparative force: *i.e.* Pilate 'was very much afraid'.

9. Back inside the *praetorium* (*cf.* 18:28), Pilate seeks to alleviate his own fear by questioning Jesus about his origins: *Where do you come from?* Jesus *gave him no answer*, a silence which is a Johannine parallel to Mark 14:61; 15:5 (*cf.* Is. 53:7). Neither in John nor in Mark is the silence absolute: in both, Jesus speaks again. But the question as Pilate phrases it cannot rightly be answered with a word, a phrase, a clause – at least, not if Pilate is to understand it. And Pilate has shown no interest in real understanding: he has contemptuously dismissed Jesus' claim to testify to the truth (18:37–38), so why should Jesus think the governor is any more prepared for truth now? What answer, long or brief, could Jesus have provided for the Roman prefect who is more interested in political manoeuvering than in justice, who displays superstitious fear but no remorse, who (in the next verses) still struts on the stage of human power but is enslaved by the political threats of his frenzied opposition?

10. Jesus' silence irritates Pilate. That silence was much worse than the modern crime of contempt of court, for as long as Pilate held the imperial commission he retained in his power both sweeping executive power and, for non-citizens, final judicial authority. Pilate interprets Jesus' silence as at best stupidity, at worse a baiting sullenness.

11. Behind Pilate's 'power' (*exousia*, 'authority'), however, Jesus discerns the hand of God. Typical of biblical compatibilism, even the worst evil cannot escape the outer boundaries of God's sovereignty – yet God's sovereignty never mitigates the responsibility and guilt of moral agents who operate under divine sovereignty, while their voluntary decisions and their evil rebellion never render God utterly contingent (*e.g.* Gn. 50:19–20; Is. 5:10ff.; Acts 4:27–28). Especially in writing of events that lead up to the cross, New Testament writers are bound to see the hand of God bringing all things to their dramatic purpose (*cf.* Carson, 'OT', esp. pp. 247–248), no matter how vile the secondary causalities may be; for the alternatives are unthinkable. If God merely outwits his enemies, whose evil sets both the agenda and the pace, then the mission of the Son to die for fallen sinners is reduced to a mere after-thought; if God's sovereignty capsizes all human responsibility, then it is hard to see why the mission of the Son should be undertaken at all, since in that case there are no sins for the Lamb of God to take away.

Pilate's authority, then, was given to him *from above* (*anōthen*; cf. notes on 3:3, 5). *Therefore* (*dia touto*) *the one who handed me over to you is guilty of a greater sin.* The force of the *Therefore* is not immediately clear, and some suggestions are almost certainly wrong. Morris (p. 797), for instance, plausibly argues that Caiaphas is the betrayer, the one who handed Jesus over to Pilate, and that Caiaphas is 'ultimately responsible' since Judas was merely 'a tool' and Pilate was serving under the delegated authority of God himself. But if Judas was a tool, he was a *culpable* tool; moreover, if God's sovereignty mitigates Pilate's responsibility, why should it not similarly attenuate the responsibility of Caiaphas (*cf.* 11:49–52!)?

The way forward turns on three observations:

(1) The text does not exonerate Pilate; his sin is only relatively less than that of the person who handed Jesus over to him. The fact that he would not have had *any* authority over Jesus apart from heaven's sanction therefore does *not* absolve him of *all* responsibility.

(2) The identity of the person *guilty of a greater sin* is uncertain. Because he is described as *the one who handed* [Jesus] *over* (*ho paradous*) to Pilate, and that verb, often rendered in some form of the verb 'to betray', is regularly attached to Judas (*e.g.* 6:71; 13:21; 18:2), it is natural to think of Iscariot. On the other hand, Judas plays no part in the plot after 18:13, and, technically speaking, he was not responsible for handing Jesus over to Pilate. The verb is twice used with reference to Jesus' accusers handing him over to Pilate (18:30, 35), but the singular form of the expression in this verse encourages us to think of one person. On the whole, it seems best to fasten on Caiaphas, since he not only took an active if not determinative part in the plot against Jesus (11:49–53) and, as high priest presiding over the Sanhedrin, he took a leading part in formulating the charges against Jesus (*cf.* Mk. 14:61–64), charges of which John demonstrates his thorough awareness. The critical point, however, is this: whether the person *guilty of a greater sin* refers to Judas or to Caiaphas, the distinguishing feature in that sin is its initiative, the active role of handing Jesus over.

(3) Most important, what God ('from above') gives to Pilate (*i.e.* the antecedent of *it*) is not 'authority' or 'power' (*exousia*), since this Greek word is feminine while 'it were . . . given' (*ēn dedomenon*) is neuter. In other words, although it is true that all civil authority is mediated authority from God himself (*cf.* Pr. 8:15; Rom. 13), that is not the point here. The neuter verbal form suggests that what is given to Pilate is the entire turn of events, or, more precisely, the event of the betrayal

itself.[1] It is not God's sovereign hand behind Pilate's authority that mitigates his guilt: that would be to disown the compatibilism of which the biblical writers are so fond, and would imply that God is less than sovereign over the person with the greater guilt. Rather, Pilate's guilt is mitigated because he takes a *relatively* passive role. True, Pilate remains responsible for his spineless, politically-motivated judicial decision; but he did not initiate the trial or engineer the betrayal that brought Jesus into court. Judas, Caiaphas and Pilate all acted under God's sovereignty. But Pilate would not have had judicial authority over Jesus unless the event of the betrayal itself had been given to him *from above* (and thus God was in some mysterious sense behind the action of the one who handed Jesus over to Pilate). *Therefore* the one who handed Jesus over to Pilate, the one who from the human vantage point took the initiative to bring Jesus down, is guilty of the greater sin.

12. *From then on* (*ek toutou*, which could be causal, 'For this reason', instead of temporal), *i.e.* from the time Jesus gave the response of v. 11, Pilate *tried to set Jesus free* (whether by dismissing the case or by attempting to manipulate the crowds into applying the amnesty to Jesus; the text does not specify). This does not mean that Pilate had a full grasp of what Jesus was saying; it means that Pilate was convinced that Jesus had done nothing worthy of death. Neither the charge of sedition nor the additional charge of blasphemy held up in Pilate's eyes.

But then a new and sensitive issue is introduced. The Jews expose the desperate weakness of Pilate's authority by shouting, *If you let this man go, you are no friend of Caesar*. Pilate had ample reason to fear the implicit threat. Tiberius Caesar was known to be quick to entertain suspicions against his subordinates, and swift to exact ruthless punishment (*cf.* Additional Note). On earlier occasions the Jewish authorities had communicated their displeasure with Pilate to the Emperor; Pilate had no reason to think they would refrain from doing so in this case. What defence of himself could be possibly give to a somewhat paranoid ruler, against the charge that he had failed to convict and execute a man arraigned on well-substantiated charges of sedition – brought up on charges put forward by the Sanhedrin, no less, the highest court in the land and known to be less than enthusiastic about the Emperor's rule? Whether or not *friend of Caesar* was at this point a technical term, everyone knew that even the claim to be a king (unless some kind of vassal-king status was granted by the Emperor himself) signalled opposition to Caesar.

The verse is saturated with irony. In order to execute Jesus, the Jewish

---

[1]So, rightly, Hoskyns, p. 524; Lagrange, p. 483; Carson, pp. 129–130. The handing over of Jesus to the Roman governor is determined by God, and if Pilate finds himself in a position of authority it is therefore because of God's action. It is only in this sense that v. 11 circumscribes Pilate's authority, not by an argument that affirms that all human authority finds its source and limitation in the divine will (as many contend: *e.g.* Bauer, p. 219). Though this latter point is doubtless in some sense true, it is not in view in this verse.

authorities make themselves out to be more loyal subjects of Caesar than the hated Roman official Pilate is. They thereby demonstrate their slavery not only to sin (8:34) but to the political thraldom they earlier disavowed (8:33). Jesus *claims to be a king,* but king of such a nature (18:36–37) that he is far less of an immediate threat to Caesar than are the people who are levelling the charge – as is made clear by the Jewish revolt, which lay ahead of the crucifixion but was almost certainly behind John the Evangelist when he wrote. And when the Jews eventually revolted, they were ruthlessly crushed and their temple was razed, while even as John writes the kingship of the crucified Master is running from strength to strength.

13. Confronted with such pressure, Pilate capitulates. Judgment must be declared, and on the original charge of sedition. Correspondingly, *he brought Jesus out (cf.* notes on 18:28–29) *and sat down on the judge's seat* (*bēma*) – assuming this is the correct rendering (*cf.* Additional Note). This seat was placed on the spot known as *The Stone Pavement* (*lithostrōtos*), called *Gabbatha* (and the meaning of this Aramaic word is sharply disputed; *cf.* notes on 5:2). An area paved with stones, originally about 3000 square feet in size, has been discovered in a building identified as the Fortress of Antonia, but it is far from certain that Jesus' trial actually took place in Antonia (*cf.* notes on 18:28; *ISBE* 2. 373). Be that as it may, the actual *bēma* was far more important than the paving stones: here is the personal representative of Rome offering his judicial decision on the one who alone is the promised Messiah, the one to whom the Father himself entrusted all (eschatological) judgment (5:22).

14a. The precise referent of *day of Preparation* (*paraskeuē*) is disputed. If this refers to the day before the Passover, *i.e.* the day in which one prepares for the Passover, then John is presenting Jesus as being sent to execution about the same time the Passover lambs are being slaughtered. That would mean that the meal Jesus and his disciples enjoyed the night before was not the Passover supper; and that in turn brings us into sharp contradiction with the Synoptic witness, which makes it clear that Jesus and his disciples ate the Passover (*cf.* notes on 13:1, 27; 18:28). The attractiveness of this theory, despite the clash with the Synoptists, rests in the assumption that John introduces this time factor here as a symbolic way of saying that the true Passover lamb was none other than Jesus himself: he was sentenced to be slaughtered just as the slaughter of the lambs began.

One would have thought, however, that if this were John's intent he would have achieved much more dramatic power by inserting this time notice just after v. 16a. Moreover, a better way of reading the passage turns on recognizing that *paraskeuē* ('Preparation') regularly refers to Friday – *i.e.* the Preparation of the Sabbath is Friday.[1] Despite the fact

---

[1] *Cf.* C. C. Torrey, *JBL* 50, 1931, p. 241; A. J. B. Higgins, *NTS* 1, 1954–55, pp. 206ff.; Morris, pp. 776–777.

that Barrett (p. 545) confidently insists *paraskeuē tou pascha* must refer to the Preparation day of (*i.e.* before) the Passover, he does not offer any evidence of a single instance where *paraskeuē* refers to the day before any feast day other than Sabbath.[1] If this latter identification is correct, then *tou pascha* must be taken to mean, not 'of the Passover', but 'of the Passover Feast' or 'of the Passover week'. This is a perfectly acceptable rendering, since 'Passover' can refer to the Passover meal, the day of the Passover meal, or (as in this case) the entire Passover week (*i.e.* Passover day plus the immediately ensuing Feast of Unleavened Bread: *cf.* Jos., *Ant.* xiv. 21; xvii. 213; *Bel.* ii. 10; Lk. 22:1; *cf.* notes on 18:28). Hence *paraskeuē tou pascha* probably means 'Friday of Passover week' (*cf.* also notes on v. 31). In this view, John and the Synoptics agree that the last supper was eaten on Thursday evening (*i.e.* the onset of Friday, by Jewish reckoning), and was a Passover meal.

We must nevertheless advance a reason as to why the day is here introduced. The strength of the view that *paraskeuē* refers to the day before Passover turns less on linguistic arguments than on its (alleged) explanatory power: it makes possible the view that John is affirming that Jesus himself is the slaughtered Passover lamb. But another reason can be given for this insertion of the day. This is preparation for vv. 31–37, where the piercing of Jesus' side by a spear, and the 'sudden flow of blood and water', turns on the need to ensure that Jesus and those crucified with him be taken down from the cross promptly, since it was already *paraskeuē* (v. 31) and the next day, the Sabbath, was a special Sabbath (since it fell within the Passover week). This pattern – an advance time notice to anticipate the development of a theological theme that turns on this time notice – is already found in ch. 5: John remarks in passing that the healing of the man who had been paralysed for thirty-eight years took place on a Sabbath (v. 9), and thus prepares for the Sabbath-controversy recorded a little farther on in the chapter (vv. 16ff.).

As for the time of day, this final decision and sentencing took place *about the sixth hour*. If we reckon the hours from sunrise to sundown, that would place it about noon. Mark 15:25 informs us, however, that Jesus was crucified at 'the third hour', about 9.00 a.m. Assuming that this is a correct reading of Mark's sentence division,[2] the discrepancy is

---

[1]Barrett simply affirms that *paraskeuē tou pascha* is the Greek equivalent of the Hebrew for 'the eve of Passover', but that is the very point that must be demonstrated. The fact remains that *paraskeuē* refers to Friday, the day before the Sabbath, in Josephus (*Ant.* xvi. 163), not to mention second-century sources (*Didache* viii. 1; *Martyrdom of Polycarp* vii. 1).

[2]A. Mahoney (*CBQ* 28, 1966, pp. 292–299) argues, however, that in Mark the words 'at the third hour' refer not to Jesus' crucifixion but to the preceding sentence (Mk. 15:24) dealing with the soldiers casting lots for Jesus' clothes – an event which, he argues, took place earlier than the crucifixion, when Jesus was beaten. That removes the discrepancy between Mark and John, but at the expense of upsetting the sequence of Mark's narrative. France (pp. 117–123) attempts a resolution by finding symbolic significance in John's 'sixth hour'.

apparent. Westcott (2. 324–326) attempts to resolve the problem by arguing that John used a 'Roman' method of computing time, beginning the day with midnight and thus taking *about the sixth hour* to refer to 6.00 a.m. This is barely possible, but it makes the chronology extremely tight. In any case, there is no convincing evidence that this 'Roman' system of time-keeping was used 'other than in legal matters like leases' (*cf.* notes on 1:39; Morris, pp. 800f. – his discussion of the evidence is helpful). Barrett (p. 545) thinks it possible that there was an early transcriptional error introduced into the manuscript tradition by the confusion of the Greek numerals *gamma* Γ (3) and *diagamma* F (6). Again, this is possible, but no manuscript evidence supports it. The theory that John changed the time to the sixth hour (*i.e.* noon) to bring Jesus' sentencing into chronological line with the slaughtering of the Passover lambs falls away if *paraskeuē* ('Preparation') is understood to refer to Friday. Moreover, that theory cannot explain why the sixth hour is associated with Jesus' *sentencing* rather than with his *death*.

More than likely we are in danger of insisting on a degree of precision in both Mark and John which, in days before watches, could not have been achieved. The reckoning of time for most people, who could not very well carry sundials and astronomical charts, was necessarily approximate. If the sun was moving toward mid-heaven, two different observers might well have glanced up and decided, respectively, that it was 'the third hour' or 'about the sixth hour'. Mark's concern is to set a time frame in which the three hours of darkness occur (Mk. 15:25, 33). By contrast, John's point appears to be that the proceedings had dragged on quite a long time, beginning with the 'early morning' (18:28) commencement of the proceedings before Pilate. During all this time it became ever clearer that justice demanded Jesus be released while evil's tide rolled inexorably on and brought him to the cross – the evil of the Jews, the evil of Pilate, the evil of all those for whom the Lamb of God died.

14b. Pilate knows he cannot escape the political trap that has been set for him, but he taunts his hated opponents once more. Without a trace of remorse for the shame and scorn that both he and his opponents are heaping on Jesus, he mockingly acclaims Jesus, as if at a coronation: *Here is your king*. Pilate is no fool. He is perfectly aware that the ostensible allegiance of the Jewish authorities to Caesar (v. 12) is no more than political hypocrisy deployed to ensure that he will condemn Jesus to the cross. By this acclamation of Jesus, he simultaneously throws up with bitter irony the spurious charge of sedition in their face, and mocks their vassal status by saying that this bloodied and helpless prisoner is the only king they are likely to have. But again, the Evangelist sees still deeper irony. Like Caiaphas before him (11:49–52), Pilate spoke better than he knew. The long-awaited king of the Jews stood before them, and they did not recognize him.

15. Pilate's tactics simply infuriate the crowd: *Take him away! Take him away! Crucify him!* With mock concern and more taunting, Pilate asks,

'Shall I crucify *your king*?' He thereby drives the chief priests to their own blasphemy: *We have no king*[1] *but Caesar*. The Hebrew Scriptures repeatedly insist that the only true king of Israel is God himself (*e.g.* Jdg. 8:23; 1 Sa. 8:7); the Davidic kings are legitimate, at least in theory, only because they are vassal monarchs in liege to the LORD and bound by the covenant. By vehemently insisting they have no king but Caesar, they are not only rejecting Jesus' messianic claims, they are abandoning Israel's messianic hope as a matter of principle, rejecting *any* claimant ('We have *no king* but Caesar'), and finally disowning the kingship of the LORD himself. 'Their repudiation of Jesus in the name of a pretended loyalty to the emperor entailed their repudiation of the promise of the kingdom of God, with which the gift of the Messiah is inseparably bound in Jewish faith, and Israel's vocation to be its heir, its instrument, and its proclaimer to the nations' (Beasley-Murray, p. 343). This is the ultimate evidence in support of the Prologue's pronouncement, 'He came to that which was his own, but his own did not receive him' (1:11), and of the terrible blindness depicted in 12:37ff.

Even so, throughout this degenerating series of exchanges (18:28 – 19:16a) between Pilate and 'the Jews' (*cf.* notes on 1:19), it is the Jewish authorities that are always in view – sometimes explicitly (*e.g.* 'the chief priests and their officials', 19:6), as here ('the chief priests'), and sometimes implicitly. This is part of early Christianity's most important apologetic, *especially in the evangelization of Jews*. Christians, whether Jews or Gentiles, had to explain *to Jews* how it came about that so many Jews, and especially the Jewish leadership, did not accept Jesus, and how this understanding undergirds the Christians' claim to be the true locus of the people of God. 'Writing as a Jew for other Jews, [John] is concerned from beginning to end to present the condemnation of Jesus, the *true* king of Israel, as the great betrayal of the nation by its own leadership' (Robinson, *John*, pp. 273–274).

16a. The actual death sentence is not pronounced, but is implied not only by Pilate's sitting down on the tribunal (v. 13) but also by his decisive control of the 'notice' on the cross (vv. 19–22). It is not entirely clear what is meant by 'Pilate handed him over *to them* (*autois*) to be crucified'. The preceding verse suggests that *them* refers to the Jewish authorities, but John knows full well that the Jews did not have the right, delegated or not, to crucify anyone: it is the soldiers, Roman auxiliaries, who perform the execution (vv. 23, 24). It seems best to understand *autois* as a dative of advantage: Pilate hands Jesus over [*sc.* to the soldiers] *to satisfy the demands of the Jews* (*cf.* NEB: 'Then at last, to satisfy them, [Pilate] handed Jesus over to be crucified'). This reading is confirmed by Luke 23:24: 'So Pilate decided to grant their demand' (lit. he 'handed Jesus over to their will [*tō thelēmati autōn*]').

---

[1]The Latin word for 'king' (*rex*) was not applied to Caesar, but Greek *basileus* means either 'king' or 'emperor'.

Additional notes

12. 'Friend of Caesar' was virtually an official title by the time of the Emperor Vespasian (AD 69–71), but its exact status in Jesus' day is disputed. It probably enjoyed at least semi-technical force,[1] being applied to a select number of distinguished persons amongst the leading men of Rome. A further fascinating conjecture has often been put forward. Pilate was a favoured acquaintance of Aelius Sejanus, prefect of the praetorian guard and highly influential in court circles; perhaps, too, he was his protégé (though this suggestion is based on an uncertain inference from Philo (*Leg. Gaium* 159–161). It is possible that Pilate secured 'Friend of Caesar' status under his sponsorship: the Roman historian Tacitus is frequently cited, 'the closer a man's with Sejanus, the stronger his claim to the emperor's friendship' (*Annals* VI. viii). In the autumn of AD 31, however, Sejanus fell from power, and Tiberius Caesar executed not only Sejanus but many of his closest friends and supporters. If the trial of Jesus took place after the fall of Sejanus, certainly Pilate and probably Caiaphas (who was no mean politician) would have known of Pilate's precarious position, and the implicit threat of v. 12 assumes terrifying proportions.

As attractive as this reconstruction is, it stalls on the uncertainty as to the date of Jesus' trial and death. Those who detect a connection with Sejanus are inclined to place Jesus' death in AD 33, a calendrically suitable year. The majority, however, probably rightly, place his death in AD 30. On balance, it seems best to regard *friend of Caesar* in v. 12 as a semi-technical honorific that Pilate may or may not have enjoyed. If he did (*cf.* discussion in *NewDocs* 3. § 75), the threat would have been taunting and severe, even if Sejanus had not yet fallen. Indeed, even if Pilate could not claim the honorific, the implicit threat of the Jewish authorities ('If you let this man go, you are no friend of Caesar') would be perceived as a profound understatement soaked in vicious irony, a threat reminding Pilate of bad reports that had previously gone to the Emperor.

13. The interpretation of v. 13 offered above assumes that the rendering of the NIV and most English versions is correct: *Pilate . . . sat down* (*ekathisen*) *on the judge's seat* (*bēma*). But it is linguistically possible to read the verb transitively: 'Pilate . . . *set* [Jesus] *down* on the judge's seat (*bēma*)'.[2] Although it is hard to imagine that any Roman governor, not least Pilate, would actually set a suspect on his own seat, it has been shown that *bēma* properly means 'tribunal', the platform on which not only the governor sat but also his clerks and advisors. The argument, then, is that Pilate had Jesus sit down on another chair on the tribunal, primarily to irritate his Jewish opponents; and in so doing contributed,

---

[1] *Cf.* E. Bammel, *TLZ* 77, 1952, pp. 205–210.
[2] Of the minority of commentators who hold this view, the most articulate and convincing is I. de la Potterie, *Bib* 41, 1960, pp. 217–247.

however unwittingly, to the profound irony of the proceedings. Pilate's 'Here is your king!' (v. 14) now implicitly adds, 'on the *bēma*'. Moreover, John is intensely interested in the theme of judgment (*e.g.* 3:18–21; 5:22, 27; 12:48), and this interpretation brings the themes of kingship and judgment together: while the Jews cry 'Take him away! Crucify him!' (v. 15), Jesus confronts them as their judge – their judge because they will not accept him as their king.

As attractive as this view is, it should probably be rejected (*cf.* especially Dauer, pp. 269–274). Although *ekathisen* can be taken transitively, that is not the most common usage. In other passages in the New Testament where the verb is used in connection with kings and governors, the intransitive meaning prevails. More importantly, although the kingship of Jesus is a strong theme throughout this chapter, the theme of Jesus as judge is not. And if Pilate merely sets Jesus down on *another* chair on the tribunal, it would be an extraordinary act but would not in itself be a symbol of a judging role: it might symbolize the role of a court clerk! For unabashed symbolism of judging, Jesus would have to sit not only on the tribunal but in the governor's seat. Historically, that is most implausible; contextually, it does not quite fit; syntactically, it is possible but no more. The case for this alternative interpretation is not persuasive.

7. Jesus crucified (19:16b–30)

In main outline, John's account of Jesus' death parallels that of Mark rather closely. Nevertheless, he omits some details, and introduces several features not reported elsewhere, including the controversy caused by the inscription on the cross (vv. 19–22), several fulfilment quotations (vv. 24, 28–29, 36–37), the care of Jesus for his mother (vv. 25–27) and the last cry before his death (v. 30). The significance of these distinctive elements is treated below.

16b–17. The Greek text simply reads '*They* took charge of Jesus'. The referent must be the soldiers (vv. 23, 25). At this point they probably administered the terrible scourging, the *verberatio* (*cf.* notes on v. 1). *Carrying his own cross* (lit. 'carrying the cross for himself' [*heautō*]) confirms what we know of Roman practice: 'Each criminal as part of his punishment carries his cross on his back' (Plutarch, *The Divine Vengeance*, 554 A/B). This refers to the cross-member, the horizontal bar (Lat. *patibulum*). The condemned criminal bore it on his shoulders to the place of execution, where the upright beam of the gibbet was already fastened in the ground. The victim was then made to lie on his back on the ground, where his arms were stretched out and either tied or nailed to the *patibulum*. The cross-member was then hoisted up, along with the victim, and fastened to the vertical beam. The victim's feet were tied or nailed to the upright, to which was also sometimes attached a piece of wood that served as a kind of seat (Lat. *sedecula*) that partially supported the body's weight. This was designed to increase the agony, not relieve it (*cf.* notes on vv. 18, 31ff.).

The Synoptics report (Mt. 27:32; Mk. 15:21; Lk. 23:26) that the soldiers commandeered Simon of Cyrene to carry the cross for Jesus. The traditional harmonization is almost certainly correct. Despite the brutal beatings, Jesus 'went out' (sc. from the *praetorium*, 18:28) and carried the cross-member as far as the gate of the city, where he collapsed in weakness from pain and loss of blood, and where the soldiers impressed Simon who (Mark says) was 'on his way in from the country'. If the *praetorium* refers to the Fortress of Antonia, and the traditional *Via Dolorosa* is approximately the route that Jesus went, it is perhaps worth noting that tradition places the intervention of the soldiers and of Simon at the fifth station of the cross. Dodd (*HTFG*, p. 125) judges the harmonization to be 'a perfectly reasonable interpretation of the evidence'.

Even so, it is important to ask why John omits mention of Simon of Cyrene. The brief answer is that it does not lend support to his central themes, and would therefore be distracting. It is possible to think of Jesus' death in terms of his resolution, his obedience to the Father, his Father's plan; it is also possible to think of Jesus' death in terms of Jesus' suffering, struggle, weakness and anguish. Both perspectives are correct (*cf.* notes on v. 28); both are in some measure taught in each of the four Gospels. But John, even though he makes room for the suffering (*e.g.* 12:27–28), greatly emphasizes the sovereign plan of the Father and the Son's obedience. And so he reports, rightly, that Jesus carried his own cross.

Other connections may have been in the Evangelist's mind, but are much harder to demonstrate. The church Fathers tend to see in this event the antitype to Isaac carrying wood to the place of sacrifice, almost his own sacrifice (Gn. 22:6). Even some Jewish scholars thought the Isaac episode evocative of crucifixion: Isaac carried the wood 'like one carries his stake [= cross] on his shoulder' (*Genesis Rabbah* 56:3 [on Gn. 22:6]). How much John could have expected his readers to infer is very difficult to determine. Again, the second-century gnostic heretic Basilides in his commentary on John argues that Simon the Cyrene took Jesus' place and died on the cross in his stead[1] – the common view of Muslims to this day. If that view were rising in John's day (and there is no evidence that it was), it is possible that John might find it expedient simply to omit mention of the Cyrene. But we are rapidly approaching the borders of uncontrolled speculation.

Golgotha is an English transliteration of the Greek, itself a transliteration of the Aramaic *gulgoltâ*, which means 'skull'. Our more common 'Calvary' derives from Latin *calvaria*, which also means 'skull' and which was used in the (Latin) Vulgate version in all four Gospels. *The place of the Skull* probably derived its name from its appearance, though this is uncertain. The site is in doubt. Gordon's Calvary is not an

---

[1] So Irenaeus, *Against Heresies* II. xxiv. 4, though some doubt that Irenaeus rightly represents Basilides. *Cf.* also *The Second Treatise of the Great Seth*, in J. M. Robinson (ed.), *The Nag Hammadi Library in English* (Harper and Row, 1977), p. 332.

option.[1] The most likely site is near the Church of the Holy Sepulchre, just outside the northern wall, and not far from a road (Mt. 27:39; Jn. 19:20).

18. *Here*, in this public place where all could see him, the soldiers *crucified him*. In the ancient world, this most terrible of punishments is always associated with shame and horror.[2] It was so brutal that no Roman citizen could be crucifed without the sanction of the Emperor. Stripped naked and beaten to pulpy weakness (*cf.* notes on v. 1), the victim could hang in the hot sun for hours, even days. To breathe, it was necessary to push with the legs and pull with the arms to keep the chest cavity open and functioning. Terrible muscle spasm wracked the entire body; but since collapse meant asphyxiation, the strain went on and on. This is also why the *sedecula* (*cf.* notes on vv. 16b–17) prolonged life and agony: it partially supported the body's weight, and therefore encouraged the victim to fight on.

All four Gospels mention that Jesus was crucified with two others. Matthew and Mark call them *lēstai*, probably 'guerrilla fighters' (John applies the same word to Barabbas in 18:40); Luke (23:40–43) reports the repentance of one of them. John mentions only that Jesus was crucified between them. It is hard to imagine that the Evangelist who uses Isaiah 53 so effectively in John 12 is not now thinking of Isaiah 53:12: Jesus 'was numbered with the transgressors'. But the matter is uncertain (*cf.* Moo, pp. 154–155).

19–22. It was the custom for the crime of which the person doomed to crucifixion had been found guilty to be written on a tablet or placard and hung around his neck or carried before him as he made his way to the place of execution. Once the prisoner was crucified, the placard was often *fastened to the cross*. The Greek text says that Pilate 'wrote' it (*egrapsen*): this does not necessarily mean that he took the stylus in his own hand, but that he caused it to be written (NIV 'had a notice prepared') and controlled the content, as the ensuing verses show (*cf.* notes on 21:24–25). The Latin word for such a placard was *titulus*, which generated *titlos* in Greek, and accounts for 'title' in many English versions (NIV 'notice').[3]

The charge on the notice read *Jesus of Nazareth, the King of the Jews*. The Synoptics say much the same (Mt. 27:37; Mk. 15:26; Lk. 23:38); minor differences in wording may owe something to the trilingual form in which it was written. Aramaic (*cf.* notes on 5:2) was the language in common use in Judea; Latin was the official language of the army; and Greek was the *lingua franca* of the Empire, and well known in Galilee. Multilingual crucifixion notices are reported in other sources (*cf.* Bauer,

---

[1] *Cf.* André Parrot, *Golgotha and the Church of the Holy Sepulchre* (tr. E. Hudson; SCM, 1957), pp. 59–65.

[2] *Cf.* Martin Hengel, *Crucifixion* (SCM/Fortress, 1977).

[3] *Cf.* E. Bammel, 'The *titulus*', in E. Bammel and C. F. D. Moule (eds.), *Jesus and the Politics of His Day* (Cambridge University Press, 1984), pp. 353–364.

p. 173). The reason for such linguistic enthusiasm is obvious: the Romans had a vested interest in publicizing the nature of the crime that resulted in such punishment, as a warning to every segment of the populace.

If we recall how the theme of Jesus' kingship has been developing throughout chs. 18 – 19, there can be little doubt that this episode functions in the narrative at several levels. First, it makes clear that the charge on which Jesus was eventually found guilty was the first one, the charge of sedition (18:33). Second, the wording is Pilate's last act of revenge in the case. He has already taunted the Jews with Jesus' king-ship (vv. 14–15); here he does so again, mocking their convenient allegiance to Caesar by insisting that Jesus is their king, and snickering at their powerless status before the might of Rome by declaring this wretched victim their king. Doubtless his own sense of powerlessness before their manipulation (v. 12) contributed to his unyielding insistence that the wording remain as he prepared it. The protest of the chief priests shows they feel the sting of Pilate's savage irony; but their suggestion of an insertion, '*I am* the King of the Jews', to make the matter one of Jesus' claims and no more, would strip the governor of his last revenge. And so he stands firm. Thus Pilate's firmness is not motivated by principle and strength of character, but by the hurt obstinacy and bitter rage of a man who feels set upon. It is not, as Dauer (p. 275) argues, that Pilate refuses to change the truth into a lie, but that he is determined to humilate those who have humiliated him. This view of Pilate is confirmed by other sources: *e.g.* Philo (*Leg. Gaium* 301) describes Pilate as 'naturally inflexible, a blend of self-will and relent-lessness'.

But at a third level, Pilate's malice serves God's ends. The Lord Jesus is indeed the King of the Jews; the cross is the means of his exaltation and the very manner of his glorification. Even the trilingual notice may serve as a symbol for the proclamation of the kingship of Jesus to the whole world: 'Thus did Pilate *Tell it out among the heathen that the Lord is King*' (Hoskyns, p. 628, emphasis his, adopting the language of Ps. 96:10 AV). Thus the two men most actively and immediately responsible for Jesus' death, Caiaphas (11:49–52) and Pilate, are unwittingly furthering God's redemptive purposes, unwittingly serving as prophets of the King they execute. 'The Crucified One is the true king, the kingliest king of all; because it is he who is stretched on the cross, he turns an obscene instrument of torture into a throne of glory and "reigns from the tree" '[1] (Bruce, p. 369).

23–24. By custom the clothes of an executed criminal were the per-quisite of the executioners. Suggestions that this episode was created out of whole cloth in order to 'find' a suitable 'fulfilment' for Psalm 22:18

---

[1]The theme of Christ 'reigning from the tree' was much loved by second-century Christians (*cf.* Justin, *Dialogue with Trypho* 73), and turned in part on a gloss on the LXX text of Ps. 96:10: 'Say among the nations, "The LORD reigned *from the tree*." '

are therefore unwarranted. The division of the spoils shows that the execution squad was made up of four soldiers (*cf.* Acts 12:4). Normally a Jew in Palestine wore a tunic (*chitōn*) next to the skin, and an outer garment, something like a robe (*to himation*, always in the singular). Here John tells us that they divided Jesus *clothes* (*himatia, i.e.* the plural form) into four parts. If, somewhat anomalously, we are to think this plural form refers to the outer garment, then presumably the soldiers divided it into four parts, probably at the seams. But it is more likely that the plural expression refers to Jesus' clothes, including a belt, sandals and head covering. These three plus the outer robe gave the soldiers one item each. That left the tunic (*chitōn*, NIV 'undergarment', but it was not equivalent to our undergarments, even though it was worn next to the skin, but to our suit, over which an outer garment might be worn), and it was decided to gamble for that item so it would not have to be dismembered – a sad loss since this garment *was seamless, woven in one piece from top to bottom.*

However customary this merciless bit of byplay was at ancient executions, in the case of Jesus' death it was nothing less than the fulfilment of prophecy: it occurred *that the scripture might be fulfilled.* This does not mean that the soldiers wittingly complied with Scripture, but that God's mysterious sovereignty so operated in the event that it occurred, and occurred just this way, in order to fulfil Scripture. Indeed, it has often been remarked that John deploys more and more 'that the Scripture might be fulfilled' statements the closer he gets to the passion.[1] Of the four Evangelists, only John adduces Scripture here. It is as if he is saying that, whereas all of the details of the Messiah's life, ministry, death and exaltation are in conformity with the Father's plan and frequently in fulfilment of revealed Scripture, it is especially important that this be seen to be the case in the substance and details of his passion. So the point will not be overlooked, John adds, after the quotation from Scripture, *So this is what the soldiers did.* The concern to tie the sufferings of this messianic claimant to the will of God would be especially urgent in the evangelization of Jews and proselytes.

The Scripture cited is Psalm 22:18 (LXX 21:19), following exactly the words of the LXX. The psalmist is afflicted by both physical distress and the mockery of his opponents, and apparently uses the symbolism of an execution scene, in which the executioners distribute the victim's clothes, to elaborate the depth of his sense of abandonment. Davidic typology, a central motif in early Christianity, assures that this will have final reference to Christ, a connection made all the easier in this instance by the fact that Jesus himself drew attention to the relevance of Psalm 22 by citing the first verse on the cross: 'My God, my God, why have you forsaken me?' (Mt. 27:46; Mk. 15:34).

---

[1] *Cf.* Craig A. Evans, 'Obduracy and the Lord's Servant: Some Observations on the Use of the Old Testament in the Fourth Gospel', in Craig A. Evans and William F. Stinespring

The language of the quotation has generated no little discussion as to whether the Evanglist has manipulated the text. Both the LXX and John read:

'They divided my garments (*ta himatia*) among them,
and cast lots (*ebalon klēron*) for my clothing (*ton himatismon*).'

The parallelism of the underlying Hebrew poetry means it is probable that the 'garments' in the first line refer to the same thing as the 'clothing' in the second. But John, it is argued, apparently *distinguishes* the two, the first referring either to the *himation*, the outer robe, or to the clothes apart from the tunic, while the second line refers to the tunic, the *chitōn* for which the soldiers drew lots. He thus preserves the integrity of the eyewitness evidence (*cf.* vv. 25–27), but demonstrates his ignorance of Hebrew poetry and misapplies Scripture. By contrast, Lindars (*NTA*, p. 91) argues that 'John must not be held ignorant of the most common characteristic of Hebrew poetry' – to which Barrett (pp. 550–551) responds by saying that, judging by the misapplication of the Psalm, the view of Lindars 'comes near to accusing [John] of saying what he knew to be untrue.' Moo (pp. 256–257) simply says that, granted John's knowledge of what actually transpired, 'not unnaturally, he sees in this incident a fulfilment of the other half of the psalm verse and accordingly records it'.

In fact, the problem thus erected may be a false one. Several important studies in recent years have pointed out that Hebrew synonymous parallelism is frequently far from exact in its equivalencies, even in its referents. This enables the second or third line to do more than say more or less the same thing in different words; subsequent lines may say something complementary in more or less the same words. Even before these studies, Hoskyns (p. 629) pointed out that the psalm verse allows itself the possibility of being divided into two parts, since the LXX switches from the plural (*ta himatia*) to the singular of another word (*ton himatismon*), a distinction that could conceivably be taken of outer and inner clothes respectively.

Better still, if the parallelism is quite tight, and *ta himatia* and *ton himatismon* both refer to the inner tunic,[1] by the same logic 'divided' (line 1) and 'cast lots' (line 2) refer to the same activity. After all, how would the executioners decide to 'divide' the clothes of the criminal? An outer robe, a belt, and a headpiece would not all have the same value; the fairest form of division might well be to cast lots. Thus John may be applying the Old Testament text in its entirety *only* to the *second* part of the division at the foot of Jesus' cross. Alternatively, even the four

---

(eds.), *Early Jewish and Christian Exegesis: Studies in Memory of William Hugh Brownlee* (Scholars, 1987), esp. pp. 225f.

[1]That is possible: the two nouns are certainly not always differentiated in the Greek of the period: *cf.* MM, *s.v.*: *NewDocs* 3. § 41.

soldiers who crucified Jesus may have carried out the initial division of clothes by means of casting lots (*cf*. Hengstenberg, 2. 412: 'As the value of the four parts was unequal, the first distribution was probably by lot.'). In that case, the seamless garment is treated differently (vv. 23b–24) not because it was the only garment of clothing to have its ownership decided by lot, but because, since it was seamless, the soldiers thought best to use the lot to assign it to *one* soldier instead of distributing it amongst themselves. In this view, the Evangelist sees in the *entire* distribution of Jesus' clothes a fulfilment of *both* lines of Psalm 22:18,[1] but mentions the peculiarity of the decision about the tunic because he was an eyewitness, and possibly because he saw something symbolic in the seamless garment.

But what symbolism? Two views have dominated the interpretation of this passage.

(1) From the fact that Josephus (*Ant*. iii. 161) describes a high priest's robe (which he calls a *chitōn*) as 'woven from a single length of thread', Jesus' seamless tunic has been taken as a symbol for his high priestly ministry (*e.g.* Macgregor, p. 346). But the priestly garment was not an inner 'tunic' but a robe. Further, *chitōn* was not the normal word for referring to it, and, unlike the Epistle to the Hebrews, the Fourth Gospel does not dwell on Jesus' high priestly ministry.

(2) From the fact that Philo (*De Fug. et Inv.* 110–112) can use a robe as a symbol of the *logos* ('Word'; *cf*. notes on 1:1) which binds all things into a unity, Jesus' seamless tunic has been taken to represent the unity of the church (*e.g.* Hoskyns, p. 630). Certainly the unity of those given to Jesus is an important theme in John (*cf*. esp. ch. 17), but John's use of *logos* as a Christological title (1:1, 14) is conceptually far removed from Philo (*cf*. notes on 1:1), and in any case there is no transparent reason in the Gospel of John for making this association. Moreover, here Jesus has his tunic (= church?) taken from him!

Still other suggestions have been made, but when commentators admit, as they frequently do, that 'we have no way of knowing whether such references were in the evangelist's mind' (Brown, 2. 922), it is an admission that *the text itself* does not sanction such associations, since that is the only access we have to the Evangelist's mind. The one association that has some merit, precisely because Jesus' clothes and Jesus' death come together in both passages, is the one that ties 19:23–24 to the footwashing (13:1–20). Jesus laid aside his garments, his outer garments, when he washed his disciples' feet, in an act that anticipated the cleansing that would issue from his death. So here he loses his

---

[1]The fact that the Evangelist uses *lachōmen* for 'Let's decide by lot' instead of some form of the LXX's *ebalon klēron* ('They . . . cast lots'), and uses *chitōn* for Jesus' inner tunic instead of *ton himatismon* in the second line of the Psalm quotation, constitutes evidence not only that John is not simply 'creating' the event out of his reading of Scripture, but also that he is probably not dividing the two stichs of the Psalm into separate events in his own mind, the second applying only to the *chitōn* (NIV 'undergarment', tunic).

clothes, all his clothes. The same self-humbling operates, but here to the last degree, as he lays aside his glory, and by this act, in the divine paradox, is glorified. Yet while his last earthly possessions are stripped from him, he remains under his Father's sovereign care, even as his tunic is not torn and destroyed (*cf.* Schnackenburg, 3. 274).

25. The Greek syntax[1] suggests a contrast between the soldiers (v. 24) and the women here introduced. While the soldiers carry out their barbaric task and coolly profit from the exercise, the women wait in faithful devotion to the one whose death they can still understand only as tragedy.[2]

How many women John enumerates has been disputed. It is possible to read the list as two, three or four: (a) Two: his mother and his mother's sister, namely 'Mary of Clopas' (which probably means *Mary the wife of Clopas*, as in the NIV) and Mary Magdalene. This is highly unlikely, for it would mean not only that Mary had remarried after the death of Joseph, but also that there were two women with the name 'Mary' in the same family. (b) Three: In this view Jesus' mother's sister is 'Mary of Clopas', but this too presupposes two women with the same name in one family. (c) Four: This is more likely, and assumes that John has listed two women without naming them, and two others by name.

The Synoptists mention several women at the cross, but they are standing afar, and they are introduced only after Jesus has died (Mt. 27:55–56; Mk. 15:40; Lk. 23:49; the latter mentions no names). That John should introduce them earlier is not surprising: he is preparing for vv. 26–27, which necessarily takes place while Jesus is still alive. Nor should John's '*Near* the cross' be seen as a contradiction of the Synoptic witness. It was natural, perhaps inevitable, that during the long vigil some who loved him would venture closer, and, revulsed by the suffering, drift away again – only to return. E. Stauffer[3] has adduced evidence that crucified persons were often surrounded by friends, relatives and enemies. Barrett's objection (p. 551) that the concerns for military security at the crucifixion of a rebel king outweighs such evidence, his insistence that the soldiers would keep people away and therefore that vv. 25–27 must be judged inauthentic, cannot bear much weight. True, there are recorded instances of people taking a friend down from a cross, the victim surviving, and the presence of the soldiers was to ensure security against such an eventuality. But apart from the fact that four Roman auxiliaries were unlikely to be terrified by a few women in deep mourning, the Roman authorities, if we are to judge by Pilate, were well aware that neither Jesus nor his disciples posed much of a

---

[1]*Hoi men oun stratiōtai* ... *Heistēkeisan de.* ... At the risk of overtranslating: 'So the soldiers, on the one hand, did these things; on the other hand, there stood near the cross of Jesus. ...'

[2]*Cf.* Morris, p. 811 n. 60: 'In the light of Matt. 27:55 and Luke 8:2f. it is not impossible that these women had provided the very clothes over which the soldiers gambled.'

[3]E. Stauffer, *Jesus and His Story* (tr. D. M. Barton; SCM, 1960), pp. 111, 179 n. 1.

threat. More important, the 'notice' (v. 19) was meant to be read. If people could be close enough to the cross to read a sign, close enough (according to all four Gospels) to hear some of Jesus' utterances, it is difficult to see why vv. 25–27 should be assessed so negatively.

If we attempt to correlate the four people to whom John refers with the three listed in Matthew and Mark, Mary Magdalene (*i.e.* Mary of Magdala, a village on the west shore of Galilee two or three miles north of Tiberias) appears in all four lists. John has not mentioned her before, but she figures prominently in the resurrection accounts (20:1ff.). Only Luke 8:2 offers additional information: she was one of those women who ministered to Jesus, and seven demons had gone out of her, presumably in consequence of Jesus' ministry. The mother of Jesus appears only in John's list. Of the other two women in John's list, there is something to be said for supposing that Mary the wife of Clopas is to be identified with Mary the mother of James and Joses. That means that Salome (Mk. 15:40) is the mother of James and John the sons of Zebedee (Mt. 27:56–57), and is none other than the sister of Mary the mother of Jesus. The primary reason why these identifications cannot be certain is that Mark tells us, 'Many other women who had come up with him to Jerusalem were also there' (Mk. 15:41), and therefore the lists should not necessarily be mapped onto each other. In favour of the traditional identification, however, are two details: (a) assuming that John is the beloved disciple (*cf.* vv. 26–27) who stands behind the Fourth Gospel, it is remarkable that he alone of the Evangelists mentions neither his own name nor the name of his brother – which makes it unsurprising that his mother, the sister of Mary the mother of Jesus, is also unnamed; (b) Jesus' assignation of a connection between his mother and the beloved disciple (vv. 26–27) becomes somewhat easier on the assumption that John is his cousin on his mother's side, his mother's nephew.

26–27. The disciple whom Jesus loved (*cf.* notes on 13:23) was not mentioned in the previous verse, but is here introduced.[1] The Greek behind *Dear woman* (*gynai*) is as difficult to translate as at 2:4, the only other place where Jesus' mother appears in the Fourth Gospel (except for brief mention at 2:12; 6:42).

The words Jesus uses, *here is your son . . . Here is your mother*, are reminiscent of legal adoption formulae, but such formulae would have been cast in the second person (*e.g.* 'You are my son'). If Jesus was the breadwinner of the family before he embarked on his public ministry, and if every mention of Mary during Jesus' years of ministry involves Jesus in a quiet self-distancing from the constraints of a merely human family, and this not least for his mother's good (*cf.* notes on 2:2–4), it is wonderful to remember that even as he hung dying on a Roman cross, suffering as the Lamb of God, he took thought of and made provision

---

[1] Morris, p. 812: 'Is this perhaps the touch of one who remembers who were there, but records them as he saw them and thus does not mention himself?'

for his mother. Some have found it surprising that Jesus' brothers did not take over this responsibility. But quite apart from the fact that they were at this point quite unsympathetic to their older brother (7:5), they may not even have been in Jerusalem: their home was in Capernaum (*cf.* notes on 2:12). Barrett (p. 552) objects that their lack of faith (7:5) 'could not annul their legal claim'. True enough, but this is not a legal scene. Jesus displays his care for his mother as both she and the beloved disciple are passing through their darkest hour, on their way to full Christian faith.[1] *From that time* (*hōra*, 'hour') *on*, from the 'hour' of Jesus' death/exaltation (*cf.* notes on 2:4; 12:23; 17:1), *this disciple took her into his home*.[2]

The more difficult question is whether this relationship that the dying Jesus establishes between his mother and the beloved disciple is symbolic, and if so, of what. There have been any number of suggestions, most of them anachronistically tied either to later developments in historical theology, or to an unlikely interpretation of 2:1–11, or to both. Roman Catholic exegesis has tended not so much to see Mary coming under the care of the beloved disciple, as the reverse; and if the beloved disciple is also taken as an idealization of all true disciples, the way is cleared to think of Mary as the mother of the church. For some scholars, this theme is tied to 'new Eve' typology – Mary as the antitype of the first woman, who can say, 'With the help of the LORD I have brought forth a man' (Gn. 4:1). Indeed, for Brown (2. 925–926), this is virtually the climax of Jesus' mission, since the next verse (v. 28) discloses that Jesus now knows that all things have been completed.

Apart from the question of the meaning of v. 28, however (for which see below), the fact that the beloved disciple took Mary into his home, rather than the reverse, rather favours the view that he was commissioned to look after her. Thus, the *theological* reading favoured by many Catholic exegetes tends to move in a direction contrary to an *historical* reading of the text. Certainly it is true that John uses history to teach theology, and that both Jesus and John use historical events, institutions and utterances in symbolic ways to teach deeper truths to those with eyes to see. But such theological readings are *in line* with the historical reading. In this instance, however, the Fourth Gospel focuses on the exclusiveness of the Son, the finality of his cross-work, the promise of

---

[1]That both Mary and Jesus' brothers are found with the apostles and the rest of the one hundred and twenty in the period between the ascension and Pentecost (Acts 1:14), even though the brothers, at least, were thoroughly sceptical a few months earlier (7:5) and even Mary may have had her doubts (*cf.* Mk. 3:20–35), is best accounted for by the information Paul provides: after his resurrection Jesus appeared to James (1 Cor. 15:7).

[2]The last phrase, 'into his home', renders *eis ta idia*, lit. 'into his own [things]', an expression also found in 1:11. It is difficult to imagine that there is any direct allusion, however, not only because the contexts of each occurrence are so different but also because the same phrase occurs in 16:32 without any possibility of an allusion to the Prologue. On the possibility that John the son of Zebedee had a place of his own in Jerusalem, *cf.* Introduction, § IV.

the Paraclete as the definitive aid to the believers after Jesus has been glorified, and correspondingly de-emphasizes Mary by giving her almost no part to play in the narrative, and by reporting a rebuke, however gentle, that Jesus administered to her (2:4). With such themes lying on the surface of the text, it is most natural to see in vv. 26–27 an expression of Jesus' love and care for his mother, a thoughtful provision for her needs at the hour of supreme devastation (cf. Dauer, pp. 322–326). To argue, then, that this scene is symbolic of a continuing role for Mary as the church comes under her care is without adequate contextual control. It is so anachronistic an interpretation that is difficult to imagine how it could have gained such sway apart from the developments of centuries of later traditions.

Others have taken the beloved disciple to represent the ideal Christian, and Mary to represent the faithful remnant of Israel that accepted Jesus as the promised Messiah. The remnant of Israel is thus the 'mother' from which the church is born. But it is hard to see how the remnant comes under the care of the church, or vice versa. Bultmann (p. 673) sees in the beloved disciple a representation of Gentile Christianity, and in Mary a representative of Jewish Christianity: thus that part of the Jews that tarries by the cross overcomes the offence of the cross and learns to feel at home in the increasingly Gentile church, while Gentile Christianity is charged with making the Jewish remnant feel at home.[1] But this ill suits the thrust of the narrative. The beloved disciple is himself a Jew, and at this stage of the Gospel he has not yet come to believe in the resurrection (cf. 20:8). When most of these interpretations are canvassed, it is hard not to sympathize with Dodd (IFG, p. 423), who dismisses the lot as 'singularly unconvincing' (similarly Schlatter, p. 351).

If a symbolic reading is to be sanctioned, it must be constrained by the themes of the Fourth Gospel, and perhaps secondarily by possible parallels in the Synoptics. The suggestion of Gourgues[2] is attractive. In John 2:1–11, Mary approaches Jesus as a mother and is somewhat rebuffed. If she demonstrates the first signs of faith, it must be the faith of a disciple, not a mother. Here she stands near the cross with other disciples, and once she has assumed that stance she may again be assigned a role as mother – but not as mother of Jesus, but of another fellow-disciple. The blessing she receives is a peculiar manifestation of a truth articulated elsewhere: 'And everyone who has left houses or brothers or sisters or father or mother or children or fields for my sake will receive a hundred times as much and will inherit eternal life' (Mt. 19:29).

28. Others may unconsciously play their part in the divine plan of redemption (e.g. vv. 23–24; cf. Acts 13:29), but not Jesus. This does not

---

[1]Minear (pp. 143–152) has developed this view yet farther.
[2]M. Gourgues, NRT 108, 1986, pp. 174–191.

mean his cry *I am thirsty* was a bit of manipulative histrionics: a man scourged, bleeding, and hanging on a cross under the Near-Eastern sun would be so desperately dehydrated that thirst would be part of the torture.[1] But Jesus' mind is so steeped in Scripture that he understands the relevance of the Davidic texts to himself. He knew that *all was now completed* (*ēdē panta tetelestai*). This cannot be taken so mechanically that there is nothing whatsoever left to fulfil in the divine plan, not even Jesus' death. The very next line displays one more fulfilment, and v. 30 connects the moment of Jesus' death with the final fulfilment. Rather, Jesus' knowledge *that all was now completed* is the awareness that all the steps that had brought him to this point of pain and impending death were in the design of his heavenly Father, and death itself was imminent.[2]

Although some have tried to connect the *so that the Scripture would be fulfilled* clause with what precedes ('Jesus, knowing that all things had been accomplished in order to fulfil Scripture, said "I thirst"'), it is best to read it with what follows (reading 'Jesus, knowing that all things had been accomplished, in order to fulfil Scripture said "I thirst"'; *cf.* Moo, pp. 275–278). Even if this is what is meant, the Old Testament passage to which reference is made is not obvious. Some have promoted Psalm 22:15, where the fact that the psalmist's tongue sticks to the roof of his mouth presumably means he is thirsty. The suggestion has additional force because Psalm 22 has just been quoted (v. 24). Others opt for Psalm 42:2 or 63:1 ('My soul thirsts for God'), but this means that John 19:28 must be taken in a highly symbolic fashion, since Jesus thirsts for water, not for God. Better still is Psalm 69:21 ('They . . . gave me vinegar for my thirst'). This Psalm has already twice been cited in this Gospel (2:17; 15:25), and the particular verse, Psalm 69:21, not only includes specific reference to thirst, but is apparently alluded to in John 19:29–30 (see below).

Indeed, it has been suggested[3] that the link to Psalm 69:21 may be even tighter. If we grant that Jesus knew he was fulfilling this Scripture, presumably he knew that by verbally confessing his thirst he would precipitate the soldiers' effort to give him some wine vinegar. In that case, the fulfilment clause could be rendered. 'Jesus, knowing that all things had been accomplished, in order to fulfil [the] Scripture [which says "They . . . gave me vinegar for my thirst"] said "I thirst"'. Either way, John wants to make his readers understand that every part of Jesus' passion was not only in the Father's plan of redemption but a

---

[1]*Cf.* Beasley-Murray, p. 351: 'One may no more assume that John's emphasis on the cross as the exaltation of Jesus excludes his desolation of spirit than his emphasis on the deity of the Son excludes the Son's true humanity.'

[2]John's summary of Jesus' knowledge is a more urgent and ominous form of the repeated declaration that the hour had arrived (12:23; 17:1): both statements are slightly proleptic, the latter more so than the former. For this reason, the attempt to make vv. 26–27 the climax of the narrative on the basis of v. 28a fails (*cf.* note on vv. 26–27).

[3]Prof. C. F. D. Moule, in a personal letter dated 2 Sept. 1988.

consequence of the Son's direct obedience to it (*cf.* notes on 5:19–30). And either way, the hermeneutical assumption is that David and his experiences constitute a prophetic model, a 'type', of 'great David's greater son'.

This truth may also by highlighted by the strange choice of verb for *would be fulfilled* (*teleiōthē*). In fulfilment formulae, John elsewhere uses the verb preferred by others, *plēroō* ('to fulfil'), but here resorts to *teleioō* (more properly 'to complete'). Almost certainly this is because he is drawing attention to the use of the same verb in the preceding clause ('that all *was* now *completed*', *tetelestai*) and in v. 30 ('It is finished', *tetelestai*). The completion of his work is necessarily the fulfilment of Scripture and the performance of the Father's will. Jesus' cry *I am thirsty*, the final instance of his active, self-conscious obedience in the Fourth Gospel, and so tied to 'It is finished', thus represents 'not the isolated fulfilling of a particular trait in the scriptural picture, but the perfect completion of the whole prophetic image' (Westcott, 2. 315; *cf.* Reim, p. 49).

29. The drink offered here is not to be confused with the 'wine mixed with myrrh' which some charitable people offered him on the way to the cross (Mk. 15:23). That was a sedative designed to dull the agony, and Jesus refused to drink it. He was fully resolved to drink, instead, the cup of suffering the Father had assigned him. The episode in John 19:29 finds its parallel rather in Mark 15:36. Far from being a sedative, it would prolong life and therefore prolong pain. The 'wine vinegar' (*oxos*) was a cheap, sour wine used by soldiers; the use of this word recalls Psalm 69:21, where the same noun appears. The use of a sponge to carry some to Jesus' lips is also reported in Mark 15:36 par.

Only John, however, mentions that the sponge was placed on a branch of hyssop (Gk. *hyssōpō*). The hyssop (NEB mg. 'marjoram') is a little plant, a sprig of which is ideal for sprinkling – the use to which it was regularly put in Old Testament times (*e.g.* the sprinkling of blood on the doorposts and lintel at Passover, Ex. 12:22). By the same token, the plant is frequently judged too small and light to serve the purpose assigned to it here.

This has prompted commentators to favour one of two other approaches:

(1) Some think that John chooses the term 'hyssop' even though some other stick was in fact used by the soldiers (Mk. 15:36 speaks of a 'stick', *kalamos*), in order to forge additional links to the Passover. But giving Jesus a drink of wine vinegar soaked in a sponge perched on a bit of hyssop that couldn't hold its weight is a remote parallel from a sprig of hyssop used to sprinkle blood. A rising number of commentators are now rejecting this view (*e.g.* Schnackenburg, 3. 284; Haenchen, 2. 194).

(2) Others have followed the suggestion of Joachim Camerarius in the sixteenth century. He conjectured that the original word was not *hyssōpō* ('on hyssop') but *hyssō* ('on a javelin'); and two cursive

manuscripts were later found to support his suggestion.[1] Some therefore wonder if an error could have occurred early enough in the transmission of the Gospel that it affected virtually all the manuscript evidence. The fact that *soldiers* offer this drink to Jesus might be taken to support the suggestion. However, G. D. Kilpatrick[2] has shown that the *hyssos* (Lat. *pilum*) was not any kind of javelin, but one at this time reserved for Roman legionary troops, not the auxiliary troops stationed in Judea, and therefore no *hyssos* would have been available.

Of course, an individual *hyssos* might have made its way to Jerusalem, but this improbability compounded with the weakness of the textual evidence makes for an implausible case. Meanwhile, others have argued that although a *branch* of hyssop would not support a sodden sponge, a *stalk* of hyssop could.[3] Indeed, the branches of hyssop at the end of a stalk could form a little 'nest' to cradle the sponge. Roman crosses were not very high; the soldiers needed to raise the sponge barely above their own heads.

30. However the drink reached him, Jesus completed his part in fulfilling the prophecy. *When he had received the drink*, Jesus cried out once more – possibly the 'loud cry' of Mark 15:37, the content of which is not there reported. If the content is recorded here, it may be because the beloved disciple was close enough to hear it.

In the Greek text, the cry itself is one word, *tetelestai* (*cf.* notes on v. 28). As an English translation, *It is finished* captures only part of the meaning, the part that focuses on completion. Jesus' work was done. But this is no cry of defeat; nor is it merely an announcement of imminent death (though it is not less than that). The verb *teleō* from which this form derives denotes the carrying out of a task, and in religious contexts bears the overtone of fulfilling one's religious obligations. Accordingly, in the light of the impending cross, Jesus could earlier cry, 'I have brought you glory on earth by completing (*teleiōsas*; *i.e.* by accomplishing) the work you gave me to do' (17:4). 'Having loved his own who were in the world, he loved them *eis telos*' – not only 'to the end' but to to the full extent mandated by his mission. And so, on the brink of death, Jesus cries out, *It is accomplished!*

With that, Jesus *bowed his head and gave up* (*paredōken*, he 'handed over') *his spirit* (*cf.* Lk. 23:46). No-one took his life from him; he had the authority to lay it down of his own accord (10:17, 18), the culminating act of filial obedience (8:29; 14:31). The suggestion that this means he handed over the Holy Spirit to his followers is contradicted by the flow of the argument in ch. 20.

One of the best summaries of the significance of Jesus' death, a little

---

[1]The possibility of textual corruption is even more plausible in uncial script. The evidence is nicely set out in Beasley-Murray, p. 318, n. *q*.

[2]*Journal of Transactions of the Victoria Institute* 89, 1957, pp. 98–99.

[3]SB 2. 581; *cf.* E. Nestle, *ZNW* 14, 1913, pp. 263–265.

poem by S. W. Gandy, is particularly appropriate here, because it mirrors John's use of irony to help his readers see:

> He hell in hell laid low;
> Made sin, he sin o'erthrew;
> Bowed to the grave, destroyed it so,
> And death, by dying, slew.

8. The piercing of Jesus' side (19:31–37)

31. If *paraskeuē* ('Preparation') here refers to the same day as does its use in v. 14, and the reasoning in the notes on that verse are correct, then this sentence tells us that Jesus was crucified on Friday, the day before (*i.e.* the 'Preparation' of) the Sabbath. The next day, Sabbath (= Saturday), would by Jewish reckoning begin at sundown Friday evening. It was a *special Sabbath*, not only because it fell during the Passover Feast, but because the second paschal day, in this case falling on the Sabbath, was devoted to the very important sheaf offering (Lv. 23:11; *cf.* SB 2. 582).[1]

The normal Roman practice was to leave crucified men and women on the cross until they died – and this could take days – and then leave their rotting bodies hanging there to be devoured by vultures. If there were some reason to hasten their deaths, the soldiers would smash the legs of the victim with an iron mallet (a practice called, in Latin, *crurifragium*). Quite apart from the shock and additional loss of blood, this step prevented the victim from pushing with his legs to keep his chest cavity open. Strength in the arms was soon insufficient, and asphyxia followed.[2]

By contrast, the Mosaic law insisted that anyone hanged on a gibbet (usually after execution) should not remain there overnight (Dt. 21:22, 23). Such a person was under God's curse, and to leave him exposed would be to 'desecrate the land'. Presumably this would be viewed as doubly offensive if the day on which the desecration took place was a 'special Sabbath'.[3] So *the Jews* (clearly here a reference to the Jewish

---

[1] Those who understand the 'Preparation' in v. 14 to refer to the day before Passover, rather than the Friday of Passover week, usually adopt one of two stances in v. 31. Either they say that this use of 'Preparation' still refers to the day before Passover, and that 'special Sabbath' then refers to Passover rather than to Sabbath, or they say that this use of 'Preparation', unlike the one in v. 14, does refer to Friday. Some coalesce the two views, and suggest that Passover in that year fell on Saturday; but this produces calendrical difficulties not always taken into account. Reasons for the position adopted here have been summarized in the notes on v. 14.

[2] For independent evidence, *cf.* N. Haas (*IEJ* 20, 1970, pp. 38–59), who reports that archaeologists have uncovered the body of a man crucified in the first century north of Jerusalem. One of his legs was fractured, the other smashed to pieces.

[3] On the other hand, there was nothing to prohibit the execution itself from taking place on the Passover itself. Indeed, Mishnah (*Sanhedrin* 11:4) insists that the execution of a rebellious teacher *should* take place on one of the three principal feasts, as a salutary lesson to the people (*cf.* also Dt. 17:13; SB 2. 826).

authorities; *cf.* notes on 1:19) *asked Pilate to have the legs broken and the bodies taken down.* They may also have been hoping that this further mutilation would in the eyes of the people make Jesus appear to be plainly accursed and abandoned by God.

32–33. Apparently the soldiers began by working from either side; John has already explained that Jesus was crucified between the two others (v. 18). They found Jesus already dead – an unusually speedy death that may well have been hastened by double floggings (*cf.* notes on vv. 1, 16a) – and therefore *did not break his legs.* The Scriptural significance of this is unpacked in v. 36.

34. Instead of breaking Jesus' legs, one soldier *pierced Jesus' side with a spear.*[1] The verb *enyxen* ('pierced') could in itself suggest nothing more than a 'stab' to see if Jesus was alive, but the rest of the verse shows that there was significant penetration: the wound brought *a sudden flow of blood and water.* Medical experts disagree on what was pierced. The two most common theories are these: (a) The spear pierced Jesus' heart, and the blood from the heart mingled with the fluid from the pericardial sac to produce the 'flow of blood and water'.[2] (b) By contrast, it has been argued that fluid from the pericardial sac could not so readily escape from the body by such a wound; it would fill up the chest cavity, filling the space around the lung and then oozing into the lung itself through the wound the spear made. In tests performed on cadavers, it has been shown that where a chest has been severely injured but without penetration, hemorrhagic fluid, up to two litres of it, gathers between the pleura lining the rib cage and the lining of the lung. This separates, the clearer serum at the top, the deep red layer at the bottom. If the chest cavity were then pierced at the bottom, both layers would flow out.[3]

However the medical experts work this out, there can be little doubt that the Evangelist is emphasizing Jesus' death, his death as a man, his death beyond any shadow of doubt (*cf.* Richter, *Studien,* p. 125; Bernard, 2. 647; Bultmann, p. 678 n. 1; Beasley-Murray, pp. 356–357). This is of importance to him, as the next verse makes clear; it is the counterpoint to the Prologue: 'The Word *became flesh*' (1:14). Already by the time this Gospel was written, there were docetic influences at work – influences that became much worse by the time the Epistles of John were written (*cf.* 1 Jn. 2:22; 4:1–4; 5:6–9). The docetists denied that the Christ was truly a man, Jesus; he only *seemed* (*dokeō*, 'it seems') to take on human form. And by the same token, he never really died; it only *appeared* to be so.[4] John will have none of it: blood and water flowed

---

[1]Gk. *longchē,* a spear, lance or javelin, but not a *hyssos,* confirming the notes on v. 29, above.

[2]Pierre Barbet, *A Doctor at Calvary: the Passion of our Lord Jesus Christ as Described by a Surgeon* (Doubleday, 1953); W. D. Edwards, W. J. Gabel, F. E. Hosmer, *Journal of the American Medical Association* 255, 1986, pp. 1455–1463.

[3]A. F. Sava, *CBQ* 19, 1960, pp. 343–346.

[4]Islam continues to take this view: *cf.* the Qur'ān, *Sura* 4. 156: 'they did not kill him,

from Jesus' side, and in many strands of both Jewish and hellenistic thought at the time, the human body consists of blood and water.

Granted that this is the primary reason why John records the flow of blood and water, it must be asked if John intends some further symbolism. The most common suggestion, from Chrysostom on, has been that the water represents baptism and the blood represents the Lord's table.[1] In this view, Jesus' death sanctions these rites and empowers them. The plausibility of this symbolism turns in part on how John 3:1–21 and 6:25–71 are read. But even if one were to find a more enthusiastic sacramentalism in those passages than is defended in this commentary, a sacramental reading of the flow of water from Jesus' side still faces problems. Nowhere in Scripture does 'blood' by itself signal holy communion. Even if this blood from Jesus' side is linked to the blood of Jesus that is the true drink (6:55), it is exceedingly difficult to make the analogous connection between water from Jesus' side and baptism. For this reason Richter (*Studien*, p. 139) rightly rules out such symbolism at even the second or third levels of overtone.

If there is a secondary level of symbolism in the verse, the comments of Dodd (*IFG*, p. 428) and Schnackenburg (3. 294) are most suggestive. The flow of blood and water from Jesus' side may be a 'sign' of the life and cleansing that flow from Jesus' death. The blood of Jesus Christ, *i.e.* his sacrificial and redemptive death, is the basis of eternal life in the believer (6:53–54), and purifies us from every sin (1 Jn. 1:7), while water is symbolic of cleansing (Jn. 3:5), life (4:14) and the Spirit (7:38, 39). All of these incomparable blessings are conditioned by the death of the Lamb of God; they 'flow' from the 'lifting up' of the Son. In the combination of this verse and the theme 'Near the cross' (v. 25) lies the inspiration for the first verse of the hymn by Fanny J. Crosby (1820–1915):

> *Jesus, keep me near the cross:*
> *There a precious fountain,*
> *Free to all, a healing stream,*
> *Flows from Calv'ry's mountain.*

It is also possible, but not certain, that the Evangelist is alluding to Exodus 17, esp. v. 6: 'Strike the rock, and water will come out of it for the people to drink.' John has already used water to refer to the Holy Spirit, and has apparently alluded to the two water-from-the-rock episodes (Ex. 17; Nu. 20) as mediated by Nehemiah 9 (*cf.* notes on 7:37–39). The long-suffering Yahweh, himself the Rock of his people (*e.g.* Pss.

---

neither did they crucify him; it only seemed to be so'. As Bruce (p. 382 n. 38) notes, it is commonly recognized that Muhammed's knowledge of Christianity was mediated through docetic sources.

[1]For a convenient summary of the patristic evidence, *cf.* Westcott, 2. 328–333. Perhaps Brown (2. 946–953) is the most articulate defender of the view that there is *probably* a double sacramental reference in this verse.

18:31, 46; 95:1), discloses himself in his Word, his Self-Expression, who becomes a man (1:1, 14) and is stricken for his people, that they may receive the promised Spirit (*cf.* Burge, pp. 93–95, 133–135). So the church sings:

> *Rock of Ages, cleft for me,*
> *Let me hide myself in Thee;*
> *Let the water and the blood,*
> *From Thy riven side which flowed,*
> *Be of sin the double cure,*
> *Cleanse me from its guilt and power.*

Augustus M. Toplady (1740–78)

35. The importance of v. 34 is emphasized by the inclusion of v. 35: there was nothing less than eyewitness testimony to Jesus' death, to the flow of blood and water, to his escape from *crurifragium*. Just as John the Baptist saw and testified that Jesus is the Son of God (the verbs first come together in 1:34), so also did the witness see and testify what has been described in v. 34; *and his testimony is true.* It is generally inferred, probably rightly, that this witness is the beloved disciple (vv. 25–27), responsible for the Fourth Gospel as a whole: 'This is the disciple who testifies to these things and who wrote them down' (21:24). In fact, the issue is compounded by several other variables, including what is meant by the demonstrative pronoun *ekeinos* in the second half of the verse: 'He knows that he tells the truth'. The principal possibilities are the following:

(1) The pronoun *ekeinos* (NIV 'He') refers to Christ (*e.g.* 3:5, 16) or to God (*e.g.* 1:33; 5:19; 8:42): that is, none less than the Son or the Father attests the veracity of the witness (*i.e.* 'God knows that the witness tells the truth'). This is exceedingly artificial when we bear in mind that the Fourth Gospel, while it uses *ekeinos* to refer to Deity, uses the same pronoun to refer to others (*e.g.* John the Baptist, 5:35; Moses, 5:46; Peter, 18:17, 25; and, most importantly in this context, the beloved disciple, 13:25; 21:7, 23). The context must decide.

(2) The pronoun *ekeinos* (NIV 'He') refers to the Evangelist, but the eyewitness is someone else. In this view, the eyewitness communicated the information regarding what he saw *to* the Evangelist, not *as* the Evangelist. Speculation has ranged far as to who this particular eyewitness could be, the most recent proposal being the soldier who pierced Jesus' side.[1] This still makes for rough reading: 'He knows [*i.e.* I the Evangelist know] that he [*i.e.* the eyewitness] tells the truth.' This view is often made to depend on the assumption that the beloved disciple

---

[1] Paul S. Minear, 'Diversity and Unity: A Johannine Case-Study', in Ulrich Luz and Hans Weder (eds.), *Die Mitte des Neuen Testaments: Einheit und Vielfalt neutestamentlicher Theologie* (*Fs.* Eduard Schweizer; Vandenhoeck und Ruprecht, 1983), pp. 162–175.

was no longer present at the cross when the flow of blood and water took place, since by this time he had taken Jesus' mother Mary home (v. 27). This reads too much into v. 27. There is nothing to suggest that the beloved disciple took Mary home *that instant, i.e.* before Jesus had died. Indeed, *From that time on* (v. 27) might more literally be rendered 'From that hour [*hōra*] on' – and 'hour' is so consistently a pregnant term in John referring to the entire death/exaltation of the Son (*cf.* notes on 2:4; 12:23) that it is easy to suppose that Mary and the beloved disciple left only after Jesus had died. Thus, there is no justification from v. 27 for the supposition that the beloved disciple was absent at the effusion of blood and water.[1] In short, this second view is without adequate contextual defence.

(3) By the pronoun *ekeinos* (NIV 'He') the eyewitness refers to himself. This is certainly the easiest way to untangle the pronouns; *ekeinos* then resumes the referent in the preceding clause, 'and *his* testimony is true'. Certainly *ekeinos* can be used by an author about himself (*cf.* Jos., *Bel.* iii. 202; Bernard, 2. 649). In this case, the most likely person is the beloved disciple himself – not only because he is in the vicinity (v. 27) but also because this verse bears formal similarity to 21:24 where the beloved disciple is contextually identified.

The issue has become more complex in recent discussion because a growing number of commentators have suggested that this verse was written by the same editorial hand, different from the beloved disciple and probably from the Evangelist, that composed 21:24. Certainty is impossible, but this theory appears unnecessarily cumbersome, a means for inserting various 'layers' between the beloved disciple and the readers that does not seem warranted. In 21:24, there is an apparent distinction made between the 'we' who attest the veracity of the witness of the beloved disciple, and the beloved disciple himself. The demands of publication may well have encouraged such public attestation (*cf.* notes on 21:24, and Introduction, §IV). But that distinction is precisely what the most natural reading of 19:35 does *not* support. Here the witness and the Evangelist are one, and the most compelling assumption, as we have seen, is that he is also the beloved disciple. This last connection becomes yet more likely when we recall the critical announcement in the Prologue, often overlooked in this discussion: *we have seen his glory*. In the theology of the Fourth Gospel, the glory of the Son is nowhere more brilliantly displayed to a fallen world than in the shame and suffering of the cross (*cf.* notes on 1:14). For the Evangelist not to have been present at the supreme display of the Son's glory would be a betrayal of the anticipation called forth by the Prologue. The theme of eyewitness testimony thus links not only 1:14 and 21:24, but 19:35 as well, especially since this is the hour for the Son of Man to be glorified (12:23).

---

[1]Thus there is no need to resort to the suggestion of Temple (p. 367) that the beloved disciple took Mary to his home and then returned to the cross for the final hour.

Whoever the witness may be, his purpose is plain: *that you also may believe* (*cf.* notes on 20:30–31, where not only the same thought occurs, but the same textual variant, *pisteuēte* [present subjunctive] or *pisteusēte* [aorist subjunctive]). The benefits that flow from the death of the Son are appropriated by faith, and the witness of the Evangelist is given to foster such saving faith.

36. The events of vv. 31–33 happened in order to fulfil[1] two passages from the Bible (vv. 36–37; *cf.* Freed, pp. 108–116). Negatively, the fact that Jesus was spared the *crurifragium* fulfils one Scripture: *Not one of his bones will be broken*. The wording does not coincide precisely with any one Old Testament passage, but three texts are possible.

(1) Two are related. The source of the quotation may be Exodus 12:46 or Numbers 9:12, both of which specify that no bone of the Passover lamb may be broken. Certainly these chapters in John are laced with the Passover motif – indeed, the same could be said for much of the Fourth Gospel, even if we dissent from those who argue that in John Jesus dies at the time the Passover lambs are being killed in the temple complex. Elsewhere in the New Testament Jesus is portrayed as the Passover lamb slain for his people (1 Cor. 5:7; 1 Pet. 1:19).

(2) Alternatively, Psalm 34:20 describes God's care for the righteous man: 'he protects all his bones, not one of them will be broken'. In the context of this Psalm, this is a metaphorical way of declaring God's care over the righteous. If this is the text being applied to Jesus, the Evangelist is telling us that the fact Jesus was spared the *crurifragium* is a symbolic way of declaring that God's providential care over his righteous, suffering Servant never wavered – a kind of Johannine equivalent to the witness recorded in Luke 23:47: 'Surely this was a righteous man.'

If one must choose between the two options, the former is preferable because it turns more immediately on a literal sense (granted the Passover typology!), the same literal sense with which 19:32–33, 36 must be read. Lindars (p. 590) thinks both typologies were in the Evangelist's mind.

37. Positively, the fact that Jesus' side was pierced fulfils Zechariah 12:10. In the context of the prophecy, God speaks after the defeat of the Gentile nations who have laid siege to Jerusalem at the end-time, and says, 'And I will pour out on the house of David and the inhabitants of Jerusalem a spirit of grace and supplication. *They shall look on me, on him whom they have pierced* [so, rightly, NEB, reflecting the strange mix of pronouns in the Hebrew MT], and mourn for him as one mourns for an only child. . . .' The interplay between *on me* and *on him* has prompted many commentators, probably rightly, to understand that God is 'pierced' when his representative, the Shepherd ('Strike the shepherd,

---

[1]Once again this does not imply that the soldiers acted as they did with the intention of fulfilling Scripture, but that God so providentially overruled that their actions did in fact fulfil Scripture. *Cf.* notes on vv. 24, 28; *cf.* B. Hemelsoet, 'L'Ensévelissement selon Saint Jean', in Sevenster, esp. pp. 51–53.

and the sheep will be scattered', Zc. 13:7; *cf.* 11:4, 8–9, 15–17), is pierced. What is less clear is the reason why the people mourn, but it appears that their tears have less to do with desperation and despair than with contrition and repentance for their past sins when God mercifully comes and rescues them from their enemies (*cf.* also Zc. 13:1–2). When Zechariah 12:10 is quoted in Matthew 24:30 (*cf.* also Rev. 1:7) with reference to the parousia, the argument appears to be *a fortiori* (*cf.* Carson, *Matt,* p. 505): just as the Jews in Zechariah 12 wept in contrition and repentance when they saw the one whom they pierced, *how much more* will the nations of the earth mourn at the parousia when they see the exalted and returning Christ coming in glory, the Christ whose followers they have been persecuting, the Christ whom they pierced since it was their sins that sent him to the cross?

As John cites the text, however, the focus is on the piercing, now literally fulfilled in the spear-thrust of the soldier: that is the point of the introductory *and, as another Scripture says.* John does not explore *when* 'They will look on the one they have pierced'. If John has in mind a referent for *They,* he does not tell us; yet as at the cross both executioners and disciples saw the wound but in time perceived quite different significance in that wound, so also both in this world and at its end men and women are confronted by the one whom they have pierced and perceive very different things. One day, however, all will look on him and mourn, whether in deep contrition or grim despair.[1]

But if there is uncertainty in the referent of *They,* and debate as to when all will see the one they have pierced, there is little doubt about John's Christological purpose. John's first readers, familiar with their Bibles, would remember the references in Zechariah to God's promised shepherd, and remember that Jesus said, 'I am the good shepherd. The good shepherd lays down his life for his sheep' (10:11). They might also remember that the next chapter of Zechariah begins with the words, 'On that day a fountain will be opened to the house of David and the inhabitants of Jerusalem, to cleanse them from sin and impurity.'[2] And it would be hard for them not to reflect on the flow of blood and water from Jesus' side, the promise of the Spirit (7:37–39) and the cleansing and life that issue from these new covenant promises (3:3, 5).

9. The burial of Jesus (19:38–42)

38. Joseph of Arimathea appears in all four Gospels, and only in connection with the burial of Jesus. The Synoptists tell us he was a member of the Sanhedrin (Mk. 15:43 par.), that he was rich (Mt. 27:57), and that he was looking for the kingdom of God (Mk. 15:43; Lk. 23:51). Matthew (27:57) and John refer to him as a disciple of Jesus; John alone

---

[1]This seems more faithful to John's Gospel than the interpretation (*e.g.* in Schnackenburg, 4. 164–173) that the salvation of the people by gazing on Christ is exclusively in view.

[2]*Cf.* Paul S. Minear, 'Diversity and Unity', esp. pp. 168–169.

adds, *but secretly because he feared the Jews*.[1] Normally this would condemn him in John's eyes (12:42–43), but Joseph exculpates himself by the courageous action he now undertakes.

Almost as if his previous faintheartedness was shamed by the crisis of the cross, Joseph *asked Pilate for the body of Jesus*. Under Roman law, the bodies of executed criminals were normally handed over to their next of kin, but not so in the case of those crucified for sedition. They were left to the vultures, the culminating indignity and shame. The Jews never refused to bury any executed criminal, but instead of allowing the bodies of such sinners to be placed in family tombs, where they might desecrate those already buried, they provided a burial site for criminals just outside the city (*cf.* Jos., *Ant.* v. 44). Doubtless the request of the authorities that the bodies be taken down (v. 31) assumed that they be buried in this common grave. As a member of the Sanhedrin, however, Joseph used his rank to gain access to Pilate, and thus stood out from his fellow councillors. Joseph would have known that, if Jesus' brothers were present in Jerusalem, they would not have dared to approach Pilate even if they wanted to, and in any case they would have been refused. Joseph's act doubtless made him a pariah in some quarters of the Sanhedrin; it was doubly courageous since the charge under which Jesus had been executed was sedition.[2] That Pilate acceded to the request probably reflects the governor's conviction that Jesus was not really guilty, and may have been a final snub against the Jewish authorities.

39. Only John mentions the part Nicodemus played. Nicodemus was most likely himself a member of the Sanhedrin (*cf.* notes on 3:1), and the Evangelist takes pains to call to mind one of his previous appearances in the Fourth Gospel – he is *the man who earlier had visited Jesus at night* (3:1–15; *cf.* 7:50–52). If *at night* (3:2) there has the moral overtones suggested by the context of ch. 3 (*cf.* esp. 3:19–21), John may be telling us that by this action Nicodemus shows he is stepping out of the darkness and emerging into the light.

The mixture of spices brought by Nicodemus, one hundred *litrai* (*cf.* notes on 12:3), was a little less than the *seventy-five pounds* specified by the NIV – 65.45 pounds, to be more precise (hence NEB's 'more than half a hundredweight', where a hundredweight is 112 pounds avoirdupois). Mention of so large an amount is neither an error nor an exaggeration (despite Lagrange, p. 503; Dodd, *HTFG*, p. 139 n. 2). Five hundred

---

[1] Observe, in passing, this use of *the Jews*: the reference is clearly to the Jewish authorities (*cf.* notes on 1:19), and can scarcely be based on radical prejudice since both Joseph of Arimathea and the Evangelist are Jews.

[2] This historical reconstruction renders implausible the theory of Dennis D. Sylva (*NTS* 34, 1988, pp. 148–151) that Joseph of Arimathea and Nicodemus are portrayed as participating 'in the handing of Jesus to the power of death' (p. 149). After all, Jesus was already dead when they made their request. That they did not yet understand that Jesus had to rise is beside the point: their action was courageous and honouring to the one they had come to love.

servants bearing spices participated in the funeral procession of Herod the Great (Jos., *Ant.* xvii. 199). In the fifth decade of the first century, Onkelos burned about eighty pounds of spices at the funeral of Gamaliel the elder (SB 2. 584; *cf.* also 2 Ch. 16:14). The implication in the present narrative is that two wealthy men used their servants to carry the spices, help take Jesus' body down from the cross, and then prepare him for burial. At a guess, Joseph saw to the legal steps while Nicodemus secured the spices.

As used by Egyptians in embalming, myrrh was a fragrant resin. The Jews turned it into powdered form, and mixed it with aloes, a powder of aromatic sandalwood. The mixture provided a pleasant fragrance in a variety of circumstances (*e.g.* Ps. 45:8; Pr. 7:17; Song 4:14). Used in connection with burial, its purpose was not to embalm (since the Jews did not remove internal organs and fill the space with spices, as the Egyptians did) but to stifle the smell of putrefaction.

40. The spices were apparently laid the length of the *strips of linen* (*othonia*), which were then wound around Jesus' body. More spices were laid under the body, and perhaps packed around it (*cf.* Robinson, *John*, p. 283). Some have objected that John's use of *othonia* (NIV 'strips of linen'), a word found only in John (*cf.* 20:5, 6, 7) and in a variant in Luke 24:12, generates an inevitable conflict with Mark 15:46 par., which states that Joseph wrapped Jesus' body in a *sindōn*. But a *sindōn* can refer either to a single piece of cloth, or to the material used (hence NIV's suitably ambiguous 'some linen cloth', Mk. 15:46). Conversely, some suggest that the plural *othonia* can be a plural of category, thus referring to only one object, or a plural of extension, reflecting the size of the piece, and Brown (2. 942) goes so far as to argue that the Jews never used strips of cloth like those used to wrap Egyptian mummies. There appears to be insufficient evidence to reach a firm decision.[1]

41–42. Only John tells us that at the place (*topos*, as in vv. 17, 20) where Jesus was crucified *there was a garden* and *a new tomb* (almost certainly an artificial cave). We are not told in the canonical Gospels that the garden and its tomb belonged to Joseph of Arimathea (although that is asserted in the apocryphal *Gospel of Peter* 24). Sabbath was almost upon them (on 'Preparation' *cf.* notes on vv. 14, 31), sundown on Friday evening, when all work would have to cease, and so the nearness of the tomb was a great help (*since the tomb was near by, they laid Jesus there*).[2] John emphasizes not only that the tomb was new, but that *no-one had ever been laid* in it. From the perspective of the Jewish authorities, this was doubtless less offensive than burying a crucified sinner in an occupied

[1] Beasley-Murray (p. 360), tongue firmly in cheek, comments, 'For enthusiastic contenders for the genuineness of the Turin shroud, the question is acute, but for most others not so.'

[2] Probably it would have been permitted, under emergency conditions, to wash and anoint the body even after sundown had begun (Mishnah *Shabbath* 23: 4–5), but this was hardly desirable; and the carrying of so large a supply of spices would certainly not have been condoned, nor the moving of the body itself.

tomb (*cf*. notes on v. 38); but the Evangelist's concern is unlikely to have been to mollify their scruples. More likely his purpose is to prepare for ch. 20: if on the third day the tomb was empty, only one body had disappeared, and only one person could have been resurrected. The word for 'garden' (*kēpos*) suggests something substantial, an orchard or a plantation (*cf*. 18:1), and this prepares the way for mention of a gardener (20:15).

The site is almost certainly not the 'garden tomb' to which tourists are directed (though that is the sort of appearance the genuine tomb doubtless had in the first century), but the Church of the Holy Sepulchre. In the fourth century the Emperor Constantine tore down the temple of Venus erected there by Hadrian after the destruction of Jerusalem in AD 135, and built in its stead the Church of the Resurrection, now replaced by the Church of the Holy Sepulchre (which goes back to Crusading times).

John does not mention that Joseph rolled a stone across the tomb's mouth, or that Mary Magdalene and Mary the mother of Joses saw where Jesus was laid (Mk. 15:46–47 par.), but both details are assumed by the opening verses of the next chapter.

F. THE RESURRECTION OF JESUS *(20:1–31)*

The dramatic 'It is finished' (19:30) did not mean that *everything* connected with the 'lifting up' of the Son was finished, but only that Jesus' suffering was finished, his obedience perfect and the will of the Father accomplished up to the decisive juncture of Jesus' death. After all, events that took place *after* Jesus had died are also said to fulfil Scripture (19:36, 37). Of nothing is this truer than of the resurrection of Jesus Christ (20:9), even though the first witnesses did not understand this at the time. For John, nothing could be more disastrous than to consider the cross in isolation from the resurrection, for nothing is more certain in his mind than that the cross is the route Jesus took to return to his Father (14:28–31; 20:17), that the ultimate glorification of the Son with the Father is accomplished through the paradoxical glorification on the cross (12:23–28).

Detailed discussion of the relationship between, on the one hand, John's descriptions of the discovery of the empty tomb and of some initial resurrection appearances, and, on the other, the corresponding reports in the Synoptics, are beyond the scope of this commentary. Useful summaries of the most important discussions are found in Brown (2. 966–978) and Beasley-Murray (pp. 367–370). Some small notice will be taken of the critical discussion in the notes below. A few preliminary remarks may not be entirely out of place.

(1) For John, as for all the early Christians, the resurrection of Jesus

was the immutable fact upon which their faith was based; and their faith in large part depended on the testimony and transformed behaviour of those who had actually seen the resurrected Jesus. Their Master was not in God's eyes a condemned criminal; the resurrection proved that he was vindicated by God, and therefore none less than the Messiah, the Son of God he claimed to be. The culminating faith that brings the disciples out of the era of the Mosaic covenant and into the era of the saving sovereignty of God mediated through the Son is based on the sheer facticity of the resurrection (20: 8, 24–29) – or, better put, such faith trusts Jesus as the resurrected Lord. Nor is John alone on the non-negotiability of the resurrection, for Paul writes, 'And if Christ has not been raised, our preaching is useless and so is your faith. More than that, we are then found to be false witnesses about God, for we have testified about God that he raised Christ from the dead. . . . And if Christ has not been raised, your faith is futile; you are still in your sins' (1 Cor. 15:14–17).

(2) Some of the alleged discrepancies are at the trivial level. John is criticized for having Mary come to the tomb alone, even though she says '*we* [plural] don't know where they have put him!' (20:2); alternatively, he is criticized for mentioning only Mary of Magdala when Mark (16:1) adds Mary the mother of James, and Salome – while Matthew (28:1) says it was Mary Magdalene and the other Mary, and Luke (24:10) specifies Mary Magdalene, Mary the mother of James, Joanna, and others who were with them. But there are more than a score of passages in the Gospels where one Evangelist reports so-and-so-many people, and a parallel report adds one or two more, or mentions only one person. We have just found this to be the case with respect to the burial of Jesus and the mention of Nicodemus (19:38–42). Only the assumptions scholars make about the nature of the descent of tradition, coupled with peculiarly modern and Western notions of precise reportage, could discern any difficulty in such variables.

Again, some have found difficulty with the fact that the beloved disciple is said to believe (v. 8) even though he did not yet understand the Scriptures that said Jesus had to rise from the dead (v. 9). But surely that is the point. Earlier the disciples understood neither the Scriptures nor, in some instances, what Jesus was saying (2:19–22). Now the faith of the beloved disciple (and doubtless the faith of other disciples followed the same route) came to rest securely on the fact of Jesus' resurrection, and other factors, including the transformation of their understanding of the Scriptures, followed later. It was not that for the first time they were then exposed to a distinctive way of reading the Scriptures. Far from it: Jesus had been teaching them throughout his ministry. But the resurrection of Jesus opened a door of understanding. It proved to be the decisive step; and, aided in due course by the Paraclete, the disciples remembered what Jesus had taught (14:25–26; 16:12–15) and embarked on their new integration of understanding, including a fresh grasp of Scripture and the articulation of their faith.

The Evangelist carefully preserves this step along the process, when, from his own experience (assuming the beloved disciple is none other than the Evangelist), he relates his own coming to faith in the once dead and now resurrected Messiah – even as he ruefully confesses the paucity of his understanding of Scripture at this juncture (*cf.* further Carson, 'Mis').

(3) Some of the difficulties and tensions in the narrative turn on too little information. For example, Mary Magdalene finds the tomb empty and, upon hearing her report Peter and the beloved disciple rush off to the tomb. Eventually they return to their own homes (v. 10), while Mary is found outside the tomb crying (v. 11). When or how did Mary get there? For almost two thousand years it has been assumed, not unreasonably, that she returned to the garden alone, or possibly in the wake of the two running men. Must a narrator report each mechanical step? This lack of information, coupled with modern assumptions about the way ancient editors and communities constantly cut up their sources and patched them together into new pieces, has led to several ingenious but unbelievable reconstructions.

Or again, largely because according to v. 20a Jesus shows his hands and side to his disciples without any report of a request to do so, G. Hartmann[1] has attempted to 'retrieve' the original source. He suggests that in this source Mary *and* Peter returned to the tomb, and v. 8 originally told of the lack of comprehension of both of them. He thinks that Mary's announcement to the disciples (v. 18) was originally followed by the blank unbelief of v. 25, but originally set in the plural, rather than being cast on Thomas' lips. Then comes the account of the risen Lord in v. 19 (v. 26 is treated as a mere doublet), and the invitation to all the disciples reported in v. 27. At this point vv. 21–23 follow on.

With a minor caveat, Beasley-Murray (pp. 368–369) adopts this reconstruction because 'it treats the tradition behind *the text* with seriousness'. Perhaps so, but it is hard to see how it treats the text with seriousness: at every point speculation is piled on speculation, where the only possible rebuttals are no less speculative, and equally futile. It is hard to imagine what possible mental processes could have possessed the editor or editors to re-shape Hartmann's 'original' text into the text of John 20 as we have it. It is far wiser to admit we do not have all the answers we would like: the sources do not provide them.

(4) Most of the contemporary discussion assumes that the writing is so late and so far removed from the historical events that there was little or no eyewitness memory to draw upon. The writing process turned on the manipulation of sources, written and perhaps oral tradition, with the dictates of the current 'school' providing the real impress. None of these assumptions is intrinsically plausible. Although the evidence is not unambiguous, the least difficult position is that the Evangelist is the

[1]*ZNW* 55, 1964, pp. 197–220.

beloved disciple, none other than the apostle John (*cf.* Introduction, § IV). Even if this were not so, it is hard to imagine any book as unified in structure, thought and vocabulary as the Fourth Gospel being little more than a pastiche of sources, so poorly woven together that after two thousand years source-criticism can so easily retrieve them.

Brown's discussion (2. 955ff.) is amongst the most comprehensive, full of thoughtful evaluation. Nevertheless, his work leads to a startling conclusion: the editors were simultaneously (a) devout Christians who were nevertheless entirely nonchalant about their cavalier handling of sources, including the knowing creation of narrative without historical referent (p. 999); (b) so unusually stupid that they never noticed the seams and warts they regularly introduced into original sources which were until then characterized by remarkable unity (pp. 1002, 1004); and (c) so slavishly deferential to the sources they received that they felt obligated to insert whole chunks of them intact, even when doing so introduced inconsistencies into the account (p. 1000). These are too many impossible things to believe before breakfast!

(5) Many scholars have rightly repeated the reflection of Vincent Taylor,[1] who offers a plausible reason why the passion narratives, for all their differences, are more integral and sequentially co-ordinated than the resurrection narratives. The account of the passion could not make sense unless at least some of the details were re-told in the same order: the arrest must precede sentencing, arraignment before the Jews must precede appearance before Pilate, flogging must precede crucifixion, and so forth. But there is little that destroys the coherence of each resurrection appearance if it is divorced from a particular sequence. True, the discovery of the empty tomb precedes the resurrection appearances, and the appearance to Thomas along with the other ten must follow the appearance to the ten; but in terms of the fundamental meaning and significance of each resurrection account, and in terms of the way they were first preached, each of Jesus' resurrection appearances could stand more or less alone: the entire sequence of appearances was not necessary to establish meaning and credibility. This means the student of the Gospels must proceed with extraordinary caution when historical or source-critical harmonizations are attempted.

The theological summary of Kysar (p. 299), though it does not comprehensively reflect the themes of John 20, is very suggestive: 'In each of the following [resurrection narratives] we will discover a pattern with the following features: (1) The beneficiaries of the appearance are engulfed in a human emotion (Mary, grief; the disciples, fear; and Thomas, doubt). (2) The risen Christ appears to them in the midst of their condition. (3) As a result, their condition is transformed (Mary, mission; the disciples, gladness; Thomas, faith). Thereby John depicts the appearances as experiences of liberation, much as Christ liberated

---

[1]*The Formation of the Gospel Tradition* (Macmillan, 1953), pp. 59–62.

Lazarus from the grip of death . . . and as his own death is a "new Passover." '[1]

1. Peter and John at the empty tomb (20:1–9)

1. It is remarkable that all four Gospels (*cf.* Mt. 28:1; Mk. 16:2; Lk. 24:1) introduce their respective resurrection accounts by specifying *the first day of the week*, rather than 'the third day' after the crucifixion (*cf.* 1 Cor. 15:3, 4), despite Jesus' passion predictions (Mk. 8:31 par.). The reason is disputed, but it may have to do with the desire to present the resurrection of Jesus as the beginning of something new.

John says the first approach to the tomb took place *while it was still dark, i.e.* early on Sunday morning. Mark specifies dawn; Luke says 'very early in the morning', and Matthew uses a complicated construction that probably means much the same (*cf.* Carson, *Matt*, pp. 587–588). If Mary Magdalene first approached the tomb alone, and then with other women (*cf.* discussion below, and notes on vv. 11–12), John's *darkness* may suggest that she went before dawn. Whether this is so or not, one is tempted to think that John emphasizes the darkness of the dawn because he is still using light/darkness symbolism (*cf.* notes on 3:2; 13:30): the darkness of the hour is the perfect counterpart to the darkness that still shrouds Mary's understanding.

Mary of Magdala (*cf.* notes on 19:25) is prominent in the first resurrection account of each of the four Gospels, but only here does she appear alone. It is quite uncertain how this report is to be reconciled with those in the Synoptics. Perhaps she went to the tomb alone (John), and then returned with some other women (Synoptics), right on the trail of Peter and the beloved disciple. If so, we are to think of her as becoming separated from the others after their arrival at the empty tomb (vv. 10–18). Many argue that the plural 'we' (v. 2) hints that Mary Magdalene was *not* alone on her first trip to the tomb (though other explanations for the 'we' are possible: *e.g.* Bultmann [p. 684 n. 1], rightly cites both Aramaic and Greek parallels where the plural is merely a mode of speech, without plural referent). Bernard (2. 262) argues that a Jewish woman in first-century Jerusalem would not be likely to walk alone, in the dark, to a place of ceremonial dirt, a place of execution; but grief may breed courage as readily as cowardice. Certainly there are Gospel parallels where one Evangelist mentions two or more people while another Evangelist mentions only the most prominent, but on the whole it seems wiser to apply this principle to Mary's second trip to the tomb (assuming there were two trips) than to the first (*cf.* notes on vv. 11–12).

---

[1]Other useful studies on the resurrection, pitched at various levels, include: B. F. Westcott, *The Gospel of the Resurrection: Thoughts on Its Relation to Reason and History* (Macmillan, 1906); G. E. Ladd, *I Believe in the Resurrection of Jesus* (Hodder and Stoughton/ Eerdmans, 1975); Daniel P. Fuller, *Easter Faith and History* (Eerdmans, 1965); W. L. Craig, 'The Bodily Resurrection of Jesus', in *GP 1*, pp. 47–74; *idem*, 'The Empty Tomb of Jesus', in *GP 2*, pp. 173–200; John Wenham, *Easter Enigma: Do the Resurrection Stories Contradict One Another?* (Paternoster, 1984).

However this matter be resolved, it is worth recalling that the Synoptists, who mention several women at the tomb, agree in naming Mary Magdalene first. This probably reflects the early church's memory of the fact that she was the first person to see the resurrected Jesus. Her witness was not as greatly utilized in the primitive preaching as was that of, say, Peter, doubtless owing to the fact that a woman's evidence was not normally admissible in court (*e.g.* Mishnah *Rosh ha-Shanah* 1:8). The Evangelists have nevertheless taken pains to honour her, and thoughtful Christians will remember that God delights to choose what the world deems foolish to shame the wise, so that no-one may boast before him (*cf.* 1 Cor. 1:27–29).

Alone or (less probably) with others, Mary *went to the tomb and saw that the stone* [not actually mentioned before now] *had been removed from the entrance.* The text does not tell us whether she looked inside, but gives the impression she did not. Had she done so, the fact that it was *still dark* would have made the cave a very black hole indeed.

2. The robbing of graves was a crime sufficiently common that the Emperor Claudius (AD 41–54) eventually ordered capital punishment to be meted out to those convicted of destroying tombs, removing bodies or even displacing the sealing stones. John records no hint of the Jewish allegation that Jesus' disciples were the ones who stole Jesus' body (*cf.* Mt. 28:13–15), but the fact that such a charge could be levelled demonstrates that grave robbery was not uncommon. So it is not surprising that the sight of the removed stone prompted Mary Magdalene to draw the conclusion she did. In distress she ran to report her news to two of the most prominent of Jesus' disciples, to Peter and the beloved disciple.[1]

The form of her report, 'They have taken *the Lord* (*ton kyrion*) out of the tomb . . .', is not yet a Christological confession of any significance (*cf.* further on vv. 11, 18, 28). Readers who have already meditated on v. 28 may nevertheless return to this spot and perceive, once again, how often the people in this Gospel speak better than they know.

3–5. Luke 24:12 mentions only Peter at the tomb. For that reason many see the mention of the beloved disciple as either inventive special pleading or a creation full of symbolism (briefly discussed below). Yet Luke 24:24 reports that Cleopas and his companion on the Emmaus road said that '*some* of our companions went to the tomb and found it just as the women had said': the plural should be given its natural force, and taken as confirmation of the witness of the Fourth Gospel.

As for the allegorical interpretations that have attached themselves to these verses, there is too little evidence to support any of them. There is no indication, for instance, that the description of the beloved disciple's

---

[1] It is possible to understand the Greek to mean 'to Peter and to another disciple whom Jesus loved [*i.e.* other than the known "beloved disciple"]', but this is a quite unnecessary refinement. The NIV has the right sense. The verb for *loved* is here *phileō*, not *agapaō* as in 13:23 where the beloved disciple is introduced. There is no difference in meaning between the two references: *cf.* notes on 3:16, 35; 5:20; 11:3, 5; 21:15–17.

fleetness of foot – swifter than Peter! – is a veiled way of insisting that in the 'Johannine church' John must be accorded greater pre-eminence than Peter. In view of 13:12–17, even the suggestion is repulsive. Bultmann (p. 685) holds that Peter represents Jewish Christianity, and the beloved disciple Gentile Christianity: the Jewish church is first on the scene (Peter enters the tomb before John), but that fact gives no precedence since both stand beside the empty grave-clothes. Indeed, the eager faith of the Gentiles is greater than that of the Jews (the beloved disciple ran faster than Peter). There are no reliable indications in the text that John assigned such symbolic value to the two disciples. The ancient explanation for the swiftness of the beloved disciple is probably the correct one: he was younger than Peter, and arrived first. Because the entire narrative is designed to explain just how and when and to what degree faith in the resurrection of Jesus was achieved (cf. vv. 29–31), the details of the eyewitness are deemed important.

The beloved disciple *bent over and looked in* (*parakypsas blepei*). The expression is consonant with either a grave dug in the ground, or a cave tomb. That he *did not go in* requires us to think of the latter. He saw *the strips of linen* (*ta othonia*; cf. notes on 19:40) *lying there*, evidence enough that no-one had simply moved the body. Nor would thieves have been likely to leave behind expensive linen and even more expensive spices.

6–7. Peter may arrive second but, true to his nature, he impetuously rushed right into the tomb. He not only saw *the strips of linen lying there*, but also *the burial cloth* (*soudarion*; cf. notes on 11:44) *that had been around Jesus' head*. Apparently this could not be seen from the entrance: the flow of the passage from v. 5 to v. 8 suggests that John did not see the latter piece of cloth until he too entered the tomb.

This cloth *was folded up by itself, separate from the linen*. Clearly, John perceives these details to be important, but their exact meaning is disputed. Some have thought that the burial cloth still retained the shape of Jesus' head, and was separated from the strips of linen by a distance equivalent to the length of Jesus' neck. Others have suggested that, owing to the mix of spices separating the layers, even the strips of linen retained the shape they had when Jesus' body filled them out. Both of these suggestions say more than the text requires. What seems clearest is the contrast with the resurrection of Lazarus (11:44). Lazarus came from the tomb wearing his grave-clothes, the additional burial cloth still wrapped around his head. Jesus' resurrection body apparently passed through his grave-clothes, spices and all, in much the same way that he later appeared in a locked room (vv. 19, 26). The description of the burial cloth that had been around Jesus' head does not suggest that it still retained the shape of the corpse, but that it had been neatly rolled up and set to one side by the one who no longer had any use for it.[1] The

---

[1] This assumes that *eis hena topon* (lit. 'in one place') here means 'in a place by itself', or, more briefly, 'by itself' (NIV). Most commentators prefer this rendering to the alternative, which takes *hena* to be equivalent to *tina*, *i.e.* 'in a certain place'.

description is powerful and vivid, not the sort of thing that would have been dreamed up; and the fact that two men saw it (v. 8) makes their evidence admissible in a Jewish court (Dt. 19:15).

8. Timid at first, the beloved disciple, doubtless emboldened by Peter, entered the tomb and saw the place where the Master lay – now nothing but linen grave-clothes and the additional burial cloth that had been around Jesus' head. With sudden intuition he perceived that the only explanation was that the Jesus who had been crucified, the Jesus who had so recently assigned him his mother, the Jesus who had been buried in this new tomb, had risen from the dead. The beloved disciple *saw and believed* – and thus the Evangelist introduces the themes of seeing and believing that reach their climax in v. 29.[1]

Most of the early witnesses came to faith in Jesus as the resurrected Lord not because they could not find his corpse but because they found Christ alive; but John testifies that he came to such faith before he saw Jesus in resurrected form. And he took this step, not simply because the tomb was empty, but because the grave-clothes were still there.

But if the empty tomb did not receive great prominence in the earliest apostolic preaching (*cf.* 1 Cor. 15:3–7), New Testament writers nevertheless recognized the strategic importance of the empty tomb for both history and theology. Historically, the preaching and the rapid growth of the early church are alike unexplainable apart from an empty tomb. Even on the doubtful supposition that all the first Christians were dupes or hallucinating enthusiasts, the Jewish authorities, though they had every incentive to do so, could not come up with the body of the man whose execution they had organized. Theologically, the empty tomb rules out any re-interpretation of 'resurrection' that makes it indistinguishable from mere immortality. The empty tomb establishes that there was continuity between Jesus' pre-death body and his post-resurrection body. However transformed the latter was (*cf.* 1 Cor. 15:35ff.), its point of continuity with the pre-death Jesus did not lie exclusively at the level of Jesus' *personality*; it lay also at the level of Jesus' *body*. Much that is said in the New Testament about the Christian's ultimate hope (*e.g.* 1 Thes. 4:13–18; 1 Cor. 15) is incoherent if this point is not absorbed.

It is normally assumed that Peter did *not* at this time come to faith (though Bultmann, p. 684, insists that both disciples believed). Strictly speaking, the Evangelist does not tell us what went on in Peter's mind. The witness of the beloved disciple *may* not be designed to contrast his faith with Peter's unbelief; it *may* simply be the confession of his *own*

---

[1] Although it has been argued that all the beloved disciple came to believe was that Mary Magdalene had told the truth and that the tomb was empty (*e.g.* Nicholson, pp. 69–71), this is unbearably trite. Moreover, it not only makes both Peter and the beloved disciple unbelievably stupid (they, unlike Mary, have to enter the tomb to find it is empty!), it also fails to account for the absolute usage of the verb 'to believe', not to mention the introduction of the relation between seeing and believing (v. 29).

faith. But the narrative reads more naturally if we assume that Peter did not at this time believe, and this is confirmed by the best text of Luke 24:12, which says that Peter 'went away, wondering to himself what had happened'. To speak of rivalry between the two men, however, not only goes beyond what this passage says, it is to fly in the face of the Fourth Gospel as a whole, where the two are presented as friends, not competitors.

Many have wondered why, if the beloved disciple at this time came to believe in the resurrection of Jesus, he did not actively witness to his faith amongst the other disciples. For some, this is sufficient reason for doubting the historicity of the early morning race to the tomb. Strictly speaking, however, the text does not say that the beloved disciple did *not* bear witness. More important, even if we assume he did, such witness was necessarily more tentative than that of the first reports of having actually seen the risen Jesus – and even these reports were at first greeted with generous scepticism (Lk. 24:36). Or perhaps the beloved disciple thought it best to hold his peace until events had confirmed or destroyed his fledgling faith. Perhaps he was not all that far removed from Peter's pondering (Lk. 24:12).

9. Neither Peter nor the beloved disciple at this point understood *from Scripture that Jesus had to rise from the dead*. By the time John wrote that was no longer the case: the church had worked out a detailed understanding of the Old Testament by which to understand and explain the life, ministry, death and resurrection of their Lord (*cf.* 1 Cor. 15:3–7). At this point, however, the fledgling faith of the beloved disciple was grounded on what he had seen (and not seen!) in the tomb. The singular *Scripture* (*graphē*) may suggest that a specific Old Testament text is in mind (Sanders, p. 422, n. 3, suggests Ps. 16:10; Bruce, p. 386, thinks of Lv. 23:11 or Ho. 6:2), but it is also possible that it refers to the entire Scripture. The failure of the disciples to grasp the teaching of Scripture at this point is confirmed by similar patterns of belief and misunderstanding reported by Luke (24:25–27, 32, 44–47; *cf.* notes on 2:19–22).

2. *Jesus appears to Mary* (20:10–18)

10. This verse is transitional. On the one hand, Peter and the beloved disciple are dismissed: the two disciples *went back to their homes* (*apēlthon . . . pros autous*); *but Mary*, on the other hand – the mild adversative in v. 11 establishes a contrast – returned to the tomb. The expression rendered *to their homes* is not that of 19:27 (*eis ta idia*); here, the expression is roughly equivalent to the French idiom 'chez eux' ('at their own [place]').

11–12. Some have wondered why the beloved disciple did not at least share his faith with Mary, but there is no particular reason to think that their paths crossed after her initial announcement (v. 2). The reason Mary returned to the tomb is not given. Her sense of grief and loss may have driven her back there; or, as the sequel suggests, she may have been hoping to find someone who could enlighten her as to who took the body, and where they put it. Standing *outside*[1] the tomb, she wept, and *bent over* (same verb as in v. 5) *to look into the tomb* – perhaps for the first time (*cf.* notes on v. 1).

Mary *saw two angels in white*, one at each end of the place where Jesus lay. How the tomb was configured to allow such an arrangement is uncertain. Several structures to accommodate the corpse were commonplace in the first century. Sometimes a kind of stone bench ran around the inside wall; sometimes a bench-arcosolium was cut out (a flat ledge under a recessed arch cut out of an inner wall); sometimes a *loculus* was cut out of the wall (a tunnel-like burial chamber hollowed out of an inner wall, not unlike the Roman catacombs); a trough-arcosolium was a sarcophagus under a recessed arch. John's account rules out the *loculus*. The fourth-century descriptions of the uncovering of the tomb in the time of Constantine (*cf.* notes on 19:41–42) suggest a trough-arcosolium, but the descriptions are not entirely clear, and some have doubted that this particular structure was used before AD 70.

Whatever the structure, if this approach of Mary is to be collated with the visit of the women reported in the Synoptics, something must be said about these two angels; for they, not the grave-clothes, capture Mary's attention. Mark 16:5 reports a 'young man' dressed in white who appears to the women; Luke 24:4 describes two 'men' dressed in 'clothes that gleamed like lightning' who 'stood beside' the women; Matthew 28:2–3 says that an angel with the appearance of lightning and wearing a garment as white as snow rolled back the stone and frightened the guards, and later talked with the women. Notwithstanding contrary opinion, in all cases, including Mark, we are to think of angels, for the white garments or the shining white garments are a symbol for visitors from the heavenly realms (so, rightly, Beasley-Murray, p. 374). Angels regularly appear as human visitors in the Old Testament. In this case, they are not merely interpretative angels, as so often in apocalyptic literature, but evidence that God himself has been at work. The difference in number (one angel or two) is of a piece with Gospel variations in other narratives (*e.g.* Mk. 10:46–52 and Mt. 20:29–34). In any case, John's point is that this empty tomb cannot be explained by appealing to grave robbers; this is nothing other than the invasion of God's power.

13. In all four Gospels, the angels make some reference to the seeking of the women. On *Woman* (*gynai*), *cf.* notes on 2:4; 19:26. The question of the angels, *why are you crying?*, is not designed to elicit information. It is gentle reproof: by this time Mary should not have been crying. Her response shows she has still not transcended the explanation to which she had earlier gravitated (v. 2).

14–15. Probably we are to think that Mary suddenly becomes aware of someone else near the tomb, and turns to that person with the same

---

[1]Some manuscripts omit 'outside' (*exō*), or place the adverb elsewhere, or read 'in the tomb'. Most textual critics agree that 'outside' is original (*cf.* Metzger, pp. 254–255).

intent – to find out if anyone knows what has happened to Jesus' body. As so often in the resurrection narratives, Jesus is not immediately recognized. The couple on the Emmaus road were 'kept from recognising him' (Lk. 24:16), and the long ending of Mark says he appeared to them 'in a different form' (Mk. 16:12); the disciples in the boat on the lake of Tiberias did not recognize the man on the shore (Jn. 21:4); Mary *did not realise that it was Jesus*. In this instance, it is possible that Mary was blinded by tears. Taken as a whole, however, the resurrection accounts provide a certain tension. On the one hand, Jesus' resurrection body can be touched and handled (v. 27; Lk. 24:39), bears the marks of the wounds inflicted on Jesus' pre-death body (Jn. 20:20, 25, 27), and not only cooks fish (21:9) but eats it (Lk. 24:41–43). On the other hand, Jesus' resurrection body apparently rose through the grave-clothes (Jn. 20:6–8), appears in a locked room (vv. 19, 26), and is sometimes not (at least initially) recognized. The closest we are likely to come to an explanation is 1 Cor. 15:35ff.

The stranger's approach is courteous: for *Woman, cf.* v. 13. Doubtless Mary takes his pair of questions to be the probing concern of a kind stranger. As she pondered them after the fact, she could not help seeing them in a different light (as John's readers must). The first (*why are you crying?*) becomes mild rebuke; the second (*Who is it you are looking for?*) becomes an invitation to reflect on the kind of Messiah she was expecting, and thus to widen her horizons and to recognize that, grand as her devotion to him was, her estimate of him was still far too small. The evangelistic implications for John's readers are transparent.

When first uttered, however, Jesus' words have only the most mundane meaning for Mary. She supposes him to be the gardener (*kēpouros; cf.* notes on 19:41): *kyrie* ('Sir') is a courtesy, not a confession of faith. Perhaps, she told herself, he had seen something – indeed, perhaps he had been involved in the moving of the body himself. If Mary thought him to be the gardener, she may have wondered if he had been under orders from the owner to remove the body of this executed criminal from the new tomb where it had been hurriedly placed. That she should offer to make the arrangements to fetch the body and give it a proper burial suggests she was a woman of some wealth and standing (as Lk. 8:2–3 attests).

16. Whatever the cause of her blindness, the single word *Mary*, spoken as Jesus had always uttered it, was enough to remove it. The good shepherd 'calls his own sheep by name . . . and his sheep follow him because they know his voice' (10:3–4). Anguish and despair are instantly swallowed up by astonishment and delight. Mary addresses him as she always has: *Rabboni!* – an Aramaic word (*cf.* notes on 5:2) which John dutifully translates for his Greek-speaking readers (*cf.* notes on 1:38, 41, and Additional Note). It may not be the highest Christological confession (*cf.* v. 28), but at this point Mary is enthralled by the restored relationship, not contemplating its theological implications.

17. This verse belongs to a handful of the most difficult passages in the

New Testament. The initial prohibition, *mē mou haptou*, can be taken several different ways: compare 'Touch me not' (AV), 'Do not hold on to me' (NIV) and 'Stop clinging to Me' (NASB). What meaning we choose turns on at least three variables: the force of the verb *haptomai* ('to touch', from which *haptou* derives), the significance of a present tense prohibition, and the relation of this prohibition to the succeeding clause. Unfortunately, the meaning of this second clause is even more disputed than the first, and the combination of difficulties breeds numerous interpretative permutations that cannot be canvassed in detail here. Four may be mentioned:

(1) Michael McGehee, supported by Porter (p. 356), has recently proposed that the word rendered *for* (*gar*) should be understood as an anticipatory *gar*, more or less the equivalent of 'since', and linking its clause not with the one that precedes it but with the one that succeeds it. McGehee re-punctuates the verse and renders it, 'Don't cling to me. Since I have not yet ascended (*anabebēka*) to the Father, go to my brothers and tell them I am ascending (*anabainō*) to my Father and your Father. . . .' Porter adds that the tenses of the two transliterated verbs, perfect and present respectively, properly understood, may confirm McGehee: 'I have not yet reached a state of ascension . . . I am in progress of ascending' (at the risk of over-translation). This cuts the prohibition off from the rest of the sentence, making it quite unnecessary to explain the prohibition in terms of the second clause.

Although this explanation has its attractions, it fails on two grounds. First, although anticipatory *gar* is not uncommon in classical Greek and is not unknown in hellenistic Greek, there is no certain example in the New Testament; and second, it leaves the initial prohibition, *Do not hold on to me* (however it is rendered) so free that one wonders what it is doing there. We are still not told *why* Jesus should insist on this prohibition, especially since it will be reversed in v. 27.

(2) Zerwick (§ 476) recognizes that the *gar* ('for') links the prohibition to something that succeeds it, but suggests that the words immediately after the *gar* are parenthetical – *i.e.* 'Do not keep hold of me, *for* (I am not yet ascended to My Father) go rather to My brethren and tell them . . .' More briefly, Jesus says, 'Let go of me *because* you must go to my brothers with a message.' This assumes that *gar* ('for') links a prohibition and an imperative, an extremely unusual combination. Moreover, the allegedly parenthetical remark simply does not read like a parenthesis. It would have helped Zerwick's case if it had been introduced by a concessive word like 'although': *e.g.* 'Do not keep hold of me, *for* (*although* I am not yet ascended) *etc.*'; but this is not the case.

(3) Increasingly, recent scholars have opted for a rather complex theological solution. The first step is to observe the difficulties on the very surface of the text. Brown (2. 992–993, 1011–1016), for instance, rightly notes that, at a superficial reading, the *for* clause explains *why* Mary is forbidden to touch or to cling to Jesus, even though Thomas is invited to touch him (v. 27): Jesus had not yet ascended when Mary

approached him, but had apparently ascended (and returned?) by the time he had to deal with Thomas. Now either the very physical demonstration of 20:27 argues that Jesus had not yet at that point ascended, or, as Thüsing (pp. 265–266) argues, the appearances to Mary and to Thomas must have been of very different types. But if something as dramatic as the ascension has taken place between v. 17 and v. 27, why is it not mentioned? And why should being ascended make a difference? If Jesus *has* ascended between v. 17 and v. 27, the implication is that the disciples are permitted to touch Jesus after the ascension but not before – exactly the reverse of what might have been expected. If someone were to suggest that it is because of some substantial difference in the resurrection body after the ascension, it must be objected that this is the sheerest speculation.

Brown, then, followed by many others, attempts to resolve the issue by making allowance 'for John's technique. He is fitting a theology of resurrection/ascension that by definition has no dimensions of time and space into a narrative that is necessarily sequential' (2. 1014). He concludes:

> Thus, in our opinion, the statement 'I am ascending to my Father' in 17b is not an exact determination of time and has no implication for the state of the risen Jesus previous to that statement. It is a theological statement contrasting the passing nature of Jesus' presence in his post-resurrectional appearances and the permanent nature of his presence in the Spirit. (2. 1014–1015)

This view is sometimes linked with the suggestion of Lagrange (p. 512) that *de* (normally 'but'; rendered 'instead' in NIV) does not apply to *Go* but to *I am returning* (*anabainō*, lit. 'I am ascending'). This has the effect of making *Go instead to my brothers and tell them* parenthetical, yielding the paraphrase: 'Stop touching me (or attempting to do so); it is true (*gar*) that I have not yet ascended to the Father but I am about to do so' (so Barrett, p. 566). The idea is that the resurrection has opened the door to a new, intimate, spiritual relationship between Jesus and his disciples. Physical contact is no longer the appropriate mode of personal contact, even though it is still possible to appeal to touch as proof of the reality of the resurrection and of the continuity between the historical Jesus and the risen Christ.

Despite some strengths, this explanation seems unlikely. It rightly understands that John thinks of the death and exaltation of the Son as, theologically speaking, one event. By his death, Jesus returns to the Father; his being lifted up on the cross is also his being lifted up to heaven. He is glorified in his crucifixion, but this is also the means of his return to the glory he had with the Father before the world began. But it is far from clear that John thinks that Jesus' death and exaltation took place at the same instant – any more than he thinks Jesus' death and resurrection took place at the same instant (*cf.* v. 1). Nor does he think the resurrection and the ascension took place at the same instant, if we are to judge by the Thomas episode. Brown's frank appeal to categories outside space and time raises questions about what John's first readers were to think. More importantly, because John's *not yet* is now made to bear the weight of a contrast between the 'passing nature of Jesus' presence in his post-resurrectional appearances and the permanent nature of his presence in the Spirit', we are forced to think of a concrete time for ascension after all, for the Fourth Gospel has repeatedly insisted that the Spirit will come only *after* Jesus has returned to the Father. Moreover, Lagrange's parenthesis is certainly not the most natural way to read the Greek text, and Barrett's rendering, rather unbelievably, treats that troublesome *gar* (NIV 'for') as a concessive: 'it is true' in his context really means 'although'. Above all, it is entirely unclear why Thomas should still be encouraged to touch, when Mary is so firmly repulsed. If this theological explanation were correct, the order of the two narratives would have to be reversed. Finally, the natural reading of 20:29, with its contrast between seeing-believing and not-seeing-believing, presupposes that Jesus ascended *subsequently* to v. 28. Attempts to avoid this point are unconvincing.

(4) On balance, it seems best to opt for another fairly common explanation. Although a prohibition using the present imperative form (*mē mou haptou*) does not *necessarily* signal the stopping of something in progress, or the preventing of something being attempted (*cf.* Porter, ch. 7), it is commonly used in instances where contextual features show that is what is meant. The verb *haptomai* (often 'to touch') can refer to many kinds of physical contact, including clinging, seizing, holding. Probably Mary had fallen to her face and grasped him by the feet (*cf.* Mt. 28:9, where the verb is *krateō*). Moreover, if the suggestion of Lagrange is set aside, *I am ascending* is part of the message Mary is to convey, not part of the reason Mary should not cling to Jesus. And finally, the present tense *I am ascending* is no more problematic than the present tense in 10:18, 'I *lay down* [my life] of my own accord': in both cases it rather misses the point to ask with a straight face, 'Right away?'

The thought, then, might be paraphrased this way: 'Stop touching me (or, Stop holding on to me), *for* (*gar*) I have not yet ascended [NIV's "returned" is too weak] to my Father – *i.e.* I am not yet in the ascended state (taking the perfect *anabebēka* with Porter), so you do not have to hang on to me as if I were about to disappear permanently. This is a time for joy and sharing the good news, not for clutching me as if I were some jealously guarded private dream-come-true. Stop clinging to me, but (*de*) go and tell my disciples that I am in process of ascending (*anabainō*) to my Father and your Father.'

This makes the contrast between the prohibition to Mary and the invitation to Thomas easier to understand. Mary is told to stop, because her enthusiastic and relieved grasping of Jesus does not really comprehend what is transpiring. She now believes him to be alive, but has understood neither that he is not about to disappear, nor that he soon will. Thomas is told to touch, because he has not yet believed that Jesus has risen from the dead.

That Jesus is in process of ascending to his Father, on the way as it were, is in conformity with the significance of the ascension described in Luke 24:51; Acts 1:9–11. After his resurrection, Jesus appeared to his disciples many times, but he was not continually with them as in the days before his crucifixion. His abode, his habitat, was no longer this earth; in his 'spiritual body' (to use the language of Paul) he was no longer constrained as in 'the days of his flesh' (Heb. 5:7 AV), but was already glorified. It is a commonplace of the New Testament writers that in the wake of his resurrection Jesus was exalted to the right hand of the Majesty on high. But as long as his resurrection appearances continued, the disciples might expect him to show up at any time. His final departure was therefore dramatic and decisive, a kind of acted farewell, so that the finality of what was taking place might be clear. In that sense, in both John and Luke/Acts, Jesus is in process of ascending to the Father until the culminating ascension. To use John's language, Jesus is not at this point in the state of ascension: he is still in process. But the farewell discourse has made it clear that he must depart to prepare a place for them (14:2), to send the promised Paraclete (16:7), and ultimately to return to take them to be with him (14:3). John 20:17 is not the virtual replacement of the language of resurrection by the language of ascension, as some have thought, but the insistence that the resurrection is so tied to the ascension, to Jesus' return to his Father, that if Mary can accept the one she must be prepared to accept the implications of the other.

The message Mary is to convey to the disciples is more than the mere announcement that Jesus is in process of ascending: 'Go . . . to *my brothers* and tell them, "I am ascending (NIV, returning) to my Father *and your Father*, to my God *and your God*."' Mary (unlike Dodd, *HTFG*, pp. 147, 324; *cf.* Mt. 28:10, 16) understands that these are not Jesus' physical brothers (as in 7:5), and goes *to the disciples* (v. 18). Because of Jesus' death/resurrection/exaltation, his disciples come to share in his sonship to the Father. The unique features of his sonship are of course presupposed (*cf.* notes on 1:12–13, 18; 5:19–30): the expressions *my Father and your Father* and *my God and your God* assume distance between Jesus and his followers, even as they establish links. But the emphasis here is on the shared privileges (*cf.* Rom. 8:15–16; Heb. 2:11–12, citing Ps. 22:22).[1]

18. Mary of Magdala (*cf.* 19:25) did as she was told, not only announcing *I have seen the Lord!* but also telling them *that he had said these things to her*. The words *the Lord* still do not constitute a confession akin to that of Thomas (*cf.* notes on vv. 2, 15, 28). At this point Mary is simply

---

[1] It is not the language, the form of address to God, that is new (*cf.* Allen Mawhinney, *JETS* 31, 1988, pp. 181–189) but the *theology* and *eschatological experience* that are new.

identifying the one she saw in the garden with the Master they all knew, and knew to have been crucified. But she spoke better than she knew.

John does not tell us how the disciples responded, but there is no reason to think that they reacted any better than they did to the women's report of the empty tomb (Lk. 24:9–11).

Additional note

16. *Rabbouni* or *rabboni* (the spelling varies in the manuscripts) appears to be an extended form of the more familiar *rabbi* (lit., 'my teacher'). The term appears elsewhere in the New Testament only at Mark 10:51 (which, strangely, NIV renders as 'Rabbi'). In rabbinical Hebrew the term is regularly applied to God (in the expression *ribbônô šel 'ôlām*, 'rabbi of the world'), and this prompts Hoskyns (p. 543) to argue that although it *may* be used *in reference* to a human rabbi, it is *never* used in *addressing* a human rabbi. Mary's address therefore becomes a form of address to God, not unlike v. 28. But it has often been pointed out that *rabboni* is used in addressing men in the Palestinian and Jerusalem Targums (Aramaic paraphrases of the Hebrew Scriptures). As far as John is concerned, he offers *Didaskale* ('Teacher') as his translation for *both* 'Rabbi' (1:38) and 'Rabboni' (20:16).

3. Jesus appears to his disciples (20:19–23)

19. Verses 19 and 20 have as their closest parallel Luke 24:36–42, also set on the evening of that first Easter day. How large a group is referred to by *the disciples* is not certain, but in the light of the circle at the last supper (made up of Jesus plus the Twelve, and then, after Judas Iscariot left, the Eleven), and in the light of the fact that Thomas is singled out as not having been present (v. 24) – though doubtless there were countless other 'disciples' less tightly connected with the Lord who were also not present – we should probably think of the Ten (*i.e.* the Twelve, less Judas and Thomas).

The *reason* the doors were locked was their *fear of the Jews*: the authorities had seen to it that their leader was executed, so it would have been relatively easy for them to pick off his followers had they decided to do so. But the *function* of the locked doors in John's narrative, both here and in v. 26, is to stress the miraculous nature of Jesus' appearance amongst his followers. As his resurrection body passed through the grave-clothes (v. 6–8), so it passed through the locked doors and simply 'materialized' (*cf.* notes on vv. 14–15). It is tempting, with Bruce (p. 391), to find in this episode the inspiration for the practice of the early church, when it met together on Sunday evenings, to invoke Christ's presence with them in the words, *Marana tha!* ('Come, O Lord!', 1 Cor. 16:22b).

At one level, the greeting *Peace be with you!* is conventional, representing Hebrew *šālōm 'ālêkem*, still in use today. Indeed, perhaps when the disciples first heard the risen Lord utter it, they thought little of it, being so astonished and overjoyed that linguistic subtleties would elude them. But the repetition of the greeting (vv. 21, 26) would eventually prompt the reflective amongst them to recall that Jesus before the cross had promised to bequeath to them his peace (14:27; 16:33). Though a common word, šālōm was also the embracing term used to denote the unqualified well-being that would characterize the people of God once the eschatological kingdom had dawned. Jesus' '"Shalom!" on Easter evening is the complement of "it is finished" on the cross, for the peace of reconciliation and life from God is now imparted . . . Not surprisingly it is included, along with "grace," in the greeting of *every* epistle of Paul in the NT' (Beasley-Murray, p. 379).

20. The doors might be shut, but Jesus proves that his appearance is that of the crucified Master, now risen from the dead: he shows them *his hands and side* (Lk. 24:39 adds his 'feet'), the parts of his body where the wounds or scars could be seen. Others who had been crucified, if somehow they had been raised, could have shown their feet and hands (*cf.* Additional Note); only he could show his side (*cf.* 19:32–35). Thus the disciples were forced to grasp what became a central confession of the church: the risen Lord is none other than the crucified sacrifice.

Temple (p. 366) reminds us that Jesus' wounds are his credentials to the suffering race of human beings. He cites the poem of Edward Shillito, 'Jesus of the Scars', published shortly after the savage butchery of the First World War:

> If we have never sought, we seek Thee now;
> Thine eyes burn through the dark, our only stars;
> We must have sight of thorn-pricks on Thy brow,
> We must have Thee, O Jesus of the Scars.
>
> The heavens frighten us; they are too calm;
> In all the universe we have no place.
> Our wounds are hurting us; where is the balm?
> Lord Jesus, by Thy Scars, we claim Thy grace.
>
> If, when the doors are shut, Thou drawest near,
> Only reveal those hands, that side of Thine;
> We know to-day what wounds are, have no fear,
> Show us Thy Scars, we know the countersign.
>
> The other gods were strong; but Thou wast weak;
> They rode, but Thou didst stumble to a throne;
> But to our wounds only God's wounds can speak,
> And not a god has wounds, but Thou alone.

The disciples *were overjoyed* when they saw the Lord. He had come to them and turned their grief to joy, just as he had promised (14:18; 16:20–22).

21. On the repetition of *Peace be with you!*, *cf.* notes on v. 19. Each Gospel includes a commission from the risen Jesus. This one builds on

17:18, 'As you sent me into the world, I have sent them into the world.' Here the verb used in the two clauses is not the same: 'As the Father has sent me (*apestalken*), I am sending (*pempō*) you'; but nothing should be made of the change,[1] as if the clue to the verse lay in two kinds of 'sending'.

In recent years this verse has generated a storm of controversy amongst Christians concerned to think through the mission of the church. On the one side, the argument has gone like this: John 20:21 does more than draw vague parallels between Jesus' mission and ours. Jesus deliberately makes his mission the *model* of ours. Thus the church should define its task in terms of its understanding of *Jesus'* task. Since the latter manifestly included healing the sick, helping the needy and preaching the gospel to the poor (Lk. 4:18, 19; 7:22), our mission must do no less. The church's mission must not be restricted to evangelism and church planting; it embraces everything that we rightly do in imitation of Christ. We are to be both salt (a preservative function) and light (a revelatory function).

The other side objects that this neglects the Johannine context, which immediately introduces the centrality of the forgiveness of sins (v. 23). Jesus came into the world as the unique Lamb of God to take away our sins; he came as the incarnate Word; and such central features intrinsic to the sending of Jesus we cannot precisely emulate. Without wanting to deny the church's obligation to do good to all men, especially those of the household of faith, this side of the discussion finds v. 21 incapable of supporting the weight that is being placed on it.

Methodologically, both approaches to the text are faulty. To appeal to several verses from Luke to establish what is central to John's understanding of mission is indefensible. If this verse has specific content, it must be deduced from the immediate context, and especially from the matrix of themes connected with the 'sending' theme in the Fourth Gospel. Here it is the perfect obedience of the Son that is especially emphasized (*e.g.* 5:19–30; 8:29), an obedience that has already been made a paradigm for the relation of the believers to Jesus (15:9–10). Jesus was sent by his Father into the world (3:17) by means of the incarnation (1:14) with the end of saving the world (1:29); now that Jesus' disciples no longer belong to the world (15:19), they must also be sent back into the world (20:21) in order to bear witness, along with the Paraclete (15:26–27) – though obviously there is no mention of incarnation along the lines of 1:14, and any parallel must be entirely derivative. In so far as Jesus was entirely obedient to and dependent upon his Father, who sealed and sanctified him and poured out the Spirit upon him without limit (1:32; 3:34; 4:34; 5:19; 6:27; 10:36; 17:4), so far also does he constitute the definitive model for his disciples: they have become children of God

---

[1]Both words are used for the sending of Christ by the Father, and for the sending of the disciples by Christ: *cf.* the compact summary in Barrett, p. 569. This is an instance of John's penchant for minor stylistic variations: *cf.* Morris, *SFG*, pp. 293ff.

(1:12–13; 3:3, 5; 20:17), the Spirit has been promised to them (chs. 14 – 16) and will soon be imparted to them (*cf.* notes on v. 22), they have been sanctified by Christ and will be sanctified by God's word (17:17) as they grow in unqualified obedience to and dependence upon their Lord.

From a missiological point of view, such emphases must also be joined with similar study of the commissions reported in the other Gospels. There is sufficient comprehensiveness both here and elsewhere to make Christians aware that they never have an excuse to rest on their laurels, or to define their task too narrowly; perfect obedience to the Son, modelled on Jesus' perfect obedience, is as daunting a challenge as the command to teach others to obey *all* that Jesus has commanded (Mt. 28:20). At the same time, what is central to the Son's mission – that he came as the Father's gift so that those who believe in him might not perish but have eternal life (3:16), experiencing new life as the children of God (1:12–13) and freedom from the slavery of sin because they have been set free by the Son of God (8:34–36) – must never be lost to view as the church defines her mission. The reader is almost immediately reminded of these centralities by the reference to the forgiveness and retention of sins (v. 23), and by the stated purpose of the Gospel (vv. 30–31).

It is probably wrong to think of the disciples simply *replacing* Jesus now that he is returning to his Father. The perfect tense in 'As the Father has sent (*apestalken*) me' suggests, at the risk of pedantry, that Jesus is in an ongoing state of 'sentness'. Just because he ascends to his Father does not mean he is no longer the 'sent one' *par excellence* (*cf.* 9:7). Thus Christ's disciples do not take over Jesus' mission; his mission continues and is effective in their ministry (14:12–14). 'The apostles were commissioned to carry on Christ's work, and not to begin a new one' (Westcott, 2. 349–350; *cf.* Schnackenburg, 3. 324). And if, as has been argued throughout this commentary (*cf.* notes on 20:30–31), John is primarily writing to evangelize Jews and proselytes, the emphases in these verses, by spelling out the privileges and responsibilities of Christians, not only provide readers with an incentive to convert to Christ, but justify the evangelistic work being undertaken even as they read.

22. *And with that* (*kai touto eipōn*, lit., 'After saying this') links v. 21 with v. 22: the commission is thereby tied to the giving of the Spirit. But what exactly is meant by *Receive the Holy Spirit*? In part, the question is raised by the concern of some scholars to establish an appropriate link with the bestowal of the Spirit at Pentecost (Acts 2). But even for those whose views of Scripture do not prompt them to ask how two such diverse accounts have come down to us, let alone to harmonize them, there are, as we shall see, several notable problems within the text of John for those who are simply content to call this John's version of Pentecost.

Many solutions have been proposed, the most important of which are these:

(1) Since *pneuma hagion* ('Holy Spirit') is without the article, it has been suggested that, unlike the Paraclete promises and unlike Acts 2, it is not

the personal Holy Spirit who is in view, but the impersonal breath of God, emblematic of power or spiritual gift (*e.g.* Johnston, p. 11). But it is precarious, not least in John, to distinguish the person from the power by appealing to the article. 'Spirit' is anarthrous in the second half of 7:39 (in the best texts), even though the word clearly refers to the personal Holy Spirit.

(2) Many take this as some sort of actual impartation of the Spirit, but define things in such a way as to allow room for Pentecost. For Calvin (2. 205), the disciples are here *sprinkled* with the grace of the Spirit, but not *saturated* with his full enduement of power until Acts 2.[1] Westcott (2. 350–351) thinks power of new life is bestowed here, and power for ministry in Acts; Bruce (pp. 391–392) seems to favour the reverse. By appealing to the Targums (Aramaic paraphrases of the Hebrew Bible – both Neofiti and Onkelos) on Genesis 2:7, Wojciechowski[2] proposes that by Jesus' exhalation the disciples received the gift of the word, including the gift of tongues, which was then not manifested until Pentecost. M. M. B. Turner[3] envisions two comings of the Spirit: John 20:22 as the complement and fulfilment of 17:17–19, and Acts 2 as the fulfilment of the Paraclete promises. Many others think of some sort of preliminary enduement in anticipation of Pentecost.

The difficulty with all of these views is threefold. First, although it is right to consider what bearing Acts 2 may have on the interpretation of John 20:22, these interpretations sound as if they are hostage to Acts 2. Second, since in John the promise of the Spirit turns on Jesus' return to his Father, a twofold coming of the Spirit somehow suggests that Jesus returned twice; or, less provocatively put, if Jesus finally returned to the Father only once (upon which the gift of the Spirit depends), what warrant is there for thinking the Spirit was bestowed twice? And third, how realistic is it to admit the proposed divorces between Spirit and Paraclete, power for ministry and power for life, and so forth?

(3) The most frequently espoused view today is that this verse is John's Pentecost, *i.e.* this is the promised endowment of the Spirit, and John knows no other (or if he does, he fails to hint at it). The Fourth Gospel has insisted that the coming of the Spirit is bound up with Jesus'

---

[1]Calvin also greatly stresses the divinity of Christ implicit in this passage, even if (we must assume) his exposition of this point is cast in terms of application:

. . . for it would be meaningless if the Spirit did not proceed from Him. So much the more hateful is the sacrilege of the Papists, who seize to themselves the honour which belongs to the Son of God. For their mitred bishops boast that in making sacrificing priests they breathe out the Spirit when they belch over them. But the fact plainly shows how different their stinking breath is from Christ's divine breathing; for all that they do is to change horses into asses. Moreover, Christ not only communicates to His disciples the Spirit whom He has received, but bestows Him as His own, as the one whom He has in common with the Father. Wherefore, all who profess to give the Spirit by breathing usurp to themselves the glory of divinity (2. 204–205).

[2]Michal Wojciechowski, *NTS* 33, 1987, pp. 289–292.

[3]*VE* 10, 1977, pp. 24–42, esp. p. 34.

glorification, which is tied to the 'hour' of the cross (7:37–39; 16:7). The hour has come; correspondingly, Jesus breathes on his followers and says, *Receive the Holy Spirit*. In terms of Johannine theology, this, it is argued, is as much as you could ask for. Moreover, that Jesus *breathed on them* is reminiscent of Genesis 2:7 and Ezekiel 37:9; this 'insufflation' (as the event is called) is the beginning of the new creation, the awakening of the dead. Further, this interpretation is often tied to the third interpretation of v. 17, discussed above: Jesus has ascended and thereby opened up a new relationship with him through the Spirit.

Those who hold this view, and they are many, divide into two camps. The one says that all attempts at harmonization with Acts are futile – perhaps (as with Barrett) because Acts is given very low marks for historical reliability. The other camp (*e.g.* Beasley-Murray, pp. 380–382; Burge, pp. 114–149) argues that John knows about Pentecost, but chooses to write it up this way, in close temporal connection with Easter, because of his peculiar theological vision that tightly ties the descent of the Spirit to Jesus' death/exaltation. Luke himself, of course, connects the gift of the Spirit with the exaltation of Christ (Acts 2:32–33); John's theological structure demands that he move the gift of the Spirit back from Pentecost to Easter, implicitly '*including the story of the Ascension in the Easter narrative*' (Beasley-Murray, p. 382, emphasis his). John's account, in other words, is theological but not chronological, and thus there is no question of two bestowals of the Spirit, one at Easter and the other at Pentecost. The fourth Evangelist's central theological vision, not to mention the fact that, unlike Luke, he wrote only one volume, not two, has determined these choices.

Though attractive in many ways, this interpretation faces more problems than are commonly recognized. Because countervailing evidence is often simultaneously support for the fourth view, it seems best to articulate that view and then marshal the evidence.

(4) Theodore of Mopsuestia, whose exegesis, admittedly, varied from the brilliant to the heretical, argued that v. 22 is to be regarded as a symbolic promise of the gift of the Spirit later to be given (*i.e.* at Pentecost). Although his view was condemned at the fifth ecumenical council at Constantinople in AD 553, and is usually given short shrift today, much can be said in its favour. (*Cf.* further, Carson, pp. 140–144.)

(a) Despite most of our English versions, the text does not say 'he breathed *on them*' but simply 'he breathed' or, perhaps, 'he exhaled' (*enephysēsen*). The lexica give as the meaning of the verb (*emphysaō*) 'he breathed in' or 'he breathed upon', but actual usage outside the New Testament (this is the only place it occurs within the New Testament) does not encourage the view that the preposition 'in' or 'upon' was part of the meaning of the verb itself. In its dozen or so uses in the LXX, for instance, there is always some additional syntactical structure to carry this prepositional force wherever it is needed. Thus in Genesis 2:7 LXX, 'he breathed into his face the breath of life' is the verb + accusative substantive (*enephysēsen eis to prosōpon autou pnoēn zōēs*). The structures may vary: *e.g.* verb +dative object; verb + preposition *epi* + accusative substantive. Even in the one passage where no such structure is found in the clause itself, it is understood from the parallelism with the previous clause: in *Wisdom* 15:11, the idolator fails to know the one who formed him

> and inspired *him* with an active soul
> and breathed [*into him*] a living spirit.

> *kai ton empneusanta <u>autō</u> psychēn energousan*
> *kai emphysēsanta pneuma zōtikon.*

There is but one passage in the LXX where there is no such structure, *viz.* *Ecclesiasticus* 43:4, and it is in only one part of the manuscript tradition. There, the writer praises God for creating the heavenly bodies, including the sun which 'breathes out fiery vapours' (*atmidas pyrōdeis emphysōn*). Here there is no question of 'breathing in' or 'breathing into' or 'breathing upon' someone. The direct object, 'fiery vapours', is what is breathed *out*. This fact is doubtless what has caused the other parts of the textual tradition at this point to use the verb *ekphysōn*, where the introductory *ek* ('of' or 'out of') more clearly emphasizes the point. What cannot be in dispute, however, is that the verb *emphysaō* itself, when not encumbered by some auxiliary expression specifying the person or thing on whom or into whom the breath is breathed, simply means 'to breathe'. Similar results arise out of the study of other relevant bodies of Greek literature.

The point of this rather technical background is that the verb *emphysaō* is absolute in John 20:22 – *i.e.* it has no auxiliary structure, not even a direct object. Apart from other compelling considerations, therefore, the verse should be translated, 'And with that he breathed, and said, "Receive the Holy Spirit."' Referring to the episode as the '*in*sufflation' is already begging the issue. There is no single English word to sum up taking a deep breath and exhaling; 'exhalation' describes only the latter half, but it is closer to what is said than 'insufflation'. Schonfield's periphrastic 'he expelled a deep breath' goes too far, but it probably has the right idea. In short, it is only the words *Receive the Holy Spirit* that have fostered the view that Jesus was somehow breathing *in* or *into* his disciples, thereby imparting the Spirit.

Although the matter is little discussed, virtually all sides would probably agree that Jesus' action was symbolic in some sense. Unless one adopts a literalistic and mechanical view of the action, understanding the Holy Spirit to be nothing less than Jesus' expelled air, one is forced to say that the 'breathing' was symbolic – an appropriate symbolism not only because 'wind' and 'breath' and 'air' could all be denoted by the same word (*cf.* notes on 3:8), but also because the gift of the Holy Spirit is certainly dependent on Jesus, on Jesus' glorification. Granted that Jesus' action is symbolic, the question becomes, What, precisely, is being symbolized? Is it the gift of the Spirit that is being imparted even as Jesus speaks, or is it the gift of the Spirit that has long been promised and that is now imminent? In short, are there contextual reasons for thinking that this is a symbolic act that anticipates the future imminent bestowal?

(b) Perhaps it is worth recalling the similar sense of 'imminence' generated by the approach of the Greeks (12:20ff.). From that time on, Jesus speaks of his 'hour' as having arrived (*e.g.* 12:23, 31; 13:31; 17:1, 5). Indeed, John 17:5 is cast in the form of an imperative: 'And now, Father, glorify me in your presence . . .'; but that does not mean the glorification takes place even as Jesus speaks. Similarly, John 13:31 ('Now is the Son of Man glorified and God is glorified in him') is followed by the new commandment, which in the nature of the case was unlikely to be the lodestar of the earliest disciples until after the resurrection and the gift of the Spirit. So there is no intrinsic reason for thinking that the imperative of 20:22, *Receive the Holy Spirit*, must be experienced immediately.

(c) There is too slight a demonstration within the Gospel of John that this alleged bestowal of the Spirit made the slightest bit of difference in the lives of Jesus' followers. The disciples still meet behind locked doors (v. 26) and the natural inference is that they are still afraid of the Jewish authorities (v. 19). When Thomas comes to faith, it is not because of the promised witness of the Spirit (15:26–27), but because he sees the risen Jesus for himself. Those who accept John 21 as part of the Gospel, even if it is cast as an epilogue, cannot fail to observe that the disciples are sidling back to their old employment (21:1–3), sorting out elementary reconciliation with the Master (21:15–19), and still playing 'let's-compare-service-record' games (21:20–22). All this is not only a far cry from the power, joy, exuberant witness, courageous preaching and delight in suffering displayed by the early Christians after Pentecost in Acts, it is no less distant from the same virtues *foretold in John's farewell discourse, where the promise of the Spirit receives such emphasis*. If John 20:22 is understood to be the Johannine Pentecost, it must be frankly admitted that the results are desperately disappointing, and the promises of John 14 – 16 vastly inflated. The alternative is surely preferable. The episode in 20:22, which most will agree is in some sense symbolic, is best understood as symbolic of the enduement *that is still to come*.

(d) Granted that John is deeply interested in the *theological* unity of Christ's cross, resurrection, ascension, exaltation and bestowal of the Spirit – a point on which all sides agree – that fact remains that he specifies that the episode of 20:22 takes place on the first Easter day (20:19). If this is a free creation, there is no reason why he should not stipulate that first Sunday, and every theological reason for doing so. But if, as Beasley-Murray argues, he knows that the enduement of the Spirit really took place at Pentecost, as Acts 2 reports, and decided to make a theological statement that connected the gift of the Spirit more dramatically with the cross and glorification of Christ than Luke attempted, why should he make the temporal specification at all?

Indeed, if John knows about Pentecost, others do as well: therefore would not some of his readers simply be confused?

(e) In Beasley-Murray's reconstruction, the cost of this 're-telling' of the Pentecost story is very high. John has not only managed to bring the gift of the Spirit into close connection with the resurrection and ascension of Jesus, he has managed to exclude Thomas from the gift. And strangely, when Thomas does come to faith, there is no mention of the Spirit. That is one reason why Beasley-Murray can entertain partition theories of ch. 20 that originally depicted only *one* resurrection appearance to the disciples. If we add to this that Beasley-Murray's primary reason for insisting that ch. 21 *could not* have originally followed ch. 20 as part of the Gospel, not even as 'postscript' or 'epilogue', turns on his interpretation of 20:17, 22 (p. 395), it begins to appear that a doubtful interpretation of these two verses is wielding too much influence on still more doubtful judgments of a critical nature. Conversely, regardless of the provenance of John 21, Beasley-Murray's judgment that John 21 'would not be in place after the Thomas incident, and still less immediately after 20:19-23' (p. 395), is tantamount to admitting that *in their present form* chs. 20 – 21 cannot be made to support his interpretation of 20:22. It is surely wiser to adopt an interpretation of 20:22, if one is available, that makes sense of chs. 20 – 21, than to indulge in the more speculative forms of source-criticism, especially if such analysis assumes that the alleged final editor was incompetent. The symbolic interpretation admirably meets these constraints.

(f) So far the argument has focused on reasons *in the Fourth Gospel* for thinking this action points ahead. If Acts 2 be admitted as useful *historical* data, the case advanced here is considerably strengthened. This is not simply because an awkward discrepancy has been eliminated and an elementary harmonization achieved (though for historians, Christians or otherwise, those are surely not unworthy goals), but because Acts 2, if historical, would be part of the common heritage of the church and therefore a point of reference.

An analogy may clarify this point. It is doubtful if today a single leader of the American Pentecostal/charismatic renewal movement would be ignorant of the Azusa Street meetings in 1906. For them and for many charismatic leaders worldwide, not to mention many charismatics who do not aspire to leadership, Azusa Street is a primary point of reference,[1] even thought it appears rarely in contemporary charismatic writings. Granted that Acts 2 is historical, Pentecost must become for Christians world-wide a point of reference – a point supported by the fact that Pentecost became a Christian feast, unlike any other of the Jewish feasts. When John writes, by any reckoning less removed by at least twenty years from Pentecost than modern charismatics are from Azusa Street, he expects his readers to share this reference point with

---

[1] *Cf.* Walter J. Hollenweger, *The Pentecostals* (SCM, 1972), pp. 22–24, 26.

him. Thus, John 20:22 is not mere symbolism anticipating an endowment of the Spirit that is nowhere mentioned, it is symbolism anticipating the endowment of the Spirit that the church at the time of writing has already experienced, and of which outsiders are inevitably aware.

(g) Thus it appears that John has preserved the theological unity of the death/exaltation of Jesus, and of the eschatological Spirit-blessings Jesus secured, *not* by sacrificing historical authenticity, but by drawing attention through this episode to what was already known amongst his readers. Jesus' 'exhalation' and command *Receive the Holy Spirit* are best understood as a kind of acted parable pointing forward to the full enduement still to come (though in the past for John's readers). A suitable Johannine analogy might be the washing of the disciples' feet: 'Unless I wash you, you have no part with me' (13:8). That can be read at a simplistic level as exhausted in the footwashing. Readers with more insight understand that the footwashing itself points forward to the spiritual washing achieved by the Lamb of God whose death takes away the sin of the world. John has repeatedly developed these anticipating steps in his narrative; it is not surprising if he uses one more to show that the story does not end with his book.

23. The reception of the Spirit is here linked with the forgiveness and retention of sins. To read this verse is to be reminded of Matthew 16:19; 18:18, and indeed many have argued that one saying stands behind all three passages.[1] That conclusion is too quickly drawn: one thing that an itinerant preacher inevitably does is repeat himself, often with minor variations.

The passive perfects *they are forgiven* (*apheōntai*) and *they are not forgiven* (*kekratēntai*) need not detain us. The construction is not as difficult as in Matthew (on which *cf.* Carson, *Matt*, pp. 370–374). If these perfects are not temporally construed, but are read aspectually,[2] they will be rendered 'they are in a state of forgiveness', *i.e.* 'they stand forgiven' and 'they do not stand forgiven'; but even so, the passive voice implies it is God who is acting. In the parallel statements in Matthew, the context suggest church discipline; in this verse, where the context is the mission of Jesus' disciples (v. 21) and the Spirit who empowers them (v. 22), the focus is on evangelism.

> There is no doubt from the context that the reference is to forgiving sins, or withholding forgiveness. But though this sounds stern and harsh, it is simply the result of the preaching of the gospel, which either brings men to repent as they hear of the ready and costly forgiveness of God, or leaves them unresponsive to the offer of forgiveness which is

[1] J. A. Emerton (*JTS* 13, 1962, pp. 325–331) argues that 'binding' and 'loosing' (Matthew) correspond to 'forgiving' and 'retaining [NIV "not forgiving"]' (John), and that behind both stands a semitic original not unlike Is. 22:22.

[2] *Cf.* Porter, pp. 471–474; *idem, FN* 1, 1988, pp. 155–173.

the gospel, and so they are left in their sins. (Marsh, pp. 641–642)

The Christian witnesses proclaim and declare, and, empowered by the Spirit, live by the message of their own proclamation; it is God who *effectively* forgives or retains the sin. Thus Christian ministry is a continuation of Jesus' ministry (*cf.* notes on v. 21): through the gift of the Spirit the authority that Jesus exercises in, say, John 9, is repeated in their lives. Jesus there gave both sight and faith to the one who knew he was blind; to those who claimed to see, he declared, 'Your guilt remains' (9:41). Thus the retention of their sin was both description and condemnation. And the Paraclete who is given as a gift to Jesus' followers (v. 22) continues the same two-edged work through them (*cf.* notes on 15:26–27; 16:7–11).

Additional note

20. When the Romans crucified someone, they either tied or nailed the victim to the cross. If the latter, they drove the nails through his wrists; the hands would not have supported the weight. But both the Hebrew word for hand (*yād*) and the Greek word (*cheir*) can include the wrist and forearm. Nails were commonly driven through the feet, one spike through both feet, one foot placed on top of the other.

4. *Jesus again appears to his disciples – including Thomas* (20:24–29)

24–25. Thomas (both his Aramaic and his Greek names are given: *cf.* notes on 11:16) appears only as a name in the Synoptics, but is fleshed out a little in John. In his previous appearances (11:16; 14:5) he has been less a doubter than a loyal but pessimistic and perhaps somewhat obtuse disciple. The rubric 'doubting Thomas' is not entirely fair: had he been present when the risen Christ first manifested himself to the disciples, doubtless he too would have believed. Why he was not present that first Easter day is not told us, but in the providence of God his absence and subsequent coming to faith have generated one of the great Christological confessions in the New Testament. That he is designated *one of the Twelve* (*cf.* notes on 6:71) argues that 'disciples' in v. 19 most probably refers to the Ten (the apostles less Judas Iscariot and Thomas).

Informed as to what his colleagues in the apostolic band have seen, Thomas remains unconvinced, and demands not only a palpable sign but the most personal and concrete evidence that the person whom he knew had been killed in a specific fashion had indeed been raised from the dead. The risen Jesus must have some sort of *physical* continuity with the Jesus who was crucified. Although it is possible to paint him in romantic shades, picturing him as a common-sense disciple all too aware of how imagination can play tricks, it is hard not to perceive in this attitude at least a little of what Jesus had earlier condemned (4:48).

26. *A week later* is an idiomatic rendering of (lit.) 'After eight days'; the inclusive reckoning brings the action back to Sunday, one week after Easter. The chronology is not sacrificed to theology (*cf.* notes on v. 22). This emphasis on the Lord's day (*cf.* Rev. 1:10)[1] may reflect peculiar theological interests of the writer. If the readers are Jews and proselytes interested in the Christian faith, it may be a subtle allusion to the origins of Christian worship on this particular day.

This meeting, with Thomas present, again takes place behind locked doors, the natural inference being that the disciples are still frightened of the Jewish authorities (v. 19).[2] On Jesus' sudden appearance and greeting, *cf.* notes on v. 19.

27. By taking up Thomas' challenge in this way, Jesus simultaneously proves that he hears his disciples even when he is not physically present, and removes all possible grounds for unbelief, even the most unreasonable. The last clause, *Stop doubting and believe* (*mē ginou apistos alla pistos*), could be rendered several ways. If both *apistos* and *pistos* are taken adjectivally, and the verb *ginou* is understood at its simplest, the clause reads (lit.), 'Do not be unbelieving but believing.' Unfortunately, neither *apistos* nor *pistos* occur elsewhere in John, but elsewhere in the New Testament they often function substantivally: 'Do not be an unbeliever, but a believer.' Since the verb often means 'to show oneself [to be something]' (*e.g.* Jn. 15:8), many have taken the clause in a softer way: 'Stop being unbelieving, but show yourself a believer.' That is possible, but perhaps too mild. Up to this point, Thomas has shown himself a loyal disciple of the Jesus who went to the cross, so far as he understood him; he has not been a believer in any distinctly Christian sense.

Whether Thomas actually took Jesus up on his challenge and touched the marks of the wounds in his 'hands' (*cf.* Additional Note on v. 20) and side we are not told. The impression given is that the sight itself proved sufficient (v. 29), that Thomas was so overcome with awe and reverence that he immediately uttered his confession.

28. The historicity of both the confession itself and the incident as a whole has come under grave suspicion. The issues are too complex to be addressed in detail here, but a few observations should be made. Are we to think that the church made up a story that pictures one of the Twelve as incredulous to the point of unreasonable obstinacy (v. 25), and that reports the Lord's public reproof of that apostle (vv. 27, 29)? Even if the narrative has an apologetic purpose, that is scant reason for assessing it

---

[1]On which *cf.* Richard Bauckham, 'The Lord's Day', in D. A. Carson (ed.), *From Sabbath to Lord's Day: A Biblical, Historical and Theological Investigation* (Paternoster/Zondervan, 1982), pp. 221–250.

[2]Despite Fenton (p. 206), who argues that fear is not mentioned in v. 26 because (in his interpretation of v. 22) the Spirit has already been given, and fear has been swallowed up by faith. Then why the locked doors? It will not do to say that this provides Jesus with an opportunity to display the miraculous powers of his resurrection body: that is to confuse the effect of the locked doors with the disciples' intention in locking them.

as unhistorical: it is surely as justifiable to conclude that the account was chosen precisely because it was so suitable. At least one part of the story (v. 25) finds a parallel elsewhere (Lk. 24:39); and the portrait of Thomas is in thorough agreement with what we learn of him from 11:16 and 14:5. The speed with which Thomas' pessimistic unbelief was transformed into joyful faith is surely consistent with the experience of the other witnesses (*e.g.* vv. 16, 20).

If it be objected that this Christological confession is too 'high' or 'developed' at this early date, several points must be observed: (1) The view which insists on this point does so on the basis of a slow evolutionary development of the rise of Christological titles, and this reconstruction, so far as the sources go, is not unassailable (*cf.* Introduction, § III). (2) Thomas, like most Jews, was doubtless familiar with Old Testament accounts of believers who conversed with what appeared to be men, only to learn, with terror, that they were heavenly visitors, possibly Yahweh himself. Moreover it is arguable that as Judaism developed after the Exile, the reaction against idolatry and the punishments it attracted generated a view of God that made him more and more transcendent, but correspondingly less personal; and into the vacuum left by this shift rushed a mounting number of intermediaries, angels and other ill-defined beings (Carson, esp. pp. 41–121). Within two hundred years of this Thomas episode, and probably much earlier, one of these could actually be referred to as 'little Yahweh'. This is not to suggest that Johannine Christology is indistinguishable from the angelology of Judaism. Christianity, by definition, is *messianic*. But it does suggest that Thomas was not devoid of categories to begin to make sense of the resurrection of Jesus. (3) The use of *kyrios* ('lord') for both common courtesy (*e.g.* v. 15) and in addressing God himself facilitated the development of Christological understanding. (4) In any case, *kyrios* is an *early* post-resurrection title (*e.g.* Rom. 10:9; 1 Cor. 12:3; Phil. 2:9–11), and because it is used of God himself in the LXX, in many of its occurrences it cannot be considered less elevated than *theos* ('God'). (5) It is hard to see why *my Lord*, an exceedingly rare pairing of words, should be ruled out of court, when the Aramaic *marana* ('our Lord') was early used as an invocation even in Greek-speaking churches (1 Cor. 16:22; *cf.* notes on Jn. 16:20).

Finally, if the Evangelist is none other than the apostle John, or even if the Evangelist is someone else who derives his information from the apostle John, then we are dealing with eyewitness testimony.

Thomas' utterance cannot possibly be taken as shocked profanity addressed to God (if to anyone), a kind of blasphemous version of a stunned 'My word!' Despite its popularity with some modern Arians, such profanity would not have been found in first-century Palestine on the lips of a devout Jew. In any case, Thomas' confession is addressed *to him*, *i.e.* to Jesus; and Jesus immediately (if implicitly) praises him for his faith, even if it is not as notable as the faith of those who believe without demanding the kind of evidence accorded Thomas. Nor are Thomas' words most easily read as a predicative statement addressed to Jesus: 'My Lord is also my God.' The overwhelming majority of grammarians rightly take the utterance as vocative address to Jesus: *My Lord and my God!* – the nouns being put not in the vocative case but in the nominative (as sometimes happens in vocatival address) to add a certain sonorous weight.

The repeated pronoun *my* does not diminish the universality of Jesus' lordship and deity, but it ensures that Thomas' words are a *personal* confession of faith. Thomas thereby not only displays his faith in the resurrection of Jesus Christ, but points to its deepest meaning; it is nothing less than the revelation of who Jesus Christ is. The most unyielding sceptic has bequeathed to us the most profound confession.

The thoughtful reader of this Gospel immediately recognizes certain connections: (1) Thomas' confession is the climactic exemplification of what it means to honour the Son as the Father is honoured (5:23). It is the crowning display of how human faith has come to recognize the truth set out in the Prologue: 'The Word was God . . .; the Word became flesh' (1:1, 14). (2) At the same time, Jesus' deity does not exhaust deity; Jesus can still talk about his God and Father in the third person. After all, this confession is set within a chapter where the resurrected Jesus himself refers to 'my Father . . . my God' (v. 17). This is entirely in accord with the careful way he delineates the nature of his unique sonship (5:16–30). (3) The reader is expected to articulate the same confession, as the next verse implies. John's readers, like Thomas, need to come to faith; and this is what coming to faith looks like. Clearly this has critical bearing on how vv. 30–31 are interpreted.

29. The editors of the Greek text (NA²⁶) take the first part of Jesus' response to Thomas as rebuke cast as a question: 'Because you have seen me, you have believed?' So also Lindars (p. 646), who compares 1:50 and 16:31. But the point of the latter passages is that the people involved do *not* really believe, whereas here Thomas has truly come to faith. It is better to understand the first part of Jesus' response as a statement (and to that extent a confirmation of Thomas's faith) – one that prepares the way for the beatitude that follows: *blessed are those who have not seen and yet have believed.*

The Fourth Gospel reports only one other beatitude (13:17), and, like most beatitudes (*e.g.* Mt. 5:3–12), both strike a note of admonition. The word *makarios* ('blessed') does not simply declare 'happy' those who meet the conditions, but pronounces them accepted by God. Thomas, like all the witnesses of the resurrection, 'saw and believed', to use the language applied to the beloved disciple (v. 8) – though all the latter saw, at least until the Sunday evening (vv. 19–20), were the grave-clothes, not the resurrected Lord. But Jesus here foresees a time when he will not provide the kind of tangible evidence afforded the beloved disciple and Thomas; in short, he will ascend to his Father permanently, and all those who believe will do so without the benefit of having seen their resurrected Lord. That is as true today as it was for those who first believed after the ascension. This does not (or should not) mean that our faith is diminished or our joy truncated: 'Though you have not seen him, you love him; and even though you do not see him now, you believe in him and are filled with an inexpressible and glorious joy, for you are receiving the goal of your faith, the salvation of your souls' (1 Pet. 1:8–9).

The major commentaries cite the saying of Rabbi Simeon ben Laqish (c. AD 250), who reportedly said (*Tanḥuma* § 6 [32a]: cf. SB 2. 586):

> The proselyte is dearer to God than all the Israelites who stood by Mount Sinai. For if all the Israelites had not seen the thunder and the flames and the lightnings and the quaking mountain and the sound of the trumpet they would not have accepted the law and taken upon themselves the kingdom of God. Yet this man has seen none of all these things yet comes and gives himself to God and takes on himself the yoke of the kingdom of God. Is there any who is dearer than this man? (tr. Barrett, p. 574)

Yet for Rabbi Simeon the contrast is stark, while Jesus' words in v. 29 are cautious and balanced. Thomas' faith is not depreciated: rather, it is as if the step of faith Thomas has taken, displayed in his unrestrained confession, triggers in Jesus' mind the next step, the coming-to-faith of those who cannot see but who will believe – and so he pronounces a blessing on them. Within the context of the Fourth Gospel as a whole, however, 'but for the fact that Thomas and the other apostles saw the incarnate Christ there would have been no Christian faith at all. Cf. 1:18, 50f.; 2:11; 4:45; 6:2; 9:37; 14:7, 9; 19:35' (Barrett, p. 573). The witness theme in the book has not been lost to view; later believers come to faith through the word of the earlier believers (17:20). Blessed, then, are those who cannot share Thomas' experience of sight, but who, in part because they read of Thomas' experience, come to share Thomas' faith.[1] For us, faith comes not by sight, but from what is heard (or read!), and what is heard comes by the word (*i.e.* the declaration) of Christ (Rom. 10:17). Indeed, that is why John himself has written, as he proceeds to make explicit.

5. Conclusion: the purpose of the Fourth Gospel (20:30–31)

30. The particles *men oun* connect vv. 30–31 with what precedes. The most common meaning of the second is 'therefore'. The flow of thought

---

[1]Thus Bultmann (p. 696) is quite mistaken when he attempts on the basis of this verse to divorce faith from the historical dimensions of the Gospel. From John's perspective, both the theology and the facts that undergird it are true and essential to the good news as he has presented it. The resurrection appearances were no more concessions to human weakness than the incarnation. These events were the climactic acts of God's revelatory self-disclosure in Christ. But precisely because they were *historical* acts, later generations *could not* have access to them except through the witness of the first disciples. That is John's point, as vv. 30–31 make clear.

seems to be: Those who have not seen the risen Christ and yet have believed are blessed; *therefore* this book has been composed, to the end that you may believe. The first of two particles (*men*) is paired with *de* introducing v. 31. Together, they frame the thought of these two verses: *On the one hand*, there are, doubtless, many more signs Jesus did that could have been reported; but, *on the other*, these have been committed to writing so that you may believe.

Those who believe that John incorporated a 'Signs Source' (*cf.* Introduction, §§ II, III) think that these two verses constitute the conclusion of that hypothetical document. Those who think there is insufficient evidence to justify such a source find no difficulty in believing that the Evangelist composed his own conclusion.

It is possible that *miraculous signs* (*sēmeia*; *cf.* notes on 2:11) refers only to the miracles reported in chs. 2 – 12. Most of these have discourses or dialogues connected with them that are designed to unpack what the miracles *signify*. But to place this conclusion here suggests that the greatest sign of them all is the death, resurrection and exaltation of the incarnate Word, the *significance* of which has been carefully set forth in the farewell discourse. This also goes some way to explaining why, when John writes down in one sentence the purpose of his book, he singles out the 'signs' (and, in the nature of the case, what they mean, what readers should see in them). As Morris (*JC*, p. 2 n. 2) puts it, '. . . on Johannine premises I do not see how the purpose of the Fourth Gospel is to be understood without reckoning with the signs.' But however far *miraculous signs* extends, clearly John, like the other Evangelists, selected only a small portion of the miracles he knew about (*cf.* the hint in 12:37).

31. What he chose to write, John tells his readers, was written *that you may believe*. This not only expresses the purpose of the book, but is 'the shortest summary of Johannine theology' (Blank, p. 191). To expound in detail each word and phrase would be to expound the book. For *believe*, *cf.* notes on 1:12–13; for *Christ*, on 1:41; for *Son of God* (an expression which for Jews functioned in many ways, including, as here, rough synonymity with 'Christ' or 'Messiah'), on 1:49; for *life*, on 1:4; 3:15, 16. In recent years, most commentators have adopted the view, based primarily on their reconstruction of the setting of the Fourth Gospel as a whole rather than on particular details in this verse, that this Gospel was written to be read by Christians, by the Johannine community (*e.g.* Whitacre, pp. 6ff.). The stated goal, *that you may believe that Jesus is the Christ, the Son of God*, is interpreted to mean that the Evangelist intends by his book to *establish* the faith of Christians, rather than to bring non-Christians to faith. Some commentaries, including this one, argue that John's primary purpose is evangelism (*cf.* Introduction, § VI). The turning points in this passage are three (for documentation and more detailed arguments, *cf.* Carson, 'Purpose'):

(1) The words *that you may believe* hide a controversial variant. The textual evidence (*cf.* Metzger, p. 256) is fairly evenly divided between

hina pisteuēte (present subjunctive) and *hina pisteusēte* (aorist subjunctive), the latter marginally favoured. It is often assumed that the former, strictly interpreted, must be taken to mean 'in order that you may continue to believe', and the latter 'that you may decisively believe' (compare NEB text, 'that you may hold the faith', and NEB margin, 'that you may come to believe'). Quite apart from the fact that this is a reductionistic analysis of what a 'strict interpretation' of the present and aorist tenses requires, it can easily be shown that John elsewhere in his Gospel can use *either* tense to refer to *both* coming to faith and continuing in the faith.

(2) In a much-cited essay, H. Riesenfeld[1] has argued that John commonly uses the present tense after *hina* ('in order that'). But most of his examples are drawn from 1 John, where demonstrably the readers *are* Christians. Within the Fourth Gospel itself, the aorist subjunctive follows *hina* approximately 88 times ('approximately' because of textual variants), the present subjunctive approximately 47 times (*cf.* Carson, 'Purpose', p. 641 n. 6). That Riesenfeld has had to resort to 1 John for so much of his evidence might even be taken as *prima facie* evidence against his thesis; that so many commentators cite his work uncritically suggests an enormous commitment to the view that the Fourth Gospel was composed with believers in mind.

(3) Above all, it can be shown that, with very high probability, the *hina*-clause must on syntactical grounds be rendered 'that you may believe that the Christ, the Son of God, is Jesus'. That means that the fundamental question being addressed by the Evangelist is not 'Who is Jesus?', which might be asked by either Christians or non-Christians, if with slightly different emphases; but 'Who is the Messiah?' If that is understood as an identity question, as it must be,[2] *Christians would not ask it because they already knew the answer*. Those who would ask it would be unconverted Jews, along with proselytes and God-fearers,[3] for the category 'Messiah' was important to them, and the concern to identify him would be of great interest. This particular coalescence of Jews and Gentiles, of course, is entirely in line with the church's evangelistic thrusts in the early decades of the church: *e.g.* 'Brothers, children of Abraham, and you God-fearing Gentiles . . .' (Acts 13:26); 'many of the Jews and devout converts to Judaism followed Paul and Barnabas' (Acts 13:43) – even if it is also true that in many circumstances the animus this aroused forced Paul and his team, at least, to turn to Gentiles. But there is no reason to think that other pillars in the church, including John (Gal.

---

[1]*ST* 19, 1965, pp. 213–220.

[2]*I.e.* as a question asking who the Messiah is, rather than a question asking what kind of person the Messiah would be: *cf.* Carson, 'Purpose', pp. 644–645.

[3]Although the exact significance of *proselytes* and *God-fearers* is occasionally disputed, they are used here to designate, respectively, Gentiles who have so converted to Judaism that they have been circumcised and have come under the covenant relationship, and Gentiles largely appreciative of Judaism's tenets and claims but who have not yet submitted to circumcision.

2:9), quickly turned to Gentiles unconnected with the synagogue.

Even if John's purpose is primarily evangelistic, it must be admitted that throughout the history of the church this Gospel has served not only as a means for reaching unbelievers but as a means for instructing, edifying and comforting believers. Still, one must not confuse purpose with result. A modern evangelist aiming at the conversion of hearers may still find that Christians who attend his ministry are greatly edified. John's *purpose* in writing was to evangelize; the impact of his Gospel, *i.e.* the *result* of his writing, has far exceeded any hope he could have entertained.

One of the reasons some have given for thinking that vv. 30–31 originally served as the conclusion of the hypothetical 'Signs Source' is that the Christology expressed here is somewhat 'lower' than what is articulated in the preceding two verses (vv. 28–29). This is a serious misunderstanding of the Fourth Gospel. In John, the nature of Jesus' deity is profoundly and repeatedly tied to the exposition of his sonship (*cf.* esp. notes on 5:16–30), which is linked with his messiahship. If one must use the somewhat question-begging categories 'higher' and 'lower', it is not that 'Son of God' has been dragged lower by its connection with 'Messiah', but that 'Messiah' has been raised higher by its connection with 'Son of God' (*cf.* de Jonge, pp. 49–76). 'The content of Christological faith in v. 31 is not to be viewed as a lower Christology than that of Thomas' confession, but must be understood in its light and filled out by it' (Beasley-Murray, p. 388).

John's purpose is not academic. He writes in order that men and women may believe certain propositional truth, the truth that the Christ, the Son of God, is Jesus, the Jesus whose portrait is drawn in this Gospel. But such faith is not an end in itself. It is directed toward the goal of personal, eschatological salvation: *that by believing you may have life in his name.* That is still the purpose of this book today, and at the heart of the Christian mission (v. 21).

V. EPILOGUE (21:1–25)

Most contemporary interpreters have concluded that John 21 was not part of the Fourth Gospel as it was first written, and that, assuming John 21 was added later, it was added by someone other than the Evangelist. There have also been some strenuous defences of the more traditional view that although 20:30–31 constitutes the conclusion of the body of the Fourth Gospel, ch. 21 was composed with the rest of the Gospel and was designed to be a kind of Epilogue that balances the Prologue (1:1–18) by tying up some loose ends and pointing the way forward.[1] The debate has turned on four areas:

(1) There are linguistic considerations. Bultmann (pp. 700–701) offers one of the more detailed analyses of the twenty-eight words that appear in ch. 21 but nowhere else in the Fourth Gospel. Most of these are so tied to the subject matter that they cannot be viewed as particularly significant: *e.g.* the Greek words for 'fish', 'net', 'feed', 'take care of [my sheep]', 'he wrapped', 'naked' and the like. A few words and constructions, however, cannot be dismissed so easily: *e.g.* in v. 12, the verb 'to ask' is *exetazō*, rather than the expected *erōtaō*; in v. 5 the disciples are addressed as *paidia* rather than the *teknia* used in 1:12; and so forth. Some of these are surely a reflection of the fact that John, as we have repeatedly observed, has a penchant for synonyms. In the case of *paidia*, the term appears frequently in 1 John, while within John 1 – 20 the alternative *teknia* is never used in direct address.

Over against these bits of evidence stand a number of places where ch. 21 exhibits vocabulary or syntactical constructions typical of chs. 1 – 20. These include not only obvious units such as the double *amēn* behind v. 18 (*cf.* notes on 1:51), and the variation of synonyms that characterize vv. 15–17, but fairly obscure constructions such as the opening words of v. 19 (*cf.* 12:33). Plummer (pp. 348–357) provides a list of twenty-five such units. Some are found in John 21 and *predominantly* in John 1 – 20 (*e.g.* the particle *mentoi* in 21:4 also occurs in Jn. 4:27; 7:13; 12:42; 20:5,

---

[1] In addition to certain commentators (*e.g.* Plummer, Hoskyns, Morris), *cf.* S. S. Smalley, *NTS* 20, 1974, pp. 275–288; and esp. (though from a quite different perspective) H. Thyen, 'Entwicklungen innerhalb der johanneischen Theologie und Kirche im Spiegel von Joh. 21 und der Lieblingsjüngertexte des Evangeliums', in *BETL*, pp. 259–299; *idem*, *ThR* 42, 1977, pp. 211–270.

and elsewhere in the New Testament is found only three times); others are found in John 21 and elsewhere *exclusively* in John 1 – 20 (*e.g.* Cana, 21:2 and 2:1; 4:46; Didymus, 21:2 and 11:16; 20:24).

As a result, even those scholars who are most thoroughly convinced that John 21 came from a different hand usually admit that these 'linguistic and stylistic considerations . . . are not in themselves sufficient to establish the belief that ch. 21 was written by a different author' (Barrett, p. 577). Moreover, there is reason to suspect that if similar tests were applied to several other chapters in John, the results would be no less ambivalent.

(2) For most scholars who are convinced that John 21 was added later, and probably came from a different hand, the crucial factor is their reading of ch. 20. John 20, it is argued, has reached not only a suitable but a triumphant conclusion (vv. 30–31). Jesus has risen, he has appeared, his ascension has been dealt with, the Spirit he promised has been bequeathed and his great commission solemnly uttered. What more is there to say? Everything else is necessarily anticlimactic. Even another resurrection appearance is unlikely to convince anyone not already convinced by the evidence displayed in ch. 20.

Yet this position, superficially overwhelming, is far from unassailable. At root, it turns on a certain reading of 20:17 and 22, and to a lesser extent on 20:28 and 30–31 – a reading already judged implausible by this commentary, and by many others. If we are to read John 20 more or less as advocated here, then John 21 no longer seems so inappropriate. True, John 20:30–31 is the climax of the book, the 'conclusion' in that sense. But as in a 'whodunit' where all the pieces have finally come together in a magnificent act of disclosure, there remains certain authorial discretion: the book may end abruptly with the act of disclosure, the solution to the mystery, or it may wind down through a postscript that tells what happens to the characters, especially if what happens to them sheds a certain light backward onto the principal plot of the work. Hoskyns (p. 656) has a point: 'a Christian gospel ends properly, not with the appearance of the risen Lord to His disciples, and their belief in Him, but with a confident statement that this mission to the world, undertaken at His command and under His authority, will be the means by which many are saved'. He argues that all three Synoptic Gospels end this way;[1] the Fourth Gospel is consonant with the pattern *only if John 21 is included*.

(3) What, then, does John 21 add? As we have seen, both sides agree that the linguistic evidence is not determinative; they disagree on their reading of John 20. We now discover that they disagree on their reading of John 21. Those who are persuaded that the chapter is not part of the original Gospel and clashes with ch. 20 tend to disparage the contribution of ch. 21, and may object that say, v. 25 is 'somewhat feebly

---

[1]His point is slightly weakened if it is believed that the proper ending of Mark is Mk. 16:8.

imitating the style of 20:30f.', or that vv. 1–14 show signs of confusion because 'No fewer than three words . . . are used for fish in different parts of the narrative' (Barrett, pp. 577, 578 – as if John were not given to synonyms!).

By contrast, those who judge John 21 to be an authentic part of the Gospel, quite apart from their different reading of ch. 20, tend to list the contributions that John 21 offers. The best of these, perhaps, are as follows:

(a) Peter is reconciled with Jesus, and given a commission; and thus an important 'loose end' is tied up.

(b) Peter and the beloved disciple reappear in vignettes that develop their characters entirely in line with what is known of them from the rest of the book, but in such a way that distinctions in role are specifically removed from the ring of competition; their complementarity is for the first time strongly affirmed.

(c) Peter's death, which has almost certainly occurred by the time the Fourth Gospel was composed, is so tied to the prophecy of Jesus and the theme of discipleship (v. 19) that it becomes a paradigm of how other Christians are to face suffering for the faith – and this as an exemplification of the teaching of Jesus in the Farewell Discourse (cf. 15:18 – 16:4).

(d) The death of Peter and its relation in God's providence to the Evangelist's long life provide an opportunity to articulate at a practical level some implications of the sustained tension throughout the Gospel between the dominant inaugurated eschatology (congruent with the Evangelist's long life and therefore with the 'delayed' parousia) and the futurist eschatology of apocalyptic expectation (Jesus *will return* vv. 22–23; cf. 5:28–29; 6:39–40; 14:1–3).

(e) As in the days before his crucifixion, Jesus is still ahead of the disciples, providing for their needs and serving them – a lesson the church must learn again and again.

(f) There is further anticipation, both in symbolic form and otherwise (cf. notes on v. 11, 15–17), of the mission of the church.

(g) The Holy Spirit is still not mentioned. This would be unconscionable under the alternative exegesis of 20:22 (cf. notes there). The tone of this chapter entirely suits the ostensible setting: Jesus is triumphant and looking to the future, but the disciples have still not been endued with the promised Spirit.

(h) There is a hint (vv. 24–25) addressing the enigma of who the beloved disciple is, who the Evangelist is. That these verses are difficult for us to interpret is beside the point; doubtless they were much clearer to the initial readers. Far from being a pale imitation of 20:30–31, they make their own contribution to the credibility of the entire book.

(4) There is no textual evidence that the book was ever published without John 21. Certainly if the first twenty chapters of the book had been published for a few years before ch. 21 was added, one would expect significant textual evidence of such independent circulation. But the less time one may reasonably allow between the alleged publication

of chs. 1 – 20 and the publication of the book as we have it, the more it is likely that, *even if* ch. 21 were added later, it was added by the same Evangelist who composed the rest (unless we hypothesize a timely death!). And *if* ch. 21 were added by the same hand, it must have been because the author thought the addition an improvement. Where, then, can one find reliable literary criteria to distinguish between the addition of an Epilogue to complete a work *at the time of composition*, and the addition of an Epilogue *some time later* by the same author? Even the possibility of a different amanuensis, or of a group of associates entrusted with writing down these last narratives as the Evangelist had repeatedly taught them, as some have suggested, does not alter these basic realities – though it might account for some of the linguistic oddities and for the 'we' in v. 24 (*cf.* notes below).

Such considerations will be weighed differently by different people. The evidence in favour of an originally integral Gospel incorporating ch. 21 seems reasonably firm, and that view is presupposed in the exposition that follows.

A. JESUS APPEARS TO HIS DISCIPLES BY THE SEA (21:1–14)

1. *Afterwards* (*meta tauta*, as in 3:22) establishes sequence but no chronological details. The disciples have left Jerusalem and returned to Galilee, probably not with the main groups of journeying pilgrims but in small groups of two or three, several days after the week-long Feast of Unleavened Bread.[1] There Jesus *appeared* (*ephanerōsen heauton*, lit. 'he revealed himself') *again to his disciples*, this time by the *Sea of Tiberias* – an alternative name for Lake Galilee, one found in the New Testament only in John (*cf.* notes on 6:1). Such 'revelation' or 'manifestation' is a common theme of the Fourth Gospel, but more commonly in reference to Jesus' manifestation in the days of his flesh: *e.g.* John the Baptist came that Jesus might *be revealed* to Israel (1:31); in the first sign, Jesus *revealed* his glory (2:11), and throughout his ministry, climaxing in the cross/ exaltation, Jesus *revealed* his Father's name (17:6). Here, in resurrection body, he reveals himself. The implication of the wording seems to be that this resurrection appearance (undertaken, like all the others in the Fourth Gospel, at Jesus' initiative) is itself a revelatory act.

2. Of the seven disciples, Simon Peter (the double name is especially common in John) appears first, probably because he was the unofficial leader, as suggested even by his initiative in the next verse. Thomas is again identified by both his Aramaic and Greek names (*cf.* 11:16; 20:24).

---

[1] *Cf.* C. F. D. Moule, *NTS* 4, 1957–58, pp. 58–61.

Nathanael has not been mentioned since 1:45–51, and only here is he said to come from Cana, the site of Jesus' first two signs in this Gospel (2:1–11; 4:46–54). The sons of Zebedee have not been identified as such before in John. The silence is remarkable, since the Synoptics portray Peter and the two sons of Zebedee, James and John, as a kind of triumvirate within the Twelve. That silence has contributed to the view that the beloved disciple (*cf.* v. 20) is none other than John. (It could not have been James, since James was martyred so early he could not have been responsible for the composition of this Gospel.) The mention of two more disciples, unnamed, makes this identification less than certain, though Haenchen overstates the matter when he insists that the unnamed pair 'make it impossible for us to determine [the beloved disciple's] name' (2. 229). This assessment would be fair if it were the only access we have to the identification of the beloved disciple. In reality, there are both internal and external reasons for making the identification (*cf.* Introduction, § IV), so such piecemeal assessment appears unjustified.

It might be tempting to suppose that these *seven* disciples represent, through the symbolism of the number, all of Jesus' followers. But since John does not habitually utilize this number, nor even in this instance mention the number – the reader must do the addition – we cannot be certain.

3. Commentators divide as to whether Peter and his friends are to be blamed for going fishing. Hoskyns (p. 552) describes the scene as 'one of complete apostasy' and 'the fulfilment of xvi.32'; Barrett (p. 579) judges it 'unthinkable' that 'Peter and his brother disciples should contemplate a return to their former occupation after the events of ch. 20'; Brown (2. 1096) speaks of 'aimless activity undertaken in desperation'. By contrast, Bruce (p. 399) insists there is no evidence that Peter was abandoning the commission he had received in order to return to fishing, and meanwhile 'it was better for him to employ his time usefully than remain idle'. And Beasley-Murray (p. 399) comments, 'Even though Jesus be crucified and risen from the dead, the disciples must still *eat!*'

The truth is probably between the two, but a good deal closer to the latter. There is no evidence that Peter and the others had gone to Galilee in order to fish. The most reasonable assumption is that they went in obedience to the Lord's command (Mk. 14:28; 16:7 par.). Moreover by this time Peter himself had seen the risen Lord (Lk. 24:34; 1 Cor. 15:5), a point confirmed by the fact that Peter so quickly threw himself into the water and swam for shore as soon as the identity of the man of the shore was pointed out. This does not read like the action of someone who is running away.

But if Peter and his friends have neither apostasized nor sunk into despair, this fishing expedition and the dialogue that ensues do not read like the lives of men on a Spirit-empowered mission. It is impossible to imagine any of this taking place in Acts, *after Pentecost*. There is a certain eagerness for the risen Jesus, still strangely halting as the reality of Jesus' resurrection is still sinking in. But most emphatically this is not the portrait of believers who have received the promised Paraclete. There is neither the joy nor the assurance, not to mention the sense of mission and the spirit of unity, that characterize the church when freshly endowed with the promised Spirit. It is this 'tone' in the chapter that confirms the exegesis of 20:22, given above, and authenticates the chapter as part of the original Gospel.

Although there is evidence that the night time was considered best for fishing on Galilee, one wonders if the Evangelist is not still employing one of his favourite symbols (*cf.* notes on 3:2, 19–21; 13:30; 20:1). They are coming to grips with the resurrection, but they still have not learned the profound truth that apart from Christ they can do nothing (15:5), and so *that night they caught nothing* (*cf.* Lk. 5:5).

4. Whether this is an instance when disciples are kept from recognizing the resurrected Christ (Lk. 24:16; *cf.* notes on 20:14, 15) is unclear. It may have been so *early in the morning* that it was impossible in the dimness to identify the figure on the shore.[1]

5–6. The word *paidia* (NIV 'Friends', frequently 'children') can be used much like British 'lads' or American 'boys' or 'guys' (*cf.* M. I. 170 n. 1). The word rendered 'fish' (*prosphagion*) is used only here in the New Testament. Strictly speaking it refers to a bit of something to eat, a titbit, which in the Galilean culture would often be a bit of fish. The *mē* that introduces the question expresses doubt or expects a negative answer: 'Lads, haven't you caught anything?'

Although *the right side*[2] of anything was widely considered in Greek circles to be a sign of good luck, it would be utterly trivial to think that this is why Jesus gave his command *Throw your net on the right side of the boat and you will find some*, or why the disciples heeded it. Why he gave the command is straightforward: he knew there was a great school of fish on the starboard side, as he had known it on another occasion (Lk. 5:1–11). What is at first more difficult is why these fishermen should pay any attention. If they had already recognized the Master, their obedience would make sense, but not v. 7, where recognition comes only after the catch; if they have not recognized him, why listen to the voice of someone calling in early dawn gloom from the shore of the lake? Indeed, Brown (2. 1090–1091) asks how Peter could go through the same situation and much of the same dialogue as on the earlier occasion, without recognizing Jesus. This difficulty is judged to be primary evidence of 'secondary' features in the story, prompting many to conclude that this is a variant account of the episode described in Luke 5:1–11.

---

[1]The expression *prōias de ēdē genomenēs* ('Early in the morning') is ambiguous. It can (but does not frequently) refer to the beginning of the working day (about full daylight): *cf.* Mt. 20:1.

[2]The word for 'side' found here (*meros*) does not have this meaning anywhere else in the New Testament, but parallels are not uncommon elsewhere (*cf. NewDocs* 2. § 2; 3. § 47).

But as Marshall[1] points out, the amount of 'common dialogue' is greatly over-estimated. It amounts to no more than the command to let down their nets. If the disciples are not *expecting* Jesus to appear, and do not recognize the man on the shore, it is hard to see how Jesus' exhortation to throw the net on the starboard side greatly differs from advice contemporary sports fishermen have to endure (and occasionally appreciate): 'Try casting over there. You often catch them over there!' (If there are some contemporary sports fishermen who have not yet experienced this delight, I recommend they take my children with them on their next trip.)

Whether in hope or in tired resignation, the men in the boat heed the advice. Immediately they are *unable to haul the net because of the large number of fish* – a rather different result from the episode of Luke 5:1–11, where two boats are so filled with fish that they are in danger of sinking.

7. Characteristically, the beloved disciple exhibits quick insight, and Peter quick action. No sooner has the former exclaimed, *It is the Lord!*, than Peter has *wrapped his outer garment around him . . . and jumped into the water*. The general picture is clear; the details are not. One does not normally put *on* a garment before swimming. The words rendered *for he had taken it off* are, literally, 'for he was naked (*gymnos*)'. If, as some think, Peter was totally naked or nearly so (*gymnos* could mean either), he may have donned his *outer garment* (*ependytēs*), even though it would impede his limbs. Alternatively, he was wearing nothing but the 'outer garment' while he was fishing, loosely draped around him, and before jumping into the water *he wrapped [it] around him*, i.e. he tucked up the lower part of the garment and either knotted it or fastened it with his girdle in order not to restrict his legs (the verb is *diezōsato* – the same verb is used to describe Jesus tying a towel around his waist preparatory to washing his disciples' feet, 13:4, 5).

8. We are to understand that Peter impetuously swims ashore and leaves his companions struggling to manoeuvre the boat to shore, *towing the net full of fish*. The distance was about two hundred cubits; a *pēchys* ('cubit') was usually about eighteen inches, hence NIV's *about a hundred yards*. The fact that the narrator's perspective stays with the boat, instead of diverting to the encounter between Jesus and Peter, is a small indication of eyewitness integrity.

9–10. When those in the boat landed, *they saw a fire of burning coals* (*anthrakia; cf.* notes on 18:18)[2] *with fish on it, and some bread*. In the days of his flesh, Jesus washes his disciples' feet (13:1–17). Now, as their risen Lord, he serves them still (*cf.* also v. 13): he meets their tiredness after a night of toil with a hot breakfast. They can begin to eat what he has

---

[1] *Cf.* I. Howard Marshall, *Commentary on Luke* (Paternoster, 1978), pp. 199–200.

[2] Since this is the second of only two places where *anthrakia* is mentioned, and the other is the setting for Peter's disowning of Jesus, some have suggested that this mention of *anthrakia* is John's subtle pointer to that earlier failure, since at this charcoal fire restoration takes place. If so, the connection is very subtle indeed.

cooked while some of the fish they have just caught are prepared. The word for 'fish' in vv. 9, 10 is *opsarion* (*cf.* notes on 6:9, 11), singular in v. 9 (was there just one large fish being cooked?) and plural in v. 10 – though the singular form can be collective, as probably in v. 13). For further comments on this word, *cf.* Introduction, § IV; *NewDocs* 2. § 64).

11. The story again links up with Peter. That he could climb aboard and haul the net ashore himself suggests that he was a physically strong man.

Large quantities of ink have gone into explaining why there should be 153 fish. At the purely historical level, it is unsurprising that someone counted them, either as part of dividing them up amongst the fishermen in preparation for sale, or because one of the men was so dumbfounded by the size of the catch that he said something like this: 'Can you believe it? I wonder how many there are?'

But such pedestrian considerations have not satisfied those who are certain there is profound significance in the number. Throughout the history of the church, the most popular solution is that advanced by Jerome, who in his commentary on Ezekiel 47 ties this miracle with the prophetic vision of the stream of living water that flows from the temple to the Dead Sea, which begins to teem with life. Jerome cites the naturalist Oppian who, he claims, avers that there are 153 different species of fish. Thus this catch of fish, effected by the risen Lord's command, becomes an acted parable of the fruitful mission of the church that draws (*helkyō*; the same verb is behind 'dragged') all human beings without distinction (12:32).[1] The trouble with this explanation is that Oppian's list, no matter how it is counted, does not yield 153; the most likely number is 157.[2] Scholars debate whether Jerome was simply mistaken in the number, misascribed the right number to some other naturalist whose work is now lost, or simply 'cooked the books'. So far as our evidence goes, however, this is no solution.

Another proposal based on Ezekiel 47 has been put forward more recently. Describing the effect of the stream from the temple, Ezekiel writes: 'There will be large numbers of fish, because this water flows there and makes the salt water fresh; so where the river flows everything will live. Fishermen will stand along the shore; from En Gedi to En Eglaim there will be places for spreading nets' (47:9–10). Now each Hebrew and Greek letter stands for a number, so every Greek or Hebrew word has a numerical value. Based on this discipline, called 'gematria', J. A. Emerton[3] has noted that in Hebrew 'En' is the word for 'spring', while 'Gedi' yields the number 17 and 'Eglaim' the number 153. Indeed, the two numbers are related: 153 is the triangular number of 17 (*i.e.* 1+2+3+. . .+17=153; for the reason why it is called 'triangular' *cf.* Hoskyns, p. 553). Thus the number represents the places where, in the

---

[1] Jerome, *Commentaria in Ezichielem, Lib.* xiv, *Cap.* 47; *cf. PL* 26. 474C.
[2] *Cf.* Robert M. Grant, *HTR* 42, 1949, pp. 273–275.
[3] *JTS* 9, 1958, pp. 86–89.

time of the fulfilment of messianic hopes, gospel fishermen are to spread their nets. Of course, this 'solution' supposes that the readers understand Hebrew. That is extremely unlikely in a book where elementary Hebrew words have to be transliterated (*e.g.* 1:37, 41). P. R. Ackroyd, noting this point, has derived 153 by adding the Greek numbers for 'Gedi' and 'Eglaim', but to do so he has had to find variant spellings in different manuscripts.[1]

That 153 is the triangular number of 17 did not escape the church Fathers. Augustine[2] noted it, and observed that 17=10+7, the 10 representing the ten commandments and the 7 the sevenfold Spirit of God (Rev. 1:4). Others break 7 down into 3+4, the number of the Trinity and the number of the new Jerusalem, the city built foursquare. Others have observed that 153=(3×50)+3, the double 3 pointing to the Trinity. Another scholar observes that in the feeding of the five thousand there were originally five little loaves of bread, from which twelve baskets of scraps were taken up, and 5+12=17 – *i.e.* there is a link between that (allegedly) eucharistic feast and this one.[3] Other solutions based on gematria have presented themselves: that 153 is the number for the words 'the church of love' in Hebrew,[4] or of 'the children of God',[5] or of Pisgah (thus making an allusion to the death of Moses, Dt. 34:1),[6] or of the Hebrew for 'Cana G' (representing 'Cana in Galilee', and thereby tying this miracle to the first two).[7]

Many other suggestions have been put forward, none very convincing. Whatever internal difficulty each might have, as a group most of them do not relate to this passage very well. They tend to offer, at best, an allusion to an admittedly Johannine theme, but nothing that flows naturally out of John 21:11. If the Evangelist has some symbolism in mind connected with the number 153, he has hidden it well.

Even so, there may be symbolism in the sheer quantity, if not the number itself, since the Evangelist draws attention to it: *but even with so many the net was not torn.* It is hard not to see an allusion to Luke 5:1–11, where the nets were torn. This may suggest that the gospel net will never break, that there is no limit to the number of converts it catches (Bruce, pp. 401–402). If such symbolism is operating, it may owe something to Jesus himself, who elsewhere promised to make his disciples 'fishers of men' (Mk. 1:17).

12–13. It was almost as if the disciples were reluctant to come, even as they were eager to be with him. Jesus must spell out the invitation: *Come*

---

[1]*JTS* 10, 1959, p. 10. J. A. Emerton (*JTS* 11, 1960, pp. 329–336) himself pointed out the difficulty of having to choose spellings from different manuscripts. More recent discussion (Bruce Grigsby, *ExpT* 95, 1984, pp. 177–178) has not escaped the problem of assuming a strongly semitic readership.
[2]*In Johan. Tract.* 122.   [3]So M. Rissi, *ThZ* 35, 1979, pp. 73–89.
[4]D. R. Ahrendts, *ZWT* 41, 1898, p. 480.
[5]J. A. Romeo, *JBL* 97, 1978, pp. 263–264.
[6]O. T. Owen, *ExpT* 100, 1988, pp. 52–54; but *cf.* J. M. Ross, *ExpT* 100, 1989, p. 375.
[7]M. Oberweis, *ZNW* 77, 1986, pp. 236–241.

and have breakfast (*aristēsate*, here used, as classically, for the first meal of the day, as v. 4 requires; more commonly in the New Testament for a later meal – *e.g.* Lk. 11:37–38; 14:12).

The second half of the verse is finely balanced, a balance that must be respected if the mood of the text is to be preserved. One might ask why, if the disciples 'knew it was the Lord', they would *want* to ask him, 'Who are you?' But the Evangelist does not merely say they *did* not ask him, he says they *dared* not ask him (lit.) 'knowing it was the Lord'. This is not the same reticence as that exhibited by the two disciples on the road to Emmaus who were kept from recognizing him (Lk. 24:16): these disciples *know* it is the Lord, and yet are still so uneasy, so hesitant, so uncertain, that they apparently long to ask him, in effect, 'Is it *really* you?', yet *dare* not do so.

Perhaps it is the lack of imaginative historical reconstruction on our part that makes us hesitate to see the compelling power of this interpretation. Our creeds make the resurrection of Jesus Christ so central that it requires considerable mental effort to put ourselves in the places of the first disciples. The evidence of ch. 20 is here presupposed. The disciples had been granted the strongest possible reasons for believing in Jesus' resurrection, and indeed did so: *they knew it was the Lord*. But whether because they could see Jesus was not simply resuscitated (like Lazarus), but appeared with new powers, or because they were still grappling with the strangeness of a crucified and resurrected Messiah, or because despite the irrefutable power of the evidence presented to them resurrection itself seemed strange, they felt considerable unease – yet suppressed their question because they knew the one before them could only be Jesus.

Thus, when *Jesus came, took the bread and gave it to them, and did the same with the fish* (v. 13), he was not primarily offering evidence of his own physical resurrection. Unlike Luke 24:41–43, there is no mention of his own eating – eating which had earlier been done less to sustain him than to establish the faith of his disciples. Here, however, he reassures them, meets their physical needs, serves them as he did before his passion. It is a time for them to adjust to the new eschatological situation; it is a time sufficiently symbol-laden, in a culture where symbols were more highly regarded than in our own, to speak to them powerfully, as they meditated upon it, about the Lord's continued presence and power with them as they prosecuted the mission with which he charged them.

Despite the fact that some Christian art in the first few centuries of the church depicts fish along with bread in representations of the eucharist, and despite the fact that some commentators make similar connections, the allusions are at best remote. One's assessment is necessarily based in part on one's prior reading of John 6. Even so, there is no hint that Jesus here gives *himself* in the bread and fish, or that in their eating they are even symbolically, let alone sacramentally, partaking of him.

14. That there was in the Evangelist's mind some evidential value in this episode in support of Jesus' resurrection is confirmed by this verse, which forms a literary *inclusio* (*cf.* notes on 1:18) with v. 1. John writes that *Jesus appeared to his disciples*: the verb (*ephanerōthē*) is the passive form of the verb used in v. 1, lit. 'Jesus was revealed' or 'Jesus was manifested'. As in v. 1, the emphasis is on Jesus' self-disclosure. The verb is stronger than the more common *ōphthē* ('he appeared'), used more commonly in the New Testament (*e.g.* Lk. 24:34; 1 Cor. 15:5-8). The expression *he was raised* (passive of *egeirō*) is one of two verbs commonly used to refer to the resurrection itself, the other being *anistēmi* (used in 20:9). There does not appear to be a great distinction in meaning.

The reference to the *third time* Jesus appeared probably enumerates only the appearances reported in this Gospel (20:19-23; 20:26-29). The appearance to Mary Magdalene is not counted, since that was not an appearance *to his disciples*. It is extremely difficult to place all the appearances reported in the New Testament into chronological order. At least three sequences are possible.

B. JESUS AND PETER AND JOHN (21:15-24)

15-17. Many contemporary commentators think of vv. 15-23 as a fundamentally different unit from what precedes. To use the language of Schnackenburg (3. 361), vv. 1-14 constitute 'a disciple pericope', and vv. 15-19 'a Peter fragment'. In the latter, the breakfast and the other disciples disappear from view, leaving only Peter, the beloved disciple, and Jesus. This is unwarranted. The opening words, *When they had finished eating*, establish the connection; there is no compelling reason for dismissing them as 'editorial' (as many do). The link is important: as Peter had boasted of his reliability in the presence of his fellow disciples (13:8, 37-38; *cf.* 18:10-11), so this restoration to public ministry is effected in a similarly public environment – regardless of whatever private forgiveness and reconciliation there may have been between Jesus and Peter when Jesus revealed himself after his resurrection to this one apostle, alone (1 Cor. 15:5; Lk. 24:34). Later in the pericope we are probably to think of Peter walking down the beach with Jesus, the beloved disciple not far behind, certainly within earshot (vv. 20-21).

The public nature of Peter's reinstatement is suggested by Jesus' initial question, *Simon son of John, do you truly love me more than these?* By itself, *more than these* (*toutōn*, genitive of comparison) could be interpreted in three ways: (1) 'Do you love me more than you love these disciples?' But this question does not cohere with any theme in the book. (2) 'Do you love me more than you love this fishing gear?' That is possible; the boat and the nets have been mentioned, and doubtless other gear was lying around. But in John 1 Peter is not called *from* his fishing, and the fishing of 21:3 has fewer negative overtones than some suppose. In any case all seven disciples went fishing: why then focus on Peter? (3) 'Do you love me more than these other disciples do?' (which of course assumes they are still present). This makes sense. Peter has always been able to advance the strongest personal boast. On the night Jesus was betrayed, while others were growing quiet, Peter could insist, 'I will lay down my life for you [not "We" and "our"!] (13:37). It was Peter who slashed at Malchus (18:10). *Cf.* Matthew 26:33. But physical courage was not enough that night, and it was Peter also, spirit willing but flesh weak, who publicly disowned the Lord. Whatever potential for future service he had therefore depended not only on forgiveness from Jesus, but also on reinstatement amongst the disciples.

Some expositions of these verses turn on the distribution of the two different verbs for 'love' that appear. When Jesus asks the question the first two times, 'Do you love me?', the verb is *agapaō*; Peter responds with 'I love you' (*phileō*). The third time, however, Jesus himself uses *phileō*; and still Peter cannot bring himself to use more than the same. Commonly it is argued that *agapaō* is the stronger form of 'to love', but so powerfully has Peter had his old self-confidence expunged from him that the most he will claim is the weaker form – even when Jesus draws attention to the point, using the weaker form himself when he asks the question for the third time. This accounts for the distinction the NIV maintains between 'truly love' and 'love'.[1]

This will not do, for at least the following reasons:

(1) We have already seen that the two verbs are used interchangeably in this Gospel. The expression 'beloved disciple', more literally 'disciple whom Jesus *loved*', can be based on either verb (*cf.* notes on 20:2). The Father loves the Son – and both verbs serve (3:35; 5:20). Jesus loved Lazarus – and again both verbs serve (11:5, 36).

(2) No reliable distinction can be based on the LXX. For instance, Jacob's preferential love for Joseph is expressed with both verbs (Gn. 37:3, 4). When Amnon incestuously rapes his sister Tamar, both verbs can be used to refer to his 'love' (2 Sam. 13). Despite one verb for 'love' in the Hebrew text of Proverbs 8:17, the LXX uses both *agapaō* and *phileō*.

(3) Convincing evidence has been advanced that the verb *agapaō* was coming into prominence throughout Greek literature from about the fourth century BC onward, as one of the standard verbs for 'to love'. One of the reasons for this change is that *phileō* has taken on the additional meaning 'to kiss', in some contexts.[2] In other words, *agapaō* does not come into play because it is a peculiarly sacred word.

---

[1] The most sophisticated contemporary defence of a semantic distinction between the two verbs in this passage is probably that of K. L. McKay, *NovT* 27, 1985, pp. 319–333.

[2] *E.g.* Mt. 26:49. Robert Joly (*Le vocabulaire chrétien de l'amour, est-il original? Φιλεῖν et Ἀγαπᾶν dans le grec antique* [Presses Universitaires de Bruxelles, 1968]) demonstrates that *phileō* acquired this new meaning because an older verb for 'to kiss', *kyneō*, was dropping out of use. The reason for this was that it sounded much like another verb, *kynō*, 'to impregnate' – especially in the aorist, where both verbs have the same form (*ekysa*). The potential for salacious puns exerted pressure on *kyneō* and gradually forced it into obsolescence. Briefly, *cf.* D. A. Carson, *Exegetical Fallacies* (Baker, 1984), pp. 51–54.

(4) Even in the New Testament, *agapaō* is not always distinguished by a good object: Demas regrettably 'loved' the present age (2 Tim. 4:10).

(5) Nor does it help to argue, with Hendriksen (2. 494–500), that because the *total* range of meaning of each verb is not the same as that of the other (*e.g. agapaō* never means 'to kiss'), therefore there is necessarily some distinction to be made here. But this conclusion is invalid. All agree that synonyms enjoy differences of association, nuance and emotional colouring within their total semantic range. 'But within any one individual passage these differences do not amount to a distinction of real theological reference: they do not specify a difference in the kind of love referred to.'[1]

(6) Amongst those who insist a distinction between the two verbs is to be maintained in each verse, there is no agreement. Thus, Trench[2] insists *agapaō* is philanthropic and altruistic, but without emotional attachment, and therefore much too cold for Peter's affection. That is why the apostle prefers *phileō*. By contrast, for Westcott (2. 367) *agapaō* denotes the higher love that will in time come to be known as the distinctively Christian love, while Peter cannot bring himself to profess more than 'the feeling of natural love', *phileō*. Bruce (p. 405) wisely comments: 'When two such distinguished Greek scholars (both, moreover, tending to argue from the standards of classical Greek) see the significance of the synonyms so differently, we may wonder if indeed we are intended to see such distinct significance.'

(7) By now it has become clear that the Evangelist constantly uses minor variations for stylistic reasons of his own (*cf.* Morris, *SFG*, pp. 293–319). This is confirmed by the present passage. In addition to the two words for 'love', John resorts to three other pairs: *boskō* and *poimainō* ('feed' and 'take care of' the sheep), *arnia* and *probata* ('lambs' and 'sheep'), and *oida* and *ginōskō* (both rendered 'you know' in v. 17). These have not stirred homiletical imaginations; it is difficult to see why the first pair should.[3]

Jesus' initial question probes Peter to the depth of his being. He does not try to answer in terms of the relative strength of his love as compared with that of other disciples. He appeals rather to the Lord's knowledge. Despite my bitter failure, he says in effect, I love you – *you know that I love you*. Jesus accepts his declaration, doubtless to Peter's relief, and commissions him: *Feed my lambs*. The emphasis is now on the

---

[1]James Barr, 'Words for Love in Biblical Greek', in L. D. Hurst and N. T. Wright (eds.), *The Glory of Christ in the New Testament* (Fs. G. B. Caird; Clarendon, 1987), pp. 3–18, esp. p. 15.

[2]R. C. Trench, *Synonyms of the New Testament* (Spottiswoode and Co., 1880), p. 40.

[3]Incidentally, it is unwarranted to try to resolve this issue by appealing to the underlying Aramaic that was probably spoken on this occasion. Although there are various Aramaic words for 'to love' or 'to like', we have no access to the actual words other than what this text provides, and despite occasional claims to the contrary John gives little evidence that this is merely *translation* Greek mechanically trying to preserve an underlying semitic source.

pastoral rather than the evangelistic (*cf.* v. 11). Peter's love for his Lord, and the evidence of his reinstatement, are both to be displayed in Peter's pastoral care for the Lord's flock (*cf.* Jn. 10).

But that is not the end of the matter. Three times Jesus asks the same question. When Peter is particularly grieved (v. 17), it is not because Jesus has changed verbs, but because the same question is being asked for the third time. As he had disowned Jesus three times, so Jesus requires this elementary yet profound confession three times. There is no trace of self-righteousness in Peter's response. He can only appeal to the fact that the Lord knows everything, and therefore knows Peter's heart: *Lord, you know all things; you know that I love you*. And that is enough. Lest there be any doubt that Peter is fully restored to future service, Jesus again commands, *Feed my lambs*. This ministry 'is described in verbs, not nouns: Tend, feed, not Be a pastor, hold the office of pastor. And the sheep are Christ's sheep, not Peter's. Not, Tend your flock, but Tend my sheep' (Barrett, *Essays*, pp. 165–166). That Peter fulfilled the terms of the service required of him receives its best attestation in 1 Peter (esp. 5:1–4).

Strangely, some Roman Catholic scholars have used this passage to establish the primacy of Peter as the first pontiff, with rights of governance and authority. It is usually argued that in the Old Testament the figure of the shepherd was often tied to kingly rule: *cf.* 2 Samuel 5:2, where David declares, 'And the LORD said to you, "You will shepherd my people Israel, and you will become their ruler"'. When John 21:15–17 is tied to the common Roman Catholic exegesis of Matthew 16:16–19, the argument gains a certain plausibility.

But quite apart from questions of succession, which are certainly not in view in either Matthew 16:13–20 or John 21:15–17, neither the ostensible link between the two passages, nor the most common Catholic exegesis of either passage, is very secure. Matthew 16:13–20 certainly establishes a unique role for Peter in the *founding* of the church – *i.e.* it establishes what has been called 'his salvation-historical primacy'.[1] It does not establish him in a position of ruling authority over other apostles. As for John 21:15–17, neither founding pre-eminence nor comparative authority is in view. It is true that the figure of the shepherd can be used to picture authority. But this passage does not establish that Peter has relatively more authority than other 'shepherds' of the flock of God. When close comparisons are made with Acts 20:28 and 1 Peter 4:1–4, it becomes clear that *each* shepherd of the flock of God, of Jesus' sheep, of the church of God, is to mirror *both* authority *and* a certain brokenness that is utterly exemplary. The Ephesian elders are to guard and shepherd the flock over which the Holy Spirit has made them overseers ('bishops' – but without any evidence to support a notion, this

[1]*Cf.* Carson, *Matt*, pp. 363–375; George R. Beasley-Murray, *Jesus and the Kingdom of God* (Paternoster/Eerdmans, 1986), pp. 179–185.

early, of *monarchical* bishops with authority over several parishes), while Peter pictures himself as a 'fellow elder' who can encourage other elders to be 'shepherds' and 'overseers' ('bishops'), 'being examples to the flock'. And all must give an account to the Chief Shepherd when he appears, the Lord Jesus himself. Thus there is nothing intrinsic to the language of John 21:15–17 that suggests a *distinctive* authority for Peter. All Christian leadership entails a certain tension between authority and meek, exemplary service, patterned finally on Jesus himself. In the context of the Fourth Gospel, these verses deal with Peter's reinstatement to service, not with his elevation to primacy.

18–19. For *I tell you the truth, cf.* notes on 1:51. Jesus' prophecy in v. 18 is often taken as an ambiguous adaptation of a proverb that originally contrasted the vigour of youth with the frailty of old age. Bultmann (p. 713) reconstructs the proverb this way: 'In youth a man is free to go where he will; in old age a man must let himself be taken where he does not will.' On this reading, the Evangelist, after the fact, applies it to Peter's death by crucifixion. Elliott goes farther, and understands *neōteros* ('younger') to refer to a new convert, and contrasts his tempestuous youth with the mature serenity of age.[1]

As popular as this view may be, Bultmann's suggestion is an hypothesis not only without evidence, but against the evidence. In this context, the *younger* Peter carries the positive connotations of freedom, while *old* here signals not serenity but restriction and martyrdom. More important is the way *stretch out your hands* was understood in the ancient world: it widely referred to crucifixion (Haenchen, 2. 226–227). Some think that improbable in this context because of the sequence: Peter is told that, when he is old, he will stretch out his hands, someone else will dress him and lead him where he does not want to go. If this 'stretching of the hands' refers to crucifixion, should it not *follow* the other items? Bauer (p. 232) proposed long ago that this 'stretching' took place when a condemned prisoner was tied to his cross-member (the *patibulum: cf.* notes on 19:17) and forced to carry his 'cross' to the place of execution. The cross-member would be placed on the prisoner's neck and shoulders, his arms tied to it, and *then* he would be led away to death. Despite the fact that many reject this explanation (even Schnackenburg [3. 482 n. 75] joins with those who write this off as 'antiquarian sophistry'!), the most detailed study of crucifixion in the ancient world describes just such horrible variations on this grisly form of execution.[2]

The Evangelist's explanation (v. 19) of Jesus' prediction (v. 18), therefore, aligns with the prediction itself: *Jesus said this to indicate the kind of death by which Peter would glorify God.* And thus he imitates Christ, not only in the kind of death he suffers (*cf.* 12:33; 18:32), but also, though to a lesser extent, in bringing glory to God by his death (*cf.* 12:27–28;

---

[1] J. H. Elliot, *CBQ* 32, 1970, p. 383.

[2] M. Hengel, *Crucifixion* (SCM/Fortress, 1977), esp. ch. 4. *Cf.* Beasley-Murray, pp. 408–409.

13:31–32; 17:1). Peter himself came to recognize the principle: whenever any Christian follows Christ to suffering and death, it is a means of bringing praise to God (1 Pet. 4:14–16). What is remarkable is that Peter lived and served three decades with this prediction hanging over him.

By the time the Fourth Gospel was written, the prediction had been fulfilled, and Peter had glorified God by his martyrdom, probably in Rome, under the emperor Nero. Extra-biblical sources for the event are not strong. Clement of Rome (*c.* AD 96) mentions Peter's martyrdom but does not reveal what form it took (*1 Clement* 5:4). Writing about AD 212, Tertullian affirms that it was when Peter was bound to the cross that he was girded by someone else (*Scorpiace* ['Antidote for the Scorpion's Sting'] 15), but it is unclear whether Tertullian has access to independent information, or is simply referring to this text. Later accounts of Peter asking to be crucified upside down, because he felt unworthy to be crucified as his Lord was, are too remote and too infected with legendary accretions to be reliable.[1] What is undisputed is that the indelible shame Peter bore for his public disowning of the Lord Jesus Christ on the night he was sentenced to death was forgiven by the Lord himself, and subsequently overwhelmed by the apostle's fruitful ministry and martyrdom.

Jesus' concluding words to Peter, *Follow me*, may invite Peter for a private walk along the beach (*cf.* v. 20). But in the context of this book, they do more: they tie this step of discipleship to Jesus' initial call (1:43), challenge Peter to consistent discipleship until the martyrdom he now faces comes due, and implicitly invite every waverer, every reader, to the same steadfast pursuit of the risen Lord. They also anticipate v. 21.

20–21. Whether Jesus and Peter begin their walk now, or have been doing so for some time, is not clear. Either way, the beloved disciple (*cf.* notes on 13:23) has left the group and is *following* them. Many think this is a subtle way of advancing the beloved disciple's interests: Peter is told to *follow* (v. 19) Jesus, but the beloved disciple is already *following* him. This rather subtle interpretation is possible only if we think that Jesus and Peter were conversing privately *before* Jesus said, 'Follow me!' Only in that case could it be thought that the beloved disciple was *already* following. If instead it is only at this point that Jesus and Peter stroll down the beach, then Peter begins to 'follow' from the moment Jesus speaks. If the beloved disciple also does, he is farther behind! Probably the entire approach is too subtle: if the beloved disciple's following is to be interpreted symbolically, then why not Peter's turning around?

That the Evangelist specifically identifies the beloved disciple by referring back to 13:24–25 is not because this is the first time he appears in the epilogue (*cf.* v. 7, where he is not so identified) but for two other reasons. First, the reminder that this disciple leaned his head on Jesus'

---

[1]*Acts of Peter* 37–39; Eusebius, *H. E.* III. i. But that victims were sometimes crucified upside down is independently attested by Seneca (*Consolation to Marcia* 20).

breast at the last supper establishes his credentials as an intimate of the Lord Jesus – an especially significant intimacy in light of the beloved disciple's distinctive role (vv. 22, 24). The point is important, for this intimacy simultaneously establishes the credentials of the Fourth Gospel. It may not be too far-fetched to think of John leaning on Jesus' breast as a kind of lesser intimacy to that of the Son with the Father, in the bosom of the Father (1:18; cf. also notes on 15:9–11).[1] Second, the episode at the last supper calls to mind that Peter signalled to John to get him to ask Jesus a question: i.e. it assumes a certain intimacy between the beloved disciple and Peter. That intimacy makes Peter's question more comprehensible, if not more justifiable. His own prognosis is not very good: for Peter the cost of discipleship will be high. What about him?

22. The burden of Jesus' reply is tart: in brief, Peter is told it is none of his business. Peter has been informed what will befall him: let him therefore obey, regardless of the specific forms of obedience others must pursue (cf. 1 Cor. 4:2–7). You must follow me (the pronoun You [sing.] is emphatic). John may be asked to remain until Jesus returns: what is that to you? Clearly in this context the verb remain (menō) means 'remain alive on earth', without any overtone of its use in John 15. The transparently futurist eschatology should not be explained away. It is in line with 5:24–25, 28–29; 6:39–40; 14:3.

There is no belittling of either disciple. One of them may be called to strategic pastoral ministry (vv. 15–17) and a martyr's crown (vv. 18–19), and the other to a long life (v. 22) and to strategic historical-theological witness, in written form (v. 24). It is this that ties v. 24 so closely to the preceding verses. And if the beloved disciple's commission is not cast in terms as explicit as those of Peter, it is the historical record that constrains the Evangelist: at this point Peter needed a fresh commission, since that was part of his restoration, while the beloved disciple did not.

23. Whatever else may be disputed in this verse, it is clear that here the beloved disciple is a real individual, not an idealization of the ideal follower or of some part of the church.[2] It is also clear that the saying of v. 22 circulated widely in at least some parts of the church before this chapter was written. The saying became an ill-advised but influential support for those whose eagerness for the parousia was not bounded by the careful restrictions imposed by, say, 1 Thessalonians 4:13–18 and 2 Thessalonians 2. As long as the beloved disciple was alive, their understanding of the imminence of the parousia could rise with the disciple's increasing age, until it reached fever pitch. Once he died (whether or not that death had taken place by the time of writing), their

---

[1] Cf. I. de la Potterie, Bib 67, 1986, pp. 343–359.

[2] E.g. Bultmann repeatedly treats the beloved disciple in chs. 13 – 20 as a mere symbol of Gentile Christianity. He recognizes that in ch. 21 the beloved disciple is represented as a real individual, but he thinks the author of ch. 21 is someone different from the Evangelist and did not properly understand chs. 1 – 20 (pp. 483, 715).

faith would suffer a rude shock, and the enemies of the Gospel could smirk on the sidelines. And so the Evangelist carefully points out what Jesus did and did not say.

But had the beloved disciple died by this point? Strong voices can be found on both sides of the question. Those who think the beloved disciple was dead at the time of writing suggest that it was his death, the death of the last eyewitness, that precipitated the need to include ch. 21 (*e.g.* Brown, 2. 1117–1119, 1142; *cf.* Smalley, p. 81). In that case, it is a trifle surprising to find v. 23 cast as it is. Under their assumptions, once the crisis of the beloved disciple's death had occurred the problem would involve the very structure of Christian eschatology. The rumour about the beloved disciple would have to be addressed, much as here, but all kinds of other evidence (like that of 2 Thes. 2) could be adduced to justify the view that Jesus' return might well be delayed. As it is, it seems simpler to think that the circulating rumour is making the rounds while the beloved disciple is still alive, but advancing in years, and he is determined to stifle it as well as he can for fear of the damage that would be done if he died before the Lord's return. If the rumour is based on a false interpretation of Jesus that is circulating round the churches, it seems reasonable to suppose that, if the beloved disciple were already dead, the falsity of that interpretation could instantly be established by pointing out the disciple's grave. The silence on this point supports the view that the beloved disciple was still alive at the time of writing. The point is strengthened if John's intended readers are Jews, proselytes and God-fearers who know something of the truth but are holding back from conversion to the risen Christ. They, too, have heard something of these rumours, and the Evangelist does not want the credibility of his witness to them, the witness that we call the Fourth Gospel (v. 24), seriously impaired by his own death.

It is possible, but not quite certain, that the Evangelist, whom the next verse identifies as the beloved disciple, is confronting the same sort of divisiveness with which Paul deals in 1 Cor. 1 – 4 (*cf.* esp. 1:10–11). Some are saying, 'I am of Peter', and others 'I am of John' (assuming John is the beloved disciple). The Evangelist is not interested in playing such games, even to his own advantage. He is perfectly aware that the form of service may differ from believer to believer. What he wants is that his readers will so follow Jesus that they will be true disciples themselves (*cf.* Lindars, p. 640). Although this could be strongly applied to a divided church, it has its own dramatic appeal to outsiders. The relationships amongst the apostles need to be understood, so that even if the church does not always live up to the teachings of its Master, potential converts may take comfort from the fact that obedience to Christ does not have to descend into party politics. The Jesus whom both Peter and the beloved disciple served in quite different ways, in ways as different as the service that will be rendered by all the converts that follow, is the Jesus passionately concerned about the unity of his people (Jn. 17), the oneness of his flock (Jn. 10).

24. Many scholars treat vv. 24 and 25 as coming from a different source or sources than the rest of ch. 21. At very least, they are read as a separate conclusion or conclusions, with little direct connection with the preceding. But v. 24 is better seen as part of the answer to Peter's question in v. 21: 'Lord, what about him?' (*cf.* Barrett, pp. 587–588, and notes also on vv. 22–23). All disciples live under the commission of 20:21. After that, there are distinctions: Peter serves by tending the flock of God and by glorifying God in his death; the beloved disciple serves by following Jesus throughout a long life, and as the trustworthy *disciple who testifies to these things and who wrote them down*. That means v. 24 has to be read as part of vv. 20–23, and v. 20 establishes that the beloved disciple is none other than the beloved disciple who appears throughout the Fourth Gospel. By the same token, *these things* to which this disciple testifies must not be the contents of ch. 21 alone, but the entire Fourth Gospel.

It is more difficult to decide to what person or persons the 'we' refers in this clause, *We know that his testimony is true*. The principal options are these:

(1) The *We* refers to the elders in the church at Ephesus (Westcott, 2. 374), or to others who are closely linked with the beloved disciple (Schlatter, p. 376), or perhaps to the church to which he belonged, without specifying Ephesus (Bultmann, pp. 717–718). The advantage of this view is that it allows full force to the plural *We*. The Muratorian Canon (11. 10–15) reports that John wrote his Gospel only after some of his disciples and fellow bishops had entreated him to do so (similarly Clement of Alexandria, as quoted by Eusebius, *H. E.* VI. xiv. 7). Again, however, we do not know if this is independent information, or informed guessing based on the exegesis of this verse. One form or another of this theory makes sense not only of the *We* but also of the fact that others than apostles should get involved with the attestation of an apostolic work. 'The "we" is to be taken with full seriousness; there exists an apostolic church whose very existence is a confirmation and affirmation of the apostolic witness' (Barrett, p. 588). What must be added is that no form of this theory *in itself* justifies the view that the Fourth Gospel was therefore a joint product, with the beloved disciple providing some memories and perspectives while others (later?) wrote them up.

Yet the view is not without difficulty. It is hard to imagine in what context other church leaders would be providing a character reference for an apostle. The problem is perhaps avoided if we take *We know that his testimony is true* either as a form of identification (it is none other than the truthful beloved disciple who wrote this, and we testify to the fact) or as a form the Christian leaders adopt for identifying themselves with John's readers (*all* of us know that what the beloved disciple attests is true). But neither is a natural interpretation of the text.

(2) It has been argued that *We know* is an indefinite expression more or less the equivalent of the modern 'as is well known' or the like.[1] Doubtless

---

[1] C. H. Dodd, *JTS* 4, 1953, pp. 212–213.

that is possible, but it is an extremely odd expression for an author to use in justification of his *own* truthfulness.

(3) John uses the *We* to refer to himself – *i.e.* it is an editorial 'we'. Certainly John sometimes uses this *plural* form on the lips of the *individual* characters he describes within the Fourth Gospel (*e.g.* 3:2, 11; 20:2), though it must be admitted that in each case crucial interpretative questions arise. Assuming the author is also the writer of the Johannine epistles, the expression becomes fairly frequent (*e.g.* 1 Jn. 1:2, 4, 5, 6, 7; 3 Jn. 12). Not all of these occurrences function the same way. Some seem to be tying the author to apostolic authority (*e.g.* 1 Jn. 1:3), others connect the author with his readers (*e.g.* 1 Jn. 1:7), others identify his opponents (*e.g.* 1 Jn. 1:6), and still others serve as a self-reference (*e.g.* 1 Jn. 1:4).

Despite these parallels, the use of 'we' in John 21:24, if taken as a self-reference by the Evangelist, remains a somewhat awkward form when the writer is understood to be attesting the truthfulness of his own witness. However, even this is not entirely without parallel in the New Testament. For instance, because Paul loathes every form of boastful self-promotion, yet finds himself in the awkward position of having to defend his spiritual credentials in the face of the attacks of the false 'super-apostles', he describes his own spectacular visions and revelations by referring to 'a man in Christ' – in the third person (2 Cor. 12:2–4). But perhaps the strongest evidence in support of this view comes from the Fourth Gospel's Prologue: *'We* have seen his glory' (1:14).

Either the first or third option is possible, the third slightly preferable. For some (*e.g.* Morris, pp. 880–881), the former option is sufficient to support apostolic authorship. For others (*e.g.* Thyen, cited at the beginning of this chapter), not even the latter will do: he thinks the unknown Evangelist created the figure of the beloved disciple and inserted him at appropriate junctures into his Gospel to give his work more credibility. Of course, this is a more damaging admission than Thyen realizes. To gain such credibility the Evangelist had to create a figure that his readers *think* is someone important, none other than the apostle John. Thus Thyen implicitly admits that the Gospel as most naturally read ascribes authorship to the apostle, but posits pseudonymity against the more natural reading of the text.

Culpepper (pp. 45–49) does something similar. Using literary categories developed in connection with the study of the nineteenth-century European novel, he lucidly demonstrates that the 'narrator' finally identifies the 'implied author' with the beloved disciple. That is exactly correct. But Culpepper then distances the 'implied author' from the real author in a way that could not be sanctioned if the literary work in question were not viewed as a piece of fiction but as a work of (theologically structured) history, where the author goes to great pains to emphasize the theme of witness and testimony (*cf.* notes on 1:7, 15; *cf.* Introduction, §§ III, IV).

Even if the beloved disciple is the one *who testifies to these things*, what is meant by the claim that he *wrote them down*? Since Bernard (2. 713), it has become popular to compare 19:19: presumably Pilate did not do the actual writing. So here: perhaps the beloved disciple caused the book to be written, but had little hand in the actual writing.

But this will not do. The context of 19:19 demonstrates that, assuming Pilate did not do the actual writing, the wording on the *titulus* accurately expressed what he wanted to say, so accurately that the addition of the one word proposed by the Jewish authorities would have changed his intent. Pilate rejected the proposal. It may be that amanuenses had some freedom of composition (Rom. 16:22 is frequently cited): the evidence is not very clear,[1] but it is reasonable to suppose that gifted amanuenses sometimes did more than take dictation. No matter: once the author (as opposed to the amanuensis) read the final product, and signed it with his own name (as Paul did with his epistles), it was his product. In any case, even if *wrote . . . down* here really means 'caused to be written down', there is no evidence whatsoever that this was used for a *later* writing of *earlier* testimony, after the witness had died; nor is there any evidence that the term 'amanuensis' is appropriate where someone ostensibly reports the thoughts and witness of an employer or teacher now deceased. Further, even if one were to insist that the verb 'to write' *can* mean 'to cause to write', and therefore allows some distance between the beloved disciple and the text, the previous clause, *who testifies to these things*, 'implies firsthand testimony' (Bruce, p. 3). 'The most natural meaning of these words, and therefore the meaning to be adopted unless very strong reasons are brought against it, is that the disciple himself not only bore witness to but also wrote down *tauta* ("these things")' (Barrett, p. 587).

In short, there are two identifications to be made: (1) the beloved disciple is the apostle John; (2) the evangelist is the beloved disciple. If both of these are true, then the evangelist is John. We have already outlined the evidence in favour of (1) (*cf.* Introduction, § IV, and notes on 13:23). Ironically, some of those most strongly supportive of (1) are those who deny (2). This verse establishes, not with absolute certainty but with reasonable clarity, the truthfulness of (2).

C. THE GREATNESS OF JESUS (21:25)

25. It is impossible to be certain, but the most natural way of reading this verse is to assume that the Evangelist, now that he has identified

---

[1]For a useful survey, *cf.* Richard N. Longenecker, 'On the Form, Function and Authority of the New Testament Letters', in Carson/Woodbridge I, pp. 101–114.

himself as the beloved disciple (= the apostle John), feels free to make an overt self-reference (*I suppose*). This view is enhanced if the 'we' in v. 24 is also a self-reference: certainly 1 John delights in going back and forth between 'we' and 'I'. On this reading, John is overtly alluding to 20:30–31: several of the clauses in v. 25 have close parallels in the earlier passage. But now the horizons are expanded. Not only are there many other 'signs' not recorded in the Fourth Gospel (20:30), there are many other things (*alla polla*) Jesus did – so many that if they were all recorded *the whole world* (one of the few 'neutral' instances of *kosmos*: *cf.* notes on 1:9) *would not have room for the books that would be written.*

Doubtless this may be taken as a pardonable exaggeration, but the stylistic and theological care of the Evangelist throughout the work argue decisively against the suggestion. If in v. 24 the Evangelist has already alluded to the Prologue (*cf.* notes above), it is best to think he is doing so again. The Jesus to whom he bears witness is not only the obedient Son and the risen Lord, he is the incarnate Word, the one through whom the universe was created. If all his deeds were described, the world would be a very small and inadequate library indeed.

It is as if John has identified himself (v. 24), but is not content to focus on himself, not even on his veracity. He must close by saying his own work is only a minute part of all the honours due the Son.

INDEX OF MODERN AUTHORS

INDEX OF BIBLICAL REFERENCES